Merriam-Webster's Pocket French-English Dictionary

Merriam-Webster, Incorporated
Springfield, Massachusetts, U.S.A.

A GENUINE MERRIAM-WEBSTER

The name *Webster* alone is no guarantee of excellence. It is used by a number of publishers and may serve mainly to mislead an unwary buyer.

Merriam-Webster™ is the name you should look for when you consider the purchase of dictionaries or other fine reference books. It carries the reputation of a company that has been publishing since 1831 and is your assurance of quality and authority.

ISBN-13: 978-0-87779-518-6
ISBN-10: 0-87779-518-5

MADE IN THE UNITED STATES OF AMERICA

4567TFP:RP0807

Contents

Preface

MERRIAM-WEBSTER'S POCKET FRENCH-ENGLISH DICTIONARY is a concise reference for the core vocabulary of French and English. Its 40,000 entries and over 50,000 translations provide up-to-date coverage of the basic vocabulary and idioms in both languages. In addition, the book includes vocabulary specific to the Canadian province of Quebec.

IPA (International Phonetic Alphabet) pronunciations are given for all words. Included as well are tables of irregular verbs in both languages and the most common French abbreviations.

This book shares many details of presentation with our larger *Merriam-Webster's French-English Dictionary,* but for reasons of conciseness it also has a number of features uniquely its own. Users need to be familiar with the following major features of this dictionary.

Main entries follow one another in strict alphabetical order, without regard to intervening spaces or hyphens.

Homographs (words spelled the same but having different meanings or parts of speech) are run on at a single main entry if they are closely related. Run-on homograph entries are replaced in the text by a boldfaced swung dash (as **devoir**. . .*vt*. . . — ~ *nm* . . .). Homographs of distinctly different origin (as **date**[1] and **date**[2]) are given separate entries.

Run-on entries for related words that are not homographs may also follow the main entry. Thus we have the main entry **calculer** *vt* followed by run-on entries for — **calcul** *nm,* — **calculateur, -trice** *adj,* and — **calculatrice** *nf.* However, if a related word falls later in the alphabet than a following unrelated main entry, it will be entered at its own place; **ear** and its run-on — **eardrum** precede the main entry **earl** which is followed by the main entry **earlobe.**

Variant spellings appear at the main entry separated by *or* (as **judgment** *or* **judgement; paralyze** *or Brit* **paralyse;** or **lis** *or* **lys**).

Inflected forms of English verbs, adjectives, adverbs, and nouns are shown when they are irregular (as **wage** . . . **waged; waging; ride** . . . **rode; ridden; good** . . . **better; best;** or **fly** . . . *n, pl* **flies**) or when there might be doubt about their spelling (as **ego** . . . *n, pl* **egos**). Inflected forms of French irregular verbs are shown in the section Conjugation of French Verbs on page 6a; numerical references to this table are included at the main entry (as **tenir** {92} *vt*). Irregular plurals of French nouns or adjectives are shown at the main entry (as **mondial, -diale** *adj, mpl* **-diaux**).

Cross-references are provided to lead the user to the appropriate main entry (as **mice → mouse** or **fausse → faux**[2]).

Pronunciation information is either given explicitly or implied for all English and French words. A full list of the pronunciation symbols used appears on page 30a.

The grammatical function of entry words is indicated by an italic **functional label** (as *vt, adj,* or *nm*). Italic **usage labels** may be added at the entry or sense as well (as **artilleur** . . . *nm Can* **:** pitcher (in baseball); **center** *or Brit* **centre** . . . *n* . . .; or **tuyau** . . . *nm* . . . **2** *fam* **:** tip, advice). These labels are also included in the translations (as **bet** . . . *n* **:** pari *m,* gageure *f Can).*

Usage notes are occasionally placed before a translation to clarify meaning or use (as **moins** . . . *prep* . . . **2** (*in expressions of time*) **:** to, of).

Synonyms may appear before the translation word(s) in order to provide context for the meaning of an entry word or sense (as **poursuivre** . . . *vt* . . . **2** CONTINUER **:** carry on with; or **meet** . . . *vt* . . . **2** SATISFY **:** satisfaire).

Bold notes are sometimes used before a translation to introduce a plural sense or a common phrase using the main entry word (as **meuble** . . . *nm* . . . **2 ~s** *nmpl* **:** furniture; or **call** . . . *vt* . . . **3 ~ off** **:** annuler). Note that when an entry word is repeated in a bold note, it is replaced by a swung dash

Conjugation of French Verbs

Simple Tenses

Tense	Regular verbs ending in -ER parler	
PRESENT INDICATIVE	je parle tu parles il parle	nous parlons vous parlez ils parlent
PRESENT SUBJUNCTIVE	je parle tu parles il parle	nous parlions vous parliez ils parlent
PRETERIT INDICATIVE	je parlai tu parlas il parla	nous parlâmes vous parlâtes ils parlèrent
IMPERFECT INDICATIVE	je parlais tu parlais il parlait	nous parlions vous parliez ils parlaient
IMPERFECT SUBJUNCTIVE	je parlasse tu parlasses il parlât	nous parlassions vous parlassiez ils parlassent
FUTURE INDICATIVE	je parlerai tu parleras il parlera	nous parlerons vous parlerez ils parleront
CONDITIONAL	je parlerais tu parlerais il parlerait	nous parlerions vous parleriez ils parleraient
IMPERATIVE	parle, parlez	parlons parlez
PRESENT PARTICIPLE (GERUND)	parlant	
PAST PARTICIPLE	parlé	

Tense	Regular verbs ending in -IR grandir	
PRESENT INDICATIVE	je grandis tu grandis il grandit	nous grandissons vous grandissez ils grandissent
PRESENT SUBJUNCTIVE	je grandisse tu grandisses il grandisse	nous grandissions vous grandissiez ils grandissent
PRETERIT INDICATIVE	je grandis tu grandis il grandit	nous grandîmes vous grandîtes ils grandirent
IMPERFECT INDICATIVE	je grandissais tu grandissais il grandissait	nous grandissions vous grandissiez ils grandissaient
IMPERFECT SUBJUNCTIVE	je grandisse tu grandisses il grandît	nous grandissions vous grandissiez ils grandissent
FUTURE INDICATIVE	je grandirai tu grandiras il grandira	nous grandirons vous grandirez ils grandiront
CONDITIONAL	je grandirais tu grandirais il grandirait	nous grandirions vous grandiriez ils grandiraient
IMPERATIVE	grandis, grandissez	grandissons grandissez
PRESENT PARTICIPLE (GERUND)	grandissant	
PAST PARTICIPLE	grandi	

Perfect Tenses

The *perfect* tenses are formed with *avoir* and the past participle:

PRESENT PERFECT

j'ai parlé, nous avons parlé, etc. (*indicative*)
j'aie parlé, nous ayons parlé, etc. (*subjunctive*)

PAST PERFECT

j'avais parlé, nous avions parlé, etc. (*indicative*)
j'eusse parlé, nous eussions parlé, etc. (*subjunctive*)

PRETERIT PERFECT

j'eus parlé, nous eûmes parlé, etc.

FUTURE PERFECT

j'aurai parlé, nous aurons parlé, etc.

CONDITIONAL PERFECT

j'aurais parlé, nous aurions parlé, etc.
or
j'eusse parlé, nous eussions parlé, etc.

PAST IMPERATIVE

aie parlé, ayons parlé, ayez parlé

The perfect tenses of the following verbs are formed with *être*:

aller, arriver, décéder, devenir, échoir, éclore, entrer, mourir, naître, partir, repartir, rentrer, rester, retourner, sortir, tomber, venir, revenir, parvenir, survenir

For example, the present perfect of *arriver* would be as follows:

je suis arrivé, nous sommes arrivés, etc. (*indicative*)

Irregular Verbs

The *imperfect subjunctive*, the *conditional*, and the first and second person plural of the *imperative* are not included in the model conjugations list but can be derived from other verb forms:

The *imperfect subjunctive* is formed by using the second person singular of the preterit indicative, removing the final *s*, and adding the following suffixes: *-sse, -sses, -t* (and adding a circumflex accent on the preceding vowel), *-ssions, -ssiez, -ssent*. *Servir* is conjugated as follows:

PRETERIT INDICATIVE, SECOND PERSON SINGULAR	servis – *s* = servi
IMPERFECT SUBJUNCTIVE	je servisse, tu servisses, il servît, nous servissions, vous servissiez, ils servissent

The *conditional* is formed by using the stem of the future indicative and adding the following suffixes: *-ais, -ais, -ait, -ions, -iez,- aient*. *Prendre* is conjugated as follows:

FUTURE INDICATIVE	je prendrai – *ai* = prendr
CONDITIONAL	je prendrais, tu prendrais, il prendrait, nous prendrions, vous prendriez, ils prendraient

The first and second person plural of the *imperative* are the same as the corresponding forms of the present indicative.

Model Conjugations of Irregular Verbs

The model conjugations below include the following simple tenses: the *present indicative* (*IND*), the *present subjunctive* (*SUBJ*), the *preterit indicative* (*PRET*), the *imperfect indicative* (*IMPF*), the *future indicative* (*FUT*), the second person singular form of the *imperative* (*IMPER*), the *present participle* or *gerund* (*PRP*), and the *past participle* (*PP*). Each set of conjugations is preceded by the corresponding infinitive form of the verb, shown in bold type. Only tenses containing irregularities are listed, and the irregular verb forms within each tense are displayed in bold type.

Also note that some conjugated verbs are labeled *defective verb*. This refers to a verb lacking one or more of the usual forms of grammatical inflection (tense, mood, etc.), for example, in French, the verbs *bruire* and *ouïr*.

Each irregular verb entry in the French-English section of this dictionary is cross-referred by number to one of the following model conjugations. These cross-reference numbers are shown in curly braces { } immediately preceding the entry's functional label.

The three main categories of verbs are:

1) Verbs ending in -ER
2) Verbs ending in -IR

Present indicative endings for verbs in these categories are:

-is, -is, -it, -issons, -issez, -issent

For example, *j'arrondis, nous arrondissons,* etc. for infinitive *arrondir*

3) Verbs ending in -IR/-OIR/-RE

Present indicative endings for verbs in these categories are:

-e, -es, -e, -ons, -ez, -ent

For example, *j'accueille, nous accueillons,* etc. for infinitive *accueillir*

or

-s(x), -s(x), -t(d), -ons, -ez, -ent

For example, *je rends, nous rendons,* etc. for infinitive *rendre*

Note that in the third group there are two different sets of endings for both the present indicative and preterit indicative depending on the verb in question, as shown above for the present indicative. For clarity, these forms are included in the model conjugations in an attempt to prevent the reader from inadvertently choosing the wrong endings.

1 **absoudre :** *IND* **j'absous, tu absous, il absout, nous absolvons, vous absolvez, ils absolvent;** *SUBJ* **j'absolve, tu absolves, il absolve, nous absolvions, vous absolviez, ils absolvent;** *PRET* (*not used*); *IMPF* **j'absolvais, tu absolvais, il absolvait, nous absolvions, vous absolviez, ils absolvaient;** *IMPER* **absous;** *PRP* **absolvant;** *PP* **absous**

2 **accroire** (*defective verb*) *Used only in the infinitive*

3 **accueillir :** *IND* **j'accueille, tu accueilles, il accueille,** nous accueillons, vous accueillez, ils accueillent; *PRET* **j'accueillis, tu accueillis, il accueillit, nous accueillîmes, vous accueillîtes, ils accueillirent;** *FUT* **j'accueillerai, tu accueilleras, il accueillera, nous accueillerons, vous accueillerez, ils accueilleront;** *IMPER* **accueille**

4 **advenir** (*defective verb*) *Used only in the infinitive and in the following tenses* **:** *IND* **il advient;** *SUBJ* **il advienne;** *PRET* **il ad-**

vint; *IMPF* **il advenait;** *FUT* **il adviendra;** *PRP* **advenant;** *PP* **advenu**

5 **aller :** *IND* **je vais, tu vas, il va, nous allons, vous allez, ils vont;** *SUBJ* **j'aille, tu ailles, il aille, nous allions, vous alliez, ils aillent;** *FUT* **j'irai, tu iras, il ira, nous irons, vous irez, ils iront;** *IMPER* **va**

6 **annoncer :** *IND* j'annonce, tu annonces, il annonce, **nous annonçons,** vous annoncez, ils annoncent; *PRET* **j'annonçai, tu annonças, il annonça, nous annonçâmes, vous annonçâtes, ils annoncèrent;** *IMPF* **j'annonçais, tu annonçais, il annonçait,** nous annoncions, vous annonciez, **ils annonçaient;** *PRP* **annonçant**

7 **apparaître :** *IND* **j'apparais, tu apparais, il apparaît, nous apparaissons, vous apparaissez, ils apparaissent;** *SUBJ* **j'apparaisse, tu apparaisses, il apparaisse, nous apparaissions, vous apparaissiez, ils apparaissent;** *PRET* **j'apparus, tu apparus, il apparut, nous apparûmes, vous apparûtes, ils apparurent;** *IMPF* **j'apparaissais, tu apparaissais, il apparaissait, nous apparaissions, vous apparaissiez, ils apparaissaient;** *IMPER* **apparais;** *PRP* **apparaissant;** *PP* **apparu**

8 **appeler :** *IND* **j'appelle, tu appelles, il appelle,** nous appelons, vous appelez, **ils appellent;** *SUBJ* **j'appelle, tu appelles, il appelle,** nous appelions, vous appeliez, **ils appellent;** *FUT* **j'appellerai, tu appelleras, il appellera, nous appellerons, vous appellerez, ils appelleront;** *IMPER* **appelle**

9 **asseoir :** *IND* **j'assieds** *or* **j'assois, tu assieds** *or* **tu assois, il assied** *or* **il assoit, nous asseyons** *or* **nous assoyons, vous asseyez** *or* **vous assoyez, ils asseyent** *or* **ils assoient;** *SUBJ* **j'asseye** *or* **j'assoie, tu asseyes** *or* **tu assoies, il asseye** *or* **il assoie, nous asseyions** *or* **nous assoyions, vous asseyiez** *or* **vous assoyiez, ils asseyent** *or* **ils assoient;** *PRET* **j'assis, tu assis, il assit, nous assîmes, vous assîtes, ils assirent;** *IMPF* **j'asseyais** *or* **j'assoyais, tu asseyais** *or* **tu assoyais, il asseyait** *or* **il assoyait, nous asseyions** *or* **nous assoyions, vous asseyiez** *or* **vous assoyiez, ils asseyaient** *or* **ils assoyaient;** *FUT* (*not used*); *IMPER* **assieds** *or* **assois;** *PRP* **asseyant** *or* **assoyant;** *PP* **assis**

10 **avoir :** *IND* **j'ai, tu as, il a, nous avons, vous avez, ils ont;** *SUBJ* **j'aie, tu aies, il ait, nous ayons, vous ayez, ils aient;** *PRET* **j'eus, tu eus, il eut, nous eûmes, vous eûtes, ils eurent;** *IMPF* **j'avais, tu avais, il avait, nous avions, vous aviez, ils**

avaient; *FUT* **j'aurai, tu auras, il aura, nous aurons, vous aurez, ils auront;** *IMPER* **aie, ayons, ayez;** *PRP* **ayant;** *PP* **eu**

11 **balayer :** *IND* **je balaie** *or* je balaye, **tu balaies** *or* tu balayes, **il balaie** *or* il balaye, nous balayons, vous balayez, **ils balaient** *or* ils balayent; *SUBJ* **je balaie** *or* je balaye, **tu balaies** *or* tu balayes, **il balaie** *or* il balaye, nous balayions, vous balayiez, **ils balaient** *or* ils balayent; *FUT* **je balaierai** *or* je balayerai, **tu balaieras** *or* tu balayeras, **il balaiera** *or* il balayera, **nous balaierons** *or* nous balayerons, **vous balaierez** *or* vous balayerez, **ils balaieront** *or* ils balayeront; *IMPER* **balaie** *or* balaye

12 **battre :** *IND* **je bats, tu bats, il bat,** nous battons, vous battez, ils battent; *PRET* **je battis, tu battis, il battit, nous battîmes, vous battîtes, ils battirent;** *IMPER* **bats;** *PP* **battu**

13 **boire :** *IND* je bois, tu bois, il boit, **nous buvons, vous buvez, ils boivent;** *SUBJ* **je boive, tu boives, il boive, nous buvions, vous buviez, ils boivent;** *PRET* **je bus, tu bus, il but, nous bûmes, vous bûtes, ils burent;** *IMPF* **je buvais, tu buvais, il buvait, nous buvions, vous buviez, ils buvaient;** *PRP* **buvant;** *PP* **bu**

14 **bouillir :** *IND* **je bous, tu bous, il bout,** nous bouillons, vous bouillez, ils bouillent; *PRET* **je bouillis, tu bouillis, il bouillit, nous bouillîmes, vous bouillîtes, ils bouillirent**; *IMPER* **bous**

15 **braire** (*defective verb*) *Used only in the infinitive and in the following tenses* **:** *IND* **il brait, ils braient;** *IMPF* **brayait, brayaient;** *FUT* **il braira, ils brairont**

16 **bruire** (*defective verb*) *Used only in the infinitive and in the following tenses* **:** *IND* **il bruit, ils bruissent;** *SUBJ* (*not used*); *PRET* (*not used*); *IMPF* **il bruissait, ils bruissaient;** *PRP* **bruissant;** *PP* **bruit**

17 **changer :** *IND* je change, tu changes, il change, **nous changeons,** vous changez, ils changent; *PRET* **je changeai, tu changeas, il changea, nous changeâmes, vous changeâtes, ils changèrent;** *IMPF* **je changeais, tu changeais, il changeait,** nous changions, vous changiez, **ils changeaient;** *PRP* **changeant**

18 **choir** (*defective verb*) *Used only in the following tenses* **:** *IND* **je chois, tu chois, il choit, ils choient;** *SUBJ* (*not used*); *PRET* **il chut;** *IMPF* (*not used*); *FUT* il choira; *IMPER* (*not used*); *PRP* (*not used*); *PP* **chu**

19 **clore** (*defective verb*) *Used only in the following tenses* **:** *IND* je clos, tu clos, **il clôt, ils closent;** *SUBJ* **je close, tu closes, il close, nous closions, vous closiez, ils closent;** *PRET* (*not used*); *IMPF* (*not used*); *FUT* (*used but regularly formed*); *PRP* **closant;** *PP* **clos**

20 **congeler :** *IND* **je congèle, tu congèles, il congèle,** nous congelons, vous congelez, **ils congèlent;** *SUBJ* **je congèle, tu congèles, il congèle,** nous congelions, vous congeliez, **ils congèlent;** *FUT* **je congèlerai, tu congèleras, il congèlera, nous congèlerons, vous congèlerez, ils congèleront;** *IMPER* **congèle**

21 **conquérir :** *IND* **je conquiers, tu conquiers, il conquiert,** nous conquérons, vous conquérez, **ils conquièrent;** *SUBJ* **je conquière, tu conquières, il conquière,** nous conquérions, vous conquériez, **ils conquièrent;** *PRET* **je conquis, tu conquis, il conquit, nous conquîmes, vous conquîtes, ils conquirent;** *FUT* **je conquerrai, tu conquerras, il conquerra, nous conquerrons, vous conquerrez, ils conquerront;** *IMPER* **conquiers;** *PP* **conquis**

22 **coudre :** *IND* je couds, tu couds, il coud, **nous cousons, vous cousez, ils cousent;** *SUBJ* **je couse, tu couses, il couse, nous cousions, vous cousiez, ils cousent;** *PRET* **je cousis, tu cousis, il cousit, nous cousîmes, vous cousîtes, ils cousirent;** *IMPF* **je cousais, tu cousais, il cousait, nous cousions, vous cousiez, ils cousaient;** *PRP* **cousant;** *PP* **cousu**

23 **courir :** *IND* **je cours, tu cours, il court,** nous courons, vous courez, ils courent; *PRET* **je courus, tu courus, il courut, nous courûmes, vous courûtes, ils coururent;** *FUT* **je courrai, tu courras, il courra, nous courrons, vous courrez, ils courront;** *IMPER* **cours;** *PP* **couru**

24 **croire :** *IND* je crois, tu crois, il croit, **nous croyons, vous croyez,** ils croient; *SUBJ* je croie, tu croies, il croie, **nous croyions, vous croyiez,** ils croient; *PRET* **je crus, tu crus, il crut, nous crûmes, vous crûtes, il crurent;** *IMPF* **je croyais, tu croyais, il croyait, nous croyions, vous croyiez, ils croyaient;** *PRP* **croyant;** *PP* **cru**

25 **croître :** *IND* **je croîs, tu croîs, il croît, nous croissons, vous croissez, ils croissent;** *SUBJ* **je croisse, tu croisses, il croisse, nous croissions, vous croissiez, ils croissent;** *PRET* **je crûs, tu crûs, il crût, nous crûmes, vous crûtes, ils crûrent;** *IMPF* **je**

croissais, tu croissais, il croissait, nous croissions, vous croissiez, ils croissaient; *IMPER* **croîs;** *PRP* **croissant;** *PP* **crû**

26 **décevoir :** *IND* **je déçois, tu déçois, il déçoit,** nous décevons, vous décevez, **ils déçoivent;** *SUBJ* **je déçoive, tu déçoives, il déçoive,** nous décevions, vous déceviez, **ils déçoivent;** *PRET* **je déçus, tu déçus, il déçut, nous déçûmes, vous déçûtes, ils déçurent;** *IMPER* **déçois;** *PP* **déçu**

27 **déchoir** (*defective verb*) *Used only in the following tenses* : *IND* je déchois, tu déchois, il déchoit *or* **il déchet, nous déchoyons, vous déchoyez, ils déchoient;** *SUBJ* je déchoie, tu déchoies, il déchoie, **nous déchoyions, vous déchoyiez, ils déchoient;** *PRET* **je déchus, tu déchus, il déchut, nous déchûmes, vous déchûtes, ils déchurent;** *IMPF* (*not used*); *FUT* (*used but regularly formed*); *IMPER* (*not used*); *PRP* (*not used*); *PP* **déchu**

28 **devoir :** *IND* **je dois, tu dois, il doit,** nous devons, vous devez, **ils doivent;** *SUBJ* **je doive, tu doives, il doive,** nous devions, vous deviez, **ils doivent;** *PRET* **je dus, tu dus, il dut, nous dûmes, vous dûtes, ils durent;** *IMPER* **dois;** *PRP* **dû**

29 **dire :** *IND* je dis, tu dis, il dit, **nous disons, vous dites, ils disent;** *SUBJ* **je dise, tu dises, il dise, nous disions, vous disiez, ils disent;** *PRET* **je dis, tu dis, il dit, nous dîmes, vous dîtes, ils dirent;** *IMPF* **je disais, tu disais, il disait, nous disions, vous disiez, ils disent;** *PRP* **disant;** *PP* **dit**

30 **dormir :** *IND* **je dors, tu dors, il dort,** nous dormons, vous dormez, ils dorment; *PRET* **je dormis, tu dormis, il dormit, nous dormîmes, vous dormîtes, ils dormirent;** *IMPER* **dors**

31 **échoir** (*defective verb*) *Used only in the following tenses* : *IND* **il échoit, ils échoient;** *SUBJ* **il échoie;** *PRET* **il échut, ils échurent;** *IMPF* (*not used*); *FUT* il échoira *or* **il écherra;** ils échoiront *or* **ils écherront;** *IMPER* (*not used*); *PRP* **échéant;** *PP* **échu**

32 **éclore** (*defective verb*) *Used only in the following tenses* : *IND* **il éclot;** *PP* **éclos**

33 **écrire :** *IND* j'écris, tu écris, il écrit, **nous écrivons, vous écrivez, ils écrivent;** *SUBJ* **j'écrive, tu écrives, il écrive, nous écrivions, vous écriviez, ils écrivent;** *PRET* **j'écrivis, tu écrivis, il écrivit, nous écrivîmes, vous écrivîtes, ils écrivirent;** *IMPF* **j'écrivais, tu écrivais, il écrivait, nous écrivions, vous écriviez, ils écrivaient;** *PRP* **écrivant;** *PP* **écrit**

34 **enclore** (*defective verb) Used only in the following tenses* : *IND* j'enclos, tu enclos, il enclot, **nous enclosons, vous enclosez, ils enclosent**; *SUBJ* **j'enclose, tu encloses, il enclose, nous enclosions, vous enclosiez, ils enclosent**; *PRET* (*not used*); *IMPF* (*not used*); *FUT* (*used but regularly formed*); *IMPER* enclos; *PRP* **enclosant**; *PP* **enclos**

35 **ensuivre (s')** (*defective verb) Used only in the following tenses* : *IND* **il s'ensuit**; *SUBJ* **il s'ensuive**; *PRET* **il s'ensuivit**; *IMPF* **il s'ensuivait**; *FUT* **il s'ensuivra**; *PP* **s'ensuivi**

36 **envoyer** : *IND* **j'envoie, tu envoies, il envoie,** nous envoyons, vous envoyez, **ils envoient**; *SUBJ* **j'envoie, tu envoies, il envoie,** nous envoyions, vous envoyiez, **ils envoient**; *FUT* **j'enverrai, tu enverras, il enverra, nous enverrons, vous enverrez, ils enverront**; *IMPER* **envoie**

37 **éteindre** : *IND* **j'éteins, tu éteins, il éteint, nous éteignons, vous éteignez, ils éteignent**; *SUBJ* **j'éteigne, tu éteignes, il éteigne, nous éteignions, vous éteigniez, ils éteignent**; *PRET* **j'éteignis, tu éteignis, il éteignit, nous éteignîmes, vous éteignîtes, ils éteignirent**; *IMPF* **j'éteignais, tu éteignais, il éteignait, nous éteignions, vous éteigniez, ils éteignaient**; *IMPER* **éteins**; *PRP* **éteignant**; *PP* **éteint**

38 **être** : *IND* **je suis, tu es, il est, nous sommes, vous êtes, ils sont**; *SUBJ* **je sois, tu sois, il soit, nous soyons, vous soyez, ils soient**; *PRET* **je fus, tu fus, il fut, nous fûmes, vous fûtes, ils furent**; *IMPF* **j'étais, tu étais, il était, nous étions, vous étiez, ils étaient**; *FUT* **je serai, tu seras, il sera, nous serons, vous serez, ils seront**; *IMPER* **sois**; *PRP* **étant**; *PP* **été**

39 **exclure** : *IND* **j'exclus, tu exclus, il exclut, nous excluons, vous excluez, ils excluent**; *PRET* **j'exclus, tu exclus, il exclut, nous exclûmes, vous exclûtes, ils exclurent**; *IMPER* **exclus**; *PP* **exclu**

40 **extraire** : *IND* j'extrais, tu extrais, il extrait, **nous extrayons, vous extrayez,** ils extraient; *SUBJ* j'extraie, tu extraies, il extraie, **nous extrayions, vous extrayiez,** ils extraient; *PRET* (*not used*); *IMPF* **j'extrayais, tu extrayais, il extrayait, nous extrayions, vous extrayiez, ils extrayaient**; *PRP* **extrayant**; *PP* **extrait**

41 **faillir** (*defective verb) Used only in the infinitive and as a PP* **failli**

42 **faire** : *IND* je fais, tu fais, il fait, **nous faisons, vous faites, ils**

font; *SUBJ* **je fasse, tu fasses, il fasse, nous fassions, vous fassiez, ils fassent;** *PRET* **je fis, tu fis, il fit, nous fîmes, vous fîtes, ils firent;** *IMPF* **je faisais, tu faisais, il faisait, nous faisions, vous faisiez, ils faisaient;** *FUT* **je ferai, tu feras, il fera, nous ferons, vous ferez, ils feront;** *PRP* **faisant;** *PP* **fait**

43 **falloir** (*defective verb*) *Used only in the following tenses* **:** *IND* **il faut;** *SUBJ* **il faille;** *PRET* **il fallut;** *IMPF* **il fallait;** *FUT* **il faudra;** *IMPER* (*not used*); *PRP* (*not used*); *PP* **fallu**

44 **forfaire** (*defective verb*) *Used only in the infinitive and in the following tenses* **:** *IND* **il forfait;** *PP* **forfait**

45 **frire** (*defective verb*) *Used only in the following tenses* **:** *IND* **je fris, tu fris, il frit;** *FUT* je frirai, tu friras, il frira, nous frirons, vous frirez, ils friront; *IMPER* **fris;** *PP* **frit**

46 **fuir :** *IND* je fuis, tu fuis, il fuit, **nous fuyons, vous fuyez, ils fuient;** *SUBJ* je fuie, tu fuies, il fuie, **nous fuyions, vous fuyiez, ils fuient;** *PRET* je fuis, tu fuis, il fuit, **nous fuîmes, vous fuîtes, ils fuirent;** *IMPF* **je fuyais, tu fuyais, il fuyait, nous fuyions, vous fuyiez, ils fuyaient;** *PRP* **fuyant;** *PP* **fui**

47 **gésir** (*defective verb*) *Used only in the following tenses* **:** *IND* **je gis, tu gis, il gît, nous gisons, vous gisez, ils gisent;** *IMPF* **je gisais, tu gisais, il gisait, nous gisions, vous gisiez, ils gisaient;** *PRP* **gisant**

48 **haïr :** *IND* **je hais, tu hais, il hait, nous haïssons, vous haïssez, ils haïssent;** *SUBJ* **je haïsse, tu haïsses, il haïsse, nous haïssions, vous haïssiez, ils haïssent;** *PRET* **je haïs, tu haïs, il haït, nous haïmes, vous haïtes, ils haïrent;** *IMPF* **je haïssais, tu haïssais, il haïssait, nous haïssions, vous haïssiez, ils haïssaient;** *IMPER* **hais;** *PRP* **haïssant;** *PP* **haï**

49 **instruire :** *IND* j'instruis, tu instruis, il instruit, **nous instruisons, vous instruisez, ils instruisent;** *SUBJ* **j'instruise, tu instruises, il instruise, nous instruisions, vous instruisiez, ils instruisent;** *PRET* **j'instruisis, tu instruisis, il instruisit, nous instruisîmes, vous instruisîtes, ils instruisirent;** *IMPF* **j'instruisais, tu instruisais, il instruisait, nous instruisions, vous instruisiez, ils instruisaient;** *PRP* **instruisant;** *PP* **instruit**

50 **joindre :** *IND* **je joins, tu joins, il joint, nous joignons, vous joignez, ils joignent;** *SUBJ* **je joigne, tu joignes, il joigne, nous joignions, vous joigniez, ils joignent;** *PRET* **je joignis, tu joignis, il joignit, nous joignîmes, vous joignîtes, ils**

joignirent; *IMPF* **je joignais, tu joignais, il joignait, nous joignions, vous joigniez, ils joignaient;** *IMPER* **joins;** *PRP* **joignant;** *PP* **joint**

51 **lire :** *IND* je lis, tu lis, il lit, **nous lisons, vous lisez, ils lisent;** *SUBJ* **je lise, tu lises, il lise, nous lisions, vous lisiez, ils lisent;** *PRET* **je lus, tu lus, il lut, nous lûmes, vous lûtes, ils lurent;** *IMPF* **je lisais, tu lisais, il lisait, nous lisions, vous lisiez, ils lisaient;** *PRP* **lisant;** *PP* **lu**

52 **mener :** *IND* **je mène, tu mènes, il mène,** nous menons, vous menez, **ils mènent;** *SUBJ* **je mène, tu mènes, il mène,** nous menions, vous meniez, **ils mènent;** *FUT* **je mènerai, tu mèneras, il mènera, nous mènerons, vous mènerez, ils mèneront;** *IMPER* **mène**

53 **mettre :** *IND* **je mets, tu mets, il met,** nous mettons, vous mettez, ils mettent; *PRET* **je mis, tu mis, il mit, nous mîmes, vous mîtes, ils mirent;** *IMPER* **mets;** *PP* **mis**

54 **moudre :** *IND* je mouds, tu mouds, il moud, **nous moulons, vous moulez, ils moulent;** *SUBJ* **je moule, tu moules, il moule, nous moulions, vous mouliez, ils moulent;** *PRET* **je moulus, tu moulus, il moulut, nous moulûmes, vous moulûtes, ils moulurent;** *IMPF* **je moulais, tu moulais, il moulait, nous moulions, vous mouliez, ils moulaient;** *PRP* **moulant;** *PP* **moulu**

55 **mourir :** *IND* **je meurs, tu meurs, il meurt,** nous mourons, vous mourez, **ils meurent;** *SUBJ* **je meure, tu meures, il meure,** nous mourions, vous mouriez, **ils meurent;** *PRET* **je mourus, tu mourus, il mourut, nous mourûmes, vous mourûtes, ils moururent;** *FUT* **je mourrai, tu mourras, il mourra, nous mourrons, vous mourrez, ils mourront;** *IMPER* **meurs;** *PRP* **mourant;** *PP* **mort**

56 **mouvoir :** *IND* **je meus, tu meus, il meut,** nous mouvons, vous mouvez, **ils meuvent;** *SUBJ* **je meuve, tu meuves, il meuve,** nous mouvions, vous mouviez, **ils meuvent;** *PRET* **je mus, tu mus, il mut, nous mûmes, vous mûtes, ils murent;** *IMPER* **meus;** *PP* **mû**

57 **naître :** *IND* **je nais, tu nais, il naît, nous naissons, vous naissez, ils naissent;** *SUBJ* **je naisse, tu naisses, il naisse, nous naissions, vous naissiez, ils naissent;** *PRET* **je naquis, tu naquis, il naquit, nous naquîmes, vous naquîtes, ils naquirent;** *IMPF* **je naissais, tu naissais, il naissait, nous**

naissions, vous naissiez, ils naissaient; *IMPER* **nais;** *PRP* **naissant;** *PP* **né**

58 **nettoyer :** *IND* **je nettoie, tu nettoies, il nettoie,** nous nettoyons, vous nettoyez, **ils nettoient;** *SUBJ* **je nettoie, tu nettoies, il nettoie,** nous nettoyions, vous nettoyiez, **ils nettoient;** *FUT* **je nettoierai, tu nettoieras, il nettoiera, nous nettoierons, vous nettoierez, ils nettoieront;** *IMPER* **nettoie**

59 **oindre** (*defective verb*) *Used only in the infinitive and as a* *PP* **oint**

60 **ouïr** (*defective verb*) *Used only in the infinitive and as a pp* **ouï**

61 **paître** (*defective verb*) *Used only in the following tenses* **:** *IND* **je pais, tu pais, il paît, nous paissons, vous paissez, ils paissent;** *SUBJ* **je paisse, tu paisses, il paisse, nous paissions, vous paissiez, ils paissent;** *PRET* (*not used*); *IMPF* **je paissais, tu paissais, il paissait, nous paissions, vous paissiez, ils paissaient;** *FUT* (*used but regular*); *IMPER* **pais;** *PRP* **paissant;** *PP* (*not used*)

62 **parfaire** (*defective verb*) *Used only in the infinitive and in the following tenses* *IND* **il parfait;** *PP* **parfait**

63 **perdre :** *IND* je perds, tu perds, **il perd**, nous perdons, vous perdez, ils perdent; *PRET* **je perdis, tu perdis, il perdit, nous perdîmes, vous perdîtes, ils perdirent;** *PP* **perdu**

64 **piéger :** *IND* **je piège, tu pièges, il piège, nous piégeons,** vous piégez, **ils piègent;** *SUBJ* **je piège, tu pièges, il piège,** nous piégions, vous piégiez, **ils piègent;** *PRET* **je piégeai, tu piégeas, il piégea, nous piégeâmes, vous piégeâtes, ils piégèrent;** *IMPF* **je piégeais, tu piégeais, il piégeait,** nous piégions, vous piégiez, **ils piégeaient;** *IMPER* **piège;** *PRP* **piégeant;** *PP* **piégé**

65 **plaindre :** *IND* je plains, tu plains, il plaint, **nous plaignons, vous plaignez, ils plaignent;** *SUBJ* **je plaigne, tu plaignes, il plaigne, nous plagnions, vous plagniez, ils plaignent;** *PRET* **je plaignis, tu plaignis, il plaignit, nous plaignîmes, vous plaignîtes, ils plaignirent;** *IMPF* **je plaignais, tu plaignais, il plaignait, nous plaignions, vous plaigniez, ils plaignaient;** *PRP* **plaignant;** *PP* **plaint**

66 **plaire :** *IND* je plais, tu plais, **il plaît, nous plaisons, vous plaisez, ils plaisent;** *SUBJ* **je plaise, tu plaises, il plaise, nous plaisions, vous plaisiez, ils plaisent;** *PRET* **je plus, tu plus, il plut, nous plûmes, vous plûtes, ils plurent;** *IMPF* **je plaisais,**

tu plaisais, il plaisait, nous plaisions, vous plaisiez, ils plaisaient; *PRP* **plaisant;** *PP* **plu**

67 **pleuvoir** (*defective verb*) *Used in the infinitive and in the following tenses* *IND* **il pleut, ils pleuvent** (*only in the figurative*); *SUBJ* **il pleuve, ils pleuvent** (*only in the figurative*); *PRET* **il plut;** *IMPF* **il pleuvait, ils pleuvaient** (*only in the figurative*); *FUT* **il pleuvra;** *IMPER* (*not used*); *PRP* **pleuvant;** *PP* **plu**

68 **pourvoir :** *IND* **je pourvois, tu pourvois, il pourvoit, nous pourvoyons, vous pourvoyez, ils pourvoient;** *SUBJ* **je pourvoie, tu pourvoies, il pourvoie, nous pourvoyions, vous pourvoyiez, ils pourvoient;** *PRET* **je pourvus, tu pourvus, il pourvut, nous pourvûmes, vous pourvûtes, ils pourvurent;** *IMPF* **je pourvoyais, tu pourvoyais, il pourvoyait, nous pourvoyions, vous pourvoyiez, ils pourvoyaient;** *FUT* **je pourvoirai, tu pourvoiras, il pourvoira, nous pourvoirons, vous pourvoirez, ils pourvoiront;** *IMPER* **pourvois;** *PRP* **pourvoyant;** *PP* **pourvu**

69 **pouvoir :** *IND* **je peux** *or* **je puis, tu peux, il peut,** nous pouvons, vous pouvez, **ils peuvent;** *SUBJ* **je puisse, tu puisses, il puisse, nous puissions, vous puissiez, ils puissent;** *PRET* **je pus, tu pus, il put, nous pûmes, vous pûtes, ils purent;** *FUT* **je pourrai, tu pourras, il pourra, nous pourrons, vous pourrez, ils pourront;** *IMPER* (*not used*); *PP* **pu**

70 **prendre :** *IND* je prends, tu prends, **il prend, nous prenons, vous prenez, ils prennent;** *SUBJ* **je prenne, tu prennes, il prenne, nous prenions, vous preniez, ils prennent;** *PRET* **je pris, tu pris, il prit, nous prîmes, vous prîtes, ils prirent;** *IMPF* **je prenais, tu prenais, il prenait, nous prenions, vous preniez, ils prenaient;** *PRP* **prenant;** *PP* **pris**

71 **prévaloir :** *IND* **je prévaux, tu prévaux, il prévaut,** nous prévalons, vous prévalez, ils prévalent; *PRET* **je prévalus, tu prévalus, il prévalut, nous prévalûmes, vous prévalûtes, ils prévalurent;** *FUT* **je prévaudrai, tu prévaudras, il prévaudra, nous prévaudrons, vous prévaudrez, ils prévaudront;** *IMPER* **prévaux;** *PP* **prévalu**

72 **rassir** (*defective verb*) *Used only in the infinitive and as a* *PP* **rassis**

73 **ravoir** (*defective verb*) *Used only in the infinitive*

74 **résoudre :** *INF* **je résous, tu résous, il résout, nous résolvons, vous résolvez, ils résolvent;** *SUBJ* **je résolve, tu résolves, il ré-**

solve, nous résolvions, vous résolviez, ils résolvent; *PRET* **je résolus, tu résolus, il résolut, nous résolûmes, vous résolûtes, ils résolurent;** *IMPF* **je résolvais, tu résolvais, il résolvait, nous résolvions, vous résolviez, ils résolvaient;** *IMPER* **résous;** *PRP* **résolvant;** *PP* **résolu**

75 **résulter** (*defective verb) Used only in the infinitive and in the following tenses* : *IND* **il résulte;** *PRP* **résultant**

76 **rire :** *IND* **je ris, tu ris, il rit, nous rions, vous riez, ils rient;** *SUBJ* je rie, tu ries, il rie, **nous riions, vous riiez,** ils rient; *PRET* **je ris, tu ris, il rit, nous rîmes, vous rîtes, ils rirent;** *IMPER* **ris;** *PP* **ri**

77 **rompre :** *IND* je romps, tu romps, **il rompt**, nous rompons, vous rompez, ils rompent; *PRET* **je rompis, tu rompis, il rompit, nous rompîmes, vous rompîtes, ils rompirent;** *PP* **rompu**

78 **saillir :** *IND* **je saille, tu sailles, il saille,** nous saillons, vous saillez, ils saillent; *PRET* **je saillis, tu sallis, il saillit, nous saillîmes, vous saillîtes, ils saillirent;** *FUT* **je saillerai, tu sailleras, il saillera, nous saillerons, vous saillerez, ils sailleront;** *IMPER* **saille**

79 **savoir :** *IND* **je sais, tu sais, il sait,** nous savons, vous savez, ils savent; *SUBJ* **je sache, tu saches, il sache, nous sachions, vous sachiez, ils sachent;** *PRET* **je sus, tu sus, il sut, nous sûmes, vous sûtes, ils surent;** *FUT* **je saurai, tu sauras, il saura, nous saurons, vous saurez, ils sauront;** *IMPER* **sache, sachons, sachez;** *PRP* **sachant;** *PP* **su**

80 **seoir** (*defective verb*) *Used only in the following tenses* : *IND* **il sied, ils siéent;** *SUBJ* **il siée, ils siéent;** *PRET* (*not used*); *IMPF* **il seyait, ils seyaient;** *FUT* **il siéra, ils siéront;** *IMPER* (*not used*); *PRP* **séant** *or* **seyant;** *PP* (*not used*)

81 **servir :** *IND* **je sers, tu sers, il sert,** nous servons, vous servez, ils servent; *PRET* **je servis, tu servis, il servit, nous servîmes, vous servîtes, ils servirent;** *FUT* **je servirai, tu serviras, il servira, nous servirons, vous servirez, ils serviront;** *IMPER* **sers;** *PP* **servi**

82 **sortir :** *IND* **je sors, tu sors, il sort,** nous sortons, vous sortez, ils sortent; *PRET* **je sortis, tu sortis, il sortit, nous sortîmes, vous sortîtes, ils sortirent;** *FUT* **je sortirai, tu sortiras, il sortira, nous sortirons, vous sortirez, ils sortiront;** *IMPER* **sors;** *PRP* **sortant;** *PP* **sorti**

83 **souffrir :** *IND* **je souffre, tu souffres, il souffre,** nous souffrons, vous souffrez, ils souffrent; *PRET* **je souffris, tu souffris, il souffrit, nous souffrîmes, vous souffrîtes, ils souffrirent;** *FUT* **je souffrirai, tu souffriras, il souffrira, nous souffrirons, vous souffrirez, ils souffriront;** *IMPER* **souffre;** *PP* **souffert**

84 **sourdre** (*defective verb*) *Used only in the infinitive and in the following tenses* **:** *IND* **il sourd, ils sourdent;** *IMPF* **il sourdait, ils sourdaient**

85 **stupéfaire** (*defective verb*) *Used only in the following tense* *PP* **stupéfié**

86 **suffire :** *IND* je suffis, tu suffis, il suffit, **nous suffisons, vous suffisez, ils suffisent;** *SUBJ* **je suffise, tu suffises, il suffise, nous suffisions, vous suffisiez, ils suffisent;** *PRET* **je suffis, tu suffis, il suffit, nous suffîmes, vous suffîtes, ils suffirent;** *IMPF* **je suffisais, tu suffisais, il suffisait, nous suffisions, vous suffisiez, ils suffisaient;** *PRP* **suffisant;** *PP* **suffi**

87 **suggérer :** *IND* **je suggère, tu suggères, il suggère,** nous suggérons, vous suggérez, **ils suggèrent;** *SUBJ* **je suggère, tu suggères, il suggère,** nous suggérions, vous suggériez, **ils suggèrent;** *IMPER* **suggère**

88 **suivre :** *IND* **je suis, tu suis, il suit,** nous suivons, vous suivez, ils suivent; *PRET* **je suivis, tu suivis, il suivit, nous suivîmes, vous suivîtes, ils suivirent;** *IMPER* **suis;** *PP* **suivi**

89 **suppléer :** *IND* **je supplée, tu supplées, il supplée, nous suppléons, vous suppléez, ils suppléent;** *SUBJ* **je supplée, tu supplées, il supplée, nous suppléions, vous suppléiez, ils suppléent;** *PRET* **je suppléai, tu suppléas, il suppléa, nous suppléâmes, vous suppléâtes, ils suppléèrent;** *FUT* **je suppléerai, tu suppléeras, il suppléera, nous suppléerons, vous suppléerez, ils suppléeront;** *IMPER* **supplée;** *PP* **suppléé**

90 **surseoir :** *IND* **je sursois, tu sursois, il sursoit, nous sursoyons, vous sursoyez, ils sursoient;** *SUBJ* **je sursoie, tu sursoies, il sursoie, nous sursoyions, vous sursoyiez, ils sursoient;** *PRET* **je sursis, tu sursis, il sursit, nous sursîmes, vous sursîtes, ils sursirent;** *IMPF* **je sursoyais, tu sursoyais, il sursoyait, nous sursoyions, vous sursoyiez, ils sursoyaient;** *FUT* **je surseoirai, tu surseoiras, il surseoira, nous surseoirons, vous surseoirez, ils surseoiront;** *IMPER* **sursois;** *PRP* **sursoyant;** *PP* **sursis**

91 **taire :** *IND* je tais, tu tais, **il tait, nous taisons, vous taisez, ils taisent;** *SUBJ* **je taise, tu taises, il taise, nous taisions, vous taisiez, ils taisent;** *PRET* **je tus, tu tus, il tut, nous tûmes, vous tûtes, ils turent;** *IMPF* **je taisais, tu taisais, il taisait, nous taisions, vous taisiez, ils taisaient;** *PRP* **taisant;** *PP* **tu**

92 **tenir :** *IND* **je tiens, tu tiens, il tient,** nous tenons, vous tenez, **ils tiennent;** *SUBJ* **je tienne, tu tiennes, il tienne,** nous tenions, vous teniez, **ils tiennent;** *PRET* **je tins, tu tins, il tint, nous tînmes, vous tîntes, ils tinrent;** *FUT* **je tiendrai, tu tiendras, il tiendra, nous tiendrons, vous tiendrez, ils tiendront;** *IMPER* **tiens;** *PP* **tenu**

93 **tressaillir :** *IND* **je tressaille, tu tressailles, il tressaille,** nous tressaillons, vous tressaillez, ils tressaillent; *PRET* **je tressaillis, tu tressaillis, il tressaillit, nous tressaillîmes, vous tressaîllites, ils tressaillirent;** *FUT* **je tressaillirai, tu tressailliras, il tressaillira, nous tressaillirons, vous tressaillirez, ils tressailliront;** *IMPF* **tressaille;** *PP* **tressailli**

94 **vaincre :** *IND* **je vaincs, tu vaincs, il vainc, nous vainquons, vous vainquez, ils vainquent;** *SUBJ* **je vainque, tu vainques, il vainque, nous vainquions, vous vainquiez, ils vainquent;** *PRET* **je vainquis, tu vainquis, il vainquit, nous vainquîmes, vous vainquîtes, ils vainquirent;** *IMPF* **je vainquais, tu vainquais, il vainquait, nous vainquions, vous vainquiez, ils vainquaient;** *IMPER* **vaincs;** *PRP* **vainquant;** *PP* **vaincu**

95 **valoir :** *IND* **je vaux, tu vaux, il vaut,** nous valons, vous valez, ils valent; *SUBJ* **je vaille, tu vailles, il vaille,** nous valions, vous valiez, **ils vaillent;** *PRET* **je valus, tu valus, il valut, nous valûmes, vous valûtes, ils valurent;** *FUT* **je vaudrai, tu vaudras, il vaudra, nous vaudrons, vous vaudrez, ils vaudront;** *IMPER* **vaux;** *PP* **valu**

96 **vérifier :** *SUBJ* je vérifie, tu vérifies, il vérifie, **nous vérifiions, vous vérifiiez,** ils vérifient; *IMPF* je vérifiais, tu vérifiais, il vérifiait, **nous vérifiions, vous vérifiiez,** ils vérifiaient

97 **vêtir :** *IND* **je vêts, tu vêts, il vêt,** nous vêtons, vous vêtez, ils vêtent; *PRET* **je vêtis, tu vêtis, il vêtit, nous vêtîmes, vous vêtîtes, ils vêtirent;** *FUT* **je vêtirai, tu vêtiras, il vêtira, nous vêtirons, vous vêtirez, ils vêtiront;** *IMPER* **vêts;** *PP* **vêtu**

98 **vivre :** *IND* **je vis, tu vis, il vit,** nous vivons, vous vivez, ils vivent; *PRET* **je vécus, tu vécus, il vécut, nous vécûmes, vous vécûtes, ils vécurent**; *IMPER* **vis;** *PP* **vécu**

99 **voir :** *IND* je vois, tu vois, il voit, **nous voyons, vous voyez,** ils voient; *SUBJ* je voie, tu voies, il voie, **nous voyions, vous voyiez,** ils voient; *PRET* **je vis, tu vis, il vit, nous vîmes, vous vîtes, ils virent;** *IMPF* **je voyais, tu voyais, il voyait, nous voyions, vous voyiez, ils voyaient;** *FUT* **je verrai, tu verras, il verra, nous verrons, vous verrez, ils verront;** *PRP* **voyant;** *PP* **vu**

100 **vouloir :** *IND* **je veux, tu veux, il veut,** nous voulons, vous voulez, **ils veulent;** *SUBJ* **je veuille, tu veuilles, il veuille,** nous voulions, vous vouliez; **ils veuillent;** *PRET* **je voulus, tu voulus, il voulut, nous voulûmes, vous voulûtes, ils voulurent;** *FUT* **je voudrai, tu voudras, il voudra, nous voudrons, vous voudrez, ils voudront;** *IMPER* **veux** *or* **veuille;** *PP* **voulu**

Irregular English Verbs

INFINITIVE	PAST	PAST PARTICIPLE
arise	arose	arisen
awake	awoke	awoken *or* awaked
be	was, were	been
bear	bore	borne
beat	beat	beaten *or* beat
become	became	become
befall	befell	befallen
begin	began	begun
behold	beheld	beheld
bend	bent	bent
beseech	beseeched *or* besought	beseeched *or* besought
beset	beset	beset
bet	bet	bet
bid	bade *or* bid	bidden *or* bid
bind	bound	bound
bite	bit	bitten
bleed	bled	bled
blow	blew	blown
break	broke	broken
breed	bred	bred
bring	brought	brought
build	built	built
burn	burned *or* burnt	burned *or* burnt
burst	burst	burst
buy	bought	bought
can	could	—
cast	cast	cast
catch	caught	caught
choose	chose	chosen
cling	clung	clung
come	came	come
cost	cost	cost
creep	crept	crept
cut	cut	cut
deal	dealt	dealt
dig	dug	dug
do	did	done
draw	drew	drawn
dream	dreamed *or* dreamt	dreamed *or* dreamt
drink	drank	drunk *or* drank

INFINITIVE	PAST	PAST PARTICIPLE
drive	drove	driven
dwell	dwelled *or* dwelt	dwelled *or* dwelt
eat	ate	eaten
fall	fell	fallen
feed	fed	fed
feel	felt	felt
fight	fought	fought
find	found	found
flee	fled	fled
fling	flung	flung
fly	flew	flown
forbid	forbade	forbidden
forecast	forecast	forecast
forego	forewent	foregone
foresee	foresaw	foreseen
foretell	foretold	foretold
forget	forgot	forgotten *or* forgot
forgive	forgave	forgiven
forsake	forsook	forsaken
freeze	froze	frozen
get	got	got *or* gotten
give	gave	given
go	went	gone
grind	ground	ground
grow	grew	grown
hang	hung	hung
have	had	had
hear	heard	heard
hide	hid	hidden *or* hid
hit	hit	hit
hold	held	held
hurt	hurt	hurt
keep	kept	kept
kneel	knelt *or* kneeled	knelt *or* kneeled
know	knew	known
lay	laid	laid
lead	led	led
leap	leaped *or* leapt	leaped *or* leapt
leave	left	left
lend	lent	lent
let	let	let
lie	lay	lain
light	lit *or* lighted	lit *or* lighted
lose	lost	lost

INFINITIVE	PAST	PAST PARTICIPLE
make	made	made
may	might	—
mean	meant	meant
meet	met	met
mow	mowed	mowed *or* mown
pay	paid	paid
put	put	put
quit	quit	quit
read	read	read
rend	rent	rent
rid	rid	rid
ride	rode	ridden
ring	rang	rung
rise	rose	risen
run	ran	run
saw	sawed	sawed *or* sawn
say	said	said
see	saw	seen
seek	sought	sought
sell	sold	sold
send	sent	sent
set	set	set
shake	shook	shaken
shall	should	—
shear	sheared	sheared *or* shorn
shed	shed	shed
shine	shone *or* shined	shone *or* shined
shoot	shot	shot
show	showed	shown *or* showed
shrink	shrank *or* shrunk	shrunk *or* shrunken
shut	shut	shut
sing	sang *or* sung	sung
sink	sank *or* sunk	sunk
sit	sat	sat
slay	slew	slain
sleep	slept	slept
slide	slid	slid
sling	slung	slung
smell	smelled *or* smelt	smelled *or* smelt
sow	sowed	sown *or* sowed
speak	spoke	spoken
speed	sped *or* speeded	sped *or* speeded
spell	spelled	spelled
spend	spent	spent
spill	spilled	spilled

INFINITIVE	PAST	PAST PARTICIPLE
spin	spun	spun
spit	spit *or* spat	spit *or* spat
split	split	split
spoil	spoiled	spoiled
spread	spread	spread
spring	sprang *or* sprung	sprung
stand	stood	stood
steal	stole	stolen
stick	stuck	stuck
sting	stung	stung
stink	stank *or* stunk	stunk
stride	strode	stridden
strike	struck	struck
swear	swore	sworn
sweep	swept	swept
swell	swelled	swelled *or* swollen
swim	swam	swum
swing	swung	swung
take	took	taken
teach	taught	taught
tear	tore	torn
tell	told	told
think	thought	thought
throw	threw	thrown
thrust	thrust	thrust
tread	trod	trodden *or* trod
wake	woke	woken *or* waked
waylay	waylaid	waylaid
wear	wore	worn
weave	wove *or* weaved	woven *or* weaved
wed	wedded	wedded
weep	wept	wept
will	would	—
win	won	won
wind	wound	wound
withdraw	withdrew	withdrawn
withhold	withheld	withheld
withstand	withstood	withstood
wring	wrung	wrung
write	wrote	written

French Numbers

Cardinal Numbers

1	un	24	vingt-quatre
2	deux	25	vingt-cinq
3	trois	26	vingt-six
4	quatre	27	vingt-sept
5	cinq	28	vingt-huit
6	six	29	vingt-neuf
7	sept	30	trente
8	huit	31	trente et un
9	neuf	40	quarante
10	dix	50	cinquante
11	onze	60	soixante
12	douze	70	soixante-dix
13	treize	80	quatre-vingts
14	quatorze	90	quatre-vingt-dix
15	quinze	100	cent
16	seize	101	cent un
17	dix-sept	200	deux cents
18	dix-huit	1 000	mille
19	dix-neuf	1 001	mille un
20	vingt	2 000	deux mille
21	vingt et un	100 000	cent mille
22	vingt-deux	1 000 000	un million
23	vingt-trois	1 000 000 000	un milliard

Ordinal Numbers

1st	premier, première	16th	seizième
2nd	deuxième *or* second	17th	dix-septième
3rd	troisième	18th	dix-huitième
4th	quatrième	19th	dix-neuvième
5th	cinquième	20th	vingtième
6th	sixième	21st	vingt et unième
7th	septième	22nd	vingt-deuxième
8th	huitième	30th	trentième
9th	neuvième	40th	quarantième
10th	dixième	50th	cinquantième
11th	onzième	60th	soixantième
12th	douzième	70th	soixante-dixième
13th	treizième	80th	quatre-vingtième
14th	quatorzième	90th	quatre-vingt-dixième
15th	quinzième	100th	centième

Abbreviations in This Work

adj adjective
adv adverb
adv phr adverbial phrase
Bel Belgium
Brit Great Britain
Can Canada
conj conjunction
conj phr conjunctive phrase
esp especially
etc et cetera
f feminine
fam familiar or colloquial
fpl feminine plural
interj interjection
m masculine
mf masculine or feminine
mpl masculine plural
n noun
nf feminine noun
nfpl feminine plural noun
nfs & pl invariable singular or plural feminine noun
nm masculine noun
nmf masculine or feminine noun
nmfpl plural noun invariable for gender
nmfs & pl noun invariable for both gender and number
nmpl masculine plural noun
nms & pl invariable singular or plural masculine noun
npl plural noun
ns & pl noun invariable for plural
pl plural
pp past participle
prep preposition
prep phr prepositional phrase
pron pronoun
qqch quelque chose (something)
qqn quelqu'un (someone)
s singular
s.o. someone
sth something
Switz Switzerland
usu usually
v verb (transitive and intransitive)
v aux auxiliary verb
vi intransitive verb
v impers impersonal verb
vr reflexive verb
vt transitive verb

Pronunciation Symbols

VOWELS

- æ ask, bat, glad
- ɑ cot, bomb
- ã *French* chant, ennui
- a *New England* aunt, *British* ask, glass
- e *French* été, aider, chez
- ɛ egg, bet, fed
- ɛ̃ *French* lapin, main
- ə about, javelin, Alabama
- *ə* when italicized as in *ə*l, *ə*m, *ə*n, indicates a syllabic pronunciation of the consonant as in bottle, prism, button
- i very, any, thirty
- i: eat, bead, bee
- ɪ id, bid, pit
- o Ohio, yellower, potato
- o: oats, own, zone, blow
- ɔ awl, maul, caught, paw
- ɔ̃ ombre, mon
- ʊ sure, should, could
- u *French* ouvert, chou, rouler
- u: boot, two, coo
- ʌ under, putt, bud
- y *French* pur, *German* fühlen
- eɪ eight, wade, bay
- aɪ ice, bite, tie
- aʊ out, gown, plow
- ɔɪ oyster, coil, boy
- ər further, stir
- ø *French* deux, *German* Höhe
- œ *French* bœuf, *German* Gött
- œ̃ *French* lundi, parfum

CONSONANTS

- b baby, labor, cab
- d day, ready, kid
- ʤ just, badger, fudge
- ð then, either, bathe
- f foe, tough, buff
- g go, bigger, bag
- h hot, aha
- j yes, vineyard
- k cat, keep, lacquer, flock
- l law, hollow, boil
- m mat, hemp, hammer, rim
- n new, tent, tenor, run
- ŋ rung, hang, swinger
- ɲ *French* digne, agneau
- p pay, lapse, top
- r rope, burn, tar
- s sad, mist, kiss
- ʃ shoe, mission, slush
- t toe, button, mat
- ţ indicates that some speakers of English pronounce this sound as a voiced alveolar flap, as in later, catty, battle
- ʧ choose, batch
- θ thin, ether, bath
- v vat, never, cave
- w wet, software
- ɥ *French* cuir, appui
- x *German* Bach, *Scottish* loch
- z zoo, easy, buzz
- ʒ azure, beige
- *h, k, p, t* when italicized indicate sounds which are present in the pronunciation of some speakers of English but absent in the pronunciation of others, so that *whence* [ˈ*h*wɛn*t*s] can be pronounced as [ˈhwɛns], [ˈhwɛnts], [ˈwɛnts], or [ˈwɛns].

OTHER SYMBOLS

- ˈ high stress **pen**manship
- ˌ low stress penman**ship**
- ʼ aspiration; when used before French words in *h*-, indicates absence of liaison, as in *le héros* [lə ʼero]
- ( ) indicate sounds that are present in the pronunciation of some speakers of French but absent in that of others, as in *cenellier* [s(ə)nelje], *but* [by(t)]

French-English Dictionary

A

a [a] *nm* : a, first letter of the alphabet
à [a] *prep* **1 :** to **2 ~ deux heures :** at two o'clock **3 ~ la :** in the manner of, like **4 ~ l'heure :** per hour **5 ~ mon avis :** in my opinion **6 ~ pied :** on foot **7 ~ vendre :** for sale **8 la femme aux yeux verts :** the woman with green eyes **9 un ami ~ moi :** a friend of mine **10 voler aux riches :** steal from the rich
abaisser [abese] *vt* **1 :** lower, reduce **2** HUMILIER : humble — **s'abaisser** *vr* **1 :** lower oneself **2 ~ à :** stoop to
abandonner [abɑ̃dɔne] *vt* : abandon — **s'abandonner** *vr* **1 :** neglect oneself **2 ~ à :** give oneself up to — **abandon** [abɑ̃dɔ̃] *nm* **1 :** abandonment, neglect **2** DÉSINVOLTURE : abandon
abasourdir [abazurdir] *vt* : stun
abat–jour [abaʒur] *nms & pl* : lampshade
abats [aba] *nmpl* **1 :** entrails **2 ~ de volaille :** giblets
abattant [abatɑ̃] *nm* : flap, leaf
abattis [abati] *nmpl* : giblets
abattoir [abatwar] *nm* : slaughterhouse
abattre [abatr] {12} *vt* **1 :** knock down, cut down **2** ÉPUISER : wear out **3** DÉMORALISER : dishearten — **s'abattre** *vr* **1 :** fall, crash **2 ~ sur :** descend on — **abattement** [abatmɑ̃] *nm* **1 :** reduction, allowance **2 :** despondency — **abattu, -tue** [abaty] *adj* : downcast
abbaye [abei] *nf* : abbey — **abbé** [abe] *nm* **1 :** abbot **2** PRÊTRE : priest
abcès [apsɛ] *nm* : abscess
abdiquer [abdike] *v* : abdicate — **abdication** [abdikasjɔ̃] *nf* : abdication
abdomen [abdɔmɛn] *nm* : abdomen — **abdominal, -nale** [abdɔminal] *adj, mpl* **-naux** [no] : abdominal
abécédaire [abesedɛr] *nm* : primer, speller
abeille [abɛj] *nf* : bee
aberrant, -rante [abɛrɑ̃, -rɑ̃t] *adj* : absurd — **aberration** [abɛrasjɔ̃] *nf* : aberration
abêtir [abɛtir] *vt* : make stupid
abhorrer [abɔre] *vt* : abhor
abîme [abim] *nm* : abyss, depths — **abîmer** [abime] *vt* : spoil, damage — **s'abîmer** *vr* **1 :** be spoiled **2 :** sink, founder
abject, -jecte [abʒɛkt] *adj* : despicable, abject
abjurer [abʒyre] *vt* : renounce, abjure
abnégation [abnegasjɔ̃] *nf* : self-denial
aboiement [abwamɑ̃] *nm* : barking — **abois** [abwa] *nmpl* **aux ~ :** at bay
abolir [abɔlir] *vt* : abolish — **abolition** [abɔlisjɔ̃] *nf* : abolition
abominable [abɔminabl] *adj* : abominable
abonder [abɔ̃de] *vi* : abound — **abondamment** [abɔ̃damɑ̃] *adv* : abundantly — **abondance** [abɔ̃dɑ̃s] *nf* : abundance — **abondant, -dante** [abɔ̃dɑ̃, -dɑ̃t] *adj* : abundant
abonner [abɔne] *vt* : subscribe to — **abonné, -née** [abɔne] *n* : subscriber —**abonnement** [abɔnmɑ̃] *nm* : subscription
aborder [abɔrde] *vt* **1 :** approach **2 :** tackle, deal with — *vi* : (reach) land — **abord** [abɔr] *nm* **1 :** approach **2 d'~ :** at first **3 ~s** *nmpl* : surroundings — **abordable** [abɔrdabl] *adj* **1 :** approachable **2 :** affordable — **abordage** [abɔrdaʒ] *nm* : boarding
aborigène [abɔriʒɛn] *nmf* : aborigine, native — **~** *adj* : aboriginal
abortif, -tive [abɔrtif, -tiv] *adj* : abortive
aboutir [abutir] *vi* **1 :** succeed **2 ~ à :** result in — **aboutissement** [abutismɑ̃] *nm* : result
aboyer [abwaje] {58} *vi* : bark
abraser [abraze] *vt* : abrade — **abrasif, -sive** [abrazif, -ziv] *adj* : abrasive
abréger [abreʒe] {64} *vt* : shorten, abridge — **abrégé** [abreʒe] *nm* : summary — **abrègement** [abrɛʒmɑ̃] *nm* : abridgment
abreuver [abrœve] *vt* **1 :** water **2 ~ de :** shower with — **s'abreuver** *vr* : drink — **abreuvoir** [abrœvwar] *nm* : watering place
abréviation [abrevjasjɔ̃] *nf* : abbreviation
abri [abri] *nm* **1 :** shelter **2 à l'~ :** under cover — **abriter** [abrite] *vt* **1 :** shelter **2** HÉBERGER : house
abricot [abriko] *nm* : apricot
abrier [abrije] {96} *vt Can* : cover
abroger [abrɔʒe] {17} *vt* : repeal

abrupt, -brupte [abrypt] *adj* **1** ESCARPÉ : steep **2** BRUSQUE : abrupt
abrutir [abrytir] *vt* : make stupid — **abruti, -tie** [abryti] *n fam* : fool, idiot
absenter [apsɑ̃te] *v* **s'absenter** *vr* : leave, go away — **absence** [apsɑ̃s] *nf* : absence — **absent, -sente** [apsɑ̃, -sɑ̃t] *adj* : absent — ~ *n* : absentee
absolu, -lue [apsɔly] *adj* : absolute — **absolu** *nm* : absolute — **absolument** [-lymɑ̃] *adv* : absolutely
absolution [apsɔlysjɔ̃] *nf* : absolution
absorber [apsɔrbe] *vt* **1** : absorb **2** : take (medicine) — **absorbant, -bante** [apsɔrbɑ̃, -bɑ̃t] *adj* **1** : absorbent **2** : engrossing — **absorption** [apsɔrpsjɔ̃] *nf* : absorption
absoudre [apsudr] {1} *vt* : absolve
abstenir [apstənir] {92} *v* **s'abstenir** *vr* **1** : abstain **2** ~ **de** : refrain from — **abstinence** [apstinɑ̃s] *nf* : abstinence
abstraction [apstraksjɔ̃] *nf* **1** : abstraction **2 faire ~ de** : set aside — **abstraire** [apstrɛr] {40} *vt* : abstract — **abstrait, -traite** [apstrɛ, -trɛt] *adj* : abstract — **abstrait** *nm* : abstract
absurde [apsyrd] *adj* : absurd — **absurdité** [apsyrdite] *nf* : absurdity
abuser [abyze] *vt* : deceive — *vi* ~ **de** **1** : misuse **2** : exploit — **s'abuser** *vr* : be mistaken — **abusif, -sive** [abyzif, -ziv] *adj* **1** EXAGÉRÉ : excessive **2** IMPROPRE : incorrect
académie [akademi] *nf* : academy — **académique** [akademik] *adj* : academic
Acadien, -dienne [akadjɛ̃, -djɛn] *n* **1** : Acadian **2** : Cajun — **acadien, -dienne** *adj* **1** : Acadian **2** : Cajun
acajou [akaʒu] *nm* : mahogany
acariâtre [akarjatr] *adj* : cantankerous
accabler [akable] *vt* **1** ÉCRASER : overwhelm **2** : condemn — **accablant, -blante** [akablɑ̃, -blɑ̃t] *adj* : overwhelming — **accablement** [akabləmɑ̃] *nm* : despondency
accalmie [akalmi] *nf* : lull
accaparer [akapare] *vt* : monopolize
accéder [aksede] {87} *vi* **1** ~ **à** : reach, obtain **2** ~ **à** : accede to
accélérer [akselere] {87} *v* : accelerate — **accélérateur** *nm* : accelerator — **accélération** [akselerasjɔ̃] *nf* : acceleration
accent [aksɑ̃] *nm* **1** : accent **2** : stress, emphasis — **accentuer** [aksɑ̃tɥe] *vt* **1** : accent, stress **2** : emphasize — **s'accentuer** *vr* : become more pronounced
accepter [aksɛpte] *vt* : accept, agree to — **acceptable** [aksɛptabl] *adj* : acceptable — **acceptation** [aksɛptasjɔ̃] *nf* : acceptance
acception [aksɛpsjɔ̃] *nf* : sense, meaning
accès [aksɛ] *nm* **1** : access **2** : entry **3** CRISE : fit, attack — **accessible** [aksɛsibl] *adj* : accessible
accession [aksɛsjɔ̃] *nf* ~ **à** : accession to, attainment of
accessoire [aksɛswar] *nm* **1** : accessory **2** : prop — ~ *adj* : incidental, secondary
accident [aksidɑ̃] *nm* : accident — **accidenté, -tée** [aksidɑ̃te] *adj* **1** : damaged, injured **2** : rough, uneven — ~ *n* : accident victim — **accidentel, -telle** [aksidɑ̃tɛl] *adj* : accidental — **accidentellement** [-tɛlmɑ̃] *adv* : accidentally
acclamer [aklame] *vt* : acclaim, cheer — **acclamation** [aklamasjɔ̃] *nf* : cheering
acclimater [aklimate] *vt* : acclimatize — **s'acclimater** *vr* : adapt
accolade [akɔlad] *nf* **1** ÉTREINTE : embrace **2** : brace sign, bracket
accommoder [akɔmɔde] *vt* : accommodate — **s'accommoder** *vr* ~ **de** : put up with — **accommodant, -dante** [akɔmɔdɑ̃, -dɑ̃t] *adj* : obliging — **accommodement** [akɔmɔdmɑ̃] *nm* : compromise
accompagner [akɔ̃pɑɲe] *vt* : accompany — **accompagnement** [akɔ̃paɲmɑ̃] *nm* : accompaniment
accomplir [akɔ̃plir] *vt* : accomplish — **s'accomplir** *vr* : take place — **accompli, -plie** [akɔ̃pli] *adj* : finished — **accomplissement** [akɔ̃plismɑ̃] *nm* : accomplishment
accordéon [akɔrdeɔ̃] *nm* : accordion
accorder [akɔrde] *vt* **1** : reconcile **2** OCTROYER : grant, bestow — **s'accorder** *vr* : be in agreement — **accord** [akɔr] *nm* **1** : agreement **2** : approval, consent **3** : chord (in music)
accoster [akɔste] *vt* : approach — *vi* : dock, land
accotement [akɔtmɑ̃] *nm* : shoulder (of a road)
accoucher [akuʃe] *vt* : deliver (a baby) — *vi* **1** : be in labor **2** ~ **de** : give birth to — **accouchement** [akuʃmɑ̃] *nm* : childbirth
accouder [akude] *v* **s'accouder** *vr* ~ **à** *or* ~ **sur** : lean (one's elbows) on — **accoudoir** [akudwar] *nm* : armrest

accoupler [akuple] *vt* : couple, link — **s'accoupler** *vr* : mate — **accouplement** [akupləmɑ̃] *nm* **1** : coupling **2** : mating

accourir [akurir] {23} *vi* : come running

accoutrement [akutrəmɑ̃] *nm* : outfit

accoutumer [akutyme] *vt* : accustom — **s'accoutumer** *vr* **~ à** : get accustomed to — **accoutumé, -mée** [akutyme] *adj* : customary

accréditer [akredite] *vt* **1** : accredit **2** : substantiate (a rumor, etc.)

accroc [akro] *nm* **1** : rip, tear **2** OBSTACLE : hitch, snag

accrocher [akrɔʃe] *vt* **1** SUSPENDRE : hang up **2** : hook, hitch **3** HEURTER : bump into **4 ~ l'œil** : catch the eye — *vi* : catch, snag — **s'accrocher** *vr* : hang on, cling — **accrochage** [akrɔʃaʒ] *nm* **1** : hanging, hooking **2** : collision **3** QUERELLE : dispute — **accrocheur, -cheuse** [akrɔʃœr, -ʃøz] *adj* **1** OPINIÂTRE : tenacious **2** ATTRAYANT : eye-catching

accroire [akrwar] {2} *vt* **en faire ~ à** : take in, dupe

accroître [akrwatr] {25} *vt* : increase — **s'accroître** *vr* : grow — **accroissement** [akrwasmɑ̃] *nm* : growth, increase

accroupir [akrupir] *v* **s'accroupir** *vr* : squat

accueillir [akœjir] {3} *vt* : greet — **accueil** [akœj] *nm* : welcome, reception — **accueillant, -lante** [akœjɑ̃, -jɑ̃t] *adj* : welcoming, hospitable

acculer [akyle] *vt* : corner

accumuler [akymyle] *vt* : accumulate — **s'accumuler** *vr* : pile up — **accumulation** [akymylasjɔ̃] *nf* : accumulation

accuser [akyze] *vt* **1** : accuse **2 ~ réception de** : acknowledge receipt of — **accusateur, -trice** [akyzatœr, -tris] *adj* : incriminating — **accusation** [akyzasjɔ̃] *nf* : accusation — **accusé, -sée** *n* : defendant, accused

acerbe [asɛrb] *adj* : acerbic

acéré, -rée [asere] *adj* : sharp

acharner [aʃarne] *v* **s'acharner** *vr* **1** S'OBSTINER : persevere **2 ~ sur** : persecute, hound — **acharné, -née** [aʃarne] *adj* : relentless — **acharnement** [aʃarnəmɑ̃] *nm* : relentlessness

achat [aʃa] *nm* **1** : purchase **2 faire des ~s** : go shopping

acheminer [aʃmine] *vt* **1** : transport **2** : forward (mail) — **s'acheminer** *vr* **~ vers** : head for — **acheminement** [aʃminmɑ̃] *nm* : dispatch, routing

acheter [aʃte] {20} *vt* : buy, purchase — **acheteur, -teuse** [aʃtœr, -tøz] *n* : buyer

achever [aʃve] {52} *vt* : complete, finish — **s'achever** *vr* : draw to a close — **achèvement** [aʃɛvmɑ̃] *nm* : completion

acide [asid] *adj & nm* : acid — **acidité** [asidite] *nf* : sourness, acidity

acier [asje] *nm* : steel — **aciérie** [asjeri] *nf* : steelworks

acné [akne] *nf* : acne

acolyte [akɔlit] *nm* : accomplice

acompte [akɔ̃t] *nm* : deposit, installment

à–côté [akote] *nm, pl* **à–côtés** : extra, perk

à–coup [aku] *nm, pl* **à–coups** : jerk, jolt

acoustique [akustik] *adj* : acoustic — **~** *nf* : acoustics

acquérir [akerir] {21} *vt* **1** : acquire **2** : purchase — **acquéreur, -reuse** [akerœr, -røz] *n* : buyer

acquiescer [akjese] {6} *vi* : agree

acquis, -quise [aki, -kiz] *adj* **1** : acquired **2** : established — **acquis** *nms & pl* : knowledge — **acquisition** [akizisjɔ̃] *nf* : acquisition

acquitter [akite] *vt* **1** : acquit **2** PAYER : pay — **s'acquitter** *vr* **~ de 1** : carry out **2** : pay off — **acquit** [aki] *nm* : receipt — **acquittement** [akitmɑ̃] *nm* : payment (of a debt)

acre [akr] *nf* : acre *Can*

âcre [akr] *adj* : acrid — **âcreté** [akrəte] *nf* : bitterness

acrobate [akrɔbat] *nmf* : acrobat — **acrobatie** [akrɔbasi] *nf* : acrobatics — **acrobatique** [akrɔbatik] *adj* : acrobatic

acrylique [akrilik] *adj & nm* : acrylic

acte [akt] *nm* **1** : action, deed **2** : act (in theater) **3** : certificate, document **4 ~s** *nmpl* : proceedings

acteur, -trice [aktœr, -tris] *n* : actor, actress *f*

actif, -tive [aktif, -tiv] *adj* : active — **actif** *nm* **1** : assets *pl* **2** : active voice

action [aksjɔ̃] *nf* **1** : action, act **2** EFFET : effect **3** : share (in finance) — **actionnaire** [aksjɔnɛr] *nmf* : shareholder — **actionner** [aksjɔne] *vt* **1** : engage, set in motion **2** : sue

activer [aktive] *vt* **1** : activate **2** HÂTER : speed up — **s'activer** *vr* : bustle about

activiste [aktivist] *adj & nmf* : activist — **activisme** [aktivism] *nm* : activism
activité [aktivite] *nf* : activity
actualité [aktɥalite] *nf* **1** : current events *pl* **2 ~s** *nfpl* : news — **actualiser** [aktɥalize] *vt* : update, modernize
actuel, -tuelle [aktɥɛl] *adj* : current, present — **actuellement** [-tɥɛlmɑ̃] *adv* : at present
acuité [akɥite] *nf* : acuteness
acupuncture [akypɔ̃ktyr] *nf* : acupuncture
adage [adaʒ] *nm* : adage
adapter [adapte] *vt* : adapt, fit — **s'adapter** *vr* : adapt — **adaptation** [adaptasjɔ̃] *nf* : adaptation — **adaptateur** [adaptatœr] *nm* : adapter
additif [aditif] *nm* : additive
addition [adisjɔ̃] *nf* **1** : addition **2** NOTE : bill, check — **additionnel, -nelle** [adisjɔnɛl] *adj* : additional — **additionner** [adisjɔne] *vt* : add (up)
adepte [adɛpt] *nmf* : follower
adéquat, -quate [adekwa, -kwat] *adj* **1** SUFFISANT : adequate **2** APPROPRIÉ : appropriate
adhérer [adere] {87} *vi* **1** : adhere **2 ~ à** : join — **adhérence** [aderɑ̃s] *nf* : adhesion, grip — **adhérent, -rente** [aderɑ̃, -rɑ̃t] *adj* : adhering, sticking — **~** *n* : member
adhésif, -sive [adezif, -ziv] *adj* : adhesive — **adhésif** *nm* : adhesive — **adhésion** [adezjɔ̃] *nf* **1** : adhesion **2** : adherence, support **3** AFFILIATION : membership
adieu [adjø] *nm, pl* **adieux** : farewell, good-bye
adjacent, -cente [adʒasɑ̃, -sɑ̃t] *adj* : adjacent
adjectif [adʒɛktif] *nm* : adjective
adjoindre [adʒwɛ̃dr] {50} *vt* **1** : appoint **2** : add, attach — **s'adjoindre** *vr* **~ qqn** : take s.o. on, hire s.o. — **adjoint, -jointe** [adʒwɛ̃, -ʒwɛ̃t] *adj & n* : assistant
adjonction [adʒɔ̃ksjɔ̃] *nf* : addition
admettre [admɛtr] {53} *vt* : admit
administrer [administre] *vt* : administer — **administrateur, -trice** [administratœr, -tris] *n* : director, administrator — **administratif, -tive** [administratif, -tiv] *adj* : administrative — **administration** [administrasjɔ̃] *nf* : administration
admirer [admire] *vt* : admire — **admirable** [admirabl] *adj* : admirable — **admirateur, -trice** [admiratœr, -tris] *n* : admirer — **admiratif, -tive** [admiratif, -tiv] *adj* : admiring — **admiration** [admirasjɔ̃] *nf* : admiration
admissible [admisibl] *adj* : acceptable, eligible — **admission** [admisjɔ̃] *nf* : admittance
admonester [admɔnɛste] *vt* : admonish
ADN [adeɛn] *nm* (*a*cide *d*ésoxyribo*n*ucléique) : DNA
adolescence [adɔlesɑ̃s] *nf* : adolescence — **adolescent, -cente** [-lesɑ̃, -sɑ̃t] *adj & n* : adolescent
adopter [adɔpte] *vt* : adopt — **adoptif, -tive** [adɔptif, -tiv] *adj* : adoptive, adopted —**adoption** [adɔpsjɔ̃] *nf* : adoption
adorer [adɔre] *vt* : adore, worship — **adorable** [adɔrabl] *adj* : adorable
adosser [adose] *vt* : lean — **s'adosser** *vr* **~ à** *or* **~ contre** : lean back against
adoucir [adusir] *vt* **1** : soften **2** : alleviate, ease — **s'adoucir** *vr* : become milder, mellow — **adoucissement** [adusismɑ̃] *nm* **1** : softening **2** : alleviation
adresser [adrese] *vt* : address — **adresse** [adrɛs] *nf* **1** : address **2** HABILETÉ : skill — **s'adresser** *vr* **~ à** : speak to
adroit, -droite [adrwa, -drwat] *adj* HABILE : skillful
adulte [adylt] *adj & nmf* : adult
adultère [adyltɛr] *nm* : adultery — **~** *adj* : adulterous
advenir [advənir] {4} *v impers* **1** : happen, occur **2 ~ de** : become of
adverbe [advɛrb] *nm* : adverb
adversaire [advɛrsɛr] *nmf* : opponent — **adverse** [advɛrs] *adj* : opposing — **adversité** [advɛrsite] *nf* : adversity
aérer [aere] {87} *vt* : air out — **s'aérer** *vr* : get some fresh air
aérien, -rienne [aerjɛ̃, -rjɛn] *adj* : air, aerial
aérobic [aerɔbik] *nm* : aerobics
aérodynamique [aerɔdinamik] *adj* : aerodynamic
aérogare [aerɔgar] *nf* : air terminal
aéroglisseur [aerɔglisœr] *nm* : hovercraft
aéroport [aerɔpɔr] *nm* : airport
aérosol [aerɔsɔl] *nm* : aerosol
affable [afabl] *adj* : affable
affaiblir [afeblir] *vt* : weaken — **s'affaiblir** *vr* **1** : become weak **2** ATTÉNUER : fade
affaire [afɛr] *nf* **1** : affair **2** CAS : mat-

ter **3** ENTREPRISE : business **4** TRANSACTION : deal **5 ~s** *nfpl* : belongings **6 ~s** *nfpl* : business **7 avoir ~ à** : deal with — **affairer** [afere] *v* **s'affairer** *vr* : be busy — **affairé, -rée** [afere] *adj* : busy

affaisser [afese] *v* **s'affaisser** *vr* : collapse, give way — **affaissement** [afɛsmɑ̃] *nm* : sagging, sinking

affaler [afale] *v* **s'affaler** *vr* : collapse

affamé, -mée [afame] *adj* : famished

affecter [afɛkte] *vt* **1** : affect **2** NOMMER : appoint **3** ASSIGNER : allocate **4** FEINDRE : feign — **affectation** [afɛktasjɔ̃] *nf* **1** : appointment **2 ~ des fonds** : allocation of funds — **affecté, -tée** [afɛkte] *adj* : mannered, affected

affectif, -tive [afɛktif, -tiv] *adj* : emotional

affection [afɛksjɔ̃] *nf* **1** : affection **2** : ailment — **affectionner** [afɛksjɔne] *vt* : be fond of — **affectueux, -tueuse** [afɛktɥø, -tɥøz] *adj* : affectionate — **affectueusement** [-tɥøzmɑ̃] *adv* : fondly

afférent, -rente [aferɑ̃, -rɑ̃t] *adj* **~ à** : pertaining to

affermir [afɛrmir] *vt* : strengthen

affiche [afiʃ] *nf* : poster, notice — **affichage** [afiʃaʒ] *nm* **1** : posting, publicizing **2 ~ numérique** : digital display — **afficher** [afiʃe] *vt* **1** : post, put up **2** : show, display

affilée [afile] **d'~** *adv phr* : in a row

affiler [afile] {96} *vt* : sharpen

affilier [afilje] *vt* : affiliate — **s'affilier** *vr* **~ à** : join

affiner [afine] *vt* : refine

affinité [afinite] *nf* : affinity

affirmatif, -tive [afirmatif, -tiv] *adj* : affirmative — **affirmative** *nf* : affirmative

affirmer [afirme] *vt* : affirm, assert — **s'affirmer** *vr* : assert oneself — **affirmation** [afirmasjɔ̃] *nf* : assertion

affliger [afliʒe] {17} *vt* : afflict, distress — **affliction** [afliksjɔ̃] *nf* : affliction — **affligeant, -geante** [afliʒɑ̃, -ʒɑ̃t] *adj* : distressing

affluer [aflye] *vi* **1** COULER : flow **2 ~ vers** : flock to — **affluence** [aflyɑ̃s] *nf* **1** : crowd **2 heure d'~** : rush hour — **affluent** [aflyɑ̃] *nm* : tributary

afflux [afly] *nm* : influx, rush

affoler [afɔle] *vt* EFFRAYER : terrify — **s'affoler** *vr* : panic — **affolé, -lée** [afɔle] *adj* : frightened — **affolement** [afɔlmɑ̃] *nm* : panic

affranchir [afrɑ̃ʃir] *vt* **1** LIBÉRER : liberate, free **2** : stamp (a letter) — **affranchissement** [afrɑ̃ʃismɑ̃] *nm* **1** : liberation **2** : stamping, postage

affréter [afrete] {87} *vt* : charter

affreux, -freuse [afrø, -frøz] *adj* : horrible — **affreusement** [afrøzmɑ̃] *adv* : horribly

affronter [afrɔ̃te] *vt* : confront — **s'affronter** *vr* : confront each other — **affront** [afrɔ̃] *nm* : affront — **affrontement** [afrɔ̃tmɑ̃] *nm* : confrontation

affûter [afyte] *vt* : sharpen — **affût** [afy] *nm* **être à l'~ de** : be on the lookout for

afin [afɛ̃] *adv* **1 ~ de** : in order to **2 ~ que** : so that

africain, -caine [afrikɛ̃, -kɛn] *adj* : African

agacer [agase] {6} *vt* : irritate — **agaçant, -çante** [agasɑ̃, -sɑ̃t] *adj* : annoying — **agacement** [agasmɑ̃] *nm* : annoyance

âge [aʒ] *nm* **1** : age (of a person) **2** : age, era — **âgé, -gée** [aʒe] *adj* **1** VIEUX : elderly **2 ~ de 10 ans** : 10 years old

agence [aʒɑ̃s] *nf* : agency, office

agencer [aʒɑ̃se] {6} *vt* : arrange, lay out — **agencement** [aʒɑ̃smɑ̃] *nm* : layout

agenda [aʒɛ̃da] *nm* : appointment book

agenouiller [aʒnuje] *v* **s'agenouiller** *vr* : kneel

agent, -gente [aʒɑ̃, -ʒɑ̃t] *n* **1** : agent **2 ~ de police** : police officer

agglomération [aglɔmerasjɔ̃] *nf* : urban area

agglutiner [aglytine] *vt* : stick together

aggraver [agrave] *vt* : aggravate, make worse — **s'aggraver** *vr* EMPIRER : worsen — **aggravation** [agravasjɔ̃] *nf* : worsening

agile [aʒil] *adj* : agile — **agilité** [aʒilite] *nf* : agility

agir [aʒir] *vi* **1** : act **2** SE COMPORTER : behave **3** : take effect (of medication) — **s'agir** *vr* **il s'agit de** : it is a question of — **agissements** [aʒismɑ̃] *nmpl* : schemes, dealings

agiter [aʒite] *vt* **1** SECOUER : shake **2** TROUBLER : disturb — **s'agiter** *vr* **1** : bustle about **2** : fidget — **agitation** [aʒitasjɔ̃] *nf* **1** : agitation **2** : (political) unrest — **agité, -tée** [aʒite] *adj* **1** : restless **2** : rough, choppy

agneau [aɲo] *nm, pl* **agneaux** : lamb

agonie [agɔni] *nf* : (death) throes *pl* — **agoniser** [agɔnize] *vi* : be dying

agrafe [agraf] *nf* **1** : hook, fastener **2**

: staple — **agrafer** [agrafe] *vt* **1** : fasten **2** : staple — **agrafeuse** [agraføz] *nf* : stapler

agrandir [agrɑ̃dir] *vt* : enlarge — **s'agrandir** *vr* : expand, grow — **agrandissement** [agrɑ̃dismɑ̃] *nm* : enlargement, expansion

agréable [agreabl] *adj* : nice, pleasant — **agréablement** [-abləmɑ̃] *adv* : pleasantly

agréer [agree] *vt* **1** : accept **2 veuillez ~ l'expression de mes sentiments distingués** : sincerely yours — **agréé, agréée** [agree] *adj* : authorized

agrégé, -gée [agreʒe] *n France* : certified teacher or professor — **agrégation** [agregasjɔ̃] *nf France* : qualifying exam for teachers or professors

agrément [agremɑ̃] *nm* **1** : charm, appeal **2 voyage d'~** : pleasure trip — **agrémenter** [agremɑ̃te] *vt* : embellish

agrès [agrɛ] *nmpl* : (gymnastic) apparatus

agresser [agrese] *vt* : attack, assault — **agresseur** [agrɛsœr] *nm* : attacker — **agressif, -sive** [agrɛsif, -siv] *adj* : aggressive — **agression** [agrɛsjɔ̃] *nf* **1** : attack **2** : aggression — **agressivité** [agrɛsivite] *nf* : aggressiveness

agricole [agrikɔl] *adj* : agricultural — **agriculteur, -trice** [agrikyltœr, -tris] *n* : farmer — **agriculture** [agricyltyr] *nf* : agriculture, farming

agripper [agripe] *vt* : clutch, grab — **s'agripper** *vr* **~ à** : cling to, clutch

agrumes [agrym] *nmpl* : citrus fruits

aguets [agɛ] **aux ~** *adv phr* : on the lookout

ah [a] *interj* : oh!, ah!

ahuri, -rie [ayri] *adj* : dumbfounded — **ahurissant, -sante** [ayrisɑ̃, -sɑ̃t] *adj* : astounding

aider [ede] *vt* : help — **aide** *nf* **1** : aid **2 à l'~ de** : with the help of — **aide** *nmf* : assistant

aïe [aj] *interj* : ouch!, ow!

aïeux [ajø] *nmpl* : ancestors

aigle [ɛgl] *nm* : eagle

aigre [ɛgr] *adj* : sour, tart — **aigre-doux, -douce** [ɛgrədu, -dus] *adj* : bittersweet — **aigreur** [ɛgrœr] *nf* : sourness — **aigri** [egri] *adj* : embittered

aigu, -guë [egy] *adj* **1** : sharp, keen **2** VIF : acute **3** STRIDENT : shrill

aiguille [egɥij] *nf* **1** : needle **2** : hand (of a clock)

aiguillon [egɥijɔ̃] *nm* **1** : goad **2** : stinger (of an insect)

aiguiser [egize] *vt* **1** : sharpen **2 ~ l'appétit** : whet the appetite

ail [aj] *nm* : garlic

aile [ɛl] *nf* **1** : wing **2** : fender (of an automobile) — **ailier** [elje] *nm* : wing, end (in sports)

ailleurs [ajœr] *adv* **1** : elsewhere **2 d'~** : besides, moreover **3 par ~** : furthermore

aimable [ɛmabl] *adj* : kind — **aimablement** [ɛmabləmɑ̃] *adv* : kindly

aimant[1]**, -mante** [ɛmɑ̃, -mɑ̃t] *adj* : loving, caring

aimant[2] *nm* : magnet

aimer [eme] *vt* **1** : love, like **2 ~ mieux** : prefer

aine [ɛn] *nf* : groin

aîné, -née [ene] *adj* **1** : older, oldest **2** : senior — **~** *n* **1** : elder child, eldest child **2 aînés** *nmpl* : elders **3 il est mon aîné** : he's older than me

ainsi [ɛ̃si] *adv* **1** : in this way, thus **2 ~ que** : just as **3 ~ que** : as well as **4 et ~ de suite** : and so on **5 pour ~ dire** : so to speak

air [ɛr] *nm* **1** : air **2** MÉLODIE : tune **3** EXPRESSION : air, look **4 avoir l'~** : look, seem

aire [ɛr] *nf* **1** : area **2 ~ d'atterrissage** : landing strip

aisance [ezɑ̃s] *nf* **1** : ease **2** PROSPÉRITÉ : affluence — **aise** *nf* **1** : ease **2 être à l'~** : be comfortable — **aisé, -sée** [eze] *adj* **1** : easy **2** RICHE : well-off — **aisément** [ezemɑ̃] *adv* : easily

aisselle [ɛsɛl] *nf* : armpit

ajourner [aʒurne] *vt* : adjourn — **ajournement** [aʒurnəmɑ̃] *nm* : adjournment

ajouter [aʒute] *vt* : add — **ajout** [aʒu] *nm* : addition

ajuster [aʒyste] *vt* : adjust — **ajustement** [aʒystəmɑ̃] *nm* : adjustment

alarmer [alarme] *vt* : alarm — **s'alarmer** *vr* : become alarmed — **alarmant, -mante** [alarmɑ̃, -mɑ̃t] *adj* : alarming — **alarme** [alarm] *nf* : alarm

album [albɔm] *nm* : album

alcool [alkɔl] *nm* : alcohol — **alcoolique** [alkɔlik] *adj & nmf* : alcoholic — **alcoolisé, -sée** [alkɔlize] *adj* : alcoholic — **alcoolisme** [-kɔlism] *nm* : alcoholism

alcôve [alkov] *nf* : alcove

aléa [alea] *nm* : risk — **aléatoire** [aleatwar] *adj* **1** : risky, uncertain **2** : random

alentour [alɑ̃tur] *adv* : around, sur-

rounding — **alentours** [alɑ̃tur] *nmpl* **aux ~ de** : around, in the vicinity of
alerter [alɛrte] *vt* : alert, warn — **alerte** [alɛrt] *adj* : alert, lively — **alerte** *nf* : alert, warning
algèbre [alʒɛbr] *nf* : algebra
algérien, -rienne [alʒerjɛ̃, -rjɛn] *adj* : Algerian
algue [alg] *nf* : seaweed
alias [aljas] *adv* : alias
alibi [alibi] *nm* : alibi
aliéner [aljene] {87} *vt* : alienate — **aliénation** [aljenasjɔ̃] *nf* : alienation
aligner [aliɲe] *vt* : align — **s'aligner** *vr* : fall into line — **alignement** [aliɲmɑ̃] *nm* : alignment
alimenter [alimɑ̃te] *vt* **1** : feed **2** APPROVISIONNER : supply — **aliment** [alimɑ̃] *nm* : food — **alimentation** [alimɑ̃tasjɔ̃] *nf* **1** : diet, nourishment **2 magasin d'~** : grocery store
alinéa [alinea] *nm* : paragraph
alité, -tée [alite] *adj* : bedridden
allaiter [alete] *vt* : nurse, breast-feed — **allaitement** [alɛtmɑ̃] *nm* : breast-feeding
allant [alɑ] *nm* : drive, spirit
allécher [aleʃe] {87} *vt* : allure, tempt — **alléchant, -chante** [aleʃɑ̃, -ʃɑ̃t] *adj* : tempting
allée [ale] *nf* **1** : path, lane, walk **2** : aisle **3 ~s et venues** : comings and goings
allégation [alegasjɔ̃] *nf* : allegation
allégeance [aleʒɑ̃s] *nf* : allegiance
alléger [aleʒe] {64} *vt* **1** : lighten **2** SOULAGER : alleviate
allègre [alɛgr] *adj* : cheerful, lively — **allégresse** [alegrɛs] *nf* : elation
alléguer [alege] {87} *vt* : allege
allemand, -mande [almɑ̃, -mɑ̃d] *adj* : German — **allemand** *nm* : German (language)
aller [ale] {5} *vi* **1** : go **2** MARCHER : work **3** : proceed, get along **4 ~ à** : fit, suit **5 allons-y** : let's go **6 comment allez-vous?** : how are you? **7 elle va bien** : she is fine — *v aux* : be going to, be about to — **s'en ~** *vr* : go away — **~** *nm* **1** *or* **~ simple** : one-way (ticket) **2 aller–retour** : round-trip (ticket)
allergie [alɛrʒi] *nf* : allergy — **allergique** [alɛrʒik] *adj* : allergic
alliage [aljaʒ] *nm* : alloy
allier [alje] {96} *vt* : combine — **s'allier** *vr* **~ à** : become allied with — **alliance** [aljɑ̃s] *nf* **1** : alliance **2** : wedding ring **3 par ~** : by marriage — **allié, -liée** *n* : ally
alligator [aligatɔr] *nm* : alligator
allô [alo] *interj* : hello
allocation [alɔkasjɔ̃] *nf* **1** : allocation **2 ~ de chômage** : unemployment benefit
allocution [alɔkysjɔ̃] *nf* : short speech, address
allonger [alɔ̃ʒe] {17} *vt* **1** : lengthen **2** ÉTIRER : stretch (out) — *vi* : get longer — **s'allonger** *vr* SE COUCHER : lie down
allouer [alwe] *vt* : allocate
allumer [alyme] *vt* **1** : light, ignite **2** : turn on, switch on — **s'allumer** *vr* : come on, light (up) — **allumage** *nm* **1** : lighting **2** : (automobile) ignition — **allumette** [alymɛt] *nf* : match
allure [alyr] *nf* **1** APPARENCE : appearance **2** : speed, pace **3 à toute ~** : at full speed
allusion [alyzjɔ̃] *nf* : allusion
almanach [almana] *nm* : almanac
alors [alɔr] *adv* **1** : then **2 ~ que** : while, when **3 ~ que** : even though **4 et ~?** : so?, so what? **5 ou ~** : or else
alouette [alwɛt] *nf* : lark
alourdir [alurdir] *vt* : weigh down — **s'alourdir** *vr* : become heavy
alphabet [alfabɛ] *nm* : alphabet — **alphabétique** [alfabetik] *adj* : alphabetical
alpin, -pine [alpɛ̃, -pin] *adj* : alpine — **alpinisme** [alpinism] *nm* : mountain climbing
altérer [altere] {87} *vt* **1** : distort **2** ABÎMER : spoil — **s'altérer** *vr* : deteriorate
alterner [altɛrne] *v* : alternate — **alternatif, -tive** [altɛrnatif, -tiv] *adj* : alternative — **alternative** [alternativ] *nf* : alternative
altesse [altɛs] *nf* **son Altesse** : His (Her) Highness
altier, -tière [altje, -tjɛr] *adj* : haughty
altitude [altityd] *nf* : altitude
altruisme [altrɥism] *nm* : altruism
aluminium [alyminjɔm] *nm* : aluminum
amabilité [amabilite] *nf* : kindness
amadouer [amadwe] *vt* : cajole
amaigrir [amegrir] *vt* : make thin — **amaigrissement** [amegrismɑ̃] *nm* : weight loss
amalgame [amalgam] *nm* : mixture
amande [amɑ̃d] *nf* **1** : almond **2** : kernel (of a fruit or nut)

amant, -mante [amɑ̃, -mɑ̃t] *n* : lover
amarrer [amare] *vt* : moor — **amarrage** [amaraʒ] *nm* : mooring
amas [ama] *nm* : pile, heap — **amasser** [amase] *vt* ACCUMULER : amass — **s'amasser** *vr* : pile up
amateur [amatœr] *nm* **1** : enthusiast **2** : amateur
ambages [ɑ̃baʒ] **sans ~** *adv phr* : plainly
ambassade [ɑ̃basad] *nf* : embassy — **ambassadeur, -drice** [ɑ̃basadœr, -dris] *n* : ambassador
ambiance [ɑ̃bjɑ̃s] *nf* : atmosphere — **ambiant, -biante** [ɑ̃bjɑ̃, -bjɑ̃t] *adj* : surrounding
ambigu, -guë [ɑ̃bigy] *adj* : ambiguous — **ambiguïté** [ɑ̃bigɥite] *nf* : ambiguity
ambitieux, -tieuse [ɑ̃bisjø, -sjøz] *adj* : ambitious — **ambition** [ɑ̃bisjɔ̃] *nf* : ambition
ambivalent, -lente [ɑ̃bivalɑ̃, -lɑ̃t] *adj* : ambivalent
ambre [ɑ̃br] *nm* : amber
ambulant, -lante [ɑ̃bylɑ̃, -lɑ̃t] *adj* : itinerant — **ambulance** [ɑ̃bylɑ̃s] *nf* : ambulance
ambulatoire [ɑ̃bylatwar] *adj* : ambulatory
âme [am] *nf* **1** : soul **2 état d'~** : state of mind
améliorer [ameljɔre] *vt* : improve — **s'améliorer** *vr* : get better — **amélioration** [ameljɔrasjɔ̃] *nf* : improvement
aménager [amenaʒe] {17} *vt* : fit out — **aménagement** [amenaʒmɑ̃] *nm* **1** : fitting out **2** : development (of a region, etc.)
amender [amɑ̃de] *vt* : amend — **amende** [amɑ̃d] *nf* : fine — **amendement** [amɑ̃dmɑ̃] *nm* : amendment
amener [amne] {52} *vt* **1** : bring **2** OCCASIONNER : cause
amenuiser [amənɥize] *v* **s'amenuiser** *vr* : dwindle
amer, -mère [amɛr] *adj* : bitter — **amèrement** [amɛrmɑ̃] *adv* : bitterly
américain, -caine [amerikɛ̃, -kɛn] *adj* : American
amérindien, -dienne [amerɛ̃djɛ̃, -djɛn] *adj* : Native American
amertume [amɛrtym] *nf* : bitterness
ameublement [amœbləmɑ̃] *nm* **1** : furnishing **2** MEUBLES : furniture
ami, -mie [ami] *n* **1** : friend **2** *or* **petit ~** : boyfriend **3** *or* **petite ~e** : girlfriend
amiable [amjabl] *adj* **à l'~** : amicable
amiante [amjɑ̃t] *nm* : asbestos
amibe [amib] *nf* : amoeba
amical, -cale [amikal] *adj, mpl* **-caux** [-ko] : friendly
amidon [amidɔ̃] *nm* : starch — **amidonner** [amidɔne] *vt* : starch
amincir [amɛ̃sir] *vt* : make thinner — **s'amincir** *vr* : get thinner
amiral [amiral] *nm, pl* **-raux** [-ro] : admiral
amitié [amitje] *nf* **1** : friendship **2 ~s** *nfpl* : best regards
ammoniaque [amɔnjak] *nf* : ammonia
amnésie [amnezi] *nf* : amnesia
amnistie [amnisti] *nf* : amnesty
amoindrir [amwɛ̃drir] *vt* : lessen — **s'amoindrir** *vr* : diminish
amollir [amɔlir] *vt* : soften
amonceler [amɔ̃sle] {18} *vt* : accumulate — **s'amonceler** *vr* : pile up — **amoncellement** [amɔ̃sɛlmɑ̃] *nm* : pile, heap
amont [amɔ̃] *nm* **en ~** : upstream
amorce [amɔrs] *nf* **1** DÉBUT : beginning(s) **2** APPÂT : bait **3** : detonator, fuse — **amorcer** [amɔrse] {6} *vt* **1** COMMENCER : begin **2** APPÂTER : bait **3** : boot (a computer) — **s'amorcer** *vr* : begin
amorphe [amɔrf] *adj* : listless
amorti [amɔrti] *nm Can* : bunt (in baseball)
amortir [amɔrtir] *vt* : cushion, deaden — **amortisseur** [amɔrtisœr] *nm* : shock absorber
amour [amur] *nm* : love — **amoureusement** [amurøzmɑ̃] *adv* : lovingly — **amoureux, -reuse** [amurø, -røz] *adj* **1** : loving **2 être ~** : be in love — **~** *n* : lover — **amour–propre** [amurprɔpr] *nm* : self-esteem
amovible [amɔvibl] *adj* : removable
amphibien [ɑ̃fibjɛ̃] *nm* : amphibian
amphithéâtre [ɑ̃fiteatr] *nm* **1** : amphitheater **2** : lecture hall
ample [ɑ̃pl] *adj* : ample — **ampleur** [ɑ̃plœr] *nf* : extent, range
amplifier [ɑ̃plifje] {96} *vt* **1** : amplify **2** : expand — **s'amplifier** *vr* : increase — **amplificateur** [ɑ̃plifikatœr] *nm* : amplifier
ampoule [ɑ̃pul] *nf* **1** : lightbulb **2** CLOQUE : blister **3** : vial (in medicine)
amputer [ɑ̃pyte] *vt* **1** : amputate **2** : cut drastically — **amputation** [ɑ̃pytasjɔ̃] *nf* **1** : amputation **2** : drastic cut
amuse–gueule [amyzgøl] *nms & pl* : appetizer
amuser [amyze] *vt* : amuse — **s'a-**

muser *vr* **1** : play **2** : enjoy oneself — **amusant, -sante** [amyzɑ̃, -zɑ̃t] *adj* : amusing — **amusement** [amyzmɑ̃] *nm* : amusement

amygdale [amidal] *nf* : tonsil

an [ɑ̃] *nm* **1** : year **2 le Nouvel An** : New Year's Day

analgésique [analʒezik] *adj & nm* : analgesic

analogie [analɔʒi] *nf* : analogy — **analogue** [analɔg] *adj* : similar

analphabète [analfabɛt] *adj* : illiterate — **analphabétisme** [analfabetism] *nm* : illiteracy

analyse [analiz] *nf* **1** : analysis **2** : (blood) test — **analyser** [analize] *vt* : analyze — **analytique** [analitik] *adj* : analytic, analytical

ananas [anana(s)] *nms & pl* : pineapple

anarchie [anarʃi] *nf* : anarchy

anatomie [anatɔmi] *nf* : anatomy — **anatomique** [anatɔmik] *adj* : anatomic(al)

ancêtre [ɑ̃sɛtr] *nmf* : ancestor

anchois [ɑ̃ʃwa] *nms & pl* : anchovy

ancien, -cienne [ɑ̃sjɛ̃, -sjɛn] *adj* **1** : former **2** VIEUX : ancient, old — **anciennement** [ɑ̃sjɛnmɑ̃] *adv* : formerly — **ancienneté** [ɑ̃sjɛnte] *nf* **1** : oldness **2** : seniority

ancre [ɑ̃kr] *nf* : anchor — **ancrer** [ɑ̃kre] *vt* : anchor

andouille [ɑ̃duj] *nf fam* **1** : andouille (sausage) **2** *fam* : fool, sap

âne [an] *nm* : ass, donkey

anéantir [aneɑ̃tir] *vt* **1** DÉTRUIRE : annihilate **2** ACCABLER : overwhelm — **anéantissement** [aneɑ̃tismɑ̃] *nm* : annihilation

anecdote [anɛkdɔt] *nf* : anecdote

anémie [anemi] *nf* : anemia — **anémique** [anemik] *adj* : anemic

ânerie [anri] *nf* : stupid mistake or remark

anesthésie [anɛstezi] *nf* : anesthesia — **anesthésique** [anɛstezik] *adj & nm* : anesthetic

aneth [anɛt] *nm* : dill

ange [ɑ̃ʒ] *nm* : angel — **angélique** [ɑ̃ʒelik] *adj* : angelic

anglais, -glaise [ɑ̃glɛ, -glɛz] *adj* : English — **anglais** *nm* : English (language)

angle [ɑ̃gl] *nm* **1** : angle **2** : corner

anglophone [ɑ̃glɔfɔn] *adj* : English-speaking

anglo–saxon, -saxonne [ɑ̃glɔsaksɔ̃, -saksɔn] *adj* : Anglo-Saxon

angoisser [ɑ̃gwase] *vt* : distress — **angoissant, -sante** [ɑ̃gwasɑ̃, -sɑ̃t] *adj* : agonizing — **angoisse** [ɑ̃gwas] *nf* : anguish

anguille [ɑ̃gij] *nf* : eel

anguleux, -leuse [ɑ̃gylø, -løz] *adj* : angular

animal [animal] *nm, pl* **-maux** [-mo] : animal

animateur, -trice [animatœr, -tris] *n* **1** : moderator **2** : (television show) host

animer [anime] *vt* : enliven — **s'animer** *vr* : come to life — **animation** [animasjɔ̃] *nf* : animation — **animé, -mée** [anime] *adj* : animated, lively

animosité [animɔzite] *nf* : animosity

anis [ani(s)] *nm* : anise

ankyloser [ɑ̃kiloze] *v* **s'ankyloser** *vr* : stiffen (up)

anneau [ano] *nm, pl* **-neaux** : ring

année [ane] *nf* **1** : year **2 ~ bissextile** : leap year

annexe [anɛks] *adj* **1** : adjoining, attached **2** : related — **~** *nf* : annex — **annexer** [anɛkse] *vt* : annex

annihiler [aniile] *vt* : annihilate — **annihilation** [aniilasjɔ̃] *nf* : annihilation

anniversaire [anivɛrsɛr] *nm* **1** : anniversary **2** : birthday

annoncer [anɔ̃se] {6} *vt* **1** : announce **2** DÉNOTER : indicate — **s'annoncer** *vr* : appear (to be) — **annonce** [anɔ̃s] *nf* **1** : announcement **2** : advertisement — **annonceur, -ceuse** [anɔ̃sœr, -søz] *n* **1** : advertiser **2** *Can* : (radio) announcer

annoter [anɔte] *vt* : annotate — **annotation** [anɔtasjɔ̃] *nf* : annotation

annuaire [anɥɛr] *nm* **1** : yearbook **2 ~ téléphonique** : telephone directory

annuel, -nuelle [anɥɛl] *adj* : annual — **annuellement** [anɥɛlmɑ̃] *adv* : annually

annulaire [anylɛr] *nm* : ring finger

annuler [anyle] *vt* **1** : cancel **2** RÉVOQUER : annul — **annulation** [anylasjɔ̃] *nf* **1** : cancellation **2** : annulment

anodin, -dine [anɔdɛ̃, -din] *adj* **1** : insignificant **2** : harmless

anomalie [anɔmali] *nf* : anomaly

anonyme [anɔnim] *adj* : anonymous — **anonymat** [anɔnima] *nm* : anonymity

anorexie [anɔrɛksi] *nf* : anorexia

anormal, -male [anɔrmal] *adj, mpl* **-maux** [-mo] : abnormal

anse [ɑ̃s] *nf* **1** : handle **2** : cove

antagoniste [ɑ̃tagɔnist] *adj* : antagonistic

antan [ɑ̃tɑ̃] **d'~** *adj phr* : of yesteryear
antarctique [ɑ̃tarktik] *adj* : antarctic
antécédent, -dente [ɑ̃tesedɑ̃, -dɑ̃t] *adj* : previous — **antécédents** *nmpl* : (medical) history, (criminal) record
antenne [ɑ̃tɛn] *nf* : antenna
antérieur, -rieure [ɑ̃terjœr] *adj* **1** PRÉCÉDENT : previous **2** : front (of a part, etc.) — **antérieurement** [ɑ̃terjœrmɑ̃] *adv* : previously
anthologie [ɑ̃tɔlɔʒi] *nf* : anthology
anthropologie [ɑ̃trɔpɔlɔʒi] *nf* : anthropology
antibiotique [antibiɔtik] *adj & nm* : antibiotic
anticiper [ɑ̃tisipe] *vt* : anticipate — *vi* : think ahead — **anticipation** [ɑ̃tisipasjɔ̃] *nf* : anticipation
anticorps [ɑ̃tikɔr] *nms & pl* : antibody
antidote [ɑ̃tidɔt] *nm* : antidote
antigel [ɑ̃tiʒɛl] *nm* : antifreeze
antilope [ɑ̃tilɔp] *nf* : antelope
antipathie [ɑ̃tipati] *nf* : antipathy
antique [ɑ̃tik] *adj* : ancient, antique — **antiquité** [ɑ̃tikite] *nf* **1** : antiquity **2** : antique
antisémite [ɑ̃tisemit] *adj* : anti-Semitic
antiseptique [ɑ̃tisɛptik] *adj & nm* : antiseptic
antonyme [ɑ̃tɔnim] *nm* : antonym
antre [ɑ̃tr] *nm* : den, lair
anus [anys] *nms & pl* : anus
anxieux, anxieuse [ɑ̃ksjø, -sjøz] *adj* : anxious — **anxiété** [ɑ̃ksjete] *nf* : anxiety
août [u(t)] *nm* : August
apaiser [apeze] *vt* : appease — **s'apaiser** *vr* : quiet down — **apaisement** [apɛzmɑ̃] *nm* : calming (down)
apanage [apanaʒ] *nm* : prerogative
apathie [apati] *nf* : apathy — **apathique** [apatik] *adj* : apathetic
apercevoir [apɛrsəvwar] {26} *vt* : perceive, see — **s'apercevoir** *vr* **1 ~ de** : notice **2 ~ que** : realize that — **aperçu** [apɛrsy] *nm* : general idea, outline
apéritif [aperitif] *nm* : aperitif
à-peu-près [apøprɛ] *nms & pl* : approximation
apeuré, -rée [apœre] *adj* : frightened
apitoyer [apitwaje] {58} *v* **s'apitoyer** *vr* **~ sur** : feel sorry for — **apitoiement** [apitwamɑ̃] *nm* : pity
aplanir [aplanir] *vt* **1** : level **2** : resolve (a problem) — **s'aplanir** *vr* : flatten out
aplatir [aplatir] *vt* : flatten
aplomb [aplɔ̃] *nm* **1** : aplomb, composure **2 d'~** : steady, balanced
apocalypse [apɔkalips] *nf* : apocalypse
apogée [apɔʒe] *nm* : peak
apostrophe [apɔstrɔf] *nf* : apostrophe — **apostropher** [apɔstrɔfe] *vt* : address rudely
apothéose [apɔteoz] *nf* : crowning moment
apôtre [apotr] *nm* : apostle
apparaître [aparɛtr] {73} *vi* : appear — *v impers* **il apparaît que** : it seems that
apparat [apara] *nm* **1** : pomp **2 d'~** : ceremonial
appareiller [aparɛje] *vi* : set sail — *vt* : match up — **appareil** [aparɛj] *nm* **1** : apparatus, appliance **2** : telephone **3 ~ auditif** : hearing aid **4 ~ digestif** : digestive system **5 ~ photo** : camera
apparence [aparɑ̃s] *nf* **1** : appearance **2 en ~** : outwardly — **apparent, -rente** [aparɑ̃, -rɑ̃t] *adj* : apparent — **apparemment** [aparamɑ̃] *adv* : apparently
apparenté, -tée [aparɑ̃te] *adj* : related
apparition [aparisjɔ̃] *nf* **1** MANIFESTATION : appearance **2** SPECTRE : apparition
appartement [apartəmɑ̃] *nm* : apartment
appartenir [apartənir] {92} *vi* **~ à** : belong to — *v impers* **il m'appartient de** : it's up to me to — **appartenance** [apartənɑ̃s] *nf* : membership, belonging
appâter [apate] *vt* **1** : bait **2** : lure, entice — **appât** [apa] *nm* : bait, lure
appauvrir [apovrir] *vt* : impoverish — **s'appauvrir** *vr* : become impoverished
appeler [aple] {8} *vt* **1** : call **2** NÉCESSITER : call for, require **3 en ~ à** : appeal to — *vi* : call — **s'appeler** *vr* : be named, be called — **appel** [apɛl] *nm* **1** : call **2** : appeal
appendice [apɑ̃dis] *nm* : appendix — **appendicite** [apɑ̃disit] *nf* : appendicitis
appentis [apɑ̃ti] *nm* : shed
appesantir [apəzɑ̃tir] *vt* : weigh down — **s'appesantir** *vr* **1** : grow heavier **2 ~ sur** : dwell on
appétit [apeti] *nm* **1** : appetite **2 bon ~!** : enjoy your meal! — **appétissant, -sante** [apetisɑ̃, -sɑ̃t] *adj* : appetizing
applaudir [aplodir] *v* : applaud — **ap-**

plaudissements [aplodismɑ̃] *nmpl* : applause
appliquer [aplike] *vt* : apply — **s'appliquer** *vr* **1** : apply oneself **2** ~ **à** CONCERNER : apply to — **applicateur** [aplikatœr] *nm* : applicator — **application** [aplikasjɔ̃] *nf* : application — **appliqué, -quée** [aplike] *adj* : industrious, painstaking
appoint [apwɛ̃] *nm* **1** : contribution, support **2 d'~** : extra **3 faire l'~** : make exact change — **appointements** [apwɛ̃tmɑ̃] *nmpl* : salary
apporter [apɔrte] *vt* **1** AMENER : bring **2** FOURNIR : provide — **apport** [apɔr] *nm* : contribution
apposer [apoze] *vt* : put, affix
apprécier [apresje] {96} *vt* **1** : appreciate **2** : appraise — **appréciation** [apresjasjɔ̃] *nf* : assessment, appraisal
appréhender [apreɑ̃de] *vt* **1** ARRÊTER : apprehend, arrest **2** : dread — **appréhension** [apreɑ̃sjɔ̃] *nf* : apprehension
apprendre [aprɑ̃dr] {70} *vt* **1** : learn **2** ENSEIGNER : teach
apprenti, -tie [aprɑ̃ti] *n* : apprentice — **apprentissage** [aprɑ̃tisaʒ] *nm* **1** : apprenticeship **2** : learning
apprêter [aprɛte] *v* **s'apprêter** *vr* : get ready
apprivoiser [aprivwaze] *vt* : tame
approbateur, -trice [aprɔbatœr, -tris] *adj* : approving — **approbation** [aprɔbasjɔ̃] *nf* : approval
approcher [aprɔʃe] *vt* : approach — *vi* : draw near — **s'approcher** *vr* ~ **de** : come up to — **approchant, -chante** [aprɔʃɑ̃, -ʃɑ̃t] *adj* : similar — **approche** [aprɔʃ] *nf* : approach
approfondir [aprɔfɔ̃dir] *vt* **1** : deepen **2** PÉNÉTRER : delve into — **approfondi, -die** [aprɔfɔ̃di] *adj* : thorough
approprier [aprɔprije] {96} *v* **s'approprier** *vr* : appropriate — **approprié, -priée** [aprɔprije] *adj* : appropriate
approuver [apruve] *vt* : approve (of)
approvisionner [aprɔvizjɔne] *vt* : supply — **s'approvisionner** *vr* : stock up — **approvisionnement** [aprɔvizjɔnmɑ̃] *nm* : supply, provision
approximation [aprɔksimasjɔ̃] *nf* : approximation — **approximatif, -tive** [aprɔksimatif, -tiv] *adj* : approximate — **approximativement** [-tivmɑ̃] *adv* : approximately
appuyer [apɥije] {58} *vt* **1** : rest, lean **2** SOUTENIR : support — *vi* ~ **sur** : push, press — **s'appuyer** *vr* **1** ~ **à** *or* ~ **contre** : lean against **2** ~ **sur** : rely on — **appui** [apɥi] *nm* : support
âpre [apr] *adj* : bitter, harsh
après [aprɛ] *adv* : afterwards — ~ *prep* **1** : after **2** : beyond **3** ~ **tout** : after all **4 d'~** : according to — **après–demain** [aprɛdmɛ̃] *adv* : the day after tomorrow — **après–midi** [aprɛmidi] *nmfs & pl* : afternoon
à–propos [aprɔpo] *nm* **1** : aptness **2** : presence of mind
apte [apt] *adj* : capable — **aptitude** [aptityd] *nf* : aptitude
aquarelle [akwarɛl] *nf* : watercolor
aquarium [akwarjɔm] *nm* : aquarium
aquatique [akwatik] *adj* : aquatic
aqueduc [akdyk] *nm* : aqueduct
arabe [arab] *adj* : Arab, Arabic — ~ *nm* : Arabic (language)
arachide [araʃid] *nf* : peanut
araignée [areɲe] *nf* : spider
arbitraire [arbitrɛr] *adj* : arbitrary
arbitre [arbitr] *nm* **1** : arbitrator **2** : referee **3 libre** ~ : free will — **arbitrer** [arbitre] *vt* **1** : arbitrate **2** : referee
arborer [arbɔre] *vt* : bear, display
arbre [arbr] *nm* **1** : tree **2** : shaft
arbrisseau [arbriso] *nm* : shrub
arbuste [arbyst] *nm* : bush
arc [ark] *nm* **1** : arc, curve **2** : bow (in archery)
arcade [arkad] *nf* : arch, archway
arc–boutant [arkbutɑ̃] *nm, pl* **arcs–boutants** : flying buttress
arc–en–ciel [arkɑ̃sjɛl] *nm, pl* **arcs–en–ciel** : rainbow
archaïque [arkaik] *adj* : archaic
arche [arʃ] *nf* **1** : arch **2** : ark
archéologie [arkeɔlɔʒi] *nf* : archaeology
archet [arʃɛ] *nm* : bow (in music)
archevêque [arʃəvɛk] *nm* : archbishop
archipel [arʃipɛl] *nm* : archipelago
architecture [arʃitɛktyr] *nf* : architecture — **architecte** [arʃitɛkt] *nmf* : architect
archives [arʃiv] *nfpl* : archives
arctique [arktik] *adj* : arctic
ardent, -dente [ardɑ̃, -dɑ̃t] *adj* **1** : burning **2** PASSIONNÉ : ardent — **ardemment** [ardamɑ̃] *adv* : ardently — **ardeur** [ardœr] *nf* **1** CHALEUR : heat **2** : ardor
ardoise [ardwaz] *nf* : slate
ardu, -due [ardy] *adj* : arduous
arène [arɛn] *nf* **1** : arena **2** ~**s** : bullring, amphitheater — **aréna** [arena] *nm Can* : arena

arête [arɛt] *nf* **1** : fish bone **2** : ridge, bridge (of the nose)
argent [arʒɑ̃] *nm* **1** : money **2** : silver **3 ~ comptant** : cash — **argenté, -tée** [arʒɑ̃te] *adj* **1** : silver-plated **2** : silvery — **argenterie** [arʒɑ̃tri] *nf* : silverware
argile [arʒil] *nf* : clay
argot [argo] *nm* : slang
argument [argymɑ̃] *nm* : argument — **argumentation** [argymɑ̃tasjɔ̃] *nf* : rationale — **argumenter** [argymɑ̃te] *vi* : argue
aride [arid] *adj* : arid
aristocrate [aristɔkrat] *nmf* : aristocrat — **aristocratique** [-kratik] *adj* : aristocratic — **aristocratie** [aristɔkrasi] *nf* : aristocracy
arithmétique [aritmetik] *nf* : arithmetic
armature [armatyr] *nf* : framework
armer [arme] *vt* **1** : arm **2** : cock (a gun) — **arme** [arm] *nf* **1** : weapon **2 ~s** *nfpl* : coat of arms — **armée** [arme] *nf* : army — **armement** [arməmɑ̃] *nm* : armament
armistice [armistis] *nm* : armistice
armoire [armwar] *nf* **1** : cupboard **2** : wardrobe, closet
armoiries [armwari] *nfpl* : coat of arms
armure [armyr] *nf* : armor
arnaquer [arnake] *vt fam* : swindle — **arnaque** [arnak] *nf fam* : swindle
aromate [arɔmat] *nm* : spice, herb
arôme [arom] *nm* **1** : aroma **2** : flavor — **aromatique** [arɔmatik] *adj* : aromatic — **aromatiser** [arɔmatize] *vt* : flavor
arpenter [arpɑ̃te] *vt* **1** : pace up and down **2** MESURER : survey
arqué, -quée [arke] *adj* : curved, arched
arrache-pied [araʃpje] **d'~** *adv phr* : relentlessly
arracher [araʃe] *vt* **1** : pull up or out **2** DÉCHIRER : tear off **3** : snatch, grab
arranger [arɑ̃ʒe] {17} *vt* **1** : arrange **2** RÉPARER : fix **3** CONVENIR : suit, please **4** RÉGLER : settle — **s'arranger** *vr* **1** : come to an agreement **2** : get better — **arrangement** [arɑ̃ʒmɑ̃] *nm* : arrangement
arrestation [arɛstasjɔ̃] *nf* : arrest
arrêter [arete] *vt* **1** : stop **2** FIXER : fix **3** APPRÉHENDER : arrest **4** DÉTERMINER : decide on — **s'arrêter** *vr* **1** : stop, cease **2 ~ de faire** : stop doing — **arrêt** [arɛ] *nm* **1** : stopping, halt **2** : decree **3 ~ d'autobus** : bus stop
arrhes [ar] *nfpl France* : deposit
arrière [arjɛr] *adj* : back, rear — **~** *nm* **1** : back, rear **2 en ~** : backwards **3 en ~ de** : behind — **arriéré, -rée** [arjere] *adj* **1** : overdue **2** : backward — **arriéré** *nm* **1** : arrears *pl* **2** : backlog — **arrière-goût** [arjɛrgu] *nm, pl* **arrière-goûts** : aftertaste — **arrière-grand-mère** [arjɛrgrɑ̃mɛr] *nf, pl* **arrière-grands-mères** : great-grandmother — **arrière-grand-père** [arjɛrgrɑ̃pɛr] *nm, pl* **arrière-grands-pères** : great-grandfather — **arrière-pays** [arjɛrpei] *nms & pl* : hinterland — **arrière-pensée** [arjɛrpɑ̃se] *nf, pl* **arrière-pensées** : ulterior motive — **arrière-plan** [arjɛrplɑ̃] *nm, pl* **arrière-plans** : background
arrimer [arime] *vt* **1** : stow **2** FIXER : secure, fix
arriver [arive] *vi* **1** : arrive, come **2** RÉUSSIR : succeed **3** SE PASSER : happen, occur **4 ~ à** ATTEINDRE : reach — **arrivée** [arive] *nf* **1** : arrival **2** *or* **ligne d'~** : finish line — **arriviste** [arivist] *adj* : pushy — **~** *nmf* : upstart
arrogant, -gante [arɔgɑ̃, -gɑ̃t] *adj* : arrogant — **arrogance** [arɔgɑ̃s] *nf* : arrogance
arroger [arɔʒe] {17} *v* **s'arroger** *vr* : claim (without right)
arrondir [arɔ̃dir] *vt* **1** : make round **2** : round off (a number)
arrondissement [arɔ̃dismɑ̃] *nm* : district
arroser [aroze] *vt* **1** : water **2** : baste (in cooking) **3** CÉLÉBRER : drink to — **arrosoir** [arozwar] *nm* : watering can
arsenal [arsənal] *nm, pl* **-naux** [-no] **1** : shipyard **2** : arsenal
arsenic [arsənik] *nm* : arsenic
art [ar] *nm* : art
artère [artɛr] *nf* **1** : artery **2** : main road
arthrite [artrit] *nf* : arthritis
artichaut [artiʃo] *nm* : artichoke
article [artikl] *nm* **1** : article **2 ~s de toilette** : toiletries
articuler [artikyle] *vt* : articulate — **articulation** [artikylasjɔ̃] *nf* **1** : articulation **2** : joint (in anatomy)
artifice [artifis] *nm* : trick, device
artificiel, -cielle [artifisjɛl] *adj* : artificial — **artificiellement** [-sjɛlmɑ̃] *adv* : artificially
artillerie [artijri] *nf* : artillery
artilleur [artijœr] *nm Can* : pitcher (in baseball)
artisan, -sane [artizɑ̃, -zan] *n* : artisan, craftsman — **artisanal, -nale** *adj, pl* **-naux** : made by craftsmen, home-

made — **artisanat** [artizana] *nm* **1** : artisans *pl* **2** : arts and crafts *pl*
artiste [artist] *nmf* : artist — **artistique** [artistik] *adj* : artistic
as [AS] *nm* : ace
ascendant, -dante [asɑ̃dɑ̃, -dɑ̃t] *adj* : ascending — **ascendant** *nm* **1** : influence **2 ~s** *nmpl* : ancestors — **ascendance** [asɑ̃dɑ̃s] *nf* : ancestry
ascenseur [asɑ̃sœr] *nm* : elevator
ascension [ASɑ̃SJɔ̃] *nf* : ascent
ascète [asɛt] *nmf* : ascetic — **ascétique** [asetik] *adj* : ascetic
asiatique [azjatik] *adj* : Asian
asile [azil] *nm* **1** : (political) asylum **2** ABRI : refuge
aspect [aspɛ] *nm* **1** : aspect **2** ALLURE : appearance
asperge [aspɛrʒ] *nf* : asparagus
asperger [aspɛrʒe] {17} *vt* : sprinkle, spray
aspérité [asperite] *nf* : bump, protrusion
asphalte [asfalt] *nm* : asphalt
asphyxier [asfiksje] {96} *vt* : asphyxiate, suffocate — **s'asphyxier** *vr* : suffocate — **asphyxie** [asfiksi] *nf* : asphyxiation
aspirer [aspire] *vt* **1** : suck up (a liquid) **2** : inhale — *vi* **~ à** : aspire to — **aspiration** [aspirasjɔ̃] *nf* **1** AMBITION : aspiration **2** : suction **3** : inhaling — **aspirateur** [aspiratœr] *nm* **1** : vacuum cleaner **2 passer l'~** : vacuum
aspirine [aspirin] *nf* : aspirin
assagir [asaʒir] *vt* : calm, quiet — **s'assagir** *vr* : quiet down
assaillir [asajir] {93} *vt* : attack — **assaillant, -lante** [asajɑ̃, -jɑ̃t] *n* : attacker
assainir [asenir] *vt* : purify, clean up
assaisonner [asɛzɔne] *vt* : season — **assaisonnement** [ɑsɛzɔnmɑ̃] *nm* : seasoning
assassiner [asasine] *vt* : murder, assassinate — **assassin** *nm* : murderer, assassin
assaut [aso] *nm* **1** : assault **2 prendre d'~** : storm
assécher [aseʃe] {87} *vt* : drain
assembler [asɑ̃ble] *vt* : assemble — **s'assembler** *vr* : gather — **assemblée** [asɑ̃ble] *nf* **1** RÉUNION : meeting **2** : (political) assembly
asséner [asene] {87} *vt* : strike (a blow)
assentiment [asɑ̃timɑ̃] *nm* : assent, consent
asseoir [aswar] {9} *vt* : seat, sit — **s'asseoir** *vr* : sit down
assermenté, -tée [asɛrmɑ̃te] *adj* : sworn
assertion [asɛrsjɔ̃] *nf* : assertion
asservir [asɛrvir] *vt* : enslave
assez [ase] *adv* **1** SUFFISAMMENT : enough **2** : rather, quite
assidu, -due [asidy] *adj* : diligent — **assiduité** [asidɥite] *nf* : diligence
assiéger [asjeʒe] {64} *vt* : besiege
assiette [asjɛt] *nf* : plate, dish — **assiettée** [asjete] *nf* : plateful
assigner [asiɲe] *vt* : assign, allot — **assignation** [asiɲasjɔ̃] *nf* **1** : allocation **2** : summons, subpoena
assimiler [asimile] *vt* **1** : assimilate **2 ~ à** : equate with, compare to — **assimilation** [asimilasjɔ̃] *nf* : assimilation
assis, -sise [asiz] *adj* : seated, sitting down
assise *nf* **1** : foundation, base **2 ~s** *nfpl* : court
assister [asiste] *vt* : assist — *vi* **~ à** : attend — **assistance** [asistɑ̃s] *nf* **1** : assistance **2** : audience — **assistant, -tante** [asistɑ̃, -tɑ̃t] *n* : assistant
associer [asɔsje] {96} *vt* **1** : associate **2 ~ qqn à** : include s.o. in — **s'associer** *vr* : join together — **association** [asɔsjasjɔ̃] *nf* : association — **associé, -ciée** [asɔsje] *n* : associate
assoiffé, -fée [aswafe] *adj* : thirsty
assombrir [asɔ̃brir] *vt* : darken — **s'assombrir** *vr* : darken
assommer [asɔme] *vt* **1** : stun, knock out **2** *fam* : bore stiff — **assommant, -mante** [asɔmɑ̃, -mɑ̃t] *adj* : boring
assortir [asɔrtir] *vt* : match — **assorti, -tie** [asɔrti] *adj* **1** : matched **2** : assorted — **assortiment** [asɔrtimɑ̃] *nm* : assortment
assoupir [asupir] *v* **s'assoupir** *vr* : doze off
assouplir [asuplir] *vt* : make supple, soften — **s'assouplir** *vr* : loosen up
assourdir [asurdir] *vt* **1** : deafen **2** ÉTOUFFER : muffle
assouvir [asuvir] *vt* : appease
assujettir [asyʒetir] *vt* **1** : subjugate **2 ~ à** : subject to
assumer [asyme] *vt* : assume, take on
assurer [asyre] *vt* **1** : assure **2** FOURNIR : provide **3** : insure (one's property, etc.) — **s'assurer** *vr* **~ de** : make sure of — **assurance** [asyrɑ̃s] *nf* **1** : assurance **2** : insurance **3 ~-vie** : life insurance — **assuré, -rée** [asyre]

adj : confident, certain — **assurément** [asyremɑ̃] *adv* : certainly
astérisque [asterisk] *nm* : asterisk
asthme [asm] *nm* : asthma
asticot [astiko] *nm* : maggot
astiquer [astike] *vt* : polish
astre [astr] *nm* : star
astreindre [astrɛ̃dr] {37} *vt* : compel — **astreignant, -gnante** [astrɛɲɑ̃, -ɲɑ̃t] *adj* : demanding
astrologie [astrɔlɔʒi] *nf* : astrology
astronaute [astrɔnot] *nmf* : astronaut
astronomie [astrɔnɔmi] *nf* : astronomy
astuce [astys] *nf* **1** : cleverness **2** TRUC : trick **3** PLAISANTERIE : joke — **astucieux, -cieuse** [astysjø, -sjøz] *adj* : astute, clever — **astucieusement** [-sjøzmɑ̃] *adv* : cleverly
atelier [atəlje] *nm* **1** : studio **2** : workshop
athée [ate] *adj* : atheistic — ~ *nmf* : atheist
athlète [atlɛt] *nmf* : athlete — **athlétique** [atletik] *adj* : athletic — **athlétisme** [atletism] *nm* : athletics
atlantique [atlɑ̃tik] *adj* : Atlantic
atlas [atlas] *nm* : atlas
atmosphère [atmɔsfɛr] *nf* : atmosphere — **atmosphérique** [atmɔsferik] *adj* : atmospheric
atome [atom] *nm* : atom — **atomique** [atɔmik] *adj* : atomic
atomiseur [atɔmizœr] *nm* : atomizer
atout [atu] *nm* **1** : trump (card) **2** AVANTAGE : asset
âtre [atr] *nm* : hearth
atroce [atrɔs] *adj* : atrocious — **atrocité** [atrɔsite] *nf* : atrocity
atrophier [atrɔfje] {96} *v* **s'atrophier** *vr* : atrophy
attabler [atable] *v* **s'attabler** *vr* : sit down at the table
attacher [ataʃe] *vt* : tie (up), fasten — **s'attacher** *vr* **1** : fasten **2** ~ **à** : attach oneself to **3** ~ **à** : apply oneself to — **attachant, -chante** [ataʃɑ̃, -ʃɑ̃t] *adj* : appealing, likeable — **attache** [ataʃ] *nf* **1** : fastener **2** LIEN : tie, bond — **attaché, -chée** [ataʃe] *n* : attaché — **attachement** [ataʃmɑ̃] *nm* : attachment
attaquer [atake] *v* : attack — **s'attaquer** *vr* ~ **à** : attack — **attaque** [atak] *nf* : attack
attarder [atarde] *v* **s'attarder** *vr* : linger — **attardé** [atarde] *adj* **1** : late **2** : retarded **3** DÉMODÉ : old-fashioned
atteindre [atɛ̃dr] {37} *vt* **1** : reach, attain **2** FRAPPER : strike, hit **3** AFFECTER : affect — **atteinte** [atɛ̃t] *nf* **1** : attack **2 hors d'**~ : out of reach **3 porter** ~ **à** : undermine
atteler [atle] {8} *vt* : harness — **s'atteler** *vr* ~ **à** : apply oneself to — **attelage** [atlaʒ] *nm* : team (of animals)
attelle [atɛl] *nf* : splint
attenant, -nante [atnɑ̃, -nɑ̃t] *adj* : adjoining
attendre [atɑ̃dr] {63} *vt* **1** : wait for **2** ESPÉRER : expect — *vi* **1** : wait **2 faire** ~ **qqn** : keep s.o. waiting **3 en attendant** : in the meantime — **s'attendre** *vr* ~ **à** : expect
attendrir [atɑ̃drir] *vt* **1** ÉMOUVOIR : move **2** : tenderize (meat) — **s'attendrir** *vr* : be moved — **attendrissant, -sante** [atɑ̃drisɑ̃, -sɑ̃t] *adj* : moving, touching
attendu, -due [atɑ̃dy] *adj* **1** : expected **2** : long-awaited — **attendu** *prep* ~ **que** : since, considering that
attente [atɑ̃t] *nf* **1** : wait **2** ESPOIR : expectation
attenter [atɑ̃te] *vi* ~ **à** : make an attempt on — **attentat** [atɑ̃ta] *nm* : attack
attention [atɑ̃sjɔ̃] *nf* **1** : attention **2** ~**!** : look out!, beware! **3 faire** ~ : pay attention — **attentionné, -née** [atɑ̃sjɔne] *adj* : considerate — **attentif, -tive** [atɑ̃tif, -tiv] *adj* **1** : attentive **2** : careful **3 être** ~ **à** : pay attention to — **attentivement** [-tivmɑ̃] *adv* : attentively
atténuer [atenɥe] *vt* **1** : tone down **2** : ease, allay — **s'atténuer** *vr* : subside
atterrer [atere] *vt* : dismay, appall
atterrir [aterir] *vi* : land — **atterrissage** [aterisaʒ] *nm* : landing
attester [atɛste] *vt* : attest, testify to — **attestation** [atɛstasjɔ̃] *nf* **1** : affidavit **2** : certificate
attirail [atiraj] *nm fam* : gear, paraphernalia
attirer [atire] *vt* : attract, draw — **attirance** [atirɑ̃s] *nf* : attraction — **attirant, -rante** [atirɑ̃, -rɑ̃t] *adj* : attractive
attiser [atize] *vt* : stir up, kindle
attitré, -trée [atitre] *adj* **1** : authorized **2** HABITUEL : regular
attitude [atityd] *nf* : attitude
attouchement [atuʃmɑ̃] *nm* : touching, fondling
attraction [atraksjɔ̃] *nf* : attraction (in science)
attrait [atrɛ] *nm* : appeal, attraction
attraper [atrape] *vt* : catch

attrayant, -trayante [atrɛjɑ̃, -trɛjɑ̃t] *adj* ATTIRANT : attractive
attribuer [atribɥe] *vt* : attribute, assign — **s'attribuer** *vr* : claim for oneself — **attribut** [atriby] *nm* : attribute — **attribution** [atribysjɔ̃] *nf* : allocation, allotment
attrister [atriste] *vt* : sadden
attrouper [atrupe] *v* **s'attrouper** *vr* : gather — **attroupement** [atrupmɑ̃] *nm* : crowd
au [o] → **à, le**
aubaine [obɛn] *nf* : good fortune, godsend
aube [ob] *nf* : dawn, daybreak
aubépine [obepin] *nf* : hawthorn
auberge [obɛrʒ] *nf* **1** : inn **2 ~ de jeunesse** : youth hostel — **aubergiste** [obɛrʒist] *nmf* : innkeeper
aubergine [obɛrʒin] *nf* : eggplant
auburn [obœrn] *adj* : auburn
aucun, -cune [okœ̃, -kyn] *adj* **1** : no, not any **2 plus qu'aucun autre** : more than any other — **~** *pron* **1** : none, not any **2** : any, anyone **3 d'aucuns** : some (people) — **aucunement** [okynmɑ̃] *adv* : not at all
audace [odas] *nf* **1** : audacity **2** COURAGE : boldness — **audacieux, -cieuse** [odasjø, -jøz] *adj* **1** : audacious **2** HARDI : daring
au–dedans [odədɑ̃] *adv* **1** : inside **2 ~ de** : within
au–dehors [odəɔr] *adv* **1** : outside **2 ~ de** : outside (of)
au–delà [odəla] *adv* **1** : beyond **2 ~ de** : beyond
au–dessous [odsu] *adv* **1** : below **2 ~ de** : below, under
au–dessus [odsy] *adv* **1** : above **2 ~ de** : above, over
au–devant [odvɑ̃] *adv* **1** : ahead **2 aller ~ de** : go to meet
audible [odibl] *adj* : audible
audience [odjɑ̃s] *nf* **1** : audience **2 ~s publiques** : public hearings
audio [odjo] *adj* : audio — **audiovisuel, -suelle** [odjɔvizɥel] *adj* : audiovisual
auditeur, -trice [oditœr, -tris] *n* : listener
audition [odisjɔ̃] *nf* **1** : hearing **2** : audition (in theater) — **auditionner** [odisjɔne] *v* : audition — **auditoire** [oditwar] *nm* : audience — **auditorium** [oditɔrjɔm] *nm* : auditorium
auge [oʒ] *nf* : trough
augmenter [ogmɑ̃te] *v* : increase — **augmentation** [ogmɑ̃tasjɔ̃] *nf* : increase, raise
augurer [ogyre] *vt* : augur — **augure** [ogyr] *nm* : omen
aujourd'hui [oʒurdɥi] *adv & nm* : today
aumône [omon] *nf* : alms *pl*
aumônier [omonje] *nm* : chaplain
auparavant [oparavɑ̃] *adv* : before(hand)
auprès [oprɛ] *adv* **~ de 1** : beside, near, next to **2** : compared with **3 ambassadeur ~ des Nations Unies** : ambassador to the United Nations
auquel, -quelle [okɛl] → **lequel**
auréole [oreɔl] *nf* **1** : halo **2** TACHE : ring
auriculaire [orikylɛr] *nm* : little finger
aurore [ɔrɔr] *nf* AUBE : dawn
ausculter [oskylte] *vt* : examine (with a stethoscope)
auspices [ospis] *nmpl* **sous les ~ de** : under the auspices of
aussi [osi] *adv* **1** : too, also, as well **2** TELLEMENT : so **3 ~ ... que** : as ... as
aussitôt [osito] *adv* **1** : immediately **2 ~ que** : as soon as
austère [ostɛr] *adj* : austere — **austérité** [osterite] *nf* : austerity
austral, -trale [ostral] *adj, mpl* **-trals** : southern
australien, -lienne [ostraljɛ̃, -jɛn] *adj* : Australian
autant [otɑ̃] *adv* **1** *or* **~ de** : as much, as many, so much, so many **2 ~ que** : as much as, as many as, as far as **3 d'~ plus** : all the more **4 pour ~** : for all that
autel [otɛl] *nm* : altar
auteur [otœr] *nm* **1** : author **2** : person responsible, perpetrator
authentique [otɑ̃tik] *adj* : authentic
auto [oto] *nf* : car, automobile
autobiographie [otɔbjɔgrafi] *nf* : autobiography
autobus [otɔbys] *nm* : bus
autocar [otɔkar] *nm* : bus, coach
autochtone [otɔktɔn] *adj & nmf* : native
autocollant, -lante [otɔkɔlɑ̃, -lɑ̃t] *adj* : self-adhesive — **autocollant** *nm* : sticker
autocuiseur [otɔkɥizœr] *nm* : pressure cooker
autodéfense [otɔdefɑ̃s] *nf* : self-defense
autodidacte [otɔdidakt] *adj* : self-taught

autodiscipline [otɔdisiplin] *nf* : self-discipline
autographe [otɔgraf] *nm* : autograph
automation [otɔmasjɔ̃] *nf* : automation — **automatique** [otɔmatik] *adj* : automatic — **automatiquement** [-tikmɑ̃] *adv* : automatically
automatiser [otɔmatize] *vt* : automate — **automatisation** [otɔmatizasjɔ̃] *nf* : automation
automne [otɔn] *nm* : autumn, fall
automobile [otɔmɔbil] *adj* : automotive — **~** *nf* : automobile, car — **automobiliste** [otɔmɔbilist] *nmf* : motorist, driver
autonome [otɔnɔm] *adj* : autonomous — **autonomie** [otɔnɔmi] *nf* : autonomy
autoportrait [otɔpɔrtrɛ] *nm* : self-portrait
autopsie [otɔpsi] *nf* : autopsy
autoriser [otɔrize] *vt* : authorize — **autorisation** [otɔrizasjɔ̃] *nf* **1** : authorization **2** PERMIS : permit
autorité [otɔrite] *nf* : authority — **autoritaire** [otɔritɛr] *adj* : authoritarian
autoroute [otɔrut] *nf* **1** : highway, freeway **2 ~ à péage** : turnpike
auto–stop [otɔstɔp] *nm* **faire de l'~** : hitchhike — **auto–stoppeur, -peuse** [otɔstɔpœr, -pøz] *n* : hitchhiker
autosuffisant, -sante [otɔsyfizɑ̃, -zɑ̃t] *adj* : self-sufficient
autour [otur] *adv* **1 ~ de** : around, about **2 tout ~** : all around
autre [otr] *adj* **1** : other, different **2 ~ chose** : something else — **~** *pron* : other, another
autrefois [otrəfwa] *adv* : in the past, formerly
autrement [otrəmɑ̃] *adv* **1** : differently **2** SINON : otherwise **3 ~ dit** : in other words
autruche [otryʃ] *nf* : ostrich
autrui [otrɥi] *pron* : others
auvent [ovɑ̃] *nm* : awning
auxiliaire [oksiljɛr] *adj & nmf* : auxiliary, assistant — **~** *nm* : auxiliary (verb)
auxquels, -quelles [okɛl] → **lequel**
avachi, -chie [avaʃi] *adj* : shapeless, limp
aval [aval] *nm* **en ~** : downstream
avalanche [avalɑ̃ʃ] *nf* : avalanche
avaler [avale] *vt* : swallow
avancer [avɑ̃se] {6} *vt* : move forward, put ahead — *vi* **1** : advance, go forward **2** : be fast (of a watch) — **s'avancer** *vr* **1** : move forward **2** : progress — **avance** [avɑ̃s] *nf* **1** : advance **2** : lead **3 à l'~** *or* **d'~** : in advance **4 en ~** : early — **avancé, -cée** [avɑ̃se] *adj* : advanced — **avancement** [avɑ̃smɑ̃] *nm* : promotion
avant [avɑ̃] *adv* **1** : before **2** : first **3 ~ de** : before **4 ~ que** : before, until — **~** *adj* : front — **~** *nm* **1** : front **2** : forward (in sports) **3 en ~** : forward, ahead **4 en ~ de** : ahead of — **~** *prep* **1** : before, by **2 ~ tout** : above all
avantager [avɑ̃taʒe] {17} *vt* **1** FAVORISER : favor **2** : flatter — **avantageux, -geuse** [avɑ̃taʒø, -ʒøz] *adj* : profitable, worthwhile — **avantage** [avɑ̃taʒ] *nm* **1** : advantage **2 ~s sociaux** : fringe benefits
avant–bras [avɑ̃bra] *nms & pl* : forearm
avant–dernier, -nière [avɑ̃dɛrnje, -njɛr] *adj* : next to last
avant–garde [avɑ̃gard] *nf, pl* **avant–gardes** : avant-garde
avant–goût [avɑ̃gu] *nm, pl* **avant–goûts** : foretaste
avant–hier [avɑ̃tjɛr] *adv* : the day before yesterday
avant–midi [avɑ̃midi] *nfs & pl Can, nms & pl Bel* : morning
avant–poste [avɑ̃pɔst] *nm, pl* **avant–postes** : outpost
avant–première [avɑ̃prəmjɛr] *nf, pl* **avant–premières** : preview
avant–propos [avɑ̃prɔpo] *nms & pl* : foreword
avant–toit [avɑ̃twa] *nm* : eaves *pl*
avare [avar] *adj* : miserly — **~** *nmf* : miser
avarié [avarje] *adj* : spoiled, rotten
avec [avɛk] *prep* : with — **~** *adv fam* : with it, with them
avenant, -nante [avnɑ̃, -nɑ̃t] *adj* : pleasant
avènement [avɛnmɑ̃] *nm* **1** : accession (to a throne) **2** DÉBUT : advent
avenir [avnir] *nm* **1** : future **2 à l'~** : in the future
avent [avɑ̃] *nm* **l'~** : Advent
aventure [avɑ̃tyr] *nf* **1** : adventure **2** : love affair — **aventurer** [avɑ̃tyre] *vt* : risk — **s'aventurer** *vr* : venture — **aventureux, -reuse** [avɑ̃tyrø, -røz] *adj* : adventurous
avenu [avny] *adj m* **nul et non ~** : null and void
avenue [avny] *nf* : avenue
avérer [avere] {87} *v* **s'avérer** *vr* : turn out to be
averse [avɛrs] *nf* : shower, storm

aversion [avɛrsjɔ̃] *nf* : aversion, dislike
avertir [avɛrtir] *vt* **1** : warn **2** INFORMER : inform — **avertissement** [avɛrtismɑ̃] *nm* : warning — **avertisseur** [avɛrtisœr] *nm* **1** : (car) horn **2** : alarm
aveu [avø] *nm, pl* **-veux** : confession, admission
aveugle [avœgl] *adj* : blind — ∼ *nmf* : blind person — **aveuglant, -glante** [avœglɑ̃, -glɑ̃t] *adj* : blinding — **aveuglement** [avœgləmɑ̃] *nm* : blindness — **aveuglément** [avœglemɑ̃] *adv* : blindly — **aveugler** [avœgle] *vt* : blind
aviateur, -trice [avjatœr, -tris] *n* : pilot — **aviation** [avjasjɔ̃] *nf* : aviation
avide [avid] *adj* **1** CUPIDE : greedy **2** ∼ **de** : eager for — **avidité** [avidite] *nf* **1** CUPIDITÉ : greed **2** : eagerness
avilir [avilir] *vt* : debase
avion [avjɔ̃] *nm* : airplane
aviron [avirɔ̃] *nm* RAME : oar
avis [avis] *nm* **1** : opinion **2** ANNONCE : notice **3** CONSEIL : advice — **aviser** [avize] *vt* : inform, notify — **avisé, -sée** [avize] *adj* : sensible
aviver [avive] *vt* : revive
avocat[1], **-cate** [avɔka, -kat] *n* : lawyer, attorney
avocat[2] *nm* : avocado
avoine [avwan] *nf* : oats *pl*
avoir [avwar] {10} *vt* **1** POSSÉDER : have **2** OBTENIR : get **3** ∼ **dix ans** : be ten years old **4** ∼ **à** : have to **5** ∼ **mal** : be hurt — *v impers* **1 il y a** : there is, there are **2 qu'est-ce qu'il y a?** : what's wrong? — *v aux* : have — ∼ *nm* : assets *pl*
avoisiner [avwazine] *vt* : be near, border on — **avoisinant, -nante** [avwazinɑ̃] *adj* : neighboring
avorter [avɔrte] *vi* : abort — **avortement** [avɔrtəmɑ̃] *nm* : abortion
avouer [avwe] *vt* : admit, confess to — **s'avouer** *vr* : confess, own up
axe [aks] *nm* **1** : axis **2** ∼ **routier** : major road — **axer** [akse] *vt* : center, focus
axiome [aksjom] *nm* : axiom
azote [azɔt] *nm* : nitrogen
azur [azyr] *nm* : sky blue

B

b [be] *nm* : b, second letter of the alphabet
babeurre [babœr] *nm* : buttermilk
babiller [babije] *vi* : babble, chatter — **babillage** [babijaʒ] *nm* : babbling — **babillard** [babijar] *nm Can* : bulletin board
babiole [babjɔl] *nf* : trinket
babouin [babwɛ̃] *nm* : baboon
baby-sitter [bebisitœr] *nmf, pl* **baby-sitters** *France* : baby-sitter — **baby-sitting** [bebisitiŋ] *nm* **faire du** ∼ *France* : baby-sit
baccalauréat [bakalɔrea] *nm* **1** *France* : school-leaving certificate **2** *Can* : bachelor's degree
bâche [baʃ] *nf* : tarpaulin
bâcler [bakle] *vt* : rush through
bacon [bekɔn] *nm* : bacon
bactéries [bakteri] *nfpl* : bacteria
badaud, -daude [bado, -dod] *n* : (curious) onlooker
badge [badʒ] *nm* : badge
badiner [badine] *vi* **1** : joke, jest **2** ∼ **avec** : toy with — **badinage** [badinaʒ] *nm* : banter, joking
bafouer [bafwe] *vt* : ridicule, scorn
bafouiller [bafuje] *v* : mumble, stammer — **bafouillage** [bafujaʒ] *nm* : mumbling, gibberish
bagage [bagaʒ] *nm* : baggage, luggage
bagarrer [bagare] *vi* : fight — **se bagarrer** *vr* : fight, brawl — **bagarre** [bagar] *nf* : fight, brawl
bagatelle [bagatɛl] *nf* : trifle, trinket
bagne [baɲ] *nm* : labor camp
bagnole [baɲɔl] *nf fam* : jalopy
bague [bag] *nf* : ring
baguette [bagɛt] *nf* **1** : stick, rod, baton **2** : baguette (loaf of French bread) **3** ∼ **de tambour** : drumstick **4** ∼**s** *nfpl* : chopsticks
baie [bɛ] *nf* **1** : bay **2** : berry
baigner [beɲe] *vt* : bathe, wash — *vi* : soak, steep — **se baigner** *vr* **1** : take a bath **2** : go swimming — **baignade** [bɛɲad] *nf* : swimming — **baigneur, -gneuse** [bɛɲœr, -ɲøz] *n* : swimmer, bather — **baignoire** [beɲwar] *nf* : bathtub
bail [baj] *nm, pl* **baux** [bo] : lease
bâiller [baje] *vi* **1** : yawn **2** : be ajar (of a door) — **bâillement** [bajmɑ̃] *nm* : yawn
bâillonner [bajɔne] *vt* : gag, muzzle — **bâillon** [bajɔ̃] *nm* : gag

bain [bɛ̃] *nm* : bath
bain–marie [bɛ̃mari] *nm, pl* **bains–marie** : double boiler
baïonnette [bajɔnɛt] *nf* : bayonet
baiser [beze] *vt* : kiss — **~** *nm* : kiss
baisser [bese] *vt* : lower, reduce (volume, light, etc.) — *vi* : drop, decline — **se baisser** *vr* : bend down — **baisse** [bɛs] *nf* : fall, drop
bal [bal] *nm* : ball, dance
balader [balade] *v* **se balader** *vr* **1** : go for a walk **2** : go for a drive — **balade** [balad] *nf* **1** : stroll, walk **2** : drive, ride
balafre [balafr] *nf* : gash, slash
balai [balɛ] *nm* : broom, brush
balancer [balɑ̃se] {6} *vt* **1** : sway, swing (one's arms, etc.) **2** : balance (an account) **3** *fam* : chuck, junk — **se balancer** *vr* : rock, sway — **balance** [balɑ̃s] *nf* : scales *pl,* balance
balancier [balɑ̃sje] *nm* : pendulum
balançoire [balɑ̃swar] *nf* **1** : child's swing **2** BASCULE : seesaw
balayer [baleje] {11} *vt* **1** : sweep **2** : scan (in computer science) — **balayage** [balɛjaʒ] *nm* : sweeping — **balayeuse** [balɛjøz] *nf* **1** : street-cleaning truck **2** *Can* : vacuum cleaner
balbutier [balbysje] {96} *v* : stammer, stutter — **balbutiement** [balbysimɑ̃] *nm* **1** : stammering, stuttering **2 ~s** *nmpl* : beginnings
balcon [balkɔ̃] *nm* : balcony
baldaquin [baldakɛ̃] *nm* : canopy
baleine [balɛn] *nf* : whale
balise [baliz] *nf* : buoy, beacon — **baliser** [balize] *vt* : mark with beacons
balistique [balistik] *adj* : ballistic
balivernes [balivɛrn] *nfpl* : nonsense
ballade [balad] *nf* : ballad
balle [bal] *nf* **1** : ball (in sports) **2** : bullet **3** *France fam* : franc
balle–molle [balmɔl] *nf Can* : softball
ballet [balɛ] *nm* : ballet — **ballerine** [balrin] *nf* : ballerina
ballon [balɔ̃] *nm* **1** : (foot)ball **2** : balloon — **ballon–panier** [balɔ̃panje] *nm Can* : basketball (game)
ballot [balo] *nm* BALUCHON : pack, bundle
ballotter [balɔte] *vt* SECOUER : shake, toss about — *vi* : toss, roll around
balloune [balun] *nf Can* : balloon
balnéaire [balneɛr] *adj* : seaside
balourd, -lourde [balur, -lurd] *adj* : awkward, clumsy
baluchon [balyʃɔ̃] *nm* : pack, bundle
balustrade [balystrad] *nf* : guardrail
bambin, -bine [bɑ̃bɛ̃, -bin] *n* : child, toddler
bambou [bɑ̃bu] *nm* : bamboo
ban [bɑ̃] *nm* **1** : round of applause **2 ~s** *nmpl* : banns **3 mettre au ~** : ostracize
banal, -nale [banal] *adj, mpl* **-nals** : commonplace, trite — **banalité** [banalite] *nf* : triviality
banane [banan] *nf* : banana
banc [bɑ̃] *nm* **1** : bench **2** : school (of fish) **3 ~ de sable** : sandbank **4 ~ de neige** *Can* : snowbank
bancaire [bɑ̃kɛr] *adj* : banking, bank
bancal, -cale [bɑ̃kal] *adj, mpl* **-cals** : wobbly, rickety
bandage [bɑ̃daʒ] *nm* **1** : bandaging **2** PANSEMENT : bandage
bande [bɑ̃d] *nf* **1** : gang, group, pack (of animals) **2** : tape, (reel of) film **3 ~ dessinée** : comic strip
bandeau [bɑ̃do] *nm, pl* **-deaux 1** : blindfold **2** : headband
bander [bɑ̃de] *vt* **1** : bandage **2 ~ les yeux à** : blindfold
banderole [bɑ̃drɔl] *nf* : banner, pennant
bandit [bɑ̃di] *nm* VOLEUR : bandit, robber
bandoulière [bɑ̃duljɛr] *nf* : shoulder strap
banlieue [bɑ̃ljø] *nf* : suburbs *pl*
bannière [banjɛr] *nf* : banner
bannir [banir] *vt* : banish, exile
banque [bɑ̃k] *nf* **1** : bank **2 travailler dans la ~** : work in banking — **banqueroute** [bɑ̃krut] *nf* : bankruptcy
banquet [bɑ̃kɛ] *nm* : banquet, feast
banquette [bɑ̃kɛt] *nf* : bench, seat (in a booth or vehicle)
banquier, -quière [bɑ̃kje, -kjɛr] *n* : banker
baptême [batɛm] *nm* : baptism — **baptiser** [batize] *vt* : baptize, christen
bar [bar] *nm* **1** : sea bass **2** CAFÉ : bar
baragouin [baragwɛ̃] *nm* : gibberish — **baragouiner** [baragwine] *vi* : talk gibberish, jabber
baraque [barak] *nf* **1** : hut, shack **2** : stall, booth (at a fair, etc.)
barbare [barbar] *adj* : barbaric — **~** *nmf* : barbarian
barbe [barb] *nf* : beard
barbecue [barbəkju] *nm* : barbecue
barbelé, -lée [barbəle] *adj* **fil barbelé** : barbed wire
barbiche [barbiʃ] *nf* : goatee
barbier [barbje] *nm Can* : barber
barbouiller [barbuje] *vt* **1** : smear **2** GRIBOUILLER : scribble

bardeau [bardo] *nm, pl* **-deaux** : shingle
barème [barɛm] *nm* : scale, table, list
baril [baril] *nm* TONNELET : barrel, keg
bariolé, -lée [barjɔle] *adj* : multicolored
barman [barman] *nm, pl* **-mans** *or* **-men** : bartender
baromètre [barɔmɛtr] *nm* : barometer
baron, -ronne [barɔ̃, -rɔn] *n* : baron *m*, baroness *f*
barque [bark] *nf* : small boat
barrage [baraʒ] *nm* **1** : dam **2** ~ **routier** : roadblock
barre [bar] *nf* **1** : bar, rod **2** NIVEAU : mark, level **3 prendre la** ~ : take the helm — **barreau** [baro] *nm, pl* **-reaux 1** : bar **2** : rung — **barrer** [bare] *vt* **1** : bar, block **2** : cross out (a word) **3** : steer (a boat) **4** *Can* : lock
barricader [barikade] *vt* : barricade — **barricade** [barikad] *nf* : barricade
barrière [barjɛr] *nf* : barrier
baryton [baritɔ̃] *nm* : baritone
bas *nms & pl* **1** : bottom, lower part **2** : stocking **3 à** ~ : down with **4 en** ~ : below **5 en** ~ **de** : at the bottom of — ~ *adv* **1** : low **2 parler tout** ~ : whisper, speak softly — **bas, basse** [ba, baz (*before a vowel or mute h*), bas] *adj* **1** : low **2** VIL : base, vile
basané, -née [bazane] *adj* : tanned, sunburned
bascule [baskyl] *nf* **1** BALANCE : balance, scales *pl* **2** BALANÇOIRE : seesaw — **basculer** [baskyle] *vi* : tip, topple
base [baz] *nf* **1** : base **2** FONDEMENT : basis **3** ~ **de données** : database
baseball *or* **base–ball** [bɛzbol] *nm* : baseball — **baseballeur, -leuse** [bɛzbolœr, -løz] *n Can* : baseball player
baser [baze] *vt* FONDER : base, found
basilic [bazilik] *nm* : basil
basilique [bazilik] *nf* : basilica
basket [baskɛt] *or* **basket–ball** [baskɛtbol] *nm* : basketball — **basketteur, -teuse** [baskɛtœr, -tøz] *n* : basketball player
basque [bask] *adj & nm* : Basque
basse [bas] *nf* : bass (in music)
bassin [basɛ̃] *nm* **1** : basin (in geography) **2** : pond, pool **3** : pelvis — **bassine** [basin] *nf* : bowl
basson [basɔ̃] *nm* : bassoon
bataille [bataj] *nf* : battle, fight — **batailler** [bataje] *vi* : fight, struggle (hard) — **batailleur, -leuse** [batajœr, -jøz] *adj* : quarrelsome — ~ *n* : fighter
bâtard, -tarde [batar, -tard] *adj & n* : bastard
bateau *nm, pl* **-teaux 1** : boat, ship **2** ~ **à voiles** : sailboat
batifoler [batifɔle] *vi* : frolic
bâtir [batir] *vt* **1** CONSTRUIRE : build, erect **2** FAUFILER : baste, tack — **bâtiment** [batimɑ̃] *nm* **1** : building, structure **2** NAVIRE : ship — **bâtisseur, -seuse** [batisœr, -søz] *n* : builder
bâton [batɔ̃] *nm* **1** : rod, stick, staff **2** *Can* : bat (in sports) **3** ~ **de rouge** : lipstick
battre [batr] {12} *vt* **1** FRAPPER : hit, strike **2** VAINCRE : defeat **3** : shuffle (cards) — *vi* : beat (of the heart) — **se battre** *vr* : fight — **battant, -tante** [batɑ̃, -tɑ̃t] *adj* **1** : beating, pounding **2 pluie battante** : pouring rain — **batte** [bat] *nf* : bat (in sports) — **battement** [batmɑ̃] *nm* **1** : beating **2** ~ **de cœur** : heartbeat — **batterie** [batri] *nf* **1** : battery (of a car) **2** ENSEMBLE : set, group **3** : drums, drum set — **batteur** [batœr, -tøz] *nm* **1** : whisk, eggbeater **2** : drummer **3** : batter (in sports)
baume [bom] *nm* : balm
baux → **bail**
bavard, -varde [bavar, -vard] *adj* : talkative — ~ *n* : chatterbox — **bavarder** [bavarde] *vi* **1** : chatter **2** : gossip — **bavardage** [bavardaʒ] *nm* : idle talk, chatter
bave [bav] *nf* : dribble, spittle — **baver** [bave] *vi* **1** : dribble, drool **2** COULER : leak — **bavoir** [bavwar] *nm* : (baby's) bib
bavure [bavyr] *nf* **1** : smudge **2** GAFFE : blunder
bazar [bazar] *nm* **1** : bazaar **2** *fam* : clutter, mess
beau [bo] (**bel** [bɛl] *before vowel or mute h*), **belle** [bɛl] *adj, mpl* **beaux** [bo] **1** : beautiful, handsome **2** : good (of a performance, etc.) **3** : considerable (in quantity) **4** ~ **temps** : nice weather — ~ *adv* **1 avoir** ~ : do (something) in vain **2 il fait** ~ : it's nice outside
beaucoup [boku] *adv* **1** : much, a lot **2** ~ **de** : much, many, a lot of **3 de** ~ : by far
beau–fils [bofis] *nm, pl* **beaux–fils 1** : son-in-law **2** : stepson — **beau–frère** [bofrɛr] *nm, pl* **beaux–frères 1** : brother-in-law **2** : stepbrother —

beau-père [bopɛr] *nm, pl* **beaux-pères 1** : father-in-law **2** : stepfather
beauté [bote] *nf* : beauty
beaux-arts [bozar] *nmpl* : fine arts
beaux-parents [boparɑ̃] *nmpl* : in-laws
bébé [bebe] *nm* : baby, infant
bec [bɛk] *nm* **1** : beak, bill **2** *fam* : mouth **3** EMBOUCHURE : mouthpiece **4** : point (of a pen) **5** : spout, lip (of a jug, etc.) **6** *Can fam* : kiss
bêche [bɛʃ] *nf* : spade — **bêcher** [beʃe] *vt* : dig (up)
bedaine [bədɛn] *nf fam* : paunch
bée *adj* [be] → **bouche**
beffroi [befrwa] *nm* : belfry
bégayer [begeje] {11} *v* : stutter, stammer
béguin [begɛ̃] *nm fam* : crush, infatuation
beige [bɛʒ] *adj & nm* : beige
beignet [bɛɲɛ] *nm* **1** : doughnut **2** : fritter — **beigne** [bɛɲ] *nm Can* : doughnut
bel [bɛl] → **beau**
bêler [bele] *vi* : bleat — **bêlement** [bɛlmɑ̃] *nm* : bleat
belette [bəlɛt] *nf* : weasel
belge [bɛlʒ] *adj* : Belgian
bélier [belje] *nm* : ram
belle [bɛl] *adj* → **beau**
belle-famille [bɛlfamij] *nf, pl* **belles-familles** : in-laws *pl* — **belle-fille** [bɛlfij] *nf, pl* **belles-filles 1** : daughter-in-law **2** : stepdaughter — **belle-mère** [bɛlmɛr] *nf, pl* **belles-mères 1** : mother-in-law **2** : stepmother — **belle-sœur** [bɛlsœr] *nf, pl* **belles-sœurs** : sister-in-law
belligérant, -rante [beliʒerɑ̃, -rɑ̃t] *adj & n* : belligerent
belliqueux, -queuse [belikø, -køz] *adj* GUERRIER : warlike
bémol [bemɔl] *adj & nm* : flat (in music)
bénédiction [benediksjɔ̃] *nf* : blessing, benediction
bénéfice [benefis] *nm* **1** AVANTAGE : benefit, advantage **2** GAIN : profit — **bénéficiaire** [benefisjɛr] *nmf* : beneficiary — **bénéficier** [benefisje] {96} *vi* **~ de** : benefit from — **bénéfique** [benefik] *adj* : beneficial
bénévole [benevɔl] *adj* : voluntary — **~** *nmf* : volunteer
bénin, -nigne [benɛ̃, beniɲ] *adj* **1** : slight, minor **2** : benign (of a tumor)
bénir [benir] *vt* : bless — **bénit, -nite** [beni, -nit] *adj* : blessed
benjamin, -mine [bɛ̃ʒamɛ̃, -min] *n* CADET : youngest child
béquille [bekij] *nf* **1** : crutch **2** : kickstand
bercer [bɛrse] {6} *vt* **1** : rock (a baby) **2** APAISER : soothe, lull — **se bercer** *vr* : rock, swing — **berceau** [bɛrso] *nm, pl* **-ceaux** : cradle — **berceuse** [bɛrsøz] *nf* **1** : lullaby **2** : rocking chair
béret [berɛ] *nm* : beret
berge [bɛrʒ] *nf* RIVE : bank (of a river, etc.)
berger, -gère [bɛrʒe, -ʒɛr] *n* : shepherd, shepherdess *f* — **berger** *nm* : sheepdog
berline [bɛrlin] *nf* : sedan
berlingot [bɛrlɛ̃go] *nm* **1** : carton (for milk, etc.) **2** : hard candy
berner [bɛrne] *vt* : fool, deceive
besogne [bəzɔɲ] *nf* : task, job
besoin [bəzwɛ̃] *nm* **1** : need **2 avoir ~ de** : need **3 dans le ~** : needy
bestiole [bɛstjɔl] *nf* : bug, tiny creature
bétail [betaj] *nm* : livestock, cattle *pl*
bête [bɛt] *nf* ANIMAL : animal, creature — **~** *adj* : stupid, silly — **bêtement** [bɛtmɑ̃] *adv* : foolishly — **bêtise** [betiz] *nf* **1** : stupidity **2** : stupid thing, nonsense
béton [betɔ̃] *nm* : concrete
bette [bɛt] *nf* : Swiss chard
betterave [bɛtrav] *nf* : beet
beugler [bøgle] *vi* **1** : moo, bellow **2** : blare (of a radio, etc.) — *vt* : bellow out
beurre [bœr] *nm* : butter — **beurrer** [bœre] *vt* : butter
bévue [bevy] *nf* : blunder
biais [bjɛ, bjɛz] *nm* **1** : means, way **2 de ~** : diagonally — **biaiser** [bjeze] *vi* : hedge, dodge the issue
bibelot [biblo] *nm* : trinket, curio
biberon [bibrɔ̃] *nm* : baby bottle
Bible [bibl] *nf* **la ~** : the Bible — **biblique** [biblik] *adj* : biblical, scriptural
bibliographie [biblijɔgrafi] *nf* : bibliography
bibliothèque [biblijɔtɛk] *nf* **1** : library **2** : bookcase — **bibliothécaire** [biblijɔtekɛr] *nmf* : librarian
bicarbonate [bikarbɔnat] *nm* **~ de soude** : baking soda
biceps [bisɛps] *nms & pl* : biceps
biche [biʃ] *nf* : doe
bicoque [bikɔk] *nf* : shack, shanty
bicyclette [bisiklɛt] *nf* : bicycle
bidon [bidɔ̃] *nm* : can, flask

bien [bjɛ̃] *adv* **1** : well, satisfactorily **2** TRÈS : very, quite **3** RÉELLEMENT : definitely, really **4** VOLONTIERS : readily, happily **5 ~ des fois** : many times **6 ~ que** : although **7 ~ sûr** : of course — **~** *adj* **1** : good, fine, satisfactory **2** : well, in good health **3** BEAU : good-looking **4** RESPECTABLE : nice **5** : comfortable (of shoes, etc.) — **~** *nm* **1** : good **2 ~s** *nmpl* : possessions, property — **~** *interj* : OK, all right, very well — **bien–aimé, -aimée** [bjɛ̃neme] *adj & n* : beloved — **bien-être** [bjɛ̃nɛtr] *nm* **1** : well-being **2** : comfort

bienfaisance [bjɛ̃fəzɑ̃s] *nf* : charity, kindness — **bienfaisant, -sante** [bjɛ̃fəzɑ̃, -zɑ̃t] *adj* **1** : charitable **2** BÉNÉFIQUE : beneficial — **bienfait** [bjɛ̃fɛ] *nm* AVANTAGE : benefit — **bienfaiteur, -trice** [bjɛ̃fɛtœr, -tris] *n* : benefactor

bientôt [bjɛ̃to] *adv* : soon, shortly

bienveillance [bjɛ̃vejɑ̃s] *nf* : kindness, benevolence — **bienveillant, -lante** [bjɛ̃vejɑ̃, -jɑ̃t] *adj* : kind, benevolent

bienvenu, -nue [bjɛ̃vny] *adj* : welcome — **~** *n* **soyez le ~** : you are welcome (here) — **bienvenue** *nf* : welcome

bière [bjɛr] *nf* : beer

biffer [bife] *vt* : cross out

bifteck [biftɛk] *nm* : steak

bifurquer [bifyrke] *vi* : to fork — **bifurcation** [bifyrkasjɔ̃] *nf* : fork (in a road)

bigot, -gote [bigo, -ɔt] *adj* : overly devout — **~** *n* : (religious) zealot

bigoudi [bigudi] *nm* : hair curler

bijou [biʒu] *nm, pl* **-joux 1** : jewel **2** MERVEILLE : gem — **bijouterie** [biʒutri] *nf* **1** BIJOUX : jewelry **2** : jewelry store — **bijoutier, -tière** [biʒutje, -tjɛr] *n* : jeweler

bilan [bilɑ̃] *nm* **1** : assessment **2** : balance sheet (in finance)

bilatéral, -rale [bilateral] *adj, mpl* **-raux** [-ro] : bilateral

bile [bil] *nf* **1** : bile **2 se faire de la ~** : worry

bilingue [bilɛ̃g] *adj* : bilingual

billard [bijar] *nm* : billiards *pl*

bille [bij] *nf* **1** : (playing) marble **2** : billiard ball

billet [bijɛ] *nm* **1** : bill, banknote **2** TICKET : ticket **3 ~ doux** : love letter — **billetterie** [bijɛtri] *nf* **1** GUICHET : ticket office **2** : automatic teller machine

billion [biljɔ̃] *nm* : trillion (US), billion (Brit)

bimensuel, -suelle [bimɑ̃sɥɛl] *adj* : semimonthly

binette [binɛt] *nf* : hoe

biochimie [bjɔʃimi] *nf* : biochemistry

biographie [bjɔgrafi] *nf* : biography — **biographe** [bjɔgraf] *nmf* : biographer — **biographique** [bjɔgrafik] *adj* : biographical

biologie [bjɔlɔʒi] *nf* : biology — **biologique** [bjɔlɔʒik] *adj* : biological

bis [bis] *adv* **1** : twice (in music) **2** : A (in an address) — **~** *nm & interj* : encore

biscotte [biskɔt] *nf* : cracker

biscuit [biskɥi] *nm* **1** : cookie **2** : sponge cake

bise [biz] *nf* **1** : north wind **2** *fam* : kiss, smack

biseau [bizo] *nm* **1** : bevel **2 en ~** : beveled

bisexuel, -sexuelle [bisɛksɥɛl] *adj* : bisexual

bison [bizɔ̃] *nm* : bison, buffalo

bissextile [bisɛkstil] *adj* **année ~** : leap year

bistouri [bisturi] *nm* : lancet

bistro *or* **bistrot** [bistro] *nm* : café

bit [bit] *nm* : bit (unit of information)

bizarre [bizar] *adj* : bizarre, strange — **bizarrement** [-zarmɑ̃] *adv* : oddly, strangely

blafard, -farde [blafar, -fard] *adj* : pale, pallid

blague [blag] *nf* PLAISANTERIE : joke — **blaguer** [blage] *vi* PLAISANTER : joke, kid around — **blagueur, -gueuse** [blagœr, -gøz] *n* : joker

blaireau [blɛro] *nm, pl* **-raux** : badger

blâmer [blame] *vt* : blame, criticize — **blâme** [blam] *nm* DÉSAPPROBATION : blame, censure

blanc, blanche [blɑ̃, blɑ̃ʃ] *adj* **1** : white **2** PÂLE : pale **3** : pure, innocent **4 page blanche** : blank sheet — **blanc** *nm* **1** : white **2** INTERVALLE : gap, blank space

blanchir [blɑ̃ʃir] *vt* **1** : whiten, bleach **2** : launder (one's clothes) **3** : blanch (vegetables) — *vi* : turn white — **blanchissage** [blɑ̃ʃisaʒ] *nm* : laundering — **blanchisserie** [blɑ̃ʃisri] *nf* : laundry

blasé, -sée [blaze] *adj* : blasé, jaded

blason [blazɔ̃] *nm* : coat of arms

blasphème [blasfɛm] *nm* : blasphemy

blatte [blat] *nf* : cockroach

blazer [blazɛr] *nm* : blazer

blé [ble] *nm* : wheat

blême [blɛm] *adj* : pale, wan

blesser [blese] *vt* : injure, wound — **blessé, -sée** [blese] *n* : casualty, injured person — **blessure** [blesyr] *nf* : injury, wound

bleu, bleue [blø] *adj* **1** : blue **2** : very rare (of steak, etc.) — **bleu** *nm* **1** : blue **2** : bruise

bleuet [bløɛ] *nm Can* : blueberry

blindé, -dée [blɛ̃de] *adj* : armored — **blindé** *nm* : armored vehicle

bloc [blɔk] *nm* **1** : block **2 en ~** : as a whole

blocage [blɔkaʒ] *nm* **1** : obstruction **2** : freezing (of prices, etc.)

blocus [blɔkys] *nm* : blockade

blond, blonde [blɔ̃, blɔ̃d] *adj & n* : blond

blonde *nf Can fam* : girlfriend

bloquer [blɔke] *vt* **1** : block (an entrance) **2** : jam on (the brakes) **3** : freeze (a bank account, etc.), stop (a check) — **se bloquer** *vr* : jam, stick

blottir [blɔtir] *v* **se blottir** *vr* : cuddle, snuggle

blouse [bluz] *nf* **1** CHEMISIER : blouse **2** SARRAU : smock

blouson [bluzɔ̃] *nm* : jacket

blue–jean [bludʒin] *nm, pl* **blue–jeans** : jeans *pl*

bluffer [blœfe] *vi* : bluff — **bluff** [blœf] *nm* : bluff

bobine [bɔbin] *nf* : reel, spool

bocal [bɔkal] *nm, pl* **-caux** [bɔko] : jar

bœuf [bœf] *nm, pl* **bœufs** [bø] : beef

bohème [bɔɛm] *adj* : bohemian — **bohémien, -mienne** [bɔemjɛ̃, -mjɛn] *n* : gypsy

boire [bwar] {13} *vt* **1** : drink **2** ABSORBER : absorb — *vi* : drink

bois [bwa] *nms & pl* **1** : wood **2** FORÊT : woods *pl* **3 ~ de chauffage** : firewood **4 ~** *nmpl* : antlers — **boisé, -sée** [bwaze] *adj* : wooded — **boisé** *nm Can* : woods *pl*

boisseau [bwaso] *nm* : bushel

boisson [bwasɔ̃] *nf* **1** : drink, beverage **2 en ~** *Can* : drunk

boîte [bwat] *nf* **1** : (tin) can **2** : box **3 ~ de nuit** : nightclub

boiter [bwate] *vi* : limp — **boiteux, -teuse** [bwatø, -tøz] *adj* **1** : lame **2** BRANLANT : wobbly, shaky — **boitiller** [bwatije] *vi* : limp slightly, hobble

boîtier [bwatje] *nm* : casing, housing

bol [bɔl] *nm* **1** : bowl **2** : bowlful

bombarder [bɔ̃barde] *vt* : bomb, bombard — **bombardement** [bɔ̃bardəmɑ̃] *nm* : bombing, bombardment — **bombardier** [bɔ̃bardje] *nm* : bomber (plane)

bombe [bɔ̃b] *nf* **1** : bomb **2** ATOMISEUR : aerosol spray

bomber [bɔ̃be] *vt* : puff out, swell

bon, bonne [bɔ̃ (bon *before a vowel or mute h*), bɔn] *adj* **1** : good **2** CORRECT : correct, proper **3 ~ marché** : inexpensive **4 ~ sens** : common sense **5 pour de ~** : for good, for keeps — **bon** *adv* **faire ~** : be nice — **~** *nm* **1** : good thing **2** : voucher, bond

bonbon [bɔ̃bɔ̃] *nm* : candy

bond [bɔ̃] *nm* **1** SAUT : bound, leap **2** : bounce (of a ball)

bondé, -dée [bɔ̃de] *adj* : crammed, packed

bondir [bɔ̃dir] *vi* : jump, leap

bonheur [bɔnœr] *nm* **1** : happiness, pleasure **2 par ~** : luckily

bonhomme [bɔnɔm] *nm, pl* **bonshommes 1** *fam* : fellow, guy **2 ~ de neige** : snowman

bonjour [bɔ̃ʒur] *nm* **1** : hello, good morning, good afternoon **2** *Can* : good-bye

bonne [bɔn] *nf* DOMESTIQUE : maid

bonnement [bɔnmɑ̃] *adv* **tout ~** : quite simply

bonnet [bɔnɛ] *nm* : cap, hat

bonneterie [bɔnɛtri] *nf* : hosiery

bonsoir [bɔ̃swar] *nm* : good evening, good night

bonté [bɔ̃te] *nf* : goodness, kindness

bord [bɔr] *nm* **1** : edge, rim **2** : bank, shore **3 à ~** : on board, aboard **4 au ~ de** : on the verge of

bordeaux [bɔrdo] *nm* : Bordeaux, claret (wine)

bordée [bɔrde] *nf* **1** : volley **2 ~ de neige** *Can* : snowstorm

bordel [bɔrdɛl] *nm fam* **1** : brothel **2** PAGAILLE : mess, shambles

border [bɔrde] *vt* **1** : border, line **2** : tuck in

bordereau [bɔrdəro] *nm, pl* **-reaux** [-ro] **1** : note (in finance) **2 ~ de dépôt** : deposit slip

bordure [bɔrdyr] *nf* : border, edge

borne [bɔrn] *nf* **1** : milestone, landmark **2 ~s** *nfpl* : limits — **borné, -née** [bɔrne] *adj* : narrow-minded — **borner** [bɔrne] *vt* RESTREINDRE : limit, restrict — **se borner** *vr* : confine oneself

bosquet [bɔske] *nm* : grove, copse

bosse [bɔs] *nf* **1** : hump (of a person or animal) **2 se faire une ~** : get a bump — **bosseler** [bɔsle] {8} *vt* : dent

(a bumper, etc.) — **bosser** [bɔse] *vi France fam* : work, slave away
botanique [bɔtanik] *nf* : botany — ~ *adj* : botanical
botte [bɔt] *nf* **1** : boot **2** : bunch (of radishes), sheaf (of hay) — **botter** [bɔte] *vt* : kick (in sports)
bottin [bɔtɛ̃] *nm* : (telephone) directory
bouche [buʃ] *nf* **1** : mouth **2** ENTRÉE : opening, entrance **3** ~ **bée** : flabbergasted **4** ~ **d'incendie** : fire hydrant — **bouchée** [buʃe] *nf* : mouthful
boucher[1] [buʃe] *vt* : stop up, block — **se boucher** *vr* : become blocked — **bouchon** [buʃɔ̃] *nm* **1** : cork, stopper **2** : float (in fishing) **3** EMBOUTEILLAGE : traffic jam
boucher[2], **-chère** [buʃe, -ʃɛr] *n* : butcher — **boucherie** [buʃri] *nf* : butcher's shop
boucler [bukle] *vt* **1** : buckle (a belt), fasten (a seat belt) **2** : complete (a task) — *vi* : curl — **boucle** [bukl] *nf* **1** : buckle **2** : curl **3** ~ **d'oreille** : earring — **bouclé, -clée** [bukle] *adj* : curly
bouclier [buklije] *nm* : shield
bouddhiste [budist] *adj & nmf* : Buddhist — **bouddhisme** [budism] *nm* : Buddhism
bouder [bude] *vt* : avoid — *vi* : sulk, pout — **bouderie** [budri] *nf* : sulkiness — **boudeur, -deuse** [budœr, -døz] *adj* : sulky
boudin [budɛ̃] *nm* : blood sausage
boue [bu] *nf* : mud — **boueux, boueuse** [buø, buøz] *adj* : muddy
bouée [bwe] *nf* : buoy
bouffant, -fante [bufɑ̃, -fɑ̃t] *adj* : baggy (of pants) — **bouffi, -fie** [bufi] *adj* : puffy, swollen
bouffe [buf] *nf fam* : grub, chow — **bouffer** [bufe] *vt fam* : eat, gobble up
bouffée [bufe] *nf* **1** : puff, gust **2** : surge, fit (of rage, etc.)
bouffon, -fonne [bufɔ̃, bufɔn] *adj* : comical — **bouffon** *nm* : clown, buffoon
bougeoir [buʒwar] *nm* : candlestick
bouger [buʒe] {17} *vt* : move — *vi* : budge, stir
bougie [buʒi] *nf* **1** : candle **2** : spark plug (of a car)
bougonner [bugɔne] *vi* : grumble — **bougon, -gonne** [bugɔ̃,-gɔn] *adj* : grumpy
bouillabaisse [bujabɛs] *nf* : fish soup
bouillir [bujir] {14} *vi* **1** : boil **2** : seethe (with anger, etc.) — **bouillie** [buji] *nf* : baby cereal, gruel — **bouilloire** [bujwar] *nf* : kettle, teakettle — **bouillon** [bujɔ̃] *nm* : broth, stock — **bouillonner** [bujɔne] *vi* **1** : bubble, foam **2** → **bouillir 2**
boulanger, -gère [bulɑ̃ʒe, -ʒɛr] *n* : baker — **boulangerie** [bulɑ̃ʒri] *nf* : bakery
boule [bul] *nf* **1** : ball **2** ~ **de neige** : snowball
bouleau [bulo] *nm, pl* **-leaux** : birch
bouledogue [buldɔg] *nm* : bulldog
boulet [bulɛ] *nm* **1** : cannonball **2** : ball and chain
boulette [bulɛt] *nf* **1** : pellet **2** : meatball
boulevard [bulvar] *nm* : boulevard
bouleverser [bulvɛrse] *vt* **1** : upset, turn upside down **2** PERTURBER : overwhelm — **bouleversant, -sante** [bulvɛrsɑ̃, -sɑ̃t] *adj* : distressing, upsetting — **bouleversement** [bulvɛrsəmɑ̃] *nm* : upheaval, upset
boulon [bulɔ̃] *nm* : bolt
boulot [bulo] *nm fam* **1** : work, task **2** EMPLOI : job — **boulot, -lotte** [bulo, -lɔt] *adj* : plump, chubby
boum [bum] *nm* **1** : bang **2** : boom (of business, etc.)
bouquet [bukɛ] *nm* : bouquet, bunch (of flowers)
bouquin [bukɛ̃] *nm fam* : book — **bouquiniste** [bukinist] *nmf* : secondhand bookseller
bourbier [burbje] *nm* : swamp, quagmire
bourde [burd] *nf* : blunder
bourdon [burdɔ̃] *nm* : bumblebee — **bourdonnement** [burdɔnmɑ̃] *nm* : buzz, hum, droning — **bourdonner** [burdɔne] *vi* : buzz, hum
bourgeois, -geoise [burʒwa, -ʒwaz] *adj & n* : bourgeois — **bourgeoisie** [burʒwazi] *nf* : bourgeoisie
bourgeon [burʒɔ̃] *nm* : bud — **bourgeonner** [burʒɔne] *vi* : bud
bourgogne [burgɔɲ] *nm* : Burgundy (wine)
bourrage [buraʒ] *nm* : filling, stuffing
bourreau [buro] *nm, pl* **-reaux 1** : executioner **2** ~ **de travail** : workaholic
bourrer [bure] *vt* : fill, stuff, cram — *vi* : be filling — **se bourrer** *vr* : stuff oneself
bourru, -rue [bury] *adj* : gruff, surly
bourse [burs] *nf* **1** PORTE-MONNAIE : purse **2** : scholarship **3 la Bourse** : the stock market — **boursier, -sière** [bursje, -sjɛr] *adj* : stock, stock-market

boursoufler [bursufle] *vt* : puff up, cause to swell — **se boursoufler** *vr* : blister — **boursouflure** [bursuflyr] *nf* : blister (of paint, etc.)

bousculer [buskyle] *vt* **1** : jostle, shove **2** PRESSER : rush — **se bousculer** *vr* : jostle — **bousculade** [buskylad] *nf* : rush, scramble

bousiller [buzije] *vt fam* : bungle, botch

boussole [busɔl] *nf* : compass

bout [bu] *nm* **1** EXTRÉMITÉ : end, tip **2** MORCEAU : bit **3 au ~ de** : after **4 à ~ portant** : point-blank

bouteille [butɛj] *nf* : bottle

boutique [butik] *nf* : shop, boutique

bouton [butɔ̃] *nm* **1** : button **2** BOURGEON : bud **3** : pimple **4** *or* **~ de porte** : doorknob — **boutonner** [butɔne] *vt* : button — **boutonnière** *nf* : buttonhole

bovins [bɔvɛ̃] *nmpl* : cattle

bowling [buliŋ] *nm* : bowling

box [bɔks] *nm, pl* **boxes** : stall (for a horse)

boxe [bɔks] *nf* : boxing — **boxer** [bɔkse] *vi* : box — **boxeur** [bɔksœr] *nm* : boxer, fighter

boyau [bwajo] *nm, pl* **boyaux 1** INTESTIN : intestine, gut **2** : inner tube (of a tire)

boycotter [bɔjkɔte] *vt* : boycott — **boycottage** [bɔjkɔtaʒ] *nm* : boycott

bracelet [braslɛ] *nm* : bracelet

braconner [brakɔne] *vi* : poach (of game)

braguette [bragɛt] *nf* : fly (of pants, etc.)

braille [braj] *nm* : braille

brailler [braje] *vi fam* : bawl, howl

braire [brɛr] {15} *vi* : bray

braise [brɛz] *nf* : embers *pl*

brancard [brɑ̃kar] *nm* CIVIÈRE : stretcher

branche [brɑ̃ʃ] *nf* **1** : branch **2** : sidepiece (of eyeglasses) — **branché, -chée** [brɑ̃ʃe] *adj fam* : trendy — **brancher** [brɑ̃ʃe] *vt* **1** : connect (a utility) **2** : plug in (a device)

branchie [brɑ̃ʃi] *nf* : gill (of a fish)

brandir [brɑ̃dir] *vt* : brandish, wave

branler [brɑ̃le] *vi* : wobble, be loose — **branlant, -lante** [brɑ̃lɑ̃, -lɑ̃t] *adj* : unsteady — **branle** [brɑ̃l] *nm* **mettre en ~** : set in motion

braquer [brake] *vt* **1** DIRIGER : aim **2** : turn (a steering wheel) **3** *fam* : point a gun at **4 ~ qqn contre qqch** : turn s.o. against sth

bras [bra] *nms & pl* : arm — **brasser** [brase] *vt* **1** : mix **2** : brew (beer) — **brasserie** [brasri] *nf* **1** : brewery **2** : restaurant — **brassière** [brasjɛr] *nf Can* : bra, brassiere

brave [brav] *adj* **1** GENTIL : good, nice **2** COURAGEUX : brave — **bravement** [busɔl] *adv* : bravely, boldly — **braver** [brave] *vt* : brave

break [brɛk] *nm France* : station wagon — **~** *nm Can* : break, rest

brebis [brəbi] *nf* : ewe

brèche [brɛʃ] *nf* : gap

bredouiller [brəduje] *v* : mumble, mutter

bref, brève [brɛf, brɛv] *adj* : brief, short — **bref** [brɛf] *adv or* **en ~** : briefly, in short

brésilien, -lienne [breziljɛ̃, -ljɛn] *adj* : Brazilian

bretelle [brətɛl] *nf* **1** : strap **2** : (access) ramp **3 ~s** *nfpl* : suspenders

breton, -tonne [brətɔ̃, brətɔn] *n* : Breton

breuvage [brœvaʒ] *nm* : beverage

brevet [brəvɛ] *nm* **1** : patent **2** : diploma, certificate — **breveter** [brəvte] {8} *vt* : patent

bribes [brib] *nfpl* : bits, pieces

bric-à-brac [brikabrak] *nms & pl* : odds and ends

bricoler [brikɔle] *vi* : do odd jobs, putter — *vt* : fix up — **bricolage** [brikɔlaʒ] *nm* : do-it-yourself work — **bricoleur, -leuse** [brikɔlœr, -løz] *n* : handyman

bride [brid] *nf* : bridle — **brider** [bride] *vt* **1** : bridle (a horse) **2** CONTENIR : keep in check

bridge [bridʒ] *nm* : bridge (card game)

brièveté [brijɛvte] *nf* : brevity — **brièvement** [brijɛvmɑ̃] *adv* : briefly

brigade [brigad] *nf* : brigade, squad

briller [brije] *vi* : shine — **brillant, -lante** [brijɑ̃, -jɑ̃t] *adj* **1** : bright, shiny **2** REMARQUABLE : brilliant, outstanding — **brillant** *nm* : gloss, shine

brimer [brime] *vt* : bully

brin [brɛ̃] *nm* **1** : blade (of grass), sprig **2** : little bit, iota **3** : strand (of thread, etc.)

brindille [brɛ̃dij] *nf* : twig

bringue [brɛ̃g] *nf fam* : binge

brio [brijo] *nm* **1** : brilliance, panache **2 avec ~** : brilliantly

brioche [brijɔʃ] *nf* **1** : brioche **2** *fam* : paunch

brique [brik] *nf* : brick

briquet [brikɛ] *nm* : (cigarette) lighter

brise [briz] *nf* : breeze

briser [brize] *vt* **1 :** break, smash **2** DÉTRUIRE : ruin, wreck — **se briser** *vr* : shatter, break

britannique [britanik] *adj* : British

broche [brɔʃ] *nf* **1 :** brooch **2 :** spit, skewer (in cooking) — **brochette** [brɔʃɛt] *nf* : skewer

brochure [brɔʃyr] *nf* : brochure, pamphlet

brocoli [brɔkɔli] *nm* : broccoli

broder [brɔde] *vt* : embroider — **broderie** [brɔdri] *nf* : embroidery

bronchite [brɔ̃ʃit] *nf* : bronchitis

bronze [brɔ̃z] *nm* : bronze — **bronzage** [brɔ̃zaʒ] *nm* : suntan — **bronzé, -zée** [brɔ̃ze] *adj* : suntanned — **bronzer** [brɔ̃ze] *vi* : get a suntan

brosse [brɔs] *nf* : brush — **brosser** [brɔse] *vt* **1 :** brush **2 :** paint (a picture) — **se brosser** *vr* **~ les cheveux :** brush one's hair

brouette [bruɛt] *nf* : wheelbarrow

brouiller [bruje] *vt* **1 :** mix up, scramble **2** TROUBLER : blur, cloud — **se brouiller** *vr* **1 :** quarrel **2 :** cloud over (of the weather) — **brouillard** [brujar] *nm* : fog, mist — **brouillon, -lonne** [brujɔ̃, -jɔn] *adj* : disorganized, untidy — **brouillon** *nm* : rough draft

broussailles [brusaj] *nfpl* : undergrowth

brousse [brus] *nf* **la ~ :** bush, wilderness

brouter [brute] *vi* : graze

broyer [brwaje] {58} *vt* : grind, crush

bru [bry] *nf* : daughter-in-law

bruine [brɥin] *nf* : drizzle — **bruiner** [brɥine] *vi* : drizzle

bruire [brɥir] {16} *vi* : rustle, murmur, hum — **bruissement** [brɥismɑ̃] *nm* : rustling, murmuring — **bruit** [brɥi] *nm* **1 :** noise **2** VACARME : commotion, fuss **3** RUMEUR : rumor

brûler [bryle] *vt* **1 :** burn, scald **2 :** run (a red light) — *vi* : burn (up) — **se brûler** *vr* : burn oneself — **brûlant, -lante** [brylɑ̃, -lɑ̃t] *adj* **1 :** burning hot **2 :** ardent — **brûleur** [brylœr] *nm* : burner — **brûlure** [brylyr] *nf* **1 :** burn **2 ~s d'estomac :** heartburn

brume [brym] *nf* : mist, haze — **brumeux, -meuse** [brymø, -møz] *adj* : misty, foggy

brun, brune [brœ̃, bryn] *adj* : brown — **brun** *n* : brunet — **~** *nm* : brown — **brunette** [brynɛt] *nf* : brunette

brusque [brysk] *adj* : brusque, abrupt — **brusquement** [bryskəmɑ̃] *adv* : abruptly, suddenly — **brusquer** [bryske] *vt* : rush, hurry

brut, brute [bryt] *adj* **1 :** raw, crude **2 :** dry (of wine) **3 poids ~ :** gross weight

brutal, -tale [brytal] *adj, mpl* **-taux** [bryto] : brutal — **brutalement** [-talmɑ̃] *adv* **1 :** brutally **2 :** suddenly — **brutaliser** [brytalize] *vt* : abuse, mistreat — **brutalité** [brytalite] *nf* : brutality — **brute** [bryt] *nf* : brute

bruyant, bruyante [brɥijɑ̃, -jɑ̃t] *adj* : noisy, loud — **bruyamment** [brɥijamɑ̃] *adv* : noisily, loudly

bruyère [bryjɛr] *nf* : heather

buanderie [byɑ̃dri] *nf* **1 :** laundry room **2** *Can* : self-service laundry

buccal, -cale [bykal] *adj, mpl* **-caux** [byko] : oral

bûche [byʃ] *nf* : log — **bûcher** [byʃe] *vi fam* : work, slave away — **bûcheron, -ronne** [byʃrɔ̃, -rɔn] *n* : logger, lumberjack

budget [bydʒɛ] *nm* : budget — **budgétaire** [bydʒetɛr] *adj* : budgetary — **budgétiser** [bydʒezite] *vt* : budget

buée [bɥe] *nf* : steam, mist

buffet [byfɛ] *nm* **1 :** sideboard **2 :** buffet

buffle [byfl] *nm* : buffalo

buisson [bɥisɔ̃] *nm* : bush, shrub

bulbe [bylb] *nm* : bulb (of a plant)

bulldozer [byldozɛr] *nm* : bulldozer

bulle [byl] *nf* : bubble

bulletin [byltɛ̃] *nm* **1 :** report, bulletin **2 ~ de vote :** ballot

bureau [byro] *nm, pl* **-reaux 1 :** office, study **2** SECRÉTAIRE : desk **3 :** department, bureau

bureaucrate [byrokrat] *nmf* : bureaucrat — **bureaucratie** [byrokrasi] *nf* : bureaucracy — **bureaucratique** [-kratik] *adj* : bureaucratic

bus [bys] *nm* AUTOBUS : bus

buste [byst] *nm* **1 :** chest, bust **2 :** bust (in sculpture)

but [by(t)] *nm* **1 :** aim, goal **2** *Can* : base (in baseball)

buter [byte] *vi* **~ contre** *or* **~ sur** : stumble on, trip over — *vt* : antagonize — **se buter** *vr* : become obstinate — **buté, -tée** [byte] *adj* : obstinate

butin [bytɛ̃] *nm* : loot

butte [byt] *nf* **1 :** small hill, mound **2 être en ~ à :** come up against

buveur, -veuse [byvœr, -vøz] *n* : drinker

C

c [se] *nm* **:** c, third letter of the alphabet
ça [sa] *pron* **1 :** that, this **2 :** it **3 ~ va? :** how's it going? **4 ~ y est :** there, that's it
cabane [kaban] *nf* **:** cabin, hut — **cabanon** [kabanɔ̃] *nm* **:** shed
cabaret [kabarɛ] *nm* **:** nightclub
cabine [kabin] *nf* **1 :** cabin, cab (of a truck, etc.) **2 ~ téléphonique :** telephone booth **3 ~ de pilotage :** cockpit
cabinet [kabinɛ] *nm* **1 :** office **2 :** cabinet (in government) **3 ~ de toilette** *France* **:** toilet
câble [kabl] *nm* **1 :** cable **2 :** cable television
cabosser [kabɔse] *vt* **:** dent
cabriole [kabrijɔl] *nf* **:** somersault
cacahouète [kakaɥɛt] *nf* **:** peanut
cacao [kakao] *nm* **:** cocoa
cache–cache [kaʃkaʃ] *nms & pl* **:** hide-and-seek
cachemire [kaʃmir] *nm* **:** cashmere
cacher [kaʃe] *vt* **:** hide, conceal — **se cacher** *vr* **:** hide
cachet [kaʃɛ] *nm* **1** COMPRIMÉ **:** tablet, pill **2** *or* **~ de la poste :** postmark **3 :** fee **4 :** character, style — **cacheter** [kaʃte] {8} *vt* **:** seal
cachette [kaʃɛt] *nf* **:** hiding place
cachot [kaʃo] *nm* **:** dungeon
cachottier, -tière [kaʃotje, -tjɛr] *adj* **:** secretive — **cachotterie** [kaʃɔtri] *nf* **:** little secret
cacophonie [kakɔfɔni] *nf* **:** cacophony
cactus [kaktys] *nms & pl* **:** cactus
cadavre [kadavr] *nm* **:** corpse
cadeau [kado] *nm, pl* **-deaux :** gift, present
cadenas [kadna] *nm* **:** padlock — **cadenasser** [-nase] *vt* **:** padlock
cadence [kadɑ̃s] *nf* **:** cadence, rhythm
cadet, -dette [kadɛ, -dɛt] *adj* **:** younger, youngest — **~** *n* **1 :** younger, youngest (son, daughter, child) **2 :** junior
cadran [kadrɑ̃] *nm* **1 :** dial, face **2** *Can fam* **:** alarm clock
cadre [kadr] *nm* **1 :** frame **2 :** setting, surroundings *pl* **3** STRUCTURE **:** framework **4 :** executive
caduc, -duque [kadyk] *adj* **1 :** obsolete **2 :** deciduous
cafard [kafar] *nm* **1 :** cockroach **2 avoir le ~ :** have the blues
café [kafe] *nm* **1 :** coffee **2 :** café, bar — **caféine** [kafein] *nf* **:** caffeine — **cafetière** [kaftjɛr] *nf* **:** coffeepot — **cafétéria** [kafeterja] *nf* **:** cafeteria
cage [kaʒ] *nf* **1 :** cage **2 ~ d'escalier :** stairwell
cageot [kaʒo] *nm* **:** crate
cagnotte [kaɲɔt] *nf* **:** pool, kitty
cagoule [kagul] *nf* **:** hood
cahier [kaje] *nm* **:** notebook, exercise book
cahoter [kaɔte] *vi* **:** bump along — **cahoteux, -teuse** [kaɔtø, -tøz] *adj* **:** bumpy
cailler [kaje] *vi* **1 :** curdle **2 :** clot (of blood) — **caillot** [kajo] *nm* **:** clot
caillou [kaju] *nm, pl* **-loux :** pebble, stone
caisse [kɛs] *nf* **1** BOÎTE **:** box, crate **2** *or* **~ enregistreuse :** cash register **3 ~ d'épargne :** savings bank **4 ~ populaire** *Can* **:** cooperative bank — **caissier, -sière** [kesje, -sjɛr] *n* **1 :** cashier **2 :** (bank) teller
cajoler [kaʒɔle] *vt* **1 :** fuss over, cuddle **2** ENJÔLER **:** cajole
cajun [kaʒœ̃] *adj* **:** Cajun
cake [kɛk] *nm* **:** fruitcake
calamité [kalamite] *nf* **:** calamity
calcaire [kalkɛr] *nm* **:** limestone — **~** *adj* **:** chalky
calciner [kalsine] *vt* **:** char
calcium [kalsjɔm] *nm* **:** calcium
calculer [kalkyle] *vt* **:** calculate — **calcul** [kalkyl] *nm* **1 :** calculation, sum **2 :** arithmetic **3 ~ bilaire :** gallstone — **calculateur, -trice** [kalkylatœr, -tris] *adj* **:** calculating — **calculatrice** *nf* **:** calculator
cale [kal] *nf* **1 :** wedge **2 :** hold (of a ship)
calé, -lée [kale] *adj fam* **:** brainy
calèche [kalɛʃ] *nf* **:** (horse-drawn) carriage
caleçon [kalsɔ̃] *nm* **1 :** boxer shorts *pl* **2 :** leggings *pl* **3** *or* **~s de bain :** swimming trunks
calembour [kalɑ̃bur] *nm* **:** pun

calendrier [kalɑ̃drije] *nm* : calendar
calepin [kalpɛ̃] *nm* : notebook
caler [kale] *vt* : wedge — *vi* : stall (of an engine)
calibre [kalibr] *nm* **1** : caliber **2** : grade, size — **calibrer** [kalibre] *vt* : calibrate, grade
califourchon [kalifurʃɔ̃] **à ∼s** *adv phr* : astride
câliner [kaline] *vt* : cuddle — **se câliner** *vr* : cuddle (up)
calmant, -mante [kalmɑ̃, -mɑ̃t] *adj* : soothing — **calmant** *nm* : sedative
calmar [kalmar] *nm* : squid
calme [kalm] *nm* **1** : calm **2 du ∼!** : quiet down! — **∼** *adj* : calm — **calmer** [kalme] *vt* : calm, soothe — **se calmer** *vr* : calm down
calomnie [kalɔmni] *nf* : slander, libel — **calomnier** [kalɔmnje] {96} *vt* : slander, libel
calorie [kalɔri] *nf* : calorie
calorifère [kalɔrifɛr] *nm* : heater, stove
calquer [kalke] *vt* **1** : trace (a drawing) **2** : copy, imitate — **calque** [kalk] *nm* : (exact) copy
calvaire [kalvɛr] *nm* : ordeal, suffering
calvitie [kalvisi] *nf* : baldness
camarade [kamarad] *nmf* **1** : friend **2 ∼ de classe** : classmate — **camaraderie** [kamaradri] *nf* : friendship
cambrer [kɑ̃bre] *vt* : curve, arch
cambrioler [kɑ̃brjɔle] *vt* : burglarize — **cambriolage** [kɑ̃brijɔlaʒ] *nm* : burglary — **cambrioleur, -leuse** [kɑ̃brijɔlør, -løz] *n* : burglar
cambrure [kɑ̃bryr] *nf* : arch, curve
camelot [kamlo] *nm Can* : paperboy
camelote [kamlɔt] *nf fam* : trash, junk
caméra [kamera] *nf* : movie or television camera
camion [kamjɔ̃] *nm* : truck — **camionnette** [kamjɔnɛt] *nf* : van — **camionneur, -neuse** [kamjɔnœr, -nøz] *n* : truck driver
camoufler [kamufle] *vt* : camouflage — **camouflage** [kamuflaʒ] *nm* : camouflage
camp [kɑ̃] *nm* **1** : camp **2** PARTI : side, team
campagne [kɑ̃paɲ] *nf* **1** : country, countryside **2** : campaign (in politics, etc.) — **campagnard, -gnarde** [kɑ̃paɲar, -ɲard] *adj* : country, rustic
camper [kɑ̃pe] *vi* : camp — **campement** [kɑ̃pmɑ̃] *nm* : encampment — **campeur, -peuse** [kɑ̃pœr, -pøz] *n* : camper — **camping** [kɑ̃piŋ] *nm* **1** : camping **2** : campground
campus [kɑ̃pys] *nm* : campus
canadien, -dienne [kanadjɛ̃, -djɛn] *adj* : Canadian — **canadien-français, canadienne-française** *adj, pl* **canadiens-français, canadiennes-françaises** : French-Canadian
canal [kanal] *nm, pl* **-naux** [kano] **1** : canal **2** : channel
canapé [kanape] *nm* : sofa, couch
canard [kanar] *nm* : duck
canari [kanari] *nm* : canary
cancer [kɑ̃sɛr] *nm* : cancer — **cancéreux, -reuse** [kɑ̃serø, -røz] *adj* : cancerous
candeur [kɑ̃dœr] *nf* : ingenuousness
candidat, -date [kɑ̃dida, -dat] *n* : candidate — **candidature** [kɑ̃didatyr] *nf* : candidacy
candide [kɑ̃did] *adj* : ingenuous, naïve
cane [kan] *nf* : (female) duck — **caneton** [kantɔ̃] *nm* : duckling
canette [kanɛt] *nf* **1** : (small) bottle **2** : can (for a beverage)
caniche [kaniʃ] *nm* : poodle
canicule [kanikyl] *nf* : heat wave
canif [kanif] *nm* : pocketknife
canine [ˈkeɪˌnaɪn] *nf* : canine (tooth)
caniveau [kanivo] *nm, pl* **-veaux** : gutter (in a street)
canne [kan] *nf* **1** : cane **2 ∼ à pêche** : fishing rod **3 ∼ à sucre** : sugarcane
canneberge [kanbɛrʒ] *nf* : cranberry
cannelle [kanɛl] *nf* : cinnamon
cannibale [kanibal] *nmf* : cannibal
canoë [kanɔe] *nm* : canoe
canon [kanɔ̃] *nm* **1** : cannon **2** : barrel (of a gun) **3** : canon, rule
canot [kano] *nm* **1** *France* : boat **2** *Can* : canoe **3 ∼ de sauvetage** : lifeboat
cantaloup [kɑ̃talu] *nm* : cantaloupe
cantine [kɑ̃tin] *nf* : canteen, cafeteria
cantique [kɑ̃tik] *nm* : hymn
canton [kɑ̃tɔ̃] *nm* **1** *France* : district, canton **2** *Can* : township
canular [kanylar] *nm* : hoax
canyon [kaɲɔ̃] *nm* : canyon
caoutchouc [kautʃu] *nm* **1** : rubber **2 ∼s** *nmpl* : galoshes — **caoutchouteux, -teuse** [kautʃutø, -tøz] *adj* : rubbery
cap [kap] *nm* **1** PROMONTOIRE : cape **2** ÉTAPE : milestone
capable [kapabl] *adj* : capable
capacité [kapasite] *nf* **1** : capacity **2** APTITUDE : ability
cape [kap] *nf* : cape, cloak
capitaine [kapitɛn] *nm* : captain

capital, -tale [kapital] *adj, mpl* **-taux** [-to] **1 :** major, crucial **2 peine capitale :** capital punishment — **capital** *nm, pl* **-taux :** capital, assets *pl* — **capitale** *nf* **:** capital (city)
capitalisme [kapitalism] *nm* **:** capitalism — **capitaliste** [kapitalist] *adj* **:** capitalist(ic)
capiteux, -teuse [kapitø, -tøz] *adj* **:** heady
caporal–chef [kapɔralʃɛf] *nm, pl* **caporaux–chefs** [-ro] **:** corporal
capot [kapo] *nm* **:** hood (of an automobile) — **capoter** [kapɔte] *vt* **:** overturn, capsize
caprice [kapris] *nm* **:** whim — **capricieux, -cieuse** [kaprisjø, -sjøz] *adj* **:** temperamental
capsule [kapsyl] *nf* **1 :** capsule **2 :** cap (of a bottle)
capter [kapte] *vt* **1 :** pick up (radio signals) **2 ~ l'attention de :** capture the attention of
captif, -tive [kaptif, -tiv] *adj & n* **:** captive — **captiver** [kaptive] *vt* **:** captivate — **captivité** [kaptivite] *nf* **:** captivity
capture [kaptyr] *nf* **1 :** capture, seizure **2** ATTRAPE **:** catch — **capturer** [kaptyre] *vt* **:** capture, catch
capuche [kapyʃ] *nf* **:** hood — **capuchon** [kapyʃɔ̃] *nm* **1 :** hood **2 :** cap, top (of a pen, etc.)
caqueter [kakte] {8} *vi* **:** cackle
car[1] [kar] *nm* **:** bus, coach
car[2] *conj* **:** for, because
carabine [karabin] *nf* **:** rifle
caractère [karaktɛr] *nm* **1 :** letter, character **2** TEMPÉRAMENT **:** character, nature — **caractériser** [karakterize] *vt* **:** characterize — **caractéristique** [karakteristik] *adj & nf* **:** characteristic
carafe [karaf] *nf* **:** carafe, decanter
caramel [karamɛl] *nm* **1 :** caramel **2 ~ mou :** fudge
carapace [karapas] *nf* **:** shell
carat [kara] *nm* **:** carat, karat
caravane [karavan] *nf* **1 :** caravan **2 :** trailer
carbone [karbɔn] *nm* **:** carbon — **carboniser** [karbɔnize] *vt* **:** burn, char
carburant [karbyrɑ̃] *nm* **:** fuel — **carburateur** [karbyratœr] *nm* **:** carburetor
carcasse [karkas] *nf* **:** carcass
cardiaque [kardjak] *adj* **:** cardiac
cardigan [kardigɑ̃] *nm* **:** cardigan
cardinal, -nale [kardinal] *adj, mpl* **-naux** [-no] **:** cardinal, chief — **cardinal** *nm, pl* **-naux 1 :** cardinal (in religion) **2 :** cardinal number
carence [karɑ̃s] *nf* **:** lack, deficiency
caresser [karese] *vt* **1 :** caress **2 :** cherish, dream of — **caresse** [karɛs] *nf* **:** caress
cargaison [kargɛzɔ̃] *nf* **:** cargo, freight — **cargo** [kargo] *nm* **:** freighter
caricature [karikatyr] *nf* **:** caricature
carie [kari] *nf* **:** tooth decay, cavity
carillon [karijɔ̃] *nm* **:** bell, chime — **carillonner** [karijɔne] *v* **:** chime
carnage [karnaʒ] *nm* **:** carnage, bloodshed
carnaval [karnaval] *nm, pl* **-vals :** carnival
carnet [karnɛ] *nm* **1 :** notebook **2 :** book (of stamps, tickets, etc.)
carotte [karɔt] *nf* **:** carrot
carré, -rée [kare] *adj* **1 :** square **2 :** straightforward — **carré** *nm* **:** square
carreau [karo] *nm, pl* **-reaux 1 :** tile **2** VITRE **:** windowpane **3 :** diamond (in playing cards) **4 à ~x :** checkered
carrefour [karfur] *nm* **:** intersection, crossroads
carreler [karle] {8} *vt* **:** tile — **carrelage** [karlaʒ] *nm* **:** tiled floor
carrément [karemɑ̃] *adv* **1 :** bluntly, directly **2 :** downright
carrière [karjɛr] *nf* **1 :** career **2 :** stone quarry
carrosse [karɔs] *nm* **:** (horse-drawn) coach
carrure [karyr] *nf* **:** build (of the body)
carte [kart] *nf* **1 :** card **2 :** (road) map **3 :** menu (in a restaurant) **4** *or* **~ à jouer :** playing card **5 ~ de crédit :** credit card **6 ~ des vins :** wine list **7 ~ postale :** postcard
cartilage [kartilaʒ] *nm* **:** cartilage, gristle
carton [kartɔ̃] *nm* **1 :** cardboard **2 :** cardboard box
cartouche [kartuʃ] *nf* **:** cartridge
cas [ka] *nms & pl* **1 :** case **2 en aucun ~ :** on no account **3 en ~ de :** in case of
cascade [kaskad] *nf* **1 :** cascade, torrent **2 :** waterfall
case [kaz] *nf* **1 :** box (on a form) **2 ~ postale** *Can* **:** post office box
caserne [kazɛrn] *nf* **1** *France* **:** barracks *pl* **2 ~ de pompiers** *France* **:** fire station
casier [kazje] *nm* **1 :** pigeonhole **2 ~ judiciaire :** police record
casino [kazino] *nm* **:** casino
casque [kask] *nm* **1 :** helmet **2 :** head-

phones *pl* — **casquette** [kaskɛt] *nf* : cap
casser [kase] *v* : break — **se casser** *vr* **1** : break (one's leg, etc.) **2 casse-toi!** *fam* : get out of here! — **cassable** [kasabl] *adj* : breakable — **casse-croûte** [kaskrut] *nms & pl* **1** : snack **2** *Can* : snack bar — **casse-noix** [kasnwa] *nms & pl* : nutcracker
casserole [kasrɔl] *nf* : saucepan
casse-tête [kastɛt] *nms & pl* **1** : puzzle **2** PROBLÈME : headache
cassette [kasɛt] *nf* : cassette
cassonade [kasɔnad] *nf* : brown sugar
cassure [kasyr] *nf* : break
castor [kastɔr] *nm* : beaver
catalogue [katalɔg] *nm* : catalog
cataracte [katarakt] *nf* : cataract
catastrophe [katastrɔf] *nf* : catastrophe — **catastrophique** [katastrɔfik] *adj* : catastrophic
catéchisme [kateʃism] *nm* : catechism
catégorie [kategɔri] *nf* : category — **catégorique** [kategɔrik] *adj* : categorical
cathédrale [katedral] *nf* : cathedral
catholique [katɔlik] *adj* : Catholic — **catholicisme** [katɔlisism] *nm* : Catholicism
catimini [katimini] **en ~** *adv phr* : on the sly
cauchemar [koʃmar] *nm* : nightmare
cause [koz] *nf* **1** : cause, reason **2** : (legal) case **3 à ~ de** : because of, on account of — **causer** [koze] *vt* PROVOQUER : cause — *vi* : chat — **causerie** [kozri] *nf* : talk, chat
caution [kosjɔ̃] *nf* **1** : surety, guarantee **2 libérer sous ~** : release on bail
cavalerie [kavalri] *nf* : cavalry — **cavalier, -lière** [kavalje, -ljɛr] *n* : rider, horseman *m*, horsewoman *f* — **cavalier** *nm* : knight (in chess)
cave [kav] *nf* : cellar
caverne [kavɛrn] *nf* GROTTE : cavern, cave
caviar [kavjar] *nm* : caviar
cavité [kavite] *nf* : cavity, hollow
CD [sede] *nm* (compact disc) : CD
ce [sə] (**cet** [sɛt] *before a vowel or mute h*), **cette** [sɛt] *adj, pl* **ces** [se] **1** : this, that, these, those **2 cette fois-ci** : this time **3 cette idée**! : what an idea! — **ce** (**c'** [s] *before a vowel*) *pron* **1** : it, that, these, those **2 ~ que, ~ qui, ~ dont** : what, which **3 c'est** : it is **4 ce sont** : they are **5 c'est cela** : that's right
ceci [səsi] *pron* : this
cécité [sesite] *nf* : blindness
céder [sede] {87} *vt* : give up, yield — *vi* : give in
cédille [sedij] *nf* : cedilla
cèdre [sɛdr] *nm* : cedar
cégep [seʒɛp] *nm* (*c*ollège d'*e*nseignement *g*énéral *e*t *p*rofessionnel) *Can* : junior college
ceinture [sɛ̃tyr] *nf* **1** : belt **2 ~ de sauvetage** : life belt **3 ~ de sécurité** : safety belt
cela [səla] *pron* : that, it
célébrer [selebre] {87} *vt* : celebrate — **célébration** [selebrasjɔ̃] *nf* : celebration — **célèbre** [selɛbr] *adj* : famous — **célébrité** [selebrite] *nf* **1** : fame, renown **2** : celebrity (person)
céleri [sɛlri] *nm* : celery
céleste [selɛst] *adj* : heavenly
célibataire [selibatɛr] *adj* : single, unmarried — **~** *nmf* : single person
celle, celles → **celui**
cellule [selyl] *nf* : cell
celui [səlɥi], **celle** [sɛl] *pron, pl* **ceux** [sø], **celles** [sɛl] : the one(s), those — **celui-ci** [səlɥisi], **celle-ci** [sɛlsi] *pron, pl* **ceux-ci** [søsi], **celles-ci** [sɛlsi] **1** : this (one), these **2** : the latter — **celui-là** [səlɥila], **celle-là** [sɛlla] *pron, pl* **ceux-là** [søla], **celles-là** [sɛlla] **1** : that (one), those **2** : the former
cendre [sɑ̃dr] *nf* : ash — **cendrier** [sɑ̃drije] *nm* : ashtray
censé, -sée [sɑ̃se] *adj* **être ~ faire** : be supposed to do
censurer [sɑ̃syre] *vt* : censor, ban — **censure** [sɑ̃syr] *nf* **1** : censorship **2** : censure
cent [sɑ̃] *adj* : a hundred, one hundred — **~** *nm* **1** : hundred **2** : cent **3 pour ~** : percent — **centaine** [sɑ̃tɛn] *nf* : about a hundred — **centenaire** [sɑ̃tnɛr] *adj* : hundred-year-old — **~** *nm* : centennial — **centième** [sɑ̃tjɛm] *adj & nmf & nm* : hundredth
centigrade [sɑ̃tigrad] *adj* : centigrade
centime [sɑ̃tim] *nm* : centime
centimètre [sɑ̃timɛtr] *nm* **1** : centimeter **2** : tape measure
central, -trale [sɑ̃tral] *adj, mpl* **-traux** [sɑ̃tro] : central — **central** *nm* **~ téléphonique** : telephone exchange — **centrale** *nf* **1** : power plant **2 ~ syndicale** : labor union —**centraliser** [sɑ̃tralize] *vt* : centralize
centre [sɑ̃tr] *nm* **1** : center **2 ~ commercial** : shopping center — **centrer** [sɑ̃tre] *vt* : center — **centre-ville**

[sɑ̃trəvil] *nm, pl* **centres–villes** : downtown
cependant [səpɑ̃dɑ̃] *conj* : however, yet
céramique [seramik] *nf* : ceramics
cerceau [sɛrso] *nm, pl* **-ceaux** : hoop
cercle [sɛrkl] *nm* **1** : circle **2** : group (of friends, etc.)
cercueil [sɛrkœj] *nm* : coffin
céréale [sereal] *nf* : cereal
cérémonie [seremɔni] *nf* **1** : ceremony **2 sans ~** : informally
cerf [sɛr] *nm* : stag
cerf–volant [sɛrvɔlɑ̃] *nm, pl* **cerfs–volants** : kite
cerise [səriz] *nf* : cherry — **cerisier** [sərizje] *nm* : cherry tree
cerner [sɛrne] *vt* **1** : surround **2** DÉFINIR : define, determine — **cerne** [sɛrn] *nm* **avoir des ~s** : have rings under one's eyes
certain, -taine [sɛrtɛ̃, -tɛn] *adj* **1** : certain, sure **2** : certain, some — **certainement** [sɛrtɛnmɑ̃] *adv* : certainly — **certains, certaines** [sɛrtɛ̃, -tɛn] *pron pl* : some (people), certain (ones)
certes [sɛrt] *adv* : of course, indeed
certifier [sɛrtifje] {96} *vt* : certify — **certificat** [sɛrtifika] *nm* : certificate
certitude [sɛrtityd] *nf* : certainty
cerveau [sɛrvo] *nm, pl* **-veaux** : brain
ces → **ce**
cesser [sese] *v* : cease, stop — **cesse** [sɛs] *nf* **sans ~** : constantly — **cessez–le–feu** [seselfø] *nms & pl* : cease-fire
c'est–à–dire [sɛtadir] *conj* : that is (to say)
cet, cette → **ce** — **ceux** → **celui** — **ceux–ci** → **celui–ci** — **ceux–là** → **celui–là**
chacun, chacune [ʃakœ̃, -kyn] *pron* **1** : each (one) **2** : everybody, everyone
chagrin [ʃagrɛ̃] *nm* PEINE : grief, sorrow — **chagriner** [ʃagrine] *vt* : grieve, distress
chahut [ʃay] *nm* : uproar, din
chaîne [ʃɛn] *nf* **1** : chain **2** : (television) channel **3** : (stereo) system — **chaînon** [ʃɛnɔ̃] *nm* : link
chair [ʃɛr] *nf* **1** : flesh **2** : meat **3 ~ de poule** : goose bumps
chaire [ʃɛr] *nf* **1** : (university) chair **2** : pulpit
chaise [ʃɛz] *nf* **1** : chair, seat **2 ~ roulante** : wheelchair
chaland [ʃalɑ̃] *nm* : barge
châle [ʃal] *nm* : shawl
chalet [ʃalɛ] *nm* **1** : chalet **2** *Can* : cottage
chaleur [ʃalœr] *nf* **1** : heat **2** : warmth — **chaleureux, -reuse** [ʃalœrø, -røz] *adj* : warm, friendly
chaloupe [ʃalup] *nf* : rowboat
chamailler [ʃamaje] *v* **se chamailler** *vr* : bicker
chambarder [ʃɑ̃barde] *vt fam* : mess up
chambre [ʃɑ̃br] *nf* **1** : room, bedroom **2** : (legislative) chamber, house
chameau [ʃamo] *nm, pl* **-meaux** : camel
champ [ʃɑ̃] *nm* **1** : field **2 ~ de bataille** : battlefield **3 ~ de courses** : racetrack
champagne [ʃɑ̃paɲ] *nm* : champagne
champêtre [ʃɑ̃pɛtr] *adj* : rural
champignon [ʃɑ̃piɲɔ̃] *nm* : mushroom
champion, -pionne [ʃɑ̃pjɔ̃, -pjɔn] *n* : champion — **championnat** [ʃɑ̃pjɔna] *nm* : championship
chance [ʃɑ̃s] *nf* **1** : luck, fortune **2** POSSIBILITÉ : chance, possibility **3 par ~** : fortunately
chanceler [ʃɑ̃sle] {8} *vi* : stagger — **chancelant, -lante** [ʃɑ̃slɑ̃, -lɑ̃t] *adj* : unsteady
chancelier [ʃɑ̃səlje] *nm* : chancellor
chanceux, -ceuse [ʃɑ̃sø, -søz] *adj* : lucky
chandail [ʃɑ̃daj] *nm* : sweater
chandelle [ʃɑ̃dɛl] *nf* : candle — **chandelier** [ʃɑ̃dəlje] *nm* : candlestick
changer [ʃɑ̃ʒe] {17} *vt* **1** REMPLACER : change **2** MODIFIER : alter — *vi* **1 ~ de** : change **2 ~ d'avis** : change one's mind — **se changer** *vr* : change one's clothes — **change** [ʃɑ̃ʒ] *nm* : exchange (in finance) — **changement** [ʃɑ̃ʒmɑ̃] *nm* : change
chanson [ʃɑ̃sɔ̃] *nf* : song — **chant** [ʃɑ̃] *nm* **1** : song, hymn **2** : singing
chantage [ʃɑ̃taʒ] *nm* : blackmail
chanter [ʃɑ̃te] *v* **1** : sing **2 faire ~** : blackmail — **chanteur, -teuse** [ʃɑ̃tœr, -tøz] *n* : singer
chantier [ʃɑ̃tje] *nm* **1** : (construction) site **2 ~ naval** : shipyard
chantonner [ʃɑ̃tɔne] *v* : hum
chanvre [ʃɑ̃vr] *nm* : hemp
chaos [kao] *nm* : chaos — **chaotique** [kaɔtik] *adj* : chaotic
chapeau [ʃapo] *nm, pl* **-peaux** : hat, cap
chapelet [ʃaplɛ] *nm* : rosary
chapelle [ʃapɛl] *nf* : chapel
chapelure [ʃaplyr] *nf* : bread crumbs *pl*
chaperon [ʃaprɔ̃] *nm* : chaperon

chapiteau [ʃapito] *nm, pl* **-teaux** : circus tent
chapitre [ʃapitr] *nm* **1** : chapter (of a book) **2** : subject matter
chaque [ʃak] *adj* : each, every
char [ʃar] *nm* **1** : chariot **2** : cart, wagon, float (in a parade) **3 ~ d'assaut** : tank
charabia [ʃarabja] *nm fam* : gibberish
charbon [ʃarbɔ̃] *nm* **1** : coal **2 ~ de bois** : charcoal
charcuterie [ʃarkytri] *nf* **1** : delicatessen **2** : cooked pork products
charger [ʃarʒe] {17} *vt* **1** : load **2** : charge (a battery) **3 ~ de** : put in charge of — **se charger** *vr* **~ de** : take care of — **charge** [ʃarʒ] *nf* **1** : load **2** RESPONSABILITÉ : responsibility **3** : (electrical) charge **4** FONCTION : office **5 ~s** : costs **6 à la ~ de** : dependent on — **chargé, -gée** [ʃarʒe] *adj* : busy — **chargement** [ʃarʒəmɑ̃] *nm* **1** : loading **2** : load, cargo
chariot [ʃarjo] *nm* : cart, wagon
charisme [karism] *nm* : charisma — **charismatique** [-rismatik] *adj* : charismatic
charité [ʃarite] *nf* : charity — **charitable** [ʃaritabl] *adj* : charitable
charlatan [ʃarlatɑ̃] *nm* : charlatan
charmer [ʃarme] *vt* : charm — **charmant, -mante** [ʃarmɑ̃, -mɑ̃t] *adj* : charming, delightful — **charme** [ʃarm] *nm* : charm, attraction — **charmeur, -meuse** [ʃarmœr, -møz] *adj* : charming — **~** *n* : charmer
charnière [ʃarnjɛr] *nf* : hinge
charnu, -nue [ʃarny] *adj* : fleshy
charpente [ʃarpɑ̃t] *nf* **1** : framework **2** : build (of the body) — **charpentier** [ʃarpɑ̃tje] *nm* : carpenter
charrette [ʃarɛt] *nf* : cart
charrue [ʃary] *nf* : plow
charte [ʃart] *nf* : charter — **charter** [ʃarte] *nm* : charter flight
chas [ʃa] *nm* : eye (of a needle)
chasser [ʃase] *vt* **1** : hunt **2** EXPULSER : chase away — **chasse** [ʃas] *nf* **1** : hunting **2** POURSUITE : chase **3** *or* **~ d'eau** : flush (of a toilet) — **chasse-neige** [ʃasnɛʒ] *nms & pl* : snowplow — **chasseur, -seuse** [ʃasœr, -søz] *n* : hunter
châssis [ʃasi] *nm* : frame (of a window)
chaste [ʃast] *adj* : chaste — **chasteté** [ʃastəte] *nf* : chastity
chat, chatte [ʃa, ʃat] *n* : cat
châtaigne [ʃatɛɲ] *nf* : chestnut
château [ʃato] *nm, pl* **-teaux** **1** : castle **2 ~ fort** : stronghold
châtier [ʃatje] {96} *vt* : chastise — **châtiment** [ʃatimɑ̃] *nm* : punishment
chaton [ʃatɔ̃] *nm* : kitten
chatouiller [ʃatuje] *vt* : tickle — **chatouilleux, -leuse** [ʃatujø, -jøz] *adj* : ticklish
châtrer [ʃatre] *vt* : castrate
chatte → **chat**
chaud, chaude [ʃo, ʃod] *adj* : warm, hot — **chaud** [ʃo] *adv* **1 avoir ~** : feel warm or hot **2 il fait ~** : it's warm, it's hot — **~** *nm* : heat, warmth — **chaudière** [ʃodjɛr] *nf* : boiler — **chaudron** [ʃodrɔ̃] *nm* : cauldron
chauffage [ʃofaʒ] *nm* : heating
chauffard [ʃofar] *nm* : reckless driver
chauffer [ʃofe] *vt* : heat, warm — *vi* : warm up — **se chauffer** *vr* : warm (oneself) up
chauffeur [ʃofœr] *nm* : driver, chauffeur
chaussée [ʃose] *nf* : roadway
chausser [ʃose] *vt* **1** : put on (shoes) **2 ~ du 7** : take size 7 (in shoes) — **chaussette** [ʃosɛt] *nf* : sock — **chausson** [ʃosɔ̃] *nm* **1** : slipper **2 ~ aux pommes** : apple turnover — **chaussure** [ʃosyr] *nf* : shoe, footwear
chauve [ʃov] *adj* : bald — **chauve–souris** [ʃovsuri] *nf, pl* **chauves–souris** : bat (animal)
chauvin, -vine [ʃovɛ̃, -vin] *adj* : chauvinistic
chaux [ʃo] *nf* **1** : lime **2 lait de ~** : whitewash
chavirer [ʃavire] *v* : capsize
chef [ʃɛf] *nm* **1** : leader, head, chief **2** *or* **~ cuisinier** : chef **3 ~ d'orchestre** : conductor **4 en ~** : (in) chief — **chef–d'œuvre** [ʃɛdœvr] *nm, pl* **chefs–d'œuvre** : masterpiece
chemin [ʃəmɛ̃] *nm* **1** : road, path **2 ~ de fer** : railroad
cheminée [ʃəmine] *nf* **1** : fireplace **2** : chimney
cheminer [ʃəmine] *vi* **1** : walk along **2** PROGRESSER : progress
chemise [ʃəmiz] *nf* **1** : shirt **2** DOSSIER : folder **3 ~ de nuit** : nightgown — **chemisier** [ʃəmizje] *nm* : blouse
chenal [ʃənal] *nm, pl* **-naux** [ʃəno] : channel
chêne [ʃɛn] *nm* : oak
chenille [ʃənij] *nf* : caterpillar
chèque [ʃɛk] *nm* : check
cher, chère [ʃɛr] *adj* **1** : dear, beloved **2** COÛTEUX : expensive — **~** *n* **mon**

cher, ma chère : my dear — **cher** *adv* **coûter ~** : cost a lot
chercher [ʃɛrʃe] *vt* : look for, seek — **chercheur, -cheuse** [ʃɛrʃœr, -ʃøz] *n* : researcher
chérir [ʃerir] *vt* : cherish — **chéri, -rie** [ʃeri] *adj & n* : darling, dear
chétif, -tive [ʃetif, -tiv] *adj* : puny, weak
cheval [ʃəval] *nm, pl* **-vaux** [ʃəvo] **1** : horse **2** *or* **cheval–vapeur** : horsepower
chevalerie [ʃəvalri] *nf* : chivalry
chevalet [ʃəvalɛ] *nm* : easel
chevalier [ʃəvalje] *nm* : knight
chevaucher [ʃəvoʃe] *vt* **1** : straddle **2** : overlap — **se chevaucher** *vr* : overlap
chevelure [ʃəvlyr] *nf* : hair — **chevelu, -lue** [ʃəvly] *adj* : hairy
chevet [ʃəvɛ] *nm* : bedside
cheveu [ʃəvø] *nm, pl* **-veux** **1** POIL : hair **2 ~x** *nmpl* : (head of) hair
cheville [ʃəvij] *nf* : ankle
chèvre [ʃɛvr] *nf* : goat — **chevreau** [ʃəvro] *nm, pl* **-vreaux** : kid (goat)
chevreuil [ʃəvrœj] *nm* : roe deer
chevron [ʃəvrɔ̃] *nm* : rafter
chez [ʃe] *prep* **1** : at (the house of) **2** PARMI : among, in **3 ~ soi** : at home
chez–soi [ʃeswa] *nms & pl* : home
chic [ʃik] *adj s & pl* **1** : stylish **2** SYMPATHIQUE : nice
chicane [ʃikan] *nf* : squabble
chicorée [ʃikɔre] *nf* **1** : endive **2** : chicory (for coffee)
chien, chienne [ʃjɛ̃, -ʃjɛn] *n* : dog, bitch *f*
chiffon [ʃifɔ̃] *nm* : rag — **chiffonner** [ʃifɔne] *vt* : crumple
chiffre [ʃifr] *nm* **1** : figure, numeral **2** : amount, sum (in finance) **3** CODE : code **4 ~ d'affaires** : turnover — **chiffrer** [ʃifre] *vt* : calculate, assess — **se chiffrer** *vr* **~ à** : amount to
chignon [ʃiɲɔ̃] *nm* : (hair) bun
chimie [ʃimi] *nf* : chemistry — **chimique** [ʃimik] *adj* : chemical — **chimiste** [ʃimist] *nmf* : chemist
chimpanzé [ʃɛ̃pɑ̃ze] *nm* : chimpanzee
chinois, -noise [ʃinwa, -nwaz] *adj* : Chinese — **chinois** *nm* : Chinese (language)
chiot [ʃjo] *nm* : puppy
chips [ʃips] *nfpl* : potato chips
chirurgie [ʃiryrʒi] *nf* : surgery — **chirurgical, -cale** [ʃiryrʒikal] *adj, mpl* **-caux** [-ko] : surgical — **chirurgien, -gienne** [ʃiryrʒjɛ̃, -ʒjɛn] *n* : surgeon
chlore [klɔr] *nm* : chlorine
choc [ʃɔk] *nm* **1** : shock **2** : impact, crash
chocolat [ʃɔkɔla] *nm* : chocolate
chœur [kœr] *nm* **1** : choir **2** : chorus
choir [ʃwar] {18} *vi* : drop, fall
choisir [ʃwazir] *vt* : choose — **choix** [ʃwa] *nm* **1** : choice **2 de ~** : choice, first-rate
cholestérol [kɔlɛsterɔl] *nm* : cholesterol
chômage [ʃomaʒ] *nm* : unemployment — **chômeur, -meuse** [ʃomœr, -møz] *n* : unemployed person
choquer [ʃɔke] *vt* : shock, offend — **choquant, -quante** [ʃɔkɑ̃, -kɑ̃t] *adj* : shocking
choral, -rale [kɔral] *adj, mpl* **-rals** or **-raux** [kɔro] : choral — **chorale** *nf* : choir
chose [ʃoz] *nf* **1** : thing **2** AFFAIRE : matter
chou [ʃu] *nm, pl* **choux** : cabbage — **chouchou, -choute** [ʃuʃu, -ʃut] *n fam* : pet, favorite — **choucroute** [ʃukrut] *nf* : sauerkraut
chouette [ʃwɛt] *nf* : owl — **~** *adj fam* : terrific, neat
chou–fleur [ʃuflœr] *nm, pl* **choux–fleurs** : cauliflower
choyer [ʃwaje] {58} *vt* : pamper
chrétien, -tienne [kretjɛ̃, -tjɛn] *adj & n* : Christian — **christianisme** [kristjanism] *nm* : Christianity
chrome [krom] *nm* **1** : chromium **2 ~s** *nmpl* : chrome
chronique [krɔnik] *adj* : chronic — **~** *nf* : (newspaper) column, (televison) report — **chroniqueur, -queuse** [krɔnikœr, -køz] *n* : columnist
chronologie [krɔnɔlɔʒi] *nf* : chronology — **chronologique** [krɔnɔlɔʒik] *adj* : chronological
chronomètre [krɔnɔmɛtr] *nm* : stopwatch — **chronométrer** [krɔnɔmetre] {87} *vt* : time
chuchoter [ʃyʃɔte] *v* : whisper — **chuchotement** [ʃyʃɔtmɑ̃] *nm* : whisper
chum [tʃɔm] *nm Can fam* : boyfriend
chut [ʃyt] *interj* : sh!, hush!
chute [ʃyt] *nf* **1** : fall **2** *or* **~ d'eau** : waterfall **3 ~ de pluie** : rainfall
ci [si] *adv* **1 ce livre-ci** : this book **2 cette fois-ci** : this time **3 ceux-ci** : these ones **4 par-ci par-là** : here and there — **~** *pron* **1 ~ et ça** : this and that **2** → **comme** — **ci–après** [siaprɛ] *adv* : hereafter — **ci–bas** [siba] *adv* : below
cible [sibl] *nf* : target

ciboule [sibul] *nf* : scallion — **ciboulette** [sibulɛt] *nf* : chive
cicatrice [sikatris] *nf* : scar — **cicatriser** [sikatrize] *v* **se cicatriser** *vr* : heal (up)
ci–contre [sikɔ̃tr] *adv* : opposite
ci–dessous [sidəsu] *adv* : below
ci–dessus [sidəsy] *adv* : above
cidre [sidr] *nm* : cider
ciel [sjɛl] *nm* **1** *pl* **ciels** : sky **2** *pl* **cieux** [sjø] : heaven
cierge [sjɛrʒ] *nm* : candle (in a church)
cigare [sigar] *nm* : cigar — **cigarette** [sigarɛt] *nf* : cigarette
cigogne [sigɔɲ] *nf* : stork
ci–inclus, -cluse [siɛ̃kly, -klyz] *adj* : enclosed — **ci–inclus** [siɛ̃kly] *adv* : enclosed
ci–joint, -jointe [siʒwɛ̃, -ʒwɛ̃t] *adj* : enclosed — **ci–joint** [siʒwɛ̃] *adv* : enclosed, herewith
cil [sil] *nm* : eyelash
cime [sim] *nf* : summit, peak
ciment [simɑ̃] *nm* : cement
cimetière [simtjɛr] *nm* : cemetery
cinéaste [sineast] *nmf* : film director
cinéma [sinema] *nm* **1** : movie theater **2 aller au ~** : go to the movies
cinglant, -glante [sɛ̃glɑ̃, -glɑ̃t] *adj* : cutting, biting
cinq [sɛ̃k] *adj* **1** : five **2** : fifth (in dates) — **~** *nms & pl* : five
cinquante [sɛ̃kɑ̃t] *adj & nms & pl* : fifty — **cinquantaine** [sɛ̃kɑ̃tɛn] *nf* **une ~ de** : about fifty — **cinquantième** [sɛ̃kɑ̃tjɛm] *adj & nmf & nm* : fiftieth
cinquième [sɛ̃kjɛm] *adj & nmf & nm* : fifth
cintre [sɛ̃tr] *nm* : coat hanger
cirage [siraʒ] *nm* : shoe polish
circoncire [sirkɔ̃sir] {86} *vt* : circumcise — **circoncision** [sirkɔ̃sizjɔ̃] *nf* : circumcision
circonférence [sirkɔ̃ferɑ̃s] *nf* : circumference
circonflexe [sirkɔ̃flɛks] *adj* **accent ~** : circumflex (accent)
circonscrire [sirkɔ̃skrir] {33} *vt* : limit, contain — **circonscription** [sirkɔ̃skripsjɔ̃] *nf* : district, ward
circonspect, -specte [sirkɔ̃spɛ, -spɛkt] *adj* : cautious, circumspect
circonstance [sirkɔ̃stɑ̃s] *nf* : circumstance, occasion
circuit [sirkɥi] *nm* **1** : circuit **2** *or* **coup de ~** *Can* : home run (in baseball)
circulaire [sirkylɛr] *adj & nf* : circular
circuler [sirkyle] *vi* **1** : circulate **2** SE DÉPLACER : move (along) **3** : run (of buses, etc.) **4 faire ~ des bruits** : spread rumors — **circulation** [sirkylasjɔ̃] *nf* **1** : circulation **2** : traffic
cire [sir] *nf* : wax — **ciré** [sire] *nm* : oilskin — **cirer** [sire] *vt* : wax, polish
cirque [sirk] *nm* **1** : circus **2** *fam* : chaos
cisailles [sizaj] *nfpl* : shears
ciseau [sizo] *nm, pl* **-seaux** **1** : chisel **2 ~x** *nmpl* : scissors — **ciseler** [sizle] {20} *vt* : chisel
citadelle [sitadɛl] *nf* : citadel
citadin, -dine [sitadɛ̃, -din] *n* : city dweller
citation [sitasjɔ̃] *nf* **1** : quotation **2** : summons (in law)
cité [site] *nf* **1** : city **2 ~ universitaire** *France* : college dormitories *pl* **3 ~ universitaire** *Can* : college campus
citer [site] *vt* **1** : quote **2** MENTIONNER : name, cite
citerne [sitɛrn] *nf* : tank, reservoir
citoyen, citoyenne [sitwajɛ̃, -jɛn] *n* : citizen — **citoyenneté** [sitwajɛnte] *nf* : citizenship
citron [sitrɔ̃] *nm* : lemon — **citronnade** [sitrɔnad] *nf* : lemonade
citrouille [sitruj] *nf* : pumpkin
civière [sivjɛr] *nf* : stretcher
civil, -vile [sivil] *adj* **1** : civil **2** : secular — **~** *n* : civilian — **civilisation** [sivilizasjɔ̃] *nf* : civilization — **civiliser** [sivilize] *vt* : civilize — **civilité** [sivilite] *nf* : civility
civique [sivik] *adj* : civic
clair, claire [klɛr] *adj* **1** : clear **2** LUMINEUX : bright **3** PÂLE : light-colored — **clair** *adv* : clearly — **clair** [klɛr] *nm* **1 ~ de lune** : moonlight **2 mettre au ~** : make clear — **clairement** [klɛrmɑ̃] *adv* : clearly — **clairière** [klɛrjɛr] *nf* : clearing
clairon [klɛrɔ̃] *nm* : bugle
clairsemé, -mée [klɛrsəme] *adj* : scattered, sparse
clamer [klame] *vt* : proclaim — **clameur** [klamœr] *nf* : clamor
clan [klɑ̃] *nm* : clan, clique
clandestin, -tine [klɑ̃dɛstɛ̃, -tin] *adj* **1** : clandestine **2 passager ~** : stowaway
clapier [klapje] *nm* : (rabbit) hutch
clapoter [klapɔte] *vi* : lap (of waves)
claque [klak] *nf* **1** : slap, smack **2 ~s** *nfpl Can* : rubbers, galoshes — **claquement** [klakmɑ̃] *nm* : bang(ing), slam(ming) — **claquer** [klake] *vt* **1**

GIFLER : slap **2** : slam (a door) — *vi* **1 faire ~ ses doigts** : snap one's fingers **2 il claque des dents** : his teeth are chattering — **claquettes** [klakɛt] *nfpl* : tap dancing

clarifier [klarifje] {96} *vt* : clarify — **clarification** [-rifikasjɔ̃] *nf* : clarification

clarinette [klarinɛt] *nf* : clarinet

clarté [klarte] *nf* **1** : light, brightness **2** NETTETÉ : clarity

classe [klas] *nf* **1** : class, category **2** : classroom **3 aller en ~** : go to school — **classement** [klasmɑ̃] *nm* **1** : classification **2** RANG : ranking, place — **classer** [klase] *vt* : class, classify — **se classer** *vr* : rank — **classeur** [klasœr] *nm* **1** : binder **2** : filing cabinet

classifier [klasifje] {96} *vt* : classify — **classification** [klasifikasjɔ̃] *nf* : classification

classique [klasik] *adj* : classic(al) — **~** *nm* : classic (of a book, etc.)

clause [kloz] *nf* : clause

claustrophobie [klostrɔfɔbi] *nf* : claustrophobia

clavecin [klavsɛ̃] *nm* : harpsichord

clavicule [klavikyl] *nf* : collarbone

clavier [klavje] *nm* : keyboard

clé *or* **clef** [kle] *nf* **1** : key **2** : clef (in music) **3 ~ anglaise** : monkey wrench — **~** *adj* : key

clément, -mente [klemɑ̃, -mɑ̃t] *adj* **1** : lenient **2** DOUX : mild, clement — **clémence** [klemɑ̃s] *nf* : leniency

clémentine [klemɑ̃tin] *nf* : tangerine

clenche [klɑ̃ʃ] *nf* : latch

clergé [klɛrʒe] *nm* : clergy

clérical, -cale [klerikal] *adj, mpl* **-caux** [-ko] : clerical

cliché [kliʃe] *nm* : cliché

client, cliente [kliɑ̃, kliɑ̃t] *n* **1** : customer, client **2** : patient — **clientèle** [kliɑ̃tɛl] *nf* **1** : customers *pl* **2** : practice (of a doctor)

cligner [kliɲe] *vi* **1 ~ de l'œil** : wink **2 ~ des yeux** : blink — **clignotant** [kliɲɔtɑ̃] *nm* : blinker, directional signal — **clignoter** [kliɲɔte] *vi* **1** : flicker, flash **2** → **cligner 2**

climat [klima] *nm* : climate — **climatisation** [klimatizasjɔ̃] *nf* : air-conditioning — **climatisé, -sée** [klimatize] *adj* : air-conditioned — **climatiseur** [klimatizœr] *nm* : air conditioner

clin [klɛ̃] *nm* **1 ~ d'œil** : wink **2 en un ~ d'œil** : in a flash

clinique [klinik] *nf* : clinic — **~** *adj* : clinical

cliquer [klike] *vi* : click (on a computer)

cliqueter [klikte] {8} *vi* : clink, jingle, clack — **cliquetis** [klikti] *nm* : jingle, clatter

clochard, -charde [klɔʃar, -ʃard] *n* : tramp

cloche [klɔʃ] *nf* : bell — **clocher** [klɔʃe] *nm* : belfry, steeple

cloison [klwazɔ̃] *nf* : partition — **cloisonner** [klwazɔne] *vt* : partition (off)

cloître [klwatr] *nm* : cloister

cloque [klɔk] *nf* : blister

clore [klor] {19} *vt* : close, conclude — **clos, close** [klo, -kloz] *adj* : closed, shut — **clôture** [klotyr] *nf* **1** : fence **2** : end, closure — **clôturer** [klotyre] *vt* **1** : enclose **2** : bring to a close

clou [klu] *nm, pl* **~s** **1** : nail **2** : high point **3** FURONCLE : boil **4 ~ de girofle** : clove — **clouer** [klue] *vt* **1** : nail **2** : pin down

clown [klun] *nm* : clown

club [klœb] *nm* : club

coaguler [kɔagyle] *v* : coagulate — **se coaguler** *vr* : coagulate, clot

coalition [kɔalisjɔ̃] *nf* : coalition

coasser [kɔase] *vi* : croak

cobaye [kɔbaj] *nm* : guinea pig

cocaïne [kɔkain] *nf* : cocaine

cocasse [kɔkas] *adj* : comical

coccinelle [kɔksinɛl] *nf* : ladybug

cocher [kɔʃe] *vt* : check (off)

cochon [kɔʃɔ̃] *nm* **1** : pig **2 ~ d'Inde** : guinea pig — **cochonnerie** [kɔʃɔnri] *nf* : junk, trash

cocktail [kɔktɛl] *nm* : cocktail

coco [kɔko] *nm or* **noix de ~** : coconut — **cocotier** [kɔkɔtje] *nm* : coconut palm

cocon [kɔkɔ̃] *nm* : cocoon

cocotte [kɔkɔt] *nf* : casserole dish

code [kɔd] *nm* **1** : code **2 ~ postal** : zip code — **coder** [kɔde] *vt* : code, encode

coéquipier, -pière [kɔekipje, -jɛr] *n* : teammate

cœur [kœr] *nm* **1** : heart **2** : center, core **3** : hearts *pl* (in playing cards) **4** COURAGE : courage **5 à ~ joie** : to one's heart's content **6 avoir mal au ~** : feel sick, feel nauseous **7 de bon ~** : willingly

coffre [kɔfr] *nm* **1** : (toy) chest **2** COFFRE-FORT : safe **3** : trunk (of a car) — **coffre-fort** [kɔfrəfɔr] *nm, pl* **cof-**

fres–forts : safe — **coffret** [kɔfrɛ] *nm* : small box, case
cognac [kɔɲak] *nm* : cognac
cogner [kɔɲe] *vt* : knock, bang — *vi* : knock — **se cogner** *vr* **1** : bump oneself **2 ~ la tête** : hit one's head
cohabiter [kɔabite] *vi* : live together
cohérent, -rente [kɔerɑ̃, -rɑ̃t] *adj* : coherent — **cohérence** [-erɑ̃s] *nf* : coherence
cohue [kɔy] *nf* : crowd
coiffe [kwaf] *nf* : headdress — **coiffer** [kwafe] *v* **se coiffer** *vr* : do one's hair — **coiffeur, -feuse** [kwafœr, -føz] *n* : hairdresser — **coiffure** [kwafyr] *nf* **1** : hairdo **2** : hairdressing
coin [kwɛ̃] *nm* **1** : corner **2** ENDROIT : place, spot
coincer [kwɛ̃se] {6} *vt* **1** : wedge, jam **2** *fam* : corner, nab — *vi* : get stuck
coïncider [kɔɛ̃side] *vi* : coincide — **coïncidence** [kɔɛ̃sidɑ̃s] *nf* : coincidence
col [kɔl] *nm* **1** : collar **2** : neck (of a bottle)
colère [kɔlɛr] *nf* **1** : anger **2 se mettre en ~** : get angry — **coléreux, -reuse** [kɔlerø, -røz] *adj* : bad-tempered, irritable — **colérique** [kɔlerik] *adj* : bad-tempered
colimaçon [kɔlimasɔ̃] *nm* **1** : snail **2 escalier en ~** : spiral staircase
colique [kɔlik] *nf* **1** : diarrhea **2** *or* **~s** *nfpl* : colic
colis [kɔli] *nms & pl* : parcel, package
collaborer [kɔlabɔre] *vi* : collaborate — **collaborateur, -trice** [kɔlabɔratœr, -tris] *n* : colleague — **collaboration** [-bɔrasjɔ̃] *nf* : collaboration
collant, -lante [kɔlɑ̃, -lɑ̃t] *adj* : sticky — **collant** *nm* **1** : panty hose *pl* **2 ~s** *mpl* : tights
collation [kɔlasjɔ̃] *nf* : snack
colle [kɔl] *nf* **1** : paste, glue **2** : trick question
collecte [kɔlɛkt] *nf* : collection — **collecter** [kɔlɛkte] *vt* : collect (funds) — **collectif, -tive** [kɔlɛktif, -tiv] *adj* : collective, joint — **collection** [kɔlɛksjɔ̃] *nf* : collection — **collectionner** [kɔlɛksjɔne] *vt* : collect — **collectionneur, -neuse** [kɔlɛksjɔnœr, -nøz] *n* : collector
collège [kɔlɛʒ] *nm* **1** *France* : junior high school **2** *Can* : vocational college — **collégial, -giale** [kɔleʒjal] *adj, mpl* **-giaux** [-ʒjo] : collegiate — **collégien, -gienne** [kɔleʒjɛ̃, -ʒjɛn] *n France* : schoolboy *m*, schoolgirl *f*
collègue [kɔlɛg] *nmf* : colleague
coller [kɔle] *vt* : stick, glue — *vi* **~ à** : stick to, adhere to
collet [kɔlɛ] *nm* **1** : collar (of a shirt) **2 être ~ monté** : be prim and proper
collier [kɔlje] *nm* **1** : necklace **2** : (animal) collar
colline [kɔlin] *nf* : hill
collision [kɔlizjɔ̃] *nf* **1** : collision **2 entrer en ~ avec** : collide with
colloque [kɔlɔk] *nm* : symposium
colombe [kɔlɔ̃b] *nf* : dove
colon [kɔlɔ̃] *nm* : settler
côlon [kolɔ̃] *nm* : colon (in anatomy)
colonel [kɔlɔnɛl] *nm* : colonel
colonie [kɔlɔni] *nf* **1** : colony **2 ~ de vacances** : summer camp — **colonial, -niale** [kɔlɔnjal] *adj, mpl* **-niaux** [-njo] : colonial — **coloniser** [kɔlɔnize] *vt* : colonize, settle
colonne [kɔlɔn] *nf* **1** : column **2 ~ vertébrale** : spine, backbone
colorer [kɔlɔre] *vt* : color, tint — **colorant** [kɔlɔrɑ̃] *nm* : dye, stain — **coloré, -rée** [kɔlɔre] *adj* **1** : colorful **2** : colored — **colorier** [kɔlɔrje] {96} *vt* : color (a drawing) — **coloris** [kɔlɔri] *nm* : shade, color
colporter [kɔlpɔrte] *vt* : hawk, peddle — **colporteur, -teuse** [kɔlpɔrtœr, -tøz] *n* : peddler
coma [kɔma] *nm* : coma
combattre [kɔ̃batr] {12} *v* : fight — **combat** [kɔ̃ba] *nm* **1** : fight(ing) **2 ~ de boxe** : boxing match — **combattant, -tante** [kɔ̃batɑ̃, -tɑ̃t] *n* **1** : combatant, fighter **2 ancien combattant** : veteran — **combatif, -tive** [kɔ̃batif, -tiv] *adj* : combative
combien [kɔ̃bjɛ̃] *adv* **1** : how much, how many **2 ~ de** : how much, how many **3 ~ de fois** : how often **4 ~ de temps** : how long
combiner [kɔ̃bine] *vt* **1** : combine **2** PRÉPARER : work out, devise — **combinaison** [kɔ̃binɛzɔ̃] *nf* **1** : combination **2** : coveralls *pl*, suit — **combiné** [kɔ̃bine] *nm* : (telephone) receiver
combler [kɔ̃ble] *vt* **1** : fill (in) **2** : satisfy, fulfill — **comble** [kɔ̃bl] *adj* : packed — **~** *nm* **le ~ de** : the height of
combustible [kɔ̃bystibl] *adj* : combustible — **~** *nm* : fuel — **combustion** [kɔ̃bystjɔ̃] *nf* : combustion
comédie [kɔmedi] *nf* : comedy — **comédien, -dienne** [kɔmedjɛ̃, -djɛn] *n* : actor *m*, actress *f*
comestible [kɔmɛstibl] *adj* : edible

comète [kɔmɛt] *nf* : comet
comique [kɔmik] *adj* : comic, funny — ~ *nmf* : comedian, comic
comité [kɔmite] *nm* : committee
commander [kɔmɑ̃de] *vt* **1** : command **2** : order (a meal, etc.) — **commandant** [kɔmɑ̃dɑ̃] *nm* **1** : commander **2** : major (in the army) **3** ~ **de bord** : captain — **commande** [kɔmɑ̃d] *nf* **1** : order **2** ~ **à distance** : remote control — **commandement** [kɔmɑ̃dmɑ̃] *nm* **1** : command, authority **2** : commandment (in religion)
comme [kɔm] *adv* : how — ~ *conj* **1** : as, like **2** : since **3** : when, as **4** ~ **ci,** ~ **ça** : so-so **5** ~ **il faut** : properly — ~ *prep* : like, as
commémorer [kɔmemɔre] *vt* : commemorate — **commémoration** [kɔmemɔrasjɔ̃] *nf* : commemoration
commencer [kɔmɑ̃se] {6} *v* : begin, start — **commencement** [kɔmɑ̃smɑ̃] *nm* : beginning, start
comment [kɔmɑ̃] *adv* **1** : how **2** : what **3** ~ **ça va?** : how is it going?
commenter [kɔmɑ̃te] *vt* : comment on — **commentaire** [kɔmɑ̃tɛr] *nm* **1** : comment **2** : commentary
commérages [kɔmeraʒ] *nmpl fam* : gossip
commerce [kɔmɛrs] *nm* : business, trade — **commercer** [kɔmɛrse] {6} *vi* : trade, deal — **commerçant, -çante** [kɔmɛrsɑ̃, -sɑ̃t] *n* : merchant, storekeeper — **commercial** [kɔmɛrsjal] *adj, mpl* **-ciaux** [-sjo] : commercial — **commercialiser** [kɔmɛrsjalize] *vt* : market
commère [kɔmɛr] *nf fam* : gossip (person)
commettre [kɔmɛtr] {53} *vt* : commit
commis [kɔmi] *nm* **1** : clerk **2** ~ **voyageur** : traveling salesman
commissaire [kɔmisɛr] *nm* : superintendent, commissioner — **commissariat** [kɔmisarja] *nm* ~ **de police** : police station
commission [kɔmisjɔ̃] *nf* **1** : committee **2** ~**s** *nfpl* : shopping
commode [kɔmɔd] *adj* **1** : handy **2** **pas** ~ : awkward — ~ *nf* : chest of drawers — **commodité** [kɔmɔdite] *nf* : convenience
commotion [kɔmɔsjɔ̃] *nf* ~ **cérébrale** : concussion
commun, -mune [kɔmœ̃, -myn] *adj* **1** : common, shared **2** : usual, ordinary — **commun** *nm* **1 en** ~ : in common **2 hors du** ~ : out of the ordinary
communauté [kɔmynote] *nf* **1** : community **2** : commune — **communautaire** [kɔmynotɛr] *adj* : communal
communication [kɔmynikasjɔ̃] *nf* **1** : communication **2** ~ **téléphonique** : telephone call
communion [kɔmynjɔ̃] *nf* : communion
communiquer [kɔmynike] *v* : communicate — **communiqué** [kɔmynike] *nm* : press release
communisme [kɔmynism] *nm* : communism — **communiste** [kɔmynist] *adj & nmf* : communist
commutateur [kɔmytatœr] *nm* : (electric) switch
compact, -pacte [kɔ̃pakt] *adj* : compact, dense — **compact** *nm* : compact disc
compagnie [kɔ̃paɲi] *nf* **1** : company **2** **tenir** ~ **à qqn** : keep s.o. company — **compagne** [kɔ̃paɲ] *nf* : (female) companion, partner — **compagnon** [kɔ̃paɲɔ̃] *nm* : companion
comparer [kɔ̃pare] *vt* : compare — **comparaison** [kɔ̃parɛzɔ̃] *nf* : comparison
compartiment [kɔ̃partimɑ̃] *nm* : compartment
compas [kɔ̃pa] *nms & pl* : compass
compassion [kɔ̃pasjɔ̃] *nf* : compassion
compatible [kɔ̃patibl] *adj* : compatible — **compatibilité** [kɔ̃patibilite] *nf* : compatibility
compatir [kɔ̃patir] *vi* : sympathize — **compatissant, -sante** [kɔ̃patisɑ̃, -sɑ̃t] *adj* : compassionate
compatriote [kɔ̃patrijɔt] *nmf* : compatriot
compenser [kɔ̃pɑ̃se] *vt* : compensate for — **compensation** [kɔ̃pɑ̃sasjɔ̃] *nf* : compensation
compétent, -tente [kɔ̃petɑ̃, -tɑ̃t] *adj* : competent — **compétence** [-petɑ̃s] *nf* : competence
compétiteur, -trice [kɔ̃petitœr, -tris] *n* : competitor, rival — **compétitif, -tive** [kɔ̃petitif, -tiv] *adj* : competitive — **compétition** [kɔ̃petisjɔ̃] *nf* : competition
complaisant, -sante [kɔ̃plɛzɑ̃, -zɑ̃t] *adj* **1** AIMABLE : obliging, kind **2** INDULGENT : indulgent
complément [kɔ̃plemɑ̃] *nm* : complement — **complémentaire** [kɔ̃plemɑ̃tɛr] *adj* : complementary
complet, -plète [kɔ̃plɛ, -plɛt] *adj* **1** : complete **2** PLEIN : full (of a hotel, etc.) — **complet** *nm* : suit — **com-**

plètement [kɔ̃plɛtmɑ̃] *adv* : completely — **compléter** [kɔ̃plete] {87} *vt* : complete
complexe [kɔ̃plɛks] *adj & nm* : complex — **complexité** [kɔ̃plɛksite] *nf* : complexity
complication [kɔ̃plikasjɔ̃] *nf* : complication
complice [kɔ̃plis] *adj* : knowing (of a look, etc.) — ~ *nmf* : accomplice
compliment [kɔ̃plimɑ̃] *nm* : compliment — **complimenter** [kɔ̃plimɑ̃te] *vt* : compliment
compliquer [kɔ̃plike] *vt* : complicate — **compliqué, -quée** [kɔ̃plike] *adj* : complicated
complot [kɔ̃plo] *nm* : plot — **comploter** [kɔ̃plɔte] *v* : plot, scheme
comporter [kɔ̃pɔrte] *vt* **1** CONTENIR : include **2** : entail (risks, etc.) — **se comporter** *vr* : behave — **comportement** [kɔ̃pɔrtəmɑ̃] *nm* : behavior
composer [kɔ̃poze] *vt* **1** : compose (music) **2** : constitute, make up **3** : dial (a number) — **se composer** *vr* ~ **de** : consist of — **composant** [kɔ̃pozɑ̃t] *nm* ÉLÉMENT : component — **composé, -sée** [kɔ̃poze] *adj* : compound — **composé** *nm* : compound — **compositeur, -trice** [kɔ̃pozitœr, -tris] *n* : composer — **composition** [kɔ̃pozisjɔ̃] *nf* : composition
compote [kɔ̃pɔt] *nf* ~ **de pommes** : apple sauce
compréhensif, -sive [kɔ̃preɑ̃sif, -siv] *adj* : understanding — **compréhension** [kɔ̃preɑ̃sjɔ̃] *nf* : understanding, comprehension
comprendre [kɔ̃prɑ̃dr] {70} *vt* **1** : consist of, comprise **2** : understand **3 mal** ~ : misunderstand
compression [kɔ̃prɛsjɔ̃] *nf* : compression
comprimer [kɔ̃prime] *vt* : compress — **comprimé** [kɔ̃prime] *nm* : tablet, pill
compris, -prise [kɔ̃pri, -priz] *adj* **1** INCLUS : included **2 y compris** : including
compromettre [kɔ̃prɔmɛtr] {53} *vt* : compromise — **compromis** [kɔ̃prɔmi] *nm* : compromise
comptable [kɔ̃tabl] *nmf* : accountant — **comptabilité** [kɔ̃tabilite] *nf* : accounting
comptant [kɔ̃tɑ̃] *adv* **payer** ~ : pay cash
compte [kɔ̃t, -tɛs] *nm* **1** : (bank) account **2 au bout du** ~ : in the end **3** ~ **à rebours** : countdown **4 se rendre** ~ **de** : realize — **compter** [kɔ̃te] *vt* **1** : count **2** ESPÉRER : expect **3** ~ **faire** : intend to do — *vi* **1** CALCULER : count **2** IMPORTER : matter **3** ~ **sur** : count on
compte–rendu [kɔ̃trɑ̃dy] *nm, pl* **comptes–rendus** : report
compteur [kɔ̃tœr] *nm* : meter
comptoir [kɔ̃twar] *nm* : counter, bar
comte, comtesse [kɔ̃t, -tɛs] *n* : count *m,* countess *f*
comté [kɔ̃te] *nm* : county
concave [kɔ̃kav] *adj* : concave
concéder [kɔ̃sede] {87} *vt* : grant, concede
concentrer [kɔ̃sɑ̃tre] *vt* : concentrate — **se concentrer** *vr* **1** : concentrate **2** ~ **sur** : center on — **concentration** [kɔ̃sɑ̃trasjɔ̃] *nf* : concentration
concept [kɔ̃sɛpt] *nm* : concept — **conception** [kɔ̃sɛpsjɔ̃] *nf* : conception
concerner [kɔ̃sɛrne] *vt* **1** : concern **2 en ce qui me concerne** : as far as I'm concerned — **concernant** [kɔ̃sɛrnɑ̃] *prep* : concerning, regarding
concert [kɔ̃sɛr] *nm* **1** : concert **2 de** ~ : together — **se concerter** [kɔ̃sɛrte] *vr* : consult, confer — **concerté, -tée** [kɔ̃sɛrte] *adj* : concerted
concession [kɔ̃sesjɔ̃] *nf* : concession — **concessionnaire** [kɔ̃sesjɔnɛr] *nmf* : dealer, agent
concevoir [kɔ̃səvwar] {26} *vt* **1** : conceive (a child) **2** IMAGINER : conceive of, design
concierge [kɔ̃sjɛrʒ] *nmf* : janitor
concilier [kɔ̃silje] {96} *vt* : reconcile — **conciliant, -liante** [kɔ̃siljɑ̃, -ljɑ̃t] *adj* : conciliatory
concis, -cise [kɔ̃si, -siz] *adj* : concise — **concision** [kɔ̃sizjɔ̃] *nf* **avec** ~ : concisely
conclure [kɔ̃klyr] {39} *vt* : conclude — **concluant, -cluante** [kɔ̃klyɑ̃, -klyɑ̃t] *adj* : conclusive — **conclusion** [kɔ̃klyzjɔ̃] *nf* : conclusion
concombre [kɔ̃kɔ̃br] *nm* : cucumber
concorder [kɔ̃kɔrde] *vi* : agree, match — **concordant, -dante** [kɔ̃kɔrdɑ̃, -dɑ̃t] *adj* : in agreement
concourir [kɔ̃kurir] {23} *vi* **1** : compete **2** ~ **à** : work toward — **concours** [kɔ̃kur] *nm* : competition, contest
concret, -crète [kɔ̃krɛ, -krɛt] *adj* : concrete — **concrétiser** [kɔ̃kretize] *vt* : give shape to — **se concrétiser** *vr* : materialize
concurrencer [kɔ̃kyrɑ̃se] {6} *vt* : rival,

compete with — **concurrence** [kɔ̃kyrɑ̃s] *nf* : competition, rivalry — **concurrent, -rente** [kɔ̃kyrɑ̃, -rɑ̃t] *adj* : competing, rival — ~ *n* : competitor

condamner [kɔ̃dane] *vt* **1** : condemn **2** : sentence (in law) — **condamnation** [kɔ̃danasjɔ̃] *nf* **1** : condemnation **2** PEINE : sentence

condenser [kɔ̃dɑ̃se] *vt* : condense — **condensation** [kɔ̃dɑ̃sasjɔ̃] *nf* : condensation

condescendant, -dante [kɔ̃desɑ̃dɑ̃, -dɑ̃t] *adj* : condescending

condiment [kɔ̃dimɑ̃] *nm* : condiment

condition [kɔ̃disjɔ̃] *nf* **1** : condition **2** **~s** *nfpl* : conditions, circumstances **3** **sous ~ que** : provided that — **conditionnel, -nelle** [kɔ̃disjɔnɛl] *adj* : conditional

condoléances [kɔ̃dɔleɑ̃s] *nfpl* : condolences

conduire[kɔ̃dɥir] {49} *vt* **1** : drive **2** **~ à** : lead to — **se conduire** *vr* : behave — **conducteur, -trice** [kɔ̃dyktœr, -tris] *n* : driver — **conducteur** *nm* : conductor (of electricity) — **conduite** [kɔ̃dɥit] *nf* **1** : behavior, conduct **2** TUYAU : pipe **3** **~ à droite** : right-hand drive

cône [kon] *nm* : cone

confection [kɔ̃fɛksjɔ̃] *nf* **1** : making **2** **la ~** : the clothing industry — **confectionner** [kɔ̃fɛksjɔne] *vt* : make (a meal, a garment, etc.)

confédération [kɔ̃federasjɔ̃] *nf* : confederation

conférence [kɔ̃ferɑ̃s] *nf* **1** : conference **2** COURS : lecture — **conférencier, -cière** [kɔ̃ferɑ̃sje, -sjɛr] *n* : lecturer

conférer [kɔ̃fere] {87} *v* : confer

confession [kɔ̃fesjɔ̃] *nf* **1** : confession **2** : denomination — **confesser** [kɔ̃fese] *vt* : confess

confettis [kɔ̃feti] *nmpl* : confetti

confiant, -fiante [kɔ̃nfjɑ̃, -fjɑ̃t] *adj* **1** : confident, trusting **2** ASSURÉ : self-confident — **confiance** [kɔ̃fjɑ̃s] *nf* **1** : confidence, trust **2** **~ en soi** : self-confidence

confidence [kɔ̃fidɑ̃s] *nf* **1** : confidence **2** **faire des ~s à** : confide in — **confident, -dente** [kɔ̃fidɑ̃, -dɑ̃t] *n* : confidant, confidante *f* — **confidentiel, -tielle** [kɔ̃fidɑ̃sjɛl] *adj* : confidential

confier [kɔ̃fje] {96} *vt* **1** **~ à qqn** : confide to s.o. **2** **~ (qqch) à qqn** : entrust (sth) to s.o. — **se confier** *vr* **~ à qqn** : confide in s.o.

confiner [kɔ̃fine] *vt* : confine — **confins** [kɔ̃fɛ̃] *nmpl* : limits, confines

confirmer [kɔ̃firme] *vt* : confirm — **confirmation** [kɔ̃firmasjɔ̃] *nf* : confirmation

confiserie [kɔ̃fizri] *nf* **1** : candy store **2** : candy

confisquer [kɔ̃fiske] *vt* : confiscate

confiture [kɔ̃fityr] *nf* : jam, preserves *pl*

conflit [kɔ̃fli] *nm* : conflict

confondre [kɔ̃fɔ̃dr] {63} *vt* **1** : confuse, mix up **2** ÉTONNER : baffle

conformer [kɔ̃fɔrme] *v* **se conformer** *vr* **~ à** : conform to — **conforme** [kɔ̃fɔrm] *adj* **1** **~ à** : in keeping with **2** **~ à** : true to — **conformément** [kɔ̃fɔrmemɑ̃] *adv* **~ à** : in accordance with — **conformité** [kɔ̃fɔrmite] *nf* : conformity

confort [kɔ̃fɔr] *nm* : comfort — **confortable** [kɔ̃fɔrtabl] *adj* : comfortable

confrère [kɔ̃frɛr] *nm* : colleague

confronter [kɔ̃frɔ̃te] *vt* **1** : confront **2** COMPARER : compare

confus [kɔ̃fy] *adj* **1** : confused **2** : embarrassed — **confusion** [kɔ̃fyzjɔ̃] *nf* **1** DÉSORDRE : confusion **2** GÊNE : embarrassment **3** ERREUR : mix-up

congé [kɔ̃ʒe] *nm* **1** VACANCES : vacation **2** : leave, time off — **congédier** [kɔ̃ʒedje] {96} *vt* : dismiss (an employee)

congeler [kɔ̃ʒle] {20} *vt* : freeze — **congélateur** [kɔ̃ʒelatœr] *nm* : freezer

congestion [kɔ̃ʒɛstjɔ̃] *nf* : congestion — **congestionner** [kɔ̃ʒɛstjɔne] *vt* : congest

congrès [kɔ̃grɛ] *nm* : congress, conference

conifère [kɔnifɛr] *nm* : conifer

conjecturer [kɔ̃ʒɛktyre] *v* : conjecture — **conjecture** [kɔ̃ʒɛktyr] *nf* : conjecture

conjoint, -jointe [kɔ̃ʒwɛ̃, -ʒwɛ̃t] *adj* : joint — ~ *n* ÉPOUX : spouse — **conjointement** [-ʒwɛ̃tmɑ̃] *adv* **~ avec** : in conjunction with

conjonction [kɔ̃ʒɔ̃ksjɔ̃] *nf* : conjunction

conjoncture [kɔ̃ʒɔ̃ktyr] *nf* : circumstances *pl*, juncture

conjugaison [kɔ̃ʒygɛzɔ̃] *nf* : conjugation

conjugal, -gale [kɔ̃ʒygal] *adj*, *mpl* **-gaux** [-go] : marital

conjuguer [kɔ̃ʒyge] *vt* : conjugate (a verb)

connaître [kɔnɛtr] {7} *vt* **1** : know **2**

ÉPROUVER : experience — **se connaître** *vr* **1** : know each other **2 s'y ~ en** : know about, be an expert in — **connaissance** [kɔnɛsɑ̃s] *nf* **1** : knowledge **2** : acquaintance **3** CONSCIENCE : consciousness **4 à ma ~** : as far as I know **5 faire ~ avec qqn** : meet s.o. **6 ~s** *nfpl* : knowledge, learning — **connaisseur, -seuse** [kɔnɛsœr, -søz] *n* : expert
connecter [kɔnɛkte] *vt* : connect
connexe [kɔnɛks] *adj* : related
connu, -nue [kɔny] *adj* : well-known
conquérir [kɔ̃kerir] {21} *vt* **1** : conquer **2** : win over — **conquérant, -rante** [kɔ̃kerɑ̃, -rɑ̃t] *n* : conqueror — **conquête** [kɔ̃kɛt] *nf* : conquest
consacrer [kɔ̃sakre] *vt* **1** : consecrate **2 ~ à** : devote to — **se consacrer** *vr* **~ à** : dedicate oneself to
conscience [kɔ̃sjɑ̃s] *nf* **1** : conscience **2** : consciousness — **consciemment** [kɔ̃sjamɑ̃] *adv* : consciously — **consciencieux, -cieuse** [kɔ̃sjɑ̃sjø, -sjøz] *adj* : conscientious — **conscient, -ciente** [kɔ̃sjɑ̃, -sjɑ̃t] *adj* : conscious, aware
consécutif, -tive [kɔ̃sekytif, -tiv] *adj* : consecutive — **consécutivement** [-tivmɑ̃] *adv* : consecutively
conseil [kɔ̃sɛj] *nm* **1** : (piece of) advice **2** : council **3 ~ d'administration** : board of directors — **conseiller** [kɔ̃seje] *vt* **1** : advise **2** RECOMMANDER : recommend — **conseiller, -lère** [kɔ̃seje, -jɛr] *n* **1** : counselor, advisor **2** : councillor
consentir [kɔ̃sɑ̃tir] {82} *vi* **~ à** : consent to, agree to — **consentant, -tante** [kɔ̃sɑ̃tɑ̃, -tɑ̃t] *adj* : willing — **consentement** [kɔ̃sɑ̃tmɑ̃] *nm* : consent
conséquence [kɔ̃sekɑ̃s] *nf* **1** : consequence **2 en ~** : consequently — **conséquent, -quente** [kɔ̃sekɑ̃, -kɑ̃t] *adj* : consistent, logical — **conséquent** *nm* **par ~** : consequently
conservateur, -trice [kɔ̃sɛrvatœr, -tris] *adj* : conservative — **~** *n* **1** : conservative **2** : curator — **conservation** [kɔ̃sɛrvasjɔ̃] *nf* : conservation
conservatoire [kɔ̃sɛrvatwar] *nm* : academy, conservatory
conserver [kɔ̃sɛrve] *vt* GARDER : keep, retain — **se conserver** *vr* : keep, stay fresh — **conserve** [kɔ̃sɛrv] *nf* **1** : canned food **2 en ~** : canned
considérable [kɔ̃siderabl] *adj* : considerable
considérer [kɔ̃sidere] {87} *vt* **1** : consider **2** ESTIMER : think highly of — **considération** [kɔ̃siderasjɔ̃] *nf* **1** : consideration **2** ESTIME : respect
consigner [kɔ̃siɲe] *vt* : check (luggage, etc.) — **consigne** [kɔ̃siɲ] *nf* **1** ORDRE : instructions *pl* **2** : checkroom
consister [kɔ̃siste] *vi* **1 ~ en** : consist of **2 ~ dans** : lie in **3 ~ à faire** : consist in doing — **consistance** [kɔ̃sistɑ̃s] *nf* : consistency — **consistant, -tante** [kɔ̃sistɑ̃, -tɑ̃t] *adj* **1** ÉPAIS : thick **2** NOURRISSANT : substantial
consoler [kɔ̃sɔle] *vt* : console, comfort — **consolation** [kɔ̃sɔlasjɔ̃] *nf* : consolation
consolider [kɔ̃sɔlide] *vt* : consolidate
consommer [kɔ̃sɔme] *vt* : consume — *vi* : have a drink — **consommateur, -trice** [kɔ̃sɔmatœr, -tris] *n* : consumer — **consommation** [kɔ̃sɔmasjɔ̃] *nf* **1** : consumption **2** BOISSON : drink — **consommé** [kɔ̃sɔme] *nm* : clear soup
consonne [kɔ̃sɔn] *nf* : consonant
conspirer [kɔ̃spire] *vi* : conspire, plot — **conspiration** [kɔ̃spirasjɔ̃] *nf* : conspiracy
constant, -tante [kɔ̃stɑ̃, -tɑ̃t] *adj* : constant, continual — **constamment** [kɔ̃stamɑ̃] *adv* : constantly
constater [kɔ̃state] *vt* REMARQUER : notice — **constatation** [kɔ̃statasjɔ̃] *nf* : observation
constellation [kɔ̃stelasjɔ̃] *nf* : constellation
consternation [kɔ̃stɛrnasjɔ̃] *nf* : dismay — **consterner** [kɔ̃stɛrne] *vt* : dismay
constipation [kɔ̃stipasjɔ̃] *nf* : constipation — **constiper** [kɔ̃stipe] *vt* : constipate
constituer [kɔ̃stitɥe] *vt* **1** COMPOSER : constitute **2** ÉLABORER : set up, form — **constitution** [kɔ̃stitysjɔ̃] *nf* **1** : constitution **2** ÉTABLISSEMENT : setting up — **constitutionnel, -nelle** [kɔ̃stitysjɔnɛl] *adj* : constitutional
constructeur, -trice [kɔ̃stryktœr, -tris] *n* : builder — **constructif, -tive** [kɔ̃stryktif, -tiv] *adj* : constructive — **construction** [kɔ̃stryksjɔ̃] *nf* : building, construction — **construire** [kɔ̃strɥir] {49} *vt* : construct, build
consulat [kɔ̃syla] *nm* : consulate
consultant, -tante [kɔ̃syltɑ̃, -tɑ̃t] *n* : consultant — **consultation** [kɔ̃syltasjɔ̃] *nf* : consultation (with a doctor, etc.) — **consulter** [kɔ̃sylte] *vt* **1** : consult **2** : refer to — **se consulter** *vr* : confer

consumer [kɔ̃syme] *vt* : burn, destroy
contact [kɔ̃takt] *nm* **1** : contact, touch **2 couper le ~** : switch off the ignition **3 rester en ~** : keep in touch — **contacter** [kɔ̃takte] *vt* : get in touch with, contact
contagieux, -gieuse [kɔtaʒjœ, -ʒjøz] *adj* : contagious
contaminer [kɔ̃tamine] *vt* **1** : contaminate **2** INFECTER : infect — **contamination** [-minasjɔ̃] *nf* : contamination
conte [kɔ̃t] *nm* **1** : tale, story **2 ~ de fées** : fairy tale
contempler [kɔ̃tɑ̃ple] *vt* : contemplate — **contemplation** [-tɑ̃plasjɔ̃] *nf* : contemplation
contemporain, -raine [kɔ̃tɑ̃pɔrɛ̃, -rɛn] *adj & n* : contemporary
contenir [kɔ̃tnir] {92} *vt* **1** : hold, contain **2** RETENIR : restrain — **se contenir** *vr* : control oneself — **contenance** [kɔ̃tnɑ̃s] *nf* ALLURE : bearing, attitude
content, -tente [kɔ̃tɑ̃, -tɑ̃t] *adj* : content, pleased — **contentement** [kɔ̃tɑ̃tmɑ̃] *nm* : satisfaction — **contenter** [kɔ̃tɑ̃te] *vt* : satisfy, please — **se contenter** *vr* **~ de** : be contented with
contentieux [kɔ̃tɑ̃sjø] *nm* **1** : dispute **2** : legal department
contenu [kɔ̃tny] *nm* : contents *pl*
conter [kɔ̃te] *vt* : tell (a story)
contester [kɔ̃tɛste] *vt* : contest, dispute — *vi* : protest — **contestation** [kɔ̃tɛstasjɔ̃] *nf* **1** DISPUTE : dispute **2** : (political) protest
conteur, -teuse [kɔ̃tœr, -tøz] *n* : storyteller
contexte [kɔ̃tɛkst] *nm* : context
contigu, -guë [kɔ̃tigy] *adj* : adjacent
continent [kɔ̃tinɑ̃] *nm* : continent — **continental, -tale** [-nɑ̃tal] *adj, mpl* **-taux** [-to] : continental
continuer [kɔ̃tinɥe] *vt* **1** : continue **2** PROLONGER : extend — *vi* : continue, go on — **continu, -nue** [kɔ̃tiny] *adj* : continuous — **continuation** [kɔ̃tinɥasjɔ̃] *nf* : continuation — **continuel, -nuelle** [kɔ̃tinɥɛl] *adj* : continuous, continual — **continuellement** [kɔ̃tinɥɛlmɑ̃] *adv* : continually — **continuité** [kɔ̃tinɥite] *nf* : continuity
contorsion [kɔ̃tɔrsjɔ̃] *nf* : contortion — **contorsionner** [kɔ̃tɔrsjɔne] *v* **se contorsionner** *vr* : contort oneself
contour [kɔ̃tur] *nm* : outline, contour — **contourner** [kɔ̃turne] *vt* **1** : bypass **2** : get around (a difficulty, etc.)
contraceptif, -tive [kɔ̃trasɛptif, -tiv] *adj* : contraceptive — **contraceptif** *nm* : contraceptive — **contraception** [kɔ̃trasɛpsjɔ̃] *nf* : contraception
contracter [kɔ̃trakte] *vt* **1** : contract (a muscle) **2** : incur (a debt) **3** : catch (a cold, etc.) — **contraction** [kɔ̃traksjɔ̃] *nf* : contraction, tensing
contradiction [kɔ̃tradiksjɔ̃] *nf* : contradiction — **contradictoire** [kɔ̃tradiktwar] *adj* : contradictory
contraindre [kɔ̃trɛ̃dr] {65} *vt* **~ à** : compel to, force to — **contrainte** [kɔ̃trɛ̃, -trɛ̃t] *nf* : constraint, coertion
contraire [kɔ̃trɛr] *adj & nm* : contrary, opposite — **contrairement** [kɔ̃trɛrmɑ̃] *adv* **~ à** : contrary to
contrarier [kɔ̃trarje] {96} *vt* : annoy, vex — **contrariant, -riante** [kɔ̃trarjɑ̃, -rjɑ̃t] *adj* : annoying — **contrariété** [kɔ̃trarjete] *nf* : annoyance
contraste [kɔ̃trast] *nm* : contrast
contrat [kɔ̃tra] *nm* : contract
contravention [kɔ̃travɑ̃sjɔ̃] *nf* : (parking) ticket
contre [kɔ̃tr] *prep* **1** : against **2** : versus (in law) **3** : (in exchange) for **4 trois ~ un** : three to one — **~** *nm* **le pour et le ~** : the pros and cons — **~** *adv* **1 par ~** : on the other hand **2 parler ~** : speak in opposition — **contre–attaque** [kɔ̃tratake] *nf, pl* **contre–attaques** : counterattack — **contrebande** [kɔ̃trəbɑ̃d] *nf* : smuggling — **contrebandier, -dière** [kɔ̃trəbɑ̃dje, -djɛr] *n* : smuggler — **contrebas** [kɔ̃trəba] **en ~** *adv phr* : (down) below — **contrebasse** [kɔ̃trəbas] *nf* : double bass — **contrecarrer** [kɔ̃trəkare] *vt* : thwart — **contrecœur** [kɔ̃trəkœr] **à ~** *adv phr* : unwillingly — **contrecoup** [kɔ̃trəku] *nm* : consequence — **contredire** [kɔ̃trədir] {29} *vt* : contradict — **se contredire** *vr* : contradict oneself — **contrefaire** [kɔ̃trəfɛr] {42} *vt* : counterfeit, forge — **contrefaçon** [kɔ̃trəfasɔ̃] *nf* : counterfeiting, forgery — **contrefort** [kɔ̃trəfɔr] *nm* **1** : buttress **2 ~s** *nmpl* : foothills — **contremaître** [kɔ̃trəmɛtr, -mɛtrɛs] *n* : foreman — **contrepartie** [kɔ̃trəparti] *nf* **1** : compensation **2 en ~** : in return — **contrepoids** [kɔ̃trəpwa] *nm* : counterbalance — **contrer** [kɔ̃tre] *vt* : counter — **contresens** [kɔ̃trəsɑ̃s] **à ~** *adv phr* : the wrong way — **contretemps** [kɔ̃trətɑ̃] *nm* : hitch, setback — **contrevenir** [kɔ̃trəvnir] {92} *vi* **~ à** : contravene

contribuer [kɔ̃tribɥe] *vi* : contribute — **contribuable** [kɔ̃tribɥabl] *nmf* : taxpayer — **contribution** [kɔ̃tribysjɔ̃] *nf* : contribution

contrit, -trite [kɔ̃tri, -trit] *adj* : contrite

contrôle [kɔ̃trol] *nm* **1** : checking, inspection **2** ~ **de soi-même** : self-control — **contrôler** [kɔ̃trole] *vt* **1** : check, inspect **2** MAÎTRISER : supervise, control — **contrôleur, -leuse** [kɔ̃trolœr, -løz] *n* : (ticket) inspector, (bus) conductor

controverse [kɔ̃trɔvɛrs] *nf* : controversy — **controversé, -sée** [kɔ̃trɔvɛrse] *adj* : controversial

contusionner [kɔ̃tyzjɔne] *vt* : bruise — **contusion** [kɔ̃tyzjɔ̃] *nf* : bruise

convaincre [kɔ̃vɛ̃kr] {94} *vt* : convince — **convaincant, -cante** [kɔ̃vɛ̃kɑ̃, -kɑ̃t] *adj* : convincing

convalescence [kɔ̃valesɑ̃s] *nf* : convalescence

convenir [kɔ̃vnir] {92} *vt* : agree, admit — *vi* ~ **à** : suit, fit — *v impers* **il convient de** : it is advisable to — **convenable** [kɔ̃vnabl] *adj* **1** ACCEPTABLE : adequate **2** : proper, decent — **convenance** [kɔ̃vnɑ̃s] *nf* **1 à votre** ~ : at your convenience **2** ~**s** *nfpl* : conventions, proprieties

convention [kɔ̃vɑ̃sjɔ̃] *nf* **1** USAGE : custom **2** ACCORD : agreement **3** ASSEMBLÉE : convention, assembly — **conventionnel, -nelle** [kɔ̃vɑ̃sjɔnɛl] *adj* : conventional

convenu, -nue [kɔ̃vny] *adj* : agreed

converger [kɔ̃vɛrʒe] {17} *vi* : converge, meet

conversation [kɔ̃vɛrsasjɔ̃] *nf* : conversation — **converser** [kɔ̃vɛrse] *vi* : converse

convertir [kɔ̃vɛrtir] *vt* : convert — **conversion** [kɔ̃vɛrsjɔ̃] *nf* : conversion

conviction [kɔ̃viksjɔ̃] *nf* CERTITUDE : conviction

convier [kɔ̃vje] {96} *vt* : invite

convive [kɔ̃viv] *nmf* : guest (at a meal)

convoi [kɔ̃vwa] *nm* **1** : convoy **2** *or* ~ **funèbre** : funeral procession

convoiter [kɔ̃vwate] *vt* : covet

convoquer [kɔ̃vɔke] *vt* **1** : convene **2** : summon

convulsion [kɔ̃vylsjɔ̃] *nf* : convulsion

coopérer [kɔɔpere] {87} *vi* : cooperate — **coopératif, -tive** [kɔɔperatif, -tiv] *adj* : cooperative — **coopération** [-perasjɔ̃] *nf* : cooperation — **coopérative** *nf* : cooperative

coordination [kɔɔrdinasjɔ̃] *nf* : coordination — **coordonner** [kɔɔrdɔne] *vt* : coordinate

copain, -pine [kɔpɛ̃, -pin] *n* **1** : friend, buddy **2** *or* **petit copain, petite copine** : boyfriend *m*, girlfriend *f*

copeau [kɔpo] *nm, pl* **-peaux** : chip (of wood, etc.)

copie [kɔpi] *nf* **1** : copy, duplicate **2** DEVOIR : paper, schoolwork — **copier** [kɔpje] {96} *vt* **1** : copy **2** ~ **sur** : copy from, crib from

copieux, -pieuse [kɔpjø, -pjøz] *adj* : plentiful, copious

copilote [kɔpilɔt] *nmf* : copilot

copine → **copain**

copropriété [kɔprɔprijete] *nf* **1** : joint ownership **2 immeuble en** ~ : condominium

coq [kɔk] *nm* : rooster

coque [kɔk] *nf* **1** : hull (of a boat) **2 œuf à la** ~ : soft-boiled egg

coquelicot [kɔkliko] *nm* : poppy

coquet, -quette [kɔke, -kɛt] *adj* **1** ÉLÉGANT : stylish **2** : attractive **3** *fam* : tidy, considerable

coquille [kɔkij] *nf* **1** : shell **2** FAUTE : misprint **3** ~ **Saint-Jacques** : scallop — **coquillage** [kɔkijaʒ] *nm* **1** : shellfish **2** COQUILLE : shell

coquin, -quine [kɔkɛ̃, -kin] *adj* : mischievous — ~ *n* : rascal, scamp

cor [kɔr] *nm* **1** : horn (in music) **2** : corn (on one's foot)

corail [kɔraj] *nm, pl* **-raux** [kɔro] : coral

Coran [kɔrɑ̃] *nm* : Koran

corbeau [kɔrbo] *nm, pl* **-beaux** : crow

corbeille [kɔrbɛj] *nf* **1** : basket **2** ~ **à papier** : wastepaper basket

corbillard [kɔrbijar] *nm* : hearse

corde [kɔrd] *nf* **1** : rope **2** : string **3** ~**s vocales** : vocal cords — **cordage** [kɔrdaʒ] *nm* **1** : rope **2** ~**s** *nmpl* : rigging

cordial, -diale [kɔrdjal] *adj, mpl* **-diaux** [-djo] : cordial — **cordialement** [-djalmɑ̃] *adv* : cordially

cordon [kɔrdɔ̃] *nm* **1** : cord (in anatomy) **2** ~ **de soulier** : shoelace — **cordonnerie** [kɔrdɔnri] *nf* : shoe repair shop — **cordonnier, -nière** [kɔrdɔnje, -njɛr] *n* : shoemaker, cobbler

coréen, -réenne [kɔreɛ̃, -reɛn] *adj* : Korean — **coréen** *nm* : Korean (language)

coriace [kɔrjas] *adj* : tough

corne [kɔrn] *nf* **1** : antler, horn **2** : horn (instrument) **3** ~ **de brume** : foghorn

cornée [kɔrne] *nf* : cornea
corneille [kɔrnɛj] *nf* : crow
cornemuse [kɔrnəmyz] *nf* : bagpipes *pl*
cornet [kɔrnɛ] *nm* **1** : cone **2 ∼ de crème glacée** : ice-cream cone
corniche [kɔrniʃ] *nf* : cliff road
cornichon [kɔrniʃɔ̃] *nm* : pickle
corporation [kɔrpɔrasjɔ̃] *nf* : corporation
corporel, -relle [kɔrpɔrɛl] *adj* : bodily
corps [kɔr] *nm* **1** : body **2** : corps (in the army, etc.) **3** : professional body **4 prendre ∼** : take shape
corpulent, -lente [kɔrpylɑ̃, -lɑ̃t] *adj* : stout
correct, -recte [kɔrɛkt] *adj* : correct — **correctement** [-rɛktəmɑ̃] *adv* : correctly — **correcteur, -trice** [kɔrɛktœr, -tris] *adj* : corrective — **correction** [kɔrɛksjɔ̃] *nf* **1** : correction **2** : grading, marking **3** PUNITION : beating
corrélation [kɔrelasjɔ̃] *nf* : correlation
correspondre [kɔrɛspɔ̃dr] {63} *vi* **1** : correspond, write **2** : communicate (by telephone, etc.) **3 ∼ à** : correspond to — **correspondance** [kɔrɛspɔ̃dɑ̃s] *nf* **1** : correspondence **2** : connection (of a plane, etc.) — **correspondant, -dante** [kɔrɛspɔ̃dɑ̃, -dɑ̃t] *n* **1** : correspondent **2** : person being called (on the telephone)
corrida [kɔrida] *nf* : bullfight
corridor [kɔridɔr] *nm* : corridor
corriger [kɔriʒe] {17} *vt* **1** : correct **2** : grade, mark
corroborer [kɔrɔbɔre] *vt* : corroborate
corroder [kɔrɔde] *vt* : corrode
corrompre [kɔrɔ̃pr] {77} *vt* **1** : corrupt **2** SOUDOYER : bribe — **corrompu, -pue** [kɔrɔ̃py] *adj* : corrupt
corrosif, -sive [kɔrɔzif, -ziv] *adj* : corrosive — **corrosion** [kɔrɔzjɔ̃] *nf* : corrosion
corruption [kɔrypsjɔ̃] *nf* **1** : corruption **2** : bribery
corsage [kɔrsaʒ] *nm* **1** : blouse **2** : bodice (of a dress)
corsé, -sée [kɔrse] *adj* : full-bodied (of wine), strong (of coffee, etc.)
corser [kɔrse] *v* **se corser** *vr* : get more complicated
cortège [kɔrtɛʒ] *nm* : procession
corvée [kɔrve] *nf* : chore
cosmétique [kɔsmetik] *nm* : cosmetic — **∼** *adj* : cosmetic
cosmique [kɔsmik] *adj* : cosmic
cosmopolite [kɔsmɔpɔlit] *adj* : cosmopolitan
cosmos [kɔsmos] *nm* : universe, cosmos
cosse [kɔs] *nf* : pod, husk
costaud, -taude [kɔsto, -tod] *adj fam* : sturdy, burly
costume [kɔstym] *nm* **1** : costume **2** COMPLET : suit — **costumer** [kɔstyme] *v* **se costumer** *vr* **∼ en** : dress up as
cote [kɔt] *nf* **1** : (stock) quotation **2** CLASSEMENT : rating **3** : call number (of a library book) **4** NIVEAU : level
côte [kot] *nf* **1** : coast **2** : rib (in anatomy) **3** : chop, cutlet **4** PENTE : hill **5 ∼ à ∼** : side by side
côté [kote] *nm* **1** : side **2** : way, direction **3 à ∼** : nearby **4 à ∼ de** : next to **5 de ∼** : sideways **6 de mon ∼** : for my part **7 mettre de ∼** : put aside
coteau [kɔto] *nm, pl* **-teaux** : hill, hillside
côtelé, -lée [kotle] *adj* **velours côtelé** : corduroy
côtelette [kotlɛt] *nf* : chop
coter [kɔte] *vt* : quote (in finance)
coterie [kɔtri] *nf* : clique
côteux, -teuse [kotø, -tøz] *adj Can* : hilly
côtier, -tière [kotje, -tjɛr] *adj* : coastal
cotiser [kɔtize] *vi* : subscribe, pay one's dues — **cotisation** [kɔtizasjɔ̃] *nf* : dues *pl*, fee
coton [kɔtɔ̃] *nm* : cotton
côtoyer [kotwaye] {58} *vt* **1** : skirt, run alongside of **2** FRÉQUENTER : mix with
cou [ku] *nm* : neck
coucher [kuʃe] *vt* **1** : put to bed **2** : lay down flat — *vi* : sleep, spend the night — **se coucher** *vr* **1** : lie down, go to bed **2** : set (of the sun) — **∼** *nm* **1** : bedtime **2 ∼ du soleil** : sunset — **couche** [kuʃ] *nf* **1** : layer, stratum **2** : coat (of paint) **3** : (baby) diaper **4 fausse ∼** : miscarriage — **couchette** [kuʃɛt] *nf* : berth, bunk
coucou [kuku] *nm* : cuckoo
coude [kud] *nm* **1** : elbow **2** COURBE : bend, angle **3 ∼ à ∼** : shoulder to shoulder
cou-de-pied [kudpje] *nm, pl* **cous-de-pied** : instep
coudre [kudr] {22} *v* : sew
couler [kule] *vt* **1** : sink **2** : cast (metal) — *vi* **1** : flow, run **2** : leak (of a faucet) **3** : sink (of a boat)

couleur [kulœr] *nf* **1 :** color **2 :** suit (of cards)
coulisser [kulise] *vi* **:** slide (in a groove) — **coulisses** [kulis] *nfpl* **:** backstage, wings
couloir [kulwar] *nm* **1 :** corridor **2 :** lane (in transportation)
coup [ku] *nm* **1 :** knock, blow **2** CHOC **:** shock **3 :** stroke, shot (in sports) **4 :** (political) coup **5 ~ de feu :** gunshot **6 ~ de foudre :** love at first sight **7 ~ de pied :** kick **8 ~ de poing :** punch **9 ~ de soleil :** sunburn **10 ~ de téléphone :** telephone call **11 ~ d'œil :** glance **12 tout à ~ :** suddenly
coupable [kupabl] *adj* **:** guilty — **~** *nmf* **:** culprit
coupant, -pante [kupɑ̃, -pɑ̃t] *adj* **1 :** sharp **2** CAUSTIQUE **:** cutting, curt
couper [kupe] *vt* **1 :** cut, cut up **2 :** cut off, block **3** CROISER **:** intersect **4** DILUER **:** dilute — *vi* **:** cut — **se couper** *vr* **1 :** cut oneself **2 :** intersect — **coupe** [kup] *nf* **1 :** fruit dish **2 :** cup (in sports) **3** *or* **~ de cheveux :** haircut **4** *or* **~ transversale :** cross section — **coupe–ongles** [kupɔ̃gl] *nms & pl* **:** nail clippers — **coupe–papier** [kuppapje] *nms & pl* **:** letter opener
couple [kupl] *nm* **:** couple — **coupler** [kuple] *vt* **:** pair (up)
coupon [kupɔ̃] *nm* **:** coupon
coupure [kupyr] *nf* **1 :** cut **2** BILLET **:** banknote
cour [kur] *nf* **1 :** court (of law) **2 :** courtyard **3 :** courtship **4 ~ de récréation :** playground
courage [kuraʒ] *nm* **:** courage — **courageux, -geuse** [kuraʒø, -ʒøz] *adj* **:** courageous
courant, -rante [kurɑ̃, -rɑ̃t] *adj* **1 :** (electric) current **2** COMMUN **:** common, usual — **courant** *nm* **1 :** (electric) current **2 :** course (of the day, etc.) **3 ~ d'air :** draft **4 être au ~ de :** know all about — **couramment** [kuramɑ̃] *adv* **1 :** fluently **2** SOUVENT **:** commonly
courbature [kurbatyr] *nf* **:** stiffness, ache — **courbaturé, -rée** [kurbatyre] *adj* **:** aching
courber [kurbe] *vt* **:** bend, curve — **se courber** *vr* **:** bend, curve — **courbe** [kurb] *nf* **:** curve
coureur, -reuse [kurœr, -røz] *n* **:** runner
courge [kurʒ] *nf* **:** gourd — **courgette** [kurʒɛt] *nf* **:** zucchini
courir [kurir] {23} *vt* **1 :** run in, compete in **2** FRÉQUENTER **:** frequent **3** PARCOURIR **:** roam through **4 :** run (a risk, etc.) — *vi* **1 :** run **2** SE PRESSER **:** rush
couronner [kurɔne] *vt* **:** crown — **couronne** [kurɔn] *nf* **1 :** crown **2 :** wreath — **couronnement** [kurɔnmɑ̃] *nm* **1 :** coronation **2 :** crowning achievement
courrier [kurje] *nm* **1 :** mail, correspondence **2 ~ électronique :** electronic mail, e-mail — **courriel** [kurjɛl] *nm Can* **:** electronic mail
courroie [kurwa] *nf* **:** strap, belt
cours [kur] *nm* **1 :** course, class **2 :** flow, current **3 au ~ de :** in the course of, during **4 ~ d'eau :** river, stream **5 ~ du soir :** night school **6 en ~ :** in progress
course [kurs] *nf* **1 :** running **2** COMPÉTITION **:** race, competition **3** COMMISSION **:** errand **4 faire des ~s :** go shopping
court, courte [kur, kurt] *adj* **:** short — **court** [kur] *adv* **1 à ~ de :** short of **2 s'arrêter ~ :** stop short **3 tout ~ :** simply — **court** *nm* **:** court (in sports) — **court–circuit** [kursirkɥi] *nm, pl* **courts–circuits :** short circuit
courtier, -tière [kurtje, -tjɛr] *n* **:** broker, agent
courtiser [kurtize] *vt* **:** court, woo
courtois, -toise [kurtwa, -twaz] *adj* **:** courteous — **courtoisie** [kurtwazi] *nf* **:** courtesy
cousin, -sine [kuzɛ̃, -zin] *n* **:** cousin
coussin [kusɛ̃] *nm* **:** cushion
coût [ku] *nm* **:** cost — **coûtant** [kutɑ̃] **à prix ~** *adv phr* **:** at cost
couteau [kuto] *nm, pl* **-teaux 1 :** knife **2 ~ de poche :** pocketknife
coûter [kute] *vt* **1 :** cost **2 ~ cher :** be expensive **3 ça coûte combien? :** how much is it? — *vi* **:** cost — **coûteux, -teuse** [kutø, -tøz] *adj* **:** costly
coutume [kutym] *nf* **:** custom — **coutumier, -mière** [kutymje, -mjɛr] *adj* **:** customary
couture [kutyr] *nf* **1 :** sewing **2 :** dressmaking **3 :** seam (of a garment) — **couturier** [kutyrje] *nm* **:** fashion designer — **couturière** [kutyrjɛr] *nf* **:** dressmaker
couvée [kuve] *nf* **:** brood
couvent [kuvɑ̃] *nm* **:** convent
couver [kuve] *vt* **1 :** hatch **2** PROTÉGER **:** overprotect **3 :** be coming down with

(an illness) — *vi* **1 :** smolder **2 :** be brewing
couvercle [kuvɛrkl] *nm* **1 :** lid, cover **2 :** top (of a spray can, etc.)
couvert, -verte [kuvɛr, -vɛrt] *adj* **1 :** covered **2** NUAGEUX **:** overcast — **couvert** *nm* **1 :** place setting (at a table) **2 ∼s** *nmpl* **:** flatware **3 à ∼ :** under cover — **couverture** [kuvɛrtyr] *nf* **1 :** cover (of a book, etc.) **2 :** blanket **3 :** roofing **4 :** news coverage
couveuse [kuvøz] *nf* **:** incubator
couvrir [kuvrir] {83} *vt* **:** cover — **se couvrir** *vr* **1 :** dress warmly **2 :** become overcast **3 ∼ de :** be covered with — **couvre–feu** [kuvrəfø] *nm, pl* **couvre–feux :** curfew — **couvre–lit** [kuvrəli] *nm, pl* **couvre–lits :** bedspread
cow–boy [kɔbɔj] *nm, pl* **cow–boys :** cowboy
coyote [kɔjɔt] *nm* **:** coyote
crabe [krab] *nm* **:** crab
cracher [kraʃe] *v* **:** spit
craie [krɛ] *nf* **:** chalk
craindre [krɛ̃dr] {65} *vt* **1** REDOUTER **:** fear, be afraid of **2 ∼ que :** regret that, fear that — **crainte** [krɛ̃t] *nf* **1 :** fear, dread **2 de ∼ que :** for fear that — **craintif, -tive** [krɛ̃tif, -tiv] *adj* **:** fearful, timid
crampe [krɑ̃p] *nf* **:** cramp
crampon [krɑ̃pɔ̃] *nm* **:** clamp — **cramponner** [krɑ̃pɔne] *v* **se cramponner** *vr* **∼ à :** cling to
cran [krɑ̃] *nm fam* **:** courage, guts
crâne [kran] *nm* **:** skull
crapaud [krapo] *nm* **:** toad
craquer [krake] *vi* **1 :** crack, snap, creak **2** SE DÉCHIRER **:** tear, rip **3** *fam* **:** break down — **craquement** [krakmɑ̃] *nm* **:** crack, creak
crasse [kras] *nf* **:** filth — **crasseux, -seuse** [krasø, -søz] *adj* **:** filthy
cratère [kratɛr] *nm* **:** crater
cravache [kravaʃ] *nf* **:** horsewhip
cravate [kravat] *nf* **:** necktie
crayon [krɛjɔ̃] *nm* **1 :** pencil **2 ∼ à bille :** ballpoint pen
créancier, -cière [kreɑ̃sje, -sjɛr] *n* **:** creditor
créateur, -trice [kreatœr, -tris] *adj* **:** creative — **∼** *n* **:** creator — **création** [kreasjɔ̃] *nf* **:** creation — **créativité** [kreativite] *nf* **:** creativity
créature [kreatyr] *nf* **:** creature
crèche [krɛʃ] *nf France* **:** nursery
crédible [kredibl] *adj* **:** credible — **crédibilité** [-dibilite] *nf* **:** credibility
crédit [kredi] *nm* **1 :** credit **2 ∼s** *nmpl* **:** funds — **créditer** [kredite] *vt* **:** credit — **créditeur, -trice** [kreditœr, -tris] *n* **:** creditor
crédule [kredyl] *adj* **:** credulous — **crédulité** [-dylite] *nf* **:** credulity
créer [kree] {89} *vt* **:** create
crémaillère [kremajɛr] *nf* **pendre la ∼ :** have a housewarming (party)
crème [krɛm] *nf* **1 :** cream **2 ∼ glacée** *Can* **:** ice cream — **crémerie** [krɛmri] *nf France* **:** dairy shop — **crémeux, -meuse** [kremø, -møz] *adj* **:** creamy
créneau [kreno] *nm, pl* **-neaux 1 :** slot, gap **2 faire un ∼ :** back into a parking space
crêpe [krɛp] *nf* **:** pancake, crepe — **∼** *nm* **:** crepe (fabric)
crépiter [krepite] *vi* **:** crackle — **crépitement** [krepitmɑ̃] *nm* **1 :** crackling **2 :** patter (of rain)
crépu, -pue [krepy] *adj* **:** frizzy
crépuscule [krepyskyl] *nm* **:** twilight, dusk
cresson [krɛsɔ̃] *nm* **:** watercress
crête [krɛt] *nf* **1 :** crest, peak **2 :** comb (of a rooster)
crétin, -tine [kretɛ̃, -tin] *n* **:** idiot
creuser [krøze] *vt* **:** dig, hollow out — **se creuser** *vr* **∼ la tête** *fam* **:** rack one's brains — **creux, creuse** [krø, krøz] *adj* **1 :** hollow **2 :** sunken (of eyes) — **creux** *nm* **1** CAVITÉ **:** hollow, cavity **2 :** pit (of the stomach)
crevaison [krəvɛzɔ̃] *nf* **:** flat tire
crevasse [krəvas] *nf* **:** crevice, crack
crever [krəve] {52} *vt* **1 :** burst, puncture **2** *fam* **:** wear out — *vi* **1 :** burst **2 ∼ de faim :** be starving — **crevé, -vée** [krəve] *adj* **1 :** punctured, flat (of a tire) **2** *fam* **:** dead tired
crevette [krəvɛt] *nf* **:** shrimp, prawn
cri [kri] *nm* **1 :** cry, shout **2 le dernier ∼ :** the latest thing — **criant, criante** [krijɑ̃, krijɑ̃t] *adj* **:** glaring, obvious — **criard, criarde** [krijar, krijard] *adj* **1 :** shrill **2 :** gaudy
cribler [krible] *vt* **1 :** sift, screen **2 ∼ de :** riddle with — **crible** [kribl] *nm* **:** sieve
cric [krik] *nm* **:** (car) jack
cricket [krikɛt] *nm* **:** cricket (sport)
crier [krije] {96} *vi* **:** shout, yell — *vt* **:** shout (out)
crime [krim] *nm* **1 :** crime **2** MEURTRE **:** murder — **criminel, -nelle** [kriminɛl] *adj* **:** criminal — **∼** *n* **1 :** criminal **2** MEURTRIER **:** murderer

crinière [krinjɛr] *nf* : mane
criquet [krikɛ] *nm* : locust (insect)
crise [kriz] *nf* **1** : crisis **2** ACCÈS : fit, outburst **3 ~ cardiaque** : heart attack
crispé, -pée [krispe] *adj* : tense, clenched
crisser [krise] *vi* : screech, squeal (of tires)
cristal [kristal] *nm, pl* **-taux** [kristo] : crystal
critère [kritɛr] *nm* : criterion
critique [kritik] *adj* : critical — **~** *nf* **1** : criticism **2** : critique, review — **~** *nmf* : critic, reviewer — **critiquer** [kritike] *vt* : criticize
croasser [krɔase] *vi* : caw, croak
croc [kro] *nm* : fang
crochet [krɔʃɛ] *nm* **1** : hook **2** : square bracket **3 faire du ~** : crochet **4 faire un ~** : make a detour — **crochu, -chue** [krɔʃy] *adj* : hooked
crocodile [krɔkɔdil] *nm* : crocodile
croire [krwar] {24} *vt* **1** : believe **2** PENSER : think, believe — *vi* **~ à** *or* **~ en** : believe in
croisade [krwazad] *nf* : crusade
croiser [krwaze] *vt* **1** : cross **2** : intersect **3** RENCONTRER : pass, meet **4** : crossbreed — *vi* : cruise (of a ship) — **se croiser** *vr* **1** : cross, cut across **2** : pass each other — **croisement** [krwazmɑ̃] *nm* **1** : junction **2** : crossbreeding — **croiseur** [krwazœr] *nm* : cruiser (ship) — **croisière** [krwazjɛr] *nf* : cruise
croître [krwatr] {25} *vi* : grow, increase — **croissant, -sante** [krwasɑ̃, -sɑ̃t] *adj* : growing, increasing — **croissant** *nm* : croissant — **croissance** [krwasɑ̃s] *nf* : growth, development
croix [krwa] *nf* : cross
croquer [krɔke] *vt* : crunch, munch — *vi* **~ dans** : bite into (an apple, etc.) — **croquant, -quante** [krɔkɑ̃, -kɑ̃t] *adj* : crunchy — **croque-monsieur** [krɔkməsjø] *nms & pl* : grilled ham and cheese sandwich
croquis [krɔki] *nm* : sketch
crosse [krɔs] *nf* : butt (of a gun)
crotte [krɔt] *nf* : droppings *pl*, dung — **crottin** [krɔtɛ̃] *nm* : (horse) manure
crouler [krule] *vi* S'EFFONDRER : crumble, collapse
croupir [krupir] *vi* **1** : stagnate **2 ~ dans** : wallow in
croustillant, -lante [krustijɑ̃, -jɑ̃t] *adj* : crisp, crispy
croûte [krut] *nf* **1** : (pie) crust **2** : scab — **croûton** [krutɔ̃] *nm* **1** : crust (of bread) **2** : crouton
croyance [krwajɑ̃s] *nf* : belief — **croyant, croyante** [krwajɑ̃, -jɑ̃t] *n* : believer
cru, crue [kry] *adj* **1** : raw, uncooked **2** OSÉ : crude **3** : harsh (of light, etc.) — **cru** *nm* **1** VIGNOBLE : vineyard **2** : vintage (of wine)
cruauté [kryote] *nf* : cruelty
cruche [kryʃ] *nf* : jug, pitcher
crucial, -ciale [krysjal] *adj, mpl* **-ciaux** [-sjo] : crucial
crucifier [krysifje] {96} *vt* : crucify — **crucifix** [krysifi] *nms & pl* : crucifix — **crucifixion** [krysifiksjɔ̃] *nf* : crucifixion
crudités [krydite] *nfpl* : raw vegetables
crue [kry] *nf* : rise in water level
cruel, cruelle [kryɛl] *adj* : cruel — **cruellement** [-ɛlmɑ̃] *adv* : cruelly
crustacés [krystase] *nmpl* : shellfish
crypte [kript] *nf* : crypt
cube [kyb] *adj* : cubic — **~** *nm* : cube — **cubique** [kybik] *adj* : cubic
cueillir [kœjir] {3} *vt* : pick, gather — **cueillette** [kœjɛt] *nf* : picking, gathering
cuillère *or* **cuiller** [kɥijɛr] *nf* **1** : spoon **2** : spoonful **3 ~ à thé** *or* **~ à café** : teaspoon — **cuillerée** [kɥijere] *nf* **1** : spoonful **2 ~ à café** : teaspoonful
cuir [kɥir] *nm* **1** : leather **2 ~ chevelu** : scalp
cuire [kɥir] {49} *vt* : cook, bake — *vi* : cook
cuisine [kɥizin] *nf* **1** : kitchen **2** : cooking, cuisine **3 faire la ~** : cook — **cuisiner** [kɥizine] *v* **1** : cook **2** *fam* : interrogate, grill — **cuisinier, -nière** [kɥizinje, -njɛr] *n* : chef, cook — **cuisinière** *nf* : stove
cuisse [kɥis] *nf* **1** : thigh **2** : leg (in cooking)
cuisson [kɥisɔ̃] *nf* : cooking, baking
cuit, cuite [kɥi, kɥit] *adj* **1** : cooked **2 bien ~** : well-done
cuivre [kɥivr] *nm* **1** : copper **2** *or* **~ jaune** : brass **3 ~s** *nmpl* : brass (musical instruments)
culbute [kylbyt] *nf* **1** : somersault **2** CHUTE : tumble, fall
cul-de-sac [kydsak] *nm, pl* **culs-de-sac** : dead end
culinaire [kylinɛr] *adj* : culinary
culminer [kylmine] *vi* : culminate, peak — **culminant, -nante** [kylminɑ̃, -nɑ̃t] *adj* **point culminant** : high point

culot [kylo] *nm fam* **avoir du ~** : have a lot of nerve
culotte [kylɔt] *nf* **1** PANTALON : pants *pl* **2** : panties *pl*
culpabilité [kylpabilite] *nf* : guilt
culte [kylt] *nm* **1** VÉNÉRATION : worship, cult **2** : religion
cultiver [kyltive] *vt* : cultivate, grow — **cultivateur, -trice** [kyltivatœr, -tris] *n* AGRICULTEUR : farmer — **cultivé, -vée** [kyltive] *adj* **1** : cultivated **2** : cultured, educated
culture [kyltyr] *nf* **1** CONNAISSANCES : culture **2** : cultivation, growing **3** : crop **4 ~ physique** : physical education — **culturel, -relle** [kyltyrɛl] *adj* : cultural — **culturisme** [kyltyrism] *nm* : bodybuilding
cumuler [kymyle] *vt* **1** : accumulate **2** : hold concurrently — **cumulatif, -tive** [kymylatif, -tiv] *adj* : cumulative
cupide [kypid] *adj* : greedy — **cupidité** [kypidite] *nf* : greed
cure [kyr] *nf* : treatment, cure
curé [kyre] *nm* : pastor, parish priest
curer [kyre] *v* **se curer** *vr* : clean (one's nails, teeth, etc.) — **cure–dent** *or* **cure–dents** [kyrdɑ̃] *nm, pl* **cure–dents** : toothpick
curieux, -rieuse [kyrjø, -rjøz] *adj* **1** : curious **2** ÉTRANGE : strange, odd — **~** *n* : onlooker — **curieusement** [kyrjøzmɑ̃] *adv* : curiously, strangely — **curiosité** [kyrjɔzite] *nf* : curiosity
curry [kyri] *nm* : curry
curseur [kyrsœr] *nm* : cursor
cuver [kyve] *vi* : ferment — **cuve** [kyv] *nf* : vat, tank — **cuvée** [kyve] *nf* : vintage — **cuvette** [kyvɛt] *nf* : basin
cyanure [sjanyr] *nm* : cyanide
cycle [sikl] *nm* : cycle — **cyclique** [siklik] *adj* : cyclic, cyclical
cycliste [siklist] *nmf* : cyclist, bicyclist — **cyclisme** [siklism] *nm* : cycling, bicycling
cyclomoteur [siklɔmɔtœr] *nm* : moped
cyclone [siklon] *nm* : cyclone
cygne [siɲ] *nm* : swan
cylindre [silɛ̃dr] *nm* : cylinder — **cylindrique** [silɛ̃drik] *adj* : cylindrical
cymbale [sɛ̃bal] *nf* : cymbal
cynique [sinik] *adj* : cynical — **~** *nmf* : cynic — **cynisme** [sinism] *nm* : cynicism
cyprès [siprɛ] *nm* : cypress

D

d [de] *nm* : d, fourth letter of the alphabet
dactylographier [daktilɔgrafje] {96} *vt* : type — **dactylo** [daktilo] *or* **dactylographe** [daktilɔgraf] *nmf* : typist
daigner [deɲe] *vt* : deign
daim [dɛ̃] *nm* **1** : deer **2** : suede
dalle [dal] *nf* : slab, paving stone
daltonien, -nienne [daltɔnjɛ̃, -njɛn] *adj* : color-blind
dame [dam] *nf* **1** : lady **2** : queen (in games) **3 ~s** *nfpl or* **jeu de ~s** : checkers — **damier** [damje] *nm* : checkerboard
dandiner [dɑ̃dine] *v* **se dandiner** *vr* : waddle
danger [dɑ̃ʒe] *nm* : danger — **dangereux, -reuse** [dɑ̃ʒrø, -røz] *adj* : dangerous
dans [dɑ̃] *prep* **1** : in **2** : into, inside **3** : from, out of **4 ~ la journée** : during the day **5 ~ les 20 ans** : in about 20 years **6 monter ~ l'auto** : get into the car
danser [dɑ̃se] *v* : dance — **danse** [dɑ̃s] *nf* : dance, dancing — **danseur, -seuse** [dɑ̃sœr, -søz] *n* : dancer
dard [dar] *nm* **1** : stinger (of an insect) **2** *Can* : dart
date [dat] *nf* : date — **dater** [date] *vi* **1** : be dated, be old-fashioned **2 ~ de** : date from
datte [dat] *nf* : date (fruit)
dauphin [dofɛ̃] *nm* : dolphin
davantage [davɑ̃taʒ] *adv* **1** PLUS : more **2** : (any) longer
de [də] (**d'** *before vowels and mute h*) *prep* **1** : of **2** (*before infinitive*) : to, of **3 de l', de la, du, des** : some, any **4 ~ Molière** : by Molière **5 ~ Montréal** : from Montreal **6 moins ~ cinq** : less than five
dé [de] *nm* **1** : die, dice *pl* **2 ~ à coudre** : thimble
déambuler [deɑ̃byle] *vi* : stroll, wander about
débâcle [debakl] *nf* : fiasco
déballer [debale] *vt* : unpack, unwrap
débandade [debɑ̃dad] *nf* : stampede
débarquer [debarke] *vt* : unload (goods) — *vi* : disembark (of passen-

gers) — **débarquement** [debarkəmɑ̃] *nm* **1** : unloading **2** : landing
débarrasser [debarase] *vt* : clear, rid — **se débarrasser** *vr* **~ de** : get rid of
débarrer [debare] *vt Can* : unlock
débattre [debatr] {12} *vt* : debate, discuss — **se débattre** *vr* : struggle — **débat** [deba] *nm* **1** : debate, discussion **2 ~s** *nmpl* : proceedings
débaucher [deboʃe] *vt* **1** CORROMPRE : corrupt **2** LICENCIER : lay off — **débauche** [deboʃ] *nf* : debauchery
débiliter [debilite] *vt* : debilitate — **débile** [debil] *adj fam* : stupid
débiter [debite] *vt* **1** : debit **2** VENDRE : sell, retail **3** FOURNIR : produce **4** : recite, reel off — **débit** [debi] *nm* **1** : debit **2** : turnover (of merchandise, etc.) **3** : (rate of) flow — **débiteur, -trice** [debitœr, -tris] *n* : debtor
déblayer [debleje] {11} *vt* : clear (away)
débloquer [deblɔke] *vt* : free, release
déboires [debwar] *nmpl* ENNUIS : difficulties
déboîter [debwate] *vt* : dislocate (a joint) — *vi* : pull out, change lanes
débonnaire [debɔnɛr] *adj* : easygoing, good-natured
déborder [debɔrde] *vi* : overflow — *vt* **1** : extend beyond **2** SUBMERGER : overwhelm — **débordé, -dée** [debɔrde] *adj* : overwhelmed
déboucher [debuʃe] *vt* : open, unblock — *vi* **~ sur** : open onto, lead to — **débouché** [debuʃe] *nm* **1** : outlet, market **2** : opportunity, prospect
débourser [deburse] *vt* : pay out
debout [dəbu] *adv* **1** : standing up **2** : upright, on end **3** : up, out of bed
déboutonner [debutɔne] *vt* : unbutton, undo
débraillé, -lée [debraje] *adj* : disheveled
débrancher [debrɑ̃ʃe] *vt* : unplug, disconnect
débrayer [debreje] {11} *vi* **1** : disengage the clutch **2** : go on strike — **débrayage** [debrɛjaʒ] *nm* **1** : disengaging the clutch **2** : strike, walkout
débris [debri] *nms & pl* **1** : fragment **2 ~** *nmpl* : rubbish, scraps
débrouiller [debruje] *vt* DÉMÊLER : disentangle — **se débrouiller** *vr* : manage, cope — **débrouillard, -larde** [debrujar, -jard] *adj* : resourceful
débuter [debyte] *v* : begin — **début** [deby] *nm* **1** : beginning **2 ~s** *nmpl* : debut, early stages — **débutant, -tante** [debytɑ̃, -tɑ̃t] *n* : beginner, novice
décacheter [dekaʃte] {8} *vt* : unseal, open
décadence [dekadɑ̃s] *nf* : decadence — **décadent, -dente** [dekadɑ̃, -dɑ̃t] *adj* : decadent
décaféiné, -née [dekafeine] *adj* : decaffeinated
décalage [dekalaʒ] *nm* **1** : gap, interval **2 ~ horaire** : time difference
décamper [dekɑ̃pe] *vi* : clear out
décaper [dekape] *vt* **1** : clean, scour **2** : strip (paint, etc.) — **décapant** [dekɑpɑ̃] *nm* : paint stripper
décapotable [dekapɔtabl] *adj & nf* : convertible
décapsuleur [dekapsylœr] *nm* : bottle opener
décéder [desede] {87} *vi* : die — **décédé, -dée** [desede] *adj* : deceased
déceler [desle] {20} *vt* **1** DÉCOUVRIR : detect **2** RÉVÉLER : reveal
décembre [desɑ̃br] *nm* : December
décence [desɑ̃s] *nf* : decency
décennie [deseni] *nf* : decade
décent, -cente [desɑ̃, -sɑ̃t] *adj* : decent
déception [desɛpsjɔ̃] *nf* : disappointment
décerner [desɛrne] *vt* : award
décès [desɛ] *nm* : death
décevoir [desəvwar] {26} *vt* : disappoint — **décevant, -vante** [desəvɑ̃, -vɑ̃t] *adj* : disappointing
déchaîner [deʃene] *vt* : unleash — **se déchaîner** *vr* : erupt, burst out — **déchaîné, -née** [deʃene] *adj* : raging, unbridled — **déchaînement** [deʃɛnmɑ̃] *nm* : outburst
décharger [deʃarʒe] {17} *vt* **1** : unload **2** : discharge (a firearm, etc.) **3** SOULAGER : relieve, unburden — **décharge** [deʃarʒ] *nf* **1** : discharge **2** : garbage dump
décharné, -née [deʃarne] *adj* : gaunt
déchausser [deʃose] *v* **se déchausser** *vr* : take off one's shoes
déchéance [deʃeɑ̃s] *nf* : decay, decline
déchet [deʃɛ] *nm* **1** : scrap **2 ~s** : waste, refuse
déchiffrer [deʃifre] *vt* : decipher
déchiqueter [deʃikte] {8} *vt* : tear into pieces
déchirer [deʃire] *vt* : tear up, tear apart — **déchirant, -rante** [deʃirɑ̃, -rɑ̃t] *adj* : heartrending — **déchirure** [deʃiryr] *nf* : tear

déchoir [deʃwar] {27} *vi* : fall, decline (in prestige)
décider [deside] *vt* **1** : decide **2** CONVAINCRE : persuade **3** ~ **de** : decide on, determine — **se décider** *vr* : make up one's mind — **décidé, -dée** [deside] *adj* **1** : decided, settled **2** DÉTERMINÉ : determined — **décidément** [desidemɑ̃] *adv* : definitely, really
décimal, -male [desimal] *adj, mpl* **-maux** [-mo] : decimal — **décimale** *nf* : decimal
décision [desizjɔ̃] *nf* **1** : decision **2** : decisiveness — **décisif, -sive** [desizif, -ziv] *adj* : decisive
déclarer [deklare] *vt* **1** PROCLAMER : declare **2** : register, report — **se déclarer** *vr* : break out (of fire, etc.) — **déclaration** [deklarasjɔ̃] *nf* : declaration, statement
déclencher [deklɑ̃ʃe] *vt* **1** : set off, trigger **2** LANCER : launch — **déclenchement** [deklɑ̃ʃmɑ̃] *nm* : onset, outbreak
déclic [deklik] *nm* : click
décliner [dekline] *v* : decline — **déclin** [deklɛ̃] *nm* : decline
décoller [dekɔle] *vt* : unstick, remove — *vi* : take off (of an airplane, etc.) — **décollage** [dekɔlaʒ] *nm* : takeoff
décolleté, -tée [dekɔlte] *adj* : low-cut
décolorer [dekɔlɔre] *vt* : bleach — **se décolorer** *vr* : fade
décombres [decɔ̃br] *nmpl* : rubble, debris
décommander [dekɔmɑ̃de] *vt* : cancel
décomposer [dekɔ̃poze] *vt* : decompose — **décomposition** [dekɔ̃pozisjɔ̃] *nf* : decomposition, rotting
décompter [dekɔ̃te] *vt* **1** : count, calculate **2** DÉDUIRE : deduct — **décompte** [dekɔ̃t] *nm* **1** : count, breakdown **2** DÉDUCTION : deduction
déconcerter [dekɔ̃sɛrte] *vt* : disconcert
décongeler [dekɔ̃ʒle] {20} *v* : thaw, defrost
déconnecter [dekɔnɛkte] *vt* : disconnect
déconseiller [dekɔ̃seje] *vt* : dissuade, advise against — **déconseillé, -lée** [dekɔ̃seje] *adj* : inadvisable
décontracté, -tée [dekɔ̃trakte] *adj* : relaxed, casual
décorer [dekɔre] *vt* ORNER : decorate — **décor** [dekɔr] *nm* **1** : decor **2** : scenery (in theater, etc.) — **décoration** [dekɔrasjɔ̃] *nf* : decoration — **décorateur, -trice** [dekɔratœr, -tris] *n* : interior decorator — **décoratif, -tive** [dekɔratif, -tiv] *adj* : decorative
décortiquer [dekɔrtike] *vt* : shell, hull
découler [dekule] *vi* : result, follow
découper [dekupe] *vt* **1** : cut up, carve **2** : cut out (a picture)
décourager [dekuraʒe] {17} *vt* : discourage — **se décourager** *vr* : lose heart — **découragement** [dekuraʒmɑ̃] *nm* : discouragement
décousu, -sue [dekusy] *adj* **1** : unstitched **2** : disjointed, disconnected
découvrir [dekuvrir] {83} *vt* **1** : discover **2** : uncover — **se découvrir** *vr* : clear up (of weather) — **découvert** [dekuvɛr] *nm* : overdraft (in banking) — **découverte** [dekuvɛrt] *nf* : discovery
décrépit, -pite [dekrepi, -pit] *adj* : decrepit
décret [dekrɛ] *nm* : decree, edict — **décréter** [dekrete] {87} *vt* : decree
décrire [dekrir] {33} *vt* : describe
décrocher [dekrɔʃe] *vt* **1** : unhook, take down **2** *fam* : get, land (a job, etc.) — *vi fam* : drop out, give up
décroître [dekrwatr] {25} *vi* : decrease, decline
déçu, -çue [desy] *adj* : disappointed
dédaigner [dedeɲe] *vt* : disdain, scorn — **dédaigneux, -neuse** [dedɛɲø, -ɲøz] *adj* : disdainful, scornful — **dédain** [dedɛ̃] *nm* MÉPRIS : disdain, scorn
dédale [dedal] *nm* : maze, labyrinth
dedans [dədɑ̃] *adv* **1** : inside, in **2 en** ~ : on the inside, within — ~ *nm* : inside, interior
dédicace [dedikas] *nf* : dedication — **dédicacer** [dedikase] {6} *vt* : inscribe, dedicate
dédier [dedje] {96} *vt* : dedicate
dédommager [dedɔmaʒe] {17} *vt* : compensate — **dédommagement** [dedɔmaʒmɑ̃] *nm* INDEMNITÉ : compensation
déduire [dedɥir] {49} *vt* **1** : deduct **2** CONCLURE : deduce, infer — **déduction** [dedyksjɔ̃] *nf* : deduction
déesse [deɛs] *nf* : goddess
défaillir [defajir] {93} *vi* : weaken, fail — **défaillance** [defajɑ̃s] *nf* : failing, weakness
défaire [defɛr] {42} *vt* **1** : undo **2** : unpack — **se défaire** *vr* **1** : come undone **2** ~ **de** : part with — **défait, -faite** [defɛ, -fɛt] *adj* **1** : undone **2** : defeated — **défaite** *nf* : defeat
défaut [defo] *nm* **1** IMPERFECTION : flaw, defect **2** FAIBLESSE : shortcom-

ing **3** MANQUE : lack **4 faire ~** : be lacking

défavoriser [defavɔrize] *vt* : put at a disadvantage — **défavorable** [defavɔrabl] *adj* : unfavorable

défectueux, -tueuse [defɛktɥø, -tɥøz] *adj* : defective, faulty — **défectuosité** [defɛktɥozite] *nf* **1** : defectiveness **2** DÉFAUT : defect, fault

défendre [defɑ̃dr] {63} *vt* **1** : defend **2** PROTÉGER : protect, uphold **3** INTERDIRE : forbid — **se défendre** *vr* : defend oneself — **défendeur, -deresse** [defɑ̃dœr, -drɛs] *n* : defendant

défense [defɑ̃s] *nf* **1** : defense **2** INTERDICTION : prohibition **3** : tusk (of an elephant, etc.) — **défenseur** [defɑ̃sœr] *nm* : defender — **défensif, -sive** [defɑ̃sif, -siv] *adj* : defensive — **défensive** *nf* : defensive

défi [defi] *nm* : challenge, dare

déficit [defisit] *nm* : deficit

défier [defje] {96} *vt* **1** : challenge, dare **2** BRAVER : defy

défigurer [defigyre] *vt* **1** : disfigure **2 ~ les faits** : distort the facts

défiler [defile] *vi* **1** : march, parade **2** : stream past **3** : scroll (on a computer) — **défilé** [defile] *nm* **1** : parade, procession **2** : stream (of visitors, etc.)

définir [definir] *vt* : define — **défini, -nie** [defini] *adj* **1** : defined **2** : definite — **définitif, -tive** [definitif, -tiv] *adj* : definitive, final — **définition** [definisjɔ̃] *nf* : definition — **définitivement** [definitivmɑ̃] *adv* : definitively, for good

défoncer [defɔ̃se] {6} *vt* : smash, break down

déformer [defɔrme] *vt* : deform, distort — **déformation** [defɔrmasjɔ̃] *nf* : distortion

défraîchi, -chie [defreʃi] *adj* : faded, worn

défrayer [defreje] {11} *vt* : pay (s.o.'s expenses)

défunt, -funte [defœ̃, -fœ̃t] *adj & n* : deceased

dégager [degaʒe] {17} *vt* **1** : free **2** DÉBARRASSER : clear (the way, etc.) **3** EXTRAIRE : bring out **4** ÉMETTRE : emit — **se dégager** *vr* **1** : clear (up) **2** : emanate **3 ~ de** : get free of — **dégagé, -gée** [degaʒe] *adj* **1** : clear, open **2** : free and easy

dégâts [dega] *nmpl* : damage

dégeler [deʒle] {20} *v* : thaw — **dégel** [deʒɛl] *nm* : thaw

dégénérer [deʒenere] {87} *vi* : degenerate

dégingandé, -dée [deʒɛ̃gɑ̃de] *adj* : lanky

dégivrer [deʒivre] *vt* : defrost

dégonfler [degɔ̃fle] *vt* : deflate — **se dégonfler** *vr* : deflate, go flat

dégoûter [degute] *vt* : disgust — **se dégoûter** *vr* **~ de** : get sick of — **dégoût** [degu] *nm* : disgust — **dégoûtant, -tante** [degutɑ̃, -tɑ̃t] *adj* : disgusting

dégoutter [degute] *vi* : drip

dégrader [degrade] *vt* : degrade

dégrafer [degrafe] *vt* : unhook

degré [dəgre] *nm* **1** : degree **2** : step (of a staircase) **3 par ~s** : gradually

dégueulasse [degœlas] *adj fam* : disgusting

déguiser [degize] *vt* : disguise — **se déguiser** *vr* **~ en** : dress up as — **déguisement** [degizmɑ̃] *nm* : disguise

déguster [degyste] *vt* **1** : taste **2** SAVOURER : savor, enjoy

dehors [dəɔr] *adv* **1** : outside **2 en ~** : (toward the) outside **3 en ~ de** : outside of, apart from — **~** *nms & pl* : outside, exterior

déjà [deʒa] *adv* : already

déjeuner [deʒœne] *nm* **1** : lunch **2** *Can* : breakfast — **~** *vi* **1** : have lunch **2** *Can* : have breakfast

déjouer [deʒwe] *vt* : thwart

delà [dəla] *adv* → **au–delà, par–delà**

délabrer [delabre] *v* **se délabrer** *vr* : become dilapidated — **délabrement** [delabrəmɑ̃] *nm* : dilapidation, disrepair

délai [delɛ] *nm* **1** : time limit **2** : extension (of time) **3** : waiting period

délaisser [delese] *vt* **1** ABANDONNER : abandon, desert **2** : neglect

délasser [delase] *vt* : relax — **se délasser** *vr* : relax

délayer [deleje] {11} *vt* **1** DILUER : dilute **2** : drag out (a speech, etc.)

déléguer [delege] {87} *vt* : delegate — **délégué, -guée** [delege] *n* : delegate — **délégation** [delegasjɔ̃] *nf* : delegation

délibérer [delibere] {87} *vi* : deliberate — **délibéré, -rée** [delibere] *adj* **1** : deliberate **2** DÉCIDÉ : determined

délicat, -cate [delika, -kat] *adj* **1** : delicate **2** : tactful **3** EXIGEANT : fussy — **délicatement** [delikatmɑ̃] *adv* **1** : delicately **2** : finely, precisely — **délicatesse** [delikatɛs] *nf* **1** : delicacy **2** : tactfulness

délice [delis] *nm* : delight — **délicieux, -cieuse** [delisjø, -sjøz] *adj* : delicious, delightful
délier [delje] {96} *vt* **1** : untie **2 ~ de** : release from
délimiter [delimite] *vt* : demarcate
délinquant, -quante [delɛ̃kɑ̃, -kɑ̃t] *adj & n* : delinquent
délire [delir] *nm* **1** : delirium **2 en ~** : delirious, frenzied — **délirant, -rante** [delirɑ̃, -rɑ̃t] *adj* **1** : delirious **2** : frenzied — **délirer** [delire] *vi* **1** : be delirious **2** : rave
délit [deli] *nm* : crime, offense
délivrer [delivre] *vt* **1** : set free **2** : issue, award **3 ~ de** : relieve of — **délivrance** [delivrɑ̃s] *nf* **1** : freeing, release **2** : delivery, issue **3** SOULAGEMENT : relief
déloger [delɔʒe] {17} *vt* **1** : evict **2** : remove, dislodge
déloyal, -loyale [delwajal] *adj, mpl* **-loyaux** [-jo] **1** : disloyal **2** : unfair — **déloyauté** [delwajote] *nf* : disloyalty
delta [dɛlta] *nm* : delta
déluge [delyʒ] *nm* **1** : deluge, flood **2** AVERSE : downpour
demain [dəmɛ̃] *adv & nm* : tomorrow
demander [dəmɑ̃de] *vt* **1** : ask for, request **2** : ask (about) **3** NÉCESSITER : call for, require — **se demander** *vr* : wonder — **demande** [dəmɑ̃d] *nf* **1** : request **2** : application (form) **3 l'offre et la ~** : supply and demand
démanger [demɑ̃ʒe] {17} *vi* : itch — **démangeaison** [demɑ̃ʒɛzɔ̃] *nf* : itch, itching
démarche [demarʃ] *nf* **1** ALLURE : gait, walk **2** REQUÊTE : step, action
démarrer [demare] *v* : start (up) — **démarreur** [demarœr] *nm* : starter
démêler [demele] *vt* : disentangle — **démêlé** [demele] *nm* **1** : quarrel **2 ~s** *nmpl* : problems, trouble
déménager [demenaʒe] {17} *v* : move, relocate — **déménagement** [demenaʒmɑ̃] *nm* : moving, relocation
démence [demɑ̃s] *nf* : madness, insanity
démener [demne] {52} *v* **se démener** *vr* : struggle, thrash about
dément, -mente [demɑ̃, -mɑ̃t] *adj* : insane, demented
démentir [demɑ̃tir] {82} *vt* : refute, deny — **démenti** [demɑ̃ti] *nm* : denial
démesuré, -rée [deməzyre] *adj* : excessive, immoderate
démettre [demɛtr] {53} *vt* : dismiss, fire — **se démettre** *vr* **1** : resign **2** : dislocate (one's shoulder, etc.)
demeurer [dəmœre] *vi* **1** (*with* **être**) : remain **2** (*with* **avoir**) : reside — **demeure** [dəmœr] *nf* : residence
demi, -mie *adj* **1** : half **2 et ~** : and a half, half past — **~** *n* : half — **demi** *nm France* : half-pint (of beer) — **à ~** *adv phr* : half, halfway
démission [demisjɔ̃] *nf* : resignation — **démissionner** [demisjɔne] *vi* : resign
démocratie [demɔkrasi] *nf* : democracy — **démocratique** [demɔkratik] *adj* : democratic
démodé, -dée [demɔde] *adj* : old-fashioned, out-of-date
demoiselle [demwazɛl] *nf* **1** : young lady **2 ~ d'honneur** : bridesmaid
démolir [demɔlir] *vt* : demolish — **démolition** [demɔlisjɔ̃] *nf* : demolition
démon [demɔ̃] *nm* : demon
démonstration [demɔ̃strasjɔ̃] *nf* : demonstration — **démonstrateur, -trice** [demɔ̃stratœr, -tris] *n* : demonstrator — **démonstratif, -tive** [demɔ̃stratif, -tiv] *adj* : demonstrative
démonter [demɔ̃te] *vt* : dismantle, take down
démontrer [demɔ̃tre] *vt* : demonstrate, show
démoraliser [demɔralize] *vt* : demoralize
démunir [demynir] *vt* : deprive
dénégation [denegasjɔ̃] *nf* : denial
dénicher [deniʃe] *vt* : unearth
dénier [denje] {96} *vt* : deny
dénigrer [denigre] *vt* : disparage
dénombrer [denɔ̃bre] *vt* : count, enumerate
dénommer [denɔme] *vt* : name, call — **dénomination** [denɔminasjɔ] *nf* : name, designation
dénoncer [denɔ̃se] {6} *vt* : denounce, inform on — **dénonciation** [denɔ̃sjasjɔ̃] *nf* : denunciation
dénoter [denɔte] *vt* : denote
dénouement [denumɑ̃] *nm* : outcome
dénouer [denwe] *vt* : untie, undo
denrée [dɑ̃re] *nf* **1** : commodity **2 ~s alimentaires** : foods
dense [dɑ̃s] *adj* : dense — **densité** [dɑ̃site] *nf* : density, denseness
dent [dɑ̃] *nf* **1** : tooth **2** : cog (of a wheel), prong (of a fork) — **dentaire** [dɑ̃tɛr] *adj* : dental
dentelé, -lée [dɑ̃tle] *adj* : jagged, serrated
dentelle [dɑ̃tɛl] *nf* : lace
dentiste [dɑ̃tist] *nmf* : dentist — **den-**

tier [dɑ̃tje] *nm* : dentures *pl* — **dentifrice** [dɑ̃tifris] *nm* : toothpaste — **dentition** [dɑ̃tisjɔ̃] *nf* : teeth *pl*
dénuder [denyde] *vt* **1** : make bare **2** : strip (off)
dénué, -nuée [denɥe] *adj* **~ de** : devoid of, lacking in
déodorant [deɔdɔrɑ̃] *adj & nm* : deodorant
dépanner [depane] *vt* **1** : fix, repair **2** : help out (s.o.) — **dépanneur** [depanœr] *nm Can* : convenience store
dépareillé, -lée [depareje] *adj* : odd, not matching
départ [depar] *nm* **1** : departure **2** : start (in sports)
départements [departəmɑ̃] *nm* : department
départir [departir] {82} *v* **se départir** *vr* **~ de** : abandon, depart from
dépassé, -sée [depase] *adj* : outdated, outmoded
dépasser [depase] *vt* **1** : pass, go past **2** EXCÉDER : exceed **3** SURPASSER : surpass **4 cela me dépasse!** : that's beyond me! — *vi* : stick out — **dépassement** [depasmɑ̃] *nm* : passing
dépayser [depeize] *vt* **1** : disorient **2** : provide with a change of scenery
dépecer [depəse] {6} *and* {52} *vt* : cut up, tear apart
dépêcher [depeʃe] *vt* : dispatch — **se dépêcher** *vr* : hurry up — **dépêche** [depɛʃ] *nf* : dispatch
dépeindre [depɛ̃dr] {37} *vt* : depict, describe
dépendre [depɑ̃dr] {63} *vi* **~ de** : depend on — *vt* : take down — **dépendance** [depɑ̃dɑ̃s] *nf* : dependence — **dépendant, -dante** [depɑ̃dɑ̃, -dɑ̃t] *adj* : dependent
dépenser [depɑ̃se] *vt* **1** : spend (money) **2** : use up, expend (energy) — **se dépenser** *vr* : exert oneself — **dépens** [depɑ̃] *nmpl* **aux ~ de** : at the expense of — **dépense** [depɑ̃s] *nf* **1** : spending, expenditure **2** : expense — **dépensier, -sière** [depɑ̃sje, -sjɛr] *adj* : extravagant
dépérir [deperir] *vi* **1** : wither (of a plant) **2** : waste away (of a person)
dépister [depiste] *vt* **1** : detect, discover **2** : track down (a criminal)
dépit [depi] *nm* **1** : spite **2 en ~ de** MALGRÉ : in spite of, despite
déplacer [deplase] {6} *vt* : move, shift — **se déplacer** *vr* : move about — **déplacé, -cée** [deplase] *adj* : out of place
déplaire [deplɛr] {66} *vi* **1** : be disliked **2 ~ à** : displease — **déplaisant, -sante** [deplɛzɑ̃, -zɑ̃t] *adj* : unpleasant
dépliant [deplijɑ̃] *nm* : brochure, pamphlet
déplier [deplije] {96} *vt* : unfold
déplorer [deplɔre] *vt* : deplore — **déplorable** [deplɔrabl] *adj* : deplorable
déployer [deplwaje] {58} *vt* **1** : deploy **2** DÉPLIER : unfold, spread out
déposer [depoze] *vt* **1** : put down **2** : deposit (a sum of money) **3** : drop off, leave **4** : register, file (a complaint) — *vi* : testify — **se déposer** *vr* : settle
dépôt [depo] *nm* **1** : deposit **2** ENTREPÔT : warehouse, store **3** : (train) station **4 ~ d'ordures** : (garbage) dump — **dépotoir** [depɔtwar] *nm* : dump
dépouiller [depuje] *vt* **~ qqn de** : deprive s.o. of
dépourvu, -vue [depurvy] *adj* **~ de** : without, lacking in — **au dépourvu** *adv phr* : by surprise
déprécier [depresje] {96} *vt* **1** : devalue **2** : disparage — **se déprécier** *vr* : depreciate — **dépréciation** [depresjasjɔ̃] *nf* : depreciation
dépression [depresjɔ̃] *nf* : depression
déprimer [deprime] *vt* : depress — **déprimant, -mante** [deprimɑ̃, -mɑ̃t] *adj* : depressing — **déprimé, -mée** [deprime] *adj* : depressed, dejected
depuis [dəpɥi] *prep* **1** : since **2** : from **3 ~ deux ans** : for two years — **~** *adv* : since (then) — **depuis que** *adv phr* : (ever) since
député, -tée [depyte] *n* : representative (in government)
déraciner [derasine] *vt* : uproot
dérailler [deraje] *vi* : derail — **déraillement** [derajmɑ̃] *nm* : derailment
déraisonnable [derɛzɔnabl] *adj* : unreasonable
déranger [derɑ̃ʒe] {17} *vt* **1** : bother, disturb **2** DÉRÉGLER : disrupt, upset — **se déranger** *vr* : put oneself out — **dérangement** [derɑ̃ʒmɑ̃] *nm* **1** : trouble, bother **2** : (stomach) upset
déraper [derape] *vi* **1** GLISSER : skid, slip **2** : get out of hand (of a situation)
dérégler [deregle] {87} *vt* **1** : put out of order **2** : upset, disturb — **se dérégler** *vr* : go wrong
dérision [derizjɔ̃] *nf* : derision, mockery — **dérisoire** [derizwar] *adj* : ridiculous, pathetic
dériver [derive] *vt* **1** : divert **2 ~ de** : derive from — *vi* : drift, be adrift —

dérivé [derive] *nm* **1** : derivation (of a word) **2** : by-product
dernier, -nière [dɛrnje, -njɛr] *adj* **1** : last, previous **2** : latest (of a novel, etc.) **3** : final, last **4** : lowest (of a step, etc.) — ~ *n* **1** : last (one) **2 ce dernier, cette dernière** : the latter — **dernièrement** [dɛrnjɛrmɑ̃] *adv* : recently
dérobé, -bée [derɔbe] *adj* : hidden — **à la dérobée** *adv phr* : on the sly
dérouler [derule] *vt* : unwind, unroll — **se dérouler** *vr* : take place — **déroulement** [derulmɑ̃] *nm* : development, progress
dérouter [derute] *vt* : disconcert, confuse — **déroute** [derut] *nf* : rout
derrière [dɛrjɛr] *adv & prep* : behind — ~ *nm* **1** : back, rear **2** *fam* : buttocks *pl,* bottom
des → **de**
dès [dɛ] *prep* **1** : from **2** ~ **lors** : from then on **3** ~ **que** : as soon as
désaccord [dezakɔr] *nm* : disagreement
désagréable [dezagreabl] *adj* DÉPLAISANT : disagreeable, unpleasant
désagréger [dezagreʒe] {64} *vt* : break up — **se désagréger** *vr* : disintegrate
désagrément [dezagremɑ̃] *nm* : annoyance
désapprouver [dezapruve] *vt* : disapprove of — **désapprobation** [dezaprɔbasjɔ̃] *nf* : disapproval
désarmer [dezarme] *vt* : disarm — **désarmement** [dezarməmɑ̃] *nm* : disarmament
désarroi [dezarwa] *nm* : confusion, distress
désastre [dezastr] *nm* : disaster — **désastreux, -treuse** [dezastrø, -trøz] *adj* : disastrous
désavantage [dezavɑ̃taʒ] *nm* : disadvantage — **désavantager** [dezavɑ̃taʒe] {17} *vt* : put at a disadvantage — **désavantageux, -geuse** [dezavɑ̃taʒø, -ʒøz] *adj* : disadvantageous
désaveu [dezavø] *nm, pl* **-veux** : repudiation, denial
désavouer [dezavwe] *vt* RENIER : deny, repudiate
descendre [dəsɑ̃dr] {63} *vt* **1** : go down (the stairs, etc.) **2** : take (sth) down — *vi* **1** : go down, come down **2** : get off (of a passenger) **3** ~ **de** : be descended from — **descendant, -dante** [desɑ̃dɑ̃, -dɑ̃t] *n* : descendant — **descente** [desɑ̃t] *nf* **1** : descent **2** : (police) raid **3** PENTE : slope
description [dɛskripsjɔ̃] *nf* : description — **descriptif, -tive** [dɛskriptif, -tiv] *adj* : descriptive
désemparé, -rée [dezɑ̃pare] *adj* **1** : distraught **2** : in distress
déséquilibrer [dezekilibre] *vt* : unbalance — **déséquilibre** [dezekilibr] *nm* : imbalance
désert, -serte [dezɛr, -zɛrt] *adj* : desert, deserted — **désert** *nm* : desert
déserter [dezɛrte] *v* : desert — **déserteur** [dezɛrtœr] *nm* : deserter
désespérer [dezɛspere] {87} *vi* : despair — *vt* : drive to despair — **désespéré, -rée** [dezɛspere] *adj* : desperate — **désespoir** [dezɛspwar] *nm* : desperation, despair
déshabiller [dezabije] *vt* : undress — **se déshabiller** *vr* : get undressed
déshonneur [dezɔnœr] *nm* : dishonor, disgrace — **déshonorant, -rante** [dezɔnɔrɑ̃, -rɑ̃t] *adj* : dishonorable — **déshonorer** [dezɔnɔre] *vt* : dishonor, disgrace
déshydrater [dezidrate] *vt* : dehydrate
désigner [deziɲe] *vt* **1** : designate, indicate **2** NOMMER : appoint
désillusion [dezilyzjɔ̃] *nf* : disillusionment — **désillusionner** [dezilyzjɔne] *vt* : disillusion
désinfecter [dezɛ̃fɛkte] *vt* : disinfect — **désinfectant** [dezɛ̃fɛktɑ] *nm* : disinfectant
désintégrer [dezɛ̃tegre] {87} *v* **se désintégrer** *vr* : disintegrate
désintéressé, -sée [dezɛ̃terese] *adj* : impartial, disinterested
désinvolte [dezɛ̃vɔlt] *adj* : casual, offhand — **désinvolture** [dezɛ̃vɔltyr] *nf* : offhand manner
désirer [dezire] *vt* : want, desire — **désir** [dezir] *nm* : desire — **désireux, -reuse** [dezirø, -røz] *adj* : anxious, eager
désobéir [dezɔbeir] *vi* : disobey — **désobéissance** [dezɔbeisɑ̃s] *nf* : disobedience — **désobéissant, -sante** [dezɔbeisɑ̃, -sɑ̃t] *adj* : disobedient
désobligeant, -geante [dezɔbliʒɑ̃, -ʒɑ̃t] *adj* : disagreeable
désoler [dezɔle] *vt* : distress — **se désoler** *vr* : be upset — **désolé, -lée** [dezɔle] *adj* **1** : desolate **2 être** ~ : be sorry
désopilant, -lante [dezɔpilɑ̃, -lɑ̃t] *adj* : hilarious
désordonné, -née [dezɔrdɔne] *adj* **1** : disorganized **2** : untidy — **désordre**

[dezɔrdr] *nm* **1** : disorder **2** : untidiness

désorganiser [dezɔrganize] *vt* : disorganize

désorienté, -tee [dezɔrjɑ̃te] *adj* : disoriented, confused

désormais [dezɔrmɛ] *adv* : henceforth, from now on

désosser [dezɔse] *vt* : bone (a fish)

desquels, desquelles → **lequel**

dessécher [deseʃe] {87} *vt* : dry up, parch

desserrer [desere] *vt* : loosen

dessert [desɛr] *nm* : dessert

desservir [desɛrvir] {81} *vt* **1** : serve (by providing transportation) **2** : clear (the table) **3** : do a disservice to

dessin [desɛ̃] *nm* **1** : drawing **2** : design, pattern **3** CONTOUR : outline **4** **∼ animé** : (animated) cartoon — **dessinateur, -trice** [desinatœr, -tris] *n* **1** : artist **2** : designer — **dessiner** [desine] *vt* **1** : draw **2** : outline — *vi* : draw, sketch — **se dessiner** *vr* **1** : stand out **2** APPARAÎTRE : appear, take shape

dessous [dəsu] *adv* : underneath — **∼** *nms & pl* **1** : underneath, underside **2** **∼** *nmpl* : underwear, lingerie **3 en ∼** : underneath, down below **4 en ∼ de** : below — **dessous–de–verre** [d(ə)ɛsudvɛr] *nms & pl* : coaster

dessus [dəsy] *adv* : on top, on (it) — **∼** *nms & pl* **1** : top **2** : upper (of a shoe) **3** : upper floor, upstairs **4 en ∼** : on top, above

destiner [dɛstine] *vt* **1** : destine **2** **∼ qqch à qqn** : intend sth for s.o. — **destin** [dɛstɛ̃] *nm* : fate, destiny — **destinataire** [dɛstinatɛr] *nmf* : addressee — **destination** [dɛstinasjɔ̃] *nf* : destination — **destinée** [dɛstine] *nf* : fate, destiny

destruction [dɛstryksjɔ̃] *nf* : destruction — **destructeur, -trice** [dɛstryktœr, -tris] *adj* : destructive

désuet, -suète [dezɥɛ, -zɥɛt] *adj* : outdated, obsolete — **désuétude** [dezɥetyd] *nf* **tomber en ∼** : fall into disuse

désunir [dezynir] *vt* : separate, divide

détacher [detaʃe] *vt* **1** : detach, tear off **2** : untie, unfasten — **se détacher** *vr* **1** : come undone **2** **∼ de** : grow apart from — **détaché, -chée** [detaʃe] *adj* : detached

détailler [detaje] *vt* **1** : sell retail **2** ÉNUMÉRER : detail, itemize — **détail** [detaj] *nm* **1** : detail **2** : retail

détecter [detɛkte] *vt* : detect — **détecteur** [detɛktœr] *nm* : detector, sensor — **détection** [detɛksjɔ̃] *nf* : detection — **détective** [detɛktiv] *nm* : detective

détendre [detɑ̃dr] {63} *vt* **1** : slacken, loosen **2** : relax, ease — **se détendre** *vr* **1** : become slack **2** : relax, unwind — **détendu, -due** [detɑ̃dy] *adj* : relaxed

détenir [detnir] {92} *vt* **1** POSSÉDER : hold, possess **2** : detain (a suspect)

détente [detɑ̃t] *nf* **1** REPOS : relaxation **2** : trigger (of a firearm)

détenteur, -trice [detɑ̃tœr, -tris] *n* : holder

détention [detɑ̃sjɔ̃] *nf* **1** : possession **2** EMPRISONNEMENT : detention

détenu, -nue [detny] *n* : prisoner

détergent [detɛrʒɑ̃] *nm* : detergent

détériorer [deterjɔre] *vt* : damage — **se détériorer** *vr* : deteriorate — **détérioration** [deterjɔrasjɔ̃] *nf* : deterioration

déterminer [detɛrmine] *vt* : determine — **se déterminer** *vr* **∼ à** : make up one's mind to — **détermination** [detɛrminasjɔ̃] *nf* : determination — **déterminé, -née** [detɛrmine] *adj* **1** : determined, resolute **2** : specified, definite

déterrer [detere] *vt* : dig up, unearth

détester [detɛste] *vt* : detest — **détestable** [detɛstabl] *adj* : hateful

détoner [detɔne] *vi* : explode — **détonation** [detɔnasjɔ̃] *nf* : explosion

détourner [deturne] *vt* **1** : divert, reroute **2** : hijack (an airplane) **3** : embezzle (funds) — **détour** [detur] *nm* : detour — **détourné, -née** [deturne] *adj* : indirect, roundabout — **détournement** [deturnəmɑ̃] *nm* **1** : diversion, rerouting **2** : hijacking **3** : embezzlement

détraquer [detrake] *vt* **1** : put out of order, break **2** *fam* : upset (one's stomach) — **se détraquer** *vr* : break down, go wrong

détresse [detrɛs] *nf* : distress

détriment [detrimɑ̃] *nm* **au ∼ de** : at the cost of

détritus [detrity(s)] *nmpl* : waste, rubbish

détroit [detrwa] *nm* : strait

détruire [detrɥir] {49} *vt* : destroy

dette [dɛt] *nf* : debt

deuil [dœj] *nm* : bereavement, mourning

deux [dø] *adj* **1** : two **2** : second (in dates) **3 ∼ fois** : twice — **∼** *nm* **1**

: two **2 tous les ~** : both (of them) — **deuxième** [døzjɛm] *adj & nmf* : second — **deuxièmement** [døzjɛmmɑ̃] *adv* : secondly, second
deux–points [døpwɛ̃] *nms & pl* : colon
dévaliser [devalize] *vt* : rob (a bank, etc.)
dévaloriser [devalɔrize] *vt* **1** : reduce the value of **2** : belittle (s.o.)
devancer [dəvɑ̃se] {6} *vt* **1** : be ahead of **2** ANTICIPER : anticipate
devant [dəvɑ̃] *adv* : in front, ahead, before — **~** *nm* : front — **~** *prep* **1** : in front of **2** : ahead of
devanture [dəvɑ̃tyr] *nf* **1** : storefront **2** : shopwindow
dévaster [devaste] *vt* : devastate
développer [devlɔpe] *vt* : develop — **se développer** *vr* : develop — **développement** [devlɔpmɑ̃] *nm* : development
devenir [dəvnir] {92} *vi* **1** : become **2 qu'est-ce que tu deviens?** : what are you up to?
déverser [deverse] *vt* : pour (out) — **se déverser** *vr* **~ dans** : flow into
déviation [devjasjɔ̃] *nf* **1** : deviation **2** DÉTOUR : detour — **dévier** [devje] {96} *vt* : deflect, divert (traffic) — *vi* **1** : veer, swerve **2 ~ de** : deviate from
deviner [dəvine] *vt* **1** : guess **2** APERCEVOIR : perceive **3** PRÉDIRE : foretell
devinette [dəvinɛt] *nf* : riddle
devis [dəvi] *nms & pl* : estimate
devise [dəviz] *nf* **1** : motto **2** : currency (money)
dévisser [devise] *vt* : unscrew
dévoiler [devwale] *vt* : unveil, reveal
devoir [dəvwar] {28} *vt* : owe — *v aux* **1** : have to, should **2** (*expressing obligation*) : must — **~** *nm* **1** : duty **2 ~s** *nmpl* : homework
dévorer [devɔre] *vt* : devour
dévot, -vote [devo, -vɔt] *adj* : devout, pious — **dévotion** [devosjɔ̃] *nf* : devotion, piety
dévouer [devwe] *vt* : devote — **se dévouer** *vr* : devote oneself — **dévoué, -vouée** [devwe] *adj* : devoted — **dévouement** [devumɑ̃] *nm* : dedication, devotion
dextérité [dɛksterite] *nf* : dexterity, skill
diabète [djabɛt] *nm* : diabetes — **diabétique** [djabetik] *adj & nmf* : diabetic
diable [djabl] *nm* : devil — **diabolique** [djabɔlik] *adj* : diabolical
diagnostic [djagnɔstik] *nm* : diagnosis — **diagnostiquer** [djagnɔstike] *vt* : diagnose
diagonal, -nale [djagɔnal] *adj, mpl* **-naux** [-no] : diagonal — **diagonale** *nf* **1** : diagonal **2 en ~** : diagonally
diagramme [djagram] *nm* : graph, chart
dialecte [djalɛkt] *nm* : dialect
dialogue [djalɔg] *nm* : dialogue
diamant [djamɑ̃] *nm* : diamond
diamètre [djamɛtr] *nm* : diameter
diaphragme [djafragm] *nm* : diaphragm
diapositive [djapɔzitiv] *nf* : slide, transparency
diarrhée [djare] *nf* : diarrhea
dictateur [diktatœr] *nm* : dictator
dicter [dikte] *vt* : dictate — **dictée** [dikte] *nf* : dictation
dictionnaire [diksjɔnɛr] *nm* : dictionary
dièse [djɛz] *nm* **1** : sharp (in music) **2** : pound sign
diesel [djezɛl] *adj & nm* : diesel
diète [djɛt] *nf* RÉGIME : diet
dieu [djø] *nm, pl* **dieux 1** : god **2 Dieu** : God
diffamer [difame] *vt* : slander, libel — **diffamation** [difamasjɔ̃] *nf* : slander, libel
différence [diferɑ̃s] *nf* **1** : difference **2 à la ~ de** : unlike — **différencier** [diferɑ̃sje] {96} *vt* : differentiate — **différend** [diferɑ̃] *nm* : disagreement — **différent, -rente** [diferɑ̃, -rɑ̃t] *adj* : different — **différer** [difere] {87} *vt* : defer, postpone — *vi* : differ, vary
difficile [difisil] *adj* : difficult — **difficilement** [difisilmɑ̃] *adv* : with difficulty — **difficulté** [difikylte] *nf* : difficulty
difforme [difɔrm] *adj* : deformed, misshapen — **difformité** [difɔrmite] *nf* : deformity
diffuser [difyze] *vt* **1** : broadcast **2** PROPAGER : spread, distribute — **diffusion** [difyzjɔ̃] *nf* **1** : broadcasting **2** : distribution
digérer [diʒere] {87} *vt* **1** : digest **2** *fam* : put up with — **digestif, -tive** [diʒɛstif, -tiv] *adj* : digestive — **digestion** [diʒɛstjɔ̃] *nf* : digestion
digital, -tale [diʒital] *adj, mpl* **-taux** [-to] : digital
digne [diɲ] *adj* **1** : dignified **2 ~ de** : worthy of — **dignité** [diɲite] *nf* : dignity
digue [dig] *nf* : dike

dilapider [dilapide] *vt* : squander
dilater [dilate] *vt* : dilate — **se dilater** *vr* : dilate
dilemme [dilɛm] *nm* : dilemma
diluer [dilɥe] *vt* : dilute
dimanche [dimɑ̃ʃ] *nm* : Sunday
dimension [dimɑ̃sjɔ̃] *nf* : dimension
diminuer [diminɥe] *vt* RÉDUIRE : lower, reduce — *vi* : diminish, decrease — **diminution** [diminysjɔ̃] *nf* : reduction, decreasing
dinde [dɛ̃d] *nf* : (female) turkey — **dindon** [dɛ̃dɔ̃] *nm* : (male) turkey
dîner [dine] *vi* **1** : dine, have dinner **2** *Can* : have lunch — **~** *nm* **1** : dinner **2** *Can* : lunch — **dîneur, -neuse** [dinœr, -nœz] *n* : diner (person)
dinosaure [dinozɔr] *nm* : dinosaur
diplomate [diplɔmat] *adj* : diplomatic, tactful — **~** *nmf* : diplomat — **diplomatie** [diplɔmasi] *nf* : diplomacy — **diplomatique** [diplɔmatik] *adj* : diplomatic
diplôme [diplom] *nm* : diploma — **diplômé, -mée** [diplome] *adj* : qualified, certified — **~** *n* : graduate
dire [dir] {29} *vt* **1** : say **2** : tell **3** **qu'en dis-tu?** : what do you think? **4** **vouloir ~** : mean — **se dire** *vr* **1** : tell oneself **2** **comment se dit ... en français?** : how do you say ... in French? — **~** *nm* **1** : statement **2** **au ~ de** : according to
direct, -recte [dirɛkt] *adj* : direct — **direct** *nm* **1** : express train **2** **en ~** : live, in person — **directement** [-təmɑ̃] *adv* : directly, straight
directeur, -trice [dirɛktœr, -tris] *adj* : directing, guiding — **~** *n* **1** : manager, director **2** **directeur général** : chief executive officer
direction [dirɛksjɔ̃] *nf* **1** : direction **2** GESTION : management **3** : steering (mechanism)
directive [dirɛktiv] *nf* : order
dirigeant, -geante [diriʒɑ̃, ʒɑ̃t] *adj* : ruling — **~** *n* : leader, director
diriger [diriʒe] {17} *vt* **1** : direct, manage **2** CONDUIRE : steer **3** MENER : conduct **4** **~ sur** : aim at — **se diriger** *vr* **~ vers** : head toward
discerner [disɛrne] *vt* : discern — **discernement** [disɛrnəmɑ̃] *nm* : discernment
disciple [disipl] *nm* : disciple
discipline [disiplin] *nf* : discipline — **discipliner** [disipline] *vt* : discipline
discorde [diskɔrd] *nf* : discord
discours [diskur] *nms & pl* : speech
discréditer [diskredite] *vt* : discredit
discret, -crète [diskrɛ, -krɛt] *adj* : discreet — **discrétion** [diskresjɔ̃] *nf* **1** : discretion **2** **à ~** : unlimited, as much as one wants
discrimination [diskriminasjɔ̃] *nf* : discrimination
disculper [diskylpe] *vt* : clear, exonerate
discussion [diskysjɔ̃] *nf* : discussion
discuter [diskyte] *vt* **1** : discuss, debate **2** CONTESTER : question — *vi* **1** : talk **2** PROTESTER : argue **3** **~ de** : discuss
diseuse [dizøz] *nf* **~ de bonne aventure** : fortune-teller
disgrâce [disgras] *nf* : disgrace
disloquer [dislɔke] *vt* LUXER : dislocate
disparaître [disparɛtr] {7} *vi* **1** : disappear **2** MOURIR : die — **disparition** [disparisjɔ̃] *nf* **1** : disappearance **2** MORT : extinction, death
disparité [disparite] *nf* : disparity
disparu, -rue [dispary] *adj* : missing — **~** *n* **1** : missing person **2** : dead person
dispenser [dispɑ̃se] *vt* **1** : exempt, excuse **2** DISTRIBUER : dispense — **se dispenser** *vr* **~ de** : avoid — **dispense** [dispɑ̃s] *nf* : exemption
disperser [dispɛrse] *vt* : disperse, scatter — **se disperser** *vr* : disperse
disponible [disponibl] *adj* : available — **disponibilité** [disponibilite] *nf* : availability
disposer [dispoze] *vt* **1** PLACER : arrange **2** INCITER : incline, dispose — *vi* **~ de** : have at one's disposal — **disposé, -sée** [dispoze] *adj* **1** : arranged **2** **~ à** : disposed to, willing to — **dispositif** [dispozitif] *nm* **1** : device, mechanism **2** PLAN : plan of action — **disposition** [dispozisjɔ̃] *nf* **1** : arrangement, layout **2** APTITUDE : aptitude **3** TENDANCE : tendency **4** **à la ~ de** : at the disposal of **5** **~s** *nfpl* : steps, measures
disproportionné, -née [disprɔpɔrsjɔne] *adj* : disproportionate
disputer [dispyte] *vt* **1** : compete in, play **2** *fam* : tell off **3** *Can* : scold — **se disputer** *vr* : quarrel, fight — **dispute** [dispyt] *nf* : argument, quarrel
disqualifier [diskalifje] {96} *vt* : disqualify
disque [disk] *nm* **1** : (phonograph) record **2** : disk — **disquette** [diskɛt] *nf* : floppy disk
disséminer [disemine] *vt* : scatter

dissentiment [disɑ̃timɑ̃] *nm* : dissent
dissertation [disɛrtasjɔ̃] *nf* : essay (in school)
dissimuler [disimyle] *vt* : conceal, hide — **se dissimuler** *vr* : hide oneself — **dissimulation** [disimylasjɔ̃] *nf* **1** : deceit **2** : concealment
dissiper [disipe] *vt* **1** : disperse **2** : squander (one's fortune) — **se dissiper** *vr* : clear (up), vanish
dissolu, -lue [disɔly] *adj* : dissolute — **dissolution** [disɔlysjɔ̃] *nf* **1** : dissolution, breakup **2** : dissolving — **dissolvant** [disɔlvɑ̃] *nm* **1** : solvent **2** : nail polish remover
dissoudre [disudr] {1} *vt* : dissolve — **se dissoudre** *vr* : dissolve
dissuader [disɥade] *vt* : dissuade, deter
distance [distɑ̃s] *nf* : distance — **distant, -tante** [distɑ̃, -tɑt] *adj* : distant
distiller [distile] *vt* : distill
distinct, -tincte [distɛ̃, -tɛ̃kt] *adj* : distinct — **distinctif, -tive** [distɛ̃ktif, -tiv] *adj* : distinctive — **distinction** [distɛ̃ksjɔ̃] *nf* : distinction
distinguer [distɛ̃ge] *v* : distinguish — **distingué, -guée** [distɛ̃ge] *adj* : distinguished
distraction [distraksjɔ̃] *nf* **1** : distraction **2** PASSE-TEMPS : recreation
distraire [distrɛr] {40} *vt* **1** : distract **2** DIVERTIR : amuse, entertain — **se distraire** *vr* : amuse oneself — **distrait, -traite** [distrɛ, -trɛt] *adj* : distracted, absentminded
distribuer [distribɥe] *vt* **1** : distribute **2** : deliver (mail) — **distributeur** [distribytœr] *nm* **1** : distributor **2** *or* **~ automatique** : dispenser, vending machine — **distribution** [distribysjɔ̃] *nf* **1** : distribution **2** : casting, cast (of actors)
district [distrikt] *nm* : district
dit, dite [di, dit] *adj* **1** : agreed upon, stated **2** : called, known as
divaguer [divage] *vi* : rave
divan [divɑ̃] *nm* : couch
divergence [-vɛrʒɑ̃s] *nf* : difference — **diverger** [divɛrʒe] {17} *vi* : diverge
divers, -verse [divɛr, -vɛrs] *adj* **1** VARIÉ : diverse **2** PLUSIEURS : various — **diversifier** [divɛrsifje] {96} *vt* : diversify — **diversion** [divɛrsjɔ̃] *nf* : diversion — **diversité** [divɛrsite] *nf* : diversity, variety
divertir [divɛrtir] *vt* : amuse, entertain — **se divertir** *vr* : amuse oneself — **divertissement** [divɛrtismɑ̃] *nm* : entertainment, pastime
dividende [dividɑ̃d] *nm* : dividend
divine, -vine [divɛ̃, -vin] *adj* : divine — **divinité** [divinite] *nf* : divinity
diviser [divize] *vt* : divide — **se diviser** *vr* : divide — **division** [divizjɔ̃] *nf* : division
divorcer [divɔrse] {6} *vi* : get a divorce — **divorce** [divɔrs] *nm* : divorce
divulguer [divylge] *vt* : divulge, disclose
dix [dis, *before a consonant* di, *before a vowel or mute h* diz] *adj* **1** : ten **2** : tenth (in dates) — **~** *nms & pl* : ten
dix-huit [dizɥit] *adj* **1** : eighteen **2** : eighteenth (in dates) — **~** *nms & pl* : eighteen — **dix-huitième** [dizɥitjɛm] *adj & nmf & nm* : eighteenth
dixième [dizjɛm] *adj & nmf & nm* : tenth
dix-neuf [diznœf] *adj* **1** : nineteen **2** : nineteenth (in dates) — **~** *nms & pl* : nineteen — **dix-neuvième** [diznœvjɛm] *adj & nmf & nm* : nineteenth
dix-sept [disɛt] *adj* **1** : seventeen **2** : seventeenth (in dates) — **~** *nms & pl* : seventeen — **dix-septième** [disɛtjɛm] *adj & nmf & nm* : seventeenth
dizaine [dizɛn] *nf* : ten, about ten
docile [dɔsil] *adj* : obedient
dock [dɔk] *nm* : dock
docteur [dɔktœr] *nm* : doctor
doctrine [dɔktrin] *nf* : doctrine
document [dɔkymɑ̃] *nm* : document — **documentation** [dɔkymɑ̃tasjɔ̃] *nf* : literature, leaflets *pl* — **documenter** [dɔkymɑ̃te] *v* **se documenter** *vr* **~ sur** : research
dodu, -due [dɔdy] *adj* : plump, chubby
dogme [dɔgm] *nm* : dogma
doigt [dwa] *nm* **1** : finger **2** **~ de pied** : toe — **doigté** [dwate] *nm* TACT : tact
dollar [dɔlar] *nm* : dollar
domaine [dɔmɛn] *nm* **1** : domain **2** PROPRIÉTÉ : estate
dôme [dom] *nm* : dome
domestique [dɔmɛstik] *adj* **1** : domestic **2** : domesticated — **~** *nmf* : servant — **domestiquer** [dɔmɛstike] *vt* APPRIVOISER : domesticate
domicile [dɔmisil] *nm* : residence, home
dominer [dɔmine] *v* : dominate — **dominant, -nante** [dɔminɑ̃, -nɑ̃t] *adj* : dominant
dommage [dɔmaʒ] *nm* **1** PRÉJUDICE : harm, injury **2** DÉGÂTS : damage **3** **c'est ~** : that's too bad
dompter [dɔ̃te] *vt* : tame
don [dɔ̃] *nm* : gift — **donateur, -trice**

[dɔnatœr, -tris] *n* : donor, giver — **donation** [dɔnasjɔ̃] *nf* : donation

donc [dɔ̃k] *conj* **1** : so, therefore, consequently **2** : so, then

donner [dɔne] *vt* **1** : give **2** : produce, yield **3** MONTRER : indicate, show **4** CAUSER : cause **5** : deal (cards) — *vi* **1** : produce a crop **2 ~ dans** : fall into **3 ~ sur** : overlook — **se donner** *vr* **~ à** : devote oneself to — **donne** [dɔn] *nf* : deal (in card games) — **donné, -née** [dɔne] *adj* **1** : given **2 c'est ~** : it's a bargain — **donnée** *nf* **1** : fact **2 ~s** *nfpl* : data — **donneur, -neuse** [dɔnœr, -nøz] *n* **1** : donor **2** : (card) dealer

dont [dɔ̃] *pron* : of which, of whom, whose

doré, -rée [dɔre] *adj* **1** : gilt **2** : golden

dorénavant [dɔrenavɑ̃] *adv* : henceforth

dorer [dɔre] *vt* **1** : gild **2** BRUNIR : tan — *vi* : brown (in cooking)

dorloter [dɔrlɔte] *vt* : pamper

dormir [dɔrmir] {30} *vi* : sleep, be asleep

dortoir [dɔrtwar] *nm* : dormitory

dorure [dɔryr] *nf* : gilding, gilt

dos [do] *nms & pl* : back

dose [doz] *nf* : dose — **doser** [doze] *vt* : measure out (a dose of medicine)

dossier [dosje] *nm* **1** : file, record **2** : back (of a chair)

doter [dɔte] *vt* **1** : endow **2** ÉQUIPER : equip

douane [dwan] *nf* **1** : customs **2** : (import) duty — **douanier, -nière** [dwanje, -njɛr] *adj* : customs — **douanier** *nm* : customs officer

double [dubl] *adv & adj* : double — **~** *nm* **1** : double **2** : copy, duplicate — **doublement** [dubləmɑ̃] *adv* : doubly — **doubler** [duble] *vt* **1** : double **2** : line (fabric) **3** : dub (a film, etc.) **4** DÉPASSER : pass, overtake — *vi* : double — **doublure** [dublyr] *nf* **1** : lining **2** : understudy

douce → **doux** — **doucement** [dusmɑ̃] *adv* **1** : gently, softly **2** LENTEMENT : slowly — **douceur** [dusœr] *nf* **1** : softness, smoothness **2** : gentleness, mildness

douche [duʃ] *nf* : shower — **doucher** [duʃe] **se doucher** *vr* : take a shower

doué, douée [dwe] *adj* **1** : gifted, talented **2 ~ de** : endowed with

douille [duj] *nf* : electric socket

douillet, -lette [dujɛ, -jɛt] *adj* CONFORTABLE : cozy

douleur [dulœr] *nf* **1** : pain **2** CHAGRIN : grief — **douloureux, -reuse** [dulurø, -røz] *adj* : painful

douter [dute] *vt* **1** : doubt **2 ~ de** : question — **se douter** *vr* **~ de** : suspect — **doute** [dut] *nm* : doubt — **douteux, -teuse** [dutø, -tøz] *adj* : doubtful

doux, douce [du, dus] *adj* **1** : sweet **2** : soft (of skin) **3** : mild, gentle

douze [duz] *adj* **1** : twelve **2** : twelfth (in dates) — **~** *nms & pl* : twelve — **douzaine** [duzɛn] *nf* : dozen — **douzième** [duzjɛm] *adj & nmf & nm* : twelfth

doyen, doyenne [dwajɛ̃, -jɛn] *n* : dean

dragon [dragɔ̃] *nm* : dragon

draguer [drage] *vt* : dredge

drainer [drene] *vt* : drain — **drainage** [drɛnaʒ] *nm* : drainage, draining

drame [dram] *nm* **1** : drama **2** : tragedy — **dramatique** [dramatik] *adj* : dramatic — **dramatiser** [dramatize] *vt* : dramatize — **dramaturge** [dramatyrʒ] *nmf* : playwright

drap [dra] *nm* **1** : sheet **2** : woolen fabric

drapeau [drapo] *nm, pl* **-peaux** : flag

draper [drape] *vt* : drape

drastique [drastik] *adj* : drastic

dresser [drese] *vt* **1** LEVER : raise **2** ÉRIGER : put up, erect **3** ÉTABLIR : draft, draw up **4** : train (an animal) **5 ~ les oreilles** : cock one's ears — **se dresser** *vr* **1** : stand up **2** : rise up, tower

dribbler [drible] *vi* : dribble (in sports)

drogue [drɔg] *nf* : drug — **drogué, -guée** [drɔge] *n* : drug addict — **droguer** [drɔge] *vt* : drug — **se droguer** *vr* : take drugs

droit [drwa] *nm* **1** : right **2** : fee, tax, duty **3 le ~** : law **4 ~s d'auteur** : copyright — **~** *adv* : straight, directly — **droit, droite** [drwa, drwat] *adj* **1** : right, right-hand **2** : straight, direct **3** VERTICAL : upright, vertical **4** HONNÊTE : honest — **droite** *nf* **1** : right, right-hand side **2 la ~** : the right (in politics) — **droitier, -tière** [drwatje, -tjɛr] *adj* : right-handed — **droiture** [drwatyr] *nf* : uprightness, integrity

drôle [drol] *adj* : funny — **drôlement** [drolmɑ̃] *adv* **1** : amusingly **2** BIZARREMENT : strangely, oddly **3** *fam* : really, awfully

dru, drue [dry] *adj* : thick (of hair, etc.)

du → **de, le**

dû, due [dy] *adj* **1** : due, owing **2 ~ à** : due to — **dû** *nm* : due

duc [dyk] *nm* : duke — **duchesse** [dyʃɛs] *nf* : duchess
duel [dɥɛl] *nm* : duel
dûment [dymɑ̃] *adv* : duly
dune [dyn] *nf* : dune
duo [dyo] *nm* **1** : duet **2** : duo, pair
dupe [dyp] *nf* : dupe — **duper** [dype] *vt* : dupe, deceive
duplex [dyplɛks] *nm* : duplex (apartment)
duplicata [dyplikata] *nms & pl* : duplicate
duquel → **lequel**
dur, dure [dyr] *adj* **1** : hard, stiff **2** DIFFICILE : difficult **3** SÉVÈRE : harsh — **dur** *adv* : hard
durable [dyrabl] *adj* : durable, lasting
durant [dyrɑ̃] *prep* **1** : for (a period of time) **2** : during
durcir [dyrsir] *v* : harden — **se durcir** *vr* : harden — **durcissement** [dyrsismɑ̃] *nm* : hardening
durée [dyre] *nf* : duration, length
durement [dyrmɑ̃] *adv* : harshly, severely
durer [dyre] *vi* : last, go on
dureté [dyrte] *nf* **1** : hardness **2** SÉVÉRITÉ : harshness
duvet [dyvɛ] *nm* **1** : down (fabric) **2** : sleeping bag
dynamique [dinamik] *adj* : dynamic
dynamite [dinamit] *nf* : dynamite — **dynamiter** [dinamite] *vt* : dynamite, blast
dynastie [dinasti] *nf* : dynasty

E

e [ø] *nm* : e, fifth letter of the alphabet
eau [o] *nf, pl* **eaux 1** : water **2 ~ de Cologne** : cologne **3 ~ douce** : freshwater **4 ~ de Javel** : bleach **5 ~ oxygénée** : hydrogen peroxide — **eau–de–vie** *nf, pl* **eaux–de–vie** : brandy
ébahir [ebair] *vt* : astound, dumbfound
ébaucher [eboʃe] *vt* : sketch out, outline — **s'ébaucher** *vr* : form, take shape — **ébauche** [eboʃ] *nf* : outline, sketch
ébène [ebɛn] *nf* : ebony — **ébéniste** [ebenist] *nmf* : cabinetmaker
éblouir [ebluir] *vt* : dazzle, stun
ébouler [ebule] *v* **s'ébouler** *vr* : cave in, collapse
ébouriffer [eburife] *vt* : tousle, ruffle
ébranler [ebrɑ̃le] *vt* **1** : shake **2** : weaken, undermine
ébrécher [ebreʃe] {87} *vt* : chip, nick — **ébréchure** [ebreʃyr] *nf* : chip, nick
ébriété [ebrijete] *nf* : inebriation, drunkenness
ébullition [ebylisjɔ̃] *nf* : boil, boiling
écailler [ekaje] *vt* **1** : scale (fish) **2** : open (a shell) **3** : chip (paint) — **s'écailler** *vr* : flake off — **écaille** [ekaj] *nf* **1** : scale (of a fish) **2** : tortoiseshell **3** FRAGMENT : flake, chip
écarlate [ekarlat] *adj & nf* : scarlet
écarquiller [ekarkije] *vt* **~ les yeux** : open one's eyes wide
écarter [ekarte] *vt* **1** : spread, open **2** ÉLOIGNER : move apart **3** EXCLURE : rule out **4** DÉTOURNER : divert, distract — **s'écarter** *vr* **1** : move away **2** SE SÉPARER : part, open — **écart** [ekar] *nm* **1** : distance, gap **2** VARIATION : difference **3** : lapse (of conduct) **4** DÉVIATION : swerve **5 à l'~** : apart, away — **écarté, -tée** [ekarte] *adj* **1** ISOLÉ : remote **2** : wide apart — **écartement** [ekartəmɑ̃] *nm* : gap
ecclésiastique [eklezjastik] *nm* : clergyman
écervelé, -lée [esɛrvəle] *adj* : scatterbrained
échafaud [eʃafo] *nm* : scaffold — **échafaudage** [eʃafodaʒ] *nm* : scaffolding
échalote [eʃalɔt] *nf* **1** : shallot **2** *Can* : scallion
échanger [eʃɑ̃ʒe] {17} *vt* : exchange — **échange** [eʃɑ̃ʒ] *nm* **1** : exchange **2** : trade, commerce — **échangeur** [eʃɑ̃ʒœr] *nm* : (highway) interchange
échantillon [eʃɑ̃tijɔ̃] *nm* : sample
échapper [eʃape] *vi* **1 ~ à** : escape (from) **2 laisser ~** : let out **3 l'~ belle** : have a narrow escape — *vt Can* : drop — **s'échapper** *vr* : escape
écharde [eʃard] *nf* : splinter
écharpe [eʃarp] *nf* **1** : scarf **2 en ~** : in a sling
échasse [eʃas] *nf* : stilt
échauffer [eʃofe] *v* **s'échauffer** *vr* : warm up
échéance [eʃeɑ̃s] *nf* **1** : due date **2** OBLIGATION : financial obligation, payment **3 à longue ~** : in the long run

— **échéant** [eʃeɑ̃] **le cas ~** *adv phr* : if need be

échec [eʃɛk] *nm* **1** : failure, setback **2 ~s** *nmpl* : chess **3 ~ et mat** : checkmate **4 en ~** : in check

échelle [eʃɛl] *nf* **1** : ladder **2** MESURE : scale — **échelon** [eʃlɔ̃] *nm* **1** : rung **2** NIVEAU : level — **échelonner** [eʃlɔne] *vt* : space out, spread out

échevelé, -lée [eʃəvle] *adj* : disheveled

échiquier [eʃikje] *nm* : chessboard

écho [eko] *nm* : echo — **échographie** [ekografi] *nf* : ultrasound

échoir [eʃwar] {31} *vi* **1** : fall due **2 ~ à qqn** : fall to s.o.

échouer [eʃwe] *vi* : fail (of an exam) — **s'échouer** *vr* : run aground

éclabousser [eklabuse] *vt* : splash, spatter — **éclaboussure** [eklabusyr] *nf* : splash

éclairer [eklere] *vt* **1** : light (up) **2** INFORMER : enlighten **3** EXPLIQUER : clarify — *vi* : give light — **s'éclairer** *vr* **1** : light up **2** : become clearer — **éclair** [eklɛr] *nm* **1** ÉCLAT : flash **2** : (flash of) lightning — **éclairage** [eklɛraʒ] *nm* : lighting, illumination — **éclaircie** [eklɛrsi] *nf* **1** : sunny spell **2** : clearing, glade — **éclaircir** [eklɛrsir] *vt* **1** : lighten **2** CLARIFIER : clarify **3** : thin (in cooking) — **s'éclaircir** *vr* : clear (up) — **éclaircissement** [eklɛrsismɑ̃] *nm* : explanation, clarification

éclaireur, -reuse [eklɛrœr, -røz] *n* : boy scout *m*, girl scout *f* — **éclaireur** *nm* : (military) scout

éclater [eklate] *vi* **1** : burst, explode **2** : break up, splinter — **éclat** [ekla] *nm* **1** : splinter, chip **2** : brilliance, shine **3** : splendor **4 ~ de rire** : burst (of laughter) — **éclatant, -tante** [eklatɑ̃, -tɑ̃t] *adj* **1** BRILLANT : brilliant **2 un succès éclatant** : a resounding success — **éclatement** [eklatmɑ̃] *nm* **1** : explosion, bursting **2** : rupture, split

éclipse [eklips] *nf* : eclipse — **éclipser** [eklipse] *v* **s'éclipser** *vr* : slip away

éclore [eklɔr] {32} *vi* **1** : hatch **2** : open out, blossom — **éclosion** [eklozjɔ̃] *nf* **1** : hatching **2** : blossoming

écluse [eklyz] *nf* : lock (of a canal)

écœurer [ekœre] *vt* : sicken, disgust — **écœurant, -rante** [ekœrɑ̃, -rɑ̃t] *adj* **1** : cloying, sickening **2** DÉGUEULASSE : disgusting

école [ekɔl] *nf* **1** : school **2 ~ secondaire** *Can* : high school **3 ~ maternelle** *Can* : kindergarten — **écolier, -lière** [ekɔlje, -ljɛr] *n* : schoolboy *m*, schoolgirl *f*

écologie [ekɔlɔʒi] *nf* : ecology — **écologique** [ekɔlɔʒik] *adj* : ecological

économie [ekɔnɔmi] *nf* **1** : economy **2** : economics **3 ~s** *nfpl* : savings — **économe** [ekɔnɔm] *adj* : thrifty, economical — **~** *nmf* : bursar — **économique** [ekɔnɔmik] *adj* : economic — **économiser** [ekɔnɔmize] *v* : save — **économiste** [ekɔnɔmist] *nmf* : economist

écorce [ekɔrs] *nf* **1** : bark (of a tree) **2** : peel (of a fruit)

écorcher [ekɔrʃe] *vt* **1** DÉPOUILLER : skin **2** ÉGRATIGNER : scratch, graze — **écorchure** [ekɔrʃyr] *nf* : graze, scratch

écossais, -saise [ekɔsɛ, -sɛz] *adj* **1** : Scottish **2** : tartan, plaid

écosser [ekɔse] *vt* : shell (peas, etc.)

écosystème [ekɔsistɛm] *nm* : ecosystem

écouler [ekule] *vt* : sell, dispose of — **s'écouler** *vr* **1** : flow (out) **2** PASSER : pass, elapse — **écoulement** [ekulmɑ̃] *nm* : flow

écourter [ekurte] *vt* : cut short, curtail

écouter [ekute] *vt* : listen to — *vi* : listen — **écouteur** [ekutœr] *nm* **1** : (telephone) receiver **2 ~s** *nmpl* : headphones

écoutille [ekutij] *nf* : hatch (of a ship)

écran [ekrɑ̃] *nm* : screen

écraser [ekraze] *vt* **1** : crush, squash, mash **2** : run over (an animal, etc.) **3** ACCABLER : overwhelm — **s'écraser** *vr* : crash (of a plane, etc.) — **écrasant, -sante** [ekrazɑ̃, -zɑ̃t] *adj* : crushing, overwhelming

écrémé, -mée [ekreme] *adj* **lait écrémé** : skim milk

écrevisse [ekrəvis] *nf* : crayfish

écrier [ekrije] {96} *v* **s'écrier** *vr* : exclaim

écrin [ekrɛ̃] *nm* : case, box

écrire [ekrir] {33} *v* : write — **s'écrire** *vr* : be spelled — **écrit** [ekri] *nm* **1** : writing(s) **2** : document **3 par ~** : in writing — **écriteau** [ekrito] *nm, pl* **-teaux** : notice, sign — **écriture** [ekrityr] *nf* : writing — **écrivain** [ekrivɛ̃] *nm* : writer — **écrivaillon** [ekrivajɔ̃] *nm fam* : hack writer

écrou [ekru] *nm* : (metal) nut

écrouler [ekrule] *v* **s'écrouler** *vr* : collapse — **écroulement** [ekrulmɑ̃] *nm* : collapse

écueil [ekœj] *nm* RÉCIF : reef
écume [ekym] *nf* **1** : foam, froth **2** : scum (in cooking) — **écumer** [ekyme] *vi* : foam, froth — **écumeux, -meuse** [ekymø, -møz] *adj* : foamy
écureuil [ekyrœj] *nm* : squirrel
écurie [ekyri] *nf* : stable
écusson [ekysɔ̃] *nm* : badge
édenté, -tée [edɑ̃te] *adj* : toothless
édifice [edifis] *nm* : building — **édifier** [edifje] {96} *vt* CONSTRUIRE : build
éditer [edite] *vt* **1** : publish **2** : edit — **éditeur, -trice** [editœr, -tris] *n* **1** : publisher **2** : editor — **édition** [edisjɔ̃] *nf* **1** : publishing **2** : edition (of a book) — **éditorial** [editɔrjal] *nm, pl* **-riaux** [-rjo] : editorial
édredon [edrədɔ̃] *nm* : comforter
éducation [edykasjɔ̃] *nf* **1** ENSEIGNEMENT : education **2** : upbringing (of children) **3 avoir de l'~** : have good manners — **éducatif, -tive** [edykatif, -tiv] *adj* : educational — **éduquer** [edyke] *vt* **1** : educate **2** ÉLEVER : bring up
effacer [efase] {6} *vt* : erase, delete — **s'effacer** *vr* **1** : fade **2** S'ÉCARTER : stand aside
effectif, -tive [efɛktif, -tiv] *adj* : real, actual — **effectivement** [efɛktivmɑ̃] *adv* **1** : indeed, in fact **2** RÉELLEMENT : really
effectuer [efɛktɥe] *vt* EXÉCUTER : carry out, make
efféminé, -née [efemine] *adj* : effeminate
effervescent, -cente [efɛrvesɑ, -sɑ̃t] *adj* : effervescent
effet [efɛ] *nm* **1** RÉSULTAT : effect, result **2 en ~** : indeed, actually **3 faire bon ~** : make a good impression
efficace [efikas] *adj* : efficient — **efficacité** [efikasite] *nf* **1** : efficiency **2** : effectiveness
effilocher [efilɔʃe] *vt* : shred, fray — **s'effilocher** *vr* : fray
effleurer [eflœre] *vt* **1** FRÔLER : touch lightly, graze **2 ça m'a effleuré l'esprit** : it crossed my mind
effondrer [efɔ̃dre] *v* **s'effondrer** *vr* : collapse — **effondrement** [efɔ̃drəmɑ̃] *nm* : collapse
efforcer [efɔrse] {6} *v* **s'efforcer** *vr* : strive, endeavor
effort [efɔr] *nm* : effort
effrayer [efreje] {11} *vt* : frighten — **effrayant, -frayante** [efrɛjɑ̃, -jɑ̃t] *adj* : frightening
effréné, -née [efrene] *adj* : wild, unrestrained
effriter [efrite] *vt* : crumble — **s'effriter** *vr* : crumble
effroi [efrwa] *nm* : terror, dread
effronté, -tée [efrɔ̃te] *adj* : impudent
effroyable [efrwajabl] *adj* : dreadful
égal, -gale [egal] *adj, mpl* **égaux** [ego] **1** : equal **2** RÉGULIER : regular, even **3 ça m'est ~** : it makes no difference to me — **~** *n* : equal — **également** [egalmɑ̃] *adv* **1** : equally **2** AUSSI : also, as well — **égaler** [egale] *vt* : equal — **égaliser** [egalize] *vt* **1** : equalize **2** : level (out) — **égalité** [egalite] *nf* : equality
égard [egar] *nm* **1** : regard, consideration **2 à cet ~** : in this respect **3 à l'~ de** : with regard to
égarer [egare] *vt* **1** : lead astray **2** PERDRE : lose, misplace — **s'égarer** *vr* **1** : lose one's way **2** : be misplaced
égayer [egeje] {11} *vt* : cheer up
églefin [egləfɛ̃] *nm* : haddock
église [egliz] *nf* : church
ego [ego] *nm* : ego — **égoïsme** [egɔism] *nm* : selfishness — **égoïste** [egɔist] *adj* : selfish
égorger [egɔrʒe] {17} *vt* : cut the throat of
égotisme [egɔtism] *nm* : egotism — **égotiste** [egɔtist] *adj* : egotistic(al)
égoutter [egute] *vt* : allow to drip, drain — **s'égoutter** *vr* : drain — **égout** [egu] *nm* : sewer — **égouttoir** [egutwar] *nm* : (dish) drainer
égratigner [egratiɲe] *vt* : scratch, graze — **égratignure** [egratiɲyr] *nf* : scratch
eh [e] *interj* **1** : hey! **2 ~ bien** : well
éhonté, -tée [eɔ̃te] *adj* : shameless, brazen
éjaculer [eʒakyle] *v* : ejaculate
éjecter [eʒɛkte] *vt* **1** : eject **2** *fam* : kick out
élaborer [elabɔre] *vt* : develop, put together — **élaboration** [elabɔrasjɔ̃] *nf* : elaboration, development
élan[1] [elɑ̃] *nm* **1** : momentum **2** : rush, surge (of energy, etc.)
élan[2] *nm* : elk
élancé, -cée [elɑ̃se] *adj* : slender
élancer [elɑ̃se] {6} *v* **s'élancer** *vr* SE PRÉCIPITER : dash, rush — **élancement** [elɑ̃smɑ̃] *nm* : shooting pain
élargir [elarʒir] *vt* : widen, broaden — **s'élargir** *vr* : expand, become broader — **élargissement** [elarʒismɑ̃] *nm* : widening, expanding

élastique [elastik] *adj* : elastic, flexible — **~** *nm* **1** : elastic **2** : rubber band
électeur, -trice [elɛktœr, -tris] *n* : voter — **élection** [elɛksjɔ̃] *nf* : election — **électoral, -rale** [elɛktɔral] *adj, mpl* **-raux** [-ro] : electoral, election — **électorat** [elɛktɔra] *nm* : electorate
électricité [elɛktrisite] *nf* : electricity — **électricien, -cienne** [elɛktrisjɛ̃, -sjɛn] *n* : electrician — **électrique** [elɛktrik] *adj* : electric(al)
électrocuter [elɛktrɔkyte] *vt* : electrocute
électron [elɛktrɔ̃] *nm* : electron — **électronique** [elɛktrɔnik] *adj* : electronic — **~** *nf* : electronics
élégance [elegɑ̃s] *nf* : elegance — **élégant, -gante** [elegɑ̃, -gɑ̃t] *adj* : elegant
élément [elemɑ̃] *nm* **1** : element **2** COMPOSANT : component, part — **élémentaire** [elemɑ̃tɛr] *adj* : elementary, basic
éléphant [elefɑ̃] *nm* : elephant
élevage [ɛlvaʒ] *nm* : breeding
élévation [elevasjɔ̃] *nf* **1** : elevation **2** AUGMENTATION : rise, increase
élève [elɛv] *nmf* : pupil, student
élever [elve] {52} *vt* **1** : raise **2** ÉRIGER : erect **3** ÉDUQUER : bring up (a child) — **s'élever** *vr* **1** : rise (up) **2 ~ à** : amount to — **élevé, -vée** [elve] *adj* **1** : high, elevated **2 bien ~** : well-mannered — **éleveur, -veuse** [elvœr, -vøz] *n* : breeder
éligible [eliʒibl] *adj* : eligible
éliminer [elimine] *vt* : eliminate — **élimination** [eliminasjɔ̃] *nf* : elimination
élire [elir] {51} *vt* : elect
élite [elit] *nf* : elite
elle [ɛl] *pron* **1** : she, it **2** : her **3 elles** *pron pl* : they, them — **elle–même** [ɛlmɛm] *pron* **1** : herself, itself **2 elles–mêmes** *pron pl* : themselves
éloge [elɔʒ] *nm* : eulogy, praise
éloigner [elwaɲe] *vt* **1** ÉCARTER : push aside, move away **2** DÉTOURNER : divert, turn away — **s'éloigner** *vr* : move or go away — **éloigné, -gnée** [elwaɲe] *adj* : distant, remote — **éloignement** [elwaɲmɑ̃] *nm* : distance, remoteness
éloquence [elɔkɑ̃s] *nf* : eloquence — **éloquent, -quente** [elɔkɑ̃, -kɑ̃t] *adj* : eloquent
élu, -lue [ely] *adj* : elected — **~** *n* : elected representative
élucider [elyside] *vt* : elucidate
éluder [elyde] *vt* : elude
émacié, -ciée [emasje] *adj* : emaciated
émail [emaj] *nm, pl* **émaux** [emo] : enamel
émanciper [emɑ̃sipe] *vt* : emancipate — **émancipation** [emɑ̃sipasjɔ̃] *nf* : emancipation
émaner [emane] *vi* **~ de** : emanate from
emballer [ɑ̃bale] *vt* **1** EMPAQUETER : pack, wrap **2** *fam* : thrill — **s'emballer** *vr* **1** : race (of an engine), bolt (of a horse) **2** *fam* : get carried away — **emballage** [ɑ̃balaʒ] *nm* : packing, wrapping
embarcadère [ɑ̃barkadɛr] *nm* : wharf, pier
embarcation [ɑ̃barkasjɔ̃] *nf* : small boat
embardée [ɑ̃barde] *nf* : swerve (of a car)
embargo [ɑ̃bargo] *nm* : embargo
embarquer [ɑ̃barke] *vt* **1** : embark **2** CHARGER : load — *vi* : board — **s'embarquer** *vr* : board — **embarquement** [ɑ̃barkəmɑ̃] *nm* **1** : boarding **2** : loading (on board)
embarrasser [ɑ̃barase] *vt* **1** ENCOMBRER : clutter **2** ENTRAVER : hinder **3** GÊNER : embarrass — **s'embarrasser** *vr* **~ de** : burden oneself with — **embarras** [ɑ̃bara] *nms & pl* **1** : difficulty **2** : embarrassment — **embarrassant, -sante** [ɑ̃barasɑ̃, -sɑ̃t] *adj* **1** : embarrassing, awkward **2** ENCOMBRANT : cumbersome
embaucher [ɑ̃boʃe] *vt* : hire — **embauche** [ɑ̃boʃ] *nf* : hiring, employment
embaumer [ɑ̃bome] *vt* **1** : embalm **2** : scent, make fragment
embellir [ɑ̃belir] *vt* **1** ENJOLIVER : beautify **2** EXAGÉRER : embellish
embêter [ɑ̃bete] *vt* **1** : annoy, bother **2** LASSER : bore — **s'embêter** *vr* : be bored — **embêtant, -tante** [ɑ̃bɛtɑ̃, -tɑ̃t] *adj* : annoying — **embêtement** [ɑ̃bɛtmɑ̃] *nm* : hassle, bother
emblée [ɑ̃ble] **d'~** *adv phr* : right away
emblème [ɑ̃blɛm] *nm* : emblem
embobiner [ɑ̃bɔbine] *vt fam* : bamboozle, trick
emboîter [ɑ̃bwate] *vt* : fit together — **s'emboîter** *vr* **~ dans** : fit into
embonpoint [ɑ̃bɔ̃pwɛ̃] *nm* : stoutness, corpulence
embouchure [ɑ̃buʃyr] *nf* **1** : mouth (of a river) **2** : mouthpiece

embourber [ɑ̃burbe] *v* **s'embourber** *vr* : get bogged down

embouteillage [ɑ̃butɛjaʒ] *nm* : traffic jam

emboutir [ɑ̃butir] *vt* HEURTER : crash into, ram

embranchement [ɑ̃brɑ̃ʃmɑ̃] *nm* : junction, fork

embraser [ɑ̃braze] *vt* : set on fire — **s'embraser** *vr* : catch fire

embrasser [ɑ̃brase] *vt* **1** : kiss **2** ÉTREINDRE : embrace, hug — **s'embrasser** *vr* : kiss

embrasure [ɑ̃brazyr] *nf* : doorway

embrayage [ɑ̃brɛjaʒ] *nm* : clutch (of an automobile) — **embrayer** [ɑ̃breje] {11} *vi* : engage the clutch

embrocher [ɑ̃brɔʃe] *vt* : skewer (meat on a spit)

embrouiller [ɑ̃bruje] *vt* **1** : tangle up **2** COMPLIQUER : confuse — **s'embrouiller** *vr* : get mixed up

embryon [ɑ̃brijɔ̃] *nm* : embryo

embûche [ɑ̃byʃ] *nf* : trap, pitfall

embuer [ɑ̃bɥe] *vt* : mist up

embuscade [ɑ̃byskad] *nf* : ambush

éméché, -chée [emeʃe] *adj fam* : tipsy

émeraude [emrod] *nf* : emerald

émerger [emɛrʒe] {17} *vi* : emerge — **émergence** [emɛrʒɑ̃s] *nf* : emergence

émeri [emri] *nm* : emery

émerveiller [emɛrveje] *vt* : amaze — **s'émerveiller** *vr* **~ de** : marvel at — **émerveillement** [emɛrvɛjmɑ̃] *nm* : amazement, wonder

émettre [emɛtr] {53} *vt* **1** : produce, give out **2** : issue (a check) **3** TRANSMETTRE : transmit, broadcast **4** EXPRIMER : express — **émetteur** [emetœr] *nm* **1** : transmitter **2** : issuer

émeute [emøt] *nf* : riot — **émeutier, -tière** [emøtje] *n* : rioter

émietter [emjete] *vt* : crumble, break up — **s'émietter** *vr* : crumble

émigrer [emigre] *vi* **1** : emigrate **2** : migrate — **émigrant, -grante** [emigrɑ̃, -grɑ̃t] *n* : emigrant — **émigration** [emigrasjɔ̃] *nf* : emigration — **émigré, -grée** [emigre] *n* : emigrant, émigré

éminence [eminɑ̃s] *nf* : eminence — **éminent, -nente** [eminɑ̃, -nɑ̃t] *adj* : eminent

émission [emisjɔ̃] *nf* **1** : emission **2** : transmission (of a message) **3** : program, broadcast **4** : issue (of a stamp, etc.)

emmagasiner [ɑ̃magazine] *vt* : store (up)

emmêler [ɑ̃mele] *vt* **1** : tangle **2** EMBROUILLER : muddle, mix up

emménager [ɑ̃menaʒe] {17} *vi* : move in

emmener [ɑ̃mne] {52} *vt* : take

emmitoufler [ɑ̃mitufle] *vt* : wrap up, bundle up — **s'emmitoufler** *vr* : bundle (up)

émoi [emwa] *nm* : excitement, turmoil

émotif, -tive [emɔtif, -tiv] *adj* : emotional — **émotion** [emosjɔ̃] *nf* : emotion — **émotionnel, -nelle** [emosjɔnɛl] *adj* : emotional

émousser [emuse] *vt* : blunt, dull

émouvoir [emuvwar] {56} *vt* : move, affect — **s'émouvoir** *vr* **1** : be moved **2 ~ de** : be concerned about — **émouvant, -vante** [emuvɑ̃, -vɑ̃t] *adj* : moving

empailler [ɑ̃paje] *vt* : stuff

empaqueter [ɑ̃pakte] {8} *vt* : package, wrap up

emparer [ɑ̃pare] *v* **s'emparer** *vr* **~ de** : seize, take hold of

empathie [ɑ̃pati] *nf* : empathy

empêcher [ɑ̃peʃe] *vt* **1** : prevent, stop **2 il n'empêche que** : nevertheless — **s'empêcher** *vr* : refrain, stop oneself — **empêchement** [ɑ̃pɛʃmɑ̃] *nm* : hitch, difficulty

empereur [ɑ̃prœr] *nm* : emperor

empester [ɑ̃peste] *vt* : stink up — *vi* : stink

empêtrer [ɑ̃petre] *v* **s'empêtrer** *vr* : become entangled

emphase [ɑ̃faz] *nf* : pomposity

empiéter [ɑ̃pjete] {87} *vi* **~ sur** : infringe on

empiffrer [ɑ̃pifre] *v* **s'empiffrer** *vr fam* : stuff oneself

empiler [ɑ̃pile] *vt* : pile, stack — **s'empiler** *vr* : pile up

empire [ɑ̃pir] *nm* **1** : empire **2 sous l'~ de** : under the influence of

empirer [ɑ̃pire] *v* : worsen

emplacement [ɑ̃plasmɑ̃] *nm* : site, location

emplette [ɑ̃plɛt] *nf* **1** ACHAT : purchase **2 faire ses ~s** : go shopping

emplir [ɑ̃plir] *vt* : fill — **s'emplir** *vr* : fill up

employer [ɑ̃plwaje] {58} *vt* **1** UTILISER : use **2** : employ, provide a job for — **s'employer** *vr* : be used — **emploi** [ɑ̃plwa] *nm* **1** : use **2** TRAVAIL : employment, job **3 ~ du temps** : schedule, timetable — **employé, -ployée** [ɑ̃plwaje] *n* : employee — **employeur,**

-ployeuse [ɑ̃plwajœr, -plwajøz] *n* : employer
empocher [ɑ̃pɔʃe] *vt* : pocket
empoigner [ɑ̃pwaɲe] *vt* : grasp, seize
empoisonner [ɑ̃pwazɔne] *vt* : poison — **empoisonnement** [ɑ̃pwazɔnmɑ̃] *nm* : poisoning
emporter [ɑ̃pɔrte] *vt* **1** : take (away) **2** ENTRAÎNER : carry away **3 l'~ sur** : beat, get the better of — **s'emporter** *vr* : lose one's temper
empreinte [ɑ̃prɛ̃t] *nf* **1** : print, imprint **2 ~ digitale** : fingerprint
empresser [ɑ̃prese] *v* **s'empresser** *vr* **1 ~ auprès de** : be attentive toward **2 ~ de** : be in a hurry to — **empressé, -sée** [ɑ̃prese] *adj* : attentive, eager (to please) — **empressement** [ɑ̃prɛsmɑ̃] *nm* **1** : attentiveness **2** : eagerness
emprise [ɑ̃priz] *nf* : influence, hold
emprisonner [ɑ̃prizɔne] *vt* : imprison — **emprisonnement** [ɑ̃prizɔnmɑ̃] *nm* : imprisonment
emprunter [ɑ̃prœ̃te] *vt* **1** : borrow **2** PRENDRE : take, follow — **emprunt** [ɑ̃prœ̃] *nm* : loan
ému, -mue [emy] *adj* : moved, touched
en [ɑ̃] *prep* **1** : in, into **2 aller ~ Belgique** : go to Belgium **3 ~ guerre** : at war **4 ~ vacances** : on vacation **5 ~ voiture** : by car **6 fait ~ plastique** : made of plastic — **~** *pron* **1** (*expressing quantity*) : some, any **2** (*representing a noun governed by* de) : it, them **3 qu'~ ferons-nous?** : what will we do of it? **4 j'~ viens** : I've just come from there
encadrer [ɑ̃kadre] *vt* **1** : frame **2** ENTOURER : surround **3** SURVEILLER : supervise — **encadrement** [ɑ̃kadrəmɑ̃] *nm* : frame
encaisser [ɑ̃kese] *vt* **1** : cash (a check), collect (money) **2** *fam* : take, tolerate
encastrer [ɑ̃kastre] *vt* : embed, build in
enceinte [ɑ̃sɛ̃t] *adj* : pregnant — **~** *nf* **1** : wall, enclosure **2 ~ acoustique** : speaker
encens [ɑ̃sɑ̃] *nm* : incense
encercler [ɑ̃sɛrkle] *vt* : surround, encircle
enchaîner [ɑ̃ʃene] *vt* **1** : chain (up) **2** LIER : link, connect — **s'enchaîner** *vr* : be connected — **enchaînement** [ɑ̃ʃɛnmɑ̃] *nm* **1** SÉRIE : series, sequence **2** LIEN : chain, link
enchanter [ɑ̃ʃɑ̃te] *vt* **1** ENSORCELER : enchant, bewitch **2** RAVIR : delight — **enchanté, -tée** [ɑ̃ʃɑ̃te] *adj* **1** : enchanted **2 ~ de vous connaître** : delighted/pleased to meet you — **enchantement** [ɑ̃ʃɑ̃tmɑ̃] *nm* **1** : enchantment **2** : delight — **enchanteur, -teresse** [ɑʃɑ̃tœr, -trɛs] *adj* : enchanting
enchère [ɑ̃ʃɛr] *nf* **1** : bid, bidding **2 vente aux ~s** : auction
enchevêtrer [ɑ̃ʃəvɛtre] *vt* : tangle — **s'enchevêtrer** *vr* : become tangled
enclencher [ɑ̃klɑ̃ʃe] *vt* : engage (a mechanism) — **s'enclencher** *vr* : engage, interlock
enclin, -cline [ɑ̃klɛ̃, -klin] *adj* **~ à** : inclined to
enclore [ɑ̃klɔr] {34} *vt* : enclose
enclos [ɑ̃klo] *nm* : enclosure
enclume [ɑ̃klym] *nf* : anvil
encoche [ɑ̃kɔʃ] *nf* : notch
encolure [ɑ̃kɔlyr] *nf* : neck (of a dress, etc.)
encombrer [ɑ̃kɔ̃bre] *vt* **1** : clutter (up) **2** OBSTRUER : block, hamper — **s'encombrer** *vr* **~ de** : burden oneself with — **encombrant, -brante** [ɑ̃kɔ̃brɑ̃, -brɑ̃t] *adj* : cumbersome — **encombre** [ɑ̃kɔ̃br] **sans ~** *adv phr* : without a hitch — **encombrement** [ɑ̃kɔ̃brəmɑ̃] *nm* **1** : clutter, congestion **2** EMBOUTEILLAGE : traffic jam
encontre [ɑ̃kɔ̃tr] **à l'~ de** *prep phr* : against, contrary to
encore [ɑ̃kɔr] *adv* **1** TOUJOURS : still **2** : more, again **3 ~ que** : although **4 pas ~** : not yet **5 si ~** : if only
encourager [ɑ̃kuraʒe] {17} *vt* : encourage — **encouragement** [ɑ̃kuraʒmɑ̃] *nm* : encouragement
encourir [ɑ̃kurir] {23} *vt* : incur
encrasser [ɑ̃krase] *vt* **1** SALIR : dirty **2** OBSTRUER : clog up
encre [ɑ̃kr] *nf* : ink — **encrer** [ɑ̃kre] *vt* : ink — **encrier** [ɑ̃krije] *nm* : inkwell
encyclopédie [ɑ̃siklɔpedi] *nf* : encyclopedia
endetter [ɑ̃dete] *v* **s'endetter** *vr* : get into debt
endeuillé, -lée [ɑ̃dœje] *adj* : in mourning, bereaved
endive [ɑ̃div] *nf* : endive, chickory
endoctriner [ɑ̃dɔktrine] *vt* : indoctrinate — **endoctrinement** [ɑ̃dɔktrinmɑ̃] *nm* : indoctrination
endommager [ɑ̃dɔmaʒe] {17} *vt* : damage
endormir [ɑ̃dɔrmir] {30} *vt* : put to sleep — **s'endormir** *vr* : fall asleep — **endormi, -mie** [ɑ̃dɔrmi] *adj* **1** : asleep **2** : sleepy

endosser [ɑ̃dɔse] *vt* **1 :** take on, assume **2 :** endorse (a check)
endroit [ɑ̃drwa] *nm* **1 :** place, spot **2 à l'∼ :** right side up
enduire [ɑ̃dɥir] {49} *vt* **:** coat, cover — **enduit** [ɑ̃dɥi] *nm* **:** coating
endurance [ɑ̃dyrɑ̃s] *nf* **:** endurance
endurcir [ɑ̃dyrsir] *vt* **:** toughen, harden — **s'endurcir** *vr* **:** harden
endurer [ɑ̃dyre] *vt* **:** endure
énergie [enɛrʒi] *nf* **:** energy — **énergique** [enɛrʒik] *adj* **:** energetic
énerver [enɛrve] *vt* **:** irritate, annoy — **s'énerver** *vr* **:** get worked up
enfance [ɑ̃fɑ̃s] *nf* **:** childhood — **enfant** [ɑ̃fɑ̃] *nmf* **:** child — **enfanter** [ɑ̃fɑ̃te] *vt* **:** give birth to — **enfantillage** [ɑ̃fɑ̃tijaʒ] *nm* **:** childishness — **enfantin, -tine** [ɑ̃fɑ̃tɛ̃, -tin] *adj* **1 :** childlike **2 :** childish
enfer [ɑ̃fɛr] *nm* **:** hell
enfermer [ɑ̃fɛrme] *vt* **:** shut up, lock up — **s'enfermer** *vr* **1 :** shut oneself away **2 ∼ dans :** retreat into
enfiler [ɑ̃file] *vt* **1 :** slip on, put on (a garment) **2 :** string, thread (a needle)
enfin [ɑ̃fɛ̃] *adv* **1 :** finally, at last **2 :** lastly **3 ∼, je crois :** at least I think so **4 mais ∼, donne-le-moi! :** come on, give it to me!
enflammer [ɑ̃flame] *vt* **1 :** ignite, set fire to **2 :** inflame (in medicine) — **s'enflammer** *vr* **:** catch fire
enfler [ɑ̃fle] *v* **:** swell — **s'enfler** *vr* **:** swell up — **enflure** [ɑ̃flyr] *nf* **:** swelling
enfoncer [ɑ̃fɔ̃se] {6} *vt* **1 :** drive or push in **2** DÉFONCER **:** break down — *vi* **:** sink — **s'enfoncer** *vr* **1 :** sink in **2** CÉDER **:** give way
enfouir [ɑ̃fwir] *vt* **1 :** bury **2** CACHER **:** hide
enfreindre [ɑ̃frɛ̃dr] {37} *vt* **:** infringe
enfuir [ɑ̃fɥir] {46} *v* **s'enfuir** *vr* **:** flee
engager [ɑ̃gaʒe] {17} *vt* **1** OBLIGER **:** bind, commit **2** RECRUTER **:** hire **3** COMMENCER **:** start **4 ∼ qqn à :** urge s.o. to **5 ∼ une vitesse :** put a car in gear — **s'engager** *vr* **1 :** commit oneself **2 :** enlist (in the army) **3 ∼ dans :** enter, turn into (a street) — **engagé, -gée** [ɑ̃gaʒe] *adj* **1 :** committed **2** *Can fam* **:** busy — **engageant, -geante** [ɑ̃gaʒɑ̃, -ʒɑ̃t] *adj* **:** engaging — **engagement** [ɑ̃gaʒmɑ̃] *nm* **1** PROMESSE **:** commitment **2** PARTICIPATION **:** involvement
engin [ɑ̃ʒɛ̃] *nm* **:** machine, device
engloutir [ɑ̃glutir] *vt* **1 :** gobble up, devour **2 :** engulf, swallow up
engorger [ɑ̃gɔrʒe] {17} *vt* **:** block, jam up
engouement [ɑ̃gumɑ̃] *nm* **:** infatuation
engouffrer [ɑ̃gufre] *vt* **:** devour
engourdir [ɑ̃gurdir] *vt* **:** numb — **s'engourdir** *vr* **:** go numb — **engourdi, -die** [ɑ̃gurdi] *adj* **:** numb
engraisser [ɑ̃grese] *vt* **:** fatten — *vi* **:** put on weight — **engrais** [ɑ̃grɛ] *nm* **:** fertilizer, manure
engrenage [ɑ̃grənaʒ] *nm* **:** gears *pl*
engueuler [ɑ̃gœle] *vt fam* **:** yell at, bawl out
énième [enjɛm] *adj* **:** nth, umpteenth
enivrer [ɑ̃nivre] *vr* **:** intoxicate, make drunk — **s'enivrer** *vr* **:** get drunk
enjamber [ɑ̃ʒɑ̃be] *vt* **1 :** step over **2 :** span — **enjambée** [ɑ̃ʒɑ̃be] *nf* **:** stride
enjeu [ɑ̃ʒø] *nm, pl* **-jeux :** stake (in games)
enjôler [ɑ̃ʒole] *vt* **:** cajole, wheedle
enjoliver [ɑ̃ʒɔlive] *vt* **:** embellish — **enjoliveur** [ɑ̃jɔlivœr] *nm* **:** hubcap
enjoué, -jouée [ɑ̃ʒwe] *adj* **:** cheerful
enlacer [ɑ̃lase] {6} *vt* **:** embrace, hug
enlaidir [ɑ̃ledir] *vt* **:** make ugly — *vi* **:** grow ugly
enlever [ɑ̃lve] {52} *vt* **1 :** remove, take away **2** KIDNAPPER **:** abduct — **enlèvement** [ɑ̃lɛvmɑ̃] *nm* **1 :** removal **2 :** abduction
enliser [ɑ̃lize] *v* **s'enliser** *vr* **:** sink, get stuck
ennemi, -mie [ɛnmi] *n* **:** enemy
ennui [ɑ̃nɥi] *nm* **1** PROBLÈME **:** trouble, problem **2 :** boredom — **ennuyant, -nuyante** [ɑ̃nɥijɑ̃, ɑ̃nɥijɑ̃t] *adj Can* **1 :** annoying **2 :** boring — **ennuyer** [ɑ̃nɥije] {58} *vt* **1** AGACER **:** annoy **2 :** bore — **s'ennuyer** *vr* **:** be bored — **ennuyeux, -nuyeuse** [ɑ̃nɥijø, ɑ̃nɥijøz] *adj* **1 :** annoying **2 :** boring
énoncer [enɔ̃se] {6} *vt* **:** express, state — **énoncé** [enɔ̃se] *nm* **1 :** statement **2** LIBELLÉ **:** wording
énorme [enɔrm] *adj* **:** enormous, huge — **énormément** [enɔrmemɑ̃] *adv* **∼ de :** a great number of
enquête [ɑ̃kɛt] *nf* **1** INVESTIGATION **:** investigation, inquiry **2** SONDAGE **:** survey — **enquêter** [ɑ̃kete] *vi* **:** investigate
enraciner [ɑ̃rasine] *vt* **:** root — **s'enraciner** *vr* **:** take root
enrager [ɑ̃raʒe] {17} *vi* **:** be furious — **enragé, -gée** [ɑ̃raʒe] *adj* **1 :** rabid (of an animal) **2 :** furious (of a person)

enrayer [ɑ̃reje] {11} *vt* **1** : check, curb **2** BLOQUER : jam
enregistrer [ɑ̃rəʒistre] *vt* **1** : record **2** INSCRIRE : register **3** : check in (baggage) — **enregistrement** [ɑ̃rəʒistrəmɑ̃] *nm* **1** : registration **2** : (tape) recording
enrhumer [ɑ̃ryme] *v* **s'enrhumer** *vr* : catch a cold
enrichir [ɑ̃riʃir] *vt* : enrich — **s'enrichir** *vr* : grow rich — **enrichissement** [ɑ̃riʃismɑ̃] *nm* : enrichment
enrober [ɑ̃rɔbe] *vt* : coat
enrôler [ɑ̃role] *vt* : enroll, enlist — **s'enrôler** *vr* : enlist
enroué, -rouée [ɑ̃rwe] *adj* : hoarse
enrouler [ɑ̃rule] *vt* : wind, coil — **s'enrouler** *vr* **~ dans** : wrap oneself in (a blanket)
ensanglanté, -tée [ɑ̃sɑ̃glɑ̃te] *adj* : bloody, bloodstained
enseignant, -gnante [ɑ̃sɛɲɑ̃, -ɲɑ̃t] *adj* : teaching — **~** *n* : teacher
enseigne [ɑ̃sɛɲ] *nf* : sign
enseigner [ɑ̃seɲe] *v* : to teach — **enseignement** [ɑ̃sɛɲmɑ̃] *nm* **1** : teaching **2** : education
ensemble [ɑ̃sɑ̃bl] *adv* : together — **~** *nm* **1** : group, set **2** TOTALITÉ : whole **3** : (musical) ensemble **4** : suit, outfit **5 dans l'~** : on the whole
ensemencer [ɑ̃səmɑ̃se] {6} *vt* : sow
ensoleillé, -lée [ɑ̃sɔleje] *adj* : sunny
ensorceler [ɑ̃sɔrsəle] {8} *vt* : bewitch, charm
ensuite [ɑ̃sɥit] *adv* **1** : then, next **2** : afterwards, later
ensuivre [ɑ̃sɥivr] {35} *v* **s'ensuivre** *vr* : ensue, follow
entailler [ɑ̃taje] *vt* : gash, cut — **entaille** [ɑ̃taj] *nf* **1** : cut, gash **2** ENCOCHE : notch
entamer [ɑ̃tame] *vt* **1** : cut into, eat into **2** : start, enter into (negotiations)
entasser [ɑ̃tase] *vt* **1** : pile (up) **2** SERRER : cram — **s'entasser** *vr* : pile up
entendre [ɑ̃tɑ̃dr] {63} *vt* **1** : hear **2** COMPRENDRE : understand **3** VOULOIR : intend — **s'entendre** *vr* **1** : agree **2 ~ avec** : get along with — **entendement** [ɑ̃tɑ̃dmɑ̃] *nm* : understanding — **entendu, -due** [ɑ̃tɑ̃dy] *adj* **1** : agreed, understood **2 bien ~** : of course — **entente** [ɑ̃tɑ̃t] *nf* **1** : harmony **2** ACCORD : agreement, understanding
entériner [ɑ̃terine] *vt* : ratify
enterrer [ɑ̃tere] *vt* : bury — **enterrement** [ɑ̃tɛrmɑ̃] *nm* **1** : burial **2** FUNÉRAILLES : funeral
en-tête [ɑ̃tɛt] *nm, pl* **en-têtes** : heading
entêter [ɑ̃tete] *v* **s'entêter** *vr* : be obstinate, persist — **entêté, -tée** [ɑ̃tete] *adj* : stubborn, obstinate — **entêtement** [ɑ̃tɛtmɑ̃] *nm* : stubbornness
enthousiasme [ɑ̃tuzjasm] *nm* : enthusiasm — **enthousiasmer** [ɑ̃tuzjasme] *vt* : fill with enthusiasm, excite — **enthousiaste** [ɑ̃tuzjast] *adj* : enthusiastic — **~** *nmf* : enthusiast, fan
entier, -tière [ɑ̃tje, -tjɛr] *adj* : entire, whole — **entier** *nm* **en ~** : totally, in its entirety — **entièrement** [ɑ̃tjɛrmɑ̃] *adv* : entirely, wholly
entité [ɑ̃tite] *nf* : entity
entonnoir [ɑ̃tɔnwar] *nm* : funnel (utensil)
entorse [ɑ̃tɔrs] *nf* : sprain
entortiller [ɑ̃tɔrtije] *vt* : twist, wind
entourer [ɑ̃ture] *vt* : surround — **entourage** [ɑ̃turaʒ] *nm* : circle (of friends or family)
entracte [ɑ̃trakt] *nm* : intermission
entraide [ɑ̃trɛd] *nf* : mutual aid
entrailles [ɑ̃traj] *nfpl* **1** : entrails **2** PROFONDEURS : depths
entrain [ɑ̃trɛ̃] *nm* : liveliness, spirit
entraîner [ɑ̃trene] *vt* **1** EMPORTER : carry away **2** OCCASIONNER : lead to, involve **3** FORMER : train, coach — **s'entraîner** *vr* : train, practice — **entraînant, -nante** [ɑ̃trɛnɑ̃, -nɑ̃t] *adj* : lively — **entraînement** [ɑ̃trɛnmɑ̃] *nm* **1** : training, coaching **2** PRATIQUE : practice — **entraîneur, -neuse** [ɑ̃trɛnœr, -nøz] *n* : trainer, coach
entraver [ɑ̃trave] *vt* : hinder — **entrave** [ɑ̃trav] *nf* : hindrance
entre [ɑ̃tr] *prep* **1** : between **2** PARMI : among
entrecôte [ɑ̃trəkot] *nf* : rib steak
entrecroiser [ɑ̃trəkrwaze] *v* **s'entrecroiser** *vr* : intersect
entrée [ɑ̃tre] *nf* **1** : entrance, entry **2** ACCÈS : admission **3** BILLET : ticket **4** : first course (of a meal) **5** : entry (in a text), input (of information)
entre-jambes [ɑ̃trəʒɑ̃b] *nms & pl* : crotch (of clothing)
entrelacer [ɑ̃trəlase] {6} *vt* : intertwine
entremêler [ɑ̃trəmele] *vt* : mix together
entremets [ɑ̃trəmɛ] *nms & pl* : dessert
entreposer [ɑ̃trəpoze] *vt* : store — **entrepôt** [ɑ̃trəpo] *nm* : warehouse
entreprendre [ɑ̃trəprɑ̃dr] {70} *vt* : undertake, start — **entreprenant, -nante** [ɑ̃trəprənɑ̃, -nɑ̃t] *adj* : enterprising — **entrepreneur, -neuse** [ɑ̃trəprənœr,

-nøz] *n* : contractor — **entreprise** [ɑ̃trəpriz] *nf* **1** : enterprise, undertaking **2** : business, firm

entrer [ɑ̃tre] *vi* **1** : enter, go in, come in **2 ça n'entre pas** : it doesn't fit **3 ~ dans** : join, go into — *vt* **1** : bring in, take in **2** : enter, input (data, etc.)

entre-temps [ɑ̃trətɑ̃] *adv* : meanwhile

entretenir [ɑ̃trətnir] {92} *vt* **1** MAINTENIR : maintain **2 ~ qqn de** : speak to s.o. about — **s'entretenir** *vr* **1 ~ avec** : consult with, converse with **2 ~ de** : discuss, talk about — **entretenu, -nue** [ɑ̃trətny] *adj* : kept, maintained — **entretien** [ɑ̃trətjɛ̃] *nm* **1** : maintenance **2** CONVERSATION : talk, interview

entrevoir [ɑ̃trəvwar] {99} *vt* **1** : glimpse, make out **2** PRÉSAGER : foresee, anticipate — **entrevue** [ɑ̃trəvy] *nf* : meeting, interview

entrouvert, -verte [ɑ̃truvɛr, -vɛrt] *adj & adv* : half open, ajar

énumérer [enymere] {87} *vt* : enumerate — **énumération** [-merasjɔ̃] *nf* : enumeration

envahir [ɑ̃vair] *vt* **1** : invade **2** : overcome (fear, etc.)

envelopper [ɑ̃vlɔpe] *vt* **1** : envelop **2** RECOUVRIR : wrap up, cover — **enveloppe** [ɑ̃vlɔp] *nf* : envelope

envergure [ɑ̃vɛrgyr] *nf* **1** : wingspan **2** IMPORTANCE : breadth, scope

envers [ɑ̃vɛr] *prep* : toward, to — **~** *nm* **1** REVERS : back, reverse **2 à l'~** : inside out, upside down, backward

envie [ɑ̃vi] *nf* **1** : envy **2** DÉSIR : desire, wish — **envier** [ɑ̃vje] {96} *vt* : envy — **envieux, -vieuse** [ɑ̃vjø, -vjøz] *adj* : envious

environ [ɑ̃virɔ̃] *adv* : about, approximately — **environnement** [ɑ̃virɔnmɑ̃] *nm* : environment, surroundings — **environnant, -nante** [ɑ̃virɔnɑ̃, -nɑ̃t] *adj* : surrounding — **environs** [ɑ̃virɔ̃] *nmpl* **1** : surroundings **2 aux ~ de** : around, about

envisager [ɑ̃vizaʒe] {17} *vt* : consider, imagine

envoi [ɑ̃vwa] *nm* **1** : sending, dispatching **2** COLIS : parcel, package

envoler [ɑ̃vɔle] *v* **s'envoler** *vr* **1** : take off (of a plane) **2** : fly away (of a bird) — **envol** [ɑ̃vɔl] *nm* : takeoff — **envolée** [ɑ̃vɔle] *nf* **1** : flight **2** AUGMENTATION : rise, surge

envoyer [ɑ̃vwaje] {36} *vt* **1** : send (out) **2** LANCER : throw **3 ~ par la poste** : mail — **envoyé, -voyée** [ɑ̃vwaje] *n* : envoy

enzyme [ɑ̃zim] *nf* : enzyme

épagneul, -gneule [epaɲœl] *n* : spaniel

épais, -paisse [epɛ, -pɛs] *adj* : thick — **épaisseur** [epɛsœr] *nf* **1** : thickness **2** : layer — **épaissir** [epesir] *v* **s'épaissir** *vr* : thicken

épancher [epɑ̃ʃe] *vt* : give vent to — **s'épancher** *vr* : pour one's heart out

épanouir [epanwir] *v* **s'épanouir** *vr* **1** : bloom **2** S'ÉCLAIRER : light up **3** SE DÉVELOPPER : develop, flourish — **épanouissement** [epanwismɑ̃] *nm* : blossoming

épargner [eparɲe] *vt* **1** ÉCONOMISER : save **2** : spare (s.o.'s life, etc.) — **s'épargner** *vr* : spare oneself — **épargne** [eparɲ] *nf* **1** : saving **2** : savings *pl*

éparpiller [eparpije] *vt* : scatter, disperse — **s'éparpiller** *vr* : dissipate — **épars, -parse** [epar, -pars] *adj* : scattered

épater [epate] *vt fam* : amaze — **épatant, -tante** [epatɑ̃, -tɑ̃t] *adj fam* : amazing

épaule [epol] *nf* : shoulder — **épaulette** [epolɛt] *nf* : shoulder strap

épave [epav] *nf* : wreck (of a ship)

épée [epe] *nf* : sword

épeler [eple] {8} *vt* : spell

éperdu, -due [epɛrdy] *adj* **1** : intense, passionate **2 ~ de peur** : overcome with fear — **éperdument** [epɛrdymɑ̃] *adv* : frantically, desperately

éperon [eprɔ̃] *nm* : spur — **éperonner** [eprɔne] *vt* : spur (on)

éphémère [efemɛr] *adj* : ephemeral

épi [epi] *nm* **1** : ear, cob **2** : tuft (of hair)

épice [epis] *nf* : spice — **épicé, -cée** [epise] *adj* : spicy — **épicer** [epise] {6} *vt* : spice — **épicerie** [episri] *nf* **1** : grocery store **2 ~s** *nfpl* : groceries *pl* — **épicier, -cière** [episje, -sjɛr] *n* : grocer

épidémie [epidemi] *nf* : epidemic — **épidémique** [-demik] *adj* : epidemic

épiderme [epidɛrm] *nm* : skin

épier [epje] {96} *vt* **1** : spy on **2** ATTENDRE : watch out for

épilepsie [epilɛpsi] *nf* : epilepsy — **épileptique** [epilɛptik] *adj & nmf* : epileptic

épiler [epile] *vt* : remove hair from, pluck

épilogue [epilɔg] *nm* **1** : epilogue **2** : conclusion, outcome

épinards [epinar] *nmpl* : spinach

épine [epin] *nf* **1** : thorn **2 ~ dorsale** : spine, backbone — **épineux, -neuse** [epinø, -nøz] *adj* : thorny

épingle [epɛ̃gl] *nf* **1** : pin **2 ~ à cheveux** : hairpin **3 ~ de sûreté** : safety pin

épique [epik] *adj* : epic

épisode [epizɔd] *nm* : episode

épitaphe [epitaf] *nf* : epitaph

épithète [epitɛt] *nf* : epithet

éplucher [eplyʃe] *vt* **1** PELER : peel **2** EXAMINER : scrutinize

éponge [epɔ̃ʒ] *nf* : sponge — **éponger** [epɔ̃ʒe] {17} *vt* : sponge up, mop up

épopée [epɔpe] *nf* : epic

époque [epɔk] *nf* **1** : age, era **2** : time, period

épouse [epuz] *nf* → **époux** — **épouser** [epuze] *vt* : marry, wed

épousseter [epuste] {8} *vt* : dust

époustouflant, -flante [epustuflɑ̃, -flɑ̃t] *adj fam* : amazing

épouvantable [epuvɑ̃tabl] *adj* : dreadful, horrible

épouvantail [epuvɑ̃taj] *nm* : scarecrow

épouvanter [epuvɑ̃te] *vt* : terrify — **épouvante** [epuvɑ̃t] *nf* : horror

époux, -pouse [epu, -puz] *n* : spouse, husband *m*, wife *f*

éprendre [eprɑ̃dr] {70} *v* **s'éprendre** *vr* **de** : fall in love with

épreuve [eprœv] *nf* **1** ESSAI : test **2** : ordeal, trial **3** : event (in sports) **4** : proof, print (in printing)

éprouver [epruve] *vt* **1** : test, try **2** RESSENTIR : feel, experience **3** AFFECTER : distress

épuiser [epɥize] *vt* : exhaust — **épuisé, -sée** [epɥize] *adj* **1** : exhausted **2** : out of stock — **épuisement** [epɥizmɑ̃] *nm* : exhaustion

épurer [epyre] *vt* **1** : purify, refine **2** : purge (in politics) — **épuration** [epyrasjɔ̃] *nf* **1** : purification **2** : purge

équateur [ekwatœr] *nm* : equator

équation [ekwasjɔ̃] *nf* : equation

équerre [ekɛr] *nf* **1** : square **2 d'~** : square, straight

équestre [ekɛstr] *adj* : equestrian

équilibre [ekilibr] *nm* : equilibrium, balance — **équilibré, -brée** [ekilibre] *adj* : well-balanced — **équilibrer** [ekilibre] *vt* : balance

équinoxe [ekinɔks] *nm* : equinox

équipage [ekipaʒ] *nm* : crew

équiper [ekipe] *vt* : equip, outfit — **équipe** [ekip] *nf* : team — **équipement** [ekipmɑ̃] *nm* : equipment — **équipier, -pière** [ekipje, -pjɛr] *n* : team member

équitable [ekitabl] *adj* : fair, equitable — **équitablement** [-tabləmɑ̃] *adv* : fairly

équitation [ekitasjɔ̃] *nf* : horseback riding

équité [ekite] *nf* : equity, fairness

équivalence [ekivalɑ̃s] *nf* : equivalence — **équivalent, -lente** [ekivalɑ̃, -lɑ̃t] *adj* : equivalent — **équivalent** *nm* : equivalent — **équivaloir** [ekivalwar] {95} *vi* **~ à** : be equivalent to

équivoque [ekivɔk] *adj* **1** : equivocal, ambiguous **2** DOUTEUX : questionable

érable [erabl] *nm* : maple

éradiquer [eradike] *vt* : eradicate

érafler [erafle] *vt* : scratch — **éraflure** [eraflyr] *nf* : scratch, scrape

ère [ɛr] *nf* : era

érection [erɛksjɔ̃] *nf* : erection

éreinter [erɛ̃te] *vt* **1** ÉPUISER : exhaust **2** CRITIQUER : criticize — **s'éreinter** *vr* : wear oneself out — **éreintant, -tante** [erɛ̃tɑ̃, -tɑ̃t] *adj* : exhausting

ergoter [ɛrgote] *vi* : quibble

ériger [eriʒe] {17} *vt* : erect — **s'ériger** *vr* **~ en** : set oneself up as

ermite [ɛrmit] *nm* : hermit

éroder [erɔde] *vt* : erode — **érosion** [erozjɔ̃] *nf* : erosion

érotique [erɔtik] *adj* : erotic — **érotisme** [erɔtism] *nm* : eroticism

errer [ɛre] *vi* : wander, roam — **erreur** [ɛrœr] *nf* : error, mistake — **erroné, -née** [ɛrɔne] *adj* : erroneous

érudit, -dite [erydi, -dit] *adj* : scholarly — **~** *n* : scholar — **érudition** [erydisjɔ̃] *nf* : learning, scholarship

éruption [erypsjɔ̃] *nf* **1** : eruption **2** : rash (in medicine)

escabeau [ɛskabo] *nm, pl* **-beaux** **1** : stool **2** ÉCHELLE : stepladder

escadre [ɛskadr] *nf* : squadron — **escadrille** [ɛskadrij] *nf* : squadron — **escadron** [ɛskadrɔ̃] *nm* : squadron, squad

escalader [ɛskalade] *vt* : climb — **escalade** [ɛskalad] *nf* : (rock) climbing

escale [ɛskal] *nf* : stopover

escalier [ɛskalje] *nm* **1** : stairs *pl*, steps *pl* **2 ~ de secours** : fire escape **3 ~ mécanique** : escalator

escalope [ɛskalɔp] *nf* : cutlet

escamoter [ɛskamɔte] *vt* **1** : fold away, retract **2** ÉVITER : evade — **escamotable** [ɛskamɔtabl] *adj* : retractable, foldaway

escargot [ɛskargo] *nm* : snail

escarmouche [ɛskarmuʃ] *nf* : skirmish
escarpé, -pée [ɛskarpe] *adj* : steep
esclaffer [ɛsklafe] *v* **s'esclaffer** *vr* : burst out laughing
esclave [ɛsklav] *adj & nmf* : slave — **esclavage** [ɛsklavaʒ] *nm* : slavery
escompter [ɛskɔ̃te] *vt* **1** : discount **2** ESPÉRER : count on, expect — **escompte** [ɛskɔ̃t] *nm* : discount
escorter [ɛskɔrte] *vt* : escort — **escorte** [ɛskɔrt] *nf* : escort
escrime [ɛskrim] *nf* : fencing
escroc [ɛskro] *nm* : swindler, crook — **escroquer** [ɛskrɔke] *vt* : swindle, defraud — **escroquerie** [ɛskrɔkri] *nf* : swindle, fraud
eskimo [ɛskimo] → **esquimau**
ésotérique [ezɔterik] *adj* : esoteric
espace [ɛspas] *nm* : space — **espacer** [ɛspase] {6} *vt* : space (out)
espadon [ɛspadɔ̃] *nm* : swordfish
espadrilles [ɛspadrij] *nfpl Can* : sneakers *pl*
espagnol, -gnole [ɛspaɲɔl] *adj* : Spanish — **espagnol** *nm* : Spanish (language)
espèce [ɛspɛs] *nf* **1** : species **2** SORTE : sort, kind **3 ~s** *nfpl* : cash
espérer [ɛspere] {87} *vt* **1** : hope for **2** ESCOMPTER : expect — **espérance** [ɛsperɑ̃s] *nf* : hope
espiègle [ɛspjɛgl] *adj* : mischievous
espion, -pionne [ɛspjɔ̃, -pjɔn] *n* : spy — **espionnage** [ɛspjɔnaʒ] *nm* : espionage — **espionner** [ɛspjɔne] *vt* : spy on
espoir [ɛspwar] *nm* : hope
esprit [ɛspri] *nm* **1** : mind **2** ATTITUDE : spirit **3** HUMOUR : wit **4** FANTÔME : ghost
esquimau, -maude [ɛskimo, -mod] *adj, mpl* **-maux** [-mo] : Eskimo
esquisse [ɛskis] *nf* : sketch — **esquisser** [ɛskise] *vt* : sketch
esquiver [ɛskive] *vt* : avoid, dodge — **esquive** [ɛskiv] *nf* : dodge
essai [esɛ] *nm* **1** TENTATIVE : attempt, try **2** ÉPREUVE : trial, test **3** : (literary) essay
essaim [esɛ̃] *nm* : swarm
essayer [eseje] {11} *vt* : try
essence [esɑ̃s] *nf* : gasoline — **essentiel, -tielle** [esɑ̃sjɛl] *adj* : essential — **essentiel** *nm* : main part, essentials *pl* — **essentiellement** [-sjɛlmɑ̃] *adv* : essentially
essieu [esjø] *nm, pl* **-sieux** : axle
essor [esɔr] *nm* **1** : flight (of a bird) **2** : expansion, growth
essouffler [esufle] *vt* : make breathless — **s'essouffler** *vr* : get out of breath
essuyer [esɥije] {58} *vt* **1** : wipe, dry **2** SUBIR : suffer, endure — **essuie-glace** [esɥiglas] *nm, pl* **essuie-glaces** : windshield wiper — **essuie-mains** [esɥimɛ̃] *nms & pl* : hand towel — **essuie-tout** [esɥitu] *nms & pl* : paper towel
est [ɛst] *adj* : east, eastern — **~** *nm* **1** : east **2 l'Est** : the East
estampe [ɛstɑ̃p] *nf* : engraving, print — **estampille** [ɛstɑ̃pij] *nf* : stamp
esthétique [ɛstetik] *adj* : aesthetic — **esthéticien, -cienne** [ɛstetisjɛ̃, -sjɛn] *n* : beautician
estimer [ɛstime] *vt* **1** : assess, evaluate **2** CALCULER : estimate **3** RESPECTER : esteem **4** CONSIDÉRER : consider — **estimation** [ɛstimasjɔ̃] *nf* : estimate — **estime** [ɛstim] *nf* : esteem, respect
estival, -vale [ɛstival] *adj, mpl* **-vaux** [-vo] : summer
estomac [ɛstɔma] *nm* : stomach
estrade [ɛstrad] *nf* : platform, stage
estragon [ɛstragɔ̃] *nm* : tarragon
estropié, -piée [ɛstrɔpje] *adj* : crippled, maimed
estuaire [ɛstɥɛr] *nm* : estuary
esturgeon [ɛstyrʒɔ̃] *nm* : sturgeon
et [e] *conj* : and
étable [etabl] *nf* : cowshed
établi [etabli] *nm* : workbench
établir [etablir] *vt* **1** : establish, set up **2** : draw up (a list, etc.) — **s'établir** *vr* : become established, get set up — **établissement** [etablismɑ̃] *nm* : establishment
étage [etaʒ] *nm* **1** : story, floor **2** : tier, level — **étagère** [etaʒɛr] *nf* : shelf, bookshelf
étai [etɛ] *nm* : prop, support
étain [etɛ̃] *nm* **1** : tin **2** : pewter
étaler [etale] *vt* **1** : display **2** ÉTENDRE : spread (out) **3** ÉCHELONNER : space out, stagger — **s'étaler** *vr* **1** S'ÉTENDRE : spread out **2** *fam* : fall flat, sprawl — **étalage** [etalaʒ] *nm* **1** : display **2** DEVANTURE : shopwindow **3 faire ~ de** : flaunt
étalon [etalɔ̃] *nm* **1** : stallion **2** MODÈLE : standard
étancher [etɑ̃ʃe] *vt* **1** : stem, staunch **2** : quench (thirst) — **étanche** [etɑ̃ʃ] *adj* : watertight, waterproof
étang [etɑ̃] *nm* : pond
étape [etap] *nf* **1** ARRÊT : stop, halt **2** : stage (of development)
état [eta] *nm* **1** : state, condition **2**

: statement (of expenses, etc.) **3** : (social) status **4** MÉTIER : profession, trade
étau [eto] *nm, pl* **-taux** : vise
étayer [eteje] {11} *vt* : prop up
été [ete] *nm* : summer
éteindre [etɛ̃dr] {37} *vt* **1** : put out, extinguish **2** : turn off, switch off — **s'éteindre** *vr* **1** : go out, die out **2** MOURIR : die
étendard [etɑ̃dar] *nm* : standard, flag
étendre [etɑ̃dr] {63} *vt* **1** ÉTALER : spread (out) **2** : hang up (laundry) **3** ALLONGER : stretch (out) **4** ACCROÎTRE : extend — **s'étendre** *vr* **1** : stretch **2** SE COUCHER : lie down **3** CROÎTRE : spread — **étendu, -due** [etɑ̃dy] *adj* : extensive, wide — **étendue** *nf* **1** : area **2** : extent
éternel, -nelle [etɛrnɛl] *adj* : eternal — **éternellement** [-nɛlmɑ̃] *adv* : eternally, forever — **éternité** [etɛrnite] *nf* : eternity
éternuer [etɛrnɥe] *vi* : sneeze — **éternuement** [etɛrnymɑ̃] *nm* : sneeze
éther [etɛr] *nm* : ether
éthique [etik] *adj* : ethical — ~ *nf* : ethics
ethnique [ɛtnik] *adj* : ethnic
étincelle [etɛ̃sɛl] *nf* : spark — **étinceler** [etɛ̃sle] {8} *vi* : sparkle
étiquette [etikɛt] *nf* **1** : label **2** PROTOCOLE : etiquette — **étiqueter** [etikte] {8} *vt* : label
étirer [etire] *vt* : stretch — **s'étirer** *vr* : stretch (out)
étoffe [etɔf] *nf* : material, fabric
étoile [etwal] *nf* : star — **étoilé, -lée** [etwale] *adj* : starry
étonner [etɔne] *vt* : astonish — **s'étonner** *vr* : be surprised — **étonnant, -nante** [etɔnɑ̃, -nɑ̃t] *adj* : astonishing — **étonnement** [etɔnmɑ̃] *nm* : surprise, astonishment
étouffer [etufe] *vt* **1** : stifle **2** ASPHYXIER : smother **3** : deaden (sound, etc.) — **s'étouffer** *vr* **1** : choke **2** : suffocate
étourderie [eturdəri] *nf* : thoughtlessness
étourdir [eturdir] *vt* **1** ASSOMMER : stun **2** : make dizzy — **étourdi, -die** [eturdi] *adj* : absentminded, scatterbrained — **étourdissant, -sante** [eturdisɑ̃, -sɑ̃t] *adj* **1** BRUYANT : deafening **2** : stunning — **étourdissement** [eturdismɑ̃] *nm* VERTIGE : dizziness
étourneau [eturno] *nm, pl* **-neaux** [-no] : starling
étrange [etrɑ̃ʒ] *adj* : strange — **étrangement** [etrɑ̃ʒmɑ̃] *adv* : oddly, strangely — **étrangeté** [etrɑ̃ʒte] *nf* : strangeness, oddity — **étranger, -gère** [etrɑ̃ʒe, -ʒɛr] *adj* **1** : foreign (of a country, etc.) **2** : unfamiliar, strange — ~ *n* **1** : foreigner **2** : stranger **3 à l'étranger** : abroad
étrangler [etrɑ̃gle] *vt* **1** : strangle **2** SERRER : constrict — **s'étrangler** *vr* : choke
être [ɛtr] {38} *vi* **1** : be, exist **2** ~ **à** : belong to — *v aux* : have — ~ *nm* **1** : being **2** PERSONNE : person
étreindre [etrɛ̃dr] {37} *vt* **1** : embrace, hug **2** SERRER : grip — **étreinte** [etrɛ̃t] *nf* **1** : embrace, hug **2 sous l'~ de** : in the grip of
étrenner [etrene] *vt* : use for the first time
étrier [etrije] *nm* : stirrup
étriqué, -quée [etrike] *adj* **1** : skimpy **2** MESQUIN : petty
étroit, -troite [etrwa, -trwat] *adj* **1** : narrow **2** SERRÉ : tight — **étroitesse** [etrwatɛs] *nf* : narrowness
étude [etyd] *nf* **1** : study, studying **2** BUREAU : office — **étudiant, -diante** [etydjɑ̃, -djɑ̃t] *adj & n* : student — **étudier** [etydje] {96} *v* : study
étui [etɥi] *nm* : case
euphémisme [øfemism] *nm* : euphemism
euphorie [øfɔri] *nf* : euphoria
euro [øro] *nm* : euro (monetary unit)
européen, -péenne [ørɔpeɛ̃, -peɛn] *adj* : European
eux [ø] *pron* : they, them — **eux-mêmes** [ømɛm] *pron pl* : themselves
évacuer [evakɥe] *vt* : evacuate — **évacuation** [evakɥasjɔ̃] *nf* : evacuation
évader [evade] *v* **s'évader** *vr* : escape — **évadé, -dée** [evade] *n* : fugitive
évaluer [evalɥe] *vt* : evaluate, assess — **évaluation** [evalɥasjɔ̃] *nf* : evaluation, assessment
évangile [evɑ̃ʒil] *nm* **1** : gospel **2 l'Évangile** : the Gospel
évanouir [evanwir] *v* **s'évanouir** *vr* : faint — **évanouissement** [evanwismɑ̃] *nm* : fainting, faint
évaporer [evapɔre] *v* **s'évaporer** *vr* : evaporate — **évaporation** [evapɔrasjɔ̃] *nf* : evaporation
évasif, -sive [evazif,-ziv] *adj* : evasive — **évasion** [evazjɔ̃] *nf* : escape
éveiller [eveje] *vt* **1** RÉVEILLER : awaken **2** : arouse (curiosity, etc.) —

s'éveiller *vr* **1** : wake up **2** : be aroused — **éveil** [evɛj] *nm* **1** : awakening **2 en ~** : on the alert — **éveillé, -lée** [eveje] *adj* **1** : awake **2** ALERTE : alert
événement [evɛnmɑ̃] *nm* : event
éventail [evɑ̃taj] *nm* **1** : fan **2** GAMME : range, spread
éventaire [evɑ̃tɛr] *nm* : stall, stand
éventé, -tée [evɑ̃te] *adj* : stale, flat
éventrer [evɑ̃tre] *vt* : tear open
éventualité [evɑ̃tɥalite] *nf* : eventuality, possibility — **éventuel, -tuelle** [evɑ̃tɥɛl] *adj* : possible — **éventuellement** [-tɥɛlmɑ̃] *adv* : possibly
évêque [evɛk] *nm* : bishop
évertuer [evɛrtɥe] *v* **s'évertuer** *vr* : strive, do one's best
éviction [eviksjɔ̃] *nf* : eviction
évidemment [evidamɑ̃] *adv* : obviously, of course
évidence [evidɑ̃s] *nf* : obviousness — **évident, -dente** [evidɑ̃, -dɑ̃t] *adj* : obvious, evident
évider [evide] *vt* : hollow out
évier [evje] *nm* : sink
évincer [evɛ̃se] {6} *vt* : oust
éviter [evite] *vt* **1** : avoid **2 ~ à qqn de faire qqch** : save s.o. from (doing) sth
évoluer [evɔlɥe] *vi* **1** : evolve, develop **2** SE DÉPLACER : maneuver, move about — **évolution** [evɔlysjɔ̃] *nf* **1** : evolution **2** CHANGEMENT : development, change
évoquer [evɔke] *vt* : evoke, call to mind
exacerber [ɛgzasɛrbe] *vt* : exacerbate
exact, exacte [ɛgzakt] *adj* **1** : exact **2** JUSTE : correct **3** PONCTUEL : punctual — **exactement** [ɛgzaktəmɑ̃] *adv* : exactly — **exactitude** [ɛgzaktityd] *nf* **1** : accuracy **2** PONCTUALITÉ : punctuality
ex aequo [ɛgzeko] *adv* : equal
exagérer [ɛgzaʒere] {87} *vt* : exaggerate — *vi* : go too far, overdo it — **exagération** [ɛgzaʒerasjɔ̃] *nf* : exaggeration — **exagéré, -rée** [ɛgzaʒere] *adj* : exaggerated, excessive
exalter [ɛgzalte] *vt* **1** : excite, stir **2** GLORIFIER : exalt — **s'exalter** *vr* : get excited
examiner [ɛgzamine] *vt* : examine — **examen** [ɛgzamɛ̃] *nm* : examination
exaspérer [ɛgzaspere] {87} *vt* : exasperate — **exaspération** [ɛgzasperasjɔ̃] *nf* : exasperation
exaucer [ɛgzose] {6} *vt* : grant
excaver [ɛkskave] *vt* : excavate — **excavation** [ɛkskavasjɔ̃] *nf* : excavation
excéder [ɛksede] {87} *vt* **1** : exceed **2** EXASPÉRER : exasperate — **excédent** [ɛksedɑ̃] *nm* : surplus, excess — **excédentaire** [ɛksedɑ̃tɛr] *adj* : surplus, excess
exceller [ɛksele] *vi* : excel — **excellence** [ɛkselɑ̃s] *nf* : excellence — **excellent, -lente** [ɛkselɑ̃, -lɑ̃t] *adj* : excellent
excentrique [ɛksɑ̃trik] *adj & nmf* : eccentric — **excentricité** [ɛksɑ̃trisite] *nf* : eccentricity
excepter [ɛksɛpte] *vt* : except, exclude — **excepté** [ɛksɛpte] *prep* SAUF : except, apart from — **exception** [ɛksɛpsjɔ̃] *nf* **1** : exception **2 à l'~ de** : except for — **exceptionnel, -nelle** [ɛksɛpsjɔnɛl] *adj* : exceptional
excès [ɛksɛ] *nm* **1** : excess **2 ~ de vitesse** : speeding — **excessif, -sive** [ɛksɛsif, -siv] *adj* : excessive
exciter [ɛksite] *vt* **1** : excite **2** STIMULER : stimulate — **s'exciter** *vr* : get excited — **excitant, -tante** [ɛksitɑ̃, -tɑ̃t] *adj* : exciting — **excitation** [ɛksitasjɔ̃] *nf* : excitement
exclamer [ɛksklame] *v* **s'exclamer** *vr* : exclaim — **exclamation** [ɛksklamasjɔ̃] *nf* : exclamation
exclure [ɛksklyr] {39} *vt* **1** : exclude **2** EXPULSER : expel — **exclusif, -sive** [ɛksklyzif, -ziv] *adj* : exclusive — **exclusivement** [-sivmɑ̃] *adv* : exclusively — **exclusion** [ɛksklyzjɔ̃] *nf* **1** : exclusion **2** EXPULSION : expulsion — **exclusivité** [ɛksklyzivite] *nf* **1** : exclusive rights *pl* **2 en ~** : exclusively
excréments [ɛkskremɑ̃] *nmpl* : excrement, feces
excroissance [ɛkskrwasɑ̃s] *nf* : outgrowth
excursion [ɛkskyrsjɔ̃] *nf* : excursion, trip
excuser [ɛkskyze] *vt* : excuse — **s'excuser** *vr* : apologize — **excuse** [ɛkskyz] *nf* **1** : excuse **2 ~s** *nfpl* : apology
exécrer [ɛgzekre] {87} *vt* : abhor, loathe — **exécrable** [ɛgzekrabl] *adj* : atrocious, awful
exécuter [ɛgzekyte] *vt* **1** : execute **2** EFFECTUER : perform — **s'exécuter** *vr* : comply — **exécutant, -tante** [ɛgzekytɑ̃, -tɑ̃t] *n* : performer — **exécutif, -tive** [ɛgzekytif, -tiv] *adj* : executive — **exécution** [ɛgzekysjɔ̃] *nf* : execution

exemple [ɛgzɑ̃pl] *nm* **1** : example **2 par ~** : for example, for instance — **exemplaire** [ɛgzɑ̃plɛr] *adj* : exemplary — **~** *nm* **1** : copy **2** : specimen, example

exempt, exempte [ɛgzɑ̃, ɛgzɑ̃t] *adj* : exempt — **exempter** [ɛgzɑ̃te] *vt* : exempt — **exemption** [ɛgzɑ̃psjɔ̃] *nf* : exemption

exercer [ɛgzɛrse] {6} *vt* **1** : exercise, train **2** : exert (control, influence, etc.) **3** : practice (a profession) — **s'exercer** *vr* : practice — **exercice** [ɛgzɛrsis] *nm* **1** : exercise **2 en ~** : in office

exhaler [ɛgzale] *vt* **1** : exhale **2** ÉMETTRE : utter, breathe

exhaustif, -tive [ɛgzostif, -tiv] *adj* : exhaustive

exhiber [ɛgzibe] *vt* : exhibit, show off — **exhibition** [ɛgzibisjɔ̃] *nf* : display, exhibition

exhorter [ɛgzɔrte] *vt* : exhort, urge

exiger [ɛgziʒe] {17} *vt* : demand, require — **exigeant, -geante** [ɛgziʒɑ̃, -ʒɑ̃t] *adj* : demanding, choosy — **exigence** [ɛgziʒɑ̃s] *nf* : demand, requirement

exigu, -guë [ɛgzigy] *adj* : cramped, tiny

exil [ɛgzil] *nm* : exile — **exilé, -lée** [ɛgzile] *n* : exile — **exiler** [ɛgzile] *vt* : exile — **s'exiler** *vr* : go into exile, isolate oneself

exister [ɛgziste] *vi* : exist — **existant, -tante** [ɛgzistɑ̃, -tɑ̃t] *adj* : existing — **existence** [ɛgzistɑ̃s] *nf* : existence

exode [ɛgzɔd] *nm* : exodus

exonérer [ɛgzɔnere] {87} *vt* : exempt — **exonération** [ɛgzɔnerasjɔ̃] *nf* : exemption

exorbitant, -tante [ɛgzɔrbitɑ̃, -tɑ̃t] *adj* : exorbitant

exotique [ɛgzɔtik] *adj* : exotic

expansion [ɛkspɑ̃sjɔ̃] *nf* : expansion — **expansif, -sive** [ɛkspɑ̃sif, -siv] *adj* : expansive

expatrier [ɛkspatrije] {96} *vt* : expatriate — **s'expatrier** *vr* : emigrate — **expatrié, -triée** [ɛkspatrije] *adj & n* : expatriate

expédient, -diente [ɛkspedjɑ̃, -djɑ̃t] *adj* : expedient — **expédient** *nm* : expedient

expédier [ɛkspedje] {96} *vt* : send, dispatch — **expéditeur, -trice** [ɛkspeditœr, -tris] *n* : sender — **expéditif, -tive** [ɛkspeditif, -tiv] *adj* : quick — **expédition** [ɛkspedisjɔ̃] *nf* **1** : sending, shipment **2** VOYAGE : expedition

expérience [ɛksperjɑ̃s] *nf* **1** : experience **2** ESSAI : experiment — **expérimental, -tale** [ɛksperimɑ̃tal] *adj, mpl* **-taux** [-to] : experimental — **expérimentation** [ɛksperimɑ̃tasjɔ̃] *nf* : experimentation — **expérimenté, -tée** [ɛksperimɑ̃te] *adj* : experienced — **expérimenter** [ɛksperimɑ̃te] *vt* : test, experiment with

expert, -perte [ɛkspɛr, -pɛrt] *adj & n* : expert — **expertise** [ɛkspɛrtiz] *nf* **1** : expert appraisal **2** COMPÉTENCE : expertise

expier [ɛkspje] {96} *vt* : atone for

expirer [ɛkspire] *vi* **1** : breathe out **2** : expire (of a contract) — *vt* : exhale — **expiration** [ɛkspirasjɔ̃] *nf* **1** ÉCHÉANCE : expiration **2** : exhalation (of breath)

explication [ɛksplikasjɔ̃] *nf* : explanation — **explicatif, -tive** [ɛksplikatif, -tiv] *adj* : explanatory

explicite [ɛksplisit] *adj* : explicit

expliquer [ɛksplike] *vt* : explain — **s'expliquer** *vr* **1** : explain oneself **2** : be explained

exploiter [ɛksplwate] *vt* **1** : exploit **2** : work (a field, a mine, etc.), run (a business, etc.) — **exploit** [ɛksplwa] *nm* : exploit — **exploitation** [ɛksplwatasjɔ̃] *nf* **1** : exploitation **2** : running, management (of a farm, mine, etc.) **3 ~ agricole** : (small) farm

explorer [ɛksplɔre] *vt* : explore — **explorateur, -trice** [ɛksplɔratœr, -tris] *n* : explorer — **exploration** [ɛksplɔrasjɔ̃] *nf* : exploration

exploser [ɛksploze] *vi* **1** : explode **2** : burst out, flare up (with anger, etc.) — **explosif, -sive** [ɛksplozif, -ziv] *adj* : explosive — **explosif** *nm* : explosive — **explosion** [ɛksplozjɔ̃] *nf* **1** : explosion **2** : outburst (of anger, joy, etc.)

exporter [ɛkspɔrte] *vt* : export — **exportateur, -trice** [ɛkspɔrtatœr, -tris] *adj* : exporting — **~** *n* : exporter — **exportation** [ɛkspɔrtasjɔ̃] *nf* : export, exportation

exposer [ɛkspoze] *vt* **1** : exhibit **2** EXPLIQUER : explain **3** ORIENTER : orient **4** : expose (to danger), risk (one's life, reputation, etc.) — **s'exposer** *vr* : expose oneself — **exposant, -sante** [ɛkspozɑ̃, -zɑ̃t] *n* : exhibitor — **exposé** [ɛkspoze] *nm* **1** : lecture, talk **2** : account, report — **exposition** [ɛkspozisjɔ̃] *nf* **1** : exhibition **2** PRÉSENTATION : exposition **3** ORIENTATION : orientation, aspect

exprès [ɛksprɛ] *adv* **1** : on purpose, intentionally **2** SPÉCIALEMENT : specially — **exprès, -presse** [ɛksprɛs] *adj* **1** : express, explicit **2** : special delivery — **express** [ɛksprɛs] *adj* : express — ~ *nm* **1** : express (train) **2** *or* **café ~** : espresso — **expressément** [ɛksprɛsemɑ̃] *adv* : expressly — **expressif, -sive** [ɛksprɛsif, -siv] *adj* : expressive — **expression** [ɛksprɛsjɔ̃] *nf* : expression

exprimer [ɛksprime] *vt* **1** : express **2** EXTRAIRE : squeeze, extract — **s'exprimer** *vr* : express oneself

expulser [ɛkspylse] *vt* : expel, evict — **expulsion** [ɛkspylsjɔ̃] *nf* : expulsion, eviction

exquis, -quise [ɛkski, -kiz] *adj* : exquisite

extase [ɛkstaz] *nf* : ecstasy — **extasier** [ɛkstazje] {96} *v* **s'extasier** *vr* : be in ecstasy — **extatique** [ɛkstatik] *adj* : ecstatic

extension [ɛkstɑ̃sjɔ̃] *nf* **1** : stretching (of a muscle, etc.) **2** ÉLARGISSEMENT : extension, expansion — **extensif, -sive** [ɛkstɑ̃sif, -siv] *adj* : extensive

exténuer [ɛkstenɥe] *vt* : exhaust, tire out — **exténuant, -ante** [ɛkstenɥɑ, -ɥɑ̃t] *adj* : exhausting

extérieur, -rieure [ɛksterjœr] *adj* **1** : exterior, outside **2** APPARENT : apparent **3** ÉTRANGER : foreign — **extérieur** *nm* **1** : exterior **2 à l'~** : abroad — **extérieurement** [ɛksterjœrmɑ̃] *adv* **1** : externally **2** APPAREMMENT : outwardly — **extérioriser** [ɛksterjɔrize] *vt* : show, express

exterminer [ɛkstɛrmine] *vt* : exterminate — **extermination** [ɛkstɛrminasjɔ̃] *nf* : extermination

externe [ɛkstɛrn] *adj* : external

extinction [ɛkstɛ̃ksjɔ̃] *nf* **1** : extinction **2** : extinguishing — **extincteur** [ɛkstɛ̃ktœr] *nm* : fire extinguisher

extirper [ɛkstirpe] *vt* : eradicate

extorquer [ɛkstɔrke] *vt* : extort — **extorsion** [ɛkstɔrsjɔ̃] *nf* : extortion

extra [ɛkstra] *adj* **1** : first-rate **2** *fam* : fantastic — ~ *nms & pl* **1** : extra person **2** : extra thing or amount

extraction [ɛstraksjɔ̃] *nf* : extraction

extrader [ɛkstrade] *vt* : extradite

extraire [ɛkstrɛr] {40} *vt* : extract — **extrait** [ɛkstrɛ] *nm* **1** : extract, essence **2** : excerpt (of a speech, etc.)

extraordinaire [ɛkstraɔrdinɛr] *adj* : extraordinary

extraterrestre [ɛkstratɛrɛstr] *adj & nmf* : extraterrestrial

extravagant, -gante [ɛkstravagɑ̃, -gɑ̃t] *adj* : extravagant — **extravagance** [-vagɑ̃s] *nf* : extravagance

extraverti, -tie [ɛkstravɛrti] *adj* : extroverted — ~ *n* : extrovert

extrême [ɛkstrɛm] *adj* : extreme — ~ *nm* : extreme — **extrêmement** [ɛkstrɛmmɑ̃] *adv* : extremely — **extrémité** [ɛkstremite] *nf* : extremity

exubérant, -rante [ɛgzyberɑ̃, -rɑ̃t] *adj* : exuberant — **exubérance** [-berɑ̃s] *nf* : exuberance

exulter [ɛgzylte] *vi* : exult

exutoire [ɛgzytwar] *nm* : outlet

F

f [ɛf] *nm* : f, sixth letter of the alphabet

fable [fabl] *nf* : fable

fabriquer [fabrike] *vt* **1** : make, manufacture **2** INVENTER : fabricate — **fabricant, -cante** [fabrikɑ̃, -kɑ̃t] *n* : manufacturer — **fabrication** [fabrikasjɔ̃] *nf* : manufacture, making — **fabrique** [fabrik] *nf* : factory

fabuleux, -leuse [fabylø, -løz] *adj* : fabulous

façade [fasad] *nf* : façade, front

face [fas] *nf* **1** VISAGE : face **2** CÔTÉ : side **3 en ~** : opposite **4 ~ à ~** : face-to-face **5 faire ~ à** : face — **facette** [fasɛt] *nf* : facet

facétieux, -tieuse [fasesjø, -sjøz] *adj* : facetious

fâcher [faʃe] *vt* : anger — **se fâcher** *vr* : get angry — **fâché, -chée** [faʃe] *adj* : angry — **fâcheux, -cheuse** [faʃø, -ʃøz] *adj* : unfortunate

facile [fasil] *adj* **1** : easy **2** : easygoing — **facilement** [fasilmɑ̃] *adv* : easily — **facilité** [fasilite] *nf* **1** : easiness **2** APTITUDE : aptitude — **faciliter** [fasilite] *vt* : facilitate

façon [fasɔ̃] *nf* **1** : way, manner **2 ~s** *nfpl* : behavior, manners **3 de ~ à** : so as to **4 de toute ~** : in any case **5 faire des ~s** : put on airs — **façonner** [fasɔne] *vt* **1** FORMER : shape **2** FABRIQUER : manufacture

fac-similé [faksimile] *nm, pl* **fac-similés** : facsimile, copy

facteur[1], **-trice** [faktœr, -tris] *n* : mailman
facteur[2] *nm* : factor
faction [faksjɔ̃] *nf* **1** GROUPE : faction **2** : guard (duty)
factuel, -tuelle [faktɥɛl] *adj* : factual
facture [faktyr] *nf* : bill, invoice — **facturer** [faktyre] *vt* : bill
facultatif, -tive [fakyltatif, -tiv] *adj* : optional
faculté [fakylte] *nf* **1** : faculty, ability **2** LIBERTÉ : option **3** : faculty (of a university)
fade [fad] *adj* : bland
faible [fɛbl] *adj* **1** : weak, feeble **2** : small (in quantity) **3** PÂLE : faint, light — **∼** *nmf* : weakling — **∼** *nm* : weakness — **faiblesse** [fɛblɛs] *nf* : weakness — **faiblir** [feblir] *vi* **1** : weaken **2** DIMINUER : die down
faïence [fajɑ̃s] *nf* : earthenware
faillir [fajir] {41} *vi* **∼ à** : fail to — *vt* **1** : narrowly miss **2** **∼ faire qqch** : nearly do sth — **faille** [faj] *nf* **1** : fault (in geology) **2** FAIBLESSE : flaw — **faillible** [fajibl] *adj* : fallible — **faillite** [fajit] *nf* **1** ÉCHEC : failure **2** **faire ∼** : go bankrupt
faim [fɛ̃] *nf* **1** : hunger **2** **avoir ∼** : be hungry
fainéant, -néante [feneɑ̃, -neɑ̃t] *adj* : lazy — **∼** *n* : loafer, idler
faire [fɛr] {42} *vt* **1** : do **2** : make **3** : equal, amount to **4** DIRE : say **5** **cela ne fait rien** : it doesn't matter **6** **∼ du football** : play football **7** **∼ mal à** : hurt **8** **∼ soleil** : be sunny **9** **∼ un rêve** : have a dream — **se faire** *vr* **1** **∼ à** : get used to **2** **s'en faire** : worry — **faire–part** [fɛrpar] *nms & pl* : announcement (of marriage, etc.) — **faisable** [fəzabl] *adj* : feasible
faisan, -sane [fəzɑ̃] *n* : pheasant
faisceau [fɛso] *nm, pl* **-ceaux** : beam (of light)
fait, faite [fɛ, fɛt] *adj* **1** : made, done **2** : ripe (of cheese) **3** **tout fait** : ready-made — **fait** *nm* **1** : fact **2** ÉVÉNEMENT : event **3** **au ∼** : by the way **4** **sur le ∼** : red-handed
faîte [fɛt] *nm* **1** SOMMET : summit, top **2** APOGÉE : pinnacle
falaise [falɛz] *nf* : cliff
falloir [falwar] {43} *v impers* **1** **comme il faut** : proper(ly) **2** **il fallait le faire** : it had to be done **3** **il fallait me le dire!** : you should have said so! **4** **il faut partir** : we must go **5** **il faut que je ...** : I need to ... — **s'en falloir** *vr* **1** **peu s'en faut** : very nearly **2** **tant s'en faut** : far from it
falsifier [falsifje] {96} *vt* : falsify
famé, -mée [fame] *adj* **mal famé** : disreputable
famélique [famelik] *adj* : starving
fameux, -meuse [famø, -møz] *adj* **1** CÉLÈBRE : famous **2** *fam* : first-rate
familial, -liale [familjal] *adj, mpl* **-liaux** [-ljo] : family — **familiale** *nf* : station wagon
familiariser [familjarize] *v* **se familiariser** *vr* : familiarize oneself — **familiarité** [familjarite] *nf* : familiarity — **familier, -lière** [familje, -ljɛr] *adj* **1** : familiar **2** : informal
famille [famij] *nf* : family
famine [famin] *nf* : famine
fanatique [fanatik] *adj* : fanatic(al) — **∼** *nmf* : fanatic — **fanatisme** [-natism] *nm* : fanaticism
faner [fane] *v* **se faner** *vr* : fade
fanfare [fɑ̃far] *nf* **1** : fanfare **2** : brass band
fanfaron, -ronne [fɑ̃farɔ̃, -rɔn] *adj* : boastful — **∼** *n* : braggart
fantaisie [fɑ̃tezi] *nf* **1** : fantasy **2** CAPRICE : whim — **fantaisiste** [fɑ̃tezist] *adj* : fanciful
fantasme [fɑ̃tasm] *nm* : fantasy — **fantasmer** [fɑ̃tasme] *vi* : fantasize — **fantasque** [fɑ̃task] *adj* **1** CAPRICIEUX : whimsical **2** BIZARRE : strange, weird — **fantastique** [fɑ̃tastik] *adj* : fantastic
fantoche [fɑ̃tɔʃ] *adj & nm* : puppet
fantôme [fɑ̃tom] *nm* : ghost
faon [fɑ̃] *nm* : fawn
farce [fars] *nf* **1** : practical joke **2** : farce (in theater) — **farceur, -ceuse** [farsœr, -søz] *n* : prankster
farcir [farsir] *vt* : stuff (in cooking)
fard [far] *nm* : makeup
fardeau [fardo] *nm, pl* **-deaux** : load, burden
farfelu, -lue [farfəly] *adj fam* : wacky
farine [farin] *nf* : flour
farouche [faruʃ] *adj* **1** SAUVAGE : wild **2** TIMIDE : shy **3** ACHARNÉ : fierce
fascicule [fasikyl] *nm* **1** : section (of a book) **2** LIVRET : booklet
fasciner [fasine] *vt* : fascinate — **fascinant, -nante** [fasinɑ̃, -nɑ̃t] *adj* : fascinating — **fascination** [fasinasjɔ̃] *nf* : fascination
fascisme [faʃism] *nm* : fascism — **fasciste** [faʃist] *adj & nmf* : fascist
faste[1] [fast] *adj* : lucky
faste[2] *nm* : pomp, splendor

fastidieux, -dieuse [fastidjø, -djøz] *adj* : tedious
fatal, -tale [fatal] *adj, mpl* **-tals 1** MORTEL : fatal **2** INÉVITABLE : inevitable — **fatalement** [fatalmɑ̃] *adv* : inevitably — **fatalité** [fatalite] *nf* **1** SORT : fate **2** : inevitability
fatidique [fatidik] *adj* : fateful
fatiguer [fatige] *vt* **1** : fatigue, tire **2** ENNUYER : annoy **3** : strain (an engine, etc.) — *vi* : grow tired — **se fatiguer** *vr* : wear oneself out — **fatigant, -gante** [fatigɑ̃, -gɑ̃t] *adj* **1** : tiring **2** ENNUYEUX : tiresome — **fatigue** [fatig] *nf* : fatigue — **fatigué, -guée** [fatige] *adj* : tired
faubourg [fobur] *nm* : suburb
faucher [foʃe] *vt* **1** : mow, cut **2** *fam* : swipe, pinch — **fauché, -chée** [foʃe] *adj fam* : broke, penniless
faucille [fosij] *nf* : sickle
faucon [fokɔ̃] *nm* : falcon, hawk
faufiler [fofile] *vt* : baste (in sewing) — **se faufiler** *vr* : weave one's way
faune [fon] *nf* : fauna, wildlife
faussaire [fosɛr] *nmf* : forger
fausse → **faux**[2]
fausser [fose] *vt* **1** : distort **2** DÉFORMER : bend — **faussement** [fosmɑ̃] *adv* **1** : falsely **2** : wrongfully — **fausseté** [foste] *nf* **1** : falseness **2** DUPLICITÉ : duplicity
faute [fot] *nf* **1** : fault **2** ERREUR : mistake **3 ~ de** : for lack of
fauteuil [fotœj] *nm* **1** : armchair **2 ~ roulant** : wheelchair
fautif, -tive [fotif, -tiv] *adj* **1** COUPABLE : at fault **2** ERRONÉ : faulty
fauve [fov] *nm* : big cat
faux[1] [fo] *nfs & pl* : scythe
faux[2], **fausse** [fos] *adj* **1** : false **2** INCORRECT : wrong **3** FALSIFIÉ : counterfeit, fake **4 fausse couche** : miscarriage **5 faire un faux pas** : stumble **6 faux nom** : alias — **~** *nm* : forgery — **~** *adv* : out of tune — **faux-filet** [fofilɛ] *nm, pl* **faux-filets** : sirloin — **faux-monnayeur** [fomɔnɛjœr] *nm, pl* **faux-monnayeurs** : forger
faveur [favœr] *nf* **1** : favor **2 en ~ de** : in favor of — **favorable** [favɔrabl] *adj* : favorable — **favori, -rite** [favɔri, -rit] *adj & n* : favorite — **favoris** [favɔri] *nmpl* : sideburns — **favoriser** [favɔrize] *vt* **1** : favor **2** ENCOURAGER : promote — **favoritisme** [favɔritism] *nm* : favoritism
fax [faks] *nm* : fax — **faxer** [fakse] *vt* : fax
fébrile [febril] *adj* : feverish
fécond, -conde [fekɔ̃, -kɔ̃d] *adj* : fertile — **féconder** [fekɔ̃de] *vt* : fertilize, impregnate — **fécondité** [fekɔ̃dite] *nf* : fertility
fécule [fekyl] *nf* : starch — **féculent, -lente** [fekylɑ̃, -lɑ̃t] *adj* : starchy — **féculent** [fekylɑ̃] *nm* : starchy food
fédéral, -rale [federal] *adj, mpl* **-raux** [-ro] : federal — **fédération** [federasjɔ̃] *nf* : federation
fée [fe] *nf* : fairy — **féerie** [fe(e)ri] *nf* : enchantment — **féerique** [fe(e)rik] *adj* : magical, enchanting
feindre [fɛ̃dr] {37} *vt* : feign — *vi* : pretend — **feinte** [fɛ̃t] *nf* : trick, ruse
fêler [fele] *vt* : crack
féliciter [felisite] *vt* : congratulate — **félicitations** [felisitasjɔ̃] *nfpl* : congratulations
félin, -line [felɛ̃, -lin] *adj & nm* : feline
fêlure [felyr] *nf* : crack
femelle [fəmɛl] *adj & nf* : female
féminin, -nine [feminɛ̃, -nin] *adj* : feminine — **féminisme** [feminism] *nm* : feminism — **féministe** [feminist] *adj & nmf* : feminist — **féminité** [feminite] *nf* : femininity
femme [fam] *nf* **1** : woman **2** ÉPOUSE : wife **3 ~ au foyer** : homemaker **4 ~ d'affaires** : businesswoman
fendre [fɑ̃dr] {63} *vt* : split, break — **se fendre** *vr* : crack
fenêtre [fənɛtr] *nf* : window
fenouil [fənuj] *nm* : fennel
fente [fɑ̃t] *nf* **1** : slit, slot **2** FISSURE : crack
féodal, -dale [feɔdal] *adj, mpl* **-daux** [-do] : feudal
fer [fɛr] *nm* **1** : iron **2 ~ à cheval** : horseshoe **3 ~ à repasser** : iron (for clothes)
férié, -riée [ferje] *adj* **jour férié** : holiday
ferme [fɛrm] *adj* : firm — **~** *adv* : firmly, hard — **~** *nf* : farm — **fermement** [fɛrməmɑ̃] *adv* : firmly
fermé, -mée [fɛrme] *adj* **1** : closed, shut (off) **2** EXCLUSIF : exclusive
fermenter [fɛrmɑ̃te] *vi* : ferment — **fermentation** [fɛrmɑ̃tasjɔ̃] *nf* : fermentation
fermer [fɛrme] *vt* **1** : close, shut **2** : close down (a factory, etc.) **3** ÉTEINDRE : turn off **4 ~ à clef** : lock up — **se fermer** *vr* : close (up)
fermeté [fɛrməte] *nf* : firmness
fermeture [fɛrmətyr] *nf* **1** : closing, shutting **2 ~ à glissière** : zipper

fermier, -mière [fɛrmje, -mjɛr] *n* : farmer
fermoir [fɛrmwar] *nm* : clasp
féroce [ferɔs] *adj* : ferocious — **férocité** [ferɔsite] *nf* : ferocity, ferociousness
ferraille [fɛraj] *nf* : scrap iron
ferronnerie [fɛrɔnri] *nf* **1** : ironworks **2** : wrought iron
ferroviaire [fɛrɔvjɛr] *adj* : rail, railroad
ferry–boat [fɛribot] *nm, pl* **ferry–boats** : ferry
fertile [fɛrtil] *adj* : fertile — **fertiliser** [fɛrtilize] *vt* : fertilize — **fertilité** [fɛrtilite] *nf* : fertility
fervent, -vente [fɛrvɑ̃, -vɑ̃t] *adj* : fervent — **~** *n* : enthusiast — **ferveur** [fɛrvœr] *nf* : fervor
fesses [fɛs] *nfpl* : buttocks — **fessée** [fese] *nf* : spanking — **fesser** [fese] *vt* : spank
festin [fɛstɛ̃] *nm* : feast
festival [fɛstival] *nm, pl* **-vals** : festival — **festivités** [fɛstivite] *nfpl* : festivities
fête [fɛt] *nf* **1** : holiday **2** : party **3** FOIRE : fair **4 de ~** : festive **5 faire la ~** : have a good time — **fêter** [fete] *vt* : celebrate
fétiche [fetiʃ] *nm* : fetish
fétide [fetid] *adj* : fetid
feu[1] [fø] *nm, pl* **feux 1** : fire **2** *or* **~ de circulation** : traffic light **3** : burner (of a stove) **4** : light (for a cigarette, etc.) **5** TIR : fire, shooting **6 ~ de joie** : bonfire **7 feux d'artifice** : fireworks **8 mettre le ~ à** : set fire to **9 prendre ~** : catch fire
feu[2], **feue** [fø] *adj* : late, deceased
feuille [fœj] *nf* **1** : leaf **2** : sheet (of paper, etc.) — **feuillage** [fœjaʒ] *nm* : foliage — **feuillet** [fœjɛ] *nm* : page, leaf — **feuilleter** [fœjte] {8} *vt* : leaf through — **feuilleton** [fœjtɔ̃] *nm* : series, serial
feutre [føtr] *nm* : felt — **feutré, -trée** [føtre] *adj* : muffled, hushed
fève [fɛv] *nf* : broad bean
février [fevrije] *nm* : February
fiable [fjabl] *adj* : reliable — **fiabilité** [fjabilite] *nf* : reliability
fiancer [fijɑ̃se] {6} *v* **se fiancer** *vr* : get engaged — **fiançailles** [fijɑ̃saj] *nfpl* : engagement — **fiancé, -cée** [fijɑ̃se] *n* : fiancé *m*, fiancée *f*
fibre [fibr] *nf* **1** : fiber **2 ~ de verre** : fiberglass — **fibreux, -breuse** [fibrø, -brøz] *adj* : fibrous
ficelle [fisɛl] *nf* : string, twine — **ficeler** [fisle] {8} *vt* : tie up
fiche [fiʃ] *nf* **1** : index card **2** FORMULAIRE : form **3** : (electric) plug
ficher [fiʃe] *vt* **1** : drive (in) **2** *fam* : do **3** *fam* : give **4 ~ qqn dehors** *fam* : kick s.o. out — **se ficher** *vr* **1 ~ de** *fam* : make fun of **2 je m'en fiche** *fam* : I don't give a damn
fichier [fiʃje] *nm* : file, index
fichu[1], **-chue** [fiʃy] *adj fam* **1** : lousy, awful **2** CONDAMNÉ : done for
fichu[2] *nm* : scarf, kerchief
fiction [fiksjɔ̃] *nf* : fiction — **fictif, -tive** [fiktif, -tiv] *adj* : fictional, fictitious
fidèle [fidɛl] *adj* : faithful — **~** *nmf* **1** : follower **2** : regular (customer) **3 les ~s** : the faithful — **fidèlement** [-dɛlmɑ̃] *adv* : faithfully — **fidélité** [fidelite] *nf* : fidelity
fier[1] [fje] *v* **se fier** *vr* **~ à** : trust, rely on
fier[2], **fière** [fjɛr] *adj* : proud — **fièrement** [fjɛrmɑ̃] *adv* : proudly — **fierté** [fjɛrte] *nf* : pride
fièvre [fjɛvr] *nf* : fever — **fiévreux, -vreuse** [fjɛvrø, -vrøz] *adj* : feverish
figer [fiʒe] {17} *v* **se figer** *vr* : coagulate
figue [fig] *nf* : fig
figure [figyr] *nf* **1** VISAGE : face **2** PERSONNAGE : figure **3** ILLUSTRATION : illustration — **figurant, -rante** [figyrɑ̃, -rɑ̃t] *n* : extra (in theater) — **figurer** [figyre] *vi* : appear — *vt* : represent — **se figurer** *vr* : imagine
fil [fil] *nm* **1** : thread **2** : wire **3 au ~ de** : in the course of **4 coup de ~** *fam* : phone call **5 ~ dentaire** : dental floss — **file** [fil] *nf* **1** : line, file, row **2** : lane (of a highway) **3 en ~** *or* **à la ~** : one after another — **filer** [file] *vt* **1** : spin (yarn) **2** SUIVRE : shadow **3** *fam* : give — *vi* **1** : run (of stockings) **2** *fam* : dash off **3** *fam* : fly by, slip away **4 ~ bien** *Can fam* : be doing fine
filet [filɛ] *nm* **1** : net **2** : fillet (of beef, etc.) **3** : trickle (of water)
filiale [filjal] *nf* : subsidiary (company)
filière [filjɛr] *nf* : (official) channels *pl*
filigrane [filigran] *nm* : watermark
fille [fij] *nf* **1** : girl **2** : daughter — **fillette** [fijɛt] *nf* : little girl
filleul, -leule [fijœl] *n* : godchild, godson *m*, goddaughter *f*
film [film] *nm* : film — **filmer** [filme] *vt* : film
filon [filɔ̃] *nm* : vein, lode
fils [fis] *nm* : son

filtre [filtr] *nm* : filter — **filtrer** [filtre] *vt* **1** : filter **2** : screen (visitors, etc.) — *vi* : filter through
fin[1], **fine** [fɛ̃, fin] *adj* **1** : fine **2** MINCE : thin **3** : excellent (in quality) **4** : sharp, keen **5** *Can* : nice — **fin** *adv* : finely
fin[2] *nf* **1** : end **2 à la ~** : in the end **3 prendre ~** : come to an end **4 sans ~** : endless(ly)
final, -nale [final] *adj, mpl* **-nals** *or* **-naux** [fino] : final — **finale** *nf* : finals *pl* (in sports) — **finalement** [finalmɑ̃] *adv* **1** : finally **2** : after all — **finaliste** [finalist] *nmf* : finalist
finance [finɑ̃s] *nf* **1** : finance **2 ~s** *nfpl* : finances — **financer** [finɑ̃se] {6} *vt* : finance — **financier, -cière** [finɑ̃sje,-sjɛr] *adj* : financial
finesse [finɛs] *nf* **1** : finesse, delicacy **2** PERSPICACITÉ : shrewdness
finir [finir] *vt* : finish — *vi* **1** : finish **2 en ~ avec** : be done with **3 ~ par faire** : end up doing — **fini, -nie** [fini] *adj* **1** : finished **2** : finite — **finition** [finisjɔ̃] *nf* : finish
fiole [fjɔl] *nf* : vial
firme [firm] *nf* : firm
fisc [fisk] *nm* : tax collection agency — **fiscal, -cale** [fiskal] *adj, mpl* **-caux** [fisko] : fiscal — **fiscalité** [fiskalite] *nf* : tax system
fissure [fisyr] *nf* : crack
fiston [fistɔ̃] *nm fam* : son, youngster
fixe [fiks] *adj* **1** IMMOBILE : fixed **2** INVARIABLE : invariable, set — **fixer** [fikse] *vt* **1** ATTACHER : fix, fasten **2** DÉCIDER : determine **3** ÉTABLIR : establish **4 ~ son regard sur** : stare at — **se fixer** *vr* **1** : settle down **2** SE DÉCIDER : decide
flacon [flakɔ̃] *nm* : small bottle
flageller [flaʒɛle] *vt* : flog, whip
flagrant [flagrɑ̃] *adj* **1** : flagrant **2 en ~ délit** : red-handed
flairer [flɛre] *vt* **1** : sniff, smell **2** DISCERNER : detect, sense — **flair** [flɛr] *nm* **1** : sense of smell **2** INTUITION : intuition
flamand, -mande [flamɑ̃, -mɑ̃d] *adj* : Flemish
flamant [flamɑ̃] *nm* : flamingo
flambant, -bante [flɑ̃bɑ̃, -bɑ̃t] *adj* **flambant neuf** : brand-new
flambeau [flɑ̃bo] *nm, pl* **-beaux** : torch
flamber [flɑ̃be] *vi* : burn, blaze — **flambée** [flɑ̃be] *nf* **1** : blaze, fire **2** : outburst (of anger, etc.)
flamboyer [flɑ̃bwaje] {58} *vi* : blaze, flame — **flamboyant, -boyante** [flɑ̃bwajɑ̃, -bwajɑ̃t] *adj* : blazing
flamme [flam] *nf* **1** : flame **2** FERVEUR : passion, fervor **3 en ~s** : on fire
flan [flɑ̃] *nm* : baked custard
flanc [flɑ̃] *nm* : side, flank
flancher [flɑ̃ʃe] *vi fam* **1** : give in **2** : give out, fail
flanelle [flanɛl] *nf* : flannel
flâner [flane] *vi* **1** SE BALADER : stroll **2** PARESSER : loaf around
flanquer [flɑ̃ke] *vt* **1** : flank **2 ~ par terre** : fling to the ground **3 ~ un coup à** *fam* : punch
flaque [flak] *nf* : puddle, pool
flash [flaʃ] *nm, pl* **flashs** *or* **flashes** [flaʃ] **1** : flash (in photography) **2** : news flash
flasque [flask] *adj* : flabby, limp
flatter [flate] *vt* **1** : flatter **2** CARESSER : stroke — **se flatter** *vr* : pride oneself — **flatterie** [flatri] *nf* : flattery — **flatteur, -teuse** [flatœr, -tøz] *adj* : flattering — **~** *n* : flatterer
fléau [fleo] *nm, pl* **fléaux** : calamity, scourge
flèche [flɛʃ] *nf* **1** : arrow **2** : spire (of a church) — **fléchette** [fleʃɛt] *nf* : dart
fléchir [fleʃir] *vt* PLIER : bend, flex — *vi* **1** : bend, give way **2** FAIBLIR : weaken
flegme [flɛgm] *nm* : composure — **flegmatique** [flɛgmatik] *adj* : phlegmatic
flemme [flɛm] *nf France fam* : laziness
flétan [fletɑ̃] *nm* : halibut
flétrir [fletrir] *v* **se flétrir** *vr* : wither, fade
fleur [flœr] *nf* **1** : flower **2 en ~** : in blossom — **fleuri, -rie** [flœri] *adj* **1** : flowered **2** : flowery — **fleurir** [flœrir] *vi* **1** : flower, blossom **2** PROSPÉRER : flourish — **fleuriste** [flœrist] *nmf* : florist
fleuve [flœv] *nm* : river
flexible [flɛksibl] *adj* : flexible — **flexibilité** [flɛksibilite] *nf* : flexibility — **flexion** [flɛksjɔ̃] *nf* : bending, flexing
flic [flik] *nm fam* : cop
flirter [flœrte] *vi* : flirt
flocon [flɔkɔ̃] *nm* **1** : flake **2 ~ de neige** : snowflake **3 ~s de maïs** : cornflakes
floraison [flɔrɛzɔ̃] *nf* : flowering, blossoming — **floral, -rale** [flɔral] *adj, mpl* **-raux** [flɔro] : floral — **flore** [flɔr] *nf* : flora — **florissant, -sante** [flɔrisɑ̃, -sɑ̃t] *adj* : flourishing
flot [flo] *nm* **1** : flood, stream **2 à ~** : afloat
flotter [flɔte] *vi* **1** : float **2** : flutter (of

a flag) — **flotte** [flɔt] *nf* : fleet — **flotteur** [flɔtœr] *nm* : float

flou, floue [flu] *adj* **1** : blurred **2** : vague, hazy (of ideas, etc.)

fluctuer [flyktɥe] *vi* : fluctuate — **fluctuation** [flyktɥasjɔ̃] *nf* : fluctuation

fluide [flɥid] *adj* **1** : fluid **2** : flowing freely — **~** *nm* : fluid — **fluidité** [flɥidite] *nf* : fluidity

fluor [flyɔr] *nm* : fluorine

fluorescent, -cente [flyɔresɑ̃, -sɑ̃t] *adj* : fluorescent — **fluorescence** [-sɑ̃s] *nf* : fluorescence

flûte [flyt] *nf* **1** : flute **2** : baguette — **~** *interj* **~ alors**! : nonsense!

fluvial, -viale [flyvjal] *adj, mpl* **-viaux** [-vjo] : river

flux [fly] *nm* **1** : flow **2** MARÉE : flood tide **3 le ~ et le reflux** : the ebb and flow

fœtus [fetys] *nms & pl* : fetus

foi [fwa] *nf* **1** : faith **2 bonne ~** : honesty, sincerity **3 digne de ~** : reliable **4 ma ~ !** : well!

foie [fwa] *nm* : liver

foin [fwɛ̃] *nm* : hay

foire [fwar] *nf* : fair, market

fois [fwa] *nf* **1** : time, occasion **2 à la ~** : at the same time, together **3 des ~** : sometimes **4 il était une ~** : once upon a time

foison [fwazɔ̃] **à ~** *adv phr* : in abundance — **foisonner** [fwazɔne] *vi* : abound

fol → **fou**

folâtrer [fɔlatre] *vi* : frolic — **folâtre** [fɔlatr] *adj* : playful, frisky

folie [fɔli] *nf* **1** : craziness, madness **2 à la ~** : madly

folklore [fɔlklɔr] *nm* : folklore — **folklorique** [fɔlklɔrik] *adj* : folk (of music, dance, etc.)

folle → **fou** — **follement** [fɔlmɑ̃] *adv* : madly, wildly

foncer [fɔ̃se] {6} *vt* : darken — *vi* **~ sur** : rush at — **foncé, -cée** [fɔ̃se] *adj* : dark (of colors)

foncier, -cière [fɔ̃sje, -sjɛr] *adj* **1** : land, property **2** FONDAMENTAL : fundamental — **foncièrement** [fɔ̃sjɛrmɑ̃] *adv* : fundamentally

fonction [fɔ̃ksjɔ̃] *nf* **1** : function **2** EMPLOI : job, post **3 faire ~ de** : serve as **4 en ~ de** : according to **5 ~ publique** : civil service — **fonctionnaire** [fɔ̃ksjɔnɛr] *nmf* : official, civil servant — **fonctionnel, -nelle** [fɔ̃ksjɔnɛl] *adj* : functional — **fonctionnement** [fɔ̃ksjɔnmɑ̃] *nm* : functioning, working — **fonctionner** [fɔ̃ksjɔne] *vi* : function, work

fond [fɔ̃] *nm* **1** : bottom, back **2** CŒUR : heart, root **3** ARRIÈRE-PLAN : background **4 à ~** : thoroughly **5 au ~** : in fact **6 au ~ de** : at the bottom of, in the depths of

fondamental, -tale [fɔ̃damɑ̃tal] *adj, mpl* **-taux** [-to] : fundamental — **fondamentalement** [-talmɑ̃] *adv* : basically

fonder [fɔ̃de] *vt* **1** : found **2** BASER : base — **se fonder** *vr* **~ sur** : be based on — **fondateur, -trice** [fɔ̃datœr, -tris] *n* : founder — **fondation** [fɔ̃dasjɔ̃] *nf* : foundation — **fondé, -dée** [fɔ̃de] *adj* : well-founded — **fondement** [fɔ̃dmɑ̃] *nm* **1** : foundation **2 sans ~** : groundless

fondre [fɔ̃dr] {63} *vt* **1** : melt, smelt **2** : cast (a statue, etc.) — *vi* **1** : melt **2 ~ en larmes** : dissolve into tears

fonds [fɔ̃] *nms & pl* **1** : fund **2 ~** *nmpl* : funds, capital **3** *or* **~ de commerce** : business

fontaine [fɔ̃tɛn] *nf* **1** : fountain **2** SOURCE : spring

fonte [fɔ̃t] *nf* **1** : melting, smelting **2** : thawing (of snow) **3** : cast iron

football [futbol] *nm* **1** : soccer **2** *Can* : football **3 ~ américain** *France* : football — **footballeur, -leuse** [futbolœr, -løz] *n* : soccer player, football player

footing [futiŋ] *nm France* : jogging

forage [fɔraʒ] *nm* : drilling

forçat [fɔrsa] *nm* : convict

force [fɔrs] *nf* **1** : force **2** PUISSANCE : strength **3 à ~ de** : as a result of **4 les ~s armées** : the armed forces — **forcé, -cée** [fɔrse] *adj* **1** : forced **2** INÉVITABLE : inevitable — **forcément** [fɔrsemɑ̃] *adv* : inevitably — **forcer** [fɔrse] {6} *vt* **1** : force, compel **2** : force open **3** : strain, overtax (one's voice, etc.) — *vi* : overdo it — **se forcer** *vr* : force oneself

forer [fɔre] *vt* : drill, bore

forêt [fɔrɛ] *nf* : forest — **foresterie** [fɔrɛstəri] *nf* : forestry — **forestier, -tière** [fɔrɛstje, -tjɛr] *adj* : forest

forfaire [fɔrfɛr] {44} *vi* **~ à** : fail in

forfait [fɔrfɛ] *nm* **1** : fixed price **2 déclarer ~** : withdraw — **forfaitaire** [fɔrfɛtɛr] *adj* : inclusive

forge [fɔrʒ] *nf* : forge — **forger** [fɔrʒe] {16} *vt* : forge — **forgeron** [fɔrʒərɔ̃] *nm* : blacksmith

formaliser [fɔrmalize] *v* **se formaliser** *vr* : take offense
formalité [fɔrmalite] *nf* : formality
format [fɔrma] *nm* : format — **formater** [fɔrmate] *vt* : format (a computer disk)
formation [fɔrmasjɔ̃] *nf* **1** : formation **2** APPRENTISSAGE : education, training — **forme** [fɔrm] *nf* **1** : form, shape **2** **~s** *nfpl* : (human) figure **3** **~s** *nfpl* : proprieties **4** **en ~** : fit, in shape — **formel, -melle** [fɔrmɛl] *adj* **1** : formal **2** CATÉGORIQUE : definitive — **formellement** [-mɛlmɑ̃] *adv* : strictly, absolutely — **former** [fɔrme] *vt* **1** : form **2** : train, educate, develop
formidable [fɔrmidabl] *adj* **1** : tremendous **2** *fam* : great, terrific
formulaire [fɔrmylɛr] *nm* : form, questionnaire
formule [fɔrmyl] *nf* **1** : formula **2** MÉTHODE : way, method **3** FORMULAIRE : form **4** **~ de politesse** : polite phrase, closing (of a letter) — **formuler** [fɔrmyle] *vt* : formulate, express
fort, forte [fɔr, fɔrt] *adj* **1** PUISSANT : strong **2** : loud **3** CONSIDÉRABLE : large **4** DOUÉ : gifted — **fort** [fɔr] *adv* **1** : strongly, loudly, hard **2** TRÈS : very — **fort** *nm* **1** : fort, fortress **2** : strong point — **forteresse** [fɔrtərɛs] *nf* : fortress — **fortifier** [fɔrtifje] {96} *vt* : fortify, strengthen — **fortification** [fɔrtifikasjɔ̃] *nf* : fortification
fortuit, -tuite [fɔrtɥi, -tɥit] *adj* : fortuitous, chance
fortune [fɔrtyn] *nf* : fortune — **fortuné, -née** [fɔrtyne] *adj* : wealthy
forum [fɔrɔm] *nm* : forum
fosse [fos] *nf* **1** : pit **2** TOMBE : grave **3** **~ septique** : septic tank — **fossé** [fose] *nm* **1** : ditch, trench **2** **~ de générations** : generation gap — **fossette** [fosɛt] *nf* : dimple
fossile [fosil] *nm* : fossil
fou [fu] (**fol** [fɔl] *before a vowel or mute h*), **folle** [fɔl] *adj* **1** : mad, crazy **2** *fam* : tremendous — **~** *n* : crazy person, lunatic — **fou** *nm* **1** : fool, jester **2** : bishop (in chess)
foudre [fudr] *nf* : lightning — **foudroyant, -droyante** [fudrwajɑ̃, fudrwajɑ̃t] *adj* **1** : overwhelming **2** SOUDAIN : sudden — **foudroyer** [fudrwaje] {58} *vt* : strike down
fouet [fwɛ] *nm* **1** : whip **2** : whisk **3** **de plein ~** : head-on — **fouetter** [fwete] *vt* : whip
fougère [fuʒɛr] *nf* : fern
fougue [fug] *nf* : ardor, spirit — **fougueux, -geuse** [fugø, -gøz] *adj* : fiery
fouiller [fuje] *vt* **1** : search **2** CREUSER : excavate, dig — *vi* **~ dans** : rummage through — **fouille** [fuj] *nf* **1** : search **2** **~s** *nfpl* : excavations — **fouillis** [fuji] *nm* : jumble
fouiner [fwine] *vi fam* : snoop around
foulard [fular] *nm* : scarf
foule [ful] *nf* **1** : crowd **2** **une ~ de** : masses of, lots of
fouler [fule] *vt* : press, tread on — **se fouler** *vr* : sprain (one's ankle, etc.) — **foulée** [fule] *nf* **dans la ~ de** : in the aftermath of — **foulure** [fulyr] *nf* : sprain
four [fur] *nm* **1** : oven **2** *fam* : flop (in theater, etc.)
fourbu, -bue [furby] *adj* : exhausted
fourche [furʃ] *nf* **1** : pitchfork **2** : fork (of a road) — **fourchette** [furʃɛt] *nf* : fork
fourgon [furgɔ̃] *nm* : van, truck — **fourgonnette** [furgɔnɛt] *nf* : minivan
fourmi [furmi] *nf* : ant — **fourmilière** [furmiljɛr] *nf* : anthill — **fourmiller** [furmije] *vi* **1** : swarm **2** **~ de** : be teeming with
fourneau [furno] *nm, pl* **-neaux** [furno] **1** : stove **2** CUISINIÈRE : furnace
fournée [furne] *nf* : batch
fournir [furnir] *vt* **1** : supply, provide (with) **2** **~ un effort** : make an effort — **fourni, -nie** [furni] *adj* : thick, bushy — **fournisseur, -seuse** [furnisœr, -søz] *n* : supplier — **fournitures** [furnityr] *nfpl* : equipment, supplies
fourrage [furaʒ] *nm* : fodder — **fourrager** [furaʒe] {17} *vi* : forage
fourré [fure] *nm* : thicket
fourreau [furo] *nm, pl* **-reaux** : sheath
fourrer [fure] *vt* **1** : stuff, fill **2** *fam* : thrust, stick — **fourre-tout** [furtu] *nms & pl* : tote bag, carryall
fourrière [furjɛr] *nf* : pound (for animals or vehicles)
fourrure [furyr] *nf* : fur
fourvoyer [furvwaje] {58} *v* **se fourvoyer** *vr* **1** : lead astray **2** **~ dans** : get involved in
foyer [fwaje] *nm* **1** : hearth **2** DOMICILE : home **3** RÉSIDENCE : residence, hall **4** : foyer (of a theater) **5** **lunettes à double ~** : bifocals
fracas [fraka] *nms & pl* : crash, din — **fracasser** [frakase] *vt* : shatter, smash
fraction [fraksjɔ̃] *nf* : fraction

fracture [fraktyr] *nf* : fracture — **fracturer** [fraktyre] *vt* : fracture
fragile [fraʒil] *adj* **1** : fragile **2** FAIBLE : frail — **fragilité** [fraʒilite] *nf* **1** : fragility **2** FAIBLESSE : frailty
fragment [fragmɑ̃] *nm* : fragment
frais, fraîche [frɛ, frɛʃ] *adj* **1** : fresh **2** : cool (of weather) **3 peinture fraîche** : wet paint — **frais** *nm* **1 mettre au ~** : put in a cool place **2 prendre le ~** : take a breath of fresh air **3 frais** *nmpl* : expenses, fees — **~** [frɛ] *adv* **1** : freshly **2 il fait ~** : it's cool outside — **fraîcheur** [frɛʃœr] *nf* **1** : freshness **2** : coolness — **fraîchir** [frɛʃir] *vi* : cool off (of weather)
fraise [frɛz] *nf* : strawberry
framboise [frɑ̃bwaz] *nf* : raspberry
franc, franche [frɑ̃, frɑ̃ʃ] *adj* **1** HONNÊTE : frank **2** VÉRITABLE : utter, downright — **franc** [frɑ̃] *nm* : franc
français, -çaise [frɑ̃sɛ, -sɛz] *adj* : French — **français** *nm* : French (language)
franchement [frɑ̃ʃmɑ̃] *adv* **1** SINCÈREMENT : frankly **2** NETTEMENT : clearly **3** VRAIMENT : downright, really
franchir [frɑ̃ʃir] *vt* **1** : cross (over) **2** : cover (a distance)
franchise [frɑ̃ʃiz] *nf* **1** SINCÉRITÉ : frankness **2** EXONÉRATION : exemption, allowance **3** : franchise
franco–canadien, -dienne [frɑ̃kokanadjɛ̃, -djɛn] *adj* : French-Canadian
francophone [frɑ̃kɔfɔn] *adj* : French-speaking
frange [frɑ̃ʒ] *nf* **1** : fringe **2** : bangs (of hair)
frapper [frape] *vt* **1** : strike, hit **2** IMPRESSIONNER : impress — *vi* : bang, knock — **frappant, -pante** [frapɑ̃, -pɑ̃t] *adj* : striking
fraternel, -nelle [fratɛrnɛl] *adj* : fraternal, brotherly — **fraterniser** [fraternize] *vi* : fraternize — **fraternité** [fratɛrnite] *nf* : fraternity, brotherhood
fraude [frod] *nf* : fraud — **frauder** [frode] *v* : cheat — **fraudeur, -deuse** [frodœr, -døz] *n* : cheat, swindler — **frauduleux, -leuse** [frodylø, -løz] *adj* : fraudulent
frayer [frɛje] {11} *v* **se frayer** *vr* **~ un chemin** : make one's way
frayeur [frɛjœr] *nf* : fright
fredonner [frədɔne] *vt* : hum
frégate [fregat] *nf* : frigate
frein [frɛ̃] *nm* **1** : brake **2 mettre un ~ à** : curb, block — **freiner** [frene] *vt* : slow down, check — *vi* : brake
frêle [frɛl] *adj* : frail
frelon [frəlɔ̃] *nm* : hornet
frémir [fremir] *vi* **1** FRISSONNER : shiver **2** TREMBLER : quiver, flutter **3** : simmer (in cooking)
frêne [frɛn] *nm* : ash (tree or wood)
frénésie [frenezi] *nf* : frenzy — **frénétique** [frenetik] *adj* : frantic, frenzied
fréquenter [frekɑ̃te] *vt* **1** : frequent **2** : attend (school, etc.) **3** COTOYER : associate with, see — **fréquemment** [frekamɑ̃] *adv* : frequently — **fréquence** [frekɑ̃s] *nf* : frequency — **fréquent, -quente** [frekɑ̃, -kɑ̃t] *adj* : frequent — **fréquentation** [frekɑ̃tasjɔ̃] *nf* **1** : frequenting **2** PRÉSENCE : attendance **3** RELATION : acquaintance
frère [frɛr] *nm* **1** : brother **2** : friar
fresque [frɛsk] *nf* : fresco
fret [frɛ] *nm* : freight
fretin [frətɛ̃] *nm* **menu ~** : small fry
friable [frijabl] *adj* : crumbly
friand, friande [frijɑ̃, -jɑ̃d] *adj* **~ de** : fond of
friandise [frijɑ̃diz] *nf* **1** : delicacy **2 ~s** *nfpl* : sweets
fric [frik] *nm fam* : dough, cash
friction [friksjɔ̃] *nf* **1** : friction **2** MASSAGE : massage — **frictionner** [friksjɔne] *vt* : rub, massage
frigide [friʒid] *adj* : frigid
frigo [frigo] *nm fam* : fridge
frileux, -leuse [frilø, -løz] *adj* **1** : sensitive to cold **2** PRUDENT : cautious
frimer [frime] *vi fam* : show off
fringale [frɛ̃gal] *nf* **avoir la ~** *fam* : be ravenous
fringant, -gante [frɛ̃gɑ̃, -gɑ̃t] *adj* : dashing
fripon, -ponne [fripɔ̃, -pɔn] *adj* : mischievous — **~** *n* : rascal
fripouille [fripuj] *nf fam* : scoundrel
frire [frir] {45} *v* : fry
friser [frize] *vt* **1** BOUCLER : curl **2** : border on, be close to — *vi* : curl — **frisé, -sée** [frize] *adj* : curly, curly-haired
frisquet, -quette [friskɛ, -kɛt] *adj* : chilly, nippy
frisson [frisɔ̃] *nm* : shiver, shudder — **frissonner** [frisɔne] *vi* : shiver, shudder
friture [frityr] *nf* **1** : frying **2** : deep fat, oil **3** : fried food — **frites** [frit] *nfpl* : french fries

frivole [frivɔl] *adj* : frivolous — **frivolité** [frivɔlite] *nf* : frivolity
froid, froide [frwa, frwad] *adj* : cold — **froid** [frwa] *adv* **il fait ~** : it's cold (outside) — **~** *nm* **1** : cold **2 être en ~ avec** : be on bad terms with **3 prendre ~** : catch cold — **froidement** [frwadmɑ̃] *adv* : coldly, coolly — **froideur** [frwadœr] *nf* : coldness, coolness
froisser [frwase] *vt* **1** : crumple, crease **2** BLESSER : offend — **se froisser** *vr* **1** : crease, crumple (up) **2 ~ un muscle** : strain a muscle
frôler [frole] *vt* : brush against, touch lightly
fromage [frɔmaʒ] *nm* **1** : cheese **2 ~ blanc** : cottage cheese — **fromagerie** [frɔmaʒri] *nf* : cheese shop
fronce [frɔ̃s] *nf* : gather, crease — **froncement** [frɔ̃smɑ̃] *nm* **~ de sourcils** : frown
froncer [frɔ̃se] {6} *vt* **1** : gather (fabric) **2 ~ les sourcils** : frown
fronde [frɔ̃d] *nf* **1** : rebellion, revolt **2** LANCE-PIERRES : slingshot
front [frɔ̃] *nm* **1** : forehead **2** : front (in politics, war, etc.) **3** AUDACE : audacity, cheek **4 de ~** : head-on **5 faire ~ à** : confront — **frontal, -tale** [frɔ̃tal] *adj, mpl* **-taux** [frɔ̃to] : frontal — **frontalier, -lière** [frɔ̃talje, -ljɛr] *adj* : frontier — **frontière** [frɔ̃tjɛr] *nf* : frontier, border
frotter [frɔte] *vt* **1** : rub **2** NETTOYER : polish, scrub — *vi* : rub — **frottement** [frɔtmɑ̃] *nm* **1** : rubbing **2 ~s** *nmpl* : friction, disagreement
frousse [frus] *nf fam* : scare, fright
fructueux, -tueuse [fryktɥø, -tɥøz] *adj* : fruitful
frugal, -gale [frygal] *adj, mpl* **-gaux** [frygo] : frugal — **frugalité** [frygalite] *nf* : frugality
fruit [frɥi] *nm* **1** : fruit **2 ~s de mer** : seafood — **fruité, -tée** [frɥite] *adj* : fruity — **fruitier, -tière** [frɥitje, -tjɛr] *adj* : fruit
frustrer [frystre] *vt* **1** : frustrate **2 ~ de** : deprive of — **frustrant, -trante** [frystrɑ̃, -trɑ̃t] *adj* : frustrating — **frustration** [frystrasjɔ̃] *nf* : frustration
fugace [fygas] *adj* : fleeting
fugitif, -tive [fyʒitif, -tiv] *n* : fugitive, runaway
fugue [fyg] *nf* **1 faire une ~** : run away **2 ~ amoureuse** : elopement
fuir [fɥir] {46} *vi* **1** : flee **2** SUINTER : leak — *vt* : avoid, shun — **fuite** [fɥit] *nf* **1** : flight, escape **2** : leak (of water, information, etc.)
fulgurant, -rante [fylgyrɑ̃, -rɑ̃t] *adj* : dazzling, vivid
fulminer [fylmine] *vi* : be enraged
fumer [fyme] *vt* : smoke — *vi* **1** : smoke **2** : give off steam — **fumé, -mée** [fyme] *adj* **1** : smoked **2** : tinted (of glass, etc.) — **fumée** *nf* **1** : smoke **2** VAPEUR : steam — **fumeur, -meuse** [fymœr, -møz] *n* : smoker
fumier [fymje] *nm* : dung, manure
fumigation [fymigasjɔ̃] *nf* : fumigation
funambule [fynɑ̃byl] *nmf* : tightrope walker
funèbre [fynɛbr] *adj* **1** : funeral **2** LUGUBRE : gloomy — **funérailles** [fyneraj] *nfpl* : funeral — **funéraire** [fynerɛr] *adj* : funeral
funeste [fynɛst] *adj* DÉSASTREUX : disastrous
fur [fyr] **au ~ et à mesure** *adv phr* : little by little
furet [fyrɛ] *nm* : ferret
fureter [fyrte] {20} *vi* : pry
fureur [fyrœr] *nf* **1** : rage, fury **2 faire ~** : be all the rage
furibond, -bonde [fyribɔ̃, -bɔ̃d] *adj* : furious — **furie** [fyri] *nf* : fury, rage — **furieux, -rieuse** [fyrjø, -jøz] *adj* : furious
furoncle [fyrɔ̃kl] *nm* : boil
furtif, -tive [fyrtif, -tiv] *adj* : furtive, sly
fusain [fyzɛ̃] *nm* : charcoal
fuseau [fyzo] *nm, pl* **-seaux** **1** : spindle **2 ~ horaire** : time zone
fusée [fyze] *nf* **1** : rocket **2 ~ éclairante** : flare
fuselé, -lée [fyzle] *adj* : slender, tapering
fusible [fyzibl] *nm* : fuse
fusil [fyzi] *nm* : gun, rifle — **fusillade** [fyzijad] *nf* : gunfire — **fusiller** [fyzije] *vt* : shoot
fusion [fyzjɔ̃] *nf* : fusion — **fusionner** [fyzɔnje] *v* : merge
fût [fy] *nm* : barrel, cask
futé, -tée [fyte] *adj* : cunning, crafty
futile [fytil] *adj* : futile — **futilité** [fytilite] *nf* : futility
futur, -ture [fytyr] *adj & nm* : future
fuyant, fuyante [fɥijɑ̃, fɥijɑ̃t] *adj* : elusive, shifty

G

g [ʒe] *nm* : g, seventh letter of the alphabet
gabarit [gabari] *nm* **1** : size, dimensions *pl* **2** *fam* : caliber, type
gâcher [gaʃe] *vt* : spoil, ruin
gâchette [gaʃɛt] *nf* : trigger
gâchis [gaʃi] *nm* **1** DÉSORDRE : mess **2** GASPILLAGE : waste
gadget [gadʒɛt] *nm* : gadget
gadoue [gadu] *nf* : mud, muck
gaffe [gaf] *nf fam* : blunder — **gaffer** [gafe] *vi fam* : blunder, goof (up)
gage [gaʒ] *nm* **1** : security **2** GARANTIE : pledge, guarantee **3** **∼s** *nmpl* : wages, pay **4** **en ∼ de** : as a token of **5** **mettre en ∼** : pawn — **gager** [gaʒe] {17} *vt* **1** : bet, wager **2** : guarantee (a loan, etc.) — **gageure** [gaʒœr] *nf* **1** : challenge **2** *Can* : bet, wager
gagner [gaɲe] *vt* **1** : win **2** : earn (one's living, etc.) **3** : gain (speed, etc.) **4** : save (time, space, etc.) **5** ATTEINDRE : reach — *vi* **1** : win **2** **∼ en** : increase in **3** **y ∼** : be better off — **gagnant, -gnante** [gaɲɑ̃, -ɲɑ̃t] *adj* : winning — **∼** *n* : winner — **gagne–pain** [gaɲpɛ̃] *nms & pl* : job, livelihood
gai, gaie [gɛ] *adj* : cheerful, merry — **gaieté** [gete] *nf* : cheerfulness
gaillard, -larde [gajar, -jard] *adj* **1** : sprightly **2** GRIVOIS : ribald — **∼** *nmf* : vigorous person
gain [gɛ̃] *nm* **1** : earnings *pl* **2** PROFIT : gain **3** ÉCONOMIE : saving
gaine [gɛn] *nf* **1** : girdle **2** : sheath (of a dagger)
gala [gala] *nm* : gala, reception
galant, -lante [galɑ̃, -lɑ̃t] *adj* : courteous, gallant
galaxie [galaksi] *nf* : galaxy
galbe [galb] *nm* : curve, shapeliness
galerie [galri] *nf* **1** : gallery **2** : balcony (in a theater) **3** : roof rack (of an automobile)
galet [galɛ] *nm* : pebble
galette [galɛt] *nf* : flat round cake
gallois, -loise [galwa, -lwaz] *adj* : Welsh — **gallois** *nm* : Welsh (language)
gallon [galɔ̃] *nm* : gallon
galoper [galɔpe] *vi* : gallop — **galop** [galo] *nm* : gallop
galopin [galɔpɛ̃] *nm* : rascal
galvaniser [galvanize] *vt* : galvanize
galvauder [galvode] *vt* : sully, tarnish
gambade [gɑ̃bad] *nf* : leap, skip — **gambader** [gɑ̃bade] *vi* : leap about
gamelle [gamɛl] *nf* : mess kit
gamin, -mine [gamɛ̃, -min] *adj* : mischievous — **∼** *n* : kid, youngster
gamme [gam] *nf* **1** : scale (in music) **2** SÉRIE : range, gamut
ganglion [gɑ̃glijɔ̃] *nm* **avoir des ∼s** : have swollen glands
gangrène [gɑ̃grɛn] *nf* : gangrene
gangster [gɑ̃gstɛr] *nm* : gangster
gant [gɑ̃] *nm* **1** : glove **2** **∼ de toilette** : washcloth
garage [garaʒ] *nm* : garage — **garagiste** [garaʒist] *nmf* **1** : garage owner **2** : (garage) mechanic
garant, -rante [garɑ̃, -rɑ̃t] *n* : guarantor — **garant** *nm* : guarantee (in law) — **garantie** [garɑ̃ti] *nf* : guarantee, warranty — **garantir** [garɑ̃tir] *vt* **1** : guarantee **2** **∼ de** : protect from
garçon [garsɔ̃] *nm* **1** : boy, young man **2** SERVEUR : waiter **3** **∼ manqué** : tomboy
garder [garde] *vt* **1** : keep **2** SURVEILLER : watch over **3** **∼ de** : protect from — **se garder** *vr* **1** : keep **2** **∼ de** : be careful not to — **garde** [gard] *nm* **1** : guard **2** **∼ du corps** : bodyguard — **∼** *nf* **1** : nurse **2** : (military) guard **3** : custody, care **4** **de ∼** : on duty **5** **mettre en ∼** : warn **6** **prendre ∼** : be careful — **garde–fou** [gardəfu] *nm, pl* **garde–fous** : railing — **garde–manger** [gardəmɑ̃ʒe] *nms & pl* : pantry — **garderie** [gardəri] *nf* : day-care center — **garde–robe** [gardərɔb] *nf, pl* **garde–robes** : wardrobe, closet — **gardien, -dienne** [gardjɛ̃, -djɛn] *n* **1** : warden, custodian **2** PROTECTEUR : guardian — **gardien** *nm* **1** **∼ de but** : goalkeeper **2** **∼ de la paix** *France* : police officer — **gardienne** *nf* **∼ d'enfants** : day-care worker
gare[1] [gar] *nf* **1** : station **2** **∼ routière** *France or* **∼ d'autobus** *Can* : bus station
gare[2] *interj* **1** **∼ à toi!** : watch out! **2** **sans crier ∼** : without warning
garer [gare] *vt* STATIONNER : park — **se**

garer *vr* **1** : park **2** S'ÉCARTER : move away
gargariser [gargarize] *v* **se gargariser** *vr* : gargle
gargouiller [garguje] *vi* : gurgle, rumble
garnement [garnəmɑ̃] *nm* : rascal
garnir [garnir] *vt* **1** REMPLIR : fill **2** COUVRIR : cover **3** DÉCORER : decorate, trim — **garni, -nie** [garni] *adj* : served with vegetables
garnison [garnizɔ̃] *nf* : garrison
garniture [garnityr] *nf* **1** : filling (in cooking) **2** DÉCORATION : trimming, garnish
gars [ga] *nm fam* **1** : boy, lad **2** TYPE : guy, fellow
gaspiller [gaspije] *vt* : waste, squander — **gaspillage** [gaspijaʒ] *nm* : waste
gastrique [gastrik] *adj* : gastric
gastronomie [gastrɔnɔmi] *nf* : gastronomy
gâteau [gato] *nm, pl* **-teaux 1** : cake **2 ~ sec** *France* : cookie
gâter [gate] *vt* **1** : pamper **2** ABÎMER : spoil, ruin — **se gâter** *vr* **1** : go bad **2** SE DÉTÉRIORER : deteriorate
gâterie [gatri] *nf* : little treat, delicacy
gâteux, -teuse [gatø, -tøz] *adj* : senile
gauche [goʃ] *adj* **1** : left **2** MALADROIT : clumsy — **~** *nf* **1** : left **2 la ~** : the left (wing) — **gaucher, -chère** [goʃe, -ʃɛr] *adj* : left-handed — **gaucherie** [goʃri] *nf* : awkwardness
gaufre [gofr] *nf* : waffle — **gaufrette** [gofrɛt] *nf* : wafer
gausser [gose] *v* **se gausser** *vr* **~ de** : deride, make fun of
gaver [gave] *v* **se gaver** *vr* : stuff oneself
gay [gɛ] *adj* : gay (homosexual)
gaz [gaz] *nms & pl* : gas
gaze [gaz] *nf* : gauze
gazer [gaze] *vi fam* **ça gaze?** : how are things going?
gazette [gazɛt] *nf* : newspaper
gazeux, -zeuse [gazø, -zøz] *adj* : fizzy, carbonated
gazon [gazɔ̃] *nm* **1** : grass, turf **2** PELOUSE : lawn
gazouiller [gazuje] *vi* **1** : chirp **2** : gurgle, babble (of a baby)
geai [ʒɛ] *nm* : jay
géant, géante [ʒeɑ̃, -ɑ̃t] *adj* : giant, gigantic — **~** *n* : giant
geler [ʒəle] {20} *v* : freeze — *v impers* **on gèle!** : it's freezing! — **gel** [ʒɛl] *nm* **1** : frost **2** : gel **3** : freezing (of prices, etc.) — **gélatine** [ʒelatin] *nf* : gelatin — **gelée** *nf* **1** : (hoar)frost **2** : jelly — **gelure** [ʒəlyr] *nf* : frostbite
gémir [ʒemir] *vi* : groan, moan — **gémissement** [ʒemismɑ̃] *nm* : groan(ing), moan(ing)
gemme [ʒɛm] *nf* : gem
gênant, -nante [ʒenɑ̃, -nɑ̃t] *adj* **1** : embarrassing **2** ENCOMBRANT : cumbersome **3** ENNUYEUX : annoying
gencives [ʒɑ̃siv] *nfpl* : gums
gendarme [ʒɑ̃darm] *nm* : police officer — **gendarmerie** [ʒɑ̃darməri] *nf* **1** *France* : police force **2** *France* : police station **3** *Can* : federal police force
gendre [ʒɑ̃dr] *nm* : son-in-law
gène [ʒɛn] *nm* : gene
généalogie [ʒenealɔʒi] *nf* : genealogy
gêner [ʒene] *vt* **1** : embarrass, make uncomfortable **2** DÉRANGER : bother **3** ENCOMBRER : hamper — **se gêner** *vr* : put oneself out — **gêne** [ʒɛn] *nf* **1** : inconvenience **2** : embarrassment **3** : (physical) discomfort — **gêné, -née** [ʒene] *adj* **1** : embarrassed **2** *Can* : shy
général, -rale [ʒeneral] *adj, mpl* **-raux** [-ro] : general — **général** *nm, pl* **-raux** : general — **généralement** [-ralmɑ̃] *adv* : generally, usually — **généraliser** [ʒeneralize] *v* : generalize — **se généraliser** *vr* : become widespread — **généraliste** [ʒeneralist] *nmf* : general practitioner — **généralité** [ʒeneralite] *nf* : majority
générateur [ʒeneratœr] *nm* : generator
génération [ʒenerasjɔ̃] *nf* : generation
génératrice [ʒeneratris] *nf* : (electric) generator
générer [ʒenere] {87} *vt* : generate
généreux, -reuse [ʒenerø, -røz] *adj* : generous — **généreusement** [-røzmɑ̃] *adv* : generously
générique [ʒenerik] *adj* : generic — **~** *nm* : credits *pl* (in movies)
générosité [ʒenerɔzite] *nf* : generosity
génétique [ʒenetik] *adj* : genetic — **~** *nf* : genetics
génie [ʒeni] *nm* **1** : genius **2** INGÉNIERIE : engineering — **génial, -niale** [ʒenjal] *adj, mpl* **-niaux** [-njo] **1** : brilliant **2** *fam* : fantastic, great
génisse [ʒenis] *nf* : heifer
génital, -tale [ʒenital] *adj, mpl* **-taux** [-to] : genital
genou [ʒənu] *nm, pl* **-noux 1** : knee **2 se mettre à ~x** : kneel down
genre [ʒɑ̃r] *nm* **1** SORTE : kind, type **2** ATTITUDE : style, manner **3** : gender (in grammar)

gens [ʒɑ̃] *nmfpl* **1** : people **2 ~ d'affaires** : businesspeople **3 jeunes ~** : teenagers
gentil, -tille [ʒɑ̃ti, -tij] *adj* **1** : kind, nice **2** SAGE : well-behaved — **gentillesse** [ʒɑ̃tijɛs] *nf* : kindness, niceness — **gentiment** [ʒɑ̃timɑ̃] *adv* : nicely, kindly
géographie [ʒeɔgrafi] *nf* : geography — **géographique** [ʒeɔgrafik] *adj* : geographic(al)
geôlier, -lière [ʒolje, -ljɛr] *n* : jailer
géologie [ʒeɔlɔʒi] *nf* : geology — **géologique** [ʒeɔlɔʒik] *adj* : geologic(al)
géométrie [ʒeɔmetri] *nf* : geometry — **géométrique** [ʒeɔmetrik] *adj* : geometric(al)
géranium [ʒeranjɔm] *nm* : geranium
gérant, -rante [ʒerɑ̃, -rɑ̃t] *n* : manager
gerbe [ʒɛrb] *nf* **1** : sheaf (of wheat) **2** : bunch (of flowers, etc.)
gercer [ʒɛrse] {6} *v* **se gercer** *vr* : chap, crack — **gerçure** [ʒɛrsyr] *nf* : crack (in the skin)
gérer [ʒere] {87} *vt* : manage
germain, -maine [ʒɛrmɛ̃, -mɛn] *adj* **cousin germain** : first cousin
germe [ʒɛrm] *nm* **1** : germ **2** POUSSE : sprout — **germer** [ʒɛrme] *vi* **1** : sprout, germinate **2** : form (of ideas, etc.)
gésier [ʒezje] *nm* : gizzard
gésir [ʒezir] {47} *vi* : lie, be lying
gestation [ʒɛstasjɔ̃] *nf* : gestation
geste [ʒɛst] *nm* : gesture, movement
gestion [ʒɛstjɔ̃] *nf* : management — **gestionnaire** [ʒɛstjɔnɛr] *nmf* : administrator
geyser [ʒezɛr] *nm* : geyser
gibet [ʒibɛ] *nm* : gallows
gibier [ʒibje] *nm* **1** : game (animals) **2** *fam* : prey
giboulée [ʒibule] *nf* : sudden shower
gicler [ʒikle] *vi* : spurt, squirt, spatter — **giclée** [ʒikle] *nf* : spurt, squirt
gifle [ʒifl] *nf* : slap (in the face) — **gifler** [ʒifle] *vt* : slap
gigantesque [ʒigɑ̃tɛsk] *adj* : gigantic, huge
gigot [ʒigo] *nm* : leg (of lamb) — **gigoter** [ʒigɔte] *vi fam* : wriggle, fidget
gilet [ʒilɛ] *nm* **1** : vest **2** : cardigan (sweater) **3 ~ de sauvetage** : life jacket
gin [dʒin] *nm* : gin
gingembre [ʒɛ̃ʒɑ̃br] *nm* : ginger
girafe [ʒiraf] *nf* : giraffe
giratoire [ʒiratwar] *adj* **sens ~** : rotary, traffic circle
girofle [ʒirɔfl] *nm* **clou de ~** : clove
girouette [ʒirwɛt] *nf* : weather vane
gisement [ʒizmɑ̃] *nm* : deposit (in geology)
gitan, -tane [ʒitɑ̃, -tan] *n* : Gypsy
gîte [ʒit] *nm* **1** : shelter, lodging **2 le ~ et le couvert** : room and board
givre [ʒivr] *nm* : frost — **givrer** [ʒivre] *v* **se givrer** *vr* : frost (up)
glabre [glabr] *adj* : hairless
glacer [glase] {6} *vt* **1** : freeze, chill **2** : frost (a cake) — **glaçage** [glasaʒ] *nm* : frosting — **glace** [glas] *nf* **1** : ice **2** *France* : ice cream **3** MIROIR : mirror **4** VITRE : glass — **glacé, -cée** [glase] *adj* **1** : icy, chilly **2** : iced — **glacial, -ciale** [glasjal] *adj, mpl* **-cials** *or* **-ciaux** [-sjo] : icy, frigid — **glacier** [glasje] *nm* : glacier — **glacière** [glasjɛr] *nf* : cooler, icebox — **glaçon** [glasɔ̃] *nm* **1** : block of ice **2** : icicle **3** : ice cube
glaise [glɛz] *nf* : clay
gland [glɑ̃] *nm* **1** : acorn **2** : tassel (ornament)
glande [glɑ̃d] *nf* : gland
glapir [glapir] *vi* : yelp
glas [gla] *nm* **sonner le ~** : toll the bell
glauque [glok] *adj* : gloomy, dreary
glisser [glise] *vi* **1** : slide, slip **2** DÉRAPER : skid — *vt* : slip, slide — **se glisser** *vr* **~ dans** : slip into, creep into — **glissant, -sante** [glisɑ̃, -sɑ̃t] *adj* : slippery — **glissement** [glismɑ̃] *nm* **1** : sliding, gliding **2** ÉVOLUTION : shift — **glissière** [glisjɛr] *nf* **1** : slide, groove, chute **2 à ~** : sliding — **glissoire** [gliswar] *nf* : slide
globe [glɔb] *nm* **1** : globe **2 ~ oculaire** : eyeball **3 le ~ terrestre** : the earth — **global, -bale** [glɔbal] *adj, mpl* **-baux** [glɔbo] : overall, total — **globalement** [glɔbalmɑ̃] *adv* : as a whole
gloire [glwar] *nf* **1** : glory, fame **2** MÉRITE : credit — **glorieux, -rieuse** [glɔrjø, -rjøz] *adj* : glorious — **glorifier** [glɔrifje] {96} *vt* : glorify
glossaire [glɔsɛr] *nm* : glossary
glousser [gluse] *vi* **1** : cluck **2** : chuckle — **gloussement** [glusmɑ̃] *nm* **1** : cluck, clucking **2** : chuckling
glouton, -tonne [glutɔ̃, -tɔn] *adj* : gluttonous, greedy — **~** *n* : glutton — **gloutonnerie** [glutɔnri] *nf* : gluttony
gluant, gluante [glyɑ̃, glyɑ̃t] *adj* : sticky

glucose [glykoz] *nm* : glucose
gobelet [gɔblɛ] *nm* : tumbler, beaker
gober [gɔbe] *vt* **1** : swallow whole **2** *fam* : swallow, fall for
godasse [gɔdas] *nf fam* : shoe
goéland [gɔelɑ̃] *nm* : gull
goguenard, -narde [gognar, -nard] *adj* : mocking
goinfre [gwɛ̃fr] *nm fam* : pig, glutton
golf [gɔlf] *nm* : golf
golfe [gɔlf] *nm* : gulf, bay
gomme [gɔm] *nf* **1** : gum, resin **2** : eraser **3 ~ à mâcher** : chewing gum — **gommer** [gɔme] *vt* : erase
gond [gɔ̃] *nm* : hinge
gondole [gɔ̃dɔl] *nf* : gondola
gondoler [gɔ̃dɔle] *v* **se gondoler** *vr* : warp, buckle
gonfler [gɔ̃fle] *vt* **1** : swell **2** : blow up, inflate (a balloon, etc.) **3** GROSSIR : exaggerate — *vi* : swell — **se gonfler** *vr* **1** : swell up **2 ~ de** : swell up with, be filled with — **gonflé, -flée** [gɔ̃fle] *adj* : swollen, bloated — **gonflement** [gɔ̃fləmɑ̃] *nm* : swelling
gorge [gɔrʒ] *nf* **1** : throat **2** POITRINE : bosom, chest **3** : gorge (in geography) — **gorgée** [gɔrʒe] *nf* : mouthful, sip — **gorger** [gɔrʒe] {17} *v* **se gorger** *vr* : gorge oneself
gorille [gɔrij] *nm* : gorilla
gosier [gozje] *nm* : throat
gosse [gɔs] *nmf France fam* : kid, youngster
gothique [gɔtik] *adj* : Gothic
goudron [gudrɔ̃] *nm* : tar — **goudronner** [gudrɔne] *vt* : tar (a road)
gouffre [gufr] *nm* : gulf, abyss
goujat [guʒa] *nm* : boor
goulot [gulo] *nm* **1** : neck (of a bottle) **2 ~ d'étranglement** : bottleneck
goulu, -lue [guly] *adj* : greedy
gourde [gurd] *nf* **1** : flask **2** : gourd **3** *fam* : dope, dumbbell
gourdin [gurdɛ̃] *nm* : cudgel, club
gourmand, -mande [gurmɑ̃, -mɑ̃d] *adj* GLOUTON : greedy — **~** *n* : glutton — **gourmandise** [gurmɑ̃diz] *nf* **1** : greed **2 ~s** *nfpl* : sweets, delicacies
gousse [gus] *nf* **~ d'ail** : clove of garlic
goût [gu] *nm* **1** : taste **2** SAVEUR : flavor **3** GRÉ : fondness, liking **4 de bon ~** : tasteful — **goûter** [gute] *vt* : taste — *vi* **1** : have an afternoon snack **2 ~ à** *or* **~ de** : try out, sample — **~** *nm* : afternoon snack
goutte [gut] *nf* : drop (of water, etc.) — **gouttelette** [gutlɛt] *nf* : droplet — **goutter** [gute] *vi* : drip — **gouttière** [gutjɛr] *nf* : gutter (on a roof)
gouvernail [guvɛrnaj] *nm* **1** : rudder **2** BARRE : helm
gouverner [guvɛrne] *vt* : govern, rule — **gouvernante** [guvɛrnɑ̃t] *nf* **1** : governess **2** : housekeeper — **gouvernement** [guvɛrnəmɑ̃] *nm* : government — **gouvernemental, -tale** [-mɑ̃tal] *adj* : governmental — **gouverneur** [guvɛrnœr] *nm* : governor
grâce [gras] *nf* **1** : gracefulness **2** FAVEUR : favor **3** PARDON : mercy, pardon **4 de bonne ~** : willingly **5 ~ à** : thanks to — **gracier** [grasje] {96} *vt* : pardon — **gracieux, -cieuse** [grasjø, -sjøz] *adj* **1** : graceful **2** AIMABLE : gracious **3** GRATUIT : free
grade [grad] *nm* **1** : rank **2 monter en ~** : be promoted
gradin [gradɛ̃] *nm* **1** : tier **2 ~s** *nmpl* : bleachers, stands
graduel, -duelle [gradɥɛl] *adj* : gradual — **graduellement** [-dɥɛlmɑ̃] *adv* : gradually
graduer [gradɥe] *vt* **1** : graduate (a measuring instrument) **2** : increase gradually
graffiti [grafiti] *nmpl* : graffiti
grain [grɛ̃] *nm* **1** : (cereal) grain **2** : speck, particle (of sand, salt, dust, etc.) **3 ~ de café** : coffee bean **4 ~ de poivre** : peppercorn **5 ~ de beauté** : mole — **graine** [grɛn] *nf* : seed
graisse [grɛs] *nf* **1** : fat **2** LUBRIFIANT : grease — **graisser** [grɛse] *vt* : lubricate, grease — **graisseux, -seuse** [grɛsø, -søz] *adj* : greasy
grammaire [gramɛr] *nf* : grammar — **grammatical, -cale** [gramatikal] *adj, mpl* **-caux** [-ko] : grammatical
gramme [gram] *nm* : gram
grand, grande [grɑ̃, grɑ̃d] *adj* **1** : tall **2** GROS : big, large **3** IMPORTANT : great, important **4** : elder, older, grown-up — **grand** [grɑ̃] *adv* **1** : wide **2 ~ ouvert** : wide-open — **grand–chose** [grɑ̃ʃoz] *pron* **pas ~** : not much — **grandeur** [grɑ̃dœr] *nf* **1** DIMENSION : size **2** : greatness — **grandiose** [grɑ̃djoz] *adj* : grandiose — **grandir** [grɑ̃dir] *vt* **1** : make (look) taller **2** EXAGÉRER : exaggerate — *vi* **1** : grow **2** AUGMENTER : increase — **grand–mère** [grɑ̃mɛr] *nf, pl* **grands–mères** : grandmother — **grand–père** [grɑ̃pɛr] *nm, pl* **grands–pères**

: grandfather — **grands–parents** [grɑ̃parɑ̃] *nmpl* : grandparents

grange [grɑ̃ʒ] *nf* : barn

granit *or* **granite** [granit] *nm* : granite

granulé [granyle] *nm* : tablet (in medicine) — **granuleux, -leuse** [granylø, -løz] *adj* : granular

graphique [grafik] *adj* : graphic — **~** *nm* : graph, chart

grappe [grap] *nf* : cluster (of grapes, etc.)

grappin [grapɛ̃] *nm* **1** : grapnel **2 mettre le ~ sur** : get one's hooks into

gras, grasse [gra, gras] *adj* **1** : fatty **2** GROS : fat (of persons) **3** HUILEUX : greasy, oily **4** VULGAIRE : crude, coarse **5** : bold (of type) — **gras** *nm* **1** : (animal) fat **2** : grease — **grassouillet, -lette** [grasujɛ, -jɛt] *adj* : pudgy, plump

gratifier [gratifje] {96} *vt* **~ de** : reward with — **gratification** [gratifikasjɔ̃] *nf* : bonus

gratin [gratɛ̃] *nm* : dish baked with cheese or crumb topping

gratis [gratis] *adv* : free

gratitude [gratityd] *nf* : gratitude

gratte–ciel [gratsjɛl] *nms & pl* : skyscraper

gratter [grate] *vt* : scratch, scrape — **se gratter** *vr* : scratch oneself

gratuit, -tuite [gratɥi, -tɥit] *adj* **1** : free **2** : gratuitous — **gratuitement** [-tɥitmɑ̃] *adv* : free (of charge)

gravats [grava] *nmpl* : rubble

grave [grav] *adj* **1** : serious, grave **2** SOLENNEL : solemn **3 voix ~** : deep voice — **gravement** [gravmɑ̃] *adv* : seriously

graver [grave] *vt* **1** : engrave **2** : carve **3** ENREGISTRER : cut, record

gravier [gravje] *nm* : gravel

gravillon [gravijɔ̃] *nm* : (fine) gravel, grit

gravir [gravir] *vt* : climb (up)

gravité [gravite] *nf* **1** : gravity (in physics) **2** IMPORTANCE : seriousness — **graviter** [gravite] *vi* : gravitate

gravure [gravyr] *nf* **1** : engraving **2** : print (of a picture), plate (in a book)

gré [gre] *nm* **1** VOLONTÉ : will **2** GOÛT : taste, liking **3 à votre ~** : as you wish

grec, grecque [grɛk] *adj* : Greek — **grec** *nm* : Greek (language)

greffe [grɛf] *nf* **1** : graft (in botany) **2** : graft, transplant (in medicine) — **greffer** [grɛfe] *vt* **1** : graft **2** : transplant (an organ)

greffier, -fière [grɛfje, -fjɛr] *n* : clerk of court

grêle[1] [grɛl] *adj* **1** : lanky, lean **2** AIGU : shrill

grêle[2] *nf* : hail — **grêler** [grele] *v impers* **il grêle** : it's hailing — **grêlon** [grɛlɔ̃] *nm* : hailstone

grelot [grəlo] *nm* : small bell — **grelotter** [grəlɔte] *vi* : shiver

grenade [grənad] *nf* **1** : pomegranate **2** : grenade (weapon)

grenier [grənje] *nm* : attic, loft

grenouille [grənuj] *nf* : frog

grès [grɛ] *nm* **1** : sandstone **2** POTERIE : stoneware

grésiller [grezije] *vi* : crackle, sizzle

grève [grɛv] *nf* **1** RIVAGE : shore **2** : strike — **gréviste** [grevist] *nmf* : striker

gribouiller [gribuje] *v* : scribble — **gribouillage** [gribujaʒ] *nm* : scribble, scrawl

grief [grijɛf] *nm* : grievance — **grièvement** [grijɛvmɑ̃] *adv* : seriously, severely

griffe [grif] *nf* **1** : claw **2** : signature, label (of a product) — **griffer** [grife] *vt* : scratch — **griffonner** [grifɔne] *vt* : scribble, jot down

grignoter [griɲɔte] *vt* **1** : nibble **2** AMOINDRIR : erode, eat away (at)

gril [gril] *nm* **1** : broiler **2** : grill (for cooking) — **grillade** [grijad] *nf* : grilled meat, grill

grille [grij] *nf* **1** : metal fencing, gate, bars *pl* **2** : grate (of a sewer, etc.) **3** : grid (in games) — **grillage** [grijaʒ] *nm* : wire fencing

griller [grije] *vt* **1** : toast, grill, broil **2** : burn out (a fuse, etc.) — *vi* : broil — **grille–pain** [grijpɛ̃] *nms & pl* : toaster

grillon [grijɔ̃] *nm* : cricket

grimace [grimas] *nf* : grimace — **grimacer** [grimase] {6} *vi* : grimace

grimper [grɛ̃pe] *v* : climb

grincer [grɛ̃se] {6} *vi* **1** : creak, grate **2 ~ des dents** : grind one's teeth — **grincement** [grɛ̃smɑ̃] *nm* : creak, squeak

grincheux, -cheuse [grɛ̃ʃø, -ʃøz] *adj* : grumpy

grippe [grip] *nf* **1** : flu, influenza **2 prendre qqn en ~** : take a sudden dislike to s.o. — **grippé, -pée** [gripe] *adj* **être ~** : have the flu

gris, grise [gri, griz] *adj* **1** : gray **2** MORNE : dull, dreary **3** *fam* : tipsy — **gris** *nm* : gray — **grisaille** [grizaj] *nf*

1 : grayness (of weather) **2** MONOTONIE : dullness
griser [grize] *vt* : intoxicate — **grisant, -sante** [grizɑ̃, -zɑ̃t] *adj* : intoxicating, heady
grisonner [grizɔne] *vi* : turn gray, go gray
grive [griv] *nf* : thrush
grivois, -voise [grivwa, -waz] *adj* : bawdy
grogner [grɔɲe] *vi* **1** : growl **2** : grumble — **grognement** [grɔɲmɑ̃] *nm* **1** : growling **2** : rumbling, roar — **grognon, -gnonne** [grɔɲɔ̃, -ɲɔn] *adj* : grumpy, grouchy
groin [grwɛ̃] *nm* : snout
grommeler [grɔmle] {8} *v* : mutter
gronder [grɔ̃de] *vt* : scold — *vi* **1** : rumble, roar **2** GROGNER : growl — **grondement** [grɔ̃dmɑ̃] *nm* **1** : roar, rumble **2** GROGNEMENT : growling
gros, grosse [gro, gros] *adj* **1** : big, large **2** ÉPAIS : thick **3** CORPULENT : fat **4** GRAVE : serious **5** LOURD : heavy **6** **~ lot** : jackpot — **gros** [gro] *adv* BEAUCOUP : a lot — **~** *nm* **1 en ~** : roughly, in general **2 le ~ de** : the bulk of
groseille [grozɛj] *nf* **1** : currant **2 ~ à maquereau** : gooseberry
grossir [grosir] *vt* **1** AUGMENTER : increase **2** EXAGÉRER : exaggerate **3** AGRANDIR : magnify — *vi* **1** : put on weight **2** : grow larger — **grossesse** [grosɛs] *nf* : pregnancy — **grosseur** [grosœr] *nf* **1** : fatness **2** VOLUME : size **3** : lump (in medicine) — **grossier, -sière** [grosje, -sjɛr] *adj* **1** APPROXIMATIF : coarse, rough **2** VULGAIRE : crude, vulgar **3** FLAGRANT : gross, glaring — **grossièrement** [grosjɛrmɑ̃] *adv* **1** APPROXIMATIVEMENT : roughly **2** VULGAIREMENT : crudely — **grossièreté** [grosjɛrte] *nf* **1** : coarseness **2** : rudeness — **grossiste** [grosist] *nmf* : wholesaler
grosso modo [grosomodo] *adv* : more or less, roughly
grotesque [grɔtɛsk] *adj* **1** : grotesque **2** RIDICULE : absurd, ridiculous
grotte [grɔt] *nf* : cave
grouiller [gruje] *vi* **~ de** : swarm with — **se grouiller** *vr fam* : hurry, get a move on
groupe [grup] *nm* **1** : group **2 ~ sanguin** : blood type — **groupement** [grupmɑ̃] *nm* : grouping, group — **grouper** [grupe] *vt* : group — **se grouper** *vr* : gather, get together
gruau [gryo] *nm Can* : oatmeal
grue [gry] *nf* : crane
grumeau [grymo] *nm, pl* **-meaux** : lump (in sauce, etc.)
gruyère [gryjɛr] *nm* : Gruyère (cheese)
gué [ge] *nm* : ford, crossing
guenilles[gənij] *nfpl* : rags and tatters
guenon [gənɔ̃] *nf* : female monkey
guépard [gepar] *nm* : cheetah
guêpe [gɛp] *nf* : wasp — **guêpier** [gepje] *nm* **1** : wasps' nest **2** : tight spot, trap
guère [gɛr] *adv* **ne . . . guère** : hardly, scarcely, rarely
guérilla [gerija] *nf* : guerilla warfare — **guérillero** [gerijero] *nm* : guerilla
guérir [gerir] *vt* : cure, heal — *vi* : get better, heal — **guérison** [gerizɔ̃] *nf* **1** : cure, healing **2** RÉTABLISSEMENT : recovery
guérite [gerit] *nf* : sentry box
guerre [gɛr] *nf* : war — **guerrier, -rière** [gɛrje, -jɛr] *adj* : warlike — **~** *n* : warrior
guetter [gete] *vt* **1** : watch (intently) **2** ATTENDRE : watch out for **3** MENACER : threaten — **guet** [gɛ] *nm* **faire le ~** : be on the lookout — **guet–apens** [gɛtapɑ̃] *nm, pl* **guets–apens** : ambush
gueule [gœl] *nf* **1** : mouth (of an animal, a tunnel, etc.) **2** *fam* : face **3 ta ~!** *fam* : shut up! **4 ~ de bois** : hangover — **gueuler** [gœle] *v fam* : bawl, bellow
gui [gi] *nm* : mistletoe
guichet [giʃɛ] *nm* **1** : window, counter **2** : box office **3 ~ automatique** : automatic teller machine — **guichetier, -tière** [giʃtje, -tjɛr] *n* : counter clerk, teller
guide [gid] *nm* **1** : guide **2** : guidebook — **guider** [gide] *vt* : guide — **guides** *nfpl* : reins
guidon [gidɔ̃] *nm* : handlebars *pl*
guignol [giɲɔl] *nm* **1** : puppet show **2 faire le ~** : clown around
guillemets [gijmɛ] *nmpl* : quotation marks
guilleret, -rette [gijrɛ, -rɛt] *adj* : sprightly, perky
guillotine [gijɔtin] *nf* : guillotine
guimauve [gimov] *nf* : marshmallow
guindé, -dée [gɛ̃de] *adj* : stiff, prim
guirlande [girlɑ̃d] *nf* **1** : garland **2 ~s de Noël** : tinsel
guise [giz] *nf* **1 à ta ~** : as you wish **2 en ~ de** : by way of

guitare [gitar] *nf* : guitar — **guitariste** [gitarist] *nmf* : guitarist
gymnase [ʒimnaz] *nm* : gymnasium — **gymnaste** [ʒimnast] *nmf* : gymnast
gymnastique [ʒimnastik] *nf* : gymnastics
gynécologie [ʒinekɔlɔʒi] *nf* : gynecology — **gynécologue** [ʒinekɔlɔg] *nmf* : gynecologist

H

h [aʃ] *nm* : h, eighth letter of the alphabet
habile [abil] *adj* : skillful, clever — **habilement** [abilmɑ̃] *adv* : skillfully, cleverly — **habileté** [abilte] *nf* : skill, cleverness
habilité, -tée [abilite] *adj* **~ à** : entitled to
habiller [abije] *vt* : dress, clothe — **s'habiller** *vr* **1** : get dressed **2 ~ en** : dress up as — **habillé, -lée** [abije] *adj* **1** : dressed **2** ÉLÉGANT : dressy — **habillement** [abijmɑ̃] *nm* : clothes *pl*, clothing
habit [abi] *nm* **1** : outfit, costume **2** : (religious) habit **3** *or* **~ de soirée** : evening dress, tails *pl* **4 ~s** *nmpl* : clothes
habiter [abite] *vt* : live in, inhabit — *vi* : live, reside — **habitant, -tante** [abitɑ̃, tɑ̃t] *n* **1** : inhabitant **2** : occupant — **habitat** [abita] *nm* **1** : habitat **2** : housing — **habitation** [abitasjɔ̃] *nf* **1** : house, home **2 conditions d'~** : living conditions
habitude [abityd] *nf* **1** : habit **2** COUTUME : custom **3 comme d'~** : as usual **4 d'~** : usually — **habitué, -tuée** [abitɥe] *n* : regular (customer) — **habituel, -tuelle** [abitɥɛl] *adj* : usual, regular — **habituellement** [-tɥɛlmɑ̃] *adv* : usually — **habituer** [abitɥe] *vt* : accustom — **s'habituer** *vr* **~ à** : get used to
hache ['aʃ] *nf* : ax — **haché, -chée** ['aʃe] *adj* **1** : chopped, minced, ground **2** SACCADÉ : jerky — **hacher** ['aʃe] *vt* : chop, mince, grind — **hachette** [aʃɛt] *nf* : hatchet — **hachis** ['aʃi] *nms & pl* : ground or minced food — **hachoir** ['aʃwar] *nm* **1** : meat grinder **2** : chopper, cleaver **3** : cutting board
hagard, -garde ['agar, -gard] *adj* : distraught, wild
haie ['ɛ] *nf* **1** : hedge **2** : hurdle (in sports) **3** : line, row (of persons)
haillons ['ajɔ̃] *nmpl* : rags, tatters
haïr ['air] {48} *vt* : hate — **haine** ['ɛn] *nf* : hatred, hate — **haineux, -neuse** ['ɛnø, -nøz] *adj* : full of hatred
haïtien, -tienne [aisjɛ̃, -sjɛn] *adj* : Haitian
hâle ['al] *nm* : suntan — **hâlé, -lée** ['ale] *adj* : (sun)tanned
haleine [alɛn] *nf* **1** : breath **2 hors d'~** : out of breath
haleter ['alte] {20} *vi* : pant, gasp — **haletant, -tante** ['altɑ̃, -tɑ̃t] *adj* : panting, breathless — **halètement** ['alɛtmɑ̃] *nm* : gasp
hall ['ol] *nm* : hall, lobby
halle ['al] *nf France* : covered market
hallucination [alysinasjɔ̃] *nf* : hallucination
halte ['alt] *nf* **1** ARRÊT : stop, halt **2** : stopping place **3 ~ routière** *Can* : rest area (on a highway)
haltère [altɛr] *nm* : dumbbell — **haltérophilie** [alterɔfili] *nf* : weightlifting
hamac ['amak] *nm* : hammock
hamburger ['ɑ̃bœrgœr] *nm* : hamburger (cooked)
hameçon [amsɔ̃] *nm* : fishhook
hamster ['amstɛr] *nm* : hamster
hanche ['ɑ̃ʃ] *nf* : hip
handball ['ɑdbal] *nm* : handball
handicap ['ɑ̃dikap] *nm* : handicap — **handicapé, -pée** ['ɑ̃dikape] *adj* : handicapped — **~** *n* : handicapped person — **handicaper** ['ɑ̃dikape] *vt* : handicap
hangar ['ɑ̃gar] *nm* **1** : (large) shed **2** *or* **~ d'aviation** : hangar
hanter ['ɑ̃te] *vt* : haunt — **hantise** ['ɑ̃tiz] *nf* : dread
happer ['ape] *vt* **1** : seize, snatch **2 être happé par** : be hit by (a car, etc.)
harceler ['arsəle] {8 *and* 20} *vt* : harass — **harcèlement** ['arsɛlmɑ̃] *nm* : harassment
hardi, -die ['ardi] *adj* : bold, daring — **hardiesse** ['ardjɛs] *nf* : boldness, audacity — **hardiment** ['ardimɑ̃] *adv* : boldly
hareng ['arɑ̃] *nm* : herring

hargne ['arɲ] *nf* : aggressiveness — **hargneux, -neuse** ['arɲø, -ɲøz] *adj* : aggressive, bad-tempered
haricot ['ariko] *nm* **1** : bean **2 ~ vert** : string bean
harmonica [armɔnika] *nm* : harmonica
harmonie [armɔni] *nf* : harmony — **harmonieux, -nieuse** [armɔnjø, -njøz] *adj* : harmonious — **harmoniser** [armɔnize] *vt* : harmonize — **s'harmoniser** *vr* : go well together
harnais ['arnɛ] *nm* : harness — **harnacher** ['arnaʃe] *vt* : harness (an animal)
harpe ['arp] *nf* : harp
harpon ['arpɔ̃] *nm* : harpoon — **harponner** ['arpɔne] *vt fam* : nab, collar
hasard ['azar] *nm* **1** : chance, luck **2 ~s** *nmpl* : hazards, danger **3 au ~** : at random — **hasarder** ['azarde] *vt* : risk, venture — **se hasarder** *vr* **~ à faire** : risk doing — **hasardeux, -deuse** ['azardø, -døz] *adj* : risky
hâte ['at] *nf* **1** : haste, hurry **2 avoir ~ de** : be eager to — **hâter** ['ate] *vt* : hasten, hurry — **se hâter** *vr* : hurry — **hâtif, -tive** ['atif, -tiv] *adj* **1** : hasty, rash **2** PRÉCOCE : early
hausser ['ose] *vt* **1** : raise **2 ~ les épaules** : shrug one's shoulders — **se hausser** *vr* : stand up, reach up — **hausse** ['os] *nf* **1** : rise, increase **2 à la ~** *or* **en ~** : rising, up
haut, haute ['o, 'ot] *adj* **1** : high **2** : high-ranking — **haut** ['o] *adv* **1** : high **2** FORT : loud, loudly — **~** *nm* **1** SOMMET : top **2 des ~s et des bas** : ups and downs **3 en ~** : upstairs **4 en ~ de** : on top of **5 un mètre de ~** : one meter high — **hautain, -taine** ['otɛ̃, -tɛn] *adj* : haughty — **hautbois** ['obwa] *nms & pl* : oboe — **hautement** ['otmɑ̃] *adv* : highly — **hauteur** ['otœr] *nf* **1** : height **2** ARROGANCE : haughtiness — **haut-le-cœur** ['olkœr] *nms & pl* **avoir des ~** : retch, gag — **haut-parleur** ['oparlœr] *nm, pl* **haut-parleurs** : loudspeaker
hâve ['av] *adj* : gaunt
havre ['avr] *nm* : haven
hayon ['ajɔ̃] *nm* : tailgate
hé ['e] *interj* : hey
hebdomadaire [ɛbdɔmadɛr] *adj & nm* : weekly
héberger [ebɛrʒe] {17} *vt* : accommodate, put up — **hébergement** [ebɛrʒəmɑ̃] *nm* : accommodations *pl*
hébété, -tée [ebete] *adj* : dazed — **hébétude** [ebetyd] *nf* : stupor
hébreu [ebrø] *adj m, pl* **-breux** : Hebrew — **~** *nm* : Hebrew (language) — **hébraïque** [ebraik] *adj* : Hebrew, Hebraic
hein ['ɛ̃] *interj* : eh?, what?
hélas ['elas] *interj* : alas!
héler ['ele] {87} *vt* : hail, summon
hélice [elis] *nf* : propeller
hélicoptère [elikɔptɛr] *nm* : helicopter
hémisphère [emisfɛr] *nm* : hemisphere
hémorragie [emɔraʒi] *nf* : bleeding, hemorrhage
hémorroïdes [emɔrɔid] *nfpl* : hemorrhoids
hennir ['enir] *vi* : neigh — **hennissement** ['enismɑ̃] *nm* : neighing
hépatite [epatit] *nf* : hepatitis
herbe [ɛrb] *nf* **1** : grass **2** : herb (in cooking) **3 en ~** : budding **4 mauvaise ~** : weed — **herbage** [ɛrbaʒ] *nm* : pasture — **herbeux, -beuse** [ɛrbø, -bøz] *adj* : grassy — **herbicide** [ɛrbisid] *nm* : weed killer
héréditaire [ereditɛr] *adj* : hereditary — **hérédité** [eredite] *nf* : heredity
hérésie [erezi] *nf* : heresy
hérisser ['erise] *vt* **1** : ruffle up (fur, feathers, etc.) **2 ~ qqn** *fam* : irritate s.o. — **se hérisser** *vr* **1** : stand on end **2** *fam* : bristle (with annoyance) — **hérisson** ['erisɔ̃] *nm* : hedgehog
hériter [erite] *vi* **~ de** : inherit — *vt* : inherit — **héritage** [eritaʒ] *nm* **1** : inheritance **2** : (cultural) heritage — **héritier, -tière** [eritje, -tjɛr] *n* : heir, heiress *f*
hermétique [ɛrmetik] *adj* **1** ÉTANCHE : airtight, watertight **2** OBSCUR : obscure
hernie ['ɛrni] *nf* : hernia
héroïne [erɔin] *nf* **1** : heroine **2** : heroin — **héroïque** [erɔik] *adj* : heroic — **héroïsme** [erɔism] *nm* : heroism
héron ['erɔ̃] *nm* : heron
héros ['ero] *nm* : hero
hésiter [ezite] *vi* : hesitate — **hésitant, -tante** [ezitɑ̃, -tɑ̃t] *adj* : hesitant — **hésitation** [ezitasjɔ̃] *nf* : hesitation
hétérogène [eterɔʒɛn] *adj* : heterogeneous
hétérosexuel, -sexuelle [eterɔsɛksyɛl] *adj & n* : heterosexual
hêtre ['ɛtr] *nm* : beech
heure [œr] *nf* **1** : time **2** : hour **3 ~ de pointe** : rush hour **4 ~s supplémentaires** : overtime **5 quelle ~ est-il?** : what time is it? **6 tout à l'~** : later on
heureux, -reuse [œrø, -røz] *adj* **1**

: happy **2** SATISFAIT : glad, pleased **3** CHANCEUX : fortunate, lucky — **heureusement** [œrøzmɑ̃] *adv* : fortunately, luckily

heurter ['œrte] *vt* **1** : strike, collide with **2** OFFENSER : offend, go against — *vi* : hit, collide — **se heurter** *vr* **~ à** : come up against — **heurt** ['œr] *nm* **1** : collision, crash **2** CONFLIT : conflict

hexagone [ɛgzagɔn] *nm* : hexagon

hiberner [ibɛrne] *vi* : hibernate

hibou ['ibu] *nm, pl* **-boux** [ibu] : owl

hic ['ik] *nm fam* **1** : snag **2 voilà le ~** : that's the trouble

hideux, -deuse ['idø, -døz] *adj* : hideous

hier [ijɛr] *adv* : yesterday

hiérarchie ['jerarʃi] *nf* : hierarchy — **hiérarchique** ['jerarʃik] *adj* : hierarchical

hilarité [ilarite] *nf* : hilarity, mirth — **hilarant, -rante** [ilarɑ̃, -rɑ̃t] *adj* : hilarious — **hilare** [ilar] *adj* : mirthful, merry

hindou, -doue [ɛ̃du] *adj* : Hindu

hippie *or* **hippy** ['ipi] *nmf, pl* **-pies** : hippie

hippique [ipik] *adj* : equestrian, horse — **hippodrome** [ipɔdrom] *nm* : racecourse

hippopotame [ipɔpɔtam] *nm* : hippopotamus

hirondelle [irɔ̃dɛl] *nf* : swallow

hirsute [irsyt] *adj* : hairy, shaggy

hispanique [ispanik] *adj* : Hispanic

hisser ['ise] *vt* : hoist, haul up — **se hisser** *vr* : raise oneself up

histoire [istwar] *nf* **1** : history **2** RÉCIT : story **3** AFFAIRE : affair, matter **4 ~s** *nfpl* : trouble, problems — **historien, -rienne** [istɔrjɛ̃, -rjɛn] *n* : historian — **historique** [istɔrik] *adj* : historical, historic

hiver [ivɛr] *nm* : winter — **hivernal, -nale** [ivɛrnal] *adj, mpl* **-naux** [-no] : winter, wintry

hocher ['ɔʃe] *vt* **~ la tête** : nod, shake one's head

hochet ['ɔʃɛ] *nm* : rattle

hockey ['ɔkɛ] *nm* : hockey

hollandais, -daise ['ɔlɑ̃dɛ, -dɛz] *adj* : Dutch

holocauste [ɔlɔkost] *nm* : holocaust

homard ['ɔmar] *nm* : lobster

homélie [ɔmeli] *nf* : homily

homéopathie [ɔmeɔpati] *nf* : homeopathy

homicide [ɔmisid] *nm* : homicide

hommage [ɔmaʒ] *nm* **1** : homage **2 rendre ~ à** : pay tribute to

homme [ɔm] *nm* **1** : man **2 l'~** : man, mankind **3 ~ d'affaires** : businessman

homme-grenouille [ɔmgrənuj] *nm, pl* **hommes-grenouilles** : frogman

homogène [ɔmɔʒɛn] *adj* : homogeneous

homologue [ɔmɔlɔg] *nmf* : counterpart

homologuer [ɔmɔlɔge] *vt* : ratify, approve

homonyme [ɔmɔnim] *nm* **1** : homonym **2** : namesake

homosexuel, -sexuelle [ɔmɔsɛksyɛl] *adj & n* : homosexual — **homosexualité** [ɔmɔsɛksyalite] *nf* : homosexuality

honnête [ɔnɛt] *adj* **1** : honest **2** JUSTE : reasonable, fair — **honnêtement** [ɔnɛtmɑ̃] *adv* **1** : honestly **2** DÉCEMMENT : fairly, decently — **honnêteté** [ɔnɛtte] *nf* : honesty

honneur [ɔnœr] *nm* **1** : honor **2** MÉRITE : credit

honorer [ɔnɔre] *vt* **1** : honor **2** : be a credit to **3** PAYER : pay (a debt) — **honorable** [ɔnɔrabl] *adj* **1** : honorable **2** CONVENABLE : respectable, decent — **honorablement** [-rabləmɑ̃] *adv* **1** : honorably **2** SUFFISAMMENT : respectably, decently — **honoraire** [ɔnɔrɛr] *adj* : honorary — **honoraires** *nmpl* : fees — **honorifique** [ɔnɔrifik] *adj* : honorary

honte ['ɔ̃t] *nf* **1** : shame **2 avoir ~** : be ashamed — **honteux, -teuse** ['ɔ̃tø, -tøz] *adj* **1** : ashamed **2** DÉSHONORANT : shameful

hôpital [ɔpital] *nm, pl* **-taux** [-to] : hospital

hoquet ['ɔkɛ] *nm* **1** : hiccup **2 avoir le ~** : have the hiccups — **hoqueter** ['ɔkte] {8} *vi* : hiccup

horaire [ɔrɛr] *adj* : hourly — **~** *nm* : timetable, schedule

horizon [ɔrizɔ̃] *nm* **1** : horizon **2** : view, vista — **horizontal, -tale** [ɔrizɔ̃tal] *adj, mpl* **-taux** [-to] : horizontal

horloge [ɔrlɔʒ] *nf* : clock — **horloger, -gère** [ɔrlɔrʒe, -ʒɛr] *n* : watchmaker

hormone [ɔrmɔn] *nf* : hormone

horoscope [ɔrɔskɔp] *nm* : horoscope

horreur [ɔrœr] *nf* **1** : horror **2 avoir ~ de** : detest — **horrible** [ɔribl] *adj* : horrible — **horrifiant, -fiante** [ɔrifjɑ̃, -fjɑ̃t] *adj* : horrifying — **horrifier** [ɔrifje] {96} *vt* : horrify

hors ['ɔr] *prep* **1** : except for, save **2 ~ de** : out of, outside, beyond **3 être ~ de soi** : be beside oneself — **hors-bord** ['ɔrbɔr] *nms & pl* **1** : outboard motor **2** : speedboat — **hors-d'œuvre** ['ɔrdœvr] *nms & pl* : hors d'oeuvre — **hors-la-loi** ['ɔrlalwa] *nms & pl* : outlaw

horticulture [ɔrtikyltyr] *nf* : horticulture

hospice [ɔspis] *nm France* **1** : home (for the elderly, etc.) **2** : hospice

hospitalier, -lière [ɔspitalje, -jɛr] *adj* **1** : hospital **2** ACCUEILLANT : hospitable — **hospitaliser** [ɔspitalize] *vt* : hospitalize — **hospitalité** [ɔspitalite] *nf* : hospitality

hostie [ɔsti] *nf* : host (in religion)

hostile [ɔstil] *adj* : hostile — **hostilité** [ɔstilite] *nf* **1** : hostility **2 ~s** *nfpl* : hostilities, war

hot-dog ['ɔtdɔg] *nm, pl* **hot-dogs** : hot dog

hôte, hôtesse [ot, otɛs] *n* : host, hostess *f* — **hôte** *nmf* : guest

hôtel [otɛl] *nm* **1** : hotel **2 ~ de ville** : town hall — **hôtelier, -lière** [otəlje, -jɛr] *adj* : hotel — **~** *n* : hotel manager, innkeeper — **hôtellerie** [otɛlri] *nf* : hotel business

hôtesse [otɛs] *nf* **1** → **hôte 2** : receptionist **3 ~ de l'air** : stewardess

hotte ['ɔt] *nf* **1** : basket (carried on the back) **2** : hood (of a chimney or stove)

houblon ['ublɔ̃] *nm* : hops *pl*

houe ['u] *nf* : hoe

houille ['uj] *nf* : coal — **houiller, -lère** ['uje, -jɛr] *adj* : coal, coal-mining — **houillère** *nf* : coal mine

houle ['ul] *nf* : swell, surge

houlette ['ulɛt] *nf* **sous la ~ de** : under the guidance of

houleux, -leuse ['ulø, -løz] *adj* : stormy

houppe ['up] *or* **houppette** ['upɛt] *nf* : powder puff

hourra ['ura] *nm & interj* : hurrah

housse ['us] *nf* : cover, dust cover

houx ['u] *nms & pl* : holly

huard *or* **huart** ['yar] *nm Can* : loon

hublot ['yblo] *nm* : porthole

huche ['yʃ] *nf* **~ à pain** : bread box

huer ['ɥe] *vt* : boo — *vi* : hoot — **huées** ['ɥe] *nfpl* : boos, booing

huile [ɥil] *nf* **1** : oil **2** : oil painting — **huiler** [ɥile] *vt* : oil — **huileux, -leuse** [ɥilø, -løz] *adj* : oily — **huilier** [ɥilje] *nm* : cruet

huis [ɥi] *nm* **à ~ clos** : behind closed doors

huissier [ɥisje] *nm* **1** : usher **2** *or* **~ de justice** : bailiff

huit ['ɥit, *before consonant* 'ɥi] *adj* **1** : eight **2** : eighth (in dates) — **~** *nms & pl* : eight —**huitaine** ['ɥitɛn] *nf* **une ~ (de jours)** : about a week — **huitième** ['ɥitjɛm] *adj & nmf & nm* : eighth

huître [ɥitr] *nf* : oyster

hululer ['ylyle] *vi* : hoot — **hululement** ['ylylmɑ̃] *nm* : hoot (of an owl)

humain, -maine [ymɛ̃, -mɛn] *adj* **1** : human **2** BIENVEILLANT : humane — **humain** *nm* : human being — **humanitaire** [ymanitɛr] *adj* : humanitarian — **humanité** [ymanite] *nf* : humanity

humble [œ̃bl] *adj* : humble — **humblement** [œ̃bləmɑ̃] *adv* : humbly

humecter [ymɛkte] *vt* : dampen, moisten

humer ['yme] *vt* **1** : breathe in, inhale **2** : smell

humeur [ymœr] *nf* **1** : mood, humor **2** CARACTÈRE : temperament

humide [ymid] *adj* **1** : moist, damp **2** : humid — **humidité** [ymidite] *nf* **1** : dampness **2** : humidity

humilier [ymilje] {96} *vt* : humiliate — **s'humilier** *vr* : humble oneself — **humiliant, -liante** [ymiljɑ̃, -jɑ̃t] *adj* : humiliating — **humiliation** [ymiljasjɔ̃] *nf* : humiliation — **humilité** [ymilite] *nf* : humility

humour [ymur] *nm* **1** : humor, wit **2 avoir de l'~** : have a sense of humor — **humoriste** [ymɔrist] *nmf* : humorist — **humoristique** [ymɔristik] *adj* : humorous

huppé, -pée ['ype] *adj fam* : posh, high-class

hurler ['yrle] *vt* : yell out — *vi* **1** : howl, roar **2** CRIER : yell, shout — **hurlement** ['yrləmɑ̃] *nm* : howl, yell

hutte ['yt] *nf* : hut

hybride [ibrid] *adj & nm* : hybrid

hydratant, -tante [idratɑ̃, -tɑ̃t] *adj* : moisturizing — **hydratant** *nm* : moisturizer

hydrate [idrat] *nm* **~ de carbon** : carbohydrate

hydraulique [idrolik] *adj* : hydraulic

hydroélectrique *or* **hydro-électrique** [idrɔelɛktrik] *adj* : hydroelectric

hydrogène [idrɔʒɛn] *nm* : hydrogen

hyène [jɛn] *nf* : hyena

hygiène [iʒjɛn] *nf* : hygiene — **hygiénique** [iʒjenik] *adj* : hygienic

hymne [imn] *nm* **1** : hymn **2 ~ nationale** : national anthem
hyperactif, -tive *adj* : hyperactive
hypermétrope [ipɛrmetrɔp] *adj* : farsighted
hypertension [ipɛrtɑ̃sjɔ̃] *nf* : high blood pressure
hypnotiser [ipnɔtize] *vt* : hypnotize — **hypnose** [ipnoz] *nf* : hypnosis
hypocrisie [ipɔkrizi] *nf* : hypocrisy — **hypocrite** [ipɔkrit] *adj* : hypocritical — **~** *nmf* : hypocrite
hypothèque [ipɔtɛk] *nf* : mortgage — **hypothéquer** [ipɔteke] {87} *vt* : mortgage
hypothèse [ipɔtɛz] *nf* : hypothesis — **hypothétique** [ipɔtetik] *adj* : hypothetical
hystérie [isteri] *nf* : hysteria — **hystérique** [isterik] *adj* : hysterical

I

i [i] *nm* : i, ninth letter of the alphabet
iceberg [ajsbɛrg] *nm* : iceberg
ici [isi] *adv* **1** : here **2** : now **3 d'~ là** : by then **4 par ~** : this way
icône [ikon] *nf* : icon
idéal, idéale [ideal] *adj, mpl* **idéals** *or* **idéaux** [ideo] : ideal — **idéal** *nm* : ideal — **idéaliser** [idealize] *vt* : idealize — **idéaliste** [idealist] *adj* : idealistic — **~** *nmf* : idealist
idée [ide] *nf* : idea
identifier [idɑ̃tifje] {96} *vt* : identify — **s'identifier** *vr* **~ à** : identify with — **identification** [idɑ̃tifikasjɔ̃] *nf* : identification — **identique** [idɑ̃tik] *adj* : identical — **identité** [idɑ̃tite] *nf* : identity
idéologie [ideɔlɔʒi] *nf* : ideology — **idéologique** [ideɔlɔʒik] *adj* : ideological
idiome [idjom] *nm* : idiom (language) — **idiomatique** [idjɔmatik] *adj* : idiomatic
idiot, -diote [idjo, -djɔt] *adj* : idiotic — **~** *n* : idiot, fool — **idiotie** [idjɔsi] *nf* : idiocy
idole [idɔl] *nf* : idol — **idolâtrer** [idɔlatre] *vt* : idolize
idyllique [idilik] *adj* : idyllic
igloo [iglu] *nm* : igloo
ignifuge [iɲifyʒ] *adj* : fireproof
ignoble [iɲɔbl] *adj* : base, vile
ignorance [iɲɔrɑ̃s] *nf* : ignorance — **ignorant, -rante** [iɲɔrɑ̃, -rɑ̃t] *adj* : ignorant — **ignorer** [iɲɔre] *vt* **1** : be unaware of **2** : ignore
il [il] *pron* **1** : he, it **2** (*as subject of an impersonal verb*) : it **3 ils** *pron pl* : they **4 il y a** : there is, there are
île [il] *nf* : island, isle
illégal, -gale [ilegal] *adj, mpl* **-gaux** [-go] : illegal — **illégalité** [ilegalite] *nf* : illegality
illégitime [ileʒitim] *adj* : illegitimate — **illégitimité** [ileʒitimite] *nf* : illegitimacy
illettré, -trée [iletre] *adj & n* : illiterate
illicite [ilisit] *adj* : illicit
illimité, -tée [ilimite] *adj* : boundless, unlimited
illisible [ilizibl] *adj* : illegible
illogique [ilɔʒik] *adj* : illogical
illuminer [ilymine] *vt* : illuminate, light up — **illumination** [ilyminasjɔ̃] *nf* : illumination
illusion [ilyzjɔ̃] *nf* : illusion — **illusoire** [ilyzwar] *adj* : illusory
illustration [ilystrasjɔ̃] *nf* : illustration — **illustre** [ilystr] *adj* : illustrious, renowned — **illustré, -trée** [ilystre] *adj* : illustrated — **illustrer** [ilystre] *vt* : illustrate
îlot [ilo] *nm* **1** : small island **2** : block (of houses)
ils [il] → **il**
image [imaʒ] *nf* **1** : image **2** DESSIN : picture
imaginer [imaʒine] *vt* **1** : imagine **2** INVENTER : devise, think up — **s'imaginer** *vr* : picture oneself — **imaginaire** [imaʒinɛr] *adj* : imaginary — **imaginatif, -tive** [imaʒinatif, -tiv] *adj* : imaginative — **imagination** [imaʒinasjɔ̃] *nf* : imagination
imbattable [ɛ̃batabl] *adj* : unbeatable
imbécile [ɛ̃besil] *adj* : stupid, idiotic — **~** *nmf* : fool, idiot — **imbécillité** [ɛ̃besilite] *nf* : idiocy, stupidity
imbiber [ɛ̃bibe] *vt* : soak — **s'imbiber** *vr* : get soaked
imbuvable [ɛ̃byvabl] *adj* : undrinkable
imiter [imite] *vt* **1** COPIER : imitate, mimic **2** : look (just) like — **imitateur, -trice** [imitatœr, -tris] *n* **1** : imitator **2** : impersonator — **imitation** [imitasjɔ̃] *nf* **1** : imitation **2** : impersonation
immaculé, -lée [imakyle] *adj* : immaculate

immangeable [ɛ̃mɑ̃ʒabl] *adj* : inedible
immanquable [ɛ̃mɑ̃kabl] *adj* **1** : impossible to miss **2** INÉVITABLE : inevitable
immatriculer [imatrikyle] *vt* : register — **immatriculation** [imatrikylasjɔ̃] *nf* **1** : registration **2 plaque d'~** : license plate
immature [imatyr] *adj* : immature — **immaturité** [imatyrite] *nf* : immaturity
immédiat, -diate [imedja, -djat] *adj* : immediate — **immédiatement** [-djatmɑ̃] *adv* : immediately
immense [imɑ̃s] *adj* : immense — **immensité** [imɑ̃site] *nf* : immensity
immerger [imɛrʒe] {17} *vt* : immerse, submerge — **immersion** [imɛrsjɔ̃] *nf* : immersion
immeuble [imœbl] *nm* : building
immigrer [imigre] *vi* : immigrate — **immigrant, -grante** [imigrɑ̃, -grɑ̃t] *adj & n* : immigrant — **immigration** [imigrasjɔ̃] *nf* : immigration — **immigré, -grée** [imigre] *n* : immigrant
imminent, -nente [iminɑ̃, -nɑ̃t] *adj* : imminent — **imminence** [iminɑ̃s] *nf* : imminence
immiscer [imise] {6} *v* **s'immiscer** *vr* **~ dans** : interfere with
immobile [imɔbil] *adj* : motionless
immobilier, -lière [imɔbilje, -ljɛr] *adj* : real estate, property
immobiliser [imɔbilize] *vt* **1** : immobilize **2** ARRÊTER : bring to a halt — **s'immobiliser** *vr* : stop — **immobilité** [imɔbilite] *nf* : immobility, stillness
immodéré, -rée [imɔdere] *adj* : immoderate, excessive
immonde [imɔ̃d] *adj* : foul, filthy
immoral, -rale [imɔral] *adj, mpl* **-raux** [-ro] : immoral — **immoralité** [imɔralite] *nf* : immorality
immortalité [imɔrtalite] *nf* : immortality — **immortel, -telle** [imɔrtɛl] *adj* : immortal
immuable [imɥabl] *adj* : unchanging
immuniser [imynize] *vt* : immunize — **immunisation** [-nizasjɔ̃] *nf* : immunization — **immunité** [imynite] *nf* : immunity
impact [ɛ̃pakt] *nm* : impact
impair, -paire [ɛ̃pɛr] *adj* : odd, uneven — **impair** *nm* : blunder
impardonnable [ɛ̃pardɔnabl] *adj* : unforgivable
imparfait, -faite [ɛ̃parfɛ, -fɛt] *adj* : imperfect — **imparfait** *nm* : imperfect (tense)
impartial, -tiale [ɛ̃parsjal] *adj, mpl* **-tiaux** [-sjo] : unbiased, impartial — **impartialité** [ɛ̃parsjalite] *nf* : impartiality
impartir [ɛ̃partir] *vt* : grant, bestow
impasse [ɛ̃pas] *nf* **1** : impasse, deadlock **2** CUL-DE-SAC : dead end
impassible [ɛ̃pasibl] *adj* : impassive
impatient, -tiente [ɛ̃pasjɑ̃, -sjɑ̃t] *adj* : impatient — **impatiemment** [ɛ̃pasjamɑ̃] *adv* : impatiently — **impatience** [-sjɑ̃s] *nf* : impatience — **impatienter** [ɛ̃pasjɑ̃te] *vt* : annoy — **s'impatienter** *vr* : lose patience
impeccable [ɛ̃pekabl] *adj* : impeccable, faultless
impénétrable [ɛ̃penetrabl] *adj* **1** : impenetrable **2** : inscrutable
impénitent, -tente [ɛ̃penitɑ̃, -tɑ̃t] *adj* : unrepentant
impensable [ɛ̃pɑ̃sabl] *adj* : unthinkable
impératif, -tive [ɛ̃peratif, -tiv] *adj* : imperative — **impératif** *nm* : imperative (mood)
impératrice [ɛ̃peratris] *nf* : empress
imperceptible [ɛ̃pɛrsɛptibl] *adj* : imperceptible
imperfection [ɛ̃pɛrfɛksjɔ̃] *nf* : imperfection
impérial, -riale [ɛ̃perjal] *adj, mpl* **-riaux** [-rjo] : imperial — **impérialisme** [ɛ̃perjalism] *nm* : imperialism
impérieux, -rieuse [ɛ̃perjø, -jøz] *adj* **1** : imperious **2** PRESSANT : urgent
impérissable [ɛ̃perisabl] *adj* : imperishable
imperméable [ɛ̃pɛrmeabl] *adj* : waterproof — **~** *nm* : raincoat
impersonnel, -nelle [ɛ̃pɛrsɔnɛl] *adj* : impersonal
impertinent, -nente [ɛ̃pɛrtinɑ̃, -nɑ̃t] *adj* : impertinent — **impertinence** [-tinɑ̃s] *nf* : impertinence
imperturbable [ɛ̃pɛrtyrbabl] *adj* : unflappable
impétueux, -tueuse, [ɛ̃petɥø, -tɥøz] *adj* : impetuous
impitoyable [ɛ̃pitwajabl] *adj* : merciless, pitiless
implacable [ɛ̃plakabl] *adj* : implacable
implanter [ɛ̃plɑ̃te] *vt* **1** : establish **2** : implant (in medicine) — **s'implanter** *vr* : be set up — **implantation** [ɛ̃plɑ̃tasjɔ̃] *nf* : establishment
implication [ɛ̃plikasjɔ̃] *nf* : implication
implicite [ɛ̃plisit] *adj* : implicit
impliquer [ɛ̃plike] *vt* **1** : implicate **2** SUPPOSER : imply **3** ENTRAÎNER : entail,

involve — **s'impliquer** *vr* : become involved
implorer [ɛ̃plɔre] *vt* : implore
imploser [ɛ̃ploze] *vi* : implode
impoli, -lie [ɛ̃pɔli] *adj* : impolite, rude — **impolitesse** [ɛ̃pɔlitɛs] *nf* : rudeness
impopulaire [ɛ̃pɔpylɛr] *adj* : unpopular
importer[1] [ɛ̃pɔrte] *vi* **1** : matter, be important **2 n'importe qui** : anyone, anybody **3 n'importe quoi** : anything **4 peu importe** : no matter — **importance** [ɛ̃pɔrtɑ̃s] *nf* : importance — **important, -tante** [ɛ̃pɔrtɑ̃, -tɑ̃t] *adj* **1** : important **2** LARGE : considerable — **important** *nm* **l'~** : the important thing, the main thing
importer[2] *vt* : import — **importateur, -trice** [ɛ̃pɔrtatœr, -tris] *n* : importer — **importation** [ɛ̃pɔrtasjɔ̃] *nf* **1** : importing **2** : import
importun, -tune [ɛ̃pɔrtœ̃, -tyn] *adj* : troublesome, unwelcome — **~** *n* : nuisance, pest — **importuner** [ɛ̃pɔrtyne] *vt* : pester
imposer [ɛ̃poze] *vt* **1** : impose **2** TAXER : tax — **s'imposer** *vr* **1** : be essential **2** : stand out — **imposable** [ɛ̃pozabl] *adj* : taxable — **imposant, -sante** [ɛ̃pozɑ̃, -zɑ̃t] *adj* : imposing
impossible [ɛ̃pɔsibl] *adj* : impossible — **~** *nm* **l'~** : the impossible — **impossibilité** [ɛ̃pɔsibilite] *nf* : impossibility
imposteur [ɛ̃pɔstœr] *nm* : impostor
impôt [ɛ̃po] *nm* : tax, duty
impotent, -tente [ɛ̃pɔtɑ̃, -tɑ̃t] *adj* : infirm, disabled
impraticable [ɛ̃pratikabl] *adj* : impassable (of a road, etc.)
imprécis, -cise [ɛ̃presi, -siz] *adj* : imprecise — **imprécision** [ɛ̃presizjɔ̃] *nf* : imprecision
imprégner [ɛ̃preɲe] {87} *vt* IMBIBER : impregnate, soak — **s'imprégner** *vr* **~ de** : become filled with
impression [ɛ̃presjɔ̃] *nf* **1** : impression **2** : printing — **impressionnable** [ɛ̃presjɔnabl] *adj* : impressionable — **impressionnant, -nante** [ɛ̃presjɔnɑ̃, -nɑ̃t] *adj* : impressive — **impressionner** [ɛ̃presjɔne] *vt* : impress
imprévisible [ɛ̃previzibl] *adj* : unpredictable
imprévoyance [ɛ̃prevwajɑ̃s] *nf* : lack of foresight — **imprévu, -vue** [ɛ̃prevy] *adj* : unforeseen, unexpected
imprimer [ɛ̃prime] *vt* **1** : print **2** : imprint — **imprimante** [ɛ̃primɑ̃t] *nf* : printer — **imprimé, -mée** [ɛ̃prime] *adj* : printed (of fabric, etc.) — **imprimerie** [ɛ̃primri] *nf* **1** : printing **2** : print shop — **imprimeur, -meuse** [ɛ̃primœr, -møz] *n* : printer
improbable [ɛ̃prɔbabl] *adj* : improbable, unlikely — **improbabilité** [-babilite] *nf* : unlikelihood
impromptu, -tue [ɛ̃prɔ̃pty] *adj* : impromptu
impropre [ɛ̃prɔpr] *adj* **1** INCORRECT : incorrect **2** INADAPTÉ : unsuitable
improviser [ɛ̃prɔvize] *v* : improvise — **improvisation** [ɛ̃prɔvizasjɔ̃] *nf* : improvisation
improviste [ɛ̃prɔvist] **à l'~** *adv phr* : unexpectedly
imprudent, -dente [ɛ̃prydɑ̃, -dɑ̃t] *adj* : rash, careless — **imprudemment** [ɛ̃prydamɑ̃] *adv* : carelessly — **imprudence** [ɛ̃prydɑ̃s] *nf* : carelessness
impudent, -dente [ɛ̃pydɑ̃, -dɑ̃t] *adj* : impudent — **impudence** [ɛ̃pydɑ̃s] *nf* : impudence
impudique [ɛ̃pydik] *adj* : immodest, indecent
impuissance [ɛ̃pɥisɑ̃s] *nf* **1** : helplessness **2** : (physical) impotence — **impuissant, -sante** [ɛ̃pɥisɑ̃, -sɑ̃t] *adj* **1** : helpless **2** : impotent (in medicine)
impulsion [ɛ̃pylsjɔ̃] *nf* **1** : impulse **2** POUSSÉE : impetus — **impulsif, -sive** [ɛ̃pylsif, -siv] *adj* : impulsive — **impulsivité** [ɛ̃pylsivite] *nf* : impulsiveness
impuni, -nie [ɛ̃pyni] *adj* : unpunished — **impunément** [ɛ̃pynemɑ̃] *adv* : with impunity — **impunité** [ɛ̃pynite] *nf* : impunity
impur, -pure [ɛ̃pyr] *adj* : impure — **impureté** [ɛ̃pyrte] *nf* : impurity
imputer [ɛ̃pyte] *vt* : impute
inabordable [inabɔrdabl] *adj* : inaccessible
inacceptable [inaksɛptabl] *adj* : unacceptable
inaccessible [inaksesibl] *adj* : inaccessible
inaccoutumé, -mée [inakutyme] *adj* : unaccustomed
inachevé, -vée [inaʃve] *adj* : unfinished
inaction [inaksjɔ̃] *nf* : inaction, inactivity — **inactif, -tive** [inaktif, -tiv] *adj* : inactive — **inactivité** [inaktivite] *nf* : inactivity
inadapté, -tée [inadapte] *adj* **1** : maladjusted **2 ~ à** : unsuited to, unsuitable for

inadéquat, -quate [inadekwa, -kwat] *adj* : inadequate
inadmissible [inadmisibl] *adj* : unacceptable
inadvertance [inadvɛrtɑ̃s] *nf* **par ~** : inadvertently
inaltérable [inalterabl] *adj* : stable, unchanging
inamovible [inamɔvibl] *adj* : fixed, permanent
inanimé, -mée [inanime] *adj* **1** : inanimate **2** INCONSCIENT : unconscious
inaperçu, -çue [inapɛrsy] *adj* : unseen, unnoticed
inapplicable [inaplikabl] *adj* : inapplicable
inapte [inapt] *adj* : unfit, unsuited
inarticulé, -lée [inartikyle] *adj* : inarticulate
inassouvi, -vie [inasuvi] *adj* : unsatisfied, unfulfilled
inattaquable [inatakabl] *adj* **1** : irreproachable **2** IRRÉFUTABLE : irrefutable
inattendu, -due [inatɑ̃dy] *adj* : unexpected
inattention [inatɑ̃sjɔ̃] *nf* **1** : inattention **2 faute d'~** : careless error — **inattentif, -tive** [inatɑ̃tif, -tiv] *adj* : inattentive, distracted
inaudible [inodibl] *adj* : inaudible
inaugurer [inogyre] *vt* : inaugurate — **inaugural, -rale** [inogyral] *adj, mpl* **-raux** [-ro] : inaugural — **inauguration** [inogyrasjɔ̃] *nf* : inauguration
incalculable [ɛ̃kalkylabl] *adj* : incalculable, countless
incapable [ɛ̃kapabl] *adj* : incapable, unable — **incapacité** [ɛ̃kapasite] *nf* : incapacity, inability
incarcérer [ɛ̃karsere] {87} *vt* : incarcerate
incarner [ɛ̃karne] *vt* : play (a role)
incassable [ɛ̃kasabl] *adj* : unbreakable
incendie [ɛ̃sɑ̃di] *nm* : fire — **incendiaire** [ɛ̃sɑ̃djɛr] *adj* : inflammatory
incendier [ɛ̃sɑ̃dje] {96} *vt* : set on fire
incertain, -taine [ɛ̃sɛrtɛ̃, -tɛn] *adj* **1** : uncertain **2** VAGUE : indistinct — **incertitude** [ɛ̃sɛrtityd] *nf* : uncertainty
incessant, -sante [ɛ̃sesɑ̃, -sɑ̃t] *adj* : incessant
inceste [ɛ̃sɛst] *nm* : incest — **incestueux, -tueuse** [ɛ̃sɛstɥø, -tɥøz] *adj* : incestuous
inchangé, -gée [ɛ̃ʃɑ̃ʒe] *adj* : unchanged
incidence [ɛ̃sidɑ̃s] *nf* : effect, impact
incident [ɛ̃sidɑ] *nm* : incident
incinérer [ɛ̃sinere] {87} *vt* **1** : incinerate **2** : cremate — **incinérateur** [ɛ̃sineratœr] *nm* : incinerator — **incinération** [ɛ̃sinerasjɔ̃] *nf* **1** : incineration **2** : cremation
incision [ɛ̃sizjɔ̃] *nf* : incision
inciter [ɛ̃site] *vt* : incite
incliner [ɛ̃kline] *vt* **1** PENCHER : tilt, bend **2** INCITER : incline, prompt — *vi* **~ à** : be inclined to — **s'incliner** *vr* **1** : tilt, lean **2 ~ devant** : bow to — **inclinaison** [ɛ̃klinɛzɔ̃] *nf* : incline, slope — **inclination** [ɛ̃klinasjɔ̃] *nf* **1** : nod, bow **2** TENDANCE : inclination, tendency
inclure [ɛ̃klyr] {39} *vt* **1** : include **2** JOINDRE : enclose — **inclus, -cluse** [ɛ̃kly, -klyz] *adj* : inclusive — **inclusion** [ɛ̃klyzjɔ̃] *nf* : inclusion
incognito [ɛ̃kɔɲito] *adv & adj* : incognito
incohérent, -rente [ɛ̃kɔerɑ̃, -rɑ̃t] *adj* : incoherent — **incohérence** [ɛ̃kɔerɑ̃s] *nf* : incoherence
incolore [ɛ̃kɔlɔr] *adj* : colorless
incommensurable [ɛ̃kɔmɑ̃syrabl] *adj* : immeasurable
incommode [ɛ̃kɔmɔd] *adj* **1** : inconvenient **2** INCONFORTABLE : uncomfortable — **incommoder** [ɛ̃kɔmɔde] *vt* : inconvenience
incomparable [ɛ̃kɔ̃parabl] *adj* : incomparable
incompatible [ɛ̃kɔ̃patibl] *adj* : incompatible
incompétent, -tente [ɛ̃kɔ̃petɑ̃, -tɑ̃t] *adj* : incompetent — **incompétence** [ɛ̃kɔ̃petɑ̃s] *nf* : incompetence
incomplet, -plète [ɛ̃kɔ̃plɛ, -plɛt] *adj* : incomplete
incompréhensible [ɛ̃kɔ̃preɑ̃sibl] *adj* : incomprehensible — **incompréhension** [ɛ̃kɔ̃preɑ̃sjɔ̃] *nf* : lack of understanding — **incompris, -prise** [ɛ̃kɔ̃pri, -priz] *adj* : misunderstood
inconcevable [ɛ̃kɔ̃svabl] *adj* : inconceivable
inconciliable [ɛ̃kɔ̃siljabl] *adj* : irreconcilable
inconditionnel, -nelle [ɛ̃kɔ̃disjɔnɛl] *adj* : unconditional — **~** *n* : enthusiast
inconduite [ɛ̃kɔ̃dɥit] *nf* : misconduct
inconfort [ɛ̃kɔ̃fɔr] *nm* : discomfort — **inconfortable** [ɛ̃kɔ̃fɔrtabl] *adj* : uncomfortable
incongru, -grue [ɛ̃kɔ̃gry] *adj* **1** : incongruous **2** : unseemly, inappropriate
inconnu, -nue [ɛ̃kɔny] *adj* : unknown

— ~ *n* 1 : unknown (person) 2 ÉTRANGER : stranger
inconscient, -ciente [ɛ̃kɔ̃sjɑ̃, -sjɑ̃t] *adj* 1 : unaware 2 : unconscious — **inconsciemment** [ɛ̃kɔ̃sjamɑ̃] *adv* 1 : unconsciously 2 : thoughtlessly — **inconscience** [ɛ̃kɔ̃sjɑ̃s] *nf* 1 : unconsciousness 2 : thoughtlessness
inconsidéré, -rée [ɛ̃kɔ̃sidere] *adj* : thoughtless
inconsistant, -tante [ɛ̃kɔ̃sistɑ̃, -tɑ̃t] *adj* : flimsy, weak
inconsolable [ɛ̃kɔ̃sɔlabl] *adj* : inconsolable
inconstant, -stante [ɛ̃kɔ̃stɑ̃, -stɑ̃t] *adj* : fickle
incontestable [ɛ̃kɔ̃tɛstabl] *adj* : unquestionable, indisputable — **incontesté, -tée** [ɛ̃kɔ̃tɛste] *adj* : undisputed
incontournable [ɛ̃kɔ̃turnabl] *adj* : essential, that cannot be ignored
inconvenant, -nante [ɛ̃kɔ̃vnɑ̃, -nɑ̃t] *adj* : improper, unseemly — **inconvenance** [ɛ̃kɔ̃vnɑ̃s] *nf* : impropriety
inconvénient [ɛ̃kɔ̃venjɑ̃] *nm* : disadvantage, drawback
incorporer [ɛ̃kɔrpɔre] *vt* : incorporate
incorrect, -recte [ɛ̃kɔrɛkt] *adj* 1 ERRONÉ : incorrect 2 INCONVENANT : improper — **incorrectement** [ɛ̃kɔrɛktəmɑ̃] *adv* : wrongly
incorrigible [ɛ̃kɔriʒibl] *adj* : incorrigible
incrédule [ɛ̃kredyl] *adj* : incredulous
incriminer [ɛ̃krimine] *vt* : incriminate — **incrimination** [ɛ̃kriminasjɔ̃] *nf* : incrimination
incroyable [ɛ̃krwajabl] *adj* : unbelievable, incredible — **incroyant, -croyante** [ɛ̃krwajɑ̃, -jɑ̃t] *n* : unbeliever
inculper [ɛ̃kylpe] *vt* : indict, charge — **inculpation** [ɛ̃kylpasjɔ̃] *nf* : indictment, charge — **inculpé, -pée** [ɛ̃kylpe] *n* : accused, defendant
inculquer [ɛ̃kylke] *vt* : instill
inculte [ɛ̃kylt] *adj* 1 : uncultivated 2 : uneducated
incurable [ɛ̃kyrabl] *adj* : incurable
incursion [ɛ̃kyrsjɔ̃] *nf* : incursion, foray
indécent, -cente [ɛ̃desɑ̃, -sɑ̃t] *adj* : indecent — **indécence** [ɛ̃desɑ̃s] *nf* : indecency
indéchiffrable [ɛ̃deʃifrabl] *adj* : indecipherable
indécis, -cise [ɛ̃desi, -siz] *adj* 1 : indecisive 2 INCERTAIN : undecided — **indécision** [ɛ̃desizjɔ̃] *nf* : indecision
indéfini, -nie [ɛ̃defini] *adj* 1 : indefinite 2 VAGUE : ill-defined — **indéfinissable** [ɛ̃definisabl] *adj* : indefinable
indélébile [ɛ̃delebil] *adj* : indelible
indélicat, -cate [ɛ̃delika, -kat] *adj* 1 : indelicate 2 MALHONNÊTE : dishonest
indemne [ɛ̃dɛmn] *adj* : unharmed
indemnité [ɛ̃dɛmnite] *nf* 1 : indemnity 2 ALLOCATION : allowance — **indemniser** [ɛ̃dɛmnize] *vt* : indemnify, compensate
indéniable [ɛ̃denjabl] *adj* : undeniable
indépendant, -dante [ɛ̃depɑ̃dɑ̃, -dɑ̃t] *adj* : independent — **indépendamment** [ɛ̃depɑ̃damɑ̃] *adv* : independently — **indépendance** [-pɑ̃dɑ̃s] *nf* : independence
indescriptible [ɛ̃dɛskriptibl] *adj* : indescribable
indésirable [ɛ̃dezirabl] *adj* : undesirable
indestructible [ɛ̃dɛstryktibl] *adj* : indestructible
indéterminé, -née [ɛ̃detɛrmine] *adj* : indeterminate, unspecified
index [ɛ̃dɛks] *nm* 1 : index 2 : forefinger, index finger — **indexer** [ɛ̃dekse] *vt* : index
indication [ɛ̃dikasjɔ̃] *nf* 1 : indication 2 RENSEIGNEMENT : information 3 ~s *nfpl* : instructions, directions — **indicateur, -trice** [ɛ̃dikatœr, -tris] *adj* → **panneau, poteau** — ~ *n* : informer — **indicateur** *nm* 1 GUIDE : guide, directory 2 : gauge, meter — **indicatif, -tive** [ɛ̃dikatif, -tiv] *adj* : indicative — **indicatif** *nm* : indicative (mood)
indice [ɛ̃dis] *nm* 1 SIGNE : sign, indication 2 : clue 3 : index (of prices, etc.) 4 ÉVALUATION : rating
indicible [ɛ̃disibl] *adj* : inexpressible
indien, -dienne [ɛ̃djɛ̃, -djɛn] *adj* : Indian
indifférent, -rente [ɛ̃diferɑ̃, -rɑ̃t] *adj* : indifferent — **indifférence** [ɛ̃diferɑ̃s] *nf* : indifference
indigène [ɛ̃diʒɛn] *adj* : indigenous, native — ~ *nmf* : native
indigent, -gente [ɛ̃diʒɑ̃, -ʒɑ̃t] *adj* : destitute
indigestion [ɛ̃diʒɛstjɔ̃] *nf* : indigestion — **indigeste** [ɛ̃diʒɛst] *adj* : indigestible
indignation [ɛ̃diɲasjɔ̃] *nf* : indignation — **indigne** [ɛ̃diɲ] *adj* 1 : unworthy 2 MÉPRISABLE : shameful — **indigné, -gnée** [ɛ̃diɲe] *adj* : indignant — **indigner** [ɛ̃diɲe] *vt* : outrage — **s'indigner** *vr* : be indignant — **indi-**

gnité [ɛ̃diɲite] *nf* **1** : unworthiness **2** : indignity

indigo [ɛ̃digo] *adj & nm* : indigo

indiquer [ɛ̃dike] *vt* **1** : indicate, point out **2** DIRE : give, state — **indiqué, -quée** [ɛ̃dike] *adj* **1** : given, specified **2** RECOMMANDÉ : advisable **3** APPROPRIÉ : appropriate

indirect, -recte [ɛ̃dirɛkt] *adj* : indirect — **indirectement** [-rɛktəmɑ̃] *adv* : indirectly

indiscipliné, -née [ɛ̃disipline] *adj* : undisciplined, unruly

indiscrétion [ɛ̃diskresjɔ̃] *nf* : indiscretion — **indiscret, -crète** [ɛ̃diskrɛ, -krɛt] *adj* : indiscreet

indispensable [ɛ̃dispɑ̃sabl] *adj* : indispensable

indisponible [ɛ̃dispɔnibl] *adj* : unavailable

indisposer [ɛ̃dispoze] *vt* : upset, make ill — **indisposé, -sée** [ɛ̃dispoze] *adj* : unwell — **indisposition** [ɛ̃dispozisjɔ̃] *nf* : ailment, indisposition

indissociable [ɛ̃disɔsjabl] *adj* : inseparable

indistinct, -tincte [ɛ̃distɛ̃(kt), -tɛ̃kt] *adj* : indistinct

individu [ɛ̃dividy] *nm* : individual — **individualité** [ɛ̃dividɥalite] *nf* : individuality — — **individuel, -duelle** [ɛ̃dividɥɛl] *adj* **1** : individual **2** PARTICULIER : personal, private — **individuellement** [ɛ̃dividɥɛlmɑ̃] *adv* : individually

indolent, -lente [ɛ̃dɔlɑ̃, -lɑ̃t] *adj* : lazy — **indolence** [ɛ̃dɔlɑ̃s] *nf* : laziness

indolore [ɛ̃dɔlɔr] *adj* : painless

indomptable [ɛ̃dɔ̃tabl] *adj* : indomitable

indu, -due [ɛ̃dy] *adj* : unseemly, ungodly

induire [ɛ̃dɥir] {49} *vt* **1** INCITER : incite, induce **2** CONCLURE : infer, conclude

indulgence [ɛ̃dylʒɑ̃s] *nf* : indulgence — **indulgent, -gente** [ɛ̃dylʒɑ, -ʒɑ̃t] *adj* : indulgent

indûment [ɛ̃dymɑ̃] *adv* : unduly

industrie [ɛ̃dystri] *nf* : industry — **industrialiser** [ɛ̃dystrijalize] *vt* : industrialize — **industriel, -trielle** [ɛ̃dystrijɛl] *adj* : industrial — **industrieux, -trieuse** [ɛ̃dystrijø, -trijøz] *adj* : industrious

inébranlable [inebrɑ̃labl] *adj* : unshakeable

inédit, -dite [inedi, -dit] *adj* **1** : unpublished **2** ORIGINAL : novel, original

inefficace [inefikas] *adj* **1** : inefficient **2** : ineffective — **inefficacité** [inefikasite] *nf* **1** : inefficiency **2** : ineffectiveness

inégal, -gale [inegal] *adj, mpl* **-gaux** [-go] **1** : unequal **2** IRRÉGULIER : uneven — **inégalé, -lée** [inegale] *adj* : unequaled — **inégalité** [inegalite] *nf* **1** : inequality **2** IRRÉGULARITÉ : unevenness, irregularity

inéligible [ineliʒibl] *adj* : ineligible

inéluctable [inelyktabl] *adj* : inescapable

inepte [inɛpt] *adj* : inept

inépuisable [inepɥizabl] *adj* : inexhaustible

inerte [inɛrt] *adj* **1** : inert, lifeless **2** APATHIQUE : apathetic — **inertie** [inɛrsi] *nf* **1** : inertia **2** APATHIE : apathy

inespéré, -rée [inɛspere] *adj* : unhoped for, unexpected

inestimable [inɛstimabl] *adj* : inestimable

inévitable [inevitabl] *adj* : inevitable — **inévitablement** [-tabləmɑ̃] *adv* : inevitably

inexact, -exacte [inɛgza(kt), -ɛgzakt] *adj* : inaccurate, incorrect

inexcusable [inɛkskyzabl] *adj* : inexcusable

inexistant, -tante [inɛgzistɑ̃, -tɑ̃t] *adj* : nonexistent

inexpérience [inɛksperjɑ̃s] *nf* : inexperience — **inexpérimenté, -tée** [inɛksperimɑ̃te] *adj* : inexperienced

inexplicable [inɛksplikabl] *adj* : inexplicable — **inexpliqué, -quée** [inɛksplike] *adj* : unexplained

inexprimable [inɛksprimabl] *adj* : inexpressible

infaillible [ɛ̃fajibl] *adj* : infallible

infâme [ɛ̃fam] *adj* : vile — **infamie** [ɛ̃fam] *adj* : infamy

infanterie [ɛ̃fɑ̃tri] *nf* : infantry

infantile [ɛ̃fɑ̃til] *adj* : infantile, childish

infarctus [ɛ̃farktys] *nm or* **~ myocarde** : heart attack

infatigable [ɛ̃fatigabl] *adj* : tireless

infect, -fecte [ɛ̃fɛkt] *adj* : revolting, foul — **infecter** [ɛ̃fɛkte] *vt* **1** : infect **2** : contaminate — **s'infecter** *vr* : become infected — **infectieux, -tieuse** [ɛ̃fɛksjø, -tjøz] *adj* : infectious — **infection** [ɛ̃fɛksjɔ̃] *nf* **1** : infection **2** PUANTEUR : stench

inférieur, -rieure [ɛ̃ferjœr] *adj & n* : inferior — **infériorité** [ɛ̃ferjɔrite] *nf* : inferiority

infernal, -nale [ɛ̃fɛrnal] *adj, mpl* **-naux** [-no] : infernal
infertile [ɛ̃fɛrtil] *adj* : infertile — **infertilité** [-tilite] *nf* : infertility
infester [ɛ̃fɛste] *vt* : infest
infidèle [ɛ̃fidɛl] *adj* : unfaithful — **infidélité** [ɛ̃fidelite] *nf* : infidelity
infiltrer [ɛ̃filtre] *vt* : infiltrate — **s'infiltrer** *vr* **~ dans** : seep into, penetrate — **infiltration** [ɛ̃filtrasjɔ̃] *nf* : infiltration
infime [ɛ̃fim] *adj* : minute, tiny
infini, -nie [ɛ̃fini] *adj* : infinite — **infini** *nm* **1** : infinity **2 à l'~** : endlessly — **infinité** [ɛ̃finite] *nf* **1** : infinity **2** : infinite number
infinitif [ɛ̃finitif] *nm* : infinitive
infirme [ɛ̃firm] *adj* : disabled, infirm — **~** *nmf* : disabled person — **infirmerie** [ɛ̃firməri] *nf* : infirmary — **infirmier, -mière** [ɛ̃firmje, -mjɛr] *n* : nurse — **infirmité** [ɛ̃firmite] *nf* : disability
inflammable [ɛ̃flamabl] *adj* : inflammable, flammable — **inflammation** [ɛ̃flamasjɔ̃] *nf* : inflammation
inflation [ɛ̃flasjɔ̃] *nf* : inflation — **inflationniste** [ɛ̃flasjɔnist] *adj* : inflationary
inflexible [ɛ̃flɛksibl] *adj* : inflexible, unbending — **inflexion** [ɛ̃flɛksjɔ̃] *nf* **1** : inflection (of the voice) **2** : nod (of the head)
infliger [ɛ̃fliʒe] {17} *vt* **1** : inflict **2** : impose (a penalty, etc.)
influence [ɛ̃flyɑ̃s] *nf* : influence — **influencer** [ɛ̃flyɑ̃se] {6} *vt* : influence — **influent, -fluente** [ɛ̃flyɑ̃, -flyɑ̃t] *adj* : influential — **influer** [ɛ̃flye] *vi* **~ sur** : have an influence on
informateur, -trice [ɛ̃fɔrmatœr, -tris] *n* : informant, informer
informaticien, -cienne [ɛ̃fɔrmatisjɛ̃, -sjɛn] *n* : computer programmer
information [ɛ̃fɔrmasjɔ̃] *nf* **1** : information **2 ~s** *nfpl* : news — **informatif, -tive** [ɛ̃fɔrmatif, -tiv] *adj* : informative
informatique [ɛ̃fɔrmatik] *adj* : computer — **~** *nf* : computer science — **informatiser** [ɛ̃fɔrmatize] *vt* : computerize
informe [ɛ̃fɔrm] *adj* : shapeless
informer [ɛ̃fɔrme] *vt* : inform — **s'informer** *vr* : inquire
infortune [ɛ̃fɔrtyn] *nf* : misfortune — **infortuné, -née** [ɛ̃fɔrtyne] *adj* : unfortunate
infraction [ɛ̃fraksjɔ̃] *nf* : breach (in law)
infranchissable [ɛ̃frɑ̃ʃisabl] *adj* **1** : insurmountable **2** IMPRACTICABLE : impassable
infrarouge [ɛ̃fraruʒ] *adj* : infrared
infrastructure [ɛ̃frastryktyr] *nf* : infrastructure
infructueux, -tueuse [ɛ̃fryktɥø, -tɥøz] *adj* : fruitless
infuser [ɛ̃fyze] *v* **1** : infuse **2** : brew (tea, etc.) — **infusion** [ɛ̃fyzjɔ̃] *nf* : infusion
ingénieur, -nieure [ɛ̃ʒenjœr] *n* : engineer — **ingénierie** [ɛ̃ʒeniri] *nf* : engineering
ingénieux, -nieuse [ɛ̃ʒenjø, -njøz] *adj* : ingenious — **ingéniosité** [ɛ̃ʒenjɔzite] *nf* : ingenuity
ingénu, -nue [ɛ̃ʒeny] *adj* : ingenuous, naive
ingérence [ɛ̃ʒerɑ̃s] *nf* : interference
ingratitude [ɛ̃gratityd] *nf* : ingratitude — **ingrat, -grate** [ɛ̃gra, -grat] *adj* **1** : ungrateful **2** : thankless
ingrédient [ɛ̃gredjɑ̃] *nm* : ingredient
inhabitable [inabitabl] *adj* : uninhabitable — **inhabité, -tée** [inabite] *adj* : uninhabited
inhabituel, -tuelle [inabitɥɛl] *adj* : unusual
inhaler [inale] *vt* : inhale — **inhalation** [-alasjɔ̃] *nf* : inhaling
inhérent, -rente [inerɑ̃, -rɑ̃t] *adj* : inherent
inhiber [inibe] *vt* : inhibit — **inhibition** [inibisjɔ̃] *nf* : inhibition
inhumain, -maine [inymɛ̃, -mɛn] *adj* : inhuman — **inhumanité** [inymanite] *nf* : inhumanity
inhumer [inyme] *vt* : bury — **inhumation** [inymasjɔ̃] *nf* : burial
initial, -tiale [inisjal] *adj, mpl* **-tiaux** [-sjo] : initial — **initiale** *nf* : initial
initiative [inisjativ] *nf* : initiative
initier [inisje] {96} *vt* : initiate — **initiateur, -trice** [inisjatœr, -tris] *n* **1** : initiator **2** NOVATEUR : innovator — **initiation** [inisjasjɔ̃] *nf* : initiation
injecter [ɛ̃ʒɛkte] *vt* : inject — **injection** [ɛ̃ʒɛksjɔ̃] *nf* : injection
injonction [ɛ̃ʒɔ̃ksjɔ̃] *nf* : order, injunction
injure [ɛ̃ʒyr] *nf* : insult, abuse — **injurier** [ɛ̃ʒyrje] {96} *vt* : insult — **injurieux, -rieuse** [ɛ̃ʒyrjø, -rjøz] *adj* : insulting, abusive
injuste [ɛ̃ʒyst] *adj* : unjust, unfair — **injustice** [ɛ̃ʒystis] *nf* : injustice
injustifié, -fiée [ɛ̃ʒystifje] *adj* : unjustified

inlassable [ɛ̃lasabl] *adj* : tireless
inné, -née [ine] *adj* : innate, inborn
innocent, -cente [inɔsɑ̃, -sɑ̃t] *adj & n* : innocent — **innocence** [inɔsɑ̃s] *nf* : innocence — **innocenter** [inɔsɑ̃te] *vt* : clear, exonerate
innombrable [inɔ̃brabl] *adj* : innumerable, countless
innover [inɔve] *v* : innovate — **innovateur, -trice** [inɔvatœr, -tris] *adj* : innovative — ~ *n* : innovator — **innovation** [inɔvasjɔ̃] *nf* : innovation
inoccupé, -pée [inɔkype] *adj* : unoccupied
inoculer [inɔkyle] *vt* : inoculate — **inoculation** [-kylasjɔ̃] *nf* : inoculation
inodore [inɔdɔr] *adj* : odorless
inoffensif, -sive [inɔfɑ̃sif, -siv] *adj* : inoffensive, harmless
inonder [inɔ̃de] *vt* : flood, inundate — **inondation** [inɔ̃dasjɔ̃] *nf* : flood
inopiné, -née [inɔpine] *adj* : unexpected
inopportun, -tune [inɔpɔrtœ̃, -tyn] *adj* : untimely
inoubliable [inublijabl] *adj* : unforgettable
inouï, inouïe [inwi] *adj* : incredible, unheard of
inquiet, -quiète [ɛ̃kjɛ, -kjɛt] *adj* : anxious, worried — **inquiétant, -tante** [ɛ̃kjetɑ̃, -tɑ̃t] *adj* : worrisome — **inquiéter** [ɛ̃kjete] {87} *vt* **1** : worry **2** DÉRANGER : bother, disturb — **s'inquiéter** *vr* : be worried — **inquiétude** [ɛ̃kjetyd] *nf* : worry, anxiety
inquisition [ɛ̃kizisjɔ̃] *nf* : inquisition
insaisissable [ɛ̃sezisabl] *adj* : elusive
insalubre [ɛ̃salybr] *adj* : unhealthy
insanité [ɛ̃sanite] *nf* : insanity
insatiable [ɛ̃sasjabl] *adj* : insatiable
insatisfait, -faite [ɛ̃satisfɛ, -fɛt] *adj* : dissatisfied — **insatisfaction** [ɛ̃satisfaksjɔ̃] *nf* : dissatisfaction
inscrire [ɛ̃skrir] {33} *vt* **1** ÉCRIRE : write down **2** ENREGISTRER : register, enroll — **s'inscrire** *vr* : register, enroll — **inscription** [ɛ̃skripsjɔ̃] *nf* **1** : inscription **2** : registration, enrollment
insecte [ɛ̃sɛkt] *nm* : insect — **insecticide** [ɛ̃sɛktisid] *nm* : insecticide
insécurité [ɛ̃sekyrite] *nf* : insecurity
insensé, -sée [ɛ̃sɑ̃se] *adj* : crazy, foolish
insensible [ɛ̃sɑ̃sibl] *adj* : insensitive — **insensibilité** [ɛ̃sɑ̃sibilite] *nf* : insensitivity
inséparable [ɛ̃separabl] *adj* : inseparable
insérer [ɛ̃sere] {87} *vt* : insert
insidieux, -dieuse [ɛ̃sidjø, -djøz] *adj* : insidious
insigne [ɛ̃siɲ] *nm* **1** : badge **2** *or* ~**s** *nmpl* : insignia
insignifiant, -fiante [ɛ̃siɲifjɑ̃, -fjɑ̃t] *adj* : insignificant — **insignifiance** [-ɲifjɑ̃s] *nf* : insignificance
insinuation [ɛ̃sinɥasjɔ̃] *nf* : insinuation — **insinuer** [ɛ̃sinɥe] *vt* : insinuate — **s'insinuer** *vr* ~ **dans** : insinuate oneself into, penetrate
insipide [ɛ̃sipid] *adj* : insipid
insister [ɛ̃siste] *vi* **1** : insist **2** ~ **sur** : emphasize, stress — **insistance** [ɛ̃sistɑ̃s] *nf* : insistence — **insistant, -tante** [ɛ̃sistɑ̃, -tɑ̃t] *adj* : insistent
insociable [ɛ̃sɔsjabl] *adj* : unsociable
insolation [ɛ̃sɔlasjɔ̃] *nf* : sunstroke
insolent, -lente [ɛ̃sɔlɑ̃, -lɑ̃t] *adj* : insolent — **insolence** [ɛ̃sɔlɑ̃s] *nf* : insolence
insolite [ɛ̃sɔlit] *adj* : unusual, bizarre
insoluble [ɛ̃sɔlybl] *adj* : insoluble
insolvable [ɛ̃sɔlvabl] *adj* : insolvent
insomnie [ɛ̃sɔmni] *nf* : insomnia
insondable [ɛ̃sɔ̃dabl] *adj* **1** : bottomless **2** IMPÉNÉTRABLE : unfathomable
insonoriser [ɛ̃sɔnɔrize] *vt* : soundproof
insouciant, -ciante [ɛ̃susjɑ̃, -sjɑ̃t] *adj* : carefree — **insouciance** [ɛ̃susjɑ̃s] *nf* : carefree attitude
insoutenable [ɛ̃sutnabl] *adj* **1** : untenable **2** INTOLÉRABLE : unbearable
inspecter [ɛ̃spɛkte] *vt* : inspect — **inspecteur, -trice** [ɛ̃spɛktœr, -tris] *n* : inspector — **inspection** [ɛ̃spɛksjɔ̃] *nf* : inspection
inspirer [ɛ̃spire] *vt* : inspire — *vi* : inhale — **s'inspirer** *vr* ~ **de** : be inspired by — **inspirant, -rante** [ɛ̃spirɑ̃, -rɑ̃t] *adj* : inspirational — **inspiration** [ɛ̃spirasjɔ̃] *nf* **1** : inspiration **2** : breathing in
instable [ɛ̃stabl] *adj* **1** BRANLANT : unsteady **2** : unstable, unsettled — **instabilité** [ɛ̃stabilite] *nf* : instability
installer [ɛ̃stale] *vt* : install, set up — **s'installer** *vr* : settle (in) — **installation** [ɛ̃stalasjɔ̃] *nf* **1** : installation **2** ~**s** *nfpl* : installations, facilities
instance [ɛ̃stɑ̃s] *nf* **1** AUTORITÉ : authority **2** : legal proceedings **3 en** ~ : pending
instant [ɛ̃stɑ̃, -tɑ̃t] *nm* : instant, moment — **instantané, -née** [ɛ̃stɑ̃tane] *adj* : instantaneous, instant — **instantané** *nm* : snapshot

instar [ɛ̃star] **à l'∼ de** *prep phr* : following the example of, like
instaurer [ɛ̃store] *vt* : institute, establish — **instauration** [ɛ̃storasjɔ̃] *nf* : institution
instigateur, -trice [ɛ̃stigatœr, -tris] *n* : instigator — **instigation** [ɛ̃stigasjɔ̃] *nf* : instigation
instinct [ɛ̃stɛ̃] *nm* : instinct — **instinctif, -tive** [ɛ̃stɛ̃ktif, -tiv] *adj* : instinctive, instinctual
instituer [ɛ̃stitɥe] *vt* **1** : institute, establish **2** NOMMER : appoint — **institut** [ɛ̃stity] *nm* : institute — **instituteur, -trice** [ɛ̃stitytœr, -tris] *n* : schoolteacher — **institution** [ɛ̃stitysjɔ̃] *nf* : institution
instruction [ɛ̃stryksjɔ̃] *nf* **1** : instruction, education **2** **∼s** *nfpl* : instructions — **instruire** [ɛ̃strɥir] {49} *vt* **1** : instruct **2** **∼ de** : inform of — **s'instruire** *vr* **1** : educate oneself **2** **∼ de** : find out about — **instruit, -truite** [ɛ̃strɥi, -trɥit] *adj* : learned, educated
instrument [ɛ̃strymɑ̃] *nm* : instrument — **instrumental, -tale** [ɛ̃strymɑ̃tal] *adj, mpl* **-taux** [-to] : instrumental
insu [ɛ̃sy] **à l'∼ de** *prep phr* : without the knowledge of, unknown to
insuffisant, -sante [ɛ̃syfizɑ̃, -zɑ̃t] *adj* : insufficient, inadequate — **insuffisance** [ɛ̃syfizɑ̃s] *nf* : inadequacy
insulaire [ɛ̃sylɛr] *adj* : island, insular — **∼** *nmf* : islander
insuline [ɛ̃sylin] *nf* : insulin
insulter [ɛ̃sylte] *vt* : insult — **insulte** [ɛ̃sylt] *nf* : insult
insupportable [ɛ̃sypɔrtabl] *adj* : unbearable
insurger [ɛ̃syrʒe] {17} *v* **s'insurger** *vr* : rebel, rise up — **insurgé, -gée** [ɛ̃syrʒe] *n* : insurgent, rebel
insurmontable [ɛ̃syrmɔ̃tabl] *adj* : insurmountable
insurrection [ɛ̃syrɛksjɔ̃] *nf* : insurrection
intact, -tacte [ɛ̃takt] *adj* : intact
intangible [ɛ̃tɑ̃ʒibl] *adj* : intangible
intarissable [ɛ̃tarisabl] *adj* : inexhaustible
intégral, -grale [ɛ̃tegral] *adj, mpl* **-graux** [-gro] **1** : complete **2** : unabridged — **intégralité** [ɛ̃tegralite] *nf* : whole — **intégrant, -grante** [ɛ̃tegrɑ̃, -grɑ̃t] *adj* **faire partie intégrante de** : be an integral part of
intègre [ɛ̃tɛgr] *adj* : honest, upright
intégrer [ɛ̃tegre] {87} *vt* : integrate — **s'intégrer** *vr* : integrate
intégrité [ɛ̃tegrite] *nf* : integrity
intellect [ɛ̃telɛkt] *nm* : intellect — **intellectuel, -tuelle** [ɛ̃telɛktɥɛl] *adj & n* : intellectual
intelligent, -gente [ɛ̃teliʒɑ̃, -ʒɑ̃t] *adj* : intelligent — **intelligence** [ɛ̃teliʒɑ̃s] *nf* **1** : intelligence **2** COMPRÉHENSION : understanding — **intelligible** [ɛ̃teliʒibl] *adj* : intelligible, comprehensible
intempéries [ɛtɑ̃peri] *nfpl* : bad weather
intempestif, -tive [ɛ̃tɑ̃pɛstif, -tiv] *adj* : untimely
intense [ɛ̃tɑ̃s] *adj* : intense — **intensément** [ɛ̃tɑ̃semɑ̃] *adv* : intensely — **intensif, -sive** [ɛ̃tɑ̃sif, -siv] *adj* : intensive — **intensifier** [ɛ̃tɑ̃sifje] {96} *vt* : intensify — **intensité** [ɛ̃tɑ̃site] *nf* : intensity
intenter [ɛ̃tɑ̃te] *vt* : initiate, pursue (legal action)
intention [ɛ̃tɑ̃sjɔ̃] *nf* : intention, intent — **intentionnel, -nelle** [ɛ̃tɑ̃sjɔnɛl] *adj* : intentional
interactif, -tive [ɛ̃tɛraktif, -tiv] *adj* : interactive — **interaction** [ɛ̃tɛraksjɔ̃] *nf* : interaction
intercaler [ɛ̃tɛrkale] *vt* : insert
intercéder [ɛ̃tɛrsede] {87} *vi* : intercede
intercepter [ɛ̃tɛrsɛpte] *vt* : intercept
interchangeable [ɛ̃tɛrʃɑ̃ʒabl] *adj* : interchangeable
intercontinental, -tale [ɛ̃tɛrkɔ̃tinɑ̃tal] *adj, mpl* **-taux** [-to] : intercontinental
interdire [ɛ̃tɛrdir] {29} *vt* **1** : ban, prohibit **2** EMPÊCHER : prevent — **interdiction** [ɛ̃tɛrdiksjɔ̃] *nf* : ban, prohibition — **interdit, -dite** [ɛ̃tɛrdi, -dit] *adj* **1** : prohibited **2** STUPÉFAIT : dumbfounded
intéresser [ɛ̃terese] *vt* **1** : interest **2** CONCERNER : concern — **s'intéresser** *vr* **∼ à** : be interested in — **intéressant, -sante** [ɛ̃terɛsɑ̃, -sɑ̃t] *adj* **1** : interesting **2** AVANTAGEUX : attractive, worthwhile — **intéressé, -sée** *adj* **1** : self-interested **2** CONCERNÉ : concerned — **∼** *n* : interested party — **intérêt** [ɛ̃terɛ] *nm* : interest
interface [ɛ̃tɛrfas] *nf* : interface
interférence [ɛ̃tɛrferɑ̃s] *nf* : interference — **interférer** [ɛ̃tɛrfere] {87} *vi* : interfere
intérieur, -rieure [ɛ̃terjœr] *adj* **1** : inner, inside **2** : internal, domestic (in politics) — **intérieur** *nm* **1** : inside (of a drawer, etc.) **2** : interior, home **3** **à l'∼** : indoors **4** **d'∼** : indoor — **in-**

térieurement [ɛ̃tɛrjœrmɑ̃] *adv* : inwardly, internally
intérim [ɛ̃terim] *nm* **1** : interim (period) **2** : temporary activity — **intérimaire** [ɛ̃terimɛr] *adj* : temporary, acting — ~ *nmf* : temporary employee
interjection [ɛ̃tɛrʒɛksjɔ̃] *nf* : interjection
interlocuteur, -trice [ɛ̃tɛrlɔkytœr, -tris] *n* : speaker
intermède [ɛ̃tɛrmɛd] *nm* : interlude
intermédiaire [ɛ̃tɛrmedjɛr] *adj* : intermediate — ~ *nmf* : intermediary, go-between
interminable [ɛ̃tɛrminabl] *adj* : interminable
intermittent, -tente [ɛ̃tɛrmitɑ̃, -tɑ̃t] *adj* : intermittent, sporadic — **intermittence** [ɛ̃tɛrmitɑ̃s] *nf* **par** ~ : intermittently
international, -nale [ɛ̃tɛrnasjɔnal] *adj, mpl* **-naux** [-no] : international
interne [ɛ̃tɛrn] *adj* : internal
interner [ɛ̃tɛrne] *vt* **1** : intern (in politics) **2** : confine (in medicine)
interpeller [ɛ̃tɛrpəle] *vt* **1** : shout at, call out to **2** INTERROGER : question
interphone [ɛ̃tɛrfɔn] *nm* : intercom
interposer [ɛ̃tɛrpoze] *v* **s'interposer** *vr* : intervene
interpréter [ɛ̃tɛrprete] {87} *vt* **1** : interpret **2** : perform, play (a role) — **interprétation** [ɛ̃tɛrpretasjɔ̃] *nf* : interpretation — **interprète** [ɛ̃tɛrprɛt] *nmf* **1** : interpreter **2** REPRÉSENTANT : spokesperson **3** : performer (in theater, etc.)
interroger [ɛ̃terɔʒe] {17} *vt* : interrogate, question — **s'interroger** *vr* ~ **sur** : wonder about — **interrogateur, -trice** [ɛ̃terɔgatœr, -tris] *adj* : questioning — **interrogatif, -tive** [ɛ̃terɔgatif, -tiv] *adj* : interrogative — **interrogation** [ɛ̃terɔgasjɔ̃] *nf* **1** : interrogation **2** : test (in school) — **interrogatoire** [ɛ̃terɔgatwar] *nm* : interrogation, questioning
interrompre [ɛ̃terɔ̃pr] {77} *v* : interrupt — **s'interrompre** *vr* : break off — **interrupteur** [ɛ̃terypœr] *nm* : switch — **interruption** [ɛ̃terypsjɔ̃] *nf* **1** : interruption **2 sans** ~ : continuously
intersection [ɛ̃tɛrsɛksjɔ̃] *nf* : intersection
interurbain, -baine [ɛ̃teryrbɛ̃, -bɛn] *adj* : long-distance — **interurbain** *nm* **l'**~ : long-distance telephone service
intervalle [ɛ̃tɛrval] *nm* **1** : space, gap **2** : interval (of time) **3 dans l'**~ : in the meantime
intervenir [ɛ̃tɛrvənir] {92} *vi* **1** : intervene **2** SURVENIR : take place **3** : operate (in medicine) — **intervention** [ɛ̃tɛrvɑ̃sjɔ̃] *nf* **1** : intervention **2** OPERATION : (medical) operation
intervertir [ɛ̃tɛrvɛrtir] *vt* : invert, reverse
interview [ɛ̃tɛrvju] *nf* : interview — **interviewer** [ɛ̃tɛrvjuve] *vt* : interview
intestin [ɛ̃tɛstɛ̃] *nm* : intestine — **intestinal, -nale** [ɛ̃tɛstinal] *adj, mpl* **-naux** [-no] : intestinal
intime [ɛ̃tim] *adj* **1** : intimate **2** PERSONNEL : private — ~ *nmf* : close friend
intimider [ɛ̃timide] *vt* : intimidate — **intimidant, -dante** [ɛ̃timidɑ̃, -dɑ̃t] *adj* : intimidating — **intimidation** [-midasjɔ̃] *nf* : intimidation
intimité [ɛ̃timite] *nf* : intimacy
intituler [ɛ̃tityle] *vt* : call, title — **s'intituler** *vr* : be called
intolérable [ɛ̃tɔlerabl] *adj* : intolerable, unbearable — **intolérant, -rante** [ɛ̃tɔlerɑ̃, -rɑ̃t] *adj* : intolerant — **intolérance** [-rɑ̃s] *nf* : intolerance
intonation [ɛ̃tɔnasjɔ̃] *nf* : intonation
intoxiquer [ɛ̃tɔksike] *vt* EMPOISONNER : poison — **intoxication** [ɛ̃tɔksikasjɔ̃] *nf* : poisoning
intransigeant, -geante [ɛ̃trɑ̃ziʒɑ, -ʒɑ̃t] *adj* : uncompromising
intransitif, -tive [ɛ̃trɑ̃zitif, -tiv] *adj* : intransitive
intraveineux, -neuse [ɛ̃travɛnø, -nøz] *adj* : intravenous
intrépide [ɛ̃trepid] *adj* : intrepid, fearless
intriguer [ɛ̃trige] *vt* : intrigue, puzzle — *vi* : plot, scheme — **intrigue** [ɛ̃trig] *nf* **1** : intrigue **2** : plot (of a story)
intrinsèque [ɛ̃trɛ̃sɛk] *adj* : intrinsic
introduire [ɛ̃trɔdɥir] {49} *vt* **1** : introduce **2** : show in, bring in **3** INSÉRER : insert **4** : enter, input (data) — **s'introduire** *vr* : penetrate, get in — **introduction** [ɛ̃trɔdyksjɔ̃] *nf* **1** : introduction **2** : insertion
introuvable [ɛ̃truvabl] *adj* : unobtainable, nowhere to be found
introverti, -tie [ɛ̃trɔvɛrti] *adj* : introverted — ~ *n* : introvert
intrusion [ɛ̃tryzjɔ̃] *nf* : intrusion — **intrus, -truse** [ɛ̃try, -tryz] *n* : intruder
intuition [ɛ̃tɥisjɔ̃] *nf* : intuition — **intuitif, -tive** [ɛ̃tɥitif, -tiv] *adj* : intuitive
inuit [inɥi] *adj* : Inuit

inusable [inyzabl] *adj* : durable
inusité, -tée [inyzite] *adj* : unusual, uncommon
inutile [inytil] *adj* **1** : useless **2** SUPERFLU : pointless — **inutilement** [inytilmɑ̃] *adv* : needlessly — **inutilisable** [inytilizabl] *adj* : unusable — **inutilité** [inytilite] *nf* : uselessness
invalide [ɛ̃valid] *adj* : disabled — **~** *nmf* : disabled person — **invalidité** [ɛ̃validite] *nf* : disability
invariable [ɛ̃varjabl] *adj* : invariable
invasion [ɛ̃vazjɔ̃] *nf* : invasion
inventaire [ɛ̃vɑ̃tɛr] *nm* **1** : inventory **2** **faire l'~** : take stock
invention [ɛ̃vɑ̃sjɔ̃] *nf* : invention — **inventer** [ɛ̃vɑ̃te] *vt* : invent — **inventeur, -trice** [ɛ̃vɑ̃tœr, -tris] *n* : inventor — **inventif, -tive** [ɛ̃vɑ̃tif, -tiv] *adj* : inventive
inverse [ɛ̃vɛrs] *adj* : reverse, opposite — **~** *nm* : reverse, opposite — **inversement** [ɛ̃vɛrsəmɑ̃] *adv* : conversely — **inverser** [ɛ̃vɛrse] *vt* : reverse, invert
invertébré, -brée [ɛ̃vɛrtebre] *adj* : invertebrate — **invertébré** *nm* : invertebrate
investigation [ɛ̃vɛstigasjɔ̃] *nf* : investigation
investir [ɛ̃vɛstir] *v* : invest — **investissement** [ɛ̃vɛstismɑ̃] *nm* : investment — **investisseur, -seuse** [ɛ̃vɛstisœr, -søz] *n* : investor
invétéré, -rée [ɛ̃vetere] *adj* : inveterate
invincible [ɛ̃vɛ̃sibl] *adj* : invincible
invisible [ɛ̃vizibl] *adj* : invisible
inviter [ɛ̃vite] *vt* : invite — **invitation** [ɛ̃vitasjɔ̃] *nf* : invitation — **invité, -tée** [ɛ̃vite] *n* : guest
involontaire [ɛ̃vɔlɔ̃tɛr] *adj* : involuntary
invoquer [ɛ̃vɔke] *vt* : invoke
invraisemblable [ɛ̃vrɛsɑ̃blabl] *adj* : improbable, unlikely
invulnérable [ɛ̃vylnerabl] *adj* : invulnerable
iode [jɔd] *nm* : iodine
ion [jɔ̃] *nm* : ion
iris [iris] *nm* : iris
irlandais, -daise [irlɑ̃dɛ, -dɛz] *adj* : Irish
ironie [irɔni] *nf* : irony — **ironique** [irɔnik] *adj* : ironic(al)
irradier [iradje] {96} *vt* : irradiate — *vi* : radiate
irrationnel, -nelle [irasjɔnɛl] *adj* : irrational
irréalisable [irealizabl] *adj* : unworkable
irréconciliable [irekɔ̃siljabl] *adj* : irreconcilable
irrécupérable [irekyperabl] *adj* : irretrievable, beyond repair
irréel, -réelle [ireɛl] *adj* : unreal
irréfléchi, -chie [irefleʃi] *adj* : thoughtless, rash
irréfutable [irefytabl] *adj* : irrefutable
irrégulier, -lière [iregylje, -ljɛr] *adj* : irregular — **irrégularité** [iregylarite] *nf* : irregularity
irrémédiable [iremedjabl] *adj* : irreparable
irremplaçable [irɑ̃plasabl] *adj* : irreplaceable
irréparable [ireparabl] *adj* : irreparable
irréprochable [ireprɔʃabl] *adj* : irreproachable, blameless
irrésistible [irezistibl] *adj* : irresistible
irrésolu, -lue [irezɔly] *adj* **1** INDÉCIS : irresolute **2** : unresolved (of a problem)
irrespectueux, -tueuse [irɛspɛktɥø, -tɥøz] *adj* : disrespectful
irresponsable [irɛspɔ̃sabl] *adj* : irresponsible — **irresponsabilité** [irɛspɔ̃sabilite] *nf* : irresponsibility
irrigation [irigasjɔ̃] *nf* : irrigation — **irriguer** [irige] *vt* : irrigate
irriter [irite] *vt* : irritate — **s'irriter** *vr* : get irritated — **irritable** [iritabl] *adj* : irritable — **irritation** [iritasjɔ̃] *nf* : irritation
irruption [irypsjɔ̃] *nf* : bursting in
islam [islam] *nm* : Islam — **islamique** [islamik] *adj* : Islamic
isoler [izɔle] *vt* **1** : isolate **2** : insulate — **s'isoler** *vr* : isolate oneself — **isolation** [izɔlasjɔ̃] *nf* : insulation — **isolement** [izɔlmɑ̃] *nm* **1** : isolation **2** ISOLATION : insulation — **isolément** [izɔlemɑ̃] *adv* : separately, individually
israélien, -lienne [israeljɛ̃, -ljɛn] *adj* : Israeli
issu, -sue [isy] *adj* **~ de 1** : descended from **2** : resulting from
issue *nf* **1** SORTIE : exit **2** SOLUTION : solution **3** FIN : ending, outcome
isthme [ism] *nm* : isthmus
italien, -lienne [italjɛ̃, -ljɛn] *adj* : Italian — **italien** *nm* : Italian (language)
italique [italik] *nm* : italics *pl*
itinéraire [itinerɛr] *nm* : itinerary
itinérant, -rante [itinerɑ̃, -rɑ̃t] *adj* : itinerant
ivoire [ivwar] *adj & nm* : ivory
ivre [ivr] *adj* : drunk — **ivresse** [ivrɛs] *nf* : drunkenness — **ivrogne, ivrognesse** [ivrɔɲ, -ɲɛs] *n* : drunkard

J

j [ʒi] *nm* : j, 10th letter of the alphabet
jacasser [ʒakase] *vi* : chatter, jabber
jachère [ʒaʃɛr] *nf* : fallow land
jacinthe [ʒasɛ̃t] *nf* : hyacinth
jadis [ʒadis] *adv* : in times past, formerly
jaillir [ʒajir] *vi* **1** : spurt out, gush (out) **2** APPARAÎTRE : spring up, emerge
jais [ʒɛ] *nms & pl* **1** : jet (stone) **2 de ~** : jet-black
jalon [ʒalɔ̃] *nm* : marker, milestone — **jalonner** [ʒalɔne] *vt* **1** : mark out (a route, etc.) **2** LONGER : line
jaloux, -louse [ʒalu, -luz] *adj* : jealous — **jalouser** [ʒaluze] *vt* : be jealous of — **jalousie** [ʒaluzi] *nf* **1** : jealousy **2** : venetian blind
jamais [ʒamɛ] *adv* **1** : ever **2 ne ... ~** : never **3 à ~** *or* **pour ~** : forever
jambe [ʒɑ̃b] *nf* : leg
jambon [ʒɑ̃bɔ̃] *nm* : ham
jante [ʒɑ̃t] *nf* : rim (of a wheel)
janvier [ʒɑ̃vje] *nm* : January
japonais, -naise [ʒapɔnɛ, -nɛz] *adj* : Japanese — **japonais** *nm* : Japanese (language)
japper [ʒape] *vi* : yap, yelp
jaquette [ʒakɛt] *nf* **1** : dust jacket **2** : jacket (for women)
jardin [ʒardɛ̃] *nm* **1** : garden **2 ~ d'enfants** *France* : kindergarten **3 ~ zoologique** : zoo — **jardinage** [ʒardinaʒ] *nm* : gardening — **jardiner** [ʒardine] *vi* : garden — **jardinier, -nière** *n* : gardener — **jardinière** *nf* : plant stand, window box
jargon [ʒargɔ̃] *nm* **1** : jargon **2** CHARABIA : gibberish
jarre [ʒar] *nf* : (earthenware) jar
jarret [ʒarɛ] *nm* **1** : back of the knee **2** : shank (in cooking) — **jarretelle** [ʒartɛl] *nf* : garter belt — **jarretière** [ʒartjɛr] *nf* : garter
jaser [ʒaze] *vi* **1** : chatter, prattle **2** MÉDIRE : gossip
jatte [ʒat] *nf* : bowl, basin
jauge [ʒoʒ] *nf* **1** : capacity **2** INDICATEUR : gauge — **jauger** [ʒoʒe] {17} *vt* : gauge
jaune [ʒon] *adj* : yellow — **~** *nm* **1** : yellow **2** *or* **~ d'œuf** : egg yolk — **jaunir** [ʒonir] *v* : turn yellow — **jaunisse** [ʒonis] *nf* : jaundice
Javel [ʒavɛl] *nf* → **eau**
javelot [ʒavlo] *nm* : javelin
jazz [dʒaz] *nm* : jazz
je [ʒə] (j' *before vowel or mute h*) *pron* : I
jean [dʒin] *nm* **1** : denim **2** : (blue) jeans *pl*
jeep [dʒip] *nf* : jeep
jersey [ʒɛrzɛ] *nm* : jersey (fabric)
Jésus [ʒezy] *nm* : Jesus
jeter [ʒəte] {8} *vt* **1** LANCER : throw **2** : throw away **3** ÉMETTRE : give off **4 ~ l'éponge** : throw in the towel **5 ~ un coup d'œil** : take a look at **6 ~ un sort** : cast a spell — **se jeter** *vr* **1 ~ dans** : flow into **2 ~ sur** : pounce on — **jet** [ʒɛ] *nm* **1** : jet, spurt **2** LANCER : throw, throwing **3** : jet (airplane) **4 ~ d'eau** : fountain — **jetable** [ʒətabl] *adj* : disposable — **jetée** [ʒəte] *nf* : pier, jetty
jeton [ʒətɔ̃] *nm* : token, counter
jeu [ʒø] *nm, pl* **jeux 1** DIVERTISSEMENT : play **2** : game **3** : set (of chess, etc.), deck (of playing cards) **4 ~ de dames** : checkers **5 ~ de mots** : pun **6 en ~** : at stake **7 le ~** : gambling
jeudi [ʒødi] *nm* : Thursday
jeun [ʒœ̃] **à ~** *adv phr* : on an empty stomach
jeune [ʒœn] *adj* **1** : young **2** CADET : younger **3** RÉCENT : new, recent — **~** *nmf* **1** : young person **2 les ~s** : young people
jeûner [ʒøne] *vi* : fast — **jeûne** [ʒøn] *nm* : fast
jeunesse [ʒœnɛs] *nf* **1** : youth **2** : youthfulness **3** JEUNES : young people
joaillier, -lière [ʒɔaje, -jɛr] *n* : jeweler — **joaillerie** [ʒɔajri] *nf* **1** : jewelry store **2** : jewelry
job [dʒɔb] *nm fam* : job
jockey [ʒɔkɛ] *nm* : jockey
jogging [dʒɔgiŋ] *nm* **1** : jogging **2** : sweat suit
joie [ʒwa] *nf* : joy
joindre [ʒwɛ̃dr] {50} *vt* **1** : join, link, combine **2** INCLURE : enclose, attach **3** CONTACTER : reach, contact — **se joindre** *vr* **1** : join together **2 ~ à** : join in — **joint** [ʒwɛ̃] *nm* **1** : joint **2** : seal, washer

joker [ʒɔkɛr] *nm* : joker (in playing cards)
joli, -lie [ʒɔli] *adj* **1** BEAU : pretty, attractive **2** : nice — **joliment** [ʒɔlimɑ̃] *adv* **1** : nicely **2** *fam* : really, awfully
jonc [ʒɔ̃] *nm* **1** : reed, rush **2** : (wedding) band
joncher [ʒɔ̃ʃe] *vt* **~ de** : strew with, litter with
jonction [ʒɔ̃ksjɔ̃] *nf* : junction
jongler [ʒɔ̃gle] *vi* : juggle — **jongleur, -gleuse** [ʒɔ̃glœr, -gløz] *n* : juggler
jonquille [ʒɔ̃kij] *nf* : daffodil
joue [ʒu] *nf* : cheek
jouer [ʒwe] *vi* **1** : play **2** : act, perform **3** PARIER : gamble **4 faire ~** : flex — *vt* **1** : play **2** PARIER : bet, wager **3** : perform — **jouet** [ʒwɛ] *nm* : toy, plaything — **joueur, joueuse** [ʒwœr, ʒwøz] *n* **1** : player **2** : gambler
joufflu, -flue [ʒufly] *adj* : chubby-cheeked
joug [ʒu] *nm* : yoke
jouir [ʒwir] *vi* **~ de** : enjoy — **jouissance** [ʒwisɑ̃s] *nf* **1** : pleasure **2** : use, (legal) possession
jour [ʒur] *nm* **1** : day **2** : daylight, daytime **3** ASPECT : aspect, light **4 ~ de l'An** : New Year's Day **5 de nos ~s** : nowadays **6 donner le ~ à** : give birth to **7 mettre à ~** : update
journal [ʒurnal] *nm, pl* **-naux 1** : diary, journal **2** : newspaper **3 ~ télévisé** : television news
journalier, -lière [ʒurnalje, -ljɛr] *adj* : daily — **~** *n* : day worker, laborer
journaliste [ʒurnalist] *nmf* : journalist — **journalisme** [ʒurnalism] *nm* : journalism
journée [ʒurne] *nf* **1** : day **2 toute la ~** : all day long
jovial, -viale [ʒɔvjal] *adj, mpl* **-vials** *or* **-viaux** [-vjo] : jovial
joyau [ʒwajo] *nm, pl* **joyaux** : jewel, gem
joyeux, joyeuse [ʒwajø, -jøz] *adj* **1** : joyful, happy **2 Joyeux Noël!** : Merry Christmas!
jubiler [ʒybile] *vi* : rejoice, be jubilant — **jubilé** [ʒybile] *nm* : jubilee — **jubilation** [ʒybilasjɔ̃] *nf* : jubilation
jucher [ʒyʃe] *v* **se jucher** *vr* **~ sur** : perch on
judaïque [ʒydaik] *adj* : Judaic — **judaïsme** [ʒydaism] *nm* : Judaism
judiciaire [ʒydisjɛr] *adj* : judicial — **judicieux, -cieuse** [ʒydisjø, -sjøz] *adj* : judicious
judo [ʒydo] *nm* : judo
juger [ʒyʒe] {17} *vt* **1** ÉVALUER : judge **2** CONSIDÉRER : think, consider **3** : try (in law) **4 ~ de** : assess — **se juger** *vr* : consider oneself — **juge** [ʒyʒ] *nm* : judge — **jugement** [ʒyʒmɑ̃] *nm* **1** : judgment, opinion **2** VERDICT : verdict, sentence
juguler [ʒygyle] *vt* : stifle, suppress
juif, juive [ʒɥif, ʒɥiv] *adj* : Jewish
juillet [ʒɥijɛ] *nm* : July
juin [ʒɥɛ̃] *nm* : June
jumeau, -melle [ʒymo, -mɛl] *adj & n, mpl* **-meaux** : twin — **jumeler** [ʒymle] {8} *vt* : twin, couple — **jumelles** [ʒymɛl] *nfpl* : binoculars, field glasses
jument [ʒymɑ̃] *nf* : mare
jungle [ʒœ̃gl] *nf* : jungle
junior [ʒynjɔr] *adj & nmf* : junior
jupe [ʒyp] *nf* : skirt — **jupon** [ʒypɔ̃] *nm* : slip, petticoat
jurer [ʒyre] *vt* : swear, vow — *vi* **1** : swear, curse **2 ~ avec** : clash with **3 ~ de** : swear to — **juré, -rée** [ʒyre] *n* : juror
juridiction [ʒyridiksjɔ̃] *nf* : jurisdiction
juridique [ʒyridik] *adj* : legal
juriste [ʒyrist] *nmf* : legal expert, lawyer
juron [ʒyrɔ̃] *nm* : swearword
jury [ʒyri] *nm* : jury
jus [ʒy] *nms & pl* **1** : juice **2** : gravy
jusque [ʒyskə] (**jusqu'** [ʒysk] *before a vowel*) *prep* **1** : even **2** *or* **jusqu'à** : up to, as far as **3 jusqu'à** *or* **jusqu'en** : until **4 jusqu'à présent** : up to now **5 jusqu'où?** : how far?
justaucorps [ʒystokɔr] *nms & pl* : leotard
juste [ʒyst] *adj* **1** ÉQUITABLE : just, fair **2** EXACT : correct, accurate **3** SERRÉ : tight **4 au ~** : exactly, precisely — **~** *adv* **1** : just, exactly **2** : in tune **3** *or* **tout ~** : only just, barely — **justement** [ʒystəmɑ̃] *adv* **1** EXACTEMENT : exactly, precisely **2** ÉQUITABLEMENT : justly **3** : just now — **justesse** [ʒystɛs] *nf* **1** PRÉCISION : accuracy **2** : soundness (of reasoning, etc.) **3 de ~** : just barely
justice [ʒystis] *nf* **1** ÉQUITÉ : fairness **2** : law, justice
justifier [ʒystifje] {96} *vt* : justify — *vi* **~ de** : give proof of — **se justifier** *vr* : justify oneself — **justification** [ʒustifikasjɔ̃] *nf* : justification
juteux, -teuse [ʒytø, -tøz] *adj* : juicy
juvénile [ʒyvenil] *adj* : youthful, juvenile
juxtaposer [ʒykstapoze] *vt* : juxtapose

K

k [ka] *nm* : k, 11th letter of the alphabet
kaki [kaki] *adj* : khaki
kangourou [kɑ̃guru] *nm* : kangaroo
karaté [karate] *nm* : karate
kascher [kaʃɛr] *adj* : kosher
kayak *or* **kayac** [kajak] *nm* : kayak
kermesse [kɛrmɛs] *nf* : fair, bazaar
kérosène [kerɔzɛn] *nm* : kerosene
ketchup [kɛtʃœp] *nm* : ketchup
kidnapper [kidnape] *vt* : kidnap — **kidnappeur, -peuse** [kidnapœr, -pøz] *n* : kidnapper
kilo [kilo] *nm* : kilo — **kilogramme** [kilɔgram] *nm* : kilogram — **kilomètre** [kilɔmɛtr] *nm* : kilometer — **kilométrage** [kilɔmetraʒ] *nm* : distance in kilometers, mileage — **kilowatt** [kilɔwat] *nm* : kilowatt
kimono [kimɔno] *nm* : kimono
kinésithérapie [kineziterapi] *nf* : physical therapy
kiosque [kjɔsk] *nm* **1** : kiosk, stall **2** **~ à musique** : bandstand
kiwi [kiwi] *nm* : kiwi
klaxon [klaksɔn] *nm* : horn — **klaxonner** [klaksɔne] *vi* : honk
kyrielle [kirjɛl] *nf* **une ~ de** : a string of
kyste [kist] *nm* : cyst

L

l [ɛl] *nm* : l, 12th letter of the alphabet
l' *pron & art* → **le**
la *pron & art* → **le**
là [la] *adv* **1** (*indicating a place*) : there, here **2** : then **3** (*indicating a situation or a certain point*) : when **4 de ~** : hence **5 ~ où** : where **6 par ~** : over there, that way — **là-bas** [laba] *adv* : over there
label [labɛl] *nm* : label
labeur [labœr] *nm* : toil, labor
laboratoire [labɔratwar] *nm* : laboratory
laborieux, -rieuse [labɔrjø, -rjøz] *adj* **1** : laborious **2** INDUSTRIEUX : hard-working
labourer [labure] *vt* : plow — **labour** [labur] *nm* : plowing
labyrinthe [labirɛ̃t] *nm* : labyrinth, maze
lac [lak] *nm* : lake
lacer [lase] {6} *vt* : lace up
lacérer [lasere] {87} *vt* : tear up, shred
lacet [lasɛ] *nm* **1** : shoelace **2** : sharp bend (in a road)
lâcher [laʃe] *vt* **1** RELÂCHER : loosen **2** LIBÉRER : release **3** : let out (a word, etc.) **4** *fam* : drop (someone) — *vi* : give way — **lâche** [laʃ] *adj* **1** : loose, slack **2** POLTRON : cowardly — **~** *nmf* : coward — **lâcheté** [laʃte] *nf* : cowardice
laconique [lakɔnik] *adj* : laconic
lacrymogène [lakrimɔʒɛn] *adj* **gaz ~** : tear gas
lacune [lakyn] *nf* : gap
là-dedans [laddɑ̃] *adv* : in here, in there
là-dessous [ladsu] *adv* : under here, under there
là-dessus [ladsy] *adv* **1** : on here, on there **2 il n'y a aucun doute ~** : there's no doubt about it
ladite → **ledit**
lagune [lagyn] *nf* : lagoon
là-haut [lao] *adv* **1** : up there **2** : upstairs
laïc [laik] *nm* **les ~s** : the laity
laid, laide [lɛ, lɛd] *adj* **1** : ugly **2** : despicable (of an action) — **laideur** [lɛdœr] *nf* : ugliness
laine [lɛn] *nf* : wool — **lainage** [lɛnaʒ] *nm* **1** : woolen fabric **2** : woolen garment
laïque [laik] *adj* : lay, secular — **~** *nmf* : layman, laywoman
laisse [lɛs] *nf* : lead, leash
laisser [lɛse] *vt* : leave — *v aux* **1** : let, allow **2 ~ faire** : not interfere — **se laisser** *vr* **1** : allow oneself **2 ~ aller** : let oneself go — **laisser-aller** [lɛseale] *nms & pl* : carelessness — **laissez-passer** [lɛsepase] *nms & pl* : pass, permit

lait [lɛ] *nm* : milk — **laiterie** [lɛtri] *nf* **1** : dairy industry **2** : dairy — **laiteux, -teuse** [lɛtø, -tøz] *adj* : milky — **laitier, -tière** [lɛtje, -tjɛr] *adj* : dairy — ~ *n* **1** : milkman **2** : dairyman
laiton [lɛtɔ̃] *nm* : brass
laitue [lety] *nf* : lettuce
lambeau [lɑ̃bo] *nm, pl* **-beaux 1** : rag, scrap **2 en ~x** : in tatters
lambiner [lɑ̃bine] *vi fam* : dawdle
lambris [lɑ̃bri] *nms & pl* : paneling
lame [lam] *nf* **1** : strip, slat **2 ~ de rasoir** : razor blade — **lamelle** [lamɛl] *nf* : thin strip
lamenter [lamɑ̃te] *v* **se lamenter** *vr* : lament — **lamentable** [lamɑ̃tabl] *adj* **1** : deplorable **2** PITOYABLE : pitiful, pathetic
lampe [lɑ̃p] *nf* **1** : lamp **2 ~ de poche** : flashlight — **lampadaire** [lɑ̃padɛr] *nm* **1** : floor lamp **2** : streetlight — **lampion** [lɑ̃pjɔ̃] *nm* : Chinese lantern
lance [lɑ̃s] *nf* **1** : spear, lance **2** *or* **~ à eau** : hose
lancée [lɑ̃se] *nf* **1** : momentum **2 continuer sur sa ~** : keep going
lancer [lɑ̃se] {6} *vt* **1** : throw, hurl **2** : launch **3** ÉMETTRE : issue, give out **4** : start up (a motor) — **se lancer** *vr* **~ dans** : launch into — ~ *nm* : throw, throwing — **lancement** [lɑ̃smɑ̃] *nm* **1** : throwing **2** : launching — **lance–pierres** [lɑ̃spjɛr] *nms & pl* : slingshot
lanciner [lɑ̃sine] *vi* : throb — *vt* : haunt, obsess — **lancinant, -nante** [lɑ̃sinɑ̃, -nɑ̃t] *adj* : shooting, throbbing
landau [lɑ̃do] *nm France* : baby carriage
lande [lɑ̃d] *nf* ; moor, heath
langage [lɑ̃gaʒ] *nm* : language
lange [lɑ̃ʒ] *nm* : baby blanket
langouste [lɑ̃gust] *nf* : crayfish — **langoustine** [lɑ̃gustin] *nf* : prawn
langue [lɑ̃g] *nf* **1** : tongue **2** : language — **languette** [lɑ̃gɛt] *nf* **1** : tongue (of a shoe) **2** : strip
langueur [lɑ̃gœr] *nf* : languor, lethargy — **languir** [lɑ̃gir] *vi* **1** : languish, pine **2** : flag (of conversation, etc.) — **languissant, -sante** [lɑ̃gisɑ̃, -sɑ̃t] *adj* : languid, listless
lanière [lanjɛr] *nf* : strap, lash, thong
lanterne [lɑ̃tɛrn] *nf* **1** LAMPE : lantern **2** : parking light
laper [lape] *vt* : lap up
lapider [lapide] *vt* : stone
lapin, -pine [lapɛ̃, -pin] *n* **1** : rabbit **2 poser un ~ à qqn** : stand s.o. up
laps [laps] *nms & pl* : lapse (of time) — **lapsus** [lapsys] *nms & pl* : slip, error
laque [lak] *nf* **1** : lacquer **2** : hair spray
laquelle → **lequel**
larcin [larsɛ̃] *nm* : petty theft
lard [lar] *nm* **1** : fat, lard **2** : bacon
large [larʒ] *adj* **1** : wide, broad **2** CONSIDÉRABLE : extensive **3** AMPLE : loose-fitting **4** GÉNÉREUX : generous — ~ *nm* **1 de ~** : wide, in width **2 le ~** : the open sea — ~ *adv* : on a large scale, generously — **largement** [larʒəmɑ̃] *adv* **1** : widely **2** DE BEAUCOUP : greatly, by far **3** GÉNÉREUSEMENT : generously **4** AU MOINS : easily — **largesse** [larʒɛs] *nf* : generosity — **largeur** [larʒœr] *nf* **1** : width, breadth **2 ~ d'esprit** : broad-mindedness
larguer [large] *vt* **1** : release, drop **2** *fam* : ditch, get rid of
larme [larm] *nf* **1** : tear **2** *fam* : drop, small quantity — **larmoyant, -moyante** [larmwajɑ̃, -mwajɑ̃t] *adj* : tearful
larve [larv] *nf* : larva
larynx [larɛ̃ks] *nms & pl* : larynx — **laryngite** [larɛ̃ʒit] *nf* : laryngitis
las, lasse [la, las] *adj* : weary
lasagne [lazaɲ] *nf* : lasagna
laser [lazɛr] *nm* : laser
lasser [lase] *vt* **1** : weary, tire out **2** ENNUYER : bore — **se lasser** *vr* **~ de** : grow weary of — **lassitude** [lasityd] *nf* : weariness
latent, -tente [latɑ̃, -tɑ̃t] *adj* : latent
latéral, -rale [lateral] *adj, mpl* **-raux** [-ro] : side, lateral
latex [latɛks] *nms & pl* : latex
latin, -tine [latɛ̃, -tin] *adj* : Latin — **latin** *nm* : Latin (language)
latitude [latityd] *nf* : latitude
latte [lat] *nf* : lath, floorboard
lauréat, -réate [lɔrea, -reat] *n* : prizewinner
laurier [lɔrje] *nm* **1** : laurel **2 feuille de ~** : bay leaf
lavable [lavabl] *adj* : washable
lavabo [lavabo] *nm* **1** : (bathroom) sink **2 ~s** *nmpl France* : toilets
lavage [lavaʒ] *nm* **1** : wash, washing **2 ~ de cerveau** : brainwashing
lavande [lavɑ̃d] *nf* : lavender
lave [lav] *nf* : lava
laver [lave] *vt* : wash — **se laver** *vr* **1** : wash oneself **2 ~ les mains** : wash one's hands — **lave–linge** [lavlɛ̃ʒ] *nms & pl France* : washing machine — **laverie** [lavri] *nf* : self-service laundry — **lavette** [lavɛt] *nf* : dishcloth — **laveur, -veuse** [lavœr, -vøz] *n* : wash-

er, cleaner — **lave–vaisselle** [lavvesɛl] *nms & pl* : dishwasher — **lavoir** [lavwar] *nm Can* : self-service laundry

laxatif [laksatif] *nm* : laxative

le, la [lə, la] (**l'** [l] *before a vowel or mute h*) *pron, pl* **les** [le] : him, her, it, them — ~ *art* **1** : the **2** : a, an, per

lécher [leʃe] {87} *vt* : lick, lap — **se lécher** *vr* : lick (one's fingers, etc.) — **lèche–vitrines** [lɛʃvitrin] *nms & pl* **faire du ~** : window-shop

leçon [ləsɔ̃] *nf* : lesson

lecteur, -trice [lɛktœr, -tris] *n* : reader — **lecteur** *nm* **1 ~ de disquettes** : disk drive **2 ~ laser** : CD player — **lecture** [lɛktyr] *nf* : reading

ledit, ladite [lədi, ladit] *adj, pl* **lesdits, lesdites** [ledi, ledit] : the aforesaid

légal, -gale [legal] *adj, mpl* **-gaux** [lego] : legal, lawful — **légaliser** [legalize] *vt* : legalize — **légalité** [legalite] *nf* : lawfulness

légende [leʒɑ̃d] *nf* **1** : legend, tale **2** : caption (of an illustration) — **légendaire** [leʒɑ̃dɛr] *adj* : legendary

léger, -gère [leʒe, -ʒɛr] *adj* **1** : light **2** FAIBLE : slight, faint **3** IMPRUDENT : thoughtless **4 à la légère** : rashly — **légèrement** [leʒɛrmɑ̃] *adv* **1** : lightly **2** : slightly — **légèreté** [leʒɛrte] *nf* **1** : lightness **2** : thoughtlessness

légiférer [leʒifere] {87} *vi* : legislate

légion [leʒjɔ̃] *nf* : legion

législation [leʒislasjɔ̃] *nf* : legislation — **législateur, -trice** [leʒislatœr, -tris] *n* : legislator, lawmaker — **législatif, -tive** [leʒislatif, -tiv] *adj* : legislative — **législatif** *nm* : legislature — **législature** [leʒislatyr] *nf* : term (of office)

légitime [leʒitim] *adj* **1** LÉGAL : lawful **2** : rightful, legitimate **3 ~ défense** : self-defense

legs [lɛg] *nms & pl* : legacy — **léguer** [lege] {87} *vt* **1** : bequeath **2** TRANSMETTRE : pass on

légume [legym] *nm* : vegetable

lendemain [lɑ̃dmɛ̃] *nm* **1** : next day **2 au ~ de** : just after, following **3 du jour au ~** : in a very short time **4 le ~ matin** : the next morning

lent, lente [lɑ̃, lɑ̃t] *adj* : slow — **lenteur** [lɑ̃tœr] *nf* : slowness

lentille [lɑ̃tij] *nf* **1** : lentil **2** : (optical) lens

léopard [leɔpar] *nm* : leopard

lèpre [lɛpr] *nf* : leprosy

lequel, laquelle [ləkɛl, lakɛl] *pron, pl* **lesquels, lesquelles** [lekɛl] (*with* **à** *and* **de** *contracted to* **auquel, auxquels, auxquelles; duquel, desquels, desquelles**) **1** : which **2** : who, whom **3 lequel préférez-vous?** : which one do you prefer?

les → **le**

lesbienne [lɛsbjɛn] *nf* : lesbian

lesdits, lesdites → **ledit**

léser [leze] {87} *vt* **1** : wrong **2** BLESSER : injure

lésiner [lezine] *vi* **~ sur** : skimp on

lésion [lezjɔ̃] *nf* : lesion

lesquels, lesquelles → **lequel**

lessive [lɛsiv] *nf* **1** LAVAGE : washing, wash **2** : laundry detergent — **lessiver** [lɛsive] *vt* **1** : wash, scrub **2 être lessivé** *fam* : be exhausted

lest [lɛst] *nm* : ballast

leste [lɛst] *adj* : nimble

léthargie [letarʒi] *nf* : lethargy — **léthargique** [letarʒik] *adj* : lethargic

lettre [lɛtr] *nf* **1** : letter (of the alphabet) **2** CORRESPONDANCE : letter **3 ~s** *nfpl* : arts, humanities **4 à la ~** : exactly **5 en toutes ~s** : in full — **lettré, -trée** [lɛtre] *adj* : well-read

leucémie [løsemi] *nf* : leukemia

leur [lœr] *adj, pl* **leurs** : their — **~** *pron* **1** : (to) them **2 le ~, la ~, les ~s** : theirs

leurre [lœr] *nm* **1** : (fishing) lure **2** ILLUSION : illusion, deception — **leurrer** [lœre] *vt* : deceive, delude — **se leurrer** *vr* : delude oneself

levain [ləvɛ̃] *nm* **1** : leaven **2 sans ~** : unleavened

lever [ləve] {52} *vt* **1** : lift **2** : raise **3** : close (a meeting), lift (a ban) — *vi* **1** : come up (of plants) **2** : rise (in cooking) — **se lever** *vr* **1** : get up **2** : stand up **3** : rise (of the sun) **4 le jour se lève** : day is breaking — **~** *nm* **1** : rising, rise **2 ~ du soleil** : sunrise — **levée** [ləve] *nf* **1** SUPPRESSION : lifting **2** : collection (of mail, etc.)

levier [ləvje] *nm* **1** : lever **2 ~ de vitesse** : gearshift

lèvre [lɛvr] *nf* : lip

lévrier [levrije] *nm* : greyhound

levure [ləvyr] *nf* **1** : yeast **2 ~ chimique** : baking powder

lexique [lɛksik] *nm* **1** : glossary, lexicon **2** VOCABULAIRE : vocabulary

lézard [lezar] *nm* : lizard

lézarder [lezarde] *v* **se lézarder** *vr* : crack

liaison [ljɛzɔ̃] *nf* : liaison

liant, liante [ljɑ̃, ljɑ̃t] *adj* : sociable

liasse [ljas] *nf* : bundle, wad

libanais, -naise [libanɛ, -nɛz] *adj* : Lebanese

libeller [libele] *vt* : draw up (a document), make out (a check)
libellule [libelyl] *nf* : dragonfly
libéral, -rale [liberal] *adj & n, mpl* **-raux** [-ro] : liberal
libérer [libere] {87} *vt* : free, release, liberate — **se libérer** *vr* : free oneself — **libération** [liberasjɔ̃] *nf* : liberation, freeing — **libéré, -rée** [libere] *adj* **~ de** : free from
liberté [liberte] *nf* **1** : freedom, liberty **2 en ~ conditionnelle** : on probation **3 mettre en ~** : set free
libido [libido] *nf* : libido
libraire [librɛr] *nmf* : bookseller — **librairie** [librɛri] *nf* : bookstore
libre [libr] *adj* **1** : free **2** DISPONIBLE : available, unoccupied **3** DÉGAGÉ : clear, free **4 ~ arbitre** : free will — **libre-échange** [libreʃɑ̃ʒ] *nm, pl* **libres-échanges** [librəzeʃɑ̃ʒ] : free trade — **librement** [librəmɑ̃] *adv* : freely — **libre-service** [librəsɛrvis] *nm, pl* **libres-services** : self-service
licence [lisɑ̃s] *nf* **1** : (bachelor's) degree **2** : license, permit **3 prendre des ~s avec** : take liberties with — **licencié, -ciée** [lisɑ̃sje] *n* : (university) graduate
licencier [lisɑ̃sje] {96} *vt* : lay off, dismiss — **licenciement** [lisɑ̃simɑ̃] *nm* : layoff, dismissal
lichen [likɛn] *nm* : lichen
licite [lisit] *adj* : lawful
lie [li] *nf* : sediment, dregs
liège [ljɛʒ] *nm* : cork
lien [ljɛ̃] *nm* **1** ATTACHE : bond, strap **2** RAPPORT : link **3** RELATION : tie, relationship — **lier** [lje] {96} *vt* **1** : bind, tie up **2** RELIER : link up **3** : strike up (a friendship, etc.) **4** UNIR : unite — **se lier** *vr* **~ avec** : become friends with
lierre [ljɛr] *nm* : ivy
liesse [ljɛs] *nf* : jubilation
lieu [ljø] *nm, pl* **lieux 1** ENDROIT : place **2 au ~ de** : instead of **3 avoir ~** : take place **4 avoir ~ de** : have reason to **5 en premier ~** : in the first place **6 tenir ~ de** : serve as **7 ~x** *nmpl* : premises — **lieu-dit** *or* **lieudit** [ljødi] *nm, pl* **lieux-dits** *or* **lieudits** : locality
lieutenant [ljøtnɑ̃] *nm* : lieutenant
lièvre [ljɛvr] *nm* : hare
ligament [ligamɑ̃] *nm* : ligament
ligne [liɲ] *nf* **1** : line **2** PARCOURS : route **3 en ~** : online (in computers) **4 ~ droite** : beeline — **lignée** [liɲe] *nf* **1** : line, lineage **2** DESCENDANTS : descendants *pl*
ligoter [ligɔte] *vt* : tie up, bind
ligue [lig] *nf* : league, alliance — **liguer** [lige] *v* **se liguer** *vr* **1** : join forces **2 ~ contre** : conspire against
lilas [lila] *nms & pl* : lilac
limace [limas] *nf* : slug (mollusk)
lime [lim] *nf* **1** : file **2 ~ à ongles** : nail file — **limer** [lime] *vt* : file — **se limer** *vr* **~ les ongles** : file one's nails
limiter [limite] *vt* : limit — **limitation** [limitasjɔ̃] *nf* : limitation — **limite** [limit] *adj* **1 cas ~** : borderline case **2 date ~** : deadline **3 vitesse ~** : speed limit — **~** *nf* **1** : limit **2** : border, boundary
limitrophe [limitrɔf] *adj* : bordering, adjacent
limoger [limɔʒe] {17} *vt* : dismiss
limon [limɔ̃] *nm* : silt
limonade [limɔnad] *nf* : lemonade
limousine [limuzin] *nf* : limousine
limpide [lɛ̃pid] *adj* : (crystal) clear — **limpidité** [lɛ̃pidite] *nf* : clearness
lin [lɛ̃] *nm* **1** : flax **2** : linen
linceul [lɛ̃sœl] *nm* : shroud
linéaire [lineɛr] *adj* : linear
linge [lɛ̃ʒ] *nm* **1** : (household) linen **2** LESSIVE : wash, washing **3** CHIFFON : cloth **4** *or* **~ de corps** : underwear **5** *Can fam* : clothes *pl*, clothing — **lingerie** [lɛ̃ʒri] *nf* **1** : lingerie **2** *Can* : linen closet
lingot [lɛ̃go] *nm* : ingot
linguistique [lɛ̃gɥistik] *adj* : linguistic — **~** *nf* : linguistics — **linguiste** [lɛ̃gɥist] *nmf* : linguist
linoléum [linɔleɔm] *nm* : linoleum
lion, lionne [ljɔ̃, ljɔn] *n* : lion, lioness *f* — **lionceau** [ljɔ̃so] *nm, pl* **-ceaux** : lion cub
liqueur [likœr] *nf* **1** : liqueur **2** *Can* : soft drink
liquide [likid] *adj* : liquid — **~** *nm* **1** : liquid **2** ARGENT : cash — **liquidation** [likidasjɔ̃] *nf* **1** : liquidation **2** : clearance sale — **liquider** [likide] *vt* **1** : liquidate **2** : eliminate — **liquidités** [likidite] *nfpl* : liquid assets
lire [lir] {51} *vt* : read
lis *or* **lys** [lis] *nms & pl* : lily
lisible [lizibl] *adj* : legible — **lisibilité** [-zibilite] *nf* : legibility
lisière [lizjɛr] *nf* : edge, outskirts *pl*
lisse [lis] *adj* : smooth, sleek
liste [list] *nf* : list
lit [li] *nm* **1** : bed **2 ~ de camp** : cot —

literie [litri] *nf* : bedding — **litière** [litjɛr] *nf* : litter
litige [litiʒ] *nm* : dispute
litre [litr] *nm* : liter
littérature [literatyr] *nf* : literature — **littéraire** [literɛr] *adj* : literary — **littéral, -rale** [literal] *adj, mpl* **-raux** [-ro] : literal
littoral [litɔral] *nm* : coast(line) — ~ *adj* : coastal
liturgie [lityrʒi] *nf* : liturgy — **liturgique** [lityrʒik] *adj* : liturgical
livide [livid] *adj* : pallid, pale
livraison [livrɛzɔ̃] *nf* : delivery
livre[1] [livr] *nm* **1** : book **2** ~ **de poche** : paperback **3** ~ **de recettes** : cookbook
livre[2] *nf* **1** : pound **2** *or* ~ **sterling** : pound (monetary unit)
livrer [livre] *vt* **1** : deliver **2** REMETTRE : hand over — **se livrer** *vr* **1** ~ **à** : devote oneself to **2** ~ **à** : surrender to **3** ~ **à** : confide in
livret [livrɛ] *nm* : booklet
livreur, -vreuse [livrœr, -vrøz] *n* : deliveryman *m*, delivery woman *f*
lobe [lɔb] *nm* : lobe
local, -cale [lɔkal] *adj, mpl* **-caux** [lɔko] : local — **local** *nm, pl* **-caux** : place, premises *pl* — **localiser** [lɔkalize] *vt* **1** SITUER : locate **2** LIMITER : localize — **localité** [lɔkalite] *nf* : locality
location [lɔkasjɔ̃] *nf* **1** : renting, leasing **2** : rented property — **locataire** [lɔkatɛr] *nmf* : tenant
locomotive [lɔkɔmɔtiv] *nf* : locomotive, engine
locution [lɔkysjɔ̃] *nf* : phrase, idiom
loge [lɔʒ] *nf* **1** : dressing room **2** : box (at the theater) **3** : lodge
loger [lɔʒe] {17} *vt* **1** : lodge **2** CONTENIR : accommodate — **se loger** *vr* **1** : find accommodations **2** ~ **dans** : lodge itself in — **logement** [lɔʒmɑ̃] *nm* **1** : accommodation **2** : apartment **3** HABITAT : housing
logiciel [lɔʒisjɛl] *nm* : software
logique [lɔʒik] *adj* : logical — ~ *nf* : logic
logis [lɔʒi] *nms & pl* : dwelling, abode
logistique [lɔʒistik] *nf* : logistics
loi [lwa] *nf* : law
loin [lwɛ̃] *adv* **1** : far **2** : a long time ago **3** ~ **de** : far from **4** **plus** ~ : further — ~ *nm* **1** **au** ~ : in the distance **2** **de** ~ : from a distance **3** **de** ~ : by far — **lointain, -taine** [lwɛ̃tɛ̃, -tɛn] *adj* : distant — **lointain** *nm* : distance
loisir [lwazir] *nm* **1** : leisure **2** ~**s** *nmpl* : leisure activities
long, longue [lɔ̃, lɔ̃g] *adj* : long — **long** [lɔ̃] *adv* : much, a lot — ~ *nm* **1** : length **2** **de** ~ : long, in length **3** **le** ~ **de** : along — **à la longue** *adv phr* : in the long run
longer [lɔ̃ʒe] {17} *vt* **1** : walk along, follow **2** LIMITER : border
longévité [lɔ̃ʒevite] *nf* : longevity
longitude [lɔ̃ʒityd] *nf* : longitude
longtemps [lɔ̃tɑ̃] *adv* **1** : a long time **2** **avant** ~ : before long
longue → **long** — **longuement** [lɔ̃gmɑ̃] *adv* **1** : for a long time **2** : at length — **longueur** [lɔ̃gœr] *nf* **1** : length **2** **à** ~ **de journée** : all day long **3** ~ **d'onde** : wavelength **4** ~**s** *nfpl* : tedious parts (of a film, etc.) — **longue–vue** [lɔ̃gvy] *nf, pl* **longues–vues** : telescope
lopin [lɔpɛ̃] *nm* ~ **de terre** : plot of land
loquace [lɔkas] *adj* : talkative
loque [lɔk] *nf* **1** : wreck (person) **2** ~**s** *nfpl* : rags
loquet [lɔkɛ] *nm* : latch
lorgner [lɔrɲe] *vt* : eye, ogle
lors [lɔr] *adv* ~ **de 1** : at the time of **2** : during
lorsque [lɔrskə] (**lorsqu'** [lɔrsk] *before a vowel or mute h*) *conj* : when
losange [lɔzɑ̃ʒ] *nm* **1** : lozenge, diamond shape **2** *Can* : (baseball) diamond
lot [lo] *nm* **1** SORT : fate, lot **2** PRIX : prize **3** PART : share
loterie [lɔtri] *nf* : lottery
lotion [losjɔ̃] *nf* : lotion
lotissement [lɔtismɑ̃] *nm* : (housing) development
louange [lwɑ̃ʒ] *nf* : praise — **louable** [lwabl] *adj* : praiseworthy
louche[1] [luʃ] *nf* : ladle
louche[2] *adj* : shady, suspicious — **loucher** [luʃe] *vi* **1** : be cross-eyed **2** : squint
louer[1] [lwe] *vt* : praise — **se louer** *vr* ~ **de** : be satisfied about
louer[2] *vt* : rent, lease — **se louer** *vr* : be for rent
loufoque [lufɔk] *adj fam* : crazy, zany
loup [lu] *nm* : wolf
loupe [lup] *nf* : magnifying glass
louper [lupe] *vt fam* **1** : bungle, mess up **2** : miss (a train, etc.)
lourd, lourde [lur, lurd] *adj* : heavy — **lourd** *adv* **peser** ~ : be heavy —

lourdement [lurdəmɑ̃] *adv* : heavily — **lourdeur** [lurdœr] *nf* : heaviness
loutre [lutr] *nf* : otter
louvoyer [luvwaje] {58} *vi* : hedge, equivocate
loyal, loyale [lwajal] *adj, mpl* **loyaux** [lwajo] **1** : loyal **2** HONNÊTE : fair — **loyauté** [lwajote] *nf* **1** : loyalty **2** : fairness
loyer [lwaje] *nm* : rent
lu [ly] *pp* → **lire**
lubie [lybi] *nf* : whim
lubrifier [lybrifje] {96} *vt* : lubricate — **lubrifiant** [lybrifjɑ̃] *nm* : lubricant
lucarne [lykarn] *nf* : skylight
lucide [lysid] *adj* : lucid — **lucidité** [lysidite] *nf* : lucidity
lucratif, -tive [lykratif, -tiv] *adj* : lucrative, profitable
ludique [lydik] *adj* : play, playing
lueur [lɥœr] *nf* **1** : faint light **2** : glimmer (of hope, etc.)
luge [lyʒ] *nf* : sled
lugubre [lygybr] *adj* : gloomy, dismal
lui [lɥi] *pron* **1** (*used as indirect object*) : (to) him, (to) her, (to) it **2** (*used as object of a preposition*) : him, it **3** (*used as subject or for emphasis*) : he **4** (*used as a reflexive pronoun*) : himself — **lui–même** [lɥimɛm] *pron* : himself, itself
luire [lɥir] {49} *vi* : shine, gleam — **luisant, -sante** [lɥizɑ̃, -zɑ̃t] *adj* : shining, gleaming
lumière [lymjɛr] *nf* : light — **luminaire** [lyminɛr] *nm* : lamp, light — **lumineux, -neuse** [lyminø, -nøz] *adj* **1** : luminous **2** RADIEUX : radiant, bright
lunaire [lynɛr] *adj* : lunar, moon
lunatique [lynatik] *adj* : whimsical
lunch [lœ̃ʃ] *nm, pl* **lunchs** *or* **lunches** **1** BUFFET : buffet **2** *Can* : lunch
lundi [lœ̃di] *nm* : Monday
lune [lyn] *nf* **1** : moon **2 ~ de miel** : honeymoon
lunette [lynɛt] *nf* **1** : telescope **2 ~ arrière** : rear window (of an automobile) **3 ~s** *nfpl* : glasses **4 ~s bifocales** : bifocals
lurette [lyrɛt] *nf* **il y a belle ~** *fam* : ages ago
lustre [lystr] *nm* **1** : luster, sheen **2** : chandelier — **lustré, -trée** [lystre] *adj* : shiny, glossy
luth [lyt] *nm* : lute
lutin [lytɛ̃] *nm* : imp, goblin
lutrin [lytrɛ̃] *nm* : lectern
lutte [lyt] *nf* **1** : fight, struggle **2** : wrestling — **lutter** [lyte] *vi* **1** SE BATTRE : fight, struggle **2** : wrestle — **lutteur, -teuse** [lytœr, -tøz] *n* **1** : fighter **2** : wrestler
luxation [lyksasjɔ̃] *nf* : dislocation (of a joint)
luxe [lyks] *nm* : luxury
luxer [lykse] *v* **se luxer** *vr* : dislocate (one's shoulder, etc.)
luxueux, -xueuse [lyksɥø, -sɥøz] *adj* : luxurious
luxure [lyksyr] *nf* : lust — **luxurieux, -rieuse** [lyksyrjø, -rjøz] *adj* : lustful
luzerne [lyzɛrn] *nf* : alfalfa
lycée [lise] *nm France* : high school — **lycéen, -céenne** [liseɛ̃, -seɛn] *n France* : high school student
lynx [lɛ̃ks] *nm* : lynx
lyrique [lirik] *adj* : lyric(al)
lys → **lis**

M

m [ɛm] *nm* : m, 13th letter of the alphabet
ma → **mon**
macabre [makabr] *adj* : macabre
macaron [makarɔ̃] *nm* **1** : macaroon **2** INSIGNE : badge, sticker
macaronis [makarɔni] *nmpl* : macaroni
macédoine [masedwan] *nf* : mixture (of fruits or vegetables)
macérer [masere] {87} *v* : steep, soak
mâcher [maʃe] *vt* : chew
machin [maʃɛ̃] *nm fam* : thingamajig, thing
machine [maʃin] *nf* **1** : machine **2** : engine (of a ship, a train, etc.) **3 ~ à écrire** : typewriter **4 ~ à laver** : washing machine — **machiniste** [maʃinist] *nmf* : (bus) driver
mâchoire [maʃwar] *nf* : jaw
mâchonner [maʃɔne] *vt* : chew
maçon [masɔ̃] *nm* : bricklayer, mason — **maçonnerie** [masɔnri] *nf* : masonry
maculer [makyle] *vt* : stain
madame [madam] *nf, pl* **mesdames** [medam] **1** : Mrs., Ms., Madam **2** : lady — **mademoiselle** [madmwazɛl] *nf, pl* **mesdemoiselles** [medmwazɛl] **1** : Miss, Ms. **2** : young lady

mafia *or* **maffia** [mafja] *nf* : Mafia
magasin [magazɛ̃] *nm* **1** : shop, store **2** ENTREPÔT : warehouse **3** : magazine (of a gun or camera) **4 grand ~** : department store
magazine [magazin] *nm* REVUE : magazine
magie [maʒi] *nf* : magic — **magicien, -cienne** [maʒisjɛ̃, -sjɛn] *n* : magician — **magique** [maʒik] *adj* : magic(al)
magistral, -trale [maʒistral] *adj, mpl* **-traux** [-tro] **1** : brilliant, masterly **2 cours magistral** : lecture
magistrat [maʒistra] *nm* : magistrate
magnanime [maɲanim] *adj* : magnanimous
magnat [maɲa] *nm* : magnate, tycoon
magnétique [maɲetik] *adj* : magnetic — **magnétiser** [maɲetize] *vt* : magnetize — **magnétisme** [maɲetism] *nm* : magnetism
magnétophone [maɲetɔfɔn] *nm* : tape recorder
magnétoscope [maɲetɔskɔp] *nm* : videocassette recorder, VCR
magnifique [maɲifik] *adj* : magnificent
magnolia [maɲɔlja] *nm* : magnolia
mai [mɛ] *nm* : May
maigre [mɛgr] *adj* **1** MINCE : thin **2** INSUFFISANT : meager **3** : low-fat, lean (of meat) — **maigrir** [megrir] *vi* : lose weight, reduce
maille [maj] *nf* **1** : stitch (in knitting) **2** : mesh (of a net)
maillot [majo] *nm* **1** : jersey **2 ~ de bain** : bathing suit
main [mɛ̃] *nf* **1** : hand **2** SAVOIR-FAIRE : know-how, skill **3 de première ~** : firsthand **4 donner un coup de ~ à** : lend a helping hand to **5 ~ courante** : handrail — **main–d'œuvre** [mɛ̃dœvr] *nf, pl* **mains–d'œuvre** : manpower, workforce
maint, mainte [mɛ̃, mɛ̃t] *adj* : many a
maintenant [mɛ̃tnɑ̃] *adv* **1** : now **2** : nowadays
maintenir [mɛ̃tnir] {92} *vt* **1** : maintain **2** SOUTENIR : support — **se maintenir** *vr* : remain, persist — **maintien** [mɛ̃tjɛ̃] *nm* **1** : maintaining, maintenance **2** PORT : bearing, deportment
maire, mairesse [mɛr, merɛs] *n* : mayor — **mairie** [meri] *nf* : town hall, city hall
mais [mɛ] *conj* **1** : but **2 ~ oui** : certainly, of course
maïs [mais] *nm* : corn, maize
maison [mɛzɔ̃] *nf* **1** : house, home **2** SOCIÉTÉ : firm — **~** *adj* **1** : home-made **2** : in-house (of an employee) — **maisonnée** [mɛzɔne] *nf* : household
maître, -tresse [mɛtr, -trɛs] *n* **1** : master, mistress **2 ~ d'école** : schoolteacher — **~** *adj* : main, key — **maître** [mɛtr] *nm* **1** : master (of a pet, etc.) **2** EXPERT : expert — **maîtrise** [metriz] *nf* **1** : skill, mastery **2** : master's degree **3 ~ de soi** : self-control — **maîtriser** [metrize] *vt* **1** : master **2** CONTENIR : control, restrain
majesté [maʒɛste] *nf* : majesty — **majestueux, -tueuse** [maʒɛstɥø, -tɥøz] *adj* : majestic
majeur, -jeure [maʒœr] *adj* **1** : major, main **2** : of age (in law) — **majeur** *nm* : middle finger — **majorité** [maʒɔrite] *nf* : majority
majuscule [maʒyskyl] *adj* : capital, uppercase — **~** *nf* : capital letter
mal [mal] *adv* **1** : poorly, badly **2** INCORRECTEMENT : wrongly **3 aller ~** : be unwell — **~** *adj* **1** : wrong **2** MAUVAIS : bad — **~** *nm, pl* **maux** [mo] **1** DOULEUR : pain **2** MALADIE : sickness **3** DOMMAGE : harm **4** : evil **5** PEINE : trouble, difficulty
malade [malad] *adj* : sick, ill — **~** *nmf* : sick person, patient — **maladie** [maladi] *nf* : illness, disease — **maladif, -dive** [maladif, -div] *adj* : sickly
maladresse [maladrɛs] *nf* **1** : clumsiness **2** BÉVUE : blunder — **maladroit, -droite** [maladrwa, -drwat] *adj* : clumsy, awkward
malaise [malɛz] *nm* **1** : dizziness **2** GÊNE : uneasiness, malaise
malaxer [malakse] *vt* **1** : knead **2** MÉLANGER : mix
malchance [malʃɑ̃s] *nf* : bad luck, misfortune — **malchanceux, -ceuse** [malʃɑ̃sø, -søz] *adj* : unfortunate
mâle [mal] *adj* **1** : male **2** : manly — **~** *nm* : male
malédiction [malediksjɔ̃] *nf* : curse
maléfique [malefik] *adj* : evil
malencontreux, -treuse [malɑ̃kɔ̃trø, -trøz] *adj* : unfortunate, untoward
malentendu [malɑ̃tɑ̃dy] *nm* : misunderstanding
malfaçon [malfasɔ̃] *nf* : fault, defect
malfaisant, -sante [malfəzɑ̃, -zɑ̃t] *adj* : evil, harmful — **malfaiteur** [malfɛtœr] *nm* : criminal
malgré [malgre] *prep* **1** : in spite of, despite **2 ~ tout** : nevertheless, even so
malheur [malœr] *nm* : misfortune — **malheureux, -reuse** [malœrø, -røz]

adj **1** : unhappy **2** MALCHANCEUX : unfortunate — ∼ *n* : unfortunate person — **malheureusement** [malœrøzmɑ̃] *adv* : unfortunately

malhonnête [malɔnɛt] *adj* : dishonest — **malhonnêteté** [malɔnɛtte] *nf* : dishonesty

malice [malis] *nf* : mischief, mischievousness — **malicieux, -cieuse** [malisjø, -sjøz] *adj* : mischievous

malin, -ligne [malɛ̃, -liɲ] *adj* **1** : clever **2** *fam* : difficult **3** MÉCHANT : malicious **4** : malignant (in medicine)

malle [mal] *nf* : trunk

malléable [maleabl] *adj* : malleable

mallette [malɛt] *nf* : small suitcase, valise

malnutrition [malnytrisjɔ̃] *nf* : malnutrition

malodorant, -rante [malɔdɔrɑ̃, -rɑ̃t] *adj* : foul-smelling, smelly

malpropre [malprɔpr] *adj* : dirty — **malpropreté** [malprɔprəte] *nf* : dirtiness

malsain, -saine [malsɛ̃, -sɛn] *adj* : unhealthy

malt [malt] *nm* : malt

maltraiter [maltrete] *vt* : mistreat

malveillance [malvɛjɑ̃s] *nf* : spite, malevolence — **malveillant, -lante** [malvɛjɑ̃, -jɑ̃t] *adj* : spiteful

maman [mamɑ̃] *nf* : mom, mommy

mamelle [mamɛl] *nf* **1** : teat **2** PIS : udder — **mamelon** [mamɛlɔ̃] *nm* : nipple

mammifère [mamifɛr] *nm* : mammal

mammouth [mamut] *nm* : mammoth

manche [mɑ̃ʃ] *nf* **1** : sleeve (of a shirt) **2** : round (in sports), set (in tennis) **3** *Can* : inning (in baseball) **4 la Manche** : the English Channel — ∼ *nm* **1** : handle, neck, shaft **2** ∼ **à balai** : broomstick — **manchette** [mɑ̃ʃɛt] *nf* **1** : cuff **2** : headline (in the press)

manchot [mɑ̃ʃo] *nm* : penguin

mandarine [mɑ̃darin] *nf* : tangerine, mandarin orange

mandat [mɑ̃da] *nm* **1** : mandate **2** *or* ∼ **d'arrêt** : (arrest) warrant **3** *or* ∼ **postal** : money order — **mandataire** [mɑ̃datɛr] *nmf* **1** REPRÉSENTANT : representative, agent **2** : proxy (in politics)

manège [manɛʒ] *nm* **1** : riding school **2** : merry-go-round

manette [manɛt] *nf* : lever

manger [mɑ̃ʒe] {17} *vt* **1** : eat **2** DÉPENSER : consume, use up — *vi* : eat — ∼ *nm* : food — **mangeable** [mɑ̃ʒabl] *adj* : edible — **mangeoire** [mɑ̃ʒwar] *nf* : feeding trough

mangue [mɑ̃g] *nf* : mango

maniable [manjabl] *adj* : easy to handle, manageable

maniaque [manjak] *adj* : fussy — ∼ *nmf* **1** : fussy person **2** : fanatic — **manie** [mani] *nf* **1** HABITUDE : habit **2** : quirk, obsession

manier [manje] {96} *vt* **1** MANIPULER : handle **2** UTILISER : use — **maniement** [manimɑ̃] *nm* : handling, use, operation

manière [manjɛr] *nf* **1** : manner, way **2 de** ∼ **à** : so as to **3 de toute** ∼ : in any case, anyway **4** ∼**s** *nfpl* : manners — **maniéré, -rée** [manjere] *adj* : affected, mannered

manifester [manifɛste] *vt* **1** : express **2** RÉVÉLER : reveal, show — *vi* : demonstrate — **se manifester** *vr* : appear — **manifestation** [manifɛstasjɔ̃] *nf* **1** : (political) demonstration **2** MARQUE : indication **3** : appearance (of an illness, etc.) — **manifestant, -tante** [manifɛstɑ̃, -tɑ̃t] *n* : demonstrator — **manifeste** [manifɛst] *adj* : obvious — ∼ *nm* : manifesto

manigance [manigɑ̃s] *nf* : scheme, trick — **manigancer** [manigɑ̃se] {6} *vt* : plot

manipuler [manipyle] *vt* **1** MANIER : handle **2** : manipulate — **manipulation** [manipylasjɔ̃] *nf* **1** MANIEMENT : handling **2** : manipulation

manivelle [manivɛl] *nf* : crank

mannequin [mankɛ̃] *nm* **1** : dummy, mannequin **2** : (fashion) model

manœuvre [manœvr] *nf* : maneuver — **manœuvrer** [manœvre] *vt* **1** : maneuver **2** : operate (a machine, etc.) **3** MANIPULER : manipulate — *vi* : maneuver

manoir [manwar] *nm* : manor

manquer [mɑ̃ke] *vt* : miss (an opportunity, etc.) — *vi* **1** : lack, be missing **2** ÉCHOUER : fail **3** : be absent (of a student, etc.) **4** ∼ **de** : be short of — **manque** [mɑ̃k] *nm* **1** : lack **2** LACUNE : gap — **manqué, -quée** [mɑ̃ke] *adj* **1** : failed **2** : missed

mansarde [mɑ̃sard] *nf* : attic

manteau [mɑ̃to] *nm, pl* **-teaux** [-to] : coat

manucure [manykyr] *nf* : manicure — ∼ *nmf* : manicurist

manuel, -elle [manɥɛl] *adj* : manual — **manuel** *nm* : manual, handbook

manufacture [manyfaktyr] *nf* : factory — **manufacturer** [manyfaktyre] *vt* : manufacture
manuscrit, -scrite [manyskri, -skrit] *adj* : handwritten — **manuscrit** *nm* : manuscript
manutention [manytɑ̃sjɔ̃] *nf* **1** : handling **2 frais de ~** : handling charges
maquereau [makro] *nm, pl* **-reaux** [-ro] : mackerel
maquette [makɛt] *nf* : (scale) model
maquiller [makije] *vt* : make up (one's face) — **se maquiller** *vr* : put on makeup — **maquillage** [makijaʒ] *nm* : makeup
maquis [maki] *nm France* : brush, undergrowth
marais [marɛ] *nm* : marsh, swamp
marasme [marasm] *nm* **1** : dejection, depression **2** : (economic) stagnation
marathon [maratɔ̃] *nm* : marathon
marauder [marode] *vi* VOLER : pilfer, thieve
marbre [marbr] *nm* **1** : marble **2** *Can* : home plate (in baseball)
marchand, -chande [marʃɑ̃, -ʃɑ̃d] *n* : storekeeper, merchant — **~** *adj* : market — **marchander** [marʃɑ̃de] *vt* : haggle over — *vi* : haggle, bargain — **marchandises** [marʃɑ̃diz] *nfpl* : goods, merchandise
marche [marʃ] *nf* **1** : step, stair **2** PROMENADE : walk, walking **3** RYTHME : pace **4** : march (in music) **5 ~ arrière** : reverse **6 en ~** : running, operating **7 mettre en ~** : start up
marché [marʃe] *nm* **1** : market **2** ACCORD : deal **3 bon ~** : cheap **4 ~ noir** : black market
marchepied [marʃəpje] *nm* : step, steps *pl*
marcher [marʃe] *vi* **1** : walk, march **2 ~ sur** : step on, tread on **3** FONCTIONNER : work, go, run — **marcheur, -cheuse** [marʃœr, -ʃøz] *n* : walker
mardi [mardi] *nm* **1** : Tuesday **2 ~ gras** : Mardi Gras
mare [mar] *nf* **1** : pond **2 ~ de** : pool of
marécage [marekaʒ] *nm* : marsh, swamp — **marécageux, -geuse** [marekaʒø, -ʒøz] *adj* : marshy, swampy
maréchal [mareʃal] *nm, pl* **-chaux** [-ʃo] : marshal
marée [mare] *nf* **1** : tide **2 ~ noire** : oil slick
marelle [marɛl] *nf* : hopscotch
margarine [margarin] *nf* : margarine
marge [marʒ] *nf* : margin — **marginal, -nale** [marʒinal] *adj, mpl* **-naux** [-no] : marginal
marguerite [margərit] *nf* : daisy
marier [marje] {96} *vt* **1** : marry **2** : blend (colors, etc.) — **se marier** *vr* : get married — **mari** [mari] *nm* : husband — **mariage** [marjaʒ] *nm* **1** : marriage **2** : wedding — **marié, -riée** [marje] *adj* : married — **~** *n* **1** : groom *m*, bride *f* **2 les mariés** : the newlyweds
marin, -rine [marɛ̃, -rin] *adj* : sea, marine — **marin** *nm* : sailor — **marine** *nf* : navy
mariner [marine] *v* : marinate
marionnette [marjɔnɛt] *nf* **1** : puppet **2 ~ à fils** : marionette
maritime [maritim] *adj* : maritime, coastal
marmelade [marməlad] *nf* **1** : stewed fruit **2** : marmalade
marmite [marmit] *nf* : cooking pot
marmonner [marmɔne] *v* : mutter, mumble
marmot [marmo] *nm fam* : kid, brat
marmotte [marmɔt] *nf* : woodchuck
marmotter [marmɔte] *v* : mutter, mumble
marocain, -caine [marɔkɛ̃, -kɛn] *adj* : Moroccan
marotte [marɔt] *nf* : craze, fad
marquer [marke] *vt* **1** : mark **2** INDIQUER : show, indicate **3** ÉCRIRE : note (down) **4** : score (in sports) — *vi* **1** : leave a mark **2** : stand out (of an event, etc.) — **marquant, -quante** [markɑ̃, -kɑ̃t] *adj* : memorable, outstanding — **marque** [mark] *nf* **1** : mark, trace **2** : brand, make **3** : score (in sports) **4 ~ déposée** : registered trademark — **marqué, -quée** [marke] *adj* : marked, distinct
marquisse [markiz] *nf* : canopy, marquee
marraine [marɛn] *nf* : godmother
marrant, -rante [marɑ̃, -rɑ̃t] *adj fam* : amusing, funny
marre [mar] *adv* **en avoir ~** *fam* : be fed up
marron, -ronne [marɔ̃, -rɔn] *adj* : brown — **marron** *nm* **1** : chestnut **2** : brown — **marronnier** [marɔnje] *nm* : chestnut tree
mars [mars] *nm* : March
Mars *nf* : Mars (planet)
marsouin [marswɛ̃] *nm* : porpoise
marteau [marto] *nm, pl* **-teaux** [marto] **1** : hammer **2 ~ pneumatique**

: pneumatic drill — **marteau–piqueur** [martopikœr] *nm, pl* **marteaux–piqueurs** : jackhammer — **marteler** [martəle] {20} *vt* : hammer
martial, -tiale [marsjal] *adj, mpl* **-tiaux** [-sjo] : martial
martyr, -tyre [martir] *n* : martyr — **martyriser** [martirize] *vt* : martyr
mascarade [maskarad] *nf* : masquerade
mascotte [maskɔt] *nf* : mascot
masculin, -line [maskylɛ̃, -lin] *adj* : male, masculine — **masculin** *nm* : masculine
masque [mask] *nm* : mask — **masquer** [maske] *vt* : mask, conceal
massacrer [masakre] *vt* : massacre — **massacre** [masakr] *nm* : massacre
massage [masaʒ] *nm* : massage
masse [mas] *nf* **1** : mass, body (of water, etc.) **2** : sledgehammer **3 les ∼s** : the masses
masser [mase] *vt* **1** : massage **2** ASSEMBLER : gather — **masseur, -seuse** [masœr, -søz] *n* : masseur *m,* masseuse *f*
massif, -sive [masif, -siv] *adj* **1** : massive **2** : solid (of gold, silver, etc.) — **massif** *nm* : clump (of trees)
massue [masy] *nf* : club, bludgeon
mastic [mastik] *nm* : putty — **mastiquer** [mastike] *vt* : chew
masturber [mastyrbe] *v* **se masturber** *vr* : masturbate — **masturbation** [mastyrbasjɔ̃] *nf* : masturbation
mat, mate [mat] *adj* **1** : dull, matte (of a finish, etc.) **2** : checkmated (in chess)
mât [ma] *nm* **1** : mast **2** POTEAU : pole, post
match [matʃ] *nm* : match, game
matelas [matla] *nm* : mattress — **matelasser** [matlase] *vt* REMBOURRER : pad
matelot [matlo] *nm* : sailor, seaman
mater [mate] *vt* DOMPTER : subdue, curb
matériaux [materjo] *nmpl* : materials
matériel, -rielle [materjɛl] *adj* : material — **matériel** *nm* **1** : equipment, material(s) **2** : computer hardware — **matérialiser** [materjalize] *vt* : realize, make happen — **se matérialiser** *vr* : materialize — **matérialiste** [materjalist] *adj* : materialistic
maternel, -nelle [maternɛl] *adj* : maternal, motherly — **maternelle** *nf or* **école ∼** : nursery school — **maternité** [maternite] *nf* **1** : maternity **2** GROSSESSE : pregnancy
mathématique [matematik] *adj* : mathematical — **mathématicien, -cienne** [matematisjɛ̃, -sjɛn] *n* : mathematician — **mathématiques** [matematik] *nfpl* : mathematics — **maths** *or* **math** [mat] *nfpl fam* : math
matière [matjɛr] *nf* **1** : matter, substance **2** SUJET : subject **3 ∼s premières** : raw materials
matin [matɛ̃] *nm* : morning — **matinal, -nale** [matinal] *adj, mpl* **-naux** [-no] **1** : morning **2 être ∼** : be up early — **matinée** [matine] *nf* **1** : morning **2** : matinee
matraque [matrak] *nf* : club — **matraquer** [matrake] *vt* **1** : club, bludgeon **2** : plug (a product)
matrice [matris] *nf* : matrix
matricule [matrikyl] *nf* : register, roll
matrimonial, -niale [matrimɔnjal] *adj, mpl* **-niaux** [-njo] : matrimonial
maturité [matyrite] *nf* : maturity
maudire [modir] *vt* : curse, damn — **maudit, -dite** [modi, -dit] *adj* : damned
maugréer [mogree] {89} *vi* GROGNER : grumble
maussade [mosad] *adj* **1** MOROSE : sullen **2 temps ∼** : dismal weather
mauvais, -vaise [movɛ, -vɛz] *adj* **1** : bad (of a grade, etc.) **2** : wrong (of an answer, etc.) **3** DÉPLAISANT : nasty, unpleasant
mauve [mov] *adj & nm* : mauve
mauviette [movjɛt] *nf* : weakling
maux → **mal**
maxillaire [maksilɛr] *nm* : jawbone
maxime [maksim] *nf* ADAGE : maxim, proverb
maximum [maksimɔm] *adj & nm, pl* **mums** [-mɔm] *or* **-ma** [-ma] : maximum
mayonnaise [majɔnɛz] *nf* : mayonnaise
mazout [mazut] *nm* : heating oil
me [mə] *pron* (**m'** [m] *before a vowel or mute h*) **1** : me, to me **2** : myself, to myself
mec [mɛk] *nm fam* : guy
mécanique [mekanik] *nf* **1** : mechanics **2** : mechanism — **∼** *adj* : mechanical — **mécanicien, -cienne** [mekanisjɛ̃, -sjɛn] *n* **1** : mechanic **2** : (railway or flight) engineer — **mécanisme** [mekanism] *nm* : mechanism
méchant, -chante [meʃɑ̃, -ʃɑ̃t] *adj* **1** : nasty, malicious **2** : naughty, bad (of a child) **3** : vicious (of a dog) — **∼** *n* **1** : villain (in a book or film) **2**

: naughty child — **méchamment** [meʃamɑ̃] *adv* : nastily — **méchanceté** [meʃɑ̃ste] *nf* : nastiness
mèche [mɛʃ] *nf* **1** : wick (of a candle) **2** : lock (of hair) **3** : bit (of a drill)
méconnaissable [mekɔnɛsabl] *adj* : unrecognizable
mécontent, -tente [mekɔ̃tɑ̃, -tɑ̃t] *adj* : discontented, dissatisfied — **mécontentement** [mekɔ̃tɑ̃tmɑ̃] *nm* : discontent, dissatisfaction
médaille [medaj] *nf* : medal — **médaillé, -lée** [medaje] *n* : medalist — **médaillon** [medajɔ̃] *nm* **1** : medallion **2** : locket
médecin [medsɛ̃] *nm* : doctor, physician — **médecine** [medsin] *nf* : medicine
média [medja] *nm* **1** : medium **2 les ~s** : the media
médian, -diane [medjɑ̃, -djan] *adj* : median
médiation [medjasjɔ̃] *nf* : mediation, arbitration — **médiateur, -trice** [medjatœr, -tris] *n* : mediator, arbitrator
médical, -cale [medikal] *adj, mpl* **-caux** [-ko] : medical — **médicament** [medikamɑ̃] *nm* : medicine, drug — **médication** [medikasjɔ̃] *nf* : medication — **médicinal, -nale** [medisinal] *adj, mpl* **-naux** [-no] : medicinal
médiéval, -vale [medjeval] *adj, mpl* **-vaux** [-vo] : medieval
médiocre [medjɔkr] *adj* : mediocre — **médiocrité** [medjɔkrite] *nf* : mediocrity
méditer [medite] *vt* : reflect on, think over — *vi* : meditate — **méditation** [meditasjɔ̃] *nf* : meditation
médium [medjɔm] *nm* : medium, psychic
méduse [medyz] *nf* : jellyfish
meeting [mitiŋ] *nm* **1** : meeting **2** : meet (in sports)
méfait [mefɛ] *nm* **1** : misdeed, misdemeanour **2 ~s** *nmpl* : ravages
méfier [mefje] {96} *v* **se méfier** *vr* **1** : be careful, beware **2 ~ de** : distrust — **méfiance** [mefjɑ̃s] *nf* : distrust — **méfiant, -fiante** [mefjɑ̃, -fjɑ̃t] *adj* : distrustful
mégarde [megard] *nf* **par ~** : inadvertently
mégot [mego] *nm* : cigarette butt
meilleur, -leure [mɛjœr] *adj* **1** : better **2** : best — **~** *n* : best (one) — **meilleur** *adv* : better
mélancolie [melɑ̃kɔli] *nf* : melancholy — **mélancolique** [melɑ̃kɔlik] *adj* : melancholy
mélanger [melɑ̃ʒe] {17} *vt* **1** : mix, blend **2** CONFONDRE : mix up, confuse — **se mélanger** *vr* **1** : blend (with) **2** : get mixed up — **mélange** [melɑ̃ʒ] *nm* **1** : mixing, blending **2** : mixture, blend
mélasse [melas] *nf* : molasses
mêlée [mele] *nf* **~ générale** : free-for-all
mêler [mele] *vt* : mix — **se mêler** *vr* **1** : mix, mingle **2 mêlez-vous de vos affaires** : mind your own business
mélodie [melɔdi] *nf* : melody
mélomane [melɔman] *nmf* : music lover
melon [melɔ̃] *nm* : melon
membrane [mɑ̃bran] *nf* : membrane
membre [mɑ̃br] *nm* **1** : limb **2** : member (of a group)
même [mɛm] *adj* **1** : same, identical **2** *(used as an intensifier)* : very, actual **3** → **elle–même, lui–même, eux–mêmes** — **~** *pron* **le ~, la ~, les ~s** : the same (one, ones) — **~** *adv* **1** : even **2 de ~** : likewise, the same
mémère [memɛr] *nf fam* **1** : grandma **2** *Can* : gossip
mémoire [memwar] *nf* : memory — **~** *nm* **1** : dissertation, thesis **2 ~s** *nmpl* : memoirs
mémorable [memɔrabl] *adj* : memorable
mémorandum [memɔrɑ̃dɔm] *nm* : memorandum
mémoriser [memɔrize] *vt* : memorize
menacer [mənase] {6} *v* : threaten — **menaçant, -çante** [mənasɑ̃, -sɑ̃t] *adj* : threatening — **menace** [mənas] *nf* : threat
ménage [menaʒ] *nm* **1** : household, family **2 faire le ~** : do the housework **3 un heureux ~** : a happy couple — **ménagement** [menaʒmɑ̃] *nm* : consideration, care — **ménager** [menaʒe] {17} *vt* **1** ÉPARGNER : save **2** : handle or treat with care — **se ménager** *vr* : take it easy — **ménager, -gère** [menaʒe, -ʒɛr] *adj* : household, domestic — **ménagère** [menaʒɛr] *nf* : housewife
mendier [mɑ̃dje] {96} *v* : beg — **mendiant, -diante** [mɑ̃djɑ̃, -djɑ̃t] *n* : beggar
menées [məne] *nfpl* : scheming, intrigues
mener [məne] {52} *vt* **1** : lead **2** DIRIGER : conduct, run **3 ~ qqch à**

terme : see sth through — **meneur, -neuse** [mənœr, -nøz] *n* **1** : leader **2** **meneuse de claque** *Can* : cheerleader
méningite [menɛ̃ʒit] *nf* : meningitis
ménopause [menɔpoz] *nf* : menopause
menottes [mənɔt] *nfpl* : handcuffs
mensonge [mɑ̃sɔ̃ʒ] *nm* **1** : lie **2 le ～** : lying — **mensonger, -gère** [mɑ̃sɔ̃ʒe, -ʒɛr] *adj* : false, misleading
menstruation [mɑ̃stryasjɔ̃] *nf* RÈGLES : menstruation — **menstruel, -struelle** [mɑ̃stryɛl] *adj* : menstrual
mensuel, -suelle [mɑ̃sɥɛl] *adj* : monthly — **mensuel** *nm* : monthly (magazine)
mensurations [mɑ̃syrasjɔ̃] *nfpl* : measurements
mental, -tale [mɑ̃tal] *adj, mpl* **-taux** [-to] : mental — **mentalité** [mɑ̃talite] *nf* : mentality
menteur, -teuse [mɑ̃tœr, -tøz] *adj* : untruthful, false — **～** *n* : liar
menthe [mɑ̃t] *nf* : mint
mention [mɑ̃sjɔ̃] *nf* **1** : mention **2** : (academic) distinction — **mentionner** [mɑ̃sjɔne] *vt* : mention
mentir [mɑ̃tir] {82} *vi* : lie
menton [mɑ̃tɔ̃] *nm* : chin
menu, -nue [məny] *adj* **1** PETIT : tiny **2** : minor, trifling — **menu** *adv* : finely — **～** *nm* : menu
menuiserie [mənɥizri] *nf* : woodworking, carpentry — **menuisier** [mənɥizje] *nm* : woodworker, carpenter
méprendre [meprɑ̃dr] {70} *v* **se méprendre** *vr* **～ sur** : be mistaken about
mépris [mepri] *nm* **1** DÉDAIN : contempt **2 au ～ de** : regardless of — **méprisable** [meprizabl] *adj* : despicable, contemptible — **méprisant, -sante** [meprizɑ̃, -zɑ̃t] *adj* : contemptuous, scornful — **mépriser** [meprize] *vt* : despise, scorn
mer [mɛr] *nf* **1** : sea **2** MARÉE : tide
mercenaire [mɛrsənɛr] *adj & nmf* : mercenary
mercerie [mɛrsəri] *nf* : notions *pl*
merci [mɛrsi] *interj* : thank you!, thanks! — **～** *nm* : thank-you — **～** *nf* : mercy
mercredi [mɛrkrədi] *nm* : Wednesday
mercure [mɛrkyr] *nm* : mercury
Mercure *nf* : Mercury (planet)
mère [mɛr] *nf* : mother
méridional, -nale [meridjɔnal] *adj, mpl* **-naux** [-no] : southern
meringue [mərɛ̃g] *nf* : meringue
mérite [merit] *nm* : merit, credit — **mériter** [merite] *vt* : deserve, merit — **méritoire** [meritwar] *adj* : commendable
merle [mɛrl] *nm* : blackbird
merveille [mɛrvɛj] *nf* **1** : wonder, marvel **2 à ～** : wonderfully — **merveilleux, -leuse** [mɛrvɛjø, -jøz] *adj* : wonderful, marvelous
mes → **mon**
mésaventure [mezavɑ̃tyr] *nf* : misfortune, mishap
mesdames → **madame**
mesdemoiselles → **mademoiselle**
mésentente [mezɑ̃tɑ̃t] *nf* DÉSACCORD : misunderstanding, disagreement
mesquin, -quine [mɛskɛ̃, -kin] *adj* **1** : mean, petty **2** : cheap, stingy — **mesquinerie** [mɛskinri] *nf* **1** : pettiness **2** AVARICE : stinginess
message [mɛsaʒ] *nm* : message — **messager, -gère** [mɛsaʒe, -ʒɛr] *n* : messenger — **messagerie** [mɛsaʒri] *nf* : parcel delivery service
messe [mɛs] *nf* : Mass
mesure [məzyr] *nf* **1** : measure, measurement **2** RETENUE : moderation **3 à la ～ de** : worthy of **4 à ～ que** : as **5 dans la ～ où** : insofar as — **mesuré, -rée** [məzyre] *adj* : measured, restrained — **mesurer** [məzyre] *vt* **1** : measure **2** ÉVALUER : assess
métabolisme [metabɔlism] *nm* : metabolism
métal [metal] *nm, pl* **-taux** [meto] : metal — **métallique** [metalik] *adj* : metallic
métamorphose [metamɔrfoz] *nf* : metamorphosis
métaphore [metafɔr] *nf* : metaphor
météo [meteo] *nf fam* : weather forecast
météore [meteɔr] *nm* : meteor
météorologie [meteɔrɔlɔʒi] *nf* : meteorology — **météorologique** [meteɔrɔlɔʒik] *adj* : meteorological, weather — **météorologiste** [meteɔrɔlɔʒist] *nmf* : meteorologist
méthode [metɔd] *nf* **1** : method, system **2** MANUEL : primer — **méthodique** [metɔdik] *adj* : methodical
méticuleux, -leuse [metikylø, -løz] *adj* : meticulous
métier [metje] *nm* **1** : job, profession **2** : experience, skill **3** *or* **～ à tisser** : loom
métis, -tisse [metis] *adj & n* : halfbreed, half-caste

métrage [metraʒ] *nm* **1** : length (of an object) **2** : footage (of a film)
mètre [mɛtr] *nm* **1** : meter **2 ~ ruban** : tape measure — **métrique** [metrik] *adj* : metric
métro [metro] *nm* : subway
métropole [metrɔpɔl] *nf* : city, metropolis — **métropolitain, -taine** [metrɔpɔlitɛ̃, -tɛn] *adj* : metropolitan
mets [mɛ] *nm* PLAT : dish
metteur [mɛtœr] *nm* **~ en scène** : producer, director
mettre [mɛtr] {53} *vt* **1** PLACER : put, place **2** : put on, wear **3** AJOUTER : add (in), put in **4** DISPOSER : prepare, arrange **5 ~ au point** : develop, finalize **6 ~ en marche** : turn on, switch on — **se mettre** *vr* **1** : become, get **2** : put on, wear **3 ~ à faire** : start doing **4 ~ à table** : sit down at the table
meuble [mœbl] *nm* **1** : piece of furniture **2 ~s** *nmpl* : furniture — **meublé, -blée** [mœble] *adj* : furnished — **meubler** [mœble] *vt* : furnish
meugler [møgle] *vi* : moo, low — **meuglement** [møgləmɑ̃] *nm* : mooing, lowing
meule [møl] *nf* **1** : millstone **2 ~ de foin** : haystack
meurtre [mœrtr] *nm* : murder — **meurtrier, -trière** [mœrtrije, -trijɛr] *adj* : deadly — **~** *n* ASSASSIN : murderer
meurtrir [mœrtrir] *vt* : bruise — **meurtrissure** [mœrtrisyr] *nf* : bruise
meute [møt] *nf* : pack (of hounds)
mexicain, -caine [meksikɛ̃, -kɛn] *adj* : Mexican
miaou [mjau] *nm* : meow — **miauler** [mjole] *vi* : meow
mi–bas [miba] *nms & pl* : kneesock
miche [miʃ] *nf* : round loaf of bread
mi–chemin [miʃmɛ̃] **à ~** *adv phr* : halfway, midway
microbe [mikrɔb] *nm* : germ, microbe
microfilm [mikrɔfilm] *nm* : microfilm
micro–ondes [mikrɔɔ̃d] *nms & pl* : microwave oven
microphone [mikrɔfɔn] *nm* : microphone
microscope [mikrɔskɔp] *nm* : microscope — **microscopique** [mikrɔskɔpik] *adj* : microscopic
microsillon [mikrɔsijɔ̃] *nm* : long-playing record
midi [midi] *nm* **1** : midday, noon **2** : lunchtime **3** SUD : south
mie [mi] *nf* : inside, soft part (of a loaf of bread)
miel [mjɛl] *nm* : honey — **mielleux, -leuse** [mjɛlø, -løz] *adj* : sickly sweet
mien, mienne [mjɛ̃, mjɛn] *adj* : mine, my own — **~** *pron* **le mien, la mienne, les miens, les miennes** : mine
miette [mjɛt] *nf* **1** : crumb **2 en ~s** : in pieces
mieux [mjø] *adv & adj* **1** (*comparative of* **bien**) : better **2** (*superlative of* **bien**) **le ~, la ~, les ~** : the best — **~** *nm* **1** : best **2 il y a du ~** : there's some improvement
mignon, -gnonne [miɲɔ̃, -ɲɔn] *adj* **1** : sweet, cute **2** GENTIL : nice, kind
migraine [migrɛn] *nf* : headache, migraine
migration [migrasjɔ̃] *nf* : migration — **migrateur, -trice** [migratœr, -tris] *adj* : migratory
mijoter [miʒɔte] *vt* **1** : simmer **2** MANIGANCER : plot, cook up — *vi* : simmer, stew
mil [mil] → **mille**
mile [majl] *nm* : mile
milice [milis] *nf* : militia
milieu [miljø] *nm, pl* **-lieux 1** CENTRE : middle **2** ENTOURAGE : environment **3 au ~ de** : among, in the midst of
militaire [militɛr] *adj* : military — **~** *nm* SOLDAT : soldier, serviceman
militant, -tante [militɑ̃, -tɑ̃t] *adj & n* : militant
millage [milaʒ] *nm Can* : mileage (of a motor vehicle)
mille [mil] *adj* : one thousand — **~** *nm or* **~ marin** : nautical mile
millénaire [milenɛr] *nm* : millennium
mille–pattes [milpat] *nms & pl* **1** : centipede **2** : millipede
millésime [milezim] *nm* **1** : year (of manufacture) **2** : vintage year
millet [mijɛ] *nm* : millet
milliard [miljar] *nm* : billion — **milliardaire** [miljardɛr] *nmf* : billionaire
millier [milje] *nm* : thousand
milligramme [miligram] *nm* : milligram
millimètre [milimɛtr] *nm* : millimeter
million [miljɔ̃] *nm* : million — **millionnaire** [miljɔnɛr] *nmf* : millionaire
mime [mim] *nmf* : mime — **mimer** [mime] *vt* : mimic
mimique [mimik] *nf* GRIMACE : face
minable [minabl] *adj* : shabby
mince [mɛ̃s] *adj* **1** : thin, slender **2** INSIGNIFIANT : meager, scanty —

minceur [mɛ̃sœr] *nf* : thinness, slenderness
mine[1] [min] *nf* : appearance, look
mine[2] *nf* **1** : (coal) mine **2** : (pencil) lead — **miner** [mine] *vt* : undermine, weaken — **minerai** [minrɛ] *nm* : ore
minéral, -rale [mineral] *adj, mpl* **-raux** [-ro] : mineral — **minéral** *nm* : mineral
minet, -nette [minɛ, -nɛt] *n fam* : pussycat
mineur[1], **-neure** [minœr] *adj & nmf* : minor
mineur[2] *nm* : miner
miniature [minjatyr] *adj & nf* : miniature
minimal, -male [minimal] *adj, mpl* **-maux** [-mo] : minimal, minimum — **minime** [minim] *adj* : minimal, negligible — **minimiser** [minimize] *vt* : minimize — **minimum** [minimɔm] *adj & nm, pl* **-mums** [-mɔm] *or* **-ma** [-ma] : minimum
ministère [ministɛr] *nm* **1** : department, ministry **2** CABINET : government — **ministériel, -rielle** [ministerjɛl] *adj* : governmental — **ministre** [ministr] *nm* : minister, secretary
minorité [minɔrite] *nf* : minority — **minoritaire** [minɔritɛr] *adj* : minority
minou [minu] *nm fam* : pussycat
minuit [minɥi] *nm* : midnight
minuscule [minyskyl] *adj* : minute, tiny — **~** *nf* : small (lowercase) letter
minute [minyt] *nf* : minute — **minuter** [minyte] *vt* : time — **minuterie** [minytri] *nf* : timer
minutieux, -tieuse [minysjø, -sjøz] *adj* **1** MÉTICULEUX : meticulous **2** : detailed (of work, etc.) — **minutie** [minysi] *nf* : meticulousness
miracle [mirakl] *nm* : miracle — **miraculeux, -leuse** [mirakylø, -løz] *adj* : miraculous
mirage [miraʒ] *nm* : mirage
mire [mir] *nf* **point de ~** : target
miroir [mirwar] *nm* : mirror
miroiter [mirwate] *vi* BRILLER : sparkle, shimmer — **miroitement** [mirwatmɑ̃] *nm* : sparkling, shimmering
mis, mise [mi, miz] *adj* **1** : clad **2 bien ~** : well-dressed
mise [miz] *nf* **1** : putting, placing **2** : stake (in games of chance) **3** TENUE : dress, attire — **miser** [mize] *vt* : bet — *vi* **~ sur** : bet on, count on
misérable [mizerabl] *adj* **1** PITOYABLE : wretched, pitiful **2** INSIGNIFIANT : meager, paltry — **~** *nmf* **1** : wretch **2** : scoundrel — **misère** [mizɛr] *nf* **1** : poverty **2** : misery
miséricorde [mizerikɔrd] *nf* : mercy, forgiveness
missile [misil] *nm* : missile
mission [misjɔ̃] *nf* : mission — **missionnaire** [misjɔnɛr] *adj & nmf* : missionary
mitaine [mitɛn] *nf Can, Switz* : mitten
mite [mit] *nf* : clothes moth
mi-temps [mitɑ̃] *nms & pl* : part-time job — **~** *nfs & pl* : halftime (in sports)
miteux, -teuse [mitø, -tøz] *adj* : seedy, shabby
mitigé, -gée [mitiʒe] *adj* **1** : lukewarm, reserved **2 sentiments mitigés** : mixed feelings
mitoyen, -toyenne [mitwajɛ̃, -jɛn] *adj* : common, dividing
mitrailleuse [mitrajøz] *nf* : machine gun
mi-voix [mivwa] **à ~** *adv phr* : in a low voice
mixeur [miksœr] *or* **mixer** [miksɛr] *nm* : mixer, blender
mixte [mikst] *adj* **1** : mixed **2 école ~** : coeducational school
mobile [mɔbil] *adj* **1** : mobile, moving **2 feuilles ~s** : loose-leaf paper — **~** *nm* **1** : motive (of a crime) **2** : (paper) mobile — **mobilier** [mɔbilje] *nm* MEUBLES : furniture
mobiliser [mɔbilize] *vt* : mobilize
mobilité [mɔbilite] *nf* : mobility
mocassin [mɔkasɛ̃] *nm* : moccasin
moche [mɔʃ] *adj fam* **1** : ugly **2** MAUVAIS : lousy
modalité [mɔdalite] *nf* : form, mode
mode [mɔd] *nm* **1** : mode, method **2 ~ d'emploi** : directions for use — **~** *nf* : fashion
modèle [mɔdɛl] *nm* : model — **~** *adj* : model, exemplary — **modeler** [mɔdle] {20} *vt* : mold, shape
modem [mɔdɛm] *nm* : modem
modérer [mɔdere] {87} *vt* : moderate, restrain — **modérateur, -trice** [mɔderatœr, -tris] *adj* : moderating — **modération** [mɔderasjɔ̃] *nf* MESURE : moderation, restraint — **modéré, -rée** [mɔdere] *adj* : moderate
moderne [mɔdɛrn] *adj* : modern — **moderniser** [mɔdɛrnize] *vt* : modernize
modeste [mɔdɛst] *adj* : modest — **modestie** [mɔdɛsti] *nf* : modesty
modifier [mɔdifje] {96} *vt* : modify — **se modifier** *vr* : change — **modification** [mɔdifikasjɔ̃] *nf* : modification

modique [mɔdik] *adj* : modest, low
moduler [mɔdyle] *vt* : modulate, adjust
moelle [mwal] *nf* **1** : marrow **2** ~ **épinière** : spinal cord — **moelleux, -leuse** [mwalø, -løz] *adj* **1** DOUX : soft **2** : moist (of a cake)
mœurs [mœr(s)] *nfpl* **1** : morals **2** USAGES : customs, habits
moi [mwa] *pron* **1** : I **2** : me **3** **à** ~ : mine — ~ *nm* **le** ~ : the self, the ego — **moi-même** [mwamɛm] *pron* : myself
moindre [mwɛ̃dr] *adj* **1** : lesser, smaller, lower **2** **le** ~, **la** ~ : the least, the slightest
moine [mwan] *nm* : monk
moineau [mwano] *nm, pl* **-neaux** : sparrow
moins [mwɛ̃] *adv* **1** : less **2** **le** ~ : least, the least **3** ~ **de** : less than, fewer **4** **à** ~ **que** : unless **5** **en** ~ : missing — ~ *nm* **1** : minus (sign) **2** **au** ~ *or* **du** ~ : at least **3** **pour le** ~ : at (the very) least — ~ *prep* **1** : minus **2** (*in expressions of time*) : to, of **3** (*in expressions of temperature*) : below
mois [mwa] *nm* : month
moisi, -sie [mwazi] *adj* : moldy — **moisi** *nm* : mold, mildew — **moisir** [mwazir] *vi* **1** : become moldy **2** *fam* : stagnate — **moisissure** [mwazisyr] *nf* : mold, mildew
moisson [mwasɔ̃] *nf* : harvest, crop — **moissonner** [mwasɔne] *vt* : harvest, reap — **moissonneuse** [mwasɔnøz] *nf* : harvester, reaper — **moissonneuse-batteuse** [mwasɔnøzbatøz] *nf, pl* **moissonneuses-batteuses** : combine (harvester)
moite [mwat] *adj* : damp, clammy
moitié [mwatje] *nf* **1** : half **2** **à** ~ : half, halfway — **moitié-moitié** *adv* : fifty-fifty
moka [moka] *nm* : mocha
mol → **mou**
molaire [mɔlɛr] *nf* : molar
molécule [mɔlekyl] *nf* : molecule
molle → **mou** — **mollesse** [mɔlɛs] *adj* **1** : softness **2** INDOLENCE : indolence, apathy — **mollement** [mɔlmɑ̃] *adv* **1** DOUCEMENT : softly, gently **2** : weakly, feebly
mollet [mɔlɛ] *nm* : calf (of the leg)
mollir [mɔlir] *vi* **1** : soften, go soft **2** FAIBLIR : weaken, slacken
mollusque [mɔlysk] *nm* : mollusk
môme [mom] *nmf France fam* : kid, youngster
moment [mɔmɑ̃] *nm* **1** : moment, while **2** INSTANT : minute, instant **3** OCCASION : time, occasion **4** : present (time) **5** **du** ~ **que** : since — **momentané, -née** [mɔmɑ̃tane] *adj* : momentary, temporary — **momentanément** [-nemɑ̃] *adv* **1** : momentarily **2** : at the moment
momie [mɔmi] *nf* : mummy
mon [mɔ̃], **ma** [ma] *adj, pl* **mes** [mɛ] : my
monarchie [mɔnarʃi] *nf* : monarchy — **monarque** [mɔnark] *nm* : monarch
monastère [mɔnastɛr] *nm* : monastery
monceau [mɔ̃so] *nm, pl* **-ceaux** [mɔ̃so] : heap, pile
mondain, -daine [mɔ̃dɛ̃, -dɛn] *adj* **1** : society, social **2** RAFFINÉ : fashionable
monde [mɔ̃d] *nm* **1** : world **2** : society, people *pl* **3** **tout le** ~ : everyone — **mondial, -diale** [mɔ̃djal] *adj, mpl* **-diaux** [-djo] **1** : world **2** : worldwide, global — **mondialement** [mɔ̃djalmɑ̃] *adv* : throughout the world
monétaire [mɔnetɛr] *adj* : monetary
moniteur, -trice [mɔnitœr, -tris] *n* : instructor, coach — **moniteur** *nm* : monitor, screen
monnaie [mɔnɛ] *nf* **1** : money, currency **2** PIÈCE : coin — **monnayer** [mɔnɛje] {11} *vt* **1** : convert into cash **2** : capitalize on (experience, etc.) — **monnayeur** [mɔnɛjœr] *nm* → **faux-monnayeur**
monocorde [mɔnɔkɔrd] *adj* : droning, monotonous
monogramme [mɔnɔgram] *nm* : monogram
monologue [mɔnɔlɔg] *nm* : monologue, soliloquy
monopole [mɔnɔpɔl] *nm* : monopoly — **monopoliser** [mɔnɔpɔlize] *vt* : monopolize
monotone [mɔnɔtɔn] *adj* : monotonous, dull — **monotonie** [mɔnɔtɔni] *nf* : monotony
monsieur [məsjø] *nm, pl* **messieurs** [mɛsjø] **1** : Mr., sir **2** : man, gentleman
monstre [mɔ̃str] *nm* : monster — ~ *adj* : huge, colossal — **monstrueux, -trueuse** [mɔ̃stryø, -tryøz] *adj* **1** : monstrous, huge **2** TERRIBLE : hideous — **monstruosité** [mɔ̃stryozite] *nf* : monstrosity
mont [mɔ̃] *nm* : mount, mountain
montage [mɔ̃taʒ] *nm* **1** : editing (of a film) **2** **chaîne de** ~ : assembly line

montagne [mɔ̃taɲ] *nf* **1** : mountain **2 la ~** : the mountains **3 ~s russes** : roller coaster — **montagneux, -gneuse** [mɔ̃taɲø, -ɲøz] *adj* : mountainous
montant, -tante [mɔ̃tɑ̃, -tɑ̃t] *adj* : uphill, rising — **montant** *nm* **1** : upright, post **2** SOMME : total, sum
mont–de–piété [mɔ̃dpjete] *nm, pl* **monts–de–piété** *France* : pawnshop
monte–charge [mɔ̃tʃarʒ] *nms & pl* : freight elevator
monter [mɔ̃te] *vi* **1** : go up, come up, climb (up) **2** : rise (of temperature, etc.) **3 ~ à** : ride (a bicycle, etc.) **4 ~ dans** : get into, board **5 ~ sur** : mount, get on (a horse) — *vt* (*with auxiliary verb* **avoir**) **1** : take up, bring up **2** : raise, turn up (volume, etc.) **3** : go up, climb (up) **4** : assemble, put together **5 ~ à cheval** : ride a horse — **se monter** *vr* **~ à** : amount to — **montée** [mɔ̃te] *nf* **1** : rise, rising **2** : ascent, climb **3** PENTE : slope
montre [mɔ̃tr] *nf* **1** : watch **2 faire ~ de** : show, display
montréalais, -laise [mɔreale, -lez] *adj* : of or from Montreal
montre–bracelet [mɔ̃trəbraslɛ] *nf, pl* **montres–bracelets** : wristwatch
montrer [mɔ̃tre] *vt* **1** : show, reveal **2** INDIQUER : point out — **se montrer** *vr* **1** : show oneself **2** : prove to be
monture [mɔ̃tyr] *nf* **1** : mount, horse **2** : setting (for jewelry) **3** : frames *pl* (for eyeglasses)
monument [mɔnymɑ̃] *nm* : monument — **monumental, -tale** [mɔnymɑ̃tal] *adj, mpl* **-taux** [-to] : monumental
moquer [mɔke] *v* **se moquer** *vr* **1 ~ de** : make fun of, mock **2 je m'en moque** : I couldn't care less — **moquerie** [mɔkri] *nf* : mockery
moquette [mɔkɛt] *nf* : wall-to-wall carpeting
moqueur, -queuse [mɔkœr, -køz] *adj* : mocking
moral, -rale [mɔral] *adj, mpl* **-raux** [mɔro] : moral — **moral** *nm* : morale, spirits *pl* — **morale** *nf* **1** : morals *pl*, morality **2** : moral (of a story) — **moralisateur, -trice** [mɔralizatœr, -tris] *adj* : moralizing — **moralité** [mɔralite] *nf* : morality
morbide [mɔrbid] *adj* : morbid
morceau [mɔrso] *nm, pl* **-ceaux** : piece, bit — **morceler** [mɔrsəle] {8} *vt* : break up, divide
mordant, -dante [mɔrdɑ̃, -dɑ̃t] *adj* : biting, scathing — **mordant** *nm* : bite, punch
mordiller [mɔrdije] *vt* : nibble at
mordre [mɔrdr] {63} *v* : bite — **se mordre** *vr* **~ la langue** : bite one's tongue — **mordu, -due** *adj* : smitten (with love) — **~** *n fam* : fan, buff
morfondre [mɔrfɔ̃dr] {63} *v* **se morfondre** *vr* **1** : mope **2** *Can* : wear oneself out
morgue [mɔrg] *nf* **1** : morgue, mortuary **2** ARROGANCE : arrogance
morille [mɔrij] *nf* : type of mushroom
morne [mɔrn] *adj* **1** SOMBRE : gloomy, glum **2** MAUSSADE : dismal, dreary
morose [mɔroz] *adj* : morose, sullen
morphine [mɔrfin] *nf* : morphine
mors [mɔr] *nm* : bit (of a bridle)
morse [mɔrs] *nm* **1** : walrus **2** : Morse code
morsure [mɔrsyr] *nf* : bite
mort, morte [mɔr, mɔrt] *adj* : dead — **~** *n* **1** : dead person, corpse **2** VICTIME : fatality — **mort** *nf* : death — **mortalité** [mɔrtalite] *nf* : mortality — **mortel, -telle** [mɔrtɛl] *adj* **1** : mortal **2** FATAL : fatal — **~** *n* : mortal
mortier [mɔrtje] *nm* : mortar
mortifier [mɔrtifje] {96} *vt* : mortify
mortuaire [mɔrtɥɛr] *adj* **1** FUNÈBRE : funeral **2 salon ~** *Can* : funeral home
morue [mɔry] *nf* : cod
mosaïque [mɔzaik] *adj & nf* : mosaic
mosquée [mɔske] *nf* : mosque
mot [mo] *nm* **1** : word **2** : note, line **3 ~ de passe** : password **4 ~s croisés** : crossword puzzle
motel [mɔtɛl] *nm* : motel
moteur [mɔtœr] *nm* : engine, motor — **moteur, -trice** [mɔtœr, -tris] *adj* **1** : motor **2 force motrice** : driving force
motif [mɔtif] *nm* **1** RAISON : motive, grounds *pl* **2** DESSIN : pattern, design
motion [mosjɔ̃] *nf* : motion (in politics)
motiver [mɔtive] *vt* **1** : motivate **2** EXPLIQUER : justify, explain — **motivation** [mɔtivasjɔ̃] *nf* : motivation, incentive
moto [mɔto] *nf* : bike, motorbike — **motocyclette** [mɔtɔsiklɛt] *nf* : motorcycle
motoriser [mɔtɔrize] *vt* : motorize
motte [mɔt] *nf* : clod, lump (of earth, etc.)
mou [mu] (**mol** [mɔl] *before vowel or mute h*), **molle** [mɔl] *adj* **1** : soft **2** FLASQUE : flabby, limp **3** LÂCHE : slack

4 avoir les jambes molles : be weak in the knees
mouchard, -charde [muʃar, -ʃard] *n fam* : informer, stool pigeon
mouche [muʃ] *nf* : fly
moucher [muʃe] *v* **se moucher** *vr* : blow one's nose
moucheron [muʃrɔ̃] *nm* : gnat
moucheté [muʃte] *adj* : speckled, flecked
mouchoir [muʃwar] *nm* : handkerchief
moudre [mudr] {54} *vt* : grind
moue [mu] *nf* **1** : pout **2 faire la ～** : pout
mouette [mwɛt] *nf* : gull, seagull
mouffette *or* **moufette** [mufɛt] *nf* : skunk
moufle [mufl] *nf* : mitten
mouiller [muje] *vt* **1** : wet, moisten **2 ～ l'ancre** : drop anchor — **se mouiller** *vr* **1** : get wet **2** *fam* : become involved — **mouillage** [mujaʒ] *nm* : anchorage, berth — **mouillé, -lée** [muje] *adj* : wet
moulage [mulaʒ] *nm* **1** : molding, casting **2 faire un ～ de** : take a cast of
moulant, -lante [mulɑ̃, -lɑ̃t] *adj* : tight-fitting (of clothes, etc.)
moule[1] [mul] *nf* : mussel
moule[2] *nm* **1** : mold, matrix **2 ～ à gâteaux** : cake pan — **mouler** [mule] *vt* **1** : mold **2** : cast (a statue)
moulin [mulɛ̃] *nm* **1** : mill **2 ～ à café** : coffee grinder **3 ～ à paroles** *fam* : chatterbox — **moulinet** [mulinɛ] *nm* : reel, winch
moulu, -lue [muly] *adj* **1** : ground (of coffee, etc.) **2** *fam* : worn-out
moulure [mulyr] *nf* : molding
mourir [murir] {55} *vi* **1** : die **2** : die out (of a sound, etc.) **3 ～ de faim** : be dying of hunger — **mourant, -rante** [murɑ̃, -rɑ̃t] *n* : dying person
mousquet [muskɛ] *nm* : musket — **mousquetaire** [muskətɛr] *nm* : musketeer
mousse [mus] *nf* **1** : moss (in botany) **2** : foam, lather **3** : mousse (in cooking) — **moussant, -sante** [musɑ̃, -sɑ̃t] *adj* : foaming — **mousser** [muse] *vi* : foam, froth, lather — **mousseux, -seuse** [musø, -søz] *adj* **1** : foaming, frothy **2 vin ～** : sparkling wine
moustache [mustaʃ] *nf* **1** : mustache **2 ～s** *nfpl* : whiskers (of an animal)
moustique [mustik] *nm* : mosquito — **moustiquaire** [mustikɛr] *nf* **1** : mosquito net **2** : screen (for a window, etc.)
moutarde [mutard] *nf* : mustard
mouton [mutɔ̃] *nm* **1** : sheep, sheepskin **2** : mutton (in cooking)
mouvement [muvmɑ̃] *nm* **1** : movement **2** ACTIVITÉ : activity, bustle **3** IMPULSION : impulse, reaction — **mouvementé, -tée** [muvmɑ̃te] *adj* **1** : eventful, hectic **2** ACCIDENTÉ : rough, uneven — **mouvoir** [muvwar] {56} *vt* : move, prompt
moyen, moyenne [mwajɛ̃, -jɛn] *adj* **1** : medium **2** : average **3 Moyen Âge** : Middle Ages *pl* — **moyen** *nm* **1** : way, means *pl* **2** : possibility **3 ～s** *nmpl* : means, resources — **moyenne** *nf* : average — **moyennement** [mwajɛnmɑ̃] *adv* MODÉRÉMENT : fairly, moderately
moyeu [mwajø] *nm, pl* **moyeux** : hub (of a wheel)
muer [mɥe] *vi* **1** : molt, shed **2** : change, break (of the voice) — **mue** [my] *nf* : molting, shedding
muet, muette [mɥɛ, mɥɛt] *adj* **1** : dumb **2** SILENCIEUX : silent — **～** *n* : mute, dumb person
muffin [mɔfœn] *nm Can* : muffin
muguet [mygɛ] *nm* : lily of the valley
mule [myl] *nf* : female mule — **mulet** [mylɛ] *nm* : male mule
multicolore [myltikɔlɔr] *adj* : multicolored
multimédia [myltimedja] *adj* : multimedia
multinational, -nale [myltinasjɔnal] *adj, mpl* **-naux** [-no] : multinational
multiple [myltipl] *adj* **1** : multiple **2** DIVERS : many — **～** *nm* : multiple — **multiplication** [myltiplikasjɔ̃] *nf* : multiplication — **multiplier** [myltiplije] {96} *vt* : multiply — **se multiplier** *vr* : proliferate
multitude [myltityd] *nf* : multitude, mass
municipal, -pale [mynisipal] *adj, mpl* **-paux** [-po] : municipal, town — **municipalité** [mynisipalite] *nf* **1** : municipality, town **2** : town council
munir [mynir] *vt* : equip, provide — **se munir** *vr* **～ de** : equip oneself with
munitions [mynisjɔ̃] *nfpl* : ammunition, munitions
mur [myr] *nm* : wall
mûr, mûre [myr] *adj* **1** : ripe (of a fruit) **2** : mature (of a person)
muraille [myraj] *nf* : (high) wall — **mural, -rale** [myral] *adj, mpl* **-raux** [myro] : wall, mural — **murale** [myral] *nf* : mural

mûre [myr] *nf* : blackberry
mûrir [myrir] *v* **1** : ripen **2** ÉVOLUER : mature, develop
murmure [myrmyr] *nm* : murmur — **murmurer** [myrmyre] *v* : murmur
muscade [myskad] *nf or* **noix ~** : nutmeg
muscle [myskl] *nm* : muscle — **musclé, -clée** [myskle] *adj* : muscular, powerful — **musculaire** [myskylɛr] *adj* : muscular — **musculature** [mysklatyr] *nf* : muscles *pl*
muse [myz] *nf* : muse
museau [myzo] *nm, pl* **-seaux** : muzzle, snout
musée [myze] *nm* : museum
museler [myzle] {8} *vt* : muzzle — **muselière** [myzəljɛr] *nf* : muzzle
musique [myzik] *nf* : music — **musical, -cale** [myzikal] *adj* **-caux** [-ko] : musical — **musicien, -cienne** [myzisjɛ̃, -sjɛn] *n* : musician
musulman, -mane [myzylmɑ̃, -man] *adj & n* : Muslim
mutant, -tante [mytɑ̃, -tɑ̃t] *adj & n* : mutant — **mutation** [mytasjɔ̃] *nf* **1** : transformation **2** : transfer (of an employee) — **muter** [myte] *vt* : transfer (an employee)
mutiler [mytile] *vt* : mutilate
mutiner [mytine] *v* **se mutiner** *vr* : mutiny, rebel — **mutinerie** [mytinri] *nf* RÉBELLION : mutiny, rebellion
mutuel, -tuelle [mytɥɛl] *adj* : mutual
myope [mjɔp] *adj* : nearsighted — **myopie** [mjɔpi] *nf* : myopia, nearsightedness
myrtille [mirtil] *nf France* : blueberry
mystère [mistɛr] *nm* : mystery — **mystérieux, -rieuse** [misterjø, -rjøz] *adj* : mysterious
mystifier [mistifje] {96} *vt* DUPER : deceive, dupe
mystique [mistik] *adj* : mystic, mystical
mythe [mit] *nm* : myth — **mythique** [mitik] *adj* : mythic(al) — **mythologie** [mitɔlɔʒi] *nf* : mythology

N

n [ɛn] *nm* : n, 14th letter of the alphabet
nacre [nakr] *nf* : mother-of-pearl — **nacré, -crée** [nakre] *adj* : pearly
nager [naʒe] {17} *v* : swim — **nage** [naʒ] *nf* **1** : swimming **2** : stroke (in swimming) **3 en ~** : dripping with sweat — **nageoire** [naʒwar] *nf* : fin, flipper — **nageur, -geuse** [naʒœr, -ʒøz] *n* : swimmer
naguère [nagɛr] *adv* **1** RÉCEMMENT : recently **2** AUTREFOIS : formerly
naïf, naïve [naif, naiv] *adj* **1** INGÉNU : naive **2** CRÉDULE : gullible
nain, naine [nɛ̃, nɛn] *n* : dwarf, midget
naître [nɛtr] {57} *vi* **1** : be born **2** : rise, originate — **naissance** [nɛsɑ̃s] *nf* **1** : birth **2 donner ~ à** : give rise to — **naissant, -sante** [nɛsɑ̃, -sɑ̃t] *adj* : incipient
naïveté [naivte] *nf* : naïveté
nantir [nɑ̃tir] *vt* **~ de** : provide with — **nanti, -tie** [nɑ̃ti] *adj* : affluent, well-to-do — **nantissement** [nɑ̃tismɑ̃] *nm* : collateral
nappe [nap] *nf* **1** : tablecloth **2** : layer, sheet (of water, oil, etc.) — **napper** [nape] *vt* : coat, cover — **napperon** [naprɔ̃] *nm* : mat, doily
narcotique [narkɔtik] *nm* : narcotic
narguer [narge] *vt* : mock, taunt
narine [narin] *nf* : nostril
narquois, -quoise [narkwa, -kwaz] *adj* : sneering, derisive
narrer [nare] *vt* : narrate, tell — **narrateur, -trice** [naratœr, -tris] *n* : narrator — **narration** [narasjɔ̃] *nf* : narration, narrative
nasal, -sale [nazal] *adj, mpl* **-saux** [nazo] : nasal — **naseau** [nazo] *nm, pl* **-seaux** : nostril (of an animal) — **nasillard, -larde** [nazijar, -jard] *adj* : nasal (in tone)
natal, -tale [natal] *adj, mpl* **-tals** : native (of a country, etc.) — **natalité** [natalite] *nf* : birthrate
natation [natasjɔ̃] *nf* : swimming
natif[1], -tive [natif, -tiv] *adj* **~ de** : be born in
natif[2], -tive *n* : native
nation [nasjɔ̃] *nf* : nation — **national, -nale** [nasjɔnal] *adj, mpl* **-naux** [-no] : national — **nationale** *nf France* : highway — **nationaliser** [nasjɔnalize] *vt* : nationalize — **nationalisme** [nasjɔnalism] *nm* : nationalism — **nationalité** [nasjɔnalite] *nf* : nationality
nativité [nativite] *nf* : nativity
natte [nat] *nf* **1** : (straw) mat **2** : braid (of hair) — **natter** [nate] *vt* : braid, plait

naturaliser [natyralize] *vt* : naturalize
nature [natyr] *nf* **1** : nature **2** ~ **morte** : still life — ~ *adj* : plain (of yogurt, etc.) — **naturel, -relle** [natyrɛl] *adj* : natural — **naturel** *nm* **1** : nature, disposition **2** AISANCE : naturalness — **naturellement** [natyrɛlmɑ̃] *adv* **1** : naturally **2** : of course
naufrage [nofraʒ] *nm* : shipwreck — **naufragé, -gée** [nofraʒe] *adj & n* : castaway
nausée [noze] *nf* : nausea — **nauséabond, -bonde** [nozeabɔ̃, -bɔnd] *adj* : nauseating, revolting
nautique [notik] *adj* : nautical
naval, -vale [naval] *adj, mpl* **-vals** : naval
navet [navɛ] *nm* **1** : turnip **2** *fam* : third-rate film, novel, etc.
navette [navɛt] *nf* **1** : shuttle **2 faire la** ~ : shuttle back and forth, commute
naviguer [navige] *vi* : sail, navigate — **navigable** [navigabl] *adj* : navigable — **navigateur, -trice** [navigatœr, -tris] *n* : navigator — **navigation** [navigasjɔ̃] *nf* : navigation
navire [navir] *nm* : ship, vessel
navrant, -vrante [navrɑ̃, -vrɑ̃t] *adj* **1** : upsetting, distressing **2** REGRETTABLE : unfortunate — **navré, -vrée** [navre] *adj* **être** ~ **de** : be sorry about
ne [nə] (**n'** *before a vowel or mute h*) *adv* **1** ~ **pas** : not **2** ~ **jamais** : never **3** ~ **plus** : no longer **4** ~ **que** : only
né, née [ne] *adj* : born
néanmoins [neɑ̃mwɛ̃] *adv* : nevertheless, yet
néant [neɑ̃] *nm* : emptiness, nothingness
nébuleux, -leuse [nebylø, -løz] *adj* **1** : cloudy (of the sky) **2** VAGUE : nebulous
nécessaire [nesesɛr] *adj* : necessary — ~ *nm* **1** : necessity, need **2** TROUSSE : bag, kit — **nécessairement** [nesesɛrmɑ̃] *adv* : necessarily — **nécessité** [nesesite] *nf* : necessity, need — **nécessiter** [nesesite] *vt* EXIGER : require, call for
nécrologie [nekrɔlɔʒi] *nf* : obituary
nectar [nɛktar] *nm* : nectar
nectarine [nɛktarin] *nf* : nectarine
nef [nɛf] *nf* : nave
néfaste [nefast] *adj* NUISIBLE : harmful
négatif, -tive [negatif, -tiv] *adj* : negative — **négatif** *nm* : negative (in photography) — **négative** *nf* **répondre par la** ~ : reply in the negative — **négation** [negasjɔ̃] *nf* : negative (in grammar)
négliger [negliʒe] {17} *vt* **1** : neglect **2** IGNORER : disregard — **négligé, -gée** [negliʒe] *adj* : untidy (of appearance, etc.) — **négligé** *nm* : negligee — **négligeable** [negliʒabl] *adj* : negligible — **négligence** [negliʒɑ̃s] *nf* : negligence, carelessness — **négligent, -gente** [negliʒɑ̃, -ʒɑ̃t] *adj* : negligent
négoce [negɔs] *nm* : business, trade — **négociant, -ciante** [negɔsjɑ̃, -sjɑ̃t] *n* : merchant
négocier [negɔsje] {96} *v* : negotiate — **négociable** [negɔsjabl] *adj* : negotiable — **négociateur, -trice** [negɔsjatœr, -tris] *n* : negotiator — **négociation** [negɔsjasjɔ̃] *nf* : negotiation
nègre, négresse [nɛgr, negrɛs] *adj & n* (*sometimes considered offensive*) : Negro
neige [nɛʒ] *nf* **1** : snow **2** ~ **fondue** : slush — **neiger** [neʒe] {17} *v impers* : snow — **neigeux, -geuse** [nɛʒø, -ʒøz] *adj* : snowy
nénuphar [nenyfar] *nm* : water lily
néon [neɔ̃] *nm* : neon
néophyte [neɔfit] *nmf* : novice, beginner
Neptune [nɛptyn] *nf* : Neptune (planet)
nerf [nɛr] *nm* **1** : nerve **2** VIGUEUR : vigor, spirit — **nerveux, -veuse** [nɛrvø, -vøz] *adj* : nervous, tense — **nervosité** [nɛrvozite] *nf* : nervousness
nervure [nɛrvyr] *nf* : vein (of a leaf)
n'est–ce pas [nɛspa] *adv* : no?, isn't that right?, isn't it?
net, nette [nɛt] *adj* **1** PROPRE : clean, tidy **2** CLAIR : clear, distinct — **net** *adv* : plainly, flatly — **nettement** [nɛtmɑ̃] *adv* **1** : clearly, distinctly **2** : definitely — **netteté** [nɛtte] *nf* **1** : cleanness **2** : clearness, sharpness
nettoyer [nɛtwaje] {58} *vt* **1** : clean (up) **2** ~ **à sec** : dry-clean — **nettoyage** [netwajaʒ] *nm* : cleaning — **nettoyant** [netwajɑ̃] *nm* : cleaning agent
neuf[1] [nœf] *adj* **1** : nine **2** : ninth (in dates) — ~ *nms & pl* : nine
neuf[2], **neuve** [nœf, nœv] *adj* : new — **neuf** *nm* **quoi de** ~**?** : what's new?
neurologie [nørɔlɔʒi] *nf* : neurology
neutre [nøtr] *adj* **1** : neuter (in grammar) **2** : neutral — **neutraliser** [nøtralize] *vt* : neutralize — **neutralité** [nøtralite] *nf* : neutrality
neutron [nøtrɔ̃] *nm* : neutron
neuvième [nœvjɛm] *adj & nmf & nm* : ninth

neveu [nəvø] *nm, pl* **-veux** : nephew
névrosé, -sée [nevroze] *adj & n* : neurotic — **névrotique** [nevrɔtik] *adj* : neurotic
nez [ne] *nm* : nose
ni [ni] *conj* **1 ~ . . . ~** : neither . . . nor **2 ~ plus ~ moins** : no more, no less
niais, niaise [njɛ, njɛz] *adj* : simple, foolish — **niaiserie** [njɛzri] *nf* : foolishness
niche [niʃ] *nf* **1** : niche, recess **2** : kennel — **nicher** [niʃe] *vi* : nest
nickel [nikɛl] *nm* : nickel
nicotine [nikɔtin] *nf* : nicotine
nid [ni] *nm* **1** : nest **2 ~ de brigands** : den of thieves
nièce [njɛs] *nf* : niece
nier [nje] {96} *vt* : deny
nigaud, -gaude [nigo, -god] *n* : simpleton, fool
niveau [nivo] *nm, pl* **-veaux** [nivo] **1** : level **2 ~ de vie** : standard of living — **niveler** [nivle] {8} *vt* : level
noble [nɔbl] *adj* : noble — **~** *nmf* : noble, nobleman *m*, noblewoman *f* — **noblesse** [nɔblɛs] *nf* : nobility
noce [nɔs] *nf* **1** : wedding, wedding party **2 ~s** *nfpl* : wedding
nocif, -cive [nɔsif, -siv] *adj* : noxious, harmful
nocturne [nɔktyrn] *adj* : nocturnal, night
Noël [nɔɛl] *nm* **1** : Christmas **2 père ~** : Santa Claus
nœud [nø] *nm* **1** : knot, tie **2** : knot (nautical speed) **3 ~ coulant** : noose **4 ~ papillon** : bow tie
noir, noire [nwar] *adj* **1** : black **2** SALE : dirty, grimy **3** OBSCUR : dark — **noir** *nm* **1** : black **2 dans le ~** : in the dark, in darkness — **Noir, Noire** *n* : black man, black woman — **noirceur** [nwarsœr] *nf* **1** : blackness **2** *Can* : darkness — **noircir** [nwarsir] *vi* : grow dark, darken — *vt* : blacken
noisette [nwazɛt] *nf* : hazelnut
noix [nwa] *nfs & pl* **1** : nut, walnut **2** : piece, lump (of butter, etc.) **3 ~ de cajou** : cashew (nut)
nom [nɔ̃] *nm* **1** : name **2** : (proper) noun
nomade [nɔmad] *nmf* : nomad — **~** *adj* : nomadic
nombre [nɔ̃br] *nm* : number — **nombreux, -breuse** [nɔ̃brø, -brøz] *adj* : numerous
nombril [nɔ̃bril] *nm* : navel
nominal, -nale [nɔminal] *adj, mpl* **-naux** [-no] : nominal
nommer [nɔme] *vt* **1** : name, call **2** : appoint, nominate **3** CITER : mention — **se nommer** *vr* **1** S'APPELER : be named **2** : introduce oneself — **nommément** [nɔmemɑ̃] *adv* : by name, namely
non [nɔ̃] *adv* **1** : no **2 je pense que ~** : I don't think so **3 ~ plus** : neither, either — **~** *nm* : no
nonchalance [nɔ̃ʃalɑ̃s] *nf* : nonchalance — **nonchalant, -lante** [nɔ̃ʃalɑ̃, -lɑ̃t] *adj* : nonchalant
non-sens [nɔsɑ̃s] *nms & pl* ABSURDITÉ : nonsense, absurdity
nord [nɔr] *adj* : north, northern — **~** *nm* **1** : north **2 le Nord** : the North
nord-est [nɔrɛst] *adj s & pl* : northeast, northeastern — **~** *nm* : northeast
nord-ouest [nɔrwɛst] *adj s & pl* : northwest, northwestern — **~** *nm* : northwest
normal, -male [nɔrmal] *adj, mpl* **-maux** [nɔrmo] : normal — **normale** *nf* **1** : average **2** NORME : norm — **normalement** [nɔrmalmɑ̃] *adv* : normally, usually — **normaliser** [nɔrmalize] *vt* : normalize, standardize — **normalité** [nɔrmalite] *nf* : normality — **norme** [nɔrm] *nf* : norm, standard
nos → **notre**
nostalgie [nɔstalʒi] *nf* : nostalgia — **nostalgique** [nɔstalʒik] *adj* : nostalgic
notable [nɔtabl] *adj & nm* : notable
notaire [nɔtɛr] *nm* : notary public
notamment [nɔtamɑ̃] *adv* : especially, particularly
notation [nɔtasjɔ̃] *nf* : notation
note [nɔt] *nf* **1** : note **2** ADDITION : bill, check **3** : mark, grade (in school) — **noter** [nɔte] *vt* **1** REMARQUER : note, notice **2** MARQUER : mark, write (down) **3** : mark, grade (an exam)
notice [nɔtis] *nf* : instructions *pl*
notifier [nɔtifje] {96} *vt* : notify
notion [nɔsjɔ̃] *nf* : notion, idea
notoire [nɔtwar] *adj* **1** CONNU : well-known **2** : notorious (of a criminal) — **notoriété** [nɔtɔrjete] *nf* : notoriety
notre [nɔtr] *adj, pl* **nos** [no] : our
nôtre [notr] *pron* **le ~, la ~, les ~s** : ours
nouer [nwe] *vt* : tie, knot — **noueux, noueuse** [nwø, nwøz] *adj* : gnarled
nougat [nuga] *nm* : nougat
nouille [nuj] *nf* **1** *fam* : nitwit, idiot **2 ~s** *nfpl* : noodles, pasta
nourrir [nurir] *vt* **1** ALIMENTER : feed, nourish **2** : provide for (a family, etc.)

3 : nurse, harbor (a grudge, etc.) — **se nourrir** *vr* : eat — **nourrice** [nuris] *nf* : wet nurse — **nourrissant, -sante** [nurisɑ̃, -sɑ̃t] *adj* : nourishing, nutritious — **nourrisson** [nurisɔ̃] *nm* : infant — **nourriture** [nurityr] *nf* : food
nous [nu] *pron* **1** : we **2** : us **3** **~-mêmes** : ourselves
nouveau [nuvo] (**-vel** [-vɛl] *before a vowel or mute h*), **-velle** [-vɛl] *adj, mpl* **-veaux** [nuvo] **1** : new **2 de ~** *or* **à ~** : again, once again **3 ~ venu** : newcomer — **nouveau** *nm* **1 du ~** : something new **2 le ~** : the new — **nouveau–né, -née** [nuvone] *adj & n, mpl* **nouveau–nés** : newborn — **nouveauté** [nuvote] *nf* **1** : newness, novelty **2** INNOVATION : innovation
nouvelle [nuvɛl] *nf* **1** : piece of news **2** : short story **3 ~s** *nfpl* : news — **nouvellement** [nuvɛlmɑ̃] *adv* : newly, recently
novateur, -trice [nɔvatœr, -tris] *adj* : innovative — **~** *n* : innovator
novembre [nɔvɑ̃br] *nm* : November
novice [nɔvis] *adj* : inexperienced — **~** *nmf* : novice, beginner
noyau [nwajo] *nm, pl* **noyaux** [nwajo] **1** : pit, stone (of a fruit) **2** : nucleus, core (in science)
noyauter [nwajote] *vt* : infiltrate
noyer[1] [nwaje] {58} *vt* **1** : drown **2** : flood (an engine) — **se noyer** *vr* : drown — **noyé, noyée** [nwaje] *n* : drowning victim
noyer[2] *nm* : walnut tree
nu, nue [ny] *adj* **1** : naked, nude **2** : plain, bare (of a wall) — **nu** *nm* **1** : nude **2 à ~** : bare, exposed
nuage [nɥaʒ] *nm* : cloud — **nuageux, -geuse** [nɥaʒø, -ʒøz] *adj* : cloudy
nuance [nɥɑ̃s] *nf* **1** TON : hue, shade **2** SUBTILITÉ : nuance — **nuancer** [nɥɑ̃se] {6} *vt* : qualify (opinions, etc.)
nucléaire [nykleɛr] *adj* : nuclear
nudité [nydite] *nf* : nudity, nakedness
nuée [nɥe] *nf* : horde, swarm
nuire [nɥir] {49} *vi* **~ à** : harm, injure — **nuisible** [nɥizibl] *adj* : harmful
nuit [nɥi] *nf* **1** : night, nighttime **2 faire ~** : be dark out
nul, nulle [nyl] *adj* **1** AUCUN : no **2** : null, invalid **3 être nul en maths** : be hopeless in math **5 nulle part** : nowhere — **nul** *pron* : no one, nobody — **nullement** [nylmɑ̃] *adv* : by no means
numéraire [nymerɛr] *nm* : cash
numéral, -rale [nymeral] *adj, mpl* **-raux** [-ro] : numeral — **numéral** *nm, pl* **-raux** : numeral — **numérique** [nymerik] *adj* **1** : numerical **2** : digital — **numéro** [nymero] *nm* **1** : number **2** : issue (of a periodical) — **numéroter** [nymerɔte] *vt* : number
nuptial, -tiale [nypsjal] *adj, mpl* **-tiaux** [-sjo] : nuptial, wedding
nuque [nyk] *nf* : nape of the neck
nutrition [nytrisjɔ̃] *nf* : nutrition — **nutritif, -tive** [nytritif, -tiv] *adj* **1** : nutritious **2** : nutritional
nylon [nilɔ̃] *nm* : nylon
nymphe [nɛ̃f] *nf* : nymph

O

o [o] *nm* : o, 15th letter of the alphabet
oasis [ɔazis] *nf* : oasis
obéir [ɔbeir] *vi* **~ à 1** : obey **2** : respond to — **obéissance** [ɔbeisɑ̃s] *nf* : obedience — **obéissant, -sante** [ɔbeisɑ̃, -sɑ̃t] *adj* : obedient
obélisque [ɔbelisk] *nm* : obelisk
obèse [ɔbɛz] *adj* : obese — **obésité** [ɔbezite] *nf* : obesity
objecter [ɔbʒɛkte] *vt* **1** : raise as an objection **2** PRÉTEXTER : plead (as an excuse) — **objectif, -tive** [ɔbʒɛktif, -tiv] *adj* : objective — **objectif** *nm* **1** BUT : objective, goal **2** : lens (of an optical instrument) — **objectivité** [ɔbʒɛktivite] *nf* : objectivity — **objection** [ɔbʒɛksjɔ̃] *nf* : objection — **objet** [ɔbʒɛ] *nm* **1** : object, thing **2** : subject, topic **3** BUT : aim, purpose **4 complément d'~** : object (in grammar)
obligation [ɔbligasjɔ̃] *nf* **1** : obligation **2** : (savings) bond — **obligatoire** [ɔbligatwar] *adj* : compulsory, obligatory — **obligatoirement** [ɔbligatwarmɑ̃] *adv* : necessarily
obliger [ɔbliʒe] {17} *vt* **1** : oblige **2** CONTRAINDRE : force, compel — **obligé, -gée** [ɔbliʒe] *adj* **1 c'est obligé** *fam* : it's bound to happen, it's inevitable **2 être obligé de** : have to — **obligeance** [ɔbliʒɑ̃s] *nf* AMABILITÉ : kindness — **obligeant, -geante** [ɔbliʒɑ̃, -ʒɑ̃t] *adj* : obliging, kind
oblique [ɔblik] *adj* **1** : oblique **2 en ~**

: crosswise, diagonally — **obliquer** [ɔblike] *vi* : bear, turn (off)
oblitérer [ɔblitere] {87} *vt* : cancel (a stamp)
oblong, oblongue [ɔblɔ̃, ɔblɔ̃g] *adj* : oblong
obscène [ɔpsɛn] *adj* : obscene — **obscénité** [ɔpsenite] *nf* : obscenity
obscur, -cure [ɔpskyr] *adj* **1** SOMBRE : dark **2** VAGUE : obscure — **obscurcir** [ɔpskyrsir] *vt* **1** ASSOMBRIR : darken **2** : obscure, blur — **s'obscurcir** *vr* **1** : grow dark **2** : become obscure — **obscurité** [ɔpskyrite] *nf* **1** : darkness **2** : obscurity
obséder [ɔpsede] {87} *vt* : obsess — **obsédant, -dante** [ɔpsedɑ̃, -dɑ̃t] *adj* : haunting, obsessive — **obsédé, -dée** [ɔpsede] *n* : obsessive, fanatic
obsèques [ɔpsɛk] *nfpl* : funeral
observer [ɔpsɛrve] *vt* : observe — **observateur, -trice** [ɔpsɛrvatœr, -tris] *adj* : observant, perceptive — ~ *n* : observer — **observation** [ɔpsɛrvasjɔ̃] *nf* **1** : observance **2** : observation — **observatoire** [ɔpsɛrvatwar] *nm* **1** : observatory **2** : observation post
obsession [ɔpsesjɔ̃] *nf* : obsession — **obsessionnel, -nelle** [ɔpsesjɔnɛl] *adj* : obsessive
obsolète [ɔpsɔlɛt] *adj* : obsolete
obstacle [ɔpstakl] *nm* : obstacle
obstétrique [ɔpstetrik] *nf* : obstetrics
obstiner [ɔpstine] *v* **s'obstiner** *vr* ~ **à** : persist in — **obstiné, -née** [ɔpstine] *adj* ENTÊTÉ : obstinate, stubborn
obstruction [ɔpstryksjɔ̃] *nf* : obstruction — **obstruer** [ɔpstrye] *vt* : obstruct
obtenir [ɔptənir] {92} *vt* : obtain, get — **obtention** [ɔptɑ̃sjɔ̃] *nf* : obtaining
obturer [ɔptyre] *vt* **1** : seal, stop up **2** : fill (a tooth)
obtus, -tuse [ɔpty, -tyz] *adj* : obtuse
obus [ɔby] *nm* **1** : (mortar) shell **2** **éclats d'~** : shrapnel
occasion [ɔkazjɔ̃] *nf* **1** : opportunity **2** CIRCONSTANCE : occasion **3** : bargain **4** **d'~** : secondhand — **occasionnel, -nelle** [ɔkazjɔnɛl] *adj* : occasional — **occasionnel, -nelle** *n Can* : temp, temporary employee — **occasionner** [ɔkazjɔne] *vt* CAUSER : cause
occident [ɔksidɑ̃] *nm* **1** : west **2** **l'Occident** : the West — **occidental, -tale** [ɔksidɑ̃tal] *adj, mpl* **-taux** [-to] : western, Western
occulte [ɔkylt] *adj* : occult
occuper [ɔkype] *vt* **1** : occupy **2** REMPLIR : take up, fill **3** ~ **un poste** : hold a job — **s'occuper** *vr* **1** : keep busy **2** ~ **de** : handle, take care of — **occupant, -pante** [ɔkypɑ̃,-pɑ̃t] *n* : occupant — **occupation** [ɔkypasjɔ̃] *nf* **1** : occupation **2** : occupancy — **occupé, -pée** [ɔkype] *adj* **1** : busy **2** **zone occupée** : occupied zone
occurrence [ɔkyrɑ̃s] *nf* **1** : instance, occurrence **2** **en l'~** : in this case
océan [ɔseɑ̃] *nm* : ocean — **océanique** [ɔseanik] *adj* : oceanic, ocean
ocre [ɔkr] *nmf* : ocher, ochre
octave [ɔktav] *nf* : octave
octet [ɔktɛ] *nm* : byte
octobre [ɔktɔbr] *nm* : October
octogone [ɔktɔgɔn] *nm* : octagon
octroyer [ɔktrwaje] {58} *vt* : grant, bestow
oculaire [ɔkylɛr] *adj* : ocular, eye — **oculiste** [ɔkylist] *nmf* : oculist
ode [ɔd] *nf* : ode
odeur [ɔdœr] *nf* : odor, smell
odieux, -dieuse [ɔdjø, -djøz] *adj* EXÉCRABLE : odious, hateful
odorant, -rante [ɔdɔrɑ̃, -rɑ̃t] *adj* PARFUMÉ : fragrant
odorat [ɔdɔra] *nm* : sense of smell
œil [œj] *nm, pl* **yeux** [jø] **1** : eye **2** **coup d'~** : glance — **œillade** [œjad] *nf* : wink — **œillères** [œjɛr] *nfpl* : blinders — **œillet** [œjɛ] *nm* : carnation
œsophage [ezɔfaʒ] *nm* : esophagus
œstrogène [ɛstrɔʒɛn] *nm* : estrogen
œuf [œf] *nm, pl* **œufs** [ø] : egg
œuvre [œvr] *nm* : (body of) work — ~ *nf* **1** : work, undertaking, task **2** ~ **d'art** : work of art — **œuvrer** [œvre] *vi* : work
offense [ɔfɑ̃s] *nf* : insult, offense — **offenser** [ɔfɑ̃se] *vt* : offend — **s'offenser** *vr* ~ **de** : take offense at — **offensif, -sive** [ɔfɑ̃sif, -siv] *adj* : offensive, attacking — **offensive** *nf* : offensive
office [ɔfis] *nm* **1** : service (in religion) **2** **faire** ~ **de** : act as
officiel, -cielle [ɔfisjɛl] *adj & n* : official — **officialiser** [ɔfisjalize] *vt* : make official — **officier** [ɔfisje] *nm* : officer (in the armed forces) — **officieux, -cieuse** [ɔfisjø, -sjøz] *adj* : unofficial, informal
offrande [ɔfrɑ̃d] *nf* : offering
offre [ɔfr] *nf* **1** : offer, bid **2** **l'~ et la demande** : supply and demand
offrir [ɔfrir] {83} *vt* : offer, give — **s'offrir** *vr* **1** : treat oneself to **2** SE PRÉSENTER : present itself

offusquer [ɔfyske] *vt* : offend — **s'offusquer** *vr* : take offense
ogive [ɔʒiv] *nf* : warhead
ogre, ogresse [ɔgr, ɔgrɛs] *n* : ogre
oh [o] *interj* : oh — **ohé** [ɔe] *interj* : hey
oie [wa] *nf* : goose
oignon [ɔɲɔ̃] *nm* **1** : onion **2** : bulb (of a tulip, etc.) **3** : bunion (in medicine)
oindre [wɛ̃dr] {59} *vt* : anoint
oiseau [wazo] *nm, pl* **oiseaux** : bird
oisif, -sive [wazif, -ziv] *adj* : idle — **oisiveté** [wazivte] *nf* : idleness
oisillon [wazijɔ̃] *nm* : fledgling
oléoduc [ɔleɔdyk] *nm* : (oil) pipeline
olfactif, -tive [ɔlfaktif, -tiv] *adj* : olfactory
olive [ɔliv] *nf* : olive
olympique [ɔlɛ̃pik] *adj* : Olympic
ombilical, -cale [ɔ̃bilikal] *adj, mpl* **-caux** [-ko] : umbilical
ombrage [ɔ̃braʒ] *nm* **1** OMBRE : shade **2 porter ~ à** : offend — **ombragé, -gée** [ɔ̃braʒe] *adj* : shady, shaded — **ombre** [ɔ̃br] *nf* **1** : shadow **2** SOUPÇON : hint, trace **3 à l'~** : in the shade
omelette [ɔmlɛt] *nf* : omelet
omettre [ɔmɛtr] {53} *vt* : omit, leave out — **omission** [ɔmisjɔ̃] *nf* : omission
omnibus [ɔmnibys] *nm* : local train
omnipotent, -tente [ɔmnipɔtɑ̃, -tɑ̃t] *adj* : omnipotent
omoplate [ɔmɔplat] *nf* : shoulder blade
on [ɔ̃] *pron* **1** : one, we, you **2** : they, people **3** QUELQU'UN : someone
once [ɔ̃s] *nf* : ounce
oncle [ɔ̃kl] *nm* : uncle
onctueux, -tueuse [ɔ̃ktɥø, -tɥøz] *adj* : smooth, creamy
onde [ɔ̃d] *nf* : wave
on–dit [ɔ̃di] *nms & pl* : rumor
onduler [ɔ̃dyle] *vi* **1** : undulate, sway **2** : be wavy (of hair) — **ondulation** [ɔ̃dylasjɔ̃] *nf* : undulation, wave — **ondulé, -lée** [ɔ̃dyle] *adj* **1** : wavy **2 carton ondulé** : corrugated cardboard
onéreux, -reuse [ɔnerø, -røz] *adj* COÛTEUX : costly
ongle [ɔ̃gl] *nm* : nail, fingernail
onguent [ɔ̃gɑ̃] *nm* : ointment
onyx [ɔniks] *nm* : onyx
onze [ɔ̃z] *adj* **1** : eleven **2** : eleventh (in dates) — **~** *nms & pl* : eleven — **onzième** [ɔ̃zjɛm] *adj & nmf & nm* : eleventh
opale [ɔpal] *nf* : opal
opaque [ɔpak] *adj* : opaque
opéra [ɔpera] *nm* **1** : opera **2** : opera house
opération [ɔperasjɔ̃] *nf* **1** : operation **2** : transaction (in banking, etc.) — **opérateur, -trice** [ɔperatœr, -tris] *n* : operator — **opérationnel, -nelle** [ɔperasjɔnɛl] *adj* : operational — **opérer** [ɔpere] {87} *vt* : operate on (a patient) — *vi* **1** : take effect, work **2** INTERVENIR : act
opiner [ɔpine] *vi* **~ de la tête** : nod in agreement
opiniâtre [ɔpinjatr] *adj* OBSTINÉ : stubborn, persistent
opinion [ɔpinjɔ̃] *nf* : opinion, belief
opium [ɔpjɔm] *nm* : opium
opportun, -tune [ɔpɔrtœ̃, -tyn] *adj* : opportune, timely — **opportunisme** [ɔpɔrtynism] *nm* : opportunism — **opportuniste** [ɔpɔrtynist] *adj* : opportunist, opportunistic — **~** *nmf* : opportunist
opposer [ɔpoze] *vt* **1** : put up (an objection, etc.) **2** : contrast (ideas, etc.) **3** DIVISER : divide — **s'opposer** *vr* **1** : clash, conflict **2 ~ à** : be opposed to — **opposant, -sante** [ɔpozɑ̃, -zɑ̃t] *n* ADVERSAIRE : opponent — **opposé, -sée** [ɔpoze] *adj* **1** : opposing **2** : opposite **3 ~ à** : opposed to — **opposé** *nm* **1** : opposite **2 à l'~ de** : contrary to — **opposition** [ɔpozisjɔ̃] *nf* **1** : opposition **2** : objection (in law)
oppresser [ɔprese] *vt* : oppress, burden — **oppressif, -sive** [ɔpresif, -siv] *adj* : oppressive — **oppresseur** [ɔpresœr] *nm* : oppressor — **oppression** [ɔpresjɔ̃] *nf* : oppression
opprimer [ɔprime] *vt* : oppress
opter [ɔpte] *vi* **~ pour** : opt for, choose
opticien, -cienne [ɔptisjɛ̃, -sjɛn] *n* : optician
optimisme [ɔptimism] *nm* : optimism — **optimiste** [ɔptimist] *adj* : optimistic — **~** *nmf* : optimist
optimum [ɔptimɔm] *adj & nm* : optimum
option [ɔpsjɔ̃] *nf* : option, choice — **optionnel, -nelle** [ɔpsjɔnɛl] *adj* FACULTATIF : optional
optique [ɔptik] *adj* : optic(al) — **~** *nf* **1** : optics **2** PERSPECTIVE : viewpoint
opulent, -lente [ɔpylɑ̃, -lɑ̃t] *adj* : opulent — **opulence** [-lɑ̃s] *nf* : opulence
or[1] [ɔr] *nm* : gold
or[2] *conj* **1** : but, yet **2** : now
oracle [ɔrakl] *nm* : oracle
orage [ɔraʒ] *nm* : storm, thunderstorm — **orageux, -geuse** [ɔraʒø, -ʒøz] *adj* : stormy
oral, -rale [ɔral] *adj, mpl* **oraux** [ɔro] : oral

orange [ɔrɑ̃ʒ] *adj* : orange — ~ *nf* : orange (fruit) — ~ *nm* : orange (color) — **oranger** [ɔrɑ̃ʒe] *nm* : orange tree
orateur, -trice [ɔratœr, -tris] *n* : orator, speaker
orbite [ɔrbit] *nf* **1** : orbit **2** : eye socket
orchestre [ɔrkɛstr] *nm* : orchestra
orchidée [ɔrkide] *nf* : orchid
ordinaire [ɔrdinɛr] *adj* **1** : ordinary, common **2** HABITUEL : usual — ~ *nm* **1 l'~** : the ordinary **2 d'~** : usually, as a rule — **ordinairement** [-nɛrmɑ̃] *adv* : usually
ordinateur [ɔrdinatœr] *nm* : computer
ordonnance [ɔrdɔnɑ̃s] *nf* **1** : order **2** : (medical) prescription
ordonner [ɔrdɔne] *vt* **1** : put in order, arrange **2** COMMANDER : order **3** : ordain (in religion) — **ordonné, -née** [ɔrdɔne] *adj* : tidy, orderly
ordre [ɔrdr] *nm* **1** : order **2** PROPRETÉ : tidiness **3** NATURE : nature, sort **4 ~ du jour** : agenda
ordure [ɔrdyr] *nf* **1** : filth **2 ~s** *nfpl* : trash, garbage — **ordurier, -rière** [ɔrdyrje] *adj* : filthy
oreille [ɔrej] *nf* **1** : ear **2** OUÏE : hearing
oreiller [ɔrɛje] *nm* : pillow
oreillons [ɔrɛjɔ̃] *nmpl* : mumps
orfèvre [ɔrfɛvr] *nm* : goldsmith
organe [ɔrgan] *nm* : organ (of the body) — **organique** [ɔrganik] *adj* : organic
organiser [ɔrganize] *vt* : organize — **s'organiser** *vr* : get organized — **organisateur, -trice** [ɔrganizatœr, -tris] *n* : organizer — **organisation** [ɔrganizasjɔ̃] *nf* : organization
organisme [ɔrganism] *nm* **1** : organism (in biology) **2** : organization, body
organiste [ɔrganist] *nmf* : organist
orgasme [ɔrgasm] *nm* : orgasm
orge [ɔrʒ] *nf* : barley
orgelet [ɔrʒəlɛ] *nm* : sty (in medicine)
orgie [ɔrʒi] *nf* : orgy
orgue [ɔrg] *nm* : organ (musical instrument)
orgueil [ɔrgœj] *nm* : pride — **orgueilleux, -leuse** [ɔrgœjø, -jøz] *adj* : proud
orient [ɔrjɑ̃] *nm* **1** : east **2 l'Orient** : the Orient, the East — **oriental, -tale** [ɔrjɑ̃tal] *adj, mpl* **-taux** [-to] **1** : eastern **2** : oriental
orienter [ɔrjɑ̃te] *vt* **1** : position, orient **2** GUIDER : guide, direct — **s'orienter** *vr* : find one's bearings — **orientation** [ɔrjɑ̃tasjɔ̃] *nf* **1** : orientation, direction, aspect **2** : guidance, (career) counseling
orifice [ɔrifis] *nm* : orifice
originaire [ɔriʒinɛr] *adj* **être ~ de** : be a native of
original, -nale [ɔriʒinal, -nal] *adj, mpl* **-naux** [-no] **1** : original **2** EXCENTRIQUE : eccentric — ~ *n* : character, eccentric — **original** *nm, pl* **-naux** : original — **originalité** [ɔriʒinalite] *nf* **1** : originality **2** : eccentricity — **origine** [ɔriʒin] *nf* **1** : origin **2 à l'~** : originally — **originel, -nelle** [ɔriʒinɛl] *adj* : original, primary
orignal [ɔriɲal] *nm, pl* **-naux** [-ɲo] : moose
orme [ɔrm] *nm* : elm
orner [ɔrne] *vt* DÉCORER : decorate, adorn — **orné, -née** [ɔrne] *adj* : ornate, flowery — **ornement** [ɔrnəmɑ̃] *nm* : ornament, adornment — **ornemental, -tale** [ɔrnəmɑ̃tal] *adj, mpl* **-taux** [-to] : ornamental
ornière [ɔrnjɛr] *nf* : rut
ornithologie [ɔrnitɔlɔʒi] *nf* : ornithology
orphelin, -line [ɔrfəlɛ̃, -lin] *n* : orphan
orteil [ɔrtɛj] *nm* : toe
orthodoxe [ɔrtɔdɔks] *adj* : orthodox — **orthodoxie** [ɔrtɔdɔksi] *nf* : orthodoxy
orthographe [ɔrtɔgraf] *nf* : spelling, orthography — **orthographier** [ɔrtɔgrafje] {96} *vt* : spell
orthopédie [ɔrtɔpedi] *nf* : orthopedics — **orthopédique** [ɔrtɔpedik] *adj* : orthopedic
ortie [ɔrti] *nf* : nettle
os [ɔs] *nm* : bone
osciller [ɔsile] *vi* **1** : oscillate **2** HÉSITATE : vacillate, waver — **oscillation** [ɔsilasjɔ̃] *nf* : oscillation
oser [oze] *vt* **1** : dare **2 si j'ose dire** : if I may say so — **osé, -sée** [oze] *adj* : daring, bold
osier [ozje] *nm* **1** : willow (tree) **2** : wicker (furniture)
osmose [ɔsmoz] *nf* : osmosis
ossature [ɔsatyr] *nf* **1** : skeleton, bone structure **2** : frame(work) — **ossements** [ɔsmɑ̃] *nmpl* : remains, bones — **osseux, -seuse** [ɔsø, -søz] *adj* : bony
ostensible [ɔstɑ̃sibl] *adj* : conspicuous, obvious — **ostentation** [ɔstɑ̃tasjɔ̃] *nf* : ostentation
ostéopathe [ɔsteɔpat] *nmf* : osteopath
ostracisme [ɔstrasism] *nm* : ostracism
otage [ɔtaʒ] *nm* : hostage
ôter [ote] *vt* **1** RETIRER : remove, take away **2** SOUSTRAIRE : subtract
otite [ɔtit] *nf* : ear infection

ou [u] *conj* **1** : or **2 ou . . . ou . . .** : either . . . or . . .
où [u] *adv* **1** : where, wherever **2 d'~** : from which, from where — ~ *pron* : where, that, in which, on which, to which
ouate [wat] *nf* **1** : absorbent cotton **2** BOURRE : padding, wadding — **ouaté, -tée** [wate] *adj* : padded, quilted
oublier [ublije] {96} *vt* : forget — **s'oublier** *vr* **1** : be forgotten **2** : forget oneself — **oubli** [ubli] *nm* **1** : forgetfulness **2** : oversight — **oublieux, -blieuse** [ublijø, -blijøz] *adj* : forgetful
ouest [wɛst] *adj* : west, western — ~ *nm* **1** : west **2 l'Ouest** : the West
oui [wi] *adv & nms & pl* : yes
ouïe [wi] *nf* **1** : (sense of) hearing **2 ~s** *nfpl* : gills — **ouï-dire** [widir] *nms & pl* : hearsay
ouïr [wir] {60} *vt* : hear
ouragan [uragɑ̃] *nm* : hurricane
ourler [urle] *vt* : hem — **ourlet** [urlɛ] *nm* : hem
ours [urs] *nm* **1** : bear **2 ~ blanc** *or* **~ polaire** : polar bear — **ourse** [urs] *nf* : she-bear
outil [uti] *nm* : tool — **outillage** [utijaʒ] *nm* **1** : set of tools **2** : equipment — **outiller** [utije] *vt* ÉQUIPER : equip
outrager [utraʒe] {17} *vt* INSULTER : offend, insult — **outrage** [utraʒ] *nm* : insult
outrance [utrɑ̃s] *nf* : excess — **outrancier, -cière** [utrɑ̃sje, -sjɛr] *adj* : excessive, extreme
outre [utr] *adv* **1 en ~** : in addition, besides **2 ~ mesure** : overly, unduly **3 passer ~ à** : disregard — ~ *prep* : besides, in addition to — **outre-mer** [utrəmɛr] *adv* : overseas — **outrepasser** [utrəpase] *vt* : exceed, overstep
outrer [utre] *vt* **1** EXAGÉRER : exaggerate **2** INDIGNER : outrage
ouvert, -verte [uvɛr, -vɛrt] *adj* **1** : open **2** : on, running (of a light, a faucet, etc.) — **ouverture** [uvɛrtyr] *nf* **1** : opening **2** : overture (in music) **3 ~ d'esprit** : open-mindedness
ouvrable [uvrabl] *adj* **1 jour ~** : weekday, working day **2 heures ~s** : business hours
ouvrage [uvraʒ] *nm* : work
ouvre-boîtes [uvrəbwat] *nms & pl* : can opener — **ouvre-bouteilles** [uvrəbutɛj] *nms & pl* : bottle opener
ouvreur, -vreuse [uvrœr, -vrøz] *n* : usher, usherette *f*
ouvrier, -vrière [uvrije, -vrijɛr] *n* : worker — ~ *adj* : working-class
ouvrir [uvrir] {83} *vt* **1** : open **2** : turn on (a light, a radio, etc.) — *vi* : open — **s'ouvrir** *vr* : open (up)
ovaire [ɔvɛr] *nm* : ovary
ovale [ɔval] *adj & nm* : oval
ovation [ɔvasjɔ̃] *nf* : ovation
overdose [ɔvœrdoz] *nf* : overdose
oxyde [ɔksid] *nm* **~ de carbone** : carbon monoxide — **oxyder** [ɔkside] *v* **s'oxyder** *vr* : rust
oxygène [ɔksiʒɛn] *nm* : oxygen
ozone [ozɔn] *nm* : ozone

P

p [pe] *nm* : p, 16th letter of the alphabet
pacifier [pasifje] {96} *vt* : pacify, calm — **pacifique** [pasifik] *adj* **1** : peaceful **2 l'océan Pacifique** : the Pacific Ocean — **pacifiste** [pasifist] *nmf* : pacifist
pacotille [pakɔtij] *nf* **1** : shoddy goods **2 de ~** : cheap
pacte [pakt] *nm* ACCORD : pact, agreement
pagaie [pagɛ] *nf* : paddle
pagaille *or* **pagaïe** [pagaj] *nf fam* **1** : mess, chaos **2 en ~** : in great quantities
pagayer [pagaje] {11} *vi* : paddle
page [paʒ] *nf* : page
paie [pɛ] *nf* : pay, wages *pl* — **paiement** [pɛmɑ̃] *nm* : payment
païen, païenne [pajɛ̃, pajɛn] *adj & n* : pagan, heathen
paillard, -larde [pajar, -jard] *adj* : bawdy
paillasson [pajasɔ̃] *nm* : doormat
paille [paj] *nf* **1** : (piece of) straw **2** : (drinking) straw
paillette [pajɛt] *nf* : sequin
pain [pɛ̃] *nm* **1** : bread **2** : loaf (of bread) **3** : cake, bar (of soap, etc.)
pair, paire [pɛr] *adj* : even — **pair** *nm* **1** : peer **2 aller de ~** : go hand in hand **3 hors ~** : without equal — **paire** [pɛr] *nf* : pair

paisible [pezibl] *adj* : peaceful, quiet
paître [pɛtr] {61} *vi* : graze
paix [pɛ] *nf* : peace
palace [palas] *nm* : luxury hotel
palais [palɛ] *nms & pl* **1** : palace **2** : palate **3 ~ de justice** : courts of law
palan [palɑ̃] *nm* : hoist
pale [pal] *nf* : blade (of a propeller, etc.)
pâle [pal] *adj* **1** BLÊME : pale **2** CLAIR : light, pale
palet [palɛ] *nm* : puck (in ice hockey)
paletot [palto] *nm* : short coat
palette [palɛt] *nf* **1** : palette **2** : shoulder (of pork, etc.)
pâleur [palœr] *nf* : paleness
palier [palje] *nm* **1** : landing, floor **2** NIVEAU : level, stage
pâlir [palir] *vi* : turn pale
palissade [palisad] *nf* : fence
pallier [palje] {96} *vt* : alleviate, compensate for
palmarès [palmarɛs] *nms & pl* : list of winners
palme [palm] *nf* **1** : palm leaf **2** NAGEOIRE : flipper **3 remporter la ~** : be victorious
palmé, -mée [palme] *adj* : webbed
palmier [palmje] *nm* : palm tree
palourde [palurd] *nf* : clam
palper [palpe] *vt* : feel, finger — **palpable** [palpabl] *adj* : tangible
palpiter [palpite] *vi* : palpitate, throb — **palpitant, -tante** [palpitɑ̃, -tɑ̃t] *adj* : thrilling, exciting
paludisme [palydism] *nm* : malaria
pâmer [pame] *v* **se pâmer** *vr* : be ecstatic, swoon
pamphlet [pɑ̃flɛ] *nm* : lampoon
pamplemousse [pɑ̃pləmus] *nmf* : grapefruit
pan [pɑ̃] *nm* **1** : section, piece **2** : tail (of a garment)
panacée [panase] *nf* : panacea
panais [panɛ] *nm* : parsnip
pancarte [pɑ̃kart] *nf* : sign, placard
pancréas [pɑ̃kreas] *nm* : pancreas
panda [pɑ̃da] *nm* : panda
paner [pane] *vt* : coat with breadcrumbs
panier [panje] *nm* : basket
panique [panik] *nf* : panic — **paniquer** [panike] *vi* : panic
panne [pan] *nf* **1** : breakdown **2 ~ d'électricité** : power failure, blackout
panneau [pano] *nm, pl* **-neaux 1** : panel **2** : sign, signpost **3 ~ de signalisation** : road sign **4 ~ publicitaire** : billboard
panoplie [panɔpli] *nf* **1** GAMME : array, range **2** DÉGUISEMENT : outfit, costume
panorama [panɔrama] *nm* : panorama — **panoramique** [panɔramik] *adj* : panoramic
panser [pɑ̃se] *vt* **1** : groom (a horse) **2** : dress, bandage (a wound) — **pansement** [pɑ̃smɑ̃] *nm* : dressing, bandage
pantalon [pɑ̃talɔ̃] *nm* : pants *pl*, trousers *pl*
panthère [pɑ̃tɛr] *nf* : panther
pantin [pɑ̃tɛ̃] *nm* FANTOCHE : puppet (person)
pantomime [pɑ̃tɔmim] *nf* : pantomime
pantoufle [pɑ̃tufl] *nf* : slipper
panure [panyr] *nf* : bread crumbs *pl*
paon [pɑ̃] *nm* : peacock
papa [papa] *nm fam* : dad, daddy
pape [pap] *nm* : pope
paperasse [papras] *nf* : papers *pl*, paperwork
papeterie [papɛtri] *nf* : stationery
papier [papje] *nm* **1** : paper **2** : document, paper **3 ~ d'aluminium** : aluminum foil, tinfoil **4 ~ hygiénique** : toilet paper **5 ~ mouchoir** *Can* : tissue **6 ~ peint** : wallpaper **7 ~s** *nmpl* : (identification) papers
papillon [papijɔ̃] *nm* **1** : butterfly **2 ~ de nuit** : moth
papoter [papɔte] *vi* : gab, chatter
Pâque [pak] *nf* : Passover
paquebot [pakbo] *nm* : liner, ship
pâquerette [pakrɛt] *nf* : daisy
Pâques [pak] *nm & nfpl* : Easter
paquet [pakɛ] *nm* **1** : package, parcel **2** : pack (of cigarettes, etc.) **3 un ~ de** : a heap of, a pile of
par [par] *prep* **1** : through **2** : by, by means of **3** : as, for **4** : at, during **5 ~ avion** : by airmail **6 ~ exemple** : for example **7 ~ ici** : around here **8 ~ moments** : at times **9 ~ personne** : per person **10 de ~** : throughout
parabole [parabɔl] *nf* : parable
parachever [paraʃve] {52} *vt* : complete, perfect
parachute [paraʃyt] *nm* : parachute — **parachutiste** [paraʃytist] *nmf* : paratrooper
parade [parad] *nf* : parade — **parader** [parade] *vi* : strut, show off
paradis [paradi] *nm* : paradise, heaven
paradoxe [paradɔks] *nm* : paradox — **paradoxal, -xale** [paradɔksal] *adj, mpl* **-xaux** [-kso] : paradoxical
paraffine [parafin] *nf* : paraffin (wax)
parages [paraʒ] *nmpl* **dans les ~** : in the vicinity

paragraphe [paragraf] *nm* : paragraph
paraître [parɛtr] {7} *vi* **1** : appear **2** : show, be visible **3** SEMBLER : seem, look **4 à ~** : forthcoming — *v impers* **il paraît que** : it seems that, apparently
parallèle [paralɛl] *adj* : parallel — **~** *nm* **1** : parallel **2 mettre en ~** : compare — **~** *nf* : parallel (line)
paralyser [paralyze] *vt* : paralyze — **paralysie** [paralizi] *nf* : paralysis
paramètre [paramɛtr] *nm* : parameter
paranoïa [paranɔja] *nf* : paranoia
parapet [parapɛ] *nm* : parapet
paraphe [paraf] *nm* **1** : initials *pl* **2** : signature — **parapher** [parafe] *vt* : initial
paraphrase [parafraz] *nf* : paraphrase
parapluie [paraplɥi] *nm* : umbrella
parascolaire [paraskɔlɛr] *adj* : extracurricular
parasite [parazit] *nm* **1** : parasite **2 ~s** *nmpl* : (radio) interference
parasol [parasɔl] *nm* : parasol, sunshade
paravent [paravɑ̃] *nm* : screen, partition
parc [park] *nm* **1** : park **2** : grounds *pl* **3** ENCLOS : pen, playpen **4** : fleet (of automobiles) **5 ~ d'attractions** : amusement park
parcelle [parsɛl] *nf* **1** : fragment **2** : plot (of land)
parce que [parskə] *conj* : because
parchemin [parʃəmɛ̃] *nm* : parchment
parcimonieux, -nieuse [parsimɔnjø, -njøz] *adj* : parsimonious
par-ci, par-là [parsiparla] *adv* : here and there
parcmètre [parkmɛtr] *nm France* : parking meter
parcomètre [parkɔmɛtr] *nm Can* : parking meter
parcourir [parkurir] {23} *vt* **1** : cover (a distance), travel through **2** : leaf through (a text)
parcours [parkur] *nm* **1** : course (of a river), route (of a bus, etc.) **2** : course (in sports)
par-delà *or* **par delà** [pardəla] *prep* : beyond
par-dessous [pardəsu] *adv & prep* : underneath
pardessus [pardəsy] *nms & pl* : overcoat
par-dessus [pardəsy] *adv* : over, above, on top — **~** *prep* **1** : over, above **2 ~ bord** : overboard **3 ~ tout** : above all
par-devant [pardəvɑ̃] *adv* : in front, at the front
pardonner [pardɔne] *vt* **1** : forgive, pardon **2 pardonnez-moi** : excuse me — **pardon** [pardɔ̃] *nm* **1** : forgiveness, pardon **2 ~?** : pardon?, what did you say? **3 ~** : pardon me, sorry
pare-balles [parbal] *adj s & pl* : bulletproof
pare-brise [parbriz] *nms & pl* : windshield
pare-chocs [parʃɔk] *nms & pl* : bumper
pareil, -reille [parɛj] *adj* **1** SEMBLABLE : similar, alike **2** TEL : such — **~** *n* **1** ÉGAL : equal, peer **2 sans pareil** : unequaled — **pareil** [parɛj] *adv fam* : in the same way
parent, -rente [parɑ̃, -rɑ̃t] *adj* : similar, related — **~** *n* **1** : relative, relation **2 parents** *nmpl* : parents — **parenté** [parɑ̃te] *nf* **1** : relationship **2** : family, relations *pl*
parenthèse [parɑ̃tɛz] *nf* : parenthesis, bracket
parer [pare] *vt* **1** : adorn, array **2** : ward off , parry — *vi* **~ à** : deal with
paresser [parɛse] *vi* : laze around — **paresse** [parɛs] *nf* : laziness, idleness — **paresseux, -seuse** [parəsø, -søz] *adj* : lazy — **paresseux** *nm* : sloth (animal)
parfaire [parfɛr] {62} *vt* : perfect, refine — **parfait, -faite** [parfɛ, -fɛt] *adj* **1** : perfect **2** TOTAL : absolute, complete — **parfaitement** [-fɛtmɑ̃] *adv* **1** : perfectly **2** ABSOLUMENT : definitely
parfois [parfwa] *adv* : sometimes
parfumer [parfyme] *vt* **1** : scent, perfume **2** : flavor (ice cream, etc.) — **se parfumer** *vr* : wear perfume — **parfum** [parfœ̃] *nm* **1** : scent, fragrance **2** : perfume **3** GOÛT : flavor — **parfumé, -mée** [parfyme] *adj* **1** : fragrant, scented **2** : flavored — **parfumerie** [parfymri] *nf* : perfume shop
pari [pari] *nm* : bet, wager — **parier** [parje] {96} *vt* : bet, wager
paria [parja] *nm* : outcast
parisien, -sienne [parizjɛ̃, -zjɛn] *adj* : Parisian
parjurer [parʒyre] *v* **se parjurer** *vr* : perjure oneself
parking [parkiŋ] *nm* : parking lot
parlant, -lante [parlɑ̃, -lɑ̃t] *adj* : vivid, eloquent
parlement [parləmɑ̃] *nm* : parliament — **parlementaire** [parləmɑ̃tɛr] *adj*

: parliamentary — **parlementer** [parləmɑ̃te] *vi* : negotiate
parler [parle] *vt* : talk, speak — *vi* **1** : talk, speak **2** ~ **à** : talk to **3** ~ **de** : mention, refer to — **se parler** *vr* **1** : speak to each other **2** : be spoken (of a language) — ~ *nm* : speech, way of speaking
parloir [parlwar] *nm* : parlor
parmi [parmi] *prep* : among
parodie [parɔdi] *nf* : parody — **parodier** [parɔdje] {96} *vt* : parody, mimic
paroi [parwa] *nf* **1** : partition **2** : wall (in anatomy, etc.) **3** ~ **rocheuse** : rock face
paroisse [parwas] *nf* : parish — **paroissien, -sienne** [parwasjɛ̃, -sjɛn] *n* : parishioner
parole [parɔl] *nf* **1** : (spoken) word **2** PROMESSE : word, promise **3** : speech **4** ~**s** *nfpl* : lyrics **5 prendre la** ~ : speak
paroxysme [parɔksism] *nm* : height, climax
parquer [parke] *vt* **1** : pen (cattle, etc.) **2** GARER : park
parquet [parkɛ] *nm* : parquet (floor)
parrain [parɛ̃] *nm* **1** : godfather **2** : sponsor, patron — **parrainer** [parɛne] *vt* : sponsor
parsemer [parsəme] {52} *vt* ~ **de** : scatter with, strew with
part [par] *nf* **1** : portion, piece **2** : part, share **3** : side, position **4 à** ~ : apart from **5 de la** ~ **de** : on behalf of **6 de toutes** ~**s** : from all sides **7 d'une** ~ : on (the) one hand **8 faire sa** ~ : do one's share **9 prendre** ~ **à** : take part in
partager [partaʒe] {17} *vt* **1** : divide up **2** RÉPARTIR : share — **se partager** *vr* : share — **partage** [partaʒ] *nm* : sharing, dividing
partance [partɑ̃s] *nf* **1 en** ~ : ready to depart **2 en** ~ **pour** : bound for — **partant, -tante** [partɑ̃, -tɑ̃t] *adj* : ready, willing
partenaire [partənɛr] *nmf* : partner
parterre [partɛr] *nm* **1** : flower bed **2** : orchestra section (in a theater)
parti [parti] *nm* **1** : group, camp **2** : (political) party **3** ~ **pris** : bias **4 prendre** ~ : take a stand **5 prendre son** ~ : make up one's mind **6 tirer** ~ **de** : take advantage of — **parti, -tie** [parti] *adj fam* : intoxicated, high
partial, -tiale [parsjal] *adj, mpl* **-tiaux** [-sjo] : biased, partial
participe [partisip] *nm* : participle
participer [partisipe] *vi* ~ **à 1** : participate in **2** : contribute to — **participant, -pante** [partisipɑ̃, -pɑ̃t] *n* : participant — **participation** [partisipasjɔ̃] *nf* **1** : participation **2** : contribution
particule [partikyl] *nf* : particle
particulier, -lière [partikylje, -ljɛr] *adj* **1** : particular, specific **2** SINGULIER : peculiar **3** PRIVÉ : private, personal **4 en** ~ : especially, in particular — **particularité** [partikylarite] *nf* : idiosyncrasy — **particulier** [partikylje] *nm* : individual — **particulièrement** [partikyljɛrmɑ̃] *adv* : especially, particularly
partie [parti] *nf* **1** : part **2** : game, match **3** : party, participant **4** SORTIE : outing **5 en** ~ : partly, in part **6 faire** ~ **de** : be a part of — **partiel, -tielle** [parsjɛl] *adj* : partial
partir [partir] {82} *vi* **1** : leave, depart **2** : start up, go off **3** COMMENCER : start **4** S'ENLEVER : come out (of a stain, etc.) **5 à** ~ **de** : from
partisan, -sane [partizɑ̃, -zan] *adj & n* : partisan
partition [partisjɔ̃] *nf* : score (in music)
partout [partu] *adv* **1** : everywhere **2** : all (in sports)
parure [paryr] *nf* **1** : finery **2** ENSEMBLE : set
parution [parysjɔ̃] *nf* : publication, launch
parvenir [parvənir] {92} *vi* **1** ~ **à** : reach, arrive at **2** ~ **à faire** : manage to do
parvis [parvi] *nm* : square (in front of a church)
pas[1] [pa] *adv* **1** → **ne 2** : not **3** ~ **du tout** : not at all **4** ~ **mal de** : quite a lot of
pas[2] *nms & pl* **1** : step, footstep **2** : footprint **3** : pace, gait **4** : step (in dancing) **5 de ce** ~ : right away **6** ~ **de la porte** : doorstep
passable [pasabl] *adj* : passable, fair — **passablement** [pasabləmɑ̃] **1** : quite, rather **2** : reasonably well
passage [pasaʒ] *nm* **1** : passing, crossing **2** SÉJOUR : stay, visit **3** CHEMIN : route, way **4** : passage (in a text) **5** ~ **pour piétons** : pedestrian crossing **6** ~ **interdit** : do not enter — **passager, -gère** [pasaʒe, -ʒɛr] *adj* : passing, temporary — ~ *n* **1** : passenger **2** ~ **clandestin** : stowaway — **passant, -sante** [pasɑ̃, -sɑ̃t] *adj* : busy, crowded — ~ *n* : passerby

passe [pas] *nf* **1** : pass (in sports) **2 mauvaise ~** : difficult time

passé, -sée [pase] *adj* **1** : last, past **2** DÉCOLORÉ : faded — **passé** *nm* **1** : past **2** : past tense — **~** *prep* : after, beyond

passe–partout [paspartu] *nms & pl* : master key

passeport [paspɔr] *nm* : passport

passer [pase] *vt* **1** : cross, go over **2** : pass, go past **3** : hand over **4** : put through to (on the telephone) **5** : take (an exam, etc.) **6** : spend (time) **7** : skip, pass over **8** ENFILER : slip on **9** : show (a film), play (a cassette, etc.) — *vi* **1** : pass, go past, go by **2** : drop by **3** ALLER : go **4 en passant** : incidentally **5 laissez-moi passer** : let me through — **se passer** *vr* **1** : take place **2** SE DÉROULER : turn out **3** : pass, go by (of time) **4 ~ de** : dispense with, do without

passereau [pasro] *nm, pl* **-reaux** : sparrow

passerelle [pasrɛl] *nf* **1** : footbridge **2** : gangplank

passe–temps [pastɑ̃] *nms & pl* : hobby, pastime

passeur, -seuse [pasœr, -søz] *n* : smuggler

passible [pasibl] *adj* **~ de** : liable to

passif, -sive [pasif, -siv] *adj* : passive — **passif** *nm* **1** : passive voice **2** : liabilities *pl*

passionner [pasjɔne] *vt* : fascinate, captivate — **se passionner** *vr* **~ pour** : have a passion for — **passion** [pasjɔ̃] *nf* : passion — **passionnant, -nante** [pasjɔnɑ̃, -nɑ̃t] *adj* : exciting, fascinating — **passionné, -née** [pasjɔne] *adj* : passionate — **~** *n* : enthusiast

passoire [paswar] *nf* : sieve, colander

pastel [pastɛl] *adj & nm* : pastel

pastèque [pastɛk] *nf* : watermelon

pasteur [pastœr] *nm* : minister, pastor

pasteuriser [pastœrize] *vt* : pasteurize

pastille [pastij] *nf* : lozenge

patate [patat] *nf* **1** *fam* : potato **2** *or* **~ douce** : sweet potato

patauger [patoʒe] {17} *vi* : splash about, paddle

pâte [pat] *nf* **1** : dough, batter **2 ~ à modeler** : modeling clay **3 ~ dentifrice** : toothpaste **4 ~s** *nfpl* : pasta

pâté [pate] *nm* **1** : pâté **2** *or* **~ de maisons** : block (of houses)

patelin [patlɛ̃] *nm fam* : little village

patent, -tente [patɑ̃, -tɑ̃t] *adj* : obvious, patent

patère [patɛr] *nf* : peg, hook

paternel, -nelle [patɛrnɛl] *adj* : paternal, fatherly — **paternité** [patɛrnite] *nf* : fatherhood

pâteux, -teuse [patø, -tøz] *adj* **1** : pasty, doughy **2 avoir la langue pâteuse** : have a coated tongue

pathologie [patɔlɔʒi] *nf* : pathology

patience [pasjɑ̃s] *nf* **1** : patience **2 jeu de ~** : solitaire — **patient, -tiente** [pasjɑ̃, -sjɑ̃t] *adj & n* : patient — **patiemment** [pasjamɑ̃] *adv* : patiently — **patienter** [pasjɑ̃te] *vi* : wait

patin [patɛ̃] *nm* **1** : skate **2 ~s à glace** : ice skates **3 ~s à roulettes** : roller skates — **patinage** [patinaʒ] *nm* : skating — **patiner** [patine] *vi* **1** : skate **2** : skid — **patineur, -neuse** [patinœr, -nøz] *n* : skater — **patinoire** [patinwar] *nf* : skating rink

pâtisserie [patisri] *nf* **1** : cake, pastry **2** : pastry shop, bakery

patrie [patri] *nf* : homeland

patrimoine [patrimwan] *nm* **1** : inheritance **2** HÉRITAGE : heritage

patriote [patrijɔt] *adj* : patriotic — **~** *nmf* : patriot — **patriotique** [patrijɔtik] *adj* : patriotic

patron, -tronne [patrɔ̃, -trɔn] *n* : boss, manager — **patron** *nm* : pattern (in sewing) — **patronner** [patrɔne] *vt* : support, sponsor

patrouille [patruj] *nf* : patrol — **patrouiller** [patruje] *vi* : patrol

patte [pat] *nf* **1** : paw, hoof, foot **2** *fam* : leg, foot (of a person) **3** : tab, flap

pâturage [patyraʒ] *nm* : pasture

paume [pom] *nf* : palm (of the hand)

paumer [pome] *v fam* : lose — **se paumer** *vr fam* : get lost

paupière [popjɛr] *nf* : eyelid

pause [poz] *nf* **1** : pause **2** : break (from work)

pauvre [povr] *adj* : poor — **~** *nmf* : poor man, poor woman — **pauvreté** [povrəte] *nf* : poverty

pavaner [pavane] *v* **se pavaner** *vr* : strut about

paver [pave] *vt* : pave — **pavé** [pave] *nm* **1** : pavement **2** : cobblestone

pavillon [pavijɔ̃] *nm* **1** : pavilion **2** *France* : (detached) house **3** : ward, wing (in a hospital) **4** : flag (on a ship)

pavoiser [pavwaze] *vi fam* : rejoice

pavot [pavo] *nm* : poppy

paye [pɛj] → **paie**

payement [pɛmɑ̃] → **paiement**

payer [peje] {11} *vt* : pay (for) — *vi* : pay — **se payer** *vr* : treat oneself
pays [pei] *nm* **1** : country **2** : region, area **3 du ~** : local — **paysage** [peizaʒ] *nm* : scenery, landscape — **paysan, -sanne** [peizɑ̃, -zan] *adj* **1** : agricultural, farming **2** : rural, rustic — **~** *n* **1** : small farmer **2** : peasant
péage [peaʒ] *nm* **1** : toll **2** : tollbooth
peau [po] *nf, pl* **peaux 1** : (human) skin **2** : hide, pelt **3** : peel, skin (of a fruit) **4 petites peaux** : cuticle
pêche [pɛʃ] *nf* **1** : peach **2** : fishing
péché [peʃe] *nm* : sin — **pécher** [peʃe] {87} *vi* : sin
pêcher[1] [peʃe] *vt* **1** : fish for **2** *fam* : get, dig up — *vi* : fish
pêcher[2] [peʃe] *nm* : peach tree
pécheur[1], **-cheresse** [peʃœr, -ʃrɛs] *n* : sinner
pêcheur[2], **-cheuse** [pɛʃœr, -ʃøz] *n* **1** : fisherman **2 pêcheur à la ligne** : angler
pécule [pekyl] *nm* : savings *pl*
pécuniaire [pekynjɛr] *adj* : financial
pédagogie [pedagɔʒi] *nf* : education — **pédagogique** [pedagɔʒik] *adj* : educational
pédale [pedal] *nf* : pedal — **pédaler** [pedale] *vi* : pedal — **pédalo** [pedalo] *nm* : pedal boat
pédant, -dante [pedɑ̃, -dɑ̃t] *adj* : pedantic — **~** *n* : pedant
pédestre [pedɛstr] *adj* **randonnée ~** : hike
pédiatre [pedjatr] *nmf* : pediatrician
pédicure [pedikyr] *nmf* : chiropodist
pègre [pɛgr] *nf* : (criminal) underworld
peigne [pɛɲ] *nm* : comb — **peigner** [peɲe] *vt* : comb — **se peigner** *vr* : comb one's hair — **peignoir** [pɛɲwar] *nm* : bathrobe
peindre [pɛ̃dr] {37} *vt* **1** : paint **2** DÉCRIRE : depict, portray
peine [pɛn] *nf* **1** : sorrow, sadness **2** EFFORT : trouble **3** : punishment **4 à ~** : hardly, barely — **peiner** [pene] *vt* ATTRISTER : sadden, distress — *vi* **1** : struggle **2** : labor (of an engine, etc.)
peintre [pɛ̃tr] *nm* : painter — **peinture** [pɛ̃tyr] *nf* **1** : paint **2** : painting
péjoratif, -tive [peʒɔratif, -tiv] *adj* : derogatory
pelage [pəlaʒ] *nm* : coat, fur (of an animal)
pêle–mêle [pɛlmɛl] *adv* : every which way
peler [pəle] {20} *v* : peel
pèlerin, -rine [pɛlrɛ̃] *n* : pilgrim — **pèlerinage** [pɛlrinaʒ] *nm* : pilgrimage — **pèlerine** [pɛlrin] *nf* : cape
pélican [pelikɑ̃] *nm* : pelican
pelle [pɛl] *nf* **1** : shovel **2 ~ à poussière** : dustpan — **pelletée** [pɛlte] *nf* : shovelful — **pelleter** [pɛlte] {8} *vt* : shovel
pellicule [pelikyl] *nf* **1** : (photographic) film **2** : thin layer, film **3 ~s** *nfpl* : dandruff
pelote [pəlɔt] *nf* : ball (of string, etc.) — **peloton** [plɔtɔ̃] *nm* **1** : pack, group **2** : squad, platoon **3 ~ de tête** : front runners — **pelotonner** [pəlɔtɔne] *v* **se pelotonner** *vr* : curl up (into a ball)
pelouse [pəluz] *nf* **1** : lawn, grass **2** : field (in sports)
peluche [pəlyʃ] *nf* **1** : plush **2 ~s** *nfpl* : fluff, lint **3** *or* **animal en ~** : stuffed animal
pelure [pəlyr] *nf* : peel, skin
pénal, -nale [penal] *adj, mpl* **-naux** [peno] : penal — **pénaliser** [penalize] *vt* : penalize — **pénalité** [penalite] *nf* : penalty
penaud, -naude [pəno, -nod] *adj* : sheepish
penchant [pɑ̃ʃɑ̃] *nm* : tendency, inclination
pencher [pɑ̃ʃe] *vt* INCLINER : tilt, tip — *vi* **1** : slant, lean **2 ~ pour** : favor — **se pencher** *vr* : hunch over
pendaison [pɑ̃dɛzɔ̃] *nf* **1** : hanging **2 ~ de crémaillère** : housewarming
pendant, -dante [pɑ̃dɑ̃, -dɑ̃t] *adj* : hanging, dangling — **pendant** *nm* **1** *or* **~ d'oreille** : drop earring **2** CONTREPARTIE : counterpart — **~** *prep* **1** : during, for **2 ~ que** : while — **pendentif** [pɑ̃dɑ̃tif] *nm* : pendant
penderie [pɑ̃dri] *nf* : closet, wardrobe
pendre [pɑ̃dr] {63} *v* : hang — **se pendre** *vr* : hang oneself
pendule [pɑ̃dyl] *nm* : pendulum — **~** *nf* : clock
pêne [pɛn] *nm* : bolt (of a lock)
pénétrer [penetre] {87} *vt* : penetrate — *vi* **~ dans** : enter
pénible [penibl] *adj* **1** : painful, distressing **2** ARDU : difficult — **péniblement** [penibləmɑ̃] *adv* : with difficulty
péniche [peniʃ] *nf* **1** : barge **2 ~ aménagée** : houseboat
pénicilline [penisilin] *nf* : penicillin
péninsule [penɛ̃syl] *nf* : peninsula
pénis [penis] *nm* : penis
pénitent, -tente [penitɑ̃, -tɑ̃t] *adj* : re-

pentant — **pénitencier** [penitɑ̃sje] *nm* : penitentiary

pénombre [penɔ̃br] *nf* : half-light

pensée [pɑ̃se] *nf* **1** IDÉE : thought **2** ESPRIT : mind **3** : pansy — **penser** [pɑ̃se] *vt* **1** : think **2** CROIRE : believe, suppose **3 ~ faire** : plan on doing — *vi* **~ à** : think about — **pensif, -sive** [pɑ̃sif, -siv] *adj* : pensive

pension [pɑ̃sjɔ̃] *nf* **1** : pension **2** : boardinghouse **3** : room and board **4 ~ alimentaire** : alimony — **pensionnaire** [pɑ̃sjɔnɛr] *nmf* : boarder, roomer — **pensionnat** [pɑ̃sjɔna] *nm* : boarding school

pentagone [pɛ̃tagɔn] *nm* : pentagon

pente [pɑ̃t] *nf* **1** : slope **2 en ~** : sloping

pénurie [penyri] *nf* : shortage, scarcity

pépé [pepe] *nm France fam* : grandpa

pépier [pepje] {96} *vi* : chirp, tweet — **pépiement** [pepimɑ̃] *nm* : peep (of a bird)

pépin [pepɛ̃] *nm* **1** : seed (of a fruit) **2** *fam* : snag, hitch — **pépinière** [pepinjɛr] *nf* : (tree) nursery

pépite [pepit] *nf* : nugget

perçant, -çante [pɛrsɑ̃, -sɑ̃t] *adj* **1** : piercing **2** : sharp, keen (of vision)

percée [pɛrse] *nf* **1** : opening, gap **2** DÉCOUVERTE : breakthrough

percepteur [pɛrsɛptœr] *nm* : tax collector

perceptible [pɛrsɛptibl] *adj* : perceptible, noticeable

perception [pɛrsɛpsjɔ̃] *nf* **1** : perception **2** RECOUVREMENT : collection (of taxes)

percer [pɛrse] {6} *vt* **1** : pierce, puncture **2** PÉNÉTRER : penetrate **3 ~ ses dents** : be teething — *vi* **1** : break through **2** : come through (of a tooth) — **perceuse** [pɛrsøz] *nf* : drill

percevoir [pɛrsəvwar] {26} *vt* **1** : perceive **2** : collect (taxes)

perche [pɛrʃ] *nf* **1** : pole, rod **2** : perch, bass (fish)

percher [pɛrʃe] *v* **se percher** *vr* : perch, roost — **perchoir** [pɛrʃwar] *nm* : perch, roost

percussion [pɛrkysjɔ̃] *nf* : percussion

percuter [pɛrkyte] *vt* : strike, crash into — **percutant, -tante** [pɛrkytɑ̃, -tɑ̃t] *adj* : forceful, striking

perdre [pɛrdr] {63} *vt* **1** : lose **2** GASPILLER : waste **3** MANQUER : miss **4** : ruin (one's reputation, etc.) — *vi* : lose — **se perdre** *vr* : get lost — **perdant, -dante** [pɛrdɑ̃, -dɑ̃t] *adj* : losing — **~** *n* : loser

perdrix [pɛrdri] *nfs & pl* : partridge

perdu, -due [pɛrdy] *adj* **1** : lost **2 temps perdu** : wasted time

père [pɛr] *nm* **1** : father **2 ~s** *nmpl* : ancestors

perfectionner [pɛrfɛksjɔne] *vt* : perfect, improve — **se perfectionner** *vr* : improve — **perfection** [pɛrfɛksjɔ̃] *nf* **1** : perfection **2 à la ~** : perfectly — **perfectionné, -née** [pɛrfɛksjɔne] *adj* : sophisticated — **perfectionnement** [pɛrfɛksjɔnmɑ̃] *nm* : improvement

perforer [pɛrfɔre] *vt* : perforate, pierce

performance [pɛrfɔrmɑ̃s] *nf* **1** : performance **2** RÉUSSITE : achievement — **performant, -mante** [pɛrfɔrmɑ̃, -mɑ̃t] *adj* : high-performance

péril [peril] *nm* : peril, danger — **périlleux, -leuse** [perijø, -jøz] *adj* : perilous

périmé, -mée [perime] *adj* : out-of-date, expired

périmètre [perimɛtr] *nm* : perimeter

période [perjɔd] *nf* **1** : period, time **2 par ~s** : periodically — **périodique** [perjɔdik] *adj* : periodic, periodical — **~** *nm* : periodical

péripétie [peripesi] *nf* : incident, event

périphérie [periferi] *nf* **1** : periphery, circumference **2** : outskirts *pl* (of a city) — **périphérique** [periferik] *adj* **1** : peripheral **2** : outlying (areas)

périple [peripl] *nm* : journey

périr [perir] *vi* : perish

périssable [perisabl] *adj* : perishable

perle [pɛrl] *nf* **1** : pearl **2** : gem, treasure (of a person)

permanent, -nente [pɛrmanɑ̃, -nɑ̃t] *adj* : permanent — **permanente** *nf* : perm, permanent — **permanence** [pɛrmanɑ̃s] *nf* : permanence

permettre [pɛrmɛtr] {53} *vt* **1** : allow, permit **2** : enable, make possible — **se permettre** *vr* **1** : allow oneself **2 ~ de** : take the liberty of — **permis** [pɛrmi] *nm* : license, permit — **permission** [pɛrmisjɔ̃] *nf* **1** : permission **2** : leave (in the military)

permuter [pɛrmyte] *vt* : switch around — *vi* : switch places

pernicieux, -cieuse [pɛrnisjø, -sjøz] *adj* : pernicious

peroxyde [pɛrɔksid] *nm* : peroxide

perpendiculaire [pɛrpɑ̃dikylɛr] *adj* : perpendicular

perpétrer [pɛrpetre] {87} *vt* : perpetrate, commit

perpétuer [pɛrpetɥe] *vt* : perpetuate — **perpétuel, -tuelle** [pɛrpetɥɛl] *adj* **1** : perpetual **2** : permanent — **perpétuité** [pɛrpetɥite] *nf* **à ~** : for life

perplexe [pɛrplɛks] *adj* : perplexed, puzzled — **perplexité** [pɛrplɛksite] *nf* : perplexity

perquisition [pɛrkizisjɔ̃] *nf* : (police) search

perron [perɔ̃] *nm* : (front) steps

perroquet [perɔkɛ] *nm* : parrot

perruche [peryʃ] *nf* : parakeet

perruque [peryk] *nf* : wig

persécuter [pɛrsekyte] *vt* **1** : persecute **2** HARCELER : harass — **persécution** [pɛrsekysjɔ̃] *nf* : persecution

persévérer [pɛrsevere] {87} *vi* : persevere, persist — **persévérance** [pɛrseverɑ̃s] *nf* : perseverance

persienne [pɛrsjɛn] *nf* : shutter

persil [pɛrsi] *nm* : parsley

persister [pɛrsiste] *vi* : persist — **persistant, -tante** [pɛrsistɑ̃, -tɑ̃t] *adj* : persistent — **persistance** [-tɑ̃s] *nf* : persistence

personnage [pɛrsɔnaʒ] *nm* **1** : (fictional) character **2** : character, individual

personnalité [pɛrsɔnalite] *nf* **1** : personality **2** : celebrity

personne [pɛrsɔn] *nf* : person — **~** *pron* **1** : no one, nobody **2** : anyone, anybody — **personnel, -nelle** [pɛrsɔnɛl] *adj* : personal, private — **personnel** *nm* : personnel, staff

perspective [pɛrspɛktiv] *nf* **1** : perspective (in art) **2** : point of view **3** POSSIBILITÉ : outlook, prospect

perspicace [pɛrspikas] *adj* : insightful, shrewd — **perspicacité** [pɛrspikasite] *nf* : shrewdness

persuader [pɛrsɥade] *vt* : persuade, convince — **persuasion** [pɛrsɥazjɔ̃] *nf* : persuasion

perte [pɛrt] *nf* **1** : loss **2** GASPILLAGE : waste **3 à ~ de vue** : as far as the eye can see

pertinent, -nente [pɛrtinɑ̃, -nɑ̃t] *adj* : pertinent — **pertinence** [pɛrtinɑ̃s] *nf* : pertinence

perturber [pɛrtyrbe] *vt* **1** INTERROMPRE : disrupt **2** DÉRANGER : disturb, upset — **perturbation** [pɛrtyrbasjɔ̃] *nf* : disruption

pervertir [pɛrvɛrtir] *vt* : pervert, corrupt — **pervers, -verse** [pɛrvɛr, -vɛrs] *adj* : perverse

peser [pəze] {52} *vt* **1** : weigh **2** EXAMINER : consider — *vi* **1** : weigh **2** INFLUER : carry weight **3 ~ sur** : press, push — **pesamment** [pəzamɑ̃] *adv* : heavily — **pesant, -sante** [pəzɑ̃, -zɑ̃t] *adj* **1** : heavy **2** : burdensome — **pesanteur** [pəzɑ̃tœr] *nf* **1** : gravity (in physics) **2** LOURDEUR : heaviness, weight — **pesée** [pəze] *nf* : weighing

pèse-personne [pɛzpɛrsɔn] *nm, pl* **pèse-personnes** : (bathroom) scales

pessimiste [pesimist] *adj* : pessimistic — **~** *nmf* : pessimist — **pessimisme** [pesimism] *nm* : pessimism

peste [pɛst] *nf* **1** : plague **2** : pest (person)

pesticide [pɛstisid] *nm* : pesticide

pétale [petal] *nm* : petal

pétarader [petarade] *vi* : backfire — **pétard** [petar] *nm* : firecracker

péter [pete] {87} *vi fam* : go off, explode — *vt fam* : bust, break

pétiller [petije] *vi* **1** : sparkle **2** : bubble, fizz **3** : crackle (of fire) — **pétillant, -lante** [petijɑ̃, -jɑ̃t] *adj* **1** : sparkling **2** : bubbly

petit, -tite [p(ə)ti, -tit] *adj* **1** : small, little **2** COURT : short **3** : young (of an animal) **4 ma petite sœur** : my little sister **5 petit ami, petite amie** : boyfriend, girlfriend **6 petit déjeuner** : breakfast — **~** *n* : little boy *m*, little girl *f* — **petit** *nm* : cub

petit-fils, petite-fille [p(ə)tifis, p(ə)titfij] *n* : grandson *m*, granddaughter *f*

pétition [petisjɔ̃] *nf* : petition

petits-enfants [p(ə)tizɑ̃fɑ̃] *nmpl* : grandchildren

pétrifier [petrifje] {96} *vt* : petrify

pétrin [petrɛ̃] *nm fam* : fix, jam

pétrir [petrir] *vt* : knead

pétrole [petrɔl] *nm* **1** : oil, petroleum **2** *or* **~ lampant** : kerosene — **pétrolier, -lière** [petrɔlje, -ljɛr] *adj* : oil, petroleum — **pétrolier** *nm* **1** : oil tanker **2** : oilman

pétulant, -lante [petylɑ̃, -lɑ̃t] *adj* : vivacious

peu [pø] *adv* **1** : little, not much **2** : not very **3 ~ après** : shortly after — **~** *nm* **1 ~ à ~** : little by little **2 le ~ de** : the few, the little **3 un ~** : a little, a bit — **~** *pron* **1** : few (people) **2 ~ de** : few

peupler [pœple] *vt* : populate, inhabit — **se peupler** *vr* : become populated — **peuple** [pœpl] *nm* : people *pl*

peuplier [pøplije] *nm* : poplar

peur [pœr] *nf* **1** : fear **2 avoir ~ de** : be afraid of **3 de ~ que** : lest **4 faire ~ à** : frighten — **peureux,**

-reuse [pœrø, -røz] *adj* : fearful, afraid
peut–être [pøtɛtr] *adv* : perhaps, maybe
pharaon [faraɔ̃] *nm* : pharaoh
phare [far] *nm* **1** : lighthouse **2** : headlight
pharmacie [farmasi] *nf* : pharmacy, drugstore — **pharmacien, -cienne** [farmasjɛ̃, -sjɛn] *n* : pharmacist
phase [faz] *nf* : phase, stage
phénomène [fenɔmɛn] *nm* : phenomenon
philanthrope [filɑ̃trɔp] *nmf* : philanthropist
philatélie [filateli] *nf* : stamp collecting
philosophe [filɔzɔf] *nmf* : philosopher — **philosophie** [filɔzɔfi] *nf* : philosophy
phobie [fɔbi] *nf* : phobia
phonétique [fɔnetik] *adj* : phonetic — ~ *nf* : phonetics
phoque [fɔk] *nm* : seal
phosphore [fɔsfɔr] *nm* : phosphorous
photo [fɔto] *nf* : photo
photocopie [fɔtɔkɔpi] *nf* : photocopy — **photocopier** [fɔtɔkɔpje] {96} *vt* : photocopy — **photocopieur** [fɔtɔkɔpjœr] *nm or* **photocopieuse** [fɔtɔkɔpjøz] *nf* : photocopier
photographie [fɔtɔgrafi] *nf* **1** : photography **2** : photograph — **photographe** [fɔtɔgraf] *nmf* : photographer — **photographier** [fɔtɔgrafje] {96} *vt* : photograph
phrase [fraz] *nf* : sentence
physicien, -cienne [fizisjɛ̃, -sjɛn] *n* : physicist
physiologie [fizjɔlɔʒi] *nf* : physiology
physionomie [fizjɔnɔmi] *nf* : face
physique [fizik] *adj* : physical — ~ *nm* : physique — ~ *nf* : physics
piailler [pjaje] *vi* : squawk
piano [pjano] *nm* **1** : piano **2** ~ **à queue** : grand piano — **pianiste** [pjanist] *nmf* : pianist
pic [pik] *nm* **1** : woodpecker **2** CIME : peak **3** : pick(axe)
pichet [piʃɛ] *nm* : pitcher, jug
pickpocket [pikpɔkɛt] *nm* : pickpocket
picorer [pikɔre] *v* : peck
picoter [pikɔte] *vi* : prickle, sting — **picotement** [pikɔtmɑ̃] *nm* : prickling, stinging
pie [pi] *nf* **1** : magpie **2** *fam* : chatterbox
pièce [pjɛs] *nf* **1** : piece, bit **2** : part, item **3** : room, bedroom **4** : piece (in music) **5** ~ **de théâtre** : play **6** *or* ~ **de monnaie** : coin **7** ~ **jointe** : enclosure (in correspondence)
pied [pje] *nm* **1** : foot **2** : base, bottom, leg (of a table, etc.) **3** : stalk, head (of lettuce) **4 aux ~s nus** : barefoot **5 coup de ~** : kick **6 mettre sur ~** : set up, get off the ground — **piédestal** [pjedɛstal] *nm, pl* **-taux** [-to] : pedestal
piège [pjɛʒ] *nm* **1** : trap, snare **2** : pitfall **3 prendre au ~** : entrap — **piéger** [pjeʒe] {64} *vt* **1** : trap **2** : booby-trap
pierre [pjɛr] *nf* **1** : stone **2** ~ **de touche** : touchstone **3** ~ **tombale** : tombstone — **pierreries** [pjɛrri] *nfpl* : precious stones, gems — **pierreux, -reuse** [pjɛrø, -røz] *adj* : stony
piété [pjete] *nf* : piety
piétiner [pjetine] *vt* : trample on — *vi* **1** : stamp one's feet **2** STAGNER : make no headway
piéton, -tonne [pjetɔ̃, -tɔn] *n* : pedestrian — **piétonnier, -nière** [pjetɔnje, -njɛr] *adj* : pedestrian
piètre [pjɛtr] *adj* : poor, wretched
pieu [pjø] *nm, pl* **pieux** : post, stake
pieuvre [pjøvr] *nf* : octopus
pieux, pieuse [pjø, pjøz] *adj* : pious
pige [piʒ] *nf* **à la ~** : freelance
pigeon [piʒɔ̃] *nm* : pigeon
piger [piʒe] {17} *vt fam* **1** : understand **2** *Can* : to pick (a card, a number, etc.) **3 tu piges?** : get it?
pigment [pigmɑ̃] *nm* : pigment
pignon [piɲɔ̃] *nm* **1** : gable **2** : cogwheel
pile [pil] *nf* **1** : pile, heap **2** : (storage) battery **3** ~ **ou face?** : heads or tails? — ~ *adv fam* **1** : abruptly **2** JUSTE : exactly, right **3 à l'heure ~** : on the dot
piler [pile] *vt* **1** : crush, pound **2** *Can* : mash (potatoes, etc.)
pilier [pilje] *nm* : pillar, column
piller [pije] *vt* : loot, pillage — **pillage** [pijaʒ] *nm* : looting — **pillard, -larde** [pijar, -jard] *n* : looter
pilon [pilɔ̃] *nm* **1** : pestle **2** : (chicken) drumstick — **pilonner** [pilɔne] *vt* **1** : crush, pound **2** : bombard, shell
pilote [pilɔt] *adj* : pilot, test — ~ *nm* **1** : pilot, driver **2** GUIDE : guide — **pilotage** [pilɔtaʒ] *nm* : piloting, flying — **piloter** [pilɔte] *vt* **1** : pilot, fly, drive **2** GUIDER : show around
pilule [pilyl] *nf* : pill
piment [pimɑ̃] *nm* **1** : pepper **2** ~

rouge : hot pepper **3 ~ doux** : sweet pepper
pin [pɛ̃] *nm* : pine
pinard [pinar] *nm fam* : (cheap) wine
pince [pɛ̃s] *nf* **1** : pliers *pl* **2** : tongs *pl* **3** : pincer, claw **4** : dart, fold **5 ~ à épiler** : tweezers *pl* **6 ~ à linge** : clothespin
pinceau [pɛ̃so] *nm, pl* **-ceaux** : paintbrush
pincer [pɛ̃se] {6} *vt* **1** : pinch **2** : nip at, sting (of wind, etc.) **3** *fam* : nab — *vi* : be nippy (of weather) — **pincé, -cée** [pɛ̃se] *adj* : forced, stiff — **pincée** [pɛ̃se] *nf* : pinch, small amount — **pincement** [pɛ̃smɑ̃] *nm* **1** : pinch **2** : twinge — **pincettes** [pɛ̃sɛt] *nfpl* **1** : small tweezers **2** : (fire) tongs
pinède [pinɛd] *nf* : pine forest
pingouin [pɛ̃gwɛ̃] *nm* : auk
pingre [pɛ̃gr] *adj* : stingy
pintade [pɛ̃tad] *nf* : guinea fowl
pinte [pɛ̃t] *nf* : pint
pioche [pjɔʃ] *nf* : pickax, pick — **piocher** [pjɔʃe] *vt* : dig (up)
pion, pionne [pjɔ̃, pjɔn] *n France fam* : student monitor — **pion** *nm* **1** : pawn (in chess) **2** : piece (in checkers)
pionnier, -nière [pjɔnje, -njɛr] *n* : pioneer
pipe [pip] *nf* : pipe
pipeline [pajplajn] *nm* : pipeline
piquant, -quante [pikɑ̃, -kɑ̃t] *adj* **1** : prickly, bristly **2** ÉPICÉ : hot, spicy — **piquant** *nm* **1** : prickle, thorn **2** : spine, quill
pique [pik] *nm* : spade (in playing cards) — **~** *nf* : cutting remark
pique–assiette [pikasjɛt] *nmfs & pl* : freeloader
pique–nique [piknik] *nm, pl* **pique–niques** : picnic
piquer [pike] *vt* **1** : prick, puncture **2** : sting, bite **3** : stick (into) **4** ÉVEILLER : arouse (interest, etc.) **5** *fam* : pinch, swipe **6** *fam* : nab, catch — *vi* **1** : sting, burn **2** : dive, swoop down — **se piquer** *vr* **~ de** : pride oneself on — **piquet** [pikɛ] *nm* **1** : post, stake, peg **2 ~ de grève** : picket line — **piqûre** [pikyr] *nf* **1** : prick **2** : sting, bite **3** : injection, shot
pirate [pirat] *nm* **1** : pirate **2 ~ de l'air** : hijacker
pire [pir] *adj* **1** : worse **2 le ~, la ~, les ~s** : the worst — **~** *nm* **1 le ~** : the worst **2 au ~** : at the worst
pis [pi] *adv* **1** : worse **2 de mal en ~** : from bad to worse — **~** *adj* : worse — **~** *nms & pl* **1** : udder **2 le ~** : the worst
pis–aller [pizale] *nms & pl* : last resort
piscine [pisin] *nf* : swimming pool
pissenlit [pisɑ̃li] *nm* : dandelion
pistache [pistaʃ] *nf* : pistachio
piste [pist] *nf* **1** TRACE : track, trail **2** : path, route **3** : (ski) slope **4** : racetrack **5** INDICE : lead, clue **6** *or* **~ d'atterrissage** : runway, airstrip
pistolet [pistɔlɛ] *nm* **1** : pistol, handgun **2** : spray gun
piston [pistɔ̃] *nm* : piston
pitié [pitje] *nf* : pity, mercy — **piteux, -teuse** [pitø, -tøz] *adj* : pitiful
piton [pitɔ̃] *nm* **1** : eye, hook **2** *Can fam* : button, switch
pitoyable [pitwajabl] *adj* : pitiful
pitre [pitr] *nm* : clown
pittoresque [pitɔrɛsk] *adj* : picturesque
pivot [pivo] *nm* : pivot — **pivoter** [pivɔte] *vi* : pivot, revolve
pizza [pidza] *nf* : pizza — **pizzeria** [pidzerja] *nf* : pizzeria
placage [plakaʒ] *nm* : veneer
placard [plakar] *nm* **1** : cupboard, closet **2** AFFICHE : poster — **placarder** [plakarde] *vt* : post, put up
placer [plase] {6} *vt* **1** : place, set, put **2** : seat (s.o.) **3** : put in, interject **4** : invest (money, etc.) — **se placer** *vr* **1** : position oneself **2** : get a job **3 ~ premier** : finish first — **place** [plas] *nf* **1** : place, spot **2** : room, space **3** : seat (at the theater) **4** : rank, position **5** : (public) square **6** EMPLOI : job, position **7 à la ~ de** : instead of **8 mettre en ~** : set up — **placement** [plasmɑ̃] *nm* **1** : investment **2 bureau de ~** : placement agency
placide [plasid] *adj* : placid, calm
plafond [plafɔ̃] *nm* : ceiling — **plafonner** [plafɔne] *vi* : reach a maximum, peak
plage [plaʒ] *nf* **1** : beach, shore **2** : seaside resort
plagier [plaʒje] {96} *vt* : plagiarize — **plagiat** [plaʒja] *nm* : plagiarism
plaider [plede] *vi* : plead, litigate — *vt* : plead (a case)
plaie [plɛ] *nf* : wound, cut
plaignant, -gnante [plɛɲɑ̃, -ɲɑ̃t] *n* : plaintiff
plaindre [plɛ̃dr] {65} *vt* : pity — **se plaindre** *vr* **1** : moan **2 ~ de** : complain about — **plainte** [plɛ̃t] *nf* **1** : moan **2** : complaint
plaire [plɛr] {66} *vi* **1** : be pleasing **2**

~ à : please, suit — *v impers* **1** : please **2 s'il vous plaît** : please — **se plaire** *vr* **~ à** : like, enjoy — **plaisance** [plɛzɑ̃s] *nf or* **navigation de ~** : sailing, boating — **plaisant, -sante** [plɛzɑ̃, -zɑ̃t] *adj* **1** AGRÉABLE : pleasant **2** AMUSANT : amusing, funny — **plaisanter** [plɛzɑ̃te] *vi* : joke, jest — **plaisanterie** [plɛzɑ̃tri] *nf* **1** BLAGUE : joke, jest **2** FARCE : prank — **plaisantin** [plɛzɑ̃tɛ̃] *nm* : practical joker — **plaisir** [plezir] *nm* **1** : pleasure **2 au ~** : see you soon **3 avec ~!** : of course! **4 faire ~ à** : please

plan, plane [plɑ̃, plan] *adj* : flat, level — **plan** *nm* **1** : plane (in geometry) **2** : plan, strategy **3** : map, diagram **4 premier ~** : foreground

planche [plɑ̃ʃ] *nf* **1** : board, plank **2 ~ à repasser** : ironing board **3 ~ à roulettes** : skateboard — **plancher** [plɑ̃ʃe] *nm* : floor

planer [plane] *vi* **1** : glide, soar **2 ~ sur** : hover over

planète [planɛt] *nf* : planet — **planétaire** [planetɛr] *adj* : planetary

planeur [planœr] *nm* : glider

planifier [planifje] {96} *vt* : plan — **planification** [planifikasjɔ̃] *nf* : planning

planque [plɑ̃k] *nf fam* : hideout — **planquer** [plɑ̃ke] *vt fam* : hide away, stash

planter [plɑ̃te] *vt* **1** : plant **2** ENFONCER : drive in **3** INSTALLER : put up, set up **4** *fam* : ditch, drop — **se planter** *vr* **1** *fam* : stand, plant oneself **2** *fam* : get it wrong, mess up — **plant** [plɑ̃] *nm* : seedling, young plant — **plantation** [plɑ̃tasjɔ̃] *nf* **1** : planting **2** : plantation — **plante** [plɑ̃t] *nf* **1** : sole (of the foot) **2** : plant

plaquer [plake] *vt* **1** : veneer, plate **2** APLATIR : stick (down), flatten **3** : tackle (in football) **4** *fam* : ditch, get rid of — **plaque** [plak] *nf* **1** : plate, sheet **2** : plaque, nameplate **3** : patch (of ice, etc.) **4 ~ chauffante** : hotplate **5 ~ d'immatriculation** : license plate — **plaqué, -quée** [plake] *adj* : plated — **plaquette** [plakɛt] *nf* **1** : slab (of butter, etc.) **2** : pamphlet

plastique [plastik] *adj & nm* : plastic

plat, plate [pla, plat] *adj* **1** : flat, level **2** : dull, bland — **plat** *nm* **1** : plate, dish **2** : course (of a meal) **3 à ~** : flat down **4 à ~** : dead (of a battery) **5 ~ de résistance** : main course

platane [platan] *nm* : plane tree

plateau [plato] *nm, pl* **-teaux 1** : tray, platter **2** : plateau (in geography) **3** : stage, set (in theater)

plate–bande [platbɑ̃d] *nf, pl* **plates–bandes** : flower bed

plate–forme [platfɔrm] *nf, pl* **plates–formes** : platform

platine[1] [platin] *nm* : platinum

platine[2] *nf* : turntable

platitude [platityd] *nf* : trite remark

platonique [platɔnik] *adj* : platonic

plâtre [platr] *nm* **1** : plaster **2** : plaster cast — **plâtrer** [platre] *vt* **1** : plaster **2** : put in a (plaster) cast

plausible [plozibl] *adj* : plausible, likely

plein, pleine [plɛ̃, plɛn] *adj* **1** REMPLI : full, filled (up) **2** : rounded, full **3** : pregnant (of an animal) **4 en plein jour** : in broad daylight **5 le plein air** : the outdoors — **plein** *nm* **1 à ~** : fully, totally **2 faire le ~** : fill up — **plénitude** [plenityd] *nf* : fullness

pleurer [plœre] *vt* **1** : weep for, mourn **2** : shed (tears) — *vi* **1** : cry, weep **2** : water (of eyes) **3 ~ sur** : bemoan — **pleurnicher** [plœrniʃe] *vi fam* : whine, snivel — **pleurs** [plœr] *nfpl* **en ~** : in tears

pleuvoir [pløvwar] {67} *v impers* **1** : rain **2 il pleut** : it's raining — *vi* : rain down, pour down

plier [plije] {96} *vt* **1** : fold (up) **2** : bend — *vi* **1** : bend, sag **2** : yield, give in — **se plier** *vr* **1** : fold **2 ~ à** : submit to — **pli** [pli] *nm* **1** : fold, pleat, crease **2** HABITUDE : habit **3 sous ce ~** : enclosed — **pliant, pliante** [plijɑ̃, plijɑ̃t] *adj* : folding, collapsible

plinthe [plɛ̃t] *nf* : baseboard

plisser [plise] *vt* **1** : pleat, fold, crease **2** FRONCER : wrinkle (one's brow), pucker (one's lips)

plomb [plɔ̃] *nm* **1** : lead **2** : (lead) pellet **3** FUSIBLE : fuse — **plombage** [plɔ̃baʒ] *nm* : filling (of a tooth) — **plomber** [plɔ̃be] *vt* **1** : weight with lead **2** : fill (a tooth) — **plomberie** [plɔ̃bri] *nf* : plumbing — **plombier** [plɔ̃bje] *nm* : plumber

plonger [plɔ̃ʒe] {17} *vt* : thrust, plunge — *vi* **1** : dive **2 ~ dans** : plunge into — **se plonger** *vr* **~ dans** : immerse oneself into — **plongeant, -geante** [plɔ̃ʒɑ̃, -ʒɑ̃t] *adj* **1** : plunging **2 vue plongeante** : bird's-eye view — **plongée** [plɔ̃ʒe] *nf* **1** : diving **2 ~ sous–marine** : skin diving — **plon-**

geoir [plɔ̃ʒwar] *nm* : diving board — **plongeon** [plɔ̃ʒɔ̃] *nm* **1** : dive **2** : loon (bird) — **plongeur, -geuse** [plɔ̃ʒœr, -ʒøz] *n* **1** : diver **2** : dishwasher (person)

plouf [pluf] *nm* : splash

ployer [plwaje] {58} *v* : bow, bend

pluie [plɥi] *nf* **1** : rain, rainfall **2 une ~ de** : a stream of

plume [plym] *nf* **1** : feather **2** : quill pen — **plumage** [plymaʒ] *nm* : feathers *pl* — **plumeau** [plymo] *nm, pl* **-meaux** [plymo] : feather duster — **plumer** [plyme] *vt* : pluck

plupart [plypar] *nf* **1 la ~ des** : most, the majority of **2 pour la ~** : for the most part, mostly

pluriel, -rielle [plyrjɛl] *adj & nm* : plural — **pluriel** *nm* : plural

plus [ply(s)] *adv* **1** : more **2** (*used with* **ne**) : no more, no longer **3 ~ de** : more (than) **4 de ~** : in addition, furthermore **5 de ~ en ~** : increasingly **6 en ~** : as well **7 le ~** : the most **8 non ~** : neither, either — **~** *nm* **1** : plus (sign) **2** *fam* : plus, advantage — **~** *conj* : plus (in calculations)

plusieurs [plyzjœr] *adj & pron* : several

plutôt [plyto] *adv* **1** : rather, instead **2 ~ que** : rather than

pluvieux, -vieuse [plyvjø, -vjøz] *adj* : rainy, wet

pneu [pnø] *nm, pl* **pneus** : tire — **pneumatique** [pnømatik] *adj* : inflatable

pneumonie [pnømɔni] *nf* : pneumonia

poche [pɔʃ] *nf* **1** : pocket (in clothing) **2 ~s** *nfpl* CERNES : bags (under the eyes) — **pocher** [pɔʃe] *vt* : poach (in cooking) — **pochette** [pɔʃɛt] *nf* **1** : folder, case, sleeve **2** : book (of matches) **3** : pocket handkerchief

poêle [pwal] *nm* : stove — **~** *nf or* **~ à frire** : frying pan

poème [pɔɛm] *nm* : poem — **poésie** [pɔezi] *nf* **1** : poetry **2** : poem — **poète** [pɔɛt] *nmf* : poet — **poétique** [pɔetik] *adj* : poetic(al)

poids [pwa] *nms & pl* **1** : weight, heaviness **2** FARDEAU : burden **3** IMPORTANCE : meaning, influence **4 ~ et mesures** : weights and measures **5 ~ et haltères** : weight lifting

poignant, -gnante [pwaɲɑ̃, -ɲɑ̃t] *adj* : moving, poignant

poignard [pwaɲar] *nm* : dagger — **poignarder** [pwaɲarde] *vt* : stab

poigne [pwaɲ] *nf* **1** : grip, grasp **2 à ~** : firm, forceful

poignée [pwaɲe] *nf* **1** : handful **2** : handle, knob **3 ~ de main** : handshake

poignet [pwaɲɛ] *nm* **1** : wrist **2** : cuff

poil [pwal] *nm* **1** : hair **2** : fur, coat **3** : bristle (of a brush) **4 à ~** *fam* : stark naked — **poilu, -lue** [pwaly] *adj* : hairy

poinçon [pwɛ̃sɔ̃] *nm* **1** : awl, punch **2** MARQUE : hallmark, stamp — **poinçonner** [pwɛ̃sɔne] *vt* : punch, perforate

poing [pwɛ̃] *nm* **1** : fist **2 coup de ~** : punch

point [pwɛ̃] *nm* **1** : point, position **2** DEGRÉ : degree, extent **3** : period (in punctuation) **4** QUESTION : matter **5** : point (in sports) **6** : stitch (in sewing) **7 à ~** : just right, just in time **8 mettre au ~** : adjust, perfect **9 ~ culminant** : highlight **10 ~ de vue** : point of view **11 ~ du jour** : daybreak **12 ~ mort** : neutral (gear) **13 ~s cardinaux** : points of the compass — **~** *adv* **1** (*used with* **ne**) : not **2 ~ du tout** : not at all

pointe [pwɛ̃t] *nf* **1** : point, tip **2** SOUPÇON : touch, hint **3 de ~** : state-of-the-art **4 heures de ~** : rush hour **5 sur la ~ des pieds** : on tiptoe

pointer [pwɛ̃te] *vt* **1** COCHER : check, mark off **2** : aim (a rifle at), point (a finger at) — *vi* **1** : clock in **2** : break, dawn (of a new day) — **se pointer** *vr fam* : show up

pointillé [pwɛ̃tije] *nm* : dotted line

pointilleux, -leuse [pwɛ̃tijø, -jøz] *adj* : finicky, fussy

pointu, -tue [pwɛ̃ty] *adj* : pointed, sharp

pointure [pwɛ̃tyr] *nf* : size (of clothing)

point-virgule [pwɛ̃virgyl] *nm, pl* **points-virgules** : semicolon

poire [pwar] *nf* : pear

poireau [pwaro] *nm, pl* **-reaux** : leek — **poireauter** [pwarote] *vi fam* : hang around

poirier [pwarje] *nm* : pear tree

pois [pwa] *nms & pl* **1** : pea **2 à ~** : spotted, polka-dot

poison [pwazɔ̃] *nm* : poison

poisse [pwas] *nf fam* : bad luck

poisseux, -seuse [pwasø, -søz] *adj* : sticky

poisson [pwasɔ̃] *nm* **1** : fish **2 ~ d'avril!** : April fool! — **poissonnerie** [pwasɔnri] *nf* : fish market — **pois-**

sonnier, -nière [pwasɔnje, -njɛr] *n* : fish merchant
poitrine [pwatrin] *nf* **1** : chest **2** : breasts *pl,* bosom **3** : breast (in cooking)
poivre [pwavr] *nm* : pepper — **poivré, -vrée** [pwavre] *adj* : peppery — **poivrer** [pwavre] *vt* : pepper — **poivrier** [pwavrije] *nm or* **poivrière** [pwavrijɛr] *nf* : pepper shaker — **poivron** [pwavrɔ̃] *nm* : pepper (vegetable)
poker [pɔkɛr] *nm* : poker
pôle [pol] *nm* : pole — **polaire** [pɔlɛr] *adj* : polar
polémique [pɔlemik] *adj* : controversial — ~ *nf* : debate, controversy
poli, -lie [pɔli] *adj* **1** COURTOIS : polite **2** LISSE : polished, smooth
police [pɔlis] *nf* **1** : police, police force **2** ~ **d'assurance** : insurance policy — **policier, -cière** [pɔlisje, -sjɛr] *adj* **1** : police **2 roman policier** : detective novel — **policier** *nm* : police officer
poliomyélite [pɔljɔmjelit] *nf* : poliomyelitis
polir [pɔlir] *vt* : polish, shine
polisson, -sonne [pɔlisɔ̃, -sɔn] *n* : naughty child, rascal
politesse [pɔlitɛs] *nf* **1** : politeness **2** : polite remark
politique [pɔlitik] *adj* : political — ~ *nf* **1** : politics **2** : policy, procedure — **politicien, -cienne** [pɔlitisjɛ̃, -sjɛn] *n* : politician
pollen [pɔlɛn] *nm* : pollen
polluer [pɔlɥe] *vt* : pollute — **polluant** [pɔlɥɑ̃] *nm* : pollutant — **pollution** [pɔlysjɔ̃] *nf*
polo [pɔlo] *nm* **1** : polo **2** : polo shirt
poltron, -tronne [pɔltrɔ̃, -trɔn] *adj* : cowardly — ~ *n* : coward
polyester [pɔliɛstɛr] *nm* : polyester
polyvalent, -lente [pɔlivalɑ̃, -lɑ̃t] *adj* : versatile, multipurpose
pommade [pɔmad] *nf* : ointment
pomme [pɔm] *nf* **1** : apple **2** ~ **d'Adam** : Adam's apple **3** ~ **de pin** : pinecone **4** ~ **de terre** : potato **5** ~**s frites** : French fries — **pommeau** [pɔmo] *nm* : knob (of a cane) — **pommette** [pɔmɛt] *nf* : cheekbone — **pommier** [pɔmje] *nm* : apple tree
pompe [pɔ̃p] *nf* **1** : pump **2** APPARAT : pomp, ceremony **3** ~**s funèbres** : funeral home — **pomper** [pɔ̃pe] *vt* : pump
pompette [pɔ̃pɛt] *adj fam* : tipsy
pompeux, -peuse [pɔ̃pø, -pøz] *adj* : pompous
pompier [pɔ̃pje] *nm* : firefighter, fireman
pompiste [pɔ̃pist] *nmf* : service station attendant
pompon [pɔ̃pɔ̃] *nm* : pompom
pomponner [pɔ̃pɔne] *v* **se pomponner** *vr* : get all dressed up
poncer [pɔ̃se] {6} *vt* : sand (down)
ponctualité [pɔ̃ktɥalite] *nf* : punctuality
ponctuation [pɔ̃ktɥasjɔ̃] *nf* : punctuation
ponctuel, -tuelle [pɔ̃ktɥɛl] *adj* **1** : prompt, punctual **2** : limited, selective
ponctuer [pɔ̃ktɥe] *vt* : punctuate
pondéré, -rée [pɔ̃dere] *adj* : levelheaded, sensible
pondre [pɔ̃dr] {63} *vt* : lay (eggs)
poney [ponɛ] *nm* : pony
pont [pɔ̃] *nm* **1** : bridge **2** : deck (of a ship)
ponte [pɔ̃t] *nf* : laying (of eggs)
pont–levis [pɔ̃lәvi] *nm, pl* **ponts–levis** : drawbridge
ponton [pɔ̃tɔ̃] *nm* : pontoon
pop [pɔp] *adj s & pl* : pop
pop–corn [pɔpkɔrn] *nms & pl* : popcorn
popote [pɔpɔt] *nf* **1** : mess (in the military) **2** *fam* : cooking
populaire [pɔpylɛr] *adj* **1** : popular **2** : working-class — **popularité** [pɔpylarite] *nf* : popularity
population [pɔpylasjɔ̃] *nf* : population — **populeux, -leuse** [pɔpylø, -løz] *adj* : densely populated
porc [pɔr] *nm* **1** : pig, hog **2** : pork (in cooking)
porcelaine [pɔrsәlɛn] *nf* **1** : porcelain **2** : china, chinaware
porc–épic [pɔrkepik] *nm, pl* **porcs–épics** : porcupine
porche [pɔrʃ] *nm* : porch
porcherie [pɔrʃәri] *nf* : pigpen, pigsty
pore [pɔr] *nm* : pore — **poreux, -reuse** [pɔrø, -røz] *adj* : porous
pornographie [pɔrnɔgrafi] *nf* : pornography — **pornographique** [-grafik] *adj* : pornographic
port [pɔr] *nm* **1** : port, harbor **2** : wearing, carrying (of arms, etc.) **3** MAINTIEN : bearing **4** ~ **payé** : postpaid
portable [pɔrtabl] *adj* : portable
portail [pɔrtaj] *nm* : gate
portant, -tante [pɔrtɑ̃, -tɑ̃t] *adj* **bien portant** : in good health
portatif, -tive [pɔrtatif, -tiv] *adj* : portable

porte [pɔrt] *nf* **1** : door, doorway **2** : gate (at an airport, etc.) **3 ~ de sortie** : exit, way out
porte–avions [pɔrtavjɔ̃] *nms & pl* : aircraft carrier
porte–bagages [pɔrtbagaʒ] *nms & pl* : luggage rack
porte–bonheur [pɔrtbɔnœr] *nms & pl* : lucky charm
porte–clés *or* **porte–clefs** [pɔrtəkle] *nms & pl* : key ring
porte–documents [pɔrtdɔkymɑ̃] *nms & pl* : briefcase
portée [pɔrte] *nf* **1** : range **2** : impact, significance **3** : litter (of kittens, etc.) **4 à ~ de** : within reach of
portefeuille [pɔrtəfœj] *nm* **1** : wallet **2** : portfolio (in finance or politics)
portemanteau [pɔrtmɑ̃to] *nm, pl* **-teaux** [-to] : coat rack
porte–monnaie [pɔrtmɔnɛ] *nms & pl* : change purse
porte–parole [pɔrtparɔl] *nms & pl* : spokesperson
porter [pɔrte] *vt* **1** TRANSPORTER : carry **2** : wear, have on **3** APPORTER : bring **4** : bear (responsibility, etc.) **5 être porté à** : be inclined to — *vi* **1** : carry (of a voice) **2 ~ sur** CONCERNER : be about — **se porter** *vr* **1** : be worn **2 ~ bien** : be (feel, go) well
porte–savon [pɔrtsavɔ̃] *nms & pl* : soap dish
porte–serviettes [pɔrtsɛrvjɛt] *nms & pl* : towel rack
porteur, -teuse [pɔrtœr, -tøz] *n* **1** : porter **2** : holder, bearer (of news, etc.) **3** : carrier (of disease)
porte–voix [pɔrtəvwa] *nms & pl* : megaphone
portier, -tière [pɔrtje, -tjɛr] *n* : doorman
portière *nf* : door (of an automobile)
portillon [pɔrtijɔ̃] *nm* : gate
portion [pɔrsjɔ̃] *nf* : portion
porto [pɔrto] *nm* : port (wine)
portrait [pɔrtrɛ] *nm* : portrait
portuaire [pɔrtɥɛr] *adj* : harbor, port
portugais, -gaise [pɔrtygɛ, -gɛz] *adj* : Portuguese — **portugais** *nm* : Portuguese (language)
poser [poze] *vt* **1** : put (down), place **2** INSTALLER : put up, install **3** : pose (a problem) **4 ~ sa candidature** : apply (for a job) — *vi* : pose, sit — **se poser** *vr* **1** : land, alight **2** : arise, come up — **pose** [poz] *nf* **1** : installing **2** : pose, posture — **posé, -sée** [poze] *adj* : composed, calm
positif, -tive [pɔzitif, -tiv] *adj* : positive
position [pozisjɔ] *nf* **1** : position **2 prendre ~** : take a stand — **positionner** [pozisjɔne] *vt* : position, place
posologie [pozɔlɔʒi] *nf* : dosage
posséder [pɔsede] {87} *vt* **1** AVOIR : possess, have **2** MAÎTRISER : know thoroughly — **possesseur** [pɔsesœr] *nm* : owner, possessor — **possessif, -sive** [pɔsesif, -siv] *adj* : possessive — **possession** [pɔsesjɔ̃] *nf* : ownership, possession
possible [pɔsibl] *adj* : possible — **~** *nm* **1 dans la mesure du ~** : as far as possible **2 faire son ~** : do one's utmost — **possibilité** [pɔsibilite] *nf* **1** : possibility **2 ~s** *nfpl* : means, resources
poste [pɔst] *nm* **1** : job, position **2** : post, station **3** : (telephone) extension **4 ~ d'essence** : gas station **5 ~ de pilotage** : cockpit **6 ~ de pompiers** *Can* : fire station **7 ~ de télévision** : television set — **~** *nf* **1** : mail service **2** : post office — **postal, -tale** [pɔstal] *adj, mpl* **-taux** [pɔsto] : postal, mail — **poster** [pɔste] *vt* **1** : post, station **2** : mail
postérieur, -rieure [pɔsterjœr] *adj* **1** : later (of a date, etc.) **2** : rear, back — **postérieur** *nm fam* : bottom, buttocks *pl*
postérité [pɔsterite] *nf* : posterity
posthume [pɔstym] *adj* : posthumous
postiche [pɔstiʃ] *adj* : false, fake
postier, -tière [pɔstje, -tjɛr] *n* : postal worker
post–scriptum [pɔstskriptɔm] *nms & pl* : postscript
postuler [pɔstyle] *vt* : apply for (a position) — **postulant, -lante** [pɔstylɑ̃, -lɑ̃t] *n* : candidate, contestant
posture [pɔstyr] *nf* : posture
pot [po] *nm* **1** : pot, jar, container **2** *fam* : drink, glass **3 ~ d'échappement** : muffler (of an automobile)
potable [pɔtabl] *adj* **1** : drinkable **2** *fam* : fair, passable
potage [pɔtaʒ] *nm* : soup — **potager** [pɔtaʒe] *adj* **jardin ~** : vegetable garden
pot–au–feu [pɔtofø] *nms & pl* : beef stew
pot–de–vin [podvɛ̃] *nm, pl* **pots–de–vin** : bribe
pote [pɔt] *nm fam* : pal, buddy
poteau [pɔto] *nm, pl* **-teaux 1** : post, pole **2 ~ indicateur** : signpost
potelé, -lée [pɔtle] *adj* : chubby, plump

potence [pɔtɑ̃s] *nf* : gallows
potentiel, -tielle [pɔtɑ̃sjɛl] *adj & nm* : potential
poterie [pɔtri] *nf* : pottery
potin [pɔtɛ̃] *nm fam* **1** *France* : noise, racket **2 ~s** *nmpl* : gossip
potion [pɔsjɔ̃] *nf* : potion
potiron [pɔtirɔ̃] *nm* : large pumpkin
pot–pourri [popuri] *nm, pl* **pots–pourris** : potpourri
pou [pu] *nm, pl* **poux** : louse
poubelle [pubɛl] *nf* : garbage can
pouce [pus] *nm* **1** : thumb **2** : big toe **3** : inch (measurement) **4 faire du ~** *Can* : hitchhike
poudre [pudr] *nf* : powder — **poudrer** [pudre] *vt* : powder — **poudrerie** [pudrəri] *nf Can* : (snow) flurries *pl* — **poudreux, -dreuse** [pudrø, -drøz] *adj* : powdery — **poudrier** [pudrije] *nm* : (powder) compact
pouffer [pufe] *vi* **~ de rire** : burst out laughing
pouilleux, -leuse [pujø, -jøz] *adj* **1** : lousy, flea-ridden **2** : seedy (of a neighborhood)
poulailler [pulaje] *nm* : henhouse, chicken coop
poulain [pulɛ̃] *nm* **1** : colt, foal **2** PROTÉGÉ : protégé
poule [pul] *nf* **1** : hen **2** : fowl (in cooking) — **poulet** [pulɛ] *nm* : chicken
pouliche [puliʃ] *nf* : filly
poulie [puli] *nf* : pulley
pouls [pu] *nm* : pulse
poumon [pumɔ̃] *nm* : lung
poupe [pup] *nf* : stern
poupée [pupe] *nf* : doll
poupon [pupɔ̃] *nm* **1** : tiny baby **2** : baby doll — **pouponnière** [pupɔnjɛr] *nf* : nursery (for babies)
pour [pur] *prep* **1** : for **2** : to, in order to **3 ~ cent** : percent **4 ~ que** : in order that, so that — **~** *nm* **le ~ et le contre** : the pros and cons
pourboire [purbwar] *nm* : tip
pourcentage [pursɑ̃taʒ] *nm* : percentage
pourchasser [purʃase] *vt* : pursue, hunt down
pourparlers [purparle] *nmpl* : talks, negotiations
pourquoi [purkwa] *adv & conj* : why — **~** *nms & pl* : reason, cause
pourrir [purir] *v* : rot, decay — **pourri, -rie** [puri] *adj* : rotten — **pourriture** [purityr] *nf* : rot, decay
poursuivre [pursɥivr] {88} *vt* **1** : pursue, chase **2** CONTINUER : carry on with **3 ~ en justice** : sue, prosecute **4** HARCELER : hound — *vi* : continue — **poursuite** [pursɥit] *nf* **1** : pursuit **2 ~s** *nfpl* : legal proceedings, lawsuit — **poursuivant, -vante** [pursɥivɑ̃, -vɑ̃t] *n* **1** : pursuer **2** : plaintiff
pourtant [purtɑ̃] *adv* : however, yet
pourtour [purtur] *nm* : perimeter
pourvoir [purvwar] {68} *vt* **~ de** : provide with — *vi* **~ à** : provide for — **pourvu** [purvy] *conj* **~ que 1** : provided that **2** : let's hope (that)
pousser [puse] *vt* **1** : push, shove **2** INCITER : encourage, urge **3** POURSUIVRE : pursue, continue (with) **4** : let out (a scream) — *vi* **1** : push **2** CROÎTRE : grow — **se pousser** *vr* : move over — **pousse** [pus] *nf* **1** : growth **2** BOURGEON : shoot, sprout — **poussé, -sée** [puse] *adj* : advanced, extensive — **poussée** [puse] *nf* **1** : pressure **2** IMPULSION : push **3** AUGMENTATION : upsurge **4** ACCÈS : attack, outbreak (in medicine) — **poussette** [pusɛt] *nf* : stroller
poussière [pusjɛr] *nf* : dust — **poussiéreux, -reuse** [pusjerø, -røz] *adj* : dusty
poussin [pusɛ̃] *nm* : chick
poutre [putr] *nf* : beam, girder
pouvoir [puvwar] {69} *v aux* **1** : be able to **2** : be permitted to — *v impers* : be possible — *vt* **1** : be able to do **2 je n'en peux plus!** : I can't take anymore! — **se pouvoir** *v impers* : be possible — **~** *nm* : power
pragmatique [pragmatik] *adj* : pragmatic
prairie [preri] *nf* : meadow
pratiquer [pratike] *vt* **1** : practice **2** : play (a sport) **3** : use, apply **4** EFFECTUER : carry out — **praticable** [pratikabl] *adj* **1** : feasible **2** : passable (of a road, etc.) — **praticien, -cienne** [pratisjɛ̃, -sjɛn] *n* : practitioner — **pratiquant, -quante** [pratikɑ̃, -kɑ̃t] *adj* : practicing — **~** *n* : churchgoer, follower — **pratique** [pratik] *adj* : practical — **~** *nf* : practice
pré [pre] *nm* : meadow
préalable [prealabl] *adj* **1** : preliminary **2 sans avis ~** : without prior notice — **~** *nm* **1** : prerequisite **2 au ~** : beforehand
préambule [preɑ̃byl] *nm* **1** : preamble **2 sans ~** : without warning
préau [preo] *nm, pl* **préaux** [preo] : (covered) playground, courtyard

préavis [preavi] *nm* : (prior) notice

précaire [prekɛr] *adj* : precarious

précaution [prekosjɔ̃] *nf* **1** : precaution **2** PRUDENCE : caution, care

précéder [presede] {87} *vt* : precede — **précédemment** [presedamɑ̃] *adv* : previously — **précédent, -dente** [presedɑ̃, -dɑ̃t] *adj* : previous, prior — **précédent** *nm* : precedent

prêcher [preʃe] *v* : preach

précieux, -cieuse [presjø, -sjøz] *adj* **1** : precious **2** UTILE : valuable

précipice [presipis] *nm* : abyss, chasm

précipiter [presipite] *vt* **1** : hurl, throw **2** HÂTER : hasten, speed up — **se précipiter** *vr* **1** : hasten, rush **2** ~ **sur** : throw oneself on — **précipitation** [presipitasjɔ̃] *nf* **1** : hurry, haste **2** ~**s** *nfpl* : precipitation (in meteorology) — **précipité, -tée** [presipite] *adj* **1** : rapid **2** HÂTIF : hasty, rash

préciser [presize] *vt* : specify, make clear — **se préciser** *vr* : become clearer — **précis, -cise** [presi, -siz] *adj* **1** : precise, accurate **2** : clear, specific — **précis** *nms & pl* **1** : summary **2** MANUEL : handbook — **précisément** [presizemɑ̃] *adv* : precisely, exactly — **précision** [presizjɔ̃] *nf* **1** : precision **2** : clarity

précoce [prekɔs] *adj* **1** : early **2** : precocious (of a child, etc.)

préconçu, -cue [prekɔ̃sy] *adj* : preconceived

préconiser [prekɔnize] *vt* : recommend, advocate

précurseur [prekyrsœr] *nm* : forerunner

prédateur [predatœr] *nm* : predator

prédécesseur [predesɛsœr] *nm* : predecessor

prédilection [predilɛksjɔ̃] *nf* **1** : partiality **2 de** ~ : favorite

prédire [predir] {29} *vt* : predict — **prédiction** [prediksjɔ̃] *nf* : prediction

prédisposer [predispoze] *vt* : predispose

prédominant, -nante [predɔminɑ̃, -nɑ̃t] *adj* : predominant

préfabriqué, -quée [prefabrike] *adj* : prefabricated

préface [prefas] *nf* : preface

préfecture [prefɛktyr] *nf* ~ **de police** *France* : police headquarters

préférer [prefere] {87} *vt* : prefer — **préférable** [preferabl] *adj* : preferable — **préféré, -rée** [prefere] *adj & n* : favorite — **préférence** [preferɑ̃s] *nf* : preference

préfet [prefɛ] *nm* ~ **de police** *France* : police commissioner

préfixe [prefiks] *nm* : prefix

préhistorique [preistɔrik] *adj* : prehistoric

préjudice [preʒydis] *nm* **1** : harm, damage **2 porter** ~ **à** : cause harm to — **préjudiciable** [preʒydisjabl] *adj* : harmful, detrimental

préjugé [preʒyʒe] *nm* : prejudice

prélasser [prelase] *v* **se prélasser** *vr* : lounge (around)

prélever [prelәve] {52} *vt* **1** : withdraw, deduct **2** : take (a sample of) — **prélèvement** [prelɛvmɑ̃] *nm* **1** : withdrawal, deduction **2** : (blood) sample

préliminaire [preliminɛr] *adj* : preliminary

prélude [prelyd] *nm* : prelude

prématuré, -rée [prematyre] *adj* : premature

prémédité [premedite] *adj* : premeditated

premier, -mière [prәmje, -mjɛr] *adj* **1** : first **2** : top, leading **3 premier ministre** : prime minister — ~ *n* : first (one) — **premier** *nm* : first (in dates) — **première** *nf* **1** : first class **2** : premiere (of a show) — **premièrement** [prәmjɛrmɑ̃] *adv* : in the first place, firstly

prémunir [premynir] *v* **se prémunir** *vr* ~ **contre** : protect oneself against

prendre [prɑ̃dr] {70} *vt* **1** : take **2** ACHETER : get, pick up **3** : take on (responsibility) **4** ATTRAPER : catch, capture **5** : put on, gain (weight) **6** : have (a meal) — *vi* **1** : set, thicken **2** : break out (of fire) **3** ~ **à droite** : bear right **4** ~ **sur soi** : take upon oneself — **se prendre** *vr* **1** : be taken **2** : get caught **3** ~ **les doigts dans** : catch one's fingers in **4** ~ **pour** : consider oneself **5 s'en** ~ **à** : attack — **preneur, -neuse** [prәnœr, -nøz] *n* : buyer, taker

prénom [prenɔ̃] *nm* : given name, first name

préoccuper [preɔkype] *vt* : worry, preoccupy — **préoccupation** [preɔkypasjɔ̃] *nf* : worry, concern

préparer [prepare] *vt* **1** : prepare, make ready **2** ~ **qqn à** : prepare s.o. for — **se préparer** *vr* : prepare oneself, get ready — **préparatifs** [preparatif] *nmpl* : preparations — **préparation** [preparasjɔ̃] *nf* : preparation

prépondérant, -rante [prepɔ̃derɑ̃, -rɑ̃t] *adj* : predominant

préposer [prepoze] *vt* **~ à** : put in charge of — **préposé, -sée** [prepoze] *n* **1** : employee, clerk **2** *France* : mailman
préposition [prepɔzisjɔ̃] *nf* : preposition
prérogative [prerɔgativ] *nf* : prerogative
près [prɛ] *adv* **1** : close, near(by) **2** : near, soon **3 à . . . ~** : more or less, within about **4 à peu ~** : almost, just about **5 de ~** : closely **6 ~ de** : near
présage [prezaʒ] *nm* : omen — **présager** [prezaʒe] {17} *vt* **1** : foresee **2** : portend, bode
presbyte [prɛsbit] *adj* : farsighted
presbytère [prɛsbitɛr] *nm* : rectory
prescrire [prɛskrir] {33} *vt* : prescribe — **prescription** [prɛskripsjɔ̃] *nf* : prescription
préséance [preseɑ̃s] *nf* : precedence
présent, -sente [prezɑ̃, -zɑ̃t] *adj* : present — **~** *nm* : present (time) — **présence** [prezɑ̃s] *nf* **1** : presence **2 en ~** : face to face **3 ~ d'esprit** : presence of mind — **présentement** [prezɑ̃tmɑ̃] *adv* : at the moment, now
présenter [prezɑ̃te] *vt* **1** MONTRER : present, show **2** : introduce (to) **3** : pay, offer (one's condolences) **4** : submit (a proposal, etc.) — **se présenter** *vr* **1** : go, come, appear **2** : introduce oneself **3 ~ à** : run for (an office) — **présentateur, -trice** [prezɑ̃tatœr, -tris] *n* : newscaster, anchor — **présentation** [prezɑ̃tasjɔ̃] *nf* **1** : presentation **2** : introduction — **présentoir** [prezɑ̃twar] *nm* : display shelf
préserver [prezɛrve] *vt* **1** : protect **2** CONSERVER : preserve — **préservatif** [prezɛrvatif] *nm* : condom — **préservation** [prezɛrvasjɔ̃] *nf* : protection, preservation
présider [prezide] *vt* : preside over, chair — *vi* **~ à** : rule over, govern — **président, -dente** [prezidɑ̃, -dɑ̃t] *n* **1** : president **2** : chairperson — **présidence** [prezidɑ̃s] *nf* **1** : presidency **2** : chairmanship — **présidentiel, -tielle** [prezidɑ̃sjɛl] *adj* : presidential
présomption [prezɔ̃psjɔ̃] *nf* : presumption — **présomptueux, -tueuse** [prezɔ̃ptɥø, -tɥøz] *adj* : presumptuous
presque [prɛsk] *adv* : almost, nearly
presqu'île [prɛskil] *nf* : peninsula
pressant, -sante [prɛsɑ̃, -sɑ̃t] *adj* : urgent, pressing
presse [prɛs] *nf* : press
pressé, -sée [prese] *adj* **1** : hurried **2** : urgent **3** : freshly squeezed
pressentir [presɑ̃tir] {82} *vt* : sense, have a premonition about — **pressentiment** [presɑ̃timɑ̃] *nm* : premonition
presse–papiers [prɛspapje] *nms & pl* : paperweight
presser [prese] *vt* **1** : press, squeeze **2** INCITER : urge **3** HÂTER : hurry, rush — *vi* : be pressing, be urgent — **se presser** *vr* **1** SE HÂTER : hurry up **2 ~ contre** *or* **~ sur** : snuggle up against — **pression** [prɛsjɔ̃] *nf* : pressure
prestance [prɛstɑ̃s] *nf* : (imposing) presence
prestation [prɛstasjɔ̃] *nf* : benefit, allowance — **prestataire** [prɛstatɛr] *nm* : recipient
prestidigitateur, -trice [prɛstidiʒitatœr, -tris] *n* : magician, conjurer
prestige [prɛstiʒ] *nm* : prestige — **prestigieux, -gieuse** [prɛstiʒjø, -ʒjøz] *adj* : prestigious
présumer [prezyme] *vt* : presume, suppose — *vi* **~ de** : overestimate, overrate
prêt[1], **prête** [prɛ, prɛt] *adj* **1** : ready, prepared **2** DISPOSÉ : willing
prêt[2] *nm* : loan
prêt–à–porter [prɛtapɔrte] *nm, pl* **prêts–à–porter** : ready-to-wear (clothing)
prétendre [pretɑ̃dr] {63} *vt* **1** : claim, maintain **2** VOULOIR : intend — **prétendant, -dante** [pretɑ̃dɑ̃, -dɑ̃t] *n* : pretender (to a throne) — **prétendant** *nm* : suitor — **prétendu, -due** [pretɑ̃dy] *adj* : so-called, alleged
prétention [pretɑ̃sjɔ̃] *nf* : pretentiousness — **prétentieux, -tieuse** [pretɑ̃sjø, -sjøz] *adj* : pretentious
prêter [prete] *vt* **1** : lend **2 ~ à** : attribute to **3 ~ attention** : pay attention **4 ~ l'oreille** : listen — *vi* **~ à** : give rise to, cause — **se prêter** *vr* **~ à** : lend itself to, suit — **prêteur, -teuse** [prɛtœr, -tøz] *n* **prêteur sur gages** : pawnbroker
prétexte [pretɛkst] *nm* : pretext, excuse — **prétexter** [pretɛkste] *vt* : use as an excuse
prêtre [prɛtr] *nm* : priest
preuve [prœv] *nf* **1** : proof, evidence **2 faire ~ de** : show
prévaloir [prevalwar] {71} *vi* : prevail — **se prévaloir** *vr* **1 ~ de** : take advantage of **2 ~ de** : boast of
prévenant, -nante [prevnɑ̃, -nɑ̃t] *adj* : considerate, thoughtful

prévenir [prevnir] {92} *vt* **1** ÉVITER : prevent **2** AVISER : tell, inform **3** AVERTIR : warn **4** ANTICIPER : anticipate — **prévention** [prevɑ̃sjɔ̃] *nf* : prevention — **prévenu, -nue** [prevny] *n* : defendant, accused

prévoir [prevwar] {99} *vt* **1** : predict, anticipate **2** : plan (on), schedule **3** : provide for, allow (for) — **prévisible** [previzibl] *adj* : foreseeable — **prévision** [previzjɔ̃] *nf* **1** : prediction **2** **~s** *nfpl* : forecast — **prévoyant, -voyante** [prevwajɑ̃, -vwajɑ̃t] *adj* : provident, farsighted — **prévoyance** [prevwajɑ̃s] *nf* : foresight

prier [prije] {96} *vi* : pray — *vt* **1** **~ de** : ask to, request to **2** **je vous en prie** : please **3** **je vous en prie** : don't mention it, you're welcome — **prière** [prijɛr] *nf* : prayer

primaire [primɛr] *adj* : primary, elementary

prime[1] [prim] *adj* **1** : early, first **2** **de ~ abord** : at first

prime[2] *nf* **1** : premium, allowance **2** RÉCOMPENSE : bonus, gift

primer [prime] *vt* : prevail over — *vi* : be of primary importance

primeurs [primœr] *nfpl* : early produce

primevère [primvɛr] *nf* : primrose

primitif, -tive [primitif, -tiv] *adj* : primitive

primordial, -diale [primɔrdjal] *adj, mpl* **-diaux** [-djo] : essential, vital

prince [prɛ̃s] *nm* : prince — **princesse** [prɛ̃sɛs] *nf* : princess

principal, -pale [prɛ̃sipal] *adj, mpl* **-paux** [-po] : main, principal — **principal** *nm* ESSENTIEL : main thing — **principalement** [prɛ̃sipalmɑ̃] *adv* : primarily, mainly

principe [prɛ̃sip] *nm* : principle, rule

printemps [prɛ̃tɑ̃] *nm* : spring

priorité [prijɔrite] *nf* **1** : priority **2** : right-of-way **3** **en ~** : first

pris[1] [pri] *pp* → **prendre**

pris[2], **prise** [pri, priz] *adj* **1** : taken, sold **2** OCCUPÉ : busy **3** **~ de** : afflicted with

prise [priz] *nf* **1** : capture, catch **2** : hold, grip **3** *Can* : strike (in baseball) **4** **~ de courant** : (electrical) outlet **5** **~ de sang** : blood test

priser [prize] *vt* : prize, value

prison [prizɔ̃] *nf* : prison — **prisonnier, -nière** [prizɔnje, -njɛr] *adj* : captive — **~** *n* : prisoner

priver [prive] *vt* : deprive — **se priver** *vr* **~ de** : go without — **privé, -vée** [prive] *adj* : private — **privé** *nm* **1** : private sector **2** **en ~** : in private

privilégier [privileʒje] {96} *vt* : privilege, favor — **privilège** [privilɛʒ] *nm* : privilege

prix [pri] *nms & pl* **1** : price, cost **2** : prize **3** **à tout ~** : at all costs

probable [prɔbabl] *adj* : probable, likely — **probabilité** [prɔbabilite] *nf* : probability — **probablement** [prɔbabləmɑ̃] *adv* : probably

problème [prɔblɛm] *nm* : problem

procéder [prɔsede] {87} *vi* **1** : proceed **2** **~ à** : carry out — **procédé** [prɔsede] *nm* : process, procedure — **procédure** [prɔsedyr] *nf* **1** : procedure **2** : proceedings *pl* (in law)

procès [prɔsɛ] *nm* **1** : lawsuit **2** : (criminal) trial

procession [prɔsesjɔ̃] *nf* : procession

processus [prɔsesys] *nms & pl* : process, system

procès-verbal [prɔsɛvɛrbal] *nm, pl* **procès-verbaux** [-vɛrbo] **1** : minutes *pl* (of a meeting) **2** *France* : (parking) ticket

prochain, -chaine [prɔʃɛ̃, -ʃɛn] *adj* **1** SUIVANT : next, following **2** PROCHE : imminent, forthcoming **3** **à la prochaine!** *fam* : see you!, until next time! — **prochain** *nm* : fellowman — **prochainement** [prɔʃɛnmɑ̃] *adv* : soon, shortly

proche [prɔʃ] *adj* **1** : near(by) **2** : imminent, near **3** **~ de** : close to — **proches** [prɔʃ] *nmpl* : close relatives

proclamer [prɔklame] *vt* : proclaim, declare — **proclamation** [prɔklamasjɔ̃] *nf* : proclamation, declaration

procuration [prɔkyrasjɔ̃] *nf* : proxy (in an election)

procurer [prɔkyre] *vt* : provide, give — **se procurer** *vr* : get, obtain — **procureur** [prɔkyrœr] *nm or* **~ général** : prosecutor

prodige [prɔdiʒ] *nm* : prodigy — **prodigieux, -gieuse** [prɔdiʒjø, -ʒjøz] *adj* : prodigious, extraordinary

prodigue [prɔdig] *adj* **1** : extravagant **2** GÉNÉREUX : lavish — **prodiguer** [prɔdige] *vt* : lavish

produire [prɔdɥir] {49} *vt* **1** : produce **2** CAUSER : bring about — **se produire** *vr* **1** : occur, happen **2** : perform (on stage) — **producteur** [prɔdyktœr] *nm* : producer — **production** [prɔdyksjɔ̃] *nf* : production — **produit** [prɔdɥi] *nm* : product

profaner [prɔfane] *vt* : defile, desecrate

— **profane** [prɔfan] *adj* : secular — ~ *nmf* : layperson
proférer [prɔfere] {87} *vt* : utter
professer [prɔfese] *vt* : profess
professeur [prɔfesœr] *nm* **1** : (school)-teacher **2** : professor
profession [prɔfesjɔ̃] *nf* : occupation, trade — **professionnel, -nelle** [prɔfɛsjɔnɛl] *adj & n* : professional
profil [prɔfil] *nm* : profile
profit [prɔfi] *nm* **1** : profit **2** AVANTAGE : benefit — **profiter** [prɔfite] *vi* **1** ~ **à** : be of benefit to **2** ~ **de** : take advantage of
profond, -fonde [prɔfɔ̃, -fɔ̃d] *adj* **1** : deep **2** : profound — **profondément** [prɔfɔ̃demɑ̃] *adv* : profoundly, deeply — **profondeur** [prɔfɔ̃dœr] *nf* : depth
profusion [prɔfyzjɔ̃] *nf* : profusion
progéniture [prɔʒenityr] *nf* : offspring
programme [prɔgram] *nm* **1** : program **2** : plan, schedule **3** : curriculum, syllabus (in academics) — **programmer** [prɔgrame] *vt* **1** : program (a computer) **2** : plan, schedule — **programmeur, -meuse** [prɔgramœr, -møz] *n* : (computer) programmer
progrès [prɔgrɛ] *nm* : progress — **progresser** [prɔgrese] *vi* : make progress — **progressif, -sive** [prɔgresif, -siv] *adj* : progressive — **progressivement** [-sivmɑ̃] *adv* : progressively, gradually
prohiber [prɔibe] *vt* : prohibit — **prohibition** [prɔibisjɔ] *nf* : prohibition
proie [prwa] *nf* : prey
projecteur [prɔʒɛktœr] *nm* **1** : projector **2** : spotlight — **projectile** [prɔʒɛktil] *nm* : missile, projectile — **projection** [prɔʒɛksjɔ̃] *nf* : projection, showing
projeter [prɔʃte] {8} *vt* **1** LANCER : throw **2** : project, show (a film, etc.) **3** : cast, project (light) **4** PRÉVOIR : plan — **projet** [prɔʒɛ] *nm* **1** : plan, project **2** ÉBAUCHE : draft, outline
proliférer [prɔlifere] {87} *vi* : proliferate — **prolifération** [-ferasjɔ̃] *nf* : proliferation — **prolifique** [prɔlifik] *adj* : prolific
prologue [prɔlɔg] *nm* : prologue
prolonger [prɔlɔ̃ʒe] {17} *vt* : prolong, extend — **se prolonger** *vr* : continue — **prolongation** [prɔlɔ̃gasjɔ̃] *nf* : extension (of time) — **prolongement** [prɔlɔ̃ʒmɑ̃] *nm* : extension (of a road, etc.)
promener [prɔmne] {52} *vt* : take for a walk — **se promener** *vr* : go for a walk — **promenade** [prɔmnad] *nf* **1** : walk, stroll **2** : trip, ride (in a car, etc.) **3** : walkway, promenade — **promeneur, -neuse** [prɔmnœr, -nøz] *n* : walker
promettre [prɔmɛtr] {53} *v* : promise — **se promettre** *vr* ~ **de** : resolve to — **promesse** [prɔmɛs] *nf* : promise — **prometteur, -teuse** [prɔmɛtœr, -tøz] *adj* : promising
promontoire [prɔmɔ̃twar] *nm* : headland
promouvoir [prɔmuvwar] {56} *vt* : promote — **promotion** [prɔmɔsjɔ̃] *nf* : promotion
prompt, prompte [prɔ̃, prɔ̃t] *adj* : prompt, quick
prôner [prone] *vt* : advocate
pronom [prɔnɔ̃] *nm* : pronoun
prononcer [prɔnɔ̃se] {6} *vt* : pronounce — *vi* : hand down a decision (in law) — **se prononcer** *vr* : give one's opinion — **prononciation** [prɔnɔ̃sjasjɔ̃] *nf* : pronunciation
pronostic [prɔnɔstik] *nm* **1** : prognosis **2** PRÉVISION : forecast
propagande [prɔpagɑ̃d] *nf* : propaganda
propager [prɔpaʒe] {17} *vt* : propagate, spread — **se propager** *vr* : spread — **propagation** [prɔpagasjɔ̃] *nf* : propagation
prophète [prɔfɛt] *nm* : prophet — **prophétie** [prɔfesi] *nf* : prophecy — **prophétique** [prɔfetik] *adj* : prophetic — **prophétiser** [prɔfetize] *vt* : prophesy
propice [prɔpis] *adj* : favorable
proportion [prɔpɔrsjɔ̃] *nf* **1** : proportion, ratio **2** ~**s** *nfpl* : dimensions, size — **proportionnel, -nelle** [prɔpɔrsjɔnɛl] *adj* : proportional
proposer [prɔpoze] *vt* **1** : suggest, propose **2** OFFRIR : offer **3** : nominate (for election) — **se proposer** *vr* ~ **de** : intend to — **propos** [prɔpo] *nms & pl* **1** : subject **2** BUT : intention, point **3** ~ *nmpl* : comments, talk **4 à** ~ : appropriate **5 à** ~ **de** : regarding, about — **proposition** [prɔpozisjɔ̃] *nf* **1** : suggestion **2** OFFRE : offer, proposal
propre [prɔpr] *adj* **1** : clean, neat **2** : proper, correct (of a word) **3** ~ **à** : characteristic of **4** ~ **à** : suitable for **5 par sa** ~ **faute** : through his own fault — **proprement** [prɔprəmɑ̃] *adv* **à** ~ **parler** : strictly speaking — **propreté** [prɔprəte] *nf* : cleanliness, neatness

propriété [prɔprijete] *nf* **1** : property **2** : ownership — **propriétaire** [prɔprijetɛr] *nmf* **1** : owner **2** : landlord, landlady *f*
propulser [prɔpylse] *vt* : propel
prorata [prɔrata] *nms & pl* **au ~ de** : in proportion to
proscrire [prɔskrir] {33} *vt* **1** INTERDIRE : ban, prohibit **2** BANNIR : banish — **proscrit, -scrite** [prɔskri, -skrit] *n* : outcast
prose [proz] *nf* : prose
prospectus [prɔspɛktys] *nms & pl* : leaflet
prospérer [prɔspere] {87} *vi* : flourish, thrive — **prospérité** [prɔsperite] *nf* : prosperity
prosterner [prɔstɛrne] *v* **se prosterner** *vr* : bow down
prostituée [prɔstitɥe] *nf* : prostitute — **prostitution** [prɔstitysjɔ̃] *nf* : prostitution
prostré, -trée [prɔstre] *adj* : prostrate
protagoniste [prɔtagɔnist] *nmf* : protagonist
protéger [prɔteʒe] {64} *vt* **1** : protect **2** PATRONNER : support — **se protéger** *vr* **~ de** : protect oneself from — **protecteur, -trice** [prɔtɛktœr, -tris] *adj* : protective — **~** *n* **1** : protector **2** : patron — **protection** [prɔtɛksjɔ̃] *nf* : protection
protéine [prɔtein] *nf* : protein
protestant, -tante [prɔtɛstɑ̃, -tɑ̃t] *adj & n* : Protestant
protester [prɔtɛste] *vi* : protest — **protestation** [prɔtɛstasjɔ̃] *nf* : protest
prothèse [prɔtɛz] *nf* **1** : prosthesis **2** **~ dentaire** : denture
protocole [prɔtɔkɔl] *nm* : protocol
protubérant, -rante [prɔtyberɑ̃, -rɑ̃t] *adj* : protruding — **protubérance** [prɔtyberɑ̃s] *nf* : protuberance
proue [pru] *nf* : prow, bow (of a ship)
prouesse [pruɛs] *nf* : feat
prouver [pruve] *vt* **1** ÉTABLIR : prove **2** MONTRER : show, demonstrate
provenance [prɔvnɑ̃s] *nf* **1** : source, origin **2 en ~ de** : from
provenir [prɔvnir] {92} *vi* **~ de 1** : come from **2** : result from
proverbe [prɔvɛrb] *nm* : proverb
providence [prɔvidɑ̃s] *nf* : providence
province [prɔvɛ̃s] *nf* : province — **provincial, -ciale** [-vɛ̃sjal] *adj, mpl* **-ciaux** [-sjo] : provincial
proviseur [prɔvizœr] *nm France* : principal (of a school)
provision [prɔvizjɔ̃] *nf* **1** : stock, supply **2 ~s** *nfpl* : provisions, food
provisoire [prɔvizwar] *adj* : temporary
provoquer [prɔvɔke] *vt* **1** : give rise to **2** DÉFIER : provoke — **provocant, -cante** [prɔvɔkɑ̃, -kɑ̃t] *adj* : provocative — **provocation** [prɔvɔkasjɔ̃] *nf* : provocation
proximité [prɔksimite] *nf* : closeness, proximity
prude [pryd] *nf* : prude
prudent, -dente [prydɑ̃, -dɑ̃t] *adj* : careful, cautious — **prudemment** [prydamɑ̃] *adv* : carefully, cautiously — **prudence** [prydɑ̃s] *nf* : care, caution
prune [pryn] *nf* : plum — **pruneau** [pryno] *nm, pl* **-neaux** : prune
prunelle [prynɛl] *nf* : pupil (of the eye)
psaume [psom] *nm* : psalm
pseudonyme [psødɔnim] *nm* : pseudonym
psychanalyser [psikanalize] *vt* : psychoanalyze — **psychanalyse** [psikanaliz] *nf* : psychoanalysis — **psychanalyste** [-list] *nmf* : psychoanalyst
psychiatrie [psikjatri] *nf* : psychiatry — **psychiatre** [psikjatr] *nmf* : psychiatrist — **psychiatrique** [psikjatrik] *adj* : psychiatric
psychologie [psikɔlɔʒi] *nf* : psychology — **psychologique** [psikɔlɔʒik] *adj* : psychological — **psychologue** [psikɔlɔg] *nmf* : psychologist
puant, puante [pɥɑ̃, -ɑ̃t] *adj* : foul, stinking — **puanteur** [pɥɑ̃tœr] *nf* : stink, stench
puberté [pybɛrte] *nf* : puberty
public, -blique [pyblik] *adj* : public — **public** *nm* **1** : public **2** : audience, spectators *pl*
publication [pyblikasjɔ̃] *nf* : publication
publicité [pyblisite] *nf* **1** : publicity **2** : (television) commercial — **publicitaire** [pyblisitɛr] *adj* : advertising
publier [pyblije] {96} *vt* : publish
puce [pys] *nf* **1** : flea **2** : computer chip
pudeur [pydœr] *nf* : modesty — **pudique** [pydik] *adj* : modest, decent
puer [pɥe] *vi* : smell, stink — *vt* : reek of
puéril, -rile [pɥeril] *adj* : childish
puis [pɥi] *adv* : then, afterwards
puiser [pɥize] *vt* **~ dans** : draw from, dip into
puisque [pɥiskə] *conj* : since, as, because
puissant, -sante [pɥisɑ̃, -sɑ̃t] *adj*

: powerful — **puissance** [pɥisɑ̃s] *nf* : power
puits [pɥi] *nm* **1** : well **2** : (mine) shaft
pull *or* **pull–over** [pyl, pylɔvɛr] *nm France* : pullover sweater
pulpe [pylp] *nf* : pulp
pulsation [pylsasjɔ̃] *nf* BATTEMENT : beat
pulsion [pylsjɔ̃] *nf* : drive, urge
pulvériser [pylverize] *vt* **1** : pulverize **2** VAPORISER : spray
punaise [pynɛz] *nf* **1** : (bed)bug **2** : thumbtack
punch [pɔ̃ʃ] *nm* : punch (drink)
punir [pynir] *vt* : punish — **punition** [pynisjɔ̃] *nf* : punishment
pupille[1] [pypij] *nmf* : ward (of the court)
pupille[2] *nf* : pupil (of the eye)
pupitre [pypitr] *nm* **1** : music stand **2** BUREAU : desk
pur, pure [pyr] *adj* : pure — **pureté** [pyrte] *nf* : purity
purée [pyre] *nf* **1** : puree **2 ~ de pommes de terre** : mashed potatoes
purgatoire [pyrgatwar] *nm* : purgatory
purger [pyrʒe] {17} *vt* **1** : drain (a radiator, etc.) **2** : rid of, purge **3** : serve (a sentence) — **purge** [pyrʒ] *nf* : purge
purifier [pyrifje] {96} *vt* : purify — **purification** [pyrifikasjɔ̃] *nf* : purification
puritain, -taine [pyritɛ̃, -tɛn] *n* : puritan — **~** *adj* : puritanical
pur–sang [pyrsɑ̃] *nms & pl* : Thoroughbred
pus [py] *nm* : pus
putride [pytrid] *adj* : rotten
puzzle [pœzl] *nm* : (jigsaw) puzzle
pyjama [piʒama] *nm* : pajamas *pl*
pylône [pilon] *nm* : pylon
pyramide [piramid] *nf* : pyramid
pyromane [pirɔman] *nmf* : arsonist
python [pitɔ̃] *nm* : python

Q

q [ky] *nm* : q, 17th letter of the alphabet
quadriller [kadrije] *vt* : surround, take control of — **quadrillage** [kadrijaʒ] *nm* : crisscross pattern, grid — **quadrillé, -lée** [kadrije] *adj* : squared
quadrupède [k(w)adrypɛd] *nm* : quadruped
quadruple [k(w)adrypl] *adj* : quadruple
quai [kɛ] *nm* **1** : quay, wharf **2** : platform (at a railway station)
qualifier [kalifje] {96} *vt* **1** : qualify **2** DÉCRIRE : describe — **qualification** [kalifikasjɔ̃] *nf* : qualification
qualité [kalite] *nf* **1** : quality, excellence **2** : quality, property **3 en ~ de** : in one's role as
quand [kɑ̃] *adv & conj* **1** : when **2 ~ même** : all the same, even so
quant [kɑ̃] **~ à** *prep phr* : as for, as to, regarding
quantité [kɑ̃tite] *nf* : quantity
quarantaine [karɑ̃tɛn] *nf* **1** : quarantine **2 une ~ de** : about forty
quarante [karɑ̃t] *adj & nms & pl* : forty — **quarantième** [karɑ̃tjɛm] *adj & nmf & nm* : fortieth
quart [kar] *nm* **1** : quarter, fourth **2 un ~ d'heure** : fifteen minutes
quartier [kartje] *nm* **1** : piece, segment, quarter **2** : area, district **3 ~ général** : (military) headquarters
quartz [kwarts] *nm* : quartz
quasi [kazi] *adv* : nearly, almost
quatorze [katɔrz] *adj* **1** : fourteen **2** : fourteenth (in dates) — **~** *nms & pl* : fourteen — **quatorzième** [katɔrzjɛm] *adj & nmf & nm* : fourteenth
quatre [katr] *adj* **1** : four **2** : fourth (in dates) — **~** *nms & pl* : four
quatre–vingt–dix [katrəvɛ̃dis] *adj & nms & pl* : ninety
quatre–vingts [katrəvɛ̃] (**quatre-vingt** *with another numeral adjective*) *adj & nms & pl* : eighty
quatrième [katrijɛm] *adj & nmf* : fourth
quatuor [kwatɥɔr] *nm* : quartet
que [kə] *conj* **1** : that **2 plus ~ nécessaire** : more than necessary **3 qu'il fasse soleil ou non** : whether it's sunny or not **4** → **ne** — **~** *pron* **1** : who, whom, that **2** : which **3 ~ faire?** : what should we do? — **~** *adv* : how (much), how (many)
québécois, -coise [kebekwa, -kwaz] *adj* : Quebecer, Quebecois
quel, quelle [kɛl] *adj* **1** : what, which **2** : whatever, whichever, whoever — **~** *pron* : who, which one
quelconque [kɛlkɔ̃k] *adj* **1** : some sort of, any **2 un être ~** : an ordinary person
quelque [kɛlk(ə)] *adj* **1** : a few, several, some **2 ~ chose** : something **3 ~**

part : somewhere **4 ~ peu** : somewhat — **~** *adv* : about, approximately
quelquefois [kɛlkəfwa] *adv* : sometimes
quelques-uns, quelques-unes [kɛlkəzœ̃, kɛlkəzyn] *pron* : some, a few
quelqu'un [kɛlkœ̃] *pron* **1** : someone, somebody **2** : anyone, anybody **3 y a-t-il quelqu'un?** : is anybody there?
quémander [kemɑ̃de] *vt* : beg for
qu'en-dira-t-on [kɑ̃diratɔ̃] *nms & pl* : gossip
querelle [kərɛl] *nf* : quarrel — **quereller** [kərele] *v* **se quereller** *vr* : quarrel — **querelleur, -leuse** [kərɛlœr, -løz] *adj* : quarrelsome
question [kɛstjɔ̃] *nf* **1** : question **2** : matter, issue — **questionnaire** [kɛstjɔnɛr] *nm* : questionnaire — **questionner** [kɛstjɔne] *vt* : question
quête [kɛt] *nf* **1** : quest, search **2** : collection (of money) — **quêter** [kete] *vt* : look for, seek — *vi* : take a collection
queue [kø] *nf* **1** : tail **2** : tail end, rear, bottom **3** : handle (of a pot) **4 ~ de billard** : cue (stick) **5 ~ de cheval** : ponytail **6 faire la ~** : stand in line
qui [ki] *pron* **1** : who, whom **2** : which, that **3 ~ que** : whoever, whomever
quiconque [kikɔ̃k] *pron* **1** : whoever, whomever **2** : anyone, anybody
quiétude [kjetyd] *nf* : quiet, tranquility
quille [kij] *nf* **1** : keel **2 ~s** *nfpl* : ninepins
quincaillerie [kɛ̃kajri] *nf* **1** : hardware **2** : hardware store
quinte [kɛ̃t] *nf or* **~ de toux** : coughing fit
quintuple [kɛ̃typl] *adj* : fivefold
quinzaine [kɛ̃zɛn] *nf* **1 une ~ de** : about fifteen **2 une ~ de jours** : two weeks
quinze [kɛ̃z] *adj* **1** : fifteen **2** : fifteenth (in dates) — **~** *nms & pl* : fifteen — **quinzième** [kɛ̃zjɛm] *adj & nmf & nm* : fifteenth
quiproquo [kiprɔko] *nm* : misunderstanding
quittance [kitɑ̃s] *nf* : receipt
quitte [kit] *adj* **1** : even, quits **2 ~ à** : even if, at the risk of
quitter [kite] *vt* **1** : leave, depart from **2** : take off (a hat, etc.) **3 ne quittez pas** : hold the (telephone) line — **se quitter** *vr* : part, separate
qui-vive [kiviv] *nms & pl* **être sur le ~** : be on the alert
quoi [kwa] *pron* **1** : what **2** (*after a pronoun*) : which **3 ~ que** : whatever
quoique [kwakə] *conj* : although, though
quota [kɔta] *nm* : quota
quotidien, -dienne [kɔtidjɛ̃, -djɛn] *adj* **1** : daily **2** : everyday, routine — **quotidien** *nm* **1** : daily (newspaper) **2 au ~** : on a daily basis — **quotidiennement** [kɔtidjɛnmɑ̃] *adv* : daily
quotient [kɔsjɑ̃] *nm* : quotient

R

r [ɛr] *nm* : r, 18th letter of the alphabet
rabâcher [rabaʃe] *vt* : repeat over and over
rabaisser [rabɛse] *vt* **1** : reduce **2** DÉPRÉCIER : belittle, degrade — **rabais** [rabɛ] *nms & pl* RÉDUCTION : reduction, discount
rabat [raba] *nm* : flap
rabat-joie [rabaʒwa] *nms & pl* : killjoy, spoilsport
rabattre [rabatr] {12} *vt* **1** : reduce, diminish **2** : bring down, pull down — **se rabattre** *vr* **1** : fold up, shut **2 ~ sur** : make do with
rabbin [rabɛ̃] *nm* : rabbi
rabot [rabo] *nm* : plane (tool) — **raboter** [rabɔte] *vt* : plane
raboteux, -teuse [rabɔtø, -tøz] *adj* INÉGAL : rough, uneven
rabougri, -grie [rabugri] *adj* **1** : stunted **2** : shriveled (up)
rabrouer [rabrue] *vt* : snub
raccommoder [rakɔmɔde] *vt* : mend, patch up
raccompagner [rakɔ̃paɲe] *vt* : take (someone) back, see home
raccorder [rakɔrde] *vt* : connect, link up — **raccord** [rakɔr] *nm* : link, connection — **raccordement** [rakɔrdəmɑ̃] *nm* : linking, connection
raccourcir [rakursir] *vt* : shorten — *vi* : become shorter, shrink — **raccourci** [rakursi] *nm* **1** : shortcut **2 en ~** : in short, briefly
raccrocher [rakrɔʃe] *vt* **~ le récepteur** : hang up (a telephone receiver) — *vi* : hang up (on s.o.) — **se raccrocher** *vr* **~ à** : hang on to

race [ras] *nf* **1** : (human) race **2** : breed (of animals) **3 de ~** : thoroughbred
racheter [raʃte] {20} *vt* **1** : buy back **2** : buy more of **3** : redeem (in religion) **4** COMPENSER : make up for — **rachat** [raʃa] *nm* : buying back
racial, -ciale [rasjal] *adj, mpl* **-ciaux** [rasjo] : racial
racine [rasin] *nf* : root
racisme [rasism] *nm* : racism — **raciste** [rasist] *adj & nmf* : racist
racler [rakle] *vt* : scrape (off) — **raclée** [rakle] *nf fam* : beating, thrashing
racoler [rakɔle] *vt* : solicit
raconter [rakɔ̃te] *vt* **1** CONTER : tell, relate **2** : say, talk about — **racontars** [rakɔ̃tar] *nmpl* : gossip — **raconteur, -teuse** [rakɔ̃tœr, -tøz] *n* : storyteller
radar [radar] *nm* : radar
rade [rad] *nf* **en ~** : stranded
radeau [rado] *nm, pl* **-deaux** : raft
radiateur [radjatœr] *nm* **1** : radiator **2** : heater
radical, -cale [radikal] *adj, mpl* **-caux** [-ko] : radical — **~** *n* : radical
radier [radje] {96} *vt* : cross off
radieux, -dieuse [radjø, -djøz] *adj* : radiant, dazzling
radin, -dine [radɛ̃] *adj fam* : stingy — **~** *n fam* : cheapskate
radio [radjo] *nf* **1** : radio **2** RADIOGRAPHIE : X ray
radioactif, -tive [radjɔaktif, -tiv] *adj* : radioactive
radiodiffuser [radjɔdifyze] *vt* : broadcast — **radiodiffusion** [radjɔdifyzjɔ̃] *nf* : broadcasting
radiographie [radjɔgrafi] *nf* : X ray — **radiographier** [radjɔgrafje] {96} *vt* : X-ray
radis [radi] *nm* : radish
radoter [radɔte] *vi* : ramble on
radoucir [radusir] *vt* : soften (up) — **se radoucir** *vr* : grow milder
rafale [rafal] *nf* **1** : gust (of wind, etc.) **2** : burst (of gunfire)
raffermir [rafɛrmir] *vt* : firm up, tone up
raffiner [rafine] *vt* : refine — **raffinage** [rafinaʒ] *nm* : refining — **raffiné, -née** [rafine] *adj* : refined — **raffinement** [rafinmɑ̃] *nm* : refinement — **raffinerie** [rafinri] *nf* : refinery
raffoler [rafɔle] *vi* **~ de** : adore, be crazy about
rafistoler [rafistɔle] *vt fam* : patch up, fix up
rafler [rafle] *vt fam* : swipe, steal — **rafle** [rafl] *nf* : (police) raid
rafraîchir [rafrɛʃir] *vt* : refresh, cool — **se rafraîchir** *vr* **1** : get cooler **2** : freshen up — **rafraîchissant, -sante** [rafrɛʃisɑ̃, -sɑ̃t] *adj* : refreshing — **rafraîchissement** [rafrɛʃismɑ̃] *nm* **1** : cooling **2 ~s** *nmpl* : cool drinks, refreshments
rage [raʒ] *nf* **1** : rabies **2** FUREUR : rage — **rager** [raʒe] {17} *vi* : rage, fume
ragot [rago] *nm fam* : gossip
ragoût [ragu] *nm* : ragout, stew
raide [rɛd] *adj* **1** : stiff (of muscles) **2** : tight, taut (of a rope) **3** : steep (of a hill) **4** : straight (of hair) — **~** *adv* : steeply — **raideur** [rɛdœr] *nf* **1** : stiffness **2** : steepness — **raidir** [rɛdir] *vt* : stiffen, tighten — **se raidir** *vr* : tighten, tense up
raie [rɛ] *nf* **1** : stripe **2** : part (in hair)
raifort [rɛfɔr] *nm* : horseradish
rail [raj] *nm* : rail, track
railler [raje] *vt* : make fun of — **raillerie** [rajri] *nf* : mockery — **railleur, -leuse** [rajœr, -jøz] *adj* MOQUEUR : mocking
rainure [rɛnyr] *nf* : groove, slot
raisin [rɛzɛ̃] *nm* **1** : grape **2 ~ de Corinthe** : currant **3 ~ sec** : raisin
raison [rɛzɔ̃] *nf* **1** : reason **2 avoir ~** : be right **3 en ~ de** : because of **4 perdre la ~** : lose one's mind — **raisonnable** [rɛzɔnabl] *adj* : sensible, reasonable — **raisonnement** [rɛzɔnmɑ̃] *nm* **1** : reasoning **2** : argument — **raisonner** [rɛzɔne] *vi* : reason — *vt* : reason with
rajeunir [raʒœnir] *vt* : make look younger — *vi* : look younger
rajouter [raʒute] *vt* **1** : add **2 en ~** : exaggerate — **rajout** [raʒu] *nm* : addition
rajuster [raʒyste] *vt* : (re)adjust
râle [ral] *nm* : groan
ralentir [ralɑ̃tir] *v* : slow down — **ralenti, -tie** [ralɑ̃ti] *adj* : slow — **ralenti** *nm* **1** : slow motion **2** : idling speed (of a car) — **ralentissement** [ralɑ̃tismɑ̃] *nm* : slowing down
râler [rale] *vi* **1** : groan **2** *fam* : grumble
rallier [ralje] {96} *vt* : rally (troops) — **se rallier** *vr* : rally
rallonger [ralɔ̃ʒe] {17} *vt* : lengthen — *vi* : get longer — **rallonge** [ralɔ̃ʒ] *nf* : extension (cord)
rallumer [ralyme] *vt* **1** : turn back on **2** RANIMER : revive
ramasser [ramase] *vt* **1** : pick up, collect **2** CUEILLIR : pick, gather — **se ramasser** *vr* : crouch — **ramassage** [ramasaʒ] *nm* : picking up, collection

rambarde [rɑ̃bard] *nf* : guardrail
rame [ram] *nf* **1** AVIRON : oar **2** : (subway) train **3** : ream (of paper)
rameau [ramo] *nm, pl* **-meaux** : branch, bough
ramener [ramne] {52} *vt* **1** : bring back, take back **2** RÉDUIRE : reduce
ramer [rame] *vi* : row
ramification [ramifikasjɔ̃] *nf* : offshoot
ramollir [ramɔlir] *vt* : soften — **se ramollir** *vr* : soften
ramoner [ramɔne] *vt* : sweep (a chimney), clean out (pipes) — **ramoneur** [ramɔnœr] *nm* : chimney sweep
rampe [rɑ̃p] *nf* **1** : (access) ramp **2** : banister, handrail **3** : footlights *pl* **4** **~ de lancement** : launching pad
ramper [rɑ̃pe] *vi* **1** : crawl, creep **2** S'ABAISSER : grovel
rancart [rɑ̃kar] *nm* **mettre au ~** *fam* : discard, scrap
rance [rɑ̃s] *adj* : rancid — **rancir** [rɑ̃sir] *vi* : turn rancid
rancœur [rɑ̃kœr] *nf* RESSENTIMENT : rancor, resentment
rançon [rɑ̃sɔ̃] *nf* : ransom — **rançonner** [rɑ̃sɔne] *vt* : hold to ransom
rancune [rɑ̃kyn] *nf* **1** : rancor, resentment **2** **garder ~ à** : hold a grudge against
randonnée [rɑ̃dɔne] *nf* **1** : ride, trip **2** : walk, hike — **randonneur, -neuse** [rɑ̃dɔnœr, -nøz] *n* : hiker
rang [rɑ̃] *nm* **1** RANGÉE : row **2** : rank (in a hierarchy) — **rangée** [rɑ̃ʒe] *nf* : row, line — **rangement** [rɑ̃ʒmɑ̃] *nm* **1** : tidying up **2** : storage space — **ranger** [rɑ̃ʒe] {17} *vt* **1** : tidy up **2** CLASSER : put in order **3** : put away (objects), park (a vehicle) — **se ranger** *vr* **1** : line up **2** SE GARER : park **3** S'ASSAGIR : settle down **4** **~ à** : go along with
ranimer [ranime] *vt* **1** : revive **2** : rekindle (a fire)
rapace [rapas] *adj* : rapacious — **~** *nm* : bird of prey
rapatrier [rapatrije] {96} *vt* : repatriate, send home
râper [rape] *vt* : grate (cheese, etc.) — **râpe** [rap] *nf* : grater
rapetisser [raptise] *vt* : shorten — *vi* : shrink — **se rapetisser** *vr* : shrink
râpeux, -peuse [rapø, -pøz] *adj* : rough
rapide [rapid] *adj* **1** : quick, rapid **2** : steep — **~** *nm* **1** : rapids *pl* **2** : express train — **rapidement** [rapidmɑ̃] *adv* : rapidly, swiftly — **rapidité** [rapidite] *nf* : rapidity, speed
rapiécer [rapjese] {6} *vt* : patch (up)
rappeler [raple] {8} *vt* **1** : remind **2** : call back — **se rappeler** *vr* : remember, recall — **rappel** [rapɛl] *nm* **1** : reminder **2** : recall
rapporter [rapɔrte] *vt* **1** : bring back, take back **2** : yield (in finance) **3** RELATER : tell, report — *vi* **1** : yield a profit **2** *fam* : tell tales — **se rapporter** *vr* **~ à** : relate to — **rapport** [rapɔr] *nm* **1** : report **2** LIEN : connection **3** RENDEMENT : return, yield **4** PROPORTION : ratio **5** **~s** *nmpl* : relations **6** **~s** *nmpl* : sexual intercourse — **rapporteur, -teuse** [rapɔrtœr, -tøz] *n* : tattletale
rapprocher [raprɔʃe] *vt* **1** : bring closer **2** COMPARER : compare — **se rapprocher** *vr* **1** **~ de** : approach, come closer to **2** **~ de** : resemble — **rapproché, -chée** [raprɔʃe] *adj* : close
raquette [rakɛt] *nf* **1** : (tennis) racket **2** : snowshoe
rare [rar] *adj* **1** : rare, uncommon **2** : infrequent **3** CLAIRSEMÉ : sparse — **rarement** [rarmɑ̃] *adv* : seldom, rarely — **rareté** [rarte] *nf* : rarity, scarcity
ras [ra] *adv* : short — **ras, rase** [ra, raz] *adj* : short (of hair)
raser [raze] {87} *vt* **1** : shave **2** DÉTRUIRE : raze **3** FRÔLER : graze, skim — **se raser** *vr* : shave — **rasage** [razaʒ] *nm* : shaving — **rasoir** [razwar] *nm* : razor
raseur, -seuse [razœr, -zøz] *n fam* : bore
rassasier [rasazje] {96} *vt* : satisfy — **se rassasier** *vr* : eat one's fill
rassembler [rasɑ̃ble] *vt* : gather, collect — **se rassembler** *vr* : gather, assemble — **rassemblement** [rasɑ̃bləmɑ̃] *nm* : gathering, assembly
rasseoir [raswar] {9} *v* **se rasseoir** *vr* : sit down again
rassir [rasir] {72} *vi* : go stale
rassis, -sise [rasi, -siz] *adj* : stale
rassurer [rasyre] *vt* : reassure — **rassurant, -rante** [rasyrɑ̃, -rɑ̃t] *adj* : reassuring
rat [ra] *nm* : rat
ratatiner [ratatine] *v* **se ratatiner** *vr* : shrivel up
rate [rat] *nf* : spleen
râteau [rato] *nm, pl* **-teaux** : rake
rater [rate] *vt* **1** MANQUER : miss **2** : fail (an exam, etc.) — *vi* ÉCHOUER : fail, go wrong
ratifier [ratifje] {96} *vt* : ratify — **ratification** [-tifikasjɔ̃] *nf* : ratification

ration [rasjɔ̃] *nf* : share, ration
rationaliser [rasjɔnalize] *vt* : rationalize — **rationnel, -nelle** [rasjɔnɛl] *adj* : rational
rationner [rasjɔne] *vt* : ration
ratisser [ratise] *vt* : rake
raton [ratɔ̃] *nm* **~ laveur** : raccoon
rattacher [rataʃe] *vt* **1** : tie up again **2** RELIER : link, connect
rattraper [ratrape] *vt* **1** : recapture **2** : catch up with (s.o.) **3 ~ le temps perdu** : make up for lost time
raturer [ratyre] *vt* BIFFER : delete — **rature** [ratyr] *nf* : deletion
rauque [rok] *adj* ENROUÉ : hoarse
ravager [ravaʒe] {17} *vt* : ravage, devastate — **ravages** [ravaʒ] *nmpl* **faire des ~** : wreak havoc
ravaler [ravale] *vt* **1** : restore (a building) **2** : stifle (one's anger)
ravi, -vie [ravi] *adj* ENCHANTÉ : delighted
ravin [ravɛ̃] *nm* : ravine
ravir [ravir] *vt* : delight
raviser [ravise] *v* **se raviser** *vr* : change one's mind
ravisseur, -seuse [ravisœr, -søz] *n* : kidnapper
ravitailler [ravitaje] *vt* **1** : supply (with food) **2** : refuel
raviver [ravive] *vt* : revive
ravoir [ravwar] {73} *vt* : get back
rayer [rɛje] {11} *vt* **1** ÉRAFLER : scratch **2** BARRER : cross out, erase — **rayé, rayée** [rɛje] *adj* : striped
rayon [rɛjɔ̃] *nm* **1** : ray **2** : radius (of a circle) **3** : range, scope **4** ÉTAGÈRE : shelf **5** : department (in a store) **6 ~ de miel** : honeycomb
rayonnant, -nante [rɛjɔnɑ̃, -nɑ̃t] *adj* : radiant
rayonne [rɛjɔn] *nf* : rayon
rayonner [rɛjɔne] *vi* **1** : radiate **2** BRILLER : shine **3** : tour around **4 ~ sur** : exert influence on — **rayonnement** [rɛjɔnmɑ̃] *nm* : radiation
rayure [rɛjyr] *nf* **1** : stripe **2** ÉRAFLURE : scratch
raz-de-marée [radmare] *nms & pl* : tidal wave
réagir [reaʒir] *vi* : react — **réacteur** [reaktœr] *nm* **1** : jet engine **2** : (nuclear) reactor — **réaction** [reaksjɔ̃] *nf* **1** : reaction **2 à ~** : jet-propelled — **réactionnaire** [reaksjɔnɛr] *adj & nmf* : reactionary
réaliser [realize] *vt* **1** : carry out, execute **2** ACCOMPLIR : achieve **3** : direct (a film) **4** : realize (a profit) — **se réaliser** *vr* : materialize, come true — **réalisateur, -trice** [realizatœr, -tris] *n* : director (in movies, television, etc.) — **réalisation** [realizasjɔ̃] *nf* **1** EXÉCUTION : execution, carrying out **2** : accomplishment **3** : production (of a film)
réaliste [realist] *adj* : realistic
réalité [realite] *nf* **1** : reality **2 en ~** : in fact, actually
réanimer [reanime] *vt* : resuscitate
réapparaître [reaparɛtr] {7} *vi* : reappear
rébarbatif, -tive [rebarbatif, -tiv] *adj* : forbidding, daunting
rebâtir [rəbatir] *vt* : rebuild
rebattu, -tue [rəbaty] *adj* : hackneyed
rebelle [rəbɛl] *nmf* : rebel — **~** *adj* : rebellious — **rebeller** [rəbɛle] *v* **se rebeller** *vr* : rebel — **rébellion** [rebɛljɔ̃] *nf* : rebellion
rebondir [rəbɔ̃dir] *vi* **1** : bounce, rebound **2** : start (up) again — **rebond** [rəbɔ̃] *nm* : bounce, rebound
rebord [rəbɔr] *nm* : edge, sill (of a window)
rebours [rəbur] **à ~** *adv phr* : the wrong way
rebrousse-poil [rəbruspwal] **à ~** *adv phr* : the wrong way
rebrousser [rəbruse] *vt* **1** : brush back **2 ~ chemin** : turn back
rebuffade [rəbyfad] *nf* : rebuff, snub
rebut [rəby] *nm* **1** : trash, scrap **2 mettre au ~** : discard — **rebutant, -tante** [rəbytɑ̃, -tɑ̃t] *adj* : repellent, disagreeable — **rebuter** [rəbyte] *vt* : put off, discourage
récalcitrant, -trante [rekalsitrɑ̃, -trɑ̃t] *adj* : stubborn
récapituler [rekapityle] *vt* RÉSUMER : recapitulate, sum up
recel [rəsɛl] *nm* : possession of stolen goods
récemment [resamɑ̃] *adv* DERNIÈREMENT : recently
recensement [rəsɑ̃smɑ̃] *nm* : census
récent, -cente [resɑ̃, -sɑ̃t] *adj* : recent
récépissé [resepise] *nm* : receipt
récepteur [resɛptœr] *nm* : receiver
réception [resɛpsjɔ̃] *nf* : reception — **réceptionniste** [resɛpsjɔnist] *nmf* : receptionist
récession [resesjɔ̃] *nf* : recession
recette [rəsɛt] *nf* **1** : recipe (in cooking) **2** : take, receipts *pl*
recevoir [rəsəvwar] {26} *vt* **1** : receive, get **2** ACCUEILLIR : welcome **3** : see (a client, etc.) **4** : accommodate, hold —

receveur, -veuse [rəsəvœr, -vøz] *n* **1** *Can* : catcher (in sports) **2 ~ des contributions** : tax collector
rechange [rəʃɑ̃ʒ] *nm* **de ~ 1** : spare, extra **2** : alternative
réchapper [reʃape] *vi* **~ de** : come through, survive
recharger [rəʃarʒe] {17} *vt* **1** : refill **2** : recharge — **recharge** [rəʃarʒ] *nf* **1** : refill **2** : recharging
réchaud [reʃo] *nm* : (portable) stove
réchauffer [reʃofe] *vt* : reheat — **se réchauffer** *vr* : warm up, get warmer
rêche [rɛʃ] *adj* : rough, prickly
rechercher [rəʃɛrʃe] *vt* : search for, seek — **recherche** [rəʃɛrʃ] *nf* **1** : search **2** : (academic) research — **recherché, -chée** [rəʃɛrʃe] *adj* : sought-after, in demand
rechigner [rəʃiɲe] *vi* **1** : grumble **2 ~ à** : balk at
rechute [rəʃyt] *nf* : relapse
récif [resif] *nm* : reef
récipient [resipjɑ̃] *nm* : container
réciproque [resiprɔk] *adj* : reciprocal
réciter [resite] *vt* : recite — **récit** [resi] *nm* : account, story — **récital** [resital] *nm, pl* **-tals** : recital
réclamer [reklame] *vt* **1** : call for, demand **2** REVENDIQUER : claim — **réclamation** [reklamasjɔ̃] *nf* PLAINTE : complaint — **réclame** [reklam] *nf* **1** : advertisement **2** : advertising
reclus, -cluse [rəkly, -klyz] *n* : recluse
recoin [rəkwɛ̃] *nm* : nook, corner
récolte [rekɔlt] *nf* **1** : harvesting **2** : harvest, crop — **récolter** [rekɔlte] *vt* **1** : harvest **2** RAMASSER : gather, collect
recommander [rəkɔmɑ̃de] *vt* **1** : recommend **2** : register (a letter, etc.) — **recommandation** [rəkɔmɑ̃dasjɔ̃] *nf* : recommendation
recommencer [rəkɔmɑ̃se] {6} *v* : begin again
récompenser [rekɔ̃pɑ̃se] *vt* : reward — **récompense** [rekɔ̃pɑ̃s] *nf* : reward
réconcilier [rekɔ̃silje] {96} *vt* : reconcile — **réconciliation** [rekɔ̃siljasjɔ̃] *nf* : reconciliation
reconduire [rəkɔ̃dɥir] {49} *vt* RACCOMPAGNER : see home, accompany
réconforter [rekɔ̃fɔrte] *vt* : comfort — **réconfort** [rekɔ̃fɔr] *nm* : comfort — **réconfortant, -tante** [rekɔ̃fɔrtɑ̃, -tɑ̃t] *adj* : comforting, heartwarming
reconnaître [rəkɔnɛtr] {7} *vt* **1** : recognize **2** ADMETTRE : acknowledge — **reconnaissance** [rɛkɔnɛsɑ̃s] *nf* **1** : recognition **2** GRATITUDE : gratitude — **reconnaissable** [rəkɔnɛsabl] *adj* : recognizable — **reconnaissant, -sante** [rəkɔnɛsɑ̃, -sɑ̃t] *adj* : grateful — **reconnu, -nue** [rəkɔny] *adj* : well-known
reconsidérer [rəkɔ̃sidere] {87} *vt* : reconsider
reconstituer [rəkɔ̃stitɥe] *vt* : recreate, reconstruct
reconstruire [rəkɔ̃strɥir] {49} *vt* : reconstruct, rebuild
record [rəkɔr] *nm* : record
recouper [rəkupe] *v* **se recouper** *vr* : tally, match up
recourbé, -bée [rəkurbe] *adj* : curved, hooked
recourir [rəkurir] {23} *vi* **~ à** : resort to — **recours** [rəkur] *nm* : recourse, resort
recouvrer [rəkuvre] *vt* : recover, regain
recouvrir [rəkuvrir] {83} *vt* : cover (up)
récréation [rekreasjɔ̃] *nf* **1** LOISIRS : recreation **2** : recess, break — **récréatif, -tive** [rekreatif, -tiv] *adj* : recreational
recréer [rəkree] {89} *vt* : re-create
récrier [rekrije] {96} *v* **se récrier** *vr* : exclaim
récrimination [rekriminasjɔ̃] *nf* : reproach
récrire [rekrir] {33} *vt* : rewrite
recroqueviller [rəkrɔkvije] *v* **se recroqueviller** *vr* **1** : curl up **2** : shrivel up
recruter [rəkryte] *vt* : recruit — **recrue** [rəkry] *nf* : recruit — **recrutement** [rəkrytmɑ̃] *nm* : recruitment
rectangle [rɛktɑ̃gl] *nm* : rectangle — **rectangulaire** [-tɑ̃gylɛr] *adj* : rectangular
rectifier [rɛktifje] {96} *vt* : rectify, correct — **rectification** [rɛktifikasjɔ̃] *nf* : correction
recto [rɛkto] *nm* : right side (of a page)
rectum [rɛktɔm] *nm* : rectum
reçu, -cue [rəsy] *adj* : accepted, approved — **reçu** *nm* : receipt
recueillir [rəkœjir] {3} *vt* **1** : collect, gather **2** : obtain (information) — **se recueillir** *vr* : meditate — **recueil** [rəkœj] *nm* : collection
reculer [rəkyle] *vt* **1** REPOUSSER : move back, push back **2** DIFFÉRER : postpone — *vi* **1** : move back, back up **2 ~ devant** : shrink from — **recul** [rəkyl] *nm* **1** : recoil (of a fire arm) **2 avec le ~** : with hindsight — **reculons** [rəkylɔ̃] **à ~** *adv phr* : backward

récupérer [rekypere] {87} *vt* **1** : recover, get back **2** : salvage **3** : make up (hours of work, etc.) — *vi* SE RÉTABLIR : recover, recuperate
récurer [rekyre] *vt* : scour
recycler [rəsikle] *vt* **1** : retrain (personnel) **2** : recycle — **se recycler** *vr* : retrain
rédacteur, -trice [redaktœr, -tris] *n* : editor — **rédaction** [redaksjɔ̃] *nf* **1** : writing, editing **2** : editorial staff
reddition [redisjɔ̃] *nf* : surrender
rédemption [redɑ̃psjɔ̃] *nf* : redemption
redevable [rədəvabl] *adj* **être ~ à** : be indebted to — **redevance** [rədəvɑ̃s] *nf* : dues *pl*, fees *pl*
rédiger [rediʒe] {17} *vt* : draw up, write
redire [rədir] {29} *vt* RÉPÉTER : repeat
redondant, -dante [rədɔ̃dɑ̃, -dɑ̃t] *adj* SUPERFLU : redundant
redonner [rədɔne] *vt* **1** RENDRE : give back **2** RÉTABLIR : restore (confidence)
redoubler [rəduble] *vt* **1** DOUBLER : double **2** : repeat (a year in school) **3 ~ ses efforts** : intensify one's efforts
redouter [rədute] *vt* : fear — **redoutable** [rədutabl] *adj* : formidable
redresser [rədrɛse] *vt* **1** : straighten (up) **2** : rectify, redress (wrongs, etc.) — **se redresser** *vr* : straighten up
réduction [redyksjɔ̃] *nf* : reduction
réduire [redɥir] {49} *vt* **1** : reduce **2 ~ en** : crush to — **réduit, -duite** [redɥi, -dɥit] *adj* **1** : reduced (of speed) **2** : small, limited — **réduit** *nm* : recess, nook
rééduquer [reedyke] *vt* : rehabilitate — **rééducation** [reedykasjɔ̃] *nf* : rehabilitation
réel, -elle [reɛl] *adj* : real — **réel** *nm* : reality — **réellement** [reɛlmɑ̃] *adv* : really
refaire [rəfɛr] {42} *vt* : do again, redo — **réfection** [refɛksjɔ̃] *nf* : repair
référence [referɑ̃s] *nf* : reference
référendum [referɛ̃dɔm] *nm* : referendum
référer [refere] {87} *v* **se référer** *vr* **~ à** : refer to
réfléchir [refleʃir] *vt* : reflect — *vi* PENSER : think — **réfléchi, -chie** [refleʃi] *adj* **1** : thoughtful **2** : reflexive (of a verb)
refléter [rəflete] {87} *vt* : reflect, mirror — **reflet** [rəflɛ] *nm* : reflection, image
réflexe [reflɛks] *adj & nm* : reflex
réflexion [reflɛksjɔ̃] *nf* **1** : reflection (of light, etc.) **2** PENSÉE : thought
refluer [rəflye] *vi* **1** : ebb, flow back **2** : surge back (of crowds, etc.) — **reflux** [rəflys] *nm* : ebb
réformer [refɔrme] *vt* : reform — **réformateur, -trice** [refɔrmatœr, -tris] *n* : reformer — **réforme** [refɔrm] *nf* : reform
refouler [rəfule] *vt* **1** : drive back (a crowd) **2 ~ ses larmes** : hold back tears
réfractaire [refraktɛr] *adj* **~ à** : resistant to
refrain [rəfrɛ̃] *nm* : refrain, chorus
refréner [rəfrene] *or* **réfréner** [refrene] {87} *vt* : curb, check
réfrigérer [refriʒere] {87} *vt* : refrigerate — **réfrigérateur** [refriʒeratœr] *nm* : refrigerator
refroidir [rəfrwadir] *v* : cool (down) — **refroidissement** [rəfrwadismɑ̃] *nm* **1** : cooling **2** RHUME : cold, chill
refuge [rəfyʒ] *nm* : refuge — **réfugié, -giée** [refyʒje] *n* : refugee — **réfugier** [rəfyʒje] {96} *v* **se réfugier** *vr* : take refuge
refuser [rəfyze] *vt* : refuse — **refus** [rəfy] *nm* : refusal
réfuter [refyte] *vt* : refute
regagner [rəgaɲe] *vt* **1** : win back **2 ~ son domicile** : return home
régal [regal] *nm, pl* **-gals** DÉLICE : delight, treat — **régaler** [regale] *vt* : treat — **se régaler** *vr* **1** : enjoy oneself **2 ~ de** : feast on
regard [rəgar] *nm* **1** : look **2 au ~ de** : in regard to — **regarder** [rəgarde] *vt* **1** : look at, watch **2** CONSIDÉRER : consider **3** CONCERNER : concern — *vi* : look — **se regarder** *vr* **1** : look at oneself **2** : look at each other
régénérer [reʒenere] {87} *vt* : regenerate
régie [reʒi] *nf* **1** *France* : public corporation **2** *Can* : provincial public-service agency
régime [reʒim] *nm* **1** : (political) regime **2** : system **3** : cluster, bunch (of bananas) **4 au ~** : on a diet
région [reʒjɔ̃] *nf* : region, area — **régional, -nale** [reʒjɔnal] *adj, mpl* **-naux** [-no] : regional
régir [reʒir] *vt* : govern
registre [rəʒistr] *nm* : register
réglable [reglabl] *adj* **1** : adjustable **2** : payable — **réglage** [reglaʒ] *nm* : adjustment
règle [rɛgl] *nf* **1** : ruler (instrument) **2** LOI : rule **3 ~s** *nfpl* : menstrual period **4 en ~** : in order, valid — **réglé,**

-glée [regle] *adj* ORGANISÉ : orderly, organized — **règlement** [rɛgləmɑ̃] *nm* **1** : regulations *pl* **2** RÉSOLUTION : settlement — **réglementation** [rɛgləmɑ̃tasjɔ̃] *nf* : regulation — **régler** [regle] {87} *vt* **1** : adjust, regulate **2** : settle (a dispute)

réglisse [reglis] *nf* : licorice

régner [reɲe] {87} *vi* : reign — **règne** [rɛɲ] *nm* : reign, rule

regorger [rəgɔrʒe] {17} *vi* **~ de** : overflow with

regretter [rəgrete] *vt* **1** : regret, be sorry about **2** : miss (s.o.) — **regret** [rəgrɛ] *nm* : regret

régularité [regylarite] *nf* : regularity — **régulier, -lière** [regylje, -ljɛr] *adj* **1** : regular **2** CONSTANT : even, steady

réhabiliter [reabilite] *vt* **1** : rehabilitate **2** RÉNOVER : renovate — **réhabilitation** [reabilitasjɔ̃] *nf* : rehabilitation

rein [rɛ̃] *nm* **1** : kidney **2 ~s** *nmpl* DOS : back

reine [rɛn] *nf* : queen

réinsérer [reɛ̃sere] {87} *vt* : rehabilitate

réitérer [reitere] {87} *vt* : reiterate, repeat

rejeter [rəʒte] {8} *vt* **1** RENVOYER : throw back **2** REFUSER : reject — **rejet** [rəʒɛ] *nm* : rejection

rejoindre [rəʒwɛ̃dr] {50} *vt* **1** RENCONTRER : join, meet **2** RATTRAPER : catch up with **3** REGAGNER : return to — **se rejoindre** *vr* : meet

réjouir [reʒwir] *vt* : delight — **se réjouir** *vr* : rejoice, be delighted — **réjouissance** [reʒwisɑ̃s] *nf* **1** : rejoicing **2 ~s** *nfpl* : festivities — **réjouissant, -sante** [reʒwisɑ̃, -sɑ̃t] *adj* : cheering, delightful

relâcher [rəlaʃe] *vt* **1** DESSERRER : loosen (up), slacken **2** LIBÉRER : release — **se relâcher** *vr* **1** : loosen **2** : become lax — **relâche** [rəlaʃ] *nf* : respite

relais [rəlɛ] *nm* **1** : relay **2 ~ routier** : truck stop

relancer [rəlɑ̃se] {6} *vt* **1** : throw back **2** : revive, boost (the economy, etc.) — **relance** [rəlɑ̃s] *nf* : boost

relatif, -tive [rəlatif, -tiv] *adj* : relative — **relativité** [rəlativite] *nf* : relativity

relation [rəlasjɔ̃] *nf* **1** : connection, relation **2** : relationship **3** CONNAISSANCE : acquaintance **4 ~s** *nfpl* : relations

relaxer [rəlakse] *vt* : relax — **relaxation** [rəlaksasjɔ̃] *nf* : relaxation

relayer [rəlɛje] {11} *vt* : relieve — **se relayer** *vr* : take turns

reléguer [rəlege] {87} *vt* : relegate

relent [rəlɑ̃] *nm* : stench

relève [rəlɛv] *nf* **1** : relief **2 prendre la ~** : take over

relever [rəlve] {52} *vt* **1** : pick up, raise (up) **2** AUGMENTER : increase **3** RELAYER : relieve **4** : bring out, enhance — **se relever** *vr* : get up (again) — **relevé** [rəlɛve] *nm* **1** : (bank) statement **2** : reading (of a meter)

relief [rəljɛf] *nm* **1** : relief **2 mettre en ~** : highlight

relier [rəlje] {96} *vt* **1** : link, join **2** : bind (a book)

religion [rəliʒjɔ̃] *nf* : religion — **religieux, -gieuse** [rəliʒjø, -ʒjøz] *adj* : religious — **~** *n* : monk *m*, nun *f*

relique [rəlik] *nf* : relic

reliure [rəljyr] *nf* : binding

reluire [rəlɥir] {49} *vi* BRILLER : glisten, shine — **reluisant, -sante** [rəlɥizɑ̃, -zɑ̃t] *adj* : gleaming

remanier [rəmanje] {96} *vt* : revise, modify

remarquer [rəmarke] *vt* **1** : remark, observe **2** CONSTATER : notice — **remarquable** [rəmarkabl] *adj* : remarkable — **remarque** [rəmark] *nf* : remark

remblai [rɑ̃blɛ] *nm* : embankment

rembobiner [rɑ̃bɔbine] *vt* : rewind

rembourrer [rɑ̃bure] *vt* : pad

rembourser [rɑ̃burse] *vt* **1** : repay (a debt) **2** : refund, reimburse — **remboursement** [rɑ̃bursəmɑ̃] *nm* : refund, reimbursement

remède [rəmɛd] *nm* : remedy, cure — **remédier** [rəmedje] {96} *vi* **~ à** : remedy, cure

remercier [rəmɛrsje] {96} *vt* **1** : thank **2** CONGÉDIER : dismiss, fire — **remerciement** [rəmɛrsimɑ̃] *nm* **1** : thanking **2 ~s** *nmpl* : thanks

remettre [rəmɛtr] {53} *vt* **1** REMPLACER : replace **2** RAJOUTER : add **3** : put back (on) **4** DONNER : deliver, hand over **5** : postpone **6** RECONNAÎTRE : recognize, place — **se remettre** *vr* **1** : go back, get back **2** : put on again **3** : recover, get better **4 ~ à** : begin again **5 ~ de** : get over — **remise** [rəmiz] *nf* **1** : postponement **2** LIVRAISON : delivery **3** : remission (of a debt, etc.) **4** RABAIS : discount **5** : shed — **rémission** [remisjɔ̃] *nf* : remission

remonter [rəmɔ̃te] *vt* **1** : take back up, bring back up, raise up (again) **2** : go back up (the stairs, etc.) **3** : cheer up, invigorate — *vi* **1** : go back up, rise (again) **2 ~ à** : date back to — **remontée** [rəmɔ̃te] *nf* **1** : climb, ascent **2 ~ mécanique** : ski lift — **remonte–pente** [rəmɔ̃tpɑ̃t] *nm, pl* **remonte–pentes** : ski lift

remords [rəmɔr] *nm* : remorse

remorquer [rəmɔrke] *vt* : tow — **remorque** [rəmɔrk] *nf* : trailer — **remorqueuse** [rəmɔrkøz] *nf Can* : tow truck

remous [rəmu] *nm* : (back)wash

remplacer [rɑ̃plase] {6} *vt* : replace — **remplaçant, -çante** [rɑ̃plasɑ̃, -sɑ̃t] *n* : substitute — **remplacement** [rɑ̃plasmɑ̃] *nm* : replacement

remplir [rɑ̃plir] *vt* **1** : fill (up) **2** : fill out (a form, etc.) **3** : carry out, fulfill — **remplissage** [rɑ̃plisaʒ] *nm* : filling, filler

remporter [rɑ̃pɔrte] *vt* **1** REPRENDRE : take back **2** : win (a prize, etc.)

remue–ménage [rəmymenaʒ] *nms & pl* : commotion, fuss

remuer [rəmɥe] *vt* **1** MÉLANGER : stir, mix **2 ~ la queue** : wag its tail — *vi* : fidget, squirm

rémunérer [remynere] {87} *vt* : pay (for) — **rémunération** [remynerasjɔ̃] *nf* : payment

renâcler [rənakle] *vi* **1** : snort **2 ~ à** : balk at

renaître [rənɛtr] {57} *vi* : be reborn — **renaissance** [rənɛsɑ̃s] *nf* : rebirth, revival

renard [rənar] *nm* : fox

renchérir [rɑ̃ʃerir] *vi* **1** : become more expensive **2 ~ sur** : go (one step) further than

rencontrer [rɑ̃kɔ̃tre] *vt* **1** : meet **2** TROUVER : come across, encounter — **se rencontrer** *vr* **1** : meet **2** SE TROUVER : be found — **rencontre** [rɑ̃kɔ̃tr] *nf* **1** : meeting, encounter **2** : match, game

rendement [rɑ̃dmɑ̃] *nm* **1** : output **2** RAPPORT : yield

rendez–vous [rɑ̃devu] *nms & pl* **1** : appointment, meeting **2** : meeting place

rendre [rɑ̃dr] {63} *vt* **1** : give back, return **2** : pronounce (a verdict) **3** EXPRIMER : convey **4 ~ grâces** : give thanks — *vi* VOMIR : vomit — **se rendre** *vr* **1** : surrender **2 ~ à** : go to **3 ~ compte de** : realize, be aware of

rêne [rɛn] *nf* : rein

renfermer [rɑ̃fɛrme] *vt* : contain — **se renfermer** *vr* : withdraw (into oneself) — **renfermé** [rɑ̃fɛrme] *nm* : mustiness

renfler [rɑ̃fle] *v* **se renfler** *vr* : bulge, swell — **renflement** [rɑ̃fləmɑ̃] *nm* : bulge

renforcer [rɑ̃fɔrse] {6} *vt* : reinforce — **renfort** [rɑ̃fɔr] *nm* : reinforcement

renfrogné, -gnée [rɑ̃frɔɲe] *adj* : sullen, scowling

rengaine [rɑ̃gɛn] *nf* **la même ~** : the same old story

renier [rənje] {96} *vt* : deny, disown

renifler [rənifle] *v* : sniff

renne [rɛn] *nm* : reindeer

renom [rənɔ̃] *nm* : renown, fame — **renommé, -mée** [rənɔme] *adj* : renowned — **renommée** *nf* : fame, renown

renoncer [rənɔ̃se] {6} *vi* **~ à** : renounce, give up — **renonciation** [rənɔ̃sjasjɔ̃] *nf* : renunciation

renouer [rənwe] *vt* REPRENDRE : renew, resume

renouveau [rənuvo] *nm, pl* **-veaux** : revival

renouveler [rənuvle] {8} *vt* : renew — **renouvellement** [rənuvɛlmɑ̃] *nm* : renewal

rénover [renɔve] *vt* : renovate — **rénovation** [renɔvasjɔ̃] *nf* : renovation

renseigner [rɑ̃seɲe] *vt* : inform — **se renseigner** *vr* : ask, make inquiries — **renseignement** [rɑ̃sɛɲəmɑ̃] *nm* : information

rentable [rɑ̃tabl] *adj* : profitable

rente [rɑ̃t] *nf* **1** : (private) income **2 ~ viagère** : annuity

rentrer [rɑ̃tre] *vi* **1** : go in, get in **2** : go back in **3** RETOURNER : return — *vt* **1** : bring in, take in **2** : pull in (one's stomach) — **rentrée** [rɑ̃tre] *nf* **1** : return (to work, etc.) **2 ~ scolaire** : start of the new school year

renverser [rɑ̃vɛrse] *vt* **1** : knock down, overturn **2** RÉPANDRE : spill **3** : overthrow (a regime) **4** STUPÉFIER : astonish — **se renverser** *vr* : fall over, overturn — **renversement** [rɑ̃vɛrsəmɑ̃] *nm* : reversal

renvoyer [rɑ̃vwaje] {36} *vt* **1** : send back, throw back **2** CONGÉDIER : dismiss **3** REMETTRE : postpone **4 ~ à** : refer to **5** *Can fam* : throw up — **renvoi** [rɑ̃vwa] *nm* **1** : return (of a package) **2** LICENCIEMENT : dismissal **3** : cross-reference **4** REMISE : postponement **5** : belch, burp

réorganiser [reɔrganize] *vt* : reorganize

repaire [rəpɛr] *nm* : den, lair
répandre [repɑ̃dr] {63} *vt* **1** : spill **2** : shed (blood, tears, etc.) **3** : spread (the news) **4** : give off, emit — **se répandre** *vr* **1** : spill **2** SE PROPAGER : spread — **répandu, -due** [repɑ̃dy] *adj* : widespread
réparer [repare] *vt* **1** : repair **2** : make up for (an error) — **réparation** [reparasjɔ̃] *nf* : repair, repairing
repartir [rəpartir] {82} *vt* : retort — *vi* **1** : leave again **2** : start again
répartir [repartir] *vt* **1** : divide up, distribute **2** : spread (out) — **se répartir** *vr* : divide — **répartition** [repartisjɔ̃] *nf* : distribution
repas [rəpa] *nm* : meal
repasser [rəpase] *vt* **1** : pass again, take again, show again **2** : iron, press **3** : go (back) over — *vi* : pass by again, come again — **repassage** [rəpasaʒ] *nm* : ironing
repentir [rəpɑ̃tir] {82} *v* **se repentir** *vr* : repent — ~ *nm* : repentance
répercuter [reperkyte] *v* **se répercuter** *vr* **1** : echo **2** ~ **sur** : have repercussions on — **répercussion** [reperkysjɔ̃] *nf* : repercussion
repère [rəpɛr] *nm* **1** : line, mark **2** **point de** ~ : landmark — **repérer** [rəpere] {87} *vt* **1** : mark **2** SITUER : locate — **se repérer** *vr* : find one's way
répertoire [repɛrtwar] *nm* **1** : list, index **2** : repertoire (in theater) **3** ~ **d'adresses** : address book **4** ~ **téléphonique** : telephone directory
répéter [repete] {87} *vt* **1** : repeat **2** : rehearse (in theater) — **répétitif, -tive** [repetitif, -tiv] *adj* : repetitive, repetitious — **répétition** [repetisjɔ̃] *nf* **1** : repetition **2** : rehearsal
répit [repi] *nm* : respite
replacer [rəplase] {6} *vt* : replace
replier [rəplije] {96} *vt* : fold up, fold over — **se replier** *vr* **1** : fold up **2** ~ **sur soi-même** : withdraw into oneself
répliquer [replike] *vt* RÉPONDRE : reply — *vi* **1** : respond **2** RIPOSTER : retort — **réplique** [replik] *nf* **1** : reply **2** : line (in a play) **3** : replica (in art)
répondre [repɔ̃dr] {63} *v* : answer, reply — **répondeur** [repɔ̃dœr] *nm* : answering machine — **réponse** [repɔ̃s] *nf* : answer, response
report [rəpɔr] *nm* RENVOI : postponement
reportage [rəpɔrtaʒ] *nm* : report
reporter[1] [rəpɔrte] *vt* **1** : take back **2** REMETTRE : postpone **3** : carry forward (a calculation, etc.)
reporter[2] [rəpɔrtɛr] *nm* : reporter
reposer [rəpoze] *v* : rest — **se reposer** *vr* **1** : rest **2** ~ **sur** : rely on — **repos** [rəpo] *nm* : rest — **reposant, -sante** [rəpozɑ̃, -zɑ̃t] *nm* : restful
repousser [rəpuse] *vi* : grow back — *vt* **1** : push back **2** DÉGOÛTER : disgust **3** : turn down (an offer) **4** REPORTER : postpone — **repoussant, -sante** [rəpusɑ̃, -sɑ̃t] *adj* DÉGOÛTANT : repulsive
reprendre [rəprɑ̃dr] {70} *vt* **1** : take (up) again **2** : take back, return **3** RETROUVER : regain **4** RECOMMENCER : resume **5** : repair, alter (a garment) — *vi* **1** : pick up, improve **2** : resume
représailles [rəprezaj] *nfpl* : reprisals
représenter [rəprezɑ̃te] *vt* **1** : represent **2** JOUER : perform — **représentant, -tante** [rəprezɑ̃tɑ̃, -tɑ̃t] *n* : representative — **représentatif, -tive** [rəprezɑ̃tatif, -tiv] *adj* : representative — **représentation** [rəprezɑ̃tasjɔ̃] *nf* **1** : representation **2** : performance (in theater)
réprimander [reprimɑ̃de] *vt* : reprimand — **réprimande** [reprimɑ̃d] *nf* : reprimand
réprimer [reprime] *vt* : repress, suppress
reprise [rəpriz] *nf* **1** : recapture **2** : resumption **3** : repeat, revival **4** : recovery **5** : trade-in (of goods) **6** : round (in sports) **7** : darn, mend — **repriser** [rəprize] *vt* : darn, mend
reprocher [rəprɔʃe] *vt* ~ **à** : reproach — **reproche** [rəprɔʃ] *nm* : reproach
reproduire [rəprɔdɥir] {49} *vt* : reproduce — **se reproduire** *vr* **1** : reproduce **2** SE RÉPÉTER : recur — **reproduction** [rəprɔdyksjɔ̃] *nf* : reproduction
réprouver [repruve] *vt* : condemn
reptile [rɛptil] *nm* : reptile
repu, -pue [rəpy] *adj* : satiated, full
république [repyblik] *nf* : republic — **républicain, -caine** [repyblikɛ̃, -kɛn] *adj & n* : republican
répudier [repydje] {96} *vt* : repudiate
répugner [repyɲe] *vt* : disgust — *vi* ~ **à** : be averse to — **répugnance** [repyɲɑ̃s] *nf* **1** : repugnance **2** : reluctance — **répugnant, -gnante** [repyɲɑ̃, -ɲɑ̃t] *adj* : repugnant
réputation [repytasjɔ̃] *nf* : reputation — **réputé, -tée** [repyte] *adj* : renowned, famous

requérir [rəkerir] {21} *vt* : require
requête [rəkɛt] *nf* : request
requin [rəkɛ̃] *nm* : shark
requis, -quise [rəki, -kiz] *adj* : required
rescapé, -pée [rɛskape] *n* : survivor
rescousse [rɛskus] *nf* : rescue, aid
réseau [rezo] *nm, pl* **-seaux** : network
réserver [rezɛrve] *vt* : reserve — **réservation** [rezɛrvasjɔ̃] *nf* : reservation — **réserve** [rezɛrv] *nf* **1** PROVISION : stock **2** RETENUE : reserve **3** : (Indian) reservation **4** : (game) preserve **5** **sous ~ de** : subject to — **réservé, -vée** [rezɛrve] *adj* : reserved
réservoir [rezɛrvwar] *nm* **1** : tank **2** : reservoir
résidence [rezidɑ̃s] *nf* : residence — **résident, -dente** [rezidɑ̃, -dɑ̃t] *n* : resident — **résidentiel, -tielle** [rezidɑ̃sjɛl] *adj* : residential — **résider** [rezide] *vi* : reside
résidu [rezidy] *nm* : residue
résigner [reziɲe] *vt* : resign — **se résigner** *vr* **~ à** : resign oneself to — **résignation** [reziɲasjɔ̃] *nf* : resignation
résilier [rezilje] {96} *vt* : terminate
résine [rezin] *nf* : resin
résister [reziste] *vi* **~ à** : resist — **résistance** [rezistɑ̃s] *nf* : resistance — **résistant, -tante** [rezistɑ̃, -tɑ̃t] *adj* : tough, durable
résolu, -lue [rezɔly] *adj* : resolute, resolved — **résolution** [rezɔlysjɔ̃] *nf* **1** : resolution **2** DÉTERMINATION : resolve
résonner [rezɔne] *vi* : resound — **résonance** [rezɔnɑ̃s] *nf* : resonance — **résonnant, -nante** [rezɔnɑ̃, -nɑ̃t] *adj* : resonant
résorber [rezɔrbe] *vt* : absorb, reduce
résoudre [rezudr] {74} *vt* : solve, resolve — **se résoudre** *vr* **~ à** : decide to
respect [rɛspɛ] *nm* : respect — **respectable** [rɛspɛktabl] *adj* : respectable — **respecter** [rɛspɛkte] *vt* : respect
respectif, -tive [rɛspɛktif, -tiv] *adj* : respective
respectueux, -tueuse [rɛspɛktɥø, -tɥøz] *adj* : respectful
respirer [rɛspire] *v* : breathe — **respiration** [rɛspirasjɔ̃] *nf* : breathing
resplendir [rɛsplɑ̃dir] *vi* : shine — **resplendissant, -sante** [rɛsplɑ̃disɑ̃, -sɑ̃t] *adj* : radiant
responsable [rɛspɔ̃sabl] *adj* : responsible — **responsabilité** [rɛspɔ̃sabilite] *nf* **1** : responsibility **2** : liability
resquiller [rɛskije] *vi fam* **1** : sneak in (without paying) **2** : cut in line
ressaisir [rəsezir] *v* **se ressaisir** *vr* : pull oneself together
ressasser [rəsase] *vt* : keep going over
ressembler [rəsɑ̃ble] *vi* **~ à** : resemble — **se ressembler** *vr* : resemble each other, look alike — **ressemblance** [rəsɑ̃blɑ̃s] *nf* **1** : resemblance, likeness **2** SIMILITUDE : similarity
ressentir [rəsɑ̃tir] {82} *vt* : feel — **se ressentir** *vr* : feel the effects of — **ressentiment** [rəsɑ̃timɑ̃] *nm* : resentment
resserrer [rəsere] *vt* : tighten (a knot, etc.) — **se resserrer** *vr* **1** : tighten (up) **2** : narrow
ressortir [rəsɔrtir] {82} *vt* : take out again, bring out again — *vi* **1** : go out again **2** : stand out — *v impers* : emerge, be evident — **ressort** [rəsɔr] *nm* **1** : spring (of a mattress, etc.) **2** : impulse, motivation **3 en dernier ~** : as a last resort — **ressortissant, -sante** [rəsɔrtisɑ̃, -sɑ̃t] *n* : national
ressource [rəsurs] *nf* : resource
ressusciter [resysite] *vt* : resuscitate — *vi* : come back to life, revive
restant, -tante [rɛstɑ̃, -tɑ̃t] *adj* : remaining — **restant** *nm* : remainder
restaurant [rɛstɔrɑ̃] *nm* : restaurant
restaurer [rɛstɔre] *vt* : restore
rester [rɛste] *vi* **1** : stay, remain **2** : be left — *v impers* **il reste** : there remains — **reste** [rɛst] *nm* **1** : remainder, rest **2 au ~** *or* **du ~** : besides, moreover **3 ~s** *nmpl* : leftovers **4 ~s** *nmpl* : remains
restituer [rɛstitɥe] *vt* **1** : restore, return **2** : reproduce (sound, etc.)
restreindre [rɛstrɛ̃dr] {37} *vt* : restrict
restrictif, -tive [rɛstriktif, -tiv] *adj* : restrictive — **restriction** [rɛstriksjɔ̃] *nf* : restriction
résultat [rezylta] *nm* : result — **résulter** [rezylte] {75} *vi* **~ de** : result from — *v impers* **il résulte** : it follows
résumer [rezyme] *vt* : summarize, sum up — **résumé** [rezyme] *nm* **1** : summary **2 en ~** : in short
résurrection [rezyrɛksjɔ̃] *nf* : resurrection
rétablir [retablir] *vt* : restore — **se rétablir** *vr* **1** : be restored **2** GUÉRIR : recover — **rétablissement** [retablismɑ̃] *nm* **1** : restoration **2** GUÉRISON : recovery

retarder [rətarde] *vt* **1** : delay **2** RE-PORTER : postpone **3** : set back (a clock, etc.) — *vi* : be slow — **retard** [rətar] *nm* **1** : lateness, delay **2** : backwardness — **retardataire** [rətardatɛr] *nmf* : latecomer

retenir [rətənir] {92} *vt* **1** : hold back, stop **2** RETARDER : keep, detain **3** GARDER : retain **4** RÉSERVER : reserve, book **5** SE RAPPELER : remember **6** : carry (in mathematics) — **se retenir** *vr* **1** : restrain oneself **2** ~ **à** : hold on to

retentir [rətɑ̃tir] *vi* : ring, resound — **retentissant, -sante** [rətɑ̃tisɑ̃, -sɑ̃t] *adj* : resounding — **retentissement** [rətɑ̃tismɑ̃] *nm* : effect, impact

retenue [rətəny] *nf* **1** : deduction **2** : detention (in school) **3** RÉSERVE : reserve, restraint

réticent, -cente [retisɑ̃, -sɑ̃t] *adj* : reticent, reluctant — **réticence** [-tisɑ̃s] *nf* : reticence, reluctance

rétine [retin] *nf* : retina

retiré, -rée [rətire] *adj* : remote, secluded

retirer [rətire] *vt* **1** : take off (clothing, etc.) **2** : take away, remove **3** : withdraw (money, support, etc.) **4** : collect (baggage, etc.) **5** *Can* : retire, put out (in baseball) — **se retirer** *vr* : withdraw, retreat

retomber [rətɔ̃be] *vi* : fall again, fall back — **retombées** [rətɔ̃be] *nfpl* : repercussions, consequences

rétorquer [retɔrke] *vt* : retort

rétorsion [retɔrsjɔ̃] *nf* : retaliation

retoucher [rətuʃe] *vt* **1** : touch up **2** : alter (a dress, etc.) — **retouche** [rətuʃ] *nf* **1** : touching up **2** : alteration

retour [rətur] *nm* **1** : return **2 de** ~ : back

retourner [rəturne] *vt* **1** : turn over **2** : return (a compliment, etc.) — *vi* REVENIR : return — **se retourner** *vr* **1** : turn around **2** : overturn (of a boat, etc.) **3** ~ **contre** : turn against

retrait [rətrɛ] *nm* **1** : withdrawal **2 en** ~ : set back **3** *Can* : out (in baseball)

retraite [rətrɛt] *nf* **1** : retirement **2** : retreat (in religion, etc.) **3** PENSION : pension

retransmettre [rətrɑ̃smɛtr] {53} *vt* : broadcast — **retransmission** [rətrɑ̃smisjɔ̃] *nf* : broadcast

rétrécir [retresir] *vi* : shrink

rétribuer [retribɥe] *vt* : pay — **rétribution** [retribysjɔ̃] *nf* RÉMUNÉRATION : payment

rétroactif, -tive [retrɔaktif, -tiv] *adj* : retroactive

rétrograder [retrɔgrade] *vt* : demote — *vi* : downshift (of a gear)

retrousser [rətruse] *vt* : turn up, roll up

retrouvailles [rətruvaj] *nfpl* : reunion

retrouver [rətruve] *vt* **1** : find (again) **2** REVOIR : see again **3** SE RAPPELER : remember — **se retrouver** *vr* **1** : meet again **2** : find one's way

rétroviseur [retrɔvizœr] *nm* : rearview mirror

réunir [reynir] *vt* RASSEMBLER : gather, collect — **se réunir** *vr* : meet — **réunion** [reynjɔ̃] *nf* : meeting

réussir [reysir] *vi* : succeed — *vt* **1** : make a success of **2** : pass (an exam) — **réussi, -sie** [reysi] *adj* : successful — **réussite** [reysit] *nf* : success

revanche [rəvɑ̃ʃ] *nf* **1** : revenge **2 en** ~ : on the other hand

rêve [rɛv] *nm* : dream

réveiller [reveje] *vt* **1** : wake up **2** : awaken — **se réveiller** *vr* : wake up — **réveil** [revɛj] *nm* **1** : waking up, awakening **2** : alarm clock — **réveille–matin** [revɛjmatɛ̃] *nms & pl* : alarm clock

révéler [revele] {87} *vt* **1** : reveal **2** INDIQUER : show — **se révéler** *vr* : prove to be —**révélation** [revelasjɔ̃] *nf* : revelation

revendiquer [rəvɑ̃dike] *vt* **1** : claim **2** EXIGER : demand — **revendication** [rəvɑ̃dikasjɔ̃] *nf* : claim

revendre [rəvɑ̃dr] {63} *vt* : sell

revenir [rəvnir] {92} *vi* **1** : come back, return **2** ~ **à** : return to, go back to **3** ~ **à** : come down to, amount to **4** ~ **de** : get over

revente [rəvɑ̃t] *nf* : resale

revenu [rəvəny] *nm* : revenue, income

rêver [rɛve] *v* : dream

réverbère [revɛrbɛr] *nm* : streetlight

révérence [reverɑ̃s] *nf* **1** VÉNÉRATION : reverence **2** : bow, curtsy

révérend, -rende [reverɑ̃, -rɑ̃d] *adj* : reverend

rêverie [rɛvri] *nf* : daydreaming

revers [rəvɛr] *nm* **1** ENVERS : back, reverse **2** : lapel (of a jacket), cuff (of trousers) **3** : backhand (in tennis) **4** ÉCHEC : setback

réversible [revɛrsibl] *adj* : reversible

revêtement [rəvɛtmɑ̃] *nm* **1** : facing (in construction) **2** : surface (of a road)

rêveur, -veuse [rɛvœr, -vøz] *adj* : dreamy — ~ *n* : dreamer
revirement [rəvirmɑ̃] *nm* : reversal, turnabout
réviser [revize] *vt* **1** : revise, review **2** : overhaul (a vehicle) — **révision** [revizjɔ̃] *nf* **1** : review, revision **2** : service (of a vehicle)
révocation [revɔkasjɔ̃] *nf* **1** : dismissal **2** : repeal
revoir [rəvwar] {99} *vt* **1** : see again **2** RÉVISER : review — **se revoir** *vr* : meet (each other) again — ~ *nm* **au ~** : goodbye
révolter [revɔlte] *vt* : revolt, outrage — **se révolter** *vr* : rebel — **révolte** [revɔlt] *nf* : revolt
révolu, -lue [revɔly] *adj* : past
révolution [revɔlysjɔ̃] *nf* : revolution — **révolutionnaire** [revɔlysjɔnɛr] *adj & nmf* : revolutionary — **révolutionner** [revɔlysjɔne] *vt* : revolutionize
revolver [revɔlvɛr] *nm* : revolver
révoquer [revɔke] *vt* **1** : dismiss **2** : revoke (a privilege, etc.)
revue [rəvy] *nf* **1** : magazine **2 passer en ~** : go over
rez–de–chaussée [redʃose] *nms & pl* : first floor, ground floor
rhabiller [rabije] *v* **se rhabiller** *vr* : get dressed again
rhétorique [retɔrik] *adj* : rhetorical — ~ *nf* : rhetoric
rhinocéros [rinɔserɔs] *nm* : rhinoceros
rhubarbe [rybarb] *nf* : rhubarb
rhum [rɔm] *nm* : rum
rhumatisme [rymatism] *nm* : rheumatism
rhume [rym] *nm* : cold
ricaner [rikane] *vi* : snicker, giggle
riche [riʃ] *adj* : rich — ~ *nmf* : rich person — **richesse** [riʃɛs] *nf* **1** : wealth **2** : richness
ricocher [rikɔʃe] *vi* : ricochet — **ricochet** [rikɔʃɛ] *nm* : ricochet
ride [rid] *nf* **1** : wrinkle **2** : ripple (on water)
rideau [rido] *nm, pl* **-deaux** : curtain
rider [ride] *vt* **1** : wrinkle **2** : ripple (water)
ridicule [ridikyl] *adj* ABSURDE : ridiculous — ~ *nm* : ridicule — **ridiculiser** [ridikylize] *vt* : ridicule
rien [rjɛ̃] *pron* **1** : nothing **2** : anything **3 de ~** : don't mention it, you're welcome **4 ~ que** : only, just — ~ *nm* : trifle
rigide [riʒid] *adj* **1** : rigid **2** RIGOUREUX : strict — **rigidité** [riʒidite] *nf* : rigidity
rigoler [rigɔle] *vi fam* **1** : have fun **2** PLAISANTER : laugh, joke — **rigolo, -lote** [rigɔlɔ, -lɔt] *adj fam* : funny, comical
rigueur [rigœr] *nf* **1** SÉVÉRITÉ : rigor, harshness **2** : precision **3 à la ~** : if absolutely necessary **4 de ~** : obligatory — **rigoureux, -reuse** [rigurø, -røz] *adj* **1** : rigorous **2** : harsh (of climate)
rimer [rime] *vi* : rhyme — **rime** [rim] *nf* : rhyme
rincer [rɛ̃se] {6} *vt* : rinse — **rinçage** [rɛ̃saʒ] *nm* : rinsing, rinse
riposte [ripɔst] *nf* **1** RÉPLIQUE : retort **2** CONTRE-ATTAQUE : counterattack — **riposter** [ripɔste] *vt* : retort — *vi* : counter, retaliate
rire [rir] {76} *vi* **1** : laugh **2** S'AMUSER : joke, have fun **3 ~ de** : mock, make fun of — ~ *nm* : laugh, laughter
risque [risk] *nm* : risk — **risqué, -quée** [riske] *adj* : risky — **risquer** [riske] *vt* **1** : risk **2 ça risque d'arriver** : it may very well happen — **se risquer** *vr* : venture
rissoler [risɔle] *v* : brown (in cooking)
ristourne [risturn] *nf* REMISE : discount
rite [rit] *nm* : rite, ritual — **rituel, -tuelle** [ritɥɛl] *adj* : ritual — **rituel** *nm* : rite, ritual
rivage [rivaʒ] *nm* : shore
rival, -vale [rival] *adj & n, mpl* **-vaux** [rivo] : rival — **rivaliser** [rivalize] *vi* **~ avec** : compete with, rival — **rivalité** [rivalite] *nf* : rivalry
rive [riv] *nf* : bank, shore
river [rive] *vt* : rivet
riverain, -raine [rivrɛ̃, -rɛn] *n* : resident (on a street)
rivet [rivɛ] *nm* : rivet
rivière [rivjɛr] *nf* : river
rixe [riks] *nf* BAGARRE : brawl, fight
riz [ri] *nm* : rice — **rizière** [rizjɛr] *nf* : (rice) paddy
robe [rɔb] *nf* **1** : dress **2** PELAGE : coat **3 ~ de mariée** : wedding gown **4 ~ de nuit** *Can* : nightgown
robinet [rɔbinɛ] *nm* : faucet
robot [rɔbo] *nm* : robot
robuste [rɔbyst] *adj* : robust
roc [rɔk] *nm* : rock — **roche** [rɔʃ] *nf* : rock — **rocher** [rɔʃe] *nm* : rock — **rocheux, -cheuse** [rɔʃø, -ʃøz] *adj* : rocky
roder [rɔde] *vt* **1** : break in (a vehicle) **2** *fam* : polish up (a performance, etc.)
rôder [rode] *vi* **1** : prowl **2** ERRER

: wander about — **rôdeur, -deuse** [rodœr, -døz] *n* : prowler
rogne [rɔɲ] *nf fam* : anger
rognon [rɔɲɔ̃] *nm* : kidney (in cooking)
roi [rwa] *nm* : king
rôle [rol] *nm* : role, part
roman [rɔmɑ̃] *nm* : novel — **romancier, -cière** [rɔmɑ̃sje, -sjɛr] *n* : novelist
romantique [rɔmɑ̃tik] *adj* : romantic
rompre [rɔ̃pr] {77} *vt* : break (off) — *vi* : break up
ronce [rɔ̃s] *nf* : bramble
rond, ronde [rɔ̃, rɔ̃d] *adj* : round — **rond** *nm* **1** : circle, ring **2** : (round) slice **3** *Can* : burner (of a stove) — **ronde** *nf* : rounds *pl*, patrol
rondelet, -lette [rɔ̃dlɛ, -lɛt] *adj fam* : plump
rondelle [rɔ̃dɛl] *nf* **1** : washer **2** TRANCHE : slice **3** *Can* : (hockey) puck
rondeur [rɔ̃dœr] *nf* : roundness
rondin [rɔ̃dɛ̃] *nm* : log
rond–point [rɔ̃pwɛ̃] *nm, pl* **ronds–points** : traffic circle, rotary
ronfler [rɔ̃fle] *vi* : snore — **ronflement** [rɔ̃fləmɑ̃] *nm* : snore, snoring
ronger [rɔ̃ʒe] {17} *vt* **1** : gnaw, nibble **2** : eat away at — **se ronger** *vr* **~ les ongles** : bite one's nails — **rongeur** [rɔ̃ʒœr] *nm* : rodent
ronronner [rɔ̃rɔne] *vi* **1** : purr **2** : hum (of an engine, etc.)
rosbif [rɔzbif] *nm* : roast beef
rose [roz] *nf* : rose — **~** *adj & nm* : rose, pink (color) — **rosé, -sée** [roze] *adj* : rosy, pinkish
roseau [rozo] *nm, pl* **-seaux** : reed
rosée [roze] *nf* : dew
rosier [rozje] *nm* : rosebush
rosser [rɔse] *vt* : beat, thrash
rossignol [rɔsiɲɔl] *nm* : nightingale
rotatif, -tive [rɔtatif, -tiv] *adj* : rotary — **rotation** [rɔtasjɔ̃] *nf* : rotation
roter [rote] *vi fam* : burp, belch
rôti [roti] *nm* : roast (meat)
rotin [rɔtɛ̃] *nm* : rattan
rôtir [rotir] *v* : roast — **rôtissoire** [rotiswar] *nf* : rotisserie
rotule [rɔtyl] *nf* : kneecap
rouage [rwaʒ] *nm* **1** : cogwheel **2 ~s** *nmpl* : workings
roucouler [rukule] *vi* : coo
roue [ru] *nf* **1** : wheel **2 grande ~** : Ferris wheel
rouer [rwe] *vt* **~ de coups** : thrash, beat
rouet [rue] *nm* : spinning wheel
rouge [ruʒ] *adj* : red — **~** *n* **1** : red **2 ~ à lèvres** : lipstick — **rougeâtre** [ruʒatr] *adj* : reddish — **rougeaud, -geaude** [ruʒo, -ʒod] *adj* : ruddy
rouge–gorge [ruʒgɔrʒ] *nm, pl* **rouges–gorges** : robin
rougeole [ruʒɔl] *nf* : measles
rougeoyer [ruʒwaje] {58} *vi* : turn red, glow
rougeur [ruʒœr] *nf* **1** : redness **2 ~s** *nfpl* : red blotches (on skin)
rougir [ruʒir] *vt* : make red — *vi* **1** : redden, turn red **2** : blush (with shame, etc.)
rouille [ruj] *nf* : rust — **rouillé, -lée** [ruje] *adj* : rusty — **rouiller** [ruje] *v* : rust
rouler [rule] *vt* : roll (up) — *vi* **1** : roll **2** : go, run (of a car) **3** CONDUIRE : drive — **roulant, -lante** [rulɑ̃, -lɑ̃t] *adj* : on wheels — **rouleau** [rulo] *nm, pl* **-leaux 1** : roller **2** : roll (of paper) — **roulement** [rulmɑ̃] *nm* **1** : roll, rolling **2** : rumble (of thunder) **3** : turnover (in finance) **4 ~ à billes** : ball bearing **5 ~ de tambour** : drum roll
roulette [rulɛt] *nf* : roulette
roulotte [rulɔt] *nf Can* : trailer, camper
rouspéter [ruspete] {87} *vi fam* RONCHONNER : grumble — **rouspéteur, -teuse** [ruspetœr, -tøz] *n* : grouch
roussir [rusir] *vt* : scorch, singe
route [rut] *nf* **1** : road **2** : route, highway **3** CHEMIN : way, path **4 bonne ~ !** : have a good trip! **5 se mettre en ~** : set out, get going
routier, -tière [rutje, -tjɛr] *adj* : road — **routier** *nm* **1** : truck driver **2** : truck stop
routine [rutin] *nf* : routine — **routinier, -nière** [rutinje, -njɛr] *adj* : routine
roux, rousse [ru, rus] *adj* : russet, red — **~** *n* : redhead
royal, royale [rwajal] *adj, mpl* **royaux** [rwajo] : royal, regal — **royaume** [rwajom] *nm* : kingdom, realm — **royauté** [rwajɔte] *nf* : royalty
ruban [rybɑ̃] *nm* **1** : ribbon **2 ~ adhésif** : adhesive tape
rubéole [rybeɔl] *nf* : German measles
rubis [rybi] *nms & pl* : ruby
rubrique [rybrik] *nf* **1** : column (in a newspaper) **2** : heading
ruche [ryʃ] *nf* : hive, beehive
rude [ryd] *adj* **1** : rough (of a surface, etc.) **2** PÉNIBLE : hard, tough **3** : severe, harsh (of winter) — **rudement** [rydmɑ̃] *adv* **1** : roughly, harshly **2** *fam* DRÔLEMENT : awfully, terribly

rudimentaire [rydimɑ̃tɛr] *adj* : rudimentary — **rudiments** [rydimɑ̃] *nmpl* : rudiments
rue [ry] *nf* : street
ruée [rɥe] *nf* : rush
ruelle [rɥɛl] *nf* : alley(way)
ruer [rɥe] *vi* : buck (of a horse) — **se ruer** *vr* **1 ~ sur** : fling oneself at **2 ~ vers** : rush toward
rugir [ryʒir] *vt* : bellow out — *vi* : roar — **rugissement** [ryʒismɑ̃] *nm* **1** : roar **2** : howling
ruine [rɥin] *nf* **1** : ruin **2 tomber en ~** : fall into ruin — **ruiner** [rɥine] *vt* **1** : ruin **2** DÉTRUIRE : wreck
ruisseau [rɥiso] *nm, pl* **-seaux** : stream, creek
ruisseler [rɥisle] {8} *vi* : stream, flood
rumeur [rymœr] *nf* : rumor
ruminer [rymine] *vt* : ponder — *vi* : brood
rupture [ryptyr] *nf* **1** : break, breaking **2** : breakup (of a relationship) **3** : breach (of contract)
rural, -rale [ryral] *adj, mpl* **-raux** [ryro] : rural
ruse [ryz] *nf* **1** : trick **2** : cunning — **rusé, -sée** [ryze] *adj* MALIN : cunning
russe [rys] *adj* : Russian — **~** *nm* : Russian (language)
rustique [rystik] *adj* : rustic
rythme [ritm] *nm* **1** : rhythm, beat **2** : rate, pace — **rythmique** [ritmik] *adj* : rhythmic, rhythmical

S

s [ɛs] *nm* : s, 19th letter of the alphabet
sa → **son**
sabbat [saba] *nm* : Sabbath
sable [sabl] *nm* **1** : sand **2 ~s mouvants** : quicksand — **sablé** [sable] *nm* : shortbread (cookie) — **sabler** [sable] *vt* : sand — **sablonneux, -neuse** [sablɔnø, -nøz] *adj* : sandy
saborder [sabɔrde] *vt* : scuttle (a ship)
sabot [sabo] *nm* **1** : clog, wooden shoe **2** : hoof
saboter [sabɔte] *vt* **1** : sabotage **2** : botch up — **sabotage** [sabɔtaʒ] *nm* : sabotage — **saboteur, -teuse** [sabɔtœr, -tøz] *n* : saboteur
sabre [sabr] *nm* : saber
sac [sak] *nm* **1** : sack, bag **2 ~ à dos** : backpack, knapsack **3 ~ à main** : handbag, purse
saccade [sakad] *nf* : jerk, jolt — **saccadé, -dée** [sakade] *adj* : jerky
saccager [sakaʒe] {17} *vt* **1** : sack **2** DÉVASTER : devastate, wreck
sacerdoce [sasɛrdɔs] *nm* **1** : priesthood **2** : vocation
sachet [saʃɛ] *nm* **1** : packet, small bag **2** : sachet
sacoche [sakɔʃ] *nf* : bag, satchel
sacrer [sakre] *vt* **1** : crown **2** : consecrate — **sacre** [sakr] *nm* **1** : coronation **2** : consecration — **sacré, -crée** [sakre] *adj* **1** : sacred, holy **2** *fam* : damned, heck of a — **sacrement** [sakrəmɑ̃] *nm* : sacrament
sacrifier [sakrifje] {96} *vt* : sacrifice — *vi* **~ à** : conform to — **se sacrifier** *vr* : sacrifice oneself — **sacrifice** [sakrifis] *nm* : sacrifice
sacrilège [sakrilɛʒ] *nm* : sacrilege — **~** *adj* : sacrilegious
sadique [sadik] *adj* : sadistic — **sadisme** [sadism] *nm* : sadism
safari [safari] *nm* : safari
sagace [sagas] *adj* : shrewd
sage [saʒ] *adj* **1** : wise **2** DOCILE : well-behaved — **~** *n* : wise person, sage — **sage–femme** [saʒfam] *nf, pl* **sages–femmes** : midwife — **sagesse** [saʒɛs] *nf* : wisdom
saigner [seɲe] *v* : bleed — **saignant, -gnante** [seɲɑ̃, -ɲɑ̃t] *adj* : rare, undercooked — **saignement** [seɲmɑ̃] *nm* : bleeding
saillir [sajir] {78} *vi* : project — **saillant, -lante** [sajɑ̃, -jɑ̃t] *adj* **1** : projecting **2** : salient — **saillie** [saji] *nf* **1** : projection **2 faire ~** : project
sain, saine [sɛ̃, sɛn] *adj* **1** : healthy, sound **2** : wholesome
saindoux [sɛ̃du] *nm* : lard
saint, sainte [sɛ̃, sɛ̃t] *adj* : holy — **~** *n* : saint
saisir [sezir] *vt* **1** : seize, grab **2** COMPRENDRE : grasp **3** IMPRESSIONNER : strike, impress **4** : enter (data) — **se saisir** *vr* **~ de** : seize — **saisie** [sezi] *nf* : seizure (of property) — **saisissant, -sante** [sezisɑ̃, -sɑ̃t] *adj* : striking
saison [sɛzɔ̃] *nf* : season — **saisonnier, -nière** [sɛzɔnje, -njɛr] *adj* : seasonal
salade [salad] *nf* : salad — **saladier** [saladje] *nm* : salad bowl

salaire [salɛr] *nm* : salary, wages — **salarié, -riée** [salarje] *n* : salaried employee
salaud [salo] *nm usu vulgar* : bastard
sale [sal] *adj* : dirty — **saleté** [salte] *nf* **1** : dirt **2** : dirtiness **3** *fam* : dirty trick
saler [sale] *vt* : salt — **salé, -lée** [sale] *adj* **1** : salty **2** : salted **3** *fam* : steep — **salière** [saljɛr] *nf* : saltshaker
salir [salir] *vt* : soil — **se salir** *vr* : get dirty
salive [saliv] *nf* : saliva
salle [sal] *nf* **1** : room **2** : auditorium, hall **3 ~ à manger** : dining room **4 ~ de bains** : bathroom
salon [salɔ̃] *nm* **1** : living room **2** : (beauty) salon **3** EXPOSITION : exhibition, show
salopette [salɔpɛt] *nf* : overalls *pl*
salubre [salybr] *adj* : healthy
saluer [salɥe] *vt* **1** : greet **2** : say goodbye to **3** : salute — **salut** [saly] *nm* **1** : greeting **2** : salute **3** : safety **4** : salvation **5 ~!** : hello!, good-bye! — **salutation** [salytasjɔ̃] *nf* : greeting
samedi [samdi] *nm* : Saturday
sanction [sɑ̃ksjɔ̃] *nf* : sanction — **sanctionner** [sɑ̃ksjɔne] *vt* **1** : sanction **2** : punish
sanctuaire [sɑ̃ktɥɛr] *nm* : sanctuary
sandale [sɑ̃dal] *nf* : sandal
sandwich [sɑ̃dwitʃ] *nm, pl* **-wiches** *or* **-wichs** [-witʃ] : sandwich
sang [sɑ̃] *nm* : blood — **sang-froid** [sɑ̃frwa] *nms & pl* **1** : composure, calm **2 de ~** : in cold blood — **sanglant, -glante** [sɑ̃glɑ̃, -glɑ̃t] *adj* **1** : bloody **2** : cruel
sangle [sɑ̃gl] *nf* : strap
sanglot [sɑ̃glo] *nm* : sob — **sangloter** [sɑ̃glɔte] *vi* : sob
sangsue [sɑ̃sy] *nf* : leech
sanguin, -guine [sɑ̃gɛ̃, -gin] *adj* **1** : blood **2** : sanguine
sanitaire [sanitɛr] *adj* **1** : sanitary **2** : health — **~s** *nmpl* : bathroom
sans [sɑ̃] *adv & prep* **1** : without **2 ~ que** : without
santé [sɑ̃te] *nf* **1** : health **2 à votre ~!** : to your health!, cheers!
saper [sape] *vt* MINER : undermine
sapeur-pompier [sapœrpɔ̃pje] *nm, pl* **sapeurs-pompiers** *France* : firefighter
saphir [safir] *nm* : sapphire
sapin [sapɛ̃] *nm* : fir
sarcastique [sarkastik] *adj* : sarcastic — **sarcasme** [sarkasm] *nm* : sarcasm
sarcler [sarkle] *vt* : weed
sardine [sardin] *nf* : sardine
satellite [satelit] *nm* : satellite
satin [satɛ̃] *nm* : satin
satire [satir] *nf* : satire — **satirique** [satirik] *adj* : satirical
satisfaire [satisfɛr] {42} *vt* : satisfy — *vi* **~ à** : satisfy — **se satisfaire** *vr* **~ de** : be content with — **satisfaction** [satisfaksjɔ̃] *nf* : satisfaction — **satisfaisant, -sante** [satisfəzɑ̃, -zɑ̃t] *adj* **1** : satisfactory **2** : satisfying — **satisfait, -faite** [satisfɛ, -fɛt] *adj* : satisfied
saturer [satyre] *vt* : saturate
Saturne [satyrn] *nf* : Saturn
sauce [sos] *nf* : sauce
saucisse [sosis] *nf* : sausage — **saucisson** [sosisɔ̃] *nm* : sausage, cold cut
sauf, sauve [sof, sov] *adj* : safe — **sauf** *prep* **1** : except (for), apart from **2 ~ si** : unless
sauge [soʒ] *nf* : sage (herb)
saugrenu, -nue [sogrəny] *adj* : preposterous
saule [sol] *nm* : willow
saumon [somɔ̃] *nm* : salmon
sauna [sona] *nm* : sauna
saupoudrer [sopudre] *vt* : sprinkle
saut [so] *nm* **1** : jump, leap **2 faire un ~ chez qqn** : drop in on s.o. — **sauter** [sote] *vt* **1** : jump over **2** OMETTRE : skip — *vi* **1** BONDIR : jump, leap **2** EXPLOSER : blow up — **sauterelle** [sotrɛl] *nf* : grasshopper — **sauteur, -teuse** [sotœr, -tøz] *n* : jumper — **sautiller** [sotije] *vi* : hop
sauvage [sovaʒ] *adj* **1** CRUEL : savage **2** : wild **3** FAROUCHE : shy — **~** *nmf* : savage — **sauvagerie** [sovaʒri] *nf* **1** : savagery **2** : unsociability
sauvegarde [sovgard] *nf* **1** : safeguard **2** : backup (of a computer file) — **sauvegarder** [sovgarde] *vt* **1** : safeguard **2** : save (a computer file)
sauver [sove] *vt* : save, rescue — **se sauver** *vr* **1** : escape **2** *fam* : leave, rush off — **sauve-qui-peut** [sovkipø] *nms & pl* : stampede, panic — **sauvetage** [sovtaʒ] *nm* : rescue — **sauveteur** [sovtœr] *nm* : rescuer, lifesaver — **sauvette** [sovɛt] **à la ~** *adv phr* : hastily — **sauveur** [sovœr] *nm* : savior
savant, -vante [savɑ̃, -vɑ̃t] *adj* : learned, scholarly — **~** *n* : scholar — **savant** *nm* : scientist
saveur [savœr] *nf* : flavor, savor
savoir [savwar] {79} *vt* **1** : know **2** : be able to, know how to — **~** *nm* **1** : learning, knowledge **2 à ~** : namely

— **savoir–faire** [savwarfɛr] *nms & pl* : know-how, expertise
savon [savɔ̃] *nm* : soap — **savonner** [savɔne] *vt* : soap (up), lather — **savonnette** [savɔnɛt] *nf* : bar of soap — **savonneux, -neuse** [savɔnø, -nøz] *adj* : soapy
savourer [savure] *vt* : savor — **savoureux, -reuse** [savurø, -røz] *adj* : savory, tasty
saxophone [saksɔfɔn] *nm* : saxophone
scandale [skɑ̃dal] *nf* **1** : scandal **2** SCÈNE : scene, row — **scandaleux, -leuse** [skɑ̃dalø, -løz] *adj* : scandalous — **scandaliser** [skɑ̃dalize] *vt* : scandalize
scandinave [skɑ̃dinav] *adj* : Scandinavian
scarabée [skarabe] *nm* : beetle
scarlatine [skarlatin] *nf* : scarlet fever
sceau [so] *nm* **1** : seal **2** : hallmark, stamp
scélérat, -rate [selera, -rat] *n* : villain
sceller [sele] *vt* : seal — **scellé** [sele] *nm* : seal
scène [sɛn] *nf* **1** : scene **2** : stage (in theater) — **scénario** [senarjo] *nm* : scenario
sceptique [sɛptik] *adj* : skeptical — **~** *nmf* : skeptic
schéma [ʃema] *nm* : diagram — **schématique** [ʃematik] *adj* : schematic
schisme [ʃism] *nm* : schism
scie [si] *nf* : saw
sciemment [sjamɑ̃] *adv* : knowingly
science [sjɑ̃s] *nf* **1** : science **2** SAVOIR : learning, knowledge — **scientifique** [sjɑ̃tifik] *adj* : scientific — **~** *nmf* : scientist
scier [sje] {96} *vt* : saw — **scierie** [siri] *nf* : sawmill
scinder [sɛ̃de] *vt* : split, divide — **se scinder** *vr* : be divided, split up
scintiller [sɛ̃tije] *vi* : sparkle — **scintillement** [sɛ̃tijmɑ̃] *nm* : sparkling, twinkling
scission [sisjɔ̃] *nf* : split
scolaire [skɔlɛr] *adj* : school — **scolarité** [skɔlarite] *nf* : schooling
score [skɔr] *nm* : score
scotch [skɔtʃ] *nm* : Scotch whiskey
scrupule [skrypyl] *nm* : scruple — **scrupuleux, -leuse** [skrypylø, -løz] *adj* : scrupulous
scruter [skryte] *vt* : scrutinize — **scrutin** [skrytɛ̃] *nm* **1** : ballot **2** : polls *pl*
sculpter [skylte] *vt* : sculpt, sculpture — **sculpteur** [skyltœr] *nm* : sculptor — **sculpture** [skyltyr] *nf* : sculpture
se [sə] (**s'** *before a vowel or mute h*) *pron* **1** : oneself, himself, herself, themselves, itself **2** : each other, one another
séance [seɑ̃s] *nf* **1** : session, meeting **2** : performance
seau [so] *nm, pl* **seaux** : bucket, pail
sec, sèche [sɛk, sɛʃ] *adj* **1** : dry **2** : dried (of fruit) **3** DUR : harsh, sharp — **sec** [sɛk] *adv* BRUSQUEMENT : abruptly, hard — **~** *nm* **1** : dryness **2 à ~** : dried up **3 à ~** *fam* : broke — **sèche–cheveux** [sɛʃʃəvø] *nms & pl* : hairdryer — **sécher** [seʃe] {87} *vt* **1** : dry **2** *France fam* : skip (a class, etc.) — *vi* : dry (up), dry out — **sécheresse** [sɛʃrɛs] *nf* **1** : drought **2** : dryness — **séchoir** [seʃwar] *nm* : dryer
second, -conde [səgɔ̃, -gɔ̃d] *adj & nmf* : second — **second** *nm* **1** : assistant, helper **2** : third floor — **secondaire** [səgɔ̃dɛr] *adj* : secondary — **seconde** [səgɔ̃d] *nf* : second — **seconder** [səgɔ̃de] *vt* : assist
secouer [səkwe] *vt* **1** : shake (one's head, etc.) **2** : shake off
secourir [səkurir] {23} *vt* **1** : help, aid **2** : rescue — **secouriste** [səkurist] *nmf* : first aid worker — **secours** [səkur] *nms & pl* **1** : help, aid **2 au ~!** : help! **3 de ~** : (for) emergency **4 premiers ~** : first aid **5 secours** *nmpl* : rescuers
secousse [səkus] *nf* **1** SACCADE : jolt, jerk **2** CHOC : shock **3** : tremor
secret, -crète [səkrɛ, -krɛt] *adj* : secret — **secret** *nm* **1** : secret **2** : secrecy
secrétaire [səkretɛr] *nmf* : secretary — **secrétariat** [səkretarjat] *nm* : secretary's office
sécréter [sekrete] {87} *vt* : secrete — **sécrétion** [-resjɔ̃] *nf* : secretion
secte [sɛkt] *nm* : sect
secteur [sɛktœr] *nm* : sector, area
section [sɛksjɔ̃] *nf* : section — **sectionner** [sɛksjɔne] *vt* **1** DIVISER : divide **2** : sever
séculaire [sekylɛr] *adj* : age-old
sécurité [sekyrite] *nf* **1** : security **2** : safety — **sécuriser** [sekyrize] *vt* : reassure
sédatif, -tive [sedatif, -tiv] *adj* : sedative — **sédatif** *nm* : sedative
sédentaire [sedɑ̃tɛr] *adj* : sedentary
sédiment [sedimɑ̃] *nm* : sediment
séduire [sedɥir] {49} *vt* **1** : seduce **2** : charm **3** : appeal to — **séducteur,**

-trice [sedyktœr, -tris] *adj* : seductive — ~ *n* : seducer — **séduction** [sedyksjɔ̃] *nf* **1** : seduction **2** : charm, appeal — **séduisant, -sante** [sedɥizɑ̃, -zɑ̃t] *adj* : seductive, attractive

segment [sɛgmɑ̃] *nm* : segment

ségrégation [segregasjɔ̃] *nf* : segregation

seigle [sɛgl] *nm* : rye

seigneur [sɛɲœr] *nm* **1** : lord **2 le Seigneur** : the Lord

sein [sɛ̃] *nm* **1** : breast, bosom **2 au ~ de** : within

séisme [seism] *nm* : earthquake

seize [sɛz] *adj* **1** : sixteen **2** : sixteenth (in dates) — ~ *nms & pl* : sixteen — **seizième** [sɛzjɛm] *adj & nmf & nm* : sixteenth

séjour [seʒur] *nm* : stay — **séjourner** [seʒurne] *vi* : stay (at a hotel, etc.)

sel [sɛl] *nm* : salt

sélection [selɛksjɔ̃] *nf* : selection — **sélectionner** [selɛksjɔne] *vt* : select, choose

selle [sɛl] *nf* : saddle

sellette [sɛlɛt] *nf* **être sur la ~** : be in the hot seat

selon [səlɔ̃] *prep* **1** : according to **2 ~ que** : depending on whether

semaine [səmɛn] *nf* : week

sémantique [semɑ̃tik] *adj* : semantic — ~ *nf* : semantics

sembler [sɑ̃ble] *vi* : seem — *v impers* **il semble que** : it seems that — **semblable** [sɑ̃blabl] *adj* **1** : similar, like **2** TEL : such — ~ *nmf* : fellow creature — **semblant** [sɑ̃blɑ̃] *nm* **1** : semblance, appearance **2 faire ~** : pretend

semelle [səmɛl] *nf* : sole

semer [səme] {52} *vt* **1** : sow, seed **2** RÉPANDRE : scatter — **semence** [səmɑ̃s] *nf* : seed

semestre [səmɛstr] *nm* : semester — **semestriel, -trielle** [səmɛstrijɛl] *adj* : semiannual

séminaire [seminɛr] *nm* **1** : seminary **2** : seminar

semi-remorque [səmirəmɔrk] *nm, pl* **semi-remorques** : semitrailer

semis [səmi] *nm* **1** : seedling **2** : seedbed

semonce [səmɔ̃s] *nf* RÉPRIMANDE : reprimand

semoule [səmul] *nf* : semolina

sénat [sena] *nm* : senate — **sénateur** [senatœr] *nm* : senator

sénile [senil] *adj* : senile — **sénilité** [senilite] *nf* : senility

sens [sɑ̃s] *nms & pl* **1** : sense **2** SIGNIFICATION : meaning **3** DIRECTION : direction, way **4 à mon ~** : in my opinion **5 ~ dessus dessous** : upside down

sensation [sɑ̃sasjɔ̃] *nf* : sensation — **sensationnel, -nelle** [sɑ̃sasjɔnɛl] *adj* : sensational

sensé, -sée [sɑ̃se] *adj* : sensible

sensibiliser [sɑ̃sibilize] *vt* **~ à** : make sensitive to — **sensibilité** [sɑ̃sibilite] *nf* : sensitivity — **sensible** [sɑ̃sibl] *adj* **1** : sensitive **2** APPRÉCIABLE : noticeable — **sensiblement** [sɑ̃sibləmɑ̃] *adv* **1** : noticeably **2** : approximately

sensoriel, -rielle [sɑ̃sɔrjɛl] *adj* : sensory

sensuel, -suelle [sɑ̃sɥɛl] *adj* : sensual, sensuous — **sensualité** [sɑ̃sɥalite] *nf* : sensuality

sentence [sɑ̃tɑ̃s] *nf* JUGEMENT : sentence

senteur [sɑ̃tœr] *nf* : scent

sentier [sɑ̃tje] *nm* : path

sentiment [sɑ̃timɑ̃] *nm* **1** : sentiment, feeling **2 recevez l'expression de mes ~s respectueux** : yours truly — **sentimental, -tale** [sɑ̃timɑ̃tal] *adj, mpl* **-taux** [-to] : sentimental — **sentimentalité** [-talite] *nf* : sentimentality

sentinelle [sɑ̃tinɛl] *nf* : sentinel

sentir [sɑ̃tir] {82} *vt* **1** : smell, taste **2** : feel **3** : appreciate **4** PRESSENTIR : sense — *vi* : smell — **se sentir** *vr* : feel (tired, sick, etc.)

seoir [swar] {80} *vi* **~ à** : suit

séparer [separe] *vt* **1** DÉTACHER : separate **2** : divide — **se séparer** *vr* **1** : separate **2 ~ de** : part with, be without — **séparation** [separasjɔ̃] *nf* : separation — **séparé, -rée** [separe] *adj* **1** : separate **2** : separated — **séparément** [separemɑ̃] *adv* : separately

sept [sɛt] *adj* **1** : seven **2** : seventh (in dates) — ~ *nms & pl* : seven

septante [sɛptɑ̃t] *adj Bel, Switz* **1** : seventy **2** : seventieth — ~ *nms & pl Bel, Switz* : seventy

septembre [sɛptɑ̃br] *nm* : September

septième [sɛtjɛm] *adj & nmf & nm* : seventh

sépulture [sepyltyr] *nf* TOMBE : grave

séquelle [sekɛl] *nf* **1** : consequence **2 ~s** *nfpl* : aftereffects

séquence [sekɑ̃s] *nf* : sequence

séquestrer [sekɛstre] *nm* : confine, sequester

serein, -reine [sərɛ̃, -rɛn] *adj* CALME

: serene, calm — **sérénité** [serenite] *nf* : serenity

sergent [sɛrʒɑ̃] *nm* : sergeant

série [seri] *nf* **1** : series **2** : set **3 de ~** : mass-produced, standard **4 fabrication en ~** : mass production

sérieux, -rieuse [serjø, -rjøz] *adj* : serious — **sérieux** *nm* **1** : seriousness **2 prendre au ~** : take seriously — **sérieusement** [serjøzmɑ̃] *adv* : seriously

serin [sərɛ̃] *nm* : canary

seringue [sərɛ̃g] *nf* : syringe

serment [sɛrmɑ̃] *nm* **1** : oath **2** : vow, promise

sermon [sɛrmɔ̃] *nm* : sermon

serpent [sɛrpɑ̃] *nm* **1** : snake **2 ~ à sonnettes** : rattlesnake — **serpenter** [sɛrpɑ̃te] *vi* : meander — **serpentin** [sɛrpɑ̃tɛ̃] *nm* : streamer

serre [sɛr] *nf* **1** : greenhouse, hothouse **2 ~s** *nfpl* : claws

serré, -rée [sere] *adj* **1** : tight **2** : crowded, cramped, dense

serrer [sere] *vt* **1** : squeeze, grip **2** : clench (one's fists, etc.) **3** : tighten (a knot, etc.) **4** : stay close to **5** : push closer together — **se serrer** *vr* **1** : huddle up **2** : tighten (up) **3 ~ la main** : shake hands

serrure [sɛryr] *nf* : lock — **serrurier** [sɛryrje] *nm* : locksmith

sérum [serɔm] *nm* : serum

serveur, -veuse [sɛrvœr, -vøz] *n* : waiter *m*, waitress *f* — **serveur** *nm* : (computer) server

serviable [sɛrvjabl] *adj* : helpful, obliging

service [sɛrvis] *nm* **1** : service **2** FAVEUR : favor **3** : serving, course **4** : department **5** : (coffee) set **6** : serve (in sports) **7 hors ~** : out of order

serviette [sɛrvjɛt] *nf* **1** : napkin **2** : towel **3** : briefcase **4 ~ hygiénique** : sanitary napkin

servir [sɛrvir] {81} *vt* **1** : serve **2** : wait on, attend to — *vi* **1** : be useful, serve **2 ~ de** : serve as — **se servir** *vr* **1** : serve oneself, help oneself **2 ~ de** : make use of

serviteur [sɛrvitœr] *nm* : servant

ses → **son**

session [sesjɔ̃] *nf* : session

seuil [sœj] *nm* : threshold

seul, seule [sœl] *adj* **1** : alone **2** : lonely **3** UNIQUE : only, sole — **~** *pron* : only one, single one — **seulement** [sœlmɑ̃] *adv* **1** : only **2** MÊME : even — **~** *conj* : but, only

sève [sɛv] *nf* : sap

sévère [sevɛr] *adj* : severe — **sévérité** [severite] *nf* : severity

sévir [sevir] *vi* **1** : rage **2 ~ contre** : punish

sevrer [səvre] *vt* : wean

sexe [sɛks] *nm* **1** : sex **2** : sex organs, genitals — **sexisme** [sɛksism] *nm* : sexism — **sexiste** [sɛksist] *adj & nmf* : sexist — **sexualité** [sɛksɥalite] *nf* : sexuality — **sexuel, sexuelle** [sɛksɥɛl] *adj* : sexual

seyant, seyante [sɛjɑ̃, -jɑ̃t] *adj* : becoming, flattering

shampooing [ʃɑ̃pwɛ̃] *nm* : shampoo

shérif [ʃerif] *nm* : sheriff

short [ʃɔrt] *nm* : shorts *pl*

si[1] [si] *adv* **1** TELLEMENT : so, such, as **2** : yes **3 ~ bien que** : with the result that, so

si[2] *conj* : if, whether

sida [sida] *nm* : AIDS

sidérer [sidere] {87} *vt fam* : stagger, amaze

sidérurgie [sideryrʒi] *nf* : steel industry

siècle [sjɛkl] *nm* : century

siège [sjɛʒ] *nm* **1** : seat **2** : siege **3** *or* **~ social** : headquarters — **siéger** [sjeʒe] {64} *vi* **1** : sit (in an assembly) **2** : have its headquarters

sien, sienne [sjɛ̃, sjɛn] *adj* : his, hers, its, one's — **~** *pron* **le sien, la sienne, les siens, les siennes** : his, hers, its, one's, theirs

sieste [sjɛst] *nf* : siesta, nap

siffler [sifle] *vt* **1** : whistle **2** : whistle for, whistle at **3** : boo — *vi* **1** : whistle **2** : hiss **3** : wheeze — **sifflement** [sifləmɑ̃] *nm* : whistling — **sifflet** [siflɛ] *nm* **1** : whistle **2 ~s** *nmpl* : boos — **siffloter** [siflɔte] *v* : whistle

sigle [sigl] *nm* : acronym

signaler [siɲale] *vt* **1** : signal **2** : point out — **se signaler** *vr* : distinguish oneself — **signal** [siɲal] *nm, pl* **-gnaux** [-ɲo] : signal — **signalement** [siɲalmɑ̃] *nm* : description — **signalisation** [siɲalizasjɔ̃] *nf* : signals *pl*, signs *pl*

signature [siɲatyr] *nf* **1** : signature **2** : signing

signe [siɲ] *nm* **1** : sign **2** : (punctuation) mark — **signer** [siɲe] *vt* : sign — **se signer** *vr* : cross oneself

signifier [siɲifje] {96} *vt* : signify, mean — **significatif, -tive** [siɲifikatif, -tiv] *adj* : significant — **signification** [siɲifikasjɔ̃] *nf* : significance, meaning

silence [silɑ̃s] *nm* **1** : silence **2** : rest

(in music) — **silencieux, -cieuse** [silɑ̃sjø, -sjøz] *adj* : silent, quiet — **silencieux** *nm* : muffler
silex [silɛks] *nm* : flint
silhouette [silwɛt] *nf* : silhouette, outline
silicium [silisjɔm] *nm* : silicon
sillage [sijaʒ] *nm* : wake (of a ship)
sillon [sijɔ̃] *nm* **1** : furrow **2** : groove (of a disc, etc.) — **sillonner** [sijɔne] *vt* **1** CREUSER : furrow **2** : crisscross
silo [silo] *nm* : silo
simagrée [simagre] *nf* **faire des ~s** : put on airs
similaire [similɛr] *adj* : similar — **similitude** [similityd] *nf* : similarity
simple [sɛ̃pl] *adj* **1** : simple **2** : mere **3 aller ~** : one-way ticket — **~** *nm* : singles (in tennis) — **simplement** [sɛ̃pləmɑ̃] *adv* : simply — **simplicité** [sɛ̃plisite] *nf* : simplicity — **simplifier** [sɛ̃plifje] {96} *vt* : simplify
simulacre [simylakr] *nm* : sham, pretense
simuler [simyle] *vt* : simulate — **simulation** [simylasjɔ̃] *nf* : simulation
simultané, -née [simyltane] *adj* : simultaneous
sincère [sɛ̃sɛr] *adj* : sincere — **sincèrement** [-sɛrmɑ̃] *adv* : sincerely — **sincérité** [sɛ̃serite] *nf* : sincerity
singe [sɛ̃ʒ] *nm* : monkey — **singer** [sɛ̃ʒe] {17} *vt* **1** IMITER : mimic **2** FEINDRE : feign — **singeries** [sɛ̃ʒri] *nfpl* : antics
singulariser [sɛ̃gylarize] *vt* : draw attention to — **se singulariser** *vr* : call attention to oneself
singularité [sɛ̃gylarite] *nf* : peculiarity
singulier, -lière [sɛ̃gylje, -ljɛr] *adj* : singular — **singulier** *nm* : singular (in grammar) — **singulièrement** [sɛ̃gyljɛrmɑ̃] *nm* **1** : strangely **2** NOTAMMENT : particularly
sinistre [sinistr] *adj* : sinister — **~** *nm* DÉSASTRE : disaster — **sinistré, -trée** [sinistre] *adj* : damaged, stricken — **~** *n* : disaster victim
sinon [sinɔ̃] *conj* **1** : or else **2** : if not **3 ~ que** : except that
sinueux, -nueuse [sinɥø, -nɥøz] *adj* : winding, meandering
siphon [sifɔ̃] *nm* : siphon
sirène [sirɛn] *nf* **1** : mermaid **2** : siren, alarm
sirop [siro] *nm* : syrup
siroter [sirɔte] *vt fam* : sip
sis, sise [si, siz] *adj* : located (in law)
site [sit] *nm* **1** : site **2** : setting
sitôt [sito] *adv* **1** : as soon as **2 ~ après** : immediately after
situer [sitɥe] *vt* : situate, locate — **situation** [sitɥasjɔ̃] *nf* **1** : situation **2 ~ de famille** : marital status
six [sis, *before consonant* si, *before vowel* siz] *adj* **1** : six **2** : sixth (in dates) — **~** *nms & pl* : six — **sixième** [sizjɛm] *adj & nmf & nm* : sixth
ski [ski] *nm* **1** : ski **2** : skiing **3 ~ nautique** : waterskiing — **skier** [skje] {96} *vi* : ski — **skieur, skieuse** [skjœr, skjøz] *n* : skier
slip [slip] *nm* **1** : briefs *pl* **2** : panties *pl*
smoking [smɔkiŋ] *nm* : tuxedo
snob [snɔb] *adj* : snobbish — **~** *nmf* : snob — **snober** [snɔbe] *vt* : snub — **snobisme** [snɔbism] *nm* : snobbery
sobre [sɔbr] *adj* : sober — **sobriété** [sɔbrijete] *nf* : sobriety
soccer [sɔkɛr] *nm Can* : soccer
sociable [sɔsjabl] *adj* : sociable
social, -ciale [sɔsjal] *adj, mpl* **-ciaux** [-sjo] : social — **socialisme** [sɔsjalism] *nm* : socialism — **socialiste** [-sjalist] *adj & nmf* : socialist — **société** [sɔsjete] *nf* **1** : society **2** COMPAGNIE : company, firm
sociologie [sɔsjɔlɔʒi] *nf* : sociology — **sociologique** [sɔsjɔlɔʒik] *adj* : sociological — **sociologue** [sɔsjɔlɔg] *nmf* : sociologist
socle [sɔkl] *nm* : base, pedestal
soda [sɔda] *nm* : soda, soft drink
sodium [sɔdjɔm] *nm* : sodium
sœur [sœr] *nf* **1** : sister **2** : nun
sofa [sɔfa] *nm* : sofa
soi [swa] *pron* : oneself, himself, herself, itself — **soi–disant** [swadizɑ̃] *adv* : supposedly — **~** *adj* : so-called
soie [swa] *nf* **1** : silk **2** : bristle
soif [swaf] *nf* **1** : thirst **2 avoir ~** : be thirsty
soigner [swaɲe] *vt* **1** : treat, nurse, look after **2** : do with care — **se soigner** *vr* : take care of oneself — **soigné, -gnée** [swaɲe] *adj* **1** : carefully done **2** : neat — **soigneux, -gneuse** [swaɲø, -ɲøz] *adj* **1** : careful **2** : neat, tidy
soi–même [swamɛm] *pron* : oneself
soin [swɛ̃] *nm* **1** : care **2 ~s** *nmpl* : care **3 premiers ~s** : first aid **4 prendre ~ de** : take care of
soir [swar] *nm* : evening, night — **soirée** [sware] *nf* **1** : evening **2** FÊTE : party
soit [swa] *adv* : so be it, very well — **~** *conj* **1** : that is, in other words **2 soit . . . soit . . .** : either . . . or . . .

soixante [swasɑ̃t] *adj & nms & pl* : sixty — **soixante–dix** [swasɑ̃tdis] *adj & nms & pl* : seventy — **soixante–dixième** [swasɑ̃tdizjɛm] *adj & nmf & nm* : seventieth — **soixantième** [swasɑ̃tjɛm] *adj & nmf & nm* : sixtieth
soja [sɔʒa] *nm* : soybean
sol [sɔl] *nm* **1** : ground, floor **2** PLANCHER : flooring **3** TERRE : soil
solaire [sɔlɛr] *adj* **1** : solar **2** : sun
soldat [sɔlda] *nm* : soldier
solde[1] [sɔld] *nf* : pay
solde[2] *nm* **1** : balance (in finance) **2** *or* **~s** *nmpl* : sale — **solder** [sɔlde] *vt* **1** : settle (an account, etc.) **2** : sell off, put on sale — **se solder** *vr* **~ par** : end in
sole [sɔl] *nf* : sole (fish)
soleil [sɔlɛj] *nm* **1** : sun **2** : sunshine, sunlight
solennel, -nelle [sɔlanɛl] *adj* **1** : solemn **2** : formal — **solennité** [sɔlanite] *nf* : solemnity
solidaire [sɔlidɛr] *adj* **1** : united **2** : interdependent — **solidarité** [sɔlidarite] *nf* : solidarity
solide [sɔlid] *adj* : solid — **~** *nm* : solid — **solidement** [sɔlidmɑ̃] *adv* : solidly — **solidifier** [sɔlidifje] {96} *v* **se solidifier** *vr* : solidify — **solidité** [sɔlidite] *nf* : solidity
solitaire [sɔlitɛr] *adj* : solitary — **~** *nmf* : loner, recluse — **~** *nm* : solitaire — **solitude** [sɔlityd] *nf* **1** : solitude **2** : loneliness
solliciter [sɔlisite] *vt* **1** : solicit, seek **2** : appeal to, approach — **sollicitude** [sɔlisityd] *nf* : solicitude, concern
solo [sɔlo] *nm, pl* **solos** *or* **soli** : solo
soluble [sɔlybl] *adj* : soluble — **solution** [sɔlysjɔ̃] *nf* : solution
solvable [sɔlvabl] *adj* : solvent
sombre [sɔ̃br] *adj* **1** OBSCUR : dark **2** TRISTE : gloomy
sombrer [sɔ̃bre] *vi* COULER : sink
sommaire [sɔmɛr] *adj* **1** : brief, concise **2** : summary — **~** *nm* : summary
somme[1] [sɔm] *nf* **1** : sum **2 en ~** : in short, all in all
somme[2] *nm* : short nap, catnap
sommeil [sɔmɛj] *nm* : sleep — **sommeiller** [sɔmɛje] *vi* **1** : doze **2** : lie dormant
sommer [sɔme] *vt* : summon
sommet [sɔmɛ] *nm* : summit, top
sommier [sɔmje] *nm* : base (of a bed), bedsprings *pl*
somnambule [sɔmnɑ̃byl] *nmf* : sleepwalker
somnifère [sɔmnifɛr] *nm* : sleeping pill
somnolence [sɔmnɔlɑ̃s] *nf* : drowsiness — **somnolent, -lente** [sɔmnɔlɑ̃, -lɑ̃t] *adj* : drowsy — **somnoler** [sɔmnɔle] *vi* : doze
somptueux, -tueuse [sɔ̃ptɥø, -tɥøz] *adj* : sumptuous
son[1], **sa** [sɔ̃, sa] *adj, pl* **ses** [se] : his, her, its, one's
son[2] *nm* **1** : sound **2** : volume **3** : (wheat) bran
sonde [sɔ̃d] *nf* **1** : probe **2** : sounding line — **sondage** [sɔ̃daʒ] *nm* : poll, survey — **sonder** [sɔ̃de] *vt* **1** : survey, poll **2** : sound, probe
songe [sɔ̃ʒ] *nm* : dream — **songer** [sɔ̃ʒe] {17} *vt* : consider, imagine — *vi* **1** : dream **2 ~ à** : think about — **songeur, -geuse** [sɔ̃ʒœr, -ʒøz] *adj* : pensive
sonner [sɔne] *v* **1** : ring **2** : strike, sound — **sonnant, -nante** [sɔnɑ̃, -nɑ̃t] *adj* **à cinq heures sonnantes** : at five o'clock sharp — **sonné, -née** [sɔne] *adj* **1** *fam* : groggy **2** *fam* : crazy, nuts **3 il est minuit sonné** : it's past midnight — **sonnerie** [sɔnri] *nf* **1** : ringing, ring **2** : alarm (bell)
sonnet [sɔnɛ] *nm* : sonnet
sonnette [sɔnɛt] *nf* : bell, doorbell
sonore [sɔnɔr] *adj* **1** : resonant **2** : sound — **sonorisation** [sɔnɔrizasjɔ̃] *nf* : sound system — **sonorité** [sɔnɔrite] *nf* **1** : tone **2** : resonance, acoustics
sophistiqué, -quée [sɔfistike] *adj* : sophisticated
soporifique [sɔpɔrifik] *adj* : soporific
soprano [sɔprano] *nmf* : soprano
sorbet [sɔrbɛ] *nm* : sorbet
sorcier, -cière [sɔrsje, -sjɛr] *n* : sorcerer, witch — **sorcellerie** [sɔrsɛlri] *nf* : sorcery, witchcraft
sordide [sɔrdid] *adj* **1** : sordid **2** : squalid
sornettes [sɔrnɛt] *nfpl* : nonsense
sort [sɔr] *nm* **1** : fate, lot **2** : spell, hex
sortant, -tante [sɔrtɑ̃, -tɑ̃t] *adj* : outgoing, resigning
sorte [sɔrt] *nf* **1** ESPÈCE : sort, kind **2 de ~ que** : so that **3 en quelque ~** : in a way
sortie [sɔrti] *nf* **1** : exit **2** DÉPART : departure **3** : launch, release (of a book, etc.) **4** EXCURSION : outing
sortilège [sɔrtilɛʒ] *nm* : spell
sortir [sɔrtir] {82} *vt* **1** : take out, bring out **2** : launch, release — *vi* **1** : go out, come out **2** PARTIR : leave, exit **3 ~ de** : come from, come out of — **se**

sortir *vr* **1 ~ de** : get out of **2 s'en sortir** : get by, pull through
sosie [sɔzi] *nm* : double
sot, sotte [so, sɔt] *adj* : foolish, silly — **~** *n* : fool — **sottise** [sɔtiz] *nf* **1** : foolishness **2** : foolish act or remark
sou [su] *nm* **être sans le ~** : be penniless
soubresaut [subrəso] *nm* : jolt, start
souche [suʃ] *nf* **1** : stump (of a tree) **2** : stock, descent
soucier [susje] {96} *v* **se soucier** *vr* : worry, be concerned — **souci** [susi] *nm* : worry, concern — **soucieux, -cieuse** [susjø, -sjøz] *adj* : anxious, concerned
soucoupe [sukup] *nf* **1** : saucer **2 ~ volante** : flying saucer
soudain, -daine [sudɛ̃, -dɛn] *adj* : sudden — **soudainement** [-dɛnmɑ̃] *adv* : suddenly
soude [sud] *nf* : soda
souder [sude] *vt* : weld, solder
soudoyer [sudwaje] {58} *vt* : bribe
soudure [sudyr] *nf* **1** : solder **2** : soldering
souffler [sufle] *vt* **1** : blow **2** ÉTEINDRE : blow out **3** CHUCHOTER : whisper — *vi* **1** : blow **2** HALETER : pant, puff — **souffle** [sufl] *nm* **1** : breath, breathing **2** : puff, gust — **soufflé** [sufle] *nm* : soufflé — **soufflet** [suflɛ] *nm* : bellows
souffrir [sufrir] {83} *vt* **1** SUPPORTER : tolerate **2** PERMETTRE : allow — *vi* : suffer — **souffrance** [sufrɑ̃s] *nf* **1** : suffering **2 en ~** : pending — **souffrant, -frante** [sufrɑ̃, -frɑ̃t] *adj* : unwell
soufre [sufr] *nm* : sulfur
souhait [swɛ] *nm* **1** : wish **2 à vos ~s!** : bless you! — **souhaitable** [swɛtabl] *adj* : desirable — **souhaiter** [swete] *vt* : wish, hope for
souiller [suje] *vt* : soil
soûl, soûle [su, sul] *adj* : drunk
soulager [sulaʒe] {17} *vt* : relieve — **soulagement** [sulaʒmɑ̃] *nm* : relief
soûler [sule] *vt* : make drunk, intoxicate — **se soûler** *vr* : get drunk
soulever [sulve] {52} *vt* **1** : lift, raise **2** PROVOQUER : stir up — **se soulever** *vr* **1** : rise up **2** : lift oneself up — **soulèvement** [sulɛvmɑ̃] *nm* : uprising
soulier [sulje] *nm* : shoe
souligner [suliɲe] *vt* **1** : underline **2** : emphasize
soumettre [sumɛtr] {53} *vt* **1** : subjugate **2** PRÉSENTER : submit **3 ~ à** : subject to — **se soumettre** *vr* : submit — **soumis, -mise** [sumi, -miz] *adj* : submissive — **soumission** [sumisjɔ̃] *nf* : submission
soupape [supap] *nf* : valve
soupçon [supsɔ̃] *nm* **1** : suspicion **2** : hint, touch — **soupçonner** [supsɔne] *vt* : suspect — **soupçonneux, -neuse** [supsɔnø, -nøz] *adj* : suspicious
soupe [sup] *nf* : soup
souper [supe] *vi Can* : have supper — **~** *nm Can* : supper
soupeser [supəze] {52} *vt* **1** : feel the weight of **2** PESER : weigh, consider
soupière [supjɛr] *nf* : tureen
soupirer [supire] *vi* : sigh — **soupir** [supir] *nm* : sigh
souple [supl] *adj* : supple, flexible — **souplesse** [suplɛs] *nf* : suppleness, flexibility
source [surs] *nf* **1** : source **2** : spring (of water)
sourcil [sursi] *nm* : eyebrow — **sourciller** [sursije] *vi* **sans ~** : without batting an eyelid — **sourcilleux, -leuse** [sursijø, -jøz] *adj* **1** : finicky **2** : supercilious
sourd, sourde [sur, surd] *adj* : deaf — **~** *nmf* : deaf person — **sourd–muet, sourde–muette** [surmɥɛ, surdmɥɛt] *n* : deaf-mute
sourdre [surdr] {84} *vi* MONTER : well up
sourire [surir] {76} *vi* : smile — **~** *nm* : smile — **souriant, -riante** [surjɑ̃, -rjɑ̃t] *adj* : smiling, cheerful
souris [suri] *nf* : mouse
sournois, -noise [surnwa, -nwaz] *adj* : sly, underhanded
sous [su] *prep* **1** : under, beneath **2** : during **3 ~ peu** : shortly
sous–alimenté, -tée [suzalimɑ̃te] *adj* : malnourished
sous–bois [subwa] *nms & pl* : undergrowth
souscrire [suskrir] {33} *vi* **~ à** : subscribe to — **souscription** [suskripsjɔ̃] *nf* : subscription
sous–développé, -pée [sudevlɔpe] *adj* : underdeveloped
sous–entendre [suzɑ̃tɑ̃dr] {63} *vt* : imply, infer — **sous–entendu** [suzɑ̃tɑ̃dy] *nm* : insinuation
sous–estimer [suzɛstime] *vt* : underestimate
sous–jacent, -cente [suʒasɑ̃, -sɑ̃t] *adj* : underlying
sous–louer [sulwe] *vt* : sublet
sous–marin, -rine [sumarɛ̃, -rin] *adj*

: underwater — **sous-marin** *nm* : submarine
sous-officier [suzɔfisje] *nm* : noncommissioned officer
sous-produit [suprɔdɥi] *nm* : by-product
sous-sol [susɔl] *nm* : basement, cellar
sous-titre [sutitr] *nm* : subtitle
soustraire [sustrɛr] {40} *vt* **1** : subtract **2** : remove, take away — **se soustraire** *vr* **~ à** : escape from — **soustraction** [sustraksjɔ̃] *nf* : subtraction
sous-vêtement [suvɛtmɑ̃] *nm* **1** : undergarment **2 ~s** *nmpl* : underwear
soutane [sutan] *nf* : cassock
soute [sut] *nf* : hold (of a ship)
soutenir [sutnir] {92} *vt* **1** MAINTENIR : support, hold up **2** RÉSISTER : withstand **3** : sustain — **soutenu, -nue** [sutny] *adj* **1** : formal **2** : sustained
souterrain, -raine [sutɛrɛ̃, -rɛn] *adj* : underground — **souterrain** *nm* : underground passage
soutien [sutjɛ̃] *nm* : support
soutien-gorge [sutjɛ̃gɔrʒ] *nm, pl* **soutiens-gorge** : bra, brassiere
soutirer [sutire] *vt* **~ à** : extract from
souvenir [suvnir] {92} *v* **se souvenir** *vr* **1 ~ de** : remember **2 ~ que** : remember that — **~** *nm* **1** : memory **2** : souvenir **3 mes meilleurs ~s à** : my best regards to
souvent [suvɑ̃] *adv* : often
souverain, -raine [suvrɛ̃, -rɛn] *adj* **1** : supreme **2** : sovereign — **~** *n* : sovereign — **souveraineté** [suvrɛnte] *nf* : sovereignty
soviétique [sɔvjetik] *adj* : Soviet
soyeux, soyeuse [swajø, swajøz] *adj* : silky
spacieux, -cieuse [spasjø, -sjøz] *adj* : spacious
spaghetti [spagɛti] *nmpl* : spaghetti
sparadrap [sparadra] *nm* : adhesive tape
spasme [spasm] *nm* : spasm
spatial, -tiale [spasjal] *adj, mpl* **-tiaux 1** : spatial **2 vaisseau spatial** : spaceship
speaker, -kerine [spikœr, -krin] *n France* : announcer (on radio, TV, etc.)
spécial, -ciale [spesjal] *adj, mpl* **-ciaux** [-sjo] **1** : special **2** BIZARRE : odd, peculiar — **spécialement** [spesjalmɑ̃] *adv* **1** EXPRÈS : specially **2** : especially — **spécialiser** [spesjalize] *v* **se spécialiser** *vr* : specialize — **spécialiste** [spesjalist] *nmf* : specialist — **spécialité** [spesjalite] *nf* : specialty
spécifier [spesifje] {96} *vt* : specify — **spécifique** [spesifik] *adj* : specific
spécimen [spesimɛn] *nm* : specimen
spectacle [spɛktakl] *nm* **1** : spectacle, sight **2** : show — **spectaculaire** [spɛktakylɛr] *adj* : spectacular — **spectateur, -trice** [spɛktatœr, -tris] *n* **1** : spectator **2** : observer, onlooker
spectre [spɛktr] *nm* **1** : specter, ghost **2** : spectrum
spéculer [spekyle] *vi* : speculate — **spéculation** [spekylasjɔ̃] *nf* : speculation
sperme [spɛrm] *nm* : sperm
sphère [sfɛr] *nf* : sphere — **sphérique** [sferik] *adj* : spherical
spirale [spiral] *nf* : spiral
spirituel, -tuelle [spiritɥɛl] *adj* : spiritual — **spiritualité** [spiritɥalite] *nf* : spirituality
splendeur [splɑ̃dœr] *nf* : splendor — **splendide** [splɑ̃did] *adj* : splendid
spongieux, -gieuse [spɔ̃ʒjø, -ʒjøz] *adj* : spongy
spontané, -née [spɔ̃tane] *adj* : spontaneous — **spontanéité** [spɔ̃taneite] *nf* : spontaneity — **spontanément** [-nemɑ̃] *adv* : spontaneously
sporadique [spɔradik] *adj* : sporadic
sport [spɔr] *adj* : sport, sports — **~** *nm* **1** : sport **2 ~s d'équipes** : team sports — **sportif, -tive** [spɔrtif, -tiv] *adj* **1** : sport, sports **2** : sportsmanlike **3** : athletic — **~** *n* : sportsman *m*, sportswoman *f*
spot [spɔt] *nm* **1** : spotlight **2** PUBLICITÉ : commercial
sprint [sprint] *nm* : sprint
square [skwar] *nm France* : small public garden
squelette [skəlɛt] *nm* : skeleton
stabiliser [stabilize] *vt* : stabilize — **stabilité** [stabilite] *nf* : stability — **stable** [stabl] *adj* : stable, steady
stade [stad] *nm* **1** : stadium **2** ÉTAPE : stage, phase
stage [staʒ] *nm* **1** : internship **2** : (training) course — **stagiaire** [staʒjɛr] *nmf* : trainee, intern
stagner [stagne] *vi* : stagnate — **stagnant, -gnante** [stagnɑ̃, -gnɑ̃t] *adj* : stagnant
stalle [stal] *nf* : stall
stand [stɑ̃d] *nm* **1** : stand, stall, booth **2 ~ de tir** : shooting range
standard [stɑ̃dar] *adj* : standard — **~** *nm* **1** : standard **2** : (telephone)

switchboard — **standardiste** [stɑ̃dardist] *nmf* : switchboard operator
standing [stɑ̃diŋ] *nm* : standing, status
star [star] *nf* VEDETTE : star
station [stasjɔ̃] *nf* **1** : station **2** ~ **d'autobus** : bus stop **3** ~ **balnéaire** : seaside resort — **stationnaire** [stasjɔnɛr] *adj* : stationary — **stationner** [stasjɔne] *vi* : park — **stationnement** [stasjɔnmɑ̃] *nm* : parking — **station–service** [stasjɔ̃sɛrvis] *nf, pl* **stations–service** : gas station, service station
statistique [statistik] *adj* : statistical — ~ *nf* **1** : statistic **2** : statistics
statue [staty] *nf* : statue
statuer [statɥe] *vi* : decree, ordain
stature [statyr] *nf* : stature
statut [staty] *nm* **1** : statute **2** : status — **statutaire** [statytɛr] *adj* : statutory
steak [stɛk] *nm* : steak
stéréo [stereo] *adj & nf* : stereo
stéréotype [stereɔtip] *nm* **1** : stereotype **2** : cliché
stérile [steril] *adj* : sterile — **stérilisation** [-lizasjɔ̃] *nf* : sterilization — **stériliser** [sterilize] *vt* : sterilize — **stérilité** [sterilite] *nf* : sterility
stéthoscope [stetɔskɔp] *nm* : stethoscope
stigmate [stigmat] *nm* : mark, stigma — **stigmatiser** [stigmatize] *vt* : stigmatize
stimuler [stimyle] *vt* : stimulate — **stimulation** [-mylasjɔ̃] *nf* : stimulation — **stimulant, -lante** [stimylɑ̃, -lɑ̃t] *adj* : stimulating — **stimulant** *nm* **1** : stimulant **2** : stimulus
stipuler [stipyle] *vt* : stipulate
stock [stɔk] *nm* : stock, goods — **stocker** [stɔke] *vt* : stock
stoïque [stɔik] *adj* : stoic, stoical — ~ *nmf* : stoic
stop [stɔp] *nm* **1** : stop sign **2** : brake light — ~ *interj* : stop — **stopper** [stɔpe] *vt* **1** : stop, halt **2** : mend — *vi* : stop
store [stɔr] *nm* **1** : awning **2** : blind, window shade
strapontin [strapɔ̃tɛ̃] *nm* : folding seat
stratagème [strataʒɛm] *nm* : stratagem — **stratégie** [strateʒi] *nf* : strategy — **stratégique** [strateʒik] *adj* : strategic
stress [strɛs] *nms & pl* : stress — **stressant, -sante** [strɛsɑ̃, -sɑ̃t] *adj* : stressful
strict, stricte [strikt] *adj* **1** : strict **2** : austere, plain
strident, -dente [stridɑ̃, -dɑ̃t] *adj* : strident, shrill
strier [strije] {96} *vt* : streak
strophe [strɔf] *nf* : stanza
structure [stryktyr] *nf* : structure — **structural, -rale** [stryktyral] *adj, mpl* **-raux** [-ro] : structural — **structurer** [stryktyre] *vt* : structure
studieux, -dieuse [stydjø, -djøz] *adj* : studious
studio [stydjo] *nm* **1** : studio **2** : studio apartment
stupéfier [stypefje] {96} *vt* : astonish, stun — **stupéfaction** [stypefaksjɔ̃] *nf* : astonishment — **stupéfait, -faite** [stypefɛ, -fɛt] *adj* : amazed, astounded — **stupéfiant, -fiante** [stypefjɑ̃, -fjɑ̃t] *adj* : amazing, astounding — **stupéfiant** *nm* : drug, narcotic
stupeur [stypœr] *nf* **1** : astonishment **2** : stupor
stupide [stypid] *adj* : stupid — **stupidité** [stypidite] *nf* : stupidity
style [stil] *nm* : style
stylo [stilo] *nm* **1** : pen **2** ~ **à bille** : ballpoint (pen)
suave [sɥav] *adj* **1** : sweet **2** : smooth, suave
subalterne [sybaltɛrn] *adj & nmf* : subordinate
subconscient, -ciente [sybkɔ̃sjɑ̃, -sjɑ̃t] *adj & nm* : subconscious
subdiviser [sybdivize] *vt* : subdivide
subir [sybir] *vt* **1** : undergo **2** : suffer **3** SUPPORTER : put up with **4** : take (an exam)
subit, -bite [sybi, -bit] *adj* : sudden — **subitement** [-bitmɑ̃] *adv* : suddenly
subjectif, -tive [sybʒɛktif, -tiv] *adj* : subjective — **subjectivité** [sybʒɛktivite] *nf* : subjectivity
subjonctif [sybʒɔ̃ktif] *nm* : subjunctive
subjuguer [sybʒuge] *vt* : captivate
sublime [syblim] *adj* : sublime
submerger [sybmɛrʒe] {17} *vt* **1** : submerge, flood **2** : overwhelm
subordonner [sybɔrdɔne] *vt* : subordinate — **subordonné, -née** [sybɔrdɔne] *adj & n* : subordinate
subreptice [sybrɛptis] *adj* : surreptitious
subséquent, -quente [sybsekɑ̃, -kɑ̃t] *adj* : subsequent
subside [sypsid] *nm* : grant, subsidy
subsidiaire [sybzidjɛr] *adj* : subsidiary
subsister [sybziste] *vi* **1** SURVIVRE : subsist, survive (on) **2** DURER : remain
substance [sypstɑ̃s] *nf* : substance —

substantiel, -tielle [sypstɑ̃sjɛl] *adj* : substantial
substantif [sypstɑ̃tif] *nm* : noun
substituer [sypstitɥe] *vt* : substitute — **se substituer** *vr* ~ **à** : substitute for, replace — **substitut** [sypstity] *nm* : substitute — **substitution** [sypstitysjɔ̃] *nf* : substitution
subterfuge [syptɛrfyʒ] *nm* : ploy, subterfuge
subtil, -tile [syptil] *adj* : subtle — **subtilité** [syptilite] *nf* : subtlety
subvenir [sybvənir] {92} *vi* ~ **à** : provide for, meet — **subvention** [sybvɑ̃sjɔ̃] *nf* : subsidy — **subventionner** [sybvɑ̃sjɔne] *vt* : subsidize
subversif, -sive [sybvɛrsif, -siv] *adj* : subversive — **subversion** [sybvɛrsjɔ̃] *nf* : subversion
suc [syk] *nm* **1** : juice **2** : sap
succédané [syksedane] *nm* : substitute
succéder [syksede] {87} *vi* ~ **à** : succeed, follow — **se succéder** *vr* : follow one another
succès [syksɛ] *nm* : success
successeur [syksesœr] *nm* : successor — **successif, -sive** [syksesif, -siv] *adj* : successive — **succession** [syksesjɔ̃] *nf* : succession
succinct, -cincte [sykse᷉, -sɛ̃t] *adj* : succinct
succion [syksjɔ̃, sysjɔ̃] *nf* : suction, sucking
succomber [sykɔ̃be] *vi* **1** : die **2** ~ **à** : succumb to
succulent, -lente [sykylɑ̃, -lɑ̃t] *adj* : succulent
succursale [sykyrsal] *nf* : branch (of a bank, etc.)
sucer [syse] {6} *vt* : suck
sucette [sysɛt] *nf* **1** : lollipop **2** : pacifier
sucre [sykr] *nm* : sugar — **sucré, -crée** [sykre] *adj* : sweet, sweetened — **sucrer** [sykre] *vt* : sweeten, add sugar to
sud [syd] *adj* : south, southern, southerly — ~ *nm* **1** : south **2 le Sud** : the South
sud–africain, -caine [sydafrikɛ̃, -kɛn] *adj* : South African
sud–américain, -caine [sydamerikɛ̃, -kɛn] *adj* : South American
sud–est [sydɛst] *adj s & pl* : southeast, southeastern — ~ *nm* : southeast
sud–ouest [sydwɛst] *adj s & pl* : southwest, southwestern — ~ *nm* : southwest
suédois, -doise [sɥedwa, -dwaz] *adj* : Swedish — **suédois** *nm* : Swedish (language)
suer [sɥe] *vi* : sweat — *vt* : sweat, ooze — **sueur** [sɥœr] *nf* : sweat
suffire [syfir] {86} *vi* : suffice — **se suffire** *vr or* ~ **à soi–même** : be self-sufficient — **suffisamment** [syfizamɑ̃] *adv* : sufficiently — **suffisance** [syfizɑ̃s] *nf* : self-importance — **suffisant, -sante** [syfizɑ̃, -zɑ̃t] *adj* **1** : sufficient **2** : conceited
suffixe [syfiks] *nm* : suffix
suffoquer [syfɔke] *v* : suffocate, choke
suffrage [syfraʒ] *nm* : suffrage, vote
suggérer [sygʒere] {86} *vt* : suggest — **suggestion** [sygʒɛstjɔ̃] *nf* : suggestion
suicide [sɥisid] *nm* : suicide — **suicider** [sɥiside] *v* **se suicider** *vr* : commit suicide
suie [sɥi] *nf* : soot
suinter [sɥɛ̃te] *vi* : ooze, seep
suisse [sɥis] *adj* : Swiss
suite [sɥit] *nf* **1** : suite **2** : continuation, sequel **3** SÉRIE : series, sequence **4** CONSÉQUENCE : result **5 par la** ~ : later, afterwards **6 par** ~ **de** : due to, as a result of
suivre [sɥivr] {88} *vt* **1** : follow **2** : take (a course) **3** : keep up with — *vi* **1** : follow **2** : keep up **3 faire** ~ : forward (mail) — **se suivre** *vr* : follow one another — **suivant, -vante** [sɥivɑ̃, -vɑ̃t] *adj* : following, next — ~ *n* : next one, following one — **suivant** *prep* : according to — **suivi, -vie** [sɥivi] *adj* **1** : regular, steady **2** : coherent
sujet, -jette [syʒɛ, -ʒɛt] *adj* ~ **à** : subject to, prone to — ~ *n* : subject (of a state or country) — **sujet** *nm* **1** : subject, topic **2** RAISON : cause
summum [sɔmɔm] *nm* : height, peak
super [sypɛr] *adj s & pl fam* : great, super
superbe [sypɛrb] *adj* : superb
supercherie [sypɛrʃəri] *nf* TROMPERIE : deception
superficie [sypɛrfisi] *nf* : area, surface — **superficiel, -cielle** [sypɛrfisjɛl] *adj* : superficial
superflu, -flue [sypɛrfly] *adj* : superfluous
supérieur, -rieure [syperjœr] *adj* **1** : superior **2** : upper, top **3** ~ **à** : higher than — ~ *n* : superior — **supériorité** [syperjɔrite] *nf* : superiority
superlative [sypɛrlatif] *nm* : superlative

supermarché [sypɛrmarʃe] *nm* : supermarket
superstitieux, -tieuse [sypɛrstisjø, -sjøz] *adj* : superstitious — **superstition** [sypɛrstisjɔ̃] *nf* : superstition
superviser [sypɛrvize] *vt* : supervise
supplanter [syplɑ̃te] *vt* : supplant
suppléer [syplee] {89} *vt* **1** REMPLACER : replace, fill in for **2** : supplement — *vi* ∼ **à** : make up for — **suppléant, -pléante** [sypleɑ̃, -pleɑ̃t] *adj & n* : substitute, replacement
supplément [syplemɑ̃] *nm* **1** : supplement **2** : extra charge — **supplémentaire** [syplemɑ̃tɛr] *adj* : additional, extra
supplication [syplikasjɔ̃] *nf* : plea
supplice [syplis] *nm* : torture — **supplicier** [syplisje] {96} *vt* TORTURER : torture
supplier [syplije] {96} *vt* : implore, beg
supporter[1] [sypɔrte] *vt* **1** SOUTENIR : support, hold up **2** ENDURER : tolerate, bear — **support** [sypɔr] *nm* : support, prop — **supportable** [sypɔrtabl] *adj* : bearable, tolerable
supporter[2] [sypɔrtɛr] *nm* : supporter, fan
supposer [sypoze] *vt* **1** : suppose, assume **2** IMPLIQUER : imply — **supposition** [sypozisjɔ̃] *nf* : supposition
suppositoire [sypozitwar] *nm* : suppository
supprimer [syprime] *vt* **1** : abolish **2** : take out, delete — **suppression** [syprɛsjɔ̃] *nf* **1** : removal, elimination **2** : deletion
suppurer [sypyre] *vi* : fester
suprême [syprɛm] *adj* : supreme — **suprématie** [sypremasi] *nf* : supremacy
sur[1] [syr] *prep* **1** : on, upon **2** : over, above **3** : about, on **4** PARMI : out of **5** : by (in measurements)
sur[2]**, sure** [syr] *adj* : sour
sûr, sûre [syr] *adj* **1** CERTAIN : sure, certain **2** FIABLE : reliable **3** : safe, secure **4** : sound **5** ∼ **de soi** : self-confident
surabondance [syrabɔ̃dɑ̃s] *nf* : overabundance
suranné, -née [syrane] *adj* : outdated
surcharger [syrʃarʒe] {17} *vt* **1** : overload **2** : alter — **surcharge** [syrʃarʒ] *nf* : overload
surchauffer [syrʃofe] *vt* : overheat
surclasser [syrklase] *vt* : outclass
surcroît [syrkrwa] *nm* **1** : increase **2** **de** ∼ : in addition
surdité [syrdite] *nf* : deafness
surélever [syrelve] {52} *vt* : raise, heighten
sûrement [syrmɑ̃] *adv* **1** : surely **2** : safely **3** ∼ **pas** : certainly not
surenchérir [syrɑ̃ʃerir] *vi* : bid higher
surestimer [syrɛstime] *vt* : overestimate, overrate
sûreté [syrte] *nf* **1** SÉCURITÉ : safety **2** : surety, guarantee (in law)
surexcité, -tée [syrɛksite] *adj* : overexcited
surf [sœrf] *nm* : surfing
surface [syrfas] *nf* : surface
surgelé [syrʒəle] *adj* : frozen (of food)
surgir [syrʒir] *vi* : appear suddenly, arise
surhumain, -maine [syrymɛ̃, -mɛn] *adj* : superhuman
sur-le-champ [syrləʃɑ̃] *adv* : immediately
surlendemain [syrlɑ̃dmɛ̃] *nm* **le** ∼ : two days later
surmener [syrməne] {52} *vt* : overwork — **surmenage** [syrmənaʒ] *nm* : overwork
surmonter [syrmɔ̃te] *vt* **1** : overcome **2** : surmount, top
surnager [syrnaʒe] {17} *vi* : float
surnaturel, -relle [syrnatyrɛl] *adj & nm* : supernatural
surnom [syrnɔ̃] *nm* : nickname
surnombre [syrnɔ̃br] *nm* **en** ∼ : excess, too many
surnommer [syrnɔme] *vt* : nickname
surpasser [syrpase] *vt* : surpass, outdo
surpeuplé, -plée [syrpœple] *adj* : overpopulated
surplomber [syrplɔ̃be] *v* : overhang
surplus [syrply] *nm* : surplus
surprendre [syrprɑ̃dr] {70} *vt* **1** ÉTONNER : surprise **2** : catch, take by surprise **3** : overhear — **surprenant, -nante** [syrprənɑ̃, -nɑ̃t] *adj* : surprising — **surprise** [syrpriz] *nf* : surprise
sursaut [syrso] *nm* : start, jump — **sursauter** [syrsote] *vi* : start, jump
surseoir [syrswar] {90} *vi* ∼ **à** : postpone, defer
sursis [syrsi] *nm* : reprieve
surtaxe [syrtaks] *nf* : surcharge
surtout [syrtu] *adv* **1** : above all **2** : especially, particularly
surveiller [syrvɛje] *vt* **1** : watch (over) **2** : supervise — **surveillance** [syrvɛjɑ̃s] *nf* **1** : supervision **2** : watch, surveillance — **surveillant, -lante** [syrvɛjɑ̃, -jɑ̃t] *n* **1** : supervisor, overseer **2** ∼ **de prison** : prison guard

survenir [syrvənir] {92} *vi* : occur, take place

survivre [syrvivr] {98} *vi* **1** : survive **2** ~ **à** : outlive — **survie** [syrvi] *nf* : survival — **survivant, -vante** [syrvivɑ̃, -vɑ̃t] *n* : survivor

survoler [syrvɔle] *vi* **1** : fly over **2** : skim through

sus [sy(s)] *adv* **1 en** ~ : extra **2 en** ~ **de** : in addition to

susceptible [sysɛptibl] *adj* **1** : sensitive, touchy **2** ~ **de** : likely to — **susceptibilité** [sysɛptibilite] *nf* : susceptibility

susciter [sysite] *vt* : arouse, give rise to

suspect, -pecte [syspɛ, -pɛkt] *adj* : suspicious, suspect — ~ *n* : suspect — **suspecter** [syspɛkte] *vt* : suspect

suspendre [syspɑ̃dr] {63} *vt* **1** INTERROMPRE : suspend, interrupt **2** PENDRE : hang up — **se suspendre** *vr* ~ **à** : hang from — **suspens** [syspɑ̃] *nm* **en** ~ : unresolved, uncertain

suspense [syspɑ̃s] *nm* : suspense

suspicion [syspisjɔ̃] *nf* : suspicion

suture [sytyr] *nf* **1** : suture **2 point de** ~ : stitch

svelte [zvɛlt] *adj* : slender, svelte

syllabe [silab] *nf* : syllable

symbole [sɛ̃bɔl] *nm* : symbol — **symbolique** [sɛ̃bɔlik] *adj* : symbolic — **symboliser** [sɛ̃bɔlize] *vt* : symbolize — **symbolisme** [sɛ̃bɔlism] *nm* : symbolism

symétrie [simetri] *nf* : symmetry — **symétrique** [simetrik] *adj* : symmetrical, symmetric

sympathie [sɛ̃pati] *nf* **1** : liking **2** CONDOLÉANCES : condolences — **sympathique** [sɛ̃patik] *adj* : nice, likeable — **sympathiser** [sɛ̃patize] *vi* ~ **avec** : get along with

symphonie [sɛ̃fɔni] *nf* : symphony — **symphonique** [sɛ̃fɔnik] *adj* : symphonic

symptôme [sɛ̃ptom] *nm* : symptom

synagogue [sinagɔg] *nf* : synagogue

syndicat [sɛ̃dika] *nm* : union, labor union — **syndiquer** [sɛ̃dike] *vt* : unionize — **se syndiquer** *vr* : join a union

syndrome [sɛ̃drom] *nm* : syndrome

synonyme [sinɔnim] *nm* : synonym — ~ *adj* : synonymous

syntaxe [sɛ̃taks] *nf* : syntax

synthèse [sɛ̃tɛz] *nf* : synthesis — **synthétique** [sɛ̃tetik] *adj* : synthetic

système [sistɛm] *nm* : system — **systématique** [sistematik] *adj* : systematic

T

t [te] *nm* : t, 20th letter of the alphabet

tabac [taba] *nm* **1** : tobacco **2** ~ **à priser** : snuff **3** *France* : tobacco shop

table [tabl] *nf* **1** : table **2 se mettre à** ~ : sit down to eat **3** ~ **de matières** : table of contents

tableau [tablo] *nm, pl* **-leaux 1** PEINTURE : painting **2** : picture, scene **3** : table, chart **4** ~ **d'affichage** : bulletin board **5** ~ **de bord** : dashboard **6** ~ **noir** : blackboard

tabler [table] *vt* ~ **sur** : count on

tablette [tablɛt] *nf* **1** : shelf **2** : bar (of candy), stick (of gum)

tablier [tablije] *nm* : apron

tabou, -boue [tabu] *adj* : taboo — **tabou** *nm* : taboo

tabouret [taburɛ] *nm* : stool

tache [taʃ] *nf* **1** : stain, spot **2** ~ **de rousseur** : freckle — **tacher** [taʃe] *vt* SALIR : stain, spot

tâche [taʃ] *nf* : task — **tâcher** [taʃe] *vi* ~ **de** : try to

tacheté [taʃte] *adj* : speckled

tacite [tasit] *adj* : tacit

tact [takt] *nm* : tact

tactique [taktik] *adj* : tactical — ~ *nf* STRATÉGIE : tactics *pl*

taie [tɛ] *nf or* ~ **d'oreiller** : pillowcase

tailler [taje] *vt* **1** : cut, prune, trim **2** : sharpen (a pencil) — **taille** [taj] *nf* **1** : cutting, pruning **2** : size (of clothing, etc.) **3** HAUTEUR : height **4** : waist — **tailleur** [tajœr] *nm* **1** : woman's suit **2** : tailor

taire [tɛr] {91} *vt* : hush up, keep secret — **se taire** *vr* **1** : be quiet **2** : fall silent

talc [talk] *nm* : talcum powder

talent [talɑ̃] *nm* : talent — **talentueux, -tueuse** [talɑ̃tɥø, -tɥøz] *adj* : talented

talon [talɔ̃] *nm* **1** : heel **2** : stub (of a check) — **talonner** [talɔne] *vt* **1** : follow closely **2** : harass

talus [taly] *nms & pl* : embankment, slope

tambour [tɑ̃bur] *nm* : drum — **tambouriner** [tɑ̃burine] *vt* : drum

tamia [tamja] *nm* : chipmunk
tamis [tami] *nms & pl* : sieve, sifter — **tamiser** [tamize] *vt* **1** : sift **2** : filter
tampon [tɑ̃pɔ̃] *nm* **1** BOUCHON : plug **2** : buffer (of a railway car) **3** : rubber stamp **4 ~ encreur** : ink pad **5 ~ hygiénique** : tampon — **tamponner** [tɑ̃pɔne] *vt* **1** : dab **2** HEURTER : crash into **3** : stamp (a document)
tandis [tɑ̃di] **~ que** *conj phr* **1** : while **2** : whereas
tangente [tɑ̃ʒɑ̃t] *nf* : tangent
tangible [tɑ̃ʒibl] *adj* : tangible
tango [tɑ̃go] *nm* : tango
tanguer [tɑ̃ge] *vi* : pitch (of a ship, etc.)
tanière [tanjɛr] *nf* : lair, den
tanner [tane] *vt* **1** : tan (leather, etc.) **2** *fam* : pester, annoy
tant [tɑ̃] *adv* **1** : so much, so many **2 en ~ que** : as, in so far as **3 ~ mieux!** : so much the better! **4 ~ pis!** : too bad! **5 ~ que** : as much as, as long as
tante [tɑ̃t] *nf* : aunt
tantôt [tɑ̃to] *adv* **1** : sometimes **2** *Can* : later **3** *France* : this afternoon
tapage [tapaʒ] *nm* **1** : uproar, din **2** SCANDALE : scandal — **tapageur, -geuse** [tapaʒœr, -ʒøz] *adj* **1** : rowdy **2** TAPE-À-L'ŒIL: flashy
tape [tap] *nf* : slap — **tape–à–l'œil** [tapalœj] *adj* : flashy
taper [tape] *vt* **1** : hit, slap **2** : type — *vi* **1** : hit, bang **2** : beat down (of the sun)
tapir [tapir] *v* **se tapir** *vr* : crouch
tapis [tapi] *nms & pl* **1** : carpet **2 ~ roulant** : moving walkway, conveyor belt — **tapisser** [tapise] *vt* **1** : wallpaper **2 ~ de** : cover with — **tapisserie** [tapisri] *nf* **1** : tapestry **2** : wallpaper
tapoter [tapɔte] *vt* : tap, pat
taquiner [takine] *vt* : tease — **taquinerie** [takinri] *nf* : teasing
tarabiscoté, -tée [tarabiskɔte] *adj* : fussy, overelaborate
tard [tar] *adv* : late — **tarder** [tarde] *vi* : take a long time — **tardif, -dive** [tardif, -div] *adj* : late
tare [tar] *nf* DÉFAUT : defect
tarif [tarif] *nm* **1** : rate, fare **2** : price, schedule of prices **3 ~ douanier** : tariff, customs duty
tarir [tarir] *v* : dry up
tarte [tart] *nf* : tart, pie
tartine [tartin] *nf* : slice of bread (and butter) — **tartiner** [tartine] *vt* : spread (with butter, etc.)
tartre [tartr] *nm* : tartar
tas [ta] *nms & pl* **1** : heap, pile **2 des ~ de** : a lot of, piles of
tasse [tas] *nf* : cup
tasser [tase] *vt* **1** : pack down **2** ENTASSER : cram, squeeze **3** *Can* : move over — **se tasser** *vr* **1** : shrink **2** : cram (into a car)
tâter [tate] *vt* **1** : feel **2 ~ le terrain** : check out the lay of the land — *vi* **~ de** : try one's hand at
tatillon, -lonne [tatijɔ̃, -jɔn] *adj* : fussy, finicky
tâtonner [tatɔne] *vi* : grope about — **tâtons** [tatɔ̃] **à ~** *adv phr* **avancer à ~** : feel one's way
tatouer [tatwe] *vt* : tattoo — **tatouage** [tatwaʒ] *nm* **1** : tattoo **2** : tattooing
taudis [todi] *nms & pl* : hovel, slum
taule [tol] *nf fam* : prison
taupe [top] *nf* : mole
taureau [tɔro] *nm, pl* **-reaux** : bull
taux [to] *nms & pl* **1** : rate **2** : level **3 ~ de change** : exchange rate **4 ~ de cholestérol** : cholesterol level
taverne [tavɛrn] *nf* : inn, tavern
taxe [taks] *nf* : tax — **taxer** [takse] *vt* : tax
taxi [taksi] *nm* : taxi, taxicab
te [tə] (**t'** *before a vowel or mute h*) *pron* **1** : you, to you **2** (*used as a reflexive pronoun*) : yourself
technique [tɛknik] *nf* : technique — **~** *adj* : technical — **technicien, -cienne** [tɛknisjɛ̃, -sjɛn] *n* : technician
technologie [tɛknɔlɔʒi] *nf* : technology — **technologique** [tɛknɔlɔʒik] *adj* : technological
tee–shirt [tiʃœrt] *nm, pl* **tee–shirts** : T-shirt
teindre [tɛ̃dr] {37} *vt* : dye — **teint** [tɛ̃] *nm* : complexion — **teinte** [tɛ̃t] *nf* **1** : shade, hue **2 une ~ de** : a tinge of — **teinter** [tɛ̃te] *vt* : tint, stain — **teinture** [tɛ̃tyr] *nf* **1** : dye **2** : dyeing — **teinturerie** [tɛ̃tyrri] *nf* **1** : dyeing **2** : dry cleaner's — **teinturier, -rière** [tɛ̃tyrje, -rjɛr] *n* : dry cleaner
tel, telle [tɛl] *adj* **1** : such **2** : such and such, a certain **3 ~ que** : such as, like **4 tel quel** : as (it) is — **~** *pron* **1** : a certain one, someone **2 un tel, une telle** : so-and-so
télé [tele] *nf fam* : TV
télécommande [telekɔmɑ̃d] *nf* : remote control
télécommunication [telekɔmynikasjɔ̃] *nf* : telecommunication
télécopie [telekɔpi] *nf* : fax — **télé-**

copieur [telekɔpjœr] *nm* : fax machine
télégramme [telegram] *nm* : telegram
télégraphe [telegraf] *nm* : telegraph
téléphone [telefɔn] *nm* : telephone — **téléphoner** [telefɔne] *vt* : telephone, call — **téléphonique** [telefɔnik] *adj* : telephone
télescope [teleskɔp] *nm* : telescope — **télescoper** [teleskɔpe] *v* **se télescoper** *vr* **1** : collide **2** : overlap — **télescopique** [teleskɔpik] *adj* : telescopic
télésiège [telesjɛʒ] *nm* : chairlift
téléski [teleski] *nm* : ski lift
téléviser [televize] *vt* : televise — **téléviseur** [televizœr] *nm* : television set — **télévision** [televizjɔ̃] *nf* **1** : television **2** TÉLÉVISEUR : television set
tellement [tɛlmɑ̃] *adv* **1** : so, so much **2 ~ de** : so many, so much
téméraire [temerɛr] *adj* : rash, reckless — **témérité** [temerite] *nf* : rashness, recklessness
témoin [temwɛ̃] *nm* **1** : witness **2** : baton (in a relay race) — **témoignage** [temwaɲaʒ] *nm* **1** RÉCIT : account, story **2** : testimony (in court) **3** PREUVE : evidence — **témoigner** [temwaɲe] *vt* **1** : testify, attest **2** MONTRER : show — *vi* : testify
tempe [tɑ̃p] *nf* : temple
tempérament [tɑ̃peramɑ̃] *nm* CARACTÈRE : temperament
température [tɑ̃peratyr] *nf* : temperature
tempéré, -rée [tɑ̃pere] *adj* : temperate
tempête [tɑ̃pɛt] *nf* : storm
temple [tɑ̃pl] *nm* **1** : temple **2** : (protestant) church
temporaire [tɑ̃pɔrɛr] *adj* : temporary
temporel, -relle [tɑ̃pɔrɛl] *adj* : temporal, worldly
temps [tɑ̃] *nms & pl* **1** : time **2** : weather **3** : tense (in grammar) **4 à plein ~** : full-time **5 de ~ à autre** : from time to time **6 quel ~ fait-il?** : what's the weather like?
tenace [tənas] *adj* : tenacious, stubborn — **tenacité** [tənasite] *nf* : tenacity
tenailles [tənaj] *nfpl* : pincers, tongs
tendance [tɑ̃dɑ̃s] *nf* **1** : tendency **2** COURANT : trend
tendon [tɑ̃dɔ̃] *nm* : tendon, sinew
tendre[1] [tɑ̃dr] {63} *vt* **1** : tense, tighten (a rope, etc.) **2 ~ la main** : hold out one's hand **3 ~ un piège à** : set a trap for — *vi* **1 ~ à** : tend to **2 ~ vers** : strive for — **se tendre** *vr* **1** : tighten **2** : become strained — **tendu, -due** [tɑ̃dy] *adj* **1** : tight, taut **2** : tense, strained **3** : outstretched (of a hand)
tendre[2] *adj* **1** : tender, soft **2** : gentle, loving — **tendresse** [tɑ̃drɛs] *nf* : tenderness, affection
ténèbres [tenɛbr] *nfpl* : darkness — **ténébreux, -breuse** [tenebrø, -brøz] *adj* OBSCUR : dark
teneur [tənœr] *nf* : content
tenir [tənir] {92} *vt* **1** : hold, keep **2** : have, catch **3** : run, manage (a hotel, store, etc.) **4** : take up (a space) **5** CONSIDÉRER : hold, regard — *vi* **1** : hold, stay in place **2** DURER : hold up, last **3** : fit (into a space) **4 ~ à** : be fond of **5 ~ à** : be anxious to **6 ~ de** : take after — *v impers* : depend — **se tenir** *vr* **1** : hold, hold up, hold onto **2** RESTER : remain **3** : behave (oneself) **4 ~ debout** : stand still
tennis [tenis] *nm* **1** : tennis **2 ~** *nmpl France* : sneakers
ténor [tenɔr] *nm* : tenor
tension [tɑ̃sjɔ̃] *nf* : tension
tentacule [tɑ̃takyl] *nm* : tentacle
tentation [tɑ̃tasjɔ̃] *nf* : temptation
tentative [tɑ̃tativ] *nf* : attempt
tente [tɑ̃t] *nf* : tent
tenter [tɑ̃te] *vt* **1** : tempt **2** ESSAYER : attempt
tenu, -nue [təny] *adj* **1** : obliged **2 bien ~** : well-kept, tidy
ténu, -nue [teny] *adj* : tenuous
tenue *nf* **1** : conduct, manners *pl* **2** MAINTIEN : posture **3** : clothes *pl*, dress **4 ~ de livres** : bookkeeping
terme [tɛrm] *nm* **1** : term, word **2** ÉCHÉANCE : deadline **3 mettre un ~ à** : put an end to
terminer [tɛrmine] *v* FINIR : finish — **se terminer** *vr* : end — **terminaison** [tɛrminɛzɔ̃] *nf* : ending — **terminal, -nale** [tɛrminal] *adj, mpl* **-naux** [-no] : final, terminal — **terminal** *nm, pl* **-naux** : terminal
terminologie [tɛrminɔlɔʒi] *nf* : terminology
terminus [tɛrminys] *nms & pl* : terminus
terne [tɛrn] *adj* **1** FADE : drab **2** ENNUYEUX : dull
ternir [tɛrnir] *vt* : tarnish
terrain [tɛrɛ̃] *nm* **1** : ground **2** PARCELLE : plot (of land) **3** : land, terrain **4 ~ d'aviation** : airfield **5 ~ de camping** : campsite
terrasse [tɛras] *nf* : terrace — **terrasser** [tɛrase] *vt* : knock down, floor
terre [tɛr] *nf* **1** TERRAIN : land **2** : dirt,

soil **3 :** earth, world **4 aller à ~ :** go ashore **5 la Terre :** the Earth **6 par ~ :** on the ground, on the floor **7 sous ~ :** underground **8 terre–à–terre :** down-to-earth, matter-of-fact

terrestre [tɛrɛstr] *adj* **1 :** earth, terrestrial **2 :** earthly, worldly

terreur [tɛrœr] *nf* **:** terror

terreux, -reuse [tɛrø, -røz] *adj* **:** earthy

terrible [tɛribl] *adj* **1 :** terrible **2** *fam* FORMIDABLE **:** terrific, great

terrier [tɛrje] *nm* **1 :** hole, burrow **2** CHIEN **:** terrier

terrifier [tɛrifje] {96} *vt* ÉPOUVANTER **:** terrify

territoire [tɛritwar] *nm* **:** territory — **territorial, -riale** [tɛritɔrjal] *adj, mpl* **-riaux** [-rjo] **:** territorial

terroriser [tɛrɔrize] *vt* **:** terrorize — **terrorisme** [tɛrɔrism] *nm* **:** terrorism — **terroriste** [-rɔrist] *adj & nmf* **:** terrorist

tes → **ton**[1]

tesson [tɛsɔ̃] *nm* **:** fragment, shard

test [tɛst] *nm* **:** test

testament [tɛstamɑ̃] *nm* **1 :** will, testament **2 Ancien Testament :** Old Testament

tester [tɛste] *vt* **:** test

testicule [tɛstikyl] *nm* **:** testicle

tétanos [tetanos] *nms & pl* **:** tetanus

têtard [tɛtar] *nm* **:** tadpole

tête [tɛt] *nf* **1 :** head **2** VISAGE **:** face **3** MENEUR **:** leader **4 :** top (of a class, etc.) **5** ESPRIT **:** mind, brain **6 faire la ~ :** sulk **7 tenir ~ à :** stand up to — **tête–à–queue** [tɛtakø] *nms & pl* **:** spin (of an automobile) — **tête–à–tête** [tɛtatɛt] *nms & pl* **:** tête-à-tête

téter [tete] {87} *vt* **:** suck (at) — *vi* **:** suckle, nurse — **tétine** [tetin] *nf* **1 :** teat **2 :** nipple (on a baby's bottle), pacifier

têtu, -tue [tety] *adj* **:** stubborn

texte [tɛkst] *nm* **:** text

textile [tɛkstil] *nm* **:** textile

texture [tɛkstyr] *nf* **:** texture

thé [te] *nm* **:** tea

théâtre [teatr] *nm* **:** theater — **théâtral, -trale** [teatral] *adj, mpl* **-traux** [-tro] **:** theatrical

théière [tejɛr] *nf* **:** teapot

thème [tɛm] *nm* **:** theme

théologie [teɔlɔʒi] *nf* **:** theology

théorie [teɔri] *nf* **:** theory — **théorique** [teɔrik] *adj* **:** theoretical

thérapie [terapi] *nf* **:** therapy — **thérapeute** [terapøt] *nmf* **:** therapist — **thérapeutique** [terapøtik] *adj* **:** therapeutic

thermal, -male [tɛrmal] *adj, mpl* **-maux** [tɛrmo] **:** thermal — **thermique** [tɛrmik] *adj* **:** thermal

thermomètre [tɛrmɔmɛtr] *nm* **:** thermometer

thermos [tɛrmos] *nmfs & pl* **:** thermos

thermostat [tɛrmɔsta] *nm* **:** thermostat

thèse [tɛz] *nf* **:** thesis

thon [tɔ̃] *nm* **:** tuna

thym [tɛ̃] *nm* **:** thyme

tibia [tibja] *nm* **:** shin(bone)

tic [tik] *nm* **1 :** tic, twitch **2** HABITUDE **:** mannerism

ticket [tikɛ] *nm* BILLET **:** ticket

tiède [tjɛd] *adj* **:** lukewarm — **tiédir** [tjedir] *vi* **:** warm up, cool down

tien, tienne [tjɛ̃, tjɛn] *adj* **:** yours, of yours — **~** *pron* **le tien, la tienne, les tiens, les tiennes :** yours

tiers, tierce [tjɛr, tjɛrs] *adj* **:** third — **tiers** *nm* **1 :** third **2 :** third party

tige [tiʒ] *nf* **1 :** stem, stalk **2 :** (metal) rod

tigre [tigr] *nm* **:** tiger — **tigresse** [tigrɛs] *nf* **:** tigress

tilleul [tijœl] *nm* **:** linden (tree)

timbale [tɛ̃bal] *nf* **:** tumbler, cup

timbre [tɛ̃br] *nm* **1 :** (postage) stamp **2** SONNETTE **:** bell **3** TON **:** timbre, tone — **timbrer** [tɛ̃bre] *vt* **:** stamp, postmark

timide [timid] *adj* **:** timid, shy — **timidité** [timidite] *nf* **:** shyness

tintamarre [tɛ̃tamar] *nm* **:** din, racket

tinter [tɛ̃te] *vt* **:** ring, toll — *vi* **1 :** ring, chime **2 :** jingle, tinkle — **tintement** [tɛ̃tmɑ̃] *nm* **:** ringing, chiming

tir [tir] *nm* **:** shooting, firing

tirage [tiraʒ] *nm* **1 :** printing, printout **2 :** circulation (of a newspaper, etc.) **3 :** drawing (in a lottery)

tirailler [tiraje] *vt* **:** pull at, tug at

tiré, -rée [tire] *adj* **:** drawn, haggard

tire–bouchon [tirbuʃɔ̃] *nm, pl* **tire–bouchons :** corkscrew

tirelire [tirlir] *nf* **:** piggy bank

tirer [tire] *vt* **1 :** pull, tug **2 :** fire, shoot **3 ~ de :** pull out of, draw away from **4 ~ la langue :** stick out one's tongue **5 ~ une ligne :** draw a line — *vi* **1 :** pull **2 :** fire, shoot **3 ~ au sort :** draw lots — **se tirer** *vr* **1 ~ de :** get through, escape from **2 s'en tirer** *fam* **:** cope, manage

tiret [tirɛ] *nm* **:** dash, hyphen

tireur, -reuse [tirœr, -røz] *n* **:** gunman

tiroir [tirwar] *nm* **:** drawer

tisane [tizan] *nf* : herbal tea
tisonnier [tizɔnje] *nm* : poker
tisser [tise] *vt* : weave — **tissage** [tisaʒ] *nm* **1** : weaving **2** : weave
tissu [tisy] *nm* **1** : material, fabric **2** : tissue (in biology)
titre [titr] *nm* **1** : title (of a book, etc.) **2** : rank, qualification **3** *or* **gros ~** : headline **4** : security, bond **5 à ~ d'exemple** : as an example
tituber [titybe] *vi* : stagger
titulaire [titylɛr] *adj* : tenured, permanent — **~** *nmf* **1** : holder **2** : tenured professor
toast [tost] *nm* : toast
toboggan [tɔbɔgɑ̃] *nm* : toboggan, sleigh
toge [tɔʒ] *nf* : gown, robe (of a judge, etc.)
toi [twa] *pron* **1** : you **2** TOI-MÊME : yourself
toile [twal] *nf* **1** : cloth, fabric **2** TABLEAU : canvas, painting **3 ~ d'araignée** : spiderweb, cobweb
toilette [twalɛt] *nf* **1** : washing up **2** TENUE : clothing, outfit **3** *Can* : toilet, bathroom **4 ~s** *nfpl* : toilet, bathroom
toi-même [twamɛm] *pron* : yourself
toison [twazɔ̃] *nf* : fleece
toit [twa] *nm* : roof — **toiture** [twatyr] *nf* : roofing
tôle [tol] *nf* **1** : sheet metal **2 ~ ondulée** : corrugated iron
tolérer [tɔlere] {87} *vt* : tolerate — **tolérance** [tɔlerɑ̃s] *nf* : tolerance — **tolérant, -rante** [tɔlerɑ̃, -rɑ̃t] *adj* : tolerant
tollé [tɔle] *nm* : outcry
tomate [tɔmat] *nf* : tomato
tombant, -bante [tɔ̃bɑ̃, -bɑ̃t] *adj* : sloping, drooping
tombe [tɔ̃b] *nf* SÉPULTURE : grave, tomb — **tombeau** [tɔ̃bo] *nm, pl* **-beaux** : tomb, mausoleum
tomber [tɔ̃be] *vi* **1** : fall, drop **2** : die down, subside **3** : droop, sag **4 ~ amoureux** : fall in love **5 ~ malade** : fall ill **6 ~ sur** : run into, come across **7 laisser ~** : give up — **tombée** [tɔ̃be] *nf* **à la ~ du jour** *or* **à la ~ de la nuit** : at nightfall, at the close of day
tome [tɔm] *nm* : volume (of a book)
ton[1] [(tɔn *before a vowel or mute h*)], **ta** [ta] *adj, pl* **tes** [te] : your
ton[2] *nm* **1** : tone, pitch **2** : hue, shade — **tonalité** [tɔnalite] *nf* **1** : tone **2** : tonality, key (in music) **3** : dial tone
tondre [tɔ̃dr] {63} *vt* **1** : mow (the lawn) **2** : shear, clip (hair) — **tondeuse** [tɔ̃døz] *nf* **1** *or* **~ à gazon** : lawn mower **2** : clippers *pl*, shears *pl*
tonifier [tɔnifje] {96} *vt* REVIGORER : tone up, invigorate — **tonique** [tɔnik] *nm* : tonic
tonne [tɔn] *nf* : ton
tonneau [tɔno] *nm, pl* **-neaux 1** : barrel, cask **2** : rollover (of an automobile) — **tonnelet** [tɔnlɛ] *nm* : keg
tonner [tɔne] *vi* : thunder — **tonnerre** [tɔnɛr] *nm* : thunder
tonton [tɔ̃tɔ̃] *nm fam* : uncle
tonus [tɔnys] *nms & pl* **1** : (muscle) tone **2** : energy, vigor
toqué, -quée [tɔke] *adj fam* : crazy
torche [tɔrʃ] *nf* : torch
torchon [tɔrʃɔ̃] *nm* **1** CHIFFON : rag **2 ~ à vaisselle** : dishcloth — **torcher** [tɔrʃe] *vt fam* : wipe
tordre [tɔrdr] {63} *vt* : twist, wring — **se tordre** *vr* **1** : twist **2** : double up (with pain, laughter, etc.) — **tordu, -due** [tɔrdy] *adj* : twisted, warped
torero [tɔrero] *nm* : bullfighter
tornade [tɔrnad] *nf* : tornado
torpeur [tɔrpœr] *nf* : lethargy
torpille [tɔrpij] *nf* : torpedo
torrent [tɔrɑ̃] *nm* : torrent
torride [tɔrid] *adj* : torrid
torsade [tɔrsad] *nf* : twist, coil
torse [tɔrs] *nm* : torso, chest
tort [tɔr] *nm* **1** : wrong **2 à ~** : wrongly **3 avoir ~** : be wrong **4 faire du ~ à** : harm
torticolis [tɔrtikɔli] *nms & pl* : stiff neck
tortiller [tɔrtije] *vt* : twist — **se tortiller** *vr* : wriggle, squirm
tortue [tɔrty] *nf* : turtle, tortoise
tortueux , -euse [tɔrtɥø, -øz] *adj* **1** : winding (of a road) **2** : convoluted, tortuous
torture [tɔrtyr] *nf* : torture — **torturer** [tɔrtyre] *vt* : torture
tôt [to] *adv* **1** : soon **2** : early **3 ~ ou tard** : sooner or later
total, -tale [tɔtal] *adj, mpl* **-taux** [tɔto] : total — **total** *nm, pl* **-taux** : total — **totaliser** [tɔtalize] *vt* : total — **totalitaire** [tɔtalitɛr] *adj* : totalitarian — **totalité** [tɔtalite] *nf* **1 en ~** : completely **2 la ~ de** : all of
toucher [tuʃe] *vt* **1** : touch, handle **2** : hit, strike **3** CONCERNER : affect **4** ÉMOUVOIR : move, touch **5** : receive, earn (a salary) — *vi* **~ à 1** : touch upon, bring up **2** : relate to — **se**

toucher *vr* : touch each other — **~** *nm* **1** : sense of touch **2** SENSATION : feel — **touchant, -chante** [tuʃɑ̃, -ʃɑ̃t] *adj* ÉMOUVANT : touching — **touche** [tuʃ] *nf* **1** : key (on a keyboard) **2** TRACE : trace, hint
touffe [tuf] *nf* : tuft, clump — **touffu, -fue** [tufy] *adj* : bushy
toujours [tuʒur] *adv* **1** : always, forever **2** ENCORE : still
toupet [tupɛ] *nm fam* : nerve, cheek
toupie [tupi] *nf* : top (toy)
tour[1] [tur] *nm* **1** : tour, circuit **2** : walk, ride **3 ~ de taille** : girth (of a person) **4 attendre son ~** : wait one's turn **5 jouer un ~ à qqn** : play a trick on s.o. **6** : lathe (in carpentry)
tour[2] *nf* **1** : tower **2** : castle (in chess)
tourbe [turb] *nf* : peat
tourbillon [turbijɔ̃] *nm* **1** : whirlwind, whirlpool **2** : whirl, bustle — **tourbillonner** [turbijɔne] *vi* : whirl, swirl
tourelle [turɛl] *nf* : turret
touriste [turist] *nmf* : tourist — **tourisme** [turism] *nm* : tourism — **touristique** [turistik] *adj* : tourist
tourment [turmɑ̃] *nm* : torment — **tourmenter** [turmɑ̃te] *vt* : torment — **se tourmenter** *vr* S'INQUIÉTER : worry
tourner [turne] *vt* **1** : turn, rotate **2** : stir (a sauce), toss (a salad) **3** : shoot, film — *vi* **1** : turn, revolve, spin **2** : run (of an engine, etc.) **3** : make a film **4** : go bad, sour (of milk) **5 bien ~** : turn out well — **se tourner** *vr* : turn around — **tournant, -nante** [turnɑ̃, -nɑ̃t] *adj* : turning, revolving — **tournant** *nm* **1** : bend **2** : turning point — **tournée** [turne] *nf* **1** : tour **2** *fam* : round (of drinks)
tournesol [turnəsɔl] *nm* : sunflower
tournevis [turnəvis] *nms & pl* : screwdriver
tourniquet [turnikɛ] *nm* : turnstile
tournoi [turnwa] *nm* : tournament
tournoyer [turnwaje] {58} *vi* : whirl, spin
tournure [turnyr] *nf* **1** : turn (of events) **2** : expression
tourterelle [turtərɛl] *nf* : turtledove
tousser [tuse] *vi* : cough
tout [tu] (**toute(s)** [tut] *before feminine adjectives beginning with a consonant or an aspirate h*) *adv* **1** COMPLÈTEMENT : completely **2** : quite, very, all **3 ~ à coup** : suddenly **4 ~ à fait** : completely, entirely **5 ~ de suite** : immediately — **tout, toute** *adj, pl* **tous, toutes 1** : all **2** : each, every **3 à tout âge** : at any age **4 à toute vitesse** : at full speed **5 tout le monde** : everyone, everybody — **tout** *nm* **1 le ~** : the whole **2 pas du ~** : not at all — **tout** *pron, pl* **tous, toutes 1** : all, everything **2** : anyone, everyone
toutefois [tutfwa] *adv* : however
toux [tu] *nfs & pl* : cough
toxicomane [tɔksikɔman] *nmf* : drug addict
toxique [tɔksik] *adj* : toxic, poisonous
trac [trak] *nm* : stage fright, jitters *pl*
tracasser [trakase] *vt* : worry, bother — **se tracasser** *vr* : worry, fret — **tracas** [traka] *nms & pl* **1** : worry **2 ~** *nmpl* ENNUIS : troubles, problems
tracer [trase] {6} *vt* **1** : trace **2** DESSINER : draw **3 ~ le chemin** : pave the way — **trace** [tras] *nf* **1** : track, trail **2** : trace, vestige **3 ~s de pas** : footprints **4 suivre les ~s de qqn** : follow in s.o.'s footsteps — **tracé** [trase] *nm* PLAN : plan, layout
trachée [traʃe] *nf* : trachea, windpipe
tract [trakt] *nm* : leaflet
tractations [traktasjɔ̃] *nfpl* : negotiations
tracteur [traktœr] *nm* : tractor
traction [traksjɔ̃] *nf* **1** : traction **2 ~ avant** : front-wheel drive
tradition [tradisjɔ̃] *nf* : tradition — **traditionnel, -nelle** [tradisjɔnɛl] *adj* : traditional
traduire [tradɥir] {49} *vt* : translate — **traducteur, -trice** [tradyktœr, -tris] *n* : translator — **traduction** [tradyksjɔ̃] *nf* : translation
trafic [trafik] *nm* **1** : traffic **2** : (drug) trafficking — **trafiquant, -quante** [trafikɑ̃, -kɑ̃t] *n* : dealer, trafficker — **trafiquer** [trafike] *vt* : doctor, tamper with — *vi* : traffic, trade
tragédie [traʒedi] *nf* : tragedy — **tragique** [traʒik] *adj* : tragic
trahir [trair] *vt* : betray — **trahison** [traizɔ̃] *nf* **1** : betrayal **2** : treason
train [trɛ̃] *nm* **1** : (passenger) train **2** : pace, rate **3** : set, series **4 en ~ de** : in the process of **5 ~ de vie** : lifestyle
traîner [trene] *vt* **1** : pull, drag **2 ~ les pieds** : drag one's feet — *vi* **1** : drag **2** : dawdle, lag behind **3** : be lying around (of clothes, etc.) — **se traîner** *vr* : drag oneself, crawl — **traîne** [trɛn] *nf* **1** : train (of a dress) **2** *Can* : toboggan, sled — **traîneau** [trɛno] *nm, pl* **-neaux** : sled, sleigh —

traînée [trene] *nf* **1** : streak **2** TRACE : trail **3** : drag (of an airplane, etc.)
train–train [trɛ̃trɛ̃] *nms & pl* ROUTINE : routine
traire [trɛr] {40} *vt* : milk (an animal)
trait [trɛ] *nm* **1** : (character) trait **2** : stroke, line **3 avoir ~ à** : relate to **4 d'un ~** : in one gulp **5 ~ d'union** : hyphen **6 ~s** *nmpl* : features
traite [trɛt] *nf* **1** : milking **2 d'une ~** : in one go **3 ~ bancaire** : bank draft
traité [trete] *nm* **1** : treaty **2** : treatise
traiter [trete] *vt* **1** : treat **2** : process (data) **3 ~ qqn de menteur** : call s.o. a liar — *vi* **~ de** : deal with — **traitement** [trɛtmɑ̃] *nm* **1** : treatment **2 ~ de texte** : word processing
traiteur [trɛtœr] *nm* : caterer
traître, -tresse [trɛtr, -trɛs] *n* : traitor — **~** *adj* : treacherous
trajectoire [traʒɛktwar] *nf* : trajectory
trajet [traʒɛ] *nm* **1** PARCOURS : route **2** VOYAGE : journey
trancher [trɑ̃ʃe] *vt* **1** COUPER : cut **2** : resolve (an issue) — *vi* **1** : stand out **2** : come to a decision — **tranchant, -chante** [trɑ̃ʃɑ̃, -ʃɑ̃t] *adj* : sharp, cutting — **tranchant** *nm* : cutting edge — **tranche** [trɑ̃ʃ] *nf* **1** : slice (of bread) **2** PARTIE : portion, section **3** : edge (of a book) — **tranchée** *nf* : trench
tranquille [trɑ̃kil] *adj* **1** : calm, quiet **2 tiens-toi ~!** : sit still! — **tranquillisant** [trɑ̃kilizɑ] *nm* : tranquilizer — **tranquilliser** [trɑ̃kilize] *vt* RASSURER : reassure — **tranquillité** [trɑ̃kilite] *nf* CALME : peacefulness, tranquillity
transaction [trɑ̃zaksjɔ̃] *nf* : transaction
transcrire [trɑ̃skrir] {33} *vt* : transcribe — **transcription** [trɑ̃skripsjɔ̃] *nf* : transcription
transe [trɑ̃s] *nf* : trance
transférer [trɑ̃sfere] *vt* : transfer — **transfert** [trɑ̃sfɛr] *nm* : transfer
transformer [trɑ̃sfɔrme] *vt* : transform, change — **se transformer** *vr* **~ en** : turn into — **transformateur** [trɑ̃sfɔrmatœr] *nm* : transformer — **transformation** [trɑ̃sfɔrmasjɔ̃] *nf* : transformation
transfusion [trɑ̃sfyzjɔ̃] *nf* : transfusion
transgresser [trɑ̃sgrese] *vt* ENFREINDRE : infringe, violate
transir [trɑ̃zir] *vt* **1** : chill (to the bone) **2** : paralyse (with fear)
transistor [trɑ̃zistɔr] *nm* : transistor
transit [trɑ̃zit] *nm* : transit
transitif, -tive [trɑ̃zitif, -tiv] *adj* : transitive
transition [trɑ̃zisjɔ̃] *nf* : transition — **transitoire** [trɑ̃zitwar] *adj* : transitory, transient
translucide [trɑ̃slysid] *adj* : translucent
transmettre [trɑ̃smɛtr] {53} *vt* **1** : transmit (signals, data, etc.) **2** : pass on, convey **3** : broadcast (a show) — **transmission** [trɑ̃smisjɔ̃] *nf* **1** : transmission **2** : broadcasting
transparent, -rente [trɑ̃sparɑ̃, -rɑ̃t] *adj* : transparent — **transparence** [trɑ̃sparɑ̃s] *nf* : transparency
transpercer [trɑ̃spɛrse] {6} *vt* : pierce
transpirer [trɑ̃spire] *vt* : perspire — **transpiration** [trɑ̃spirasjɔ̃] *nf* : perspiration
transplanter [trɑ̃splɑ̃te] *vt* : transplant — **transplantation** [trɑ̃splɑ̃tasjɔ̃] *nm* : transplant
transporter [trɑ̃spɔrte] *vt* : transport, carry — **transport** [trɑ̃spɔr] *nm* : transport — **transporteur** [trɑ̃spɔrtœr] *nm* : carrier, transporter
transposer [trɑ̃spoze] *vt* : transpose
transversal, -sale [trɑ̃svɛrsal] *adj, mpl* **-saux** [-so] : cross (of a beam)
trapèze [trapɛz] *nm* **1** : trapezoid **2** : trapeze
trappe [trap] *nf* **1** PIÈGE : trap **2** : trapdoor
trapu, -pue [trapy] *adj* : stocky, squat
traquer [trake] *vt* POURSUIVRE : track down
traumatiser [tromatize] *vt* : traumatize — **traumatisant, -sante** [tromatizɑ̃, -zɑ̃t] *adj* : traumatic — **traumatisme** [tromatism] *nm* : trauma
travailler [travaje] *vt* **1** : work **2** PRATIQUER : work on **3** TRACASSER : worry — *vi* : work — **travail** [travaj] *nm, pl* **-vaux** [travo] **1** : work **2** TÂCHE : task, job **3** EMPLOI : work, employment **4 travaux** *nmpl* : works, work — **travailleur, -leuse** [travajœr, -jøz] *adj* : hardworking, industrious — **~** *n* : worker
travée [trave] *nf* **1** : row (of seats) **2** : span (of a bridge)
travers [travɛr] *nms & pl* **1 à ~** *or* **au ~** : through **2 de ~** : askew, wrongly **3 en ~** : across, sideways — **traverser** [travɛrse] *vt* **1** : cross (the road, etc.) **2** : run through, pass through — **traversée** [travɛrse] *nf* : crossing
trébucher [trebyʃe] *vi* : stumble
trèfle [trɛfl] *nm* **1** : clover, shamrock **2** : clubs *pl* (in playing cards)
treillis [trɛji] *nms & pl* : trellis, lattice

treize [trɛz] *adj* **1** : thirteen **2** : thirteenth (in dates) — **~** *nms & pl* : thirteen — **treizième** [trɛzjɛm] *adj & nmf & nm* : thirteenth

trembler [trɑ̃ble] *vi* **1** : shake, tremble **2** : quiver (of the voice) — **tremblement** [trɑ̃bləmɑ̃] *nm* **1** : trembling **2** FRISSON : shiver **3 ~ de terre** : earthquake — **trembloter** [trɑ̃blɔte] *vi* : quaver

trémousser [tremuse] *v* **se trémousser** *vr* : wriggle around

tremper [trɑ̃pe] *vt* **1** : soak **2** : dip, dunk — **trempe** [trɑ̃p] *nf* : caliber, quality — **trempé, -pée** [trɑ̃pe] *adj* : soaked

tremplin [trɑ̃plɛ̃] *nm* **1** : springboard **2** *or* **~ à ski** : ski jump

trente [trɑ̃t] *adj* **1** : thirty **2** : thirtieth (in dates) — **~** *nms & pl* : thirty — **trentième** [trɑ̃tjɛm] *adj & nmf & nm* : thirtieth

trépied [trepje] *nm* : tripod

trépigner [trepiɲe] *vi* : stamp one's feet

très [trɛ] *adv* : very

trésor [trezɔr] *nm* : treasure

tressaillir [tresajir] {93}*vi* **1** : start (with surprise, etc.), wince (with pain) **2** TREMBLER : quiver, tremble — **tressaillement** [tresajmɑ̃] *nm* : start, wince

tresse [trɛs] *nf* : braid, plait — **tresser** [trese] *vt* **1** : braid, plait **2** : weave (a basket, etc.)

treuil [trœj] *nm* : winch

trêve [trɛv] *nf* **1** : truce **2** : respite

tri [tri] *nm* : sorting (out)

triangle [trijɑ̃gl] *nm* : triangle — **triangulaire** [trijɑ̃gylɛr] *adj* : triangular

tribal, -bale [tribal] *adj, mpl* **-baux** [tribo] : tribal

tribord [tribɔr] *nm* : starboard

tribu [triby] *nf* : tribe

tribulations [tribylasjɔ̃] *nfpl* : tribulations

tribunal [tribynal] *nm, pl* **-naux** [-no] : court

tribune [tribyn] *nf* **1** : gallery, grandstand **2** : rostrum, platform **3** DÉBAT : forum

tribut [triby] *nm* : tribute

tributaire [tribytɛr] *adj* **être ~ de** : be dependent on

tricher [triʃe] *vi* : cheat — **tricherie** [triʃri] *nf* : cheating — **tricheur, -cheuse** [triʃœr, -ʃøz] *n* : cheat

tricoter [trikɔte] *v* : knit — **tricot** [triko] *nm* **1** : knitting **2** : knitted fabric **3** CHANDAIL : sweater

tricycle [trisikl] *nm* : tricycle

trier [trije] {96} *vt* **1** : sort (out) **2** CHOISIR : select

trimbaler *or* **trimballer** [trɛ̃bale] *vt fam* : cart around

trimestre [trimɛstr] *nm* **1** : quarter (in economics, etc.) **2** : term (in school) — **trimestriel, -trielle** [trimɛstrijɛl] *adj* : quarterly

tringle [trɛ̃gl] *nf* : rod

trinité [trinite] *nf* : trinity

trinquer [trɛ̃ke] *vi* : clink glasses, drink (a toast)

trio [trijo] *nm* : trio

triomphe [trijɔ̃f] *nm* : triumph — **triompher** [trijɔ̃fe] *vi* : triumph

tripes [trip] *nfpl* **1** : tripe **2** *fam* : guts

triple [tripl] *adj & nm* : triple, treble — **tripler** [triple] *v* : triple — **triplés, -plées** [triple] *npl* : triplets

tripoter [tripɔte] *vt* : fiddle with

trique [trik] *nf* : cudgel

triste [trist] *adj* **1** : sad **2** : dismal **3** LAMENTABLE : deplorable, sorry — **tristesse** [tristɛs] *nf* : sadness, gloominess

triton [tritɔ̃] *nm* : newt

troc [trɔk] *nm* : swap

trognon [trɔɲɔ̃] *nm* : core (of an apple, etc.)

trois [trwa] *adj* **1** : three **2** : third (in dates) — **~** *nms & pl* : three — **troisième** [trwazjɛm] *adj & nmf* : third

trombe [trɔ̃b] *nf* **1** : waterspout **2 ~s d'eau** : downpour

trombone [trɔ̃bɔn] *nm* **1** : trombone **2** : paper clip

trompe [trɔ̃p] *nf* **1** : horn **2** : trunk (of an elephant)

tromper [trɔ̃pe] *vt* **1** DUPER : deceive **2** : be unfaithful to (one's spouse) — **se tromper** *vr* : make a mistake — **tromperie** [trɔ̃pri] *nf* : deception, deceit

trompette [trɔ̃pɛt] *nf* : trumpet

trompeur, -peuse [trɔ̃pœr, -pøz] *adj* **1** : deceitful **2** : misleading

tronc [trɔ̃] *nm* **1** : trunk (of a tree) **2** TORSE : torso

tronçon [trɔ̃sɔ̃] *nm* : section — **tronçonneuse** [trɔ̃sɔnøz] *nf* : chain saw

trône [tron] *nm* : throne

tronquer [trɔ̃ke] *vt* : truncate

trop [tro] *adv* **1** : too **2 ~ de** : too many, too much **3 de ~** *or* **en ~** : too many, extra

trophée [trɔfe] *nm* : trophy

tropique [trɔpik] *nm* **1** : tropic **2 ~s** *nmpl* : tropics — **tropical, -cale**

[trɔpikal] *adj, mpl* **-caux** [-ko] : tropical
trop–plein [trɔplɛ̃] *nm, pl* **trop–pleins** **1** : overflow **2** SURPLUS : excess, surplus
troquer [trɔke] *vt* : trade, barter
trotter [trɔte] *vi* : trot
trotteuse [trɔtøz] *nf* : second hand (of a watch)
trottiner [trɔtine] *vi* : scurry along
trottinette [trɔtinɛt] *nf* : scooter
trottoir [trɔtwar] *nm* : sidewalk
trou [tru] *nm* **1** : hole **2** : gap (of time) **3 ~ de mémoire** : memory lapse **4 ~ de (la) serrure** : keyhole
troubler [truble] *vt* **1** : disturb **2** BROUILLER : blur, cloud **3** INQUIÉTER : trouble — **trouble** [trubl] *adj* **1** : cloudy **2** FLOU : blurred, unclear — **~** *nm* **1** : confusion **2** : trouble **3 ~s** *nmpl* : disorder (in medicine) **4 ~s** *nmpl* : unrest
trouer [true] *vt* : make a hole in, pierce — **trouée** [true] *nf* : gap
trouille [truj] *nf fam* : fear, fright
troupe [trup] *nf* **1** : troop **2 ~ de théâtre** : theater company
troupeau [trupo] *nm, pl* **-peaux** : herd, flock
trousse [trus] *nf* **1** : kit, case **2 aux ~s de** : on the heels of
trousseau [truso] *nm, pl* **-seaux** **1** : trousseau **2 ~ de clefs** : bunch of keys
trouver [truve] *vt* **1** : find **2** ESTIMER : think — **se trouver** *vr* **1** : be (found) **2** : find oneself **3** SE SENTIR : feel — *v impers* **il se trouve que** : it turns out that — **trouvaille** [truvaj] *nf* DÉCOUVERTE : find
truand [tryɑ̃] *nm* : gangster, crook
truc [tryk] *nm* **1** : trick **2** *fam* MACHIN : thing, thingamajig
truelle [tryɛl] *nf* : trowel
truffe [tryf] *nf* : truffle
truite [trɥit] *nf* : trout
truquer [tryke] *vt* : fix, rig
trust [trœst] *nm* : trust, cartel
tsar [tsar, dzar] *nm* : czar
t–shirt [tiʃœrt] *nm* → **tee–shirt**
tu [ty] *pron* : you
tuba [tyba] *nm* **1** : tuba **2** : snorkel
tube [tyb] *nm* **1** : tube **2** *fam* : hit (song)
tuberculose [tybɛrkyloz] *nf* : tuberculosis
tuer [tɥe] *vt* **1** : kill **2** ÉPUISER : exhaust — **se tuer** *vr* **1** : be killed, die **2** : kill oneself — **tuerie** [tyri] *nf* CARNAGE : slaughter — **tueur, tueuse** [tɥœr, tɥøz] *n* : killer
tue–tête [tytɛt] **à ~** *adv phr* : at the top of one's lungs
tuile [tɥil] *nf* **1** : tile **2** *fam* : bad luck
tulipe [tylip] *nf* : tulip
tumeur [tymœr] *nf* : tumor
tumulte [tymylt] *nm* : tumult, commotion — **tumultueux, -tueuse** [tymyltɥø, -tɥøz] *adj* : stormy, turbulent
tunique [tynik] *nf* : tunic
tunnel [tynɛl] *nm* : tunnel
tuque [tyk] *nf Can* : stocking cap
turban [tyrbɑ̃] *nm* : turban
turbine [tyrbin] *nf* : turbine
turbulence [tyrbylɑ̃s] *nf* : turbulence — **turbulent, -lente** [tyrbylɑ̃, -lɑ̃t] *adj* **1** : unruly **2** : turbulent
turc, turque [tyrk] *adj* : Turkish — **turc** *nm* : Turkish (language)
turquoise [tyrkwaz] *adj* : turquoise
tutelle [tytɛl] *nf* **1** : guardianship **2** : care, protection
tuteur, -trice [tytœr, -tris] *n* **1** : guardian **2** : tutor — **tuteur** *nm* : stake
tutoyer [tytwaje] {58} *vt* : address someone as *tu*
tuyau [tɥijo] *nm, pl* **tuyaux** **1** : pipe, tube **2** *fam* : tip, advice — **tuyauterie** [tɥijotri] *nf* : pipes *pl,* plumbing
tympan [tɛ̃pɑ̃] *nm* : eardrum
type [tip] *nm* **1** : type, kind **2** : example, model **3** : (physical) type **4** *fam* : guy, fellow
typhon [tifɔ̃] *nm* : typhoon
typique [tipik] *adj* : typical
tyran [tirɑ̃] *nm* : tyrant — **tyrannie** [tirani] *nf* : tyranny

U

u [y] *nm* : u, 21st letter of the alphabet
ulcère [ylsɛr] *nm* : ulcer
ultérieur, -rieure [ylterjœr] *adj* : later, subsequent — **ultérieurement** [ylterjœrmɑ̃] *adv* : subsequently
ultimatum [yltimatɔm] *nm* : ultimatum — **ultime** [yltim] *adj* : ultimate, final
ultraviolet, -lette [yltravjolɛ, -lɛt] *adj* : ultraviolet
un, une [œ̃ (œn *before a vowel or mute* h), yn] *adj* : a, an, one — ~ *n & pron* **1** : one **2 une par une** : one by one — ~ *art, pl* **des 1** (*used in the singular*) : a, an **2** (*used in the plural*) : some — **un** *nm* : (number) one
unanime [ynanim] *adj* : unanimous — **unanimité** [ynanimite] *nf* : unanimity
uni, -nie [yni] *adj* **1** : united **2** LISSE : smooth **3** : solid (of a color) **4** : close-knit (of a family)
unifier [ynifje] {96} *vt* : unite, unify — **unification** [ynifikasjɔ̃] *nf* : unification
uniforme [ynifɔrm] *adj* : uniform, even — ~ *nm* : uniform — **uniformiser** *vt* : make uniform, standardize — **uniformité** [ynifɔrmite] *nf* : uniformity
unilatéral, -rale [ynilateral] *adj, pl* **-raux** [-ro] : unilateral
union [ynjɔ̃] *nf* : union
unique [ynik] *adj* **1** : unique **2 enfant** ~ : only child **3 sens** ~ : one-way — **uniquement** [ynikmɑ̃] *adv* : only, solely
unir [ynir] *vt* **1** : unite, connect **2** COMBINER : combine — **s'unir** *vr* : unite
unisson [ynisɔ̃] *nm* : unison
unité [ynite] *nf* **1** : unity **2** : unit
univers [ynivɛr] *nm* : universe — **universel, -selle** [ynivɛrsɛl] *vt* : universal
universitaire [ynivɛrsitɛr] *adj* : university, academic — **université** [ynivɛrsite] *nf* : university
uranium [yranjɔm] *nm* : uranium
Uranus [yranys] *nm* : Uranus
urbain, -baine [yrbɛ̃, -bɛn] *adj* : urban, city — **urbanisme** [yrbanism] *nm* : city planning
urgence [yrʒɑ̃s] *nf* **1** : urgency **2** : emergency **3 d'**~ : urgently, immediately — **urgent, -gente** [yrʒɑ̃, -ʒɑ̃t] *adj* : urgent
urine [yrin] *nf* : urine — **uriner** [yrine] *vi* : urinate — **urinoir** [yrinwar] *nm* : urinal
urne [yrn] *nf* **1** : urn **2** : ballot box
urticaire [yrtikɛr] *nf* : hives
usage [yzaʒ] *nm* **1** : use **2** : usage (of a word) **3** COUTUME : habit, custom — **usagé, -gée** [yzaʒe] *adj* **1** : worn **2** : used, secondhand — **usager** [yzaʒe] *nm* : user
user [yze] *vt* **1** CONSOMMER : use **2** : wear out, to use up — *vi* **1** ~ **de** : exercise (one's rights, etc.) **2** ~ **de** : make use of — **usé, -sée** [yze] *adj* **1** : worn-out **2** : hackneyed, trite
usine [yzin] *nf* : factory
usité, -tée [yzite] *adj* : commonly used
ustensile [ystɑ̃sil] *nm* : utensil
usuel, -suelle [yzɥɛl] *adj* : common, usual — **usuellement** [yzɥɛlmɑ̃] *adv* : usually, ordinarily
usure [yzyr] *nm* : wear (and tear)
usurper [yzyrpe] *vt* : usurp
utérus [yterys] *nms & pl* : uterus
utile [ytil] *adj* : useful — **utilisable** [ytilizabl] *adj* : usable — **utiliser** [ytilize] *vt* : use — **utilisateur, -trice** [ytilizatœr, -tris] *n* : user — **utilisation** [ytilizasjɔ̃] *nf* : use — **utilité** [ytilite] *nf* : usefulness
utopie [ytɔpi] *nf* : utopia — **utopique** [ytɔpik] *adj* : utopian

V

v [ve] *nm* : v, 22d letter of the alphabet
va [va], *etc.* → **aller**
vacances [vakɑ̃s] *nfpl* : vacation — **vacancier, -cière** [vakɑ̃sje, -sjɛr] *n* : vacationer — **vacant, -cante** [vakɑ̃, -kɑ̃t] *adj* : vacant
vacarme [vakarm] *nm* : racket, din
vaccin [vaksɛ̃] *nm* : vaccine — **vacciner** [vaksine] *vt* : vaccinate — **vaccination** [vaksinasjɔ̃] *nf* : vaccination
vache [vaʃ] *nf* : cow — **~** *adj fam* : mean, nasty — **vachement** [vaʃmɑ̃] *adv fam* : really, very — **vacherie** [vaʃri] *nf fam* **1** : nastiness **2** : dirty trick
vaciller [vasije] *vi* **1** : stagger, sway **2** : flicker (of a light) **3** : falter, fail — **vacillant, -lante** [vasijɑ̃, -jɑ̃t] *adj* **1** : unsteady, shaky **2** : wavering, faltering — **vacillement** [vasijmɑ̃] *nm* **1** : flicker **2** : faltering
va–et–vient [vaevjɛ̃] *nms & pl* **1** : comings and goings **2** : to-and-fro motion
vagabond, -bonde [vagabɔ̃, -bɔ̃d] *n* : vagrant, tramp — **vagabonder** [vagabɔ̃de] *vi* : roam, wander
vagin [vaʒɛ̃] *nm* : vagina
vague[1] [vag] *adj* : vague, indistinct — **~** *nm* : vagueness — **vaguement** [vagmɑ̃] *adv* : vaguely, slightly
vague[2] *nf* : wave
vaillant, -lante [vajɑ̃, -jɑ̃t] *adj* **1** : valiant, brave **2** : healthy, robust — **vaillamment** [vajamɑ̃] *adv* : courageously
vain, vaine [vɛ̃, vɛn] *adj* **1** : vain, futile **2 en ~** : in vain
vaincre [vɛ̃kr] {94} *vt* **1** BATTRE : defeat **2** SURMONTER : overcome — **vaincu, -cue** [vɛ̃ky] *adj* : defeated — **vainqueur** [vɛ̃kœr] *nm* : victor, winner
vaisseau [vɛso] *nm, pl* **-seaux** **1** : (blood) vessel **2** : vessel, ship **3 ~ spatial** : spaceship
vaisselle [vɛsɛl] *nf* : crockery, dishes *pl*
valable [valabl] *adj* **1** VALIDE : valid **2** BON : good, worthwhile
valet [valɛ] *nm* **1** : servant **2** : jack (in playing cards)
valeur [valœr] *nf* **1** : value **2** MÉRITE : merit, worth **3 objets de ~** : valuables **4 ~s** *nfpl* : stocks, securities
valide [valid] *adj* : valid — **valider** [valide] *vt* : validate — **validité** [validite] *nf* : validity
valise [valiz] *nf* : suitcase
vallée [vale] *nf* : valley — **vallon** [valɔ̃] *nm* : small valley — **vallonné, -née** [valɔne] *adj* : hilly
valoir [valwar] {95} *vi* **1** : have a (certain) cost **2** : be worth **3** : apply, be valid **4 ça vaut combien?** : how much is it worth? **5 faire ~** : point out, assert — *vt* **1** PROCURER : earn, bring (to) **2 ~ la peine** : be worth the trouble — *v impers* **il vaut mieux** : it's better (to) — **se valoir** *vr* : be equivalent
valoriser [valɔrize] *vt* : increase the value of
valse [vals] *nf* : waltz — **valser** [valse] *vi* : waltz
valve [valv] *nf* : valve
vampire [vɑ̃pir] *nm* : vampire
vandale [vɑ̃dal] *nmf* : vandal — **vandalisme** [vɑ̃dalism] *nm* : vandalism
vanille [vanij] *nf* : vanilla
vanité [vanite] *nf* : vanity — **vaniteux, -teuse** [vanitø, -tøz] *adj* : conceited, vain
vanne [van] *nf* **1** : floodgate **2** *fam* : dig, gibe
vanter [vɑ̃te] *vt* : vaunt, praise — **se vanter** *vr* **1** : boast **2 ~ de** : pride oneself on — **vantard, -tarde** [vɑ̃tar, -tard] *adj* : boastful — **~** *n* : braggart — **vantardise** [vɑ̃tardiz] *nf* : boast
va–nu–pieds [vanypje] *nmfs & pl* : beggar
vapeur [vapœr] *nf* **1** : steam **2 ~s** *nfpl* : fumes
vaporiser [vapɔrize] *vt* : spray — **vaporisateur** [vapɔrizatœr] *nm* : spray, atomizer
vaquer [vake] *vi* **~ à** : attend to, see to
varappe [varap] *nf* : rock climbing
variable [varjabl] *adj* : variable, changeable — **variante** [varjɑ̃t] *nf* : variant — **variation** [varjasjɔ̃] *nf* : variation
varice [varis] *nf* : varicose vein
varicelle [varisɛl] *nf* : chicken pox
varier [varje] {96} *v* : vary — **varié, -riée** [varje] *adj* **1** : varied, varying **2**

: various, diverse — **variété** [varjete] *nf* : variety
variole [varjol] *nf* : smallpox
vase[1] [vaz] *nm* : vase
vase[2] *nf* BOUE : mud, silt — **vaseux, -seuse** [vazø, -zøz] *adj* BOUEUX : muddy
vaste [vast] *adj* : vast, immense
vaurien, -rienne [vorjɛ̃, -rjɛn] *n* : good-for-nothing
vautour [votur] *nm* : vulture
vautrer [votre] *v* **se vautrer** *vr* **~ dans** : wallow in
veau [vo] *nm, pl* **veaux 1** : calf **2** : veal
vécu [veky] *pp* → **vivre** — **vécu, -cue** [veky] *adj* : real, true
vedette [vədɛt] *nf* **1** : star, celebrity **2 mettre en ~** : put in the spotlight, feature
végétal, -tale [veʒetal] *adj, mpl* **-taux** : vegetable, plant — **végétal** *nm* : vegetable, plant — **végétarien, -rienne** [veʒetarjɛ̃, -rjɛn] *adj & n* : vegetarian — **végéter** [veʒete] {87} *vi* : vegetate — **végétation** [veʒetasjɔ̃] *nf* : vegetation
véhément, -mente [veemɑ̃, -mɑ̃t] *adj* : vehement — **véhémence** [veemɑ̃s] *nf* : vehemence
véhicule [veikyl] *nm* : vehicle
veiller [veje] *vt* : sit up with, watch over — *vi* **1** : stay awake **2** : keep watch **3** : be vigilant **4 ~ à** : see to — **veille** [vɛj] *nf* **1** : day before, eve **2** : watch, vigil — **veillée** [veje] *nf* **1** SOIRÉE : evening **2 ~ funèbre** : wake — **veilleur, -leuse** [vejœr, -jøz] *n* **1** : lookout, sentry **2 ~ de nuit** : night watchman — **veilleuse** *nf* **1** : nightlight **2** : pilot light
veine [vɛn] *nf* **1** : vein **2** *fam* : luck
vélo [velo] *nm* : bike, bicycle
vélomoteur [velɔmɔtœr] *nm* : moped
velours [vəlur] *nm* **1** : velvet, velour **2 ~ côtelé** : corduroy — **velouté, -tée** [vəlute] *adj* : velvety, smooth
velu, -lue [vəly] *adj* : hairy
venaison [vənɛzɔ̃] *nf* : venison
vendange [vɑ̃dɑ̃ʒ] *nf* : grape harvest
vendre [vɑ̃dr] {63} *vt* **1** : sell **2 à ~** : for sale — **se vendre** : sell — **vendeur, -deuse** [vɑ̃dœr, -døz] *n* : salesperson
vendredi [vɑ̃drədi] *nm* : Friday
vénéneux, -neuse [venenø, -nøz] *adj* : poisonous
vénérer [venere] {87} *vt* : venerate — **vénérable** [venerabl] *adj* : venerable
vénérien, -rienne [venerjɛ̃, -rjɛn] *adj* : venereal
venger [vɑ̃ʒe] {17} *vt* : avenge — **se venger** *vr* : take revenge — **vengeance** [vɑ̃ʒɑ̃s] *nf* : vengeance, revenge — **vengeur, -geresse** [vɑ̃ʒœr, -ʒrɛs] *adj* : vengeful — **~** *n* : avenger
venin [vənɛ̃] *nm* : venom, poison — **venimeux, -meuse** [vənimø, -møz] *adj* : poisonous
venir [vənir] {92} *vi* **1** : come **2 ~ de** : come from **3 en ~ à** : come to (a conclusion, etc.) **4 faire ~** : send for — *v aux* **1** : come and, come to **2 ~ de** : have just
vent [vɑ̃] *nm* **1** : wind **2 il y a du ~** *or* **il fait du ~** : it's windy — **venteux, -teuse** [vɑ̃tø, -tøz] *adj* : windy
vente [vɑ̃t] *nf* **1** : sale, selling **2 en ~** : for sale
ventiler [vɑ̃tile] *vt* : ventilate — **ventilateur** [vɑ̃tilatœr] *nm* : (electric) fan, ventilator — **ventilation** [vɑ̃tilasjɔ̃] *nf* : ventilation
ventouse [vɑ̃tuz] *nf* **1** : suction cup **2** : plunger
ventre [vɑ̃tr] *nm* **1** : stomach, belly **2** : womb **3 avoir mal au ~** : have a stomachache
ventriloque [vɑ̃trilɔk] *nmf* : ventriloquist
venu [vəny] *pp* → **venir** — **venu, -nue** [vəny] *adj* **1 bien venu** : timely **2 mal venu** : ill-advised, unwelcome — **venue** *nf* : coming, arrival
Vénus [venys] *nf* : Venus (planet)
ver [vɛr] *nm* **1** : worm **2 ~ de terre** : earthworm
véranda [verɑ̃da] *nf* : veranda, porch
verbe [vɛrb] *nm* : verb — **verbal, -bale** [vɛrbal] *adj, mpl* **-baux** [-bo] : verbal
verdeur [vɛrdœr] *nf* : vigor, vitality
verdict [vɛrdikt] *nm* : verdict
verdir [vɛrdir] *v* : turn green — **verdoyant, -doyante** [vɛrdwajɑ̃, -dwajɑ̃t] *adj* : green, verdant — **verdure** [vɛrdyr] *nf* : greenery
verge [vɛrʒ] *nf* : rod, stick
verger [vɛrʒe] *nm* : orchard
verglacé, -cée [vɛrglase] *adj* : icy — **verglas** [vɛrgla] *nm* : black ice
vergogne [vɛrgɔɲ] *nf* **sans ~** : shamelessly
véridique [veridik] *adj* : truthful
vérifier [verifje] {96} *vt* : verify, check — **vérification** [verifikasjɔ̃] *nf* : verification, check
vérité [verite] *nf* **1** : truth **2 en ~** : in fact — **véritable** [veritabl] *adj* **1** RÉEL

: true, actual **2** AUTHENTIQUE : genuine **3** (*used as an intensive*) : real — **véritablement** [-tabləmɑ̃] *adv* : actually, really

vermine [vɛrmin] *nf* : vermin

vernis [vɛrni] *nms & pl* **1** : varnish **2** : glaze (on pottery) **3** : veneer, facade **4 ~ à ongles** : nail polish — **vernir** [vɛrnir] *vt* : varnish — **vernissage** [vɛrnisaʒ] *nm* **1** : varnishing **2** : opening (of an art exhibition) — **vernisser** [vɛrnise] *vt* : glaze (ceramics)

verre [vɛr] *nm* **1** : glass **2** : (drinking) glass **3 ~s** *nmpl* : eyeglasses, lenses **4 prendre un ~** : have a drink — **verrerie** [vɛrri] *nf* : glassware — **verrière** [vɛrjɛr] *nf* **1** : glass roof **2** : glass wall

verrou [vɛru] *nm* : bolt — **verrouiller** [vɛruje] *vt* : bolt, lock

verrue [vɛry] *nf* : wart

vers[1] [vɛr] *nms & pl* : line, verse (of poetry)

vers[2] *prep* **1** : toward, towards **2** : about, around, near

versant [vɛrsɑ̃] *nm* : slope, side (of a hill, etc.)

versatile [vɛrsatil] *adj* : fickle

verser [vɛrse] *vt* **1** : pour, serve **2** PAYER : pay **3** RÉPANDRE : shed (tears, etc.) — *vi* **1** : overturn **2 ~ dans** : lapse into — **verse** [vɛrs] *nf* **pleuvoir à ~** : pour (rain) — **versé, -sée** [vɛrse] *adj* **~ dans** : (well-)versed in — **versement** [vɛrsəmɑ̃] *nm* **1** : payment **2** : installment

verset [vɛrsɛ] *nm* : verse

version [vɛrsjɔ̃] *nf* : version

verso [vɛrso] *nm* : back (of a page)

vert, verte [vɛr, vɛrt] *adj* **1** : green **2** : unripe **3** GAILLARD : sprightly, vigorous — **vert** *nm* : green

vertèbre [vɛrtɛbr] *nf* : vertebra — **vertébral, -brale** [vɛrtebral] *adj, mpl* **-braux** [-bro] : vertebral

vertement [vɛrtəmɑ̃] *adv* : sharply, severely

vertical, -cale [vɛrtikal] *adj, mpl* **-caux** [-ko] : vertical — **verticale** *nf* **à la ~** : vertically — **verticalement** [-kalmɑ̃] *adv* : vertically

vertige [vɛrtiʒ] *nm* : dizziness — **vertigineux, -neuse** [vɛrtiʒinø, -nøz] *adj* **1** : dizzy **2** : breathtaking

vertu [vɛrty] *nf* **1** : virtue **2 en ~ de** : by virtue of — **vertueux, -tueuse** [vɛrtɥø, -tɥøz] *adj* : virtuous

verve [vɛrv] *nf* : humor, wit

vésicule [vezikyl] *nf* **~ biliaire** : gallbladder

vessie [vesi] *nf* : bladder

veste [vɛst] *nf* **1** : jacket **2** *Can* : vest

vestiaire [vɛstjɛr] *nm* : locker room

vestibule [vɛstibyl] *nm* : hall

vestige [vɛstiʒ] *nm* **1** : vestige **2** : relic, remains

veston [vɛstɔ̃] *nm* : (man's) jacket

vêtement [vɛtmɑ̃] *nm* **1** : garment, article of clothing **2 ~s** *nmpl* : clothes, clothing

vétéran [veterɑ̃] *nm* : veteran

vétérinaire [veterinɛr] *nmf* : veterinarian

vêtir [vetir] {97} *vt* HABILLER : dress — **se vêtir** *vr* : get dressed — **vêtu, -tue** [vɛty] *adj* : dressed

veto [veto] *nms & pl* : veto

veuf, veuve [vœf, vœv] *adj* : widowed — **~** *n* : widower *m*, widow *f*

vexer [vɛkse] *vt* : vex, upset — **se vexer** *vr* : take offense — **vexant, -xante** [vɛksɑ̃, -ksɑ̃t] *adj* : hurtful

via [vja] *prep* : via

viable [vjabl] *adj* : viable

viaduc [vjadyk] *nm* : viaduct

viande [vjɑ̃d] *nf* **1** : meat **2 ~ hachée** : hamburger

vibrer [vibre] *vi* : vibrate — **vibrant, -brante** [vibrɑ̃, -brɑ̃t] *adj* : vibrant — **vibration** [vibrɑsjɔ̃] *nf* : vibration

vicaire [vikɛr] *nm* : vicar, curate

vice [vis] *nm* **1** DÉBAUCHE : vice **2** DÉFAUT : defect

vice-président, -dente [visprezidɑ̃, -dɑ̃t] *n* : vice president

vice versa *or* **vice-versa** [vis(e)vɛrsa] *adv* : vice versa

vicier [visje] {96} *vt* : pollute, taint

vicieux, -cieuse [visjø, -sjøz] *adj* : perverse, depraved

victime [viktim] *nf* : victim

victoire [viktwar] *nf* : victory — **victorieux, -rieuse** [viktɔrjø, -rjøz] *adj* : victorious

vidange [vidɑ̃ʒ] *nf* **1** : emptying, draining **2** : oil change — **vidanger** [vidɑ̃ʒe] {17} *vt* : empty, drain

vide [vid] *adj* : empty — **~** *nm* **1** : emptiness, void **2** LACUNE : gap

vidéo [video] *adj s & pl* : video — **~** *nf* : video

vidéocassette [videɔkasɛt] *nf* : videocassette, videotape

vider [vide] *vt* **1** : empty **2** : vacate (the premises) **3** : clean (a fowl), gut (a fish) — **videur** [vidœr] *nm* : bouncer

vie [vi] *nf* **1** : life **2** : lifetime **3** : livelihood, living **4 à ~** : for life **5 être en ~** : be alive **6 jamais de la ~!** : never!

vieil → **vieux**

viellard [vjɛjar] *nm* : old man
vieille → **vieux**
vieillir [vjejir] *vt* : make (someone) old, age — *vi* **1** : grow old, age **2** : become outdated — **vieillesse** [vjɛjɛs] *nf* : old age
vierge [vjɛrʒ] *adj* **1** : virgin **2** : empty, blank (of a tape, etc.) — ~ *nf* : virgin
vieux [vjø] (**vieil** [vjɛj] *before a vowel or mute h*), **vieille** [vjɛj] *adj, mpl* **vieux** **1** : old **2 vieille fille** : old maid **3 vieux jeu** : old-fashioned — ~ *n* : old man *m,* old woman *f*
vif, vive [vif, viv] *adj* **1** : lively, animated **2** AIGU : sharp, keen **3** : vivid (of a color) **4** : brisk, bracing (of the wind) — **vif** *nm* **1 à** ~ : open, exposed **2 le** ~ **du sujet** : the heart of the matter **3 sur le** ~ : on the spot, from life
vigilant, -lante [viʒilɑ̃, -lɑ̃t] *adj* : vigilant — **vigilance** [viʒilɑ̃s] *nf* : vigilance
vigne [viɲ] *nf* **1** : grapevine **2** : vineyard — **vigneron, -ronne** [viɲrɔ̃, -rɔn] *n* : winegrower
vignette [viɲɛt] *nf* : label, sticker
vignoble [viɲɔbl] *nm* : vineyard
vigueur [vigœr] *nf* **1** : vigor **2 en** ~ : in force — **vigoureux, -reuse** [vigurø, -røz] *adj* **1** : vigorous, sturdy **2** : forceful, energetic
VIH [veiaʃ] *nm* (*V*irus de l'*I*mmunodéficience *H*umaine) : HIV
vil, vile [vil] *adj* : vile, base
vilain, -laine [vilɛ̃, -lɛn] *adj* **1** LAID : ugly **2** MÉCHANT : naughty
villa [vila] *nf* : villa
village [vilaʒ] *nm* : village — **villageois, -geoise** [vilaʒwa, -ʒwaz] *n* : villager
ville [vil] *nf* **1** : city, town **2 en** ~ : downtown
villégiature [vileʒjatyr] *nf* **1** : vacation **2** *or* **lieu de** ~ : resort
vin [vɛ̃] *nm* : wine
vinaigre [vinɛgr] *nm* : vinegar — **vinaigrette** [vinɛgrɛt] *nf* : vinaigrette
vindicatif, -tive [vɛ̃dikatif, -tiv] *adj* : vindictive
vingt [vɛ̃ (vɛ̃t *before a vowel, mute h, and the numbers 22-29*)] *adj* **1** : twenty **2** : twentieth (in dates) — ~ *nms & pl* : twenty — **vingtaine** [vɛ̃tɛn] *nf* : about twenty — **vingtième** [vɛ̃tjɛm] *adj & nmf & nm* : twentieth
vinicole [vinikɔl] *adj* : wine, winegrowing
vinyle [vinil] *nm* : vinyl
viol [vjɔl] *nm* : rape — **violation** [vjɔlasjɔ̃] *nf* : violation
violent, -lente [vjɔlɑ̃, -lɑ̃t] *adj* : violent — **violemment** [vjɔlamɑ̃] *adv* : violently — **violence** [vjɔlɑ̃s] *nf* : violence
violer [vjɔle] *vt* **1** : rape **2** : violate, break (a law, etc.)
violet, -lette [vjɔlɛ, -lɛt] *adj* : purple, violet — **violet** *nm* : purple, violet — **violette** *nf* : violet (flower)
violon [vjɔlɔ̃] *nm* : violin — **violoncelle** [vjɔlɔ̃sɛl] *nm* : cello — **violoniste** [vjɔlɔnist] *nmf* : violinist
vipère [vipɛr] *nf* : adder, viper
virer [vire] *vt* **1** : transfer (funds) **2** *fam* : fire, expel — *vi* **1** : veer, turn **2** : change color — **virage** [viraʒ] *nm* **1** COURBE : bend, turn **2** : change, shift (in direction) — **virée** [vire] *nf fam* : outing, trip — **virement** [virmɑ̃] *nm* : (bank) transfer
virevolter [virvɔlte] *vi* : twirl
virginité [virʒinite] *nf* : virginity
virgule [virgyl] *nf* **1** : comma **2** : (decimal) point
viril, -rile [viril] *adj* : virile, manly — **virilité** [virilite] *nf* : virility
virtuel, -tuelle [virtɥɛl] *adj* : virtual
virtuose [virtɥoz] *nmf* : virtuoso
virulent, -lente [virylɑ̃, -lɑ̃t] *adj* : virulent
virus [virys] *nms & pl* : virus
vis [vi] *nfs & pl* : screw
visa [viza] *nm* : visa
visage [vizaʒ] *nm* : face
vis-à-vis [vizavi] *adv* ~ **de 1** : opposite, facing **2** : towards, with respect to — ~ *nms & pl* **en** ~ : facing each other
viscères [visɛr] *nmpl* : innards
viser [vize] *vt* : aim for, aim at — *vi* **1** : aim **2** ~ **à** : aim at, intend to — **visée** [vize] *nf* : aim, design
visible [vizibl] *adj* **1** : visible **2** : obvious — **visibilité** [vizibilite] *nf* : visibility
visière [vizjɛr] *nf* : visor (of a cap, etc.)
vision [vizjɔ̃] *nf* : vision — **visionnaire** [vizjɔnɛr] *adj & nmf* : visionary — **visionner** [vizjɔne] *vt* : view
visite [vizit] *nf* **1** : visit **2** VISITEUR : visitor **3** : examination, inspection **4 rendre** ~ **à qqn** : visit s.o. — **visiter** [vizite] *vt* **1** : visit **2** EXAMINER : examine, inspect — **visiteur, -teuse** [vizitœr, -tøz] *n* : visitor
vison [vizɔ̃] *nm* : mink

visqueux, -queuse [viskø, -køz] *adj* : viscous
visser [vise] *vt* : screw (on)
visuel, -suelle [vizɥɛl] *adj* : visual — **visualiser** [vizɥalize] *vt* : visualize
vital, -tale [vital] *adj, mpl* **-taux** [vito] : vital — **vitalité** [vitalite] *nf* : vitality
vitamine [vitamin] *nf* : vitamin
vite [vit] *adv* **1** RAPIDEMENT : fast, quickly **2** TÔT : soon — **vitesse** [vitɛs] *nf* **1** : speed **2** : gear (of a car)
viticole [vitikɔl] *adj* : wine, wine-growing — **viticulture** [vitikyltyr] *nf* : wine growing
vitre [vitr] *nf* **1** : pane, windowpane **2** : window (of a car, train, etc.) — **vitrail** [vitraj] *nm, pl* **-traux** [vitro] : stained-glass window — **vitré, -trée** [vitre] *adj* : glass, glazed — **vitrer** [vitre] *vt* : glaze — **vitreux, -treuse** [vitrø, -trøz] *adj* : glassy — **vitrine** [vitrin] *nf* **1** : shop window **2** : display case
vivable [vivabl] *adj* : bearable
vivacité [vivasite] *nf* **1** : vivacity, liveliness **2** AGILITÉ : quickness **3** : sharpness, vividness
vivant, -vante [vivɑ̃, -vɑ̃t] *adj* **1** : alive, living **2** ANIMÉ : lively — **vivant** *nm* **1 du ~ de** : during the lifetime of **2 les ~s** : the living
vivats [viva] *nmpl* : cheers
vive → **vif** — **~** [viv] *interj* : long live, three cheers for — **vivement** [vivmɑ̃] *adv* **1** : quickly **2** : greatly
vivier [vivje] *nm* : fishpond
vivifier [vivifje] {96} *vt* : invigorate — **vivifiant, -fiante** [vivifjɑ̃, -fjɑ̃t] *adj* : invigorating
vivre [vivr] {98} *vt* : live through, experience — *vi* **1** : live **2 ~ de** : live on, live by — **vivres** [vivr] *nmpl* : provisions, food
vocabulaire [vɔkabylɛr] *nm* : vocabulary
vocation [vɔkasjɔ̃] *nf* : vocation, calling
vociférer [vɔsifere] {87} *v* : shout, scream
vodka [vɔdka] *nf* : vodka
vœu [vø] *nm, pl* **vœux 1** SOUHAIT : wish **2** SERMENT : vow **3 meilleurs ~x** : best wishes
vogue [vɔg] *nf* : vogue, fashion
voici [vwasi] *prep* **1** : here is, here are **2** : this is, these are **3 me ~** : here I am **4 ~ trois jours** : three days ago
voie [vwa] *nf* **1** : road, route, way **2** : lane (of a highway) **3** : way, course **4** *or* **~ ferrée** : railroad track, railroad **5 en ~ de** : in the process of **6 la Voie lactée** : the Milky Way
voilà [vwala] *prep* **1** : there is, there are **2** : that is, those are **3** VOICI : here is, here are **4 ~ tout!** : that's all! **5 ~ un an** : a year ago
voile [vwal] *nm* : veil — **~** *nf* **1** : sail **2** : sailing — **voiler** [vwale] *vt* **1** : veil **2** DISSIMULER : conceal — **se voiler** *vr* : warp (of wood) — **voilier** [vwalje] *nm* : sailboat — **voilure** [vwalyr] *nf* : sails *pl*
voir [vwar] {99} *vt* **1** : see **2 faire ~** *or* **laisser ~** : show — *vi* **1** : see **2 ~ à** : see to, make sure that **3 voyons** : let's see — **se voir** *vr* **1** : see oneself **2** : see each other **3 ça se voit** : that's obvious, it shows
voire [vwar] *adv* : indeed, or even
voirie [vwari] *nf* : highway department
voisin, -sine [vwazɛ̃, -zin] *adj* **1** : neighboring, adjoining **2 ~ de** : similar to — **~** *n* : neighbor — **voisinage** [vwazinaʒ] *nm* **1** : neighborhood **2** ENVIRONS : vicinity
voiture [vwatyr] *nf* **1** AUTOMOBILE : car, automobile **2** WAGON : (railroad) car, coach **3 ~ d'enfant** : baby carriage
voix [vwa] *nfs & pl* **1** : voice **2** VOTE : vote **3 à haute ~** : out loud
vol [vɔl] *nm* **1** : (plane) flight **2** : flock (of birds) **3** : theft, robbery
volage [vɔlaʒ] *adj* : fickle, flighty
volaille [vɔlaj] *nf* **1** : poultry **2** : fowl
volant [vɔlɑ̃] *nm* **1** : steering wheel **2** : shuttlecock **3** : flounce (of a skirt)
volcan [vɔlkɑ̃] *nm* : volcano — **volcanique** [vɔlkanik] *adj* : volcanic
volée [vɔle] *nf* **1** : volley **2** VOL : flock, flight
voler[1] [vɔle] *vt* **1** : steal **2** : rob **3 ~ à l'étalage** : shoplift
voler[2] *vi* : fly — **volet** [vɔlɛ] *nm* **1** : shutter, flap **2** : (detachable) section — **voleter** [vɔlte] {8} *vi* : flutter, flit
voleur, -leuse [vɔlœr, -løz] *adj* : dishonest — **~** *n* : thief, robber
volière [vɔljɛr] *nf* : aviary
volley [vɔlɛ] *or* **volley-ball** [vɔlɛbol] *nm* : volleyball
volontaire [vɔlɔ̃tɛr] *adj* **1** : voluntary **2** : deliberate **3** DÉTERMINÉ : willful — **~** *nmf* : volunteer — **volontairement** [vɔlɔ̃tɛrmɑ̃] *adv* **1** : voluntarily **2** : deliberately — **volonté** [vɔlɔ̃te] *nf* **1** : will **2** : willpower **3 à ~** : at will **4 bonne ~** : goodwill — **volontiers** [vɔlɔ̃tje] *adv* : willingly, gladly

volt [vɔlt] *nm* : volt — **voltage** [vɔltaʒ] *nm* : voltage
volte–face [vɔltəfas] *nfs & pl* : about-face
voltiger [vɔltiʒe] {17} *vi* : flutter about — **voltige** [vɔltiʒ] *nf* : acrobatics
volubile [vɔlybil] *adj* : voluble
volume [vɔlym] *nm* : volume — **volumineux, -neuse** [vɔlyminø, -nøz] *adj* : bulky
volupté [vɔlypte] *nf* : sensual pleasure — **voluptueux, -tueuse** [vɔlyptɥø, -tɥøz] *adj* : voluptuous
volute [vɔlyt] *nf* : coil (of smoke, etc.)
vomir [vɔmir] *vt* : vomit — *vi* : vomit
vorace [vɔras] *adj* : voracious
vote [vɔt] *nm* **1** : vote **2** : voting — **voter** [vɔte] *vi* : vote — *vt* : vote for
votre [vɔtr] *adj, pl* **vos** [vo] : your
vôtre [votr] *pron* **le ~, la ~, les ~s** : yours, your own
vouer [vwe] *vt* **1** PROMETTRE : vow, pledge **2** CONSACRER : dedicate, devote **3 voué à** : doomed to
vouloir [vulwar] {100} *vt* **1** : want, wish for **2** CONSENTIR À : agree to, be willing to **3 ~ dire** : mean **4 en ~ à** : bear a grudge against **5 veuillez patienter** : please wait — **voulu, -lue** [vuly] *adj* **1** DÉLIBÉRÉ : intentional **2** REQUIS : required
vous [vu] *pron* **1** (*as subject or direct object*) : you **2** (*as indirect object*) : you, to you **3** : yourself **4 à ~** : yours — **vous–même** [vumɛm] *pron, pl* **vous–mêmes** : yourself
voûte [vut] *nf* : vault, arch — **voûté, -tée** [vute] *adj* **1** : arched **2** : stooped, bent over
vouvoyer [vuvwaje] {58} *vt* : address as *vous*
voyage [vwajaʒ] *nm* **1** : trip, voyage **2 avoir son ~** *Can fam* : to be fed up — **voyager** [vwajaʒe] {17} *vi* : travel — **voyageur, -geuse** [vwajaʒœr, -ʒøz] *n* **1** : traveler **2** : passenger
voyance [vwajɑ̃s] *nf* : clairvoyance — **voyant, voyante** [vwajɑ̃, vwajɑ̃t] *adj* : loud, gaudy — **~** *n* : clairvoyant — **voyant** *nm* : warning light
voyelle [vwajɛl] *nf* : vowel
voyou [vwaju] *nm* : thug, hoodlum
vrac [vrak] *adv* **1 en ~** : loose, in bulk **2 en ~** : haphazardly
vrai, vraie [vrɛ] *adj* **1** : true **2** : real **3 à vrai dire** : to tell the truth — **vraiment** [vrɛmɑ̃] *adv* : really
vraisemblable [vrɛzɑ̃blabl] *adj* : likely, probable — **vraisemblance** [vrɛzɑ̃blɑ̃s] *nf* : likelihood, probability
vrombir [vrɔ̃bir] *vi* **1** : hum, buzz **2** : roar (of an engine) — **vrombissement** [vrɔ̃bismɑ̃] *nm* : humming, buzzing, roaring
vu [vy] *pp* → **voir** — **~** *prep* : in view of, considering — **vu, vue** [vy] *adj* **1** : seen, regarded **2 bien vu** : well thought of — **vue** *nf* **1** : sight, eyesight **2** : view, vista **3** IDÉE : opinion, view — **vu que** *conj phr* : seeing that, inasmuch as
vulgaire [vylgɛr] *adj* **1** GROSSIER : vulgar **2** ORDINAIRE : common — **vulgariser** [vylgarize] *vt* : popularize — **vulgarité** [vylgarite] *nf* : vulgarity
vulnérable [vylnerabl] *adj* : vulnerable — **vulnérabilité** [vylnerabilite] *nf* : vulnerability

WXYZ

w [dubləve] *nm* : w, 23d letter of the alphabet
wagon [vagɔ̃] *nm* : car (of a train)
wagon–lit [vagɔ̃li] *nm, pl* **wagons–lits** : sleeping car
wagon–restaurant [vagɔ̃rɛstɔrɑ̃] *nm, pl* **wagons–restaurants** : dining car
wallon, -lonne [walɔ̃, -lɔn] *adj* : Walloon
watt [wat] *nm* : watt
w-c [vese] *nmpl* : toilet
week–end [wikɛnd] *nm, pl* **week–ends** : weekend
western [wɛstɛrn] *nm* : western
whisky [wiski] *nm, pl* **-kies** : whiskey
x [iks] *nm* : x, 24th letter of the alphabet
xénophobie [gzenɔfɔbi] *nf* : xenophobia
xérès [gzerɛs, kserɛs] *nm* : sherry
xylophone [ksilɔfɔn] *nm* : xylophone
y [igrɛk] *nm* : y, 25th letter of the alphabet
y [i] *adv* **1** : there **2 ça ~ est !** : finally! **3 il ~ a** : there is, there are — **~** *pron* **1** : it, about it, on it, in it **2** : them, about them, on them, in them **3 j'y suis!** : I've got it!
yacht [jot] *nm* : yacht
yaourt [jaurt] *nm* : yogurt
yeux [jø] → **œil**
yoga [jɔga] *nm* : yoga
yogourt *or* **yoghourt** [jɔgurt] → **yaourt**
yo–yo *or* **yoyo** [jojo] *nm* : yo-yo
z [zɛd] *nm* : z, 26th letter of the alphabet
zèbre [zɛbr] *nm* : zebra — **zébrure** [zebryr] *nf* **1** : stripe **2** : welt
zèle [zɛl] *nm* : zeal — **zélé, -lée** [zele] *adj* : zealous
zénith [zenit] *nm* : zenith
zéro [zero] *adj* **1** : zero **2** : nil, worthless — **~** *nm* : zero, naught
zézayer [zezeje] *vi* : lisp
zigzag [zigzag] *nm* : zigzag — **zigzaguer** [zigzage] *vi* : zigzag
zinc [zɛ̃g] *nm* : zinc
zizanie [zizani] *nf* : discord, conflict
zodiaque [zɔdjak] *nm* : zodiac
zona [zona] *nm* : shingles
zone [zon] *nf* : zone, area — **zonage** [zonaʒ] *nm* : zoning
zoo [zo(o)] *nm* : zoo — **zoologie** [zɔɔlɔʒi] *nf* : zoology
zoom [zum] *nm* **1** : zoom lens **2 faire un ~** : zoom in
zut [zyt] *interj fam* : darn!, damn it!

English-French Dictionary

A

a[1] [ˈeɪ] *n, pl* **a's** or **as** [ˈeɪz] : a *m,* première lettre de l'alphabet
a[2] [ə, ˈeɪ] *art* (**an** [ən, ˈæn] *before a vowel or silent h*) **1** : un *m,* une *f* **2** PER : par
aback [əˈbæk] *adv* **taken ~** : déconcerté
abandon [əˈbændən] *vt* : abandonner — **~** *n* : abandon *m*
abashed [əˈbæʃt] *adj* : décontenancé
abate [əˈbeɪt] *vi* **abated; abating** : s'apaiser, se calmer
abbey [ˈæbi] *n, pl* **-beys** : abbaye *f* — **abbot** [ˈæbət] *n* : abbé *m*
abbreviate [əˈbriːviˌeɪt] *vt* **-ated; -ating** : abréger — **abbreviation** [əˌbriːviˈeɪʃən] *n* : abréviation *f*
abdicate [ˈæbdɪˌkeɪt] *v* **-cated; -cating** : abdiquer
abdomen [ˈæbdəmən, æbˈdoːmən] *n* : abdomen *m* — **abdominal** [æbˈdɑmənəl] *adj* : abdominal
abduct [æbˈdʌkt] *vt* : enlever — **abduction** [æbˈdʌkʃən] *n* : enlèvement *m*
aberration [ˌæbəˈreɪʃən] *n* : aberration *f*
abhor [əbˈhɔr, æb-] *vt* **-horred; -horring** : abhorrer, détester
abide [əˈbaɪd] *v* **abode** [əˈboːd] *or* **abided; abiding** *vt* : supporter — *vi* **~ by** : respecter, se conformer à
ability [əˈbɪləṭi] *n, pl* **-ties** **1** : aptitude *f* **2** SKILL : habileté *f,* talent *m*
ablaze [əˈbleɪz] *adj* : en feu
able [ˈeɪbəl] *adj* **abler; ablest** **1** CAPABLE : capable **2** SKILLED : habile — **ably** [ˈeɪbəli] *adv* : habilement
abnormal [æbˈnɔrməl] *adj* : anormal — **abnormality** [ˌæbnərˈmæləṭi, -nɔr-] *n, pl* **-ties** : anormalité *f,* anomalie *f*
aboard [əˈbord] *adv* : à bord — **~** *prep* : à bord de, dans
abode [əˈboːd] *n* : demeure *f,* domicile *m*
abolish [əˈbɑlɪʃ] *vt* : abolir — **abolition** [ˌæbəˈlɪʃən] *n* : abolition *f*
abominable [əˈbɑmənəbəl] *adj* : abominable
aborigine [ˌæbəˈrɪʤəni] *n* : aborigène *mf*
abort [əˈbɔrt] *vt* : faire avorter — **abortion** [əˈbɔrʃən] *n* : avortement *m*
abound [əˈbaʊnd] *vi* **~ in** : abonder en
about [əˈbaʊt] *adv* **1** APPROXIMATELY : vers, environ **2** AROUND : autour **3** NEARBY : près **4 be ~ to** : être sur le point de — **~** *prep* **1** AROUND : autour de **2** CONCERNING : sur, de
above [əˈbʌv] *adv* **1** OVERHEAD : au-dessus, en haut **2** PREVIOUSLY : ci-dessus — **~** *prep* **1** OVER : au-dessus de **2** EXCEEDING : plus de **3 ~ all** : surtout
abrasive [əˈbreɪsɪv] *adj* : abrasif
abreast [əˈbrɛst] *adv* **1** : de front, côte à côte **2 ~ of** : au courant de
abridge [əˈbrɪʤ] *vt* **abridged; abridging** : abréger
abroad [əˈbrɔd] *adv* **1** : à l'étranger **2** WIDELY : de tous côtés
abrupt [əˈbrʌpt] *adj* **1** SUDDEN : brusque **2** STEEP : abrupt
abscess [ˈæbˌsɛs] *n* : abcès *m*
absence [ˈæbsənts] *n* **1** : absence *f* **2** LACK : manque *m* — **absent** [ˈæbsənt] *adj* : absent — **absentee** [ˌæbsənˈtiː] *n* : absent *m,* -sente *f* — **absentminded** [ˌæbsəntˈmaɪndəd] *adj* : distrait
absolute [ˈæbsəˌluːt, ˌæbsəˈluːt] *adj* : absolu — **absolutely** [ˈæbsəˌluːtli, ˌæbsəˈluːtli] *adv* : absolument
absolve [əbˈzɑlv, æb-, -ˈsɑlv] *vt* **-solved; -solving** : absoudre
absorb [əbˈzɔrb, æb-, -ˈsɔrb] *vt* : absorber — **absorbent** [əbˈzɔrbənt, æb-, -ˈsɔr-] *adj* : absorbant — **absorption** [əbˈzɔrpʃən, æb-, -ˈsɔrp-] *n* : absorption *f*
abstain [əbˈsteɪn, æb-] *vi* **~ from** : s'abstenir de — **abstinence** [ˈæbstənənts] *n* : abstinence *f*
abstract [æbˈstrækt, ˈæbˌ-] *adj* : abstrait — **~** *n* SUMMARY : résumé *m*
absurd [əbˈsərd, -ˈzərd] *adj* : absurde — **absurdity** [əbˈsərdəṭi, -ˈzər-] *n, pl* **-ties** : absurdité *f*
abundant [əˈbʌndənt] *adj* : abondant — **abundance** [əˈbʌndənts] *n* : abondance *f*
abuse [əˈbjuːz] *vt* **abused; abusing** **1** MISUSE : abuser de **2** MISTREAT : maltraiter **3** INSULT : injurier — **~** [əˈbjuːs] *n* **1** MISUSE : abus *m* **2** MISTREATMENT : mauvais traitement *m* **3** INSULTS : insultes *fpl,* injures *fpl* — **abusive** [əˈbjuːsɪv] *adj* : injurieux

abut [ə'bʌt] *vi* **abutted; abutting ~ on** : être contigu à

abyss [ə'bɪs, 'æbɪs] *n* : abîme *m*

academy [ə'kædəmi] *n, pl* **-mies 1** SCHOOL : école *f,* collège *m* **2** SOCIETY : académie *f* — **academic** [ˌækə'dɛmɪk] *adj* **1** : universitaire **2** THEORETICAL : théorique

accelerate [ɪk'sɛləˌreɪt, æk-] *v* **-ated; -ating** : accélérer — **acceleration** [ɪkˌsɛlə'reɪʃən, æk-] *n* : accélération *f*

accent ['ækˌsɛnt, æk'sɛnt] *vt* : accentuer — **~** ['ækˌsɛnt, -sənt] *n* : accent *m* — **accentuate** [ɪk'sɛntʃuˌeɪt, æk-] *vt* **-ated; -ating** : accentuer

accept [ɪk'sɛpt, æk-] *vt* : accepter — **acceptable** [ɪk'sɛptəbəl, æk-] *adj* : acceptable — **acceptance** [ɪk'sɛptənts, æk-] *n* **1** : acceptation *f* **2** APPROVAL : approbation *f*

access ['ækˌsɛs] *n* : accès *m* — **accessible** [ɪk'sɛsəbəl, æk-] *adj* : accessible

accessory [ɪk'sɛsəri, æk-] *n, pl* **-ries 1** : accessoire *m* **2** ACCOMPLICE : complice *mf*

accident ['æksədənt] *n* **1** : accident *m* **2 by ~** : par hasard — **accidental** [ˌæksə'dɛntəl] *adj* : accidentel — **accidentally** [ˌæksə'dɛntəli, -'dɛntli] *adv* : accidentellement, par hasard

acclaim [ə'kleɪm] *vt* : acclamer — **~** *n* : acclamation *f*

acclimate [ə'klaɪməˌeɪt] *vt* **-mated; -mating** : acclimater

accommodate [ə'kɑməˌdeɪt] *vt* **-dated; -dating 1** ADAPT : accommoder **2** SATISFY : satisfaire **3** LODGE : loger **4** HOLD : contenir — **accommodation** [əˌkɑmə'deɪʃən] *n* **1** : accommodation *f* **2 ~s** *npl* LODGING : logement *m*

accompany [ə'kʌmpəni, -'kɑm-] *vt* **-nied; -nying** : accompagner

accomplice [ə'kɑmpləs, -'kʌm-] *n* : complice *mf*

accomplish [ə'kɑmplɪʃ, -'kʌm-] *vt* **1** : accomplir **2** REALIZE : réaliser — **accomplishment** [ə'kɑmplɪʃmənt, -'kʌm-] *n* : accomplissement *m*

accord [ə'kɔrd] *n* **1** AGREEMENT : accord *m* **2 of one's own ~** : de son plein gré — **accordance** [ə'kɔrdənts] *n* **in ~ with** : conformément à — **accordingly** [ə'kɔrdɪŋli] *adv* : en conséquence — **according to** [ə'kɔrdɪŋ] *prep* : selon, d'après

accordion [ə'kɔrdiən] *n* : accordéon *m*

account [ə'kaʊnt] *n* **1** : compte *m* **2** REPORT : compte *m* rendu **3** WORTH : importance *f* **4 on ~ of** : à cause de **5 on no ~** : en aucun cas **6 take into ~** : tenir compte de — **~** *vi* **~ for** : expliquer — **accountable** [ə'kaʊntəbəl] *adj* : responsable — **accountant** [ə'kaʊntənt] *n* : comptable *mf* — **accounting** [ə'kaʊntɪŋ] *n* : comptabilité *f*

accrue [ə'kru:] *vi* **-crued; -cruing** : s'accumuler

accumulate [ə'kju:mjəˌleɪt] *v* **-lated; -lating** *vt* : accumuler — *vi* s'accumuler — **accumulation** [əˌkju:mjə'leɪʃən] *n* : accumulation *f*

accurate ['ækjərət] *adj* : exact, précis — **accurately** *adv* : exactement, avec précision — **accuracy** ['ækjərəsi] *n, pl* **-cies** : exactitude *f,* précision *f*

accuse [ə'kju:z] *vt* **-cused; -cusing** : accuser — **accusation** [akyzasjɔ̃] *n* : accusation *f*

accustom [ə'kʌstəm] *vt* : accoutumer — **accustomed** [ə'kʌstəmd] *adj* **1** CUSTOMARY : habituel **2 become ~ to** : s'habituer à

ace ['eɪs] *n* : as *m*

ache [eɪk] *vi* **ached; aching** : faire mal — **~** *n* : douleur *f*

achieve [ə'tʃi:v] *vt* **achieved; achieving** : accomplir, atteindre — **achievement** [ə'tʃi:vmənt] *n* : accomplissement *m,* réussite *f*

acid ['æsəd] *adj* : acide — **~** *n* : acide *m*

acknowledge [ɪk'nɑlɪdʒ, æk-] *vt* **-edged; -edging 1** ADMIT : admettre **2** RECOGNIZE : reconnaître **3 ~ receipt of** : accuser réception de — **acknowledgment** [ɪk'nɑlɪdʒmənt, æk-] *n* **1** : reconnaissance *f* **2 ~ of receipt** : accusé *m* de réception

acne ['ækni] *n* : acné *f*

acorn ['eɪˌkɔrn, -kərn] *n* : gland *m*

acoustic [ə'ku:stɪk] *or* **acoustical** [ə'ku:stɪkəl] *adj* : acoustique — **acoustics** [ə'ku:stɪks] *ns & pl* : acoustique *f*

acquaint [ə'kweɪnt] *vt* **1 ~ s.o. with** : mettre qqn au courant de **2 be ~ed with** : connaître (une personne) — **acquaintance** [ə'kweɪntənts] *n* : connaissance *f*

acquire [ə'kwaɪr] *vt* **-quired; -quiring** : acquérir — **acquisition** [ˌækwə'zɪʃən] *n* : acquisition *f*

acquit [ə'kwɪt] *vt* **-quitted; -quitting** : acquitter

acre ['eɪkər] *n* : acre *f* — **acreage** ['eɪkərɪdʒ] *n* : superficie *f*

acrid ['ækrəd] *adj* : âcre
acrobat ['ækrə,bæt] *n* : acrobate *mf* — **acrobatic** [,ækrə'bætɪk] *adj* : acrobatique — **acrobatics** [,ækrə'bætɪks] *ns & pl* : acrobatie *f*
across [ə'krɔs] *adv* **1** : de large, d'un côté à l'autre **2 ~ from** : en face de **3 go ~** : traverser — **~** *prep* **1 ~ the street** : de l'autre côté de la rue **2 lie ~ sth** : être en travers de qqch
acrylic [ə'krɪlɪk] *n* : acrylique *m*
act ['ækt] *vi* **1** : agir **2** PERFORM : jouer, faire du théâtre **3 ~ as** : servir de — *vt* : jouer (un rôle) — **~** *n* **1** ACTION : acte *m* **2** DECREE : loi *f* **3** : acte *m* (d'une pièce de théâtre), numéro *m* (de variétés) **4 put on an ~** : jouer la comédie — **acting** *adj* : intérimaire
action ['ækʃən] *n* **1** : action *f* **2** DEED : acte *m* **2** LAWSUIT : procès *m*, action *f*
activate ['æktə,veɪt] *vt* **-vated; -vating** : activer
active ['æktɪv] *adj* : actif — **activity** [æk'tɪvəti] *n, pl* **-ties** : activité *f*
actor ['æktər] *n* : acteur *m*, -trice *f* — **actress** ['æktrəs] *n* : actrice *f*
actual ['æktʃuəl] *adj* **1** : réel, véritable **2** VERY : même — **actually** ['æktʃuəli, -ʃəli] *adv* **1** REALLY : vraiment **2** IN FACT : en fait
acupuncture ['ækju,pʌŋktʃər] *n* : acupuncture *f*
acute [ə'kju:t] *adj* **acuter; acutest 1** : aigu **2** KEEN : fin
ad ['æd] *n* → **advertisement**
adamant ['ædəmənt, -,mænt] *adj* : inflexible
adapt [ə'dæpt] *vt* : adapter — *vi* : s'adapter — **adaptable** [ə,dæptəbəl] *adj* : adaptable — **adaptation** [,æ-,dæp'teɪʃən, -dəp-] *n* : adaptation *f* — **adapter** [ə'dæptər] *n* : adapteur *m*
add ['æd] *vt* **1** : ajouter **2 ~ up** : additionner — *vi* : additionner
addict ['ædɪkt] *n or* **drug ~** : toxicomane *mf;* drogué *m*, -guée *f* — **addiction** [ə'dɪkʃən] *n* **1** : dépendance *f* **2 drug ~** : toxicomanie *f*
addition [ə'dɪʃən] *n* **1** : addition *f* **2 in ~** : en plus — **additional** [ə'dɪʃənəl] *adj* : additionnel, supplémentaire — **additive** ['ædətɪv] *n* : additif *m*
address [ə'drɛs] *vt* **1** : adresser (une lettre, etc.) **2** : s'adresser à (une personne), aborder (un problème) — **~** [ə'drɛs, 'æ,drɛs] *n* **1** : adresse *f* **2** SPEECH : discours *m*
adept [ə'dɛpt] *adj* : habile
adequate ['ædɪkwət] *adj* : adéquat, suffisant — **adequately** ['ædɪkwətli] *adv* : suffisamment
adhere [æd'hir, əd-] *vi* **-hered; -hering 1** STICK : adhérer **2 ~ to** KEEP : adhérer à, observer — **adherence** [æd-'hɪrənts, əd-] *n* : adhésion *f* — **adhesion** [æd'hiʒən, əd-] *n* : adhésion *f*, adhérence *f* — **adhesive** [æd'hi:sɪv, əd-, -zɪv] *adj* : adhésif — **~** *n* : adhésif *m*
adjacent [ə'dʒeɪsənt] *adj* : adjacent, contigu
adjective ['ædʒɪktɪv] *n* : adjectif *m*
adjoining [ə'dʒɔɪnɪŋ] *adj* : contigu
adjourn [ə'dʒərn] *vt* : ajourner — *vi* : suspendre la séance
adjust [ə'dʒʌst] *vt* : ajuster — *vi* ADAPT : s'adapter — **adjustable** [ə'dʒʌstəbəl] *adj* : réglable, ajustable — **adjustment** [ə'dʒʌstmənt] *n* **1** : ajustement *m* **2** ADAPTATION : adaptation *f*
ad–lib ['æd'lɪb] *vt* **ad–libbed; ad–libbing** : improviser
administer [æd'mɪnəstər, əd-] *vt* : administrer — **administration** [æd-,mɪnə'streɪʃən, əd-] *n* : administration *f* — **administrative** [æd'mɪnə,streɪtɪv, əd-] *adj* : administratif — **administrator** [æd'mɪnə,streɪtər, əd-] *n* : administrateur *m*, -trice *f*
admirable ['ædmərəbəl] *adj* : admirable
admiral ['ædmərəl] *n* : amiral *m*
admire [æd'maɪr] *vt* **-mired; -miring** : admirer — **admiration** [,ædmə'reɪʃən] *n* : admiration *f* — **admirer** [æd-'maɪrər] *n* : admirateur *m*, -trice *f* — **admiring** [æd'maɪrɪŋ] *adj* : admiratif
admit [æd'mɪt, əd-] *vt* **-mitted; -mitting 1** : admettre **2** ACKNOWLEDGE : reconnaître **3** CONFESS : avouer — **admission** [æd'mɪʃən] *n* **1** ADMITTANCE : admission *f* **2** FEE : entrée *f* **3** CONFESSION : aveu *m* — **admittance** [æd-'mɪtənts, əd-] *n* : entrée *f*
admonish [æd'mɑnɪʃ, əd-] *vt* : réprimander
ado [ə'du:] *n* **1** : agitation *f* **2 without further ~** : sans plus de cérémonie
adolescent [,ædəl'ɛsənt] *n* : adolescent *m*, -cente *f* — **adolescence** [,ædəl'ɛsənts] *n* : adolescence *f*
adopt [ə'dɑpt] *vt* : adopter — **adoption** [ə'dɑpʃən] *n* : adoption *f*
adore [ə'dor] *vt* **adored; adoring** : adorer — **adorable** [ə'dorəbəl] *adj* : adorable — **adoration** [,ædə'reɪʃən] *n* : adoration *f*
adorn [ə'dɔrn] *vt* : orner

adrift [ə'drɪft] *adv & adj* : à la dérive
adroit [ə'drɔɪt] *adj* : adroit, habile
adult [ə'dʌlt, 'æ,dʌlt] *adj* : adulte — ~ *n* : adulte *mf*
adultery [ə'dʌltəri] *n, pl* **-teries** : adultère *m*
advance [æd'vænts, əd-] *v* **-vanced; -vancing** *vt* : avancer — *vi* **1** : avancer **2** IMPROVE : progresser — ~ *n* **1** : avance *f* **2 in ~** : à l'avance, d'avance — **advancement** [æd'væntsmənt, əd-] *n* : avancement *m*
advantage [əd'væntɪʤ, æd-] *n* **1** : avantage *m* **2 take ~ of** : profiter de — **advantageous** [,æd,væn'teɪʤəs, -vən-] *adj* : avantageux
advent ['æd,vɛnt] *n* **1** : avènement *m* **2 Advent** : Avent *m*
adventure [æd'vɛnʧər, əd-] *n* : aventure *f* — **adventurous** [æd'vɛnʧərəs, əd-] *adj* : aventureux
adverb ['æd,vərb] *n* : adverbe *m*
adversary ['ædvər,sɛri] *n, pl* **-saries** : adversaire *mf*
adverse [æd'vɛrs, 'æd,-] *adj* : défavorable — **adversity** [æd'vərsəṭi, əd-] *n, pl* **-ties** : adversité *f*
advertise ['ædvər,taɪz] *v* **-tised; -tising** *vt* : faire de la publicité pour — *vi* : passer une annonce (dans un journal) — **advertisement** ['ædvər,taɪzmənt, æd'vərṭəzmənt] *n* : publicité *f*, annonce *f* — **advertiser** ['ædvər,taɪzɛr] *n* : annonceur *m* — **advertising** ['ædvər,taɪzɪŋ] *n* : publicité *f*
advice [æd'vaɪs] *n* : conseils *mpl*
advise [æd'vaɪz, əd-] *vt* **-vised; -vising** **1** : conseiller **2** RECOMMEND : recommander **3** INFORM : aviser — **advisable** [æd'vaɪzəbəl, əd-] *adj* : recommandé, prudent — **adviser** [æd'vaɪzər, əd-] *n* : conseiller *m*, -lère *f* — **advisory** [æd'vaɪzəri, əd-] *adj* : consultatif
advocate ['ædvə,keɪt] *vt* **-cated; -cating** : préconiser — ~ ['ædvəkət] *n* **1** SUPPORTER : défenseur *m* **2** LAWYER : avocat *m*, -cate *f*
aerial ['æriəl] *adj* : aérien — ~ *n* : antenne *f*
aerobics [,ær'o:bɪks] *ns & pl* : aérobic *m*
aerodynamic [,æro:daɪ'næmɪk] *adj* : aérodynamique
aerosol ['ærə,sɔl] *n* : aérosol *m*
aesthetic [ɛs'θɛṭɪk] *adj* : esthétique
afar [ə'fɑr] *adv* **from ~** : de loin
affable ['æfəbəl] *adj* : affable
affair [ə'fær] *n* **1** : affaire *f* **2** *or* **love ~** : liaison *f*, affaire *f* de cœur
affect [ə'fɛkt, æ-] *vt* : affecter — **affection** [ə'fɛkʃən] *n* : affection *f* — **affectionate** [ə'fɛkʃənət] *adj* : affectueux
affirm [ə'fərm] *vt* : affirmer — **affirmative** [ə'fərməṭɪv] *adj* : affirmatif
affix [ə'fɪks] *vt* : apposer (une signature), coller (un timbre)
afflict [ə'flɪkt] *vt* : affliger — **affliction** [ə'flɪkʃən] *n* : affliction *f*
affluent ['æ,flu:ənt; æ'flu:-, ə-] *adj* : riche
afford [ə'ford] *vt* **1** : avoir les moyens d'acheter **2 ~ to do** : se permettre de faire
affront [ə'frʌnt] *n* : affront *m*
afloat [ə'flo:t] *adj & adv* : à flot
afoot [ə'fʊt] *adv & adj* : en train, en cours
afraid [ə'freɪd] *adj* **1 be ~ of** : avoir peur de, craindre **2 be ~ that** : regretter que **3 I'm ~ not** : hélas, non
African ['æfrɪkən] *adj* : africain
after ['æftər] *adv* **1** AFTERWARD : après **2** BEHIND : en arrière — ~ *conj* : après que — ~ *prep* **1** : après **2 ~ all** : après tout **3 it's ten ~ five** : il est cinq heures dix
aftereffect ['æftərɪ,fɛkt] *n* : répercussion *f*
aftermath ['æftər,mæθ] *n* : suites *fpl*
afternoon [,æftər'nu:n] *n* : après-midi *mf*
afterward ['æftərwərd] *or* **afterwards** [-wərdz] *adv* : après, ensuite
again [ə'gɛn, -gɪn] *adv* **1** : encore (une fois), de nouveau **2 ~ and ~** : maintes et maintes fois **3 then ~** : d'autre part
against [ə'gɛntst, -'gɪntst] *prep* **1** : contre **2 go ~** : aller à l'encontre
age ['eɪʤ] *n* **1** : âge *m* **2** ERA : ère *f*, époque *f* **3 come of ~** : atteindre la majorité **4 for ~s** : depuis longtemps **5 old ~** : vieillesse *f* — ~ *v* **age; aging** : vieillir — **aged** ['eɪʤəd, 'eɪʤd] *adj* **1** : âgé de **2** ['eɪʤd] OLD : vieux, âgé
agency ['eɪʤəntsi] *n, pl* **-cies** : agence *f*
agenda [ə'ʤɛndə] *n* : ordre *m* du jour, programme *m*
agent ['eɪʤənt] *n* : agent *m*
aggravate ['ægrə,veɪt] *vt* **-vated; -vating** **1** WORSEN : aggraver **2** ANNOY : agacer, énerver
aggregate ['ægrɪgət] *adj* : total, global — ~ *n* : ensemble *m*, total *m*
aggression [ə'grɛʃən] *n* : agression *f* —

aggressive [ə'grɛsɪv] *adj* : agressif — **aggressor** [ə'grɛsər] *n* : agresseur *m*
aghast [ə'gæst] *adj* : horrifié
agile ['ædʒəl] *adj* : agile — **agility** [ə'dʒɪləṭi] *n, pl* **-ties** : agilité *f*
agitate ['ædʒəˌteɪt] *vt* **-tated; -tating 1** SHAKE : agiter **2** TROUBLE : inquiéter — **agitation** [ˌædʒə'teɪʃən] *n* : agitation *f*
ago [ə'go:] *adv* **1** : il y a **2 long ~** : il y a longtemps
agony ['ægəni] *n, pl* **-nies** : angoisse *f*, souffrance *f* — **agonize** ['ægəˌnaɪz] *vi* **-nized; -nizing** : se tourmenter — **agonizing** ['ægəˌnaɪzɪŋ] *adj* : déchirant
agree [ə'gri:] *v* **agreed; agreeing** *vt* **1** ADMIT : convenir **2 ~ that** : reconnaître que — *vi* **1** : être d'accord **2** CORRESPOND : concorder **3 ~ to** : consentir à — **agreeable** [ə'gri:əbəl] *adj* **1** PLEASING : agréable **2** WILLING : consentant — **agreement** [ə'gri:mənt] *n* : accord *m*
agriculture ['ægrɪˌkʌltʃər] *n* : agriculture *f* — **agricultural** [ˌægrɪ'kʌltʃərəl] *adj* : agricole
aground [ə'graund] *adv* **run ~** : s'échouer
ahead [ə'hɛd] *adv* **1** IN FRONT : en avant, devant **2** BEFOREHAND : à l'avance **3** LEADING : en avance **4 go ~!** : allez-y! — **ahead of** *prep* **1** IN FRONT OF : devant **2 ~ time** : avant l'heure
aid ['eɪd] *vt* : aider — **~** *n* : aide *f*, secours *m*
AIDS ['eɪdz] *n* (*a*cquired *i*mmuno*d*eficiency *s*yndrome) : sida *m*
ail ['eɪl] *vi* : être souffrant — **ailment** ['eɪlmənt] *n* : maladie *f*
aim ['eɪm] *vt* : braquer (une arme à feu), diriger (une remarque, etc.) — *vi* **1 ~ to** : avoir l'intention de **2 ~ at** *or* **~ for** : viser — **~** *n* : but *m* — **aimless** ['eɪmləs] *adj* : sans but
air ['ær] *vt* **1** : aérer **2** EXPRESS : exprimer **3** BROADCAST : diffuser — **~** *n* **1** : air *m* **2 on the ~** : à l'antenne — **air-conditioned** [ˌærkən'dɪʃənd] *adj* : climatisé — **air-conditioning** [ˌærkən'dɪʃənɪŋ] *n* : climatisation *f* — **aircraft** ['ærˌkræft] *ns & pl* : avion *m* — **air force** *n* : armée *f* de l'air — **airline** ['ærˌlaɪn] *n* : compagnie *f* aérienne — **airmail** ['ærˌmeɪl] *n* **1** : poste *f* aérienne **2 by ~** : par avion — **airplane** ['ærˌpleɪn] *n* : avion *m* — **airport** ['ærˌport] *n* : aéroport *m* — **airstrip** ['ærˌʃtrɪp] *n* : piste *f* d'atterrissage — **airtight** ['ær'taɪt] *adj* : hermétique — **airy** ['æri] *adj* **airier; -est** : aéré
aisle ['aɪl] *n* : allée *f* (d'un théâtre, etc.), couloir *m* (d'un avion)
ajar [ə'dʒɑr] *adj & adv* : entrouvert
akin [ə'kɪn] *adj* **~ to** : semblable à
alarm [ə'lɑrm] *n* **1** : alarme *f* **2** ANXIETY : inquiétude *f* — **~** *vt* : alarmer — **alarm clock** *n* : réveille-matin *m*
alas [ə'læs] *interj* : hélas!
album ['ælbəm] *n* : album *m*
alcohol ['ælkəˌhɔl] *n* : alcool *m* — **alcoholic** [ˌælkə'hɔlɪk] *adj* : alcoolisé, alcoolique — **~** *n* : alcoolique *mf* — **alcoholism** ['ælkəhɔˌlɪzəm] *n* : alcoolisme *m*
alcove ['ælˌko:v] *n* : alcôve *f*
ale ['eɪl] *n* : bière *f*
alert [ə'lərt] *adj* **1** WATCHFUL : vigilant **2** LIVELY : alerte, éveillé — **~** *n* : alerte *f* — **~** *vt* : alerter — **alertness** [ə'lərtnəs] *n* **1** : vigilance *f* **2** : vivacité *f*
alfalfa [æl'fælfə] *n* : luzerne *f*
alga ['ælgə] *n, pl* **-gae** ['ælˌdʒi:] : algue *f*
algebra ['ældʒəbrə] *n* : algèbre *f*
Algerian [æl'dʒɪriən] *adj* : algérien
alias ['eɪliəs] *adv* : alias — **~** *n* : nom *m* d'emprunt, faux nom *m*
alibi ['æləˌbaɪ] *n* : alibi *m*
alien ['eɪliən] *adj* : étranger — **~** *n* **1** FOREIGNER : étranger *m*, -gère *f* **2** EXTRATERRESTRIAL : extraterrestre *mf* — **alienate** ['eɪliəˌneɪt] *vt* **-ated; -ating** : aliéner — **alienation** [ˌeɪliə'neɪʃən] *n* : aliénation *f*
alight [ə'laɪt] *vi* : descendre, se poser
align [ə'laɪn] *vt* : aligner — **alignment** [ə'laɪnmənt] *n* : alignement *m*
alike [ə'laɪk] *adv* : de la même façon — **~** *adj* **1** : semblable **2 be ~** : se ressembler
alimony ['æləˌmo:ni] *n, pl* **-nies** : pension *f* alimentaire
alive [ə'laɪv] *adj* **1** LIVING : vivant, en vie **2** LIVELY : vif, animé
all ['ɔl] *adv* **1** COMPLETELY : tout, complètement **2 ~ at once** : tout d'un coup **3 ~ the better** : tant mieux — **~** *adj* : tout — **~** *pron* **1** EVERYTHING : tout **2** EVERYONE : tous, toutes **3 ~ in ~** : tout compte fait — **all-around** [ˌɔlə'raund] *adj* VERSATILE : complet
allay [ə'leɪ] *vt* : calmer, apaiser
allege [ə'lɛdʒ] *vt* **-leged; -leging** : alléguer, prétendre — **allegation** [ˌælɪ'geɪʃən] *n* : allégation *f* — **alleged** [ə'lɛdʒd, ə'lɛdʒəd] *adj* : présumé, pré-

tendu — **allegedly** [ə'lɛʤədli] *adv* : prétendument
allegiance [ə'li:ʤənts] *n* : allégeance *f*
allergy ['ælərʤi] *n, pl* **-gies** : allergie *f* — **allergic** [ə'lərʤɪk] *adj* : allergique
alleviate [ə'li:vi,eɪt] *vt* **-ated; -ating** : soulager, alléger
alley ['æli] *n, pl* **-leys** : ruelle *f*, allée *f*
alliance [ə'laɪənts] *n* : alliance *f*
alligator ['ælə,geɪtər] *n* : alligator *m*
allocate ['ælə,keɪt] *vt* **-cated; -cating** : allouer, assigner
allot [ə'lɑt] *vt* **allotted; allotting 1** ASSIGN : attribuer **2** DISTRIBUTE : répartir — **allotment** [ə'lɑtmənt] *n* : allocation *f*
allow [ə'laʊ] *vt* **1** PERMIT : permettre **2** CONCEDE : admettre **3** GRANT : accorder — *vi* **~ for** : tenir compte de — **allowance** [ə'laʊənts] *n* **1** : allocation *f* **2** : argent *m* de poche (pour les enfants) **3 make ~s for** : tenir compte de
alloy ['æ,lɔɪ] *n* : alliage *m*
all right *adv* **1** YES : d'accord **2** WELL : bien **3** CERTAINLY : bien, sans doute — **~** *adj* : pas mal, bien
allude [ə'lu:d] *vi* **-luded; -luding ~ to** : faire allusion à
allure [ə'lʊr] *vt* **-lured; -luring** : attirer
allusion [ə'lu:ʒən] *n* : allusion *f*
ally [ə'laɪ, 'æ,laɪ] *vt* **-lied; -lying 1** : allier **2 ~ oneself with** : s'allier avec — **~** ['æ,laɪ, ə'laɪ] *n, pl* **allies** : allié *m*, -liée *f*
almanac ['ɔlmə,næk, 'æl-] *n* : almanach *m*
almighty [ɔl'maɪṭi] *adj* : tout puissant, formidable
almond ['ɑmənd, 'ɑl-, 'æ-, 'æl-] *n* : amande *f*
almost ['ɔl,mo:st, ɔl'mo:st] *adv* : presque
alms ['ɑmz, 'ɑlmz, 'ælmz] *ns & pl* : aumône *f*
alone [ə'lo:n] *adv* **1** : seul **2 leave ~** : laisser tranquille — **~** *adj* : seul
along [ə'lɔŋ] *adv* **1 all ~** : tout le temps **2 ~ with** : avec, accompagné de — **~** *prep* **1** : le long de **2** ON : sur — **alongside** [ə,lɔŋ'saɪd] *adv* : à côté — **~** *or* **~ of** *prep* : à côté de
aloof [ə'lu:f] *adj* : distant
aloud [ə'laʊd] *adv* : à haute voix
alphabet ['ælfə,bɛt] *n* : alphabet *m* — **alphabetic** [,ælfə'bɛtɪk] *or* **alphabetical** [-tɪkəl] *adj* : alphabétique
already [ɔl'rɛdi] *adv* : déjà
also ['ɔl,so:] *adv* : aussi
altar ['ɔltər] *n* : autel *m*
alter ['ɔltər] *vt* **1** : changer, modifier **2** : retoucher (un vêtement) — **alteration** [,ɔltə'reɪʃən] *n* **1** : changement *m*, modification *f* **2 ~s** *npl* : retouches *fpl*
alternate ['ɔltərnət] *adj* : alternatif — **~** ['ɔltər,neɪt] *v* **-nated; -nating** *vt* : faire alterner — *vi* : alterner — **alternating current** ['ɔltər,neɪṭɪŋ] *n* : courant *m* alternatif — **alternative** [ɔl'tərnəṭɪv] *adj* : alternatif — **~** *n* : alternative *f*
although [ɔl'ðo:] *conj* : bien que, quoique
altitude ['æltə,tu:d, -,tju:d] *n* : altitude *f*
altogether [,ɔltə'gɛðər] *adv* **1** COMPLETELY : entièrement, tout à fait **2** ON THE WHOLE : dans l'ensemble **3 how much ~?** : combien en tout?
aluminum [ə'lu:mənəm] *n* : aluminium *m*
always ['ɔlwiz, -,weɪz] *adv* **1** : toujours **2** FOREVER : pour toujours
am → **be**
amass [ə'mæs] *vt* : amasser
amateur ['æmətʃər, -tər, -,tʊr, -,tjʊr] *adj* : amateur — **~** *n* : amateur *m*
amaze [ə'meɪz] *vt* **amazed; amazing** : étonner, stupéfier — **amazement** [ə'meɪzmənt] *n* : stupéfaction *f* — **amazing** [ə'meɪzɪŋ] *adj* : étonnant
ambassador [æm'bæsə,dər] *n* : ambassadeur *m*, -drice *f*
amber ['æmbər] *n* : ambre *m*
ambiguous [æm'bɪgjʊəs] *adj* : ambigu — **ambiguity** [,æmbə'gju:əṭi] *n, pl* **-ties** : ambiguïté *f*
ambition [æm'bɪʃən] *n* : ambition *f* — **ambitious** [æm'bɪʃəs] *adj* : ambitieux
ambivalence [æm'bɪvələnts] *n* : ambivalence *f* — **ambivalent** [æm'bɪvələnt] *adj* : ambivalent
amble ['æmbəl] *vi* **-bled; -bling** : déambuler
ambulance ['æmbjələnts] *n* : ambulance *f*
ambush ['æmbʊʃ] *vt* : tendre une embuscade à — **~** *n* : embuscade *f*
amenable [ə'mi:nəbəl, -'mɛ-] *adj* **1** : accommodant **2 ~ to** : disposé à
amend [ə'mɛnd] *vt* : amender, modifier — **amendment** [ə'mɛndmənt] *n* : amendement *m* — **amends** [ə'mɛndz] *ns & pl* **make ~** : réparer ses torts
amenities [ə'mɛnəṭis, -'mi:-] *npl* : équipements *mpl*, aménagements *mpl*
American [ə'mɛrɪkən] *adj* : américain

amiable ['eɪmi:əbəl] *adj* : aimable
amicable ['æmɪkəbəl] *adj* : amical
amid [ə'mɪd] *or* **amidst** [ə'mɪdst] *prep* : au milieu de, parmi
amiss [ə'mɪs] *adv* **1** : mal **2 take sth ~** : prendre qqch de travers — **~** *adj* **something is ~** : quelque chose ne va pas
ammonia [ə'mo:njə] *n* : ammoniaque *f*
ammunition [ˌæmjə'nɪʃən] *n* : munitions *fpl*
amnesia [æm'ni:ʒə] *n* : amnésie *f*
amnesty ['æmnəsti] *n, pl* **-ties** : amnistie *f*
amoeba [ə'mi:bə] *n, pl* **-bas** *or* **-bae** [-bi:] : amibe *f*
among [e'mʌŋ] *prep* : parmi, entre
amount [ə'maʊnt] *vi* **1 ~ to** TOTAL : s'élever à **2 that ~s to the same thing** : cela revient au même — **~** *n* **1** : quantité *f* **2** SUM : somme *f,* montant *m*
amphibian [æm'fɪbiən] *n* : amphibien *m* — **amphibious** [æm'fɪbiəs] *adj* : amphibie
amphitheater ['æmfəˌθi:əṭər] *n* : amphithéâtre *m*
ample ['æmpəl] *adj* **-pler; -plest 1** SPACIOUS : ample **2** PLENTIFUL : abondant
amplify ['æmpləˌfaɪ] *vt* **-fied; -fying** : amplifier — **amplifier** ['æmpləˌfaɪər] *n* : amplificateur *m*
amputate ['æmpjəˌteɪt] *v* **-tated; -tating** : amputer — **amputation** [ˌæmpjə'teɪʃən] *n* : amputation *f*
amuse [ə'mju:z] *vt* **amused; amusing** : amuser — **amusement** [ə'mju:zmənt] *n* **1** ENJOYMENT : amusement *m* **2** DIVERSION : divertissement *m*
an → **a**[2]
analgesic [ˌænəl'ʤi:zɪk, -sɪk] *n* : analgésique *m*
analogy [ə'næləʤi] *n, pl* **-gies** : analogie *f* — **analogous** [ə'næləgəs] *adj* : analogue
analysis [ə'næləsəs] *n, pl* **-yses** [-ˌsi:z] : analyse *f* — **analytic** [ˌænə'lɪtɪk] *or* **analytical** [-ṭɪkəl] *adj* : analytique — **analyze** *or Brit* **analyse** ['ænəˌlaɪz] *vt* **-lyzed** *or Brit* **-lysed; -lyzing** *or Brit* **-lysing** : analyser
anarchy ['ænərki, -ˌnɑr-] *n* : anarchie *f*
anatomy [ə'næṭəmi] *n, pl* **-mies** : anatomie *f* — **anatomic** [ˌænə'tɑmɪk] *or* **anatomical** [-mɪkəl] *adj* : anatomique
ancestor ['ænˌsɛstər] *n* : ancêtre *mf* — **ancestral** [æn'sɛstrəl] *adj* : ancestral — **ancestry** ['ænˌsɛstri] *n* **1** LINEAGE : ascendance *f* **2** ANCESTORS : ancêtres *mpl*
anchor ['æŋkər] *n* **1** : ancre *f* **2** : présentateur *m,* -trice *f* (à la télévision) — **~** *vt* : ancrer — *vi* : jeter l'ancre
anchovy ['ænˌʧo:vi, æn'ʧo:-] *n, pl* **-vies** *or* **-vy** : anchois *m*
ancient ['eɪntʃənt] *adj* : ancien
and ['ænd] *conj* **1** : et **2 come ~ see** : venez voir **3 more ~ more** : de plus en plus **4 try ~ finish it soon** : tâchez de l'achever bientôt
anecdote ['ænɪkˌdo:t] *n* : anecdote *f*
anemia [ə'ni:miə] *n* : anémie *f* — **anemic** [ə'ni:mɪk] *adj* : anémique
anesthesia [ˌænəs'θi:ʒə] *n* : anesthésie *f* — **anesthetic** ['ænəs'θɛṭɪk] *adj* : anesthésique — **~** *n* : anesthésique *m*
anew [ə'nu:, -'nju:] *adv* : encore, de nouveau
angel ['eɪnʤəl] *n* : ange *m* — **angelic** [æn'ʤɛlɪk] *or* **angelical** [-lɪkəl] *adj* : angélique
anger ['æŋgər] *vt* : fâcher, mettre en colère — **~** *n* : colère *f*
angle ['æŋgəl] *n* **1** : angle *m* **2 at an ~** : de biais — **angler** ['æŋglər] *n* : pêcheur *m,* -cheuse *f* à la ligne
Anglo-Saxon [ˌaŋglo'sæksən] *adj* : anglo-saxon
angry ['æŋgri] *adj* **-grier; -est** : fâché, en colère — **angrily** ['æŋgrəlɪ] *adv* : avec colère
anguish ['æŋgwɪʃ] *n* : angoisse *f*
angular ['æŋgjələr] *adj* : anguleux
animal ['ænəməl] *n* : animal *m*
animate ['ænəˌmeɪt] *vt* **-mated; -mating** : animer, stimuler — **~** ['ænəmət] *adj* ALIVE : vivant — **animated** ['ænəˌmeɪṭəd] *adj* **1** : animé **2 ~ cartoon** : dessin *m* animé — **animation** [ˌænə'meɪʃən] *n* : animation *f*
animosity [ˌænə'mɑsəṭi] *n, pl* **-ties** : animosité *f*
anise ['ænəs] *n* : anis *m*
ankle ['æŋkəl] *n* : cheville *f*
annex [ə'nɛks, 'æˌnɛks] *vt* : annexer — **~** ['æˌnɛks, -nɪks] *n* : annexe *f*
annihilate [ə'naɪəˌleɪt] *vt* **-lated; -lating** : anéantir, annihiler — **annihilation** [əˌnaɪə'leɪʃən] *n* : anéantissement *m*
anniversary [ˌænə'vərsəri] *n, pl* **-ries** : anniversaire *m*
annotate ['ænəˌteɪt] *vt* **-tated; -tating** : annoter
announce [ə'naunts] *vt* **-nounced;**

-nouncing : annoncer — **announcement** [ə'naʊntsmənt] *n* **1** : annonce *f* **2** NOTIFICATION : avis *m* **3** : faire-part *m* (de mariage, etc.) — **announcer** [ə'naʊntsər] *n* : présentateur *m*, -trice *f*; speaker *m*, -kerine *f France*

annoy [ə'nɔɪ] *vt* : agacer, ennuyer — **annoyance** [ə'nɔɪənts] *n* : contrariété *f* — **annoying** [ə'nɔɪɪŋ] *adj* : agaçant

annual ['ænjʊəl] *adj* : annuel

annuity [ə'nu:əţi] *n, pl* **-ties** : rente *f* (viagère)

annul [ə'nʌl] *vt* **annulled; anulling** : annuler — **annulment** [ə'nʌlmənt] *n* : annulation *f*

anoint [ə'nɔɪnt] *vt* : oindre

anomaly [ə'nɑməli] *n, pl* **-lies** : anomalie *f*

anonymous [ə'nɑnəməs] *adj* : anonyme — **anonymity** [,ænə'nɪməţi] *n* : anonymat *m*

another [ə'nʌðər] *adj* **1** : un(e) autre **2 ~ beer** : encore une bière **3 in ~ year** : dans un an — **~** *pron* **1** : un autre *m*, une autre *f* **2 one after ~** : l'un après l'autre

answer ['æntsər] *n* **1** REPLY : réponse *f* **2** SOLUTION : solution *f* — **~** *vt* **1** : répondre à **2 ~ the door** : aller ouvrir la porte — *vi* : répondre

ant ['ænt] *n* : fourmi *f*

antagonize [æn'tægə,naɪz] *vt* **-nized; -nizing** : éveiller l'hostilité de, contrarier — **antagonistic** [æn,tægə'nɪstɪk] *adj* : antagoniste

antarctic [ænt'ɑrktɪk, -'ɑrţɪk] *adj* : antarctique

antelope ['æntəl,o:p] *n, pl* **-lope** *or* **-lopes** : antilope *f*

antenna [æn'tɛnə] *n, pl* **-nae** *or* **-nas** : antenne *f*

anthem ['ænθəm] *n* : hymne *m*

anthology [æn'θɑləʤi] *n, pl* **-gies** : anthologie *f*

anthropology [,ænθrə'pɑləʤi] *n* : anthropologie *f*

antibiotic [,æntibaɪ'ɑţɪk, ,æn,taɪ-, -bi-] *adj* : antibiotique — **~** *n* : antibiotique *m*

antibody ['ænti,bɑdi] *n, pl* **-bodies** : anticorps *m*

anticipate [æn'tɪsə,peɪt] *vt* **-pated; -pating** **1** FORESEE : anticiper **2** EXPECT : s'attendre à — **anticipation** [æn,tɪsə'peɪʃən] *n* : anticipation *f*

antics ['æntɪks] *npl* : singeries *fpl*

antidote ['æntɪ,do:t] *n* : antidote *m*

antifreeze ['æntɪ,fri:z] *n* : antigel *m*

antipathy [æn'tɪpəθi] *n, pl* **-thies** : antipathie *f*

antiquated ['æntə,kweɪţəd] *adj* : dépassé

antique [æn'ti:k] *adj* : ancien, antique — **~** *n* : antiquité *f* — **antiquity** [æn'tɪkwəţi] *n, pl* **-ties** : antiquité *f*

anti–Semitic [,æntisə'mɪţɪk, ,æn,taɪ-] *adj* : antisémite

antiseptic [,æntə'sɛptɪk] *adj* : antiseptique — **~** *n* : antiseptique *m*

antisocial [,ænti'so:ʃəl, ,æn,taɪ-] *adj* UNSOCIABLE : peu sociable

antlers ['æntlərz] *npl* : bois *mpl*, ramure *f*

antonym ['æntə,nɪm] *n* : antonyme *m*

anus ['eɪnəs] *n* : anus *m*

anvil ['ænvəl, -vɪl] *n* : enclume *f*

anxiety [æŋk'zaɪəţi] *n, pl* **-ties** **1** APPREHENSION : anxiété *f* **2** EAGERNESS : impatience *f* — **anxious** ['æŋkʃəs] *adj* **1** WORRIED : inquiet, anxieux **2** EAGER : impatient — **anxiously** ['æŋkʃəsli] *adv* **1** : anxieusement **2** : avec impatience

any ['ɛni] *adv* **1** SOMEWHAT : un peu **2** AT ALL : du tout **3 do you want ~ more tea?** : voulez-vous encore du thé? **4 she doesn't smoke ~ longer** : elle ne fume plus — **~** *adj* **1** : de, de la, du, des **2** WHICHEVER : quelconque, n'importe quel **3 at ~ moment** : à tout moment **4 we don't have ~ money** : nous n'avons pas d'argent — **~** *pron* **1** WHICHEVER : n'importe lequel **2 do you have ~** : est-ce que vous en avez?

anybody ['ɛni,bʌdi, -,bɑ-] → **anyone**

anyhow ['ɛni,haʊ] *adv* **1** : de toute façon, en tout cas **2** HAPHAZARDLY : n'importe comment

anymore [,ɛni'mor] *adv* **not ~** : ne plus

anyone ['ɛni,wʌn] *pron* **1** SOMEONE : quelqu'un **2** (*in negative constructions*) : personne **3 ~ can play** : tout le monde peut jouer, n'importe qui peut jouer

anyplace ['ɛni,pleɪs] → **anywhere**

anything ['ɛni,θɪŋ] *pron* **1** WHATEVER : n'importe quoi **2** SOMETHING : quelque chose **3** (*in negative constructions*) : rien **4 ~ but** : tout sauf **5 hardly ~** : presque rien

anytime ['ɛni,taɪm] *adv* : n'importe quand

anyway ['ɛni,weɪ] → **anyhow**

anywhere ['ɛni,hwɛr] *adv* **1** : n'importe où **2** SOMEWHERE : quelque part

3 (*in negative constructions*) : nulle part **4 ~ else** : partout ailleurs

apart [ə'pɑrt] *adv* **1** ASIDE : à part, à l'écart **2** SEPARATED : éloigné **3 ~ from** : en dehors de **4 five minutes ~** : à cinq minutes d'intervalle **5 take ~** : démonter **6 tell ~** : distinguer

apartment [ə'pɑrtmənt] *n* : appartement *m*

apathy ['æpəθi] *n* : apathie *f* — **apathetic** [ˌæpə'θɛt̬ɪk] *adj* : apathique

ape ['eɪp] *n* : grand singe *m*

aperture ['æpərtʃər, -ˌtʃʊr] *n* : ouverture *f*

apex ['eɪˌpɛks] *n, pl* **apexes** *or* **apices** ['eɪpəˌsi:z, 'æ-] : sommet *m*

apiece [ə'pi:s] *adv* **1** : chacun **2 two dollars ~** : deux dollars la pièce

aplomb [ə'plɑm, -'plʌm] *n* : aplomb *m*

apology [ə'pɑləd͡ʒi] *n, pl* **-gies** : excuses *fpl* — **apologetic** [əˌpɑlə'd͡ʒɛt̬ɪk] *adj* **1** : d'excuse **2 be ~** : s'excuser — **apologize** [ə'pɑləˌd͡ʒaɪz] *vi* **-gized; -gizing** : s'excuser, faire des excuses

apostle [ə'pɑsəl] *n* : apôtre *m*

apostrophe [ə'pɑstrəˌfi:] *n* : apostrophe *f*

appall *or Brit* **appal** [ə'pɔl] *vt* **-palled; -palling** : épouvanter — **appalling** [ə'pɔlɪŋ] *adj* : épouvantable

apparatus [ˌæpə'ræt̬əs, -'reɪ-] *n, pl* **-tuses** *or* **-tus** : appareil *m*

apparel [ə'pærəl] *n* : habillement *m*

apparent [ə'pærənt] *adj* **1** OBVIOUS : évident **2** SEEMING : apparent — **apparently** [ə'pærəntli] *adv* : apparemment

apparition [ˌæpə'rɪʃən] *n* : apparition *f*

appeal [ə'pi:l] *vt* : faire appel contre (un jugement) — *vi* **1 ~ for** : lancer un appel à **2 ~ to** ATTRACT : plaire à **3 ~ to** INVOKE : faire appel à — **~** *n* **1** REQUEST : appel *m* **2** ATTRACTION : attrait *m* — **appealing** [ə'pi:lɪŋ] *adj* : attrayant, séduisant

appear [ə'pɪr] *vi* **1** : apparaître **2** SEEM : paraître, sembler **3** COME OUT : paraître, sortir — **appearance** [ə'pɪrənts] *n* **1** LOOK : apparence *f* **2** ARRIVAL : apparition *f* **3 ~s** *npl* : apparences *fpl*

appease [ə'pi:z] *vt* **-peased; -peasing** : apaiser

appendix [ə'pɛndɪks] *n, pl* **-dixes** *or* **-dices** [-dəˌsi:z] : appendice *m* — **appendicitis** [əˌpɛndə'saɪt̬əs] *n* : appendicite *f*

appetite ['æpəˌtaɪt] *n* : appétit *m* — **appetizer** ['æpəˌtaɪzər] *n* : amuse-gueule *m* — **appetizing** ['æpəˌtaɪzɪŋ] *adj* : appétissant

applaud [ə'plɔd] *v* : applaudir — **applause** [ə'plɔz] *n* : applaudissements *mpl*

apple ['æpəl] *n* : pomme *f*

appliance [ə'plaɪənts] *n* : appareil *m*

apply [ə'plaɪ] *v* **-plied; -plying** *vt* **1** : appliquer **2** EXERT : exercer **3 ~ oneself** : s'appliquer — *vi* **1** : s'appliquer **2 ~ for** : poser sa candidature pour — **applicant** ['æplɪkənt] *n* : candidat *m*, -date *f* — **application** [ˌæplə'keɪʃən] *n* **1** USE : application *f* **2** : demande *f* (d'emploi)

appoint [ə'pɔɪnt] *vt* **1** SET : fixer **2** NAME : nommer — **appointment** [ə'pɔɪntmənt] *n* **1** : nomination *f* **2** MEETING : rendez-vous *m*

apportion [ə'porʃən] *vt* : répartir

appraise [ə'preɪz] *vt* **-praised; -praising** : évaluer — **appraisal** [ə'preɪzəl] *n* : évaluation *f*

appreciate [ə'pri:ʃiˌeɪt, -'prɪ-] *vt* **-ated; -ating 1** VALUE : apprécier **2** REALIZE : comprendre, se rendre compte de **3 I ~ your help** : je vous suis reconnaissant de m'avoir aidé — **appreciation** [əˌpri:ʃi'eɪʃən, -ˌprɪ-] *n* **1** EVALUATION : appréciation *f* **2** GRATITUDE : reconnaissance *f* — **appreciative** [ə'pri:ʃət̬ɪv, -'prɪ-; ə'pri:ʃiˌeɪ-] *adj* : reconnaissant

apprehend [ˌæprɪ'hɛnd] *vt* **1** ARREST : appréhender **2** UNDERSTAND : comprendre **3** DREAD : appréhender — **apprehension** [ˌæprɪ'hɛntʃən] *n* : appréhension *f* — **apprehensive** [ˌæprɪ'hɛntsɪv] *adj* : inquiet

apprentice [ə'prɛntɪs] *n* : apprenti *m*, -tie *f* — **apprenticeship** [ə'prɛntɪsˌʃɪp] *n* : apprentissage *m*

approach [ə'pro:tʃ] *vt* **1** NEAR : s'approcher de **2** : s'adresser à (quelqu'un), aborder (un problème, etc.) — *vi* : s'approcher — **~** *n* : approche *f* — **approachable** [ə'pro:tʃəbəl] *adj* : abordable, accessible

appropriate [ə'pro:priˌeɪt] *vt* **-ated; -ating 1** SEIZE : s'approprier **2** ALLOCATE : affecter — **~** [ə'pro:priət] *adj* : approprié

approve [ə'pru:v] *vt* **-proved; -proving** *or* **~ of** : approuver — **approval** [ə'pru:vəl] *n* : approbation *f*

approximate [ə'prɑksəmət] *adj* : approximatif — **~** [ə'prɑksəˌmeɪt] *vt* **-mated; -mating** : se rapprocher de —

approximately [ə'prɑksəmətli] *adv* : à peu près, environ
apricot ['æprə,kɑt, 'eɪ-] *n* : abricot *m*
April ['eɪprəl] *n* : avril *m*
apron ['eɪprən] *n* : tablier *m*
apt ['æpt] *adj* **1** : approprié **2 be ~ to** : avoir tendance à — **aptitude** ['æptə-,tu:d, -,tju:d] *n* : aptitude *f*
aquarium [ə'kwæriəm] *n, pl* **-iums** *or* **-ia** [-iə] : aquarium *m*
aquatic [ə'kwɑṭɪk, -'kwæ-] *adj* **1** : aquatique **2** : nautique (se dit des sports)
aqueduct ['ækwə,dʌkt] *n* : aqueduc *m*
Arab ['ærəb] *or* **Arabic** ['ærəbɪk] *adj* : arabe — **Arabic** *n* : arabe *m* (langue)
arbitrary ['ɑrbə,trɛri] *adj* : arbitraire
arbitrate ['ɑrbə,treɪt] *v* **-trated; -trating** : arbitrer — **arbitration** [,ɑrbə-'treɪʃən] *n* : arbitrage *m*
arc ['ɑrk] *n* : arc *m*
arcade [ɑr'keɪd] *n* **1** : arcade *f* **2 shopping ~** : galerie *f* marchande
arch ['ɑrʧ] *n* : voûte *f*, arc *m* — **~** *vt* : arquer, courber
archaeology *or* **archeology** [,ɑrki'ɑləʤi] *n* : archéologie *f* — **archaeological** [,ɑrkiə'lɑʤɪkəl] *adj* : archéologique — **archaeologist** [,ɑrki'ɑləʤɪst] *n* : archéologue *mf*
archaic [ɑr'keɪɪk] *adj* : archaïque
archbishop [ɑrʧ'bɪʃəp] *n* : archevêque *m*
archery ['ɑrʧəri] *n* : tir *m* à l'arc
archipelago [,ɑrkə'pɛlə,go:, ,ɑrʧə-] *n, pl* **-goes** *or* **-gos** [-go:z] : archipel *m*
architecture ['ɑrkə,tɛkʧər] *n* : architecture *f* — **architect** ['ɑrkə,tɛkt] *n* : architecte *mf* — **architectural** [,ɑrkə-'tɛkʧərəl] *adj* : architectural
archives ['ɑr,kaɪvz] *npl* : archives *fpl*
archway ['ɑrʧ,weɪ] *n* : voûte *f*, arcade *f*
arctic ['ɑrktɪk, 'ɑrṭ-] *adj* : arctique
ardent ['ɑrdənt] *adj* : ardent — **ardently** ['ɑrdəntli] *adv* : ardemment — **ardor** ['ɑrdər] *n* : ardeur *f*
arduous ['ɑrʤʊəs] *adj* : ardu
are → **be**
area ['æriə] *n* **1** REGION : région *f* **2** SURFACE : aire *f* **3** FIELD : domaine *m* **4 ~ code** : indicatif *m* de zone, indicatif *m* régional *Can*
arena [ə'ri:nə] *n* : arène *f*, aréna *m Can*
aren't ['ɑrnt, 'ɑrənt] (*contraction of* **are not**) → **be**
argue ['ɑr,gju:] *v* **-gued; -guing** *vi* **1** QUARREL : se disputer **2** DEBATE : argumenter — *vt* DEBATE : discuter — **argument** ['ɑrgjəmənt] *n* **1** QUARREL : dispute *f* **2** DEBATE : discussion *f* **3** REASONING : argument *m*
arid ['ærəd] *adj* : aride
arise [ə'raɪz] *vi* **arose** [ə'ro:z]; **arisen** [ə'rɪzən]; **arising** **1** : se présenter **2 ~ from** : résulter de
aristocracy [,ærə'stɑkrəsi] *n, pl* **-cies** : aristocratie *f* — **aristocrat** [ə'rɪstə-,kræt] *n* : aristocrate *mf* — **aristocratic** [ə,rɪstə'kræṭɪk] *adj* : aristocratique
arithmetic [ə'rɪθmə,tɪk] *n* : arithmétique *f*
ark ['ɑrk] *n* : arche *f*
arm ['ɑrm] *n* **1** : bras *m* **2** WEAPON : arme *f* — **~** *vt* : armer — **armament** ['ɑrməmənt] *n* : armement *m* — **armchair** ['ɑrm,ʧɛr] *n* : fauteuil *m* — **armed** ['ɑrmd] *adj* **1** : armé **2 ~ forces** : forces *fpl* armées **3 ~ robbery** : vol *m* à main armée
armistice ['ɑrməstɪs] *n* : armistice *m*
armor *or Brit* **armour** ['ɑrmər] *n* **1** : armure *f* **2** *or* **~ plating** : blindage *m* — **armored** *or Brit* **armoured** ['ɑrmərd] *adj* : blindé — **armory** *or Brit* **armoury** ['ɑrməri] *n, pl* **-mories** : arsenal *m*
armpit ['ɑrm,pɪt] *n* : aisselle *f*
army ['ɑrmi] *n, pl* **-mies** : armée *f*
aroma [ə'ro:mə] *n* : arôme *m* — **aromatic** [,ærə'mæṭɪk] *adj* : aromatique
around [ə'raʊnd] *adv* **1** : de circonférence **2** NEARBY : là, dans les parages **3** APPROXIMATELY : environ, à peu près **4 all ~** : tout autour — **~** *prep* **1** SURROUNDING : autour de **2** THROUGHOUT : partout dans **3 ~ here** : par ici **4 ~ noon** : vers midi
arouse [ə'raʊz] *vt* **aroused; arousing** **1** AWAKE : réveiller **2** STIMULATE : éveiller
arrange [ə'reɪnʤ] *v* **-ranged; -ranging** *vt* : arranger — *vi* **~ for** : prendre des dispositions pour — **arrangement** [ə-'reɪnʤmənt] *n* **1** ORDER : arrangement *m* **2 ~s** *npl* : dispositions *fpl*
array [ə'reɪ] *n* : sélection *f*
arrears [ə'rɪrz] *npl* **1** : arriéré *m* **2 be in ~** : avoir du retard
arrest [ə'rɛst] *vt* : arrêter — **~** *n* : arrestation *f*
arrive [ə'raɪv] *vi* **-rived; -riving** **1** : arriver **2 ~ at** : parvenir à, atteindre — **arrival** [ə'raɪvəl] *n* : arrivée *f*
arrogance ['ærəgənts] *n* : arrogance *f* — **arrogant** ['ærəgənt] *adj* : arrogant
arrow ['æro] *n* : flèche *f*
arsenal ['ɑrsənəl] *n* : arsenal *m*
arsenic ['ɑrsənɪk] *n* : arsenic *m*

arson [ˈɑrsən] *n* : incendie *m* criminel
art [ˈɑrt] *n* : art *m*
artefact *Brit* → **artifact**
artery [ˈɑrt̬əri] *n, pl* **-teries** : artère *f*
artful [ˈɑrtfəl] *adj* : rusé, astucieux
arthritis [ɑrˈθraɪt̬əs] *n, pl* **-thritides** [-ˈθrɪt̬əˌdi:z] : arthrite *f* — **arthritic** [ɑrˈθrɪt̬ɪk] *adj* : arthritique
artichoke [ˈɑrt̬əˌʧo:k] *n* : artichaut *m*
article [ˈɑrtɪkəl] *n* : article *m*
articulate [ɑrˈtɪkjəˌleɪt] *vt* **-lated; -lating** : articuler — **~** [ɑrˈtɪkjələt] *adj* **be ~** : s'exprimer bien
artifact *or Brit* **artefact** [ˈɑrt̬əˌfækt] *n* : objet *m* fabriqué
artificial [ˌɑrt̬əˈfɪʃəl] *adj* : artificiel
artillery [ɑrˈtɪləri] *n, pl* **-leries** : artillerie *f*
artist [ˈɑrt̬ɪst] *n* : artiste *mf* — **artistic** [ɑrˈtɪstɪk] *adj* : artistique
as [ˈæz] *adv* **1 ~ much** : autant **2 ~ tall ~** : aussi grand que **3 ~ well** : aussi — **~** *conj* **1** LIKE : comme **2** WHILE : tandis que, alors que **3** SINCE : puisque, comme **4 ~ is** : tel quel — **~** *prep* : en tant que, comme — **~** *pron* **1** : que **2 ~ you know** : comme vous savez
asbestos [æzˈbɛstəs, æs-] *n* : amiante *m*
ascend [əˈsɛnd] *vt* : monter (à), gravir — *vi* : monter — **ascent** [əˈsɛnt] *n* : ascension *f*
ascertain [ˌæsərˈteɪn] *vt* : établir
ascribe [əˈskraɪb] *vt* **-cribed; -cribing ~ to**: attribuer à
as for *prep* : quant à
ash[1] [ˈæʃ] *n* : cendre *f*
ash[2] *n* : frêne *m* (arbre)
ashamed [əˈʃeɪmd] *adj* **1** : honteux **2 be ~** : avoir honte
ashore [əˈʃor] *adv* : à terre
ashtray [ˈæʃˌtreɪ] *n* : cendrier *m*
Asian [ˈeɪʒən, -ʃən] *adj* : asiatique
aside [əˈsaɪd] *adv* : de côté, à part — **aside from** *prep* **1** BESIDES : à part **2** EXCEPT : sauf
as if *conj* : comme si
ask [ˈæsk] *vt* **1** : demander **2** INVITE : inviter **3 ~ a question** : poser une question **4 ~ s.o.** : demandez à qqn — *vi* : demander
askance [əˈskænts] *adv* **look ~** : regarder du coin de l'œil
askew [əˈskju:] *adv & adj* : de travers
asleep [əˈsli:p] *adj* **1** : endormi **2 fall ~** : s'endormir
as of *prep* : dès, à partir de
asparagus [əˈspærəgəs] *ns & pl* : asperges *fpl*
aspect [ˈæˌspɛkt] *n* : aspect *m*
asphalt [ˈæsˌfɔlt] *n* : asphalte *m*
asphyxiate [æˈsfɪksiˌeɪt] *vt* **-ated; -ating** : asphyxier — **asphyxiation** [æˌsfɪksiˈeɪʃən] *n* : asphyxie *f*
aspire [əˈspaɪr] *vi* **-pired; -piring ~ to** : aspirer à — **aspiration** [ˌæspəˈreɪʃən] *n* : aspiration *f*
aspirin [ˈæsprən, ˈæspə-] *n, pl* **aspirin** *or* **aspirins** : aspirine *f*
ass [ˈæs] *n* **1** : âne *m* **2** FOOL : idiot *m*, -diote *f*
assail [əˈseɪl] *vt* : assaillir — **assailant** [əˈseɪlənt] *n* : assaillant *m*, -lante *f*
assassin [əˈsæsən] *n* : assassin *m* — **assassinate** [əˈsæsənˌeɪt] *vt* **-nated; -nating** : assassiner — **assassination** [əˌsæsənˈeɪʃən] *n* : assassinat *m*
assault [əˈsɔlt] *vt* : agresser — **~** *n* : agression *f*, assaut *m* (militaire)
assemble [əˈsɛmbəl] *v* **-bled; -bling** *vt* **1** CONSTRUCT : assembler **2** GATHER : rassembler — *vi* CONVENE : se rassembler — **assembly** [əˈsɛmbli] *n, pl* **-blies 1** MEETING : assemblée *f*, réunion *f* **2 ~ line** : chaîne *f* de montage
assent [əˈsɛnt] *vi* : consentir — **~** *n* : assentiment *m*
assert [əˈsərt] *vt* **1** : affirmer **2 ~ oneself** : s'imposer — **assertion** [əˈsərʃən] *n* : assertion *f* — **assertive** [əˈsərt̬ɪv] *adj* : assuré
assess [əˈsɛs] *vt* : évaluer — **assessment** [əˈsɛsmənt] *n* : évaluation *f*
asset [ˈæˌsɛt] *n* **1** : avantage *m*, atout *m* **2 ~s** *npl* : biens *mpl*, actif *m*
assiduous [əˈsɪʤuəs] *adj* : assidu
assign [əˈsaɪn] *vt* **1** ALLOT : assigner **2** APPOINT : nommer — **assignment** [əˈsaɪnmənt] *n* **1** TASK : mission *f* **2** HOMEWORK : devoir *m*
assimilate [əˈsɪməˌleɪt] *vt* **-lated; -lating** : assimiler
assist [əˈsɪst] *vt* : aider, assister — **assistance** [əˈsɪstənts] *n* : aide *f*, assistance *f* — **assistant** [əˈsɪstənt] *n* : assistant *m*, -tante *f*; adjoint *m*, -jointe *f*
associate [əˈso:ʃiˌeɪt, -si-] *v* **-ated; -ating** *vt* : associer — *vi* **~ with** : fréquenter — **~** [əˈso:ʃiət, -siət] *n* : associé *m*, -ciée *f* — **association** [əˌso:ʃiˈeɪʃən, -si-] *n* : association *f*
as soon as *conj* : aussitôt que
assorted [əˈsɔrt̬əd] *adj* : assorti — **assortment** [əˈsɔrtmənt] *n* : assortiment *m*
assume [əˈsu:m] *vt* **-sumed; -suming**

1 : assumer 2 SUPPOSE : supposer, présumer — **assumption** [əˈsʌmpʃən] *n* : supposition *f*

assure [əˈʃʊr] *vt* **-sured; -suring** : assurer — **assurance** [əˈʃʊrənts] *n* : assurance *f*

asterisk [ˈæstəˌrɪsk] *n* : astérisque *m*

asthma [ˈæzmə] *n* : asthme *m*

as though → **as if**

as to *prep* : sur, concernant

astonish [əˈstɑnɪʃ] *vt* : étonner — **astonishing** [əˈstɑnɪʃɪŋ] *adj* : étonnant — **astonishment** [əˈstɑnɪʃmənt] *n* : étonnement *m*

astound [əˈstaʊnd] *vt* : stupéfier — **astounding** [əˈstaʊndɪŋ] *adj* : stupéfiant

astray [əˈstreɪ] *adv* **1 go ~** : s'égarer **2 lead ~** : égarer

astrology [əˈstrɑləʤi] *n* : astrologie *f*

astronaut [ˈæstrəˌnɔt] *n* : astronaute *mf*

astronomy [əˈstrɑnəmi] *n, pl* **-mies** : astronomie *f* — **astronomer** [əˈstrɑnəmər] *n* : astronome *mf* — **astronomical** [ˌæstrəˈnɑmɪkəl] *adj* : astronomique

astute [əˈstuːt, -ˈstjuːt] *adj* : astucieux — **astuteness** [əˈstuːtnəs, -ˈstjuːt-] *n* : astuce *f*

as well as *conj* : en plus de — **~** *prep* : ainsi que, à part

asylum [əˈsaɪləm] *n* : asile *m*

at [ˈæt] *prep* **1** : à **2 ~ the dentist's** : chez le dentiste **3 ~ three o'clock** : à trois heures **4 ~ war** : en guerre **5 be angry ~** : être fâché contre **6 laugh ~** : rire de **7 shoot ~** : tirer sur — **at all** *adv* : du tout

ate [ˈeɪt] → **eat**

atheist [ˈeɪθiɪst] *n* : athée *mf* — **atheism** [ˈeɪθiˌɪzəm] *n* : athéisme *m*

athlete [ˈæθˌliːt] *n* : athlète *mf* — **athletic** [æθˈlɛṭɪk] *adj* : athlétique — **athletics** [æθˈlɛṭɪks] *ns & pl* : athlétisme *m*

atlas [ˈætləs] *n* : atlas *m*

atmosphere [ˈætməˌsfɪr] *n* : atmosphère *f* — **atmospheric** [ˌætməˈsfɪrɪk, -ˈsfɛr-] *adj* : atmosphérique

atom [ˈæṭəm] *n* : atome *m* — **atomic** [əˈtɑmɪk] *adj* : atomique

atomizer [ˈæṭəˌmaɪzər] *n* : atomiseur *m*

atone [əˈtoːn] *vi* **atoned; atoning ~ for** : expier — **atonement** [əˈtoːnmənt] *n* : expiation *f*

atrocious [əˈtroːʃəs] *adj* : atroce — **atrocity** [əˈtrɑsəṭi] *n, pl* **-ties** : atrocité *f*

atrophy [ˈætrəfi] *vi* **-phied; phying** : s'atrophier

attach [əˈtæʧ] *vt* **1** : attacher **2 become ~ed to** : s'attacher à — *vi* ADHERE : s'attacher — **attachment** [əˈtæʧmənt] *n* **1** AFFECTION : attachement *m* **2** ACCESSORY : accessoire *m*

attack [əˈtæk] *v* : attaquer — **~** *n* **1** : attaque *f* **2 heart ~** : crise *f* cardiaque — **attacker** [əˈtækər] *n* : agresseur *m*

attain [əˈteɪn] *vt* : atteindre — **attainment** [əˈteɪnmənt] *n* : réalisation *f*

attempt [əˈtɛmpt] *vt* : tenter — **~** *n* : tentative *f*

attend [əˈtɛnd] *vt* **1** : assister à **2 ~ church** : aller à l'église — *vi* **1 ~ to** : s'occuper de **2 ~ to** HEED : prêter attention à — **attendance** [əˈtɛndənts] *n* **1** : présence *f* **2** TURNOUT : assistance *f* — **attendant** [əˈtɛndənt] *n* **1** : gardien *m*, -dienne *f* **2 service station ~** : pompiste *mf*

attention [əˈtɛnʧən] *n* **1** : attention *f* **2 pay ~ to** : prêter attention à — **attentive** [əˈtɛntɪv] *adj* : attentif

attest [əˈtɛst] *vt* : attester — *vi* **~ to** : témoigner de

attic [ˈætɪk] *n* : grenier *m*

attitude [ˈætəˌtuːd, -ˌtjuːd] *n* : attitude *f*

attorney [əˈtərni] *n, pl* **-neys** : avocat *m*, -cate *f*

attract [əˈtrækt] *vt* : attirer — **attraction** [əˈtrækʃən] *n* **1** : attrait *f* **2** : attraction *f* (en science) — **attractive** [əˈtræktɪv] *adj* : attirant, attrayant

attribute [ˈætrəˌbjuːt] *n* : attribut *m* — **~** [əˈtrɪˌbjuːt] *vt* **-uted; -uting** : attribuer

auburn [ˈɔbərn] *adj* : auburn

auction [ˈɔkʃən] *vt* : vendre aux enchères — **~** *n* : vente *f* aux enchères

audacious [ɔˈdeɪʃəs] *adj* : audacieux — **audacity** [ɔˈdæsəṭi] *n, pl* **-ties** : audace *f*

audible [ˈɔdəbəl] *adj* : audible

audience [ˈɔdiənts] *n* : assistance *f*, public *m*

audio [ˈɔdiˌoː] *adj* : audio — **audiovisual** [ˌɔdioˈvɪʒuəl] *adj* : audiovisuel

audition [ɔˈdɪʃən] *n* : audition *f* — **~** *v* : auditionner

auditor [ˈɔdəṭər] *n* : auditeur *m*, -trice *f*

auditorium [ˌɔdəˈtoriəm] *n, pl* **-riums** *or* **-ria** [-riə] : salle *f*

augment [ɔgˈmɛnt] *vt* : augmenter

augur [ˈɔgər] *vi* **~ well** : être de bon augure

August [ˈɔgəst] *n* : août *m*

aunt [ˈænt, ˈɑnt] *n* : tante *f*

aura [ˈɔrə] *n* : aura *f*, atmosphère *f*

auspices [ˈɔspəsəz, -ˌsiːz] *npl* : auspices *mpl*
auspicious [ɔˈspɪʃəs] *adj* : favorable
austere [ɔˈstɪr] *adj* : austère — **austerity** [ɔˈstɛrət̬i] *n, pl* **-ties** : austérité *f*
Australian [ɔˈstreɪljən] *adj* : australien
authentic [əˈθɛntɪk, ɔ-] *adj* : authentique
author [ˈɔθər] *n* : auteur *m*
authority [əˈθɔrət̬i, ɔ-] *n, pl* **-ties** : autorité *f* — **authoritarian** [ɔˌθɔrəˈtɛriən, ə-] *adj* : autoritaire — **authoritative** [əˈθɔrəˌteɪt̬ɪv, ɔ-] *adj* **1** DICTATORIAL : autoritaire **2** DEFINITIVE : qui fait autorité — **authorization** [ˌɔθərəˈzeɪʃən] *n* : autorisation *f* — **authorize** [ˈɔθəˌraɪz] *vt* **-rized; -rizing** : autoriser
autobiography [ˌɔt̬oˌbaɪˈɑgrəfi] *n, pl* **-phies** : autobiographie *f* — **autobiographical** [ˌɔt̬obaɪəˈgræfɪkəl] *adj* : autobiographique
autograph [ˈɔt̬əˌgræf] *n* : autographe *m*
automate [ˈɔt̬əˌmeɪt] *v* **-mated; -mating** : automatiser — **automatic** [ˌɔt̬əˈmæt̬ɪk] *adj* : automatique — **automation** [ˌɔt̬əˈmeɪʃən] *n* : automatisation *f*
automobile [ˌɔt̬əmoˈbiːl, -ˈmoːˌbiːl] *n* : automobile *f*, voiture *f*
autonomy [ɔˈtɑnəmi] *n, pl* **-mies** : autonomie *f* — **autonomous** [ɔˈtɑnəməs] *adj* : autonome
autopsy [ˈɔˌtɑpsi, -təp-] *n, pl* **-sies** : autopsie *f*
autumn [ˈɔt̬əm] *n* : automne *m*
auxiliary [ɔgˈzɪljəri, -ˈzɪləri] *adj* : auxiliaire — ~ *n, pl* **-ries** : auxiliaire *mf*
avail [əˈveɪl] *vt* ~ **oneself of** : profiter de — ~ *n* **to no** ~ : en vain, sans résultat
available [əˈveɪləbəl] *adj* : disponible — **availability** [əˌveɪləˈbɪlət̬i] *n, pl* **-ties** : disponibilité *f*
avalanche [ˈævəˌlæntʃ] *n* : avalanche *f*
avarice [ˈævərəs] *n* : avarice *f*
avenge [əˈvɛndʒ] *vt* **avenged; avenging** : venger
avenue [ˈævəˌnuː, -ˌnjuː] *n* : avenue *f*
average [ˈævrɪdʒ, ˈævə-] *vt* **-aged; -aging** : faire en moyenne — ~ *adj* : moyen — ~ *n* : moyenne *f*
averse [əˈvərs] *adj* **be** ~ **to** : répugner à — **aversion** [əˈvərʒən] *n* : aversion *f*
avert [əˈvərt] *vt* **1** AVOID : éviter **2** ~ **one's eyes** : détourner les yeux
aviation [ˌeɪviˈeɪʃən] *n* : aviation *f*
avid [ˈævɪd] *adj* **1 be** ~ **for** : être avide de **2** ENTHUSIASTIC : passionné — **avidly** [ˈævɪdli] *adv* : avidement
avocado [ˌævəˈkɑdo, ˌɑvə-] *n, pl* **-dos** : avocat *m*
avoid [əˈvɔɪd] *vt* : éviter
await [əˈweɪt] *vt* : attendre
awake [əˈweɪk] *v* **awoke** [əˈwoːk]; **awoken** [əˈwoːkən] *or* **awaked** [əˈweɪkt]; **awaking** *vt* : réveiller, éveiller — *vi* WAKE UP : se réveiller — ~ *adj* : éveillé, réveillé — **awaken** [əˈweɪkən] → **awake**
award [əˈwɔrd] *vt* **1** GRANT : accorder **2** CONFER : décerner — ~ *n* : prix *m*
aware [əˈwær] *adj* **1** : au courant **2 be** ~ **of** : être conscient de — **awareness** [əˈwærnəs] *n* : conscience *f*
awash [əˈwɔʃ] *adj* ~ **with** : inondé de
away [əˈweɪ] *adv* **1 chatter** ~ : bavarder sans arrêt **2 give** ~ : donner **3 go** ~**!** : allez-vous en! **4 take** ~ : enlever **5 ten kilometers** ~ : à dix kilomètres d'ici **6 turn** ~ : se détourner — ~ *adj* **1** ABSENT : absent **2** ~ **game** : match *m* à l'extérieur
awe [ˈɔ] *n* : crainte *f* mêlée de respect — **awesome** [ˈɔsəm] *adj* : impressionnant
awful [ˈɔfəl] *adj* **1** : affreux **2 an** ~ **lot of** : énormément de — **awfully** [ˈɔfəli] *adv* : extrêmement
awhile [əˈhwaɪl] *adv* : un moment
awkward [ˈɔkwərd] *adj* **1** : gauche, maladroit **2** EMBARRASSING : gênant **3** DIFFICULT : difficile — **awkwardly** [ˈɔkwərdli] *adv* : maladroitement
awning [ˈɔnɪŋ] *n* : auvent *m*
awoke, awoken → **awake**
awry [əˈraɪ] *adv* **go** ~ : mal tourner
ax *or* **axe** [ˈæks] *n* : hache *f*
axiom [ˈæksiəm] *n* : axiome *m*
axis [ˈæksɪs] *n, pl* **axes** [-siːz] : axe *m*
axle [ˈæksəl] *n* : essieu *m*

B

b ['bi:] *n, pl* **b's** *or* **bs** ['bi:z] : b *m,* deuxième lettre de l'alphabet
babble ['bæbəl] *vi* **-bled; -bling 1** : babiller, gazouiller **2** MURMUR : murmurer — **~** *n* : babillage *m*
baboon [bæ'bu:n] *n* : babouin *m*
baby ['beɪbi] *n, pl* **-bies** : bébé *m* — **~** *vt* **-bied; -bying** : dorloter — **baby carriage** *n* : voiture *f* d'enfant, landau *m France* — **babyish** ['beɪbiɪʃ] *adj* : enfantin — **baby–sit** ['beɪbi,sɪt] *vi* **-sat** [-,sæt]; **-sitting** : garder des enfants, faire du baby-sitting *France* — **baby–sitter** ['beɪbi,sɪţər] *n* : gardienne *f* d'enfants, baby-sitter *mf France*
bachelor ['bæţʃələr] *n* **1** : célibataire *m* **2** GRADUATE : licencié *m,* -ciée *f*
back ['bæk] *n* **1** : dos *m* **2** REVERSE : revers *m,* dos *m* **3** REAR : derrière *m,* arrière *m,* fond *m* **4** : arrière *m* (aux sports) — **~** *adv* **1** : en arrière, vers l'arrière **2 be ~** : être de retour **3 go ~** : retourner **4 two years ~** : il y a deux ans — **~** *adj* **1** REAR : arrière, de derrière **2** OVERDUE : arriéré — **~** *vt* **1** SUPPORT : soutenir, appuyer **2** *or* **~ up** : mettre en marche arrière (un véhicule) — *vi* **1 ~ down** : céder **2 ~ up** : reculer — **backache** ['bæk,eɪk] *n* : mal *m* de dos — **backbone** ['bæk,bo:n] *n* : colonne *f* vertébrale — **backfire** ['bæk,faɪr] *vi* **-fired; -firing** : pétarader — **background** ['bæk,graʊnd] *n* **1** : arrière-plan *m,* fond *m* (d'un tableau) **2** EXPERIENCE : formation *f* — **backhand** ['bæk,hænd] *adj* : de revers — **backhanded** ['bæk,hændəd] *adj* : équivoque — **backing** ['bækɪŋ] *n* : soutien *m,* appui *m* — **backlash** ['bæk,læʃ] *n* : contrecoup *m,* répercussion *f* — **backlog** ['bæk,lɔg] *n* : accumulation *f* (de travail, etc.) — **backpack** ['bæk,pæk] *n* : sac *m* à dos — **backstage** [,bæk'steɪʤ, 'bæk,-] *adv* : dans les coulisses — **backtrack** ['bæk,træk] *vi* : revenir sur ses pas — **backup** ['bæk,ʌp] *n* **1** SUPPORT : soutien *m,* appui *m* **2** : sauvegarde *f* (en informatique) — **backward** ['bækwərd] *or* **backwards** [-wərdz] *adv* **1** : en arrière **2 bend over ~s** : faire tout son possible **3 do it ~** : fais-le à l'envers **4 fall ~** : tomber à la renverse — **backward** *adj* : en arrière
bacon [beɪkən] *n* : lard *m,* bacon *m*
bacteria [bæk'tɪriə] *npl* : bactéries *fpl*
bad ['bæd] *adj* **worse** ['wərs]; **worst** ['wərst] **1** : mauvais **2** ROTTEN : pourri **3** SEVERE : grave, aigu **4 from ~ to worse** : de mal en pis **5 too ~!** : quel dommage! — **~** *adv* → **badly**
badge ['bæʤ] *n* : insigne *m,* plaque *f*
badger ['bæʤər] *n* : blaireau *m* — **~** *vt* : harceler
badly ['bædli] *adv* **1** : mal **2** SEVERELY : gravement **3 need ~** : avoir grand besoin de
baffle ['bæfəl] *vt* **-fled; -fling** : déconcerter
bag ['bæg] *n* **1** : sac *m* **2** HANDBAG : sac *m* à main **3** SUITCASE : valise *f* — **~** *vt* **bagged; bagging** : mettre en sac
baggage ['bægɪʤ] *n* : bagages *mpl*
baggy ['bægi] *adj* **-gier; -est** : ample, trop grand
bagpipes ['bæg,paɪps] *npl* : cornemuse *f*
bail [,beɪl] *n* : caution *f* — **~** *vt* **1** *or* **~ out** : vider, écoper (un bateau) **2** *or* **~ out** RELEASE : mettre en liberté sous caution **3 ~ out** EXTRICATE : tirer d'affaire
bailiff ['beɪlif] *n* : huissier *m*
bait ['beɪt] *vt* **1** : appâter **2** HARASS : tourmenter — **~** *n* : appât *m*
bake ['beɪk] *v* **baked; baking** *vt* : faire cuire au four — *vi* : cuire (au four) — **baker** ['beɪkər] *n* : boulanger *m,* -gère *f* — **bakery** ['beɪkəri] *n, pl* **-ries** : boulangerie *f* — **baking soda** *n* : bicarbonate *m* de soude
balance ['bæləns] *n* **1** SCALES : balance *f* **2** COUNTERBALANCE : contrepoids *m* **3** EQUILIBRIUM : équilibre *m* **4** REMAINDER : reste *m* **5** *or* **bank ~** : solde *m* — **~** *v* **-anced; -ancing** *vt* **1** : faire ses comptes **2** EQUALIZE : équilibrer **3** WEIGH : peser — *vi* : être en équilibre
balcony ['bælkəni] *n, pl* **-nies** : balcon *m*
bald ['bɔld] *adj* **1** : chauve **2** WORN : usé
balk ['bɔk] *vi* **~ at** : reculer devant
ball ['bɔl] *n* **1** : balle *f,* ballon *m,* boule

f **2** DANCE : bal *m* **3 ~ of string** : pelote *f* de ficelle
ballad ['bæləd] *n* : ballade *f*
ballast ['bæləst] *n* : lest *m,* ballast *m*
ballerina [ˌbælə'ri:nə] *n* : ballerine *f*
ballet [bæ'leɪ, 'bæˌleɪ] *n* : ballet *m*
ballistic [bə'lɪstɪk] *adj* : balistique
balloon [bə'lu:n] *n* : ballon *m,* balloune *f Can*
ballot ['bælət] *n* **1** : bulletin *m* de vote **2** VOTING : scrutin *m*
ballpoint pen ['bɔlˌpɔɪnt] *n* : stylo *m* à bille
ballroom ['bɔlˌru:m, -ˌrʊm] *n* : salle *f* de danse, salle *f* de bal
balm ['bɑm, 'bɑlm] *n* : baume *m* — **balmy** ['bɑmi, 'bɑl-] *adj* **balmier; -est** : doux, agréable
baloney [bə'lo:ni] *n* NONSENSE : balivernes *fpl*
bamboo [bæm'bu:] *n* : bambou *m*
bamboozle [bæm'bu:zəl] *vt* **-zled; -zling** : embobiner *fam*
ban ['bæn] *vt* **banned; banning** : interdire — **~** *n* : interdiction *f*
banana [bə'nænə] *n* : banane *f*
band ['bænd] *n* **1** STRIP : bande *f* **2** GROUP : groupe *m,* orchestre *m* — **~** *vi* **~ together** : se réunir, se grouper
bandage ['bændɪdʒ] *n* : pansement *m,* bandage *m* — **~** *vt* : bander, panser
bandy ['bændi] *vt* **-died; -dying ~ about** : faire circuler
bang ['bæŋ] *vt* **1** STRIKE : frapper **2** SLAM : claquer — *vi* **~ on** : cogner sur — **~** *n* **1** BLOW : coup *m* **2** EXPLOSION : détonation *f* **3** SLAM : claquement *m*
bangs ['bæŋz] *npl* : frange *f*
banish ['bænɪʃ] *vt* : bannir
banister ['bænəstər] *n* : rampe *f*
bank ['bæŋk] *n* **1** : banque *f* **2** : talus *m,* rive *f* (d'un fleuve) **3** EMBANKMENT : terre-plein *m* — **~** *vt* : déposer — *vi* **1** : avoir un compte en banque **2 ~ on** : compter sur — **banker** ['bæŋkər] *n* : banquier *m* — **banking** ['bæŋkɪŋ] *n* : opérations *fpl* bancaires
bankrupt ['bæŋˌkrʌpt] *adj* : en faillite — **bankruptcy** ['bæŋˌkrʌptsi] *n, pl* **-cies** : faillite *f*
banner ['bænər] *n* : bannière *f*
banquet ['bæŋkwət] *n* : banquet *m*
banter ['bæntər] *n* : plaisanteries *fpl* — **~** *vi* : plaisanter
baptize [bæp'taɪz, 'bæpˌtaɪz] *vt* **-tized; -tizing** : baptiser — **baptism** ['bæpˌtɪzəm] *n* : baptême *m*
bar ['bɑr] *n* **1** : barre *f* (de métal), barreau *m* (d'une fenêtre) **2** BARRIER : obstacle *m,* barrière *f* **3** TAVERN : bar *m* **4 behind ~s** : sous les verrous **5 ~ of soap** : pain *m* de savon — **~** *vt* **barred; barring 1** OBSTRUCT : barrer, bloquer **2** EXCLUDE : exclure **3** PROHIBIT : interdire — **~** *prep* **1** : sauf **2 ~ none** : sans exception
barbarian [bɑr'bæriən] *n* : barbare *mf* — **barbaric** [bɑr'bærɪk] *adj* : barbare
barbecue ['bɑrbɪˌkju:] *vt* **-cued; -cuing** : griller au charbon de bois — **~** *n* : barbecue *m*
barbed wire ['bɑrbd'waɪr] *n* : fil *m* de fer barbelé
barber ['bɑrbər] *n* : coiffeur *m,* -feuse *f;* barbier *m Can*
bare ['bær] *adj* **barer; barest 1** : dénudé **2** EMPTY : vide **3** MINIMUM : essentiel — **barefaced** ['bærˌfeɪst] *adj* : éhonté — **barefoot** ['bærˌfʊt] *or* **barefooted** [-ˌfʊtəd] *adv* : pieds nus — **~** *adj* **be ~** : être nu-pieds — **barely** ['bærli] *adv* : à peine, tout juste
bargain ['bɑrgən] *n* **1** AGREEMENT : marché *m* **2** BUY : aubaine *f* — **~** *vi* **1** : négocier, marchander **2 ~ for** : s'attendre à
barge ['bɑrdʒ] *n* : chaland *m* — **~** *vi* **barged; barging ~ in** : interrompre
baritone ['bærəˌto:n] *n* : baryton *m*
bark[1] ['bɑrk] *vi* : aboyer — **~** *n* : aboiement *m* (d'un chien)
bark[2] *n* : écorce *f* (d'un arbre)
barley ['bɑrli] *n* : orge *f*
barn ['bɑrn] *n* : grange *f*
barometer [bə'rɑmətər] *n* : baromètre *m*
baron ['bærən] *n* : baron *m* — **baroness** ['bærənɪs, -nəs, -'nɛs] *n* : baronne *f*
barracks ['bærəks] *npl* : caserne *f*
barrage [bə'rɑʒ, -'rɑdʒ] *n* **1** : tir *m* de barrage **2** : déluge *m* (de questions, etc.)
barrel ['bærəl] *n* **1** : tonneau *m,* fût *m,* baril *m* **2** : canon *m* (d'une arme à feu)
barren ['bærən] *adj* : stérile
barricade *vt* ['bærəˌkeɪd, ˌbærə'-] **-caded; -cading** : barricader — **~** *n* : barricade *f*
barrier ['bæriər] *n* : barrière *f*
barring ['bɑrɪŋ] *prep* : excepté, sauf
bartender ['bɑrˌtɛndər] *n* : barman *m*
barter ['bɑrtər] *vt* : échanger, troquer — **~** *n* : échange *m,* troc *m*
base ['beɪs] *n, pl* **bases** : base *f* — **~** *vt* **based; basing** : baser, fonder — **~** *adj* **baser; basest** : bas, vil

baseball [ˈbeɪsˌbɔl] *n* : baseball *m*, base-ball *m*
basement [ˈbeɪsmənt] *n* : sous-sol *m*
bash [ˈbæʃ] *vt* : cogner, frapper — ~ *n* **1** BLOW : coup *m* **2** PARTY : fête *f*
bashful [ˈbæʃfəl] *adj* : timide, gêné *Can*
basic [ˈbeɪsɪk] *adj* : fondamental, de base — **basically** [ˈbeɪsɪkli] *adv* : au fond, fondamentalement
basil [ˈbeɪzəl, ˈbæzəl] *n* : basilic *m*
basin [ˈbeɪsən] *n* : bassin *m* (d'un fleuve)
basis [ˈbeɪsəs] *n, pl* **bases** [-ˌsi:z] : base *f*
bask [ˈbæsk] *vi* ~ **in the sun** : se chauffer au soleil
basket [ˈbæskət] *n* : corbeille *f*, panier *m* — **basketball** [ˈbæskətˌbɔl] *n* : basket *m*, basket-ball *m*, ballon-panier *m Can*
bass[1] [ˈbæs] *n, pl* **bass** *or* **basses** : perche *f*, bar *m* (poisson)
bass[2] [ˈbeɪs] *n* : basse *f* (voix, instrument)
bassoon [bəˈsu:n, bæ-] *n* : basson *m*
bastard [ˈbæstərd] *n* : bâtard *m*, -tarde *f*
baste [ˈbeɪst] *vt* **basted; basting 1** STITCH : faufiler, bâtir **2** : arroser (un rôti, etc.)
bat[1] [ˈbæt] *n* : chauve-souris *f* (animal)
bat[2] *n* : batte *f*, bâton *m Can* — ~ *vt* **batted; batting** : frapper
batch [ˈbætʃ] *n* : liasse *f* (de papiers, etc.), lot *m* (de marchandises), fournée *f* (de pain, etc.)
bath [ˈbæθ] *n, pl* **baths** [ˈbæðz, ˈbæθs] **1** : bain *m* **2** BATHROOM : salle *f* de bains **3 take a** ~ : prendre un bain — **bathe** [ˈbeɪð] *v* **bathed; bathing** *vt* : baigner — *vi* : se baigner, prendre un bain — **bathrobe** [ˈbæθˌro:b] *n* : peignoir *m* (de bain), robe *f* de chambre — **bathroom** [ˈbæθˌru:m, -ˌrʊm] *n* : salle *f* de bains — **bathtub** [ˈbæθˌtʌb] *n* : baignoire *f*
baton [bəˈtɑn] *n* : bâton *m*
battalion [bəˈtæljən] *n* : bataillon *m*
batter [ˈbæt̬ər] *vt* **1** BEAT : battre **2** MISTREAT : maltraiter — ~ *n* **1** : pâte *f* (à cuire) **2** HITTER : batteur *m* (au baseball)
battery [ˈbæt̬əri] *n, pl* **-teries** : batterie *f*, pile *f* (d'une radio, etc.)
battle [ˈbæt̬əl] *n* **1** : bataille *f* **2** STRUGGLE : lutte *f* — ~ *vi* **-tled; -tling** : lutter — **battlefield** [ˈbæt̬əlˌfi:ld] *n* : champ *m* de bataille — **battleship** [ˈbæt̬əlˌʃɪp] *n* : cuirassé *m*
bawdy [ˈbɔdi] *adj* **bawdier; -est** : paillard, grivois
bawl [ˈbɔl] *vi* : brailler *fam*
bay[1] [ˈbeɪ] *n* INLET : baie *f*
bay[2] *n or* ~ **leaf** : laurier *m*
bay[3] *vi* : aboyer — ~ *n* : aboiement *m*
bayonet [ˌbeɪəˈnɛt, ˈbeɪəˌnɛt] *n* : baïonnette *f*
bay window *n* : fenêtre *f* en saillie
bazaar [bəˈzɑr] *n* **1** : bazar *m* **2** SALE : vente *f* (de charité)
be [ˈbi:] *v* **was** [ˈwəz, ˈwɑz]; **were** [ˈwər]; **been** [ˈbɪn]; **being; am** [ˈæm]; **is** [ˈɪz]; **are** [ˈɑr] *vi* **1** : être **2** (*expressing a state*) : être, avoir **3** (*expressing age*) : avoir **4** (*expressing equality*) : faire, égaler **5** (*expressing health or well-being*) : aller, se porter — *v aux* **1** : être en train de **2** (*indicating obligation*) : devoir **3** (*used in passive constructions*) : être — *v impers* **1** (*indicating weather*) : faire **2** (*indicating time*) : être
beach [ˈbi:tʃ] *n* : plage *f*
beacon [ˈbi:kən] *n* : phare *m*, signal *m* lumineux
bead [ˈbi:d] *n* **1** : perle *f* **2** DROP : goutte *f* **3** ~**s** *npl* NECKLACE : collier *m*
beak [ˈbi:k] *n* : bec *m*
beaker [ˈbi:kər] *n* : gobelet *m*
beam [ˈbi:m] *n* **1** : poutre *f* (de bois) **2** RAY : rayon *m* — ~ *vi* SHINE : rayonner — ~ *vt* BROADCAST : diffuser, transmettre
bean [ˈbi:n] *n* **1** : haricot *m* **2** *or* **coffee** ~ : grain *m* (de café)
bear[1] [ˈbær] *n, pl* **bears** *or* **bear** : ours *m*, ourse *f*
bear[2] *v* **bore** [ˈbor]; **borne** [ˈbɔrn]; **bearing** *vt* **1** CARRY : porter **2** ENDURE : supporter — *vi* **1** ~ **in mind** : tenir compte de **2** ~ **left/right** : prendre à gauche, à droite — **bearable** [ˈbærəbəl] *adj* : supportable
beard [ˈbɪrd] *n* : barbe *f*
bearer [ˈbærər] *n* : porteur *m*, -teuse *f*
bearing [ˈbærɪŋ] *n* **1** MANNER : maintien *m* **2** SIGNIFICANCE : rapport *m* **3 get one's** ~**s** : s'orienter
beast [ˈbi:st] *n* : bête *f*
beat [ˈbi:t] *v* **beat; beaten** [ˈbi:tən] *or* **beat; beating** : battre — ~ *n* **1** : battement *m* **2** RHYTHM : rythme *m*, temps *m* — **beating** [ˈbitɪŋ] *n* **1** : raclée *f fam* **2** DEFEAT : défaite *f*
beauty [ˈbju:t̬i] *n, pl* **-ties** : beauté *f* — **beautician** [bju:ˈtɪʃən] *n* : esthéticien *m*, -cienne *f* — **beautiful** [ˈbju:t̬ɪfəl]

adj **1** : beau **2** WONDERFUL : merveilleux — **beautifully** [ˈbjuːt̬ɪfəli] *adv* WONDERFULLY : merveilleusement — **beautify** [ˈbjuːt̬ɪˌfaɪ] *vt* **-fied; -fying** : embellir

beaver [ˈbiːvər] *n* : castor *m*

because [biˈkʌz, -ˈkɔz] *conj* : parce que — **because of** *prep* : à cause de

beckon [ˈbɛkən] *vt* : faire signe à, attirer — *vi* : faire signe

become [biˈkʌm] *v* **-came** [-ˈkeɪm]; **-come; -coming** *vi* : devenir — *vt* SUIT : aller à, convenir à — **becoming** [biˈkʌmɪŋ] *adj* **1** SUITABLE : convenable **2** FLATTERING : seyant

bed [ˈbɛd] *n* **1** : lit *m* **2** BOTTOM : fond *m* (de la mer) **3 go to ~** : se coucher — **bedclothes** [ˈbɛdˌkloːz, -ˌkloːðz] *npl* : draps *mpl* et couvertures *fpl*

bedridden [ˈbɛdˌrɪdən] *adj* : alité

bedroom [ˈbɛdˌruːm, -ˌrʊm] *n* : chambre *f* (à coucher)

bedspread [ˈbɛdˌsprɛd] *n* : couvre-lit *m*

bedtime [ˈbɛdˌtaɪm] *n* : heure *f* du coucher

bee [ˈbiː] *n* : abeille *f*

beech [ˈbiːtʃ] *n, pl* **beeches** *or* **beech** : hêtre *m*

beef [ˈbiːf] *n* : bœuf *m* — **beefsteak** [ˈbifˌsteɪk] *n* : bifteck *m*

beehive [ˈbiːˌhaɪv] *n* : ruche *f*

beeline [ˈbiːˌlaɪn] *n* **make a ~ for** : se diriger droit vers

been → **be**

beep [ˈbiːp] *n* : coup *m* de klaxon, bip *m* — **~** *vi* : klaxonner, faire bip — **beeper** [ˈbiːpər] *n* : récepteur *m* de radiomessagerie

beer [ˈbɪr] *n* : bière *f*

beet [ˈbiːt] *n* : betterave *f*

beetle [ˈbiːt̬əl] *n* : scarabée *m*

before [bɪˈfor] *adv* **1** : avant, auparavant **2 the month ~** : le mois dernier — **~** *prep* **1** (*in space*) : devant **2** (*in time*) : avant **3 ~ my eyes** : sous mes yeux — **~** *conj* : avant de, avant que — **beforehand** [bɪˈforˌhænd] *adv* : à l'avance

befriend [bɪˈfrɛnd] *vt* : offrir son amitié à

beg [ˈbɛg] *v* **begged; begging** *vt* **1** : mendier **2** ENTREAT : supplier, prier — *vi* : mendier — **beggar** [ˈbɛgər] *n* : mendiant *m*, -diante *f*

begin [bɪˈgɪn] *v* **-gan** [-ˈgæn]; **-gun** [-ˈgʌn]; **-ginning** : commencer — **beginner** [bɪˈgɪnər] *n* : débutant *m*, -tante *f* — **beginning** [bɪˈgɪnɪŋ] *n* : début *m*, commencement *m*

begrudge [bɪˈgrʌdʒ] *vt* **-grudged; -grudging** **1** : accorder à regret **2** ENVY : envier

behalf [bɪˈhæf, -haf] *n* **on ~ of** : de la part de, au nom de

behave [bɪˈheɪv] *vi* **-haved; -having** : se conduire, se comporter — **behavior** *or Brit* **behaviour** [bɪˈheɪvjər] *n* : conduite *f*, comportement *m*

behind [bɪˈhaɪnd] *adv* **1** : derrière, en arrière **2 fall ~** : prendre du retard — **~** *prep* **1** : derrière, en arrière de **2** : en retard sur (l'horaire, etc.) **3 her friends are ~ her** : elle a l'appui de ses amis

behold [bɪˈhoːld] *vt* **-held; -holding** : contempler

beige [ˈbeɪʒ] *adj & nm* : beige

being [ˈbiːɪŋ] *n* **1** : être *m*, créature *f* **2 come into ~** : prendre naissance

belated [bɪˈleɪt̬əd] *adj* : tardif

belch [ˈbɛltʃ] *vi* : roter *fam* — **~** *n* : renvoi *m*

belfry [ˈbɛlfri] *n, pl* **-fries** : beffroi *m*, clocher *m*

Belgian [ˈbɛldʒən] *adj* : belge

belie [bɪˈlaɪ] *vt* **-lied; -lying** : démentir, contredire

belief [bəˈliːf] *n* **1** TRUST : confiance *f* **2** CONVICTION : croyance *f* **3** FAITH : foi *f* — **believable** [bəˈliːvəbəl] *adj* : croyable — **believe** [bəˈliːv] *v* **-lieved; -lieving** : croire — **believer** [bəˈliːvər] *n* : croyant *m*, croyante *f*

belittle [bɪˈlɪt̬əl] *vt* **-tled; -tling** : rabaisser

bell [ˈbɛl] *n* **1** : cloche *f*, clochette *f* **2** : sonnette *f* (d'une porte, etc.)

belligerent [bəˈlɪdʒərənt] *adj* : belligérant

bellow [ˈbɛˌloː] *vi* **1** : beugler **2** HOWL : brailler *fam*, hurler

belly [ˈbɛli] *n, pl* **-lies** : ventre *m*

belong [bɪˈlɔŋ] *vi* **1 ~ to** : appartenir à, être à **2 ~ to** : être membre de (un club, etc.) **3 where does it ~ ?** : où va-t-il? — **belongings** [bɪˈlɔŋɪŋz] *npl* : affaires *fpl*, effets *mpl* personnels

beloved [bɪˈlʌvəd, -ˈlʌvd] *adj* : bien-aimé — **~** *n* : bien-aimé *m*, -mée *f*

below [bɪˈloː] *adv* : en dessous, en bas — **~** *prep* : sous, au-dessous de, en dessous de

belt [ˈbɛlt] *n* **1** : ceinture *f* **2** STRAP : courroie *f* (d'une machine) **3** AREA : zone *f*, région *f* — **~** *vt* THRASH : donner un coup à

bench [ˈbɛntʃ] *n* **1** : banc *m* **2** WORKBENCH : établi *m* **3** COURT : cour *f*, tribunal *m*
bend [ˈbɛnd] *v* **bent** [ˈbɛnt]; **bending** *vt* : plier, courber — *vi* **1** : se plier, se courber **2** *or* ~ **over** : se pencher — ~ *n* : virage *m*, coude *m*
beneath [bɪˈni:θ] *adv* : au-dessous, en bas — ~ *prep* : sous, en dessous de
benediction [ˌbɛnəˈdɪkʃən] *n* : bénédiction *f*
benefactor [ˈbɛnəˌfæktər] *n* : bienfaiteur *m*, -trice *f*
benefit [ˈbɛnəfɪt] *n* **1** : avantage *m*, bénéfice *m* **2** AID : allocation *f*, prestation *f* — ~ *vt* : profiter à, bénéficier à — *vi* : profiter, tirer avantage — **beneficial** [ˌbɛnəˈfɪʃəl] *adj* : avantageux — **beneficiary** [ˌbɛnəˈfɪʃiˌɛri, -ˈfɪʃəri] *n*, *pl* **-ries** : bénéficiaire *mf*
benevolent [bəˈnɛvələnt] *adj* : bienveillant
benign [bɪˈnaɪn] *adj* **1** KIND : bienveillant, aimable **2** : bénin (en médecine)
bent [ˈbɛnt] *adj* **1** : tordu, courbé **2 be** ~ **on doing** : être décidé à faire — ~ *n* : aptitude *f*, penchant *m*
bequeath [bɪˈkwi:θ, -kwi:ð] *vt* : léguer — **bequest** [bɪˈkwɛst] *n* : legs *m*
berate [bɪˈreɪt] *vt* **-rated; -rating** : réprimander
bereaved [bɪˈri:vd] *adj* : endeuillé, attristé — **bereavement** [bɪˈri:vmənt] *n* : deuil *m*
beret [bəˈreɪ] *n* : béret *m*
berry [ˈbɛri] *n*, *pl* **-ries** : baie *f*
berserk [bərˈsərk, -ˈzərk] *adj* **1** : fou, enragé **2 go** ~ : devenir fou furieux
berth [ˈbɛrθ] *n* **1** MOORING : mouillage *m* **2** BUNK : couchette *f*
beset [bɪˈsɛt] *vt* **-set; -setting** **1** HARASS : assaillir **2** SURROUND : encercler
beside [bɪˈsaɪd] *prep* **1** : à côté de, près de **2 be** ~ **oneself** : être hors de soi — **besides** [bɪˈsaɪdz] *adv* : en plus — ~ *prep* **1** : en plus de **2** EXCEPT : sauf
besiege [bɪˈsi:dʒ] *vt* **-sieged; -sieging** : assiéger
best [ˈbɛst] *adj* (*superlative of* **good**) **1** : meilleur **2** : plus beau — ~ *adv* (*superlative of* **well**) : le mieux, le plus — ~ *n* **1 at** ~ : au mieux **2 do one's** ~ : faire de son mieux **3 the** ~ : le meilleur — **best man** *n* : garçon *m* d'honneur, témoin *n*
bestow [bɪˈsto:] *vt* : accorder, concéder
bet [ˈbɛt] *n* : pari *m*, gageure *f Can* — ~ *v* **bet; betting** *vt* : parier, gager *Can* — *vi* ~ **on sth** : parier sur qqch
betray [bɪˈtreɪ] *vt* : trahir — **betrayal** [bɪˈtreɪəl] *n* : trahison *f*
better [ˈbɛt̬ər] *adj* (*comparative of* **good**) **1** : meilleur **2 get** ~ : s'améliorer — ~ *adv* (*comparative of* **well**) **1** : mieux **2 all the** ~ : tant mieux — ~ *n* **1 the** ~ : le meilleur, la meilleure **2 get the** ~ **of** : l'emporter sur — ~ *vt* **1** IMPROVE : améliorer **2** SURPASS : surpasser, faire mieux que
between [bɪˈtwi:n] *prep* : entre — ~ *adv or* **in** ~ : au milieu
beverage [ˈbɛvrɪdʒ, ˈbɛvə-] *n* : boisson *f*
beware [bɪˈwær] *vi* ~ **of** : prendre garde à, se méfier de
bewilder [bɪˈwɪldər] *vt* : rendre perplexe, déconcerter — **bewilderment** [bɪˈwɪldərmənt] *n* : perplexité *f*, confusion *f*
bewitch [bɪˈwɪtʃ] *vt* : enchanter
beyond [biˈjɑnd] *adv* : au-delà, plus loin — ~ *prep* : au-delà de
bias [ˈbaɪəs] *n* **1** PREJUDICE : préjugé *m* **2** TENDENCY : penchant *m* — **biased** [ˈbaɪəst] *adj* : partial
bib [ˈbɪb] *n* : bavoir *m* (d'un bébé)
Bible [ˈbaɪbəl] *n* : Bible *f* — **biblical** [ˈbɪblɪkəl] *adj* : biblique
bibliography [ˌbɪbliˈɑgrəfi] *n*, *pl* **-phies** : bibliographie *f*
biceps [ˈbaɪˌsɛps] *ns & pl* : biceps *m*
bicker [ˈbɪkər] *vi* : se chamailler
bicycle [ˈbaɪsɪkəl, -ˌsɪ-] *n* : bicyclette *f*, vélo *m* — ~ *vi* **-cled; -cling** : faire de la bicyclette, faire du vélo
bid [ˈbɪd] *vt* **bade** [ˈbæd, ˈbeɪd] *or* **bid**; **bidden** [ˈbɪdən] *or* **bid; bidding** **1** OFFER : offrir **2** ~ **farewell** : dire adieu — ~ *n* **1** OFFER : offre *f*, enchère *f* **2** ATTEMPT : tentative *f*
bide [ˈbaɪd] *vt* **bode** [ˈbo:d] *or* **bided; bided; biding** ~ **one's time** : attendre le bon moment
bifocals [baɪˌfo:kəlz] *npl* : lunettes *fpl* bifocales
big [ˈbɪg] *adj* **bigger; biggest** : grand, gros
bigot [ˈbɪgət] *n* : fanatique *mf* — **bigotry** [ˈbɪgətri] *n*, *pl* **-tries** : fanatisme *m*
bike [ˈbaɪk] *n* **1** BICYCLE : vélo *m* **2** MOTORCYCLE : moto *f*
bikini [bəˈki:ni] *n* : bikini *m*
bile [ˈbaɪl] *n* : bile *f*
bilingual [baɪˈlɪŋgwəl] *adj* : bilingue
bill [ˈbɪl] *n* **1** BEAK : bec *m* (d'un oiseau) **2** INVOICE : facture *f*, compte *m*, addition *f* (au restaurant) **3** LAW : projet *m*

de loi **4** BANKNOTE : billet *m* (de banque) — **~** *vt* : facturer, envoyer la facture à

billiards ['bɪljərdz] *n* : billard *m*

billion ['bɪljən] *n, pl* **billions** *or* **billion** : milliard *m*

billow ['bɪlo] *vi* : onduler (se dit d'un drapeau)

bin ['bɪn] *n* : coffre *m,* boîte *f*

binary ['baɪnəri, -ˌnɛri] *adj* : binaire

bind ['baɪnd] *vt* **bound** ['baʊnd]; **binding** **1** TIE : lier **2** OBLIGE : obliger **3** UNITE : unir **4** : relier (un livre) — **binder** ['baɪndər] *n* FOLDER : classeur *m* — **binding** ['baɪndɪŋ] *n* : reliure *f* (d'un livre)

binge ['bɪnʤ] *n* : bringue *f fam*

bingo ['bɪŋˌgo:] *n, pl* **-gos** : bingo *m*

binoculars [bə'nɑkjələrz, baɪ-] *npl* : jumelles *fpl*

biochemistry [ˌbaɪo'kɛməstri] *n* : biochimie *f*

biography [baɪ'ɑgrəfi, bi:-] *n, pl* **-phies** : biographie *f* — **biographer** [baɪ'ɑgrəfər] *n* : biographe *mf* — **biographical** [ˌbaɪə'græfɪkəl] *adj* : biographique

biology [baɪ'ɑləʤi] *n* : biologie *f* — **biological** [-ʤɪkəl] *adj* : biologique — **biologist** [baɪ'ɑləʤɪst] *n* : biologiste *mf*

birch ['bərʧ] *n* : bouleau *m*

bird ['bərd] *n* : oiseau *m*

birth ['bərθ] *n* **1** : naissance *f* **2 give ~ to** : accoucher de — **birthday** ['bərθˌdeɪ] *n* : anniversaire *m* — **birthmark** ['bərθˌmɑrk] *n* : tache *f* de vin — **birthplace** ['bərθˌpleɪs] *n* : lieu *m* de naissance — **birthrate** ['bərθˌreɪt] *n* : natalité *f*

biscuit ['bɪskət] *n* : petit pain *m* au lait

bisexual [ˌbaɪ'sɛkʃəwəl, -'sɛkʃəl] *adj* : bisexuel

bishop ['bɪʃəp] *n* **1** : évêque *m* **2** : fou *m* (aux échecs)

bison ['baɪzən, -sən] *ns & pl* : bison *m*

bit[1] ['bɪt] *n* : mors *m* (d'une bride)

bit[2] *n* **1** : morceau *m,* bout *m* **2** : bit *m* (en informatique) **3 a ~** : un peu

bitch ['bɪʧ] *n* : chienne *f* — **~** *vi* COMPLAIN : râler *fam*

bite ['baɪt] *v* **bit** ['bɪt]; **bitten** ['bɪtən]; **biting** *vt* **1** : mordre **2** STING : piquer — *vi* : mordre — **~** *n* **1** : piqûre *f* (d'insecte), morsure *f* (de chien, etc.) **2** MOUTHFUL : bouchée *f* — **biting** *adj* **1** PENETRATING : pénétrant **2** SCATHING : mordant

bitter ['bɪṭər] *adj* **1** : amer **2 it's ~ cold** : il fait un froid glacial — **bitterness** ['bɪṭərnəs] *n* : amertume *f*

bizarre [bə'zɑr] *adj* : bizarre

black ['blæk] *adj* : noir — **~** *n* **1** : noir *m* (couleur) **2** : Noir *m,* Noire *f* (personne) — **black-and-blue** [ˌblækən'blu:] *adj* : couvert de bleus — **blackberry** ['blækˌbɛri] *n, pl* **-ries** : mûre *f* — **blackboard** ['blækˌbɔrd] *n* : tableau *m* (noir) — **blacken** ['blækən] *vt* : noircir — **blackmail** ['blækˌmeɪl] *n* : chantage *m* — **~** *vi* : faire chanter — **black market** *n* : marché *m* noir — **blackout** ['blækˌaʊt] *n* **1** : panne *f* d'électricité **2** FAINT : évanouissement *m* — **blacksmith** ['blækˌsmɪθ] *n* : forgeron *m* — **blacktop** ['blækˌtɑp] *n* : asphalte *m*

bladder ['blædər] *n* : vessie *f*

blade ['bleɪd] *n* **1** : lame *f* (de couteau) **2** : pale *f* (d'hélice, de rame, etc.) **3 ~ of grass** : brin *m* d'herbe

blame ['bleɪm] *vt* **blamed; blaming** : blâmer, reprocher — **~** *n* : faute *f,* responsabilité *f* — **blameless** ['bleɪmləs] *adj* : irréprochable

bland ['blænd] *adj* : fade, insipide

blank ['blæŋk] *adj* **1** : blanc (se dit d'une page, etc.) **2** EMPTY : vide — **~** *n* : blanc *m,* vide *m*

blanket ['blæŋkət] *n* **1** : couverture *f* (d'un lit) **2 ~ of snow** : couche *f* de neige — **~** *vt* : recouvrir

blare ['blær] *vi* **blared; blaring** : beugler

blasé [blɑ'zeɪ] *adj* : blasé

blasphemy ['blæsfəmi] *n, pl* **-mies** : blasphème *m*

blast ['blæst] *n* **1** GUST : rafale *f,* souffle *m* **2** EXPLOSION : explosion *f* **3 at full ~** : à plein volume — **~** *vt* BLOW UP : faire sauter — **blast-off** ['blæstˌɔf] *n* : lancement *m*

blatant ['bleɪtənt] *adj* : flagrant

blaze ['bleɪz] *n* **1** FIRE : incendie *f* **2** BRIGHTNESS : éclat *m* — **~** *v* **blazed; blazing** : flamber

blazer ['bleɪzər] *n* : blazer *m*

bleach ['bli:ʧ] *vt* : blanchir, décolorer — **~** *n* : décolorant *m,* eau *f* de Javel

bleachers ['bli:ʧərz] *npl* : gradins *mpl*

bleak ['bli:k] *adj* **1** DESOLATE : désolé **2** GLOOMY : triste, sombre

bleat ['bli:t] *vi* : bêler — **~** *n* : bêlement *m*

bleed ['bli:d] *v* **bled** ['blɛd]; **bleeding** : saigner

blemish ['blɛmɪʃ] *vt* : tacher, ternir — **~** *n* : tache *f,* défaut *m*

blend [ˈblɛnd] *vt* : mélanger — **~** *n* : mélange *m,* combinaison *f* — **blender** [ˈblɛndər] *n* : mixer *m*
bless [ˈblɛs] *vt* **blessed** [ˈblɛst]; **blessing** : bénir — **blessed** [ˈblɛsəd] *or* **blest** [ˈblɛst] *adj* : bénit, saint — **blessing** [ˈblɛsɪŋ] *n* : bénédiction *f*
blew → **blow**
blind [ˈblaɪnd] *adj* : aveugle — **~** *vt* **1** : aveugler **2** DAZZLE : éblouir — **~** *n* **1** : store *m* (d'une fenêtre) **2 the ~** : les non-voyants *mpl* — **blindfold** [ˈblaɪndˌfo:ld] *vt* : bander les yeux à — **~** *n* : bandeau *m* — **blindly** [ˈblaɪndli] *adv* : aveuglément — **blindness** [ˈblaɪndnəs] *n* : cécité *f*
blink [ˈblɪŋk] *vi* **1** : cligner des yeux **2** FLICKER : clignoter — **~** *n* : battement *m* des paupières — **blinker** [ˈblɪŋkər] *n* : clignotant *m*
bliss [ˈblɪs] *n* : félicité *f* — **blissful** [ˈblɪsfəl] *adj* : bienheureux
blister [ˈblɪstər] *n* **1** : ampoule *f,* cloque *f* (sur la peau) **2** : boursouflure *f* (sur une surface peinte) — **~** *vi* **1** : se couvrir d'ampoules *fpl* (se dit de la peau) **2** : se boursoufler (se dit de la peinture, etc.)
blitz [ˈblɪts] *n* : bombardement *m*
blizzard [ˈblɪzərd] *n* : tempête *f* de neige
bloated [ˈblo:t̬əd] *adj* : boursouflé, gonflé
blob [ˈblɑb] *n* **1** DROP : goutte *f* **2** SPOT : tache *f*
block [ˈblɑk] *n* **1** : bloc *m* **2** OBSTRUCTION : obstruction *f* **3** : pâté *m* de maisons, bloc *m Can* **4** *or* **building ~** : cube *m* — **~** *vt* : bloquer, boucher — **blockade** [blɑˈkeɪd] *n* : blocus *m* — **blockage** [ˈblɑkɪʤ] *n* : obstruction *f*
blond *or* **blonde** [ˈblɑnd] *adj* : blond — **~** *n* : blond *m,* blonde *f*
blood [ˈblʌd] *n* : sang *m* — **blood pressure** *n* : tension *f* artérielle — **bloodshed** [ˈblʌdˌʃɛd] *n* : carnage *m* — **bloodshot** [ˈblʌdˌʃɑt] *adj* : injecté de sang — **bloodstained** [ˈblʌdˌsteɪnd] *adj* : taché de sang — **bloodstream** [ˈblʌdˌstri:m] *n* : sang *m,* système *m* sanguin — **bloodthirsty** [ˈblʌdˌθərsti] *adj* : sanguinaire — **bloody** [ˈblʌdi] *adj* **bloodier; -est** : ensanglanté
bloom [ˈblu:m] *n* **1** : fleur *f* **2 in full ~** : en pleine floraison — **~** *vi* : fleurir, éclore
blossom [ˈblɑsəm] *n* : fleur *f* — **~** *vi* **1** : fleurir **2** MATURE : s'épanouir
blot [ˈblɑt] *n* : tache *f* (d'encre, etc.) — **~** *vt* **blotted; blotting 1** : tacher **2** DRY : sécher
blotch [ˈblɑʧ] *n* : tache *f* — **blotchy** [ˈblɑˈʧi] *adj* **blotchier; -est** : tacheté
blouse [ˈblaʊs, ˈblaʊz] *n* : chemisier *m*
blow [ˈblo:] *v* **blew** [ˈblu:]; **blown** [ˈblo:n]; **blowing** *vi* **1** : souffler **2** SOUND : sonner **3** *or* **~ out** : éclater (se dit d'un pneu), s'éteindre (se dit d'une bougie) — *vt* **1** : souffler **2** SOUND : jouer de (la trompette, etc.) **3** BUNGLE : rater **4 ~ one's nose** : se moucher — **~** *n* : coup *m* — **blowout** [ˈblo:ˌaʊt] *n* : éclatement *m* — **blow up** *vi* : exploser, sauter — *vt* **1** EXPLODE : faire sauter **2** INFLATE : gonfler
blubber [ˈblʌbər] *n* : graisse *f* de baleine
bludgeon [ˈblʌʤən] *n* : matraque *f* — **~** *vt* : matraquer
blue [ˈblu:] *adj* **bluer; bluest 1** : bleu **2** MELANCHOLY : triste — **~** *n* : bleu *m* — **blueberry** [ˈblu:ˌbɛri] *n, pl* **-ries** : myrtille *f France,* bleuet *m Can* — **bluebird** [ˈblu:ˌbərd] *n* : oiseau *m* bleu — **blue cheese** *n* : (fromage *m*) bleu *m* — **blueprint** [ˈblu:ˌprɪnt] *n* : plan *m* (de travail) — **blues** [ˈblu:z] *ns & pl* **1** : cafard *m* **2** : blues *m* (musique)
bluff [ˈblʌf] *v* : bluffer — **~** *n* **1** : falaise *f,* escarpement *m* **2** DECEPTION : bluff *m* —
blunder [ˈblʌndər] *vi* : faire une gaffe — **~** *n* : gaffe *f fam*
blunt [ˈblʌnt] *adj* **1** DULL : émoussé **2** DIRECT : brusque, franc — **~** *vt* : émousser
blur [ˈblər] *n* : image *f* floue — **~** *vt* **blurred; blurring** : brouiller, rendre flou
blurb [ˈblərb] *n* : notice *f* publicitaire
blurt [ˈblərt] *vt or* **~ out** : laisser échapper
blush [ˈblʌʃ] *n* : rougeur *f* — **~** *vi* : rougir
blustery [ˈblʌstəri] *adj* : venteux, orageux
boar [ˈbor] *n* : sanglier *m*
board [ˈbord] *n* **1** PLANK : planche *f* **2** COMMITTEE : conseil *m* **3** : tableau *m* (d'un jeu) **4 room and ~** : pension *f* complète — **~** *vt* **1** : monter à bord de (un avion, un navire), monter dans (un train) **2** LODGE : prendre en pension **3 ~ up** : couvrir de planches — **boarder** [ˈbordər] *n* : pensionnaire *mf*
boast [ˈbo:st] *n* : vantardise *f* — **~** *vi* : se vanter — **boastful** [ˈbo:stfəl] *adj* : vantard
boat [ˈbo:t] *n* : bateau *m,* barque *f*

bob [ˈbɑb] *vi* **bobbed; bobbing** *or* **~ up and down** : monter et descendre
bobbin [ˈbɑbən] *n* : bobine *f*
body [ˈbɑdi] *n, pl* **bodies 1** : corps *m* **2** CORPSE : cadavre *m* **3** : carrosserie *f* (d'une voiture) **4 ~ of water** : masse *f* d'eau — **bodily** [ˈbɑdəli] *adj* : physique, corporel —**bodyguard** [ˈbɑdiˌgɑrd] *n* : garde *m* du corps
bog [ˈbɑg, ˈbɔg] *n* : marais *m,* marécage *m* — **~** *vi* **bogged; bogging** *or* **~ down** : s'embourber
bogus [ˈboːgəs] *adj* : faux
bohemian [boːˈhiːmiən] *adj* : bohème
boil [ˈbɔɪl] *vt* : faire bouillir — *vi* : bouillir — **~** *n* **1** : ébullition *f* **2** : furoncle *m* (en médecine) — **boiler** [ˈbɔɪlər] *n* : chaudière *f*
boisterous [ˈbɔɪstərəs] *adj* : bruyant, tapageur
bold [ˈboːld] *adj* **1** DARING : hardi, audacieux **2** IMPUDENT : effronté — **boldness** [ˈboːldnəs] *n* : hardiesse *f,* audace *f*
bologna [bəˈloːni] *n* : gros *m* saucisson
bolster [ˈboːlstər] *n* : traversin *m* — **~** *vt* **-stered; -stering** *or* **~ up** : soutenir
bolt [ˈboːlt] *n* **1** LOCK : verrou *m* **2** SCREW : boulon *m* **3 ~ of lightning** : éclair *m,* coup *m* de foudre — **~** *vt* LOCK : verrouiller — *vi* FLEE : se sauver
bomb [ˈbɑm] *n* : bombe *f* — **~** *vt* : bombarder — **bombard** [bɑmˈbɑrd, bəm-] *vt* : bombarder — **bombardment** [bɑmˈbɑrdmənt] *n* : bombardement *m* — **bomber** [ˈbɑmər] *n* : bombardier *m*
bond [ˈbɑnd] *n* **1** TIE : lien *m* **2** SECURITY : bon *m* — **~** *vi* **~ with** : s'attacher à
bondage [ˈbɑndɪʤ] *n* : esclavage *m*
bone [ˈboːn] *n* : os *m,* arête *f* — **~** *vt* **boned; boning** : désosser
bonfire [ˈbɑnˌfaɪr] *n* : feu *m* de joie
bonus [ˈboːnəs] *n* : gratification *f,* prime *f*
bony [ˈboːni] *adj* **bonier; -est** : plein d'os, plein d'arêtes
boo [ˈbuː] *n, pl* **boos** : huée *f* — **~** *vt* : huer, siffler
book [ˈbʊk] *n* **1** : livre *m* **2** NOTEBOOK : cahier *m* — **~** *vt* : réserver — **bookcase** [ˈbʊkˌkeɪs] *n* : bibliothèque *f* — **bookkeeping** [ˈbʊkˌkiːpɪŋ] *n* : comptabilité *f* — **booklet** [ˈbʊklət] *n* : brochure *f* — **bookmark** [ˈbʊkˌmɑrk] *n* : signet *m* — **bookseller** [ˈbʊkˌsɛlər] *n* : libraire *mf* — **bookshelf** [ˈbʊkˌʃɛlf] *n, pl* **-shelves** : rayon *m,* étagère *f* (à livres) — **bookstore** [ˈbʊkˌstor] *n* : librairie *f*
boom [ˈbuːm] *vi* **1** : gronder, retentir **2** PROSPER : prospérer — **~** *n* **1** : grondement *m* **2** : boom *m* (économique)
boon [ˈbuːn] *n* : bienfait *m*
boost [ˈbuːst] *vt* **1** LIFT : soulever **2** INCREASE : augmenter — **~** *n* **1** INCREASE : augmentation *f* **2** ENCOURAGEMENT : encouragement *m*
boot [ˈbuːt] *n* : botte *f* — **~** *vt* **1** : donner un coup de pied à **2** *or* **~ up** : amorcer (en informatique)
booth [ˈbuːθ] *n, pl* **booths** [ˈbuːðz, ˈbuːθs] : baraque *f* (d'un marché), cabine *f* (téléphonique)
booze [ˈbuːz] *n* : alcool *m,* boissons *fpl* alcoolisées
border [ˈbɔrˌdər] *n* **1** EDGE : bord *m* **2** BOUNDARY : frontière *f* **3** : bordure *f* (d'un vêtement, etc.)
bore[1] [ˈbor] *vt* **bored; boring** DRILL : percer, forer
bore[2] *vt* TIRE : ennuyer — **~** *n* : raseur *m,* -seuse *f fam* — **boredom** [ˈbordəm] *n* : ennui *m* — **boring** [ˈborɪŋ] *adj* : ennuyeux, ennuyant *Can*
born [ˈbɔrn] *adj* **1** : né **2 be ~** : naître
borough [ˈbəro] *n* : arrondissement *m* urbain
borrow [ˈbɑro] *vt* : emprunter
bosom [ˈbʊzəm, ˈbuː-] *n* BREAST : poitrine *f* — **~** *adj* **~ friend** : ami intime
boss [ˈbɔs] *n* : patron *m,* -tronne *f;* chef *m* — **~** *vt* SUPERVISE : diriger — **bossy** [ˈbɔsi] *adj* **bossier; -est** : autoritaire
botany [ˈbɑtəni] *n* : botanique *f* — **botanical** [bəˈtænɪkəl] *adj* : botanique
botch [ˈbɑʧ] *vt or* **~ up** : bousiller *fam,* saboter
both [ˈboːθ] *adj* : les deux — **~** *conj* : à la fois — **~** *pron* : tous les deux, l'un et l'autre
bother [ˈbɑðər] *vt* **1** TROUBLE : préoccuper **2** PESTER : harceler — *vi* **~ to** : se donner la peine de — **~** *n* : ennui *m*
bottle [ˈbɑtəl] *n* **1** : bouteille *f* **2** *or* **baby ~** : biberon *m* — **~** *vt* **-tled; -tling** : mettre en bouteille — **bottleneck** [ˈbɑtəlˌnɛk] *n* : embouteillage *m*
bottom [ˈbɑţəm] *n* **1** : bas *m* (d'une page, etc.), fond *m* (d'une bouteille, d'un lac, etc.), pied *m* (d'un escalier) **2** BUTTOCKS : derrière *m fam* — **~** *adj* : du bas, inférieur — **bottomless** [ˈbɑţəmləs] *adj* : insondable

bough ['baʊ] *n* : rameau *m*
bought → **buy**
boulder ['bo:ldər] *n* : rocher *m*
boulevard ['bʊlə,vɑrd, 'bu:-] *n* : boulevard *m*
bounce ['baʊnts] *v* **bounced; bouncing** *vt* : faire rebondir — *vi* : rebondir — ~ *n* : bond *m*, rebond *m*
bound[1] ['baʊnd] *adj* ~ **for** : à destination de
bound[2] *adj* **1** OBLIGED : obligé **2 be** ~ **to** : être certain de
bound[3] *n* **out of** ~**s** : interdit — **boundary** ['baʊndri, -dəri] *n, pl* **-aries** : limite *f*, frontière *f* — **boundless** ['baʊndləs] *adj* : sans bornes
bouquet [bo:'keɪ, bu:-] *n* : bouquet *m*
bourbon ['bərbən, 'bʊr-] *n* : bourbon *m*
bourgeois ['bʊrʒ,wɑ, bʊrʒ'wɑ] *adj* : bourgeois
bout ['baʊt] *n* **1** : combat *m* (aux sports) **2** : accès *m* (de fièvre)
bow[1] ['baʊ] *vi* : s'incliner — *vt* **1** : incliner **2** ~ **one's head** : baisser la tête — ~ ['baʊ:] *n* : révérence *f*, salut *m*
bow[2] ['bo:] *n* **1** : arc *m* **2 tie a** ~ : faire un nœud
bow[3] ['baʊ] *n* : proue *f* (d'un bateau)
bowels ['baʊəlz] *npl* **1** : intestins *mpl* **2** DEPTHS : entrailles *fpl*
bowl[1] ['bo:l] *n* : bol *m*, cuvette *f*
bowl[2] *vi* : jouer au bowling — **bowling** ['bo:lɪŋ] *n* : bowling *m*
box[1] ['bɑks] *vi* FIGHT : boxer, faire de la boxe — **boxer** ['bɑksər] *n* : boxeur *m* — **boxing** ['bɑksɪŋ] *n* : boxe *f*
box[2] *n* **1** : boîte *f*, caisse *f*, coffre *m* **2** : loge *f* (au théâtre) — ~ *vt* : mettre en boîte — **box office** *n* : guichet *m*, billetterie *f*
boy ['bɔɪ] *n* : garçon *m*
boycott ['bɔɪ,kɑt] *vt* : boycotter — ~ *n* : boycott *m*, boycottage *m*
boyfriend ['bɔɪ,frɛnd] *n* : petit ami *m*
bra ['brɑ] → **brassiere**
brace ['breɪs] *n* **1** SUPPORT : support *m* **2** ~**s** *npl* : appareil *m* orthodontique — ~ *vi* ~ **oneself for** : se préparer pour
bracelet ['breɪslət] *n* : bracelet *m*
bracket ['brækət] *n* **1** SUPPORT : support *m* **2** : parenthèse *f*, crochet *m* (signe de ponctuation) **3** CATEGORY : catégorie *f* — ~ *vt* : mettre entre parenthèses, mettre entre crochets
brag ['bræg] *vi* **bragged; bragging** : se vanter
braid ['breɪd] *vt* : tresser — ~ *n* : tresse *f* (de cheveux)
braille ['breɪl] *n* : braille *m*
brain ['breɪn] *n* **1** : cerveau *m* **2** *or* ~**s** *npl* : intelligence *f* — **brainstorm** ['breɪn,stɔrm] *n* : idée *f* géniale — **brainwash** ['breɪn,wɔʃ, -,wɑʃ] *vt* : faire un lavage de cerveau à — **brainy** ['breɪni] *adj* **brainier; -est** : intelligent, calé *fam*
brake ['breɪk] *n* : frein *m* — ~ *vi* **braked; braking** : freiner
bramble ['bræmbəl] *n* : ronce *f*
bran ['bræn] *n* : son *m*
branch ['bræntʃ] *n* **1** : branche *f* (d'un arbre) **2** DIVISION : succursale *f* — ~ *vi or* ~ **off** : bifurquer
brand ['brænd] *n* **1** : marque *f* (sur un animal) **2** *or* ~ **name** : marque *f* déposée — ~ *vt* **1** : marquer (au fer rouge) **2** LABEL : étiqueter
brandish ['brændɪʃ] *vt* : brandir
brand–new ['brænd'nu:, -'nju:] *adj* : tout neuf
brandy ['brændi] *n, pl* **-dies** : cognac *m*, eau-de-vie *f*
brash ['bræʃ] *adj* : impertinent
brass ['bræs] *n* **1** : cuivre *m* (jaune), laiton *m* **2** : cuivres *mpl* (d'un orchestre)
brassiere [brə'zɪr, brɑ-] *n* : soutien-gorge *m*, brassière *f Can*
brat ['bræt] *n* : môme *mf France fam;* gosse *mf France fam*
bravado [brə'vɑdo] *n, pl* **-does** *or* **-dos** : bravade *f*
brave ['breɪv] *adj* **braver; bravest** : courageux, brave — ~ *vt* **braved; braving** : braver, défier — **bravery** ['breɪvəri] *n, pl* **-eries** : courage *m*
brawl ['brɔl] *n* : bagarre *f*
brawn ['brɔn] *n* : muscles *mpl* — **brawny** ['brɔni] *adj* **brawnier; -est** : musclé
bray ['breɪ] *vi* : braire
brazen ['breɪzən] *adj* : effronté
Brazilian [brə'zɪljən] *adj* : brésilien
breach [bri:tʃ] *n* **1** VIOLATION : infraction *f* **2** GAP : brèche *f*
bread ['brɛd] *n* **1** : pain *m* **2** ~ **crumbs** : chapelure *f*
breadth ['brɛtθ] *n* : largeur *f*
break ['breɪk] *v* **broke** ['bro:k]; **broken** ['bro:kən]; **breaking** *vt* **1** : casser, briser **2** VIOLATE : violer (la loi) **3** INTERRUPT : interrompre **4** SURPASS : battre (un record, etc.) **5** ~ **a habit** : se défaire d'une habitude **6** ~ **the news** : annoncer la nouvelle — *vi* **1** : se

casser, se briser **2 ~ away** : s'évader **3 ~ down** : tomber en panne (se dit d'une voiture) **4 ~ into** : entrer par effraction **5 ~ up** SEPARATE : rompre, se quitter — **~** *n* **1** : cassure *f,* rupture *f* **2** GAP : trouée *f,* brèche *f* **3** REST : pause *f,* break *m Can* **4 a lucky ~** : un coup de veine — **breakable** [ˈbreɪkəbˈl] *adj* : cassable — **breakdown** [ˈbreɪkˌdaʊn] *n* **1** : panne *f* (d'une machine), rupture *f* (des négociations) **2** *or* **nervous ~** : dépression *f* nerveuse

breakfast [ˈbrɛkfəst] *n* : petit déjeuner *m France,* déjeuner *Can*

breast [ˈbrɛst] *n* **1** : sein *m* (d'une femme) **2** CHEST : poitrine *f* — **breast–feed** [ˈbrɛstˌfi:d] *vt* **-fed** [-ˌfɛd]; **-feeding** : allaiter

breath [ˈbrɛθ] *n* : souffle *m,* haleine *f,* respiration *f* — **breathe** [ˈbri:ð] *v* **breathed; breathing** : respirer — **breathless** [ˈbrɛθləs] *adj* : à bout de souffle, hors d'haleine — **breathtaking** [ˈbrɛθˌteɪkɪŋ] *adj* : à couper le souffle

breed [ˈbri:d] *v* **bred** [ˈbrɛd]; **breeding** *vt* **1** : élever (du bétail) **2** CAUSE : engendrer — *vi* : se reproduire — **~** *n* **1** : race *f* **2** CLASS : espèce *f,* sorte *f*

breeze [ˈbri:z] *n* : brise *f* — **breezy** [ˈbri:zi] *adj* **breezier; -est** **1** WINDY : venteux **2** NONCHALANT : désinvolte

brevity [ˈbrɛvəṭi] *n, pl* **-ties** : brièveté *f*

brew [ˈbru:] *vt* : brasser (de la bière), faire infuser (du thé) — *vi* : fermenter (se dit de la bière), infuser (se dit du thé, etc.) — **brewery** [ˈbru:əri, ˈbrʊri] *n, pl* **-eries** : brasserie *f*

bribe [ˈbraɪb] *n* : pot-de-vin *m* — **~** *vt* **bribed; bribing** : soudoyer — **bribery** [ˈbraɪbəri] *n, pl* **-eries** : corruption *f*

brick [ˈbrɪk] *n* : brique *f* — **bricklayer** [ˈbrɪkˌleɪər] *n* : maçon *m*

bride [ˈbraɪd] *n* : mariée *f* — **bridal** [ˈbraɪdəl] *adj* : nuptial — **bridegroom** [ˈbraɪdˌgru:m] *n* : marié *m* — **bridesmaid** [ˈbraɪdzˌmeɪd] *n* : demoiselle *f* d'honneur

bridge [ˈbrɪʤ] *n* **1** : pont *m* **2** : arête *f* (du nez) **3** : bridge *m* (jeu de cartes) — **~** *vt* **bridged; bridging 1** : construire un pont sur **2 ~ the gap** : combler une lacune

bridle [ˈbraɪdəl] *n* : bride *f* — **~** *vt* **-dled; -dling** : brider

brief [ˈbri:f] *adj* : bref — **~** *n* **1** : résumé *m* **2 ~s** *npl* UNDERPANTS : slip *m* — **~** *vt* : donner des instructions à — **briefcase** [ˈbri:fˌkeɪs] *n* : serviette *f,* porte-documents *m* — **briefly** [ˈbri:fli] *adv* : brièvement

brigade [brɪˈgeɪd] *n* : brigade *f*

bright [ˈbraɪt] *adj* **1** : brillant, éclatant **2** CHEERFUL : joyeux **3** INTELLIGENT : intelligent — **brighten** [ˈbraɪtən] *vi* **1** : s'éclaircir (se dit du temps) **2** *or* **~ up** : s'animer — *vt* ENLIVEN : égayer

brilliant [ˈbrɪljənt] *adj* : brillant — **brilliance** [ˈbrɪljənts] *n* **1** BRIGHTNESS : éclat *m* **2** INTELLIGENCE : intelligence *f*

brim [ˈbrɪm] *n* : bord *m* (d'un chapeau, etc.) — **~** *vi* **brimmed; brimming** *or* **~ over** : être plein jusqu'à déborder

brine [ˈbraɪn] *n* : saumure *f*

bring [ˈbrɪŋ] *vt* **brought** [ˈbrɔt]; **bringing 1** : amener (une personne ou un animal), apporter (une chose) **2 ~ about** : occasionner **3 ~ around** PERSUADE : convaincre **4 ~ back** : rapporter **5 ~ down** : faire tomber **6 ~ on** CAUSE : provoquer **7 ~ out** : sortir **8 ~ to an end** : mettre fin à **9 ~ up** REAR : élever **10 ~ up** MENTION : mentionner

brink [ˈbrɪŋk] *n* **1** EDGE : bord *m* **2 on the ~ of** : au bord de

brisk [ˈbrɪsk] *adj* **1** FAST : rapide **2** LIVELY : vif

bristle [ˈbrɪsəl] *n* **1** : soie *f* (d'un animal) **2** : poil *m* (d'une brosse) — **~** *vi* **-tled; -tling** : se hérisser

British [ˈbrɪṭɪʃ] *adj* : britannique

brittle [ˈbrɪtəl] *adj* **-tler; -tlest** : fragile

broach [ˈbro:ʧ] *vt* : entamer

broad [ˈbrɔd] *adj* **1** WIDE : large **2** GENERAL : grand **3 in ~ daylight** : en plein jour

broadcast [ˈbrɔdˌkæst] *v* **cast; -casting** *vt* : diffuser, téléviser — *vi* : émettre — **~** *n* : émission *f*

broaden [ˈbrɔdən] *vt* : élargir — *vi* : s'élargir — **broadly** [ˈbrɔdli] *adv* : en général — **broad–minded** [ˈbrɔdˈmaɪndəd] *adj* : large d'esprit, tolérant

broccoli [ˈbrɑkəli] *n* : brocoli *m*

brochure [broˈʃʊr] *n* : brochure *f,* dépliant *m*

broil [ˈbrɔɪl] *v* : griller

broke [ˈbro:k] → **break** — **~** *adj* : fauché *fam,* cassé *Can fam* — **broken** [ˈbro:kən] *adj* : cassé, brisé — **brokenhearted** [ˌbro:kənˈhɑrṭəd] *adj* : au cœur brisé

broker [ˈbro:kər] *n* : courtier *m,* -tière *f*

bronchitis [brɑnˈkaɪṭəs, brɑŋ-] *n* : bronchite *f*

bronze [ˈbrɑnz] *n* : bronze *m*
brooch [ˈbro:tʃ, ˈbru:tʃ] *n* : broche *f*
brood [ˈbru:d] *n* : couvée *f* (d'oiseaux) — ~ *vi* **1** INCUBATE : couver **2** ~ **about** : ressasser, ruminer
brook [ˈbrʊk] *n* : ruisseau *m*
broom [ˈbru:m, ˈbrʊm] *n* : balai *m* — **broomstick** [ˈbru:mˌstɪk, ˈbrʊm-] *n* : manche *m* à balai
broth [ˈbrɔθ] *n, pl* **broths** [ˈbrɔθs, ˈbrɔðz] : bouillon *m*
brothel [ˈbrɑθəl, ˈbrɔ-] *n* : bordel *m fam*
brother [ˈbrʌðər] *n* : frère *m* — **brotherhood** [ˈbrʌðərˌhʊd] *n* : fraternité *f* — **brother–in–law** [ˈbrʌðərɪnˌlɔ] *n, pl* **brothers–in–law** : beau-frère *m* — **brotherly** [ˈbrʌðərli] *adj* : fraternel
brought → **bring**
brow [ˈbraʊ] *n* **1** EYEBROW : sourcil *m* **2** FOREHEAD : front *m* **3** : sommet *m* (d'une colline)
brown [ˈbraʊn] *adj* : brun, marron — ~ *n* : brun *m*, marron *m* — ~ *vt* : faire dorer (en cuisine)
browse [ˈbraʊz] *vi* **browsed; browsing** : regarder, jeter un coup d'œil
browser [ˈbraʊzər] *n* : navigateur *m* (en informatique)
bruise [ˈbru:z] *vt* **bruised; bruising 1** : faire un bleu à, contusionner **2** : taler (un fruit) — ~ *n* : bleu *m*, contusion *f*, prune *f Can*
brunch [ˈbrʌntʃ] *n* : brunch *m*
brunet *or* **brunette** [bru:ˈnɛt] *n* : brun *m*, brune *f*
brunt [ˈbrʌnt] *n* **bear the ~ of** : subir le plus gros de
brush [ˈbrʌʃ] *n* **1** : brosse *f* (à cheveux), pinceau *m* (de peintre) **2** UNDERGROWTH : brousses *fpl* — ~ *vt* **1** : brosser **2** GRAZE : effleurer **3** ~ **off** DISREGARD : écarter — *vi* ~ **up on** : réviser — **brush–off** [ˈbrʌʃˌɔf] *n* **give s.o. the ~** : envoyer promener qqn
brusque [ˈbrʌsk] *adj* : brusque
brutal [ˈbru:t̬əl] *adj* : brutal — **brutality** [bru:ˈtæləṭi] *n, pl* **-ties** : brutalité *f*
brute [ˈbru:t] *adj* : brutal — ~ *n* : brute *f*
bubble [ˈbʌbəl] *n* : bulle *f* — ~ *vi* **-bled; -bling** : bouillonner
buck [ˈbʌk] *n, pl* **bucks 1** *or pl* **buck** : mâle *m* (animal) **2** DOLLAR : dollar *m* — ~ *vi* **1** : ruer (se dit d'un cheval) **2** ~ **up** : ne pas se laisser abattre — *vt* OPPOSE : résister
bucket [ˈbʌkət] *n* : seau *m*
buckle [ˈbʌkəl] *n* : boucle *f* — ~ *v* **-led; -ling** *vt* **1** FASTEN : boucler **2** WARP : gauchir — *vi* BEND : se courber, se voiler
bud [ˈbʌd] *n* : bourgeon *m* (d'une feuille), bouton *m* (d'une fleur) — ~ *vi* **budded; budding** : bourgeonner
Buddhism [ˈbu:ˌdɪzəm, ˈbʊ-] *n* : bouddhisme *m* — **Buddhist** [ˈbu:ˌdɪst, ˈbʊ-] *adj* : bouddhiste — ~ *n* : bouddhiste *mf*
buddy [ˈbʌdi] *n, pl* **-dies** : copain *m*, -pine *f*
budge [ˈbʌʤ] *vi* **budged; budging 1** MOVE : bouger **2** YIELD : céder
budget [ˈbʌʤət] *n* : budget *m* — ~ *vt* : budgétiser — *vi* : dresser un budget — **budgetary** [ˈbʌʤəˌtɛri] *adj* : budgétaire
buff [ˈbʌf] *n* **1** : chamois *m* (couleur) **2** ENTHUSIAST : mordu *m*, -due *f fam;* fanatique *mf* — ~ *adj* : chamois, beige — ~ *vt* POLISH : polir
buffalo [ˈbʌfəˌlo:] *n, pl* **-lo** *or* **-loes** : buffle *m*, bison *m* (d'Amérique)
buffer [ˈbʌfər] *n* : tampon *m*
buffet [ˌbʌˈfeɪ, ˌbu:-] *n* : buffet *m* (repas ou meuble)
buffoon [ˌbʌˈfu:n] *n* : bouffon *m*
bug [ˈbʌg] *n* **1** INSECT : insecte *m*, bestiole *f* **2** FLAW : défaut *m* **3** GERM : microbe *m* **4** : bogue *m* (en informatique) — ~ *vt* **bugged; bugging 1** : installer un microphone dans (une maison, etc.) **2** PESTER : embêter
buggy [ˈbʌgi] *n, pl* **-gies 1** CARRIAGE : calèche *f* **2** *or* **baby ~** : voiture *f* d'enfant, landau *m France*
bugle [ˈbju:ˌgəl] *n* : clairon *m*
build [ˈbɪld] *v* **built** [ˈbɪlt]; **building** *vt* **1** : construire, bâtir **2** DEVELOP : établir — *vi* **1** *or* ~ **up** INTENSIFY : augmenter, intensifier **2** *or* ~ **up** ACCUMULATE : s'accumuler — ~ *n* PHYSIQUE : carrure *f*, charpente *f* — **builder** [ˈbɪldər] *n* : entrepreneur *m* — **building** [ˈbɪldɪŋ] *n* **1** : bâtiment *m*, immeuble *m* **2** CONSTRUCTION : construction *f* — **built–in** [ˈbɪltˈɪn] *adj* : encastré
bulb [ˈbʌlb] *n* **1** : bulbe *m* **2** LIGHTBULB : ampoule *f*
bulge [ˈbʌlʤ] *vi* **bulged; bulging** : être gonflé, se renfler — ~ *n* : renflement *m*
bulk [ˈbʌlk] *n* **1** : masse *f*, volume *m* **2** **in ~** : en gros — **bulky** [ˈbʌlki] *adj* **bulkier; -est** : volumineux
bull [ˈbʊl] *n* **1** : taureau *m* **2** MALE : mâle *m*
bulldog [ˈbʊlˌdɔg] *n* : bouledogue *m*

bulldozer [ˈbʊlˌdo:zər] *n* : bulldozer *m*
bullet [ˈbʊlət] *n* : balle *f* (d'un fusil)
bulletin [ˈbʊlətən, -lətən] *n* : bulletin *m* — **bulletin board** *n* : tableau *m* d'affichage, babillard *m Can*
bulletproof [ˈbʊlətˌpru:f] *adj* : pare-balles
bullfight [ˈbʊlˌfaɪt] *n* : corrida *f* — **bullfighter** [ˈbʊlˌfaɪtər] *n* : torero *m*
bull's-eye [ˈbʊlzˌaɪ] *n, pl* **bull's-eyes** : centre *m* (de la cible)
bully [ˈbʊli] *n, pl* **-lies** : tyran *m* — ~ *vt* **-lied; -lying** : malmener, maltraiter
bum [ˈbʌm] *n* : clochard *m*, -charde *f*
bumblebee [ˈbʌmbəlˌbi:] *n* : bourdon *m*
bump [ˈbʌmp] *n* **1** BULGE : bosse *f*, protubérance *f* **2** IMPACT : coup *m*, choc *m* **3** JOLT : secousse *f* — ~ *vt* : heurter, cogner — *vi* ~ **into** MEET : tomber sur — **bumper** [ˈbʌmpər] *n* : pare-chocs *m* — ~ *adj* : exceptionnel — **bumpy** [ˈbʌmpi] *adj* **bumpier; -est** **1** : cahoteux (se dit d'un chemin) **2 a ~ flight** : un vol agité
bun [ˈbʌn] *n* : petit pain *m* (au lait)
bunch [ˈbʌntʃ] *n* **1** : bouquet *m* (de fleurs), grappe *f* (de raisins), botte *f* (de légumes, etc.) **2** GROUP : groupe *m* — ~ *vt* ~ **together** : mettre ensemble — *vi* ~ **up** : s'entasser
bundle [ˈbʌndəl] *n* **1** : liasse *f* (de papiers, etc.) **2** PARCEL : paquet *m* — ~ *vi* **-dled; -dling** ~ **up** : s'emmitoufler
bungalow [ˈbʌŋgəˌlo:] *n* : maison *f* sans étage
bungle [ˈbʌŋgəl] *vt* **-gled; -gling** : gâcher
bunion [ˈbʌnjən] *n* : oignon *m*
bunk [ˈbʌŋk] *n* **1** : couchette *f* **2** ~ **bed** : lits *mpl* superposés
bunny [ˈbʌni] *n, pl* **-nies** : lapin *m*
buoy [ˈbu:i, ˈbɔɪ] *n* : bouée *f* — ~ *vt or* ~ **up** : revigorer — **buoyant** [ˈbɔɪənt, ˈbu:jənt] *adj* **1** : qui flotte **2** LIGHTHEARTED : allègre, optimiste
burden [ˈbərdən] *n* : fardeau *m* — ~ *vt* ~ **sth with** : accabler qqn de — **burdensome** [ˈbərdənsəm] *adj* : lourd
bureau [ˈbjʊro] *n* **1** : commode *f* (meuble) **2** : service *m* (gouvernemental) **3** AGENCY : agence *f* — **bureaucracy** [bjʊˈrɑkrəsi] *n, pl* **-cies** : bureaucratie *f* — **bureaucrat** [ˈbjʊrəˌkræt] *n* : bureaucrate *mf* — **bureaucratic** [ˌbjʊrəˈkrætɪk] *adj* : bureaucratique
burglar [ˈbərglər] *n* : cambrioleur *m*, -leuse *f* — **burglarize** [ˈbərgləˌraɪz] *vt* **-ized; -izing** : cambrioler — **burglary** [ˈbərgləri] *n, pl* **-glaries** : cambriolage *m*
Burgundy [ˈbərgəndi] *n, pl* **-dies** : bourgogne *m* (vin)
burial [ˈbɛriəl] *n* : enterrement *m*
burly [ˈbərli] *adj* **-lier; -est** : costaud *fam*
burn [ˈbərn] *v* **burned** [ˈbərnd, ˈbərnt] *or* **burnt** [ˈbərnt]; **burning** : brûler — ~ *n* : brûlure *f* — **burner** [ˈbərnər] *n* : brûleur *m* (d'une cuisinière), rond *m Can*
burnish [ˈbərnɪʃ] *vt* : polir
burp [ˈbərp] *vi* : avoir des renvois, roter *fam* — ~ *n* : renvoi *m*
burrow [ˈbəro] *n* : terrier *m* — ~ *vt* : creuser — *vi* ~ **into** : fouiller dans
burst [ˈbərst] *v* **burst** *or* **bursted; bursting** *vi* **1** : crever, éclater **2** ~ **into tears** : fondre en larmes **3** ~ **out laughing** : éclater de rire — ~ *vt* : crever, faire éclater — ~ *n* **1** EXPLOSION : explosion *f* **2** OUTBURST : élan *m* (d'enthousiasme), éclat *m* (de rire)
bury [ˈbɛri] *vt* **buried; burying** **1** : enterrer **2** HIDE : enfouir, cacher
bus [ˈbʌs] *n, pl* **buses** *or* **busses** : bus *m*, autobus *m* — ~ *v* **bused** *or* **bussed** [ˈbʌst]; **busing** *or* **bussing** [ˈbʌsɪŋ] *vt* : transporter en autobus — *vi* : voyager en autobus
bush [ˈbʊʃ] *n* SHRUB : buisson *m*
bushel [ˈbʊʃəl] *n* : boisseau *m*
bushy [ˈbʊʃi] *adj* **bushier; -est** : touffu
busily [ˈbɪzəli] *adv* : activement
business [ˈbɪznəs, -nəz] *n* **1** COMMERCE : affaires *fpl* **2** COMPANY : entreprise *f* **3 it's none of your ~** : ce n'est pas de vos affaires — **businessman** [ˈbɪznəsˌmæn, -nəz-] *n, pl* **-men** : homme *m* d'affaires — **businesswoman** [ˈbɪznəsˌwʊmən, -nəz-] *n, pl* **-women** : femme *f* d'affaires
bust[1] [ˈbʌst] *vt* BREAK : briser
bust[2] *n* **1** : buste *m* (en sculpture) **2** BREASTS : seins *fpl*, poitrine *f*
bustle [ˈbʌsəl] *vi* **-tled; -tling** *or* ~ **about** : s'affairer — ~ *n or* **hustle and ~** : agitation *f*, activité *f*
busy [ˈbɪzi] *adj* **busier; -est** **1** : occupé **2** BUSTLING : animé
but [ˈbʌt] *conj* : mais — ~ *prep* : sauf, excepté
butcher [ˈbʊtʃər] *n* : boucher *m*, -chère *f* — ~ *vt* **1** : abattre **2** BOTCH : bousiller *fam*
butler [ˈbʌtlər] *n* : maître *m* d'hôtel
butt [ˈbʌt] *vi* ~ **in** : interrompre — ~

n **1** : crosse *f* (d'un fusil) **2** : mégot *m fam* (de cigarette)
butter [ˈbʌt̬ər] *n* : beurre *m* — **~** *vt* : beurrer
butterfly [ˈbʌt̬ərˌflaɪ] *n, pl* **-flies** : papillon *m*
buttermilk [ˈbʌt̬ərˌmɪlk] *n* : babeurre *m*
buttocks [ˈbʌt̬əks, -ˌtɑks] *npl* : fesses *fpl*
button [ˈbʌtən] *n* : bouton *m* — **~** *vt* : boutonner — *vi or* **~ up** : se boutonner — **buttonhole** [ˈbʌtənˌhoːl] *n* : boutonnière *f*
buttress [ˈbʌtrəs] *n* : contrefort *m*
buy [ˈbaɪ] *vt* **bought** [ˈbɔt]; **buying** : acheter — **~** *n* : achat *m* — **buyer** [ˈbaɪər] *n* : acheteur *m*, -teuse *f*
buzz [ˈbʌz] *vi* : bourdonner — **~** *n* : bourdonnement *m*
buzzer [ˈbʌzər] *n* : sonnette *f*
by [ˈbaɪ] *prep* **1** NEAR : près de, à côté de **2** VIA : par, en **3** PAST : devant, à côté de **4** DURING : pendant **5** (*in expressions of time*) : avant **6** (*indicating cause or agent*) : par — **~** *adv* **1 ~ and ~** : bientôt **2 ~ and large** : en général **3 go ~** : passer **4 stop ~** : arrêter
bygone [ˈbaɪˌgɔn] *adj* **1** : passé, d'autrefois **2 let ~s be ~s** : enterrer le passé
bypass [ˈbaɪˌpæs] *n* : route *f* de contournement — **~** *vt* : contourner
by–product [ˈbaɪˌprɑdəkt] *n* : sous-produit *m*, dérivé *m*
bystander [ˈbaɪˌstændər] *n* : spectateur *m*, -trice *f*
byte [ˈbaɪt] *n* : octet *m*

C

c [ˈsiː] *n, pl* **c's** *or* **cs** : c *m*, troisième lettre de l'alphabet
cab [ˈkæb] *n* **1** : taxi *m* **2** : cabine *f* (d'un camion, etc.)
cabbage [ˈkæbɪʤ] *n* : chou *m*
cabin [ˈkæbən] *n* **1** : cabane *f* **2** : cabine *f* (d'un navire, d'un avion, etc.)
cabinet [ˈkæbnət] *n* **1** CUPBOARD : armoire *f* **2** : cabinet *m* (en politique) **3** *or* **medicine ~** : pharmacie *f*
cable [ˈkeɪbəl] *n* : câble *m* — **cable television** *n* : câble *m*
cackle [ˈkækəl] *vi* **-led; -ling** : caqueter, glousser
cactus [ˈkæktəs] *n, pl* **cacti** [-ˌtaɪ] *or* **-tuses** : cactus *m*
cadence [ˈkeɪdənts] *n* : cadence *f*, rythme *m*
cadet [kəˈdɛt] *n* : élève *mf* officier
café [kæˈfeɪ, kə-] *n* : café *m*, bistrot *m* — **cafeteria** [ˌkæfəˈtɪriə] *n* : cafétéria *f*
caffeine [kæˈfiːn] *n* : caféine *f*
cage [ˈkeɪʤ] *n* : cage *f*
cajole [kəˈʤoːl] *vt* **-joled; -joling** : cajoler, enjôler
Cajun [ˈkeɪʤən] *adj* : acadien, cajun
cake [ˈkeɪk] *n* **1** : gâteau *m* **2** BAR : pain *m* (de savon) — **caked** [ˈkeɪkt] *adj* **~ with** : couvert de
calamity [kəˈlæmət̬i] *n, pl* **-ties** : calamité *f*
calcium [ˈkælsiəm] *n* : calcium *m*
calculate [ˈkælkjəˌleɪt] *v* **-lated; -lating** : calculer — **calculating** [ˈkælkjəˌleɪt̬ɪŋ] *adj* : calculateur — **calculation** [ˌkælkjəˈleɪʃən] *n* : calcul *m* — **calculator** [ˈkælkjəˌleɪt̬ər] *n* : calculatrice *f*
calendar [ˈkæləndər] *n* : calendrier *m*
calf[1] [ˈkæf] *n, pl* **calves** [ˈkævz] : veau *m* (de bovin)
calf[2] *n, pl* **calves** : mollet *m* (de la jambe)
caliber *or* **calibre** [ˈkæləbər] *n* : calibre *m*
call [ˈkɔl] *vi* **1** : appeler **2** VISIT : passer, faire une visite **3 ~ for** : demander — *vt* **1** : appeler **2 ~ back** : rappeler **3 ~ off** : annuler — **~** *n* **1** : appel *m* **2** SHOUT : cri *m* **3** VISIT : visite *f* **4** NEED : demande *f* — **calling** [ˈkɔlɪŋ] *n* : vocation *f*
callous [ˈkæləs] *adj* : dur, sans cœur
calm [ˈkɑm, ˈkɑlm] *n* : calme *m*, tranquillité *f* — **~** *vt* : calmer, apaiser — *vi or* **~ down** : se calmer — **~** *adj* : calme, tranquille
calorie [ˈkæləri] *n* : calorie *f*
came → **come**
camel [ˈkæməl] *n* : chameau *m*
camera [ˈkæmrə, ˈkæmərə] *n* : appareil *m* photo, caméra *f*
camouflage [ˈkæməˌflɑʒ, -ˌflɑʤ] *n* : camouflage *m* — **~** *vt* **-flaged; -flaging** : camoufler
camp [ˈkæmp] *n* **1** : camp *m* **2** FACTION : parti *m* — **~** *vi* : camper, faire du camping
campaign [kæmˈpeɪn] *n* : campagne *f* — **~** *vi* : faire campagne
camping [ˈkæmpɪŋ] *n* : camping *m*

campus ['kæmpəs] *n* : campus *m,* cité *f* universitaire *Can*
can[1] ['kæn] *v aux, past* **could** ['kʊd]; *present s & pl* **can 1** (*expressing possibility or permission*) : pouvoir **2** (*expressing knowledge or ability*) : savoir **3 that cannot be** : cela n'est pas possible
can[2] *n* : boîte *f* (d'aliments), canette *f* (de boisson gazeuse), bidon *m* (d'essence, etc.) — ~ *vt* **canned; canning** : mettre en boîte
Canadian [kə'neɪdiən] *adj* : canadien
canal [kə'næl] *n* : canal *m*
canary [kə'nɛri] *n, pl* **-naries** : canari *m,* serin *m*
cancel ['kæntsəl] *vt* **-celed** *or* **-celled; -celing** *or* **-celling** : annuler — **cancellation** [,kæntsə'leɪʃən] *n* : annulation *f*
cancer ['kæntsər] *n* : cancer *m* — **cancerous** ['kæntsərəs] *adj* : cancéreux
candid ['kændɪd] *adj* : franc, sincère
candidate ['kændə,deɪt, -dət] *n* : candidat *m,* -date *f* — **candidacy** ['kændədəsi] *n, pl* **-cies** : candidature *f*
candle ['kændəl] *n* : bougie *f,* chandelle *f* — **candlestick** ['kændəl,stɪk] *n* : chandelier *m,* bougeoir *m*
candor *or Brit* **candour** ['kændər] *n* : franchise *f*
candy ['kændi] *n, pl* **-dies 1** : bonbon *m* **2** ~ **store** : confiserie *f*
cane ['keɪn] *n* : canne *f* — ~ *vt* **caned; caning** FLOG : fouetter
canine ['keɪ,naɪn] *n or* ~ **tooth** : canine *f* — ~ *adj* : canin
canister ['kænəstər] *n* : boîte *f*
cannibal ['kænəbəl] *n* : cannibale *mf*
cannon ['kænən] *n, pl* **-nons** *or* **-non** : canon *m*
cannot (**can not**) ['kæn,ɑt, kə'nɑt] → **can**[1]
canoe [kə'nu:] *n* : canoë *m,* canot *m* *Can*
canon ['kænən] *n* : canon *m,* règle *f*
can opener *n* : ouvre-boîtes *m*
canopy ['kænəpi] *n, pl* **-pies** : auvent *m,* baldaquin *m*
can't ['kænt, 'kant] (*contraction of* **can not**) → **can**[1]
cantaloupe ['kæntəl,o:p] *n* : cantaloup *m*
cantankerous [kæn'tæŋkərəs] *adj* : acariâtre
canteen [kæn'ti:n] *n* CAFETERIA : cantine *f*
canter ['kæntər] *vi* : aller au petit galop — ~ *n* : petit galop *m*
canvas ['kænvəs] *n* : toile *f*
canvass ['kænvəs] *vt* : solliciter les voix de (les électeurs) — ~ *n* : démarchage *m* électoral
canyon ['kænjən] *n* : canyon *m*
cap ['kæp] *n* **1** : casquette *f* **2** : capsule *f* (d'une bouteille), capuchon *m* (d'un stylo, etc.) — ~ *vt* **capped; capping** COVER : couvrir
capable ['keɪpəbəl] *adj* : capable — **capability** [,keɪpə'bɪləṭi] *n, pl* **-ties** : aptitude *f,* capacité *f*
capacity [kə'pæsəṭi] *n, pl* **-ties 1** : capacité *f* **2** ROLE : qualité *f*
cape[1] ['keɪp] *n* : cap *m* (en géographie)
cape[2] *n* CLOAK : cape *f,* pèlerine *f*
caper ['keɪpər] *n* : câpre *f*
capital ['kæpəṭəl] *adj* **1** : capital, principal **2** : majuscule (se dit d'une lettre) — ~ *n* **1** *or* ~ **city** : capitale *f* **2** WEALTH : capital *m,* fonds *mpl* **3** *or* ~ **letter** : majuscule *f* — **capitalism** ['kæpəṭəl,ɪzəm] *n* : capitalisme *m* — **capitalist** ['kæpəṭəlɪst] *or* **capitalistic** ['kæpəṭəl'ɪstɪk] *adj* : capitaliste — **capitalize** ['kæpəṭəl,aɪz] *v* **-ized; -izing** *vt* : écrire avec une majuscule — *vi* ~ **on** : tirer profit de
capitol ['kæpəṭ'l] *n* : capitole *m*
capsize ['kæp,saɪz, kæp'saɪz] *v* **-sized; -sizing** *vt* : faire chavirer — *vi* : chavirer
capsule ['kæpsəl, -,su:l] *n* : capsule *f*
captain ['kæptən] *n* : capitaine *m*
caption ['kæpʃən] *n* **1** : légende *f* (d'une illustration) **2** SUBTITLE : sous-titre *m*
captivate ['kæptə,veɪt] *vt* **-vated; -vating** : captiver, fasciner
captive ['kæptɪv] *adj* : captif — ~ *n* : captif *m,* -tive *f* — **captivity** [kæp'tɪvəṭi] *n* : captivité *f*
capture ['kæpʃər] *n* : capture *f,* prise *f* — ~ *vt* **-tured; -turing 1** SEIZE : capturer **2** : captiver (l'imagination), capter (l'attention)
car ['kɑr] *n* **1** : voiture *f,* automobile *f* **2** *or* **railroad** ~ : wagon *m*
carafe [kə'ræf, -'rɑf] *n* : carafe *f*
caramel ['kɑrməl; 'kærəməl, -,mɛl] *n* : caramel *m*
carat ['kærət] *n* : carat *m*
caravan ['kærə,væn] *n* : caravane *f*
carbohydrate [,kɑrbo'haɪ,dreɪt, -drət] *n* : hydrate *m* de carbone
carbon ['kɑrbən] *n* : carbone *m*
carburetor ['kɑrbə,reɪṭər, -bjə-] *n* : carburateur *m*
carcass ['kɑrkəs] *n* : carcasse *f*

card [ˈkard] *n* : carte *f* — **cardboard** [ˈkard,bord] *n* : carton *m*
cardiac [ˈkardi,æk] *adj* : cardiaque
cardigan [ˈkardɪgən] *n* : cardigan *m*
cardinal [ˈkardənəl] *n* : cardinal *m* — ~ *adj* : cardinal, essentiel
care [ˈkær] *n* **1** : soin *m* **2** WORRY : préoccupation *f* — ~ *vi* **cared; caring 1** : se préoccuper, se soucier **2** ~ **for** TEND : prendre soin de **3** ~ **for** LIKE : aimer **4 I don't** ~ : ça m'est égal
career [kəˈrɪr] *n* : carrière *f*, profession *f*
carefree [ˈkær,fri:, ,kærˈ-] *adj* : insouciant
careful [ˈkærfəl] *adj* **1** : prudent **2 be** ~! : fais attention! — **carefully** [ˈkærfəli] *adv* : prudemment, avec soin — **careless** [ˈkærləs] *adj* : négligent — **carelessness** [ˈkærləsnəs] *n* : négligence *f*
caress [kəˈrɛs] *n* : caresse *f* — ~ *vt* : caresser
cargo [ˈkar,go:] *n, pl* **-goes** *or* **-gos** : chargement *m*, cargaison *f*
Caribbean [,kærəˈbi:ən, kəˈrɪbiən] *adj* : des Caraïbes
caricature [ˈkærɪkə,ʧʊr] *n* : caricature *f*
caring [ˈkærɪŋ] *adj* : aimant, affectueux
carnage [ˈkarnɪʤ] *n* : carnage *m*
carnation [karˈneɪʃən] *n* : œillet *m*
carnival [ˈkarnəvəl] *n* : carnaval *m*
carol [ˈkærəl] *n* : chant *m* de Noël
carpenter [ˈkarpəntər] *n* : charpentier *m*, menuisier *m* — **carpentry** [ˈkarpəntri] *n* : charpenterie *f*, menuiserie *f*
carpet [ˈkarpət] *n* : tapis *m*
carriage [ˈkærɪʤ] *n* **1** : transport *m* (de marchandises) **2** BEARING : maintien *m* **3** → **baby carriage 4** *or* **horse-drawn** ~ : calèche *f*, carrosse *m*
carrier [ˈkæriər] *n* **1** : transporteur *m* **2** : porteur *m*, -teuse *f* (d'une maladie)
carrot [ˈkærət] *n* : carotte *f*
carry [ˈkæri] *v* **-ried; -rying** *vt* **1** : porter **2** TRANSPORT : transporter **3** STOCK : vendre **4** ENTAIL : comporter **5** ~ **oneself** : se présenter — *vi* : porter (se dit de la voix) — **carry away** *vt* **get carried away** : s'emballer — **carry on** *vt* CONDUCT : réaliser — *vi* **1** : mal se comporter **2** CONTINUE : continuer — **carry out** *vt* **1** : réaliser, effectuer **2** FULFILL : accomplir
cart [ˈkart] *n* : charette *f* — ~ *vt or* ~ **around** : trimbaler *fam*
carton [ˈkartən] *n* : boîte *f* de carton
cartoon [karˈtu:n] *n* **1** : dessin *m* humoristique **2** COMIC STRIP : bande *f* dessinée **3** *or* **animated** ~ : dessin *m* animé
cartridge [ˈkartrɪʤ] *n* : cartouche *f*
carve [ˈkarv] *vt* **carved; carving 1** : tailler (le bois, etc.) **2** : découper (de la viande)
case [ˈkeɪs] *n* **1** : boîte *f*, caisse *f* **2 in any** ~ : en tout cas **3 in** ~ **of** : au cas de **4 just in** ~ : au cas où
cash [ˈkæʃ] *n* : espèces *fpl*, argent *m* liquide — ~ *vt* : encaisser
cashew [ˈkæ,ʃu:, kəˈʃu:] *n* : noix *f* de cajou
cashier [kæˈʃɪr] *n* : caissier *m*, -sière *f*
cashmere [ˈkæʒ,mɪr, ˈkæʃ-] *n* : cachemire *m*
cash register *n* : caisse *f* enregistreuse
casino [kəˈsi:,no:] *n, pl* **-nos** : casino *m*
cask [ˈkæsk] *n* : fût *m*, tonneau *f*
casket [ˈkæskət] *n* : cercueil *m*
casserole [ˈkæsə,ro:l] *n* : ragoût *m*
cassette [kəˈsɛt, kæ-] *n* : cassette *f*
cast [ˈkæst] *vt* **cast; casting 1** THROW : jeter, lancer **2** : donner un rôle à (au cinéma, etc.) **3** MOLD : couler (du métal) **4** ~ **one's vote** : voter — ~ *n* **1** : distribution *f* (d'acteurs) **2** *or* **plaster** ~ : plâtre *m*
cast iron *n* : fonte *f*
castle [ˈkæsəl] *n* : château *m*
castrate [ˈkæs,treɪt] *vt* **-trated; -trating** : châtrer
casual [ˈkæʒʊəl] *adj* **1** : nonchalant **2** INFORMAL : décontracté — **casually** [ˈkæʒʊəli, ˈkæʒəli] *adv* **1** : nonchalamment **2** ~ **dressed** : habillé simplement
casualty [ˈkæʒʊəlti, ˈkæʒəl-] *n, pl* **-ties 1** : accident *m* grave, désastre *m* **2** VICTIM : blessé *m*, -sée *f*; accidenté *m*, -tée *f*; mort *m*, morte *f*
cat [ˈkæt] *n* : chat *m*, chatte *f*
catalog *or* **catalogue** [ˈkæţə,lɔg] *n* : catalogue *m*
cataract [ˈkæţə,rækt] *n* : cataracte *f*
catastrophe [kəˈtæstrə,fi:] *n* : catastrophe *f*
catch [ˈkæʧ, ˈkɛʧ] *v* **caught** [ˈkɔt]; **catching** *vt* **1** CAPTURE, TRAP : attraper **2** SURPRISE : surprendre **3** GRASP : saisir **4** SNAG : accrocher **5** : prendre (le train, etc.) **6** ~ **one's breath** : reprendre son souffle — *vi* **1** SNAG : s'accrocher **2** ~ **fire** : prendre feu — ~ *n* **1** : prise *f*, capture *f* **2** PITFALL : piège *f* — **catching** [ˈkæʧɪŋ, ˈkɛ-] *adj* : contagieux — **catchy** [ˈkæʧi, ˈkɛ-] *adj* **catchier; -est** : entraînant

category [ˈkæt̬əˌgori] *n, pl* **-ries** : catégorie *f*, classe *f* — **categorical** [ˌkæt̬əˈgɔrɪkəl] *adj* : catégorique
cater [ˈkeɪt̬ər] *vi* **1** : fournir des repas **2 ~ to** : pourvoir à — **caterer** [ˈkeɪt̬ərər] *n* : traiteur *m*
caterpillar [ˈkæt̬ərˌpɪlər] *n* : chenille *f*
cathedral [kəˈθi:drəl] *n* : cathédrale *f*
catholic [ˈkæθəlɪk] *adj* **1** : universel **2 Catholic** : catholique — **catholicism** [kəˈθɑləˌsɪzəm] *n* : catholicisme *m*
cattle [ˈkæt̬əl] *npl* : bétail *m*, bovins *mpl*
caught → **catch**
cauldron [ˈkɔldrən] *n* : chaudron *m*
cauliflower [ˈkɑlɪˌflaʊər, ˈkɔ-] *n* : chou-fleur *m*
cause [ˈkɔz] *n* **1** : cause *f* **2** REASON : raison *f*, motif *m* — **~** *vt* **caused; causing** : causer, occasionner
caution [ˈkɔʃən] *n* **1** WARNING : avertissement *m* **2** CARE : prudence *f* — **~** *vt* : avertir, mettre en garde — **cautious** [ˈkɔʃəs] *adj* : prudent, avisé — **cautiously** [ˈkɔʃəsli] *adv* : prudemment
cavalier [ˌkævəˈlɪr] *adj* : cavalier, désinvolte
cavalry [ˈkævəlri] *n, pl* **-ries** : cavalerie *f*
cave [ˈkeɪv] *n* : grotte *f*, caverne *f* — **~** *vi* **caved; caving** *or* **~ in** : s'affaisser, s'effondrer
cavern [ˈkævərn] *n* : caverne *f*
caviar *or* **caviare** [ˈkæviˌɑr, ˈkɑ-] *n* : caviar *m*
cavity [ˈkævət̬i] *n, pl* **-ties** **1** : cavité *f* **2** : carie *f* (dentaire)
CD [ˌsi:ˈdi:] *n* : CD *m*, disque *m* compact
cease [ˈsi:s] *v* **ceased; ceasing** : cesser — **cease-fire** [ˈsi:sˈfaɪr] *n* : cessez-le-feu *m* — **ceaseless** [ˈsi:sləs] *adj* : incessant, continuel
cedar [ˈsi:dər] *n* : cèdre *m*
cedilla [sɪˈdɪlə] *n* : cédille *nf*
ceiling [ˈsi:lɪŋ] *n* : plafond *m*
celebrate [ˈsɛləˌbreɪt] *v* **-brated; -brating** *vt* : fêter, célébrer — *vi* : faire le fête — **celebrated** [ˈsɛləˌbreɪt̬əd] *adj* : célèbre — **celebration** [ˌsɛləˈbreɪʃən] *n* **1** : célébration *f* **2** FESTIVITY : fête *f* — **celebrity** [səˈlɛbrət̬i] *n, pl* **-ties** : célébrité *f*
celery [ˈsɛləri] *n, pl* **-eries** : céleri *m*
cell [ˈsɛl] *n* : cellule *f*
cellar [ˈsɛlər] *n* : cave *f*
cello [ˈʧɛˌlo:] *n, pl* **-los** : violoncelle *m*
cellular [ˈsɛljələr] *adj* : cellulaire
cement [sɪˈmɛnt] *n* : ciment *m*
cemetery [ˈsɛməˌtɛri] *n, pl* **-teries** : cimetière *m*
censor [ˈsɛntsər] *vt* : censurer — **censorship** [ˈsɛntsərˌʃɪp] *n* : censure *f* — **censure** [ˈsɛnʧər] *n* : censure *f*, blâme *m* — **~** *vt* **-sured; -suring** : critiquer, blâmer
census [ˈsɛntsəs] *n* : recensement *m*
cent [ˈsɛnt] *n* : cent *m*
centennial [sɛnˈtɛniəl] *n* : centenaire *m*
center *or Brit* **centre** [ˈsɛntər] *n* : centre *m* — **~** *v* **centered** *or Brit* **centred; centering** *or Brit* **centring** *vt* : centrer — *vi* **~ on** : se concentrer sur
centigrade [ˈsɛntəˌgreɪd, ˈsɑn-] *adj* : centigrade
centimeter [ˈsɛntəˌmi:t̬ər, ˈsɑn-] *n* : centimètre *m*
centipede [ˈsɛntəˌpi:d] *n* : mille-pattes *m*
central [ˈsɛntrəl] *adj* : central — **centralize** [ˈsɛntrəˌlaɪz] *vt* **-ized; -izing** : centraliser
centre → **center**
century [ˈsɛnʧəri] *n, pl* **-ries** : siècle *m*
ceramics [səˈræmɪks] *n* : céramique *f*
cereal [ˈsɪriəl] *n* : céréale *f*
ceremony [ˈsɛrəˌmo:ni] *n, pl* **-nies** : cérémonie *f*
certain [ˈsərtən] *adj* **1** : certain **2 be ~ of** : être assuré de **3 for ~** : au juste — **certainly** [ˈsərtənli] *adv* : certainement, bien sûr — **certainty** [ˈsərtənti] *n, pl* **-ties** : certitude *f*
certify [ˈsərt̬əˌfaɪ] *vt* **-fied; -fying** : certifier — **certificate** [sərˈtɪfɪkət] *n* : certificat *m*
chafe [ˈʧeɪf] *vi* **chafed; chafing** **1** RUB : frotter **2 ~ at** : s'irriter de
chain [ˈʧeɪn] *n* **1** : chaîne *f* **2 ~ of events** : série *f* d'événements — **~** *vt* : enchaîner
chair [ˈʧɛr] *n* **1** : chaise *f* **2** : chaire *f* (d'une université) — **~** *vt* : présider — **chairman** [ˈʧɛrmən] *n, pl* **-men** [-mən, -ˌmɛn] : président *m* — **chairperson** [ˈʧɛrˌpərsən] *n* : président *m*, -dente *f*
chalk [ˈʧɔk] *n* : craie *f*
challenge [ˈʧælɪnʤ] *vt* **-lenged; -lenging** **1** DISPUTE : contester **2** DARE : défier — **~** *n* : défi *m* — **challenging** [ˈʧælɪnʤɪŋ] *adj* : stimulant
chamber [ˈʧeɪmbər] *n* : chambre *f* (de commerce, etc.)
champagne [ʃæmˈpeɪn] *n* : champagne *m*
champion [ˈʧæmpiən] *n* : champion *m*,

-pionne *f* — **championship** ['ʧæmpiən,ʃɪp] *n* : championnat *m*
chance ['ʧænts] *n* **1** LUCK : hasard *m* **2** OPPORTUNITY : occasion *f* **3** LIKELIHOOD : chances *fpl* **4 by ~** : par hasard **5 take a ~** : prendre un risque — **~** *vt* **chanced; chancing** : hasarder, risquer — **~** *adj* : fortuit
chandelier [,ʃændə'lɪr] *n* : lustre *m*
change ['ʧeɪnʤ] *v* **changed; changing** *vt* **1** : changer **2** SWITCH : changer de — *vi* **1** : changer **2** *or* **~ clothes** : se changer — **~** *n* **1** : changement *m* **2** COINS : monnaie *f* — **changeable** ['ʧeɪnʤəbəl] *adj* : changeant
channel ['ʧænəl] *n* **1** : canal *m* **2** : chenal *m* (dans un fleuve, etc.) **3** : chaîne *f* (de télévision)
chant ['ʧænt] *n* : chant *m*
chaos ['keɪ,ɑs] *n* : chaos *m* — **chaotic** [keɪ'ɑṭɪk] *adj* : chaotique
chap[1] ['ʧæp] *vi* **chapped; chapping** : se gercer
chap[2] *n* : type *m fam,* bonhomme *m fam*
chapel ['ʧæpəl] *n* : chapelle *f*
chaperon *or* **chaperone** ['ʃæpə,ro:n] *n* : chaperon *m*
chaplain ['ʧæplɪn] *n* : aumônier *m*
chapter ['ʧæptər] *n* : chapitre *m*
char ['ʧɑr] *vt* **charred; charring** : carboniser
character ['kærɪktər] *n* **1** : caractère *m* **2** : personnage *m* (d'un roman, etc.) — **characteristic** [,kærɪktə'rɪstɪk] *adj* : caractéristique — **~** *n* : caractéristique *f* — **characterize** ['kærɪktə,raɪz] *vt* **-ized; -izing** : caractériser
charcoal ['ʧɑr,ko:l] *n* : charbon *m* de bois
charge ['ʧɑrʤ] *n* **1** : charge *f* (électrique) **2** COST : prix *m,* frais *mpl* **3** ACCUSATION : inculpation *f* **4 be in ~** : être responsable — **~** *v* **charged; charging** *vt* **1** : charger (une batterie) **2** ENTRUST : charger, confier **3** ACCUSE : inculper **4** : payer par carte de crédit — *vi* **1** : se précipiter, foncer **2 ~ too much** : demander trop (d'argent)
charisma [kə'rɪzmə] *n* : charisme *m* — **charismatic** [,kærəz'mæṭɪk] *adj* : charismatique
charity ['ʧærəṭi] *n, pl* **-ties 1** : organisation *f* caritative **2** GOODWILL : charité *f*
charlatan ['ʃɑrlətən] *n* : charlatan *m*
charm ['ʧɑrm] *n* : charme *m* — **~** *vt* : charmer, captiver — **charming** ['ʧɑrmɪŋ] *adj* : charmant
chart ['ʧɑrt] *n* : graphique *m,* tableau *m*
charter ['ʧɑrṭər] *n* : charte *f* — **~** *vt* : affréter (un vol, etc.)
chase ['ʧeɪs] *n* : poursuite *f* — **~** *vt* **chased; chasing 1** : poursuivre, courir après **2** *or* **~ away** : chasser
chasm ['kæzəm] *n* : gouffre *m,* abîme *m*
chaste ['ʧeɪst] *adj* **chaster; chastest** : chaste — **chastity** ['ʧæstəṭi] *n* : chasteté *f*
chat ['ʧæt] *vi* **chatted; chatting** : bavarder, causer — **~** *n* : causerie *f* — **chatter** ['ʧæṭər] *vi* **1** : bavarder **2** : claquer (se dit des dents) — **~** *n* : bavardage *m* — **chatterbox** ['ʧæṭər,bɑks] *n* : moulin *m* à paroles *fam* — **chatty** ['ʧæṭi] *adj* **chattier; -est** : bavard
chauffeur ['ʃo:fər, ʃo'fər] *n* : chauffeur *m*
chauvinist ['ʃo:vənɪst] *or* **chauvinistic** [,ʃo:və'nɪstɪk] *adj* : chauvin
cheap ['ʧi:p] *adj* **1** INEXPENSIVE : bon marché **2** SHODDY : de mauvaise qualité — **~** *adv* : à bon marché
cheat ['ʧi:t] *vt* : frauder, tromper — *vi* **1** : tricher **2 ~ on s.o.** : tromper qqn — **~** *or* **cheater** ['ʧi:ṭər] *n* : tricheur *m,* -cheuse *f*
check ['ʧɛk] *n* **1** HALT : arrêt *m* **2** RESTRAINT : limite *f,* frein *m* **3** INSPECTION : contrôle *m* **4** *or Brit* **cheque** DRAFT : chèque *m* **5** BILL : addition *f* — **~** *vt* **1** HALT : freiner, arrêter **2** RESTRAIN : retenir, contenir **3** VERIFY : vérifier **4 ~ in** : se présenter à la réception (à l'hôtel) **5** *or* **~ off** MARK : cocher **6 ~ out** : quitter (l'hôtel) **7 ~ out** VERIFY : vérifier — **checkbook** ['ʧɛk,bʊk] *n* : carnet *m* de chèques
checkers ['ʧɛkərz] *n* : jeu *m* de dames
checkmate ['ʧɛk,meɪt] *n* : échec *m* et mat
checkpoint ['ʧɛk,pɔɪnt] *n* : poste *m* de contrôle
checkup ['ʧɛk,ʌp] *n* : examen *m* médical
cheek ['ʧik] *n* : joue *f*
cheer ['ʧɪr] *n* **1** : gaieté *f* **2** APPLAUSE : acclamation *f* **3 ~s!** : à votre santé! — **~** *vt* **1** COMFORT : encourager **2** APPLAUD : acclamer — **cheerful** ['ʧɪrfəl] *adj* : de bonne humeur
cheese ['ʧi:z] *n* : fromage *m*
cheetah ['ʧi:ṭə] *n* : guépard *m*
chef ['ʃɛf] *n* : cuisinier *m,* -nière *f;* chef *m* (cuisinier)
chemical ['kɛmɪkəl] *adj* : chimique — **~** *n* : produit *m* chimique — **chemist**

['kɛmɪst] *n* : chimiste *mf* — **chemistry** ['kɛmɪstri] *n, pl* **-tries** : chimie *f*

cheque *Brit* → **check**

cherish ['ʧɛrɪʃ] *vt* **1** : chérir, aimer **2** HARBOR : caresser, nourrir (un espoir, etc.)

cherry ['ʧɛri] *n, pl* **-ries** : cerise *f*

chess ['ʧɛs] *n* : échecs *mpl*

chest ['ʧɛst] *n* **1** BOX : coffre *m* **2** : poitrine *f* (du corps) **3** *or* ~ **of drawers** : commode *f*

chestnut ['ʧɛst,nʌt] *n* : marron *m*, châtaigne *f*

chew ['ʧu:] *vt* : mastiquer, mâcher — **chewing gum** *n* : chewing-gum *m France*, gomme *f* à mâcher

chick ['ʧɪk] *n* : poussin *m* — **chicken** ['ʧɪkən] *n* : poulet *m* — **chicken pox** *n* : varicelle *f*

chicory ['ʧɪkəri] *n, pl* **-ries 1** : endive *f* **2** : chicorée *f*

chief ['ʧi:f] *adj* : principal, en chef — ~ *n* : chef *m* — **chiefly** ['ʧi:fli] *adv* : principalement, surtout

child ['ʧaɪld] *n, pl* **children** ['ʧɪldrən] **1** : enfant *mf* **2** OFFSPRING : fils *m*, fille *f* — **childbirth** ['ʧaɪld,bərθ] *n* : accouchement *m* — **childhood** ['ʧaɪld,hʊd] *n* : enfance *f* — **childish** ['ʧaɪldɪʃ] *adj* : puéril, enfantin — **childlike** ['ʧaɪld,laɪk] *adj* : innocent, d'enfant — **childproof** ['tlaɪld,pru:f] *adj* : de sécurité pour enfants

chili *or* **chile** *or* **chilli** ['ʧɪli] *n, pl* **chilies** *or* **chiles** *or* **chillies 1** *or* ~ **pepper** : piment *m* fort **2** : chili *m* con carne

chill ['ʧɪl] *n* **1** : froid *m* **2 catch a** ~ : attraper un coup de froid **3 there's a** ~ **in the air** : il fait un peu froid — ~ *vt* : refroidir, réfrigérer — **chilly** ['ʧɪli] *adj* **chillier; -est** : frais, froid

chime ['ʧaɪm] *v* **chimed; chiming** : carillonner — ~ *n* : carillon *m*

chimney ['ʧɪmni] *n, pl* **-neys** : cheminée *f*

chimpanzee ['ʧɪm,pæn'zi:, ,ʃɪm-; ʧɪm'pænzi, ʃɪm-] *n* : chimpanzé *m*

chin ['tlɪn] *n* : menton *m*

china ['ʧaɪnə] *n* : porcelaine *f*

Chinese ['ʧaɪ'ni:z, -ni:s] *adj* : chinois — ~ *n* : chinois *m* (langue)

chip ['ʧɪp] *n* **1** : éclat *m* (de verre), copeau *m* (de bois) **2** : jeton *m* (de poker, etc.) **3** NICK : ébréchure *f* **4** *or* **computer** ~ : puce *f* — ~ *v* **chipped; chipping** *vt* : ébrécher (de la vaisselle, etc.), écailler (de la peinture) — *vi* ~ **in** : contribuer

chipmunk ['ʧɪp,mʌŋk] *n* : tamia *m*

chiropodist [kə'rɑpədɪst, ʃə-] *n* : pédicure *mf*

chiropractor ['kaɪrə,præktər] *n* : chiropracteur *m*

chirp ['ʧərp] *vi* : pépier

chisel ['ʧɪzəl] *n* : ciseau *m* — ~ *vt* **-eled** *or* **-elled; -eling** *or* **-elling** : ciseler

chitchat ['ʧɪt,ʧæt] *n* : bavardage *m*

chivalry ['ʃɪvəlri] *n, pl* **-ries** : chevalerie *f*

chive ['ʧaɪv] *n* : ciboulette *f*

chlorine ['klor,i:n] *n* : chlore *m*

chock–full ['ʧɑk'fʊl, 'ʧʌk-] *adj* : bondé, plein à craquer

chocolate ['ʧɑkələt, 'ʧɔk-] *n* : chocolat *m*

choice ['ʧɔɪs] *n* : choix *m* — ~ *adj* **choicer; choicest** : de choix, de première qualité

choir ['kwaɪr] *n* : chœur *m*

choke ['ʧo:k] *v* **choked; choking** *vt* **1** : étrangler, étouffer **2** BLOCK : boucher — *vi* : s'étouffer (en mangeant) — ~ *n* : starter *m* (d'une voiture)

cholesterol [kə'lɛstə,rɔl] *n* : cholestérol *m*

choose ['ʧu:z] *v* **chose** ['ʧo:z]; **chosen** ['ʧo:zən]; **choosing** *vt* **1** SELECT : choisir **2** DECIDE : décider — *vi* : choisir — **choosy** *or* **choosey** ['ʧu:zi] *adj* **choosier; -est** : exigeant

chop ['ʧɑp] *vt* **chopped; chopping 1** : couper (du bois), hacher (des légumes, etc.) **2** ~ **down** : abattre — ~ *n* : côtelette *f* (de porc, etc.) — **choppy** ['ʧɑpi] *adj* **-pier; -est** : agité (se dit de la mer)

chopsticks ['ʧɑp,stɪks] *npl* : baguettes *fpl*

chord ['kɔrd] *n* : accord *m* (en musique)

chore ['ʧor] *n* **1** : corvée *f* **2 household** ~**s** : travaux *mpl* ménagers

choreography [,kori'ɑgrəfi] *n, pl* **-phies** : chorégraphie *f*

chorus ['korəs] *n* **1** : chœur *m* (de chanteurs) **2** REFRAIN : refrain *m*

chose, chosen → **choose**

christen ['krɪsən] *vt* : baptiser — **christening** ['krɪsənɪŋ] *n* : baptême *m*

Christian ['krɪsʧən] *adj* : chrétien — ~ *n* : chrétien *m*, -tienne *f* — **Christianity** [,krɪsʧi'ænəṭi, ,krɪs'ʧæ-] *n* : christianisme *m*

Christmas ['krɪsməs] *n* : Noël *m*

chrome ['kro:m] *n* : chrome *m* — **chromium** ['kro:miəm] *n* : chrome *m*

chronic ['krɑnɪk] *adj* : chronique

chronicle [ˈkrɑnɪkəl] *n* : chronique *f*
chronology [krəˈnɑlədʒi] *n, pl* **-gies** : chronologie *f* — **chronological** [ˌkrɑnəlˈɑdʒɪkəl] *adj* : chronologique
chrysanthemum [krɪˈsænθəməm] *n* : chrysanthème *m*
chubby [ˈtʃʌbi] *adj* **-bier; -est** : potelé, dodu
chuck [ˈtʃʌk] *vt* : tirer, lancer
chuckle [ˈtʃʌkəl] *vi* **-led; -ling** : glousser, rire tout bas — ~ *n* : petit rire *m*
chum [ˈtʃʌm] *n* : copain *m*, -pine *f;* camarade *mf*
chunk [ˈtʃʌŋk] *n* : (gros) morceau *m*
church [ˈtʃərtʃ] *n* : église *f*
churn [ˈtʃərn] *vt* **1** : battre (du beurre) **2** STIR : agiter, remuer **3** ~ **out** : produire en série
cider [ˈsaɪdər] *n* : cidre *m*
cigar [sɪˈgɑr] *n* : cigare *m* — **cigarette** [ˌsɪgəˈrɛt, ˈsɪgəˌrɛt] *n* : cigarette *f*
cinch [ˈsɪntʃ] *n* **it's a** ~ : c'est du gateau
cinema [ˈsɪnəmə] *n* : cinéma *m*
cinnamon [ˈsɪnəmən] *n* : cannelle *f*
cipher [ˈsaɪfər] *n* **1** ZERO : zéro *m* **2** CODE : chiffre *m*
circa [ˈsərkə] *prep* : environ, vers
circle [ˈsərkəl] *n* : cercle *m* — ~ *vt* **-cled; -cling 1** : faire le tour de **2** SURROUND : entourer, encercler
circuit [ˈsərkət] *n* : circuit *m* — **circuitous** [ˌsərˈkjuːət̬əs] *adj* : détourné, indirect
circular [ˈsərkjələr] *adj* : circulaire — ~ *n* LEAFLET : circulaire *f*
circulate [ˈsərkjəˌleɪt] *v* **-lated; -lating** : circuler — **circulation** [ˌsərkjəˈleɪʃən] *n* **1** FLOW : circulation *f* **2** : tirage *m* (d'un journal)
circumcise [ˈsərkəmˌsaɪz] *vt* **-cised; -cising** : circoncire — **circumcision** [ˌsərkəmˈsɪʒən, ˈsərkəmˌ-] *n* : circoncision *f*
circumference [sərˈkʌmpfrənts] *n* : circonférence *f*
circumflex [ˈsərkəmˌflɛks] *n* : accent *m* circonflexe
circumspect [ˈsərkəmˌspɛkt] *adj* : circonspect, prudent
circumstance [ˈsərkəmˌstænts] *n* **1** : circonstance *f* **2 under no** ~**s** : en aucun cas
circus [ˈsərkəs] *n* : cirque *m*
cistern [ˈsɪstərn] *n* TANK : citerne *f*
cite [ˈsaɪt] *vt* **cited; citing** : citer — **citation** [saɪˈteɪʃən] *n* : citation *f*
citizen [ˈsɪt̬əzən] *n* : citoyen *m*, -toyenne *f* — **citizenship** [ˈsɪt̬əzənˌʃɪp] *n* : citoyenneté *f*
citrus [ˈsɪtrəs] *n, pl* **-rus** *or* **-ruses** *or* ~ **fruit** : agrumes *mpl*
city [ˈsɪt̬i] *n, pl* **-ties** : ville *f* — **city hall** *n* : hôtel *m* de ville
civic [ˈsɪvɪk] *adj* : civique — **civics** [ˈsɪvɪks] *ns & pl* : instruction *f* civique
civil [ˈsɪvəl] *adj* **1** : civil **2** ~ **rights** : droits *mpl* civiques **3** ~ **service** : fonction *f* publique — **civilian** [səˈvɪljən] *n* : civil *m*, -vile *f* — **civility** [səˈvɪlət̬i] *n, pl* **-ties** : civilité *f*, courtoisie *f* — **civilization** [ˌsɪvələˈzeɪʃən] *n* : civilisation *f* — **civilize** [ˈsɪvəˌlaɪz] *vt* **-lized; -lizing** : civiliser
clad [ˈklæd] *adj* ~ **in** : vêtu de, habillé de
claim [ˈkleɪm] *vt* **1** DEMAND : revendiquer, réclamer **2** MAINTAIN : prétendre — ~ *n* **1** : revendication *f* **2** ASSERTION : affirmation *f*
clam [ˈklæm] *n* : palourde *f*
clamber [ˈklæmbər] *vi* : grimper (avec difficulté)
clammy [ˈklæmi] *adj* **-mier; -est** : moite
clamor *or Brit* **clamour** [ˈklæmər] *n* : clameur *f*, cris *mpl* — ~ *vi* : vociférer
clamp [ˈklæmp] *n* : crampon *m* — ~ *vt* : attacher, fixer
clan [ˈklæn] *n* : clan *m*
clandestine [klænˈdɛstɪn] *adj* : clandestin, secret
clang [ˈklæŋ] *n* : bruit *m* métallique
clap [ˈklæp] *v* **clapped; clapping** : applaudir — ~ *n* : applaudissement *m*
clarify [ˈklærəˌfaɪ] *vt* **-fied; -fying** : clarifier, éclaircir — **clarification** [ˌklærəfəˈkeɪʃən] *n* : clarification *f*
clarinet [ˌklærəˈnɛt] *n* : clarinette *f*
clarity [ˈklærət̬i] *n* : clarté *f*
clash [ˈklæʃ] *vi* : s'opposer, se heurter — ~ *n* : conflit *m*
clasp [ˈklæsp] *n* : fermoir *m*, boucle *f* — ~ *vt* **1** FASTEN : attacher **2** HOLD : serrer
class [ˈklæs] *n* **1** : classe *f* **2** COURSE : cours *m* — ~ *vt* : classer, classifier
classic [ˈklæsɪk] *or* **classical** [ˈklæsɪkəl] *adj* : classique — **classic** *n* : classique *m*
classify [ˈklæsəˌfaɪ] *vt* **-fied; -fying** : classer, classifier — **classification** [ˌklæsəfəˈkeɪʃən] *n* : classification *f* — **classified** [ˈklæsəˌfaɪd] *adj* **1** : confidentiel **2** ~ **ads** : petites annonces *fpl*

classmate [ˈklæsˌmeɪt] *n* : compagnon *m*, compagne *f* de classe
classroom [ˈklæsˌru:m] *n* : salle *f* de classe
clatter [ˈklæt̬ər] *vi* : cliqueter — ∼ *n* : bruit *m*, cliquetis *m*
clause [ˈklɔz] *n* : clause *f*
claustrophobia [ˌklɔstrəˈfo:biə] *n* : claustrophobie *f*
claw [ˈklɔ] *n* : griffe *f* (d'un chat, etc.), pince *f* (d'un crustacé)
clay [ˈkleɪ] *n* : argile *f*
clean [ˈkli:n] *adj* **1** : propre **2** UNADULTERATED : pur — ∼ *vt* : nettoyer, laver — **cleanliness** [ˈklɛnlinəs] *n* : propreté *f* — **cleanse** [ˈklɛnz] *vt* **cleansed; cleansing** : nettoyer, purifier
clear [ˈkli:r] *adj* **1** : clair **2** TRANSPARENT : transparent **3** OPEN : libre, dégagé — ∼ *vt* **1** : débarrasser (un espace, etc.), dégager (une voie) **2** ∼ **a check** : encaisser un chèque **3** ∼ **up** RESOLVE : résoudre — *vi* **1** ∼ **up** BRIGHTEN : s'éclaircir (se dit du temps, etc.) **2** ∼ **up** VANISH : disparaître (se dit d'un symptôme, etc.) — ∼ *adv* **1** **hear loud and** ∼ : entendre très clairement **2 make oneself** ∼ : s'expliquer — **clearance** [ˈklɪrən*t*s] *n* **1** SPACE : espace *m* libre **2** AUTHORIZATION : autorisation *f* **3** ∼ **sale** : liquidation *f* — **clearing** [ˈklɪrɪŋ] *n* : clairière *f* — **clearly** [ˈklɪrli] *adv* **1** DISTINCTLY : clairement **2** OBVIOUSLY : évidemment
cleaver [ˈkli:vər] *n* : couperet *m*
clef [ˈklɛf] *n* : clé *f* (en musique)
clement [ˈklɛmənt] *adj* : doux, clément — **clemency** [ˈklɛmən*t*si] *n, pl* **-cies** : clémence *f*
clench [ˈklɛntʃ] *vt* : serrer
clergy [ˈklərdʒi] *n, pl* **-gies** : clergé *m* — **clergyman** [ˈklərdʒimən] *n, pl* **-men** [-mən, -ˌmɛn] : ecclésiastique *m* — **clerical** [ˈklɛrɪkəl] *adj* **1** : clérical, du clergé **2** ∼ **work** : travail *m* de bureau
clerk [ˈklərk, *Brit* ˈklɑrk] *n* **1** : employé *m*, -ployée *f* de bureau **2** SALESPERSON : vendeur *m*, -deuse *f*
clever [ˈklɛvər] *adj* **1** SKILLFUL : habile, adroit **2** SMART : astucieux — **cleverly** [ˈklɛvərli] *adv* **1** : habilement **2** : astucieusement — **cleverness** [ˈklɛvərnəs] *n* **1** SKILL : habileté *f* **2** INTELLIGENCE : intelligence *f*
cliché [kliˈʃeɪ] *n* : cliché *m*
click [ˈklɪk] *vt* : faire claquer — *vi* **1** : faire un déclic **2** : cliquer (en informatique) — ∼ *n* : déclic *m*
client [ˈklaɪənt] *n* : client *m*, cliente *f* — **clientele** [ˌklaɪənˈtɛl, ˌkli:-] *n* : clientèle *f*
cliff [ˈklɪf] *n* : falaise *f*
climate [ˈklaɪmət] *n* : climat *m*
climax [ˈklaɪˌmæks] *n* : point *m* culminant, apogée *m*
climb [ˈklaɪm] *vt* : monter, gravir — *vi* RISE : monter, augmenter — ∼ *n* : montée *f*, ascension *f*
cling [ˈklɪŋ] *vi* **clung** [ˈklʌŋ]; **clinging** ∼ **to** : s'accrocher à
clinic [ˈklɪnɪk] *n* : clinique *f* — **clinical** [ˈklɪnɪkəl] *adj* : clinique
clink [ˈklɪŋk] *vi* : cliqueter
clip [ˈklɪp] *vt* **clipped; clipping** **1** : couper, tailler **2** FASTEN : attacher (avec un trombone) — ∼ *n* FASTENER : attache *f*, pince *f* — **clippers** [ˈklɪpərz] *npl* **1** *or* **nail** ∼ : coupe-ongles *m* **2** SHEARS : tondeuse *f*
cloak [ˈklo:k] *vt* : cape *f*
clock [ˈklɑk] *n* **1** : horloge *f*, pendule *f* **2 around the** ∼ : d'affilée — **clockwise** [ˈklɑkˌwaɪz] *adv & adj* : dans le sens des aiguilles d'une montre
clog [ˈklɑg] *n* : sabot *m* — ∼ *v* **clogged; clogging** *vt* : boucher, bloquer — *vi or* ∼ **up** : se boucher
cloister [ˈklɔɪstər] *n* : cloître *m*
close[1] [ˈklo:z] *v* **closed; closing** *vt* : fermer — *vi* **1** : fermer, se fermer **2** TERMINATE : prendre fin, se terminer **3** ∼ **in** : se rapprocher — ∼ *n* : fin *f*, conclusion *f*
close[2] [ˈklo:s] *adj* **closer; closest** **1** NEAR : proche **2** INTIMATE : intime **3** STRICT : rigoureux, étroit **4 a** ∼ **game** : une partie serrée — ∼ *adv* : près — **closely** [ˈklo:sli] *adv* : de près — **closeness** [ˈklo:snəs] *n* **1** : proximité *f* **2** INTIMACY : intimité *f*
closet [ˈklɑzət] *n* : placard *m*, garde-robe *f*
closure [ˈklo:ʒər] *n* : fermeture *f*, clôture *f*
clot [ˈklɑt] *n* : caillot *m* — ∼ *vi* **clotted; clotting** : cailler, (se) coaguler
cloth [ˈklɔθ] *n, pl* **cloths** [ˈklɔðz, ˈklɔθs] : tissu *m*
clothe [ˈklo:ð] *vt* **clothed** *or* **clad** [ˈklæd]; **clothing** : habiller, vêtir — **clothes** [ˈklo:z, ˈklo:ðz] *npl* **1** : vêtements *mpl* **2 put on one's** ∼ : s'habiller — **clothespin** [ˈklo:zˌpɪn] *n* : pince *f* (à linge) — **clothing** [ˈklo:ðɪŋ] *n* : vêtements *mpl*

cloud ['klaʊd] *n* : nuage *m* — **~** *vi or* **~ over** : se couvrir de nuages — **cloudy** ['klaʊdi] *adj* **cloudier; -est** : nuageux, couvert
clout ['klaʊt] *n* : influence *m,* poids *m*
clove ['klo:v] *n* **1** : clou *m* de girofle **2** *or* **garlic ~** : gousse *f* d'ail
clover ['klo:vər] *n* : trèfle *m*
clown ['klaʊn] *n* : clown *m* — **~** *vi or* **~ around** : faire le clown
cloying ['klɔɪɪŋ] *adj* : mièvre
club ['klʌb] *n* **1** : massue *f,* matraque *f* **2** ASSOCIATION : club *m,* groupe *m* **3** **~s** *npl* : trèfle *m* (aux cartes) — **~** *vt* **clubbed; clubbing** : matraquer
cluck ['klʌk] *vi* : glousser
clue ['klu:] *n* **1** : indice *m* **2 I haven't got a ~** : je n'ai aucune idée
clump ['klʌmp] *n* : massif *m* (d'arbres), touffe *f* (d'herbe)
clumsy ['klʌmzi] *adj* **-sier; -est** : maladroit, gauche
cluster ['klʌstər] *n* : groupe *m* (de personnes), grappe *f* (de raisins, etc.) — *vi* : se rassembler, se grouper
clutch ['klʌʧ] *vt* : saisir, étreindre — *vi* **~ at** : s'agripper à — **~** *n* : embrayage *m* (d'une voiture)
clutter ['klʌţər] *vt* : encombrer — **~** *n* : désordre *m,* fouillis *m*
coach ['ko:ʧ] *n* **1** CARRIAGE : carrosse *m* **2** : voiture *f,* wagon *m* (d'un train) **3** BUS : autocar *m* **4** : billet *m* d'avion de deuxième classe **5** TRAINER : entraîneur *m,* -neuse *f* — **~** *vt* **1** : entraîner (une équipe sportive) **2** TUTOR : donner des leçons à
coagulate [ko'ægjə,leɪt] *v* **-lated; -lating** *vt* : coaguler — *vi* : se coaguler
coal ['ko:l] *n* : charbon *m*
coalition [,ko:ə'lɪʃən] *n* : coalition *f*
coarse [,kors] *adj* **coarser; coarsest** **1** : gros (se dit du sable, du sel, etc.) **2** CRUDE : grossier, vulgaire — **coarseness** ['korsnəs] *n* **1** ROUGHNESS : rudesse *f* **2** CRUDENESS : grossièreté *f*
coast ['ko:st] *n* : côte *f* — **coastal** ['ko:stəl] *adj* : côtier, littoral
coaster ['ko:stər] *n* : dessous-de-verre *m*
coast guard *n* : gendarmerie *f* maritime *France,* garde *f* côtière *Can*
coastline ['ko:st,laɪn] *n* : littoral *m*
coat ['ko:t] *n* **1** : manteau *m* **2** : pelage *m* (d'un animal) **3** : couche *f* (de peinture) — **~** *vt* **~ with** : couvrir de, recouvrir de — **coat hanger** *n* : cintre *m* — **coating** ['ko:ţɪŋ] *n* : couche *f,* revêtement *m* — **coat of arms** *n* : blason *m,* armoiries *fpl*
coax ['ko:ks] *vt* : amadouer, cajoler
cob ['kɑb] → **corncob**
cobblestone ['kɑbəl,sto:n] *n* : pavé *m*
cobweb ['kɑb,wɛb] *n* : toile *f* d'araignée
cocaine [ko:'keɪn, 'ko:,keɪn] *n* : cocaïne *f*
cock ['kɑk] *n* ROOSTER : coq *m* — **~** *vt* **1** : armer (un fusil) **2** TILT : pencher (la tête, etc.) — **cockeyed** ['kɑk,aɪd] *adj* **1** ASKEW : de travers **2** ABSURD : insensé
cockpit ['kɑk,pɪt] *n* : poste *m* de pilotage
cockroach ['kɑk,ro:ʧ] *n* : cafard *m*
cocktail ['kɑk,teɪl] *n* : cocktail *m*
cocoa ['ko:,ko:] *n* : cacao *m*
coconut ['ko:kə,nʌt] *n* : noix *f* de coco
cocoon [kə'ku:n] *n* : cocon *m*
cod ['kɑd] *ns & pl* : morue *f*
coddle ['kɑdəl] *vt* **-dled; -dling** : dorloter
code ['ko:d] *n* : code *m* — **~** *vt* : coder
coeducational [,ko:,ɛʤə'keɪʃənəl] *adj* : mixte
coerce [ko'ərs] *vt* **-erced; -ercing** : contraindre — **coercion** [ko'ərʒən, -ʃən] *n* : contrainte *f*
coffee ['kɔfi] *n* : café *m* — **coffeepot** ['kɔfi,pɑt] *n* : cafetière *f*
coffer ['kɔfər] *n* : coffre *m,* caisse *f*
coffin ['kɔfən] *n* : cercueil *m,* bière *f*
cog ['kɑg] *n* : dent *f* (d'une roue)
cogent ['ko:ʤənt] *adj* : convaincant, persuasif
cognac ['ko:n,jæk] *n* : cognac *m*
cogwheel ['kɑg,hwi:l] *n* : pignon *m*
coherent [ko'hɪrənt] *adj* : cohérent
coil ['kɔɪl] *vt* : enrouler — *vi* : s'enrouler — **~** *n* **1** : rouleau *m* **2** : volute *f* (de fumée)
coin ['kɔɪn] *n* : pièce *f* de monnaie
coincide [,ko:ɪn'saɪd, 'ko:ɪn,saɪd] *vi* **-cided; -ciding** : coïncider — **coincidence** [ko'ɪntsədənts] *n* : coïncidence *f*
colander ['kɑləndər, 'kʌ-] *n* : passoire *f*
cold ['ko:ld] *adj* **1** : froid **2 be ~** : avoir froid **3 it's ~ today** : il fait froid aujourd'hui — **~** *n* **1** : froid *m* **2** : rhume *m* (en médecine) **3 catch a ~** : s'enrhumer
coleslaw ['ko:l,slɔ] *n* : salade *f* de chou cru
colic ['kɑlik] *n* : coliques *fpl*
collaborate [kə'læbə,reɪt] *vi* **-rated; -rating** : collaborer, coopérer — **col-**

laboration [kəˌlæbəˈreɪʃən] *n* : collaboration *f*
collapse [kəˈlæps] *vi* **-lapsed; -lapsing** : s'effondrer, s'écrouler — ~ *n* : effondrement *m,* écroulement *m* — **collapsible** [kəˈlæpsəbəl] *adj* : pliant
collar [ˈkɑlər] *n* : col *m* — **collarbone** [ˈkɑlərˌbo:n] *n* : clavicule *f*
collateral [kəˈlæṭərəl] *n* : nantissement *m*
colleague [ˈkɑˌli:g] *n* : collègue *mf*
collect [kəˈlɛkt] *vt* **1** GATHER : ramasser, recueillir **2** : percevoir (des impôts), encaisser (une somme d'argent) **3** : collectionner (des objets) — *vi* **1** ASSEMBLE : se rassembler, se réunir **2** ACCUMULATE : s'accumuler — ~ *adv* **call** ~ : téléphoner en PCV *France,* téléphoner à frais virés *Can* — **collection** [kəˈlɛkʃən] *n* **1** : collection *f* (de livres, etc.) **2** : quête *f* (à l'église) — **collective** [kəˈlɛktɪv] *adj* : collectif
college [ˈkɑlɪʤ] *n* : établissement *m* d'enseignement supérieur
collide [kəˈlaɪd] *vi* **-lided; -liding** : se heurter, entrer en collision — **collision** [kəˈlɪʒən] *n* : collision *f*
colloquial [kəˈlo:kwiəl] *adj* : familier
cologne [kəˈlo:n] *n* : eau *f* de Cologne
colon[1] [ˈko:lən] *n, pl* **colons** *or* **cola** [-lə] : côlon *m* (en anatomie)
colon[2] *n, pl* **colons** : deux-points *m*
colonel [ˈkərnəl] *n* : colonel *m*
colony [ˈkɑləni] *n, pl* **-nies** : colonie *f* — **colonial** [kəˈlo:niəl] *adj* : colonial — **colonize** [ˈkɑləˌnaɪz] *vt* **-nized; -nizing** : coloniser
color *or Brit* **colour** [ˈkʌlər] *n* : couleur *f* — ~ *vt* : colorer — **color–blind** *or Brit* **colour–blind** [ˈkʌlərˌblaɪnd] *adj* : daltonien — **colored** *or Brit* **coloured** [ˈkʌlərd] *adj* : coloré — **colorful** *or Brit* **colourful** [ˈkʌlərfəl] *adj* : coloré — **colorless** *or Brit* **colourless** [ˈkʌlərləs] *adj* : incolore
colossal [kəˈlɑsəl] *adj* : colossal
colt [ˈko:lt] *n* : poulain *m*
column [ˈkɑləm] *n* **1** : colonne *f* **2** : rubrique *f* (dans la presse) — **columnist** [ˈkɑləmnɪst, -ləmɪst] *n* : chroniqueur *m,* -queuse *f*
coma [ˈko:mə] *n* : coma *m*
comb [ˈko:m] *n* **1** : peigne *m* **2** : crête *f* (d'un coq) — ~ *vt* : (se) peigner
combat [ˈkɑmˌbæt] *n* : combat *m* — ~ [kəmˈbæt, ˈkɑmˌbæt] *vt* **-bated** *or* **-batted; -bating** *or* **-batting** : combattre — **combatant** [kəmˈbætənt] *n* : combattant *m,* -tante *f*
combine [kəmˈbaɪn] *vt* **-bined; -bining** : combiner — ~ [ˈkɑmˌbaɪn] *n* HARVESTER : moisonneuse-batteuse *f* — **combination** [ˌkɑmbəˈneɪʃən] *n* : combinaison *f*
combustion [kəmˈbʌsʧən] *n* : combustion *f*
come [ˈkʌm] *vi* **came** [ˈkeɪm]; **come; coming 1** : venir **2** ARRIVE : arriver **3** ~ **about** : se produire **4** ~ **back** : revenir **5** ~ **from** : provenir de **6** ~ **in** : entrer **7** ~ **out** : sortir **8** ~ **to** REVIVE : revenir à soi **9** ~ **on!** : allez! **10** ~ **up** OCCUR : se présenter **11 how** ~? : comment ça se fait? — **comeback** [ˈkʌmˌbæk] *n* **1** RETURN : rentrée *f* **2** RETORT : réplique *f*
comedy [ˈkɑmədi] *n, pl* **-dies** : comédie *f* — **comedian** [kəˈmi:diən] *n* : comique *mf*
comet [ˈkɑmət] *n* : comète *f*
comfort [ˈkʌmpfərt] *vt* : consoler, réconforter — ~ *n* **1** : confort *m* **2** SOLACE : consolation *f,* réconfort *m* — **comfortable** [ˈkʌmpfərṭəbəl, ˈkʌmpftə-] *adj* : confortable
comic [ˈkɑmɪk] *or* **comical** [ˈkɑmɪkəl] *adj* : comique — ~ *n* : comique *mf* — **comic strip** *n* : bande *f* dessinée
coming [ˈkʌmɪŋ] *adj* : à venir
comma [ˈkɑmə] *n* : virgule *f*
command [kəˈmænd] *vt* **1** ORDER : ordonner, commander **2** ~ **respect** : inspirer le respect — *vi* : donner des ordres — ~ *n* **1** ORDER : ordre *m* **2** MASTERY : maîtrise *f* — **commander** [kəˈmændər] *n* : commandant *m* — **commandment** [kəˈmændmənt] *n* : commandement *m* (en religion)
commemorate [kəˈmɛməˌreɪt] *vt* **-rated; -rating** : commémorer — **commemoration** [kəˌmɛməˈreɪʃən] *n* : commémoration *f*
commence [kəˈmɛnts] *v* **-menced; -mencing** : commencer — **commencement** [kəˈmɛntsmənt] *n* : remise *f* des diplômes
commend [kəˈmɛnd] *vt* : louer — **commendable** [kəˈmɛndəbəl] *adj* : louable
comment [ˈkɑˌmɛnt] *n* : commentaire *m,* remarque *f* — ~ *vi* : faire des commentaires — **commentary** [ˈkɑmənˌtɛri] *n, pl* **-taries** : commentaire *m* — **commentator** [ˈkɑmənˌteɪṭər] *n* : commentateur *m,* -trice *f*
commerce [ˈkɑmərs] *n* : commerce *m* — **commercial** [kəˈmərʃəl] *adj* : commercial — ~ *n* : annonce *f* publici-

taire — **commercialize** [kə'mərʃə,laɪz] *vt* **-ized; -izing** : commercialiser

commiserate [kə'mɪzə,reɪt] *vi* **-ated; -ating** : compatir

commission [kə'mɪʃən] *n* : commission *f*, comité *m* — ~ *vt* : commander (une œuvre d'art) — **commissioner** [kə'mɪʃənər] *n* : commissaire *m*

commit [kə'mɪt] *vt* **-mitted; -mitting 1** ENGAGE : confier **2** : commettre (un crime, etc.) **3** ~ **oneself** : s'engager — **commitment** [kə'mɪtmənt] *n* **1** PROMISE : engagement *m* **2** OBLIGATION : obligation *f*

committee [kə'mɪṭi] *n* : comité *m*

commodity [kə'mɑdəṭi] *n, pl* **-ties** : marchandise *f*, denrée *f*

common ['kɑmən] *adj* **1** : commun **2** WIDESPREAD : universel — ~ *n* **in** ~ : en commun — **commonly** ['kɑmənli] *adv* : communément — **commonplace** ['kɑmən,pleɪs] *adj* : commun, banal — **common sense** *n* : bon sens *m*

commotion [kə'mo:ʃən] *n* : vacarme *m*, brouhaha *m*

commune ['kɑ,mju:n, kə'mju:n] *n* : communauté *f* — **communal** [kə'mju:nəl] *adj* : communautaire

communicate [kə'mju:nə,keɪt] *v* **-cated; -cating** : communiquer — **communication** [kə,mju:nə'keɪʃən] *n* : communication *f*

communion [kə'mju:njən] *n* : communion *f*

Communism ['kɑmjə,nɪzəm] *n* : communisme *m* — **Communist** ['kɑmjə,nɪst] *adj* : communiste

community [kə'mju:nəṭi] *n, pl* **-ties** : communauté *f*

commute [kə'mju:t] *vi* **-muted; -muting** : faire la navette, faire un trajet journalier

compact [kəm'pækt, 'kɑm,pækt] *adj* : compact — ~ ['kɑm,pækt] *n* **1** *or* ~ **car** : voiture *f* compacte **2** *or* **powder** ~ : poudrier *m* — **compact disc** ['kɑm,pækt'dɪsk] *n* : disque *m* compact, compact *m*

companion [kəm'pænjən] *n* : compagnon *m*, compagne *f* — **companionship** [kəm'pænjən,ʃɪp] *n* : compagnie *f*

company ['kʌmpəni] *n, pl* **-nies 1** : compagnie *f*, société *f* **2** : troupe *f* (de théâtre) **3** GUESTS : invités *mpl*

compare [kəm'pær] *v* **-pared; -paring** *vt* : comparer — *vi* ~ **with** : être comparable à — **comparative** [kəm'pærəṭɪv] *adj* : comparatif, relatif — **comparison** [kəm'pærəsən] *n* : comparaison *f*

compartment [kəm'pɑrtmənt] *n* : compartiment *m*

compass ['kʌmpəs, 'kɑm-] *n* **1** : boussole *f* **2 points of the** ~ : points *mpl* cardinaux

compassion [kəm'pæʃən] *n* : compassion *f* — **compassionate** [kəm'pæʃənət] *adj* : compatissant

compatible [kəm'pæṭəbəl] *adj* : compatible — **compatibility** [kəm,pæṭə'bɪləṭi] *n* : compatibilité *f*

compel [kəm'pɛl] *vt* **-pelled; -pelling** : contraindre, obliger — **compelling** [kəm'pɛlɪŋ] *adj* : irrésistible

compensate ['kɑmpən,seɪt] *v* **-sated; -sating** *vi* ~ **for** : compenser — *vt* : indemniser — **compensation** [,kɑmpən'seɪʃən] *n* : compensation *f*

compete [kəm'pi:t] *vi* **-peted; -peting** : faire concurrence, rivaliser — **competent** ['kɑmpəṭənt] *adj* : compétent — **competition** [,kɑmpə'tɪʃən] *n* **1** : concurrence *f* **2** CONTEST : compétition *f* — **competitor** [kəm'pɛṭəṭər] *n* : concurrent *m*, -rente *f*

compile [kəm'paɪl] *vt* **-piled; -piling** : dresser (une liste, etc.)

complacency [kəm'pleɪsəntsi] *n* : satisfaction *f* de soi, suffisance *f* — **complacent** [kəm'pleɪsənt] *adj* : content de soi

complain [kəm'pleɪn] *vi* : se plaindre — **complaint** [kəm'pleɪnt] *n* : plainte *f*

complement ['kɑmpləmənt] *n* : complément *m* — ~ ['kɑmplə,mɛnt] *vt* : aller bien avec — **complementary** [,kɑmplə'mɛntəri] *adj* : complémentaire

complete [kəm'pli:t] *adj* **-pleter; -est 1** WHOLE : complet, intégral **2** FINISHED : achevé **3** TOTAL : complet, absolu — ~ *vt* **-pleted; -pleting 1** : compléter (un puzzle, etc.), remplir (un questionnaire) **2** FINISH : achever — **completely** [kəm'pli:tli] *adv* : complètement — **completion** [kəm'pli:ʃən] *n* : achèvement *m*

complex [kɑm'plɛks, kəm-; 'kɑm,plɛks] *adj* : complexe — ~ ['kɑm,plɛks] *n* : complexe *m*

complexion [kəm'plɛkʃən] *n* : teint *m*

complexity [kəm'plɛksəṭi, kɑm-] *n, pl* **-ties** : complexité *f*

compliance [kəm'plaɪənts] *n* **1** : conformité *f* **2 in** ~ **with** : conformément

à — **compliant** [kəm'plaɪənt] *adj* : soumis
complicate ['kamplə,keɪt] *vt* **-cated; -cating** : compliquer — **complicated** ['kamplə,keɪṭəd] *adj* : compliqué — **complication** [,kamplə'keɪʃən] *n* : complication *f*
compliment ['kampləmənt] *n* : compliment *m* — ~ ['kamplə,mɛnt] *vt* : complimenter — **complimentary** [,kamplə'mɛntəri] *adj* **1** FLATTERING : flatteur **2** FREE : gratuit
comply [kəm'plaɪ] *vi* **-plied; -plying** ~ **with** : se conformer à, respecter
component [kəm'po:nənt, 'kam,po:-] *n* : composant *m*, élément *m*
compose [kəm'po:z] *vt* **-posed; -posing 1** : composer **2** ~ **oneself** : retrouver son calme — **composer** [kəm'po:zər] *n* : compositeur *m*, -trice *f* — **composition** [,kampə'zɪʃən] *n* : composition *f* — **composure** [kəm'po:ʒər] *n* : calme *m*, sang-froid *m*
compound[1] [kam'paʊnd,kəm-; 'kam,paʊnd] *adj* : composé — ~ ['kam,paʊnd] *n* : composé *m* (en chimie)
compound[2] ['kam,paʊnd] *n* ENCLOSURE : enceinte *f*, enclos *m*
comprehend [,kamprɪ'hɛnd] *vt* : comprendre — **comprehension** [,kamprɪ'hɛntʃən] *n* : compréhension *f* — **comprehensive** [,kamprɪ'hɛntsɪv] *adj* : complet, détaillé
compress [kəm'prɛs] *vt* : comprimer — **compression** [kəm'prɛʃən] *n* : compression *f*
comprise [kəm'praɪz] *vt* **-prised; -prising** : comprendre
compromise ['kamprə,maɪz] *n* : compromis *m* — ~ *v* **-mised; -mising** *vi* : faire un compromis — *vt* : compromettre
compulsion [kəm'pʌlʃən] *n* URGE : envie *f* — **compulsory** [kəm'pʌlsəri] *adj* : obligatoire
compute [kəm'pju:t] *vt* **-puted; -puting** : calculer — **computer** [kəm'pju:ṭər] *n* **1** : ordinateur *m* **2** ~ **science** : informatique *f* — **computerize** [kəm'pju:ṭə,raɪz] *vt* **-ized; -izing** : informatiser
con ['kan] *vt* **conned; conning** : duper, escroquer — ~ *n* **the pros and** ~**s** : le pour et le contre
concave [kan'keɪv, 'kan,keɪv] *adj* : concave
conceal [kən'si:l] *vt* : dissimuler, cacher
concede [kən'si:d] *vt* **-ceded; -ceding** : accorder, concéder
conceit [kən'si:t] *n* : suffisance *f*, vanité *f* — **conceited** [kən'si:təd] *adj* : suffisant, vaniteux
conceive [kən'si:v] *v* **-ceived; -ceiving** *vt* : concevoir — *vi* ~ **of** : concevoir
concentrate ['kantsən,treɪt] *v* **-trated; -trating** *vt* : concentrer — *vi* : se concentrer — **concentration** [,kantsən'treɪʃən] *n* : concentration *f*
concept ['kan,sɛpt] *n* : concept *m* — **conception** [kən'sɛpʃən] *n* : conception *f*
concern [kən'sərn] *vt* **1** : concerner **2** ~ **oneself about** : s'inquiéter de — ~ *n* **1** BUSINESS : affaire *f* **2** WORRY : inquiétude *f* — **concerned** [kən'sərnd] *adj* **1** ANXIOUS : inquiet **2 as far as I'm** ~ : en ce qui me concerne — **concerning** [kən'sərnɪŋ] *prep* : concernant
concert ['kan,sərt] *n* : concert *m* — **concerted** [kən'sərṭəd] *adj* : concerté
concession [kən'sɛʃən] *n* : concession *f*
concise [kən'saɪs] *adj* : concis
conclude [kən'klu:d] *v* **-cluded; -cluding** *vt* : conclure — *vi* : s'achever, se terminer — **conclusion** [kən'klu:ʒən] *n* : conclusion *f* — **conclusive** [kən'klu:sɪv] *adj* : concluant
concoct [kən'kakt, kan-] *vt* **1** PREPARE : confectionner **2** DEVISE : fabriquer — **concoction** [kən'kakʃən] *n* : mélange *m*
concrete [kan'kri:t, 'kan,kri:t] *adj* **1** : de béton **2** REAL : concret, réel — ~ ['kan,kri:t, kan'kri:t] *n* : béton *m*
concur [kən'kər] *vi* **-curred, -curring** : être d'accord
concussion [kən'kʌʃən] *n* : commotion *f* cérébrale
condemn [kən'dɛm] *vt* : condamner — **condemnation** [,kan,dɛm'neɪʃən] *n* : condamnation *f*
condense [kən'dɛnts] *vt* **-densed; -densing** : condenser — **condensation** [,kan,dɛn'seɪʃən, -dən-] *n* : condensation *f*
condescending [,k'ndɪ'sɛndɪŋ] *adj* : condescendant
condiment ['kandəmənt] *n* : condiment *m*
condition [kən'dɪʃən] *n* **1** : condition *f* **2 in good** ~ : en bon état— **conditional** [kən'dɪʃənəl] *adj* : conditionnel
condolences [kən'do:ləntsəz] *npl* : condoléances *fpl*
condom ['kandəm] *n* : préservatif *m*

condominium [ˌkɑndəˈmɪniəm] *n, pl* **-ums** : immeuble *m* en copropriété
condone [kənˈdo:n] *vt* **-doned; -doning** : excuser
conducive [kənˈdu:sɪv, -ˈdju:-] *adj* : propice, favorable
conduct [ˈkɑnˌdʌkt] *n* : comportement *m,* conduite *f* — **~** [kənˈdʌkt] *vt* **1** : conduire, diriger **2 ~ oneself** : se comporter — **conductor** [kənˈdʌktər] *n* **1** : conducteur *m* (d'électricité) **2** : chef *m* d'orchestre **3** : contrôleur *m* (de train, etc.)
cone [ˈko:n] *n* **1** : cône *m* **2** *or* **ice-cream ~** : cornet *m* (de crème glacée)
confection [kənˈfɛkʃən] *n* : confiserie *f,* bonbon *m*
confederation [kənˌfɛdəˈreɪʃən] *n* : confédération *f*
confer [kənˈfɛr] *v* **-ferred; -ferring** *vt* : conférer — *vi* **~ with** : conférer avec, s'entretenir avec — **conference** [ˈkɑnfrənts, -fərənts] *n* : conférence *f*
confess [kənˈfɛs] *vt* : confesser, avouer — *vi* **~ to** : admettre — **confession** [kənˈfɛʃən] *n* : confession *f*
confetti [kənˈfɛt̬i] *n* : confettis *mpl*
confide [kənˈfaɪd] *v* **-fided; -fiding** *vt* : confier — *vi* **~ in** : se confier à — **confidence** [ˈkɑnfədənts] *n* **1** TRUST : confiance *f* **2** SELF-ASSURANCE : confiance *f* en soi, assurance *f* **3** SECRET : confidence *f* — **confident** [ˈkɑnfədənt] *adj* **1** SURE : confiant, sûr **2** SELF-ASSURED : sûr de soi — **confidential** [ˌkɑnfəˈdɛntʃəl] *adj* : confidentiel
confine [kənˈfaɪn] *vt* **-fined; -fining 1** LIMIT : confiner, limiter **2** IMPRISON : enfermer — **confines** [ˈkɑnˌfaɪnz] *npl* : confins *mpl*, limites *fpl*
confirm [kənˈfərm] *vt* : confirmer — **confirmation** [ˌkɑnfərˈmeɪʃən] *n* : confirmation *f*
confiscate [ˈkɑnfəˌskeɪt] *vt* **-cated; -cating** : confisquer
conflict [ˈkɑnˌflɪkt] *n* : conflit *m* — **~** [kənˈflɪkt] *vi* : être en conflit, s'opposer
conform [kənˈfɔrm] *vi* **~ with** : se conformer à, être conforme à — **conformity** [kənˈfɔrmət̬i] *n, pl* **-ties** : conformité *f*
confound [kənˈfaʊnd, kɑn-] *vt* : confondre, déconcerter
confront [kənˈfrʌnt] *vt* : affronter, faire face à — **confrontation** [ˌkɑnfrənˈteɪʃən] *n* : confrontation *f*
confuse [kənˈfju:z] *vt* **-fused; -fusing** : troubler, déconcerter — **confusing** [kənˈfju:zɪŋ] *adj* : déroutant — **confusion** [kənˈfju:ʒən] *n* : confusion *f*
congenial [kənˈdʒi:niəl] *adj* : sympathique
congested [kənˈdʒɛstəd] *adj* **1** : congestionné (en médecine) **2** OBSTRUCTED : encombré — **congestion** [kənˈdʒɛstʃən] *n* : congestion *f*
Congolese [ˌkɑŋgəˈli:z,-ˈli:s] *adj* : congolais
congratulate [kənˈgrædʒəˌleɪt, -ˈgrætʃə-] *vt* **-lated; -lating** : féliciter — **congratulations** [kənˌgrædʒəˈleɪʃənz, -ˌgrætʃə-] *npl* : félicitations *fpl*
congregate [ˈkɑŋgrɪˌgeɪt] *vi* **-gated; -gating** : se rassembler, se réunir — **congregation** [ˌkɑŋgrɪˈgeɪʃən] *n* : assemblée *f* (de fidèles)
congress [ˈkɑŋgrəs] *n* : congrès *m* — **congressman** [ˈkɑŋgrəsmən] *n, pl* **-men** [-mən, -ˌmɛn] : membre *m* d'un congrès
conjecture [kənˈdʒɛktʃər] *n* : conjecture *f,* supposition *f* — **~** *vt* **-tured; -turing** : conjecturer, présumer
conjugate [ˈkɑndʒəˌgeɪt] *vt* **-gated; -gating** : conjuguer — **conjugation** [ˌkɑndʒəˈgeɪʃən] *n* : conjugaison *f*
conjunction [kənˈdʒʌŋkʃən] *n* : conjonction *f* (en grammaire)
conjure [ˈkɑndʒər, ˈkʌn-] *vt* **-jured; -juring ~ up** : invoquer, évoquer
connect [kəˈnɛkt] *vi* : assurer la correspondance (avec un train, etc.) — *vt* **1** JOIN : relier **2** ASSOCIATE : associer **3** : brancher (en électricité) — **connection** [kəˈnɛkʃən] *n* **1** : lien *m,* rapport *m* **2** : correspondance *f* (de train, etc.) **3 ~s** *npl* : relations *fpl* (sociales)
connote [kəˈno:t] *vt* **-noted; -noting** : évoquer, indiquer
conquer [ˈkɑŋkər] *vt* : conquérir, vaincre — **conqueror** [ˈkɑŋkərər] *n* : conquérant *m,* -rante *f* — **conquest** [ˈkɑnˌkwɛst, ˈkɑŋ-] *n* : conquête *f*
conscience [ˈkɑntʃənts] *n* : conscience *f* — **conscientious** [ˌkɑntʃiˈɛntʃəs] *adj* : consciencieux
conscious [ˈkɑntʃəs] *adj* **1** AWARE : conscient **2** INTENTIONAL : délibéré — **consciously** [ˈkɑntʃəsli] *adv* : consciemment — **consciousness** [ˈkɑntʃəsnəs] *n* **1** AWARENESS : conscience *f* **2 lose ~** : perdre connaissance
consecrate [ˈkɑntsəˌkreɪt] *vt* **-crated; -crating** : consacrer
consecutive [kənˈsɛkjət̬ɪv] *adj* : consécutif

consensus [kən'sɛntsəs] *n* : consensus *m*
consent [kən'sɛnt] *vi* : consentir — ~ *n* : consentement *m,* accord *m*
consequence ['kɑntsəˌkwɛnts, -kwənts] *n* **1** : conséquence *f* **2 of no ~** : sans importance — **consequently** ['kɑntsəkwəntli, -ˌkwɛnt-] *adv* : par conséquent
conserve [kən'sərv] *vt* **-served; -serving** : conserver, préserver — **conservation** [ˌkɑntsər'veɪʃən] *n* : conservation *f* — **conservative** [kən'sərvət̬ɪv] *adj* **1** : conservateur **2** CAUTIOUS : modéré, prudent — ~ *n* : conservateur *m,* -trice *f* — **conservatory** [kən'sərvəˌtori] *n, pl* **-ries** : conservatoire *m*
consider [kən'sɪdər] *vt* : considérer — **considerable** [kən'sɪdərəbəl] *adj* : considérable — **considerate** [kən'sɪdərət] *adj* : attentionné, prévenant — **consideration** [kənˌsɪdə'reɪʃən] *n* : considération *f* — **considering** [kən'sɪdərɪŋ] *prep* : étant donné, vu
consign [kən'saɪn] *vt* SEND : expédier, envoyer — **consignment** [kən'saɪnmənt] *n* : envoi *m*
consist [kən'sɪst] *vi* **1 ~ in** : consister à **2 ~ of** : se composer de, consister en — **consistency** [kən'sɪstəntsi] *n, pl* **-cies 1** TEXTURE : consistance *f* **2** COHERENCE : cohérence *f* — **consistent** [kən'sɪstənt] *adj* **1** : constant, régulier **2 ~ with** : en accord avec
console [kən'so:l] *vt* **-soled; -soling** : consoler, réconforter — **consolation** [ˌkɑntsə'leɪʃən] *n* : consolation *f*
consolidate [kən'sɑləˌdeɪt] *vt* **-dated; -dating** : consolider — **consolidation** [kənˌsɑlə'deɪʃən] *n* : consolidation *f*
consonant ['kɑntsənənt] *n* : consonne *f*
conspicuous [kən'spɪkjuəs] *adj* **1** OBVIOUS : évident, visible **2** STRIKING : voyant
conspire [kən'spaɪr] *vi* **-spired; -spiring** : conspirer, comploter — **conspiracy** [kən'spɪrəsi] *n, pl* **-cies** : conspiration *f*
constant ['kɑntstənt] *adj* : constant — **constantly** ['kɑntstəntli] *adv* : constamment
constellation [ˌkɑntstə'leɪʃən] *n* : constellation *f*
constipated ['kɑntstəˌpeɪtəd] *adj* : constipé — **constipation** [ˌkɑntstə'peɪʃən] *n* : constipation *f*
constituent [kən'stɪtʃuənt] *n* **1** COMPONENT : composant *m* **2** VOTER : électeur *m,* -trice *f*
constitute ['kɑntstəˌtu:t, -tju:t] *vt* **-tuted; -tuting** : constituer — **constitution** [ˌkɑntstə'tu:ʃən, -'tju:-] *n* : constitution *f* — **constitutional** [ˌkɑntstə'tu:ʃənəl, -'tju:-] *adj* : constitutionnel
constraint [kən'streɪnt] *n* : contrainte *f*
construct [kən'strʌkt] *vt* : construire, bâtir — **construction** [kən'strʌkʃən] *n* : construction *f* — **constructive** [kən'strʌktɪv] *adj* : constructif
construe [kən'stru:] *vt* **-strued; -struing** : interpréter
consulate ['kɑntsələt] *n* : consulat *m*
consult [kən'sʌlt] *vt* : consulter — **consultant** [kən'sʌltənt] *n* : consultant *m,* -tante *f* — **consultation** [ˌkɑntsəl'teɪʃən] *n* : consultation *f*
consume [kən'su:m] *vt* **-sumed; -suming** : consommer — **consumer** [kən'su:mər] *n* : consommateur *m,* -trice *f* — **consumption** [kən'sʌmpʃən] *n* : consommation *f*
contact ['kɑnˌtækt] *n* **1** TOUCHING : contact *m* **2 be in ~ with** : être en rapport avec **3 business ~** : relation *f* de travail — ~ ['kɑnˌtækt, kən'-] *vt* : contacter — **contact lens** ['kɑnˌtækt'lɛnz] *n* : lentille *f* (de contact), verre *m* de contact
contagious [kən'teɪdʒəs] *adj* : contagieux
contain [kən'teɪn] *vt* **1** : contenir **2 ~ oneself** : se contenir, se maîtriser — **container** [kən'teɪnər] *n* : récipient *m*
contaminate [kən'tæməˌneɪt] *vt* **-nated; -nating** : contaminer — **contamination** [kənˌtæmə'neɪʃən] *n* : contamination *f*
contemplate ['kɑntəmˌpleɪt] *v* **-plated; -plating** *vt* **1** : contempler **2** CONSIDER : envisager, considérer — *vi* : réfléchir — **contemplation** [ˌkɑntəm'pleɪʃən] *n* : contemplation *f,* réflexion *f*
contemporary [kən'tɛmpəˌrɛri] *adj* : contemporain — ~ *n, pl* **-raries** : contemporain *m,* -raine *f*
contempt [kən'tɛmpt] *n* : mépris *m,* dédain *m* — **contemptible** [kən'tɛmptəbəl] *adj* : méprisable — **contemptuous** [kən'tɛmptʃuəs] *adj* : méprisant
contend [kən'tɛnd] *vi* **1** COMPETE : rivaliser **2 ~ with** : faire face à — *vt* : soutenir, maintenir — **contender** [kən'tɛndər] *n* : concurrent *m,* -rente *f*

content[1] [ˈkɑn,tɛnt] *n* **1** : contenu *m* **2 table of ~s** : table *f* des matières

content[2] [kənˈtɛnt] *adj* : content — **~** *vt* **~ oneself with** : se contenter de, être satisfait de — **contented** [kənˈtɛntəd] *adj* : content, satisfait

contention [kənˈtɛntʃən] *n* **1** ARGUMENT : dispute *f*, discussion *f* **2** OPINION : affirmation *f*, assertion *f*

contentment [kənˈtɛntmənt] *n* : contentement *m*

contest [kənˈtɛst] *vt* : contester, disputer — **~** [ˈkɑn,tɛst] *n* **1** STRUGGLE : lutte *f* **2** COMPETITION : concours *m*, compétition *f* — **contestant** [kənˈtɛstənt] *n* : concurrent *m*, -rente *f*

context [ˈkɑn,tɛkst] *n* : contexte *m*

continent [ˈkɑntənənt] *n* : continent *m* — **continental** [,kɑntənˈɛntəl] *adj* : continental

contingency [kənˈtɪndʒəntsi] *n, pl* **-cies** : éventualité *f*

continue [kənˈtɪnju:] *v* **-ued; -uing** *vt* **1** KEEP UP : continuer (à) **2** RESUME : reprendre — *vi* : continuer — **continual** [kəˈtɪnjuəl] *adj* : continuel — **continuation** [kən,tɪnjʊˈeɪʃən] *n* : continuation *f* — **continuity** [,kɑntənˈu:əti, -ˈju:-] *n, pl* **-ties** : continuité *f* — **continuous** [kənˈtɪnjuəs] *adj* : continu

contort [kənˈtɔrt] *vt* : tordre — **contortion** [kənˈtɔrʃən] *n* : contorsion *f*

contour [ˈkɑn,tʊr] *n* : contour *m*

contraband [ˈkɑntrə,bænd] *n* : contrebande *f*

contraception [,kɑntrəˈsɛpʃən] *n* : contraception *f* — **contraceptive** [,kɑntrəˈsɛptɪv] *adj* : contraceptif — **~** *n* : contraceptif *m*

contract [ˈkɑn,trækt] *n* : contrat *m* — **~** [kənˈtrækt] *vt* : contracter — *vi* : se contracter — **contraction** [kənˈtrækʃən] *n* : contraction *f* — **contractor** [ˈkɑn,træktər, kənˈtræk-] *n* : entrepreneur *m*, -neuse *f*

contradiction [,kɑntrəˈdɪkʃən] *n* : contradiction *f* — **contradict** [,kɑntrəˈdɪkt] *vt* : contredire — **contradictory** [,kɑntrəˈdɪktəri] *adj* : contradictoire

contraption [kənˈtræpʃən] *n* : truc *m fam*, machin *m fam*

contrary [ˈkɑn,trɛri] *n, pl* **-traries 1** : contraire *m* **2 on the ~** : au contraire — **~** *adj* **1** : contraire, opposé **2 ~ to** : contrairement à

contrast [kənˈtræst] *vi* : contraster — **~** [ˈkɑn,træst] *n* : contraste *m*

contribute [kənˈtrɪbjət] *v* **-uted; -uting** *vi* : contribuer — *vt* : apporter, donner — **contribution** [,kɑntrəˈbju:ʃən] *n* : contribution *f* — **contributor** [kənˈtrɪbjətər] *n* : collaborateur *m*, -trice *f*

contrite [ˈkɑn,traɪt, kənˈtraɪt] *adj* : contrit

contrive [kənˈtraɪv] *vt* **-trived; -triving 1** DEVISE : inventer, imaginer **2 ~ to** : parvenir à, réussir à

control [kənˈtro:l] *vt* **-trolled; -trolling 1** RULE, RUN : diriger **2** REGULATE : contrôler, régler **3** RESTRAIN : maîtriser — **~** *n* **1** : contrôle *m*, régulation *f* **2** RESTRAINT : maîtrise *f* **3 remote ~** : commande *f* à distance

controversy [ˈkɑntrə,vərsi] *n, pl* **-sies** : controverse *f* — **controversial** [,kɑntrəˈvərʃəl, -siəl] *adj* : controversé

convalescence [,kɑnvəˈlɛsənts] *n* : convalescence *f*

convene [kənˈvi:n] *v* **-vened; -vening** *vt* : convoquer — *vi* : se réunir

convenience [kənˈvi:njənts] *n* **1** : commodité *f*, confort *m* **2 at your ~** : quand cela vous conviendra — **convenient** [kənˈvi:njənt] *adj* : commode

convent [ˈkɑnvənt, -,vɛnt] *n* : couvent *m*

convention [kənˈvɛntʃən] *n* **1** : convention *f* **2** CUSTOM : usage *m* — **conventional** [kənˈvɛntʃənəl] *adj* : conventionnel

converge [kənˈvərdʒ] *vi* **-verged; -verging** : converger

converse[1] [kənˈvɛrs] *vi* **-versed; -versing ~ with** : s'entretenir avec — **conversation** [,kɑnvərˈseɪʃən] *n* : conversation *f*

converse[2] [kənˈvɛrs, ˈkɑn,vɛrs] *n* : contraire *m*, inverse *m* — **conversely** [kənˈvərsli, ˈkɑn,vərs-] *adv* : inversement

conversion [kənˈvərʒən] *n* : conversion *f* — **convert** [kənˈvɛrt] *vt* : convertir — **convertible** [kənˈvərtəbəl] *n* : décapotable *f*

convex [kɑnˈvɛks, ˈkɑn,-, kənˈ-] *adj* : convexe

convey [kənˈveɪ] *vt* **-veyed; -veying** : transmettre, exprimer

convict [kənˈvɪkt] *vt* : déclarer coupable — **~** [ˈkɑn,vɪkt] *n* : détenu *m*, -nue *f* — **conviction** [kənˈvɪkʃən] *n* **1** : condamnation *f* **2** BELIEF : conviction *f*

convince [kənˈvɪnts] *vt* **-vinced; -vincing** : convaincre, persuader — **convincing** [kənˈvɪntsɪŋ] *adj* : convaincant

convoluted [ˈkɑnvəˌluːţəd] *adj* : compliqué

convulsion [kənˈvʌlʃən] *n* : convulsion *f*

cook [ˈkʊk] *n* : cuisinier *m*, -nière *f* — ~ *vi* : cuisiner, faire la cuisine — *vt* : préparer (de la nourriture) — **cookbook** [ˈkʊkˌbʊk] *n* : livre *m* de recettes

cookie *or* **cooky** [ˈkʊki] *n, pl* **-ies** : biscuit *m*, gâteau *m* sec

cooking [ˈkʊkɪŋ] *n* : cuisine *f*

cool [ˈkuːl] *adj* **1** : frais **2** CALM : calme **3** UNFRIENDLY : indifférent, froid — ~ *vt* : refroidir — *vi or* ~ **down** : se refroidir — ~ *n* **1** : fraîcheur *m* **2 lose one's** ~ : perdre son sang-froid — **cooler** [ˈkuːlər] *n* : glacière *f* — **coolness** [ˈkuːlnəs] *n* : fraîcheur *f*

coop [ˈkuːp, ˈkʊp] *n or* **chicken** ~ : poulailler *m* — ~ *vt or* ~ **up** : enfermer

cooperate [koˈɑpəˌreɪt] *vi* **-ated; -ating** : coopérer — **cooperation** [koˌɑpəˈreɪʃən] *n* : coopération *f* — **cooperative** [koˈɑpərəţɪv, -ˈɑpəˌreɪţɪv] *adj* : coopératif

coordinate [koˈɔrdənˌeɪt] *vt* **-nated; -nating** : coordonner — **coordination** [koˌɔrdənˈeɪʃən] *n* : coordination *f*

cop [ˈkɑp] *n* **1** : flic *m fam* **2 the** ~**s** : la police *fam*

cope [ˈkoːp] *vi* **coped; coping 1** : se débrouiller **2** ~ **with** : faire face à

copious [ˈkoːpiəs] *adj* : copieux

copper [ˈkɑpər] *n* : cuivre *m*

copy [ˈkɑpi] *n, pl* **copies 1** : copie *f*, reproduction *f* **2** : exemplaire *m* (d'un livre, etc.) — ~ *vt* **copied; copying 1** : faire une copie de **2** IMITATE : copier — **copyright** [ˈkɑpiˌraɪt] *n* : droits *mpl* d'auteur

coral [ˈkɔrəl] *n* : corail *m*

cord [ˈkɔrd] *n* : corde *f*, cordon *m*

cordial [ˈkɔrʤəl] *adj* : cordial, amical

corduroy [ˈkɔrdəˌrɔɪ] *n* : velours *m* côtelé

core [ˈkor] *n* **1** : trognon *m* (d'un fruit) **2** CENTER : cœur *m*, centre *m*

cork [ˈkɔrk] *n* **1** : liège *m* **2** : bouchon *m* (d'une bouteille) — **corkscrew** [ˈkɔrkˌskruː] *n* : tire-bouchon *m*

corn [ˈkɔrn] *n* **1** : grain *m* (de blé, etc.) **2** *or* **Indian** ~ : maïs *m* **3** : cor *m* (sur le pied) — **corncob** [ˈkɔrnˌkɑb] *n* : épi *m* de maïs

corner [ˈkɔrnər] *n* **1** : coin *m*, angle *m* **2 around the** ~ : à deux pas d'ici — **cornerstone** [ˈkɔrnərˌstoːn] *n* : pierre *f* angulaire

cornmeal [ˈkɔrnˌmiːl] *n* : farine *f* de maïs — **cornstarch** [ˈkɔrnˌstɑrʧ] *n* : fécule *f* de maïs

corny [ˈkɔrni] *adj* **cornier; -est** : banal, à l'eau de rose

coronary [ˈkɔrəˌnɛri] *n, pl* **-naries** : infarctus *m*

coronation [ˌkɔrəˈneɪʃən] *n* : couronnement *m*

corporal [ˈkɔrpərəl] *n* : caporal-chef *m*

corporation [ˌkɔrpəˈreɪʃən] *n* : compagnie *f* commerciale, société *f* — **corporate** [ˈkɔrpərət] *adj* : d'entreprise

corps [ˈkor] *n, pl* **corps** [ˈkorz] : corps *m*

corpse [ˈkɔrps] *n* : cadavre *m*

corpulent [ˈkɔrpjələnt] *adj* : corpulent, gras

corral [kəˈræl] *n* : corral *m*

correct [kəˈrɛkt] *vt* : corriger — ~ *adj* **1** : juste, correct **2 that's** ~ : c'est exact — **correction** [kəˈrɛkʃən] *n* : correction *f*

correlation [ˌkɔrəˈleɪʃən] *n* : corrélation *f*

correspond [ˌkɔrəˈspɑnd] *vi* : correspondre — **correspondence** [ˌkɔrəˈspɑndənts] *n* : correspondance *f* — **correspondent** [ˌkɔrəˈspɑndənt] *n* **1** : correspondant *m*, -dante *f* **2** REPORTER : journaliste *mf*

corridor [ˈkɔrədər, -ˌdɔr] *n* : corridor *m*

corroborate [kəˈrɑbəˌreɪt] *vt* **-rated; -rating** : corroborer

corrode [kəˈroːd] *vt* **-roded; -roding** : corroder — **corrosion** [kəˈroɪʃˈn] *n* : corrosion *f*

corrugated [ˈkɔrəˌgeɪţəd] *adj* : ondulé

corrupt [kəˈrʌpt] *vt* : corrompre — ~ *adj* : corrumpu — **corruption** [kəˈrʌpʃən] *n* : corruption *f*

cosmetic [kɑzˈmɛţɪk] *n* : cosmétique *f* — ~ *adj* : cosmétique

cosmic [ˈkɑzmɪk] *adj* : cosmique

cosmopolitan [ˌkɑzməˈpulətən] *adj* : cosmopolite

cosmos [ˈkɑzməs, -ˌmoːs, -ˌmɑs] *n* : cosmos *m*, univers *m*

cost [ˈkɔst] *n* : coût *m*, prix *m* — ~ *vi* **cost; costing 1** : coûter **2 how much does it** ~**?** : combien ça coûte? — **costly** [ˈkɔstli] *adj* **-lier; -est** : coûteux, cher

costume [ˈkɑsˌtuːm, -ˌtjuːm] *n* : costume *m*

cot [ˈkɑt] *n* : lit *m* de camp

cottage ['kɑṭɪʤ] *n* : petite maison *f* — **cottage cheese** *n* : fromage *m* blanc
cotton ['kɑtən] *n* : coton *m*
couch ['kaʊʧ] *n* : canapé *m*, sofa *m*
cough ['kɔf] *vi* : tousser — ~ *n* : toux *f*
could ['kʊd] → **can**[1]
council ['kaʊntsəl] *n* : conseil *m*, assemblée *f* — **councillor** *or* **councilor** ['kaʊntsələr] *n* : conseiller *m*, -lère *f*
counsel ['kaʊntsəl] *n* **1** ADVICE : conseil *m* **2** LAWYER : avocat *m*, -cate *f* — ~ *vt* **-seled** *or* **-selled; -seling** *or* **-selling** : conseiller, guider — **counselor** *or* **counsellor** ['kaʊntsələr] *n* **1** : conseiller *m*, -lère *f* **2** *or* **camp** ~ : moniteur *m*, -trice *f*
count[1] ['kaʊnt] *vt* : compter, énumérer — *vi* **1** : compter **2** ~ **on** : compter sur — ~ *n* : compte *m*, décompte *m*
count[2] *n* : comte *m* (noble)
counter[1] ['kaʊntər] *n* **1** : comptoir *m* **2** TOKEN : jeton *m*
counter[2] *vt* : s'opposer à, contrecarrer — *vi* : riposter — ~ *adv* ~ **to** : à l'encontre de — **counteract** [ˌkaʊntər'ækt] *vt* : neutraliser — **counterattack** ['kaʊntərəˌtæk] *n* : contre-attaque *f* — **counterbalance** [ˌkaʊntər'bælənts] *n* : contrepoids *m* — **counterclockwise** [ˌkaʊntər'klɑkˌwaɪz] *adv & adj* : dans le sens contraire des aiguilles d'une montre — **counterfeit** ['kaʊntərˌfɪt] *vt* : contrefaire — ~ *adj* : faux — **counterpart** ['kaʊntərˌpɑrt] *n* : homologue *mf* (d'une personne), équivalent *m* (d'une chose)
countess ['kaʊntɪs] *n* : comtesse *f*
countless ['kaʊntləs] *adj* : innombrable, incalculable
country ['kʌntri] *n, pl* **-tries** **1** NATION : pays *m*, patrie *f* **2** COUNTRYSIDE : campagne *f* — ~ *adj* : champêtre, rural — **countryside** ['kʌntriˌsaɪd] *n* : campagne *f*
county ['kaʊnti] *n, pl* **-ties** : comté *m*
coup ['ku:] *n, pl* **coups** ['ku:z] *or* ~ **d'état** : coup *m* d'état
couple ['kʌpəl] *n* **1** : couple *m* **2 a** ~ **of** : deux ou trois — ~ *v* **-pled; -pling** *vt* : accoupler — *vi* : s'accoupler
coupon ['ku:ˌpɑn, 'kju:-] *n* : coupon *m*
courage ['kərɪʤ] *n* : courage *m* — **courageous** [kə'reɪʤəs] *adj* : courageux
courier ['kʊriər, 'kəriər] *n* : messager *m*, -gère *f*
course ['kors] *n* **1** : cours *m* **2** : service *m*, plat *m* (au restaurant) **3** ~ **of action** : ligne *f* de conduite **4 golf** ~ : terrain *m* de golf **5 in the** ~ **of** : au cours de **6 of** ~ : bien sûr
court ['kort] *n* **1** : cour *f* (d'un souverain, etc.) **2** : court *m*, terrain *m* (de sports) **3** TRIBUNAL : cour *f*, tribunal *m* — ~ *vt* : courtiser, faire la cour à
courteous ['kərṭiəs] *adj* : courtois, poli — **courtesy** ['kərṭəsi] *n, pl* **-sies** : courtoisie *f*
courthouse ['kortˌhaʊs] *n* : palais *m* de justice — **courtroom** ['kortˌru:m] *n* : salle *f* de tribunal
courtship ['kortˌʃɪp] *n* : cour *f*
courtyard ['kortˌjɑrd] *n* : cour *f*, patio *m*
cousin ['kʌzən] *n* : cousin *m*, -sine *f*
cove ['ko:v] *n* : anse *f*
covenant ['kʌvənənt] *n* : contrat *m*, convention *f*
cover ['kʌvər] *vt* **1** : couvrir, recouvrir **2** *or* ~ **up** : cacher **3** DEAL WITH : traiter **4** : parcourir (une distance) **5** INSURE : assurer — ~ *n* **1** LID : couvercle *m* **2** SHELTER : abri *m*, refuge *m* **3** : couverture *f* (d'un livre) **4** ~**s** *npl* BEDCLOTHES : couvertures *fpl* — **coverage** ['kʌvərɪʤ] *n* : reportage *m*, couverture *f* — **covert** ['ko:ˌvərt, 'kʌvərt] *adj* : voilé, secret — **cover–up** ['kʌvərˌʌp] *n* : opération *f* de camouflage
covet ['kʌvət] *vt* : convoiter — **covetous** ['kʌvəṭəs] *adj* : avide, cupide
cow ['kaʊ] *n* : vache *f*
coward ['kaʊərd] *n* : lâche *mf*; poltron *m*, -tronne *f* — **cowardice** ['kaʊərdɪs] *n* : lâcheté *f* — **cowardly** ['kaʊərdli] *adj* : lâche
cowboy ['kaʊˌbɔɪ] *n* : cow-boy *m*
cower ['kaʊər] *vi* : se recroqueviller
coy ['kɔɪ] *adj* : faussement timide
coyote [kaɪ'o:ṭi, 'kaɪˌo:t] *n, pl* **coyotes** *or* **coyote** : coyote *m*
cozy ['ko:zi] *adj* **-zier; -est** : douillet, confortable
crab ['kræb] *n* : crabe *m*
crack ['kræk] *vt* **1** SPLIT : fêler, fendre **2** : casser (un œuf, etc.) **3** : faire claquer (un fouet) **4** ~ **down on** : sévir contre — *vi* **1** SPLIT : se fêler, se fendre **2** BREAK : se casser, muer (se dit de la voix) — ~ *n* **1** : craquement *m*, bruit *m* sec **2** CREVICE : crevasse *f*, fissure *f*
cracker ['krækər] *n* : biscuit *m* salé
crackle ['krækəl] *vi* **-led; -ling** : crépiter, pétiller — ~ *n* : crépitement *m*
cradle ['kreɪdəl] *n* : berceau *m* — ~ *vt* **-dled; -dling** : bercer (un enfant)
craft ['kræft] *n* **1** TRADE : métier *m*, art

m **2** CUNNING : ruse *f* **3** *pl usu* **craft** BOAT : embarcation *f* — **craftsman** [ˈkræftsmən] *n, pl* **-men** [-mən, -ˌmɛn] : artisan *m,* -sane *f* — **craftsmanship** [ˈkræftsmənˌʃɪp] *n* : artisanat *m* — **crafty** [ˈkræfti] *adj* **craftier; -est** : astucieux, rusé

cram [ˈkræm] *v* **crammed; cramming** *vt* : fourrer, entasser — *vi* : étudier à la dernière minute

cramp [ˈkræmp] *n* : crampe *f*

cranberry [ˈkrænˌbɛri] *n, pl* **-ries** : canneberge *f*

crane [ˈkreɪn] *n* : grue *f* — ~ *vt* **craned; craning** : tendre (le cou, etc.)

crank [ˈkræŋk] *n* **1** : manivelle *f* **2** ECCENTRIC : excentrique *mf* — **cranky** [ˈkræŋki] *adj* **crankier; -est** : irritable

crash [ˈkræʃ] *vi* **1** : se fracasser, s'écraser **2** : faire faillite (se dit d'une banque), s'effondrer (se dit du marché) — *vt* ~ **one's car** : avoir un accident de voiture — ~ *n* **1** : fracas *m,* bruit *m* sourd **2** COLLISION : accident *m*

crass [ˈkræs] *adj* : grossier

crate [ˈkreɪt] *n* : cageot *m,* caisse *f*

crater [ˈkreɪt̬ər] *n* : cratère *m*

crave [ˈkreɪv] *vt* **craved; craving** : désirer, avoir très envie de — **craving** [ˈkreɪvɪŋ] *n* : envie *f* (incontrôlable), soif *f*

crawl [ˈkrɔl] *vi* : ramper, marcher à quatre pattes — ~ *n* **at a** ~ : à un pas de tortue

crayon [ˈkreɪˌɑn, -ən] *n* : crayon *m* de cire

craze [ˈkreɪz] *n* : mode *f* passagère

crazy [ˈkreɪzi] *adj* **-zier; -est** **1** : fou **2** **go** ~ : devenir fou — **craziness** [ˈkreɪzinəs] *n* : folie *f*

creak [ˈkri:k] *vi* : grincer, craquer — ~ *n* : grincement *m*

cream [ˈkri:m] *n* : crème *f* — **creamy** [ˈkri:mi] *adj* **creamier; -est** : crémeux

crease [ˈkri:s] *n* : (faux) pli *m* — ~ *v* **creased; creasing** *vt* : froisser — *vi* : se froisser

create [kriˈeɪt] *vt* **-ated; -ating** : créer — **creation** [kriˈeɪʃən] *n* : création *f* — **creative** [kriˈeɪt̬ɪv] *adj* : créateur — **creator** [kriˈeɪt̬ər] *n* : créateur *m,* -trice *f*

creature [ˈkri:ʧər] *n* : créature *f*

credence [ˈkri:dənts] *n* **give** ~ **to** : accorder du crédit à

credentials [krɪˈdɛnʧəlz] *npl* : références *fpl*

credible [ˈkrɛdəbəl] *adj* : crédible — **credibility** [ˌkrɛdəˈbɪlət̬i] *n* : crédibilité *f*

credit [ˈkrɛdɪt] *n* **1** : crédit *m* **2** RECOGNITION : mérite *m* **3** **to his** ~ : à son honneur — ~ *vt* **1** : créditer (un compte de banque) **2** ~ **with** : attribuer à — **credit card** *n* : carte *f* de crédit — **creditor** [ˈkrɛdɪt̬ər] *n* : créancier *m,* -cière *f*

credulous [ˈkrɛʤələs] *adj* : crédule

creed [ˈkri:d] *n* : credo *m*

creek [ˈkri:k, ˈkrɪk] *n* : ruisseau *m*

creep [ˈkri:p] *vi* **crept** [ˈkrɛpt]; **creeping** **1** CRAWL : ramper **2** : avancer sans un bruit — ~ *n* **1** ~**s** *npl* : frissons *mpl,* chair *f* de poule **2** **move at a** ~ : avancer au ralenti

cremate [ˈkri:ˌmeɪt] *vt* **-mated; -mating** : incinérer

crescent [ˈkrɛsənt] *n* : croissant *m*

cress [ˈkrɛs] *n* : cresson *m*

crest [ˈkrɛst] *n* : crête *f*

crevice [ˈkrɛvɪs] *n* : fissure *f,* fente *f*

crew [ˈkru:] *n* **1** : équipage *m* (d'un navire) **2** TEAM : équipe *f*

crib [ˈkrɪb] *n* : lit *m* d'enfant

cricket [ˈkrɪkət] *n* **1** : grillon *m* (insecte) **2** : cricket *m* (jeu)

crime [ˈkraɪm] *n* : crime *m,* délit *m* — **criminal** [ˈkrɪmənəl] *adj* : criminel — ~ *n* : criminel *m,* -nelle *f*

cringe [ˈkrɪnʤ] *vi* **cringed; cringing** : reculer (devant)

crinkle [ˈkrɪŋkəl] *vt* **-kled; -kling** : froisser, chiffonner

cripple [ˈkrɪpəl] *vt* **-pled; -pling** **1** DISABLE : estropier **2** INCAPACITATE : paralyser

crisis [ˈkraɪsɪs] *n, pl* **-ses** [-ˌsi:z] : crise *f*

crisp [ˈkrɪsp] *adj* : croustillant, croquant — **crispy** [ˈkrɪspi] *adj* **crispier; -est** : croustillant, croquant

crisscross [ˈkrɪsˌkrɔs] *vt* : entrecroiser

criterion [kraɪˈtɪriən] *n, pl* **-ria** [-riə] : critère *m*

critic [ˈkrɪt̬ɪk] *n* : critique *mf* — **critical** [ˈkrɪt̬ɪkəl] *adj* : critique — **criticism** [ˈkrɪt̬əˌsɪzəm] *n* : critique *f* — **criticize** [ˈkrɪt̬əˌsaɪz] *vt* **-cized; -cizing** : critiquer

croak [ˈkro:k] *vi* : coasser

crockery [ˈkrɑkəri] *n* : faïence *f*

crocodile [ˈkrɑkəˌdaɪl] *n* : crocodile *m*

crony [ˈkro:ni] *n, pl* **-nies** : copain *m,* -pine *f*

crook [ˈkrʊk] *n* **1** STAFF : houlette *f* (d'un berger) **2** THIEF : escroc *m* **3** BEND : courbe *f* — **crooked** [ˈkrʊkəd]

adj **1** BENT : crochu, courbé **2** DISHONEST : malhonnête
crop [ˈkrɑp] *n* **1** HARVEST : récolte *f*, moisson *f* **2** PRODUCE : culture *f* — **~** *v* **cropped; cropping** *vt* TRIM : tailler — *vi* **~ up** : surgir, se présenter
cross [ˈkrɔs] *n* : croix *f* — **~** *vt* **1** : traverser (la rue, etc.) **2** CROSSBREED : croiser **3** OPPOSE : contrarier **4** : croiser (les bras, etc.) **5 ~ out** : rayer — **~** *adj* **1** ANGRY : fâché, contrarié **2 ~ street** : rue *f* transversale — **crossbreed** [ˈkrɔsˌbri:d] *vt* **-bred** [-bred]; **-breeding** : croiser (deux espèces) — **cross–eyed** [ˈkrɔsˌaɪd] *adj* : qui louche — **cross fire** *n* : feux *mpl* croisés — **crossing** [ˈkrɔsɪŋ] *n* **1** : croisement *m* **2** → **crosswalk** — **cross–reference** [ˌkrɔsˈrɛfrənts, -ˈrɛfərənts] *n* : renvoi *m* — **crossroads** [ˈkrɔsˌro:dz] *n* : carrefour *m* — **cross section** *n* **1** : coupe *f* transversale **2** SAMPLE : échantillon *m* — **crosswalk** [ˈkrɔsˌwɔk] *n* : passage *m* pour piétons — **crossword puzzle** [ˈkrɔsˌwərd] *n* : mots *mpl* croisés
crotch [ˈkrɑʧ] *n* : entre-jambes *m*
crouch [ˈkraʊʧ] *vi* : s'accroupir
crow [ˈkro:] *n* : corbeau *m* — **~** *vi* **crowed** *or Brit* **crew; crowing** : chanter (se dit du coq)
crowbar [ˈkro:ˌbɑr] *n* : (pince à) levier *m*
crowd [ˈkraʊd] *vi* : se presser, s'entasser — *vt* : serrer, entasser — **~** *n* : foule *f*
crown [ˈkraʊn] *n* : couronne *f* — **~** *vt* : couronner
crucial [ˈkru:ʃəl] *adj* : crucial
crucify [ˈkru:səˌfaɪ] *vt* **-fied; -fying** : crucifier — **crucifix** [ˈkru:səˌfɪks] *n* : crucifix *m* — **crucifixion** [ˌkru:səˈfɪkʃən] *n* : crucifixion *f*
crude [ˈkru:d] *adj* **cruder; crudest 1** RAW : brut **2** VULGAR : grossier **3** ROUGH : rudimentaire
cruel [ˈkru:əl] *adj* **-eler** *or* **-eller; -elest** *or* **-ellest** : cruel — **cruelty** [ˈkru:əlti] *n, pl* **-ties** : cruauté *f*
cruet [ˈkru:ɪt] *n* : huilier *m*, vinaigrier *m*
cruise [ˈkru:z] *vi* **cruised; cruising** : rouler à sa vitesse de croisière — **~** *n* : croisière *f* — **cruiser** [ˈkru:zər] *n* **1** WARSHIP : croiseur *m* **2** *or* **police ~** : véhicule *m* de police
crumb [ˈkrʌm] *n* : miette *f*
crumble [ˈkrʌmbəl] *v* **-bled; -bling** *vt* : émietter — *vi* : s'émietter, s'effriter
crumple [ˈkrʌmpəl] *vt* **-pled; -pling** : froisser, chiffonner
crunch [ˈkrʌnʧ] *vt* : croquer — **crunchy** [ˈkrʌnʧi] *adj* **crunchier; -est** : croquant
crusade [kru:ˈseɪd] *n* : croisade *f*, campagne *f*
crush [ˈkrʌʃ] *vt* : écraser, aplatir — **~** *n* **have a ~ on s.o.** : avoir le béguin pour qqn
crust [ˈkrʌst] *n* : croûte *f*
crutch [ˈkrʌʧ] *n* : béquille *f*
crux [ˈkrʌks, krʊks] *n* : point *m* crucial, cœur *m*
cry [ˈkraɪ] *vi* **cried; crying 1** SHOUT : crier, pousser un cri **2** WEEP : pleurer — **~** *n, pl* **cries** : cri *m*
crypt [ˈkrɪpt] *n* : crypte *f*
crystal [ˈkrɪstəl] *n* : cristal *m*
cub [ˈkʌb] *n* : petit *m* (d'un animal)
cube [ˈkju:b] *n* : cube *m* — **cubic** [ˈkju:bɪk] *adj* : cube, cubique
cubicle [ˈkju:bɪkəl] *n* : box *m*
cuckoo [ˈku:ˌku:, ˈkʊ-] *n, pl* **-oos** : coucou *m* (oiseau)
cucumber [ˈkju:ˌkʌmbər] *n* : concombre *m*
cuddle [ˈkʌdəl] *v* **-dled; -dling** *vt* : caresser, câliner — *vi* : se câliner
cudgel [ˈkʌʤəl] *n* : gourdin *m*, trique *f*
cue[1] [ˈkju:] *n* SIGNAL : signal *m*
cue[2] *n or* **~ stick** : queue *f* de billard
cuff [ˈkʌf] *n* : poignet *m* (de chemise), revers *m* (de pantalon)
cuisine [kwɪˈzi:n] *n* : cuisine *f*
culinary [ˈkʌləˌnɛri, ˈkju:lə-] *adj* : culinaire
cull [ˈkʌl] *vt* : choisir, sélectionner
culminate [ˈkʌlməˌneɪt] *vi* **-nated; -nating** : culminer — **culmination** [ˌkʌlməˈneɪʃən] *n* : point *m* culminant
culprit [ˈkʌlprɪt] *n* : coupable *mf*
cult [ˈkʌlt] *n* : culte *m*
cultivate [ˈkʌltəˌveɪt] *vt* **-vated; -vating** : cultiver — **cultivation** [ˌkʌltəˈveɪʃən] *n* : culture *f* (de la terre)
culture [ˈkʌlʧər] *n* : culture *f* — **cultural** [ˈkʌlʧərəl] *adj* : culturel — **cultured** [ˈkʌltlərd] *adj* : cultivé
cumbersome [ˈkʌmbərsəm] *adj* : encombrant
cumulative [ˈkju:mjələṭɪv, -ˌleɪṭɪv] *adj* : cumulatif
cunning [ˈkʌnɪŋ] *adj* : astucieux — **~** *n* : ruse *f*, astuce *f*
cup [ˈkʌp] *n* **1** : tasse *f* **2** TROPHY : coupe *f*
cupboard [ˈkʌbərd] *n* : placard *m*, armoire *f*

curator [ˈkjʊrˌeɪt̬ər, kjʊˈreɪt̬ər] *n* : conservateur *m*, -trice *f*
curb [ˈkərb] *n* **1** RESTRAINT : contrainte *f*, frein *m* **2** : bord *m* du trottoir — ~ *vt* : mettre un frein à
curdle [ˈkərdəl] *vi* **-dled; -dling** : (se) cailler
cure [ˈkjʊr] *n* : remède *m* — ~ *vt* **cured; curing** : guérir
curfew [ˈkərˌfju:] *n* : couvre-feu *m*
curious [ˈkjʊriəs] *adj* : curieux — **curiosity** [ˌkjʊriˈɑsət̬i] *n, pl* **-ties** : curiosité *f*
curl [ˈkərl] *vt* **1** : friser, boucler **2** COIL : enrouler — *vi* **1** : boucler (se dit des cheveux) **2** ~ **up** : se pelotonner — ~ *n* : boucle *f* (de cheveux) — **curler** [ˈkərlər] *n* : bigoudi *m* — **curly** [ˈkərli] *adj* **curlier; -est** : bouclé, frisé
currant [ˈkərənt] *n* **1** BERRY : groseille *f* **2** RAISIN : raisin *m* de Corinthe
currency [ˈkərəntsi] *n, pl* **-cies 1** : monnaie *f*, devise *f* **2 gain** ~ : se répandre
current [ˈkərənt] *adj* **1** PRESENT : en cours **2** PREVALENT : courant, commun — ~ *n* : courant *m*
curriculum [kəˈrɪkjələm] *n, pl* **-la** [-lə] : programme *m* (scolaire)
curry [ˈkəri] *n, pl* **-ries** : curry *m*
curse [ˈkərs] *n* : malédiction *f* — ~ *v* **cursed; cursing** *vt* : maudire — *vi* SWEAR : sacrer, jurer
cursor [ˈkərsər] *n* : curseur *m*
cursory [ˈkərsəri] *adj* : superficiel, hâtif
curt [ˈkərt] *adj* : brusque
curtail [kərˈteɪl] *vt* : écourter
curtain [ˈkərtən] *n* : rideau *m*
curtsy [ˈkərtsi] *vi* **-sied;** *or* **-seyed;** *or* **-sying** *or* **-seying** : faire une révérence — ~ *n* : révérence *f*
curve [ˈkərv] *v* **curved; curving** *vt* : courber — *vi* : se courber, faire une courbe — ~ *n* : courbe *f*
cushion [ˈkʊʃən] *n* : coussin *m* — ~ *vt* : amortir
custard [ˈkʌstərd] *n* : flan *m*
custody [ˈkʌstədi] *n, pl* **-dies 1** CARE : garde *f* **2 be in** ~ : être en détention
custom [ˈkʌstəm] *n* : coutume *f*, tradition *f* — ~ *adj* : fait sur commande — **customary** [ˈkʌstəˌmɛri] *adj* : habituel, coutumier — **customer** [ˈkʌstəmər] *n* : client *m*, cliente *f* — **customs** [ˈkʌstˈmz] *npl* : douane *f*
cut [ˈkʌt] *v* **cut; cutting** *vt* **1** : couper **2** REDUCE : réduire **3** ~ **oneself** : se couper (le doigt, etc.) **4** *or* ~ **up** : découper — *vi* **1** : couper **2** ~ **in** : interrompre — ~ *n* **1** : coupure *f* **2** REDUCTION : réduction *f*
cute [ˈkju:t] *adj* **cuter; cutest** : mignon, joli
cutlery [ˈkʌtləri] *n* : couverts *mpl*
cutlet [ˈkʌtlət] *n* : escalope *f*
cutting [ˈkʌt̬ɪŋ] *adj* **1** : cinglant (se dit du vent) **2** CURT : mordant, tranchant
cyanide [ˈsaɪəˌnaɪd, -nɪd] *n* : cyanure *m*
cycle [ˈsaɪkəl] *n* : cycle *m* — ~ *vi* **-cled; -cling** : faire de la bicyclette — **cyclic** [ˈsaɪklɪk, ˈsɪ-] *or* **cyclical** [-klɪkəl] *adj* : cyclique — **cyclist** [ˈsaɪklɪst] *n* : cycliste *mf*
cyclone [ˈsaɪˌklo:n] *n* : cyclone *m*
cylinder [ˈsɪləndər] *n* : cylindre *m* — **cylindrical** [səˈlɪndrɪkəl] *adj* : cylindrique
cymbal [ˈsɪmbəl] *n* : cymbale *f*
cynic [ˈsɪnɪk] *n* : cynique *mf* — **cynical** [ˈsɪnɪkəl] *adj* : cynique — **cynicism** [ˈsɪnəˌsɪzəm] *n* : cynisme *m*
cypress [ˈsaɪprəs] *n* : cyprès *m*
cyst [ˈsɪst] *n* : kyste *m*
czar [ˈzɑr, ˈsɑr] *n* : tsar *m*

D

d [ˈdi:] *n, pl* **d's** *or* **ds** [ˈdi:z] : d *m*, quatrième lettre de l'alphabet
dab [ˈdæb] *n* : touche *f*, petite quantité *f* — ~ *vt* **dabbed; dabbing** : appliquer délicatement
dabble [ˈdæbəl] *vi* **-bled; -bling** ~ **in** : s'intéresser superficiellement à
dad [ˈdæd] *n* : papa *m fam* — **daddy** [ˈdædi] *n, pl* **-dies** : papa *m fam*
daffodil [ˈdæfəˌdɪl] *n* : jonquille *f*
dagger [ˈdægər] *n* : poignard *m*
daily [ˈdeɪli] *adj* : quotidien — ~ *adv* : quotidiennement
dainty [ˈdeɪnti] *adj* **-tier; -est** : délicat
dairy [ˈdæri] *n, pl* **dairies** : laiterie *f*, crémerie *f France*
daisy [ˈdeɪzi] *n, pl* **-sies** : marguerite *f*
dam [ˈdæm] *n* : barrage *m*
damage [ˈdæmɪʤ] *n* **1** : dégâts *mpl* **2** ~**s** *npl* : dommages *mpl* et intérêts *mpl* — ~ *vt* **-aged; -aging** : endommager (des objets), abîmer (sa santé)

damn ['dæm] *vt* **1** CONDEMN : condamner **2** CURSE : maudire — **~** *n* **not give a ~** : s'en ficher *fam* — **~** *or* **damned** ['dæmd] *adj* : fichu *fam*, sacré *fam*
damp ['dæmp] *adj* : humide, moite — **dampen** ['dæmpən] *vt* **1** MOISTEN : humecter **2** DISCOURAGE : décourager — **dampness** ['dæmpnəs] *n* : humidité *f*
dance ['dænts] *v* **danced; dancing** : danser — **~** *n* : danse *f* — **dancer** ['dæntsər] *n* : danseur *m*, -seuse *f*
dandelion ['dænd'l,aɪən] *n* : pissenlit *m*
dandruff ['dændrəf] *n* : pellicules *fpl*
danger ['deɪndʒər] *n* : danger *m* — **dangerous** ['deɪndʒərəs] *adj* : dangereux
dangle ['dæŋgəl] *v* **-gled; -gling** *vi* HANG : pendre — *vt* : balancer, laisser pendre
dank ['dæŋk] *adj* : froid et humide
dare ['dær] *v* **dared; daring** *vt* : défier — *vi* : oser — **~** *n* : défi *m* — **daring** ['deɪrɪŋ] *adj* : audacieux, hardi
dark ['dɑrk] *adj* **1** : noir **2** : foncé (se dit des cheveux, etc.) **3** GLOOMY : sombre **4 get ~** : faire nuit — **darken** ['dɑrkən] *vt* : obscurcir — *vi* : s'obscurcir — **darkness** ['dɑrknəs] *n* : obscurité *f*, noirceur *f Can*
darling ['dɑrlɪŋ] *n* BELOVED : chéri *m*, -rie *f* — **~** *adj* : chéri
darn ['dɑrn] *vt* : repriser (en couture) — **~** *adj* : sacré
dart ['dɑrt] *n* **1** : fléchette *f*, dard *m Can* **2 ~s** *npl* : fléchettes *fpl* (jeu) — **~** *vi* : se précipiter, s'élancer
dash ['dæʃ] *vt* **~ off** : terminer à la hâte — *vi* : se précipiter — **~** *n* **1** : tiret *m* (signe de ponctuation) **2** PINCH : pincée *f*, soupçon *m* **3** RUSH : course *f* folle — **dashboard** ['dæʃ,bord] *n* : tableau *m* de bord — **dashing** ['dæʃɪŋ] *adj* : fringant, élégant
data ['deɪṭə, 'dæ-, 'dɑ-] *ns & pl* : données *fpl* — **database** ['deɪṭə,beɪs, 'dæ-, 'dɑ-] *n* : base *f* de données
date[1] ['deɪt] *n* : datte *f* (fruit)
date[2] *n* **1** : date *f* **2** APPOINTMENT : rendez-vous *m* — **~** *v* **dated; dating** *vt* **1** : dater (un chèque, etc.) **2** : sortir avec (qqn) — *vi* **~ from** : dater de, remonter à — **dated** ['deɪṭəd] *adj* : démodé
daughter ['dɔṭər] *n* : fille *f* — **daughter-in-law** ['dɔṭərɪn,lɔ] *n, pl* **daughters-in-law** : belle-fille *f*, bru *f*
daunt ['dɔnt] *vt* : décourager
dawdle ['dɔdəl] *vi* **-dled; -dling** : lambiner *fam*, traîner
dawn ['dɔn] *vi* **1** : se lever (se dit du jour) **2 it ~ed on him that** : il s'est rendu compte que — **~** *n* : aube *f*
day ['deɪ] *n* **1** : jour *m* **2** *or* **working ~** : journée *f* (de travail) **3 the ~ before** : la veille **4 the ~ before yesterday** : avant-hier **5 the ~ after** : le lendemain **6 the ~ after tomorrow** : après-demain — **daybreak** ['deɪ,breɪk] *n* : aube *f* — **daydream** ['deɪ,dri:m] *n* : rêve *m*, rêverie *f* — **~** *vi* : rêver — **daylight** ['deɪ,laɪt] *n* : lumière *f* du jour — **daytime** ['deɪ,taɪm] *n* : jour *m*, journée *f*
daze ['deɪz] *vt* **dazed; dazing** : abasourdir — **~** *n* **in a ~** : hébété
dazzle ['dæzəl] *vt* **-zled; -zling** : éblouir
dead ['dɛd] *adj* : mort — **~** *n* **the ~** : les morts — **~** *adv* COMPLETELY : complètement — **deaden** ['dɛdən] *vt* **1** : calmer (une douleur) **2** MUFFLE : assourdir — **dead end** ['dɛd'ɛnd] *n* : cul-de-sac *m*, impasse *f* — **deadline** ['dɛd,laɪn] *n* : date *f* limite — **deadly** ['dɛdli] *adj* **-lier; -est** : mortel — **dealings** ['di:lɪŋz] *npl* : transactions *fpl*, affaires *fpl*
deaf ['dɛf] *adj* : sourd — **deafen** ['dɛfən] *vt* : assourdir — **deafness** ['dɛfnəs] *n* : surdité *f*
deal ['di:l] *n* **1** TRANSACTION : affaire *f*, marché *m* **2** : donne *f* (aux cartes) — **~** *v* **dealt; dealing** *vt* **1** : donner **2** : distribuer (des cartes) **3 ~ a blow** : assener un coup — *vi* **~ with** CONCERN : traiter de — **dealer** ['di:lər] *n* : marchand *m*, -chande *f*; négociant *m*, -ciante *f*
dean ['di:n] *n* : doyen *m*, doyenne *f*
dear ['dɪr] *adj* : cher — **~** *n* : chéri *m*, -rie *f* — **dearly** ['dɪrli] *adv* : beaucoup
death ['dɛθ] *n* : mort *f*
debate [di'beɪt] *n* : débat *m*, discussion *f* — **~** *v* **-bated; -bating** : discuter
debit ['dɛbɪt] *vt* : débiter — **~** *n* : débit *m*
debris [də'bri:, deɪ-; 'deɪ,bri:] *n, pl* **-bris** [-'bri:z, -,bri:z] : décombres *mpl*
debt ['dɛt] *n* : dette *f*
debug [,di:'bʌg] *vt* : déboguer
debut [deɪ'bju:, 'deɪ,bju:] *n* : débuts *mpl* — **~** *vi* : débuter
decade ['dɛ,keɪd, dɛ'keɪd] *n* : décennie *f*
decadence ['dɛkədənts] *n* : décadence *f* — **decadent** ['dɛkədənt] *adj* : décadent

decanter [di'kæntər] *n* : carafe *f*
decay [di'keɪ] *vi* **1** DECOMPOSE : se décomposer, pourrir **2** : se carier (se dit d'une dent) — **~** *n* **1** : pourriture *f* **2** *or* **tooth ~** : carie *f* (dentaire)
deceased [di'si:st] *adj* : décédé, défunt — **~** *n* **the ~** : le défunt, la défunte
deceive [di'si:v] *vt* **-ceived; -ceiving** : tromper — **deceit** [di'si:t] *n* : tromperie *f* — **deceitful** [di'si:tfəl] *adj* : trompeur
December [di'sɛmbər] *n* : décembre *m*
decent ['di:sənt] *adj* **1** : décent, convenable **2** KIND : bien, aimable — **decency** ['disəntsi] *n, pl* **-cies** : décence *f*
deception [di'sɛpʃən] *n* : tromperie *f* — **deceptive** [di'sɛptɪv] *adj* : trompeur
decide [di'saɪd] *v* **-cided; -ciding** *vt* : décider — *vi* : se décider — **decided** [di'saɪdəd] *adj* RESOLUTE : décidé
decimal ['dɛsəməl] *adj* : décimal — **~** *n* : décimale *f* — **decimal point** *n* : virgule *f*
decipher [di'saɪfər] *vt* : déchiffrer
decision [dɪ'sɪʒən] *n* : décision *f* — **decisive** [dɪ'saɪsɪv] *adj* **1** RESOLUTE : décidé **2** CONCLUSIVE : décisif
deck ['dɛk] *n* **1** : pont *m* (d'un navire) **2** *or* **~ of cards** : jeu *m* de cartes
declare [di'klær] *vt* **-clared; -claring** : déclarer — **declaration** [ˌdɛklə'reɪʃən] *n* : déclaration *f*
decline [di'klaɪn] *v* **-clined; -clining** : décliner — **~** *n* **1** DETERIORATION : déclin *m* **2** DECREASE : baisse *f*
decompose [ˌdi:kəm'po:z] *vt* **-posed; -posing** : décomposer — *vi* : se décomposer
decongestant [ˌdi:kən'ʤɛstənt] *n* : décongestif *m*
decorate ['dɛkəˌreɪt] *vt* **-rated; -rating** : décorer — **decor** *or* **décor** [deɪ'kɔr, 'deɪˌkɔr] *n* : décor *m* — **decoration** [ˌdɛkə'reɪʃən] *n* : décoration *f* — **decorative** ['dɛkərəţɪv, -ˌreɪ-] *adj* : décoratif — **decorator** ['dɛkəˌreɪţər] *n* : décorateur *m*, -trice *f*
decoy ['diˌkɔɪ, di'-] *n* : appeau *m*
decrease [di'kri:s] *v* **-creased; -creasing** : diminuer — **~** ['di:ˌkri:s] *n* : diminution *f*
decree [di'kri:] *n* : décret *m* — **~** *vt* **-creed; -creeing** : décréter
decrepit [di'krɛpɪt] *adj* **1** FEEBLE : décrépit **2** DILAPIDATED : délabré
dedicate ['dɛdɪˌkeɪt] *vt* **-cated; -cating** **1** : dédier **2** **~ oneself to** : se consacrer à — **dedication** [dɛdɪ'keɪʃən] *n* **1** DEVOTION : dévouement *m* **2** INSCRIPTION : dédicace *f*
deduce [di'du:s, -'dju:s] *vt* **-duced; -ducing** : déduire — **deduct** [di'dʌkt] *vt* : déduire — **deduction** [di'dʌkʃən] *n* : déduction *f*
deed ['di:d] *n* : action *f*, acte *m*
deem ['di:m] *vt* : juger, considérer
deep ['di:p] *adj* : profond — **~** *adv* **1** DEEPLY : profondément **2** **~ down** : au fond — **deepen** ['di:pən] *vt* : approfondir — *vi* : devenir plus profond — **deeply** ['di:pli] *adv* : profondément
deer ['dɪr] *ns & pl* : cerf *m*
default [di'fɔlt, 'di:ˌfɔlt] *n* **by ~** : par défaut — **~** *vi* **1** : ne pas s'acquitter (d'une dette) **2** : déclarer forfait (aux sports)
defeat [di'fi:t] *vt* : battre, vaincre — **~** *n* : défaite *f*
defect ['di:ˌfɛkt, di'fɛkt] *n* : défaut *m* — **defective** [di'fɛktɪv] *adj* : défectueux
defence *Brit* → **defense**
defend [di'fɛnd] *vt* : défendre — **defendant** [di'fɛndənt] *n* : défendeur *m*, -deresse *f*; accusé *m*, -sée *f* — **defense** *or Brit* **defence** [di'fɛnts, 'di:ˌfɛnts] *n* : défense *f* — **defensive** [di'fɛntsɪv] *adj* : défensif — **~** *n* **on the ~** : sur la défensive
defer [di'fər] *v* **-ferred; -ferring** *vt* : différer — *vi* **~ to** : s'en remettre à
defiance [di'faɪənts] *n* **1** : défi *m* **2** **in ~ of** : au mépris de — **defiant** [di'faɪənt] *adj* : de défi
deficient [di'fɪʃənt] *adj* **1** INADEQUATE : insuffisant **2** FAULTY : défectueux — **deficiency** [di'fɪʃəntsi] *n, pl* **-cies** **1** LACK : carence *f* **2** FLAW : défaut *m*
deficit ['dɛfəsɪt] *n* : déficit *m*
defile [di'faɪl] *vt* **-filed; -filing** DESECRATE : profaner
define [di'faɪn] *vt* **-fined; -fining** : définir — **definite** ['dɛfənɪt] *adj* **1** : défini, précis **2** CERTAIN : certain, sûr — **definitely** ['dɛfənɪtli] *adv* : certainement — **definition** [ˌdɛfə'nɪʃən] *n* : définition *f* — **definitive** [də'fɪnəţɪv] *adj* : définitif
deflate [di'fleɪt] *v* **-flated; -flating** *vt* : dégonfler (un pneu, etc.) — *vi* : se dégonfler
deflect [di'flɛkt] *vt* : faire dévier — *vi* : dévier
deform [di'fɔrm] *vt* : déformer — **deformity** [di'fɔrməţi] *n, pl* **-ties** : difformité *f*
defraud [di'frɔd] *vt* : frauder, escroquer
defrost [di'frɔst] *vt* THAW : décongeler

defy [diˈfaɪ] *vt* **-fied; -fying 1** CHALLENGE : défier **2** RESIST : résister à
degenerate [diˈʤɛnəˌreɪt] *vi* **-ated; -ating** : dégénérer
degrade [diˈgreɪd] *vt* **-graded; -grading** : dégrader — **degrading** *adj* : dégradant
degree [diˈgri:] *n* **1** : degré *m* **2** *or* **academic ~** : diplôme *m*
dehydrate [diˈhaɪˌdreɪt] *vt* **-drated; -drating** : déshydrater
deign [ˈdeɪn] *vi* **~ to** : daigner
deity [ˈdi:əṭi, ˈdeɪ-] *n, pl* **-ties** : dieu *m,* déesse *f*
dejected [diˈʤɛktəd] *adj* : abattu — **dejection** [diˈʤɛkʃən] *n* : abattement *m*
delay [diˈleɪ] *n* : retard *m,* délai *m* — **~** *vt* **1** POSTPONE : différer **2** HOLD UP : retarder
delectable [diˈlɛktəbəl] *adj* : délicieux
delegate [ˈdɛlɪgət, -ˌgeɪt] *n* : délégué *m,* -guée *f* — **~** [ˈdɛlɪˌgeɪt] *v* **-gated; -gating** : déléguer — **delegation** [ˌdɛlɪˈgeɪʃən] *n* : délégation *f*
delete [diˈli:t] *vt* **-leted; -leting** : supprimer, effacer
deliberate [dɪˈlɪbəˌreɪt] *v* **-ated; -ating** *vt* : délibérer sur — *vi* : délibérer — **~** [dɪˈlɪbərət] *adj* : délibéré — **deliberately** [dɪˈlɪbərətli] *adv* : exprès
delicacy [ˈdɛlɪkəsi] *n, pl* **-cies 1** : délicatesse *f* **2** FOOD : mets *m* fin — **delicate** [ˈdɛlɪkət] *adj* : délicat
delicatessen [ˌdɛlɪkəˈtɛsən] *n* : charcuterie *f*
delicious [diˈlɪʃəs] *adj* : délicieux
delight [diˈlaɪt] *n* : plaisir *m,* joie *f* — **~** *vt* : réjouir — *vi* **~ in** : prendre plaisir à — **delightful** [diˈlaɪtfəl] *adj* : charmant, ravissant
delinquent [diˈlɪŋkwənt] *adj* : délinquant — **~** *n* : délinquant *m,* -quante *f*
delirious [diˈlɪriəs] *adj* : délirant, en délire — **delirium** [diˈlɪriəm] *n* : délire *m*
deliver [diˈlɪvər] *vt* **1** DISTRIBUTE : livrer **2** FREE : libérer **3** : mettre au monde (un enfant) **4** : prononcer (un discours, etc.) **5** DEAL : asséner (un coup, etc.) — **delivery** [diˈlɪvəri] *n, pl* **-eries 1** DISTRIBUTION : livraison *f,* distribution *f* **2** LIBERATION : délivrance *f* **3** CHILDBIRTH : accouchement *m*
delude [diˈlu:d] *vt* **-luded; -luding 1** : tromper **2 ~ oneself** : se faire des illusions
deluge [ˈdɛlˌju:ʤ, -ju:ʒ] *n* : déluge *m*
delusion [diˈlu:ʒən] *n* : illusion *f*
deluxe [diˈlʌks, -ˈlʊks] *adj* : de luxe
delve [ˈdɛlv] *vi* **delved; delving 1** : creuser **2 ~ into** PROBE : fouiller dans
demand [diˈmænd] *n* **1** REQUEST : demande *f* **2** CLAIM : réclamation *f* **3** → **supply** — **~** *vt* : exiger — **demanding** [ˈdiˈmændɪŋ] *adj* : exigeant
demean [diˈmi:n] *vt* **~ oneself** : s'abaisser
demeanor *or Brit* **demeanour** [diˈmi:nər] *n* : comportement *m*
demented [diˈmɛntəd] *adj* : dément, fou
democracy [diˈmɑkrəsi] *n, pl* **-cies** : démocratie *f* — **democrat** [ˈdɛməˌkræt] *n* : démocrate *mf* — **democratic** [ˌdɛməˈkræṭɪk] *adj* : démocratique
demolish [diˈmɑlɪʃ] *vt* : démolir — **demolition** [ˌdɛməˈlɪʃən, ˌdi:-] *n* : démolition *f*
demon [ˈdi:mən] *n* : démon *m*
demonstrate [ˈdɛmənˌstreɪt] *v* **-strated; -strating** *vt* : démontrer — *vi* RALLY : manifester — **demonstration** [dɛmənˈstreɪʃən] *n* **1** : démonstration *f* **2** RALLY : manifestation *f* — **demonstrative** [diˈmɑntstrəṭɪv] *adj* : démonstratif — **demonstrator** [ˈdɛmənˌstreɪṭər] *n* PROTESTOR : manifestant *m,* -tante *f*
demoralize [diˈmɔrəˌlaɪz] *vt* **-ized; -izing** : démoraliser
demote [diˈmo:t] *vt* **-moted; -moting** : rétrograder
demure [diˈmjʊr] *adj* : modeste, réservé
den [ˈdɛn] *n* LAIR : antre *m,* tanière *f*
denial [diˈnaɪəl] *n* **1** : démenti *m,* dénégation *f* **2** REFUSAL : refus *m*
denim [ˈdɛnəm] *n* : jean *m*
denomination [dɪˌnɑməˈneɪʃən] *n* **1** : confession *f* (religieuse) **2** : valeur *f* (monétaire)
denote [diˈno:t] *vt* **-noted; -noting** : dénoter
denounce [diˈnaʊnts] *vt* **-nounced; -nouncing** : dénoncer
dense [ˈdɛnts] *adj* **denser; -est 1** THICK : dense **2** STUPID : bête, obtus — **density** [ˈdɛntsəṭi] *n, pl* **-ties** : densité *f*
dent [ˈdɛnt] *vt* : cabosser — **~** *n* : bosse *f*
dental [ˈdɛntəl] *adj* : dentaire — **dental floss** *n* : fil *m* dentaire — **dentist** [ˈdɛntɪst] *n* : dentiste *mf* — **dentures** [ˈdɛnʧərz] *npl* : dentier *m*

denunciation [di,nʌntsi'eɪʃən] *n* : dénonciation *f*
deny [di'naɪ] *vt* **-nied; -nying 1** : nier **2** REFUSE : refuser
deodorant [di'o:dərənt] *n* : déodorant *m*
depart [di'pɑrt] *vi* **1** : partir **2 ~ from** : s'écarter de
department [di'pɑrtmənt] *n* : ministère *m* (gouvernemental), service *m* (d'un hôpital, etc.), rayon *m* (d'un magasin) — **department store** *n* : grand magasin *m*
departure [di'pɑrtʃər] *n* **1** : départ *m* **2** DEVIATION : écart *m*
depend [di'pɛnd] *vi* **1 ~ on** : dépendre de, compter sur **2 ~ on s.o.** : compter sur qqn **3 that ~s** : tout dépend — **dependable** [di'pɛndəbəl] *adj* : digne de confiance — **dependence** [di'pɛndənts] *n* : dépendance *f* — **dependent** [di'pɛndənt] *adj* : dépendant
depict [di'pɪkt] *vt* **1** PORTRAY : représenter **2** DESCRIBE : dépeindre
deplete [di'pli:t] *vt* **-pleted; -pleting** : épuiser, réduire
deplore [di'plor] *vt* **-plored; -ploring** : déplorer — **deplorable** [di'plorəbəl] *adj* : déplorable
deploy [di'plɔɪ] *vt* : déployer
deport [di'port] *vt* : expulser (d'un pays) — **deportation** [,di,por'teɪʃən] *n* : expulsion *f*
deposit [di'pɑzət] *vt* **-ited; -iting** : déposer — **~** *n* **1** : dépôt *m* **2** DOWN PAYMENT : acompte *m,* arrhes *fpl France*
depreciate [di'pri:ʃi,eɪt] *vi* **-ated; -ating** : se déprécier — **depreciation** [di,pri:ʃi'eɪʃən] *n* : dépréciation *f*
depress [di'prɛs] *vt* **1** PRESS : appuyer sur **2** SADDEN : déprimer — **depressed** [di'prɛst] *adj* : déprimé — **depressing** [di'prɛsɪŋ] *adj* : déprimant — **depression** [di'prɛʃən] *n* : dépression *f*
deprive [di'praɪv] *vt* **-prived; -priving** : priver
depth ['dɛpθ] *n, pl* **depths** : profondeur *f*
deputy ['dɛpjuṭi] *n, pl* **-ties** : adjoint *m,* -jointe *f*
derail [di'reɪl] *vi* : dérailler — **derailment** [di'reɪlmənt] *n* : déraillement *m*
deride [di'raɪd] *vt* **-rided; -riding** : railler — **derision** [di'rɪʒən] *n* : dérision *f*
derive [di'raɪv] *vi* **-rived; -riving ~ from** : provenir de
derogatory [di'rɑgə,tori] *adj* : désobligeant
descend [di'sɛnd] *v* : descendre — **descendant** [di'sɛndənt] *n* : descendant *m,* -dante *f* — **descent** [di'sɛnt] *n* **1** : descente *f* **2** LINEAGE : descendance *f*
describe [di'skraɪb] *vt* **-scribed; -scribing** : décrire — **description** [di'skrɪpʃən] *n* : description *f* — **descriptive** [di'skrɪptɪv] *adj* : descriptif
desecrate ['dɛsɪ,kreɪt] *vt* **-crated; -crating** : profaner
desert ['dɛzərt] *n* : désert *m* — **~** *adj* **~ island** : île *f* déserte — **~** [di'zərt] *vt* : abandonner — *vi* : déserter — **deserter** [di'zərṭər] *n* : déserteur *m*
deserve [di'zərv] *vt* **-served; -serving** : mériter
design [di'zaɪn] *vt* **1** DEVISE : concevoir **2** DRAW : dessiner — **~** *n* **1** : conception *f* **2** PLAN : plan *m* **3** SKETCH : dessin *m* **4** PATTERN : motif *m*
designate ['dɛzɪg,neɪt] *vt* **-nated; -nating** : désigner
designer [di'zaɪnər] *n* : dessinateur *m,* -trice *f*
desire [di'zaɪr] *vt* **-sired; -siring** : désirer — **~** *n* : désir *m*
desk ['dɛsk] *n* : bureau *m,* pupitre *m* (d'un élève)
desolate ['dɛsələt, -zə-] *adj* : désolé
despair [di'spær] *vi* : désespérer — **~** *n* : désespoir *m*
desperate ['dɛspərət] *adj* : désespéré — **desperation** [,dɛspə'reɪʃən] *n* : désespoir *m*
despise [di'spaɪz] *vt* **-spised; -spising** : mépriser — **despicable** [di'spɪkəbəl, 'dɛspɪ-] *adj* : méprisable
despite [də'spaɪt] *prep* : malgré
dessert [di'zərt] *n* : dessert *m*
destination [,dɛstɪ'neɪʃən] *n* : destination *f* — **destined** ['dɛstənd] *adj* **1** : destiné **2 ~ for** : à destination de — **destiny** ['dɛstəni] *n, pl* **-nies** : destin *m,* destinée *f*
destitute ['dɛstə,tu:t, -,tju:t] *adj* : indigent
destroy [di'strɔɪ] *vt* : détruire — **destruction** [di'strʌkʃən] *n* : destruction *f* — **destructive** [di'strʌktɪv] *adj* : destructeur
detach [di'tætʃ] *vt* : détacher — **detached** [di'tætʃt] *adj* : détaché
detail [di'teɪl, 'di:,teɪl] *n* : détail *m* — **~** *vt* : détailler — **detailed** [di'teɪld, 'di:,teɪld] *adj* : détaillé

detain [di'teɪn] *vt* **1** : détenir (un prisonnier) **2** DELAY : retenir

detect [di'tɛkt] *vt* : détecter, déceler — **detection** [di'tɛkʃən] *n* : détection *f* — **detective** [di'tɛktɪv] *n* : détective *m*

detention [di'tɛntʃən] *n* : détention *f*

deter [di'tər] *vt* **-terred; -terring** : dissuader

detergent [di'tərdʒənt] *n* : détergent *m*

deteriorate [di'tɪriə,reɪt] *vi* **-rated; -rating** : se détériorer — **deterioration** [di,tɪriə'reɪʃən] *n* : détérioration *f*

determine [di'tərmən] *vt* **-mined; -mining** **1** : déterminer **2** RESOLVE : décider — **determined** [di'tərmənd] *adj* RESOLUTE : déterminé — **determination** [di,tərmə'neɪʃən] *n* : détermination *f*

detest [di'tɛst] *vt* : détester

detour ['di:,tʊr, di'tʊr] *n* : détour *m* — ~ *vi* : faire un détour

devastate ['dɛvə,steɪt] *vt* **-tated; -tating** : dévaster — **devastating** ['dɛvə,steɪtɪŋ] *adj* : accablant — **devastation** [,dɛvə'steɪʃən] *n* : dévastation *f*

develop [di'vɛləp] *vt* **1** : développer **2** ~ **an illness** : contracter une maladie — *vi* **1** GROW : se développer **2** HAPPEN : se manifester — **developing** [di'vɛləpɪŋ] *adj* **1** : en expansion **2** ~ **country** : pays en voie de développement — **development** [di'vɛləpmənt] *n* : développement *m*

deviate ['di:vi,eɪt] *vi* **-ated; -ating** : dévier, s'écarter

device [di'vaɪs] *n* : appareil *m*, mécanisme *m*

devil ['dɛvəl] *n* : diable *m* — **devilish** ['dɛvəlɪʃ] *adj* : diabolique

devious ['di:viəs] *adj* CRAFTY : sournois

devise [di'vaɪz] *vt* **-vised; -vising** : inventer, concevoir

devoid [di'vɔɪd] *adj* ~ **of** : dépourvu de

devote [di'vo:t] *vt* **-voted; -voting** : consacrer, dédier — **devoted** [di'vo:ṭəd] *adj* : dévoué — **devotion** [di'vo:ʃən] *n* **1** DEDICATION : dévouement *m* **2** PIETY : dévotion *f*

devour [di'vaʊər] *vt* : dévorer

devout [di'vaʊt] *adj* **1** PIOUS : dévot **2** EARNEST : fervent

dew ['du:, 'dju:] *n* : rosée *f*

dexterity [dɛk'stɛrəṭi] *n, pl* **-ties** : dextérité *f*

diabetes [,daɪə'bi:ṭiz] *n* : diabète *m* — **diabetic** [,daɪə'bɛṭɪk] *adj* : diabétique — ~ *n* : diabétique *mf*

diabolic [,daɪə'bɑlɪk] *or* **diabolical** [-lɪkəl] *adj* : diabolique

diagnosis [,daɪɪg'no:sɪs] *n, pl* **-ses** [-'no:,si:z] : diagnostic *m* — **diagnose** ['daɪɪg,no:s, ,daɪɪg'no:s] *vt* **-nosed; -nosing** : diagnostiquer

diagonal [daɪ'ægənəl] *adj* : diagonal — **diagonally** [daɪ'ægənəli] *adv* : en diagonale

diagram ['daɪə,græm] *n* : diagramme *m*

dial ['daɪl] *n* : cadran *m* (d'une horloge), bouton *m* (d'une radio) — ~ *vt* **-aled** *or* **-alled; -aling** *or* **-alling** : faire, composer (un numéro de téléphone)

dialect ['daɪə,lɛkt] *n* : dialecte *m*

dialogue ['daɪə,lɔg] *n* : dialogue *m*

diameter [daɪ'æməṭər] *n* : diamètre *m*

diamond ['daɪmənd, 'daɪə-] *n* **1** : diamant *m* **2** : losange *m* (forme géométrique) **3** : carreau *m* (aux cartes) **4** *or* **baseball** ~ : terrain *m* de baseball, losange *m Can*

diaper ['daɪpər, 'daɪə-] *n* : couche *f* (de bébé)

diaphragm ['daɪə,fræm] *n* : diaphragme *m*

diarrhea *or Brit* **diarrhoea** [,daɪə'ri:ə] *n* : diarrhée *f*

diary ['daɪəri:] *n, pl* **-ries** : journal *m* intime

dice ['daɪs] *ns & pl* : dé *m* (à jouer)

dictate ['dɪk,teɪt, dɪk'teɪt] *vt* **-tated; -tating** : dicter — **dictation** [dɪk'teɪʃən] *n* : dictée *f* — **dictator** ['dɪk,teɪṭər] *n* : dictateur *m*

dictionary ['dɪkʃə,nɛri] *n, pl* **-naries** : dictionnaire *m*

did → **do**

die[1] ['daɪ] *vi* **died** ['daɪd]; **dying** ['daɪɪŋ] **1** : mourir, décéder **2** *or* ~ **down** SUBSIDE : diminuer **3 be dying to** : mourir d'envie de

die[2] ['daɪ] *n, pl* **dice** ['daɪs] : dé *m* (à jouer)

diesel ['di:zəl, -səl] *n* : diesel *m*

diet ['daɪət] *n* **1** FOOD : alimentation *f* **2 go on a** ~ : être au régime — ~ *vi* : suivre un régime

differ ['dɪfər] *vi* **-ferred; -ferring** : différer — **difference** ['dɪfrənts, 'dɪfərənts] *n* : différence *f* — **different** ['dɪfrənt, 'dɪfərənt] *adj* : différent — **differentiate** [dɪfə'rɛntʃi,eɪt] *v* **-ated; -ating** *vt* : différencier — *vi* ~ **between** : faire la différence entre — **differently** ['dɪfrəntli, 'dɪfərəntli] *adv* : différemment

difficult ['dɪfɪ,kʌlt] *adj* : difficile — **dif-**

ficulty ['dɪfɪˌkʌlti] *n, pl* **-ties** : difficulté *f*
dig ['dɪg] *vt* **dug** ['dʌg]; **digging 1** : creuser **2 ~ up** : déterrer
digest ['daɪˌʤɛst] *n* : résumé *m* — **~** ['daɪˌʤɛst] *vt* **1** : digérer **2** SUMMARIZE : résumer — **digestion** [daɪ'ʤɛsʧən, dɪ-] *n* : digestion *f* — **digestive** [daɪ'ʤɛstɪv, dɪ-] *adj* : digestif
digit ['dɪʤət] *n* NUMERAL : chiffre *m* — **digital** ['dɪʤətəl] *adj* : digital
dignity ['dɪgnəti] *n, pl* **-ties** : dignité *f* — **dignified** ['dɪgnəˌfaɪd] *adj* : digne
digress [daɪ'grɛs, də-] *vi* : s'écarter (du sujet)
dike ['daɪk] *n* : digue *f*
dilapidated [də'læpəˌdeɪtəd] *adj* : délabré
dilate [daɪ'leɪt, 'daɪˌleɪt] *v* **-lated; -lating** *vt* : dilater — *vi* : se dilater
dilemma [dɪ'lɛmə] *n* : dilemme *m*
diligence ['dɪləʤənts] *n* : assiduité *f* — **diligent** ['dɪləʤənt] *adj* : assidu, appliqué
dilute [daɪ'lu:t, də-] *vt* **-luted; -luting** : diluer
dim ['dɪm] *v* **dimmed; dimming** *vt* : baisser — *vi* : baisser, s'affaiblir — **~** *adj* **dimmer; dimmest 1** DARK : sombre **2** FAINT : faible, vague
dime ['daɪm] *n* : pièce *f* de dix cents
dimension [də'mɛnʧən, daɪ-] *n* : dimension *f*
diminish [də'mɪnɪʃ] *v* : diminuer
diminutive [də'mɪnjʊtɪv] *adj* : minuscule
dimple ['dɪmpəl] *n* : fossette *f*
din ['dɪn] *n* : vacarme *m,* tapage *m*
dine ['daɪn] *vi* **dined; dining** : dîner — **diner** ['daɪnər] *n* **1** : dîneur *m,* -neuse *f* **2** : petit restaurant *m* — **dining room** *n* : salle *f* à manger — **dinner** ['dɪnər] *n* : dîner *m*
dinosaur ['daɪnəˌsɔr] *n* : dinosaure *m*
dip ['dɪp] *v* **dipped; dipping** *vt* : plonger, tremper — *vi* : baisser, descendre — **~** *n* **1** DROP : déclivité *f* **2** SWIM : petite baignade *f* **3** SAUCE : sauce *f*
diploma [də'plo:mə] *n* : diplôme *m*
diplomacy [də'plo:məsi] *n* : diplomatie *f* — **diplomat** ['dɪpləˌmæt] *n* : diplomate *mf* — **diplomatic** [ˌdɪplə'mætɪk] *adj* **1** : diplomatique **2** TACTFUL : diplomate
dire ['daɪr] *adj* **direr; direst 1** : grave, terrible **2** EXTREME : extrême
direct [də'rɛkt, daɪ-] *vt* **1** : diriger **2** ORDER : ordonner — **~** *adj* **1** STRAIGHT : direct **2** FRANK : franc — **~** *adv* : directement — **direct current** *n* : courant *m* continu — **direction** [də'rɛkʃən, daɪ-] *n* **1** : direction *f* **2 ask for ~s** : demander des indications — **directly** [də'rɛktli, daɪ-] *adv* **1** STRAIGHT : directement **2** IMMEDIATELY : tout de suite — **director** [də'rɛktər, daɪ-] *n* **1** : directeur *m,* -trice *f* **2 board of ~s** : conseil *m* d'administration — **directory** [də'rɛktəri, daɪ-] *n, pl* **-ries** : annuaire *m* (téléphonique)
dirt ['dərt] *n* **1** : saleté *f* **2** SOIL : terre *f* — **dirty** ['dərti] *adj* **dirtier; -est 1** : sale **2** INDECENT : obscène, cochon *fam* — **~** *vt* **dirtied; dirtying** : salir
disability [ˌdɪsə'bɪləti] *n, pl* **-ties** : infirmité *f* — **disable** [dɪs'eɪbəl] *vt* **-abled; -abling** : rendre infirme — **disabled** [dɪs'eɪbəld] *adj* : handicapé, infirme
disadvantage [ˌdɪsəd'væntɪʤ] *n* : désavantage *m*
disagree [ˌdɪsə'gri:] *vi* **1** : ne pas être d'accord (avec qqn) **2** CONFLICT : ne pas convenir — **disagreeable** [ˌdɪsə'gri:əbəl] *adj* : désagréable — **disagreement** [ˌdɪsə'gri:mənt] *n* **1** : désaccord *m* **2** ARGUMENT : différend *m*
disappear [ˌdɪsə'pɪr] *vi* : disparaître — **disappearance** [ˌdɪsə'pi:rənts] *n* : disparition *f*
disappoint [ˌdɪsə'pɔɪnt] *vt* : décevoir — **disappointment** [ˌdɪsə'pɔɪntmənt] *n* : déception *f*
disapprove [ˌdɪsə'pru:v] *vi* **-proved; -proving ~ of** : désapprouver — **disapproval** [ˌdɪsə'pru:vəl] *n* : désapprobation *f*
disarm [dɪs'ɑrm] *v* : désarmer — **disarmament** [dɪs'ɑrməmənt] *n* : désarmement *m*
disarray [dɪsə'reɪ] *n* : désordre *m*
disaster [dɪ'zæstər] *n* : désastre *m* — **disastrous** [dɪ'zæstrəs] *adj* : désastreux
disbelief [ˌdɪsbɪ'li:f] *n* : incrédulité *f*
disc → **disk**
discard [dɪs'kɑrd, 'dɪsˌkɑrd] *vt* : se débarrasser de
discern [dɪ'sərn, -'zərn] *vt* : discerner — **discernible** [dɪ'sərnəbəl, -'zər-] *adj* : perceptible
discharge [dɪs'ʧɑrʤ, 'dɪsˌ-] *vt* **-charged; -charging 1** UNLOAD : décharger **2** DISMISS : renvoyer **3** RELEASE : libérer — **~** ['dɪsˌʧɑrʤ, dɪs'-] *n* **1** : décharge *f* (électrique) **2** FLOW : écoulement *m* **3** DISMISSAL : renvoi *m* **4** RELEASE : libération *f*

disciple [dɪˈsaɪpəl] *n* : disciple *mf*

discipline [ˈdɪsəplən] *n* : discipline *f* — ∼ *vt* **-plined; -plining 1** PUNISH : punir **2** CONTROL : discipliner

disclose [dɪsˈklo:z] *vt* **-closed; -closing** : révéler

discomfort [dɪsˈkʌmfərt] *n* **1** : malaise *m* **2** UNEASINESS : gêne *f*

disconcert [ˌdɪskənˈsərt] *vt* : déconcerter

disconnect [ˌdɪskəˈnɛkt] *vt* : débrancher (un appareil électrique), couper (l'électricité, etc.)

discontinue [ˌdɪskənˈtɪnˌju:] *vt* **-ued; -uing** : cesser, interrompre

discord [ˈdɪsˌkɔrd] *n* STRIFE : discorde *m*

discount [ˈdɪsˌkaʊnt, dɪsˈ-] *n* : rabais *m*, remise *f* — ∼ *vt* : faire une remise de

discourage [dɪsˈkərɪʤ] *vt* **-aged; -aging** : décourager — **discouragement** [dɪsˈkərɪʤmənt] *n* : découragement *m*

discover [dɪsˈkʌvər] *vt* : découvrir — **discovery** [dɪsˈkʌvəri] *n, pl* **-eries** : découverte *f*

discredit [dɪsˈkrɛdət] *vt* : discréditer

discreet [dɪˈskri:t] *adj* : discret

discrepancy [dɪsˈkrɛpəntsi] *n, pl* **-cies** : divergence *f*

discretion [dɪsˈkrɛʃən] *n* : discrétion *f*

discriminate [dɪsˈkrɪməˌneɪt] *vi* **-nated; -nating 1** ∼ **against** : être l'objet de discriminations **2** ∼ **between** : distinguer entre — **discrimination** [dɪsˌkrɪməˈneɪʃən] *n* discrimination *f*, préjugés *mpl*

discuss [dɪsˈkʌs] *vt* : discuter de, parler de — **discussion** [dɪsˈkʌʃən] *n* : discussion *f*

disdain [dɪsˈdeɪn] *n* : dédain *m* — ∼ *vt* : dédaigner

disease [dɪˈzi:z] *n* : maladie *f*

disembark [ˌdɪsɪmˈbɑrk] *vi* : débarquer

disengage [ˌdɪsɪnˈgeɪʤ] *vt* **-gaged; -gaging 1** RELEASE : dégager **2** ∼ **the clutch** : débrayer

disentangle [ˌdɪsɪnˈtæŋgəl] *vt* **-gled; -gling** : démêler

disfigure [dɪsˈfɪgjər] *vt* **-ured; -uring** : défigurer

disgrace [dɪˈskreɪs] *vt* **-graced; -gracing** : déshonorer — ∼ *n* **1** DISHONOR : disgrâce *f* **2** SHAME : honte *f* — **disgraceful** [dɪˈskreɪsfəl] *adj* : honteux

disgruntled [dɪsˈgrʌntəld] *adj* : mécontent

disguise [dɪˈskaɪz] *vt* **-guised; -guising** : déguiser — ∼ *n* : déguisement *m*

disgust [dɪˈskʌst] *n* : dégoût *m* — ∼ *vt* : dégoûter — **disgusting** [dɪˈskʌstɪŋ] *adj* : écœurant, dégoûtant

dish [ˈdɪʃ] *n* **1** : assiette *f* **2** *or* **serving** ∼ : plat *m* de service **3** ∼**es** *npl* : vaisselle *f* — ∼ *vt or* ∼ **out** : servir — **dishcloth** [ˈdɪʃˌklɔθ] *n* : torchon *m* (à vaisselle), lavette *f*

dishearten [dɪsˈhɑrtən] *vt* : décourager

disheveled *or* **dishevelled** [dɪˈʃɛvəld] *adj* : en désordre (se dit des vêtements, etc.)

dishonest [dɪˈsɑnəst] *adj* : malhonnête — **dishonesty** [dɪˈsɑnəsti] *n, pl* **-ties** : malhonnêteté *f*

dishonor [dɪˈsɑnər] *n* : déshonneur *m* — ∼ *vt* : déshonorer — **dishonorable** [dɪˈsɑnərəbəl] *adj* : déshonorant

dishwasher [ˈdɪʃˌwɔʃər] *n* : lave-vaisselle *m*

disillusion [dɪsəˈlu:ʒən] *vt* : désillusionner — **disillusionment** [ˌdɪsəˈlu:ʒənmənt] *n* : désillusion *f*

disinfect [ˌdɪsɪnˈfɛkt] *vt* : désinfecter — **disinfectant** [ˌdɪsɪnˈfɛktənt] *n* : désinfectant *m*

disintegrate [dɪsˈɪntəˌgreɪt] *vi* **-grated; -grating** : se désagréger, se désintégrer

disinterested [dɪsˈɪntərəstəd, -ˌrɛs-] *adj* : désintéressé

disjointed [dɪsˈʤɔɪntəd] *adj* : décousu, incohérent

disk *or* **disc** [ˈdɪsk] *n* : disque *m*

dislike [dɪsˈlaɪk] *n* : aversion *f*, antipathie *f* — ∼ *vt* **-liked; -liking** : ne pas aimer

dislocate [ˈdɪsloˌkeɪt, dɪsˈlo:-] *vt* **-cated; -cating** : se démettre, se luxer

dislodge [dɪsˈlɑʤ] *vt* **-lodged; -lodging** : déplacer, déloger

disloyal [dɪsˈlɔɪəl] *adj* : déloyal — **disloyalty** [dɪsˈlɔɪəlti] *n, pl* **-ties** : déloyauté *f*

dismal [ˈdɪzməl] *adj* : sombre, triste

dismantle [dɪsˈmæntəl] *vt* **-tled; -tling** : démonter

dismay [dɪsˈmeɪ] *vt* : consterner — ∼ *n* : consternation *f*

dismiss [dɪsˈmɪs] *vt* **1** DISCHARGE : renvoyer, congédier **2** REJECT : ne pas tenir compte de — **dismissal** [dɪsˈmɪsəl] *n* : renvoi *m*, licenciement *m*

disobey [ˌdɪsəˈbeɪ] *vt* : désobéir à — *vi* : désobéir — **disobedience** [ˌdɪsəˈbi:diənts] *n* : désobéissance *f* — **disobedient** [-ənt] *adj* : désobéissant

disorder [dɪsˈɔrdər] *n* **1** : désordre *m* **2** AILMENT : troubles *mpl,* maladie *f* — **disorderly** [dɪsˈɔrdərli] *adj* : désordonné
disorganize [dɪsˈɔrgəˌnaɪz] *vt* **-nized; -nizing** : désorganiser
disown [dɪsˈo:n] *vt* : renier
disparage [dɪsˈpærɪʤ] *vt* **-aged; -aging** : dénigrer
disparity [dɪsˈpærət̬i] *n, pl* **-ties** : disparité *f*
dispatch [dɪsˈpæʧ] *vt* : envoyer, expédier
dispel [dɪsˈpɛl] *vt* **-pelled; -pelling** : dissiper
dispense [dɪsˈpɛnts] *v* **-pensed; -pensing** *vt* : distribuer — *vi* **~ with** : se passer de
disperse [dɪsˈpərs] *v* **-persed; -persing** *vt* : disperser — *vi* : se disperser
display [dɪsˈpleɪ] *vt* PRESENT : exposer — **~** *n* : exposition *f,* étalage *m*
dispose [dɪsˈpo:z] *v* **-posed; -posing** *vt* : disposer — *vi* **~ of** : se débarrasser de — **disposable** [dɪsˈpo:zəbəl] *adj* : jetable — **disposal** [dɪsˈpo:zəl] *n* **1** : élimination *f* (de déchets) **2 have at one's ~** : avoir à sa disposition — **disposition** [ˌdɪspəˈzɪʃən] *n* : TEMPERAMENT : caractère *m*
dispute [dɪsˈpju:t] *vt* **-puted; -puting** : contester — **~** *n* : dispute *f,* conflit *m*
disqualify [dɪsˈkwɑləˌfaɪ] *vt* **-fied; -fying** : disqualifier
disregard [ˌdɪsrɪˈgɑrd] *vt* : ne pas tenir compte de — **~** *n* : indifférence *f*
disreputable [dɪsˈrɛpjut̬əbəl] *adj* : mal famé
disrespect [ˌdɪsrɪˈspɛkt] *n* : manque *m* de respect — **disrespectful** [ˌdɪsrɪˈspɛktfəl] *adj* : irrespectueux
disrupt [dɪsˈrʌpt] *vt* : perturber, déranger — **disruption** [dɪsˈrʌpʃən] *n* : perturbation *f*
dissatisfied [dɪsˈsæt̬əsˌfaɪd] *adj* : mécontent
disseminate [dɪˈsɛməˌneɪt] *vt* **-nated; -nating** : disséminer
dissent [dɪˈsɛnt] *vi* : différer, être en désaccord — **~** *n* : dissentiment *m*
dissertation [ˌdɪsərˈteɪʃən] *n* THESIS : thèse *f*
dissipate [ˈdɪsəˌpeɪt] *v* **-pated; -pating** *vt* DISPERSE : dissiper — *vi* : se dissiper
dissolve [dɪˈzɑlv] *v* **-solved; -solving** *vt* : dissoudre — *vi* : se dissoudre
dissuade [dɪˈsweɪd] *vt* **-suaded; -suading** : dissuader
distance [ˈdɪstənts] *n* **1** : distance *f* **2 in the ~** : au loin — **distant** [ˈdɪstənt] *adj* : distant
distaste [dɪsˈteɪst] *n* : dégoût *m* — **distasteful** [dɪsˈteɪstfəl] *adj* : déplaisant, répugnant
distill *or Brit* **distil** [dɪˈstɪl] *vt* **-tilled; -tilling** : distiller
distinct [dɪˈstɪŋkt] *adj* **1** CLEAR : distinct **2** DEFINITE : net — **distinction** [dɪˈstɪŋkʃən] *n* : distinction *f* — **distinctive** [dɪˈstɪŋktɪv] *adj* : distinctif
distinguish [dɪˈstɪŋgwɪʃ] *vt* : distinguer — **distinguished** [dɪˈstɪŋgwɪʃt] *adj* : distingué
distort [dɪˈstɔrt] *vt* : déformer — **distortion** [dɪˈstɔrʃən] *n* : déformation *f*
distract [dɪˈstrækt] *vt* : distraire — **distraction** [dɪˈstrækʃən] *n* : distraction *f*
distraught [dɪˈstrɔt] *adj* : éperdu
distress [dɪˈstrɛs] *n* **1** : angoisse *f,* affliction *f* **2 in ~** : en détresse *f* — **~** *vt* : affliger — **distressing** [dɪˈstrɛsɪŋ] *adj* : pénible
distribute [dɪˈstrɪˌbju:t, -bjut] *vt* **-uted; -uting** : distribuer, répartir — **distribution** [ˌdɪstrəˈbju:ʃən] *n* : distribution *f* — **distributor** [dɪˈstrɪbjut̬ər] *n* : distributeur *m*
district [ˈdɪsˌtrɪkt] *n* **1** AREA : région *f* **2** : quartier *m* (d'une ville) **3** : district *m* (administratif)
distrust [dɪsˈtrʌst] *n* : méfiance *f* — **~** *vt* : se méfier de
disturb [dɪˈstərb] *vt* **1** BOTHER : déranger **2** WORRY : troubler, inquiéter
disturbance [dɪˈstərbənts] *n* **to cause a ~** : faire du tapage
disuse [dɪsˈju:s] *n* **fall into ~** : tomber en désuétude
ditch [ˈdɪʧ] *n* : fossé *m*
dive [ˈdaɪv] *vi* **dived** *or* **dove** [ˈdo:v]; **dived; diving** : plonger — **~** *n* **1** : plongeon *m* **2** DESCENT : piqué *m* — **diver** [ˈdaɪvər] *n* : plongeur *m,* -geuse *f*
diverge [dəˈvərʤ, daɪ-] *vi* **-verged; -verging** : diverger
diverse [daɪˈvərs, də-, ˈdaɪˌvərs] *adj* : divers — **diversify** [daɪˈvərsəˌfaɪ, də-] *vt* **-fied; -fying** : diversifier
diversion [daɪˈvərʒən, də-] *n* **1** DEVIATION : déviation *f* **2** AMUSEMENT : divertissement *m*
diversity [daɪˈvərsət̬i, də-] *n, pl* **-ties** : diversité *f*
divert [dəˈvərt, daɪ-] *vt* **1** DEFLECT : détourner **2** AMUSE : divertir
divide [dəˈvaɪd] *v* **-vided; -viding** *vt* : diviser — *vi* : se diviser

dividend ['dɪvɪˌdɛnd, -dənd] *n* : dividende *m*
divine [də'vaɪn] *adj* **diviner; -est** : divin — **divinity** [də'vɪnət̬i] *n, pl* **-ties** : divinité *f*
division [dɪ'vɪʒən] *n* : division *f*
divorce [də'vors] *n* : divorce *m* — ~ *vi* **-vorced; -vorcing** : divorcer
divulge [də'vʌlʤ, daɪ-] *vt* **-vulged; -vulging** : divulguer
dizzy ['dɪzi] *adj* **dizzier; -est** : vertigineux — **dizziness** ['dɪzinəs] *n* : vertige *m*, étourdissement *m*
DNA [ˌdi:ˌɛn'eɪ] *n* (*d*eoxyribo*n*ucleic *a*cid) : ADN *m*
do ['du:] *v* **did** ['dɪd]; **done** ['dʌn]; **doing; does** ['dʌz] *vt* **1** : faire **2** PREPARE : préparer **3 ~ one's hair** : se coiffer — *vi* **1** BEHAVE : faire **2** MANAGE : s'en sortir **3** SUFFICE : suffire **4 ~ away with** : éliminer **5 how are you doing?** : comment-vas-tu? — *v aux* **1 does he work?** : travaille-t-il? **2 I don't know** : je ne sais pas **3 ~ be careful** : fais attention, je t'en prie **4 he reads more than I ~** : il lit plus que moi **5 you know him, don't you?** : vous le connaissez, n'est-ce pas?
dock ['dak] *n* : dock *m* — ~ *vi* : se mettre à quai
doctor ['daktər] *n* **1** : docteur *m* (de droit, etc.) **2** PHYSICIAN : médecin *m*, docteur *m*
doctrine ['daktrɪn] *n* : doctrine *f*
document ['dakjumənt] *n* : document *m* — **documentary** [ˌdakju'mɛntəri] *n, pl* **-ries** : documentaire *m*
dodge ['daʤ] *n* : ruse *f*, truc *m* — ~ *vt* **dodged; dodging** : esquiver
doe ['do:] *n, pl* **does** *or* **doe** : biche *f*
does → **do**
doesn't ['dʌzɪnt] (*contraction of* **do not**) → **do**
dog ['dɔg, 'dag] *n* : chien *m* — ~ *vt* **dogged; dogging** : poursuivre — **dogged** ['dɔgəd] *adj* : tenace
dogma ['dɔgmə] *n* : dogme *m*
doldrums ['do:ldrəmz, 'dal-] *npl* **be in the ~** : être dans le marasme
doll ['dal, 'dɔl] *n* : poupée *f*
dollar ['dalər] *n* : dollar *m*
dolphin ['dalfən, 'dɔl-] *n* : dauphin *m*
domain [do'meɪn, də-] *n* : domaine *m*
dome ['do:m] *n* : dôme *m*
domestic [də'mɛstɪk] *adj* **1** FAMILY : familial **2** HOUSEHOLD : ménager, domestique **3** INTERNAL : intérieur, du pays — ~ *n* SERVANT : domestique *mf* — **domesticate** [də'mɛstɪˌkeɪt] *vt* **-cated; -cating** : domestiquer
dominant ['damənənt] *adj* : dominant — **dominate** ['daməˌneɪt] *v* **-nated; -nating** : dominer — **domineer** [ˌd'mə'nɪr] *vi* : se montrer autoritaire
donate ['do:ˌneɪt, do:'-] *vt* **-nated; -nating** : faire (un) don de — **donation** [do:'neɪʃən] *n* : don *m*, donation *f*
done ['dʌn] → **do** — ~ *adj* **1** FINISHED : fini, terminé **2** COOKED : cuit
donkey ['daŋki, 'dʌŋ] *n, pl* **-keys** : âne *m*
donor ['do:nər] *n* **1** : donateur *m*, -trice *f* **2 blood ~** : donneur *m*, -neuse *f* de sang
don't ['do:nt] (*contraction of* **do not**) → **do**
doodle ['du:dəl] *v* **-dled; -dling** : gribouiller
doom ['du:m] *n* : perte *f*, ruine *f* — ~ *vt* : vouer, condamner
door ['dor] *n* **1** : porte *f* **2** : portière *f* (d'une voiture) **3** ENTRANCE : entrée *f* — **doorbell** ['dorˌbɛl] *n* : sonnette *f* — **doorknob** ['dorˌnab] *n* : bouton *m* de porte — **doormat** ['dorˌmæt] *n* : paillasson *m* — **doorstep** ['dorˌstɛp] *n* : pas *m* de la porte — **doorway** ['dorˌweɪ] *n* : porte *f*, embrasure *f* (de la porte)
dope ['do:p] *n* **1** DRUG : drogue *f* **2** IDIOT : imbécile *mf*
dormitory ['dɔrməˌtori] *n, pl* **-ries** : dortoir *m*
dose ['do:s] *n* : dose *f* — **dosage** ['do:sɪʤ] *n* : posologie *f*
dot ['dat] *n* **1** POINT : point *m* **2 on the ~** : pile *fam*
dote ['do:t] *vi* **doted; doting ~ on** : adorer
double ['dʌbəl] *adj* : double — ~ *v* **-bled; -bling** *vt* **1** : doubler **2** FOLD : plier (en deux) — *vi* : doubler — ~ *adv* **1** : deux fois **2 see ~** : voir double — ~ *n* : double *m* — **double bass** *n* : contrebasse *f* — **doubly** ['dʌbli] *adv* : doublement, deux fois plus
doubt ['daut] *vt* **1** : douter **2** DISTRUST : douter de — ~ *n* : doute *m* — **doubtful** ['dautfəl] *adj* : douteux
dough ['do:] *n* : pâte *f* (en cuisine) — **doughnut** ['do:ˌnʌt] *n* : beignet *m*, beigne *m Can*
douse ['daus, 'dauz] *vt* **doused; dousing 1** DRENCH : tremper **2** EXTINGUISH : éteindre
dove[1] ['do:v] → **dive**
dove[2] ['dʌv] *n* : colombe *f*

down [ˈdaʊn] *adv* **1** DOWNWARD : en bas, vers le bas **2 fall ～** : tomber **3 go ～** : descendre — **～** *prep* **1** : en bas de **2** ALONG : le long de — **～** *adj* **1** : qui descend **2** DOWNCAST : déprimé, abattu — **～** *n* : duvet *m* — **downcast** [ˈdaʊnˌkæst] *adj* : abattu — **downfall** [ˈdaʊnˌfɔl] *n* : chute *f* — **downhearted** [ˈdaʊnˌhɑrṭəd] *adj* : découragé — **downhill** [ˈdaʊnˈhɪl] *adv* **go ～** : descendre — **download** [ˈdaʊnˌlo:d] *vt* : télécharger (en informatique) — **down payment** *n* : acompte *m* — **downpour** [ˈdaʊnˌpor] *n* : averse *f* — **downright** [ˈdaʊnˌraɪt] *adv* : carrément — **～** *adj* : véritable, catégorique — **downstairs** [*adv* ˈdaʊnˈstærz, *adj* ˈdaʊnˌstærz] *adv & adj* : en bas — **downstream** [ˈdaʊnˈstri:m] *adv* : en aval — **down-to-earth** [ˌdaʊntuˈərθ] *adj* : terre à terre — **downtown** [ˌdaʊnˈtaʊn, ˈdaʊnˌtaʊn] *n* : centre-ville *m* — **～** [ˌdaʊnˈtaʊn] *adv* : en ville — **downward** [ˈdaʊnwərd] *or* **downwards** [-wərdz] *adv* : en bas, vers le bas — **downward** *adj* : vers le bas

doze [ˈdo:z] *vi* **dozed; dozing** : sommeiller, somnoler

dozen [ˈdʌzən] *n, pl* **-ens** *or* **-en** : douzaine *f*

drab [ˈdræb] *adj* **drabber; drabbest** : terne

draft [ˈdræft, ˈdrɑft] *n* **1** : courant *m* d'air **2** *or* **rough ～** : brouillon *m* **3** : conscription *f* (militaire) **4** *or* **bank ～** : traite *f* bancaire **5** *or* **～ beer** : bière *f* pression — **～** *vt* **1** OUTLINE : faire le brouillon de **2** : appeler (des soldats) sous les drapeaux — **drafty** [ˈdræfti] *adj* **draftier; -est** : plein de courants d'air

drag [ˈdræg] *v* **dragged; dragging** *vt* **1** HAUL : tirer **2** : traîner (les pieds, etc.) **3** : glisser (en informatique) — *vi* TRAIL : traîner — **～** *n* **1** RESISTANCE : résistance *f* (aérodynamique) **2 what a ～!** : quelle barbe!

dragon [ˈdrægən] *n* : dragon *m* — **dragonfly** [ˈdrægənˌflaɪ] *n, pl* **-flies** : libellule *f*

drain [ˈdreɪn] *vt* **1** EMPTY : vider, drainer **2** EXHAUST : épuiser — *vi* : s'écouler, s'égoutter (se dit de la vaisselle) — **～** *n* **1** : tuyau *m* d'écoulement **2** SEWER : égout *m* **3** DEPLETION : épuisement *m* — **drainage** [ˈdreɪnɪʤ] *n* : drainage *m* — **drainpipe** [ˈdreɪnˌpaɪp] *n* : tuyau *m* d'écoulement

drama [ˈdrɑmə, ˈdræ-] *n* : drame *m* — **dramatic** [drəˈmæṭɪk] *adj* : dramatique —**dramatize** [ˈdræməˌtaɪz, ˈdrɑ-] *vt* **-tized; -tizing** : dramatiser

drank → **drink**

drape [ˈdreɪp] *vt* **draped; draping** : draper — **drapes** *npl* CURTAINS : rideaux *mpl*

drastic [ˈdræstɪk] *adj* : sévère, énergique

draught [ˈdræft, ˈdrɑft] → **draft**

draw [ˈdrɔ] *v* **drew** [ˈdru:]; **drawn** [ˈdraʊn]; **drawing** [ˈdrɔɪŋ] *vt* **1** PULL : tirer **2** ATTRACT : attirer **3** SKETCH : dessiner **4** MAKE : faire (une distinction, etc.) **5** *or* **～ up** FORMULATE : rédiger — *vi* **1** SKETCH : dessiner **2** **～ near** : approcher — **～** *n* **1** DRAWING : tirage *m* (au sort) **2** TIE : match *m* nul **3** ATTRACTION : attraction *f* — **drawback** [ˈdrɔˌbæk] *n* : inconvénient *m* — **drawer** [ˈdrɔr, ˈdrɔər] *n* : tiroir *m* — **drawing** [ˈdrɔɪŋ] *n* **1** SKETCH : dessin *m* **2** LOTTERY : tirage *m* (au sort)

drawl [ˈdrɔl] *n* : voix *f* traînante

dread [ˈdrɛd] *vt* : redouter, craindre — **～** *n* : crainte *f*, terreur *f* — **dreadful** [ˈdrɛdfəl] *adj* : affreux, épouvantable

dream [ˈdri:m] *n* : rêve *m* — **～** *v* **dreamed** [ˈdri:md] *or* **dreamt** [ˈdrɛmpt]; **dreaming** : rêver — **dreamer** [ˈdri:mər] *n* : rêveur *m*, -veuse *f* — **dreamy** [ˈdri:mi] *adj* **dreamier; -est** : rêveur

dreary [ˈdrɪri] *adj* **drearier; -est** : morne, sombre

dredge [ˈdrɛʤ] *vt* **dredged; dredging** : draguer

dregs [ˈdrɛgz] *npl* : lie *f*

drench [ˈdrɛntʃ] *vt* : tremper

dress [ˈdrɛs] *vt* **1** CLOTHE : habiller, vêtir **2** : assaisonner (une salade) **3** BANDAGE : panser (une blessure) — *vi* **1** : s'habiller **2** *or* **～ up** : se mettre en grande toilette **3 ～ up as** : se déguiser en — **～** *n* **1** CLOTHING : tenue *f* **2** : robe *f* (de femme) — **dresser** [ˈdrɛsər] *n* : commode *f* à miroir — **dressing** [ˈdrɛsɪŋ] *n* **1** SAUCE : sauce *f*, vinaigrette *f* **2** BANDAGE : pansement *m* — **dressmaker** [ˈdrɛsˌmeɪkər] *n* : couturière *f* — **dressy** [ˈdrɛsi] *adj* **dressier; -est** : habillé, élégant

drew → **draw**

dribble [ˈdrɪbəl] *vi* **-bled; -bling** **1** TRICKLE : tomber goutte à goutte **2** DROOL : baver **3** : dribbler (aux sports)

— ~ *n* **1** TRICKLE : filet *m* **2** DROOL : bave *f*
drier, driest → **dry**
drift [ˈdrɪft] *n* **1** MOVEMENT : mouvement *m* **2** HEAP : banc *m* (de neige) *Can* — ~ *vi* **1** : dériver (sur l'eau), être emporté (par le vent) **2** ACCUMULATE : s'amonceler
drill [ˈdrɪl] *n* **1** : perceuse *f* (outil) **2** EXERCISE : exercice *m* — ~ *vt* **1** : percer, forer **2** TRAIN : entraîner
drink [ˈdrɪŋk] *v* **drank** [ˈdræŋk]; **drunk** [ˈdrʌŋk] *or* **drank; drinking** : boire — ~ *n* : boisson *f*
drip [ˈdrɪp] *vi* **dripped; dripping** : tomber goutte à goutte, dégoutter — ~ *n* DROP : goutte *f*
drive [ˈdraɪv] *v* **drove** [ˈdro:v]; **driven** [ˈdrɪvən]; **driving** *vt* **1** : conduire **2** COMPEL : inciter — *vi* : conduire, rouler — ~ *n* **1** : promenade *f* (en voiture) **2** CAMPAIGN : campagne *f* **3** VIGOR : énergie *f* **4** NEED : besoin *m* fondamental
driver [ˈdraɪvər] *n* **1** : conducteur *m*, -trice *f* **2** CHAUFFEUR : chauffeur *m*
driveway [ˈdraɪvˌweɪ] *n* : allée *f*, entrée *f* (de garage)
drizzle [ˈdrɪzəl] *n* : bruine *f* — ~ *vi* **-zled; -zling** : bruiner
drone [ˈdro:n] *n* **1** BEE : abeille *f* mâle **2** HUM : bourdonnement *m* — ~ *vi* **droned; droning 1** BUZZ : bourdonner **2** *or* ~ **on** : parler d'un ton monotone
drool [ˈdru:l] *vi* : baver — ~ *n* : bave *f*
droop [ˈdru:p] *vi* : pencher, tomber
drop [ˈdrɑp] *n* **1** : goutte *f* (de liquide) **2** DECLINE, FALL : baisse *f* **3** DESCENT : chute *f* — ~ *v* **dropped; dropping** *vt* **1** : laisser tomber **2** LOWER : baisser **3** ABANDON : abandonner **4** ~ **off** LEAVE : déposer — *vi* **1** FALL : tomber **2** DECREASE : baisser **3** ~ **by** : passer
drought [ˈdraʊt] *n* : sécheresse *f*
drove [ˈdro:v] → **drive**
droves [ˈdro:vz] *npl* **in** ~ : en masse
drown [ˈdraʊn] *vt* : noyer — *vi* : se noyer
drowsy [ˈdraʊzi] *adj* **drowsier; -est** : somnolent — **drowsiness** [ˈdraʊzinəs] *n* : somnolence *f*
drudgery [ˈdrʌʤəri] *n, pl* **-eries** : corvée *f*
drug [ˈdrʌg] *n* **1** MEDICATION : médicament *m* **2** NARCOTIC : drogue *f*, stupéfiant *m* — ~ *vt* **drugged; drugging** : droguer — **drugstore** [ˈdrʌgˌstor] *n* : pharmacie *f*
drum [ˈdrʌm] *n* **1** : tambour *m* **2** *or* **oil** ~ : bidon *m* — ~ *v* **drummed; drumming** *vi* : jouer du tambour — *vt* : tambouriner — **drumstick** [ˈdrʌmˌstɪk] *n* **1** : baguette *f* de tambour **2** : pilon *m* (de poulet)
drunk [ˈdrʌŋk] → **drink** — ~ *adj* : ivre — ~ *or* **drunkard** [ˈdrʌŋkərd] *n* : ivrogne *m*, ivrognesse *f* — **drunken** [ˈdrʌŋkən] *adj* : ivre
dry [ˈdraɪ] *adj* **drier; driest** : sec — ~ *v* **dried; drying** *vt* **1** : sécher **2** WIPE : essuyer — *vi* : sécher — **dry–clean** [ˈdraɪˌkli:n] *vt* : nettoyer à sec — **dry cleaner** *n* : teinturerie *f* — **dryer** [ˈdraɪər] *n* : séchoir *m* — **dryness** [ˈdraɪnəs] *n* : sécheresse *f*
dual [ˈdu:əl, ˈdju:-] *adj* : double
dub [ˈdʌb] *vt* **dubbed; dubbing** : doubler (un film, etc.)
dubious [ˈdu:biəs, ˈdju:-] *adj* **1** DOUBTFUL : douteux **2** QUESTIONABLE : suspect
duck [ˈdʌk] *n, pl* **ducks** *or* **duck** : canard *m* — ~ *vt* **1** PLUNGE : plonger **2** LOWER : baisser **3** AVOID, DODGE : éviter, esquiver — **duckling** [ˈdʌklɪŋ] *n* : caneton *m*
duct [ˈdʌkt] *n* : conduit *m*
due [ˈdu:, ˈdju:] *adj* **1** PAYABLE : dû, payable **2** APPROPRIATE : qui convient **3** EXPECTED : attendu **4** ~ **to** : en raison de — ~ *n* **1** : dû *m* **2** ~**s** *npl* FEE : cotisation *f* — ~ *adv* : plein, droit vers
duel [ˈdu:əl, ˈdju:-] *n* : duel *m*
duet [du:ˈɛt, dju:-] *n* : duo *m*
dug → **dig**
duke [ˈdu:k, ˈdju:k] *n* : duc *m*
dull [ˈdʌl] *adj* **1** STUPID : stupide **2** BLUNT : émoussé **3** BORING : ennuyeux **4** LACKLUSTER : terne — ~ *vt* **1** BLUNT : émousser **2** DIM, TARNISH : ternir
duly [ˈdu:li] *adv* **1** PROPERLY : dûment **2** EXPECTEDLY : comme prévu
dumb [ˈdʌm] *adj* **1** MUTE : muet **2** STUPID : bête
dumbfound *or* **dumfound** [ˌdʌmˈfaʊnd] *vt* : abasourdir
dummy [ˈdʌmi] *n, pl* **-mies 1** FOOL : imbécile *mf* **2** MANNEQUIN : mannequin *m* — ~ *adj* : faux
dump [ˈdʌmp] *vt* : déposer, jeter — ~ *n* **1** : décharge *f* (publique) **2 down in the** ~**s** : déprimé
dune [ˈdu:n, ˈdju:n] *n* : dune *f*
dung [ˈdʌŋ] *n* : fumier *m*
dungeon [ˈdʌnʤən] *n* : cachot *m*
dunk [ˈdʌŋk] *vt* : tremper

duo [ˈdu:o:, ˈdju:-] *n, pl* **duos** : duo *m*
dupe [ˈdu:p, ˈdju:p] *n* : dupe *f* — ~ *vt* **duped; duping** : duper
duplex [ˈdu:ˌplɛks, ˈdju:-] *n* : duplex *m,* maison *f* jumelée
duplicate [ˈdu:plɪkət, ˈdju:-] *adj* : en double — ~ [ˈdu:plɪˌkeɪt, ˈdju:-] *vt* **-cated; -cating** : faire un double de, copier — ~ [ˈdu:plɪkət, ˈdju:-] *n* : double *m*
durable [ˈdʊrəbəl, ˈdjʊr-] *adj* : durable, résistant
duration [dʊˈreɪʃən, djʊ-] *n* : durée *f*
during [ˈdʊrɪŋ, ˈdjʊr-] *prep* : pendant
dusk [ˈdʌsk] *n* : crépuscule *m*
dust [ˈdʌst] *n* : poussière *f* — ~ *vt* **1** : épousseter **2** SPRINKLE : saupoudrer — **dustpan** [ˈdʌstˌpæn] *n* : pelle *f* à poussière — **dusty** [ˈdʌsti] *adj* **dustier; -est** : poussiéreux
duty [ˈdu:t̬i, ˈdju:-] *n, pl* **-ties** **1** TASK : fonction *f* **2** OBLIGATION : devoir *m* **3** TAX : taxe *f,* droit *m* — **dutiful** [ˈdu:t̬ɪfəl, ˈdju:-] *adj* : obéissant
dwarf [ˈdwɔrf] *n* : nain *m,* naine *f*
dwell [ˈdwɛl] *vi* **dwelled** *or* **dwelt** [ˈdwɛlt]; **dwelling** **1** RESIDE : demeurer **2** ~ **on** : penser sans cesse à — **dweller** [ˈdwɛlər] *n* : habitant *m,* -tante *f* — **dwelling** [ˈdwɛlɪŋ] *n* : habitation *f*
dwindle [ˈdwɪndəl] *vi* **-dled; -dling** : diminuer
dye [ˈdaɪ] *n* : teinture *f* — ~ *vt* **dyed; dyeing** : teindre
dying → **die**[1]
dynamic [daɪˈnæmɪk] *adj* : dynamique
dynamite [ˈdaɪnəˌmaɪt] *n* : dynamite *f* — ~ *vt* **-mited; -miting** : dynamiter
dynasty [ˈdaɪnəsti, -næs-] *n, pl* **-ties** : dynastie *f*

E

e [ˈi:] *n, pl* **e's** *or* **es** [ˈi:z] : e *m,* cinquième lettre de l'alphabet
each [ˈi:tʃ] *adj* : chaque — ~ *pron* **1** : chacun *m,* -cune *f* **2** ~ **other** : l'un l'autre **3 they love** ~ **other** : ils s'aiment — ~ *adv* : chacun, par personne
eager [ˈi:gər] *adj* **1** ENTHUSIASTIC : avide **2** IMPATIENT : impatient — **eagerness** [ˈi:gərnəs] *n* : enthousiasme *m,* empressement *m*
eagle [ˈi:gəl] *n* : aigle *m*
ear [ˈɪr] *n* **1** : oreille *f* **2** ~ **of corn** : épi *m* de maïs — **eardrum** [ˈɪrˌdrʌm] *n* : tympan *m*
earl [ˈərl] *n* : comte *m*
earlobe [ˈɪrˌlo:b] *n* : lobe *m* de l'oreille
early [ˈərli] *adv* **-lier; -est** **1** : tôt, de bonne heure **2 as** ~ **as possible** : le plus tôt possible **3 ten minutes** ~ : en avance de dix minutes — ~ *adj* **-lier; -est** **1** FIRST : premier **2** ANCIENT : ancien **3 in the** ~ **afternoon** : au début de l'après-midi
earmark [ˈɪrˌmɑrk] *vt* : réserver, désigner
earn [ˈərn] *vt* **1** : gagner **2** DESERVE : mériter
earnest [ˈərnəst] *adj* : sérieux — ~ *n* **in** ~ : sérieusement
earnings [ˈərnɪŋz] *npl* **1** WAGES : salaire *m* **2** PROFITS : gains *mpl*
earphone [ˈɪrˌfo:n] *n* : écouteur *m*
earring [ˈɪrˌrɪŋ] *n* : boucle *f* d'oreille
earshot [ˈɪrˌʃɑt] *n* **within** ~ : à portée de voix
earth [ˈərθ] *n* **1** GROUND : terre *f,* sol *m* **2 the Earth** : la terre — **earthly** [ˈərθli] *adj* : terrestre — **earthquake** [ˈərθˌkweɪk] *n* : tremblement *m* de terre — **earthworm** [ˈərθˌwərm] *n* : ver *m* de terre — **earthy** [ˈərθi] *adj* **earthier; earthiest** : terreux
ease [ˈi:z] *n* **1** FACILITY : facilité *f* **2** COMFORT : bien-être *m* **3 feel at** ~ : être à l'aise — ~ *v* **eased; easing** *vt* **1** FACILITATE : faciliter **2** ALLEVIATE : soulager, réduire — *vi* ~ **up** : s'atténuer
easel [ˈi:zəl] *n* : chevalet *m*
easily [ˈi:zəli] *adv* **1** : facilement **2** UNQUESTIONABLY : de loin
east [ˈi:st] *adv* : vers l'est, à l'est — ~ *adj* : est — ~ *n* **1** : est *m* **2 the East** : l'Est *m,* l'Orient *m*
Easter [ˈi:stər] *n* : Pâques *m,* Pâques *fpl*
easterly [ˈi:stərli] *adv* : vers l'est — ~ *adj* : d'est, de l'est
eastern [ˈi:stərn] *adj* **1** : est, de l'est **2 Eastern** : de l'Est, oriental
easy [ˈi:zi] *adj* **easier; easiest** **1** : facile, aisé **2** RELAXED : décontracté — **easygoing** [ˌi:ziˈgo:ɪŋ] *adj* : accommodant
eat [ˈi:t] *v* **ate** [ˈeɪt]; **eaten** [ˈi:tən]; **eating** : manger
eaves [ˈi:vz] *npl* : avant-toit *m* — **eaves-**

drop ['i:vz,drɑp] *vi* **-dropped; -dropping** : écouter aux portes
ebb ['ɛb] *n* : reflux *m* — ~ *vi* **1** : refluer **2** DECLINE : décliner
ebony ['ɛbəni] *n, pl* **-nies** : ébène *f*
eccentric [ɪk'sɛntrɪk] *adj* : excentrique — ~ *n* : excentrique *mf* — **eccentricity** [,ɛk,sɛn'trɪsəṭi] *n, pl* **-ties** : excentricité *f*
echo ['ɛ,ko:] *n, pl* **echoes** : écho *m* — ~ *v* **echoed; echoing** *vt* : répéter — *vi* : se répercuter, résonner
eclipse [ɪ'klɪps] *n* : éclipse *f*
ecology [i'kɑləʤi, ɛ-] *n, pl* **-gies** : écologie *f* — **ecological** [,i:kə'lɑʤɪkəl, ,ɛkə-] *adj* : écologique
economy [i'kɑnəmi] *n, pl* **-mies** : économie *f* — **economic** [,i:kə'nɑmɪk, ,ɛkə-] *adj* : économique — **economical** [,i:kə'nɑmɪkəl, ,ɛkə-] *adj* THRIFTY : économe — **economics** [,i:kə'nɑmɪks, ,ɛkə-] *ns & pl* : sciences *fpl* économiques, économie *f* — **economist** [i'kɑnəmɪst] *n* : économiste *mf* — **economize** [i'kɑnə,maɪz] *v* **-mized; -mizing** : économiser
ecstasy ['ɛkstəsi] *n, pl* **-sies** : extase *f* — **ecstatic** [ɛk'stæṭɪk, ɪk-] *adj* : extatique
edge ['ɛʤ] *n* **1** BORDER : bord *m* **2** : tranchant *m* (d'un couteau, etc.) **3** ADVANTAGE : avantage *m* — ~ *vi* **edged; edging** : avancer lentement — **edgewise** ['ɛʤ,waɪz] *adv* : de côté — **edgy** ['ɛʤi] *adj* **edgier; edgiest** : énervé
edible ['ɛdəbəl] *adj* : comestible
edit ['ɛdɪt] *vt* **1** : réviser, corriger **2** ~ **out** : couper — **edition** [ɪ'dɪʃən] *n* : édition *f* — **editor** ['ɛdɪṭər] *n* : rédacteur *m*, -trice *f* (d'un journal); éditeur *m*, -trice *f* (d'un livre) — **editorial** [,ɛdɪ'toriəl] *n* : éditorial *m*
educate ['ɛʤə,keɪt] *vt* **-cated; -cating** : instruire, éduquer — **education** [,ɛʤə'keɪʃən] *n* **1** : éducation *f*, études *fpl* **2** TEACHING : enseignement *m*, instruction *f* — **educational** [,ɛʤə'keɪʃənəl] *adj* **1** : éducatif **2** TEACHING : pédagogique — **educator** ['ɛdʃə,keɪṭər] *n* : éducateur *m*, -trice *f*
eel ['i:l] *n* : anguille *f*
eerie ['ɪri] *adj* **eerier; -est** : étrange
effect [ɪ'fɛkt] *n* **1** : effet *m* **2 go into** ~ : entrer en vigueur — ~ *vt* : effectuer, réaliser — **effective** [ɪ'fɛktɪv] *adj* **1** : efficace **2 become** ~ : entrer en vigueur — **effectiveness** [ɪ'fɛktɪvnəs] *n* : efficacité *f*
effeminate [ə'fɛmənət] *adj* : efféminé
efficient [ɪ'fɪʃənt] *adj* : efficace — **efficiency** ['ɪfɪʃəntsi] *n pl* **-cies** : efficacité *f*
effort ['ɛfərt] *n* **1** : effort *m* **2 it's not worth the** ~ : ça ne vaut pas la peine — **effortless** ['ɛfərtləs] *adj* : facile
egg ['ɛg] *n* : œuf *m* — **eggplant** ['ɛg,plænt] *n* : aubergine *f* — **eggshell** ['ɛg,ʃɛl] *n* : coquille *f* d'œuf
ego ['i:,go:] *n, pl* **egos** **1** SELF : moi *m* **2** SELF-ESTEEM : amour-propre *m* — **egotism** ['i:gə'tɪzəm] *n* : égotisme *m* — **egotistic** [,i:gə'tɪstɪk] *or* **egotistical** [-'tɪstɪkəl] *adj* : égocentrique
Egyptian [i'ʤɪpʃən] *adj* : égyptien
eight ['eɪt] *n* : huit *m* — ~ *adj* : huit — **eighteen** [eɪt'ti:n] *n* : dix-huit *m* — ~ *adj* : dix-huit — **eighteenth** [eɪt'ti:nθ] *n* **1** : dix-huitième *mf* **2 October** ~ : le dix-huit octobre — ~ *adj* : dix-huitième — **eighth** ['eɪtθ] *n* **1** : huitième *mf* **2 February** ~ : le huit février — ~ *adj* : huitième — **eight hundred** *adj* : huit cents — **eightieth** [eɪṭiəθ] *n* : quatre-vingtième *mf* — ~ *adj* : quatre-vingtième — **eighty** [eɪṭi] *n, pl* **eighties** : quatre-vingts *m* — ~ *adj* : quatre-vingts
either ['i:ðər, 'aɪ-] *adj* **1** : l'un ou l'autre **2** EACH : chaque — ~ *pron* : l'un ou l'autre, n'importe lequel — ~ *conj* **1** : ou, soit **2** (*in negative constructions*) : ni
eject [i'ʤɛkt] *vt* : éjecter, expulser
elaborate [i'læbərət] *adj* **1** DETAILED : détaillé **2** COMPLEX : compliqué — ~ [i'læbə,reɪt] *v* **-rated; -rating** *vt* : élaborer — *vi* ~ **on** : donner des détails sur
elapse [i'læps] *vi* **elapsed; elapsing** : s'écouler
elastic [i'læstɪk] *adj* : élastique — ~ *n* : élastique *m* — **elasticity** [i,læs'tɪsəṭi, ,i:,læs-] *n, pl* **-ties** : élasticité *f*
elated [i'leɪtəd] *adj* : fou de joie — **elation** [i'leɪʃən] *n* : allégresse *f*, joie *f*
elbow ['ɛl,bo:] *n* : coude *m*
elder ['ɛldər] *adj* : aîné, plus âgé — ~ *n* : aîné *m*, aînée *f* — **elderly** ['ɛldərli] *adj* : âgé
elect [i'lɛkt] *vt* : élire — ~ *adj* : élu, futur — **election** [i'lɛkʃən] *n* : élection *f* — **electoral** [i'lɛktərəl] *adj* : électoral — **electorate** [i'lɛktərət] *n* : électorat *m*
electricity [i,lɛk'trɪsəṭi] *n, pl* **-ties** : électricité *f* — **electric** [i'lɛktrɪk] *or* **electrical** [-trɪkəl] *adj* : électrique —

electrician [i,lɛk'trɪʃən] *n* : électricien *m*, -cienne *f* — **electrocute** [i'lɛktrə,kju:t] *vt* **-cuted; -cuting** : électrocuter
electron [i'lɛk,trɑn] *n* : électron *m* — **electronic** [i,lɛk'trɑnɪk] *adj* : électronique — **electronic mail** *n* : courrier *m* électronique — **electronics** [i,lɛk'trɑnɪks] *n* : électronique *f*
elegant ['ɛlɪgənt] *adj* : élégant — **elegance** ['ɛlɪgənts] *n* : élégance *f*
element ['ɛlə,mənt] *n* **1** : élément *m* **2** ~**s** *npl* BASICS : rudiments *mpl* — **elementary** [,ɛlə'mɛntri] *adj* : élémentaire — **elementary school** *n* : école *f* primaire
elephant ['ɛləfənt] *n* : éléphant *m*
elevate ['ɛlə,veɪt] *vt* **-vated; -vating** : élever — **elevator** ['ɛlə,veɪṭər] *n* : ascenseur *m*
eleven [ɪ'lɛvən] *n* : onze *m* — ~ *adj* : onze — **eleventh** [ɪ'lɛvəntθ] *n* **1** : onzième *mf* **2 March** ~ : le onze mars — ~ *adj* : onzième
elf ['ɛlf] *n, pl* **elves** ['ɛlvz] : lutin *m*
elicit [ɪ'lɪsət] *vt* : provoquer
eligible ['ɛləʤəbəl] *adj* : éligible, admissible
eliminate [ɪ'lɪmə,neɪt] *vt* **-nated; -nating** : éliminer — **elimination** [ɪ,lɪmə'neɪʃən] *n* : élimination *f*
elite [eɪ'li:t, i-] *n* : élite *f*
elk ['ɛlk] *n* : élan *m* (d'Europe), wapiti *m* (d'Amérique)
elm ['ɛlm] *n* : orme *m*
elongate [i'lɔŋ,geɪt] *vt* **-gated; -gating** : allonger
elope [i'lo:p] *vi* **eloped; eloping** : s'enfuir (pour se marier) — **elopement** [i'lo:pmənt] *n* : fugue *f* amoureuse
eloquence ['ɛlə,kwənts] *n* : éloquence *f* — **eloquent** ['ɛlə,kwənt] *adj* : éloquent
else ['ɛls] *adv* **or** ~ : sinon, autrement — ~ *adj* **1 everyone** ~ : tous les autres **2 what** ~ : quoi d'autre — **elsewhere** ['ɛls,*h*wɛr] *adv* : ailleurs
elude [i'lu:d] *vt* **eluded; eluding** : échapper à, éluder — **elusive** [i'lu:sɪv] *adj* : insaisissable
elves → **elf**
e-mail ['i:,meɪl] *n* : courriel *m*, e-mail *m* *France*
emanate ['ɛmə,neɪt] *vi* **-nated; -nating** : émaner
emancipate [ɪ'mæntsə,peɪt] *vt* **-pated; -pating** : émanciper
embalm [ɪm'bɑm, ɛm-, -'bɑlm] *vt* : embaumer
embankment [ɪm'bæŋkmənt, ɛm-] *n* : digue *f* (d'une rivière), remblai *m* (d'une route)
embargo [ɪm'bɑrgo, ɛm-] *n, pl* **-goes** : embargo *m*
embark [ɪm'bɑrk, ɛm-] *vt* : embarquer — *vi* ~ **on** : entreprendre
embarrass [ɪm'bærəs, ɛm-] *vt* : gêner, embarrasser — **embarrassing** [ɪm'bærəsɪŋ, ɛm-] *adj* : embarrassant — **embarrassment** [ɪm'bærəsmənt, ɛm-] *n* : gêne *f*, embarras *m*
embassy ['ɛmbəsi] *n, pl* **-sies** : ambassade *f*
embed [ɪm'bɛd, ɛm-] *vt* **-bedded; -bedding** : enfoncer
embellish [ɪm'bɛlɪʃ, ɛm-] *vt* : embellir — **embellishment** [ɪm'bɛlɪʃmənt, ɛm-] *n* : ornement *m*
embers ['ɛmbərz] *npl* : braise *f*
embezzle [ɪm'bɛzəl, ɛm-] *vt* **-zled; -zling** : détourner — **embezzlement** [ɪm'bɛzəlmənt, ɛm-] *n* : détournement *m* de fonds
emblem ['ɛmbləm] *n* : emblème *m*
embody [ɪm'bɑdi, ɛm-] *vt* **-bodied; -bodying** : incarner
embrace [ɪm'breɪs, ɛm-] *v* **-braced; -bracing** *vt* : embrasser — *vi* : s'embrasser — ~ *n* : étreinte *f*
embroider [ɪm'brɔɪdər, ɛm-] *vt* : broder — **embroidery** [ɪm'brɔɪdəri, ɛm-] *n, pl* **-deries** : broderie *f*
embryo ['ɛmbri,o:] *n* : embryon *m*
emerald ['ɛmrəld, 'ɛmə-] *n* : émeraude *f*
emerge [i'mərʤ] *vi* **emerged; emerging** **1** APPEAR : apparaître **2** ~ **from** : émerger de — **emergence** [i'mərʤənts] *n* : apparition *f*
emergency [i'mərʤəntsi] *n, pl* **-cies** **1** : urgence *f* **2** ~ **exit** : sortie *f* de secours **3** ~ **room** : salle *f* des urgences
emery ['ɛməri] *n, pl* **-eries** **1** : émeri *m* **2** ~ **board** : lime *f* à ongles
emigrant ['ɛmɪgrənt] *n* : émigrant *m*, -grante *f* — **emigrate** ['ɛmə,greɪt] *vi* **-grated; -grating** : émigrer
eminence ['ɛmənənts] *n* : éminence *f* — **eminent** ['ɛmənənt] *adj* : éminent
emission [i'mɪʃən] *n* : émission *f* — **emit** [i'mɪt] *vt* **emitted; emitting** : émettre
emotion [i'mo:ʃən] *n* : émotion *f* — **emotional** [i'mo:ʃənəl] *adj* **1** : émotif **2** MOVING : émouvant
emperor ['ɛmpərər] *n* : empereur *m*
emphasis ['ɛmfəsɪs] *n, pl* **-ses** [-,si:z] : accent *m* — **emphasize** ['ɛmfə,saɪz] *vt* **-sized; -sizing** : insister sur — **em-**

phatic [ɪm'fætɪk, ɛm-] *adj* : énergique, catégorique
empire ['ɛm,paɪr] *n* : empire *m*
employ [ɪm'plɔɪ, ɛm-] *vt* : employer — **employee** [ɪm,plɔɪ'i:, ɛm-, -'plɔɪ,i:] *n* : employé *m*, -ployée *f* — **employer** [ɪm'plɔiər, ɛm-] *n* : employeur *m*, -ployeuse *f* — **employment** [ɪm'plɔɪmənt, ɛm-] *n* : emploi *m*, travail *m*
empower [ɪm'pauər, ɛm-] *vt* : autoriser
empress ['ɛmprəs] *n* : impératrice *f*
empty ['ɛmpti] *adj* **-tier; -est 1** : vide **2** MEANINGLESS : vain — ~ *v* **-tied; -tying** *vt* : vider — *vi* : se vider — **emptiness** ['ɛmptinəs] *n* : vide *m*
emulate ['ɛmjə,leɪt] *vt* **-lated; -lating** : imiter
enable [ɪ'neɪbəl, ɛ-] *vt* **-abled; -abling** : permettre
enact [ɪ'nækt, ɛ-] *vt* : promulguer (une loi, etc.)
enamel [ɪ'næməl] *n* : émail *m*
enchant [ɪn'ʧænt, ɛn-] *vt* : enchanter — **enchanting** [ɪn'ʧæntɪŋ, ɛn-] *adj* : enchanteur
encircle [ɪn'sərkəl, ɛn-] *vt* **-cled; -cling** : entourer, encercler
enclose [ɪn'klo:z, ɛn-] *vt* **-closed; -closing 1** SURROUND : entourer **2** INCLUDE : joindre (à une lettre) — **enclosure** [ɪn'klo:ʒər, ɛn-] *n* **1** : enceinte *f* **2** : pièce *f* jointe (à une lettre)
encompass [ɪn'kʌmpəs, ɛn-, -'kɑm-] *vt* **1** ENCIRCLE : entourer **2** INCLUDE : inclure
encore ['ɑn,kor] *n* : bis *m*
encounter [ɪn'kauntər, ɛn-] *vt* : rencontrer — ~ *n* : rencontre *f*
encourage [ɪn'kərɪʤ, ɛn-] *vt* **-aged; -aging** : encourager — **encouragement** [ɪn'kərɪʤmənt, ɛn-] *n* : encouragement *m*
encroach [ɪn'kro:ʧ, ɛn-] *vi* ~ **on** : empiéter sur
encyclopedia [ɪn,saɪklə'pi:diə, ɛn-] *n* : encyclopédie *f*
end ['ɛnd] *n* **1** : fin *f* **2** EXTREMITY : bout *m* **3 come to an ~** : prendre fin **4 in the ~** : finalement— ~ *vt* : terminer, mettre fin à — *vi* : se terminer
endanger [ɪn'deɪnʤər, ɛn-] *vt* : mettre en danger
endearing [ɪn'dɪrɪŋ, ɛn-] *adj* : attachant
endeavor *or Brit* **endeavour** [ɪn'dɛvər, ɛn-] *vt* ~ **to** : s'efforcer de — ~ *n* : effort *m*
ending ['ɛndɪŋ] *n* : fin *f*, dénouement *m*
endive ['ɛn,daɪv, ,ɑn'di:v] *n* : endive *f*
endless ['ɛndləs] *adj* **1** INTERMINABLE : interminable **2** INNUMERABLE : innombrable **3 ~ possibilities** : possibilités *fpl* infinies
endorse [ɪn'dɔrs, ɛn-] *vt* **-dorsed; -dorsing 1** SIGN : endosser **2** APPROVE : approuver — **endorsement** [ɪn'dɔrsmənt, ɛn-] *n* APPROVAL : approbation *f*
endow [ɪn'dau, ɛn-] *vt* : doter
endure [ɪn'dur, ɛn-, -'djur-] *v* **-dured; -during** *vt* : supporter, endurer — *vi* LAST : durer — **endurance** [ɪn'durənts, ɛn-, -'djur-] *n* : endurance *f*
enemy ['ɛnəmi] *n, pl* **-mies** : ennemi *m*, -mie *f*
energy ['ɛnərʤi] *n, pl* **-gies** : énergie *f* — **energetic** [,ɛnər'ʤɛtɪk] *adj* : énergique
enforce [ɪn'fors, ɛn-] *vt* **-forced; -forcing 1** : faire respecter (une loi) **2** IMPOSE : imposer — **enforcement** [ɪn'forsmənt, ɛn-] *n* : exécution *f*, application *f*
engage [ɪn'geɪʤ, ɛn-] *v* **-gaged; -gaging** *vt* **1** : engager (une conversation) **2 ~ the clutch** : embrayer — *vi* ~ **in** : prendre part à, s'occuper de — **engaged** [ɪn'geɪʤd, ɛn-] *adj* **get ~ to** : se fiancer à — **engagement** [ɪn'geɪʤmənt, ɛn-] *n* **1** : fiançailles *fpl* **2** APPOINTMENT : rendez-vous *m* — **engaging** [ɪn'geɪʤɪŋ, ɛn-] *adj* : engageant, attirant
engine ['ɛnʤən] *n* **1** : moteur *m* **2** LOCOMOTIVE : locomotive *f* — **engineer** [,ɛnʤə'nɪr] *n* : ingénieur *m*, -nieure *f* — **engineering** [,ɛnʤə'nɪrɪŋ] *n* : ingénierie *f*
English ['ɪŋglɪʃ, 'ɪŋlɪʃ] *adj* : anglais — ~ *n* : anglais *m* (langue) — **Englishman** ['ɪŋglɪʃmən, 'ɪŋlɪʃ-] *n* : Anglais *m* — **Englishwoman** ['ɪŋglɪʃ,wumən, 'ɪŋlɪʃ-] *n* : Anglaise *f*
engrave [ɪn'greɪv, ɛn-] *vt* **-graved; -graving** : graver — **engraving** [ɪn'greɪvɪŋ, ɛn-] *n* : gravure *f*
engross [ɪn'gro:s, ɛn-] *vt* : absorber, occuper
engulf [ɪn'gʌlf, ɛn-] *vt* : engloutir
enhance [ɪn'hænts, ɛn-] *vt* **-hanced; -hancing** : améliorer, rehausser
enjoy [ɪn'ʤɔɪ, ɛn-] *vt* **1** LIKE : aimer **2** POSSESS : jouir de **3 ~ oneself** : s'amuser — **enjoyable** [ɪn'ʤɔɪəbəl, ɛn-] *adj* : agréable — **enjoyment** [ɪn'ʤɔɪmənt, ɛn-] *n* : plaisir *m*
enlarge [ɪn'lɑrʤ, ɛn-] *vt* **-larged; -larging** : agrandir — **enlargement** [ɪn'lɑrʤmənt, ɛn-] *n* : agrandissement *m*

enlighten [ɪn'laɪtən, ɛn-] *vt* : éclairer
enlist [ɪn'lɪst, ɛn-] *vt* **1** ENROLL : enrôler **2** OBTAIN : obtenir — *vi* : s'engager, s'enrôler
enliven [ɪn'laɪvən, ɛn-] *vt* : animer
enormous [ɪ'nɔrməs] *adj* : énorme
enough [i'nʌf] *adj* : assez de — ~ *adv* : assez — ~ *pron* **have ~ of** : en avoir assez de
enquire [ɪn'kwaɪr, ɛn-], **enquiry** ['ɪn-ˌkwaɪri, 'ɛn-, -kwəri; ɪn'kwaɪri, ɛn'-] → **inquire, inquiry**
enrage [ɪn'reɪʤ, ɛn-] *vt* **-raged; -raging** : rendre furieux
enrich [ɪn'rɪʧ, ɛn-] *vt* : enrichir
enroll *or* **enrol** [ɪn'ro:l, ɛn-] *v* **-rolled; -rolling** *vt* **1** : inscrire (à l'école, etc.) **2** ENLIST : enrôler — *vi* : s'inscrire
ensue [ɪn'su:, ɛn-] *vi* **-sued; -suing** : s'ensuivre
ensure [ɪn'ʃʊr, ɛn-] *vt* **-sured; -suring** : assurer
entail [ɪn'teɪl, ɛn-] *vt* : entraîner, comporter
entangle [ɪn'tæŋgəl, ɛn-] *vt* **-gled; -gling** : emmêler
enter ['ɛntər] *vt* **1** : entrer dans **2** RECORD : inscrire — *vi* **1** : entrer **2 ~ into** : entamer
enterprise ['ɛntərˌpraɪz] *n* **1** : entreprise *f* **2** INITIATIVE : initiative *f* — **enterprising** ['ɛntərˌpraɪzɪŋ] *adj* : entreprenant
entertain [ˌɛntər'teɪn] *vt* **1** AMUSE : amuser, divertir **2** CONSIDER : considérer **3** : recevoir (des invités) — **entertainment** [ˌɛntər'teɪnmənt] *n* : divertissement *m*
enthrall *or* **enthral** [ɪn'θrɔl, ɛn-] *vt* **-thralled; -thralling** : captiver
enthusiasm [ɪn'θu:ziˌæzəm, ɛn-, -'θju:-] *n* : enthousiasme *m* — **enthusiast** [ɪn'θu:ziˌæst, ɛn-, -'θju:-, -əst] *n* : enthousiaste *mf;* passionné *m*, -née *f* — **enthusiastic** [ɪnˌθu:zi'æstɪk, ɛn-, -'θju:-] *adj* : enthousiaste
entice [ɪn'taɪs, ɛn-] *vt* **-ticed; -ticing** : attirer, entraîner
entire [ɪn'taɪr, ɛn-] *adj* : entier, complet — **entirely** [ɪn'taɪrli, ɛn-] *adv* : entièrement — **entirety** [ɪn'taɪrţi, ɛn-, -taɪrəţi] *n, pl* **-ties 1** : totalité *f* **2 in its ~** : dans son ensemble
entitle [ɪn'taɪţəl, ɛn-] *vt* **-tled; -tling 1** NAME : intituler **2** AUTHORIZE : autoriser, donner droit à — **entitlement** [ɪn-'taɪţəlmənt, ɛn-] *n* : droit *m*
entity ['ɛntəţi] *n, pl* **-ties** : entité *f*
entrails ['ɛnˌtreɪlz, -trəlz] *npl* : entrailles *fpl*
entrance¹ [ɪn'træn*t*s, ɛn-] *vt* **-tranced; -trancing** : transporter, ravir
entrance² ['ɛntrən*t*s] *n* : entrée *f*
entreat [ɪn'tri:t, ɛn-] *vt* : supplier
entrée *or* **entree** ['ɑnˌtreɪ, ˌɑn'-] *n* : entrée *f*, plat *m* principal
entrust [ɪn'trʌst, ɛn-] *vt* : confier
entry ['ɛntri] *n, pl* **-tries** ENTRANCE : entrée *f*
enumerate [ɪ'nu:məˌreɪt, ɛ-, -'nju:-] *vt* **-ated; -ating** : énumérer
enunciate [i'nʌn*t*siˌeɪt, ɛ-] *vt* **-ated; -ating 1** STATE : énoncer **2** PRONOUNCE : articuler
envelop [ɪn'vɛləp, ɛn-] *vt* : envelopper — **envelope** ['ɛnvəˌlo:p, 'ɑn-] *n* : enveloppe *f*
envious ['ɛnviəs] *adj* : envieux, jaloux — **enviously** ['ɛnviəsli] *adv* : avec envie
environment [ɪn'vaɪrənmənt, ɛn-, -'vaɪərn-] *n* : environnement *m*, milieu *m* — **environmental** [ɪnˌvaɪrən'mɛntəl, ɛn-, -ˌvaɪərn-] *adj* : de l'environnement — **environmentalist** [ɪn-ˌvaɪrən'məntəlɪst, ɛn-, -ˌvaɪərn] *n* : écologiste *mf*
envision [ɪn'vɪʒən, ɛn-] *vt* : envisager
envoy ['ɛnˌvɔɪ, 'ɑn-] *n* : envoyé *m*, -voyée *f*
envy ['ɛnvi] *n* : envie *f*, jalousie *f* — ~ *vt* **-vied; -vying** : envier
enzyme ['ɛnˌzaɪm] *n* : enzyme *f*
epic ['ɛpɪk] *adj* : épique — ~ *n* : épopée *f*
epidemic [ˌɛpə'dɛmɪk] *n* : épidémie *f* — ~ *adj* : épidémique
epilepsy ['ɛpəˌlɛpsi] *n, pl* **-sies** : épilepsie *f* — **epileptic** [ˌɛpə'lɛptɪk] *adj* : épileptique — ~ *n* : épileptique *mf*
episode ['ɛpəˌso:d] *n* : épisode *m*
epitaph ['ɛpəˌtæf] *n* : épitaphe *f*
epitome [ɪ'pɪţəmi] *n* : exemple *m* même, modèle *m* — **epitomize** [ɪ'pɪţəˌmaɪz] *vt* **-mized; -mizing** : incarner
equal ['i:kwəl] *adj* **1** SAME : égal **2 be ~ to** : être à la hauteur de — ~ *n* : égal *m*, -gale *f* — ~ *vt* **equaled** *or* **equalled; equaling** *or* **equalling** : égaler — **equality** [ɪ'kwɑləţi] *n, pl* **-ties** : égalité *f* — **equalize** ['i:kwəˌlaɪz] *vt* **-ized; -izing** : égaliser — **equally** ['i:kwəli] *adv* **1** : également **2 ~ important** : tout aussi important
equate [ɪ'kweɪt] *vt* **equated; equating ~ with** : assimiler à — **equation** [ɪ-'kweɪʒən] *n* : équation *f*

equator [ɪˈkweɪt̬ər] *n* : équateur *m*
equilibrium [ˌiːkwəˈlɪbriəm, ˌɛ-] *n, pl* **-riums** *or* **-ria** : équilibre *m*
equinox [ˈiːkwəˌnɑks, ˈɛ-] *n* : équinoxe *m*
equip [ɪˈkwɪp] *vt* **equipped; equipping** : équiper — **equipment** [ɪˈkwɪpmənt] *n* : équipement *m,* matériel *m*
equity [ˈɛkwət̬i] *n, pl* **-ties** **1** FAIRNESS : équité *f* **2 equities** *npl* STOCKS : actions *fpl* ordinaires
equivalent [ɪˈkwɪvələnt] *adj* : équivalent — **~** *n* : équivalent *m*
era [ˈɪrə, ˈɛrə, ˈiːrə] *n* : ère *f,* époque *f*
eradicate [ɪˈrædəˌkeɪt] *vt* **-cated; -cating** : éradiquer
erase [ɪˈreɪs] *vt* **erased; erasing** : effacer — **eraser** [ɪˈreɪsər] *n* : gomme *f,* efface *f Can*
erect [ɪˈrɛkt] *adj* : droit — **~** *vt* **1** BUILD : construire **2** RAISE : ériger — **erection** [ɪˈrɛkʃən] *n* **1** BUILDING : construction *f* **2** : érection *f* (en physiologie)
erode [ɪˈroːd] *vt* **eroded; eroding** : éroder, ronger — **erosion** [ɪˈroːʒən] *n* : érosion *f*
erotic [ɪˈrɑt̬ɪk] *adj* : érotique
err [ˈɛr, ˈər] *vi* : se tromper
errand [ˈɛrənd] *n* : course *f,* commission *f*
erratic [ɪˈræt̬ɪk] *adj* : irrégulier
error [ˈɛrər] *n* : erreur *f* — **erroneous** [ɪˈroːniəs, ɛ-] *adj* : erroné
erupt [ɪˈrʌpt] *vi* **1** : entrer en éruption (se dit d'un volcan) **2** : éclater (se dit de la guerre, etc.) — **eruption** [ɪˈrʌpʃən] *n* : éruption *f*
escalate [ˈɛskəˌleɪt] *vi* **-lated; -lating** **1** : s'intensifier **2** : monter en flèche (se dit des prix, etc.)
escalator [ˈɛskəˌleɪt̬ər] *n* : escalier *m* mécanique
escape [ɪˈskeɪp, ɛ-] *v* **-caped; -caping** *vt* : échapper à, éviter — *vi* : s'échapper, s'évader — **~** *n* : fuite *f,* évasion *f*
escort [ˈɛsˌkɔrt] *n* GUARD : escorte *f* — **~** [ɪˈskɔrt, ɛ-] *vt* : escorter
Eskimo [ˈɛskəˌmoː] *adj* : esquimau
especially [ɪˈspɛʃəli] *adv* : particulièrement
espionage [ˈɛspiəˌnɑʒ, -ˌnɑʤ] *n* : espionnage *m*
espresso [ɛˈsprɛˌsoː] *n, pl* **-sos** : express *m,* café *m* express
essay [ˈɛˌseɪ] *n* : essai *m* (littéraire), dissertation *f* (académique)
essence [ˈɛsənts] *n* : essence *f* — **essential** [ɪˈsɛnʧəl] *adj* : essentiel — **~** *n* **1** : objet *m* essentiel **2 the ~s** : l'essentiel *m*
establish [ɪˈstæblɪʃ, ɛ-] *vt* : établir — **establishment** [ɪˈstæblɪʃmənt, ɛ-] *n* : établissement *m*
estate [ɪˈsteɪt, ɛ-] *n* **1** POSSESSIONS : biens *mpl* **2** LAND, PROPERTY : propriété *f,* domaine *m*
esteem [ɪˈstiːm, ɛ-] *n* : estime *f* — **~** *vt* : estimer
esthetic [ɛsˈθɛt̬ɪk] → **aesthetic**
estimate [ˈɛstəˌmeɪt] *vt* **-mated; -mating** : estimer — **~** [ˈɛstəmət] *n* : estimation *f* — **estimation** [ˌɛstəˈmeɪʃən] *n* **1** JUDGMENT : jugement *m* **2** ESTEEM : estime *f*
estuary [ˈɛsʧʊˌwɛri] *n, pl* **-aries** : estuaire *m*
eternal [ɪˈtərnəl, iː-] *adj* : éternel — **eternity** [ɪˈtərnət̬i, iː-] *n, pl* **-ties** : éternité *f*
ether [ˈiːθər] *n* : éther *m*
ethical [ˈɛθɪkəl] *adj* : éthique, moral — **ethics** [ˈɛθɪks] *ns & pl* : éthique *f,* morale *f*
ethnic [ˈɛθnɪk] *adj* : ethnique
etiquette [ˈɛt̬ɪkət, -ˌkɛt] *n* : étiquette *f,* convenances *fpl*
Eucharist [ˈjuːkərɪst] *n* : Eucharistie *f*
eulogy [ˈjuːləʤi] *n, pl* **-gies** : éloge *m*
euphemism [ˈjuːfəˌmɪzəm] *n* : euphémisme *m*
euphoria [jʊˈforiə] *n* : euphorie *f*
European [ˌjuːrəˈpiːən, -piːn] *adj* : européen
evacuate [ɪˈvækjʊˌeɪt] *vt* **-ated; -ating** : évacuer — **evacuation** [ɪˌvækjʊˈeɪʃən] *n* : évacuation *f*
evade [ɪˈveɪd] *vt* **evaded; evading** : éviter, esquiver
evaluate [ɪˈvæljʊˌeɪt] *vt* **-ated; -ating** : évaluer
evaporate [ɪˈvæpəˌreɪt] *vi* **-rated; -rating** : s'évaporer
evasion [ɪˈveɪʒən] *n* : évasion *f* — **evasive** [ɪˈveɪsɪv] *adj* : évasif
eve [ˈiːv] *n* : veille *f*
even [ˈiːvən] *adj* **1** REGULAR, STEADY : régulier **2** LEVEL : uni, plat **3** EQUAL : égal **4 ~ number** : nombre *m* pair **5 get ~ with** : se venger de — **~** *adv* **1** : même **2 ~ better** : encore mieux **3 ~ so** : quand même — **~** *vt* : égaliser — *vi or* **~ out** : s'égaliser
evening [ˈiːvnɪŋ] *n* : soir *m,* soirée *f*
event [ɪˈvɛnt] *n* **1** : événement *m* **2** : épreuve *f* (aux sports) **3 in the ~ of** : en cas de — **eventful** [ɪˈvɛntfəl] *adj* : mouvementé

eventual [ɪˈvɛntʃʊəl] *adj* : final — **eventuality** [ɪˌvɛntʃʊˈæləṭi] *n, pl* **-ties** : éventualité *f* — **eventually** [ɪˈvɛntʃʊəli] *adv* : finalement, en fin de compte

ever [ˈɛvər] *adv* **1** ALWAYS : toujours **2** ~ **since** : depuis **3** **hardly** ~ : presque jamais

evergreen [ˈɛvərˌgri:n] *n* : plante *f* à feuilles persistantes

everlasting [ˌɛvərˈlæstɪŋ] *adj* : éternel

every [ˈɛvri] *adj* **1** EACH : chaque **2** ~ **month** : tous les mois — **everybody** [ˈɛvriˌbʌdi, -ˈbɑ-] *pron* : tout le monde — **everyday** [ˌɛvriˈdeɪ, ˈɛvriˌ-] *adj* : quotidien, de tous les jours — **everyone** [ˈɛvriˌwʌn] → **everybody** — **everything** [ˈɛvriˌθɪŋ] *pron* : tout — **everywhere** [ˈɛvriˌ*h*wɛr] *adv* : partout

evict [ɪˈvɪkt] *vt* : expulser — **eviction** [ɪˈvɪkʃən] *n* : expulsion *f*

evidence [ˈɛvədənts] *n* **1** PROOF : preuve *f* **2** TESTIMONY : témoignage *m* — **evident** [ˈɛvɪdənt] *adj* : évident — **evidently** [ˈɛvɪdəntli, ˌɛvɪˈdɛntli] *adv* **1** OBVIOUSLY : évidemment, manifestement **2** APPARENTLY : apparemment

evil [ˈi:vəl, -vɪl] *adj* **eviler** *or* **eviller; evilest** *or* **evillest** : mauvais, méchant — ~ *n* : mal *m*

evoke [iˈvo:k] *vt* **evoked; evoking** : évoquer

evolution [ˌɛvəˈlu:ʃən, ˌi:-] *n* : évolution *f* — **evolve** [iˈvɑlv] *vi* **evolved; evolving** : évoluer, se développer

exact [ɪgˈzækt, ɛg-] *adj* : exact, précis — ~ *vt* : exiger — **exacting** [ɪgˈzæktɪŋ, ɛg-] *adj* : exigeant — **exactly** [ɪgˈzæktli, ɛg-] *adv* : exactement

exaggerate [ɪgˈzædʒəˌreɪt, ɛg-] *v* **-ated; -ating** : exagérer — **exaggeration** [ɪgˈzædʒəˈreɪʃən, ɛg-] *n* : exagération *f*

examine [ɪgˈzæmən, ɛg-] *vt* **-ined; -ining 1** : examiner **2** QUESTION : interroger — **exam** [ɪgˈzæm, ɛg-] *n* : examen *m* — **examination** [ɪgˌzæməˈneɪʃən, ɛg-] *n* : examen *m*

example [ɪgˈzæmpəl, ɛg-] *n* : exemple *m*

exasperate [ɪgˈzæspəˌreɪt, ɛg-] *vt* **-ated; -ating** : exaspérer — **exasperation** [ɪgˌzæspəˈreɪʃən, ɛg-] *n* : exaspération *f*

excavate [ˈɛkskəˌveɪt] *vt* **-vated; -vating** : creuser, excaver

exceed [ɪkˈsi:d, ɛk-] *vt* : dépasser — **exceedingly** [ɪkˈsi:dɪŋli, ɛk-] *adv* : extrêmement

excel [ɪkˈsɛl, ɛk-] *vi* **-celled; -celling** : exceller — **excellence** [ˈɛksələnts] *n* : excellence *f* — **excellent** [ˈɛksəˌlənt] *adj* : excellent

except [ɪkˈsɛpt] *prep* **1** : sauf, excepté **2** ~ **for** : à part — ~ *vt* : excepter — **exception** [ɪkˈsɛpʃən] *n* : exception *f* — **exceptional** [ɪkˈsɛpʃənəl] *adj* : exceptionnel

excerpt [ɛkˈsərpt, ˈɛgˌzərpt] *n* : extrait *m*

excess [ɪkˈsɛs, ˈɛkˌsɛs] *n* : excès *m* — ~ [ˈɛkˌsɛs, ɪkˈsɛs] *adj* : excédentaire, en trop — **excessive** [ɪkˈsɛsɪv, ɛk-] *adj* : excessif

exchange [ɪksˈtʃeɪndʒ, ɛks-; ˈɛksˌtʃeɪndʒ] *n* **1** : échange *m* **2** : change *m* (en finances) — ~ *vt* **-changed; -changing** : échanger

excise [ˈɪkˌsaɪz, ɛk-] *n or* ~ **tax** : contribution *f* indirecte

excite [ɪkˈsaɪt, ɛk-] *vt* **-cited; -citing** : exciter — **excited** [ɪkˈsaɪṭəd, ɛk-] *adj* : excité, enthousiaste — **excitement** [ɪkˈsaɪtmənt, ɛk-] *n* : enthousiasme *m* — **exciting** [ɪkˈsaɪtɪŋ, ɛk-] *adj* : passionnant

exclaim [ɪksˈkleɪm, ɛk-] *vi* : s'exclamer — **exclamation** [ˌɛkskləˈmeɪʃən] *n* : exclamation *f* — **exclamation point** *n* : point *m* d'exclamation

exclude [ɪksˈklu:d, ɛks-] *vt* **-cluded; -cluding** : exclure — **excluding** [ɪksˈklu:dɪŋ, ɛks-] *prep* : à part, à l'exclusion de — **exclusion** [ɪksˈkluɪʃ'n, ɛks-] *n* : exclusion *f* — **exclusive** [ɪksˈklu:sɪv, ɛks-] *adj* : exclusif

excrement [ˈɛkskrəmənt] *n* : excréments *mpl*

excruciating [ɪkˈskru:ʃiˌeɪṭɪŋ, ɛk-] *adj* : atroce, insupportable

excursion [ɪkˈskərʒən, ɛk-] *n* : excursion *f*

excuse [ɪkˈskju:z, ɛk-] *vt* **-cused; -cusing 1** : excuser **2** ~ **me** : excusez-moi, pardon — ~ [ɪkˈskju:s, ɛk-] *n* : excuse *f*

execute [ˈɛksɪˌkju:t] *vt* **-cuted; -cuting** : exécuter — **execution** [ˌɛksɪˈkju:ʃən] *n* : exécution *f* — **executioner** [ˌɛksɪˈkju:ʃənər] *n* : bourreau *m*

executive [ɪgˈzɛkjəṭɪv, ɛg-] *adj* : exécutif — ~ *n* **1** MANAGER : cadre *m* **2** *or* ~ **branch** : exécutif *m*, pouvoir *m* exécutif

exemplify [ɪgˈzɛmpləˌfaɪ, ɛg-] *vt* **-fied; -fying** : illustrer — **exemplary** [ɪgˈzɛmpləri, ɛg-] *adj* : exemplaire

exempt [ɪgˈzɛmpt, ɛg-] *adj* : exempt —

~ *vt* : exempter — **exemption** [ɪg'zɛmpʃən, ɛg-] *n* : exemption *f*
exercise ['ɛksər,saɪz] *n* : exercice *m* — ~ *v* **-cised; -cising** *vt* : exercer — *vi* : faire de l'exercice
exert [ɪg'zərt, ɛg-] *vt* **1** : exercer **2** ~ **oneself** : se donner de la peine — **exertion** [ɪg'zərʃən, ɛg-] *n* : effort *m*
exhale [ɛks'heɪl] *v* **-haled; -haling** : expirer
exhaust [ɪg'zɔst, ɛg-] *vt* : épuiser — ~ *n* **1** *or* ~ **fumes** : gaz *m* d'échappement **2** *or* ~ **pipe** : tuyau *m* d'échappement — **exhaustion** [ɪg'zɔstʃən, ɛg-] *n* : épuisement *m* — **exhaustive** [ɪg'zɔstɪv, ɛg-] *adj* : exhaustif
exhibit [ɪg'zɪbət, ɛg-] *vt* **1** DISPLAY : exposer **2** SHOW : montrer — ~ *n* **1** : objet *m* exposé **2** EXHIBITION : exposition *f* — **exhibition** [,ɛksə'bɪʃən] *n* : exposition *f*
exhilarate [ɪg'zɪlə,reɪt, ɛg-] *vt* **-rated; -rating** : animer — **exhilaration** [ɪg,zɪlə'reɪʃən, ɛg-] *n* : joie *f*
exile ['ɛg,zaɪl, 'ɛk,saɪl] *n* **1** : exil *m* **2** OUTCAST : exilé *m*, -lée *f* — ~ *vt* **exiled; exiling** : exiler
exist [ɪg'zɪst, ɛg-] *vi* : exister — **existence** [ɪg'zɪstənts, ɛg-] *n* : existence *f*
exit ['ɛgzət, 'ɛksət] *n* : sortie *f* — ~ *vi* : sortir
exodus ['ɛksədəs] *n* : exode *m*
exonerate [ɪg'zɑnə,reɪt, ɛg-] *vt* **-ated; -ating** : disculper
exorbitant [ɪg'zɔrbətənt, ɛg-] *adj* : exorbitant, excessif
exotic [ɪg'zɑtɪk, ɛg-] *adj* : exotique
expand [ɪk'spænd, ɛk-] *vt* : étendre, élargir — *vi* : s'étendre, s'agrandir — **expanse** [ɪk'spænts, ɛk-] *n* : étendue *f* — **expansion** [ɪk'spæntʃən, ɛk-] *n* : expansion *f*
expatriate [ɛks'peɪtriət, -,eɪt] *n* : expatrié *m*, -triée *f* — ~ *adj* : expatrié
expect [ɪk'spɛkt, ɛk-] *vt* **1** ANTICIPATE : s'attendre à **2** AWAIT : attendre **3** REQUIRE : exiger, demander — *vi* **be expecting** : attendre un bébé, être enceinte — **expectancy** [ɪk'spɛktəntsi, ɛk-] *n, pl* **-cies** : attente *f*, espérance *f* — **expectant** [ɪk'spɛktənt, ɛk-] *adj* **1** : qui attend **2** ~ **mother** : future mère *f* — **expectation** [,ɛk,spɛk'teɪʃən] *n* : attente *f*
expedient [ɪk'spi:diənt, ɛk-] *adj* : opportun — ~ *n* : expédient *m*
expedition [,ɛkspə'dɪʃən] *n* : expédition *f*
expel [ɪk'spɛl, ɛk-] *vt* **-pelled; -pelling** : expulser, renvoyer (un élève)
expend [ɪk'spɛnd, ɛk-] *vt* : dépenser — **expendable** [ɪk'spɛndəbəl, ɛk-] *adj* : remplaçable — **expenditure** [ɪk'spɛndɪtʃər, ɛk-, -,tʃʊr] *n* : dépense *f* — **expense** [ɪk'spɛnts, ɛk-] *n* **1** : dépense *f* **2** ~**s** *npl* : frais *mpl* **3 at the** ~ **of** : aux dépens de — **expensive** [ɪk'spɛntsɪv, ɛk-] *adj* : cher, coûteux
experience [ɪk'spɪriənts, ɛk-] *n* : expérience *f* — ~ *vt* **-enced; -encing** : éprouver, connaître — **experienced** [ɪk'spɪriəntst, ɛk-] *adj* : expérimenté — **experiment** [ɪk'spɛrəmənt, ɛk-, -'spɪr-] *n* : expérience *f* — ~ *vi* : expérimenter — **experimental** [ɪk,spɛrə'mɛntəl, ɛk-, -,spɪr-] *adj* : expérimental
expert ['ɛk,spərt, ɪk'spərt] *adj* : expert — ~ ['ɛk,spərt] *n* : expert *m*, -perte *f* — **expertise** [,ɛksper'ti:z] *n* : compétence *f*
expire [ɪk'spaɪr, ɛk-] *vi* **-pired; -piring** : expirer — **expiration** [,ɛkspə'reɪʃən] *n* : expiration *f*
explain [ɪk'spleɪn, ɛk-] *vt* **1** : expliquer **2** ~ **oneself** : s'expliquer — **explanation** [,ɛksplə'neɪʃən] *n* : explication *f* — **explanatory** [ɪk'splænə,tori, ɛk-] *adj* : explicatif
explicit [ɪk'splɪsət, ɛk-] *adj* : explicite
explode [ɪk'splo:d, ɛk-] *v* **-ploded; -ploding** *vt* : faire exploser — *vi* : exploser
exploit ['ɛk,splɔɪt] *n* : exploit *m* — ~ [ɪk'splɔɪt, ɛk-] *vt* : exploiter — **exploitation** [,ɛk,splɔɪ'teɪʃən] *n* : exploitation *f*
exploration [,ɛksplə'reɪʃən] *n* : exploration *f* — **explore** [ɪk'splor, ɛk-] *v* **-plored; -ploring** : explorer — **explorer** [ɪk'splorər, ɛk-] *n* : explorateur *m*, -trice *f*
explosion [ɪk'splo:ʒən, ɛk-] *n* : explosion *f* — **explosive** [ɪk'splo:sɪv, ɛk-] *adj* : explosif — ~ *n* : explosif *m*
export [ɛk'sport, 'ɛk,sport] *vt* : exporter — ~ ['ɛk,sport] *n* : exportation *f*
expose [ɪk'spo:z, ɛk-] *vt* **-posed; -posing** **1** : exposer **2** REVEAL : révéler — **exposure** [ɪk'spo:ʒər, ɛk-] *n* : exposition *f*
express [ɪk'sprɛs, ɛk-] *adj* **1** SPECIFIC : exprès, formel **2** FAST : express — ~ *adv* **send** ~ : envoyer en exprès — ~ *n or* ~ **train** : rapide *m*, express *m* — ~ *vt* : exprimer — **expression** [ɪk-

ˈsprɛʃən, ɛk-] *n* : expression *f* — **expressive** [ɪkˈsprɛsɪv, ɛk-] *adj* : expressif — **expressly** [ɪkˈsprɛsli, ɛk-] *adv* : expressément — **expressway** [ɪkˈsprɛsˌweɪ, ɛk-] *n* : autoroute *f*
expulsion [ɪkˈspʌlʃən, ɛk-] *n* : expulsion *f,* renvoi *m* (d'un élève)
exquisite [ɛkˈskwɪzət, ˈɛkˌskwɪ-] *adj* : exquis
extend [ɪkˈstɛnd, ɛk-] *vt* **1** STRETCH : étendre **2** LENGTHEN : prolonger **3** ENLARGE : agrandir **4 ~ one's hand** : tendre la main — *vi* : s'étendre — **extension** [ɪkˈstɛntʃən, ɛk-] *n* **1** : extension *f* **2** LENGTHENING : prolongation *f* **3** ANNEX : annexe *f* **4** : poste *m* (de téléphone) **5 ~ cord** : rallonge *f* — **extensive** [ɪkˈstɛntsɪv, ɛk-] *adj* : étendu, vaste — **extent** [ɪkˈstɛnt, ɛk-] *n* **1** : étendue *f,* ampleur *f* **2** DEGREE : mesure *f,* degré *m*
exterior [ɛkˈstɪriər] *adj* : extérieur — **~** *n* : extérieur *m*
exterminate [ɪkˈstərməˌneɪt, ɛk-] *vt* **-nated; -nating** : exterminer — **extermination** [ɪkˌstərməˈneɪʃən, ɛk-] *n* : extermination *f*
external [ɪkˈstərnəl, ɛk-] *adj* : externe — **externally** [ɪkˈstərnəli, ɛk-] *adv* : extérieurement
extinct [ɪkˈstɪŋkt, ɛk-] *adj* : disparu — **extinction** [ɪkˈstɪŋkʃən, ɛk-] *n* : extinction *f*
extinguish [ɪkˈstɪŋgwɪʃ, ɛk-] *vt* : éteindre — **extinguisher** [ɪkˈstɪŋgwɪʃər, ɛk-] *n* : extincteur *m*
extol [ɪkˈsto:l, ɛk-] *vt* **-tolled; -tolling** : louer
extort [ɪkˈstɔrt, ɛk-] *vt* : extorquer — **extortion** [ɪkˈstɔrʃən, ɛk-] *n* : extorsion *f*
extra [ˈɛkstrə] *adj* : supplémentaire, de plus — **~** *n* : supplément *m* — **~** *adv* **1** : plus (que d'habitude) **2 cost ~** : coûter plus cher
extract [ɪkˈstrækt, ɛk-] *vt* : extraire, arracher — **~** [ˈɛkˌstrækt] *n* : extrait *m* — **extraction** [ɪkˈstrækʃən, ɛk-] *n* : extraction *f*
extracurricular [ˌɛkstrəkəˈrɪkjələr] *adj* : parascolaire
extraordinary [ɪkˈstrɔrdənˌɛri, ˌɛkstrəˈɔrd-] *adj* : extraordinaire
extraterrestrial [ˌɛkstrətəˈrɛstriəl] *adj* : extraterrestre — **~** *n* : extraterrestre *mf*
extravagant [ɪkˈstrævɪgənt, ɛk-] *adj* **1** : extravagant **2** WASTEFUL : prodigue —**extravagance** [ɪkˈstrævɪgənts, ɛk-] *n* **1** : extravagance *f* **2** WASTEFULNESS : prodigalité *f*
extreme [ɪkˈstri:m, ɛk-] *adj* : extrême — **~** *n* : extrême *m* — **extremity** [ɪkˈstrɛməṭi, ɛk-] *n, pl* **-ties** : extrémité *f*
extricate [ˈɛkstrəˌkeɪt] *vt* **-cated; -cating 1** : dégager **2 ~ oneself from** : s'extirper de
extrovert [ˈɛkstrəˌvərt] *n* : extraverti *m,* -tie *f* — **extroverted** [ˈɛkstrəˌvərṭəd] *adj* : extraverti
exuberant [ɪgˈzu:bərənt, ɛg-] *adj* : exubérant — **exuberance** [ɪgˈzu:bərənts, ɛg-] *n* : exubérance *f*
exult [ɪgˈzʌlt, ɛg-] *vi* : exulter
eye [ˈaɪ] *n* **1** : œil *m* **2** VISION : vision *f* **3** GLANCE : regard *m* **4 ~ of a needle** : chas *m* — **~** *vt* **eyed; eyeing** *or* **eying** : regarder — **eyeball** [ˈaɪˌbɔl] *n* : globe *m* oculaire — **eyebrow** [ˈaɪˌbraʊ] *n* : sourcil *m* — **eyeglasses** [ˈaɪˌglæsəz] *npl* : lunettes *fpl* — **eyelash** [ˈaɪˌlæʃ] *n* : cil *m* — **eyelid** [aɪˌlɪd] *n* : paupière *f* — **eyesight** [ˈaɪˌsaɪt] *n* : vue *f,* vision *f* — **eyewitness** [ˈaɪˈwɪtnəs] *n* : témoin *m* oculaire

F

f [ˈɛf] *n, pl* **f's** *or* **fs** [ˈɛfs] : f *m,* sixième lettre de l'alphabet
fable [ˈfeɪbəl] *n* : fable *f*
fabric [ˈfæbrɪk] *n* : tissu *m,* étoffe *f*
fabulous [ˈfæbjələs] *adj* : fabuleux
facade [fəˈsɑd] *n* : façade *f*
face [ˈfeɪs] *n* **1** : visage *m,* figure *f* **2** EXPRESSION : mine *f* **3** SURFACE : face *f* (d'une monnaie), façade *f* (d'un bâtiment) **4 ~ value** : valeur *f* nominale **5 in the ~ of** DESPITE : en dépit de **6 lose ~** : perdre la face **7 make a ~** : faire la grimace — **~** *vt* **faced; facing 1** CONFRONT : faire face à **2** OVERLOOK : être en face de, donner sur — **faceless** [ˈfeɪsləs] *adj* : anonyme
facet [ˈfæsət] *n* : facette *f*
face–to–face *adv* : face à face
facial [ˈfeɪʃəl] *adj* : du visage
facetious [fəˈsi:ʃəs] *adj* : facétieux
facility [fəˈsɪləṭi] *n, pl* **-ties 1** : facilité *f* **2 facilities** *npl* : installations *fpl* — **fa-**

cilitate [fə'sɪlə,teɪt] *vt* **-tated; -tating** : faciliter
facsimile [fæk'sɪməli] *n* : fac-similé *m*
fact ['fækt] *n* **1** : fait *m* **2 in ~** : en fait
faction ['fækʃən] *n* : faction *f*
factor ['fæktər] *n* : facteur *m*
factory ['fæktəri] *n, pl* **-ries** : usine *f*, fabrique *f*
factual ['fæktʃuəl] *adj* : factuel, basé sur les faits
faculty ['fækəlti] *n, pl* **-ties** : faculté *f*
fad ['fæd] *n* : mode *f* passagère, manie *f*
fade ['feɪd] *v* **faded; fading** *vi* **1** WITHER : se flétrir, se faner **2** DISCOLOR : se décolorer **3** DIM : s'affaiblir, diminuer **4** VANISH : disparaître — *vt* : décolorer
fail ['feɪl] *vi* **1** : échouer **2** WEAKEN : faiblir, baisser **3** BREAK DOWN : tomber en panne **4 ~ in** : manquer à — *vt* **1** DISAPPOINT : décevoir **2** NEGLECT : manquer, négliger **3** : échouer à (un examen) — **~** *n* **without ~** : à coup sûr — **failing** ['feɪlɪŋ] *n* : défaut *m* — **failure** ['feɪljər] *n* **1** : échec *m* **2** BREAKDOWN : panne *f*
faint ['feɪnt] *adj* **1** WEAK : faible **2** INDISTINCT : vague **3 feel ~** : se sentir mal — **~** *vi* : s'évanouir — **fainthearted** ['feɪnt'hɑrt̬əd] *adj* : timide — **faintly** ['feɪntli] *adv* **1** WEAKLY : faiblement **2** SLIGHTLY : légèrement
fair[1] ['fær] *n* : foire *f*
fair[2] *adj* **1** BEAUTIFUL : beau **2** : blond (se dit des cheveux), clair (se dit de la peau) **3** JUST : juste, équitable **4** ADEQUATE : passable **5** LARGE : grand — **fairly** ['færli] *adv* **1** HONESTLY : équitablement **2** QUITE : assez — **fairness** ['færnəs] *n* : équité *f*
fairy ['færi] *n, pl* **fairies 1** : fée *f* **2 ~ tale** *n* : conte *m* de fées
faith ['feɪθ] *n, pl* **faiths** ['feɪθs, 'feɪðz] : foi *f* — **faithful** ['feɪθfəl] *adj* : fidèle — **faithfully** *adv* : fidèlement — **faithfulness** ['feɪθfəlnəs] *n* : fidélité *f*
fake ['feɪk] *v* **faked; faking** *vt* **1** FALSIFY : falsifier **2** FEIGN : simuler — *vi* PRETEND : faire semblant — **~** *adj* : faux — **~** *n* **1** IMITATION : faux *m* **2** IMPOSTER : imposteur *m*
falcon ['fælkən, 'fɔl-] *n* : faucon *m*
fall ['fɔl] *vi* **fell** ['fɛl]; **fallen** ['fɔlən]; **falling 1** : tomber **2 ~ asleep** : s'endormir **3 ~ back** : se retirer **4 ~ back on** : avoir recours à **5 ~ behind** : prendre du retard **6 ~ in love** : tomber amoureux **7 ~ out** QUARREL : se disputer — **~** *n* **1** : chute *f* **2** AUTUMN : automne *m* **3 ~s** *npl* WATERFALL : chute *f* (d'eau), cascade *f*
fallacy ['fæləsi] *n, pl* **-cies** : erreur *f*
fallible ['fæləbəl] *adj* : faillible
fallow ['fælo] *adj* : en jachère
false ['fɔls] *adj* **falser; falsest 1** : faux **2 ~ alarm** : fausse alerte *f* **3 ~ teeth** : dentier *m* — **falsehood** ['fɔls,hʊd] *n* : mensonge *m* — **falsely** ['fɔlsli] *adv* : faussement — **falseness** ['fɔlsnəs] *n* : fausseté *f* — **falsify** ['fɔlsə,faɪ] *vt* **-fied; -fying** : falsifier
falter ['fɔltər] *vi* **1** STUMBLE : chanceler **2** WAVER : hésiter
fame ['feɪm] *n* : renommée *f*
familiar [fə'mɪljər] *adj* **1** : familier **2 be ~ with** : bien connaître — **familiarity** [fə,mɪli'ærət̬i, -,mɪl'jær-] *n, pl* **-ties** : familiarité *f* — **familiarize** [fə'mɪljə,raɪz] *vt* **-ized; -izing ~ oneself** : se familiariser
family ['fæmli, 'fæmə-] *n, pl* **-lies** : famille *f*
famine ['fæmən] *n* : famine *f*
famished ['fæmɪʃt] *adj* : affamé
famous ['feɪməs] *adj* : célèbre
fan ['fæn] *n* **1** : éventail *m*, ventilateur *m* (électrique) **2** ENTHUSIAST : enthousiaste *mf* — **~** *vt* **fanned; fanning 1** : attiser (un feu) **2 ~ oneself** : s'éventer (le visage)
fanatic [fə'næt̬ɪk] *n* : fanatique *mf* — **~** *or* **fanatical** [-t̬ɪkəl] *adj* : fanatique — **fanaticism** [fə'næt̬ə,sɪzəm] *n* : fanatisme *m*
fancy ['fæntsi] *vt* **-cied; -cying 1** LIKE : aimer **2** WANT : avoir envie de **3** IMAGINE : s'imaginer — **~** *adj* **fancier; -est 1** ELABORATE : recherché **2** LUXURIOUS : fin, de luxe — **~** *n, pl* **-cies 1** LIKING : goût *m* **2** WHIM : fantaisie *f* **3 take a ~ to** : se prendre d'affection pour — **fanciful** ['fæntsɪfəl] *adj* : fantaisiste
fanfare ['fæn,fær] *n* : fanfare *f*
fang ['fæŋ] *n* : croc *m*, crochet *m* (d'un serpent)
fantasy ['fæntəsi] *n, pl* **-sies 1** DREAM : fantasme *m* **2** IMAGINATION : fantaisie *f* — **fantasize** ['fæntə,saɪz] *vi* **-sized; -sizing** : fantasmer — **fantastic** [fæn'tæstɪk] *adj* : fantastique
far ['fɑr] *adv* **farther** ['fɑrðər] *or* **further** ['fər-]; **farthest** *or* **furthest** [-ðəst] **1** : loin **2 as ~ as** : jusqu'à **3 as ~ as possible** : autant que possible **4 by ~** : de loin **5 ~ away** : au loin **6 ~ from it!** : pas du tout! **7 ~ worse** : bien pire **8 so ~** : jusqu'ici

— ∼ *adj* **farther** *or* **further; farthest** *or* **furthest 1** : lointain **2 the ∼ right** : l'extrême droite **3 the ∼ side** : l'autre côté — **faraway** [ˈfɑrəˌweɪ] *adj* : éloigné, lointain
farce [ˈfɑrs] *n* : farce *f*
fare [ˈfær] *vi* **fared; faring** : aller — ∼ *n* **1** : tarif *m,* prix *m* **2** FOOD : nourriture *f*
farewell [færˈwɛl] *n* : adieu *m* — ∼ *adj* : d'adieu
far–fetched [ˈfɑrˈfɛtʃt] *adj* : improbable, bizarre
farm [ˈfɑrm] *n* : ferme *f* — ∼ *vt* : cultiver — *vi* : être fermier — **farmer** [ˈfɑrmər] *n* : fermier *m,* -mière *f* — **farmhand** [ˈfɑrmˌhænd] *n* : ouvrier *m,* -vrière *f* agricole — **farmhouse** [ˈfɑrmˌhaʊs] *n* : ferme *f* — **farming** [ˈfɑrmɪŋ] *n* : agriculture *f,* élevage (des animaux) — **farmyard** [ˈfɑrmˌjɑrd] *n* : cour *f* de ferme
far–off [ˈfɑrˌɔf, -ˈɔf] *adj* : lointain
far–reaching [ˈfɑrˈriːtʃɪŋ] *adj* : d'une grande portée
farsighted [ˈfɑrˌsaɪṭəd] *adj* **1** : presbyte **2** SHREWD : prévoyant
farther [ˈfɑrðər] *adv* **1** : plus loin **2** MORE : de plus — ∼ *adj* : plus éloigné, plus lointain — **farthest** [ˈfɑrðəst] *adv* : le plus loin — ∼ *adj* : le plus éloigné
fascinate [ˈfæsənˌeɪt] *vt* **-nated; -nating** : fasciner — **fascination** [ˌfæsənˈeɪʃən] *n* : fascination *f*
fascism [ˈfæʃˌɪzəm] *n* : fascisme *m* — **fascist** [ˈfæʃɪst] *adj* : fasciste — ∼ *n* : fasciste *mf*
fashion [ˈfæʃən] *n* **1** MANNER : façon *f* **2** STYLE : mode *f* **3 out of ∼** : démodé — **fashionable** [ˈfæʃənəbəl] *adj* : à la mode
fast[1] [ˈfæst] *vi* : jeûner — ∼ *n* : jeûne *m*
fast[2] *adj* **1** SWIFT : rapide **2** SECURE : ferme **3 my watch is ∼** : ma montre avance — ∼ *adv* **1** SECURELY : solidement, ferme **2** SWIFTLY : rapidement, vite **3 ∼ asleep** : profondément endormi
fasten [ˈfæsən] *vt* : attacher, fermer — *vi* : s'attacher, se fermer — **fastener** [ˈfæsənər] *n* : attache *f,* fermeture *f*
fastidious [fæsˈtɪdiəs] *adj* : méticuleux
fat [ˈfæt] *adj* **fatter; fattest 1** : gros, gras **2** THICK : épais — ∼ *n* : gras *m* (de la viande), graisse *f* (du corps)
fatal [ˈfeɪṭəl] *adj* **1** DEADLY : mortel **2** FATEFUL : fatal — **fatality** [feɪˈtæləṭi, fə-] *n, pl* **-ties** : mort *m*
fate [ˈfeɪt] *n* **1** DESTINY : destin *m* **2** LOT : sort *m* — **fateful** [ˈfeɪtfəl] *adj* : fatidique
father [ˈfɑðər] *n* : père *m* — **fatherhood** [ˈfɑðərˌhʊd] *n* : paternité *f* — **father–in–law** [ˈfɑðərɪnˌlɔ] *n, pl* **fathers–in–law** : beau-père *m* — **fatherly** [ˈfɑðərli] *adj* : paternel
fathom [ˈfæðəm] *vt* : comprendre
fatigue [fəˈtiːg] *vt* **-tigued; -tiguing** : fatiguer — ∼ *n* : fatigue *f*
fatten [ˈfætən] *vt* : engraisser — **fattening** [ˈfætənɪŋ] *n* : qui fait grossir
fatty [ˈfæti] *adj* **fattier; -est** : gras
faucet [ˈfɔsət] *n* : robinet *m*
fault [ˈfɔlt] *n* **1** FLAW : défaut *m* **2** RESPONSIBILITY : faute *f* **3** : faille *f* (géologique) — ∼ *vt* : trouver des défauts à, critiquer — **faultless** [ˈfɔltləs] *adj* : irréprochable — **faulty** [ˈfɔlti] *adj* **faultier; -est** : fautif, défectueux
fauna [ˈfɔnə] *n* : faune *f*
favor *or Brit* **favour** [ˈfeɪvər] *n* **1** APPROVAL : faveur *f* **2 do s.o. a ∼** : rendre un service à qqn **3 in ∼ of** : en faveur de, pour — ∼ *vt* **1** : favoriser **2** PREFER : préférer — **favorable** *or Brit* **favourable** [ˈfeɪvərəbəl] *adj* : favorable — **favorite** *or Brit* **favourite** [ˈfeɪvərət] *adj* : favori, préféré — ∼ *n* : favori *m,* -rite *f,* préféré *m,* -rée *f* — **favoritism** *or Brit* **favouritism** [ˈfeɪvərəˌtɪzəm] *n* : favoritisme *m*
fawn[1] [ˈfɔn] *vi* **∼ upon** : flatter servilement
fawn[2] *n* : faon *m*
fax [ˈfæks] *n* : fax *m,* télécopie *f* — ∼ *vt* : faxer, envoyer par télécopie
fear [ˈfɪr] *vt* : craindre, avoir peur de — *vi* **∼ for** : craindre pour — ∼ *n* : crainte *f,* peur *f* — **fearful** [ˈfɪrfəl] *adj* **1** FRIGHTENING : effrayant **2** AFRAID : craintif, peureux
feasible [ˌfiːzəbəl] *adj* : faisable
feast [ˈfiːst] *n* : banquet *m,* festin *m* — ∼ *vi* **∼ on** : se régaler de
feat [ˈfiːt] *n* : exploit *m,* prouesse *f*
feather [ˈfɛðər] *n* : plume *f*
feature [ˈfiːtʃər] *n* **1** : trait *m* (du visage) **2** CHARACTERISTIC : caractéristique *f* — ∼ *vt* : mettre en vedette — *vi* : figurer
February [ˈfɛbjʊˌɛri, ˈfɛbʊ-, ˈfɛbrʊ-] *n* : février *m*
feces [ˈfiːˌsiːz] *npl* : fèces *fpl*
federal [ˈfɛdrəl, -dərəl] *adj* : fédéral — **federation** [ˌfɛdəˈreɪʃən] *n* : fédération *f*
fed up [ˈfɛd] *adj* **be ∼** : en avoir assez, en avoir marre *fam*
fee [ˈfiː] *n* **1** : frais *mpl* (de scolarité),

honoraires *mpl* (médicaux) **2** *or* **entrance ~** : droit *m* d'entrée
feeble [ˈfiːbəl] *adj* **-bler; -blest 1** : faible **2 a ~ excuse** : une piètre excuse
feed [ˈfiːd] *v* **fed** [ˈfɛd]; **feeding** *vt* **1** : nourrir, donner à manger à **2** SUPPLY : alimenter — *vi* EAT : manger, se nourrir — **~** *n* : fourrage *m*
feel [ˈfiːl] *v* **felt** [ˈfɛlt]; **feeling** *vt* **1** : sentir **2** TOUCH : toucher **3** EXPERIENCE : ressentir (un sentiment) **4** BELIEVE : croire — *vi* **1** : se sentir **2** SEEM : sembler **3 ~ cold/thirsty** : avoir froid, soif **4 ~ like** WANT : avoir envie de — **~** *n* : toucher *m*, sensation *f* — **feeling** [ˈfiːlɪŋ] *n* **1** SENSATION : sensation *f* **2** EMOTION : sentiment *m* **3** OPINION : avis *m* **4 ~s** *npl* : sentiments *mpl*
feet → **foot**
feign [ˈfeɪn] *vt* : feindre
feline [ˈfiːˌlaɪn] *adj* : félin — **~** *n* : félin *m*
fell[1] → **fall**
fell[2] [ˈfɛl] *vt* : abattre (un arbre)
fellow [ˈfɛˌloː] *n* **1** COMPANION : compagnon *m* **2** MAN : gars *m fam*, type *m fam* — **fellowship** [ˈfɛloˌʃɪp] *n* **1** COMPANIONSHIP : camaraderie *f* **2** GRANT : bourse *f* universitaire
felon [ˈfɛlən] *n* : criminel *m*, -nelle *f* — **felony** [ˈfɛləni] *n, pl* **-nies** : crime *m*
felt[1] → **feel**
felt[2] [ˈfɛlt] *n* : feutre *m*
female [ˈfiːˌmeɪl] *adj* : femelle (se dit des animaux), féminin (se dit des personnes) — **~** *n* **1** : femelle *f* (animal) **2** WOMAN : femme *f*
feminine [ˈfɛmənən] *adj* : féminin — **femininity** [ˌfɛməˈnɪnəti] *n* : féminité *f* — **feminism** [ˈfɛməˌnɪzəm] *n* : féminisme *m* — **feminist** [ˈfɛmənɪst] *adj* : féministe — **~** *n* : féministe *mf*
fence [ˈfɛnts] *n* : clôture *f*, barrière *f* — **~** *v* **fenced; fencing** *vt* : clôturer — *vi* : faire de l'escrime — **fencing** [ˈfɛntsɪŋ] *n* : escrime *f*
fend [ˈfɛnd] *vt or* **~ off** : parer (un coup) — *vi* **~ for oneself** : se débrouiller tout seul
fender [ˈfɛndər] *n* : aile *f* (d'une voiture)
fennel [ˈfɛnəl] *n* : fenouil *m*
ferment [fɛrˈmɛnt] *vi* : fermenter — **fermentation** [ˌfərmənˈteɪʃən, -ˌmɛn-] *n* : fermentation *f*
fern [ˈfərn] *n* : fougère *f*
ferocious [fəˈroːʃəs] *adj* : féroce — **ferocity** [fəˈrɑsəti] *n* : férocité *f*
ferret [ˈfɛrət] *n* : furet *m* — **~** *vt* **~ out** : dénicher
Ferris wheel [ˈfɛrɪs] *n* : grande roue *f*
ferry [ˈfɛri] *vt* **-ried; -rying** : transporter — **~** *n, pl* **-ries** : ferry-boat *m*
fertile [ˈfərtəl] *adj* : fertile — **fertility** [fərˈtɪləti] *n* : fertilité *f*, fécondité *f* — **fertilize** [ˈfərtəlˌaɪz] *vt* **-ized; -izing** : fertiliser (une terre), féconder (un œuf, etc.) — **fertilizer** [ˈfərtəlˌaɪzər] *n* : engrais *m*
fervent [ˈfərvənt] *adj* : fervent — **fervor** *or Brit* **fervour** [ˈfərvər] *n* : ferveur *f*
fester [ˈfɛstər] *vi* : suppurer
festival [ˈfɛstəvəl] *n* : festival *m* — **festive** [ˈfɛstɪv] *adj* : joyeux, de fête — **festivities** [fɛsˈtɪvətiz] *npl* : réjouissances *fpl*
fetch [ˈfɛtʃ] *vt* **1** BRING : aller chercher **2** REALIZE : rapporter (de l'argent)
fetid [ˈfɛtəd] *adj* : fétide
fetish [ˈfɛtɪʃ] *n* : fétiche *m*
fetter [ˈfɛtər] *vt* : enchaîner — **fetters** [ˈfɛtərz] *npl* : fers *mpl*, chaînes *fpl*
fetus [ˈfiːtəs] *n* : fœtus *m*
feud [ˈfjuːd] *n* : querelle *f* — **~** *vi* : se quereller
feudal [ˈfjuːdəl] *adj* : féodal
fever [ˈfiːvər] *n* : fièvre *f* — **feverish** [ˈfiːvərɪʃ] *adj* : fiévreux
few [ˈfjuː] *adj* **1** : peu de **2 a ~** : quelques — **~** *pron* **1** : peu, quelques-uns, quelques-unes **2 quite a ~** : un assez grand nombre de — **fewer** [ˈfjuːər] *adj* : moins de — **~** *pron* : moins
fiancé, fiancée [ˌfiːˌɑnˈseɪ, ˌfiːˈɑnˌseɪ] *n* : fiancé *m*, -cée *f*
fiasco [fɪˈæsˌkoː] *n, pl* **-coes** : fiasco *m*
fib [ˈfɪb] *n* : petit mensonge *m* — **~** *vi* **fibbed; fibbing** : raconter des histoires
fiber *or* **fibre** [ˈfaɪbər] *n* : fibre *f* — **fiberglass** [ˈfaɪbərˌglæs] *n* : fibre *f* de verre — **fibrous** [ˈfaɪbrəs] *adj* : fibreux
fickle [ˈfɪkəl] *adj* : volage, inconstant
fiction [ˈfɪkʃən] *n* : fiction *f* — **fictional** [ˈfɪkʃənəl] *or* **fictitious** [fɪkˈtɪʃəs] *adj* : fictif
fiddle [ˈfɪdəl] *n* : violon *m* — **~** *vi* **-dled; -dling ~ with** : tripoter
fidelity [fəˈdɛləti, faɪ-] *n, pl* **-ties** : fidélité *f*
fidget [ˈfɪdʒət] *vi* : remuer — **fidgety** [ˈfɪdʒəti] *adj* : agité
field [ˈfiːld] *n* **1** : champ *m* **2** : terrain *m* (de sport) **3** SPECIALTY : domaine *m* —

field glasses *npl* : jumelles *fpl* — **field trip** : sortie *f* éducative

fiend ['fi:nd] *n* **1** : diable *m* **2** FANATIC : mordu *m* — **fiendish** ['fi:ndɪʃ] *adj* : diabolique

fierce ['fɪrs] *adj* **fiercer; -est** **1** FEROCIOUS : féroce **2** INTENSE : violent — **fierceness** ['fɪrsnəs] *n* : férocité *f*

fiery ['faɪəri] *adj* **fierier; -est** **1** BURNING : brûlant **2** SPIRITED : ardent

fifteen [fɪf'ti:n] *n* : quinze *m* — ∼ *adj* : quinze — **fifteenth** [fɪf'ti:nθ] *n* **1** : quinzième *mf* **2 November ∼** : le 15 novembre — ∼ *adj* : quinzième

fifth ['fɪfθ] *n* **1** : cinquième *mf* **2 June ∼** : le cinq juin — ∼ *adj* : cinquième

fiftieth ['fɪftiəθ] *n* : cinquantième *mf* — ∼ *adj* : cinquantième

fifty ['fɪfti] *n, pl* **-ties** : cinquante *m* — ∼ *adj* : cinquante — **fifty–fifty** [ˌfɪfti'fɪfti] *adv* : moitié-moitié — ∼ *adj* **a ∼ chance** : une chance sur deux

fig ['fɪg] *n* : figue *f*

fight ['faɪt] *v* **fought** ['fɔt]; **fighting** *vi* **1** BATTLE : se battre **2** QUARREL : se disputer **3** STRUGGLE : lutter — *vt* : se battre contre, combattre — ∼ *n* **1** BATTLE : combat *m* **2** BRAWL : bagarre *f* **3** QUARREL : dispute *f* **4** STRUGGLE : lutte *f* — **fighter** ['faɪt̬ər] *n* **1** : combattant *m*, -tante *f* **2** *or* **∼ plane** : avion *m* de chasse

figment ['fɪgmənt] *n* **∼ of the imagination** : produit *m* de l'imagination

figurative ['fɪgjərət̬ɪv, -gə-] *adj* : figuré

figure ['fɪgjər, -gər] *n* **1** : figure *f* **2** NUMBER : chiffre *m* **3** SHAPE : forme *f* **4 ∼ of speech** : façon *f* de parler **5 watch one's ∼** : surveiller sa ligne — ∼ *v* **-ured; -uring** *vt* : penser, supposer — *vi* **1** APPEAR : figurer **2 that ∼s!** : ça se comprend! — **figurehead** ['fɪgjərˌhɛd, -gər-] *n* **1** : figure *f* de proue (d'un navire) **2** : homme *m* de paille — **figure out** *vt* : comprendre

file[1] ['faɪl] *n* : lime *f* (outil) — ∼ *vt* **filed; filing** : limer

file[2] *v* **filed; filing** *vt* **1** CLASSIFY : classer **2 ∼ charges** : déposer une plainte — ∼ *n* **1** : dossier *m* **2** *or* **computer ∼** : fichier *m*

file[3] ROW : file *f* — ∼ *vi* **∼ past** : défiler devant

fill ['fɪl] *vt* **1** : remplir **2** PLUG : boucher (un trou) **3** : plomber (une dent) **4 ∼ in** INFORM : mettre au courant — *vi* **1** *or* **∼ up** : se remplir **2 ∼ in for** : remplacer — ∼ *n* **1 eat one's ∼** : se rassasier **2 have had one's ∼ of** : en avoir assez de

fillet [fɪ'leɪ, 'fɪˌleɪ, 'fɪlət] *n* : filet *m*

filling ['fɪlɪŋ] *n* **1** : garniture *f* (d'une tarte, etc.) **2** : plombage *m* (d'une dent) **3 ∼ station → service station**

filly ['fɪli] *n, pl* **-lies** : pouliche *f*

film ['fɪlm] *n* **1** : pellicule *f* **2** MOVIE : film *m* — ∼ *vt* : filmer

filter ['fɪltər] *n* : filtre *m* — ∼ *v* : filtrer

filth ['fɪlθ] *n* : saleté *f* — **filthiness** ['fɪlθinəs] *n* : saleté *f* — **filthy** ['fɪlθi] *adj* **filthier; -est** : sale, dégoûtant

fin ['fɪn] *n* : nageoire *f*

final ['faɪnəl] *adj* **1** LAST : dernier **2** CONCLUSIVE : définitif **3** ULTIMATE : final — ∼ *n* **1** *or* **∼s** : finale *f* (d'une compétition) **2 ∼s** *npl* : examens *mpl* de fin de semestre — **finalist** ['faɪnəlɪst] *n* : finaliste *mf* — **finalize** ['faɪnəlˌaɪz] *vt* **-ized; -izing** : mettre au point — **finally** ['faɪnəli] *adv* : enfin, finalement

finance [fə'nænts, 'faɪˌnænts] *n* **1** : finance *f* **2 ∼s** *npl* RESOURCES : finances *fpl* — ∼ *vt* **-nanced; -nancing** : financer — **financial** [fə'næntʃəl, faɪ-] *adj* : financier

find ['faɪnd] *vt* **found** ['faʊnd]; **finding** **1** LOCATE : trouver **2** REALIZE : s'apercevoir **3 ∼ out** : découvrir **4 ∼ guilty** : prononcer coupable — ∼ *n* : trouvaille *f* — **finding** ['faɪndɪŋ] *n* **1** FIND : découverte *f* **2 ∼s** *npl* : conclusions *fpl*

fine[1] ['faɪn] *n* : amende *f* — ∼ *vt* **fined; fining** : condamner à une amende

fine[2] *adj* **finer; -est** **1** DELICATE : fin **2** SUBTLE : subtil **3** EXCELLENT : excellent **4** : beau (se dit du temps) **5 be ∼** : aller bien **6 that's ∼ with me** : ça me va — ∼ *adv* OK : très bien — **fine arts** *npl* : beaux-arts *mpl* — **finely** ['faɪnli] *adv* **1** EXCELLENTLY : exceptionellement **2** PRECISELY : délicatement **3** MINUTELY : finement

finesse [fə'nɛs] *n* : finesse *f*

finger ['fɪŋgər] *n* : doigt *m* — ∼ *vt* : toucher, palper — **fingernail** ['fɪŋgərˌneɪl] *n* : ongle *m* — **fingerprint** ['fɪŋgərˌprɪnt] *n* : empreinte *f* digitale — **fingertip** ['fɪŋgərˌtɪp] *n* : bout *m* du doigt

finicky ['fɪnɪki] *adj* : pointilleux

finish ['fɪnɪʃ] *vt* : finir, terminer — *vi* : finir, se terminer — ∼ *n* **1** END : fin *f* **2** *or* **∼ line** : arrivée *f* **3** SURFACE : finition *f*, fini *m Can*

finite ['faɪˌnaɪt] *adj* : fini

fir ['fər] *n* : sapin *m*

fire ['faɪr] *n* **1** : feu *m* **2** BLAZE : incendie *m* **3 catch ~** : prendre feu **4 on ~** : en feu **5 open ~ on** : ouvrir le feu sur — **~** *vt* **fired; firing 1** IGNITE : incendier **2** DISMISS : renvoyer, virer **3** SHOOT : tirer — **fire alarm** *n* : avertisseur *m* d'incendie — **firearm** ['faɪr,ɑrm] *n* : arme *f* à feu — **firecracker** ['faɪr,krækər] *n* : pétard *m* — **fire engine** : pompe *f* à incendie — **fire escape** *n* : escalier *m* de secours — **fire extinguisher** *n* : extincteur *m* — **firefighter** ['faɪr,faɪṭər] *n* : pompier *m*, sapeur-pompier *m France* — **fireman** ['faɪrmən] *n, pl* **-men** [-mən, -,mɛn] → **firefighter** — **fireplace** ['faɪr,pleɪs] *n* : cheminée *f*, foyer *m* — **fireproof** ['faɪr,pru:f] *adj* : ignifuge — **fireside** ['faɪr,saɪd] *n* : coin *m* du feu — **fire station** *n* : caserne *f* de pompiers *France*, poste *m* de pompiers *Can* — **firewood** ['faɪr,wʊd] *n* : bois *m* de chauffage — **fireworks** ['faɪr,wərks] *npl* : feux *mpl* d'artifice

firm[1] ['fərm] *n* : entreprise *f*, firme *f*

firm[2] *adj* **1** : ferme **2** STEADY : solide **3 stand ~** : tenir bon — **firmly** ['fərmli] *adv* : fermement — **firmness** ['fərmnəs] *n* : fermeté *f*

first ['fərst] *adj* **1** : premier **2 at ~ sight** : à première vue — **~** *adv* **1** : d'abord **2 for the ~ time** : pour la première fois **3 ~ of all** : tout d'abord — **~** *n* **1** : premier *m*, -mière *f* **2** *or* **~ gear** : première *f* **3 at ~** : au début — **first aid** *n* : premiers secours *mpl* — **first–class** ['fərst'klæs] *adv* : en première — **~** *adj* : de première qualité, de première classe — **firstly** ['fərstli] *adv* : premièrement

fiscal ['fɪskəl] *adj* : fiscal

fish ['fɪʃ] *n, pl* **fish** *or* **fishes** : poisson *m* — **~** *vi* **1** : pêcher **2 ~ for** SEEK : chercher **3 go ~ing** : aller à la pêche — **fisherman** ['fɪʃərmən] *n, pl* **-men** [-mən, -mɛn] : pêcheur *m*, -cheuse *f* — **fishhook** ['fɪʃ,hʊk] *n* : hameçon *m* — **fishing** ['fɪʃɪŋ] *n* : pêche *f* — **fishing pole** *n* : canne *f* à la pêche — **fishy** ['fɪʃi] *adj* **fishier; -est 1** : de poisson **2** SUSPICIOUS : louche

fist ['fɪst] *n* : poing *m*

fit[1] ['fɪt] *n* : crise *f* (épileptique), accès *m* (de colère, etc.)

fit[2] *adj* **fitter; fittest 1** APPROPRIATE : convenable **2** HEALTHY : en forme **3 see ~ to** : trouver bon de — **~** *v* **fitted; fitting** *vt* **1** (*relating to clothing*) : aller à **2** MATCH : correspondre à **3** INSTALL : poser, insérer **4** EQUIP : équiper — *vi* **1** : être de la bonne taille **2** *or* **~ in** BELONG : s'intégrer — **~** *n* : coupe *f* (d'un vêtement) — **fitful** ['fɪtfəl] *adj* **1** : intermittent **2** : agité (se dit du sommeil) — **fitness** ['fɪtnəs] *n* **1** HEALTH : forme *f* physique **2** SUITABILITY : aptitude *f* — **fitting** ['fɪṭɪŋ] *adj* : approprié, convenable

five ['faɪv] *n* : cinq *m* — **~** *adj* : cinq — **five hundred** *adj* : cinq cents

fix ['fɪks] *vt* **1** ATTACH : fixer **2** REPAIR : réparer **3** PREPARE : préparer **4** RIG : truquer — **~** *n* **be in a ~** : être dans le pétrin *m* — **fixed** ['fɪkst] *adj* : fixe — **fixture** ['fɪkstʃər] *n* : installation *f*

fizz ['fɪz] *vi* : pétiller — **~** *n* : pétillement *m*

fizzle ['fɪzəl] *vi* **~ out** : s'éteindre

flabbergasted ['flæbər,gæstəd] *adj* : sidéré

flabby ['flæbi] *adj* **flabbier; -est** : mou

flaccid ['flæksəd, 'flæsəd] *adj* : flasque

flag[1] ['flæg] *vi* WEAKEN : faiblir

flag[2] *n* : drapeau *m* — **~** *vt* **flagged; flagging** : faire signe à (un taxi, etc.) — **flagpole** [,flæg,po:l] *n* : mât *m*

flagrant ['fleɪgrənt] *adj* : flagrant

flair ['flær] *n* **1** TALENT : don *m* **2** STYLE : style *m*

flake ['fleɪk] *n* : flocon *m* (de neige), écaille *f* (de peinture) — **~** *vi* **flaked; flaking** *or* **~ off** : s'écailler

flamboyant [flæm'bɔɪənt] *adj* : extravagant

flame ['fleɪm] *n* **1** : flamme *f* **2 burst into ~s** : s'embraser, s'enflammer

flamingo [flə'mɪŋgo] *n, pl* **-gos** : flamant *m*

flammable ['flæməbəl] *adj* : inflammable

flank ['flæŋk] *n* : flanc *m* — **~** *vt* : flanquer

flannel ['flænəl] *n* : flanelle *f*

flap ['flæp] *n* : rabat *m* — **~** *v* **flapped; flapping** *vt* : battre (des ailes) — *vi* **~ in the wind** : claquer au vent

flare ['flær] *vi* **flared; flaring ~ up 1** BLAZE : s'embraser **2** ERUPT : s'emporter (se dit d'une personne), éclater (se dit d'une dispute, etc.) — **~** *n* : fusée *f* éclairante

flash ['flæʃ] *vi* **1** SPARKLE : briller **2** BLINK : clignoter **3 ~ past** : passer comme un éclair — *vt* **1** PROJECT : projeter **2** SHOW : montrer **3 ~ a smile** : lancer un sourire — **~** *n* **1** éclat *m* **2**

: flash *m* (d'un appareil photographique) **3 ~ of lightning** : éclair *m* **4 in a ~** : dans un instant — **flashlight** ['flæʃ,laɪt] *n* : lampe *f* de poche — **flashy** ['flæʃi] *adj* **flashier; -est** : tape-à-l'œil, tapageur

flask ['flæsk] *n* : flacon *m*

flat ['flæt] *adj* **flatter; flattest 1** LEVEL : plat **2** DOWNRIGHT : catégorique **3** FIXED : fixe **4** MONOTONOUS : monotone **5** : éventé (se dit d'une boisson) **6** : bémol (en musique) **7 ~ tire** : crevé, à plat — **~** *n* **1** : bémol *m* (en musique) **2** *Brit* APARTMENT : appartement *m* **3** *or* **~ tire** : crevaison *f* — **~** *adv* **1** : à plat **2 ~ broke** : complètement fauché **3 in one hour ~** : dans une heure pile *fam* — **flatly** ['flætli] *adv* : catégoriquement — **flatten** ['flætən] *vt* : aplatir — *vi or* **~ out** : s'aplanir

flatter ['flæṭər] *vt* : flatter — **flatterer** ['flæṭərər] *n* : flatteur *m*, -teuse *f* — **flattering** ['flæṭərɪŋ] *adj* : flatteur — **flattery** ['flæṭəri] *n, pl* **-ries** : flatterie *f*

flaunt ['flɔnt] *vt* : faire étalage de

flavor *or Brit* **flavour** ['fleɪvər] *n* **1** : goût *m* **2** FLAVORING : parfum *m* — **~** *vt* : parfumer — **flavorful** *or Brit* **flavourful** ['fleɪvərfəl] *adj* : savoureux — **flavoring** *or Brit* **flavouring** ['fleɪvərɪŋ] *n* : parfum *m*

flaw ['flɔ] *n* : défaut *m* — **flawless** ['flɔləs] *adj* : sans défaut, parfait

flax ['flæks] *n* : lin *m*

flea ['fli:] *n* : puce *f*

fleck ['flɛk] *n* : petite tache *f*, moucheture *f*

flee ['fli:] *v* **fled** ['flɛd]; **fleeing** : fuir

fleece ['fli:s] *n* : toison *f* — **~** *vt* **fleeced; fleecing** : escroquer

fleet ['fli:t] *n* : flotte *f*

fleeting ['fli:ṭɪŋ] *adj* : bref

Flemish ['flɛmɪʃ] *adj* : flamand

flesh ['flɛʃ] *n* : chair *f* — **fleshy** ['flɛʃi] *adj* **fleshier; -est** : charnu

flew → **fly**[1]

flex ['flɛks] *vt* : fléchir — **flexible** ['flɛksəbəl] *adj* : flexible — **flexibility** ['flɛksə'bɪləṭi] *n* : flexibilité *f*

flick ['flɪk] *n* : petit coup *m* — **~** *vt* **~ a switch** : appuyer sur un bouton — *vi* **~ through** : feuilleter

flicker ['flɪkər] *vi* : vaciller — **~** *n* **1** : vacillement *m* **2 a ~ of hope** : une lueur d'espoir

flier ['flaɪər] *n* **1** PILOT : aviateur *m*, -trice *f* **2** *or* **flyer** LEAFLET : prospectus *m*

flight[1] ['flaɪt] *n* **1** FLYING : vol *m* **2 ~ of stairs** : escalier *m*

flight[2] *n* ESCAPE : fuite *f*

flimsy ['flɪmzi] *adj* **flimsier; -est 1** LIGHT : léger **2** SHAKY : peu solide **3 a ~ excuse** : une pauvre excuse

flinch ['flɪntʃ] *vi* **1** WINCE : tressaillir **2 ~ from** : reculer devant

fling ['flɪŋ] *vt* **flung** ['flʌŋ]; **flinging 1** THROW : lancer **2 ~ open** : ouvrir brusquement — **~** *n* **1** AFFAIR : affaire *f*, aventure *f* **2 have a ~ at** : essayer de faire

flint ['flɪnt] *n* : silex *m*

flip ['flɪp] *v* **flipped; flipping** *vt* **1** *or* **~ over** : faire sauter **2 ~ a coin** : jouer à pile ou face — *vi* **1** *or* **~ over** : se retourner **2 ~ through** : feuilleter — **~** *n* : saut *m* périlleux

flippant ['flɪpənt] *adj* : désinvolte

flipper ['flɪpər] *n* : nageoire *f*

flirt ['flərt] *vi* : flirter — **~** *n* : flirteur *m*, -teuse *f* — **flirtatious** [,flər'teɪʃəs] *adj* : charmeur

flit ['flɪt] *vi* **flitted; flitting** : voleter

float ['flo:t] *n* **1** RAFT : radeau *m* **2** CORK : flotteur *m* **3** : char *m* (de carnaval) — **~** *vi* : flotter — *vt* : faire flotter

flock ['flɑk] *n* **1** : volée *f* (d'oiseaux), troupeau *m* (de moutons) **2** CROWD : foule *f* — **~** *vi* : affluer, venir en foule

flog ['flɑg] *vt* **flogged; flogging** : flageller

flood ['flʌd] *n* **1** : inondation *f* **2** : déluge *m* (de paroles, de larmes, etc.) — **~** *vt* : inonder — *vi* : déborder (se dit d'une rivière) — **floodlight** ['flʌd,laɪt] *n* : projecteur *m*

floor ['flor] *n* **1** : plancher *m* **2** GROUND : sol *m* **3** STORY : étage *m* **4 dance ~** : piste *f* de danse **5 ground ~** : rez-de-chaussée *m* — **~** *vt* **1** KNOCK DOWN : terrasser **2** ASTOUND : stupéfier — **floorboard** ['flor,bord] *n* : planche *f*

flop ['flɑp] *vi* **flopped; flopping 1** : s'agiter mollement **2** *or* **~ down** COLLAPSE : s'affaler **3** FAIL : échouer — **~** *n* : fiasco *m* — **floppy** ['flɑpi] *adj* **floppier; -est** : mou — **floppy disk** *n* : disquette *f*

flora ['florə] *n* : flore *f* — **floral** ['florəl] *adj* : floral — **florid** ['florɪd] *adj* **1** FLOWERY : fleuri **2** RUDDY : rougeaud — **florist** ['florɪst] *n* : fleuriste *mf*

floss ['flɔs] → **dental floss**

flounder[1] ['flaʊndər] *n, pl* **flounder** *or* **flounders** : flet *m*

flounder[2] *vi* **1** *or* ~ **about** : patauger **2** FALTER : bredouiller
flour ['flaʊər] *n* : farine *f*
flourish ['flərɪʃ] *vi* **1** PROSPER : prospérer **2** THRIVE : s'épanouir — *vt* BRANDISH : brandir — ~ *n* : grand geste *m* — **flourishing** ['flərɪʃɪŋ] *adj* : florissant
flout ['flaʊt] *vt* : bafouer
flow ['flo:] *vi* **1** : couler **2** MOVE : s'écouler **3** CIRCULATE : circuler **4** BILLOW : flotter — ~ *n* **1** : écoulement *m* (d'un liquide) **2** MOVEMENT : circulation *f* **3** : flux *m* (de la marée)
flower ['flaʊər] *n* : fleur *f* — ~ *vi* : fleurir — **flowering** ['flaʊərɪŋ] *n* : floraison *f* — **flowerpot** ['flaʊər,pɑt] *n* : pot *m* de fleurs — **flowery** ['flaʊəri] *adj* : fleuri
flown → **fly**[1]
flu ['flu:] *n* : grippe *f*
fluctuate ['flʌktʃʊ,eɪt] *vi* **-ated; -ating** : fluctuer — **fluctuation** [,flʌktʃʊ'eɪʃən] *n* : fluctuation *f*
fluency ['flu:əntsi] *n* : aisance *f* — **fluent** ['flu:ənt] *adj* **1** : coulant, aisé **2** **be ~ in** : parler couramment — **fluently** ['flu:əntli] *adv* : couramment
fluff ['flʌf] *n* **1** DOWN : duvet *m* **2** FUZZ : peluches *fpl* — **fluffy** ['flʌfi] *adj* **fluffier; -est** : duveteux
fluid ['flu:ɪd] *adj* : fluide — ~ *n* : fluide *m*
flunk ['flʌŋk] *vt* FAIL : rater
fluorescent [,flʊr'ɛsənt, ,flɔr-] *adj* : fluorescent
flurry ['flәri] *n, pl* **-ries 1** GUST : rafale *f* **2** *or* **snow ~** : poudrerie *f Can* **3** : tourbillon *m* (d'activité)
flush ['flʌʃ] *vi* BLUSH : rougir — *vt* ~ **the toilet** : tirer la chasse d'eau — ~ *n* **1** : chasse *f* (d'eau) **2** BLUSH : rougeur *f* — ~ *adj* : au même niveau — ~ *adv* : de niveau
fluster ['flʌstər] *vt* : troubler
flute ['flu:t] *n* : flûte *f*
flutter ['flʌṭər] *vi* **1** FLAP : battre (se dit des ailes) **2** FLIT : voleter **3** ~ **about** : s'agiter — ~ *n* **1** : battement *m* (d'ailes) **2** STIR : agitation *f*, émoi *m*
flux ['flʌks] *n* **in a state of ~** : dans un état de perpétuel changement
fly[1] ['flaɪ] *v* **flew** ['flu:]; **flown** ['flo:n]; **flying** *vi* **1** : voler **2** TRAVEL : prendre l'avion **3** : flotter (se dit d'un drapeau) **4** RUSH : filer **5** FLEE : s'enfuir — *vt* : faire voler — ~ *n, pl* **flies** : braguette *f* (d'un pantalon)
fly[2] *n, pl* **flies** : mouche *f* (insecte)
flyer → **flier**
flying saucer *n* : soucoupe *f* volante
foal ['fo:l] *n* : poulain *m*
foam ['fo:m] *n* : mousse *f*, écume *f* — ~ *vi* : mousser, écumer — **foamy** ['fo:mi] *adj* **foamier; -est** : mousseux, écumeux (se dit de la mer)
focus ['fo:kəs] *n, pl* **foci** ['fo:,saɪ, -,kaɪ] **1** : foyer *m* **2** **be in ~** : être au point **3** ~ **of attention** : centre *m* d'attention — ~ *v* **-cused** *or* **-cussed; -cusing** *or* **-cussing** *vt* **1** : mettre au point (un instrument) **2** : fixer (les yeux) — *vi* ~ **on** : se concentrer sur
fodder ['fɑdər] *n* : fourrage *m*
foe ['fo:] *n* : ennemi *m*, -mie *f*
fog ['fɔg, 'fɑg] *n* : brouillard *m* — ~ *vi* **fogged; fogging** *or* ~ **up** : s'embuer — **foggy** ['fɔgi, 'fɑ-] *adj* **foggier; -est** : brumeux — **foghorn** ['fɔg,hɔrn, 'fɑg-] *n* : corne *f* de brume
foil[1] ['fɔɪl] *vt* : déjouer
foil[2] *n* : feuille *f* (d'aluminium, etc.)
fold[1] ['fo:ld] *n* **1** : parc *m* à moutons **2** **return to the ~** : rentrer au bercail
fold[2] *vt* **1** : plier **2** ~ **one's arms** : croiser les bras — *vi* **1** *or* ~ **up** : se plier **2** FAIL : échouer — ~ *n* CREASE : pli *m* — **folder** ['fo:ldər] *n* **1** FILE : chemise *f* **2** PAMPHLET : dépliant *m*
foliage ['fo:liɪdʒ, -lɪdʒ] *n* : feuillage *m*
folk ['fo:k] *n, pl* **folk** *or* **folks 1** PEOPLE : gens *mfpl* **2** ~**s** *npl* PARENTS : famille *f*, parents *mpl* — ~ *adj* : populaire, folklorique — **folklore** ['fo:k,lor] *n* : folklore *m*
follow ['fɑlo] *vt* **1** : suivre **2** PURSUE : poursuivre **3** ~ **up** : donner suite à — *vi* **1** : suivre **2** ENSUE : s'ensuivre — **follower** ['fɑloər] *n* : partisan *m*, -sane *f* — **following** ['fɑloɪŋ] *adj* : suivant — ~ *n* : partisans *mpl* — ~ *prep* : après
folly ['fɑli] *n, pl* **-lies** : folie *f*
fond ['fɑnd] *adj* **1** : affectueux **2** **be ~ of** : aimer beaucoup
fondle ['fɑndəl] *vt* **-dled; -dling** : caresser
fondness ['fɑndnəs] *n* **1** : affection *f* **2** **have a ~ for** : avoir une prédilection pour
food ['fu:d] *n* : nourriture *f* — **foodstuffs** ['fu:d,stʌfs] *npl* : denrées *fpl* alimentaires
fool ['fu:l] *n* **1** : idiot *m*, -diote *f* **2** JESTER : fou *m* — ~ *vt* DECEIVE : duper — *vi* **1** JOKE : plaisanter **2** ~ **around** : perdre son temps — **foolhardy** ['fu:l,hɑrdi] *adj* : téméraire — **foolish**

[ˈfu:lɪʃ] *adj* : bête, idiot — **foolishness** [ˈfu:lɪʃnəs] *n* : bêtise *f*, sottise *f* — **foolproof** [ˈfu:lˌpru:f] *adj* : infaillible

foot [ˈfʊt] *n, pl* **feet** [ˈfi:t] : pied *m* — **footage** [ˈfʊṭɪʤ] *n* : métrage *m* — **football** [ˈfʊtˌbɔl] *n* : football *m* américain, football *m Can* — **footbridge** [ˈfʊtˌbrɪʤ] *n* : passerelle *f* — **foothills** [ˈfʊtˌhɪlz] *npl* : contreforts *mpl* — **foothold** [ˈfʊtˌho:ld] *n* : prise *f* de pied — **footing** [ˈfʊṭɪŋ] *n* **1** → **foothold 2** STATUS : position *f* **3 on equal ~** : sur pied d'égalité — **footlights** [ˈfʊtˌlaɪts] *npl* : rampe *f* — **footnote** [ˈfʊtˌno:t] *n* : note *f* (en bas de la page) — **footpath** [ˈfʊtˌpæθ] *n* : sentier *m* — **footprint** [ˈfʊtˌprɪnt] *n* : empreinte *f* (de pied) — **footstep** [ˈfʊtˌstɛp] *n* : pas *m* — **footwear** [ˈfʊtˌwær] *n* : chaussures *fpl*

for [ˈfɔr] *prep* **1** : pour **2** BECAUSE OF : de, à cause de **3** (*indicating duration*) : pour, pendant **4** (*indicating destination*) : pour, à destination de **5 a cure ~ cancer** : un remède contre le cancer **6 ~ sale** : à vendre — **~** *conj* BECAUSE : car

forage [ˈfɔrɪʤ] *vi* **-aged; -aging** : fourrager

foray [ˈfɔrˌeɪ] *n* : incursion *f*

forbid [fərˈbɪd] *vt* **-bade** [-ˈbæd, -ˈbeɪd] *or* **-bad** [-ˈbæd]; **-bidden** [-ˈbɪdən]; **-bidding** : interdire, défendre — **forbidding** [fərˈbɪdɪŋ] *adj* : menaçant

force [ˈfors] *n* **1** : force *f* **2** *or* **~s** *npl* : forces *fpl* **3 by ~** : de force **4 in ~** : en vigueur — **~** *vt* **forced; forcing 1** : forcer **2** IMPOSE : imposer — **forceful** [ˈforsfəl] *adj* : vigoureux

forceps [ˈfɔrsəps, -ˌsɛps] *ns & pl* : forceps *m*

forcibly [ˈforsəbli] *adv* : de force

ford [ˈford] *n* : gué *m* — **~** *vt* : passer à gué

fore [ˈfor] *n* **1** : avant *m* (d'un navire) **2 come to the ~** : se mettre en évidence

forearm [ˈforˌɑrm] *n* : avant-bras *m*

foreboding [forˈbo:dɪŋ] *n* : pressentiment *m*

forecast [ˈforˌkæst] *vt* **-cast; -casting** : prévoir — **~** *n or* **weather ~** : prévisions *fpl* météorologiques, météo *f fam*

forefathers [ˈforˌfɑðərz] *npl* : ancêtres *mfpl*, aïeux *mpl*

forefinger [ˈforˌfɪŋgər] *n* : index *m*

forefront [ˈforˌfrʌnt] *n* : premier rang *m*

forego [forˈgo:] → **forgo**

foregone [forˈgɔn] *adj* **it's a ~ conclusion** : c'est gagné d'avance

foreground [ˈforˌgraʊnd] *n* : premier plan *m*

forehead [ˈfɔrəd, ˈforˌhɛd] *n* : front *m*

foreign [ˈfɔrən] *adj* **1** : étranger (se dit d'une langue, etc.) **2 ~ trade** : commerce *m* extérieur — **foreigner** [ˈfɔrənər] *n* : étranger *m*, -gère *f*

foreman [ˈformən] *n, pl* **-men** [-mən, -ˌmɛn] : contremaître *m*

foremost [ˈforˌmo:st] *adj* : principal — **~** *adv* **first and ~** : tout d'abord

forensic [fəˈrɛntsɪk] *adj* : médico-légal

forerunner [ˈforˌrʌnər] *n* : précurseur *m*

foresee [forˈsi:] *vt* **-saw; -seen; -seeing** : prévoir — **foreseeable** [forˈsi:əbəl] *adj* : prévisible

foreshadow [forˈʃædo:] *vt* : présager

foresight [ˈforˌsaɪt] *n* : prévoyance *f*

forest [ˈfɔrəst] *n* : forêt *f* — **forestry** [ˈfɔrəstri] *n* : sylviculture *f*

foretaste [ˈforˌteɪst] *n* : avant-goût *m*

foretell [forˈtɛl] *vt* **-told; -telling** : prédire

forethought [ˈforˌθɔt] *n* : prévoyance *f*

forever [fɔrˈɛvər] *adv* **1** ETERNALLY : toujours **2** CONTINUALLY : sans cesse

forewarn [forˈwɔrn] *vt* : avertir, prévenir

foreword [ˈforwərd] *n* : avant-propos *m*

forfeit [ˈfɔrfət] *n* **1** PENALTY : peine *f* **2 pay a ~** : avoir un gage — **~** *vt* : perdre

forge [ˈforʤ] *n* : forge *f* — **~** *v* **forged; forging** *vt* **1** : forger (un métal, etc.) **2** COUNTERFEIT : contrefaire, falsifier — *vi* **~ ahead** : prendre de l'avance — **forger** [ˈforʤər] *n* : faussaire *mf*, faux-monnayeur *m* — **forgery** [ˈforʤəri] *n, pl* **-eries** : faux *m*, contrefaçon *f*

forget [fərˈgɛt] *v* **-got** [-ˈgɑt]; **-gotten** [-ˈgɑtən] *or* **-got; -getting** : oublier — **forgetful** [fərˈgɛtfəl] *adj* : distrait

forgive [fərˈgɪv] *vt* **-gave** [-ˈgeɪv]; **-given** [-ˈgɪvən]; **-giving** : pardonner — **forgiveness** [fərˈgɪvnəs] *n* : pardon *m*

forgo *or* **forego** [forˈgo:] *vt* **-went; -gone; -going** : renoncer à, se priver de

fork [ˈfɔrk] *n* **1** : fourchette *f* **2** PITCHFORK : fourche *f* **3** JUNCTION : bifurcation *f* (d'une route) — **~** *vt or* **~ over** : allonger *fam* — *vi* : bifurquer

forlorn [fɔrˈlɔrn] *adj* : triste

form [ˈfɔrm] *n* **1** : forme *f* **2** DOCUMENT

: formulaire *m* — ~ *vt* : former — *vi* : se former, prendre forme

formal ['fɔrməl] *adj* **1** : officiel, solennel **2** : soigné, soutenu (se dit du langage) — ~ *n* **1** *or* ~ **dance** : bal *m* **2** *or* ~ **dress** : tenue *f* de soirée — **formality** [fɔr'mæləṭi] *n, pl* **-ties** : formalité *f*

format ['fɔr,mæt] *n* : format *m* — ~ *vt* **-matted; -matting** : formater (une diskette, etc.)

formation [fɔr'meɪʃən] *n* : formation *f*

former ['fɔrmər] *adj* **1** PREVIOUS : ancien **2** FIRST : premier — **formerly** ['fɔrmərli] *adv* : autrefois

formidable ['fɔrmədəbəl, fɔr'mɪdə-] *adj* : redoutable

formula ['fɔrmjələ] *n, pl* **-las** or **-lae** [-,li:, -,laɪ] **1** : formule *f* **2** *or* **baby** ~ : lait *m* reconstitué — **formulate** ['fɔrmjə,leɪt] *vt* **-lated; -lating** : formuler

forsake [fər'seɪk] *vt* **-sook** [-'sʊk]; **-saken** [-'seɪkən]; **-saking** : abandonner

fort ['fɔrt] *n* : fort *m*

forth ['forθ] *adv* **1 and so** ~ : et ainsi de suite **2 from this day** ~ : dorénavant **3 go back and** ~ : aller et venir — **forthcoming** [forθ'kʌmɪŋ, 'forθ-] *adj* **1** COMING : prochain, à venir **2** OPEN : communicatif — **forthright** ['forθ,raɪt] *adj* : franc, direct

fortieth ['fɔrṭiəθ] *n* : quarantième *mf* — ~ *adj* : quarantième

fortify ['fɔrṭə,faɪ] *vt* **-fied; -fying** : fortifier — **fortification** [,fɔrṭəfə'keɪʃən] *n* : fortification *f*

fortitude ['fɔrṭə,tu:d, -,tju:d] *n* : force *f* d'âme

fortnight ['fort,naɪt] *n* : quinzaine *f*, quinze jours *mpl*

fortress ['fɔrtrəs] *n* : forteresse *f*

fortunate ['fɔrtʃənət] *adj* : heureux — **fortunately** ['fɔrtʃənətli] *adv* : heureusement — **fortune** ['fɔrtʃən] *n* **1** : fortune *f* **2** LUCK : chance *f* — **fortune–teller** ['fɔrtʃən,tɛlər] *n* : diseuse *f* de bonne aventure

forty ['fɔrṭi] *n, pl* **forties** : quarante *m* — ~ *adj* : quarante

forum ['forəm] *n, pl* **-rums** : forum *m*

forward ['fɔrwərd] *adj* **1** : avant, en avant **2** BRASH : effronté — ~ *adv* : en avant, vers l'avant — ~ *n* : avant *m* (aux sports) — ~ *vt* : expédier (des marchandises), faire suivre (du courrier) — **forwards** ['fɔrwərdz] *adv* → **forward**

fossil ['fɑsəl] *n* : fossile *m*

foster ['fɔstər] *adj* : adoptif, d'accueil — ~ *vt* **1** NURTURE : nourrir **2** ENCOURAGE : encourager

fought → **fight**

foul ['faʊl] *adj* **1** : infect (se dit d'une odeur, etc.) **2** ~ **language** : langage *m* ordurier **3** ~ **play** : jeu *m* irrégulier **4** ~ **weather** : sale temps *m* — ~ *n* : faute *f* (aux sports) — ~ *vt* : salir, souiller

found[1] ['faʊnd] → **find**

found[2] *vt* : fonder, établir — **foundation** [faʊn'deɪʃən] *n* **1** : fondation *f* **2** BASIS : base *f*, fondement *m*

founder[1] ['faʊndər] *n* : fondateur *m*, -trice *f*

founder[2] *vi* **1** SINK : sombrer **2** COLLAPSE : s'effondrer

fountain ['faʊntən] *n* : fontaine *f*

four ['for] *n* : quatre *m* — ~ *adj* : quatre — **fourfold** ['for,fo:ld, -'fo:ld] *adj* : quadruple — **four hundred** *adj* : quatre cents

fourteen [for'ti:n] *n* : quatorze *m* — ~ *adj* : quatorze — **fourteenth** [for'ti:nθ] *n* **1** : quatorzième *mf* **2 June** ~ : le quatorze juin — ~ *adj* : quatorzième

fourth ['forθ] *n* **1** : quatrième *mf* (dans une série) **2** : quart *m* (en mathématiques) **3 August** ~ : le quatre août — ~ *adj* : quatrième

fowl ['faʊl] *n, pl* **fowl** *or* **fowls** : volaille *f*

fox ['fɑks] *n, pl* **foxes** : renard *m* — ~ *vt* TRICK : tromper, berner — **foxy** ['fɑksi] *adj* **foxier; -est** SHREWD : rusé

foyer ['fɔɪər, 'fɔɪ,jeɪ] *n* : vestibule *m*, foyer *m* (d'un théâtre)

fraction ['frækʃən] *n* : fraction *f*

fracture ['fræktʃər] *n* : fracture *f* — ~ *vt* **-tured; -turing** : fracturer

fragile ['frædʒəl, -,dʒaɪl] *adj* : fragile — **fragility** [frə'dʒɪləṭi] *n* : fragilité *f*

fragment ['frægmənt] *n* : fragment *m*

fragrance ['freɪgrənts] *n* : parfum *m* — **fragrant** ['freɪgrənt] *adj* : parfumé

frail ['freɪl] *adj* : frêle, fragile

frame ['freɪm] *vt* **framed; framing 1** ENCLOSE : encadrer **2** DEVISE : élaborer **3** FORMULATE : formuler **4** INCRIMINATE : monter un coup contre — ~ *n* **1** : cadre *m* (d'un tableau, etc.) **2** : charpente *f* (d'un édifice, etc.) **3** ~**s** *npl* : monture *f* (de lunettes) **4** ~ **of mind** : état *m* d'esprit — **framework** ['freɪm,wərk] *n* : structure *f*, cadre *m*

franchise ['fræn,tʃaɪz] *n* **1** : franchise *f*

(en commerce) **2** SUFFRAGE : droit *m* de vote

frank [ˈfræŋk] *adj* : franc — **frankly** [ˈfræŋkli] *adv* : franchement — **frankness** [ˈfræŋknəs] *n* : franchise *f*

frantic [ˈfræntɪk] *adj* : frénétique

fraternal [frəˈtərnəl] *adj* : fraternel — **fraternity** [frəˈtərnəṭi] *n, pl* **-ties** : fraternité *f* — **fraternize** [ˈfræṭərˌnaɪz] *vi* **-nized; -nizing** : fraterniser

fraud [ˈfrɔd] *n* **1** DECEIT : fraude *f* **2** IMPOSTOR : imposteur *m* — **fraudulent** [ˈfrɔʤələnt] *adj* : frauduleux

fraught [ˈfrɔt] *adj* **~ with** : chargé de

fray[1] [ˈfreɪ] *n* : bagarre *f*

fray[2] *vt* : mettre (les nerfs) à vif — *vi* : s'effilocher

freak [ˈfri:k] *n* **1** ODDITY : phénomène *m* **2** ENTHUSIAST : fana *mf fam* — **~** *adj* : anormal — **freakish** [ˈfri:kɪʃ] *adj* : anormal, bizarre

freckle [ˈfrɛkəl] *n* : tache *f* de rousseur

free [ˈfri:] *adj* **freer; freest 1** : libre **2** *or* **~ of charge** : gratuit **3 ~ from** : dépourvu de — **~** *vt* **freed; freeing 1** RELEASE : libérer **2** DISENGAGE : dégager — **~** *adv* **1** : librement **2 for ~** : gratuitement — **freedom** [ˈfri:dəm] *n* : liberté *f* — **freelance** [ˈfri:ˌlænts] *adv* : à la pige — **freely** [ˈfri:li] *adv* **1** : librement **2** LAVISHLY : largement — **freeway** [ˈfri:ˌweɪ] *n* : autoroute *f* — **free will** [ˈfri:ˌwɪl] *n* **1** : libre arbitre *m* **2 of one's own ~** : de sa propre volonté

freeze [ˈfri:z] *v* **froze** [ˈfro:z]; **frozen** [ˈfro:zən]; **freezing** *vt* **1** : geler (de l'eau), congeler (des aliments, etc.) **2** FIX : bloquer — *vi* : geler — **~** *n* **1** : gel *m* **2** : blocage *m* (des prix, etc.) — **freeze-dry** [ˈfri:zˈdraɪ] *vt* **-dried; -drying** : lyophiliser — **freezer** [ˈfri:zər] *n* : congélateur *m* — **freezing** [ˈfri:zɪŋ] *adj* **1** : glacial **2 it's ~** : on gèle

freight [ˈfreɪt] *n* **1** SHIPPING : transport *m* **2** GOODS : fret *m*, marchandises *fpl*

French [ˈfrɛntʃ] *adj* : français — **~** *n* **1** : français *m* (langue) **2 the ~** : les Français

French Canadian *adj* : canadien français — **~** *n* : Canadien *m* français, Canadienne *f* française

french fries [ˈfrɛnʧˌfraɪz] *npl* : frites *fpl*

Frenchman [ˈfrɛntʃmən] *n, pl* **-men** [-mən, -ˌmɛn] : Français *m* — **Frenchwoman** [ˈfrɛntʃˌwʊmən] *n, pl* **-women** [-ˌwɪmən] : Française *f*

frenzy [ˈfrɛnzi] *n, pl* **-zies** : frénésie *f* — **frenzied** [ˈfrɛnzid] *adj* : frénétique

frequency [ˈfri:kwəntsi] *n, pl* **-cies** : fréquence *f* — **frequent** [friˈkwɛnt, ˈfri:kwənt] *vt* : fréquenter — **~** [ˈfri:kwənt] *adj* : fréquent — **frequently** [ˈfri:kwəntli] *adv* : fréquemment

fresco [ˈfrɛsˌko:] *n, pl* **-coes** : fresque *f*

fresh [ˈfrɛʃ] *adj* **1** : frais **2** NEW : nouveau **3** IMPUDENT : insolent **4 ~ water** : eau *f* douce — **freshen** [ˈfrɛʃən] *vt* : rafraîchir — *vi* **~ up** : se rafraîchir — **freshly** [ˈfrɛʃli] *adv* : récemment — **freshman** [ˈfrɛʃmən] *n, pl* **-men** [-mən, -ˌmɛn] : étudiant *m*, -diante *f* de première année — **freshness** [ˈfrɛʃnəs] *n* : fraîcheur *f*

fret [ˈfrɛt] *vi* **fretted; fretting** : s'inquiéter — **fretful** [ˈfrɛtfəl] *adj* : irritable

friar [ˈfraɪər] *n* : frère *m*

friction [ˈfrɪkʃən] *n* : friction *f*

Friday [ˈfraɪˌdeɪ, -di] *n* : vendredi *m*

friend [ˈfrɛnd] *n* : ami *m*, amie *f* — **friendliness** [ˈfrɛndlinəs] *n* : gentillesse *f* — **friendly** [ˈfrɛndli] *adj* **friendlier; -est** : gentil, amical — **friendship** [ˈfrɛndˌʃɪp] *n* : amitié *f*

frigate [ˈfrɪgət] *n* : frégate *f*

fright [ˈfraɪt] *n* : peur *f*, frayeur *f* — **frighten** [ˈfraɪtən] *vt* : faire peur à, effrayer — **frightened** [ˈfraitˈnd] *adj* : apeuré, effrayé — **frightening** [ˈfraitˈnɪŋ] *adj* : effrayant — **frightful** [ˈfraɪtfəl] *adj* : terrible, affreux

frigid [ˈfrɪʤɪd] *adj* : glacial

frill [ˈfrɪl] *n* **1** RUFFLE : volant *m* (d'une jupe), jabot *m* (d'une chemise) **2** LUXURY : luxe *m*

fringe [ˈfrɪnʤ] *n* **1** : frange *f* **2** EDGE : bordure *f* **3 ~ benefits** : avantages *mpl* sociaux

frisk [ˈfrɪsk] *vt* SEARCH : fouiller — **frisky** [ˈfrɪski] *adj* **friskier; -est** : vif, folâtre

fritter [ˈfrɪṭər] *n* : beignet *m* — **~** *vt or* **~ away** : gaspiller

frivolous [ˈfrɪvələs] *adj* : frivole — **frivolity** [frɪˈvɑləṭi] *n, pl* **-ties** : frivolité *f*

frizzy [ˈfrɪzi] *adj* **frizzier; -est** : crépu

fro [ˈfro:] *adv* → **to**

frock [ˈfrɑk] *n* : robe *f*

frog [ˈfrɔg, ˈfrɑg] *n* **1** : grenouille *f* **2 have a ~ in one's throat** : avoir un chat dans la gorge — **frogman** [ˈfrɔgˌmæn, ˈfrɑg-, -mən] *n, pl* **-men** [-mən, -ˌmɛn] : homme-grenouille *m*

frolic [ˈfrɑlɪk] *vi* **-icked; -icking** : folâtrer

from [ˈfrʌm, ˈfrɑm] *prep* **1** (*indicating a starting point*) : de, à partir de **2** (*indicating a source or cause*) : de, par, à **3** ~ **now on** : à partir de maintenant **4 protection** ~ **the sun** : protection contre le soleil **5 drink** ~ **a glass** : boire dans un verre

front [ˈfrʌnt] *n* **1** : avant *m*, devant *m* **2** APPEARANCE : air *m*, contenance *f* **3** : front *m* (militaire) **4** : façade *f* (d'un bâtiment) **5 in** ~ : à l'avant **6 in** ~ **of** : devant — ~ *vi* ~ **on** : donner sur — ~ *adj* **1** : de devant, (en) avant **2** ~ **row** : premier rang *m*

frontier [ˌfrʌnˈtɪr] *n* : frontière *f*

frost [ˈfrɔst] *n* **1** : givre *m* **2** FREEZING : gel *m*, gelée *f* — ~ *vt* : glacer (un gâteau) — **frostbite** [ˈfrɔstˌbaɪt] *n* : gelure *f* — **frosting** [ˈfrɔstɪŋ] *n* ICING : glaçage *m* — **frosty** [ˈfrɔsti] *adj* **frostier; -est 1** : couvert de givre **2** FRIGID : glacial

froth [ˈfrɔθ] *n, pl* **froths** [ˈfrɔθs, ˈfrɔðz] : écume *f*, mousse *f* — **frothy** [ˈfrɔθi, -ði] *adj* **frothier; -est** : écumeux, mousseux

frown [ˈfraʊn] *vi* : froncer les sourcils — ~ *n* : froncement *m* de sourcils

froze, frozen → **freeze**

frugal [ˈfru:gəl] *adj* : économe

fruit [ˈfru:t] *n* : fruit *m* — **fruitcake** [ˈfru:tˌkeɪk] *n* : cake *m* — **fruitful** [ˈfru:tfəl] *adj* : fructueux — **fruition** [fru:ˈɪʃən] *n* **come to** ~ : se réaliser — **fruity** [ˈfru:ţi] *adj* **fruitier; -est** : fruité

frustrate [ˈfrʌsˌtreɪt] *vt* **-trated; -trating** : frustrer — **frustrating** [ˈfrʌsˌtreɪţɪŋ] *adj* : frustrant — **frustration** [ˌfrʌsˈtreɪʃən] *n* : frustration *f*

fry [ˈfraɪ] *v* **fried; frying** : frire — ~ *n, pl* **fries 1** *or* **small** ~ : menu fretin *m* **2 fries** → **french fries** — **frying pan** *n* : poêle *f*

fudge [ˈfʌʤ] *n* : caramel *m* mou — ~ *vt* FALSIFY : truquer

fuel [ˈfju:əl] *n* : combustible *m*, carburant *m* — ~ *vt* **-eled** *or* **-elled; -eling** *or* **-elling 1** : alimenter en combustible **2** STIMULATE : aviver

fugitive [ˈfju:ʤəţɪv] *n* : fugitif *m*, -tive *f*

fulfill *or* **fulfil** [fʊlˈfɪl] *vt* **-filled; -filling 1** EXECUTE : accomplir, réaliser **2** FILL, MEET : remplir — **fulfillment** [fʊlˈfɪlmənt] *n* **1** ACCOMPLISHMENT : réalisation *f* **2** SATISFACTION : contentement *m*

full [ˈfʊl, ˈfʌl] *adj* **1** FILLED : plein **2** COMPLETE : entier, total **3** : ample (se dit d'une jupe), rond (se dit d'un visage) **4** : complet (se dit d'un hotel, etc.) — ~ *adv* **1** DIRECTLY : carrément **2 know** ~ **well** : savoir très bien — ~ *n* **in** ~ : entièrement — **full–fledged** [ˈfʊlˈflɛʤd] *adj* : à part entière — **fully** [ˈfʊli] *adv* : complètement

fumble [ˈfʌmbəl] *vi* **-bled; -bling** : tâtonner, fouiller

fume [ˈfju:m] *vi* **fumed; fuming** RAGE : rager, fulminer — **fumes** [ˈfju:mz] *npl* : vapeurs *fpl*

fumigate [ˈfju:məˌgeɪt] *vt* **-gated; -gating** : désinfecter par fumigation

fun [ˈfʌn] *n* **1** : amusement *m* **2 have** ~ : s'amuser **3 for** ~ : pour rire **4 make** ~ **of** : se moquer de

function [ˈfʌŋkʃən] *n* **1** : fonction *f* **2** GATHERING : réception *f*, cérémonie *f* — ~ *vi* **1** : fonctionner **2** ~ **as** : servir de — **functional** [ˈfʌŋkʃənəl] *adj* : fonctionnel

fund [ˈfʌnd] *n* **1** : fonds *m* **2** ~**s** *npl* RESOURCES : fonds *mpl* — ~ *vt* : financer

fundamental [ˌfʌndəˈmɛntəl] *adj* : fondamental — **fundamentals** *npl* : principes *mpl* de base

funeral [ˈfju:nərəl] *n* : enterrement *m*, funérailles *fpl* — ~ *adj* : funèbre — **funeral home** *or* **funeral parlor** *n* : entreprise *f* de pompes funèbres

fungus [ˈfʌŋgəs] *n, pl* **fungi** [ˈfʌnˌʤaɪ, ˈfʌŋˌgaɪ] **1** MUSHROOM : champignon *m* **2** MOLD : moisissure *f*

funnel [ˈfʌnəl] *n* **1** : entonnoir *m* **2** SMOKESTACK : cheminée *f*

funny [ˈfʌni] *adj* **funnier; -est 1** : drôle, amusant **2** PECULIAR : bizarre — **funnies** [ˈfʌniz] *npl* : bandes *fpl* dessinées

fur [ˈfər] *n* : fourrure *f* — ~ *adj* : de fourrure

furious [ˈfjʊriəs] *adj* : furieux

furnace [ˈfərnəs] *n* : fourneau *m*

furnish [ˈfərnɪʃ] *vt* **1** SUPPLY : fournir **2** : meubler (un appartement, etc.) — **furnishings** [ˈfərnɪʃɪŋz] *npl* : ameublement *m*, meubles *mpl* — **furniture** [ˈfərnɪʧər] *n* : meubles *mpl*

furrow [ˈfəro:] *n* : sillon *m*

furry [ˈfəri] *adj* **furrier; -est** : au poil touffu (se dit d'un animal), en peluche (se dit d'un jouet, etc.)

further [ˈfərðər] *adv* **1** FARTHER : plus loin **2** MORE : davantage, plus **3** MOREOVER : de plus — ~ *adj* **1** FARTHER : plus éloigné **2** ADDITIONAL : supplémentaire **3 until** ~ **notice** : jusqu'à nouvel ordre — **furthermore**

['fərðər,mor] *adv* : en outre, de plus — **furthest** ['fərðəst] *adv & adj* → **farthest**
furtive ['fərṭɪv] *adj* : furtif
fury ['fjʊri] *n, pl* **-ries** : fureur *f*
fuse[1] *or* **fuze** ['fju:z] *n* : amorce *f*, détonateur *m* (d'une bombe, etc.)
fuse[2] *v* **fused; fusing** *vt* **1** MELT : fondre **2** UNITE : fusionner — ~ *n* **1** : fusible *m*, plomb *m* (en électricité) **2 blow a ~** : faire sauter un plomb — **fusion** ['fju:ʒən] *n* : fusion *f*
fuss ['fʌs] *n* **1** : agitation *f*, remue-ménage *m* **2 make a ~** : faire des histoires — ~ *vi* **1** : s'agiter **2** WORRY : s'inquiéter — **fussy** ['fʌsi] *adj* **fussier; -est 1** FINICKY : tatillon, pointilleux **2** ELABORATE : tarabiscoté
futile ['fju:ṭəl, 'fju:,taɪl] *adj* : futile, vain — **futility** [fju:'tɪləṭi] *n* : futilité *f*
future ['fju:ʧər] *adj* : futur — ~ *n* : avenir *m*, futur *m*
fuze *n* → **fuse**[1]
fuzz ['fʌz] *n* FLUFF : peluches *fpl* — **fuzzy** ['fʌzi] *adj* **fuzzier; -est 1** FURRY : duveteux **2** INDISTINCT : flou **3** VAGUE : confus

G

g ['ʤi:] *n, pl* **g's** *or* **gs** ['ʤi:z] : g *m*, septième lettre de l'alphabet
gab ['gæb] *vi* **gabbed; gabbing** : bavarder — ~ *n* CHATTER : bavardage *m*
gable ['geɪbəl] *n* : pignon *m*
gadget ['gæʤət] *n* : gadget *m*
gag ['gæg] *v* **gagged; gagging** *vt* : bâillonner — *vi* CHOKE : avoir des haut-le-cœur — ~ *n* **1** : bâillon *m* **2** JOKE : blague *f*
gage → **gauge**
gaiety ['geɪəṭi] *n, pl* **-eties** : gaieté *f*
gain ['geɪn] *n* **1** PROFIT : profit *m* **2** INCREASE : augmentation *f* — ~ *vt* **1** OBTAIN : gagner **2 ~ weight** : prendre du poids — *vi* **1** PROFIT : gagner **2** : avancer (se dit d'une horloge) — **gainful** ['geɪnfəl] *adj* : rémunéré
gait ['geɪt] *n* : démarche *f*
gala ['geɪlə, 'gæ-, 'gɑ-] *n* : gala *m*
galaxy ['gæləksi] *n, pl* **-axies** : galaxie *f*
gale ['geɪl] *n* : coup *m* de vent
gall ['gɔl] *n* **have the ~ to** : avoir le culot de
gallant ['gælənt] *adj* : galant
gallbladder ['gɔl,blædər] *n* : vesicule *f* biliaire
gallery ['gæləri] *n, pl* **-leries** : galerie *f*
gallon ['gælən] *n* : gallon *m*
gallop ['gæləp] *vi* : galoper — ~ *n* : galop *m*
gallows ['gæ,lo:z] *n, pl* **-lows** *or* **-lowses** [-,lo:zəz] : gibet *m*, potence *f*
gallstone ['gɔl,sto:n] *n* : calcul *m* biliaire
galore [gə'lor] *adv* : en abondance
galoshes [gə'lɑʃəz] *npl* : caoutchoucs *mpl*, claques *fpl Can*
galvanize ['gælvən,aɪz] *vt* **-nized; -nizing** : galvaniser
gamble ['gæmbəl] *v* **-bled; -bling** *vi* : jouer — *vt* WAGER : parier — ~ *n* **1** BET : pari *m* **2** RISK : entreprise *f* risquée — **gambler** ['gæmbələr] *n* : joueur *m*, joueuse *f*
game ['geɪm] *n* **1** : jeu *m* **2** MATCH : match *m*, partie *f* **3** *or* **~ animals** : gibier *m* — ~ *adj* READY : partant, prêt
gamut ['gæmət] *n* : gamme *f*
gang ['gæŋ] *n* : bande *f* — ~ *vi* **~ up on** : se liguer contre
gangplank ['gæŋ,plæŋk] *n* : passerelle *f*
gangrene ['gæŋ,gri:n, 'gæn-; gæŋ'-, gæn'-] *n* : gangrène *f*
gangster ['gæŋstər] *n* : gangster *m*
gangway ['gæŋ,weɪ] → **gangplank**
gap ['gæp] *n* **1** OPENING : trou *m* **2** INTERVAL : intervalle *m* **3** DIFFERENCE : écart *m* **4** DEFICIENCY : lacune *f*
gape ['geɪp] *vi* **gaped; gaping 1** OPEN : bâiller **2** STARE : rester bouche bée
garage [gə'rɑʒ, -'rɑʤ] *n* : garage *m*
garb ['gɑrb] *n* : costume *m*, mise *f*
garbage ['gɑrbɪʤ] *n* : ordures *fpl* — **garbage can** *n* : poubelle *f*
garble ['gɑrbəl] *vt* **-bled; -bling** : embrouiller — **garbled** ['gɑrbəld] *adj* : confus
garden ['gɑrdən] *n* : jardin *m* — ~ *vi* : jardiner — **gardener** ['gɑrdənər] *n* : jardinier *m*, -nière *f*
gargle ['gɑrgəl] *vi* **-gled; -gling** : se gargariser
garish ['gærɪʃ] *adj* : criard, voyant
garland ['gɑrlənd] *n* : guirlande *f*
garlic ['gɑrlɪk] *n* : ail *m*
garment ['gɑrmənt] *n* : vêtement *m*
garnish ['gɑrnɪʃ] *vt* : garnir — ~ *n* : garniture *f*

garret [ˈgærət] *n* : mansarde *f*
garrison [ˈgærəsən] *n* : garnison *f*
garter [ˈgɑrt̬ər] *n* : jarretière *f*
gas [ˈgæs] *n, pl* **gases** **1** : gaz *m* **2** GASOLINE : essence *f* — **~** *v* **gassed; gassing** *vt* : asphyxier au gaz — *vi* **~ up** : faire le plein d'essence — **gas station** *n* : station-service *f*
gash [ˈgæʃ] *n* : entaille *f* — **~** *vt* : entailler
gasket [ˈgæskət] *n* : joint *m* (d'étanchéité)
gasoline [ˈgæsəˌli:n, ˌgæsəˈ-] *n* : essence *f*
gasp [ˈgæsp] *vi* **1** : avoir le souffle coupé **2** PANT : haleter — **~** *n* : halètement *m*
gastric [ˈgæstrɪk] *adj* : gastrique
gastronomy [gæsˈtrɑnəmi] *n* : gastronomie *f*
gate [ˈgeɪt] *n* **1** DOOR : porte *f* **2** BARRIER : barrière *f*, grille *f* — **gateway** [ˈgeɪtˌweɪ] *n* : porte *f*, entrée *f*
gather [ˈgæðər] *vt* **1** ASSEMBLE : rassembler **2** COLLECT : ramasser **3** CONCLUDE : déduire — *vi* ASSEMBLE : se rassembler — **gathering** [ˈgæðərɪŋ] *n* : rassemblement *m*
gaudy [ˈgɔdi] *adj* **-dier; -est** : criard, tape-à-l'œil
gauge [ˈgeɪʤ] *n* **1** INDICATOR : jauge *f*, indicateur *m* **2** CALIBER : calibre *m* — **~** *vt* **gauged; gauging** **1** MEASURE : jauger **2** ESTIMATE : évaluer
gaunt [ˈgɔnt] *adj* : décharné, émacié
gauze [ˈgɔz] *n* : gaze *f*
gave → **give**
gawky [ˈgɔki] *adj* **gawkier; gawkiest** : gauche, maladroit
gay [ˈgeɪ] *adj* **1** : gai **2** HOMOSEXUAL : gay
gaze [ˈgeɪz] *vi* **gazed; gazing** : regarder (fixement) — **~** *n* : regard *m*
gazette [gəˈzɛt] *n* : journal *m* officiel
gear [ˈgɪr] *n* **1** EQUIPMENT : équipement *m* **2** POSSESSIONS : effets *mpl* personnels **3** SPEED : vitesse *f* **4** *or* **~ wheel** : roue *f* dentée — **~** *vt* : adapter — *vi* **~ up** : se préparer — **gearshift** [ˈgɪrˌʃɪft] *n* : levier *m* de vitesse
geese → **goose**
gelatin [ˈʤɛlətən] *n* : gélatine *f*
gem [ˈʤɛm] *n* : pierre *f* précieuse, gemme *f* — **gemstone** [ˈʤɛmˌsto:n] *n* : pierre *f* précieuse
gender [ˈʤɛndər] *n* **1** SEX : sexe *m* **2** : genre *m* (en grammaire)
gene [ˈʤi:n] *n* : gène *m*
genealogy [ˌʤi:niˈɑləʤi, ˌʤɛ-, -ˈæ-] *n, pl* **-gies** : généalogie *f*
general [ˈʤɛnrəl, ˈʤɛnə-] *adj* : général — **~** *n* **1** : général *m* (militaire) **2 in ~** : en général — **generalize** [ˈʤɛnrəˌlaɪz, ˈʤɛnərə-] *v* **-ized; -izing** : généraliser — **generally** [ˈʤɛnrəli, ˈʤɛnərə-] *adv* : généralement, en général — **general practitioner** *n* : généraliste *mf*
generate [ˈʤɛnəˌreɪt] *vt* **-ated; -ating** : générer — **generation** [ˌʤɛnəˈreɪʃən] *n* : génération *f* — **generator** [ˈʤɛnəˌreɪt̬ər] *n* **1** : générateur *m* **2** : génératrice *f* (d'énergie électrique)
generous [ˈʤɛnərəs] *adj* **1** : généreux **2** AMPLE : copieux — **generosity** [ˌʤɛnəˈrɑsət̬i] *n, pl* **-ties** : générosité *f*
genetic [ʤəˈnɛt̬ɪk] *adj* : génétique — **genetics** [ʤəˈnɛt̬ɪks] *n* : génétique *f*
genial [ˈʤi:niəl] *adj* : affable
genital [ˈʤɛnət̬əl] *adj* : génital — **genitals** [ˈʤɛnət̬əlz] *npl* : organes *mpl* génitaux
genius [ˈʤi:njəs] *n* : génie *m*
genocide [ˈʤɛnəˌsaɪd] *n* : génocide *m*
genteel [ʤɛnˈti:l] *adj* : distingué
gentle [ˈʤɛntəl] *adj* **-tler; -tlest** **1** MILD : doux **2** LIGHT : léger — **gentleman** [ˈʤɛntəlmən] *n, pl* **-men** [-mən, -ˌmɛn] **1** MAN : monsieur *m* **2 act like a ~** : agir en gentleman — **gentleness** [ˈʤɛntəlnəs] *n* : douceur *f*
genuine [ˌʤɛnjʊwən] *adj* **1** AUTHENTIC : authentique, véritable **2** SINCERE : sincère
geography [ʤiˈɑgrəfi] *n, pl* **-phies** : géographie *f* — **geographic** [ˌʤi:əˈgræfɪk] *or* **geographical** [-fɪkəl] *adj* : géographique
geology [ʤiˈɑləʤi] *n* : géologie *f* — **geologic** [ˌʤi:əˈlɑʤɪk] *or* **geological** [-ʤɪkəl] *adj* : géologique
geometry [ʤiˈɑmətri] *n, pl* **-tries** : géométrie *f* — **geometric** [ˌʤi:əˈmɛtrɪk] *or* **geometrical** [-trɪkəl] *adj* : géométrique
geranium [ʤəˈreɪniəm] *n* : géranium *m*
geriatric [ˌʤɛriˈætrɪk] *adj* : gériatrique — **geriatrics** [ˌʤɛriˈætrɪks] *n* : gériatrie *f*
germ [ˈʤərm] *n* **1** : germe *m* **2** MICROBE : microbe *m*
German [ˈʤərmən] *adj* : allemand — **~** *n* : allemand *m* (langue)
germinate [ˈʤərməˌneɪt] *v* **-nated; -nating** *vi* : germer — *vt* : faire germer
gestation [ʤɛˈsteɪʃən] *n* : gestation *f*
gesture [ˈʤɛsʧər] *n* : geste *m* — **~** *vi*

-tured; -turing 1 : faire des gestes **2** **~ to** : faire signe à

get [ˈgɛt] *v* **got** [ˈgɑt]; **got** *or* **gotten** [ˈgɑtən]; **getting** *vt* **1** OBTAIN : obtenir, trouver **2** RECEIVE : recevoir, avoir **3** EARN : gagner **4** FETCH : aller chercher **5** CATCH : attraper (une maladie) **6** UNDERSTAND : comprendre **7** PREPARE : préparer **8** **~ one's hair cut** : se faire couper les cheveux **9 have got to** : devoir — *vi* **1** BECOME : devenir **2** GO, MOVE : aller, arriver **3** PROGRESS : avancer **4** **~ ahead** : progresser **5** **~ at** MEAN : vouloir dire **6** **~ away** : s'échapper **7** **~ back at** : se venger de **8** **~ by** : s'en sortir **9** **~ out** : sortir **10** **~ over** : se remettre de **11** **~ together** MEET : se réunir **12** **~ up** : se lever — **get along** *vi* **1** MANAGE : aller **2 get along with** : bien s'entendre avec — **getaway** [ˈgɛt̬əˌweɪ] *n* : fuite *f* — **get–together** [ˈgɛttəˌgɛðər] *n* : réunion *f*

geyser [ˈgaɪzər] *n* : geyser *m*

ghastly [ˈgæstli] *adj* **-lier; -est** : épouvantable

ghetto [ˈgɛt̬o:] *n, pl* **-tos** *or* **-toes** : ghetto *m*

ghost [ˈgo:st] *n* : fantôme *m*, spectre *m* — **ghostly** [ˈgo:stli] *adj* **-lier; -est** : spectral

giant [ˈdʒaɪənt] *n* : géant *m*, géante *f* — **~** *adj* : géant, gigantesque

gibberish [ˈdʒɪbərɪʃ] *n* : baragouin *m*, charabia *m fam*

gibe [ˈdʒaɪb] *vi* **gibed; gibing** **~ at** : se moquer de — **~** *n* : moquerie *f*

giblets [ˈdʒɪbləts] *npl* : abats *mpl* (de volaille)

giddy [ˈgɪdi] *adj* **-dier; -est** : vertigineux — **giddiness** [ˈgɪdinəs] *n* : vertige *m*

gift [ˈgɪft] *n* **1** PRESENT : cadeau *m* **2** TALENT : don *m* — **gifted** [ˈgɪftəd] *adj* : doué

gigantic [dʒaɪˈgæntɪk] *adj* : gigantesque

giggle [ˈgɪgəl] *vi* **-gled; -gling** : rire bêtement — **~** *n* : petit rire *m*

gild [ˈgɪld] *vt* **gilded** [ˈgɪldəd] *or* **gilt** [ˈgɪlt]; **gilding** : dorer

gill [ˈgɪl] *n* : branchie *f*, ouïe *f*

gilt [ˈgɪlt] *adj* : doré

gimmick [ˈgɪmɪk] *n* : truc *m*, gadget *m*

gin [ˈdʒɪn] *n* : gin *m*

ginger [ˈdʒɪndʒər] *n* : gingembre *m* — **ginger ale** *n* : boisson *f* gazeuse au gingembre — **gingerbread** [ˈdʒɪndʒərˌbrɛd] *n* : pain *m* d'épice — **gingerly** [ˈdʒɪndʒərli] *adv* : avec précaution

giraffe [dʒəˈræf] *n* : girafe *f*

girdle [ˈgərdəl] *n* : gaine *f*

girl [ˈgərl] *n* : fille *f*, jeune fille *f* — **girlfriend** [ˈgərlˌfrɛnd] *n* : copine *f*, petite amie *f*

girth [ˈgərθ] *n* : circonférence *f*

gist [ˈdʒɪst] *n* **the ~** : l'essentiel *m*

give [ˈgɪv] *v* **gave** [ˈgeɪv]; **given** [ˈgɪvən]; **giving** *vt* **1** : donner **2** **~ out** DISTRIBUTE : distribuer **3** **~ up smoking** : arrêter de fumer — *vi* **1** YIELD : céder **2** **~ in** *or* **~ up** : se rendre — **~** *n* : élasticité *f*, souplesse *f* — **given** [ˈgɪvən] *adj* **1** SPECIFIED : donné **2** INCLINED : enclin — **given name** *n* : prénom *m*

glacier [ˈgleɪʃər] *n* : glacier *m*

glad [ˈglæd] *adj* **gladder; gladdest 1** : content **2 be ~ to** : être heureux de **3** **~ to meet you** : enchanté — **gladden** [ˈglædən] *vt* : réjouir — **gladly** [ˈglædli] *adv* : avec plaisir, volontiers

glade [ˈgleɪd] *n* : clairière *f*

glamour *or* **glamor** [ˈglæmər] *n* : charme *m* — **glamorous** [ˈglæmərəs] *adj* : séduisant

glance [ˈglænts] *vi* **glanced; glancing** **~ at** : jeter un coup d'œil à — **~** *n* : coup *m* d'œil

gland [ˈglænd] *n* : glande *f*

glare [ˈglær] *vi* **glared; glaring 1** : briller d'un éclat éblouissant **2** **~ at** : lancer un regard furieux à — **~** *n* **1** : lumière *f* éblouissante **2** STARE : regard *m* furieux — **glaring** [ˈglærɪŋ] *adj* **1** BRIGHT : éblouissant **2** FLAGRANT : flagrant

glass [ˈglæs] *n* **1** : verre *m* **2** **~es** *npl* SPECTACLES : lunettes *fpl* — **~** *adj* : en verre — **glassware** [ˈglæsˌwær] *n* : verrerie *f* — **glassy** [ˈglæsi] *adj* **glassier; glassiest** : vitreux

glaze [ˈgleɪz] *vt* **glazed; glazing** : vernisser (des céramiques) — **~** *n* **1** : vernis *m* **2** FROSTING : glaçage *m*

gleam [ˈgli:m] *n* : lueur *f* — **~** *vi* : luire, reluire

glee [ˈgli:] *n* : joie *f* — **gleeful** [ˈgli:fəl] *adj* : joyeux

glib [ˈglɪb] *adj* **glibber; glibbest** : désinvolte

glide [ˈglaɪd] *vi* **glided; gliding** : glisser (sur une surface), planer (en l'air) — **glider** [ˈglaɪdər] *n* : planeur *m*

glimmer [ˈglɪmər] *vi* : jeter une faible lueur — **~** *n* : lueur *f*

glimpse [ˈglɪmps] *vt* **glimpsed;**

glimpsing : entrevoir — ~ *n* **1** : aperçu *m* **2 catch a ~ of** : entrevoir
glint [ˈglɪnt] *vi* : étinceler — ~ *n* : reflet *m*
glisten [ˈglɪsən] *vi* : briller
glitter [ˈglɪt̬ər] *vi* : scintiller, étinceler — ~ *n* : scintillement *m*
gloat [ˈglo:t] *vi* : jubiler
globe [ˈglo:b] *n* : globe *m* — **global** [ˈglo:bəl] *adj* : mondial
gloom [ˈglu:m] *n* **1** DARKNESS : obscurité *f* **2** SADNESS : tristesse *f* — **gloomy** [ˈglu:mi] *adj* **gloomier; gloomiest 1** DARK : sombre **2** DISMAL : lugubre
glory [ˈglori] *n, pl* **-ries** : gloire *f* — **glorify** [ˈglorəˌfaɪ] *vt* **-fied; -fying** : glorifier — **glorious** [ˈgloriəs] *adj* : glorieux
gloss [ˈglɔs, ˈglɑs] *n* : brillant *m*, lustre *m*
glossary [ˈglɔsəri, ˈglɑ-] *n, pl* **-ries** : glossaire *m*
glossy [ˈglɔsi, ˈglɑ-] *adj* **glossier; glossiest** : brillant
glove [ˈglʌv] *n* : gant *m*
glow [ˈglo:] *vi* **1** : luire **2 ~ with health** : rayonner de santé — ~ *n* : lueur *f*
glue [ˈglu:] *n* : colle *f* — ~ *vt* **glued; gluing** *or* **glueing** : coller
glum [ˈglʌm] *adj* **glummer; glummest** : morne, triste
glut [ˈglʌt] *n* : surabondance *f*
glutton [ˈglʌtən] *n* : glouton *m*, -tonne *f* — **gluttonous** [ˈglʌtənəs] *adj* : glouton — **gluttony** [ˈglʌtəni] *n, pl* **-tonies** : gloutonnerie *f*
gnarled [ˈnɑrld] *adj* : noueux
gnash [ˈnæʃ] *vt* **~ one's teeth** : grincer des dents
gnat [ˈnæt] *n* : moucheron *m*
gnaw [ˈnɔ] *vt* : ronger
go [ˈgo:] *v* **went** [ˈwɛnt]; **gone** [ˈgɔn, ˈgɑn]; **going; goes** [ˈgo:z] *vi* **1** : aller **2** LEAVE : partir, s'en aller **3** EXTEND : s'étendre **4** SELL : se vendre **5** FUNCTION : marcher **6** DISAPPEAR : disparaître **7 ~ back on** : revenir sur **8 ~ for** FAVOR : aimer **9 ~ off** EXPLODE : exploser **10 ~ out** : sortir **11 ~ with** MATCH : aller avec **12 ~ without** : se passer de — *v aux* **be going to do** : aller faire — ~ *n, pl* **goes 1** ATTEMPT : essai *m*, tentative *f* **2 be on the ~** : ne jamais s'arrêter
goad [ˈgo:d] *vt* : aiguillonner (un animal), provoquer (une personne)
goal [ˈgo:l] *n* : but *m* — **goalie** [ˈgo:li] → **goalkeeper** — **goalkeeper** [ˈgo:lˌki:pər] *n* : gardien *m* de but
goat [ˈgo:t] *n* : chèvre *f*
goatee [go:ˈti:] *n* : barbiche *f*
gobble [ˈgɑbəl] *vt* **-bled; -bling** *or* **~ up** : engloutir
goblet [ˈgɑblət] *n* : verre *m* à pied
goblin [ˈgɑblən] *n* : lutin *m*
god [ˈgɑd, ˈgɔd] *n* **1** : dieu *m* **2 God** : Dieu *m* — **goddess** [ˈgɑdəs, ˈgɔ-] *n* : déesse *f* — **godchild** [ˈgɑdˌʧaɪld, ˈgɔd-] *n, pl* **-children** : filleul *m*, -leule *f* — **godfather** [ˈgɑdˌfɑðər, ˈgɔd-] *n* : parrain *m* — **godmother** [ˈgɑdˌmʌðər, ˈgɔd-] *n* : marraine *f*
goes → **go**
goggles [ˈgɑgəlz] *npl* : lunettes *fpl* (protectrices)
gold [ˈgo:ld] *n* : or *m* — **golden** [ˈgo:ldən] *adj* **1** : en or, d'or **2** : doré, couleur *f* d'or —**goldfish** [ˈgo:ldˌfɪʃ] *n* : poisson *m* rouge — **goldsmith** [ˈgo:ldˌsmɪθ] *n* : orfèvre *m*
golf [ˈgɑlf, ˈgɔlf] *n* : golf *m* — ~ *vi* : jouer au golf — **golf ball** *n* : balle *f* de golfe — **golf course** *n* : terrain *m* de golf — **golfer** [ˈgɑlfər, ˈgɔl-] *n* : joueur *m*, joueuse *f* de golf
gone [ˈgɔn] *adj* **1** PAST : passé **2** DEPARTED : parti
good [ˈgʊd] *adj* **better** [ˈbɛt̬ər]; **best** [ˈbɛst] **1** : bon **2** OBEDIENT : sage **3 be ~ at** : être bon en **4 feel ~** : se sentir bien **5 ~ evening** : bonsoir **6 ~ morning** : bonjour **7 ~ night** : bonsoir, bonne nuit **8 have a ~ time** : s'amuser — ~ *n* **1** : bien *m* **2** GOODNESS : bonté *f* **3 ~s** *npl* PROPERTY : biens *mpl* **4 ~s** *npl* WARES : marchandises *fpl* **5 for ~** : pour de bon — ~ *adv* : bien — **good-bye** *or* **good-by** [gʊdˈbaɪ] *n* : au revoir *m* — **good-looking** [ˈgʊdˈlʊkɪŋ] *adj* : beau — **goodness** [ˈgʊdnəs] *n* **1** : bonté *f* **2 thank ~ !** : Dieu merci! — **goodwill** [ˌgʊdˈwɪl] *n* : bienveillance *f* — **goody** [ˈgʊdi] *n, pl* **goodies 1 ~!** : chouette! *fam* **2 goodies** *npl* : friandises *fpl*
goof [ˈgu:f] *n* : gaffe *f fam* — ~ *vi* **1** *or* **~ up** : gaffer *fam* **2 ~ around** : faire l'imbécile
goose [ˈgu:s] *n, pl* **geese** [ˈgi:s] : oie *f* — **goose bumps** *npl* : chair *f* de poule
gopher [ˈgo:fər] *n* : gaufre *m*
gore [ˈgor] *n* BLOOD : sang *m*
gorge [ˈgorʤ] *n* RAVINE : gorge *f*, défilé *m* — ~ *vt* **gorged; gorging ~ oneself** : se gorger

gorgeous ['gɔrʤəs] *adj* : magnifique, splendide

gorilla [gə'rɪlə] *n* : gorille *m*

gory ['gori] *adj* **gorier; goriest** : sanglant

gospel ['gɑspəl] *n* **1** : évangile *m* **2 the Gospel** : l'Évangile

gossip ['gɑsɪp] *n* : commérages *mpl fam,* ragots *mpl fam* — ~ *vi* : bavarder — **gossipy** ['gɑsɪpi] *adj* : bavard

got → **get**

Gothic ['gɑθɪk] *adj* : gothique

gotten → **get**

gourmet ['gʊr,meɪ, gʊr'meɪ] *n* : gourmet *m*

govern ['gʌvərn] *v* : gouverner — **governess** ['gʌvərnəs] *n* : gouvernante *f* — **government** ['gʌvərmənt] *n* : gouvernement *m* — **governor** ['gʌvənər, 'gʌvərnər] *n* : gouverneur *m*

gown ['gaʊn] *n* **1** : robe *f* **2** : toge *f* (de juge, etc.)

grab ['græb] *vt* **grabbed; grabbing** : saisir

grace ['greɪs] *n* : grâce *f* — ~ *vt* **graced; gracing 1** HONOR : honorer **2** ADORN : orner — **graceful** ['greɪsfəl] *adj* : gracieux — **gracious** ['greɪʃəs] *adj* : courtois, gracieux

grade ['greɪd] *n* **1** QUALITY : catégorie *f,* qualité *f* **2** RANK : grade *m,* rang *m* (militaire) **3** YEAR : classe *f* (à l'école) **4** MARK : note *f* **5** SLOPE : pente *f* — ~ *vt* **graded; grading 1** CLASSIFY : classer **2** MARK : noter (un examen, etc.) — **grade school** → **elementary school**

gradual ['grædʒʊəl] *adj* : graduel, progressif — **gradually** ['grædʃʊəli, 'grædʃəli] *adv* : petit à petit

graduate ['grædʒʊət] *n* : diplômé *m,* -mée *f* — ~ ['grædʒʊ,eɪt] *vi* **-ated; -ating** : recevoir son diplôme — **graduation** [,grædʒʊ'eɪʃən] *n* : remise *f* des diplômes

graffiti [grə'fi:ţi, græ-] *npl* : graffiti *mpl*

graft ['græft] *n* : greffe *f* — ~ *vt* : greffer

grain ['greɪn] *n* **1** : grain *m* **2** CEREAL : céréales *fpl*

gram ['græm] *n* : gramme *m*

grammar ['græmər] *n* : grammaire *f* — **grammar school** → **elementary school**

grand ['grænd] *adj* **1** : grand, magnifique **2** FABULOUS : formidable *fam* — **grandchild** ['grænd,ʧaɪld] *n, pl* **-children** [-,ʧɪldrən] : petit-fils *m,* petite-fille *f* — **granddaughter** ['grænd,dɔţər] *n* : petite-fille *f* — **grandeur** ['grænʤər] *n* : grandeur *f* — **grandfather** ['grænd,fɑðər] *n* : grand-père *m* — **grandiose** ['grændi,o:s, ,grændi'-] *adj* : grandiose — **grandmother** ['grænd,mʌðər] *n* : grand-mère *f* — **grandparents** ['grænd,pærənts] *npl* : grands-parents *mpl* — **grandson** ['grænd,sʌn] *n* : petit-fils *m* — **grandstand** ['grænd,stænd] *n* : tribune *f*

granite ['grænɪt] *n* : granit *m,* granite *m*

grant ['grænt] *vt* **1** : accorder **2** ADMIT : admettre **3 take for granted** : prendre pour acquis — ~ *n* **1** SUBSIDY : subvention *f* **2** SCHOLARSHIP : bourse *f*

grape ['greɪp] *n* : raisin *m*

grapefruit ['greɪp,fru:t] *n* : pamplemousse *mf*

grapevine ['greɪp,vaɪn] *n* : vigne *f*

graph ['græf] *n* : graphique *m* — **graphic** ['græfɪk] *adj* : graphique

grapnel ['græpnəl] *n* : grappin *m*

grapple ['græpəl] *vi* **-pled; -pling** ~ **with** : lutter avec

grasp ['græsp] *vt* **1** : saisir **2** UNDERSTAND : comprendre — ~ *n* **1** : prise *f* **2** UNDERSTANDING : compréhension *f* **3 within s.o.'s** ~ : à la portée de qqn

grass ['græs] *n* **1** : herbe *f* **2** LAWN : gazon *m,* pelouse *f* — **grasshopper** ['græs,hɑpər] *n* : sauterelle *f*

grate[1] ['greɪt] *v* **grated; grating** *vt* : râper (du fromage, etc.) — *vi* : grincer

grate[2] *n* : grille *f*

grateful ['greɪtfəl] *adj* : reconnaissant — **gratefully** ['greɪtfəli] *adv* : avec reconnaissance — **gratefulness** ['greɪtfəlnəs] *n* : gratitude *f,* reconnaissance *f*

grater ['greɪţər] *n* : râpe *f*

gratify ['græţə,faɪ] *vt* **-fied; -fying 1** PLEASE : faire plaisir à **2** SATISFY : satisfaire

grating ['greɪţɪŋ] *n* : grille *f*

gratitude ['græţə,tu:d, -,tju:d] *n* : gratitude *f*

gratuitous [grə'tu:əţəs] *adj* : gratuit

gratuity [grə'tu:əţi] *n, pl* **-ities** TIP : pourboire *m*

grave[1] ['greɪv] *n* : tombe *f*

grave[2] *adj* **graver; gravest** : grave, sérieux

gravel ['grævəl] *n* : gravier *m*

gravestone ['greɪv,sto:n] *n* : pierre *f* tombale — **graveyard** ['greɪv,jard] *n* : cimetière *m*

gravity ['grævəţi] *n, pl* **-ties 1** SERIOUSNESS : gravité *f* **2** : pesanteur *f* (en physique)

gravy ['greɪvi] *n, pl* **-vies** : sauce *f* (au jus de viande)

gray [ˈgreɪ] *adj* **1** : gris **2** GLOOMY : morne — **~** *n* : gris *m* — **~** *vi or* **turn ~** : grisonner

graze[1] [ˈgreɪz] *vi* **grazed; grazing** : paître

graze[2] *vt* **1** TOUCH : frôler **2** SCRATCH : écorcher

grease [ˈgri:s] *n* : graisse *f* — **~** [ˈgri:s, ˈgri:z] *vt* **greased; greasing** : graisser — **greasy** [ˈgri:si, -zi] *adj* **greasier; greasiest 1** : graisseux **2** OILY : huileux

great [ˈgreɪt] *adj* **1** : grand **2** FANTASTIC : génial *fam,* formidable *fam* — **great–grandchild** [ˌgreɪtˈgrænd,ʧaɪld] *n, pl* **-children** [-ˌʧɪldrən] : arrière-petit-enfant *m,* arrière-petite-enfant *f* — **great–grandfather** [ˌgreɪtˈgrændˌfɑðər] *n* : arrière-grand-père *m* — **great–grandmother** [ˌgreɪtˈgrændˌmʌðər] *n* : arrière-grand-mère *f* — **greatly** [ˈgreɪtli] *adv* **1** MUCH : beaucoup **2** VERY : énormément — **greatness** [ˈgreɪtnəs] *n* : grandeur *f*

greed [ˈgri:d] *n* **1** : avarice *f,* avidité *f* **2** GLUTTONY : gloutonnerie *f* — **greedily** [ˈgri:dəli] *adv* : avidement — **greedy** [ˈgri:di] *adj* **greedier; greediest 1** : avare, avide **2** GLUTTONOUS : glouton

Greek [ˈgri:k] *adj* : grec — **~** *n* : grec *m* (langue)

green [ˈgri:n] *adj* **1** : vert **2** INEXPERIENCED : inexpérimenté — **~** *n* **1** : vert *m* (couleur) **2 ~s** *npl* : légumes *mpl* verts — **greenery** [ˈgri:nəri] *n, pl* **-eries** : verdure *f* — **greenhouse** [ˈgri:nˌhaʊs] *n* : serre *f*

greet [ˈgri:t] *vt* **1** : saluer **2** WELCOME : accueillir — **greeting** [ˈgri:t̬ɪŋ] *n* **1** : salutation *f* **2 ~s** *npl* REGARDS : salutations *fpl* **3 birthday ~s** : vœux *mpl* d'anniversaire

grenade [grəˈneɪd] *n* : grenade *f*

grew → **grow**

grey → **gray**

greyhound [ˈgreɪˌhaʊnd] *n* : lévrier *m*

grid [grɪd] *n* **1** GRATING : grille *f* **2** : quadrillage *m* (d'une carte, etc.)

griddle [ˈgrɪdəl] *n* : plaque *f* chauffante

grief [ˈgri:f] *n* : chagrin *m,* douleur *f* — **grievance** [ˈgri:vənts] *n* : grief *m* — **grieve** [ˈgri:v] *v* **grieved; grieving** *vt* DISTRESS : peiner, chagriner — *vi* **~ for** : pleurer — **grievous** [ˈgri:vəs] *adj* : grave, sérieux

grill [ˈgrɪl] *vt* **1** : griller (en cuisine) **2** INTERROGATE : cuisiner *fam* — **~** *n* : gril *m* (de cuisine) — **grille** *or* **grill** [ˈgrɪl] *n* GRATING : grille *f*

grim [ˈgrɪm] *adj* **grimmer; grimmest 1** STERN : sévère **2** GLOOMY : sinistre

grimace [ˈgrɪməs, grɪˈmeɪs] *n* : grimace *f* — **~** *vi* **-maced; -macing** : grimacer

grime [ˈgraɪm] *n* : saleté *f,* crasse *f* — **grimy** [ˈgraɪmi] *adj* **grimier; grimiest** : sale, crasseux

grin [ˈgrɪn] *vi* **grinned; grinning** : sourire — **~** *n* : (grand) sourire *m*

grind [ˈgraɪnd] *v* **ground** [ˈgraʊnd]; **grinding** *vt* **1** : moudre (du café, etc.) **2** SHARPEN : aiguiser **3 ~ one's teeth** : grincer des dents — *vi* : grincer — **~** *n* **the daily ~** : le train-train quotidien — **grinder** [ˈgraɪndər] *n* : moulin *m*

grip [ˈgrɪp] *vt* **gripped; gripping 1** : serrer, empoigner **2** CAPTIVATE : captiver — **~** *n* **1** : prise *f,* étreinte *f* **2** TRACTION : adhérence *f* **3 come to ~s with** : en venir aux prises avec

gripe [ˈgraɪp] *vi* **griped; griping** : rouspéter *fam,* ronchonner *fam* — **~** *n* : plainte *f*

grisly [ˈgrɪzli] *adj* **-lier; -est** : horrible, macabre

gristle [ˈgrɪsəl] *n* : cartilage *m*

grit [ˈgrɪt] *n* **1** : sable *m,* gravillon *m* **2 ~s** *npl* : gruau *m* de maïs — **~** *vt* **gritted; gritting ~ one's teeth** : serrer les dents

groan [ˈgro:n] *vi* : gémir — **~** *n* : gémissement *m*

grocery [ˈgro:səri, -ʃəri] *n, pl* **-ceries 1** *or* **~ store** : épicerie *f* **2 groceries** *npl* : épiceries *fpl,* provisions *fpl* — **grocer** [ˈgro:sər] *n* : épicier *m,* -cière *f*

groggy [ˈgrɑgi] *adj* **-gier; -est** : chancelant, sonné *fam*

groin [ˈgrɔɪn] *n* : aine *f*

groom [ˈgru:m, ˈgrum] *n* BRIDEGROOM : marié *m* — **~** *vt* : panser (un animal)

groove [ˈgru:v] *n* : rainure *f,* sillon *m*

grope [ˈgro:p] *vi* **groped; groping 1** : tâtonner **2 ~ for** : chercher à tâtons

gross [ˈgro:s] *adj* **1** SERIOUS : flagrant **2** TOTAL : brut **3** VULGAR : grossier — **~** *n* **~ income** : recettes *fpl* brutes — **grossly** [ˈgro:sli] *adv* : extrêmement

grotesque [gro:ˈtɛsk] *adj* : grotesque

grouch [ˈgraʊʧ] *n* : rouspéteur *m,* -teuse *f fam* — **grouchy** [ˈgraʊʧi] *adj* **grouchier; grouchiest** : grognon

ground[1] [ˈgraʊnd] → **grind**

ground[2] *n* **1** : sol *m,* terre *f* **2** *or* **~s** LAND : terrain *m* **3 ~s** *npl* REASON : raison *f* — **~** *vt* BASE : baser, fonder — **groundhog** [ˈgraʊndˌhɔg] *n* : marmotte *f* d'Amérique —**groundwork**

['graʊnd,wərk] *n* : travail *m* préparatoire

group ['gru:p] *n* : groupe *m* — ~ *vt* : grouper, réunir — *vi or* ~ **together** : se grouper

grove ['gro:v] *n* : bosquet *m*

grovel ['grɑvəl, 'grʌ-] *vi* **-eled** *or* **-elled; -eling** *or* **-elling** : ramper

grow ['gro:] *v* **grew** ['gru:]; **grown** ['gro:n]; **growing** *vi* **1** : pousser (se dit des plantes), grandir (se dit des personnes) **2** INCREASE : croître **3** BECOME : devenir — *vt* **1** CULTIVATE : cultiver **2** : laisser pousser (la barbe, etc.) — **grower** ['gro:ər] *n* : cultivateur *m*, -trice *f*

growl ['graʊl] *vi* : grogner, gronder — ~ *n* : grognement *m*, grondement *m*

grown–up ['gro:n,əp] *adj* : adulte — ~ *n* : adulte *mf*

growth ['gro:θ] *n* **1** : croissance *f* **2** INCREASE : augmentation *f* **3** TUMOR : tumeur *f*

grub ['grʌb] *n* FOOD : bouffe *f fam*

grubby ['grʌbi] *adj* **-bier; -est** : sale

grudge ['grʌʤ] *n* **1** : rancune *f* **2** **hold a** ~ : en vouloir à

grueling *or* **gruelling** ['gru:lɪŋ, gru:ə-] *adj* : exténuant, épuisant

gruesome ['gru:səm] *adj* : horrible

gruff ['grʌf] *adj* : bourru, brusque

grumble ['grʌmbəl] *vi* **-bled; -bling** : ronchonner *fam*

grumpy ['grʌmpi] *adj* **grumpier; grumpiest** : grincheux, grognon

grunt ['grʌnt] *vi* : grogner — ~ *n* : grognement *m*

guarantee [,gærən'ti:] *n* : garantie *f* — ~ *vt* **-teed; -teeing** : garantir

guarantor [,gærən'tɔr] *n* : garant *m*, -rante *f*

guard ['gɑrd] *n* **1** : garde *m* (personne) **2** **be on one's** ~ : être sur ses gardes — ~ *vt* : garder, surveiller — *vi* ~ **against** : se garder de — **guardian** ['gɑrdiən] *n* **1** : tuteur *m*, -trice *f* (d'un mineur) **2** PROTECTOR : gardien *m*, -dienne *f*

guerrilla *or* **guerilla** [gə'rɪlə] *n* **1** : guérillero *m* **2** ~ **warfare** : guérilla *f*

guess ['gɛs] *vt* **1** : deviner **2** SUPPOSE : penser — *vi* : deviner — ~ *n* : conjecture *f*

guest ['gɛst] *n* **1** VISITOR : invité *m*, -tée *f* **2** : client *m*, cliente *f* (d'un hôtel)

guide ['gaɪd] *n* **1** : guide *mf* (personne) **2** : guide *m* (livre, etc.) — ~ *vt* **guided; guiding** : guider — **guidance** ['gaɪdənts] *n* : conseils *mpl*, direction *f* — **guidebook** ['gaɪd,bʊk] *n* : guide *m* — **guideline** ['gaɪd,laɪn] *n* : ligne *f* directrice

guild ['gɪld] *n* : association *f*

guile ['gaɪl] *n* : ruse *f*

guilt ['gɪlt] *n* : culpabilité *f* — **guilty** ['gɪlti] *adj* **guiltier; guiltiest** : coupable

guinea pig ['gɪni-] *n* : cobaye *m*

guise ['gaɪz] *n* : apparence *f*

guitar [gə'tɑr, gɪ-] *n* : guitare *f*

gulf ['gʌlf] *n* : golfe *m*

gull ['gʌl] *n* : mouette *f*

gullible ['gʌlɪbəl] *adj* : crédule

gully ['gʌli] *n, pl* **-lies** : ravin *m*

gulp ['gʌlp] *vt or* ~ **down** : avaler — ~ *n* : gorgée *f*, bouchée *f*

gum[1] ['gʌm] *n* : gencive *f*

gum[2] *n* CHEWING GUM : chewing-gum *m France*, gomme *f* à mâcher

gun ['gʌn] *n* **1** FIREARM : arme *f* à feu, fusil *m* **2** *or* **spray** ~ : pistolet *m* — ~ *vt* **gunned; gunning** *or* ~ **down** : abattre — **gunfire** ['gʌn,faɪr] *n* : fusillade *f*, coups *mpl* de feu — **gunman** ['gʌnmən] *n, pl* **-men** [-mən, -,mɛn] : personne *f* armée — **gunpowder** ['gʌn,paʊdər] *n* : poudre *f* (à canon) — **gunshot** ['gʌn,ʃɑt] *n* : coup *m* de feu

gurgle ['gərgəl] *vi* **-gled; -gling** **1** : gargouiller **2** : gazouiller (se dit d'un bébé)

gush ['gʌʃ] *vi* **1** SPOUT : jaillir **2** ~ **over** : s'extasier devant

gust ['gʌst] *n* : rafale *f*

gusto ['gʌs,to:] *n, pl* **-toes** : enthousiasme *m*

gut ['gʌt] *n* **1** : intestin *m* **2** ~**s** *npl* INNARDS : entrailles *fpl* **3** ~**s** *npl* COURAGE : cran *m fam* — ~ *vt* **gutted; gutting** : détruire l'intérieur de (un édifice)

gutter ['gʌt̬ər] *n* **1** : gouttière *f* (d'un toit) **2** : caniveau *m* (d'une rue)

guy ['gaɪ] *n* : type *m fam*

guzzle ['gʌzəl] *vt* **-zled; -zling** : bâfrer *fam*, engloutir

gym ['ʤɪm] *or* **gymnasium** [ʤɪm'neɪziəm, -ʒəm] *n, pl* **-siums** *or* **-sia** [-zi:ə, -ʒə] : gymnase *m* — **gymnast** ['ʤɪmnəst, -,næst] *n* : gymnaste *mf* — **gymnastics** [ʤɪm'næstɪks] *n* : gymnastique *f*

gynecology [,gaɪnə'kɑləʤi] *n* : gynécologie *f* — **gynecologist** [,gaɪnə'kɑləʤɪst] *n* : gynécologue *mf*

Gypsy ['ʤɪpsi] *n, pl* **-sies** : gitan *m*, -tane *f*

H

h ['eɪtʃ] *n, pl* **h's** *or* **hs** ['eɪtʃəz] : h *m*, huitième lettre de l'alphabet
habit ['hæbɪt] *n* **1** CUSTOM : habitude *f*, coutume *f* **2** : habit *m* (religieux)
habitat ['hæbɪˌtæt] *n* : habitat *m*
habitual [hə'bɪtʃʊəl] *adj* **1** CUSTOMARY : habituel **2** INVETERATE : invétéré
hack[1] ['hæk] *n* **1** : cheval *m* de louage **2** *or* **~ writer** : écrivaillon *m*
hack[2] *vt* CUT : tailler — *vi* **~ into** : entrer dans (en informatique)
hackneyed ['hæknid] *adj* : rebattu
hacksaw ['hækˌsɔ] *n* : scie *f* à métaux
had → **have**
haddock ['hædək] *ns & pl* : églefin *m*
hadn't ['hædənt] (*contraction of* **had not**) → **have**
hag ['hæg] *n* : vieille sorcière *f*
haggard ['hægərd] *adj* : hâve, exténué
haggle ['hægəl] *vi* **-gled; -gling** : marchander
hail[1] ['heɪl] *vt* **1** ACCLAIM : acclamer **2** : héler (un taxi)
hail[2] ['heɪl] *n* : grêle *f* (en météorologie) — **~** *vi* : grêler — **hailstone** ['heɪlˌsto:n] *n* : grêlon *m*
hair ['hær] *n* **1** : cheveux *mpl* (sur la tête) **2** : poil *m* (de chien, sur les jambes, etc.) — **hairbrush** ['hærˌbrʌʃ] *n* : brosse *f* à cheveux — **haircut** ['hærˌkʌt] *n* : coupe *f* de cheveux — **hairdo** ['hærˌdu:] *n, pl* **-dos** : coiffure *f* — **hairdresser** ['hærˌdrɛsər] *n* : coiffeur *m*, -feuse *f* — **hairless** ['hærləs] *adj* : sans cheveux, glabre — **hairpin** ['hærˌpɪn] *n* : épingle *f* à cheveux — **hair–raising** ['hærˌreɪzɪŋ] *adj* : à vous faire dresser les cheveux sur la tête — **hair spray** *n* : laque *f* — **hairy** ['hæri] *adj* **hairier; -est** : poilu, velu
Haitian ['heɪʃən, 'heɪţiən] *adj* : haïtien
half ['hæf] *n, pl* **halves** ['hævz] **1** : moitié *f*, demi *m*, -mie *f* **2 in ~** : en deux **3** *or* **halftime** : mi-temps *f* (aux sports) — **~** *adj* **1** : demi **2 ~ an hour** : une demi-heure **3 in ~** : en deux — **~** *adv* : à demi, à moitié — **halfhearted** ['hæf'hɑrţəd] *adj* : sans enthousiasme — **halfway** ['hæf'weɪ] *adv & adj* : à mi-chemin
halibut ['hælɪbət] *ns & pl* : flétan *m*
hall ['hɔl] *n* **1** HALLWAY : couloir *m* **2** AUDITORIUM : salle *f* **3** LOBBY : entrée *f*, vestibule *m* **4** DORMITORY : résidence *f* universitaire
hallmark ['hɔlˌmɑrk] *n* : marque *f*, sceau *m*
Halloween [ˌhælə'wi:n, ˌhɑ-] *n* : Halloween *f*
hallucination [həˌlu:sən'eɪʃən] *n* : hallucination *f*
hallway ['hɔlˌweɪ] *n* **1** ENTRANCE : entrée *f*, vestibule *m* **2** CORRIDOR : couloir *m*
halo ['heɪˌlo:] *n, pl* **-los** *or* **-loes** : auréole *f*
halt ['hɔlt] *n* **1** : halte *f* **2 come to a ~** : s'arrêter — **~** *vi* : s'arrêter — *vt* : arrêter
halve ['hæv] *vt* **halved; halving 1** DIVIDE : couper en deux **2** REDUCE : réduire de moitié — **halves** → **half**
ham ['hæm] *n* : jambon *m*
hamburger ['hæmˌbərgər] *or* **hamburg** [-ˌbərg] *n* **1** : viande *f* hachée (crue) **2** : hamburger *m* (cuit)
hammer ['hæmər] *n* : marteau *m* — **~** *vt* : marteler, enfoncer (à coups de marteau)
hammock ['hæmək] *n* : hamac *m*
hamper[1] ['hæmpər] *vt* : gêner
hamper[2] *n* : panier *m* (à linge)
hamster ['hæmpstər] *n* : hamster *m*
hand ['hænd] *n* **1** : main *f* **2** : aiguille *f* (d'une montre, etc.) **3** HANDWRITING : écriture *f* **4** : main *f*, jeu *m* (aux cartes) **5** WORKER : ouvrier *m*, -vrière *f* **6 by ~** : à la main **7 give s.o. a ~** : donner un coup de main à qqn **8 on ~** : disponible **9 on the other ~** : d'autre part — **~** *vt* **1** : donner, passer **2 ~ out** : distribuer — **handbag** ['hændˌbæg] *n* : sac *m* à main — **handbook** ['hændˌbʊk] *n* : manuel *m*, guide *m* — **handcuffs** ['hændˌkʌfs] *npl* : menottes *fpl* — **handful** ['hændˌfʊl] *n* : poignée *f* — **handgun** ['hændˌgʌn] *n* : pistolet *m*, revolver *m*
handicap ['hændiˌkæp] *n* : handicap *m* — **~** *vt* **-capped; -capping** : handicaper — **handicapped** ['hændiˌkæpt] *adj* : handicapé
handicrafts ['hændiˌkræfts] *npl* : objets *mpl* artisanaux
handiwork ['hændiˌwərk] *n* : ouvrage *m*

handkerchief ['hæŋkərʧəf, -ˌʧi:f] *n, pl* **-chiefs** : mouchoir *m*
handle ['hændəl] *n* : manche *m* (d'un ustensile), poignée *f* (de porte), anse *f* (d'un panier, etc.) — **~** *vt* **-dled; -dling 1** TOUCH : toucher à, manipuler **2** MANAGE : s'occuper de — **handlebars** ['hændəlˌbarz] *npl* : guidon *m*
handmade ['hændˌmeɪd] *adj* : fait à la main
handout ['hændˌaʊt] *n* **1** ALMS : aumône *f* **2** LEAFLET : prospectus *m*
handrail ['hændˌreɪl] *n* : rampe *f*
handshake ['hændˌʃeɪk] *n* : poignée *f* de main
handsome ['hæntsəm] *adj* **handsomer; -est 1** ATTRACTIVE : beau **2** GENEROUS : généreux **3** LARGE : considérable
handwriting ['hændˌraɪṭɪŋ] *n* : écriture *f* — **handwritten** ['hændˌrɪtən] *adj* : écrit à la main
handy ['hændi] *adj* **handier; -est 1** NEARBY : à portée de la main, proche **2** USEFUL : commode, pratique **3** CLEVER : adroit — **handyman** ['hændimən] *n, pl* **-men** [-mən, -ˌmɛn] : bricoleur *m*
hang ['hæŋ] *v* **hung** ['hʌŋ]; **hanging** *vt* **1** : suspendre, accrocher **2** (*past tense often* **hanged**) EXECUTE : pendre **3 ~ one's head** : baisser la tête — *vi* **1** : être accroché, pendre **2 ~ up** : raccrocher — **~** *n* **get the ~ of** : piger *fam*
hangar ['hæŋər, 'hæŋgər] *n* : hangar *m*
hanger ['hæŋər] *n or* **coat ~** : cintre *m*
hangover ['hæŋˌo:vər] *n* : gueule *f* de bois
hanker ['hæŋkər] *vi* **~ for** : désirer, avoir envie de — **hankering** ['hæŋkərɪŋ] *n* : désir *m*, envie *f*
haphazard [hæp'hæzərd] *adj* : fait au hasard
happen ['hæpən] *vi* **1** OCCUR : arriver, se passer **2** CHANCE : arriver par hasard **3 it so happens that ...** : il se trouve que ... — **happening** ['hæpənɪŋ] *n* : événement *m*
happy ['hæpi] *adj* **happier; -est 1** : heureux **2 be ~ with** : être satisfait de — **happily** ['hæpəli] *adv* : heureusement — **happiness** ['hæpinəs] *n* : bonheur *m* — **happy-go-lucky** ['hæpigo:'lʌki] *adj* : insouciant
harass [hə'ræs, 'hærəs] *vt* : harceler — **harassment** [hə'ræsmənt, 'hærəsmənt] *n* : harcèlement *m*
harbor *or Brit* **harbour** ['harbər] *n* : port *m* — **~** *vt* **1** SHELTER : héberger **2 ~ a grudge against** : garder rancune à
hard ['hard] *adj* **1** : dur **2** DIFFICULT : difficile **3 ~ water** : eau *f* calcaire — **~** *adv* **1** : dur **2** FORCEFULLY : fort **3 take sth ~** : mal prendre qqch — **harden** ['hardən] *vt* : durcir, endurcir — *vi* : s'endurcir — **hardheaded** ['hard'hɛdəd] *adj* : têtu, entêté — **hard-hearted** ['hard'harṭəd] *adj* : dur, insensible — **hardly** ['hardli] *adv* **1** BARELY : à peine, ne ... guère **2 it's ~ surprising** : ce n'est pas surprenant — **hardness** ['hardnəs] *n* : dureté *f* — **hardship** ['hardˌʃɪp] *n* : épreuves *fpl* — **hardware** ['hardˌwær] *n* **1** : quincaillerie *f* **2** : matériel *m* (en informatique) — **hardworking** ['hard'wərkɪŋ] *adj* : travailleur, travaillant *Can*
hardy ['hardi] *adj* **hardier; -est 1** BOLD : hardi, intrépide **2** ROBUST : résistant
hare ['hær] *n, pl* **hare** *or* **hares** : lièvre *m*
harm ['harm] *n* **1** INJURY : mal *m* **2** DAMAGE : dommage *m* **3** WRONG : tort *m* — **~** *vt* : faire du mal à, nuire à — **harmful** ['harmfəl] *adj* : nuisible — **harmless** ['harmləs] *adj* : inoffensif
harmonica [har'manɪkə] *n* : harmonica *m*
harmony ['harməni] *n, pl* **-nies** : harmonie *f* — **harmonious** [har'mo:niəs] *adj* : harmonieux — **harmonize** ['harməˌnaɪz] *v* **-nized; -nizing** *vt* : harmoniser — *vi* : s'harmoniser
harness ['harnəs] *n* : harnais *m* — **~** *vt* **1** : harnacher **2** UTILIZE : exploiter
harp ['harp] *n* : harpe *f* — **~** *vi* **~ on** : rabâcher
harpoon [har'pu:n] *n* : harpon *m*
harpsichord ['harpsɪˌkord] *n* : clavecin *m*
harsh ['harʃ] *adj* **1** ROUGH : rude **2** SEVERE : dur, sévère **3** : cru (se dit des couleurs), rude (se dit des sons) — **harshness** ['harʃnəs] *n* : sévérité *f*
harvest ['harvəst] *n* : moisson *f*, récolte *f* — **~** *vt* : moissonner, récolter
has → **have**
hash ['hæʃ] *vt* **1** CHOP : hacher **2 ~ over** DISCUSS : parler de, discuter — **~** *n* **1** : hachis *m* **2** JUMBLE : gâchis *m*
hasn't ['hæzənt] (*contraction of* **has not**) → **have**
hassle ['hæsəl] *n* : embêtements *mpl*, ennuis *mpl* — **~** *vt* : tracasser
haste ['heɪst] *n* : hâte *f*, précipitation *f* — **hasten** ['heɪsən] *vt* : hâter, préci-

piter — *vi* : se hâter, se dépêcher — **hastily** ['heɪstəli] *adv* : à la hâte — **hasty** ['heɪsti] *adj* **hastier; -est** : précipité

hat ['hæt] *n* : chapeau *m*

hatch ['hætʃ] *n* : écoutille *f* (d'un navire) — ~ *vt* **1** : couver, faire éclore **2** CONCOCT : tramer (un complot) — *vi* : éclore

hatchet ['hætʃət] *n* : hachette *f*

hate ['heɪt] *n* : haine *f* — ~ *vt* **hated; hating** : haïr — **hateful** ['heɪtfəl] *adj* : odieux — **hatred** ['heɪtrəd] *n* : haine *f*

haughty ['hɔṭi] *adj* **haughtier; -est** : hautain

haul ['hɔl] *vt* : tirer, traîner — ~ *n* **1** CATCH : prise *f* **2** LOOT : butin *m* **3 it's a long ~** : la route est longue

haunch ['hɔntʃ] *n* : hanche *f* (d'une personne), derrière *m* (d'un animal)

haunt ['hɔnt] *vt* : hanter

have ['hæv, *in sense 2 as an auxiliary verb usu* 'hæf] *v* **had** ['hæd]; **having; has** ['hæz] *vt* **1** : avoir **2** WANT : vouloir, prendre **3** RECEIVE : recevoir **4** ALLOW : permettre, tolérer **5** HOLD : tenir **6 ~ a sandwich** : manger un sandwich — *v aux* **1** : avoir, être **2 ~ to** : devoir **3 you've finished, haven't you?** : tu as fini, n'est-ce pas?

haven ['heɪvən] *n* : refuge *m*, havre *m*

havoc ['hævək] *n* : ravages *mpl*, dégâts *mpl*

hawk[1] ['hɔk] *n* : faucon *m* (oiseau)

hawk[2] *vt* : colporter

hay ['heɪ] *n* : foin *m* — **hay fever** *n* : rhume *m* des foins — **haystack** ['heɪˌstæk] *n* : meule *f* de foin — **haywire** ['heɪˌwaɪr] *adj* **go ~** : se détraquer

hazard ['hæzərd] *n* **1** PERIL : risque *m* **2** CHANCE : hasard *m* — ~ *vt* : hasarder, risquer — **hazardous** ['hæzərdəs] *adj* : dangereux

haze ['heɪz] *n* : brume *f*

hazel ['heɪzəl] *n* : noisette *f* (couleur) — **hazelnut** ['heɪzəlˌnʌt] *n* : noisette *f*

hazy ['heɪzi] *adj* **hazier; -est** **1** : brumeux **2** VAGUE : vague, flou

he ['hi:] *pron* **1** : il **2** (*used for emphasis or contrast*) : lui

head ['hɛd] *n* **1** : tête *f* **2** END, TOP : bout *m* (d'une table), chevet *m* (d'un lit) **3** LEADER : chef *m* **4 ~s or tails** : pile ou face **5 per ~** : par personne — ~ *adj* MAIN : principal — ~ *vt* **1** LEAD : être en tête de **2** DIRECT : diriger — *vi* : se diriger, aller — **headache** ['hɛdˌeɪk] *n* : mal *m* de tête — **headband** ['hɛdˌbænd] *n* : bandeau *m* — **headdress** ['hɛdˌdrɛs] *n* : coiffe *f* — **headfirst** ['hɛd'fərst] *adv* : la tête la première — **heading** ['hɛdɪŋ] *n* : titre *m*, rubrique *f* — **headland** ['hɛdlənd, -ˌlænd] *n* : promontoire *m*, cap *m* — **headlight** ['hɛdˌlaɪt] *n* : phare *m* — **headline** ['hɛdˌlaɪn] *n* : (gros) titre *m* — **headlong** ['hɛd'lɔŋ] *adv* : à toute allure — **headmaster** ['hɛdˌmæstər] *n* : directeur *m* (d'école) — **headmistress** ['hɛdˌmɪstrəs, -'mɪs-] *n* : directrice *f* (d'école) — **head–on** ['hɛd'ɑn, -'ɔn] *adv & adj* : de plein fouet — **headphones** ['hɛdˌfo:nz] *npl* : casque *m* — **headquarters** ['hɛdˌkwɔrṭərz] *ns & pl* : siège *m* (d'une compagnie), quartier *m* général (militaire) — **headstrong** ['hɛdˌstrɔŋ] *adj* : têtu, obstiné — **headwaiter** ['hɛd'weɪṭər] *n* : maître *m* d'hôtel — **headway** ['hɛdˌweɪ] *n* **1** : progrès *m* **2 make ~** : avancer, progresser — **heady** ['hɛdi] *adj* **headier; -est** **1** : capiteux (se dit du vin) **2** EXCITING : grisant

heal ['hi:l] *v* : guérir

health ['hɛlθ] *n* : santé *f* — **healthy** ['hɛlθi] *adj* **healthier; -est** : sain, en bonne santé

heap ['hi:p] *n* : tas *m* — ~ *vt* : entasser

hear ['hɪr] *v* **heard** ['hərd]; **hearing** *vt* **1** : entendre **2** *or* **~ about** : apprendre — *vi* **1** : entendre **2 ~ from** : avoir des nouvelles de — **hearing** ['hɪrɪŋ] *n* **1** : ouïe *f*, audition *f* **2** : audience *f* (d'un tribunal) — **hearing aid** *n* : appareil *m* auditif — **hearsay** ['hɪrˌseɪ] *n* : ouï-dire *m*

hearse ['hərs] *n* : corbillard *m*

heart ['hɑrt] *n* **1** : cœur *m* **2 at ~** : au fond **3 by ~** : par cœur **4 lose ~** : perdre courage — **heartache** ['hɑrṭˌeɪk] *n* : chagrin *m*, peine *f* — **heart attack** *n* : crise *f* cardiaque — **heartbeat** ['hɑrtˌbi:t] *n* : battement *m* de cœur — **heartbroken** ['hɑrtˌbro:kən] *adj* **be ~** : avoir le cœur brisé — **heartburn** ['hɑrtˌbərn] *n* : brûlures *fpl* d'estomac

hearth ['hɑrθ] *n* : foyer *m*

heartily ['hɑrṭəli] *adv* **1 eat ~** : manger avec appétit **2 laugh ~** : rire de bon cœur

heartless ['hɑrtləs] *adj* : sans cœur, cruel

hearty ['hɑrṭi] *adj* **heartier; -est** **1** : cordial, chaleureux **2** : copieux (se dit d'un repas)

heat ['hi:t] *v* : chauffer — ~ *n* **1** : chaleur *f* **2** HEATING : chauffage *m* **3**

PASSION : feu *m,* ardeur *f* — **heated** [ˈhiːṭəd] *adj* : animé, passionné — **heater** [ˈhiːṭər] *n* : radiateur *m,* appareil *m* de chauffage

heath [ˈhiːθ] *n* : lande *f*

heathen [hiːðən] *adj* : païen — ~ *n, pl* **-thens** *or* **-then** : païen *m,* païenne *f*

heather [ˈhɛðər] *n* : bruyère *f*

heave [ˈhiːv] *v* **heaved** *or* **hove** [ˈhoːv]; **heaving** *vt* **1** LIFT : lever, soulever (avec effort) **2** HURL : lancer **3** ~ **a sigh** : pousser un soupir — *vi* : se soulever — ~ *n* : effort *m*

heaven [ˈhɛvən] *n* : ciel *m* — **heavenly** [ˈhɛvənli] *adj* : céleste, divin

heavy [ˈhɛvi] *adj* **heavier**; **-est** **1** : lourd, pesant **2** : gros (se dit du corps, du cœur, etc.) **3** ~ **sleep** : sommeil *m* profond **4** ~ **smoker** : grand fumeur *m* **5** ~ **traffic** : circulation *f* dense — **heavily** [ˈhɛvəli] *adv* : lourdement, pesamment — **heaviness** [ˈhɛvinəs] *n* : lourdeur *f,* pesanteur *f* — **heavyweight** [ˈhɛviˌweɪt] *n* : poids *m* lourd

Hebrew [ˈhiːˌbruː] *adj* : hébreu — ~ *n* : hébreu *m* (langue)

heckle [ˈhɛkəl] *vt* **-led; -ling** : interrompre bruyamment

hectic [ˈhɛktɪk] *adj* : mouvementé, agité

he'd [ˈhiːd] (*contraction of* **he had** *or* **he would**) → **have, would**

hedge [ˈhɛʤ] *n* : haie *f* — ~ *v* **hedged; hedging** *vt* ~ **one's bets** : se couvrir — *vi* : éviter de s'engager — **hedgehog** [ˈhɛʤˌhɔg, -ˌhɑg] *n* : hérisson *m*

heed [ˈhiːd] *vt* : faire attention à, écouter — ~ *n* **take** ~ **of** : tenir compte de — **heedless** [ˈhiːdləs] *adj* : insouciant

heel [ˈhiːl] *n* : talon *m*

hefty [ˈhɛfti] *adj* **heftier; -est** : gros, lourd

heifer [ˈhɛfər] *n* : génisse *f*

height [ˈhaɪt] *n* **1** TALLNESS : taille *f* (d'une personne), hauteur *f* (d'un objet) **2** ALTITUDE : élévation *f* **3 the** ~ **of folly** : le comble de la folie **4 what is your** ~**?** : combien mesures-tu? — **heighten** [ˈhaɪtən] *vt* : augmenter, intensifier

heir [ˈær] *n* : héritier *m,* -tière *f* — **heiress** [ˈærəs] *n* : héritière *f* — **heirloom** [ˈærˌluːm] *n* : objet *m* de famille

held → **hold**

helicopter [ˈhɛləˌkɑptər] *n* : hélicoptère *m*

hell [ˈhɛl] *n* : enfer *m* — **hellish** [ˈhɛlɪʃ] *adj* : infernal

he'll [ˈhiːl] (*contraction of* **he shall** *or* **he will**) → **shall, will**

hello [həˈloː, hɛ-] *or Brit* **hullo** [hʌˈleʊ] *interj* : bonjour!, allô! (au téléphone)

helm [ˈhɛlm] *n* : barre *f*

helmet [ˈhɛlmət] *n* : casque *m*

help [ˈhɛlp] *vt* **1** : aider, venir à l'aide de **2** PREVENT : empêcher **3** ~ **yourself** : servez-vous — ~ *n* **1** : aide *f,* secours *m* **2** STAFF : employés *mpl,* -ployées *fpl* **3** ~! : au secours! — **helper** [ˈhɛlpər] *n* : aide *mf;* assistant *m,* -tante *f* — **helpful** [ˈhɛlpfəl] *adj* : utile, serviable — **helping** [ˈhɛlpɪŋ] *n* SERVING : portion *f* — **helpless** [ˈhɛlpləs] *adj* : impuissant

hem [ˈhɛm] *n* : ourlet *m* — ~ *vt* **hemmed; hemming** : ourler

hemisphere [ˈhɛməˌsfɪr] *n* : hémisphère *m*

hemorrhage [ˈhɛmərɪʤ] *n* : hémorragie *f*

hemorrhoids [ˈhɛməˌrɔɪdz, ˈhɛmˌrɔɪdz] *npl* : hémorroïdes *fpl*

hemp [ˈhɛmp] *n* : chanvre *m*

hen [ˈhɛn] *n* : poule *f*

hence [ˈhɛnts] *adv* **1** : d'où, donc **2 ten years** ~ : d'ici dix ans — **henceforth** [ˈhɛntsˌforθ, ˌhɛntsˈ-] *adv* : dorénavant, désormais

henpeck [ˈhɛnˌpɛk] *vt* : mener par le bout du nez

hepatitis [ˌhɛpəˈtaɪtəs] *n, pl* **-titides** [-ˈtɪṭəˌdiːz] : hépatite *f*

her [ˈhər] *adj* : son, sa, ses — ~ [ˈhər, ər] *pron* **1** (*used as a direct object*) : la, l' **2** (*used as an indirect object*) : lui **3** (*used as object of a preposition*) : elle

herald [ˈhɛrəld] *vt* : annoncer

herb [ˈərb, ˈhərb] *n* : herbe *f*

herd [ˈhərd] *n* : troupeau *m* — ~ *vt* : mener, conduire — *vi or* ~ **together** : s'assembler

here [ˈhɪr] *adv* **1** : ici, là **2** NOW : alors **3** ~ **is,** ~ **are** : voici, voilà — **hereabouts** [ˈhɪrəˌbaʊts] *or* **hereabout** [-ˌbaʊt] *adv* : par ici — **hereafter** [hɪrˈæftər] *adv* : ci-après —**hereby** [hɪrˈbaɪ] *adv* : par la présente

hereditary [həˈrɛdəˌtɛri] *adj* : héréditaire — **heredity** [həˈrɛdəṭi] *n* : hérédité *f*

heresy [ˈhɛrəsi] *n, pl* **-sies** : hérésie *f*

herewith [hɪrˈwɪθ] *adv* : ci-joint

heritage [ˈhɛrəṭɪʤ] *n* : héritage *m,* patrimoine *m*

hermit ['hərmət] *n* : ermite *m*
hernia ['hərniə] *n, pl* **-nias** *or* **-niae** [-ni,i:, -ni,aɪ] : hernie *f*
hero ['hi:,ro:, 'hɪr,o:] *n, pl* **-roes** : héros *m* — **heroic** [hɪ'ro:ɪk] *adj* : héroïque — **heroine** ['hɛroən] *n* : héroïne *f* — **heroism** ['hɛro,ɪzəm] *n* : héroïsme *m*
heron ['hɛrən] *n* : héron *m*
herring ['hɛrɪŋ] *n, pl* **-ring** *or* **-rings** : hareng *m*
hers ['hərz] *pron* **1** : le sien, la sienne, les siens, les siennes **2 some friends of ~** : des amis à elle — **herself** [hər'sɛlf] *pron* **1** (*used reflexively*) : se, s' **2** (*used for emphasis*) : elle-même **3** (*used after a preposition*) : elle, elle-même
he's ['hi:z] (*contraction of* **he is** *or* **he has**) → **be, have**
hesitant ['hɛzət̬ənt] *adj* : hésitant, indécis — **hesitate** ['hɛzə,teɪt] *vi* **-tated; -tating** : hésiter — **hesitation** [,hɛzə'teɪʃən] *n* : hésitation *f*
heterogeneous [,hɛt̬ərə'dʒi:niəs, -njəs] *adj* : hétérogène
heterosexual [,hɛt̬əro'sɛkʃuəl] *adj* : hétérosexuel — **~** *n* : hétérosexuel *m*, -sexuelle *f*
hexagon ['hɛksə,gɑn] *n* : hexagone *m*
hey ['heɪ] *interj* : hé!, ohé!
heyday ['heɪ,deɪ] *n* : beaux jours *mpl*, apogée *f*
hi ['haɪ] *interj* : salut!
hibernate ['haɪbər,neɪt] *vi* **-nated; -nating** : hiberner
hiccup ['hɪkəp] *vi* **-cuped; -cuping** : hoqueter — **~** *n* **have the ~s** : avoir le hoquet
hide[1] ['haɪd] *n* : peau *f* (d'animal)
hide[2] *v* **hid** ['hɪd]; **hidden** ['hɪdən] *or* **hid; hiding** *vt* : cacher — *vi* : se cacher — **hide-and-seek** ['haɪdənd'si:k] *n* : cache-cache *m*
hideous ['hɪdiəs] *adj* : hideux, affreux
hideout ['had,aʊt] *n* : cachette *f*
hierarchy ['haɪə,rɑrki] *n, pl* **-chies** : hiérarchie *f* — **hierarchical** [,haɪə'rɑrkɪkəl] *adj* : hiérarchique
high ['haɪ] *adj* **1** : haut **2** : élevé (se dit des prix, etc.) **3** INTOXICATED : parti *fam*, drogué **4 ~ speed** : grande vitesse *f* **5 a ~ voice** : une voix aiguë — **~** *adv* : haut — **~** *n* : record *m*, niveau *m* élevé — **higher** ['haɪər] *adj* **1** : plus haut **2 ~ education** : études *fpl* supérieures — **highlight** ['haɪ,laɪt] *n* : point *m* culminant — **~** *vt* EMPHASIZE : souligner — **highly** ['haɪli] *adv* **1** VERY : très, extrêmement **2 think ~ of** : penser du bien de — **highness** ['haɪnəs] *n* **His/Her Highness** : son Altesse — **high school** *n* : lycée *m France*, école *f* secondaire *Can* — **high-strung** ['haɪ'strʌŋ] *adj* : nerveux, très tendu — **highway** ['haɪ,weɪ] *n* **1** : autoroute *f* **2** → **interstate**
hijack ['haɪ,dʒæk] *vt* : détourner (un avion) — **hijacker** ['haɪ,dʒækər] *n* : pirate *m* de l'air — **hijacking** ['haɪ,dʒækɪŋ] *n* : détournement *m*
hike ['haɪk] *v* **hiked; hiking** *vi* : faire une randonnée — *vt or* **~ up** RAISE : augmenter — **~** *n* : randonnée *f* — **hiker** ['haɪkər] *n* : randonneur *m*, -neuse *f*
hilarious [hɪ'læriəs, haɪ-] *adj* : désopilant, hilarant — **hilarity** [hɪ'lærət̬i, haɪ-] *n* : hilarité *f*
hill ['hɪl] *n* : colline *f* — **hillside** ['hɪl,saɪd] *n* : coteau *m* — **hilly** ['hɪli] *adj* **hillier; -est** : vallonné, côteux *Can*
hilt ['hɪlt] *n* : poignée *f* (d'une épée)
him ['hɪm, əm] *pron* **1** (*used as a direct object*) : le, l' **2** (*used as an indirect object or as object of a preposition*) : lui — **himself** [hɪm'sɛlf] *pron* **1** (*used reflexively*) : se, s' **2** (*used for emphasis*) : lui-même **3** (*used after a preposition*) : lui, lui-même
hind ['haɪnd] *adj* : de derrière
hinder ['hɪndər] *vt* : empêcher, entraver — **hindrance** ['hɪndrənts] *n* : entrave *f*
hindsight ['haɪnd,saɪt] *n* **in ~** : avec du recul
Hindu ['hɪn,du:] *adj* : hindou
hinge ['hɪndʒ] *n* : charnière *f*, gond *m* — **~** *vi* **hinged; hinging ~ on** : dépendre de
hint ['hɪnt] *n* **1** INSINUATION : allusion *f* **2** TRACE : soupçon *m* **3** TIP : conseil *m* — **~** *vt* : insinuer — *vi* **~ at** : faire une allusion à
hip ['hɪp] *n* : hanche *f*
hippie *or* **hippy** ['hɪpi] *n, pl* **hippies** : hippie *mf*, hippy *mf*
hippopotamus [,hɪpə'pɑt̬əməs] *n, pl* **-muses** *or* **-mi** [-,maɪ] : hippopotame *m*
hire ['haɪr] *vt* **hired; hiring 1** : engager, embaucher **2** RENT : louer — **~** *n* **1** WAGES : gages *mpl* **2 for ~** : à louer
his ['hɪz, ɪz] *adj* **1** : son, sa, ses **2 it's ~** : c'est à lui — **~** *pron* **1** : le sien, la sienne, les siens, les siennes **2 a friend of ~** : un ami à lui
Hispanic [hɪ'spænɪk] *adj* : hispanique
hiss ['hɪs] *vi* : siffler — **~** *n* : sifflement *m*

history [ˈhɪstəri] *n, pl* **-ries** **1** : histoire *f* **2** : antécédents *mpl* (médicaux, etc.) — **historian** [hɪˈstoriən] *n* : historien *m*, -rienne *f* — **historic** [hɪˈstɔrɪk] *or* **historical** [-ɪkəl] *adj* : historique

hit [ˈhɪt] *v* **hit; hitting** *vt* **1** : frapper (une balle, etc.) **2** STRIKE : heurter **3** AFFECT : toucher **4** REACH : atteindre — *vi* **1** : frapper **2** OCCUR : arriver — ~ *n* **1** : coup *m* (aux sports, etc.) **2** SUCCESS : succès *m*

hitch [ˈhɪtʃ] *vt* **1** : accrocher **2** *or* ~ **up** RAISE : remonter **3** ~ **a ride** : faire de l'auto-stop — ~ *n* PROBLEM : problème *m* — **hitchhike** [ˈhɪtʃˌhaɪk] *vi* **-hiked; -hiking** : faire de l'auto-stop — **hitchhiker** [ˈhɪtʃˌhaɪkər] *n* : auto-stoppeur *m*, -peuse *f*

hitherto [ˈhɪðərˌtuː, ˌhɪðərˈ-] *adv* : jusqu'à présent

HIV [ˌeɪtʃˌaɪˈviː] *n* (*h*uman *i*mmunodeficiency *v*irus) : VIH *m*

hive [ˈhaɪv] *n* : ruche *f*

hives [ˈhaɪvz] *ns & pl* : urticaire *f*

hoard [ˈhord] *n* : réserve *f*, provisions *fpl* — ~ *vt* : accumuler, amasser

hoarse [ˈhors] *adj* **hoarser; -est** : rauque, enroué

hoax [ˈhoːks] *n* : canular *m*

hobble [ˈhɑbəl] *vi* **-bled; -bling** : boitiller

hobby [ˈhɑbi] *n, pl* **-bies** : passe-temps *m*

hobo [ˈhoːˌboː] *n, pl* **-boes** : vagabond *m*, -bonde *f*

hockey [ˈhɑki] *n* : hockey *m*

hoe [ˈhoː] *n* : houe *f*, binette *f* — ~ *vi* **hoed; hoeing** : biner

hog [ˈhɔg, ˈhɑg] *n* : porc *m*, cochon *m* — ~ *vt* **hogged; hogging** : monopoliser

hoist [ˈhɔɪst] *vt* : hisser — ~ *n* : palan *m*

hold[1] [ˈhoːld] *v* **held** [ˈhɛld]; **holding** *vt* **1** : tenir **2** POSSESS : posséder **3** CONTAIN : contenir **4** *or* ~ **up** SUPPORT : soutenir **5** : détenir (un prisonnier, etc.) **6** ~ **the line** : ne quittez pas **7** ~ **s.o's attention** : retenir l'attention de qqn — *vi* **1** LAST : durer, continuer **2** APPLY : tenir — ~ *n* **1** GRIP : prise *f*, étreinte *f* **2 get** ~ **of** : trouver — **holder** [ˈhoːldər] *n* : détenteur *m*, -trice *f*, titulaire *mf* — **holdup** [ˈhoːldˌʌp] *n* **1** : vol *m* à main armée **2** DELAY : retard *m* — **hold up** *vt* DELAY : retarder

hold[2] *n* : cale *f* (d'un navire ou d'un avion)

hole [ˈhoːl] *n* : trou *m*

holiday [ˈhɑləˌdeɪ] *n* **1** : jour *m* férié **2** *Brit* VACATION : vacances *fpl*

holiness [ˈhoːlinəs] *n* : sainteté *f*

holler [ˈhɑlər] *vi* : gueuler *fam*, hurler — ~ *n* : hurlement *m*

hollow [ˈhɑˌloː] *n* : creux *m* — ~ *adj* **hollower; -est 1** : creux **2** FALSE : faux — ~ *vt or* ~ **out** : creuser

holly [ˈhɑli] *n, pl* **-lies** : houx *m*

holocaust [ˈhɑləˌkɔst, ˈhoː-, ˈhɔ-] *n* : holocauste *m*

holster [ˈhoːlstər] *n* : étui *m* de revolver

holy [ˈhoːli] *adj* **holier; -est 1** : saint **2** ~ **water** : eau *f* bénite

homage [ˈɑmɪdʒ, ˈhɑ-] *n* : hommage *m*

home [ˈhoːm] *n* **1** RESIDENCE : maison *f* **2** FAMILY : foyer *m*, chez-soi *m* **3** → **funeral home, nursing home** — ~ *adv* **go** ~ : rentrer à la maison, rentrer chez soi — **homeland** [ˈhoːmˌlænd] *n* : patrie *f* — **homeless** [ˈhoːmləs] *n* **the** ~ : les sans-abri — **homely** [ˈhoːmli] *adj* **homelier; -est 1** SIMPLE : simple, ordinaire **2** UGLY : laid — **homemade** [ˈhoːmˈmeɪd] *adj* : fait à la maison — **homemaker** [ˈhoːmˌmeɪkər] *n* : femme *f* au foyer — **home page** *n* : page *f* d'accueil — **home run** *n* : coup *m* de circuit *Can* — **homesick** [ˈhoːmˌsɪk] *adj* **be** ~ : avoir le mal du pays — **homeward** [ˈhoːmwərd] *or* **homewards** [-wərdz] *adv* : vers la maison — **homeward** *adj* : de retour — **homework** [ˈhoːmˌwərk] *n* : devoirs *mpl* — **homey** [ˈhoːmi] *adj* **homier; -est** COZY, INVITING : accueillant

homicide [ˈhɑməˌsaɪd, ˈhoː-] *n* : homicide *m*

homogeneous [ˌhoːməˈdʒiːniəs, -njəs] *adj* : homogène

homosexual [ˌhoːməˈsɛkʃuəl] *adj* : homosexuel — ~ *n* : homosexuel *m*, -sexuelle *f* — **homosexuality** [ˌhoːməˌsɛkʃuˈæləṭi] *n* : homosexualité *f*

honest [ˈɑnəst] *adj* : honnête — **honestly** [ˈɑnəstli] *adv* : honnêtement — **honesty** [ˈɑnəsti] *n* : honnêteté *f*

honey [ˈhʌni] *n, pl* **-eys** : miel *m* — **honeycomb** [ˈhʌniˌkoːm] *n* : rayon *m* de miel — **honeymoon** [ˈhʌniˌmuːn] *n* : lune *f* de miel

honk [ˈhɑŋk, ˈhɔŋk] *vi* : klaxonner — ~ *n* : coup *m* de klaxon

honor *or Brit* **honour** [ˈɑnər] *n* : honneur *m* — ~ *vt* : honorer — **honorable** *or Brit* **honourable** [ˈɑnərəbəl] *adj* : honorable — **honorary** ['ɑnə‚rɛri] *adj* : honoraire, honorifique

hood ['hʊd] *n* **1** : capuchon *m* (d'un vêtement) **2** : capot *m* (d'une voiture)

hoodlum ['hʊdləm, 'hu:d-] *n* : voyou *m*

hoodwink ['hʊd‚wɪŋk] *vt* : tromper

hoof ['hʊf, 'hu:f] *n, pl* **hooves** ['hʊvz, 'hu:vz] *or* **hoofs** : sabot *m* (d'un animal)

hook ['hʊk] *n* **1** : crochet *m* **2** FASTENER : agrafe *f* **3** → **fishhook** — ~ *vt* : accrocher — *vi* : s'accrocher

hoop ['hu:p] *n* : cerceau *m*

hoorah [hʊ'ra], **hooray** [hʊ'reɪ] → **hurrah**

hoot ['hu:t] *vi* **1** : hululer (se dit d'un hibou) **2** ~ **with laughter** : pouffer de rire — ~ *n* **1** : hululement *m* **2 I don't give a** ~ : je m'en fiche

hop [hɑp] *v* **hopped; hopping** *vi* : sauter, sautiller — *vt or* ~ **over** : sauter — ~ *n* : saut *m*

hope ['ho:p] *v* **hoped; hoping** : espérer — ~ *n* : espoir *m* — **hopeful** ['ho:pfəl] *adj* **1** OPTIMISTIC : plein d'espoir **2** PROMISING : encourageant — **hopefully** ['ho:pfəli] *adv* **1** : avec espoir **2** ~ **it will work** : on espère que cela marche — **hopeless** ['ho:pləs] *adj* : désespéré — **hopelessly** ['ho:pləsli] *adv* **1** : complètement **2** ~ **in love** : éperdument amoureux

hops [hɑps] *nmpl* : houblon *m*

horde ['hord] *n* : horde *f*, foule *f*

horizon [hə'raɪzən] *n* : horizon *m* — **horizontal** [‚hɔrə'zɑntəl] *adj* : horizontal

hormone ['hɔr‚mo:n] *n* : hormone *f*

horn ['hɔrn] *n* **1** : corne *f* (d'un animal) **2** : cor *m* (instrument de musique) **3** : klaxon *m* (d'un véhicule)

hornet ['hɔrnət] *n* : frelon *m*

horoscope ['hɔrə‚sko:p] *n* : horoscope *m*

horrendous [hə'rɛndəs] *adj* : épouvantable — **horrible** ['hɔrəbəl] *adj* : horrible, affreux — **horrid** ['hɔrɪd] *adj* : horrible, hideux — **horrify** ['hɔrə‚faɪ] *vt* **-fied; -fying** : horrifier — **horror** ['hɔrər] *n* : horreur *f*

hors d'oeuvre [ɔr'dərv] *n, pl* **hors d'oeuvres** [-'dərvz] : hors-d'œuvre *m*

horse ['hɔrs] *n* : cheval *m* — **horseback** ['hɔrs‚bæk] *n* **on** ~ : à cheval — **horsefly** ['hɔrs‚flaɪ] *n, pl* **-flies** : taon *m* — **horseman** ['hɔrsmən] *n, pl* **-men** [-mən, -‚mɛn] : cavalier *m* — **horsepower** ['hɔrs‚paʊər] *n* : cheval-vapeur *m* — **horseradish** ['hɔrs‚rædɪʃ] *n* : raifort *m* — **horseshoe** ['hɔrs‚ʃu:] *n* : fer *m* à cheval — **horsewoman** ['hɔrs‚wʊmən] *n, pl* **-women** [-‚wɪmən] : cavalière *f*

horticulture ['hɔrt̬ə‚kʌltʃər] *n* : horticulture *f*

hose ['ho:z] *n* **1** *pl* **hoses** : tuyau *m* (d'arrosage, etc.) **2** *pl* **hose** STOCKINGS : bas *mpl* — ~ *vt* **hosed; hosing** : arroser — **hosiery** ['ho:ʒəri, 'ho:zə-] *n* : bonneterie *f*

hospice ['hɑspəs] *n* : hospice *m*

hospital ['hɑs‚pɪt̬əl] *n* : hôpital *m* — **hospitable** [hɑs'pɪt̬əbəl, 'hɑ‚spɪ-] *adj* : hospitalier — **hospitality** [‚hɑspə'tæləti] *n, pl* **-ties** : hospitalité *f* — **hospitalize** ['hɑs‚pɪt̬ə‚laɪz] *vt* **-ized; -izing** : hospitaliser

host[1] ['ho:st] *n* **a** ~ **of** : une foule de

host[2] *n* **1** : hôte *mf* **2** : animateur *m*, -trice *f* (de radio, etc.) — ~ *vt* : animer (une émission de télévision, etc.)

host[3] *n* EUCHARIST : hostie *f*

hostage ['hɑstɪdʒ] *n* : otage *m*

hostel ['hɑstəl] *n* : auberge *f*

hostess ['ho:stəs] *n* : hôtesse *f*

hostile ['hɑstəl, -‚taɪl] *adj* : hostile — **hostility** [hɑs'tɪləti] *n, pl* **-ties** : hostilité *f*

hot ['hɑt] *adj* **hotter; hottest 1** : chaud **2** SPICY : épicé **3** ~ **news** : les dernières nouvelles **4 have a** ~ **temper** : s'emporter facilement **5 it's** ~ **today** : il fait chaud aujourd'hui

hot dog *n* : hot-dog *m*

hotel [ho:'tɛl] *n* : hôtel *m*

hotheaded ['hɑt'hɛdəd] *adj* : impétueux

hound ['haʊnd] *n* : chien *m* courant — ~ *vt* : traquer, poursuivre

hour ['aʊər] *n* : heure *f* — **hourglass** ['aʊər‚glæs] *n* : sablier *m* — **hourly** ['aʊərli] *adv & adj* : toutes les heures

house ['haʊs] *n, pl* **houses** ['haʊzəz, -səz] **1** HOME : maison *f* **2** : chambre *f* (en politique) **3 publishing** ~ : maison *f* d'édition — ~ ['haʊz] *vt* **housed; housing** : loger, héberger — **houseboat** ['haʊs‚bo:t] *n* : péniche *f* aménagée — **housefly** ['haʊs‚flaɪ] *n, pl* **-flies** : mouche *f* — **household** ['haʊs‚ho:ld] *adj* **1** : ménager **2** ~ **name** : nom *m* connu de tous — ~ *n* : ménage *m*, maison *f* — **housekeeper** ['haʊs‚ki:pər] *n* : gouvernante *f* — **housekeeping** ['haʊs‚ki:pɪŋ] *n* HOUSEWORK : ménage *m* — **housewarming** ['haʊs‚wɔrmɪŋ] *n* : pendaison *f* de crémaillère — **housewife**

[ˈhaʊs,waɪf] *n, pl* **-wives** : femme *f* au foyer, ménagère *f* — **housework** [ˈhaʊs,wərk] *n* : travaux *mpl* ménagers, ménage *m* — **housing** [ˈhaʊzɪŋ] *n* : logement *m*

hovel [ˈhʌvəl, ˈhɑ-] *n* : taudis *m*

hover [ˈhʌvər] *vi* **1** : planer **2** *or* **~ about** : rôder — **hovercraft** [ˈhʌvər,kræft] *n* : aéroglisseur *m*

how [ˈhaʊ] *adv* **1** : comment **2** (*used in exclamations*) : comme, que **3 ~ about . . . ?** : que dirais-tu de . . . ? **4 ~ come** WHY : comment, pourquoi **5 ~ much** : combien **6 ~ do you do?** : comment allez-vous? **7 ~ old are you?** : quel âge as-tu? — **~** *conj* : comment

however [haʊˈɛvər] *conj* **1** : de quelque manière que **2 ~ you like** : comme vous voulez — **~** *adv* **1** NEVERTHELESS : cependant, toutefois **2 ~ important it is** : si important que ce soit **3 ~ you want** : comme tu veux

howl [ˈhaʊl] *vi* : hurler — **~** *n* : hurlement *m*

hub [ˈhʌb] *n* **1** CENTER : centre *m* **2** : moyeu *m* (d'une roue)

hubbub [ˈhʌ,bʌb] *n* : vacarme *m*, brouhaha *m*

hubcap [ˈhʌb,kæp] *n* : enjoliveur *m*

huddle [ˈhʌdəl] *vi* **-dled; -dling** *or* **~ together** : se blottir

hue [ˈhjuː] *n* : couleur *f*, teinte *f*

huff [ˈhʌf] *n* **be in a ~** : être fâché, être vexé

hug [ˈhʌg] *vt* **hugged; hugging 1** : serrer dans ses bras, étreindre **2** : serrer, longer (un mur, etc.) — **~** *n* : étreinte *f*

huge [ˈhjuːʤ] *adj* **huger; hugest** : énorme, immense

hull [ˈhʌl] *n* : coque *f* (d'un navire)

hullo *Brit* → **hello**

hum [ˈhʌm] *v* **hummed; humming** *vi* : bourdonner — *vt* : fredonner, chantonner — **~** *n* : bourdonnement *m*

human [ˈhjuːmən, ˈjuː-] *adj* **1** : humain **2 ~ rights** : droits *mpl* de l'homme, droits *mpl* de la personne *Can* — **~** *n* : humain *m*, être *m* humain — **humane** [hjuːˈmeɪn, juː-] *adj* : humain — **humanitarian** [hjuː,mænəˈtɛriən, juː-] *adj* : humanitaire — **humanity** [hjuːˈmænəṭi, juː-] *n, pl* **-ties** : humanité *f*

humble [ˈhʌmbəl] *adj* **humbler; -blest** : humble, modeste — **~** *vt* **-bled; -bling 1** : humilier **2 ~ oneself** : s'humilier

humdrum [ˈhʌm,drʌm] *adj* : monotone, banal

humid [ˈhjuːməd, ˈjuː-] *adj* : humide — **humidity** [hjuːˈmɪdəṭi, juː-] *n, pl* **-ties** : humidité *f*

humiliate [hjuːˈmɪli,eɪt, juː-] *vt* **-ated; -ating** : humilier — **humiliating** [hjuːˈmɪli,eɪtɪŋ, juː-] *adj* : humiliant — **humiliation** [hjuː,mɪliˈeɪʃən, juː-] *n* : humiliation *f* — **humility** [hjuːˈmɪləṭi, juː-] *n* : humilité *f*

humor *or Brit* **humour** [ˈhjuːmər, ˈjuː-] *n* **1** WIT : humour *m* **2** MOOD : humeur *f* — **~** *vt* : faire plaisir à, ménager — **humorist** [ˈhjuːmərɪst, ˈjuː-] *n* : humoriste *mf* — **humorous** [ˈhjuːmərəs, ˈjuː-] *adj* : plein d'humour, drôle

hump [ˈhʌmp] *n* : bosse *f*

hunch [ˈhʌntʃ] *vi or* **~ over** : se pencher — **~** *n* : intuition *f*, petite idée *f*

hundred [ˈhʌndrəd] *n, pl* **-dreds** *or* **-dred** : cent *m* — **~** *adj* : cent — **hundredth** [ˈhʌndrədθ] *n* **1** : centième *mf* (dans une série) **2** : centième *m* (en mathématiques) — **~** *adj* : centième

hung → **hang**

hunger [ˈhʌŋgər] *n* : faim *f* — **~** *vi* **~ for** : avoir envie de — **hungry** [ˈhʌŋgri] *adj* **hungrier; -est be ~** : avoir faim

hunk [ˈhʌŋk] *n* : gros morceau *m*

hunt [ˈhʌnt] *vt* **1** : chasser **2** *or* **~ for** : chercher — **~** *n* **1** : chasse *f* (sport) **2** SEARCH : recherche *f* — **hunter** [ˈhʌntər] *n* : chasseur *m*, -seuse *f* — **hunting** [ˈhʌntɪŋ] *n* : chasse *f*

hurdle [ˈhərdəl] *n* **1** : haie *f* (aux sports) **2** OBSTACLE : obstacle *m*

hurl [ˈhərl] *vt* : lancer, jeter

hurrah [hʊˈrɑ, -ˈrɔ] *interj* : hourra!

hurricane [ˈhərə,keɪn] *n* : ouragan *m*

hurry [ˈhəri] *n* : hâte *f*, empressement *m* — **~** *v* **-ried; -rying** *vt* : presser, bousculer — *vi* **1** : se presser, se hâter **2 ~ up!** : dépêche-toi! — **hurried** [ˈhərəd] *adj* : précipité — **hurriedly** [ˈhərədli] *adv* : à la hâte

hurt [ˈhərt] *v* **hurt; hurting** *vt* **1** INJURE : faire mal à, blesser **2** OFFEND : blesser — *vi* **1** : faire mal **2 my throat ~s** : j'ai mal à la gorge — **~** *adj* : blessé — **~** *n* **1** INJURY : blessure *f* **2** PAIN : douleur *f* — **hurtful** [ˈhərtfəl] *adj* : blessant

hurtle [ˈhərṭəl] *vi* **-tled; -tling** : aller à toute vitesse

husband [ˈhʌzbənd] *n* : mari *m*

hush [ˈhʌʃ] *vt or* **~ up** : faire taire — *vi*

1 : se taire **2 ~!** : chut! — **~** *n* : silence *m*
husk ['hʌsk] *n* : enveloppe *f*
husky[1] ['hʌski] *adj* **huskier; -est** HOARSE : rauque
husky[2] *n, pl* **-kies** : chien *m* esquimau
husky[3] *n* BURLY : costaud
hustle ['həsəl] *v* **-tled; -tling** *vt* : presser, pousser — *vi* : se dépêcher — **~** *n* **~ and bustle** : agitation *f*, grande activité *f*
hut ['hʌt] *n* : hutte *f*, cabane *f*
hutch ['hʌtʃ] *n* : clapier *m*
hyacinth ['haɪə͵sɪnθ] *n* : jacinthe *f*
hybrid ['haɪbrɪd] *n* : hybride *m* — **~** *adj* : hybride
hydrant ['haɪdrənt] *n or* **fire ~** : bouche *f* d'incendie
hydraulic [haɪ'drɔlɪk] *adj* : hydraulique
hydroelectric [͵haɪdroɪ'lɛktrɪk] *adj* : hydroélectrique
hydrogen ['haɪdrəʤən] *n* : hydrogène *m*
hyena [haɪ'i:nə] *n* : hyène *f*
hygiene ['haɪ͵ʤi:n] *n* : hygiène *f* — **hygienic** [haɪ'ʤɛnɪk, -'ʤi:-; ͵haɪʤi:'ɛnɪk] *adj* : hygiénique
hymn ['hɪm] *n* : hymne *m*
hyperactive [͵haɪpər'æktɪv] *adj* : hyperactif
hyphen ['haɪfən] *n* : trait *m* d'union
hypnosis [hɪp'no:sɪs] *n, pl* **-noses** [-͵si:z] : hypnose *f* — **hypnotic** [hɪp'nɑţɪk] *adj* : hypnotique — **hypnotism** ['hɪpnə͵tɪzəm] *n* : hypnotisme *m* — **hypnotize** ['hɪpnə͵taɪz] *vt* **-tized; -tizing** : hypnotiser
hypochondriac [͵haɪpə'kɑndri͵æk] *n* : hypocondriaque *mf*
hypocrisy [hɪ'pɑkrəsi] *n, pl* **-sies** : hypocrisie *f* — **hypocrite** ['hɪpə͵krɪt] *n* : hypocrite *mf* — **hypocritical** [͵hɪpə'krɪţɪkəl] *adj* : hypocrite
hypothesis [haɪ'pɑθəsɪs] *n, pl* **-eses** [-͵si:z] : hypothèse *f* — **hypothetical** [͵haɪpə'θɛţɪkəl] *adj* : hypothétique
hysteria [hɪs'tɛriə, -'tɪr-] *n* : hystérie *f* — **hysterical** [hɪs'tɛrɪkəl] *adj* : hystérique

I

i ['aɪ] *n, pl* **i's** *or* **is** ['aɪz] : i *m*, neuvième lettre de l'alphabet
I ['aɪ] *pron* : je
ice ['aɪs] *n* **1** : glace *f* **2 ~ cube** : glaçon *m* — **~** *v* **iced; icing** *vt* : glacer — *vi or* **~ up** : se givrer — **iceberg** ['aɪs͵bərg] *n* : iceberg *m* — **icebox** ['aɪs͵bɑks] → **refrigerator** — **ice–cold** ['aɪs'ko:ld] *adj* : glacé — **ice cream** *n* : glace *f France*, crème *f* glacée *Can* — **ice–skate** *vi* **-skated; -skating** : patiner — **ice skate** ['aɪs͵skeɪt] *n* : patin *m* (à glace) — **icicle** ['aɪ͵sɪkəl] *n* : glaçon *m* — **icing** ['aɪsɪŋ] *n* : glaçage *m*
icon ['aɪ͵kɑn, -kən] *n* : icône *f* (en informatique)
icy ['aɪsi] *adj* **icier; -est 1** : verglacé (se dit d'une route) **2** FREEZING : glacial, glacé
I'd ['aɪd] (*contraction of* **I should** *or* **I would**) → **should, would**
idea [aɪ'di:ə] *n* : idée *f*
ideal [aɪ'di:əl] *adj* : idéal — **~** *n* : idéal *m* — **idealist** [aɪ'di:ə͵lɪst] *n* : idéaliste *mf* — **idealistic** [aɪ͵di:ə'lɪstɪk] *adj* : idéaliste — **idealize** [aɪ'di:ə͵laɪz] *vt* **-ized; -izing** : idéaliser
identity [aɪ'dɛntəţi] *n, pl* **-ties** : identité *f* — **identical** [aɪ'dɛntɪkəl] *adj* : identique — **identify** [aɪ'dɛntə͵faɪ] *v* **-fied; -fying** *vt* : identifier — *vi* **~ with** : s'identifier à — **identification** [aɪ͵dɛntəfə'keɪʃən] *n* **1** : identification *f* **2** *or* **~ card** : carte *f* d'identité
ideology [͵aɪdi'ɑləʤi, ͵ɪ-] *n, pl* **-gies** : idéologie *f* — **ideological** [͵aɪdiə'lɑʤɪkəl, ͵ɪ-] *adj* : idéologique
idiocy ['ɪdiəsi] *n, pl* **-cies** : idiotie *f*
idiom ['ɪdiəm] *n* **1** : expression *f* idiomatique **2** LANGUAGE : idiome *m* — **idiomatic** [͵ɪdiə'mæţɪk] *adj* : idiomatique
idiosyncrasy [͵ɪdio'sɪŋkrəsi] *n, pl* **-sies** : particularité *f*
idiot ['ɪdiət] *n* : idiot *m*, -diote *f* — **idiotic** [͵ɪdi'ɑţɪk] *adj* : idiot
idle ['aɪdəl] *adj* **idler; idlest 1** UNOCCUPIED : désœuvré, oisif **2** LAZY : paresseux **3** VAIN : vain **4 out of ~ curiosity** : par pure curiosité **5 stand ~** : être à l'arrêt — **~** *v* **idled; idling** *vi* : tourner au ralenti (se dit d'un moteur) — *vt or* **~ away** : gaspiller (son temps) — **idleness** ['aɪdəlnəs] *n* : oisiveté *f*
idol ['aɪdəl] *n* : idole *f* — **idolize** ['aɪdəl͵aɪz] *vt* **-ized; izing** : idolâtrer

idyllic [aɪˈdɪlɪk] *adj* : idyllique
if [ˈɪf] *conj* **1** : si **2** THOUGH : bien que **3** ~ **so** : dans ce cas-là **4** ~ **not** : sinon
igloo [ˈɪˌgluː] *n, pl* **-loos** : igloo *m*
ignite [ɪgˈnaɪt] *v* **-nited; -niting** *vt* : enflammer — *vi* : prendre feu, s'enflammer — **ignition** [ɪgˈnɪʃən] *n* **1** : allumage *m* **2** *or* ~ **switch** : contact *m*
ignorance [ˈɪgnərənts] *n* : ignorance *f* — **ignorant** [ˈɪgnərənt] *adj* : ignorant — **ignore** [ɪgˈnor] *vt* **-nored; -noring** : ignorer
ilk [ˈɪlk] *n* : espèce *f*
ill [ˈɪl] *adj* **worse; worst 1** SICK : malade **2** BAD : mauvais — ~ *adv* **worse** [ˈwərs]; **worst** [ˈwərst] : mal — ~ *n* : mal *m* — **ill–advised** [ˌɪlædˈvaɪzd, -əd-] *adj* : peu judicieux — **ill at ease** *adj* : mal à l'aise
I'll [ˈaɪl] (*contraction of* **I shall** *or* **I will**) → **shall, will**
illegal [ɪlˈliːgəl] *adj* : illégal
illegible [ɪlˈlɛdʒəbəl] *adj* : illisible
illegitimate [ˌɪlɪˈdʒɪt̬əmət] *adj* : illégitime — **illegitimacy** [ˌɪlɪˈdʒɪt̬əməsi] *n* : illégitimité *f*
illicit [ɪlˈlɪsət] *adj* : illicite
illiterate [ɪlˈlɪt̬ərət] *adj* : analphabète, illettré — **illiteracy** [ɪlˈlɪt̬ərəsi] *n, pl* **-cies** : analphabétisme *m*
ill–mannered [ˌɪlˈmænərd] *adj* : impoli
ill–natured [ˌɪlˈneɪtʃərd] *adj* : désagréable
illness [ˈɪlnəs] *n* : maladie *f*
illogical [ɪlˈlɑdʒɪkəl] *adj* : illogique
ill–treat [ˌɪlˈtriːt] *vt* : maltraiter
illuminate [ɪˈluːməˌneɪt] *vt* **-nated; -nating** : éclairer — **illumination** [ɪˌluːməˈneɪʃən] *n* : éclairage *m*
illusion [ɪˈluːʒən] *n* : illusion *f* — **illusory** [ɪˈluːsəri, -zəri] *adj* : illusoire
illustrate [ˈɪləsˌtreɪt] *v* **-trated; -trating** : illustrer — **illustration** [ˌɪləsˈtreɪʃən] *n* : illustration *f* — **illustrative** [ɪˈlʌstrət̬ɪv, ˈɪləˌstreɪt̬ɪv] *adj* : explicatif
illustrious [ɪˈlʌstriəs] *adj* : illustre
ill will *n* : malveillance *f*
I'm [ˈaɪm] (*contraction of* **I am**) → **be**
image [ˈɪmɪdʒ] *n* : image *f* — **imagination** [ɪˈmædʒəˈneɪʃən] *n* : imagination *f* — **imaginary** [ɪˈmædʒəˌnɛri] *adj* : imaginaire — **imaginative** [ɪˈmædʒɪnət̬ɪv] *adj* : imaginatif — **imagine** [ɪˈmædʒən] *vt* **-ined; -ining** : imaginer, s'imaginer
imbalance [ɪmˈbælənts] *n* : déséquilibre *m*
imbecile [ˈɪmbəsəl, -ˌsɪl] *n* : imbécile *mf*
imbue [ɪmˈbjuː] *vt* **-bued; -buing** : imprégner
imitation [ˌɪməˈteɪʃən] *n* : imitation *f* — ~ *adj* : artificiel, faux — **imitate** [ˈɪməˌteɪt] *vt* **-tated; -tating** : imiter — **imitator** [ˈɪməˌteɪt̬ər] *n* : imitateur *m*, -trice *f*
immaculate [ɪˈmækjələt] *adj* : impeccable
immaterial [ˌɪməˈtɪriəl] *adj* : sans importance
immature [ˌɪməˈtʃʊr, -ˈtjʊr, -ˈtʊr] *adj* : immature — **immaturity** [ˌɪməˈtʃʊrət̬i, -ˈtjʊr-, -ˈtʊr-] *n, pl* **-ties** : immaturité *f*
immediate [ɪˈmiːdiət] *adj* : immédiat — **immediately** [ɪˈmiːdiətli] *adv* **1** : immédiatement **2** ~ **before** : juste avant
immense [ɪˈmɛnts] *adj* : immense — **immensity** [ɪˈmɛntsət̬i] *n, pl* **-ties** : immensité *f*
immerse [ɪˈmərs] *vt* **-mersed; -mersing** : plonger, immerger — **immersion** [ɪˈmərʒən] *n* : immersion *f*
immigrate [ˈɪməˌgreɪt] *vi* **-grated; -grating** : immigrer — **immigrant** [ˈɪmɪgrənt] *n* : immigrant *m*, -grante *f*; immigré *m*, -grée *f* — **immigration** [ˌɪməˈgreɪʃən] *n* : immigration *f*
imminent [ˈɪmənənt] *adj* : imminent — **imminence** [ˈɪmənənts] *n* : imminence *f*
immobile [ɪˈmoːbəl] *adj* **1** FIXED : fixe **2** MOTIONLESS : immobile — **immobilize** [ɪˈmoːbəˌlaɪz] *vt* **-ized; -izing** : immobiliser
immoral [ɪˈmɔrəl] *adj* : immoral — **immorality** [ˌɪmɔˈrælət̬i, ˌɪmə-] *n* : immoralité *f*
immortal [ɪˈmɔrt̬əl] *adj* : immortel — **immortality** [ˌɪˌmɔrˈtælət̬i] *n* : immortalité *f*
immune [ɪˈmjuːn] *adj* : immunisé — **immunity** [ɪˈmjuːnət̬i] *n, pl* **-ties** : immunité *f* — **immunization** [ˌɪmjʊnəˈzeɪʃən] *n* : immunisation *f* — **immunize** [ˈɪmjʊˌnaɪz] *vt* **-nized; -nizing** : immuniser
imp [ˈɪmp] *n* **1** : lutin *m* **2** RASCAL : polisson *m*, -sonne *f*
impact [ˈɪmˌpækt] *n* : impact *m*
impair [ɪmˈpær] *vt* **1** WEAKEN : affaiblir **2** DAMAGE : détériorer
impart [ɪmˈpɑrt] *vt* : communiquer
impartial [ɪmˈpɑrʃəl] *adj* : impartial — **impartiality** [ɪmˌpɑrʃiˈælət̬i] *n* : impartialité *f*
impassable [ɪmˈpæsəbəl] *adj* : impraticable

impasse ['ɪm,pæs] *n* : impasse *f*
impassive [ɪm'pæsɪv] *adj* : impassible
impatience [ɪm'peɪʃənts] *n* : impatience *f* — **impatient** [ɪm'peɪʃənt] *adj* : impatient — **impatiently** [ɪm'peɪʃəntli] *adv* : impatiemment
impeccable [ɪm'pɛkəbəl] *adj* : impeccable
impede [ɪm'pi:d] *vt* **-peded; -peding** : entraver, gêner — **impediment** [ɪm'pɛdəmənt] *n* : entrave *f*, obstacle *m*
impel [ɪm'pɛl] *vt* **-pelled; -pelling 1** : inciter **2** PROPEL : pousser
impending [ɪm'pɛndɪŋ] *adj* : imminent
impenetrable [ɪm'pɛnətrəbəl] *adj* : impénétrable
imperative [ɪm'pɛrəţɪv] *adj* **1** COMMANDING : impérieux **2** NECESSARY : impératif — ~ *n* : impératif *m* (en grammaire)
imperceptible [,ɪmpər'sɛptəbəl] *adj* : imperceptible
imperfection [ɪm,pər'fɛkʃən] *n* : imperfection *f* — **imperfect** [ɪm'pərfɪkt] *adj* : imparfait — ~ *n or* ~ **tense** : imparfait *m*
imperial [ɪm'pɪriəl] *adj* : impérial — **imperialism** [ɪm'pɪriə,lɪzəm] *n* : impérialisme *m* — **imperious** [ɪm'pɪriəs] *adj* : impérieux
impersonal [ɪm'pərsənəl] *adj* : impersonnel
impersonate [ɪm'pərsən,eɪt] *vt* **-ated; -ating** : se faire passer pour — **impersonation** [ɪm,pərsən'eɪʃən] *n* : imitation *f* — **impersonator** [ɪm'pərsən,eɪţər] *n* : imitateur *m*, -trice *f*
impertinent [ɪm'pərtənənt] *adj* : impertinent — **impertinence** [ɪm'pərtənənts] *n* : impertinence *f*
impervious [ɪm'pərviəs] *adj* ~ **to** : imperméable à
impetuous [ɪm'pɛʧuəs] *adj* : impétueux
impetus ['ɪmpəţəs] *n* : impulsion *f*
impinge [ɪm'pɪnʤ] *vi* **-pinged; -pinging 1** ~ **on** : affecter **2** ~ **on s.o.'s rights** : empiéter sur les droits de qqn
impish ['ɪmpɪʃ] *adj* : espiègle
implant [ɪm'plænt] *vt* : implanter — ~ ['ɪm,plænt] *n* : implant *m*
implausible [ɪm'plɔzəbəl] *adj* : invraisemblable
implement ['ɪmpləmənt] *n* : outil *m*, instrument *m* — ~ ['ɪmplə,mɛnt] *vt* : mettre en œuvre, appliquer
implicate ['ɪmplə,keɪt] *vt* **-cated; -cating** : impliquer — **implication** [,ɪmplə'keɪʃən] *n* : implication *f*
implicit [ɪm'plɪsət] *adj* **1** : implicite **2** UNQUESTIONING : absolu, total
implode [ɪm'plo:d] *vi* **-ploded; -ploding** : imploser
implore [ɪm'plor] *vt* **-plored; -ploring** : implorer
imply [ɪm'plaɪ] *vt* **-plied; -plying** : impliquer
impolite [,ɪmpə'laɪt] *adj* : impoli
import [ɪm'port] *vt* : importer (des marchandises) — ~ ['ɪm,port] *n* **1** IMPORTANCE : signification *f* **2** IMPORTATION : importation *f* — **importance** [ɪm'portənts] *n* : importance *f* — **important** [ɪm'portənt] *adj* : important — **importation** [,ɪm,por'teɪʃən] *n* : importation *f* — **importer** [ɪm'porţər] *n* : importateur *m*, -trice *f*
impose [ɪm'po:z] *v* **-posed; -posing** *vt* : imposer — *vi* **1** : s'imposer **2** ~ **on** : déranger — **imposing** [ɪm'po:zɪŋ] *adj* : imposant — **imposition** [,ɪmpə'zɪʃən] *n* : imposition *f*
impossible [ɪm'pɑsəbəl] *adj* : impossible — **impossibility** [ɪm,pɑsə'bɪləţi] *n, pl* **-ties** : impossibilité *f*
impostor *or* **imposter** [ɪm'pɑstər] *n* : imposteur *m*
impotent ['ɪmpətənt] *adj* : impuissant — **impotence** ['ɪmpətənts] *n* : impuissance *f*
impound [ɪm'paʊnd] *vt* : saisir, confisquer
impoverished [ɪm'pɑvərɪʃt] *adj* : appauvri
impracticable [ɪm'præktɪkəbəl] *adj* : impraticable
impractical [ɪm'præktɪkəl] *adj* : peu pratique
imprecise [,ɪmprɪ'saɪs] *adj* : imprécis
impregnable [ɪm'prɛgnəbəl] *adj* : imprenable
impregnate [ɪm'prɛg,neɪt] *vt* **-nated; -nating 1** FERTILIZE : féconder **2** SATURATE : imprégner
impress [ɪm'prɛs] *vt* **1** IMPRINT : imprimer **2** AFFECT : impressionner **3** ~ **upon s.o.** : faire bien comprendre à qqn — **impression** [ɪm'prɛʃən] *n* : impression *f* — **impressionable** [ɪm'prɛʃənəbəl] *adj* : impressionnable — **impressive** [ɪm'prɛsɪv] *adj* : impressionnant
imprint [ɪm'prɪnt, 'ɪm,-] *vt* : imprimer — ~ ['ɪm,prɪnt] *n* MARK : empreinte *f*, marque *f*
imprison [ɪm'prɪzən] *vt* : emprisonner — **imprisonment** [ɪm'prɪzənmənt] *n* : emprisonnement *m*

improbable [ɪmˈprɑbəbəl] *adj* : improbable — **improbability** [ɪm,prɑbəˈbɪləṭi] *n, pl* **-ties** : improbabilité *f*

impromptu [ɪmˈprɑmp,tu:, -,tju:] *adj* : impromptu

improper [ɪmˈprɑpər] *adj* **1** UNSEEMLY : peu convenable **2** INCORRECT : incorrect **3** INDECENT : indécent — **impropriety** [,ɪmprəˈpraɪəṭi] *n, pl* **-ties** : inconvenance *f*

improve [ɪmˈpru:v] *v* **-proved; -proving** *vt* : améliorer — *vi* : s'améliorer, faire des progrès — **improvement** [ɪmˈpru:vmənt] *n* : amélioration *f*

improvise [ˈɪmprə,vaɪz] *v* **-vised; -vising** : improviser — **improvisation** [ɪm,prɑvəˈzeɪʃən, ,ɪmprəvə-] *n* : improvisation *f*

impudent [ˈɪmpjədənt] *adj* : impudent — **impudence** [ˈɪmpjədənts] *n* : impudence *f*

impulse [ˈɪm,pʌls] *n* : impulsion *f* — **impulsive** [ɪmˈpʌlsɪv] *adj* : impulsif — **impulsiveness** [ɪmˈpʌlsɪvnəs] *n* : impulsivité *f*

impunity [ɪmˈpju:nəṭi] *n* : impunité *f*

impure [ɪmˈpjʊr] *adj* : impur — **impurity** [ɪmˈpjʊrəṭi] *n, pl* **-ties** : impureté *f*

impute [ɪmˈpju:t] *vt* **-puted; -puting** : imputer

in [ˈɪn] *prep* **1** : dans, en, à **2 ~ 1938** : en 1938 **3 ~ an hour** : dans une heure **4 ~ Canada** : au Canada **5 ~ leather** : en cuir **6 ~ my house** : chez moi **7 ~ the hospital** : à l'hôpital **8 ~ the sun** : au soleil **9 ~ this way** : de cette manière **10 be ~ a hurry** : être pressé **11 be ~ luck** : avoir de la chance — **~** *adv* **1** INSIDE : dedans, à l'intérieur **2 be ~** : être là, être chez soi **3 come ~** : entrer **4 she's ~ for a surprise** : elle va être surprise **5 ~ power** : au pouvoir — **~** *adj* : à la mode

inability [,ɪnəˈbɪləṭi] *n, pl* **-ties** : incapacité *f*

inaccessible [,ɪnɪkˈsɛsəbəl] *adj* : inaccessible

inaccurate [ɪnˈækjərət] *adj* : inexact

inactive [ɪnˈæktɪv] *adj* : inactif — **inactivity** [,ɪn,ækˈtɪvəṭi] *n, pl* **-ties** : inactivité *f*

inadequate [ɪˈnædɪkwət] *adj* : insuffisant

inadvertently [,ɪnədˈvərtəntli] *adv* : par inadvertance

inadvisable [,ɪnædˈvaɪzəbəl] *adj* : déconseillé

inane [ɪˈneɪn] *adj* **inaner; -est** : inepte, stupide

inanimate [ɪˈnænəmət] *adj* : inanimé

inapplicable [ɪˈnæplɪkəbəl, ,ɪnəˈplɪkəbəl] *adj* : inapplicable

inappropriate [,ɪnəˈpro:priət] *adj* : inopportun, peu approprié

inarticulate [,ɪnɑrˈtɪkjələt] *adj* **1** : indistinct (se dit des mots, des sons, etc.) **2 be ~** : ne pas savoir s'exprimer

inasmuch as [,ɪnæzˈmʌtʃæz] *conj* : vu que

inaudible [ɪnˈɔdəbəl] *adj* : inaudible

inauguration [ɪ,nɔgjəˈreɪʃən, -gə-] *n* : inauguration *f* — **inaugural** [ɪˈnɔgjərəl, -gərəl] *adj* : inaugural — **inaugurate** [ɪˈnɔgjə,reɪt, -gə-] *vt* **-rated; -rating** : inaugurer

inborn [ˈɪn,bɔrn] *adj* : inné

inbred [ˈɪn,brɛd] *adj* INNATE : inné

incalculable [ɪnˈkælkjələbəl] *adj* : incalculable

incapable [ɪnˈkeɪpəbəl] *adj* : incapable — **incapacitate** [,ɪnkəˈpæsə,teɪt] *vt* **-tated; -tating** : rendre incapable — **incapacity** [,ɪnkəˈpæsəṭi] *n, pl* **-ties** : incapacité *f*

incarcerate [ɪnˈkɑrsə,reɪt] *vt* **-ated; -ating** : incarcérer

incarnation [,ɪn,kɑrˈneɪʃən] *n* : incarnation *f*

incense[1] [ˈɪnsɛnts] *n* : encens *m*

incense[2] [ɪnˈsɛnts] *vt* **-censed; -censing** : mettre en fureur

incentive [ɪnˈsɛntɪv] *n* : motivation *f*

inception [ɪnˈsɛpʃən] *n* : commencement *m*

incessant [ɪnˈsɛsənt] *adj* : incessant — **incessantly** [ɪnˈsɛsəntli] *adv* : sans cesse

incest [ˈɪn,sɛst] *n* : inceste *m* — **incestuous** [ɪnˈsɛstʃʊəs] *adj* : incestueux

inch [ˈɪntʃ] *n* : pouce *m* — **~** *v* : avancer petit à petit

incident [ˈɪntsədənt] *n* : incident *m* — **incidental** [,ɪntsəˈdɛntəl] *adj* : accessoire — **incidentally** [,ɪntsəˈdɛntəli, -ˈdɛntli] *adv* : à propos

incinerate [ɪnˈsɪnə,reɪt] *vt* **-ated; -ating** : incinérer — **incinerator** [ɪnˈsɪnə,reɪṭər] *n* : incinérateur *m*

incision [ɪnˈsɪʒən] *n* : incision *f*

incite [ɪnˈsaɪt] *vt* **-cited; -citing** : inciter

incline [ɪnˈklaɪn] *v* **-clined; -clining** *vt* **1** BEND : incliner **2 be ~d to** : avoir tendance à — *vi* **1** LEAN : s'incliner **2 ~ towards** : tendre vers — **~** [ˈɪn,klaɪn] *n* : inclinaison *f* — **inclination**

[ˌɪnklə'neɪʃən] *n* : penchant *m*, inclination *f*
include [ɪn'klu:d] *vt* **-cluded; -cluding** : inclure, comprendre — **inclusion** [ɪn'klu:ʒən] *n* : inclusion *f* — **inclusive** [ɪn'klu:sɪv] *adj* : inclus, compris
incognito [ˌɪnˌkɑg'ni:ţo, ɪn'kɑgnəˌto:] *adv & adj* : incognito
incoherence [ˌɪnko'hɪrənts, -'hɛr-] *n* : incohérence *f* — **incoherent** [ˌɪnko'hɪrənt, -'hɛr-] *adj* : incohérent
income ['ɪnˌkʌm] *n* : revenu *m* — **income tax** *n* : impôt *m* sur le revenu
incomparable [ɪn'kɑmpərəbəl] *adj* : incomparable
incompatible [ˌɪnkəm'pæţəbəl] *adj* : incompatible — **incompatibility** [ˌɪnkəmˌpæţə'bɪləţi] *n* : incompatibilité *f*
incompetent [ɪn'kɑmpəţənt] *adj* : incompétent — **incompetence** [ɪn'kɑmpəţənts] *n* : incompétence *f*
incomplete [ˌɪnkəm'pli:t] *adj* : incomplet, inachevé
incomprehensible [ˌɪnˌkɑmprɪ'hɛntsəbəl] *adj* : incompréhensible
inconceivable [ˌɪnkən'si:vəbəl] *adj* : inconcevable
inconclusive [ˌɪnkən'klu:sɪv] *adj* : peu concluant
incongruous [ɪn'kɑŋgruəs] *adj* : incongru
inconsiderate [ˌɪnkən'sɪdərət] *adj* **1** THOUGHTLESS : inconsidéré **2 be ~ toward** : manquer d'égards envers
inconsistent [ˌɪnkən'sɪstənt] *adj* **1** ERRATIC : changeant **2** CONTRADICTORY : contradictoire — **inconsistency** [ˌɪnkən'sɪstəntsi] *n, pl* **-cies** : incohérence *f*, contradiction *f*
inconspicuous [ˌɪnkən'spɪkjuəs] *adj* : qui passe inaperçu
inconvenience [ˌɪnkən'vi:njənts] *n* **1** BOTHER : dérangement *m* **2** DISADVANTAGE : inconvénient *m* — ~ *vt* **-nienced; -niencing** : déranger — **inconvenient** [ˌɪnkən'vi:njənt] *adj* : incommode
incorporate [ɪn'kɔrpəˌreɪt] *vt* **-rated; -rating** : incorporer
incorrect [ˌɪnkə'rɛkt] *adj* : incorrect
increase ['ɪnˌkri:s, ɪn'kri:s] *n* : augmentation *f* — ~ [ɪn'kri:s, 'ɪnˌkri:s] *v* **-creased; -creasing** : augmenter — **increasingly** [ɪn'kri:sɪŋli] *adv* : de plus en plus
incredible [ɪn'krɛdəbəl] *adj* : incroyable
incredulous [ɪn'krɛʤələs] *adj* : incrédule
incriminate [ɪn'krɪməˌneɪt] *vt* **-nated; -nating** : incriminer
incubator ['ɪŋkjʊˌbeɪţər, -'ɪn-] *n* : incubateur *m*, couveuse *f*
incumbent [ɪn'kʌmbənt] *n* : titulaire *mf*
incur [ɪn'kər] *vt* **-curred; -curring** : encourir (une pénalité, etc.), contracter (une dette)
incurable [ɪn'kjʊrəbəl] *adj* : incurable
indebted [ɪn'dɛţəd] *adj* ~ **to** : redevable à
indecent [ɪn'di:sənt] *adj* : indécent — **indecency** [ɪn'di:səntsi] *n, pl* **-cies** : indécence *f*
indecisive [ˌɪndɪ'saɪsɪv] *adj* : indécis
indeed [ɪn'di:d] *adv* : vraiment, en effet
indefinite [ɪn'dɛfənət] *adj* **1** : indéfini **2** VAGUE : imprécis — **indefinitely** [ɪn'dɛfənətli] *adv* : indéfiniment
indelible [ɪn'dɛləbəl] *adj* : indélébile
indent [ɪn'dɛnt] *vt* : mettre en alinéa — **indentation** [ˌɪnˌdɛn'teɪʃən] *n* DENT, NOTCH : creux *m*, bosse *f*
independent [ˌɪndə'pɛndənt] *adj* : indépendant — **independence** [ˌɪndə'pɛndənts] *n* : indépendance *f* — **independently** [ˌɪndə'pɛndəntli] *adv* : de façon indépendante
indescribable [ˌɪndɪ'skraɪbəbəl] *adj* : indescriptible
indestructible [ˌɪndɪ'strʌktəbəl] *adj* : indestructible
index ['ɪnˌdɛks] *n, pl* **-dexes** *or* **-dices** ['ɪndəˌsi:z] **1** : index *m* (d'un livre, etc.) **2** INDICATOR : indice *m* **3** *or* ~ **finger** : index *m* — ~ *vt* : classer
Indian ['ɪndiən] *adj* : indien
indication [ˌɪndə'keɪʃən] *n* : indication *f* — **indicate** ['ɪndəˌkeɪt] *vt* **-cated; -cating** : indiquer — **indicative** [ɪn'dɪkəţɪv] *adj* : indicatif — **indicator** ['ɪndəˌkeɪţər] *n* : indicateur *m*
indict [ɪn'daɪt] *vt* : inculper — **indictment** [ɪn'daɪtmənt] *n* : inculpation *f*
indifferent [ɪn'dɪfrənt, -'dɪfə-] *adj* **1** UNCONCERNED : indifférent **2** MEDIOCRE : médiocre — **indifference** [ɪn'dɪfrənts, -'dɪfə-] *n* : indifférence *f*
indigenous [ɪn'dɪʤənəs] *adj* : indigène
indigestion [ˌɪndaɪ'ʤɛsʧən, -dɪ-] *n* : indigestion *f* — **indigestible** [ˌɪndaɪ'ʤɛstəbəl, -dɪ-] *adj* : indigeste
indignation [ˌɪndɪg'neɪʃən] *n* : indignation *f* — **indignant** [ɪn'dɪgnənt] *adj* : indigné — **indignity** [ɪn'dɪgnəţi] *n, pl* **-ties** : indignité *f*
indigo ['ɪndɪˌgo:] *n, pl* **-gos** *or* **-goes** : indigo *m*

indirect [ˌɪndəˈrɛkt, -daɪ-] *adj* : indirect

indiscreet [ˌɪndɪˈskri:t] *adj* : indiscret — **indiscretion** [ˌɪndɪˈskrɛʃən] *n* : indiscrétion *f*

indiscriminate [ˌɪndɪˈskrɪmənət] *adj* **1** : sans discernement **2** RANDOM : fait au hasard

indispensable [ˌɪndɪˈspɛntsəbəl] *adj* : indispensable

indisputable [ˌɪndɪˈspju:ṭəbəl] *adj* : incontestable

indistinct [ˌɪndɪˈstɪŋkt] *adj* : indistinct

individual [ˌɪndəˈvɪʤʊəl] *adj* **1** : individuel **2** SPECIFIC : particulier — **~** *n* : individu *m* — **individuality** [ˌɪndəˌvɪʤʊˈæləṭi] *n, pl* **-ties** : individualité *f* — **individually** [ˌɪndəˈvɪʤʊəli, -ʤəli] *adv* : individuellement

indoctrinate [ɪnˈdɑktrəˌneɪt] *vt* **-nated; -nating** : endoctriner — **indoctrination** [ɪnˌdɑktrəˈneɪʃən] *n* : endoctrinement *m*

Indonesian [ˌɪndoˈni:ʒən, -ʃən] *adj* : indonésien — **~** *n* : indonésien *m* (langue)

indoor [ˈɪnˈdor] *adj* **1** : d'intérieur **2** **~ pool** : piscine *f* couverte **3** **~ sports** : sports *mpl* pratiqués en salle — **indoors** [ˈɪnˈdorz] *adv* : à l'intérieur

induce [ɪnˈdu:s, -ˈdju:s] *vt* **-duced; -ducing** **1** PERSUADE : induire **2** CAUSE : provoquer — **inducement** [ɪnˈdu:smənt, -ˈdju:s-] *n* : encouragement *m*

indulge [ɪnˈdʌlʤ] *v* **-dulged; -dulging** *vt* **1** GRATIFY : céder à **2** PAMPER : gâter — *vi* **~ in** : se permettre — **indulgence** [ɪnˈdʌlʤənts] *n* : indulgence *f* — **indulgent** [ɪnˈdʌlʤənt] *adj* : indulgent

industrial [ɪnˈdʌstriəl] *adj* : industriel — **industrialize** [ɪnˈdʌstriəˌlaɪz] *vt* **-ized; -izing** : industrialiser — **industrious** [ɪnˈdʌstriəs] *adj* : industrieux, travailleur — **industry** [ˈɪndəstri] *n, pl* **-tries** : industrie *f*

inebriated [ɪˈni:briˌeɪṭəd] *adj* : ivre

inedible [ɪˈnɛdəbəl] *adj* : immangeable

ineffective [ˌɪnɪˈfɛktɪv] *adj* : inefficace — **ineffectual** [ˌɪnɪˈfɛktʃʊəl] *adj* : inefficace

inefficient [ˌɪnɪˈfɪʃənt] *adj* **1** : inefficace **2** INCOMPETENT : incompétent — **inefficiency** [ˌɪnɪˈfɪʃəntsi] *n, pl* **-cies** : inefficacité *f*

ineligible [ɪnˈɛləʤəbəl] *adj* : inéligible

inept [ɪˈnɛpt] *adj* : inepte

inequality [ˌɪnɪˈkwɑləṭi] *n, pl* **-ties** : inégalité *f*

inert [ɪˈnərt] *adj* : inerte — **inertia** [ɪˈnərʃə] *n* : inertie *f*

inescapable [ˌɪnɪˈskeɪpəbəl] *adj* : inéluctable

inevitable [ɪnˈɛvəṭəbəl] *adj* : inévitable — **inevitably** [-bli] *adv* : inévitablement

inexcusable [ˌɪnɪkˈskju:zəbəl] *adj* : inexcusable

inexpensive [ˌɪnɪkˈspɛntsɪv] *adj* : pas cher, bon marché

inexperienced [ˌɪnɪkˈspɪriəntst] *adj* : inexpérimenté

inexplicable [ˌɪnɪkˈsplɪkəbəl] *adj* : inexplicable

infallible [ɪnˈfæləbəl] *adj* : infaillible

infamous [ˈɪnfəməs] *adj* : infâme, notoire

infancy [ˈɪnfəntsi] *n, pl* **-cies** : petite enfance *f* — **infant** [ˈɪnfənt] *n* : petit enfant *m*, petite enfant *f;* nourrisson *m* — **infantile** [ˈɪnfənˌtaɪl, -təl, -ˌti:l] *adj* : infantile

infantry [ˈɪnfəntri] *n, pl* **-tries** : infanterie *f*

infatuated [ɪnˈfæʧʊˌeɪṭəd] *adj* **be ~ with** : être épris de — **infatuation** [ɪnˌfæʧʊˈeɪʃən] *n* : engouement *m*

infect [ɪnˈfɛkt] *vt* : infecter — **infection** [ɪnˈfɛkʃən] *n* : infection *f* — **infectious** [ɪnˈfɛkʃəs] *adj* : infectieux, contagieux

infer [ɪnˈfər] *vt* **-ferred; -ferring** : déduire — **inference** [ˈɪnfərənts] *n* : déduction *f*

inferior [ɪnˈfɪriər] *adj* : inférieur — **~** *n* : inférieur *m*, -rieure *f* — **inferiority** [ɪnˌfɪriˈɔrəṭi] *n, pl* **-ties** : infériorité *f*

infernal [ɪnˈfərnəl] *adj* : infernal — **inferno** [ɪnˈfərˌno:] *n, pl* **-nos** : brasier *m*

infertile [ɪnˈfɛrṭəl, -ˌtaɪl] *adj* **1** : infertile **2** STERILE : stérile — **infertility** [ˌɪnfərˈtɪləṭi] *n* : infertilité *f*

infest [ɪnˈfɛst] *vt* : infester

infidelity [ˌɪnfəˈdɛləṭi, -faɪ-] *n, pl* **-ties** : infidélité *f*

infiltrate [ɪnˈfɪlˌtreɪt, ˈɪnfɪl-] *v* **-trated; -trating** *vt* : infiltrer — *vi* : s'infiltrer

infinite [ˈɪnfənət] *adj* : infini — **infinitive** [ɪnˈfɪnəṭɪv] *n* : infinitif *m* — **infinity** [ɪnˈfɪnəṭi] *n, pl* **-ties** : infinité *f*

infirm [ɪnˈfərm] *adj* : infirme — **infirmary** [ɪnˈfərməri] *n, pl* **-ries** : infirmerie *f* — **infirmity** [ɪnˈfərməṭi] *n, pl* **-ties** : infirmité *f*

inflame [ɪnˈfleɪm] *v* **-flamed; -flaming** *vt* : enflammer — *vi* : s'enflammer —

inflammable [ɪnˈflæməbəl] *adj* : (in)flammable — **inflammation** [ˌɪnfləˈmeɪʃən] *n* : inflammation *f* — **inflammatory** [ɪnˈflæməˌtori] *adj* : incendiaire

inflate [ɪnˈfleɪt] *v* **-flated; -flating** *vt* : gonfler — *vi* : se gonfler — **inflatable** [ɪnˈfleɪtəbəl] *adj* : gonflable — **inflation** [ɪnˈfleɪʃən] *n* : inflation *f* — **inflationary** [ɪnˈfleɪʃəˌnɛri] *adj* : inflationniste

inflexible [ɪnˈflɛksɪbəl] *adj* : inflexible

inflict [ɪnˈflɪkt] *vt* : infliger

influence [ˈɪnˌflu:ənts, ɪnˈflu:ənts] *n* **1** : influence *f* **2 under the ~ of** : sous l'effet de — **~** *vt* **-enced; -encing** : influencer, influer sur — **influential** [ˌɪnfluˈɛntʃəl] *adj* : influent

influenza [ˌɪnfluˈɛnzə] *n* : grippe *f*

influx [ˈɪnˌflʌks] *n* : afflux *m*

inform [ɪnˈfɔrm] *vt* : informer, renseigner — *vi* **~ on** : dénoncer

informal [ɪnˈfɔrməl] *adj* **1** : simple **2** CASUAL : familier, décontracté **3** UNOFFICIAL : officieux — **informally** [ɪnˈfɔrməli] *adv* : sans cérémonie, simplement

information [ˌɪnfərˈmeɪʃən] *n* : renseignements *mpl,* information *f* — **informative** [ɪnˈfɔrmət̬ɪv] *adj* : informatif — **informer** [ɪnˈfɔrmər] *n* : indicateur *m,* -trice *f*

infrared [ˌɪnfrəˈrɛd] *adj* : infrarouge

infrastructure [ˈɪnfrəˌstrʌktʃər] *n* : infrastructure *f*

infrequent [ɪnˈfri:kwənt] *adj* : rare, peu fréquent — **infrequently** [ɪnˈfri:kwəntli] *adv* : rarement

infringe [ɪnˈfrɪndʒ] *v* **-fringed; -fringing** *vt* : enfreindre — *vi* **~ on** : empiéter sur — **infringement** [ɪnˈfrɪndʒmənt] *n* : infraction *f* (à la loi)

infuriate [ɪnˈfjʊriˌeɪt] *vt* **-ated; -ating** : rendre furieux — **infuriating** [ɪnˈfjʊriˌeɪt̬ɪŋ] *adj* : exaspérant

infuse [ɪnˈfju:z] *vt* **-fused; -fusing** : infuser — **infusion** [ɪnˈfju:ʒən] *n* : infusion *f*

ingenious [ɪnˈdʒi:njəs] *adj* : ingénieux — **ingenuity** [ˌɪndʒəˈnu:ət̬i, -ˈnju:-] *n, pl* **-ties** : ingéniosité *f*

ingenuous [ɪnˈdʒɛnjʊəs] *adj* : ingénu, naïf

ingot [ˈɪŋgət] *n* : lingot *m*

ingrained [ɪnˈgreɪnd] *adj* : enraciné

ingratiate [ɪnˈgreɪʃiˌeɪt] *vt* **-ated; -ating ~ oneself with** : gagner les bonnes grâces de

ingratitude [ɪnˈgræt̬əˈtu:d, -ˈtju:d] *n* : ingratitude *f*

ingredient [ɪnˈgri:diənt] *n* : ingrédient *m*

inhabit [ɪnˈhæbət] *vt* : habiter — **inhabitant** [ɪnˈhæbət̬ənt] *n* : habitant *m,* -tante *f*

inhale [ɪnˈheɪl] *v* **-haled; -haling** *vt* : inhaler, respirer — *vi* : inspirer

inherent [ɪnˈhɪrənt, -ˈhɛr-] *adj* : inhérent — **inherently** [ɪnˈhɪrəntli, -ˈhɛr-] *adv* : fondamentalement

inherit [ɪnˈhɛrət] *vt* : hériter de — **inheritance** [ɪnˈhɛrət̬ənts] *n* : héritage *m*

inhibit [ɪnˈhɪbət] *vt* IMPEDE : entraver, gêner — **inhibition** [ˌɪnhəˈbɪʃən, ˌɪnə-] *n* : inhibition *f*

inhuman [ɪnˈhju:mən, -ˈju:-] *adj* : inhumain — **inhumane** [ˌɪnhjuˈmeɪn, -ju-] *adj* : cruel — **inhumanity** [ˌɪnhjuˈmænət̬i, -ju-] *n, pl* **-ties** : inhumanité *f*

initial [ɪˈnɪʃəl] *adj* : initial, premier — **~** *n* : initiale *f* — **~** *vt* **-tialed** *or* **-tialled; -tialing** *or* **-tialling** : parapher — **initially** [ɪˈnɪʃəli] *adv* : au départ

initiate [ɪˈnɪʃiˌeɪt] *vt* **-ated; -ating 1** BEGIN : amorcer, entreprendre **2 ~ into** : initier à — **initiation** [ɪˌnɪʃiˈeɪʃən] *n* : initiation *f* — **initiative** [ɪˈnɪʃət̬ɪv] *n* : initiative *f*

inject [ɪnˈdʒɛkt] *vt* : injecter — **injection** [ɪnˈdʒɛkʃən] *n* : injection *f*

injure [ˈɪndʒər] *vt* **-jured; -juring 1** WOUND : blesser **2** HARM : nuire à **3 ~ oneself** : se blesser — **injury** [ˈɪndʒəri] *n, pl* **-ries 1** WOUND : blessure *f* **2** WRONG : tort *m*

injustice [ɪnˈdʒʌstəs] *n* : injustice *f*

ink [ˈɪŋk] *n* : encre *f* — **inkwell** [ˈɪŋkˌwɛl] *n* : encrier *m*

inland [ˈɪnˌlænd, -lənd] *adj* : intérieur — **~** *adv* : à l'intérieur, vers l'intérieur

in–laws [ˈɪnˌlɔz] *npl* : beaux-parents *mpl*

inlet [ˈɪnˌlɛt, -lət] *n* : bras *m* de mer

inmate [ˈɪnˌmeɪt] *n* **1** PRISONER : détenu *m,* -nue *f* **2** PATIENT : interné *m,* -née *f*

inn [ˈɪn] *n* : auberge *f*

innards [ˈɪnərdz] *npl* : entrailles *fpl*

innate [ɪˈneɪt] *adj* : inné

inner [ˈɪnər] *adj* : intérieur, interne — **innermost** [ˈɪnərˌmo:st] *adj* : le plus profond

inning [ˈɪnɪŋ] *n* : tour *m* de batte, manche *f Can* (au baseball)

innocence [ˈɪnəsənts] *n* : innocence *f* — **innocent** [ˈɪnəsənt] *adj* : innocent — **~** *n* : innocent *m,* -cente *f*

innocuous [ɪ'nɑkjəwəs] *adj* : inoffensif

innovate ['ɪnəˌveɪt] *v* **-vated; -vating** : innover — **innovation** [ˌɪnə'veɪʃən] *n* : innovation *f* — **innovative** ['ɪnəˌveɪt̬ɪv] *adj* : innovateur — **innovator** ['ɪnəˌveɪt̬ər] *n* : innovateur *m*, -trice *f*

innumerable [ɪ'nu:mərəbəl, -'nju:-] *adj* : innombrable

inoculate [ɪ'nɑkjəˌleɪt] *vt* **-lated; -lating** : inoculer — **inoculation** [ɪˌnɑkjə'leɪʃən] *n* : inoculation *f*

inoffensive [ˌɪnə'fɛntsɪv] *adj* : inoffensif

inpatient ['ɪnˌpeɪʃənt] *n* : malade *m* hospitalisé, malade *f* hospitalisée

input ['ɪnˌpʊt] *n* **1** : contribution *f* **2** : entrée *f* (de données) — **~** *vt* **-putted** *or* **-put; -putting** : entrer (des données)

inquire [ɪn'kwaɪr] *v* **-quired; -quiring** *vt* : demander — *vi* **1 ~ about** : se renseigner sur **2 ~ into** : enquêter sur — **inquiry** [ɪn'kwaɪri, 'ɪnˌkwaɪri; 'ɪnkwəri, 'ɪŋ-] *n, pl* **-ries 1** QUESTION : demande *f* **2** INVESTIGATION : enquête *f* — **inquisition** [ˌɪnkwə'zɪʃən, ˌɪŋ-] *n* : inquisition *f* — **inquisitive** [ɪn'kwɪzət̬ɪv] *adj* : curieux

insane [ɪn'seɪn] *adj* : fou — **insanity** [ɪn'sænət̬i] *n, pl* **-ties** : folie *f*

insatiable [ɪn'seɪʃəbəl] *adj* : insatiable

inscribe [ɪn'skraɪb] *vt* **-scribed; -scribing 1** : inscrire **2** DEDICATE : dédicacer — **inscription** [ɪn'skrɪpʃən] *n* : inscription *f*

inscrutable [ɪn'skru:t̬əbəl] *adj* : impénétrable

insect ['ɪnˌsɛkt] *n* : insecte *m* — **insecticide** [ɪn'sɛktəˌsaɪd] *n* : insecticide *m*

insecure [ˌɪnsɪ'kjʊr] *adj* **1** UNSAFE : peu sûr **2** FEARFUL : anxieux — **insecurity** [ˌɪnsɪ'kjʊrət̬i] *n, pl* **-ties** : insécurité *f*

insensitive [ɪn'sɛntsət̬ɪv] *adj* : insensible — **insensitivity** [ɪnˌsɛntsə'tɪvət̬i] *n* : insensibilité *f*

inseparable [ɪn'sɛpərəbəl] *adj* : inséparable

insert [ɪn'sɛrt] *vt* : insérer, introduire

inside [ɪn'saɪd, 'ɪnˌsaɪd] *n* **1** : intérieur *m* **2 ~s** *npl* GUTS : entrailles *fpl* — **~** *adv* **1** : à l'intérieur **2 ~ out** : à l'envers — **~** *adj* : intérieur — **~** *prep* : à l'intérieur de

insidious [ɪn'sɪdiəs] *adj* : insidieux

insight ['ɪnˌsaɪt] *n* : perspicacité *f* — **insightful** [ɪn'saɪtfəl] *adj* : perspicace

insignia [ɪn'sɪgniə] *or* **insigne** [-ˌni:] *n, pl* **-nia** *or* **-nias** : insigne(s) *m(pl)*

insignificant [ˌɪnsɪg'nɪfɪkənt] *adj* : insignifiant

insincere [ˌɪnsɪn'sɪr] *adj* : pas sincère

insinuate [ɪn'sɪnjʊˌeɪt] *vt* **-ated; -ating** : insinuer — **insinuation** [ɪnˌsɪnjʊ'eɪʃən] *n* : insinuation *f*

insipid [ɪn'sɪpəd] *adj* : insipide

insist [ɪn'sɪst] *v* : insister — **insistent** [ɪn'sɪstənt] *adj* : insistant

insofar as [ˌɪnso'fɑræz] *conj* : dans la mesure où

insole ['ɪnˌso:l] *n* : semelle *f* (intérieure)

insolence ['ɪntsələnts] *n* : insolence *f* — **insolent** ['ɪntsələnt] *adj* : insolent

insolvent [ɪn'sɑlvənt] *adj* : insolvable

insomnia [ɪn'sɑmniə] *n* : insomnie *f*

inspect [ɪn'spɛkt] *vt* : examiner, inspecter — **inspection** [ɪn'spɛkʃən] *n* : inspection *f* — **inspector** [ɪn'spɛktər] *n* : inspecteur *m*, -trice *f*

inspire [ɪn'spaɪr] *vt* **-spired; -spiring** : inspirer — **inspiration** [ˌɪntspə'reɪʃən] *n* : inspiration *f* — **inspirational** [ˌɪntspə'reɪʃənəl] *adj* : inspirant

instability [ˌɪntstə'bɪlət̬i] *n* : instabilité *f*

install [ɪn'stɔl] *vt* **-stalled; -stalling** : installer — **installation** [ˌɪntstə'leɪʃən] *n* : installation *f* — **installment** [ɪn'stɔlmənt] *n* **1** PAYMENT : versement *m*, acompte *m* **2** : épisode *m* (d'un feuilleton)

instance ['ɪntstənts] *n* **1** : cas *m*, exemple *m* **2 for ~** : par exemple

instant ['ɪntstənt] *n* : instant *m*, moment *m* — **~** *adj* **1** IMMEDIATE : immédiat, instantané **2 ~ coffee** : café *m* instantané — **instantaneous** [ˌɪntstən'teɪniəs] *adj* : instantané — **instantly** ['ɪntstəntli] *adv* : immédiatement, sur-le-champ

instead [ɪn'stɛd] *adv* **1** : plutôt **2 I went ~** : j'y suis allé à sa place — **instead of** *prep* : au lieu de, à la place de

instep ['ɪnˌstɛp] *n* : cou-de-pied *m*

instigate ['ɪntstəˌgeɪt] *vt* **-gated; -gating** : engager, provoquer — **instigation** [ˌɪntstə'geɪʃən] *n* : instigation *f* — **instigator** ['ɪntstəˌgeɪt̬ər] *n* : instigateur *m*, -trice *f*

instill *or Brit* **instil** [ɪn'stɪl] *vt* **-stilled; -stilling** : inculquer

instinct ['ɪnˌstɪŋkt] *n* : instinct *m* — **instinctive** [ɪn'stɪŋktɪv] *or* **instinctual** [ɪn'stɪŋktʃʊəl] *adj* : instinctif

institute ['ɪnstəˌtu:t, -ˌtju:t] *vt* **-tuted; -tuting** : instituer — **~** *n* : institut *m*

— **institution** [ˌɪnstəˈtu:ʃən, -ˈtju:-] *n* : institution *f*

instruct [ɪnˈstrʌkt] *vt* **1** TEACH : instruire **2** DIRECT : charger — **instruction** [ɪnˈstrʌkʃən] *n* : instruction *f* — **instructor** [ɪnˈstrʌktər] *n* : moniteur *m*, -trice *f*

instrument [ˈɪntstrəmənt] *n* : instrument *m* — **instrumental** [ˌɪntstrəˈmentəl] *adj* **1** : instrumental **2 be ~ in** : contribuer à

insufferable [ɪnˈsʌfərəbəl] *adj* : insupportable

insufficient [ˌɪnsəˈfɪʃənt] *adj* : insuffisant

insular [ˈɪntsʊlər, -sjʊ-] *adj* **1** : insulaire **2** NARROW-MINDED : borné

insulate [ˈɪntsəˌleɪt] *vt* **-lated; -lating** : isoler — **insulation** [ˌɪntsəˈleɪʃən] *n* : isolation *f*

insulin [ˈɪntsələn] *n* : insuline *f*

insult [ɪnˈsʌlt] *vt* : insulter — **~** [ˈɪnˌsʌlt] *n* : insulte *f*, injure *f*

insure [ɪnˈʃʊr] *vt* **-sured; -suring** : assurer — **insurance** [ɪnˈʃʊrənts] *n* : assurance *f*

insurmountable [ˌɪnsərˈmaʊntəbəl] *adj* : insurmontable

intact [ɪnˈtækt] *adj* : intact

intake [ˈɪnˌteɪk] *n* **1** : consommation *f* (de nourriture) **2** ADMISSION : admission *f*

intangible [ɪnˈtænʤəbəl] *adj* : intangible

integral [ˈɪntɪgrəl] *adj* **1** : intégral **2 be an ~ part of** : faire partie intégrante de

integrate [ˈɪntəˌgreɪt] *v* **-grated; -grating** *vt* : intégrer — *vi* : s'intégrer

integrity [ɪnˈtɛgrəṭi] *n* : intégrité *f*

intellect [ˈɪntəlˌɛkt] *n* : intelligence *f* — **intellectual** [ˌɪntəˈlɛkʧʊəl] *adj* : intellectuel — **~** *n* : intellectuel *m*, -tuelle *f* — **intelligence** [ɪnˈtɛləʤənts] *n* : intelligence *f* — **intelligent** [ɪnˈtɛləʤənt] *adj* : intelligent — **intelligible** [ɪnˈtɛləʤəbəl] *adj* : intelligible

intend [ɪnˈtɛnd] *vt* **1 be ~ed for** : être destiné à **2 ~ to** : avoir l'intention de — **intended** [ɪnˈtɛndəd] *adj* **1** PLANNED : voulu **2** INTENTIONAL : intentionnel

intense [ɪnˈtɛnts] *adj* : intense — **intensely** [ɪnˈtɛntsli] *adv* **1** : intensément **2** EXTREMELY : extrêmement — **intensify** [ɪnˈtɛntsəˌfaɪ] *v* **-fied; -fying** *vt* : intensifier — *vi* : s'intensifier — **intensity** [ɪnˈtɛntsəṭi] *n, pl* **-ties** : intensité *f* — **intensive** [ɪnˈtɛntsɪv] *adj* : intensif

intent [ɪnˈtɛnt] *n* : intention *f* — **~** *adj* **1** : absorbé, attentif **2 ~ on doing** : résolu à faire — **intention** [ɪnˈtɛnʧən] *n* : intention *f* — **intentional** [ɪnˈtɛnʧənəl] *adj* : intentionnel — **intently** [ɪnˈtɛntli] *adv* : attentivement

interact [ˌɪntərˈækt] *vi* **1** : agir l'un sur l'autre **2 ~ with** : communiquer avec — **interaction** [ˌɪntərˈækʃən] *n* : interaction *f*

intercede [ˌɪntərˈsi:d] *vi* **-ceded; -ceding** : intercéder

intercept [ˌɪntərˈsɛpt] *vt* : intercepter

interchange [ˌɪntərˈʧeɪnʤ] *vt* **-changed; -changing** EXCHANGE : échanger — **~** *n* [ˈɪntərˌʧeɪnʤ] **1** EXCHANGE : échange *m* **2** JUNCTION : échangeur *m* — **interchangeable** [ˌɪntərˈʧeɪnʤəbəl] *adj* : interchangeable

intercourse [ˈɪntərˌkors] *n* : rapports *mpl* (sexuels)

interest [ˈɪntrəst, -təˌrɛst] *n* : intérêt *m* — **~** *vt* : intéresser — **interesting** [ˈɪntrəstɪŋ, -təˌrɛstɪŋ] *adj* : intéressant

interface [ˈɪntərˌfeɪs] *n* : interface *f*

interfere [ˌɪntərˈfɪr] *vi* **-fered; -fering 1** INTERVENE : intervenir **2 ~ in** : s'immiscer dans — **interference** [ˌɪntərˈfɪrənts] *n* **1** : ingérence *f* **2** : interférence *f*, parasites *mpl* (à la radio, etc.)

interim [ˌɪntərəm] *n* **1** : intérim *m* **2 in the ~** : entre-temps — **~** *adj* : provisoire

interior [ɪnˈtɪriər] *adj* : intérieur — **~** *n* : intérieur *m*

interjection [ˌɪntərˈʤɛkʃən] *n* : interjection *f*

interlock [ˌɪntərˈlɑk] *vi* : s'enclencher

intermediate [ˌɪntərˈmi:diət] *adj* : intermédiaire — **intermediary** [ˌɪntərˈmi:diˌɛri] *n, pl* **-aries** : intermédiaire *mf*

interminable [ɪnˈtərmənəbəl] *adj* : interminable

intermission [ˌɪntərˈmɪʃən] *n* **1** : pause *f* **2** : entracte *m* (au théâtre)

intermittent [ˌɪntərˈmɪtənt] *adj* : intermittent

intern[1] [ˈɪnˌtərn, ɪnˈtərn] *vt* CONFINE : interner

intern[2] [ˈɪnˌtərn] *n* : stagiaire *mf*

internal [ɪnˈtərnəl] *adj* : interne — **internally** [ɪnˈtərnəli] *adv* : intérieurement

international [ˌɪntərˈnæʃənəl] *adj* : international

Internet [ˈɪntərˌnɛt] *n* : Internet *m*

interpret [ɪnˈtərprət] *vt* : interpréter — **interpretation** [ɪnˌtərprəˈteɪʃən] *n* : interprétation *f* — **interpreter** [ɪnˈtərprətər] *n* : interprète *mf*

interrogate [ɪnˈtɛrəˌgeɪt] *vt* **-gated; -gating** : interroger — **interrogation** [ɪnˌtɛrəˈgeɪʃən] *n* QUESTIONING : interrogatoire *m* — **interrogative** [ˌɪntəˈrɑgətɪv] *adj* : interrogatif

interrupt [ˌɪntəˈrʌpt] *v* : interrompre — **interruption** [ˌɪntəˈrʌpʃən] *n* : interruption *f*

intersect [ˌɪntərˈsɛkt] *vt* : croiser, couper — *vi* : se croiser, se couper — **intersection** [ˌɪntərˈsɛkʃən] *n* JUNCTION : croisement *m,* carrefour *m*

intersperse [ˌɪntərˈspɛrs] *vt* **-spersed; -spersing ~ with** : parsemer de

interstate [ˈɪntərˌsteɪt] *n or* **~ highway** : autoroute *f*

intertwine [ˌɪntərˈtwaɪn] *vi* **-twined; -twining** : s'entrelacer

interval [ˈɪntərvəl] *n* : intervalle *m*

intervene [ˌɪntərˈviːn] *vi* **-vened; -vening 1** : intervenir **2** HAPPEN : survenir — **intervention** [ˌɪntərˈvɛntʃən] *n* : intervention *f*

interview [ˈɪntərˌvjuː] *n* **1** : entretien *m,* entrevue *f* **2** : interview *f* (à la télévision, etc.) — **~** *vt* **1** : faire passer une entrevue (pour un emploi) **2** : interviewer (à la télévision, etc.)

intestine [ɪnˈtɛstən] *n* : intestin *m* — **intestinal** [ɪnˈtɛstənəl] *adj* : intestinal

intimate[1] [ˈɪntəˌmeɪt] *vt* **-mated; -mating** : laisser entendre

intimate[2] [ˈɪntəmət] *adj* : intime — **intimacy** [ˈɪntəməsi] *n, pl* **-cies** : intimité *f*

intimidate [ɪnˈtɪməˌdeɪt] *vt* **-dated; -dating** : intimider — **intimidation** [ɪnˌtɪməˈdeɪʃən] *n* : intimidation *f*

into [ˈɪnˌtuː] *prep* **1** : en, dans **2 bump ~** : se cogner contre **3** (*used in mathematics*) **4 ~ 12 is 3** : 12 divisé par 4 fait 3

intolerable [ɪnˈtɑlərəbəl] *adj* : intolérable — **intolerance** [ɪnˈtɑlərənts] *n* : intolérance *f* — **intolerant** [ɪnˈtɑlərənt] *adj* : intolérant

intoxicate [ɪnˈtɑksəˌkeɪt] *vt* **-cated; -cating** : enivrer — **intoxicated** [ɪnˈtɑksəˌkeɪtəd] *adj* : ivre

intransitive [ɪnˈtræntsətɪv, -ˈtrænzə-] *adj* : intransitif

intravenous [ˌɪntrəˈviːnəs] *adj* : intraveineux

intrepid [ɪnˈtrɛpəd] *adj* : intrépide

intricate [ˈɪntrɪkət] *adj* : compliqué — **intricacy** [ˈɪntrɪkəsi] *n, pl* **-cies** : complexité *f*

intrigue [ˈɪnˌtriːg, ɪnˈtriːg] *n* : intrigue *f* — **~** [ɪnˈtriːg] *v* **-trigued; -triguing** : intriguer — **intriguing** [ɪnˈtriːgɪŋ] *adj* : fascinant

intrinsic [ɪnˈtrɪnzɪk, -ˈtrɪntsɪk] *adj* : intrinsèque

introduce [ˌɪntrəˈduːs, -ˈdjuːs] *vt* **-duced; -ducing 1** : introduire **2** PRESENT : présenter — **introduction** [ˌɪntrəˈdʌkʃən] *n* **1** : introduction *f* **2** PRESENTATION : présentation *f* — **introductory** [ˌɪntrəˈdʌktəri] *adj* : d'introduction, préliminaire

introvert [ˈɪntrəˌvərt] *n* : introverti *m,* -tie *f* — **introverted** [ˈɪntrəˌvərtəd] *adj* : introverti

intrude [ɪnˈtruːd] *vi* **-truded; -truding** : déranger, s'imposer — **intruder** [ɪnˈtruːdər] *n* : intrus *m,* -truse *f* — **intrusion** [ɪnˈtruːʒən] *n* : intrusion *f* — **intrusive** [ɪnˈtruːsɪv] *adj* : importun, gênant

intuition [ˌɪntʊˈɪʃən, -tjʊ-] *n* : intuition *f* — **intuitive** [ɪnˈtuːətɪv, -ˈtjuː-] *adj* : intuitif

inundate [ˈɪnənˌdeɪt] *vt* **-dated; -dating** : inonder

invade [ɪnˈveɪd] *vt* **-vaded; -vading** : envahir

invalid[1] [ɪnˈvæləd] *adj* : non valide, non valable

invalid[2] [ˈɪnvələd] *n* : infirme *mf,* invalide *mf*

invaluable [ɪnˈvæljəbəl, -ˈvæljʊə-] *adj* : inestimable, précieux

invariable [ɪnˈværiəbəl] *adj* : invariable

invasion [ɪnˈveɪʒən] *n* : invasion *f*

invent [ɪnˈvɛnt] *vt* : inventer — **invention** [ɪnˈvɛntʃən] *n* : invention *f* — **inventive** [ɪnˈvɛntɪv] *adj* : inventif — **inventor** [ɪnˈvɛntər] *n* : inventeur *m,* trice *f*

inventory [ˈɪnvənˌtɔri] *n, pl* **-ries** : inventaire *m*

invert [ɪnˈvərt] *vt* : inverser, renverser

invertebrate [ɪnˈvərtəbrət, -ˌbreɪt] *adj* : invertébré — **~** *n* : invertébré *m*

invest [ɪnˈvɛst] *v* : investir

investigate [ɪnˈvɛstəˌgeɪt] *vt* **-gated; -gating** : enquêter sur, faire une enquête sur — **investigation** [ɪnˌvɛstəˈgeɪʃən] *n* : investigation *f,* enquête *f*

investment [ɪnˈvɛstmənt] *n* : in-

vestissement *m* — **investor** [ɪnˈvɛstər] *n* : investisseur *m,* -seuse *f*
inveterate [ɪnˈvɛt̬ərət] *adj* : invétéré
invigorating [ɪnˈvɪgəˌreɪt̬ɪŋ] *adj* : vivifiant, revigorant
invincible [ɪnˈvɪntsəbəl] *adj* : invincible
invisible [ɪnˈvɪzəbəl] *adj* : invisible
invitation [ˌɪnvəˈteɪʃən] *n* : invitation *f* — **invite** [ɪnˈvaɪt] *vt* **-vited; -viting** : inviter — **inviting** [ɪnˈvaɪt̬ɪŋ] *adj* : attrayant, engageant
invoice [ˈɪnˌvɔɪs] *n* : facture *f*
invoke [ɪnˈvo:k] *vt* **-voked; -voking** : invoquer
involuntary [ɪnˈvɑlənˌtɛri] *adj* : involontaire
involve [ɪnˈvɑlv] *vt* **-volved; -volving** **1** ENTAIL : entraîner **2** CONCERN : concerner, toucher — **involved** [ɪnˈvɑlvd] *adj* INTRICATE : complexe — **involvement** [ɪnˈvɑlvmənt] *n* : participation *f*
invulnerable [ɪnˈvʌlnərəbəl] *adj* : invulnérable
inward [ˈɪnwərd] *adj* : intérieur — ∼ *or* **inwards** [ˈɪnwərdz] *adv* : vers l'intérieur
iodine [ˈaɪəˌdaɪn] *n* : iode *m,* teinture *f* d'iode
ion [ˈaɪən, ˈaɪˌɑn] *n* : ion *m*
iota [aɪˈo:t̬ə] *n* : brin *m*
IOU [ˌaɪˌoˈju:] *n* : reconnaissance *f* de dette
Iranian [ɪˈreɪniən, -ˈræ-, -ˈrɑ-; aɪˈ-] *adj* : iranien
Iraqi [ɪˈraki, -ˈræ-] *adj* : irakien
irate [aɪˈreɪt] *adj* : furieux
iris [ˈaɪrəs] *n, pl* **irises** *or* **irides** [ˈaɪrəˌdi:z, ˈɪr-] : iris *m*
Irish [ˈaɪrɪʃ] *adj* : irlandais
irksome [ˈərksəm] *adj* : irritant, agaçant
iron [ˈaɪərn] *n* **1** : fer *m* (métal) **2** : fer *m* à repasser — ∼ *vt* PRESS : repasser — **ironing** [ˈaɪərnɪŋ] *n* : repassage *m*
irony [ˈaɪrəni] *n, pl* **-nies** : ironie *f* — **ironic** [aɪˈrɑnɪk] *or* **ironical** [-nɪkəl] *adj* : ironique
irrational [ɪˈræʃənəl] *adj* : irrationnel
irreconcilable [ɪˌrɛkənˈsaɪləbəl] *adj* : irréconciliable, inconciliable
irrefutable [ˌɪrɪˈfju:t̬əbəl, ɪrˈrɛfjə-] *adj* : irréfutable
irregular [ɪˈrɛgjələr] *adj* : irrégulier — **irregularity** [ɪˌrɛgjəˈlærət̬i] *n, pl* **-ties** : irrégularité *f*
irrelevant [ɪˈrɛləvənt] *adj* : sans rapport, non pertinent
irreparable [ɪˈrɛpərəbəl] *adj* : irréparable
irreplaceable [ˌɪrɪˈpleɪsəbəl] *adj* : irremplaçable
irreproachable [ˌɪrɪˈpro:ʧəbəl] *adj* : irréprochable
irresistible [ˌɪrɪˈzɪstəbəl] *adj* : irrésistible
irresolute [ɪˈrɛzəˌlu:t] *adj* : irrésolu, indécis
irrespective of [ˌɪrɪˈspɛktɪvəv] *prep* : sans tenir compte de
irresponsible [ˌɪrɪˈspɑntsəbəl] *adj* : irresponsable — **irresponsibility** [ˌɪrɪˌspɑntsəˈbɪlət̬i] *n* : irresponsabilité *f*
irreverent [ɪˈrɛvərənt] *adj* : irrévérencieux
irrigate [ˈɪrəˌgeɪt] *vt* **-gated; -gating** : irriguer — **irrigation** [ˌɪrəˈgeɪʃən] *n* : irrigation *f*
irritate [ˈɪrəˌteɪt] *vt* **-tated; -tating** : irriter — **irritable** [ˈɪrət̬əbəl] *adj* : irritable — **irritating** [ˈɪrəˌteɪt̬ɪŋ] *adj* : irritant, agaçant — **irritation** [ˌɪrəˈteɪʃən] *n* : irritation *f*
is → **be**
Islam [ɪsˈlɑm, ɪz-, -ˈlæm; ˈɪsˌlɑm, ˈɪz-] *n* : islam *m* — **Islamic** [-mɪk] *adj* : islamique
island [ˈaɪlənd] *n* : île *f* — **isle** [ˈaɪl] *n* : île *f,* îlot *m*
isolate [ˈaɪsəˌleɪt] *vt* **-lated; -lating** : isoler — **isolation** [ˌaɪsəˈleɪʃən] *n* : isolement *m*
Israeli [ɪzˈreɪli] *adj* : israélien
issue [ˈɪˌʃu:] *n* **1** MATTER : question *f,* problème *m* **2** : publication *f* (d'un livre), émission *f* (de timbres, etc.) **3** : numéro *m* (d'une revue, etc.) **4** **make an** ∼ **of** : faire des histoires de — ∼ *v* **-sued; -suing** *vt* **1** : émettre (un chèque, etc.), distribuer (des provisions, etc.), donner (un ordre) **2** PUBLISH : publier, sortir — *vi* ∼ **from** : provenir de
isthmus [ˈɪsməs] *n* : isthme *m*
it [ˈɪt] *pron* **1** (*as subject*) : il, elle **2** (*as direct object*) : le, la l' **3** (*as indirect object*) : lui **4** (*as a nonspecific subject*) : ce, cela, ça **5** **it's snowing** : il neige **6** **that's** ∼ : c'est ça **7** **who is** ∼ **?** : qui c'est?
Italian [ɪˈtæliən, aɪ-] *adj* : italien — ∼ *n* : italien *m* (langue)
italics [ɪˈtælɪks] *npl* : italique *m*
itch [ˈɪʧ] *n* : démangeaison *f* — ∼ *vi* : avoir des démangeaisons — **itchy** [ˈɪʧi] *adj* **itchier; -est** : qui démange
it'd [ˈɪt̬əd] (*contraction of* **it had** *or* **it would**) → **have, would**
item [ˈaɪt̬əm] *n* **1** : article *m,* chose *f* **2**

: point *m* (d'un ordre du jour) **3 news ~** : nouvelle *f* — **itemize** ['aɪṭə,maɪz] *vt* **-ized; -izing** : détailler
itinerant [aɪ'tɪnərənt] *adj* : itinérant, ambulant
itinerary [aɪ'tɪnə,rɛri] *n, pl* **-aries** : itinéraire *m*
it'll ['ɪṭ'l] (*contraction of* **it shall** *or* **it will**) → **shall, will**
its ['ɪts] *adj* : son, sa, ses
it's ['ɪts] *contraction of* **it is** *or* **it has** → **be, have**
itself [ɪt,sɛlf] *pron* **1** (*used reflexively*) : se **2** (*for emphasis*) : lui-même, elle-même, soi-même
I've ['aɪv] (*contraction of* **I have**) → **have**
Ivorian ['aɪvəriən] *adj* : ivoirien
ivory ['aɪvəri] *n, pl* **-ries** : ivoire *m*
ivy ['aɪvi] *n, pl* **ivies** : lierre *m*

J

j ['ʤeɪ] *n, pl* **j's** *or* **js** ['ʤeɪz] : j *m*, dixième lettre de l'alphabet
jab ['ʤæb] *vt* **jabbed; jabbing 1** PIERCE : piquer **2** POKE : enfoncer — **~** *n* POKE : (petit) coup *m*
jabber ['ʤæbər] *vi* : jacasser, bavarder
jack ['ʤæk] *n* **1** : cric *m* (mécanisme) **2** : valet *m* (aux cartes) — **~** *vt or* **~ up** : soulever avec un cric
jackass ['ʤæk,æs] *n* : âne *m*
jacket ['ʤækət] *n* **1** : veste *f* **2** : jaquette *f* (d'un livre)
jackhammer ['ʤæk,hæmər] *n* : marteau-piqueur *m*
jackknife ['ʤæk,naɪf] *n, pl* **-knives** : couteau *m* de poche
jackpot ['ʤæk,pɑt] *n* : gros lot *m*
jaded ['ʤeɪdəd] *adj* : blasé
jagged ['ʤægəd] *adj* : dentelé
jail ['ʤeɪl] *n* : prison *f* — **~** *vt* : emprisonner, mettre en prison — **jailer** *or* **jailor** ['ʤeɪlər] *n* : geôlier *m*, -lière *f*
jam¹ ['ʤæm] *v* **jammed; jamming** *vt* **1** CRAM : entasser **2** OBSTRUCT : bloquer — *vi* : se bloquer, se coincer — **~** *n* **1** *or* **traffic ~** : embouteillage *m* **2** FIX : pétrin *m fam*
jam² *n* PRESERVES : confiture *f*
janitor ['ʤænəṭər] *n* : concierge *mf*
January ['ʤænju,ɛri] *n* : janvier *m*
Japanese [,ʤæpə'ni:z, -'ni:s] *adj* : japonais — **~** *n* : japonais *m* (langue)
jar¹ ['ʤɑr] *v* **jarred; jarring** *vi* **1** : rendre un son discordant **2 ~ on** : agacer (qqn) — *vt* JOLT : secouer — **~** *n* : secousse *f*
jar² *n* : bocal *m*, pot *m*
jargon ['ʤɑrgən] *n* : jargon *m*
jaundice ['ʤɔndɪs] *n* : jaunisse *f*
jaunt ['ʤɔnt] *n* : balade *f*
jaunty ['ʤɔnti] *adj* **-tier; -est** : allègre, insouciant
jaw ['ʤɔ] *n* : mâchoire *f* — **jawbone** ['ʤɔ,bo:n] *n* : maxillaire *m*
jay ['ʤeɪ] *n* : geai *m*
jazz ['ʤæz] *n* : jazz *m* — **~** *vt or* **~ up** : animer — **jazzy** ['ʤæzi] *adj* **jazzier; jazziest** FLASHY : voyant, tapageur
jealous ['ʤɛləs] *adj* : jaloux — **jealousy** ['ʤɛləsi] *n, pl* **-sies** : jalousie *f*
jeans ['ʤi:nz] *npl* : jean *m*, blue-jean *m*
jeer ['ʤir] *vt* BOO : huer — *vi* **~ at** : se moquer de — **~** *n* : raillerie *f*
jelly ['ʤɛli] *n, pl* **-lies** : gelée *f* — **jellyfish** ['ʤɛli,fɪʃ] *n* : méduse *f*
jeopardy ['ʤɛpərdi] *n* : danger *m*, péril *m* — **jeopardize** ['ʤɛpər,daɪz] *vt* **-dized; -dizing** : mettre en danger, compromettre
jerk ['ʤərk] *n* **1** JOLT : saccade *f*, secousse *f* **2** FOOL : idiot *m*, -diote *f* — **~** *vt* **1** YANK : tirer brusquement **2** JOLT : secouer
jersey ['ʤərzi] *n, pl* **-seys** : jersey *m* (tissu)
jest ['ʤɛst] *n* : plaisanterie *f* — **~** *vi* : plaisanter — **jester** ['ʤɛstər] *n* : bouffon *m*
Jesus ['ʤi:zəs, -zəz] *n* : Jésus *m*
jet ['ʤɛt] *n* **1** STREAM : jet *m* **2** *or* **~ airplane** : jet *m*, avion *m* à réaction — **jet–propelled** *adj* : à réaction
jettison ['ʤɛṭəsən] *vt* **1** : jeter par-dessus bord **2** DISCARD : se débarrasser de
jetty ['ʤɛṭi] *n, pl* **-ties** : jetée *f*
jewel ['ʤu:əl] *n* : bijou *m* — **jeweler** *or* **jeweller** ['ʤu:ələr] *n* : bijoutier *m*, -tière *f*; joaillier *m*, -lière *f* — **jewelry** *or Brit* **jewellery** ['ʤu:əlri] *n* : bijoux *mpl*
Jewish ['ʤu:ɪʃ] *adj* : juif
jibe ['ʤaɪb] *vi* **jibed; jibing** AGREE : concorder
jiffy ['ʤɪfi] *n, pl* **-fies** : instant *m*
jig ['ʤɪg] *n* : gigue *f* (danse)
jiggle ['ʤɪgəl] *vt* **-gled; -gling** : secouer, agiter — **~** *n* : secousse *f*

jigsaw [ˈʤɪg,sɔ] *n or* ~ **puzzle** : puzzle *m*
jilt [ˈʤɪlt] *vt* : laisser tomber
jingle [ˈʤɪŋgəl] *v* **-gled; -gling** *vi* : tinter — ~ *vt* : faire tinter — ~ *n* : tintement *m*
jinx [ˈʤɪŋks] *n* : mauvais sort *m*
jitters [ˈʤɪṭərz] *npl* **have the** ~ : être nerveux — **jittery** [ˈʤɪṭəri] *adj* : nerveux
job [ˈʤab] *n* **1** EMPLOYMENT : emploi *m* **2** TASK : travail *m,* tâche *f*
jockey [ˈʤaki] *n, pl* **-eys** : jockey *m*
jog [ˈʤag] *vi* **jogged; jogging** : faire du jogging — **jogging** [ˈʤagɪŋ] *n* : jogging *m*
join [ˈʤɔɪn] *vt* **1** UNITE : joindre, unir **2** MEET : rejoindre **3** : devenir membre de (un club, etc.) — *vi or* ~ **together** : s'unir, se joindre
joint [ʤɔɪnt] *n* **1** : articulation *f* (en anatomie) **2** : joint *m* (en menuiserie) — ~ *adj* : commun
joke [ˈʤo:k] *n* : plaisanterie *f,* blague *f* — ~ *vi* **joked; joking** : plaisanter — **joker** [ˈʤo:kər] *n* **1** : blagueur *m,* -gueuse *f* **2** : joker *m* (aux cartes)
jolly [ˈʤali] *adj* **-lier; -est** : jovial, gai
jolt [ˈʤo:lt] *vt* : secouer — ~ *n* **1** : secousse *f,* coup *m* **2** SHOCK : choc *m*
jostle [ˈʤasəl] *v* **-tled; -tling** *vt* : bousculer — *vi* : se bousculer
jot [ˈʤat] *vt* **jotted; jotting** *or* ~ **down** : prendre note de
journal [ˈʤərnəl] *n* **1** DIARY : journal *m* (intime) **2** PERIODICAL : revue *f* — **journalism** [ˈʤərnəl,ɪzəm] *n* : journalisme *m* — **journalist** [ˈdʒərnəlɪst] *n* : journaliste *mf*
journey [ˈʤərni] *n, pl* **-neys** : voyage *m*
jovial [ˈʤo:viəl] *adj* : jovial
joy [ˈʤɔɪ] *n* : joie *f* — **joyful** [ˈʤɔɪfəl] *adj* : joyeux — **joyous** [ˈʤɔɪəs] *adj* : joyeux
jubilant [ˈʤu:bələnt] *adj* : débordant de joie — **jubilee** [ˈʤu:bə,li:] *n* : jubilé *m*
Judaism [ˈʤu:də,ɪzəm, ˈʤu:di-, ˈʤu:-,deɪ-] *n* : judaïsme *m*
judge [ˈʤʌʤ] *vt* **judged; judging** : juger — ~ *n* : juge *m* — **judgment** *or* **judgement** [ˈʤʌʤmənt] *n* : jugement *m*
judicial [ʤʊˈdɪʃəl] *adj* : judiciaire — **judicious** [ʤʊˈdɪʃəs] *adj* : judicieux
jug [ˈʤʌg] *n* : cruche *f,* pichet *m*
juggle [ˈʤʌgəl] *vi* **-gled; -gling** : jongler — **juggler** [ˈʤʌgələr] *n* : jongleur *m,* -gleuse *f*
juice [ˈʤu:s] *n* : jus *m* — **juicy** [ˈʤu:si] *adj* **juicier; juiciest** : juteux
July [ʤʊˈlaɪ] *n* : juillet *m*
jumble [ˈʤʌmbəl] *vt* **-bled; -bling** : mélanger — ~ *n* : fouillis *m,* désordre *m*
jumbo [ˈʤʌm,bo:] *adj* : géant
jump [ˈʤʌmp] *vi* **1** LEAP : sauter **2** START : sursauter **3** RISE : faire un bond **4** ~ **at** : saisir (une occasion, etc.) — *vt or* ~ **over** : sauter — ~ *n* **1** LEAP : saut *m* **2** INCREASE : hausse *f* — **jumper** [ˈʤʌmpər] *n* **1** : sauteur *m,* -teuse *f* (aux sports) **2** : robe-chasuble *f* (vêtement) — **jumpy** [ˈʤʌmpi] *adj* **jumpier; jumpiest** : nerveux
junction [ˈʤʌŋkʃən] *n* **1** : jonction *f* **2** : carrefour *m,* embranchement *m* (de deux routes) — **juncture** [ˈʤʌŋkʧər] *n* : conjoncture *f*
June [ˈʤu:n] *n* : juin *m*
jungle [ˈʤʌŋgəl] *n* : jungle *f*
junior [ˈʤu:njər] *adj* **1** YOUNGER : cadet, plus jeune **2** SUBORDINATE : subalterne — ~ *n* **1** : cadet *m,* -dette *f* **2** : étudiant *m,* -diante *f* de troisième année
junk [ˈʤʌŋk] *n* : camelote *f fam*
Jupiter [ˈʤu:pəṭər] *n* : Jupiter *f*
jurisdiction [,ʤʊrəsˈdɪkʃən] *n* : juridiction *f*
jury [ˈdʒʊri] *n, pl* **-ries** : jury *m* — **juror** [ˈʤʊrər] *n* : juré *m,* -rée *f*
just [ˈʤʌst] *adj* : juste — ~ *adv* **1** BARELY : à peine **2** EXACTLY : exactement **3** ONLY : seulement **4** **he has** ~ **arrived** : il vient d'arriver **5** **it's** ~ **perfect** : c'est parfait
justice [ˈʤʌstɪs] *n* **1** : justice *f* **2** JUDGE : juge *m*
justify [ˈʤʌstə,faɪ] *vt* **-fied; -fying** : justifier — **justification** [,ʤʌstəfəˈkeɪʃən] *n* : justification *f*
jut [ˈʤʌt] *vi* **jutted; jutting** *or* ~ **out** : dépasser, faire saillie
juvenile [ˈʤu:və,naɪl, -vənəl] *adj* **1** YOUNG : jeune **2** CHILDISH : puéril — ~ *n* : jeune *mf*
juxtapose [ˈʤʌkstə,po:z] *vt* **-posed; -posing** : juxtaposer

K

k [ˈkeɪ] *n, pl* **k's** *or* **ks** [ˈkeɪz] : k *m,* onzième lettre de l'alphabet
kangaroo [ˌkæŋgəˈru:] *n, pl* **-roos** : kangourou *m*
karat [ˈkærət] *n* : carat *m*
karate [kəˈruṭi] *n* : karaté *m*
keel [ˈki:l] *n* : quille *f* — **~** *vi or* **~ over** : chavirer (se dit d'un bateau), s'écrouler (se dit d'une personne)
keen [ˈki:n] *adj* **1** PENETRATING : vif, pénétrant **2** ENTHUSIASTIC : enthousiaste
keep [ˈki:p] *v* **kept** [ˈkɛpt]; **keeping** *vt* **1** : garder **2** : tenir (une promesse, etc.) **3** DETAIN : retenir **4** PREVENT : empêcher **5 ~ up** : maintenir — *vi* **1** STAY : se tenir, rester **2** LAST : se conserver, se garder **3** *or* **~ on** CONTINUE : continuer — **~** *n* **for ~s** : pour de bon — **keeper** [ˈki:pər] *n* : gardien *m,* -dienne *f* — **keeping** [ˈki:pɪŋ] *n* **1** CARE : garde *f* **2 in ~ with** : en accord avec — **keepsake** [ˈki:pˌseɪk] *n* : souvenir *m*
keg [ˈkɛg] *n* : baril *m,* tonnelet *m*
kennel [ˈkɛnəl] *n* : niche *f*
kept → **keep**
kerchief [ˈkərtʃəf, -ˌtʃi:f] *n* : fichu *m*
kernel [ˈkərnəl] *n* **1** : amande *f* **2** CORE : noyau *m,* cœur *m*
kerosene *or* **kerosine** [ˈkɛrəˌsi:n, ˌkɛrəˈ-] *n* : kérosène *m,* pétrole *m* lampant
ketchup [ˈkɛtʃəp, ˈkæ-] *n* : ketchup *m*
kettle [ˈkɛtəl] *n* : bouilloire *f*
key [ˈki:] *n* **1** : clé *f* **2** : touche *f* (d'un clavier) — **~** *adj* : clé — **keyboard** [ˈki:ˌbord] *n* : clavier *m* — **keyhole** [ˈki:ˌho:l] *n* : trou *m* de serrure
khaki [ˈkæki, ˈku-] *adj* : kaki
kick [ˈkɪk] *vt* : donner un coup de pied à — *vi* : donner un coup de pied — **~** *n* **1** : coup *m* de pied **2** PLEASURE, THRILL : plaisir *m*
kid [ˈkɪd] *n* **1** GOAT : chevreau *m* **2** CHILD : gosse *mf France fam;* flot *m Can* — **~** *v* **kidded; kidding** *vi or* **~ around** : blaguer, plaisanter — *vt* TEASE : taquiner — **kidnap** [ˈkɪdˌnæp] *vt* **-napped** *or* **-naped** [-ˌnæpt]; **-napping** *or* **-naping** [-ˌnæpɪŋ] : kidnapper, enlever
kidney [ˈkɪdˌni] *n, pl* **-neys** : rein *m*
kill [ˈkɪl] *v* : tuer — **~** *n* **1** KILLING : mise *f* à mort **2** PREY : proie *f* — **killer** [ˈkɪlər] *n* : meurtrier *m,* -trière *f;* tueur *m,* tueuse *f* — **killing** [ˈkɪlɪŋ] *n* : meurtre *m*
kiln [ˈkɪl, ˈkɪln] *n* : four *m*
kilo [ˈki:ˌlo:] *n, pl* **-los** : kilo *m* — **kilogram** [ˈkɪləˌgræm, ˈki:-] *n* : kilogramme *m* — **kilometer** [kɪˈlamətər, ˈkɪləˌmi:-] *n* : kilomètre *m* — **kilowatt** [ˈkɪləˌwat] *n* : kilowatt *m*
kin [ˈkɪn] *n* : parents *mpl,* famille *f*
kind [ˈkaɪnd] *n* : espèce *f,* genre *m,* sorte *f* — **~** *adj* : gentil, bienveillant
kindergarten [ˈkɪndərˌgartən, -dən] *n* : jardin *m* d'enfants *France,* école *f* maternelle *Can*
kindhearted [ˈkaɪndˈharṭəd] *adj* : bon, qui a bon cœur
kindle [ˈkɪndəl] *v* **-dled; -dling** *vt* : allumer — *vi* : s'enflammer
kindly [ˈkaɪndli] *adj* **-lier; -est** : bienveillant — **~** *adv* **1** : avec gentillesse **2** OBLIGINGLY : gentiment — **kindness** [ˈkaɪndnəs] *n* : gentillesse *f,* bonté *f* — **kind of** *adv* SOMEWHAT : quelque peu
kindred [ˈkɪndrəd] *adj* **1** : apparenté **2 ~ spirit** : âme *f* sœur
king [ˈkɪŋ] *n* : roi *m* — **kingdom** [ˈkɪŋdəm] *n* : royaume *m*
kink [ˈkɪŋk] *n* **1** TWIST : nœud *m* **2** FLAW : défaut *m,* problème *m*
kinship [ˈkɪnˌʃɪp] *n* : parenté *f*
kiss [ˈkɪs] *vt* : embrasser, donner un baiser à — *vi* : s'embrasser — **~** *n* : baiser *m*
kit [ˈkɪt] *n* : trousse *f*
kitchen [ˈkɪtʃən] *n* : cuisine *f*
kite [ˈkaɪt] *n* : cerf-volant *m*
kitten [ˈkɪtən] *n* : chaton *m* — **kitty** [ˈkɪṭi] *n, pl* **-ties** FUND : cagnotte *f*
knack [ˈnæk] *n* TALENT : don *m*
knapsack [ˈnæpˌsæk] *n* : sac *m* à dos
knead [ˈni:d] *vt* : pétrir
knee [ˈni:] *n* : genou *m* — **kneecap** [ˈni:ˌkæp] *n* : rotule *f*
kneel [ˈni:l] *vi* **knelt** [ˈnɛlt] *or* **kneeled** [ˈni:ld]; **kneeling** : s'agenouiller
knew → **know**
knife [naɪf] *n, pl* **knives** [ˈnaɪvz] : couteau *m* — **~** *vt* **knifed** [naɪft]; **knifing** : donner un coup de couteau à
knight [ˈnaɪt] *n* **1** : chevalier *m* **2** : ca-

valier *m* (aux échecs) — **knighthood** [ˈnaɪtˌhuːd] *n* : titre *m* de chevalier
knit [ˈnɪt] *v* **knit** *or* **knitted** [ˈnɪţəd]; **knitting** : tricoter — **knitting** [ˈnɪtɪŋ] *n* : tricot *m*
knob [ˈnɑb] *n* : poignée *f*, bouton *m*
knock [ˈnɑk] *vt* **1** HIT : cogner, frapper **2** CRITICIZE : critiquer **3 ~ down** *or* **~ over** : renverser **4 ~ out** : assommer — *vi* **1** : frapper (à la porte) **2** : cogner (se dit d'un moteur) **3 ~ into** : heurter
knot [ˈnɑt] *n* : nœud *m* — **~** *vt* **knotted; knotting** : nouer, faire un nœud à — **knotty** [ˈnɑţi] *adj* **-tier; -est** : épineux (se dit d'un problème)
know [ˈnoː] *v* **knew** [ˈnuː, ˈnjuː]; **known** [ˈnoːn]; **knowing** *vt* **1** : savoir **2** : connaître (une personne, un lieu) **3** UNDERSTAND : comprendre — *vi* **1** : savoir **2 ~ about** : être au courant de, s'y connaître en (un sujet) — **knowing** [ˈnoːɪŋ] *adj* : entendu — **knowingly** [ˈnoːɪŋli] *adv* INTENTIONALLY : sciemment — **knowledge** [ˈnɑlɪʤ] *n* **1** : connaissance *f* **2** LEARNING : connaissances *fpl*, savoir *m* — **knowledgeable** [ˈnɑlɪʤəbəl] *adj* : bien informé
knuckle [ˈnʌkəl] *n* : jointure *f* du doigt, articulation *f* du doigt
Koran [kəˈrɑn, -ˈræn] *n* **the ~** : le Coran
Korean [kəˈriːən] *adj* : coréen — **~** *n* : coréen *m* (langue)
kosher [ˈkoːʃər] *adj* : kascher, casher

L

l [ˈɛl] *n, pl* **l's** *or* **ls** [ˈɛlz] : l *m*, douzième lettre de l'alphabet
lab [ˈlæb] → **laboratory**
label [ˈleɪbəl] *n* **1** TAG : étiquette *f* **2** BRAND : marque *f* — **~** *vt* **-beled** *or* **-belled; -beling** *or* **-belling** : étiqueter
labor *or Brit* **labour** [ˈleɪbər] *n* **1** : travail *m* **2** WORKERS : main-d'œuvre *f* **3 in ~** : en train d'accoucher — **~** *vi* **1** : travailler **2** STRUGGLE : avancer péniblement — *vt* : insister sur (un point)
laboratory [ˈlæbrəˌtori, ləˈbɔrə-] *n, pl* **-ries** : laboratoire *m*
laborer *or Brit* **labourer** [ˈleɪbərər] *n* : ouvrier *m*, -vrière *f*
laborious [ləˈboriəs] *adj* : laborieux
lace [ˈleɪs] *n* **1** : dentelle *f* **2** SHOELACE : lacet *m* — **~** *vt* **laced; lacing 1** TIE : lacer **2 be laced with** : être mêlé de (se dit d'une boisson)
lacerate [ˈlæsəˌreɪt] *vt* **-ated; -ating** : lacérer
lack [ˈlæk] *vt* : manquer de, ne pas avoir — *vi or* **be lacking** : manquer — **~** *n* : manque *m*, carence *f*
lackadaisical [ˌlækəˈdeɪzɪkəl] *adj* : apathique, indolent
lackluster [ˈlækˌlʌstər] *adj* : terne, fade
lacquer [ˈlækər] *n* : laque *m*
lacrosse [ləˈkrɔs] *n* : crosse *f*
lacy [ˈleɪsi] *adj* **lacier; -est** : de dentelle
lad [ˈlæd] *n* : gars *m*, garçon *m*
ladder [ˈlædər] *n* : échelle *f*
laden [ˈleɪdən] *adj* : chargé
ladle [ˈleɪdəl] *n* : louche *f* — **~** *vt* **-dled; -dling** : servir à la louche
lady [ˈleɪdi] *n, pl* **-dies** : dame *f*, madame *f* — **ladybug** [ˈleɪdiˌbʌg] *n* : coccinelle *f* — **ladylike** [ˈleɪdiˌlaɪk] *adj* : élégant, de dame
lag [ˈlæg] *n* **1** DELAY : retard *m* **2** INTERVAL : décalage *m* — **~** *vi* **lagged; lagging** : traîner, être en retard
lager [ˈlɑgər] *n* : bière *f* blonde
lagoon [ləˈguːn] *n* : lagune *f*
laid *pp* → **lay**[1]
lain *pp* → **lie**[1]
lair [ˈlær] *n* : tanière *f*
lake [ˈleɪk] *n* : lac *m*
lamb [ˈlæm] *n* : agneau *m*
lame [ˈleɪm] *adj* **lamer; lamest 1** : boiteux **2 a ~ excuse** : une excuse peu convaincante
lament [ləˈmɛnt] *vt* **1** MOURN : pleurer **2** DEPLORE : déplorer — **~** *n* : lamentation *f* — **lamentable** [ˈlæməntəbəl, ləˈmɛntə-] *adj* : lamentable
laminate [ˈlæməˌneɪt] *vt* **-nated; -nating** : laminer
lamp [ˈlæmp] *n* : lampe *f* — **lamppost** [ˈlæmpˌpost] *n* : réverbère *m* — **lampshade** [ˈlæmpˌʃeɪd] *n* : abat-jour *m*
lance [ˈlænts] *n* : lance *f* — **~** *vt* **lanced; lancing** : percer (en médecine)
land [ˈlænd] *n* **1** : terre *f* **2** COUNTRY : pays *m* **3** *or* **plot of ~** : terrain *m* — **~** *vt* **1** : faire un atterrissage, débarquer (des passagers) **2** CATCH : attraper (un poisson) **3** SECURE : décrocher

(un emploi, etc.) — *vi* **1** : atterrir (se dit d'un avion) **2** FALL : tomber — **landing** [ˈlændɪŋ] *n* **1** : atterrissage *m* (d'un avion) **2** : débarquement *m* (d'un navire) **3** : palier *m* (d'un escalier) — **landlady** [ˈlændˌleɪdi] *n, pl* **-dies** : propriétaire *f* — **landlord** [ˈlændˌlɔrd] *n* : propriétaire *m* — **landmark** [ˈlændˌmɑrk] *n* **1** : point *m* de repère **2** MONUMENT : monument *m* historique — **landowner** [ˈlændˌoːnər] *n* : propriétaire *m* foncier, propriétaire *f* foncière — **landscape** [ˈlændˌskeɪp] *n* : paysage *m* — ~ *vt* **-scaped; -scaping** : aménager — **landslide** [ˈlændˌslaɪd] *n* **1** : glissement *m* de terrain **2** *or* ~ **victory** : victoire *f* écrasante

lane [ˈleɪn] *n* **1** : voie *f* (d'une autoroute) **2** PATH, ROAD : chemin *m*

language [ˈlæŋgwɪdʒ] *n* **1** : langue *f* **2** SPEECH : langage *m*

languid [ˈlæŋgwɪd] *adj* : languissant — **languish** [ˈlæŋgwɪʃ] *vi* : languir

lanky [ˈlæŋki] *adj* **lankier; -est** : grand et maigre, dégingandé

lantern [ˈlæntərn] *n* : lanterne *f*

lap [ˈlæp] *n* **1** : genoux *mpl* **2** : tour *m* de piste (aux sports) — ~ *v* **lapped; lapping** *vt or* ~ **up** : boire à petites gorgées — *vi* ~ **against** : clapoter

lapel [ləˈpɛl] *n* : revers *m*

lapse [ˈlæps] *n* **1** : trou *m* (de mémoire, etc.) **2** INTERVAL : laps *m*, intervalle *m* — ~ *vi* **lapsed; lapsing 1** EXPIRE : expirer **2** ELAPSE : passer **3** ~ **into** : tomber dans

laptop [ˈlæpˌtɑp] *adj* : portable

larceny [ˈlɑrsəni] *n, pl* **-nies** : vol *m*

lard [ˈlɑrd] *n* : saindoux *m*

large [ˈlɑrdʒ] *adj* **larger; largest 1** : grand **2 at** ~ : en liberté **3 by and** ~ : en général — **largely** [ˈlɑrdʒli] *adv* : en grande partie

lark [ˈlɑrk] *n* **1** : alouette *f* (oiseau) **2 for a** ~ : comme divertissement

larva [ˈlɑrvə] *n, pl* **-vae** [-ˌviː, -ˌvaɪ] : larve *f*

larynx [ˈlærɪŋks] *n, pl* **-rynges** [ləˈrɪnˌdʒiːz] *or* **-ynxes** [ˈlærɪŋksəz] : larynx *m* — **laryngitis** [ˌlærənˈdʒaɪt̬əs] *n* : laryngite *f*

lasagna [ləˈzɑnjə] *n* : lasagnes *fpl*

laser [ˈleɪzər] *n* : laser *m*

lash [ˈlæʃ] *vt* **1** WHIP : fouetter **2** BIND : attacher — *vi* ~ **out at** : invectiver contre — ~ *n* **1** BLOW : coup *m* de fouet **2** EYELASH : cil *m*

lass [ˈlæs] *or* **lassie** [ˈlæsi] *n* : fille *f*

lasso [ˈlæˌsoː, læˈsuː] *n, pl* **-sos** *or* **-soes** : lasso *m*

last [ˈlæst] *vi* : durer — ~ *n* **1** : dernier *m*, -nière *f* **2 at** ~ : enfin, finalement — ~ *adv* **1** : pour la dernière fois, en dernière place **2 arrive** ~ : arriver dernier — ~ *adj* **1** : dernier **2** ~ **year** : l'an passé — **lastly** [ˈlæstli] *adv* : enfin, finalement

latch [ˈlætʃ] *n* : loquet *m*, serrure *f*

late [ˈleɪt] *adj* **later; latest 1** : en retard **2** : avancé (se dit de l'heure) **3** DECEASED : défunt **4** RECENT : récent — ~ *adv* **later; latest** : en retard — **lately** [ˈleɪtli] *adv* : récemment, dernièrement — **lateness** [ˈleɪtnəs] *n* **1** : retard *m* **2** : heure *f* avancée

latent [ˈleɪtənt] *adj* : latent

lateral [ˈlæt̬ərəl] *adj* : latéral

latest [ˈleɪt̬əst] *n* **at the** ~ : au plus tard

lathe [ˈleɪð] *n* : tour *m*

lather [ˈlæðər] *n* : mousse *f* — ~ *vt* : savonner — *vi* : faire mousser

Latin [ˈlætən] *adj* : latin — ~ *n* : latin *m* (langue)

latitude [ˈlæt̬əˌtuːd, -ˌtjuːd] *n* : latitude *f*

latter [ˈlæt̬ər] *adj* **1** : dernier **2** SECOND : second — ~ *pron* **the** ~ : ce dernier, cette dernière, ces derniers

lattice [ˈlæt̬əs] *n* : treillis *m*, treillage *m*

laugh [ˈlæf] *vi* : rire — ~ *n* : rire *m* — **laughable** [ˈlæfəbəl] *adj* : risible, ridicule — **laughter** [ˈlæftər] *n* : rire *m*, rires *mpl*

launch [ˈlɔntʃ] *vt* : lancer — ~ *n* : lancement *m*

launder [ˈlɔndər] *vt* **1** : laver et repasser (du linge) **2** : blanchir (de l'argent) — **laundry** [ˈlɔndri] *n, pl* **-dries 1** : linge *m* sale **2** : blanchisserie *f* (service) **3 do the** ~ : faire la lessive

lava [ˈlɑvə, ˈlæ-] *n* : lave *f*

lavatory [ˈlævəˌtori] *n, pl* **-ries** BATHROOM : toilettes *fpl*

lavender [ˈlævəndər] *n* : lavande *f*

lavish [ˈlævɪʃ] *adj* **1** EXTRAVAGANT : prodigue **2** ABUNDANT : abondant **3** LUXURIOUS : luxueux — ~ *vt* : prodiguer

law [ˈlɔ] *n* **1** : loi *f* **2** : droit *m* (profession, etc.) **3 practice** ~ : exercer le droit — **lawful** [ˈlɔfəl] *adj* : légal, légitime

lawn [ˈlɔn] *n* : pelouse *f* — **lawn mower** *n* : tondeuse *f*

lawsuit [ˈlɔˌsuːt] *n* : procès *m*

lawyer [ˈlɔɪər, ˈlɔjər] *n* : avocat *m*, -cate *f*

lax [ˈlæks] *adj* : peu strict, relâché

laxative ['læksət̬ɪv] *n* : laxatif *m*

lay[1] ['leɪ] *vt* **laid** ['leɪd]; **laying** **1** PLACE, PUT : mettre, placer **2** ~ **eggs** : pondre des œufs **3** ~ **off** : licencier (un employé) **4** ~ **out** PRESENT : présenter, exposer **5** ~ **out** DESIGN : concevoir (un plan)

lay[2] → **lie**[1]

lay[3] *adj* **1** SECULAR : laïc **2** NONPROFESSIONAL : profane

layer ['leɪər] *n* : couche *f*

layman ['leɪmən] *n, pl* **-men** [-mən, -ˌmɛn] : profane *mf,* laïque *mf* (en religion)

layoff ['leɪˌɔf] *n* : licenciement *m,* renvoi *m*

layout ['leɪˌaʊt] *n* ARRANGEMENT : disposition *f*

lazy ['leɪzi] *adj* **-zier; -est** : paresseux — **laziness** ['leɪzinəs] *n* : paresse *f*

lead[1] ['li:d] *v* **led** ['lɛd]; **leading** *vt* **1** GUIDE : conduire **2** DIRECT : diriger **3** HEAD : être à la tête de, aller au devant de — *vi* : mener, conduire (à) — ~ *n* **1** : devant *m* **2 follow s.o.'s** ~ : suivre l'exemple de qqn

lead[2] ['lɛd] *n* **1** : plomb *m* (métal) **2** : mine *f* (d'un crayon) — **leaden** ['lɛdən] *adj* **1** : de plomb **2** HEAVY : lourd

leader ['li:dər] *n* : chef *m;* dirigeant *m,* -geante *f* — **leadership** ['li:dərˌʃɪp] *n* : direction *f,* dirigeants *mpl*

leaf ['li:f] *n, pl* **leaves** ['li:vz] **1** : feuille *f* **2 turn over a new** ~ : tourner la page — ~ *vi* ~ **through** : feuilleter (se dit d'un livre, etc.) — **leaflet** ['li:flət] *n* : dépliant *m,* prospectus *m*

league ['li:g] *n* **1** : lieue *f* **2 be in** ~ **with** : être de mèche avec

leak ['li:k] *vt* **1** : faire couler (un liquide ou un gaz) **2** : divulguer (un secret) — *vi* **1** : fuir, s'échapper (se dit d'un liquide ou d'un gaz) **2** : être divulgué (se dit de l'information) — ~ *n* : fuite *f* — **leaky** ['li:ki] *adj* **leakier; -est** : qui prend l'eau

lean[1] ['li:n] *v* **leaned** *or Brit* **leant** ['lɛnt]; **leaning** ['li:nɪŋ] *vi* **1** BEND : se pencher **2** ~ **against** : s'appuyer contre — *vt* : appuyer

lean[2] *adj* : mince (se dit d'une personne), maigre (se dit de la viande)

leaning ['li:nɪŋ] *n* : tendance *f*

leanness ['li:nnəs] *n* : minceur *f* (d'une personne), maigreur *f* (de la viande)

leap ['li:p] *vi* **leaped** *or* **leapt** ['li:pt, 'lɛpt]; **leaping** : sauter, bondir — ~ *n* : saut *m,* bond *m* — **leap year** *n* : année *f* bissextile

learn ['lərn] *v* **learned** ['lərnd, 'lərnt] *or Brit* **learnt** ['lərnt]; **learning** : apprendre — **learned** ['lərnəd] *adj* : savant, érudit — **learner** ['lərnər] *n* : débutant *m,* -tante *f;* étudiant *m,* -diante *f* — **learning** ['lərnɪŋ] *n* : savoir *m,* érudition *f*

lease ['li:s] *n* : bail *m* — ~ *vt* **leased; leasing** : louer à bail

leash ['li:ʃ] *n* : laisse *f*

least ['li:st] *adj* **1** : moins **2** SLIGHTEST : moindre — ~ *n* **1 at** ~ : au moins **2 the** ~ : le moins — ~ *adv* : moins

leather ['lɛðər] *n* : cuir *m*

leave ['li:v] *v* **left** ['lɛft]; **leaving** *vt* **1** : quitter **2** : sortir de (un endroit) **3** ~ **out** : omettre — *vi* DEPART : partir — ~ *n or* ~ **of absence** : congé *m*

leaves → **leaf**

lecture ['lɛktʃər] *n* **1** TALK : conférence *f* **2** REPRIMAND : sermon *m,* réprimande *f* — ~ *v* **-tured; -turing** *vt* : sermonner — *vi* : donner un cours, donner une conférence

led → **lead**[1]

ledge ['lɛʤ] *n* : rebord *m* (d'une fenêtre, etc.), saillie *f* (d'une montagne)

leech ['li:ʧ] *n* : sangsue *f*

leek ['li:k] *n* : poireau *m*

leer ['lɪr] *vi* : jeter un regard lascif — ~ *n* : regard *m* lascif

leery ['lɪri] *adj* : méfiant

leeway ['li:ˌweɪ] *n* : liberté *f* d'action, marge *f* de manœuvre

left[1] → **leave**

left[2] ['lɛft] *adj* : gauche — ~ *adv* : à gauche — ~ *n* : gauche *f* — **left-handed** ['lɛft'handəd] *adj* : gaucher

leftovers ['lɛftˌo:vərz] *npl* : restes *mpl*

leg ['lɛg] *n* **1** : patte *f* (d'un animal), jambe *f* (d'une personne ou d'un pantalon), pied *m* (d'une table, etc.) **2** : étape *f* (d'un voyage)

legacy ['lɛgəsi] *n, pl* **-cies** : legs *m*

legal ['li:gəl] *adj* **1** LAWFUL : légitime, légal **2** JUDICIAL : juridique — **legality** [li'gælət̬i] *n, pl* **-ties** : légalité *f* — **legalize** ['li:gəˌlaɪz] *vt* **-ized; -izing** : légaliser

legend ['lɛʤənd] *n* : légende *f* — **legendary** ['lɛʤənˌdɛri] *adj* : légendaire

legible ['lɛʤəbəl] *adj* : lisible

legion ['li:ʤən] *n* : légion *f*

legislate ['lɛʤəsˌleɪt] *vi* **-lated; -lating** : légiférer — **legislation** [ˌlɛʤəs'leɪʃən] *n* : législation *f* — **legislative** ['lɛʤəsˌleɪt̬ɪv] *adj* : législatif — **legis-**

lature [ˈlɛʤəs,leɪtʃər] *n* : corps *m* législatif
legitimate [lɪˈʤɪtəmət] *adj* : légitime — **legitimacy** [lɪˈʤɪtəməsi] *n* : légitimité *f*
leisure [ˈli:ʒər, ˈlɛ-] *n* **1** : loisir *m*, temps *m* libre **2 at your ~** : à votre convenance — **leisurely** [ˈli:ʒərli, ˈlɛ-] *adv* : lentement, sans se presser — **~** *adj* : lent
lemon [ˈlɛmən] *n* : citron *m* — **lemonade** [,lɛməˈneɪd] *n* : limonade *f*
lend [ˈlɛnd] *vt* **lent** [ˈlɛnt]; **lending** : prêter
length [ˈlɛŋkθ] *n* **1** : longueur *f* **2** DURATION : durée *f* **3 at ~** FINALLY : finalement **4 at ~** EXTENSIVELY : longuement **5 go to any ~s** : faire tout son possible — **lengthen** [ˈlɛŋkθən] *vt* **1** : rallonger **2** PROLONG : prolonger — *vi* : s'allonger — **lengthways** [ˈlɛŋkθ,weɪz] *or* **lengthwise** [ˈlɛŋkθ,waɪz] *adv* : dans le sens de la longueur — **lengthy** [ˈlɛŋkθi] *adj* **lengthier; -est** : long
lenient [ˈli:niənt] *adj* : indulgent — **leniency** [ˈli:niəntsi] *n* : indulgence *f*
lens [ˈlɛnz] *n* **1** : lentille *f* (d'un instrument) **2** → **contact lens**
Lent [ˈlɛnt] *n* : carême *m*
lentil [ˈlɛntəl] *n* : lentille *f*
leopard [ˈlɛpərd] *n* : léopard *m*
leotard [ˈli:ə,tard] *n* : justaucorps *m*
lesbian [ˈlɛzbiən] *n* : lesbienne *f*
less [ˈlɛs] *adv & adj* (*comparative of* **little**) : moins — **~** *pron* : moins — **~** *prep* MINUS : moins — **lessen** [ˈlɛsən] *v* : diminuer — **lesser** [ˈlɛsər] *adj* : moindre
lesson [ˈlɛsən] *n* **1** CLASS : classe *f*, cours *m* **2 learn one's ~** : servir de leçon
lest [ˈlɛst] *conj* **~ we forget** : de peur que nous n'oublions
let [ˈlɛt] *vt* **let; letting 1** ALLOW : laisser, permettre **2** RENT : louer **3 ~'s go!** : allons-y! **4 ~ down** DISAPPOINT : décevoir **5 ~ in** : laisser entrer **6 ~ off** FORGIVE : pardonner **7 ~ up** ABATE : diminuer, arrêter
letdown [ˈlɛt,daʊn] *n* : déception *f*
lethal [ˈli:θəl] *adj* : mortel
lethargic [lɪˈθarʤɪk] *adj* : léthargique
let's [ˈlɛts] (*contraction of* **let us**) → **let**
letter [ˈlɛtər] *n* : lettre *f*
lettuce [ˈlɛtəs] *n* : laitue *f*
letup [ˈlɛt,əp] *n* : pause *f*, répit *m*
leukemia [lu:ˈki:miə] *n* : leucémie *f*
level [ˈlɛvəl] *n* **1** : niveau *m* **2 be on the ~** : être franc — **~** *vt* **-eled** *or* **-elled; -eling** *or* **-elling 1** : niveler **2** AIM : diriger **3** RAZE : raser — **~** *adj* **1** FLAT : plat, plan **2 ~ with** : au même niveau que — **levelheaded** [ˈlɛvəlˈhɛdəd] *adj* : sensé, équilibré
lever [ˈlɛvər, ˈli:-] *n* : levier *m* — **leverage** [ˈlɛvərɪʤ, ˈli:-] *n* **1** : force *f* de levier (en physique) **2** INFLUENCE : influence *f*
levity [ˈlɛvəti] *n* : légèreté *f*
levy [ˈlɛvi] *n, pl* **levies** : impôt *m* — **~** *vt* **levied; levying** : imposer, prélever (une taxe)
lewd [ˈlu:d] *adj* : lascif
lexicon [ˈlɛksɪ,kan] *n, pl* **-ica** [-kə] *or* **-icons** : lexique *m*
liable [ˈlaɪəbəl] *adj* **1** : responsable **2** LIKELY : probable **3** SUSCEPTIBLE : sujet — **liability** [,laɪəˈbɪləti] *n, pl* **-ties 1** RESPONSIBILITY : responsabilité *f* **2** DRAWBACK : désavantage *m* **3 liabilities** *npl* DEBTS : dettes *fpl*, passif *m*
liaison [ˈli:ə,zan, liˈeɪ-] *n* : liaison *f*
liar [ˈlaɪər] *n* : menteur *m*, -teuse *f*
libel [ˈlaɪbəl] *n* : diffamation *f* — **~** *vt* **-beled** *or* **-belled; -beling** *or* **-belling** : diffamer
liberal [ˈlɪbrəl, ˈlɪbərəl] *adj* : libéral — **~** *n* : libéral *m*, -rale *f*
liberate [ˈlɪbə,reɪt] *vt* **-ated; -ating** : libérer — **liberation** [,lɪbəˈreɪʃən] *n* : libération *f*
liberty [ˈlɪbərti] *n, pl* **-ties** : liberté *f*
library [ˈlaɪ,brɛri] *n, pl* **-braries** : bibliothèque *f* — **librarian** [laɪˈbrɛriən] *n* : bibliothécaire *mf*
lice → **louse**
license *or* **licence** *n* **1** PERMIT : permis *m* **2** FREEDOM : licence *f* **3** AUTHORIZATION : permission *f* — **~** [ˈlaɪsənts] *vt* **-censed; -censing** : autoriser
lick [ˈlɪk] *vt* **1** : lécher **2** DEFEAT : battre (à plate couture) — **~** *n* : coup *m* de langue
licorice *or Brit* **liquorice** [ˈlɪkərɪʃ, -rəs] *n* : réglisse *f*
lid [ˈlɪd] *n* **1** : couvercle *m* **2** EYELID : paupière *f*
lie[1] [ˈlaɪ] *vi* **lay** [ˈleɪ]; **lain** [ˈleɪn]; **lying** [ˈlaɪɪŋ] **1** *or* **~ down** : se coucher, s'allonger **2** BE : être, se trouver
lie[2] *vi* **lied; lying** [ˈlaɪɪŋ] : mentir — **~** *n* : mensonge *m*
lieutenant [lu:ˈtɛnənt] *n* : lieutenant *m*
life [ˈlaɪf] *n, pl* **lives** [ˈlaɪvz] : vie *f* — **lifeboat** [ˈlaɪf,bo:t] *n* : canot *m* de sauvetage — **lifeguard** [ˈlaɪf,gard] *n* : sauveteur *m* — **lifeless** [ˈlaɪfləs] *adj*

: sans vie — **lifelike** [ˈlaɪf͵laɪk] *adj* : naturel, réaliste — **lifelong** [ˈlaɪfˈlɔŋ] *adj* : de toute une vie — **life preserver** *n* : gilet *m* de sauvetage — **lifestyle** [ˈlaɪf͵staɪl] *n* : mode *m* de vie — **lifetime** [ˈlaɪf͵taɪm] *n* : vie *f*

lift [ˈlɪft] *vt* **1** RAISE : lever **2** STEAL : voler — *vi* **1** CLEAR UP : se dissiper **2** *or* **~ off** : décoller (se dit d'un avion, etc.) — **~** *n* **1** LIFTING : soulèvement *m* **2 give s.o. a ~** : emmener qqn en voiture — **liftoff** [ˈlɪft͵ɔf] *n* : lancement *m*

light[1] [ˈlaɪt] *n* **1** : lumière *f* **2** LAMP : lampe *f* **3** HEADLIGHT : phare *m* **4 do you have a ~?** : avez-vous du feu? — **~** *adj* **1** BRIGHT : bien illuminé **2** : clair (se dit des couleurs), blond (se dit des cheveux) — **~** *v* **lit** [ˈlɪt] *or* **lighted; lighting** *vt* **1** : allumer (un feu) **2** ILLUMINATE : éclairer — *vi or* **~ up** : s'illuminer — **lightbulb** [ˈlaɪt͵bʌlb] *n* : ampoule *f* — **lighten** [ˈlaɪtən] *vt* BRIGHTEN : éclairer — **lighter** [ˈlaɪtər] *n* : briquet *m* — **lighthouse** [ˈlaɪt͵haʊs] *n* : phare *m* — **lighting** [ˈlaɪtɪŋ] *n* : éclairage *m* — **lightning** [ˈlaɪtnɪŋ] *n* : éclairs *mpl*, foudre *f* — **light-year** [ˈlaɪt͵jɪr] *n* : année-lumière *f*

light[2] *adj* : léger — **lighten** [ˈlaɪtən] *vt* : alléger — **lightly** [ˈlaɪtli] *adv* **1** : légèrement **2 let off ~** : traiter avec indulgence — **lightness** [ˈlaɪtnəs] *n* : légèreté *f* — **lightweight** [ˈlaɪt͵weɪt] *adj* : léger

like[1] [ˈlaɪk] *v* **liked; liking** *vt* **1** : aimer (qqn) **2** WANT : vouloir — *vi* **if you ~** : si vous voulez — **likes** *npl* : préférences *fpl*, goûts *mpl* — **likable** *or* **likeable** [ˈlaɪkəbəl] *adj* : sympathique

like[2] *adj* SIMILAR : pareil — **~** *prep* : comme — **~** *conj* **1** AS : comme **2** AS IF : comme si — **likelihood** [ˈlaɪkli͵hʊd] *n* : probabilité *f* — **likely** [ˈlaɪkli] *adj* **-lier; -est** : probable — **liken** [ˈlaɪkən] *vt* : comparer — **likeness** [ˈlaɪknəs] *n* : ressemblance *f* — **likewise** [ˈlaɪk͵waɪz] *adv* **1** : de même **2** ALSO : aussi

liking [ˈlaɪkɪŋ] *n* : goût *m* (pour une chose), affection *f* (pour une personne)

lilac [ˈlaɪlək, -læk, -lɑk] *n* : lilas *m*

lily [ˈlɪli] *n, pl* **lilies** : lis *m* — **lily of the valley** *n* : muguet *m*

lima bean [ˈlaɪmə] *n* : haricot *m* de Lima

limb [ˈlɪm] *n* **1** : membre *m* (en anatomie) **2** : branche *f* (d'un arbre)

limber [ˈlɪmbər] *vi* **~ up** : s'échauffer, faire des exercices d'assouplissement

limbo [ˈlɪm͵boː] *n, pl* **-bos** : limbes *mpl*

lime [ˈlaɪm] *n* : lime *f*, citron *m* vert

limelight [ˈlaɪm͵laɪt] *n* **be in the ~** : être en vedette

limerick [ˈlɪmərɪk] *n* : poème *m* humoristique en cinq vers

limestone [ˈlaɪm͵stoːn] *n* : pierre *f* à chaux, calcaire *m*

limit [ˈlɪmət] *n* : limite *f* — **~** *vt* : limiter, restreindre — **limitation** [͵lɪməˈteɪʃən] *n* : limitation *f*, restriction *f* — **limited** [ˈlɪmətəd] *adj* : limité

limousine [ˈlɪmə͵ziːn, ͵lɪməˈ-] *n* : limousine *f*

limp[1] [ˈlɪmp] *vi* : boiter — **~** *n* **have a ~** : boiter

limp[2] *adj* : mou, flasque

line [ˈlaɪn] *n* **1** : ligne *f* **2** ROPE : corde *f* **3** ROW : rangée *f* **4** QUEUE : file *f* **5** WRINKLE : ride *f* **6 drop s.o. a ~** : écrire un mot à qqn — **~** *v* **lined; lining** *vt* **1** : doubler (un vêtement, etc.), tapisser (un mur, etc.) **2** MARK : rayer, ligner **3** BORDER : border — *vi* **~ up** : se mettre en ligne, faire la queue

lineage [ˈlɪniɪʤ] *n* : lignée *f*

linear [ˈlɪniər] *adj* : linéaire

linen [ˈlɪnən] *n* : lin *m*

liner [ˈlaɪnər] *n* **1** LINING : doublure *f* **2** SHIP : paquebot *m*

lineup [ˈlaɪn͵əp] *n* **1** *or* **police ~** : rangée *f* de suspects **2** : équipe *f* (aux sports)

linger [ˈlɪŋgər] *vi* **1** : s'attarder, flâner **2** PERSIST : persister

lingerie [͵lɑnʤəˈreɪ] *n* : vêtement *m* intime féminin, lingerie *f*

lingo [ˈlɪŋgo] *n, pl* **-goes** JARGON : jargon *m*

linguistics [lɪŋˈgwɪstɪks] *n* : linguistique *f* — **linguist** [ˈlɪŋgwɪst] *n* : linguiste *mf* — **linguistic** [lɪŋˈgwɪstɪk] *adj* : linguistique

lining [ˈlaɪnɪŋ] *n* : doublure *f*

link [ˈlɪŋk] *n* **1** : maillon *m* (d'une chaîne) **2** BOND : lien *m* **3** CONNECTION : liaison *f* — **~** *vt* : relier, lier — *vi or* **~ up** : se rejoindre, se relier

linoleum [ləˈnoːliəm] *n* : linoléum *m*, prélart *m Can*

lint [ˈlɪnt] *n* : peluches *fpl*

lion [ˈlaɪən] *n* : lion *m* — **lioness** [ˈlaɪənɪs] *n* : lionne *f*

lip [ˈlɪp] *n* **1** : lèvre *f* **2** EDGE : rebord *m* — **lipstick** [ˈlɪp͵stɪk] *n* : rouge *m* à lèvres

liqueur [lɪˈkər, -ˈkʊr, -ˈkjʊr] *n* : liqueur *f*
liquid [ˈlɪkwəd] *adj* : liquide — ~ *n* : liquide *m* — **liquidate** [ˈlɪkwəˌdeɪt] *vt* **-dated; -dating** : liquider — **liquidation** [ˌlɪkwəˈdeɪʃən] *n* : liquidation *f*
liquor [ˈlɪkər] *n* : boissons *fpl* alcoolisées
lisp [ˈlɪsp] *vi* : zézayer — ~ *n* : zézaiement *m*
list[1] [ˈlɪst] *n* : liste *f* — ~ *vt* **1** ENUMERATE : faire une liste de, énumérer **2** INCLUDE : mettre (sur une liste)
list[2] *vi* : gîter (se dit d'un bateau)
listen [ˈlɪsən] *vi* **1** : écouter **2** ~ **to reason** : entendre raison — **listener** [ˈlɪsənər] *n* : auditeur *m*, -trice *f*
listless [ˈlɪstləs] *adj* : apathique
lit [ˈlɪt] *pp* → **light**[1]
litany [ˈlɪtəni] *n, pl* **-nies** : litanie *f*
liter [ˈliːt̬ər] *n* : litre *m*
literacy [ˈlɪt̬ərəsi] *n* : alphabétisation *f*
literal [ˈlɪt̬ərəl] *adj* : littéral — **literally** [ˈlɪt̬ərəli] *adv* : littéralement, au pied de la lettre
literate [ˈlɪt̬ərət] *adj* : qui sait lire et écrire
literature [ˈlɪt̬ərəˌʧʊr, -ʧər] *n* : littérature *f* — **literary** [ˈlɪt̬əˌrɛri] *adj* : littéraire
lithe [ˈlaɪð, ˈlaɪθ] *adj* : agile et gracieux
litigation [ˌlɪt̬əˈgeɪʃən] *n* : litige *m*
litre → **liter**
litter [ˈlɪt̬ər] *n* **1** RUBBISH : ordures *fpl* **2** : portée *f* (se dit d'un animal) **3** *or* **kitty** ~ : litière *f* (de chat) — ~ *vt* : mettre du désordre dans — *vi* : jeter des déchets
little [ˈlɪt̬əl] *adj* **littler** *or* **less** [ˈlɛs] *or* **lesser** [ˈlɛsər]; **littlest** *or* **least** [ˈliːst] **1** SMALL : petit **2 a** ~ SOME : un peu de **3 he speaks ~ English** : il ne parle presque pas l'anglais — ~ *adv* **less** [ˈlɛs]; **least** [ˈliːst] : peu — ~ *pron* **1** : peu *m* **2** ~ **by** ~ : peu à peu
liturgy [ˈlɪt̬ərʤi] *n, pl* **-gies** : liturgie *f* — **liturgical** [ləˈtərʤɪkəl] *adj* : liturgique
live [ˈlɪv] *v* **lived; living** *vi* **1** : vivre **2** RESIDE : habiter **3** ~ **on** : vivre de — *vt* : vivre, mener — ~ [ˈlaɪv] *adj* **1** : vivant **2** : sous tension (se dit d'un câble électrique) **3** : en direct (se dit d'un programme de télévision, etc.) — **livelihood** [ˈlaɪvliˌhʊd] *n* : subsistance *f*, gagne-pain *m* — **lively** [ˈlaɪvli] *adj* **-lier; -est** : animé, vivant — **liven** [ˈlaɪvən] *vt or* ~ **up** : animer, égayer — *vi* : s'animer
liver [ˈlɪvər] *n* : foie *m*
livestock [ˈlaɪvˌstɑk] *n* : bétail *m*
livid [ˈlɪvəd] *adj* **1** : livide **2** ENRAGED : furieux
living [ˈlɪvɪŋ] *adj* : vivant — ~ *n* **make a** ~ : gagner sa vie — **living room** *n* : salle *f* de séjour, salon *m*
lizard [ˈlɪzərd] *n* : lézard *m*
llama [ˈlɑmə, ˈjɑ-] *n* : lama *m*
load [ˈloːd] *n* **1** CARGO : chargement *m* **2** BURDEN : charge *f*, poids *m* **3 ~s of** : beaucoup de — ~ *vt* : charger
loaf[1] [ˈloːf] *n, pl* **loaves** [ˈloːvz] : pain *m*
loaf[2] *vi* : fainéanter, paresser — **loafer** [ˈloːfər] *n* **1** : fainéant *m*, fainéante *f* **2** : mocassin *m* (soulier)
loan [ˈloːn] *n* : emprunt *m*, prêt *m* — ~ *vt* : prêter
loathe [ˈloːð] *vt* **loathed; loathing** : détester — **loathsome** [ˈloːθsəm, ˈloːð-] *adj* : odieux
lobby [ˈlɑbi] *n, pl* **-bies 1** : vestibule *m* **2** *or* **political** ~ : groupe *m* de pression, lobby *m* — ~ *vt* **-bied; -bying** : faire pression sur
lobe [ˈloːb] *n* : lobe *m*
lobster [ˈlɑbstər] *n* : homard *m*
local [ˈloːkəl] *adj* : local — ~ *n* **the ~s** *npl* : les gens du coin — **locale** [loˈkæl] *n* : lieu *m* — **locality** [loˈkæləṭi] *n, pl* **-ties** : localité *f*
locate [ˈloːˌkeɪt] *vt* **-cated; -cating 1** SITUATE : situer, établir **2** FIND : trouver — **location** [loˈkeɪʃən] *n* : emplacement *m*, endroit *m*
lock[1] [ˈlɑk] *n* : mèche *f* (de cheveux)
lock[2] *n* **1** : serrure *f* (d'une porte, etc.) **2** : écluse *f* (d'un canal) — ~ *vt* **1** : fermer (à clé) **2** *or* ~ **up** CONFINE : enfermer — *vi* **1** : se fermer à clé **2** : se bloquer (se dit d'une roue, etc.) — **locker** [ˈlɑkər] *n* : vestiaire *m* — **locket** [ˈlɑkət] *n* : médaillon *m* — **locksmith** [ˈlɑkˌsmɪθ] *n* : serrurier *m*
locomotive [ˌloːkəˈmoːt̬ɪv] *n* : locomotive *f*
locust [ˈloːkəst] *n* : criquet *m*, sauterelle *f*
lodge [ˈlɑʤ] *v* **lodged; lodging** *vt* **1** HOUSE : loger, héberger **2** FILE : déposer — *vi* : se loger — ~ *n* : pavillon *m* — **lodger** [ˈlɑʤər] *n* : locataire *mf*, pensionnaire *mf* — **lodging** [ˈlɑʤɪŋ] *n* **1** : hébergement *m* **2 ~s** *npl* : logement *m*
loft [lɔft] *n* : grenier *m* (d'une maison, à foin, etc.) — **lofty** [ˈlɔfti] *adj* **loftier; -est 1** : noble, élevé **2** HAUGHTY : hautain

log ['lɔg, 'lɑg] *n* **1** : bûche *f*, rondin *m* **2** RECORD : registre *m* de bord — ~ *vi* **logged; logging 1** : tronçonner (des arbres) **2** RECORD : enregistrer, noter **3** ~ **on** : entrer (dans le système) **4** ~ **off** : sortir (du système) — **logger** ['lɔgər, 'lɑ-] *n* : bûcheron *m*, -ronne *f*

logic ['lɑʤɪk] *n* : logique *f* — **logical** ['lɑʤɪkəl] *adj* : logique — **logistics** [lə'ʤɪstɪks, lo-] *ns & pl* : logistique *f*

logo ['lo:ˌgo:] *n, pl* **logos** [-ˌgo:z] : logo *m*

loin ['lɔɪn] *n* : filet *m*

loiter ['lɔɪt̬ər] *vi* : traîner, flâner

lollipop *or* **lollypop** ['lɑliˌpɑp] *n* : sucette *f France*, suçon *m Can*

lone ['lo:n] *adj* : solitaire — **loneliness** ['lo:nlinəs] *n* : solitude *f* — **lonely** ['lo:nli] *adj* **-lier; -est** : solitaire, seul — **loner** ['lo:nər] *n* : solitaire *mf* — **lonesome** ['lo:nsəm] *adj* : seul, solitaire

long[1] ['lɔŋ] *adj* **longer** ['lɔŋgər]; **longest** ['lɔŋgəst] : long — ~ *adv* **1** : longtemps **2 all day** ~ : toute la journée **3 as** ~ **as** : tant que **4 no** ~**er** : ne…plus **5 so** ~**!** : à bientôt! — ~ *n* **1 before** ~ : dans peu de temps **2 the** ~ **and short of it** : l'essentiel *m*

long[2] *vi* ~ **for** : avoir envie de, désirer

longevity [lɑn'ʤɛvət̬i] *n* : longévité *f*

longing ['lɔŋɪŋ] *n* : envie *f*

longitude ['lɑnʤəˌtu:d, -ˌtju:d] *n* : longitude *f*

look ['lʊk] *vi* **1** : regarder **2** SEEM : sembler **3** ~ **after** : prendre soin (de) **4** ~ **for** EXPECT : attendre **5** ~ **for** SEEK : chercher **6** ~ **into** : enquêter **7** ~ **out** : faire attention **8** ~ **over** EXAMINE : examiner **9** ~ **up to** : respecter — *vt* : regarder — ~ *n* **1** : coup *m* d'œil, regard *m* **2** APPEARANCE : aspect *m*, air *m* — **lookout** ['lʊkˌaʊt] *n* **1** : poste *m* d'observation **2** WATCHMAN : guetteur *m* **3 be on the** ~ : faire le guet

loom[1] ['lu:m] *n* : métier *m* à tisser

loom[2] *vi* **1** APPEAR : surgir **2** APPROACH : être imminent

loop ['lu:p] *n* : boucle *f* — ~ *vt* : faire une boucle avec — **loophole** ['lu:pˌho:l] *n* : échappatoire *m*

loose ['lu:s] *adj* **looser; -est 1** MOVABLE : desserré **2** SLACK : lâche **3** ROOMY : ample **4** APPROXIMATE : approximatif **5** FREE : libre **6** IMMORAL : dissolu — **loosely** ['lu:sli] *adv* **1** : sans serrer **2** ROUGHLY : approximativement — **loosen** ['lu:sən] *vt* : desserrer

loot ['lu:t] *n* : butin *m* — ~ *vt* : piller, saccager — **looter** ['lu:t̬ər] *n* : pillard *m*, -larde *f* — **looting** ['lu:t̬ɪŋ] *n* : pillage *m*

lop ['lɑp] *vt* **lopped; lopping** : couper, élaguer

lopsided ['lɑpˌsaɪdəd] *adj* : de travers, croche *Can*

lord ['lɔrd] *n* **1** : seigneur *m*, noble *m* **2 the Lord** : le Seigneur

lore ['lor] *n* : savoir *m* populaire, tradition *f*

lose ['lu:z] *v* **lost** ['lɔst]; **losing** ['lu:zɪŋ] *vt* **1** : perdre **2** ~ **one's way** : se perdre **3** ~ **time** : retarder (se dit d'une horloge) — *vi* : perdre — **loser** ['lu:zər] *n* : perdant *m*, -dante *f* — **loss** ['lɔs] *n* **1** : perte *f* **2** DEFEAT : défaite *f* **3 be at a** ~ **for words** : ne pas savoir quoi dire — **lost** ['lɔst] *adj* **1** : perdu **2 get** ~ : se perdre

lot ['lɑt] *n* **1** FATE : sort *m* **2** PLOT : parcelle *f* **3 a** ~ **of** *or* ~**s of** : beaucoup, une montagne de

lotion ['lo:ʃən] *n* : lotion *f*

lottery ['lɑt̬əri] *n, pl* **-teries** : loterie *f*

loud ['laʊd] *adj* **1** : grand, fort **2** NOISY : bruyant **3** FLASHY : criard — ~ *adv* **1** : fort **2 out** ~ : à voix haute — **loudly** ['laʊdli] *adv* : à voix haute — **loudspeaker** ['laʊdˌspi:kər] *n* : haut-parleur *m*

lounge ['laʊnʤ] *vi* **lounged; lounging 1** : se vautrer **2** ~ **about** : flâner — ~ *n* : salon *m*

louse ['laʊs] *n, pl* **lice** ['laɪs] : pou *m* — **lousy** ['laʊzi] *adj* **lousier; -est 1** : pouilleux **2** BAD : piètre, très mauvais

love ['lʌv] *n* **1** : amour *m* **2 fall in** ~ : tomber amoureux — ~ *v* **loved; loving** : aimer — **lovable** ['lʌvəbəl] *adj* : adorable — **lovely** ['lʌvli] *adj* **-lier; -est** : beau, joli — **lover** ['lʌvər] *n* : amant *m*, -mante *f* — **loving** ['lʌvɪŋ] *adj* : affectueux

low ['lo:] *adj* **lower** ['lo:ər]; **lowest 1** : bas **2** SCARCE : limité **3** DEPRESSED : déprimé — ~ *adv* **1** : bas **2 turn the lights** ~ : baisser les lumières — ~ *n* **1** : point *m* bas **2** *or* ~ **gear** : première *f* — **lower** ['lo:ər] *adj* : inférieur, plus bas — ~ *vt* : baisser — **lowly** ['lo:li] *adj* **-lier; -est** : humble

loyal ['lɔɪəl] *adj* : loyal, fidèle — **loyalty** ['lɔɪəlti] *n, pl* **-ties** : loyauté *f*

lozenge ['lɑzənʤ] *n* : pastille *f*

lubricate ['lu:brəˌkeɪt] *vt* **-cated; -cating** : lubrifier — **lubricant** ['lu:brɪkənt] *n* : lubrifiant *m* — **lubrication** [ˌlu:brə'keɪʃən] *n* : lubrification *f*
lucid ['lu:səd] *adj* : lucide — **lucidity** [lu:'sɪdəṭi] *n* : lucidité *f*
luck ['lʌk] *n* **1** : chance *f* **2 good ∼!** : bonne chance! — **luckily** ['lʌkəli] *adv* : heureusement — **lucky** ['lʌki] *adj* **luckier; -est 1** : chanceux **2 ∼ charm** : porte-bonheur *m*
lucrative ['lu:krəṭɪv] *adj* : lucratif
ludicrous ['lu:dəkrəs] *adj* : ridicule, absurde
lug ['lʌg] *vt* **lugged; lugging** : traîner
luggage ['lʌgɪdʒ] *n* : bagages *mpl*
lukewarm ['lu:k'wɔrm] *adj* : tiède
lull ['lʌl] *vt* **1** CALM : calmer **2 ∼ to sleep** : endormir — **∼** *n* : période *f* de calme, pause *f*
lullaby ['lʌləˌbaɪ] *n, pl* **-bies** : berceuse *f*
lumber ['lʌmbər] *n* : bois *m* — **lumberjack** ['lʌmbərˌdʒæk] *n* : bûcheron *m*, -ronne *f*
luminous ['lu:mənəs] *adj* : lumineux
lump ['lʌmp] *n* **1** CHUNK, PIECE : morceau *m*, motte *f* **2** SWELLING : bosse *f* **3** : grumeau *m* (dans une sauce) — **∼** *vt* *or* **∼ together** : réunir, regrouper — **lumpy** ['lʌmpi] *adj* **lumpier; -est** : grumeleux (se dit d'une sauce), bosselé (se dit d'un matelas)
lunacy ['lu:nəsi] *n, pl* **-cies** : folie *f*
lunar ['lu:nər] *adj* : lunaire
lunatic ['lu:nəˌtɪk] *n* : fou *m*
lunch ['lʌntʃ] *n* : déjeuner *m*, dîner *m* *Can*, lunch *m* *Can* — **∼** *vi* : déjeuner, dîner *Can* — **luncheon** ['lʌntʃən] *n* : déjeuner *m*
lung ['lʌŋ] *n* : poumon *m*
lunge ['lʌndʒ] *vi* **lunged; lunging 1** : se précipiter **2 ∼ at** : foncer sur
lurch[1] ['lərtʃ] *vi* **1** STAGGER : tituber **2** : faire une embardée (se dit d'une voiture)
lurch[2] *n* **leave in a ∼** : laisser en plan
lure ['lʊr] *n* **1** BAIT : leurre *m* **2** ATTRACTION : attrait *m* — **∼** *vt* **lured; luring** : attirer
lurid ['lʊrəd] *adj* **1** GRUESOME : épouvantable **2** SENSATIONAL : à sensation **3** GAUDY : criard
lurk ['lərk] *vi* : être tapi
luscious ['lʌʃəs] *adj* : délicieux, exquis
lush ['lʌʃ] *adj* : luxuriant, somptueux
lust ['lʌst] *n* **1** : luxure *f* **2** CRAVING : envie *f*, désir *m* — **∼** *vi* **∼ after** : désirer (une personne), convoiter (des richesses, etc.)
luster *or* **lustre** ['lʌstər] *n* : lustre *m*
lusty ['lʌsti] *adj* **lustier; -est** : robuste, vigoureux
luxurious [ˌlʌg'ʒʊriəs, ˌlʌk'ʃʊr-] *adj* : luxueux — **luxury** ['lʌkʃəri, 'lʌgʒə-] *n, pl* **-ries** : luxe *m*
lye ['laɪ] *n* : lessive *f*
lying → **lie**
lynch ['lɪntʃ] *vt* : lyncher
lynx ['lɪŋks] *n* : lynx *m*
lyric ['lɪrɪk] *or* **lyrical** ['lɪrɪkəl] *adj* : lyrique — **lyrics** *npl* : paroles *fpl* (d'une chanson)

M

m ['ɛm] *n, pl* **m's** *or* **ms** ['ɛmz] : m *m*, treizième lettre de l'alphabet
ma'am ['mæm] → **madam**
macabre [mə'kɑb, -'kɑbər, -'kɑbrə] *adj* : macabre
macaroni [ˌmækə'ro:ni] *n* : macaronis *mpl*
mace ['meɪs] *n* **1** : masse *f* (arme ou symbole) **2** : macis *m* (épice)
machete [mə'ʃɛṭi] *n* : machette *f*
machine [mə'ʃi:n] *n* : machine *f* — **machine gun** *n* : mitrailleuse *f* — **machinery** [mə'ʃi:nəri] *n, pl* **-eries 1** : machinerie *f* **2** WORKS : mécanisme *m*
mad ['mæd] *adj* **madder; maddest 1** INSANE : fou **2** FOOLISH : insensé **3** ANGRY : furieux
madam ['mædəm] *n, pl* **mesdames** [meɪ'dɑm] : madame *f*
madden ['mædən] *vt* : exaspérer
made → **make**
madly ['mædli] *adv* : comme un fou, follement — **madman** ['mædˌmæn, -mən] *n, pl* **-men** [-mən, -ˌmɛn] : fou *m* — **madness** ['mædnəs] *n* : folie *f*
Mafia ['mɑfiə] *n* : mafia *f*
magazine ['mægəˌzi:n] *n* **1** PERIODICAL : revue *f* **2** : magasin *m* (d'une arme à feu)
maggot ['mægət] *n* : asticot *m*
magic ['mædʒɪk] *n* : magie *f* — **∼** *or* **magical** ['mædʒɪkəl] *adj* : magique — **magician** [mə'dʒɪʃən] *n* : magicien *m*, -cienne *f*

magistrate [ˈmæʤəˌstreɪt] *n* : magistrat *m*
magnanimous [mægˈnænəməs] *adj* : magnanime
magnate [ˈmægˌneɪt, -nət] *n* : magnat *m*
magnet [ˈmægnət] *n* : aimant *m* — **magnetic** [mægˈnɛţɪk] *adj* : magnétique — **magnetism** [ˈmægnəˌtɪzəm] *n* : magnétisme *m* — **magnetize** [ˈmægnəˌtaɪz] *vt* **-tized; -tizing** : magnétiser
magnificent [mægˈnɪfəsənt] *adj* : magnifique — **magnificence** [mægˈnɪfəsənts] *n* : splendeur *f*
magnify [ˈmægnəˌfaɪ] *vt* **-fied; -fying** **1** ENLARGE : amplifier **2** EXAGGERATE : exagérer — **magnifying glass** *n* : loupe *f*
magnitude [ˈmægnəˌtu:d, -ˌtju:d] *n* : ampleur *f*
magnolia [mægˈno:ljə] *n* : magnolia *m*
mahogany [məˈhɑgəni] *n, pl* **-nies** : acajou *m*
maid [ˈmeɪd] *n* : servante *f*, bonne *f*, domestique *f* — **maiden name** *n* : nom *m* de jeune fille
mail [ˈmeɪl] *n* **1** : poste *f* **2** LETTERS : correspondence *f* — ∼ *vt* : envoyer par la poste — **mailbox** [ˈmeɪlˌbɑks] *n* : boîte *f* aux lettres — **mailman** [ˈmeɪlˌmæn, -mən] *n, pl* **-men** [-mən, -ˌmɛn] : facteur *m*
maim [ˈmeɪm] *vt* : mutiler
main [ˈmeɪn] *n* : canalisation *f* principale (d'eau ou de gaz) — ∼ *adj* : principal — **mainframe** [ˈmeɪnˌfreɪm] *n* : ordinateur *m* central — **mainland** [ˈmeɪnˌlænd, -lənd] *n* : continent *m* — **mainly** [ˈmeɪnli] *adv* : principalement — **mainstay** [ˈmeɪnˌsteɪ] *n* : soutien *m* prinicpal — **mainstream** [ˈmeɪnˌstri:m] *n* : courant *m* dominant — ∼ *adj* : dominant, conventionnel
maintain [meɪnˈteɪn] *vt* : entretenir, maintenir — **maintenance** [ˈmeɪntənənts] *n* : entretien *m*, maintien *m*
maize [ˈmeɪz] *n* : maïs *m*
majestic [məˈʤɛstɪk] *adj* : majestueux — **majesty** [ˈmæʤəsti] *n, pl* **-ties** : majesté *f*
major [ˈmeɪʤər] *adj* **1** : très important, principal **2** : majeur (en musique) — ∼ *n* **1** : commandant *m* (des forces armées) **2** : spécialité *f* (à l'université) — ∼ *vi* **-jored; -joring** : se spécialiser — **majority** [məˈʤɔrəţi] *n, pl* **-ties** : majorité *f*
make [ˈmeɪk] *v* **made** [ˈmeɪd]; **making** *vt* **1** : faire **2** MANUFACTURE : fabriquer **3** CONSTITUTE : constituer **4** PREPARE : préparer **5** RENDER : rendre **6** COMPEL : obliger **7** ∼ **a decision** : prendre une décision **8** ∼ **a living** : gagner sa vie — *vi* **1** ∼ **do** : se débrouiller **2** ∼ **for** : se diriger vers **3** ∼ **good** SUCCEED : réussir — ∼ *n* BRAND : marque *f* — **make–believe** [ˌmeɪkbəˈli:v] *n* : fantaisie *f* — ∼ *adj* : imaginaire — **make out** *vt* **1** : faire (un chèque, etc.) **2** DISCERN : distinguer **3** UNDERSTAND : comprendre — *vi* **how did you** ∼**?** : comment ça s'est passé? — **maker** [ˈmeɪkər] *n* MANUFACTURER : fabricant *m*, -cante *f* — **makeshift** [ˈmeɪkˌʃɪft] *adj* : improvisé — **makeup** [ˈmeɪkˌʌp] *n* **1** COMPOSITION : composition *f* **2** COSMETICS : maquillage *m* — **make up** *vt* **1** PREPARE : préparer **2** INVENT : inventer **3** CONSTITUTE : former — *vi* RECONCILE : faire la paix
maladjusted [ˌmæləˈʤʌstəd] *adj* : inadapté
malaria [məˈlɛriə] *n* : paludisme *m*
male [ˈmeɪl] *n* : mâle *m*, homme *m* — ∼ *adj* **1** : mâle **2** MASCULINE : masculin
malevolent [məˈlɛvələnt] *adj* : malveillant
malfunction [mælˈfʌŋkʃən] *vi* : mal fonctionner — ∼ *n* : mauvais fonctionnement *m*
malice [ˈmælɪs] *n* : mauvaise intention *f*, rancœur *f* — **malicious** [məˈlɪʃəs] *adj* : malveillant
malign [məˈlaɪn] *adj* : pernicieux — ∼ *vt* : calomnier
malignant [məˈlɪgnənt] *adj* : malveillant
mall [ˈmɔl] *n or* **shopping** ∼ : centre *m* commercial
malleable [ˈmæliəbəl] *adj* : malléable
mallet [ˈmælət] *n* : maillet *m*
malnutrition [ˌmælnʊˈtrɪʃən, -njʊ-] *n* : malnutrition *f*
malpractice [ˌmælˈpræktəs] *n* : négligence *f*
malt [ˈmɔlt] *n* : malt *m*
mama *or* **mamma** [ˈmɑmə] *n* : maman *f*
mammal [ˈmæməl] *n* : mammifère *m*
mammogram [ˈmæməˌgræm] *n* : mammographie *f*
mammoth [ˈmæməθ] *adj* : gigantesque
man [ˈmæn] *n, pl* **men** [ˈmɛn] : homme *m* — ∼ *vt* **manned; manning** : équiper en personnel

manage ['mænɪʤ] *v* **-aged; -aging** *vt* **1** HANDLE : manier **2** DIRECT : gérer, diriger — *vi* COPE : se débrouiller — **manageable** ['mænɪʤəbəl] *adj* : maniable — **management** ['mænɪʤmənt] *n* : gestion *f,* direction *f* — **manager** ['mænɪʤər] *n* : directeur *m,* -trice *f;* gérant *m,* -rante *f;* manager *m* (aux sports) — **managerial** [ˌmænəˈʤɪriəl] *adj* : de gestion

mandarin ['mændərən] *n or* ~ **orange** : mandarine *f*

mandate ['mænˌdeɪt] *n* : mandat *m*

mandatory ['mændəˌtɔri] *adj* : obligatoire

mane ['meɪn] *n* : crinière *f*

maneuver *or Brit* **manoeuvre** [məˈnu:vər, -ˈnju:-] *n* : manœuvre *f* — ~ *v* **-vered** *or Brit* **-vred; -vering** *or Brit* **-vring** : manœuvrer

mangle ['mæŋgəl] *vt* **-gled; -gling** : mutiler

mango ['mæŋˌgo:] *n, pl* **-goes** : mangue *f*

mangy ['meɪnʤi] *adj* **mangier; -est** : galeux

manhandle ['mænˌhændəl] *vt* **-dled; -dling** : malmener

manhole ['mænˌho:l] *n* : bouche *f* d'égout

manhood ['mænˌhʊd] *n* **1** : âge *m* d'homme **2** : virilité *f*

mania ['meɪniə, -njə] *n* : manie *f* — **maniac** ['meɪniˌæk] *n* : maniaque *mf*

manicure ['mænəˌkjʊr] *n* : manucure *f* — ~ *vt* **-cured; -curing** : faire les ongles de

manifest ['mænəˌfɛst] *adj* : manifeste, patent — ~ *vt* : manifester — **manifesto** [ˌmænəˈfɛsˌto:] *n, pl* **-tos** *or* **-toes** : manifeste *m*

manipulate [məˈnɪpjəˌleɪt] *vt* **-lated; -lating** : manipuler — **manipulation** [məˌnɪpjəˈleɪʃən] *n* : manipulation *f*

mankind ['mænˈkaɪnd, -ˌkaɪnd] *n* : le genre humain, humanité *f*

manly ['mænli] *adj* **-lier; -est** : viril — **manliness** ['mænlinəs] *n* : virilité *f*

mannequin ['mænɪkən] *n* : mannequin *m*

manner ['mænər] *n* **1** : manière *f* **2** KIND : sorte *f* **3** ~**s** *npl* ETIQUETTE : manières *fpl,* éducation *f* — **mannerism** ['mænəˌrɪzəm] *n* : particularité *f*

manoeuvre *Brit* → **maneuver**

manor ['mænər] *n* : manoir *m*

manpower ['mænˌpaʊər] *n* : main-d'œuvre *f*

mansion ['mænʧən] *n* : château *m*

manslaughter ['mænˌslɔt̬ər] *n* : homicide *m* involontaire

mantel ['mæntəl] *or* **mantelpiece** ['mæntəlˌpi:s] *n* : cheminée *f*

manual ['mænjʊəl] *adj* : manuel — ~ *n* : manuel *m*

manufacture [ˌmænjəˈfækʧər] *n* : fabrication *f* — ~ *vt* **-tured; -turing** : fabriquer — **manufacturer** [ˌmænjəˈfækʧərər] *n* : fabricant *m,* -cante *f*

manure [məˈnʊr, -ˈnjʊr] *n* : fumier *m*

manuscript ['mænjəˌskrɪpt] *n* : manuscrit *m*

many ['mɛni] *adj* **more** ['mor]; **most** ['mo:st] **1** : beaucoup de **2 as** ~ : autant de **3 how** ~ : combien **4 too** ~ : trop de — ~ *pron* : beaucoup

map ['mæp] *n* : carte *f,* plan *m* — ~ *vt* **mapped; mapping 1** : faire la carte de **2** *or* ~ **out** : élaborer

maple ['meɪpəl] *n* **1** : érable *m* **2** ~ **syrup** : sirop *m* d'érable

mar ['mɑr] *vt* **marred; marring** : estropier

marathon ['mærəˌθɑn] *n* : marathon *m*

marble ['mɑrbəl] *n* **1** : marbre *m* **2** : billes *fpl* (à jouer)

march ['mɑrʧ] *n* : marche *f* — ~ *vi* : marcher, défiler

March ['mɑrʧ] *n* : mars *m*

mare ['mær] *n* : jument *f*

margarine ['mɑrʤərən] *n* : margarine *f*

margin ['mɑrʤən] *n* : marge *f* — **marginal** ['mɑrʤənəl] *adj* : marginal

marigold ['mærəˌgo:ld] *n* : souci *m*

marijuana [ˌmærəˈhwɑnə] *n* : marijuana *f*

marinate ['mærəˌneɪt] *v* **-nated; -nating** : mariner

marine [məˈri:n] *adj* : marin — ~ *n* : fusilier *m* marin

marital ['mærət̬əl] *adj* **1** : conjugal **2** ~ **status** : état *m* civil

maritime ['mærəˌtaɪm] *adj* : maritime

mark ['mɑrk] *n* **1** : marque *f* **2** STAIN : tache **3** IMPRINT : trace *f* **4** TARGET : cible *f* **5** GRADE : note *f* — ~ *vt* **1** : marquer **2** STAIN : tacher **3** POINT OUT : signaler **4** : corriger (un examen, etc.) **5** COMMEMORATE : commémorer **6** CHARACTERIZE : caractériser **7** ~ **off** : délimiter — **marked** ['mɑrkt] *adj* : marqué, notable — **markedly** ['mɑrkədli] *adv* : sensiblement — **marker** ['mɑrkər] *n* **1** : repère *m* **2** PEN : marqueur *m*

market ['mɑrkət] *n* : marché *m* — ~ *vt* : vendre, commercialiser — **mar-**

ketable ['mɑrkəṭəbəl] *adj* : vendable — **marketplace** ['mɑrkət,pleɪs] *n* : marché *m*
marksman ['mɑrksmən] *n, pl* **-men** [-mən, -,mɛn] : tireur *m*, -reuse *f* d'élite — **marksmanship** ['mɑrksmən,ʃɪp] *n* : adresse *f* au tir
marmalade ['mɑrmə,leɪd] *n* : marmelade *f*
maroon[1] [mə'ru:n] *vt* : abandonner
maroon[2] *n* : rouge *m* foncé
marquee [mɑr'ki:] *n* CANOPY : marquise *f*
marriage ['mærɪʤ] *n* **1** : mariage *m* **2** WEDDING : noces *fpl* — **married** ['mærid] *adj* **1** : marié **2 get ~** : se marier
marrow ['mæro:] *n* : moelle *f*
marry ['mæri] *v* **-ried; -rying** *vt* **1** : marier **2** WED : se marier avec, épouser — *vi* : se marier
Mars ['mɑrz] *n* : Mars *f*
marsh ['mɑrʃ] *n* **1** : marécage *m* **2** *or* **salt ~** : marais *m* salant
marshal ['mɑrʃəl] *n* : maréchal *m* (militaire), commissaire *m* (de police) — **~** *vt* **-shaled** *or* **-shalled; -shaling** *or* **-shalling** : rassembler
marshmallow ['mɑrʃ,mɛlo:, -,mælo:] *n* : guimauve *f*
marshy ['mɑrʃi] *adj* **marshier; -est** : marécageux
mart ['mɑrt] *n* : marché *m*
martial ['mɑrʃəl] *adj* : martial
martyr ['mɑrṭər] *n* : martyr *m*, -tyre *f* — **~** *vt* : martyriser
marvel ['mɑrvəl] *n* : merveille *f* — **~** *vi* **-veled** *or* **-velled; -veling** *or* **-velling** : s'émerveiller — **marvelous** ['mɑrvələs] *or* **marvellous** *adj* : merveilleux
mascara [mæs'kærə] *n* : mascara *m*
mascot ['mæs,kɑt, -kət] *n* : mascotte *f*
masculine ['mæskjələn] *adj* : masculin — **masculinity** [,mæskjə'lɪnəṭi] *n* : masculinité *f*
mash ['mæʃ] *vt* **1** CRUSH : écraser, aplatir **2** PUREE : faire une purée de, piler *Can* — **mashed potatoes** *npl* : purée *f* de pommes de terre, patates *fpl Can*
mask ['mæsk] *n* : masque *m* — **~** *vt* : masquer
masochism ['mæsə,kɪzəm, 'mæzə-] *n* : masochisme *m* — **masochist** ['mæsə,kɪst, 'mæzə-] *n* : masochiste *mf* — **masochistic** [,mæsə'kɪstɪk] *adj* : masochiste
mason ['meɪsən] *n* : maçon *m* — **masonry** ['meɪsənri] *n, pl* **-ries** : maçonnerie *f*
masquerade [,mæskə'reɪd] *n* : mascarade *f* — **~** *vi* **-aded; -ading ~ as** : se déguiser en, se faire passer pour
mass ['mæs] *n* **1** : masse *f* **2** MULTITUDE : quantité *f* **3 the ~es** : les masses
Mass *n* : messe *f*
massacre ['mæsɪkər] *n* : massacre *m* — **~** *vt* **-cred; -cring** : massacrer
massage [mə'sɑʃ, -'sɑdʃ] *n* : massage *m* — **~** *vt* **-saged; -saging** : donner un massage à, masser — **masseur** [mæ'sər] *n* : masseur *m* — **masseuse** [mæ'søz, -'su:z] *n* : masseuse *f*
massive ['mæsɪv] *adj* **1** BULKY : massif **2** HUGE : énorme
mast ['mæst] *n* : mât *m*
master ['mæstər] *n* **1** : maître *m* **2 ~'s degree** : maîtrise *f* — **~** *vt* : maîtriser — **masterful** ['mæstərfəl] *adj* : magistral — **masterpiece** ['mæstər,pi:s] *n* : chef *m* d'œuvre — **mastery** ['mæstəri] *n* : maîtrise *f*
masturbate ['mæstər,beɪt] *vi* **-bated; -bating** : se masturber — **masturbation** [,mæstər'beɪʃən] *n* : masturbation *f*
mat ['mæt] *n* **1** DOORMAT : paillasson *m* **2** RUG : tapis *m*
match ['mætʃ] *n* **1** : allumette *f* **2** EQUAL : égal *m*, égale *f* **3** GAME : match *m*, combat *m* (de boxe) **4 be a good ~** : être un bon parti — **~** *vt* **1** *or* **~ up** : appareiller **2** EQUAL : égaler **3** : s'accorder avec, aller ensemble (vêtements, couleurs, etc.) — *vi* : correspondre
mate ['meɪt] *n* **1** COMPANION : compagnon *m*, -pagne *f* **2** : mâle *m*, femelle *f* (d'un animal) — **~** *vi* **mated; mating** : s'accoupler
material [mə'tɪriəl] *adj* **1** : matériel **2** IMPORTANT : important — **~** *n* **1** : matière *f* **2** FABRIC : tissu *m*, étoffe *f* — **materialistic** [mə,tɪriə'lɪstɪk] *adj* : matérialiste — **materialize** [mə'tɪriə,laɪz] *vi* **-ized; -izing** : se matérialiser
maternal [mə'tərnəl] *adj* : maternel — **maternity** [mə'tərnəṭi] *n, pl* **-ties** : maternité *f* — **~** *adj* : de maternité
math ['mæθ] → **mathematics**
mathematics [,mæθə'mæṭɪks] *ns & pl* : mathématiques *fpl* — **mathematical** [,mæθə'mæṭɪkəl] *adj* : mathématique — **mathematician** [,mæθəmə'tɪʃən] *n* : mathématicien *m*, -cienne *f*
matinee *or* **matinée** [,mætən'eɪ] *n* : matinée *f* (au cinéma)

matrimony [ˈmætrəˌmo:ni] *n* : mariage *m* — **matrimonial** [ˌmætrəˈmo:niəl] *adj* : matrimonial
matrix [ˈmeɪtrɪks] *n, pl* **-trices** [ˈmeɪtrəˌsi:z, ˈmæ-] *or* **-trixes** [ˈmeɪtrɪksəz] : matrice *f*
matte [ˈmæt] *adj* : mat
matter [ˈmæt̬ər] *n* **1** SUBSTANCE : matière *f* **2** QUESTION : affaire *f*, question *f* **3 as a ~ of fact** : en fait, en réalité **4 for that ~** : d'ailleurs **5 to make ~s worse** : pour ne rien arranger **6 what's the ~?** : qu'est-ce qu'il y a? — **~** *vi* : importer
mattress [ˈmætrəs] *n* : matelas *m*
mature [məˈtʊr, -ˈtjʊr, -ˈʧʊr] *adj* **-turer; -est** : mûr — **~** *vi* **-tured; -turing** : mûrir — **maturity** [məˈtʊrət̬i, -ˈtjʊr-, -ˈʧʊr-] *n* : maturité *f*
maul [ˈmɔl] *vt* : mutiler
mauve [ˈmo:v, ˈmɔv] *n* : mauve *m*
maxim [ˈmæksəm] *n* : maxime *f*
maximum [ˈmæksəməm] *n, pl* **-ma** [ˈmæksəmə] *or* **-mums** : maximum *m* — **~** *adj* : maximum — **maximize** [ˈmæksəˌmaɪz] *vt* **-mized; -mizing** : porter au maximum
may [ˈmeɪ] *v aux, past* **might** [ˈmaɪt]; *present s & pl* **may 1** : pouvoir **2 come what ~** : quoiqu'il arrive **3 it ~ rain** : il se peut qu'il pleuve, il va peut-être pleuvoir **4 ~ the best man win** : que le meilleur gagne
May [ˈmeɪ] *n* : mai *m*
maybe [ˈmeɪbi] *adv* : peut-être
mayhem [ˈmeɪˌhɛm, ˈmeɪəm] *n* : pagaille *f*
mayonnaise [ˈmeɪəˌneɪz] *n* : mayonnaise *f*
mayor [ˈmeɪər, ˈmɛr] *n* : maire *m*, mairesse *f*
maze [ˈmeɪz] *n* : labyrinthe *m*
me [ˈmi:] *pron* **1** : moi **2** : me, m' **3 give it to ~** : donne-le moi **4 will she come with ~?** : m'accompagnera-t-elle?
meadow [ˈmɛdo:] *n* : pré *m*, prairie *f*
meager *or* **meagre** [ˈmi:gər] *adj* : maigre
meal [ˈmi:l] *n* **1** : repas *m* **2** : farine *f* (de maïs, etc.) — **mealtime** [ˈmi:lˌtaɪm] *n* : l'heure *f* du repas
mean[1] [ˈmi:n] *vt* **meant** [ˈmɛnt]; **meaning 1** SIGNIFY : vouloir dire **2** INTEND : avoir l'intention de **3 be meant for** : être destiné à **4 he didn't ~ it** : il ne l'a pas fait exprès
mean[2] *adj* **1** UNKIND : méchant **2** STINGY : mesquin
mean[3] *adj* AVERAGE : moyen — **~** *n* : moyenne *f*
meander [miˈændər] *vi* **1** WIND : serpenter **2** WANDER : errer
meaning [ˈmi:nɪŋ] *n* : sens *m*, signification *f* — **meaningful** [ˈmi:nɪŋfəl] *adj* : significatif — **meaningless** [ˈmi:nɪŋləs] *adj* : sans signification
meanness [ˈmi:nnəs] *n* : méchanceté *f*
means [ˈmi:nz] *n* **1** : moyens *mpl* **2 by all ~** : certainement **3 by ~ of** : au moyen de **4 by no ~** : d'aucune façon
meantime [ˈmi:nˌtaɪm] *n* **1** : intervalle *m* **2 in the ~** : en attendant — **~** *adv* → **meanwhile**
meanwhile [ˈmi:nˌhwaɪl] *adv* : entretemps — **~** *n* → **meantime**
measles [ˈmi:zəlz] *npl* : rougeole *f*
measly [ˈmi:zli] *adj* **-slier; -est** : misérable, minable *fam*
measure [ˈmɛʒər, ˈmeɪ-] *n* : mesure *f* — **~** *v* **-sured; -suring** : mesurer — **measurable** [ˈmɛʒərəbəl, ˈmeɪ-] *adj* : mesurable — **measurement** [ˈmɛʒərmənt, ˈmeɪ-] *n* : mesure *f* — **measure up** *vi* **~ to** : être à la hauteur de
meat [ˈmi:t] *n* : viande *f* — **meatball** [ˈmi:tˌbɔl] *n* : boulette *f* de viande — **meaty** [ˈmi:t̬i] *adj* **meatier; -est 1** : de viande **2** SUBSTANTIAL : substantiel
mechanic [mɪˈkænɪk] *n* : mécanicien *m*, -cienne *f* — **mechanical** [mɪˈkænɪkəl] *adj* : mécanique — **mechanics** [mɪˈkænɪks] *ns & pl* **1** : mécanique *f* **2** WORKINGS : mécanisme *m* — **mechanism** [ˈmɛkəˌnɪzəm] *n* : mécanisme *m* — **mechanize** [ˈmɛkəˌnaɪz] *vt* **-nized; -nizing** : mécaniser
medal [ˈmɛdəl] *n* : médaille *f* — **medallion** [məˈdæljən] *n* : médaillon *m*
meddle [ˈmɛdəl] *vi* **-dled; -dling** : se mêler
media [ˈmi:diə] *or* **mass ~** *npl* : les médias
median [ˈmi:diən] *adj* : médian
mediate [ˈmi:diˌeɪt] *vi* **-ated; -ating** : servir de médiateur — **mediation** [ˌmi:diˈeɪʃən] *n* : médiation *f* — **mediator** [ˈmi:diˌeɪt̬ər] *n* : médiateur *m*, -trice *f*
medical [ˈmɛdɪkəl] *adj* : médical — **medicated** [ˈmɛdəˌkeɪt̬əd] *adj* : médical, traitant — **medication** [ˌmɛdəˈkeɪʃən] *n* : médicaments *mpl* — **medicinal** [məˈdɪsənəl] *adj* : médicinal — **medicine** [ˈmɛdəsən] *n* **1** : médecine *f* **2** MEDICATION : médicament *m*

medieval *or* **mediaeval** [mɪ'di:vəl, ˌmi:-, ˌmɛ-, -di'i:vəl] *adj* : médiéval
mediocre [ˌmi:di'o:kər] *adj* : médiocre — **mediocrity** [ˌmi:di'ɑkrəṭi] *n, pl* **-ties** : médiocrité *f*
meditate ['mɛdəˌteɪt] *vi* **-tated; -tating** : méditer — **meditation** [ˌmɛdə'teɪʃən] *n* : méditation *f*
Mediterranean [ˌmɛdətə'reɪniən] *adj* : méditerranéen
medium ['mi:diəm] *n, pl* **-diums** *or* **-dia** ['mi:diə] **1** MEANS : moyen *m* **2** MEAN : milieu *m* **3** → **media** — **~** *adj* : moyen
medley ['mɛdli] *n, pl* **-leys 1** : mélange *m* **2** : pot-pourri *m* (de chansons)
meek ['mi:k] *adj* : docile
meet ['mi:t] *v* **met** ['mɛt]; **meeting** *vt* **1** ENCOUNTER : rencontrer **2** SATISFY : satisfaire **3 pleased to ~ you** : enchanté de faire votre connaissance — *vi* **1** : se rencontrer **2** ASSEMBLE : se réunir **3** : faire connaissance — **~** *n* : rencontre *f* (aux sports) — **meeting** ['mi:ṭɪŋ] *n* : réunion *f*
megabyte ['mɛgəˌbaɪt] *n* : mégaoctet *m*
megaphone ['mɛgəˌfo:n] *n* : porte-voix *m,* mégaphone *m*
melancholy ['mɛlənˌkɑli] *n, pl* **-cholies** : mélancolie *f* — **~** *adj* : mélancolique, triste
mellow ['mɛlo:] *adj* **1** : doux, moelleux **2** CALM : paisible — **~** *vt* : adoucir — *vi* : s'adoucir
melody ['mɛlədi] *n, pl* **-dies** : mélodie *f*
melon ['mɛlən] *n* : melon *m*
melt ['mɛlt] *vi* : fondre — *vt* : faire fondre
member ['mɛmbər] *n* : membre *m* — **membership** ['mɛmbərˌʃɪp] *n* **1** : adhésion *f* **2** MEMBERS : membres *mpl*
membrane ['mɛmˌbreɪn] *n* : membrane *f*
memory ['mɛmri, 'mɛmə-] *n, pl* **-ries 1** : mémoire *f* **2** RECOLLECTION : souvenir *m* — **memento** [mɪ'mɛnˌto:] *n, pl* **-tos** *or* **-toes** : souvenir *m* — **memo** ['mɛmo:] *n, pl* **memos** *or* **memorandum** [ˌmɛmə'rændəm] *n, pl* **-dums** *or* **-da** [-də] : mémorandum *m* — **memoirs** ['mɛmˌwɑrz] *npl* : mémoires *mpl* — **memorable** ['mɛmərəbəl] *adj* : mémorable — **memorial** [mə'moriəl] *adj* : commémoratif — **~** *n* : monument *m* (commémoratif) — **memorize** ['mɛməˌraɪz] *vt* **-rized; -rizing** : apprendre par cœur
men → **man**
menace ['mɛnəs] *n* : menace *f* — **~** *vt* **-aced; -acing** : menacer — **menacing** ['mɛnəsɪŋ] *adj* : menaçant
mend ['mɛnd] *vt* **1** : réparer, arranger **2** DARN : raccommoder — *vi* HEAL : guérir
menial ['mi:niəl] *adj* : servile, bas
meningitis [ˌmɛnən'ʤaɪṭəs] *n, pl* **-gitides** [-'ʤɪṭəˌdi:z] : méningite *f*
menopause ['mɛnəˌpɔz] *n* : ménopause *f*
menstruate ['mɛntstruˌeɪt] *vi* **-ated; -ating** : avoir ses règles — **menstruation** [ˌmɛntstru'eɪʃən] *n* : menstruation *f,* règles *fpl*
mental ['mɛntəl] *adj* : mental — **mentality** [mɛn'tæləṭi] *n, pl* **-ties** : mentalité *f*
mention ['mɛnʧən] *n* : mention *f* — **~** *vt* **1** : mentionner **2 don't ~ it** : il n'y a pas de quoi
menu ['mɛnˌju:] *n* : menu *m*
meow [mi:'aʊ] *n* : miaulement *m,* miaou *m* — **~** *vi* : miauler
mercenary ['mərsənˌɛri] *n, pl* **-naries** : mercenaire *mf*
merchant ['mərʧənt] *n* : marchand *m,* -chande *f;* commerçant *m,* -çante *f* — **merchandise** ['mərʧənˌdaɪz, -ˌdaɪs] *n* : marchandises *fpl*
merciful ['mərsɪfəl] *adj* : miséricordieux, compatissant — **merciless** ['mərsɪləs] *adj* : impitoyable
mercury ['mərkjəri] *n* : mercure *m*
Mercury ['mərkjəri] *n* : Mercure *f*
mercy ['mərsi] *n, pl* **-cies 1** : miséricorde *f,* compassion *f* **2 at the ~ of** : à la merci de
mere ['mɪr] *adj, superlative* **merest** : simple — **merely** ['mɪrli] *adv* : simplement
merge ['mərʤ] *v* **merged; merging** *vi* : fusionner (se dit d'une compagnie), confluer (se dit d'une rivière, etc.) — *vt* : unir, fusionner — **merger** ['mərʤər] *n* : union *f,* fusion *f*
merit ['mɛrət] *n* : mérite *m* — **~** *vt* : mériter
mermaid ['mərˌmeɪd] *n* : sirène *f*
merry ['mɛri] *adj* **-rier; -est** : allègre — **merry-go-round** ['mɛrigoˌraʊnd] *n* : manège *m*
mesh ['mɛʃ] *n* : maille *f*
mesmerize ['mɛzməˌraɪz] *vt* **-ized; -izing** : hypnotiser
mess ['mɛs] *n* **1** : désordre *m* **2** MUDDLE : gâchis *m* **3** : cantine *f* (ambulante) — **~** *vt* **1 ~ up** : mettre en désordre **2** *or* **~ up** SOIL : salir **3 ~ up** BUNGLE : gâcher — *vi* **1 ~ around**

PUTTER : bricoler **2 ~ with** PROVOKE : embêter

message [ˈmɛsɪʤ] *n* : message *m* — **messenger** [ˈmɛsəndʒər] *n* : messager *m*, -gère *f*

messy [ˈmɛsi] *adj* **messier; -est** : désordonné

met → **meet**

metabolism [məˈtæbəˌlɪzəm] *n* : métabolisme *m*

metal [ˈmɛtəl] *n* : métal *m* — **metallic** [məˈtælɪk] *adj* : métallique

metamorphosis [ˌmɛtəˈmɔrfəsɪs] *n, pl* **-phoses** [-ˈsi:z] : métamorphose *f*

metaphor [ˈmɛtəˌfɔr, -fər] *n* : métaphore *f*

meteor [ˈmi:tiər, -tiˌɔr] *n* : météore *m* — **meteorological** [ˌmi:tiˌɔrəˈlɑʤɪkəl] *adj* : météorologique — **meteorologist** [ˌmi:tiəˈrɑləʤɪst] *n* : météorologue *mf* — **meteorology** [ˌmi:tiəˈrɑləʤi] *n* : météorologie *f*

meter *or Brit* **metre** [ˈmi:tər] *n* **1** : mètre *m* **2** : compteur *m* (d'électricité, etc.)

method [ˈmɛθəd] *n* : méthode *f* — **methodical** [məˈθɑdɪkəl] *adj* : méthodique

meticulous [məˈtɪkjələs] *adj* : méticuleux

metric [ˈmɛtrɪk] *or* **metrical** [-trɪkəl] *adj* : métrique

metropolis [məˈtrɑpələs] *n* : métropole *f* — **metropolitan** [ˌmɛtrəˈpɑlətən] *adj* : métropolitain

Mexican [ˈmɛksɪkən] *adj* : mexicain

mice → **mouse**

microbe [ˈmaɪˌkro:b] *n* : microbe *m*

microfilm [ˈmaɪkroˌfɪlm] *n* : microfilm *m*

microphone [ˈmaɪkrəˌfo:n] *n* : microphone *m*

microscope [ˈmaɪkrəˌsko:p] *n* : microscope *m* — **microscopic** [ˌmaɪkrəˈskɑpɪk] *adj* : microscopique

microwave [ˈmaɪkrəˌweɪv] *n or* **~ oven** : (four *m* à) micro ondes *m*

mid [ˈmɪd] *adj* **1 ~-morning** : au milieu de la matinée **2 in ~-June** : à la mi-juin **3 she is in her ~ thirties** : elle est dans la trentaine — **midair** [ˈmɪdˈær] *n* **in ~** : en plein ciel — **midday** [ˈmɪdˈdeɪ] *n* : midi *m*

middle [ˈmɪdəl] *adj* : du milieu, au milieu — **~** *n* **1** : milieu *m*, centre *m* **2 in the ~ of** : au milieu de (un espace), en train de (faire une activité) — **middle-aged** *adj* : d'un certain age — **Middle Ages** *npl* : Moyen Âge *m* — **middle class** *n* : classe *f* moyenne — **Middle Eastern** *adj* : moyen-oriental — **middleman** [ˈmɪdəlˌmæn] *n, pl* **-men** [-mən, -ˌmɛn] : intermédiaire *mf*

midget [ˈmɪʤət] *n* : nain *m*, naine *f*

midnight [ˈmɪdˌnaɪt] *n* : minuit *m*

midriff [ˈmɪdˌrɪf] *n* : diaphragme *m*

midst [ˈmɪdst] *n* **1 in the ~ of** : au milieu de **2 in our ~** : parmi nous

midsummer [ˈmɪdˈsʌmər, -ˌsʌ-] *n* : milieu *m* de l'été

midway [ˈmɪdˌweɪ] *adv* : à mi-chemin

midwife [ˈmɪdˌwaɪf] *n, pl* **-wives** [-ˌwaɪvz] : sage-femme *f*

midwinter [ˈmɪdˈwɪntər, -ˌwin-] *n* : milieu *m* de l'hiver

miff [ˈmɪf] *vt* : vexer

might[1] [ˈmaɪt] (*used to express permission or possibility or as a polite alternative to* **may**) → **may**

might[2] *n* : force *f*, pouvoir *m* — **mighty** [ˈmaɪti] *adj* **mightier; -est 1** : fort, puissant **2** GREAT : énorme — **~** *adv* : très, rudement *fam*

migraine [ˈmaɪˌgreɪn] *n* : migraine *f*

migrate [ˈmaɪˌgreɪt] *vi* **-grated; -grating** : émigrer — **migrant** [ˈmaɪgrənt] *n* : travailleur *m* saisonnier

mild [ˈmaɪld] *adj* **1** GENTLE : doux **2** LIGHT : léger

mildew [ˈmɪlˌdu:, -ˌdju:] *n* : moisissure *f*

mildly [ˈmaɪldli] *adv* : doucement, légèrement — **mildness** [ˈmaɪldnəs] *n* : douceur *f*

mile [ˈmaɪl] *n* : mille *m* — **mileage** [ˈmaɪlɪʤ] *n* : distance *f* parcourue (en milles), kilométrage *m* — **milestone** [ˈmaɪlˌsto:n] *n* : jalon *m*

military [ˈmɪləˌtɛri] *adj* : militaire — **~** *n* **the ~** : les forces armées — **militant** [ˈmɪlətənt] *adj* : militant — **~** *n* : militant *m*, -tante *f* — **militia** [məˈlɪʃə] *n* : milice *f*

milk [ˈmɪlk] *n* : lait *m* — **~** *vt* : traire (une vache, etc.) — **milky** [ˈmɪlki] *adj* **milkier; -est** : laiteux — **Milky Way** *n* **the ~** : la Voie lactée

mill [ˈmɪl] *n* **1** : moulin *m* **2** FACTORY : usine *f* — **~** *vt* : moudre — *vi or* **~ about** : grouiller

millennium [məˈlɛniəm] *n, pl* **-nia** [-niə] *or* **-niums** : millénaire *m*

miller [ˈmɪlər] *n* : meunier *m*, -nière *f*

milligram [ˈmɪləˌgræm] *n* : milligramme *m* — **millimeter** *or Brit* **millimetre** [ˈmɪləˌmi:tər] *n* : millimètre *m*

million [ˈmɪljən] *n, pl* **millions** *or* **million** : million *m* — **~** *adj* **a ~** : un million de — **millionaire** [ˌmɪljəˈnær,

ˈmɪljəˌnær] *n* : millionnaire *mf* — **millionth** [ˈmɪljənθ] *adj* : millionième

mime [ˈmaɪm] *n* **1** : mime *mf* **2** PANTOMIME : pantomime *f* — ~ *v* **mimed; miming** *vt* : imiter — *vi* : faire des mimiques — **mimic** *vt* **-icked; -icking** : imiter, singer

mince [ˈmɪnts] *vt* **minced; mincing 1** : hacher **2 not to ~ one's words** : ne pas mâcher ses mots

mind [ˈmaɪnd] *n* **1** : esprit *m* **2** INTELLECT : capacité *f* intellectuelle **3** OPINION : opinion *f* **4** REASON : raison *f* **5 have a ~ to** : avoir l'intention de — ~ *vt* **1** TEND : s'occuper de **2** OBEY : obéir à **3** WATCH : faire attention à **4 I don't ~ the heat** : la chaleur ne m'incommode pas — *vi* **1** OBEY : obéir **2 I don't ~** : ça m'est égal — **mindful** [ˈmaɪndfəl] *adj* : attentif — **mindless** [ˈmaɪndləs] *adj* **1** SENSELESS : stupide **2** DULL : ennuyeux

mine[1] [ˈmaɪn] *pron* **1** : le mien, la mienne, les miens, les miennes **2 a friend of ~** : un ami à moi

mine[2] *n* : mine *f* — ~ *vt* **mined; mining 1** : extraire (de l'or, etc.) **2** : miner (avec des explosifs) — **minefield** [ˈmaɪnˌfi:ld] *n* : champ *m* de mines — **miner** [ˈmaɪnər] *n* : mineur *m*

mineral [ˈmɪnərəl] *n* : minéral *m*

mingle [ˈmɪŋgəl] *v* **-gled; -gling** *vt* : mêler, mélanger — *vi* : se mêler (à, avec)

miniature [ˈmɪniəˌʧʊr, ˈmɪnɪˌʧʊr, -ʧər] *n* : miniature *f* — ~ *adj* : en miniature

minimal [ˈmɪnəməl] *adj* : minimal — **minimize** [ˈmɪnəˌmaɪz] *vt* **-mized; -mizing** : minimiser — **minimum** [ˈmɪnəməm] *adj* : minimum — ~ *n, pl* **-ma** [ˈmɪnəme] *or* **-mums** : minimum *m*

minister [ˈmɪnəstər] *n* **1** : pasteur *m* (d'une église) **2** : ministre *m* (en politique) — ~ *vi* ~ **to** : pourvoir à, donner des soins à — **ministerial** [ˌmɪnəˈstɪriəl] *adj* : ministériel — **ministry** [ˈmɪnəstri] *n, pl* **-tries** : ministère *m* (gouvernemental), sacerdoce *m* (religieux)

mink [ˈmɪŋk] *n, pl* **mink** *or* **minks** : vison *m*

minor [ˈmaɪnər] *adj* **1** : mineur **2** INSIGNIFICANT : sans importance — ~ *n* **1** : mineur *m*, -neure *f* **2** : matière *f* secondaire (à l'université) — **minority** [məˈnɔrət̬i, maɪ-] *n, pl* **-ties** : minorité *f*

mint[1] [ˈmɪnt] *n* **1** : menthe *f* (plante) **2** : bonbon *m* à la menthe

mint[2] *n* **1 the Mint** : l'Hôtel *m* de la Monnaie **2 worth a ~** : valoir une fortune — ~ *vt* : frapper (la monnaie) — ~ *adj* **in ~ condition** : comme neuf

minus [ˈmaɪnəs] *prep* **1** : moins **2** WITHOUT : sans — ~ *n or* ~ **sign** : moins *m*

minuscule *or* **miniscule** [ˈmɪnəsˌkju:l] *adj* : minuscule

minute[1] [ˈmɪnət] *n* **1** : minute *f* **2** MOMENT : moment *m* **3 ~s** *npl* : procès-verbal *m*

minute[2] [maɪˈnu:t, mɪ-, -ˈnju:t] *adj* **-nuter; -est 1** TINY : minuscule **2** DETAILED : minutieux

miracle [ˈmɪrɪkəl] *n* : miracle *m* — **miraculous** [məˈrækjələs] *adj* : miraculeux

mirage [mɪˈrɑʒ, *chiefly Brit* ˈmɪrˌɑʒ] *n* : mirage *m*

mire [ˈmaɪr] *n* : boue *f*, fange *f*

mirror [ˈmɪrər] *n* : miroir *m*, glace *f* — ~ *vt* : refléter, réfléchir

mirth [ˈmərθ] *n* : allégresse *f*, gaieté *f*

misapprehension [ˌmɪsˌæprəˈhɛnʧən] *n* : malentendu *m*

misbehave [ˌmɪsbiˈheɪv] *vi* **-haved; -having** : se conduire mal — **misbehavior** [ˌmɪsbiˈheɪvjər] *n* : mauvaise conduite *f*

miscalculate [mɪsˈkælkjəˌleɪt] *v* **-lated; -lating** : mal calculer

miscarriage [ˌmɪsˈkærɪʤ, ˈmɪsˌkærɪʤ] *n* **1** : fausse couche *f* **2 ~ of justice** : erreur *f* judiciaire

miscellaneous [ˌmɪsəˈleɪniəs] *adj* : divers, varié

mischief [ˈmɪsʧəf] *n* : espièglerie *f* — **mischievous** [ˈmɪsʧəvəs] *adj* : espiègle

misconception [ˌmɪskənˈsɛpʃən] *n* : concept *m* erroné

misconduct [mɪsˈkɑndəkt] *n* : mauvaise conduite *f*

misdeed [mɪsˈdi:d] *n* : méfait *m*

misdemeanor [ˌmɪsdɪˈmi:nər] *n* : délit *m* judiciaire

miser [ˈmaɪzər] *n* : avare *m*

miserable [ˈmɪzərəbəl] *adj* **1** UNHAPPY : malheureux **2** WRETCHED : misérable **3 ~ weather** : temps *m* maussade

miserly [ˈmaɪzərli] *adj* : avare

misery [ˈmɪzəri] *n, pl* **-eries 1** : souffrance *f* **2** WRETCHEDNESS : misère *f*

misfire [mɪsˈfaɪr] *vi* **-fired; -firing** : échouer

misfit [ˈmɪsˌfɪt] *n* : inadapté *m*, -tée *f*

misfortune [mɪsˈfɔrtʃən] *n* : malheur *f,* infortune *f*
misgiving [mɪsˈgɪvɪŋ] *n* : doute *m*
misguided [mɪsˈgaɪdəd] *adj* : malencontreux, peu judicieux
mishap [ˈmɪsˌhæp] *n* : contretemps *m*
misinform [ˌmɪsɪnˈfɔrm] *vt* : mal renseigner
misinterpret [ˌmɪsɪnˈtərprət] *vt* : mal interpréter
misjudge [mɪsˈdʒʌdʒ] *vt* **-judged; -judging** : mal juger
mislay [mɪsˈleɪ] *vt* **-laid** [-ˈleɪd]; **-laying** : égarer
mislead [mɪsˈli:d] *vt* **-led** [-ˈlɛd]; **-leading** : tromper — **misleading** [mɪsˈli:dɪŋ] *adj* : trompeur
misnomer [mɪsˈno:mər] *n* : terme *m* impropre
misplace [mɪsˈpleɪs] *vt* **-placed; -placing** : égarer, perdre
misprint [ˈmɪsˌprɪnt, mɪsˈ-] *n* : faute *f* typographique, coquille *f*
miss [ˈmɪs] *vt* **1** : rater, manquer (une occasion, un vol, etc.) **2** OVERLOOK : laisser passer **3** AVOID : éviter **4** OMIT : sauter **5 I ~ you** : tu me manques — **~** *n* **1** : coup *m* manqué **2** FAILURE : échec *m*
Miss [ˈmɪs] *n* : mademoiselle *f*
missile [ˈmɪsəl] *n* **1** : missile *m* **2** PROJECTILE : projectile *m*
missing [ˈmɪsɪŋ] *adj* : perdu, disparu
mission [ˈmɪʃən] *n* : mission *f* — **missionary** [ˈmɪʃəˌnɛri] *n, pl* **-aries** : missionnaire *mf*
misspell [mɪsˈspɛl] *vt* : mal orthographier, mal écrire
mist [ˈmɪst] *n* : brume *f*
mistake [mɪˈsteɪk] *vt* **-took** [-ˈstʊk]; **-taken** [-ˈsteɪkən]; **-taking 1** MISINTERPRET : mal comprendre **2** CONFUSE : confondre — **~** *n* **1** : faute *f,* erreur *f* **2 make a ~** : se tromper — **mistaken** [mɪˈsteɪkən] *adj* : erroné
mister [ˈmɪstər] *n* : monsieur *m*
mistletoe [ˈmɪsəlˌto:] *n* : gui *m*
mistreat [mɪsˈtri:t] *vt* : maltraiter
mistress [ˈmɪstrəs] *n* **1** : maîtresse *f* (de classe) **2** LOVER : amante *f*
mistrust [mɪsˈtrʌst] *n* : méfiance *f* — **~** *vt* : se méfier de
misty [ˈmɪsti] *adj* **mistier; -est** : brumeux
misunderstand [ˌmɪsˌʌndərˈstænd] *vt* **-stood** [-ˈstʊd]; **-standing** : mal comprendre — **misunderstanding** [ˌmɪsˌʌndərˈstændɪŋ] *n* : malentendu *m*
misuse [mɪsˈju:z] *vt* **-used; -using 1** : mal employer **2** MISTREAT : maltraiter — **~** [mɪsˈju:s] *n* : mauvais emploi *m,* abus *m*
mitigate [ˈmɪṭəˌgeɪt] *vt* **-gated; -gating** : atténuer
mitt [ˈmɪt] *n* : gant *m* (de baseball) — **mitten** [ˈmɪtən] *n* : moufle *f,* mitaine *f Can*
mix [ˈmɪks] *vt* **1** : mélanger **2 ~ up** : confondre — *vi* : se mélanger — **~** *n* : mélange *m* — **mixture** [ˈmɪkstʃər] *n* : mélange *m* — **mix–up** [ˈmɪksˌʌp] *n* : confusion *f*
moan [ˈmo:n] *n* : gémissement *m* — **~** *vi* : gémir
mob [ˈmɑb] *n* : foule *f* — **~** *vt* **mobbed; mobbing** : assaillir
mobile [ˈmo:bəl, -ˌbi:l, -ˌbaɪl] *adj* : mobile — **~** [ˈmo:ˌbi:l] *n* : mobile *m* — **mobile home** *n* : auto-caravane *f* — **mobility** [moˈbɪləṭi] *n* : mobilité *f* — **mobilize** [ˈmo:bəˌlaɪz] *vt* **-lized; -lizing** : mobiliser
moccasin [ˈmɑkəsən] *n* : mocassin *m*
mock [ˈmɑk, ˈmɔk] *vt* : se moquer de — **~** *adj* : faux — **mockery** [ˈmɑkəri, ˈmɔ-] *n, pl* **-eries** : moquerie *f*
mode [ˈmo:d] *n* : mode *m*
model [ˈmɑdəl] *n* **1** : modèle *m* **2** MOCK-UP : maquette *f* **3** : mannequin *m* (personne) — **~** *v* **-eled** *or* **-elled; -eling** *or* **-elling** *vt* **1** SHAPE : modeler **2** WEAR : porter — *vi* : travailler comme mannequin — **~** *adj* : modèle
modem [ˈmo:dəm, -ˌdɛm] *n* : modem *m*
moderate [ˈmɑdərət] *adj* : modéré — **~** *n* : modéré *m,* -rée *f* — **~** [ˈmɑdəˌreɪt] *v* **-ated; -ating** *vt* : modérer — *vi* : se modérer — **moderation** [ˌmɑˈdəˈreɪʃən] *n* : modération *f* — **moderator** [ˈmɑdəˌreɪṭər] *n* : animateur *m,* -trice *f*
modern [ˈmɑdərn] *adj* : moderne — **modernize** [ˈmɑdərˌnaɪz] *vt* **-nized; -nizing** : moderniser
modest [ˈmɑdəst] *adj* : modeste — **modesty** [ˈmɑdəsti] *n* : modestie *f*
modify [ˈmɑdəˌfaɪ] *vt* **-fied; -fying** : modifier
moist [ˈmɔɪst] *adj* : humide — **moisten** [ˈmɔɪsən] *vt* : humecter — **moisture** [ˈmɔɪstʃər] *n* : humidité *f* — **moisturizer** [ˈmɔɪstʃəˌraɪzər] *n* : crème *f* hydratante
molar [ˈmo:lər] *n* : molaire *f*
molasses [məˈlæsəz] *n* : mélasse *f*
mold[1] [ˈmo:ld] *n* FORM : moule *m* — **~** *vt* : mouler, former
mold[2] *n* : moisissure *f* — **moldy** [ˈmo:ldi] *adj* **moldier; -est** : moisi

mole[1] [ˈmo:l] *n* : grain *m* de beauté (sur la peau)
mole[2] *n* : taupe *f* (animal)
molecule [ˈmɑlɪˌkju:l] *n* : molécule *f*
molest [məˈlɛst] *vt* **1** HARASS : importuner **2** : abuser (sexuellement)
molt [ˈmo:lt] *vi* : muer
molten [ˈmo:ltən] *adj* : en fusion
mom [ˈmɑm] *n* : maman *f*
moment [ˈmo:mənt] *n* : instant *m*, moment *m* — **momentarily** [ˌmo:mənˈtɛrəli] *adv* **1** : momentanément **2** SOON : dans un instant, immédiatement — **momentary** [ˈmo:mənˌtɛri] *adj* : momentané
momentous [moˈmɛntəs] *adj* : très important
momentum [moˈmɛntəm] *n, pl* **-ta** [-tə] *or* **-tums** **1** : moment *m* (en physique) **2** IMPETUS : élan *m*
monarch [ˈmɑˌnɑrk, -nərk] *n* : monarque *m* — **monarchy** [ˈmɑˌnɑrki, -nər-] *n, pl* **-chies** : monarchie *f*
monastery [ˈmɑnəˌstɛri] *n, pl* **-teries** : monastère *m*
Monday [ˈmʌnˌdeɪ, -di] *n* : lundi *m*
money [ˈmʌni] *n, pl* **-eys** *or* **-ies** [-iz] : argent *m* — **monetary** [ˈmɑnəˌtɛri, ˈmʌnə-] *adj* : monétaire — **money order** *n* : mandat-poste *m*
mongrel [ˈmɑŋgrəl, ˈmʌŋ-] *n* : chien *m* métisse
monitor [ˈmɑnəţər] *n* : moniteur *m* (d'un ordinateur, etc.) — ~ *vt* : surveiller
monk [ˈmʌŋk] *n* : moine *m*
monkey [ˈmʌŋki] *n, pl* **-keys** : singe *m* — **monkey wrench** *n* : clé *f* à molette
monogram [ˈmɑnəˌgræm] *n* : monogramme *m*
monologue [ˈmɑnəˌlɔg] *n* : monologue *m*
monopoly [məˈnɑpəli] *n, pl* **-lies** : monopole *m* — **monopolize** [məˈnɑpəˌlaɪz] *vt* **-lized; -lizing** : monopoliser
monotonous [məˈnɑtənəs] *adj* : monotone — **monotony** [məˈnɑtəni] *n* : monotonie *f*
monster [ˈmɑntstər] *n* : monstre *m* — **monstrosity** [mɑnˈstrɑsəţi] *n, pl* **-ties** : monstruosité *f* — **monstrous** [ˈmɑntstrəs] *adj* **1** : monstrueux **2** HUGE : gigantesque
month [ˈmʌnθ] *n* : mois *m* — **monthly** [ˈmʌnθli] *adv* : mensuellement — ~ *adj* : mensuel
monument [ˈmɑnjəmənt] *n* : monument *m* — **monumental** [ˌmɑnjəˈmɛntəl] *adj* : monumental
moo [ˈmu:] *vi* : meugler — ~ *n* : meuglement *m*
mood [ˈmu:d] *n* : humeur *f* — **moody** [ˈmu:di] *adj* **moodier; -est** **1** GLOOMY : mélancolique, déprimé **2** IRRITABLE : de mauvaise humeur **3** TEMPERAMENTAL : d'humeur changeante
moon [ˈmu:n] *n* : lune *f* — **moonlight** [ˈmu:nˌlaɪt] *n* : clair *m* de lune
moor[1] [ˈmʊr] *n* : lande *f*
moor[2] *vt* : amarrer — **mooring** [ˈmʊrɪŋ] *n* : mouillage *m*
moose [ˈmu:s] *ns & pl* : orignal *m*
moot [ˈmu:t] *adj* : discutable
mop [ˈmɑp] *n* **1** : balai *m* à franges **2** *or* **~ of hair** : tignasse *f* — ~ *vt* **mopped; mopping** : laver (le plancher, etc.)
mope [ˈmo:p] *vi* **moped; moping** : être déprimé
moped [ˈmo:ˌpɛd] *n* : cyclomoteur *m*, vélomoteur *m*
moral [ˈmɔrəl] *adj* : moral — ~ *n* **1** : morale *f* (d'une histoire, etc.) **2** **~s** *npl* : mœurs *fpl* — **morale** [məˈræl] *n* : moral *m* — **morality** [məˈræləţi] *n, pl* **-ties** : moralité *f*
morbid [ˈmɔrbɪd] *adj* : morbide
more [ˈmor] *adj* : plus de — ~ *adv* **1** : plus, davantage **2** **~ and ~** : de plus en plus **3** **~ or less** : plus ou moins **4** **once ~** : encore une fois — ~ *n* **the ~** : le plus — ~ *pron* : plus — **moreover** [morˈo:vər] *adv* : de plus
morgue [ˈmɔrg] *n* : morgue *f*
morning [ˈmɔrnɪŋ] *n* **1** : matin *m*, avant-midi *f Can* **2** **good ~** : bonjour **3** **in the ~** : pendant la matinée
Moroccan [məˈrɑkən] *adj* : marocain
moron [ˈmorˌɑn] *n* : imbécile *mf*
morose [məˈro:s] *adj* : morose
morphine [ˈmɔrˌfi:n] *n* : morphine *f*
morsel [ˈmɔrsəl] *n* **1** BITE : bouchée *f* **2** FRAGMENT : morceau *m*
mortal [ˈmɔrţəl] *adj* : mortel — ~ *n* : mortel *m*, -telle *f* — **mortality** [mɔrˈtæləţi] *n* : mortalité *f*
mortar [ˈmɔrţər] *n* : mortier *m*
mortgage [ˈmɔrgɪʤ] *n* : hypothèque *f* — ~ *vt* **-gaged; -gaging** : hypothéquer
mortify [ˈmɔrţəˌfaɪ] *vt* **-fied; -fying** : mortifier
mosaic [moˈzeɪɪk] *n* : mosaïque *f*
Moslem [ˈmɑzləm] → **Muslim**
mosque [ˈmɑsk] *n* : mosquée *f*

mosquito [mə'ski:ţo] *n, pl* **-toes** : moustique *m,* maringouin *m Can*

moss ['mɔs] *n* : mousse *f*

most ['mo:st] *adj* **1** : la plupart de **2** **(the) ~** : le plus — **~** *adv* : plus — **~** *n* : plus *m* — **~** *pron* : la plupart — **mostly** ['mo:stli] *adv* **1** MAINLY : principalement, surtout **2** USUALLY : normalement

motel [mo'tɛl] *n* : motel *m*

moth ['mɔθ] *n* : papillon *m* de nuit, mite *f*

mother ['mʌðər] *n* : mère *f* — **~** *vt* **1** : s'occuper de **2** SPOIL : dorloter — **motherhood** ['mʌðər,hʊd] *n* : maternité *f* — **mother-in-law** ['mʌðərɪn,lɔ] *n, pl* **mothers-in-law** : belle-mère *f* — **motherly** ['mʌðərli] *adj* : maternel — **mother-of-pearl** [,mʌðərəv'pərl] *n* : nacre *f*

motif [mo'ti:f] *n* : motif *m*

motion ['mo:ʃən] *n* **1** : mouvement *m* **2** PROPOSAL : motion *f* **3 set in ~** : mettre en marche — **~** *vi* **~ to** : faire signe à — **motionless** ['mo:ʃənləs] *adj* : immobile — **motion picture** *n* : film *m*

motive ['mo:ţɪv] *n* : motif *m* — **motivate** ['mo:ţə,veɪt] *vt* **-vated; -vating** : motiver — **motivation** [,mo:ţə'veɪʃən] *n* : motivation *f*

motor ['mo:ţər] *n* : moteur *m* — **motorbike** ['mo:ţər,baɪk] *n* : moto *f* — **motorboat** ['mo:ţər,bo:t] *n* : canot *m* à moteur — **motorcycle** ['mo:ţər,saɪkəl] *n* : motocyclette *f,* moto *f* — **motorcyclist** ['mo:ţər,saɪkəlɪst] *n* : motocycliste *mf* — **motorist** ['mo:ţərɪst] *n* : automobiliste *mf*

motto ['mɑţo:] *n, pl* **-toes** : devise *f*

mould ['mo:ld] → **mold**

mound ['maʊnd] *n* **1** PILE : tas *m* **2** HILL : monticule *m*

mount[1] ['maʊnt] *n* **1** HORSE : monture *f* **2** SUPPORT : support *m* — **~** *vt* : monter sur (un cheval, etc.)

mount[2] *n* HILL : mont *m* — **mountain** ['maʊntən] *n* : montagne *f* — **mountainous** ['maʊnt'nəs] *adj* : montagneux

mourn ['morn] *vt* **~ for s.o.** : pleurer qqn — *vi* : porter le deuil — **mournful** ['mornfəl] *adj* : triste — **mourning** ['mornɪŋ] *n* : deuil *m*

mouse ['maʊs] *n, pl* **mice** ['maɪs] : souris *f* — **mousetrap** ['maʊs,træp] *n* : souricière *f*

moustache ['mʌ,stæʃ, mə'stæʃ] → **mustache**

mouth ['maʊθ] *n* : bouche *f* (d'une personne, etc.), gueule *f* (d'un animal) — **mouthful** ['maʊθ,fʊl] *n* : bouchée *f* — **mouthpiece** ['maʊθ,pi:s] *n* : bec *m,* embouchure *f* (d'un instrument de musique)

move ['mu:v] *v* **moved; moving** *vi* **1** GO : aller **2** RELOCATE : déménager **3** STIR : bouger **4** ACT : agir — *vt* **1** : déplacer **2** AFFECT : émouvoir **3** TRANSPORT : transporter **4** PROPOSE : proposer — **~** *n* **1** MOVEMENT : mouvement *m* **2** RELOCATION : déménagement *m* **3** STEP : pas *m,* étape *m* — **movable** *or* **moveable** ['mu:vəbəl] *adj* : mobile — **movement** ['mu:vmənt] *n* : mouvement *m*

movie ['mu:vi] *n* **1** : film *m* **2 ~s** *npl* : cinéma *m*

mow ['mo:] *vt* **mowed; mowed** *or* **mown** ['mo:n]; **mowing** : tondre — **mower** ['mo:ər] → **lawn mower**

Mr. ['mɪstər] *n, pl* **Messrs.** ['mɛsərz] : Monsieur *m*

Mrs. ['mɪsəz, -səs, *esp South* 'mɪzəz, -zəs] *n, pl* **Mesdames** [meɪ'dɑm, -'dæm] : Madame *f*

Ms. ['mɪz] *n* : Madame *f,* Mademoiselle *f*

much ['mʌʧ] *adj* **more; most** : beaucoup de — **~** *adv* **more** ['mor]; **most** ['mo:st] **1** : beaucoup **2 as ~** : autant **3 how ~?** : combien? **4 too ~** : trop — **~** *pron* : beaucoup

muck ['mʌk] *n* : saleté *f*

mucus ['mju:kəs] *n* : mucus *m*

mud ['mʌd] *n* : boue *f,* bouette *f Can fam*

muddle ['mʌdəl] *v* **-dled; -dling** *vt* **1** CONFUSE : confondre **2** JUMBLE : embrouiller — *vi* **~ through** : se tirer d'affaire — **~** *n* : désordre *m,* fouillis *m*

muddy ['mʌdi] *adj* **-dier; -est** : boueux

muffin ['mʌfən] *n* : muffin *m Can*

muffle ['mʌfəl] *vt* **muffled; muffling** : étouffer (des sons) — **muffler** ['mʌflər] *n* : silencieux *m* (d'un véhicule)

mug ['mʌg] *n* CUP : tasse *f* — **~** *vt* **mugged; mugging** : agresser, attaquer — **mugger** ['mʌgər] *n* : agresseur *m*

muggy ['mʌgi] *adj* **-gier; -est** : lourd et humide

mule ['mju:l] *n* : mule *f,* mulet *m*

mull ['mʌl] *vt or* **~ over** : réfléchir sur

multicolored ['mʌlti,kʌlərd, 'mʌl,taɪ-] *adj* : multicolore

multimedia [ˌmʌltiˈmi:diə, ˌmʌlˌtaɪ-] *adj* : multimédia
multinational [ˌmʌltiˈnæʃənəl, ˌmʌl-ˌtaɪ-] *adj* : multinational
multiple [ˈmʌltəpəl] *adj* : multiple — ~ *n* : multiple *m* — **multiplication** [ˌmʌltəpləˈkeɪʃən] *n* : multiplication *f* — **multiply** [ˈmʌltəˌplaɪ] *v* **-plied; -plying** *vt* : multiplier — *vi* : se multiplier
multitude [ˈmʌltəˌtu:d, -ˌtju:d] *n* : multitude *f*
mum [ˈmʌm] *adj* **keep ~** : garder le silence
mumble [ˈmʌmbəl] *vi* **-bled; -bling** : marmonner
mummy [ˈmʌmi] *n, pl* **-mies** : momie *f*
mumps [ˈmʌmps] *ns & pl* : oreillons *mpl*
munch [ˈmʌntʃ] *v* : mâcher, mastiquer
mundane [ˌmʌnˈdeɪn, ˈmʌnˌ-] *adj* : routinier, ordinaire
municipal [mjʊˈnɪsəpəl] *adj* : municipal — **municipality** [mjʊˌnɪsəˈpæləṭi] *n, pl* **-ties** : municipalité *f*
munitions [mjʊˈnɪʃənz] *npl* : munitions *fpl*
mural [ˈmjʊrəl] *n* : peinture *f* murale
murder [ˈmərdər] *n* : meurtre *m* — ~ *vt* : assassiner — **murderer** [ˈmərdərər] *n* : meurtrier *m*, -trière *f*; assassin *m* — **murderous** [ˈmərdərəs] *adj* : meurtrier
murky [ˈmərki] *adj* **murkier; -est** : obscur, sombre
murmur [ˈmərmər] *n* : murmure *m* — ~ *v* : murmurer
muscle [ˈmʌsəl] *n* : muscle *m* — ~ *vi* **-cled; -cling** *or* **~ in** : s'ingérer avec force dans — **muscular** [ˈmʌskjələr] *adj* **1** : musculaire **2** STRONG : musclé
muse[1] [ˈmju:z] *n* : muse *f*
muse[2] *vi* **mused; musing** : méditer
museum [mjʊˈzi:əm] *n* : musée *m*
mushroom [ˈmʌʃˌru:m, -ˌrʊm] *n* : champignon *m* — ~ *vi* : proliférer, se multiplier
mushy [ˈmʌʃi] *adj* **mushier; -est** **1** SOFT : mou **2** SENTIMENTAL : mièvre
music [ˈmju:zɪk] *n* : musique *f* — **musical** [ˈmju:zɪkəl] *adj* : musical — ~ *n* : comédie *f* musicale — **musician** [mjʊˈzɪʃən] *n* : musicien *m*, -cienne *f*
musket [ˈmʌskət] *n* : mousquet *m*
Muslim [ˈmʌzləm, ˈmʊs-, ˈmʊz-] *adj* : musulman — ~ *n* : musulman *m*, -mane *f*
muslin [ˈmʌzlən] *n* : mousseline *f*
mussel [ˈmʌsəl] *n* : moule *f*
must [ˈmʌst] *v aux* **1** : devoir **2 she ~ try** : elle doit essayer **3 you ~ decide** : il faut que tu te décides — ~ *n* : nécessité *f*
mustache [ˈmʌˌstæʃ, mʌˈstæʃ] *n* : moustache *f*
mustard [ˈmʌstərd] *n* : moutarde *f*
muster [ˈmʌstər] *vt* : rassembler, réunir
musty [ˈmʌsti] *adj* **mustier; -est** : qui sent le renfermé
mute [ˈmju:t] *adj* **muter; mutest** : muet — ~ *n* : muet *m*, muette *f*
mutilate [ˈmju:ṭəˌleɪt] *vt* **-lated; -lating** : mutiler
mutiny [ˈmju:tәni] *n, pl* **-nies** : mutinerie *f* — ~ *vi* **-nied; -nying** : se mutiner
mutter [ˈmʌṭər] *vi* : marmonner
mutton [ˈmʌtən] *n* : viande *f* de mouton
mutual [ˈmju:tʃʊəl] *adj* **1** : mutuel **2** COMMON : commun — **mutually** [ˈmju:tʃʊəli, -tʃəli] *adv* : mutuellement
muzzle [ˈmʌzəl] *n* **1** SNOUT : museau *m* **2** : muselière *f* (pour un chien, etc.) **3** : gueule *f* (d'une arme à feu) — ~ *vt* **-zled; -zling** : museler
my [ˈmaɪ] *adj* : mon, ma, mes
myopia [maɪˈo:piə] *n* : myopie *f* — **myopic** [maɪˈo:pɪk, -ˈɑ-] *adj* : myope
myself [maɪˈsɛlf] *pron* **1** (*reflexive*) : me **2** (*emphatic*) : moi aussi **3 by ~** : tout seul
mystery [ˈmɪstəri] *n, pl* **-teries** : mystère *m* — **mysterious** [mɪˈstɪriəs] *adj* : mystérieux
mystic [ˈmɪstɪk] *adj or* **mystical** [ˈmɪstɪkəl] : mystique
mystify [ˈmɪstəˌfaɪ] *vt* **-fied; -fying** : rendre perplexe
myth [ˈmɪθ] *n* : mythe *m* — **mythical** [ˈmɪθɪkəl] *adj* : mythique

N

n ['ɛn] *n, pl* **n's** *or* **ns** ['ɛnz] : n *m,* quatorzième lettre de l'alphabet
nab ['næb] *vt* **nabbed; nabbing** : pincer *fam*
nag ['næg] *v* **nagged; nagging** *vi* COMPLAIN : se plaindre — *vt* : harceler — **nagging** ['nægɪŋ] *adj* : persistant
nail ['neɪl] *n* **1** : clou *m* **2** FINGERNAIL : ongle *m* — **~** *vt or* **~ down** : clouer — **nail file** *n* : lime *f* à ongles — **nail polish** *n* : vernis *m* à ongles
naive *or* **naïve** [nɑ'i:v] *adj* **-iver; -est** : naïf
naked ['neɪkəd] *adj* : nu — **nakedness** ['neɪkədnəs] *n* : nudité *f*
name ['neɪm] *n* **1** : nom *m* **2** REPUTATION : réputation *f* **3 what is your ~ ?** : comment vous appelez-vous? — **~** *vt* **named; naming 1** : nommer **2** : fixer (une date, un prix, etc.) — **nameless** ['neɪmləs] *adj* : sans nom, anonyme — **namely** ['neɪmli] *adv* : c'est-à-dire, savoir — **namesake** ['neɪm,seɪk] *n* : homonyme *m*
nap ['næp] *vi* **napped; napping** : faire un somme — **~** *n* : somme *m,* sieste *f*
nape ['neɪp, 'næp] *n* : nuque *f*
napkin ['næpkən] *n* **1** : serviette *f* **2** → **sanitary napkin**
narcotic [nɑr'kɑṭɪk] *n* **1** : narcotique *m* (en pharmacie) **2** DRUG : stupéfiant *m*
narrate ['nær,eɪt] *vt* **narrated; narrating** : raconter, narrer — **narration** [næ'reɪʃən] *n* : narration *f* — **narrative** ['nærəṭɪv] *n* : récit *m* — **narrator** ['nær,eɪṭər] *n* : narrateur *m,* -trice *f*
narrow ['nær,o:] *adj* **1** : étroit **2 by a ~ margin** : de justesse — **~** *vt* : limiter, réduire — *vi* : se rétrécir — **narrowly** ['næroli] *adv* : de justesse, de peu — **narrow-minded** [,næro'maɪndəd] *adj* : étroit d'esprit
nasal ['neɪzəl] *adj* : nasal
nasty ['næsti] *adj* **-tier; -est 1** MEAN : mauvais, méchant **2** UNPLEASANT : désagréable, sale **3** SERIOUS : grave — **nastiness** ['næstinəs] *n* : méchanceté *f*
nation ['neɪʃən] *n* : pays *m,* nation *f* — **national** ['næʃənəl] *adj* : national — **nationalism** ['næʃənə,lɪzəm] *n* : nationalisme *m* — **nationality** [,næʃə'næləṭi] *n, pl* **-ties** : nationalité *f* — **nationalize** ['næʃənə,laɪz] *vt* **-ized; -izing** : nationaliser — **nationwide** ['neɪʃən'waɪd] *adj* : dans tout le pays
native ['neɪṭɪv] *adj* **1** : natal (se dit d'un pays, etc.) **2** INNATE : inné **3 ~ language** : langue *f* maternelle — **~** *n* **1** : natif *m,* -tive *f* **2 be a ~ of** : être originaire de — **Native American** *adj* : amérindien *m* — **nativity** [nə'tɪvəṭi, neɪ-] *n, pl* **-ties** : nativité *f*
natural ['nætʃərəl] *adj* **1** : naturel **2** INBORN : né, inné — **naturalize** ['nætʃərə,laɪz] *vt* **-ized; -izing** : naturaliser — **naturally** ['nætʃərəli] *adv* **1** : naturellement **2** OF COURSE : bien sûr — **nature** ['neɪtʃər] *n* : nature *f*
naught ['nɔt] *n* **1** NOTHING : rien *m* **2** ZERO : zéro *m*
naughty ['nɔti] *adj* **-tier; -est** : méchant, vilain
nausea ['nɔziə, 'nɔʃə] *n* : nausée *f* — **nauseating** ['nɔzi,eɪṭɪŋ] *adj* : écœurant, nauséabond — **nauseous** ['nɔʃəs, -ziəs] *adj* : écœuré
nautical ['nɔṭɪkəl] *adj* : nautique
naval ['neɪvəl] *adj* : naval
nave ['neɪv] *n* : nef *f* (d'une église)
navel ['neɪvəl] *n* : nombril *m*
navigate ['nævə,geɪt] *v* **-gated; -gating** *vi* : naviguer — *vt* : naviguer sur (la mer, etc.), piloter (un avion), gouverner (un bateau) — **navigable** ['nævɪgəbəl] *adj* : navigable — **navigation** [,nævə'geɪʃən] *n* : navigation *f* — **navigator** ['nævə,geɪṭər] *n* : navigateur *m,* -trice *f*
navy ['neɪvi] *n, pl* **-vies** : marine *f* — **navy blue** *adj* : bleu marine
near ['nɪr] *adv* **1** : près **2 nowhere ~ enough** : loin d'être suffisant — **~** *prep* : près de — **~** *adj* : proche — **~** *vt* : approcher de — **nearby** [nɪr'baɪ, 'nɪr,baɪ] *adv* : tout près — **~** *adj* : voisin, proche — **nearly** ['nɪrli] *adv* : presque — **nearsighted** ['nɪr,saɪṭəd] *adj* : myope
neat ['ni:t] *adj* **1** TIDY : soigné, net **2** ORDERLY : bien rangé (se dit d'une chambre, etc.) **3** SKILLFUL : habile — **neatly** ['ni:tli] *adv* **1** : soigneusement **2** SKILLFULLY : habilement — **neatness** ['ni:tnəs] *n* : ordre *m,* propreté *f*
nebulous ['nɛbjʊləs] *adj* : nébuleux

necessary [ˈnɛsə,sɛri] *adj* : nécessaire — **necessarily** [,nɛsəˈserəli] *adv* : nécessairement, forcément — **necessitate** [nɪˈsɛsə,teɪt] *vt* **-tated; -tating** : nécessiter, exiger — **necessity** [nɪˈsɛsəṭi] *n, pl* **-ties 1** : nécessité *f* **2 necessities** *npl* : choses *fpl* essentielles

neck [ˈnɛk] *n* **1** : cou *m* **2** COLLAR : col *m,* encolure *f* **3** : col *m,* goulot *m* (d'une bouteille) — **necklace** [ˈnɛkləs] *n* : collier *m* — **necktie** [ˈnɛk,taɪ] *n* : cravate *f*

nectar [ˈnɛktər] *n* : nectar *m*

nectarine [,nɛktəˈri:n] *n* : nectarine *f*

need [ˈni:d] *n* **1** : besoin *m* **2 if ~ be** : si nécessaire, s'il le faut — **~** *vt* **1** : avoir besoin de **2 ~ to** : devoir — *v aux* **not ~ to** : ne pas être obligé de

needle [ˈni:dəl] *n* : aiguille *f* — **~** *vt* **-dled; -dling** : agacer

needless [ˈni:dləs] *adj* **1** : inutile **2 ~ to say** : il va sans dire

needlework [ˈni:dəl,wərk] *n* : travaux *mpl* d'aiguille

needy [ˈni:di:] *adj* **needier; -est** : dans le besoin

negative [ˈnɛgəṭɪv] *adj* : négatif — **~** *n* **1** : négatif *m* (en photographie) **2** : négation *f* (en grammaire)

neglect [nɪˈglɛkt] *vt* : négliger — **~** *n* : négligence *f*

negligee [,nɛgləˈʒeɪ] *n* : négligé *m*

negligence [ˈnɛglɪʤənts] *n* : négligence *f*

negligent [ˈnɛglɪʤənt] *adj* : négligent

negligible [ˈnɛglɪʤəbəl] *adj* : négligeable

negotiate [nɪˈgo:ʃi,eɪt] *v* **-ated; -ating** : négocier — **negotiable** [nɪˈgo:ʃəbəl, -ʃiə-] *adj* : négociable — **negotiation** [nɪ,goʃiˈeɪshən, -siˈeɪ-] *n* : négociation *f* — **negotiator** [nɪˈgo:ʃi,eɪṭər, -si,eɪ-] *n* : négociateur *m,* -trice *f*

Negro [ˈni:,gro:] *n, pl* **-groes** *sometimes considered offensive* : nègre *m,* négresse *f*

neigh [ˈneɪ] *vi* : hennir — **~** *n* : hennissment *m*

neighbor *or Brit* **neighbour** [ˈneɪbər] *n* : voisin *m,* -sine *f* — **~** *vt* : avoisiner — *vi* **~ on** : être voisin de — **neighborhood** *or Brit* **neighbourhood** [ˈneɪbər,hʊd] *n* **1** : quartier *m,* voisinage *m* **2 in the ~ of** : environ — **neighborly** *or Brit* **neighbourly** [ˈneɪbərli] *adj* : amical

neither [ˈni:ðər, ˈnaɪ-] *conj* **1 ~ . . . nor** : ni . . . ni **2 ~ do I** : moi non plus — **~** *pron* : aucun — **~** *adj* : aucun (des deux)

neon [ˈni:,ɑn] *n* : néon *m*

nephew [ˈnɛ,fju:, *chiefly Brit* ˈne,vju:] *n* : neveu *m*

Neptune [ˈnɛp,tu:n, -,tju:n] *n* : Neptune *f*

nerve [ˈnərv] *n* **1** : nerf *m* **2** COURAGE : courage *m* **3** GALL : culot *m fam,* toupet *m fam* **4 ~s** *npl* JITTERS : nerfs *mpl* — **nervous** [ˈnərvəs] *adj* : nerveux — **nervousness** [ˈnərvəsnəs] *n* : nervosité *f* — **nervy** [ˈnərvi] *adj* **nervier; -est** : effronté

nest [ˈnɛst] *n* : nid *m* — **~** *vi* : nicher

nestle [ˈnɛsəl] *vi* **-tled; -tling** : se blottir

net[1] [ˈnɛt] *n* : filet *m* — **~** *vt* **netted; netting** : prendre au filet (des poissons)

net[2] *adj* : net — **~** *vt* **netted; netting** YIELD : rapporter

nettle [ˈnɛṭəl] *n* : ortie *f*

network [ˈnɛt,wərk] *n* : réseau *m*

neurology [nʊˈrɑləʤi, njʊ-] *n* : neurologie *f*

neurosis [nʊˈro:sɪs, njʊ-] *n, pl* **-roses** [-,si:z] : névrose *f* — **neurotic** [nʊˈrɑṭɪk, njʊ-] *adj* : névrosé

neuter [ˈnu:ṭər, ˈnju:-] *adj* : neutre — **~** *vt* : châtrer

neutral [ˈnu:ṭrəl, ˈnju:-] *adj* : neutre — **~** *n* : point *m* mort, neutre *m Can* — **neutralize** [ˈnu:trə,laɪz, ˈnju:-] *vt* **-ized; -izing** : neutraliser — **neutrality** [nu:ˈtræləṭi, nju:-] *n* : neutralité *f*

neutron [ˈnu:,trɑn, ˈnju:-] *n* : neutron *m*

never [ˈnɛvər] *adv* **1** : jamais **2 I ~ said a word** : je n'ai rien dit — **nevermore** [,nɛvərˈmor] *adv* : plus jamais, jamais plus — **nevertheless** [,nɛvərðəˈlɛs] *adv* : néanmoins

new [ˈnu:, ˈnju:] *adj* : neuf, nouveau — **newborn** [ˈnu:,bɔrn, ˈnju:-] *adj* : nouveau-né — **newcomer** [ˈnu:,kʌmər, ˈnju:-] *n* : nouveau venu *m,* nouvelle venue *f* — **newly** [ˈnu:li, ˈnju:-] *adv* : récemment — **newlywed** [ˈnu:li,wɛd, ˈnju:-] *n* : nouveau marié *m,* nouvelle mariée *f* — **news** [ˈnu:z, ˈnju:z] *n* : nouvelles *fpl* — **newscast** [ˈnu:z,kæst, ˈnju:z-] *n* : journal *m* télévisé — **newscaster** [ˈnu:z,kæstər, ˈnju:z-] *n* : présentateur *m,* -trice *f* — **newsgroup** [ˈnu:z,gru:p, ˈnju:z-] *n* : forum *m* (en informatique) — **newsletter** [ˈnu:z,lɛṭər, ˈnju:z-] *n* : bulletin *m* — **newspaper** [ˈnu:z,peɪpər, ˈnju:z-] *n* : journal *m* — **newsstand**

['nu:z,stænd, 'nju:z-] *n* : kiosque *m* à journaux

newt ['nu:t, 'nju:t] *n* : triton *m*

New Year's Day *n* : jour *m* de l'An

next ['nɛkst] *adj* **1** : prochain **2** FOLLOWING : suivant — **~** *adv* **1** : la prochaine fois **2** AFTERWARD : ensuite **3** NOW : maintenant — **next door** ['nɛkst'dor] *adv* : à côté — **next–door** *adj* : voisin, d'à côté — **next to** *prep* **1** BESIDE : à côté de **2 ~ nothing** : presque rien

nib ['nɪb] *n* : bec *m* (d'un stylo)

nibble ['nɪbəl] *vt* **-bled; -bling** : grignoter

nice ['naɪs] *adj* **nicer; nicest 1** PLEASANT : bon, agréable **2** KIND : gentil, aimable — **nicely** ['naɪsli] *adv* **1** WELL : bien **2** KINDLY : gentiment — **niceness** ['naɪsnəs] *n* : gentillesse *f* — **niceties** ['naɪsət̬iz] *npl* : subtilités *fpl*

niche ['nɪtʃ] *n* **1** : niche *f* **2 find one's ~** : trouver sa voie

nick ['nɪk] *n* **1** NOTCH : entaille *f*, encoche *f* **2 in the ~ of time** : juste à temps — **~** *vt* : faire une entaille dans

nickel ['nɪkəl] *n* **1** : nickel *m* (métal) **2** : pièce *f* de cinq cents

nickname ['nɪk,neɪm] *n* : surnom *m* — **~** *vt* : surnommer

nicotine ['nɪkə,ti:n] *n* : nicotine *f*

niece ['ni:s] *n* : nièce *f*

niggling ['nɪgəlɪŋ] *adj* **1** PETTY : insignifiant **2** NAGGING : persistant

night ['naɪt] *n* **1** : nuit *f*, soir *m* **2 at ~** : le soir **3 tomorrow ~** : demain soir — **~** *adj* : de nuit — **nightclub** ['naɪt,klʌb] *n* : boîte *f* de nuit — **nightfall** ['naɪt,fɔl] *n* : tombée *f* de la nuit — **nightgown** ['naɪt,gaʊn] *n* : chemise *f* de nuit, robe *f* de nuit *Can* — **nightingale** ['naɪtən,geɪl, 'naɪt̬ɪŋ-] *n* : rossignol *m* — **nightly** ['naɪtli] *adv & adj* : (de) tous les soirs — **nightmare** ['naɪt,mær] *n* : cauchemar *m* — **nighttime** ['naɪt,taɪm] *n* : nuit *f*

nil ['nɪl] *n* NOTHING : zéro *m* — **~** *adj* : nul

nimble ['nɪmbəl] *adj* **-bler; -blest** : agile

nine ['naɪn] *n* : neuf *m* — **~** *adj* : neuf — **nine hundred** *adj* : neuf cents — **nineteen** [naɪn'ti:n] *n* : dix-neuf *m* — **~** *adj* : dix-neuf — **nineteenth** [naɪn'ti:nθ] *n* **1** : dix-neuvième *mf* **2 January ~** : le dix-neuf janvier — **~** *adj* : dix-neuvième — **ninetieth** ['naɪnt̬iəθ] *n* : quatre-vingt-dixième *mf* — **~** *adj* : quatre-vingt-dixième — **ninety** ['naɪnt̬i] *n, pl* **-ties** : quatre-vingt-dix *m* — **ninth** ['naɪnθ] *n* **1** : neuvième *mf* **2 March ~** : le neuf mars — **~** *adj* : neuvième

nip ['nɪp] *vt* **nipped; nipping 1** BITE : mordre **2** PINCH : pincer — **~** *n* **1** BITE : morsure *f* **2** PINCH : pincement *m* **3 there's a ~ in the air** : il fait frisquet — **nippy** ['nɪpi] *adj* **-pier; -est** : frisquet

nipple ['nɪpəl] *n* **1** : mamelon *m* (d'une femme) **2** : tétine *f* (d'un biberon)

nitrogen ['naɪtrədʒən] *n* : azote *m*

nitwit ['nɪt,wɪt] *n* : imbécile *mf*

no ['no:] *adv* **1** : non **2 ~ better** : pas mieux **3 ~ bigger** : pas plus grand **4 ~ longer** : ne … plus — **~** *adj* **1** : pas de, aucun **2 ~ parking** : stationnement interdit **3 ~ smoking** : défense de fumer — **~** *n, pl* **noes** *or* **nos** ['no:z] : non *m*

noble ['nobəl] *adj* **-bler; -blest** : noble — **~** *n* : noble *mf* — **nobility** [no'bɪlət̬i] *n* : noblesse *f*

nobody ['no:bədi, -,bɑdi] *pron* : personne

nocturnal [nɑk'tərnəl] *adj* : nocturne

nod ['nɑd] *v* **nodded; nodding** *vi* **1** : faire un signe de la tête **2** *or* **~ off** : s'endormir — *vt* **~ one's head** : faire un signe de la tête — **~** *n* : signe *m* de la tête

noise ['nɔɪz] *n* : bruit *m* — **noisily** ['nɔɪzəli] *adv* : bruyamment — **noisy** ['nɔɪzi] *adj* **noisier; -est** : bruyant

nomad ['no:,mæd] *n* : nomade *mf* — **nomadic** [no'mædɪk] *adj* : nomade

nominal ['nɑmənəl] *adj* : nominal

nominate ['nɑmə,neɪt] *vt* **-nated; -nating 1** PROPOSE : proposer **2** APPOINT : nommer — **nomination** [,nɑmə'neɪʃən] *n* : nomination *f*

nonalcoholic [,nɑn,ælkə'hɔlɪk] *adj* : non alcoolisé

nonchalant [,nɑnʃə'lɑnt] *adj* : nonchalant — **nonchalance** [,nɑnʃə'lɑnts] *n* : nonchalance *f*

noncommissioned officer [,nɑnkə'mɪʃənd] *n* : sous-officier *m*

noncommittal [,nɑnkə'mɪt̬əl] *adj* : évasif

nondescript [,nɑndɪ'skrɪpt] *adj* : quelconque

none ['nʌn] *pron* : aucun, aucune — **~** *adv* **1 ~ too** : pas tellement **2 ~ the worse** : pas plus mal

nonentity [,nɑn'ɛntət̬i] *n, pl* **-ties** : être *m* insignifiant

nonetheless [ˌnʌnðəˈlɛs] *adv* : néanmoins
nonexistent [ˌnɑnɪgˈzɪstənt] *adj* : inexistant
nonfat [ˌnɑnˈfæt] *adj* : sans matière grasse
nonfiction [ˌnɑnˈfɪkʃən] *n* : œuvres *fpl* non romanesques
nonprofit [ˌnɑnˈprɑfət] *adj* : à but non lucratif
nonsense [ˈnɑnˌsɛnts, -sənts] *n* : absurdités *fpl,* sottises *fpl* — **nonsensical** [nɑnˈsɛntsɪkəl] *adj* : absurde
nonstop [ˌnɑnˈstɑp] *adj* **1** : sans arrêt **2 ~ flight** : vol *m* direct
noodle [ˈnu:dəl] *n* : nouille *f*
nook [ˈnʊk] *n* : coin *m,* recoin *m*
noon [ˈnu:n] *n* : midi *m* — **~** *adj* : de midi
no one *pron* : personne *f*
noose [ˈnu:s] *n* : nœud *m* coulant
nor [ˈnɔr] *conj* **1** : ni **2 ~ can I** : moi non plus
norm [ˈnɔrm] *n* : norme *f* — **normal** [ˈnɔrməl] *adj* : normal — **normality** [nɔrˈmælət̬i] *n* : normalité *f* — **normally** [ˈnɔrməli] *adv* : normalement
north [ˈnɔrθ] *adv* : au nord, vers le nord — **~** *adj* : nord, du nord — **~** *n* **1** : nord *m* **2 the North** : le Nord — **North American** *adj* : nord-américain — **~** *n* : Nord-Américain *m,* -caine *f* — **northeast** [nɔrθˈi:st] *adv* : au nord-est, vers le nord-est — **~** *adj* : nord-est, du nord-est — **~** *n* : nord-est *m* — **northeastern** [nɔrθˈi:stərn] *adj* : nord-est, du nord-est — **northerly** [ˈnɔrðərli] *adj* : du nord — **northern** [ˈnɔrðərn] *adj* : nord, du nord — **northwest** [nɔrθˈwɛst] *adv* : au nord-ouest, vers le nord-ouest — **~** *adj* : nord-ouest, du nord-ouest — **~** *n* : nord-ouest *m* — **northwestern** [nɔrθˈwɛstərn] *adj* : nord-ouest, du nord-ouest
Norwegian [nɔrˈwi:dʒən] *adj* : norvégien
nose [ˈno:z] *n* **1** : nez *m* **2 blow one's ~** : se moucher — **~** *vi* **nosed; nosing** *or* **~ around** : fouiner *fam* — **nosebleed** [ˈno:zˌbli:d] *n* : saignement *m* de nez — **nosedive** [ˈno:zˌdaɪv] *n* : piqué *m*
nostalgia [nɑˈstældʒə, nə-] *n* : nostalgie *f* — **nostalgic** [-dʒɪk] *adj* : nostalgique
nostril [ˈnɑstrəl] *n* : narine *f* (d'une personne), naseau *m* (d'un animal)
nosy *or* **nosey** [ˈno:zi] *adj* **nosier; -est** : curieux, fureteur
not [ˈnɑt] *adv* **1** (*used to form a negative*) : ne...pas **2** (*used to replace a negative clause*) : non, pas **3 ~ at all** : pas du tout **4 I hope ~** : j'espère que non
notable [ˈno:t̬əbəl] *adj* : notable — **~** *n* : notable *m* — **notably** [ˈno:t̬əbli] *adv* : notamment
notary public [ˈno:t̬əri] *n, pl* **notaries public** *or* **notary publics** : notaire *m*
notation [noˈteɪʃən] *n* : notation *f*
notch [ˈnɑtʃ] *n* : entaille *f,* encoche *f*
note [ˈno:t] *vt* **noted; noting 1** NOTICE : remarquer **2** *or* **~ down** : noter — **~** *n* **1** : note *f* **2** LETTER : mot *m* **3 an artist of ~** : un artiste de renom — **notebook** [ˈno:tˌbʊk] *n* : carnet *m* — **noted** [ˈno:t̬əd] *adj* : éminent, célèbre — **noteworthy** [ˈno:tˌwərði] *adj* : notable, remarquable
nothing [ˈnʌθɪŋ] *pron* : rien — **~** *adv* **~ like** : pas du tout comme — **~** *n* **1** TRIFLE : rien *m* **2** ZERO : zéro *m*
notice [ˈno:t̬ɪs] *n* **1** : avis *m,* annonce *f* **2 be given one's ~** : recevoir son congé **3 take ~ of** : faire attention à — **~** *vt* **-ticed; -ticing** : s'apercevoir de, remarquer — **noticeable** [ˈno:t̬ɪsəbəl] *adj* : visible
notify [ˈno:t̬əˌfaɪ] *vt* **-fied; -fying** : aviser, notifier — **notification** [ˌno:t̬əfəˈkeɪʃən] *n* : avis *m*
notion [ˈno:ʃən] *n* **1** : notion *f,* idée *f* **2 ~s** *npl* : mercerie *f*
notorious [noˈto:riəs] *adj* : notoire — **notoriety** [ˌno:t̬əˈraɪət̬i] *n, pl* **-ties** : notoriété *f*
notwithstanding [ˌnɑtwɪθˈstændɪŋ, -wɪð-] *adv* : néanmoins — **~** *prep* : malgré
nougat [ˈnu:gət] *n* : nougat *m*
nought [ˈnɔt, ˈnɑt] → **naught**
noun [ˈnaʊn] *n* : nom *m,* substantif *m*
nourish [ˈnərɪʃ] *vt* : nourrir — **nourishing** [ˈnərɪʃɪŋ] *adj* : nourrissant — **nourishment** [ˈnərɪʃmənt] *n* : nourriture *f,* alimentation *f*
novel [ˈnɑvəl] *adj* : nouveau, original — **~** *n* : roman *m* — **novelist** [ˈnɑvəlɪst] *n* : romancier *m,* -cière *f* — **novelty** [ˈnɑvəlt̬i] *n, pl* **-ties** : nouveauté *f*
November [noˈvɛmbər] *n* : novembre *m*
novice [ˈnɑvɪs] *n* : novice *mf;* débutant *m,* -tante *f*
now [ˈnaʊ] *adv* **1** : maintenant **2 ~ and then** : de temps à autre — **~** *conj*

~ that : maintenant que — **~** *n* **1 by ~** : déjà **2 for ~** : pour le moment **3 up until ~** : jusqu'à maintenant — **nowadays** ['naʊə,deɪz] *adv* : de nos jours

nowhere ['no:,*h*wɛr] *adv* **1** : nulle part **2 ~ near** : loin de

noxious ['nɑkʃəs] *adj* : nocif

nozzle ['nɑzəl] *n* : ajutage *m*

nuance ['nu:,ɑnts, 'nju:-] *n* : nuance *f*

nucleus ['nu:kliəs, 'nju:-] *n, pl* **-clei** [-kli,aɪ] : noyau *m* — **nuclear** ['nu:kliər, 'nju:-] *adj* : nucléaire

nude ['nu:d, 'nju:d] *adj* **nuder; nudest** : nu — **~** *n* : nu *m*

nudge ['nʌʤ] *vt* **nudged; nudging** : donner un coup de coude à — **~** *n* : coup *m* de coude

nudity ['nu:dəṭi, 'nju:-] *n* : nudité *f*

nugget ['nʌgət] *n* : pépite *f*

nuisance ['nu:sənts, 'nju:-] *n* **1** ANNOYANCE : ennui *m* **2** PEST : peste *f*

null ['nʌl] *adj* **~ and void** : nul et non avenu

numb ['nʌm] *adj* **1** : engourdi **2 ~ with fear** : paralysé par la peur — **~** *vt* : engourdir

number ['nʌmbər] *n* **1** : nombre *m*, numéro *m* **2** NUMERAL : chiffre *m* **3 a ~ of** : un certain nombre de — **~** *vt* **1** : numéroter **2** INCLUDE : compter — **numeral** ['nu:mərəl, 'nju:-] *n* : chiffre *m* — **numerical** [nʊ'mɛrɪkəl, nyʊ-] *adj* : numérique — **numerous** ['nu:mərəs, 'nju:-] *adj* : nombreux

nun ['nʌn] *n* : religieuse *f*

nuptial ['nʌpʃəl] *adj* : nuptial

nurse ['nərs] *n* : infirmier *m*, -mière *f* — **~** *v* **nursed; nursing** *vt* **1** : soigner (un malade) **2** BREAST-FEED : allaiter — *vi* SUCKLE : téter — **nursery** ['nərsəri] *n, pl* **-eries 1** : crèche *f France*, garderie *f Can* **2** : pépinière *f* (pour les plantes) — **nursing home** *n* : maison *f* de retraite, centre *m* d'accueil *Can*

nurture ['nərʧər] *vt* **-tured; -turing 1** : élever **2** : nourrir (des espoirs, etc.)

nut ['nʌt] *n* **1** : noix *f* **2** LUNATIC : fou *m*, folle *f* **3** ENTHUSIAST : mordu *m*, -due *f fam* **4 ~s and bolts** : des écrous et des boulons — **nutcracker** ['nʌt,krækər] *n* : casse-noix *m* — **nutmeg** ['nʌt,mɛg] *n* : muscade *f*

nutrient ['nu:triənt, 'nju:-] *n* : substance *f* nutritive — **nutrition** [nʊ'trɪʃən, njʊ-] *n* : nutrition *f*, alimentation *f* — **nutritional** [nʊ'trɪʃənəl, njʊ-] *adj* : nutritif — **nutritious** [nʊ'trɪʃəs, njʊ-] *adj* : nourrissant, nutritif

nuts ['nʌts] *adj* : fou, cinglé *fam*

nutshell ['nʌt,ʃɛl] *n* **1** : coquille *f* de noix **2 in a ~** : en un mot

nuzzle ['nʌzəl] *v* **-zled; -zling** *vt* : frotter son nez contre — *vi* : se blottir

nylon ['naɪ,lɑn] *n* **1** : nylon *m* **2 ~s** *npl* : bas *mpl* de nylon

nymph ['nɪm*p*f] *n* : nymphe *f*

O

o ['o:] *n, pl* **o's** *or* **os** ['o:z] **1** : o *m*, quinzième lettre de l'alphabet **2** ZERO : zéro *m*

O ['o:] → **oh**

oak ['o:k] *n, pl* **oaks** *or* **oak** : chêne *m*

oar ['or] *n* : rame *f*, aviron *m*

oasis [o'eɪsɪs] *n, pl* **oases** [-,si:z] : oasis *f*

oath ['o:θ] *n, pl* **oaths** ['o:ðz, 'o:θs] **1** : serment *m* **2** SWEARWORD : juron *m*

oats ['o:ts] *npl* : avoine *f* — **oatmeal** ['o:t,mi:l] *n* : farine *f* d'avoine

obedient [o'bi:diənt] *adj* : obéissant — **obedience** [o'bi:diənts] *n* : obéissance *f* — **obediently** [o'bi:diəntli] *adv* : docilement

obese [o'bi:s] *adj* : obèse — **obesity** [o'bi:səṭi] *n* : obésité *f*

obey [o'beɪ] *v* **obeyed; obeying** *vt* : obéir à — *vi* : obéir

obituary [ə'bɪʧʊ,ɛri] *n, pl* **-aries** : nécrologie *f*

object ['ɑbʤɪkt] *n* **1** : objet *m* **2** AIM : objectif *m*, but *m* **3** : complément *m* d'objet (en grammaire) — **~** [əb'ʤɛkt] *vi* : protester, s'opposer — *vt* : objecter — **objection** [əb'ʤɛkʃən] *n* : objection *f* — **objectionable** [əb'ʤɛkʃənəbəl] *adj* : désagréable — **objective** [əb'ʤɛktɪv] *adj* : objectif — **~** *n* : objectif *m*

oblige [ə'blaɪʤ] *vt* **obliged; obliging 1** : obliger **2 be much ~d** : être très reconnaissant **3 ~ s.o.** : rendre service à qqn — **obligation** [,ɑblə'geɪʃən] *n* : obligation *f* — **obligatory**

[ə'blɪgəˌtori] *adj* : obligatoire — **obliging** [ə'blaɪʤɪŋ] *adj* : obligeant, aimable
oblique [o'bli:k] *adj* : oblique
obliterate [ə'blɪt̬əˌreɪt] *vt* **-ated; -ating** : effacer, détruire
oblivion [ə'blɪviən] *n* : oubli *m* — **oblivious** [ə'blɪviəs] *adj* : inconscient
oblong ['ɑˌblɔŋ] *adj* : oblong
obnoxious [ɑb'nɑkʃəs, əb-] *adj* : odieux
oboe ['o:ˌbo:] *n* : hautbois *m*
obscene [ɑb'si:n, əb-] *adj* : obscène — **obscenity** [ɑb'sɛnət̬i, əb-] *n, pl* **-ties** : obscénité *f*
obscure [ɑb'skjʊr, əb-] *vt* **-scured; -scuring 1** DARKEN : obscurcir **2** HIDE : cacher — **~** *adj* : obscur — **obscurity** [ɑb'skjʊrət̬i, əb-] *n, pl* **-ties** : obscurité *f*
observe [əb'zərv] *vt* **-served; -serving** : observer — **observant** [əb'zərvənt] *adj* : observateur — **observation** [ˌɑbsər'veɪʃən, -zər-] *n* : observation *f* — **observatory** [əb'zərvəˌtori] *n, pl* **-ries** : observatoire *m* — **observer** [əb'zərvər] *n* : observateur *m*, -trice *f*
obsess [əb'sɛs] *vt* : obséder — **obsession** [ɑb'sɛʃən, əb-] *n* : obsession *f* — **obsessive** [ɑb'sɛsɪv, əb-] *adj* : obsessionnel, obsédant
obsolete [ˌɑbsə'li:t, 'ɑbsəˌ-] *adj* : obsolète, démodé
obstacle ['ɑbstɪkəl] *n* : obstacle *m*
obstetrics [əb'stɛtrɪks] *ns & pl* : obstétrique *f*
obstinate ['ɑbstənət] *adj* : obstiné
obstruct [əb'strʌkt] *vt* **1** BLOCK : obstruer **2** HINDER : entraver — **obstruction** [əb'strʌkʃən] *n* : obstruction *f*
obtain [əb'teɪn] *vt* : obtenir
obtrusive [əb'tru:sɪv] *adj* : trop voyant (se dit des choses), importun (se dit des personnes)
obtuse [ɑb'tu:s, əb-, -'tju:s] *adj* : obtus
obvious ['ɑbviəs] *adj* : évident — **obviously** ['ɑbviəsli] *adv* **1** CLEARLY : manifestement **2** OF COURSE : évidemment, bien sûr
occasion [ə'keɪʒən] *n* **1** : occasion *f* **2** EVENT : événement *m* — **~** *vt* : occasionner, provoquer — **occasional** [ə'keɪʒənəl] *adj* : occasionnel — **occasionally** [ə'keɪʒənəli] *adv* : de temps en temps
occult [ə'kʌlt, 'ɑˌkʌlt] *adj* : occulte
occupy ['ɑkjəˌpaɪ] *vt* **-pied; -pying 1** : occuper **2 ~ oneself with** : s'occuper de — **occupancy** ['ɑkjəpəntsi] *n, pl* **-cies** : occupation *f* — **occupant** ['ɑkjəpənt] *n* : occupant *m*, -pante *f* — **occupation** [ˌɑkjə'peɪʃən] *n* **1** : occupation *f* **2** JOB : profession *f*, métier *m* — **occupational** [ˌɑkjə'peɪʃənəl] *adj* **1** : professionnel **2 ~ hazard** : risque *m* du métier
occur [ə'kər] *vi* **occurred; occurring 1** HAPPEN : avoir lieu, se produire, arriver **2** APPEAR : se trouver **3 ~ to s.o.** : venir à l'esprit de qqn — **occurrence** [ə'kərənts] *n* **1** EVENT : événement *m* **2** INSTANCE : cas *m*, apparition *f*
ocean ['o:ʃən] *n* : océan *m* — **oceanic** [ˌo:ʃi'ænɪk] *adj* : océanique
ocher *or* **ochre** ['o:kər] *n* : ocre *mf*
o'clock [ə'klɑk] *adv* **1 at six ~** : à six heures **2 it's ten ~** : il est dix heures
octagon ['ɑktəˌgɑn] *n* : octogone *m*
octave ['ɑktɪv] *n* : octave *f*
October [ɑk'to:bər] *n* : octobre *m*
octopus ['ɑktəˌpʊs, -pəs] *n, pl* **-puses** *or* **-pi** [-ˌpaɪ] : pieuvre *f*
ocular ['ɑkjələr] *adj* : oculaire — **oculist** ['ɑkjəlɪst] *n* : oculiste *mf*
odd ['ɑd] *adj* **1** STRANGE : étrange, bizarre **2** : dépareillé (se dit d'une chaussette, etc.) **3 ~ jobs** : travaux *mpl* divers **4 ~ number** : nombre *m* impair **5 a hundred ~ dollars** : cent dollars et quelques — **oddity** ['ɑdət̬i] *n, pl* **-ties** : étrangeté *f* — **oddly** ['ɑdli] *adv* : étrangement — **odds** ['ɑdz] *npl* **1** RATIO : cote *f* **2** CHANCES : chances *fpl* **3 at ~s** : en conflit — **odds and ends** *npl* : objets *mpl* divers
ode ['o:d] *n* : ode *f*
odious ['o:diəs] *adj* : odieux
odor *or Brit* **odour** ['o:dər] *n* : odeur *f* — **odorless** *or Brit* **odourless** ['o:dərləs] *adj* : inodore
of ['ʌv, 'ɑv] *prep* **1** : de **2 five minutes ~ ten** : dix heures moins cinq **3 made ~ wood** : en bois **4 the eighth ~ April** : le huit avril
off ['ɔf] *adv* **1 be ~** LEAVE : s'en aller **2 come ~** : se détacher **3 cut ~** : couper **4 day ~** : jour *m* de congé **5 far ~** : éloigné **6 ~ and on** : par périodes **7 take ~** REMOVE : enlever **8 ten miles ~** : à dix milles d'ici **9 three weeks ~** : en trois semaines — **~** *prep* **1** : de **2 be ~ duty** : être libre **3 be ~ the point** : ne pas être la question **4 ~ center** : mal centré — **~** *adj* **1** OUT : éteint, fermé **2** CANCELED : annulé **3 on the ~ chance** : au cas où
offend [ə'fɛnd] *vt* : offenser — **offend-**

er [ə'fɛndər] *n* : délinquant *m,* -quante *f;* coupable *mf* — **offense** *or* **offence** [ə'fɛnts, 'ɔ,fɛnts] *n* **1** INSULT : offense *f* **2** CRIME : délit *m* **3** : attaque *f* (aux sports) **4 take ~** : s'offenser — **offensive** [ə'fɛntsɪv, 'ɔ,fɛnt-] *adj* : offensif — **~** *n* : offensive *f*

offer ['ɔfər] *vt* : offrir, présenter — **~** *n* : proposition *f,* offre *f* — **offering** ['ɔfərɪŋ] *n* : offre *f,* offrande *f* (en réligion)

offhand ['ɔf'hænd] *adv* : spontanément, au pied levé — **~** *adj* : désinvolte

office ['ɔfəs] *n* **1** : bureau *m* **2** POSITION : fonction *f,* poste *m* — **officer** ['ɔfəsər] *n* **1** *or* **police ~** : policier *m,* agent *m* (de police) **2** OFFICIAL : fonctionnaire *mf* **3** : officier *m* (dans l'armée) — **official** [ə'fɪʃəl] *adj* : officiel — **~** *n* : officiel *m,* -cielle *f*

offing ['ɔfɪŋ] *n* **in the ~** : en perspective, imminent

offset ['ɔf,sɛt] *vt* **-set; -setting** : compenser

offshore ['ɔf'ʃor] *adv* : en mer — **~** *adj* : côtier, marin

offspring ['ɔf,sprɪŋ] *ns & pl* : progéniture *f*

often ['ɔfən, 'ɔftən] *adv* **1** : souvent, fréquemment **2 every so ~** : de temps en temps

ogle ['o:gəl] *vt* **ogled; ogling** : lorgner

ogre ['o:gər] *n* : ogre *m,* ogresse *f*

oh ['o:] *interj* **1** : oh **2 ~ really?** : vraiment?

oil ['ɔɪl] *n* **1** : huile *f* (d'olive, etc.) **2** PETROLEUM : pétrole *m* **3** *or* **heating ~** : mazout *m* — **~** *vt* : huiler, lubrifier — **oilskin** ['ɔɪl,skɪn] *n* : ciré *m* — **oily** ['ɔɪli] *adj* **oilier; -est** : huileux

ointment ['ɔɪntmənt] *n* : pommade *f*

OK *or* **okay** [,o:'keɪ] *adv* **1** WELL : bien **2** YES : oui — **~** *adj* **1** ALL RIGHT : bien **2 are you ~?** : ça va? — **~** *vt* **OK'd** *or* **okayed; OK'ing** *or* **okaying** : approuver — **~** *n* **1** APPROVAL : accord *m* **2 give the ~** : donner le feu vert

okra ['o:krə, *south also* -kri] *n* : gombo *m*

old ['o:ld] *adj* **1** : vieux **2** FORMER : ancien **3 any ~** : n'importe quel **4 be ten years ~** : avoir dix ans **5 ~ age** : vieillesse *f* **6 ~ man** : vieux *m* **7 ~ woman** : vieille *f* — **~** *n* **the ~** : les vieux, les personnes âgées — **old–fashioned** ['o:ld'fæʃənd] *adj* : démodé

olive ['ɑlɪv, -ləv] *n* **1** : olive *f* (fruit) **2** *or* **~ green** : vert *m* olive

Olympic [o'lɪmpɪk] *adj* : olympique — **Olympic Games** [o'lɪmpɪk] *or* **Olympics** [-pɪks] *npl* : jeux *mpl* Olympiques

omelet *or* **omelette** ['ɑmlət, 'ɑmə-] *n* : omelette *f*

omen ['o:mən] *n* : augure *m,* présage *m*

omit [o'mɪt] *vt* **omitted; omitting** : omettre — **omission** [o'mɪʃən] *n* : omission *f*

omnipotent [ɑm'nɪpəṭənt] *adj* : omnipotent

on ['ɑn, 'ɔn] *prep* **1** : sur **2 ~ fire** : en feu **3 ~ foot** : à pied **4 ~ Friday** : vendredi **5 ~ the plane** : dans l'avion **6 ~ the right** : à droite — **~** *adv* **1 from that moment ~** : à partir de ce moment-là **2 later ~** : plus tard **3 put ~** : mettre — **~** *adj* **1** : allumé (se dit d'une lumière), en marche (se dit d'un moteur), ouvert (se dit d'un robinet) **2 be ~** : avoir lieu (se dit d'un événement)

once ['wʌnts] *adv* **1** : une fois **2** FORMERLY : autrefois — **~** *n* **1** : une seule fois **2 at ~** SIMULTANEOUSLY : en même temps **3 at ~** IMMEDIATELY : tout de suite — **~** *conj* : dès que, une fois que

oncoming ['ɑn,kʌmɪŋ, 'ɔn-] *adj* : qui approche

one ['wʌn] *n* **1** : un *m* (numéro) **2 ~ o'clock** : une heure — **~** *adj* **1** : un, une **2** ONLY : seul, unique **3** SAME : même — **~** *pron* **1** : un, une **2 ~ another** : l'un l'autre **3 ~ never knows** : on ne sait jamais **4 this ~** : celui-ci, celle-ci **5 that ~** : celui-là, celle-là **6 which ~?** : lequel?, laquelle? — **oneself** [,wən'sɛlf] *pron* **1** (*used reflexively*) : se **2** (*used for emphasis*) : soi-même **3** (*used after prepositions*) : soi **4 by ~** : seul — **one–sided** ['wʌn'saɪdəd] *adj* **1** UNEQUAL : inégal **2** BIASED : partial — **one–way** ['wʌn'weɪ] *adj* **1** : à sens unique (se dit d'une route) **2 ~ ticket** : aller *m* simple

ongoing ['ɑn,go:ɪŋ] *adj* : continu, en cours

onion ['ʌnjən] *n* : oignon *m*

online ['ɑn,laɪn, 'ɔn-] *adj or adv* : en ligne

only ['o:nli] *adj* : seul, unique — **~** *adv* **1** : seulement, ne...que **2 if ~** : si, si seulement **3 ~ too well** : trop bien — **~** *conj* BUT : mais

onset ['ɑn,sɛt] *n* : début *m*

onslaught [ˈanˌslɔt, ˈɔn-] *n* : attaque *f*
onto [ˈanˌtu:, ˈɔn-] *prep* : sur
onus [ˈo:nəs] *n* : responsabilité *f*, charge *f*
onward [ˈanwərd, ˈɔn-] *adv & adj* **1** : en avant **2 from today ~** : à partir d'aujourd'hui
onyx [ˈanɪks] *n* : onyx *m*
ooze [ˈu:z] *vi* **oozed; oozing** : suinter
opal [ˈo:pəl] *n* : opale *f*
opaque [oˈpeɪk] *adj* : opaque
open [ˈo:pən] *adj* **1** : ouvert **2** FRANK : franc, sincère **3** CLEAR : dégagé **4** PUBLIC : public **5** UNCOVERED : découvert — **~** *vt* **1** : ouvrir **2** START : commencer — *vi* **1** : s'ouvrir **2** BEGIN : commencer **3 ~ onto** : donner sur — **~** *n* **1 in the ~** OUTDOORS : au grand air, dehors **2 in the ~** KNOWN : connu — **open-air** [ˈo:pənˈær] *adj* : en plein air — **opener** [ˈo:pənər] *n* or **can ~** : ouvre-boîtes — **opening** [ˈo:pənɪŋ] *n* **1** : ouverture *f* **2** START : début *m* **3** OPPORTUNITY : occasion *f* — **~** *adj* : premier, préliminaire — **openly** [ˈo:pənli] *adv* : ouvertement, franchement
opera [ˈaprə, ˈapərə] *n* : opéra *m*
operate [ˈapəˌreɪt] *v* **-ated; -ating** *vi* **1** FUNCTION : fonctionner, marcher **2 ~ on s.o.** : opérer qqn — *vt* **1** : faire fonctionner (une machine) **2** MANAGE : diriger, gérer — **operation** [ˌapəˈreɪʃən] *n* **1** : opération *f* **2 in ~** : en marche, en service — **operational** [ˌapəˈreɪʃənəl] *adj* : opérationnel — **operative** [ˈapərət̬ɪv, -ˌreɪ-] *adj* : en vigueur — **operator** [ˈapəˌreɪt̬ər] *n* **1** : opérateur *m*, -trice *f* **2** or **telephone ~** : standardiste *mf*
opinion [əˈpɪnjən] *n* : opinion *f*, avis *m* — **opinionated** [əˈpɪnjəˌneɪt̬əd] *adj* : opiniâtre
opium [ˈo:piəm] *n* : opium *m*
opossum [əˈpasəm] *n* : opossum *m*
opponent [əˈpo:nənt] *n* : adversaire *mf*
opportunity [ˌapərˈtu:nət̬i, -ˈtju:-] *n, pl* **-ties** : occasion *f* — **opportune** [ˌapərˈtu:n, -ˈtju:n] *adj* : opportun — **opportunism** [ˌapərˈtu:ˌnɪzəm, -ˈtju:-] *n* : opportunisme *m* — **opportunist** [ˌapərˈtu:nɪst, -ˈtju:-] *n* : opportuniste *mf* — **opportunistic** [ˌapərtu:ˈnɪstik, -tju:-] *adj* : opportuniste
oppose [əˈpo:z] *vt* **-posed; -posing** : s'opposer à — **opposed** [əˈpo:zd] *adj* **~ to** : opposé à
opposite [ˈapəzət] *adj* **1** FACING : d'en face **2** CONTRARY : opposé, inverse — **~** *n* : contraire *m* — **~** *adv* : en face — **~** *prep* : en face de — **opposition** [ˌapəˈzɪʃən] *n* : opposition *f*
oppress [əˈprɛs] *vt* **1** PERSECUTE : opprimer **2** BURDEN : oppresser — **oppression** [əˈprɛʃən] *n* : oppression *f* — **oppressive** [əˈprɛsɪv] *adj* : oppressif — **oppressor** [əˈprɛsər] *n* : oppresseur *m*
opt [ˈapt] *vi* : opter
optic [ˈaptɪk] or **optical** [ˈaptɪkəl] *adj* : optique — **optician** [apˈtɪʃən] *n* : opticien *m*, -cienne *f*
optimism [ˈaptəˌmɪzəm] *n* : optimisme *m* — **optimist** [ˈaptəmɪst] *n* : optimiste *mf* — **optimistic** [ˌaptəˈmɪstɪk] *adj* : optimiste
optimum [ˈaptəməm] *adj* : optimum — **~** *n, pl* **-ma** [ˈaptəmə] : optimum *m*
option [ˈapʃən] *n* : option *f* — **optional** [ˈapʃənəl] *adj* : facultatif, optionnel
opulence [ˈapjələnts] *n* : opulence *f* — **opulent** [-lənt] *adj* : opulent
or [ˈɔr] *conj* **1** (*indicating an alternative*) : ou **2** (*following a negative*) : ni **3 ~ else** OTHERWISE : sinon
oracle [ˈɔrəkəl] *n* : oracle *m*
oral [ˈorəl] *adj* : oral
orange [ˈɔrɪndʒ] *n* **1** : orange *f* (fruit) **2** : orange *m* (couleur)
orator [ˈɔrət̬ər] *n* : orateur *m*, -trice *f*
orbit [ˈɔrbət] *n* : orbite *f* — **~** *vt* : graviter autour de
orchard [ˈɔrtʃərd] *n* : verger *m*
orchestra [ˈɔrkəstrə] *n* : orchestre *m*
orchid [ˈɔrkɪd] *n* : orchidée *f*
ordain [ɔrˈdeɪn] *vt* **1** DECREE : décréter **2** : ordonner (en religion)
ordeal [ɔrˈdi:l, ˈɔrˌdi:l] *n* : épreuve *f*
order [ˈɔrdər] *vt* **1** COMMAND : ordonner **2** REQUEST : commander (un repas, etc.) **3** ORGANIZE : organiser — **~** *n* **1** : ordre *m* **2** COMMAND, REQUEST : commande *f* **3 in good ~** : en bon état **4 in ~ to** : afin de **5 out of ~** : en panne — **orderly** [ˈɔrdərli] *adj* **1** TIDY : en ordre, ordonné **2** DISCIPLINED : discipliné
ordinary [ˈɔrdənˌɛri] *adj* **1** USUAL : normal, habituel **2** AVERAGE : ordinaire, moyen — **ordinarily** [ˌɔrdənˈɛrəli] *adv* : d'ordinaire, d'habitude
ore [ˈor] *n* : minerai *m*
oregano [əˈrɛgəˌno:] *n* : origan *m*
organ [ˈɔrgən] *n* **1** : orgue *m* (instrument de musique) **2** : organe *m* (du corps) — **organic** [ɔrˈgænɪk] *adj* **1** : organique **2** NATUREL : biologique — **organism** [ˈɔrgəˌnɪzəm] *n* : organisme

m — **organist** ['ɔrgənɪst] *n* : organiste *mf* — **organize** ['ɔrgə,naɪz] *vt* **-nized; -nizing 1** : organiser **2 get organized** : s'organiser — **organization** [,ɔrgənə'zeɪʃən] *n* : organisation *f* — **organizer** ['ɔrgə,naɪzər] *n* : organisateur *m*, -trice *f*

orgasm ['ɔr,gæzəm] *n* : orgasme *m*

orgy ['ɔrʤi] *n, pl* **-gies** : orgie *f*

Orient ['ori,ɛnt] *n* **the ~** : l'Orient *m* — **orient** *vt* : orienter — **oriental** [,ori'ɛntəl] *adj* : oriental, d'Orient — **orientation** [,oriən'teɪʃən] *n* : orientation *f*

orifice ['ɔrəfəs] *n* : orifice *m*

origin ['ɔrəʤən] *n* : origine *f* — **original** [ə'rɪʤənəl] *adj* **1** : original **2** FIRST : premier — **~** *n* : original *m* — **originality** [ə,rɪʤə'nælət̬i] *n* : originalité *f* — **originally** [ə'rɪʤənəli] *adv* : à l'origine — **originate** [ə'rɪʤə,neɪt] *v* **-nated; -nating** *vt* : donner naissance à — *vi* : provenir, prendre naissance

ornament ['ɔrnəmənt] *n* : ornement *m* — **ornamental** [,ɔrnə'mɛntəl] *adj* : ornemental — **ornate** [ɔr'neɪt] *adj* : orné

ornithology [,ɔrnə'θɑləʤi] *n, pl* **-gies** : ornithologie *f*

orphan ['ɔrfən] *n* : orphelin *m*, -line *f*

orthodox ['ɔrθə,dɑks] *adj* : orthodoxe — **orthodoxy** ['ɔrθə,dɑksi] *n, pl* **-doxies** : orthodoxie *f*

orthopedic [,ɔrθə'pi:dɪk] *adj* : orthopédique — **orthopedics** [,ɔrθə'pi:dɪks] *ns & pl* : orthopédie *f*

oscillate ['ɑsə,leɪt] *vi* **-lated; -lating** : osciller — **oscillation** [,ɑsə'leɪʃən] *n* : oscillation *f*

ostensible [ɑ'stɛntsəbəl] *adj* : apparent — **ostentation** [,ɑstən'teɪʃən] *n* : ostentation *f*

osteopath ['ɑstiə,pæθ] *n* : ostéopathe *mf*

ostracism ['ɑstrə,sɪzəm] *n* : ostracisme *m* — **ostracize** ['ɑstrə,saɪz] *vt* **-cized; -cizing** : mettre au ban de la société

ostrich ['ɑstrɪʧ, 'ɔs-] *n* : autruche *f*

other ['ʌðər] *adj* **1** : autre **2 every ~ day** : tous les deux jours **3 on the ~ hand** : d'autre part — **~** *pron* **1** : autre **2 the ~s** : les autres **3 someone or ~** : quelqu'un — **other than** *prep* : autrement que, à part — **otherwise** ['ʌðər,waɪz] *adv* **1** : autrement **2** OR ELSE : sinon — **~** *adj* : autre

otter ['ɑt̬ər] *n* : loutre *f*

ought ['ɔt] *v aux* **1** : devoir **2 you ~ to have done it** : tu aurais dû le faire

ounce ['aʊnts] *n* : once *f*

our ['ɑr, 'aʊr] *adj* : notre, nos — **ours** ['aʊrz, 'ɑrz] *pron* **1** : le nôtre, la nôtre **2 a friend of ~** : un de nos amis **3 that's ~** : c'est à nous — **ourselves** [ɑr'sɛlvz, aʊr-] *pron* **1** (*used reflexively*) : nous **2** (*used for emphasis*) : nous-mêmes

oust ['aʊst] *vt* : évincer

out ['aʊt] *adv* **1** OUTSIDE : dehors **2 cry ~** : crier **3 eat ~** : aller au restaurant **4 go ~** : sortir **5 turn ~** : éteindre — **~** *prep* → **out of** — **~** *adj* **1** ABSENT : absent, sorti **2** RELEASED : sorti **3** UNFASHIONABLE : démodé **4** EXTINGUISHED : éteint **5 the sun is ~** : il fait soleil

outboard motor ['aʊt,bord] *n* : hors-bord *m*

outbreak ['aʊt,breɪk] *n* : éruption *f* (d'une maladie, etc.), déclenchement *m* (des hostilités, etc.)

outburst ['aʊt,bərst] *n* : explosion *f*, accès *m*

outcast ['aʊt,kæst] *n* : paria *m*

outcome ['aʊt,kʌm] *n* : résultat *m*

outcry ['aʊt,kraɪ] *n, pl* **-cries** : tollé *m*

outdated [,aʊt'deɪt̬əd] *adj* : démodé

outdo [,aʊt'du:] *vt* **-did** [-'dɪd]; **-done** [-'dʌn]; **-doing** [-'du:ɪŋ]; **-does** [-'dʌz] : surpasser

outdoor ['aʊt'dor] *adj* : en plein air, de plein air — **outdoors** ['aʊt'dorz] *adv* : dehors

outer ['aʊt̬ər] *adj* : extérieur — **outer space** *n* : espace *m* cosmique

outfit ['aʊt,fɪt] *n* **1** EQUIPMENT : équipement *m* **2** COSTUME : tenue *f* **3** GROUP : équipe *f* — **~** *vt* **-fitted; -fitting** : équiper

outgoing ['aʊt,go:ɪŋ] *adj* **1** LEAVING : en partance (se dit d'un train, etc.), sortant (se dit d'une personne) **2** EXTROVERTED : ouvert **3 ~ mail** : courrier *m* à expédier

outgrow [,aʊt'gro:] *vt* **-grew** [-'gru:]; **-grown** [-'gro:n]; **-growing** : devenir trop grand pour

outing ['aʊt̬ɪŋ] *n* : excursion *f*, sortie *f*

outlandish [aʊt'lændɪʃ] *adj* : bizarre

outlast [,aʊt'læst] *vt* : durer plus longtemps que

outlaw ['aʊt,lɔ] *n* : hors-la-loi *m* — **~** *vt* : proscrire

outlay ['aʊt,leɪ] *n* : dépenses *fpl*

outlet ['aʊt,lɛt, -lət] *n* **1** EXIT : sortie *f*, issue *f* **2** MARKET : débouché *m* **3** RELEASE : exutoire *m* **4** *or* **electrical ~**

: prise *f* de courant **5** *or* **retail ~** : point *m* de vente

outline [ˈautˌlaɪn] *n* **1** CONTOUR : contour *m* **2** SKETCH : esquisse *f* — **~** *vt* **-lined; -lining 1** : souligner le contour de **2** SUMMARIZE : exposer dans ses grandes lignes

outlive [ˌautˈlɪv] *vt* **-lived; -living** : survivre à

outlook [ˈautˌlʊk] *n* : perspective *f*

outlying [ˈautˌlaɪɪŋ] *adj* : écarté, périphérique

outmoded [ˌautˈmo:dəd] *adj* : démodé

outnumber [ˌautˈnʌmbər] *vt* : surpasser en nombre

out of *prep* **1** OUTSIDE : en dehors de **2** FROM : de **3 four ~ five** : quatre sur cinq **4 made ~ plastic** : fait en plastique **5 ~ control** : hors de contrôle **6 ~ money** : sans argent **7 ~ spite** : par dépit — **out–of–date** [ˌauṭəvˈdeɪt] *adj* **1** OLD-FASHIONED : démodé **2** EXPIRED : périmé — **out–of–doors** [auṭəvˈdorz] → **outdoors**

outpost [ˈautˌpo:st] *n* : avant-poste *m*

output [ˈautˌpʊt] *n* : rendement *m*, production *f*

outrage [ˈautˌreɪʤ] *n* **1** AFFRONT : outrage *m*, affront *m* **2** ANGER : indignation *f* — **~** *vt* **-raged; -raging** : outrager — **outrageous** [ˌautˈreɪʤəs] *adj* **1** DISGRACEFUL : scandaleux **2** EXCESSIVE : outrancier

outright [ˈautˌraɪt] *adv* **1** COMPLETELY : complètement **2** INSTANTLY : sur le coup **3** FRANKLY : carrément — **~** *adj* : total, absolu

outset [ˈautˌsɛt] *n* : début *m*, commencement *m*

outside [ˌautˈsaɪd, ˈautˌ-] *n* : extérieur *m* — **~** *adj* : extérieur — **~** *adv* : à l'extérieur, dehors — **~** *prep or* **~ of** : en dehors de, à part — **outsider** [ˌautˈsaɪdər] *n* : étranger *m*, -gère *f*

outskirts [ˈautˌskərts] *npl* : banlieue *f*, périphérie *f*

outspoken [ˌautˈspo:kən] *adj* : franc, direct

outstanding [ˌautˈstændɪŋ] *adj* **1** UNPAID : impayé **2** UNRESOLVED : en suspens **3** NOTABLE : exceptionnel

outstretched [ˌautˈstrɛʧt] *adj* : tendu

outstrip [ˌautˈstrɪp] *vt* **-stripped; -stripping** : devancer

outward [ˈautwərd] *or* **outwards** [-wərdz] *adv* **1** : vers l'extérieur **2 ~ bound** : en partance — **~** *adj* : extérieur — **outwardly** [ˈautwərdli] *adv* : en apparence

outweigh [ˌautˈweɪ] *vt* : l'emporter sur

outwit [ˌautˈwɪt] *vt* **-witted; -witting** : se montrer plus malin que

oval [ˈo:vəl] *adj* : ovale — **~** *n* : ovale *m*

ovary [ˈo:vəri] *n, pl* **-ries** : ovaire *m*

ovation [oˈveɪʃən] *n* : ovation *f*

oven [ˈʌvən] *n* : four *m*

over [ˈo:vər] *adv* **1** ABOVE : au-dessus **2** MORE : de trop **3** AGAIN : encore **4 all ~** : partout **5 ask ~** : inviter **6 four times ~** : quatre fois de suite **7 ~ here** : ici **8 ~ there** : là-bas **9 start ~** : recommencer — **~** *prep* **1** ABOVE : au-dessus de, par-dessus **2** MORE THAN : plus de **3** ACROSS : de l'autre côté de **4** DURING : pendant, au cours de **5** CONCERNING : au sujet de — **~** *adj* : fini, terminé

overall [ˌo:vərˈɔl] *adv* GENERALLY : en général — **~** *adj* : d'ensemble, total — **overalls** [ˈo:vərˌɔlz] *npl* : salopette *f*

overbearing [ˌo:vərˈbærɪŋ] *adj* : impérieux, autoritaire

overboard [ˈo:vərˌbord] *adv* : pardessus bord

overburden [ˌo:vərˈbərdən] *vt* : surcharger

overcast [ˈo:vərˌkæst] *adj* : couvert

overcharge [ˌo:vərˈʧɑrʤ] *vt* **-charged; -charging** : faire payer trop cher à

overcoat [ˈo:vərˌko:t] *n* : pardessus *m*

overcome [ˌo:vərˈkʌm] *vt* **-came** [-ˈkeɪm]; **-come; -coming 1** CONQUER : vaincre, surmonter **2** OVERWHELM : accabler

overcook [ˌo:vərˈkʊk] *vt* : faire trop cuire

overcrowded [ˌo:vərˈkraudəd] *adj* : bondé

overdo [ˌo:vərˈdu:] *vt* **-did** [-ˈdɪd]; **-done** [-ˈdʌn]; **-doing; -does** [-ˈdʌz] **1** : exagérer **2** → **overcook**

overdose [ˈo:vərˌdo:s] *n* : overdose *f*

overdraw [ˌo:vərˈdrɔ] *vt* **-drew** [-ˈdru:]; **-drawn** [-ˈdrɔn]; **-drawing** : mettre à découvert — **overdraft** [ˈo:vərˌdræft] *n* : découvert *m*

overdue [ˌo:vərˈdu:] *adj* **1** UNPAID : arriéré **2** LATE : en retard

overestimate [ˌo:vərˈɛstəˌmeɪt] *vt* **-mated; -mating** : surestimer

overflow [ˌo:vərˈflo:] *v* : déborder — **~** [ˈo:vərˌflo:] *n* : trop-plein *m*, débordement *m*

overgrown [ˌo:vərˈgro:n] *adj* : envahi par la végétation

overhand [ˈo:vərˌhænd] *adv* : pardessus la tête

overhang [ˌoːvərˈhæŋ] *vt* **-hung** [-ˈhʌŋ]; **-hanging** : surplomber
overhaul [ˌoːvərˈhɔl] *vt* : réviser (un moteur, etc.), remanier (un système, etc.)
overhead [ˌoːvərˈhɛd] *adv* : au-dessus — ~ *adj* : aérien — ~ *n* : frais *mpl* généraux
overhear [ˌoːvərˈhɪr] *vt* **-heard** [-ˈhərd]; **-hearing** : entendre par hasard
overheat [ˌoːvərˈhiːt] *vt* : surchauffer
overjoyed [ˌoːvərˈdʒɔɪd] *adj* : ravi
overland [ˈoːvərˌlænd, -lənd] *adv & adj* : par voie de terre
overlap [ˌoːvərˈlæp] *v* **-lapped; -lapping** *vt* : chevaucher — *vi* : se chevaucher
overload [ˌoːvərˈloːd] *vt* : surcharger
overlook [ˌoːvərˈlʊk] *vt* **1** : donner sur (un jardin, la mer, etc.) **2** IGNORE : négliger, laisser passer
overly [ˈoːvərli] *adv* : trop
overnight [ˌoːvərˈnaɪt] *adv* **1** : (pendant) la nuit **2** SUDDENLY : du jour au lendemain — ~ [ˈoːvərˌnaɪt] *adj* **1** : de nuit, d'une nuit **2** SUDDEN : soudain
overpass [ˈoːvərˌpæs] *n* : voie *f* surélevée *Can,* pont *m* autoroutier
overpopulated [ˌoːvərˈpɑpjəˌleɪt̬əd] *adj* : surpeuplé
overpower [ˌoːvərˈpaʊər] *vt* **1** CONQUER : vaincre **2** OVERWHELM : accabler
overrate [ˌoːvərˈreɪt] *vt* **-rated; -rating** : surestimer
override [ˌoːvərˈraɪd] *vt* **-rode** [-ˈroːd]; **-ridden** [-ˈrɪdən]; **-riding** **1** : passer outre à **2** ANNUL : annuler — **overriding** [oːvərˈraɪdɪŋ] *adj* : primordial
overrule [ˌoːvərˈruːl] *vt* **-ruled; -ruling** : rejeter
overrun [ˌoːvərˈrʌn] *vt* **-ran** [-ˈræn]; **-running** **1** INVADE : envahir **2** EXCEED : dépasser
overseas [ˌoːvərˈsiːz] *adv* : à l'étranger, outre-mer — ~ [ˈoːvərˌsiːz] *adj* : à l'étranger, extérieur
oversee [ˌoːvərˈsiː] *vt* **-saw** [-ˈsɔ]; **-seen** [-ˈsiːn]; **-seeing** : surveiller
overshadow [ˌoːvərˈʃæˌdoː] *vt* : éclipser
oversight [ˈoːvərˌsaɪt] *n* : oubli *m,* omission *f*
oversleep [ˌoːvərˈsliːp] *vi* **-slept** [-ˈslɛpt]; **-sleeping** : se réveiller trop tard
overstep [ˌoːvərˈstɛp] *vt* **-stepped; -stepping** : outrepasser
overt [oˈvərt, ˈoːˌvərt] *adj* : manifeste
overtake [ˌoːvərˈteɪk] *vt* **-took** [-ˈtʊk]; **-taken** [-ˈteɪkən]; **-taking** : dépasser
overthrow [ˌoːvərˈθroː] *vt* **-threw** [-ˈθruː]; **-thrown** [-ˈθroːn]; **-throwing** : renverser
overtime [ˈoːvərˌtaɪm] *n* **1** : heures *fpl* supplémentaires **2** : prolongations *fpl* (aux sports)
overtone [ˈoːvərˌtoːn] *n* : nuance *f,* sous-entendu *m*
overture [ˈoːvərˌtʃʊr, -tʃər] *n* : ouverture *f* (en musique)
overturn [ˌoːvərˈtərn] *vt* : renverser — *vi* : se renverser
overweight [ˌoːvərˈweɪt] *adj* : trop gros, obèse
overwhelm [ˌoːvərˈhwɛlm] *vt* **1** : submerger, accabler **2** DEFEAT : écraser — **overwhelming** [ˌoːvərˈhwɛlmɪŋ] *adj* : accablant, écrasant
overwork [ˌoːvərˈwərk] *vt* : surmener — ~ *n* : surmenage *m*
overwrought [ˌoːvərˈrɔt] *adj* : à bout de nerfs
owe [ˈoː] *vt* **owed; owing** : devoir — **owing to** *prep* : à cause de
owl [ˈaʊl] *n* : hibou *m*
own [ˈoːn] *adj* : propre — ~ *vt* : posséder, avoir — *vi* ~ **up** : avouer — ~ *pron* **1 my (your, his/her, our, their)** ~ : le mien, la mienne; le tien, la tienne; le vôtre, la vôtre; le sien, la sienne; le nôtre, la nôtre; le leur, la leur **2 on one's** ~ : tout seul **3 to each his** ~ : chacun son goût — **owner** [ˈoːnər] *n* : propriétaire *mf* — **ownership** [ˈoːnərˌʃɪp] *n* : possession *f*
ox [ˈɑks] *n, pl* **oxen** [ˈɑksən] : bœuf *m*
oxygen [ˈɑksɪdʒən] *n* : oxygène *m*
oyster [ˈɔɪstər] *n* : huître *f*
ozone [ˈoːˌzoːn] *n* : ozone *m*

P

p ['pi:] *n, pl* **p's** *or* **ps** ['pi:z] : p *m,* seizième lettre de l'alphabet
pace ['peɪs] *n* **1** STEP : pas *m* **2** SPEED : allure *f* **3 keep ~ with** : suivre — ~ *v* **paced; pacing** *vt* : arpenter — *vi* ~ **to and fro** : faire les cent pas
pacify ['pæsə,faɪ] *vt* **-fied; -fying** : pacifier, apaiser — **pacifier** ['pæsə,faɪər] *n* : tétine *f,* sucette *f* — **pacifist** ['pæsəfɪst] *n* : pacifiste *mf*
pack ['pæk] *n* **1** PACKAGE : paquet *m* **2** BAG : sac *m* **3** GROUP : bande *f,* meute *f* (de chiens) **4** : jeu *m* (de cartes) — ~ *vt* **1** PACKAGE : emballer **2** FILL : remplir **3** : faire (ses bagages) — **package** ['pækɪdʒ] *vt* **-aged; -aging** : empaqueter — ~ *n* : paquet *m,* colis *m* — **packet** ['pækət] *n* : paquet *m*
pact ['pækt] *n* : pacte *m*
pad ['pæd] *n* **1** CUSHION : coussin *m* **2** TABLET : bloc *m* (de papier) **3 ink ~** : tampon *m* encreur **4 launching ~** : rampe *m* de lancement **5** : protection *f* (aux sports) — ~ *vt* **padded; padding** : rembourrer — **padding** ['pædɪŋ] *n* STUFFING : rembourrage *m*
paddle ['pædəl] *n* **1** : pagaie *f,* aviron *m Can* **2** : raquette *f* (aux sports) — ~ *vt* **-dled; -dling** : pagayer
padlock ['pæd,lɑk] *n* : cadenas *m* — ~ *vt* : cadenasser
pagan ['peɪgən] *n* : païen *m,* païenne *f* — ~ *adj* : païen
page¹ ['peɪdʒ] **paged; paging** *vt* : appeler
page² *n* : page *f* (d'un livre)
pageant ['pædʒənt] *n* : spectacle *m* — **pageantry** ['pædʒəntri] *n* : apparat *m*
paid → **pay**
pail ['peɪl] *n* : seau *m*
pain ['peɪn] *n* **1** : douleur *f* **2 take ~s** *npl* : se donner de la peine — ~ *vt* : peiner, faire souffrir — **painful** ['peɪnfəl] *adj* : douloureux — **painkiller** ['peɪn,kɪlər] *n* : analgésique *m* — **painless** ['peɪnləs] *adj* : indolore, sans douleur — **painstaking** ['peɪn,steɪkɪŋ] *adj* : soigneux, méticuleux
paint ['peɪnt] *v* : peindre, peinturer *Can* — ~ *n* : peinture *f* — **paintbrush** ['peɪnt,brʌʃ] *n* : pinceau *m* (d'un artiste), brosse *f* — **painter** ['peɪntər] *n* : peintre *m* — **painting** ['peɪntɪŋ] *n* : peinture *f*
pair ['pær] *n* **1** : paire *f* **2** COUPLE : couple *m* — ~ *vi* : accoupler
pajamas *or Brit* **pyjamas** [pə'dʒɑməz, -'dʒæ-] *npl* : pyjama *m*
pal ['pæl] *n* : copain *m,* -pine *f*
palace ['pæləs] *n* : palais *m*
palate ['pælət] *n* : palais *m* — **palatable** ['pælət̬əbəl] *adj* : savoureux
pale ['peɪl] *adj* **paler; palest** : pâle — ~ *vi* **paled; paling** : pâlir — **paleness** ['peɪlnəs] *n* : pâleur *f*
palette ['pælət] *n* : palette *f*
pallid ['pæləd] *adj* : pâle
palm¹ ['pɑm, 'pɑlm] *n* : paume *f* (de la main)
palm² *or* ~ **tree** : palmier *m* — **Palm Sunday** *n* : dimanche *m* des Rameaux
palpitate ['pælpə,teɪt] *vi* **-tated; -tating** : palpiter — **palpitation** [,pælpə'teɪʃən] *n* : palpitation *f*
paltry ['pɔltri] *adj* **-trier; -est** : dérisoire
pamper ['pæmpər] *vt* : dorloter
pamphlet ['pæmpflət] *n* : dépliant *m,* brochure *f*
pan ['pæn] *n* **1** SAUCEPAN : casserole *f* **2** FRYING PAN : poêle *f*
pancake ['pæn,keɪk] *n* : crêpe *f*
pancreas ['pæŋkriəs, 'pæn-] *n* : pancréas *m*
panda ['pændə] *n* : panda *m*
pandemonium [,pændə'mo:niəm] *n* : tumulte *m*
pander ['pændər] *vi* : flatter (bassement)
pane ['peɪn] *n* : vitre *f,* carreau *m*
panel ['pænəl] *n* **1** : panneau *m* **2** COMMITTEE : comité *m* **3** *or* **control ~** : tableau *m* (de bord) — **paneling** ['pænəlɪŋ] *n* : lambris *m*
pang ['pæŋ] *n* : tiraillement *m*
panic ['pænɪk] *n* : panique *f* — ~ *v* **-icked; -icking** : paniquer
panorama [,pænə'ræmə, -'rɑ-] *n* : panorama *m* — **panoramic** [,pænə'ræmɪk, -'rɑ-] *adj* : panoramique
pansy ['pænzi] *n, pl* **-sies** : pensée *f*
pant ['pænt] *vi* : haleter
panther ['pænθər] *n* : panthère *f*
panties ['pæntiz] *npl* : (petite) culotte *f,* slip *m France*

pantomime ['pæntə,maɪm] *n* : pantomime *f*
pantry ['pæntri] *n, pl* **-tries** : garde-manger *m*
pants ['pænts] *npl* : pantalon *m*
panty hose ['pænti,ho:z] *npl* : collant *m*
papaya [pə'paɪə] *n* : papaye *f*
paper ['peɪpər] *n* **1** : papier *m* **2** DOCUMENT : document *m* **3** NEWSPAPER : journal *m* **4** : devoir *m* (scolaire) — ~ *vt* WALLPAPER : tapisser — ~ *adj* : de papier, en papier — **paperback** ['peɪpər,bæk] *n* : livre *m* de poche — **paper clip** *n* : trombone *m* —**paperwork** ['peɪpər,wərk] *n* : paperasserie *f*
par ['pɑr] *n* **1** EQUALITY : égalité *f* **2 on a ~ with** : de pair avec
parable ['pærəbəl] *n* : parabole *f*
parachute ['pærə,ʃu:t] *n* : parachute *m*
parade [pə'reɪd] *n* **1** : défilé *m*, parade *f* (militaire) **2** DISPLAY : étalage *m* — ~ *v* **-raded; -rading** *vi* MARCH : défiler — *vt* DISPLAY : faire étalage de
paradise ['pærə,daɪs, -,daɪz] *n* : paradis *m*
paradox ['pærə,dɑks] *n* : paradoxe *m* — **paradoxical** [,pærə'dɑksɪkəl] *adj* : paradoxal
paragraph ['pærə,græf] *n* : paragraphe *m*
parakeet ['pærə,ki:t] *n* : perruche *f*
parallel ['pærə,lɛl, -ləl] *adj* : parallèle — ~ *n* **1** : parallèle *f* (en géometrie) **2** SIMILARITY : parallèle *m* — ~ *vt* MATCH : égaler
paralysis [pə'ræləsɪs] *n, pl* **-yses** [-,si:z] : paralysie *f* — **paralyze** *or Brit* **paralyse** ['pærə,laɪz] *vt* **-lyzed** *or Brit* **-lysed; -lyzing** *or Brit* **-lysing** : paralyser
parameter [pə'ræməţər] *n* : paramètre *m*
paramount ['pærə,maʊnt] *adj* : suprême
paranoia [,pærə'nɔɪə] *n* : paranoïa *f* — **paranoid** ['pærə,nɔɪd] *adj* : paranoïaque
parapet ['pærəpət, -,pɛt] *n* : parapet *m*
paraphernalia [,pærəfə'neɪljə, -fər-] *ns & pl* : attirail *m*
paraphrase ['pærə,freɪz] *n* : paraphrase *f* — ~ *vt* **-phrased; -phrasing** : paraphraser
paraplegic ['pærə'pli:dʒɪk] *n* : paraplégique *mf*
parasite ['pærə,saɪt] *n* : parasite *m*
parasol ['pærə,sɔl] *n* : parasol *m*
paratrooper ['pærə,tru:pər] *n* : parachutiste *m* (militaire)
parcel ['pɑrsəl] *n* : paquet *m*
parch ['pɑrtʃ] *vt* : dessécher
parchment ['pɑrtʃmənt] *n* : parchemin *m*
pardon ['pɑrdən] *n* **1** FORGIVENESS : pardon *m* **2** : grâce *f* (en droit) — ~ *vt* **1** FORGIVE : pardonner **2** ABSOLVE : gracier
parent ['pærənt] *n* **1** : mère *f*, père *m* **2 ~s** *npl* : parents *mpl* — **parental** [pə'rɛntəl] *adj* : parental
parenthesis [pə'rɛnθəsəs] *n, pl* **-ses** [-,si:z] : parenthèse *f*
parish ['pærɪʃ] *n* : paroisse *f* — **parishioner** [pə'rɪʃənər] *n* : paroissien *m*, -sienne *f*
Parisian [pə'rɪʒən, -'ri-] *adj* : parisien
parity ['pærəţi] *n, pl* **-ties** : parité *f*
park ['pɑrk] *n* : parc *m* — ~ *vt* : garer — *vi* : se garer, stationner
parka ['pɑrkə] *n* : parka *m*
parliament ['pɑrləmənt] *n* : parlement *m* — **parliamentary** [,pɑrlə'mɛntəri] *adj* : parlementaire
parlor *or Brit* **parlour** ['pɑrlər] *n* : salon *m*
parochial [pə'ro:kiəl] *adj* **1** : paroissial **2** PROVINCIAL : de clocher, provincial
parody ['pærədi] *n, pl* **-dies** : parodie *f* — ~ *vt* **-died; -dying** : parodier
parole [pə'ro:l] *n* : liberté *f* conditionnelle
parquet ['pɑr,keɪ, pɑr'keɪ] *n* : parquet *m*
parrot ['pærət] *n* : perroquet *m*
parry ['pæri] *vt* **-ried; -rying 1** : parer (un coup) **2** EVADE : éluder (une question)
parsley ['pɑrsli] *n* : persil *m*
parsnip ['pɑrsnɪp] *n* : panais *m*
part ['pɑrt] *n* **1** : partie *f* **2** PIECE : pièce *f* **3** ROLE : rôle *m* **4** SHARE : part *f* **5** SIDE : parti *m* **6** : raie *f* (entre les cheveux) — ~ *vi* **1** *or* **~ company** : se séparer **2 ~ with** : se défaire de — *vt* SEPARATE : séparer
partake [pɑr'teɪk, pər-] *vi* **-took** [-'tʊk]; **-taken** [-'teɪkən]; **-taking ~ in** : participer à
partial ['pɑrʃəl] *adj* **1** INCOMPLETE : partiel **2** BIASED : partial
participate [pər'tɪsə,peɪt, pɑr-] *vi* **-pated; -pating** : participer — **participant** [pər'tɪsəpənt, pɑr-] *n* : participant *m*, -pante *f*
participle ['pɑrţə,sɪpəl] *n* : participe *m*
particle ['pɑrţɪkəl] *n* : particule *f*

particular [pɑr'tɪkjələr] *adj* **1** : particulier **2** FUSSY : exigeant — ∼ *n* **1 in** ∼ : en particulier **2** ∼**s** *npl* DETAILS : détails *mpl* — **particularly** [pɑr'tɪkjələrli] *adv* : particulièrement

partisan ['pɑrţəzən, -sən] *n* : partisan *m*, -sane *f*

partition [pər'tɪʃən, pɑr-] *n* **1** DISTRIBUTION : division *f* **2** DIVIDER : cloison *f* — ∼ *vt* **1** : diviser **2** : cloisonner (une pièce)

partly ['pɑrtli] *adv* : en partie

partner ['pɑrtnər] *n* **1** ASSOCIATE : associé *m*, -ciée *f* **2** : partenaire *mf* (aux sports, en danse) — **partnership** ['pɑrtnər,ʃɪp] *n* : association *f*

party ['pɑrti] *n, pl* **-ties 1** : parti *m* (politique) **2** PARTICIPANT : partie *f* **3** GATHERING : fête *f* **4** GROUP : groupe *m*

pass ['pæs] *vi* **1** MOVE : passer **2 come to** ∼ : se passer, advenir **3** *or* ∼ **away** DIE : mourir **4** ∼ **out** FAINT : s'évanouir — *vt* **1** : passer **2** OVERTAKE : dépasser **3** : réussir (un examen) **4** ∼ **up** : laisser passer — ∼ *n* **1** PERMIT : permis *m*, laissez-passer *m* **2** : passe *f* (aux sports) **3** *or* **mountain** ∼ : col *m* de montagne — **passable** ['pæsəbəl] *adj* ACCEPTABLE : passable — **passage** ['pæsɪʤ] *n* **1** : passage *m* **2** CORRIDOR : couloir *m* — **passageway** ['pæsɪʤ,weɪ] *n* : passage *m*, couloir *m*

passenger ['pæsənʤər] *n* : passager *m*, -gère *f*

passerby [,pæsər'baɪ, 'pæsər,-] *n, pl* **passersby** : passant *m*, -sante *f*

passing ['pæsɪŋ] *adj* : passager

passion ['pæʃən] *n* : passion *f* — **passionate** ['pæʃənət] *adj* : passionné

passive ['pæsɪv] *adj* : passif

Passover ['pæs,o:vər] *n* : Pâque *f* (juive)

passport ['pæs,port] *n* : passeport *m*

password ['pæs,wərd] *n* : mot *m* de passe

past ['pæst] *adj* **1** : dernier, passé **2** FORMER : ancien — ∼ *prep* **1** BEYOND : au-delà de **2** IN FRONT OF : devant **3 half** ∼ **one** : une heure et demie — ∼ *n* : passé *m* — ∼ *adv* : devant

pasta ['pɑstə, 'pæs-] *n* : pâtes *fpl*

paste ['peɪst] *n* **1** GLUE : colle *f* **2** DOUGH : pâte *f* — ∼ *vt* **pasted; pasting** : coller

pastel [pæ'stɛl] *n* : pastel *m* — ∼ *adj* : pastel

pasteurize ['pæsʧə,raɪz, 'pæstjə-] *vt* **-ized; -izing** : pasteuriser

pastime ['pæs,taɪm] *n* : passe-temps *m*

pastor ['pæstər] *n* : pasteur *m*

pastry ['peɪstri] *n, pl* **-tries** : pâtisserie *f*

pasture ['pæsʧər] *n* : pâturage *m*

pasty ['peɪsti] *adj* **-tier; -est 1** DOUGHY : pâteux **2** PALLID : terreux

pat ['pæt] *n* **1** TAP : (petite) tape *f* **2** : noix *f* (de beurre, etc.) — ∼ *vt* **patted; patting** : tapoter — ∼ *adv* **have down** ∼ : connaître par cœur

patch ['pæʧ] *n* **1** : pièce *f* (d'étoffe) **2** : plaque *f* (de glace) — ∼ *vt* **1** REPAIR : rapiécer **2** ∼ **up** : réparer — **patchy** ['pæʧi] *adj* **patchier; patchiest** : inégal, irrégulier

patent ['pætənt] *adj* **1** *or* **patented** [-təd] : breveté **2** ['pætənt, 'peɪt-] OBVIOUS : patent, évident — ∼ ['pætənt] *n* : brevet *m* — ∼ ['pætənt] *vt* : breveter

paternal [pə'tərnəl] *adj* : paternel — **paternity** [pə'tərnəţi] *n* : paternité *f*

path ['pæθ, 'pɑθ] *n* **1** : allée *f* (dans un parc) **2** TRAIL : chemin *m*, sentier *m* **3** COURSE : trajectoire *f*

pathetic [pə'θɛţɪk] *adj* : pitoyable

pathology [pə'θɑləʤi] *n, pl* **-gies** : pathologie *f*

pathway ['pæθ,weɪ] *n* : chemin *m*, sentier *m*

patience ['peɪʃənts] *n* : patience *f* — **patient** ['peɪʃənt] *adj* : patient — ∼ *n* : patient *m*, -tiente *f*; malade *mf* — **patiently** ['peɪʃəntli] *adv* : patiemment

patio ['pæţi,o:, 'pɑt-] *n, pl* **-tios** : patio *m*

patriot ['peɪtriət, -,ɑt] *n* : patriote *mf* — **patriotic** ['peɪtri'ɑţɪk] *adj* : patriote

patrol [pə'tro:l] *n* : patrouille *f* — ∼ *vi* **-trolled; -trolling** : patrouiller

patron ['peɪtrən] *n* **1** SPONSOR : mécène *m* **2** CUSTOMER : client *m*, cliente *f* — **patronage** ['peɪtrənɪʤ, 'pæ-] *n* **1** SPONSORSHIP : patronage *m* **2** CLIENTELE : clientèle *f* — **patronize** ['peɪtrə,naɪz, 'pæ-] *vt* **-ized; -izing 1** SUPPORT : patronner, parrainer **2** : traiter avec condescendance

patter ['pæţər] *n* : crépitement *m*

pattern ['pætərn] *n* **1** MODEL : modèle *m* **2** DESIGN : dessin *m*, motif *m* **3** NORM : mode *m*, norme *f* — ∼ *vt* : modeler

paunch ['pɔnʧ] *n* : bedaine *f*

pause ['pɔz] *n* : pause *f* — ∼ *vi* **paused; pausing** : faire une pause

pave ['peɪv] *vt* **paved; paving** : paver — **pavement** ['peɪvmənt] *n* : chaussée *f*

pavilion [pə'vɪljən] *n* : pavillon *m*

paw ['pɔ] *n* : patte *f* — ~ *vt* : tripoter
pawn[1] ['pɔn] *n* : gage *m*
pawn[2] *vt* : mettre en gage — **pawnbroker** ['pɔn,bro:kər] *n* : prêteur *m*, -teuse *f* sur gages — **pawnshop** ['pɔn,ʃɑp] *n* : mont-de-piété *m France*
pay ['peɪ] *v* **paid** ['peɪd]; **paying** *vt* **1** : payer **2** ~ **attention to** : prêter attention à **3** ~ **back** : rembourser **4** ~ **one's respects** : présenter ses respects **5** ~ **s.o. a visit** : rendre visite à qqn — *vi* : payer — ~ *n* : paie *f*, salaire *m* — **payable** ['peɪebəl] *adj* : payable — **paycheck** ['peɪ,ʧɛk] *n* : chèque *m* de paie — **payment** ['peɪmənt] *n* : paiement *m*
PC [,pi:'si:] *n, pl* **PCs** *or* **PC's** COMPUTER : PC *m*, micro-ordinateur *m*
pea ['pi:] *n* : pois *m*
peace ['pi:s] *n* : paix *f* — **peaceful** ['pi:sfəl] *adj* : paisible
peach ['pi:ʧ] *n* : pêche *f*
peacock ['pi:,kɑk] *n* : paon *m*
peak ['pi:k] *n* **1** SUMMIT : sommet *m*, pic *m* **2** APEX : apogée *f* — ~ *adj* : maximal — ~ *vi* : atteindre un sommet
peanut ['pi:,nʌt] *n* : cacahouète *f*
pear ['pær] *n* : poire *f*
pearl ['pərl] *n* : perle *f*
peasant ['pɛzənt] *n* : paysan *m*, -sanne *f*
peat ['pi:t] *n* : tourbe *f*
pebble ['pɛbəl] *n* : caillou *m*
pecan [pɪ'kɑn, -'kæn, 'pi:,kæn] *n* : noix *f* de pécan *France*, noix *f* de pacane *Can*
peck ['pɛk] *vt* : picorer — ~ *n* **1** : coup *m* de bec **2** KISS : bécot *m*
peculiar [pɪ'kju:ljər] *adj* **1** DISTINCTIVE : particulier **2** STRANGE : bizarre — **peculiarity** [pɪ,kju:l'jærəṭi, -,kju:li'ær-] *n, pl* **-ties** **1** DISTINCTIVENESS : particularité *f* **2** STRANGENESS : bizarrerie *f*
pedal ['pɛdəl] *n* : pédale *f* — ~ *vt* **-aled** *or* **-alled; -aling** *or* **-alling** : pédaler
pedantic [pɪ'dæntɪk] *adj* : pédant
peddle ['pɛdəl] *vt* **-dled; -dling** : colporter — **peddler** ['pɛdlər] *n* : colporteur *m*, -teuse *f*
pedestal ['pɛdəstəl] *n* : piédestal *m*
pedestrian [pə'dɛstriən] *n* : piéton *m* — ~ *adj* ~ **crossing** : passage *m* pour piétons
pediatrics [,pi:di'ætrɪks] *ns & pl* : pédiatrie *f* — **pediatrician** [,pi:diə'trɪʃən] *n* : pédiatre *mf*
pedigree ['pɛdə,gri:] *n* : pedigree *m* (d'un animal)
peek ['pi:k] *vi* GLANCE : jeter un coup d'œil — ~ *n* : coup *m* d'œil furtif
peel ['pi:l] *vt* : peler (un fruit), éplucher (un oignon, etc.) — *vi* **1** : peler (se dit de la peau) **2** : s'écailler (se dit de la peinture) — ~ *n* : pelure *f* (de pomme), écorce *f* (d'orange), épluchure *f* (de pomme de terre)
peep[1] ['pi:p] *vi* : pépier (se dit d'un oiseau) — ~ *n* : pépiement *m* (d'un oiseau)
peep[2] *vi* PEEK : jeter un coup d'œil — ~ *n* GLANCE : coup *m* d'œil
peer[1] ['pɪr] *n* : pair *m*
peer[2] *vi* : regarder attentivement
peeve ['pi:v] *vt* **peeved; peeving** : irriter — **peevish** ['pi:vɪʃ] *adj* : grincheux
peg ['pɛg] *n* **1** HOOK : patère *f* **2** STAKE : piquet *m*
pelican ['pɛlɪkən] *n* : pélican *m*
pellet ['pɛlət] *n* **1** BALL : boulette *f* **2** SHOT : plomb *m*
pelt[1] ['pɛlt] *n* : peau *f* (d'un animal)
pelt[2] *vt* THROW : bombarder
pelvis ['pɛlvɪs] *n, pl* **-vises** [-vɪsəz] *or* **-ves** [-,vi:z] : bassin *m*
pen[1] ['pɛn] *vt* **penned; penning** ENCLOSE : enfermer — ~ *n* : parc *m*, enclos *m*
pen[2] *n* : stylo *m*
penal ['pi:nəl] *adj* : pénal — **penalize** ['pi:nəl,aɪz, 'pɛn-] *vt* **-ized; -izing** : pénaliser — **penalty** ['pɛnəlti] *n, pl* **-ties** **1** : peine *f* (en droit) **2** : pénalité *f* (aux sports)
penance ['pɛnənts] *n* : pénitence *f*
pencil ['pɛntsəl] *n* : crayon *m*
pending ['pɛndɪŋ] *adj* **1** UNDECIDED : en instance **2** IMMINENT : imminent — ~ *prep* **1** DURING : pendant **2** AWAITING : en attendant
penetrate ['pɛnə,treɪt] *v* **-trated; -trating** : pénétrer — **penetration** [,pɛnə'treɪʃən] *n* : pénétration *f*
penguin ['pɛŋgwɪn, 'pɛn-] *n* : manchot *m*
penicillin [,pɛnə'sɪlən] *n* : pénicilline *f*
peninsula [pə'nɪntsələ, -'nɪnʧulə] *n* : péninsule *f*
penis ['pi:nəs] *n, pl* **-nes** [-,ni:z] *or* **-nises** : pénis *m*
penitentiary [,pɛnə'tɛnʧəri] *n, pl* **-ries** : pénitencier *m*, prison *f*
pen name *n* : nom *m* de plume
penny ['pɛni] *n, pl* **-nies** : centime *m*, cent *m*, sou *m* — **penniless** ['pɛnɪləs] *adj* : sans le sou
pension ['pɛnʧən] *n* : pension *f*, retraite *f*

pensive ['pɛntsɪv] *adj* : pensif
pentagon ['pɛntəˌgɑn] *n* : pentagone *m*
people ['pi:pəl] *ns & pl* **1 people** *npl* : personnes *fpl,* gens *mfpl* **2** *pl* **~s** : peuple *m* — **~** *vt* **-pled; -pling** : peupler
pep ['pɛp] *n* : entrain *m*
pepper ['pɛpər] *n* **1** : poivre *m* (condiment) **2** : poivron *m* (légume) — **peppermint** ['pɛpərˌmɪnt] *n* : menthe *f* poivrée
per ['pər] *prep* **1** : par **2** ACCORDING TO : selon **3 ten miles ~ hour** : dix miles à l'heure
perceive [pər'si:v] *vt* **-ceived; -ceiving** : percevoir
percent [pər'sɛnt] *adv* : pour cent — **percentage** [pər'sɛntɪʤ] *n* : pourcentage *m*
perceptible [pər'sɛptəbəl] *adj* : perceptible
perception [pər'sɛpʃən] *n* : perception *f* — **perceptive** [pər'sɛptɪv] *adj* : perspicace
perch[1] ['pərʧ] *n* : perchoir *m* — **~** *vi* : se percher
perch[2] *n* : perche *f* (poisson)
percolate ['pərkəˌleɪt] *v* **-lated; -lating** *vi* SEEP : filtrer — *vt* : passer (du café) — **percolator** ['pərkəˌleɪţər] *n* : cafetière *f* à pression
percussion [pər'kʌʃən] *n* : percussion *f*
perennial [pə'rɛniəl] *adj* **1** RECURRING : perpétuel **2 ~ flowers** : fleurs *fpl* vivaces
perfect ['pərfɪkt] *adj* : parfait — **~** [pər'fɛkt] *vt* : perfectionner — **perfection** [pər'fɛkʃən] *n* : perfection *f* — **perfectionist** [pər'fɛkʃənɪst] *n* : perfectionniste *mf*
perforate ['pərfəˌreɪt] *vt* **-rated; -rating** : perforer
perform [pər'fɔrm] *vt* **1** CARRY OUT : exécuter, faire **2** PRESENT : jouer — *vi* **1** ACT : jouer **2** FUNCTION : fonctionner — **performance** [pər'fɔrˌmənts] *n* **1** EXECUTION : exécution *f* **2** : interprétation *f* (d'un acteur), performance *f* (d'un athlète) **3** PRESENTATION : représentation *f* — **performer** [pər'fɔrmər] *n* : interprète *mf*
perfume ['pərˌfju:m, pər'-] *n* : parfum *m*
perhaps [pər'hæps] *adv* : peut-être
peril ['pɛrəl] *n* : péril *m* — **perilous** ['pɛrələs] *adj* : périlleux
perimeter [pə'rɪməţər] *n* : périmètre *m*
period ['pɪriəd] *n* **1** : point *m* (signe de ponctuation) **2** TIME : période *f* **3** ERA : époque *f* **4** *or* **menstrual ~** : règles *fpl* — **periodic** [ˌpɪri'ɑdɪk] *adj* : périodique — **periodical** [ˌpɪri'ɑdɪkəl] *n* : périodique *m*
peripheral [pə'rɪfərəl] *adj* : périphérique
perish ['pɛrɪʃ] *vi* : périr — **perishable** ['pɛrɪʃəbəl] *adj* : périssable — **perishables** ['pɛrɪʃəbəlz] *npl* : denrées *fpl* périssables
perjury ['pərʤəri] *n* : faux témoignage *m*
perk ['pərk] *vi* **~ up** : se ragaillardir — **~** *n* : avantage *m* — **perky** ['pərki] *adj* **perkier; perkiest** : guilleret
permanence ['pərmənənts] *n* : permanence *f* — **permanent** ['pərmənənt] *adj* : permanent — **~** *n* : permanente *f*
permeate ['pərmiˌeɪt] *vt* **-ated; -ating** : pénétrer
permission [pər'mɪʃən] *n* : permission *f* — **permissible** [pər'mɪsəbəl] *adj* : permis, admissible — **permissive** [pər'mɪsɪv] *adj* : permissif — **permit** [pər'mɪt] *v* **-mitted; -mitting** : permettre — **~** ['pərˌmɪt, pər'-] *n* : permis *m*
peroxide [pə'rɑkˌsaɪd] *n* : peroxyde *m*
perpendicular [ˌpərpən'dɪkjələr] *adj* : perpendiculaire
perpetrate ['pərpəˌtreɪt] *vt* **-trated; -trating** : perpétrer — **perpetrator** ['pərpəˌtreɪţər] *n* : auteur *m* (d'un délit)
perpetual [pər'pɛʧuəl] *adj* : perpétuel
perplex [pər'plɛks] *vt* : laisser perplexe — **perplexity** [pər'plɛksəti] *n, pl* **-ties** : perplexité *f*
persecute ['pərsɪˌkju:t] *vt* **-cuted; -cuting** : persécuter — **persecution** [ˌpərsɪ'kju:ʃən] *n* : persécution *f*
persevere [ˌpərsə'vɪr] *vi* **-vered; -vering** : persévérer — **perseverance** [ˌpərsə'vɪrənts] *n* : persévérance *f*
persist [pər'sɪst] *vi* : persister — **persistence** [pər'sɪstənts] *n* : persistance *f* — **persistent** [pər'sɪstənt] *adj* : persistant
person ['pərsən] *n* : personne *f* — **personal** ['pərsənəl] *adj* : personnel — **personality** [ˌpərsən'æləţi] *n, pl* **-ties** : personnalité *f* — **personally** ['pərsənəli] *adv* : personnellement — **personnel** [ˌpərsə'nɛl] *n* : personnel *m*
perspective [pər'spɛktɪv] *n* : perspective *f*
perspiration [ˌpərspə'reɪʃən] *n* : transpiration *f* — **perspire** [pər'spaɪr] *vi* **-spired; -spiring** : transpirer
persuade [pər'sweɪd] *vt* **-suaded;**

-**suading** : persuader — **persuasion** [pər'sweɪʒən] *n* **1** : persuasion *f* **2** BELIEF : conviction *f*
pertain [pər'teɪn] *vi* ~ **to** : avoir rapport à — **pertinent** ['pərtənənt] *adj* : pertinent
perturb [pər'tərb] *vt* : troubler
pervade [pər'veɪd] *vt* **-vaded; -vading** : se répandre dans — **pervasive** [pər'veɪsɪv, -zɪv] *adj* : envahissant
perverse [pər'vərs] *adj* **1** CORRUPT : pervers **2** STUBBORN : obstiné — **pervert** ['pər,vərt] *n* : pervers *m*, -verse *f*
pessimism ['pɛsə,mɪzəm] *n* : pessimisme *m* — **pessimist** ['pɛsəmɪst] *n* : pessimiste *mf* — **pessimistic** [,pɛsə'mɪstɪk] *adj* : pessimiste
pest ['pɛst] *n* **1** : plante *f* ou animal *m* nuisible **2** NUISANCE : peste *f*
pester ['pɛstər] *vt* **-tered; -tering** : importuner, harceler
pesticide ['pɛstə,saɪd] *n* : pesticide *m*
pet ['pɛt] *n* **1** : animal *m* domestique **2** FAVORITE : chouchou *m fam* — ~ *vt* **petted; petting** : caresser
petal ['pɛtəl] *n* : pétale *m*
petition [pə'tɪʃən] *n* : pétition *f* — ~ *vt* : adresser une pétition à
petrify ['pɛtrə,faɪ] *vt* **-fied; -fying** : pétrifier
petroleum [pə'tro:liəm] *n* : pétrole *m*
petty ['pɛti] *adj* **-tier; -est 1** INSIGNIFICANT : insignifiant **2** MEAN : mesquin
petulant ['pɛtʃələnt] *adj* : irritable
pew ['pju:] *n* : banc *m* d'église
pewter ['pju:tər] *n* : étain *m*
pharmacy ['fɑrməsi] *n, pl* **-cies** : pharmacie *f* — **pharmacist** [,fɑrməsɪst] *n* : pharmacien *m*, -cienne *f*
phase ['feɪz] *n* : phase *f* — ~ *vt* **phased; phasing 1** ~ **in** : introduire graduellement **2** ~ **out** : discontinuer progressivement
phenomenon [fɪ'nɑmə,nɑn, -nən] *n, pl* **-na** [-nə] *or* **-nons** : phénomène *m* — **phenomenal** [fɪ'nɑmənəl] *adj* : phénoménal
philanthropy [fə'lænᵗθrəpi] *n, pl* **-pies** : philanthropie *f* — **philanthropist** [fə'lænᵗθrəpɪst] *n* : philanthrope *mf*
philosophy [fə'lɑsəfi] *n, pl* **-phies** : philosophie *f* — **philosopher** [fə'lɑsəfər] *n* : philosophe *mf*
phlegm ['flɛm] *n* : mucosité *f*
phobia ['fo:biə] *n* : phobie *f*
phone ['fo:n] → **telephone**
phonetic [fə'nɛtɪk] *adj* : phonétique
phony *or* **phoney** ['fo:ni] *adj* **-nier; -est** : faux — ~ *n, pl* **-nies** : charlatan *m*
phosphorus ['fɑsfərəs] *n* : phosphore *m*
photo ['fo:ṭo:] *n, pl* **-tos** : photo *f* — **photocopier** ['fo:ṭo,kɑpiər] *n* : photocopieur *m*, photocopieuse *f* — **photocopy** ['fo:ṭo,kɑpi] *n, pl* **-pies** : photocopie *f* — ~ *vt* **-copied; -copying** : photocopier — **photograph** ['fo:ṭə,græf] *n* : photographie *f*, photo *f* — ~ *vt* : photographier — **photographer** [fə'tɑgrəfər] *n* : photographe *mf* — **photographic** [,fo:ṭə'græfɪk] *adj* : photographique — **photography** [fə'tɑgrəfi] *n* : photographie *f*
phrase ['freɪz] *n* : expression *f* — ~ *vt* **phrased; phrasing** : formuler, exprimer
physical ['fɪzɪkəl] *adj* : physique — ~ *n* : examen *m* médical
physician [fə'zɪʃən] *n* : médecin *mf*
physics ['fɪzɪks] *ns & pl* : physique *f* — **physicist** ['fɪzəsɪst] *n* : physicien *m*, -cienne *f*
physiology [,fɪzi'ɑlədʒi] *n* : physiologie *f*
physique [fə'zi:k] *n* : physique *m*
piano [pi'æno:] *n, pl* **-anos** : piano *m* — **pianist** [pi'ænɪst, 'pi:ənɪst] *n* : pianiste *mf*
pick ['pɪk] *vt* **1** CHOOSE : choisir **2** GATHER : cueillir **3** REMOVE : enlever **4** ~ **a fight** : chercher la bagarre — *vi* **1** CHOOSE : choisir **2** ~ **on** : harceler — ~ *n* **1** CHOICE : choix *m* **2** BEST : meilleur *m* **3** *or* **pickax** ['pɪk,æks] : pic *m*
picket ['pɪkət] *n* **1** STAKE : piquet *m* **2** *or* ~ **line** : piquet *m* de grève — ~ *vi* : faire un piquet de grève
pickle ['pɪkəl] *n* **1** : cornichon *m* **2** JAM : pétrin *m fam* — ~ *vt* **-led; -ling** : conserver dans la saumure
pickpocket ['pɪk,pɑkət] *n* : voleur *m*, -leuse *f* à la tire
pickup ['pɪk,əp] *n or* ~ **truck** : camionnette *f* — **pick up** *vt* **1** LIFT : ramasser **2** LEARN : apprendre **3** RESUME : reprendre **4** TIDY : mettre en ordre **5** COLLECT : prendre — *vi* IMPROVE : s'améliorer
picnic ['pɪk,nɪk] *n* : pique-nique *m* — ~ *vi* **-nicked; -nicking** : pique-niquer
picture ['pɪktʃər] *n* **1** PAINTING : tableau *m* **2** DRAWING : dessin *m* **3** PHOTO : photo *f*, photographie *f* **4** IMAGE : image *f* **5** MOVIE : film *m* — ~ *vt* **-tured; -turing 1** DEPICT : dépeindre **2**

IMAGINE : s'imaginer — **picturesque** [ˌpɪktʃə'rɛsk] *adj* : pittoresque

pie ['paɪ] *n* **1** : tarte *f* (dessert) **2** : pâté *m,* tourte *f*

piece ['pi:s] *n* **1** : pièce *f* **2** FRAGMENT : morceau *m* — ~ *vt* **pieced; piecing** *or* ~ **together** : rassembler — **piecemeal** ['pi:sˌmi:l] *adv* : graduellement — ~ *adj* : fragmentaire

pier ['pɪr] *n* : jetée *f*

pierce ['pɪrs] *vt* **pierced; piercing** : percer — **piercing** ['pɪrsɪŋ] *adj* : perçant

piety ['paɪəṭi] *n, pl* **-eties** : piété *f*

pig ['pɪg] *n* : porc *m,* cochon *m*

pigeon ['pɪʤən] *n* : pigeon *m* — **pigeonhole** ['pɪʤənˌho:l] *n* : casier *m*

piggyback ['pɪgiˌbæk] *adv & adj* : sur le dos

pigment ['pɪgmənt] *n* : pigment *m*

pigpen ['pɪgˌpɛn] *n* : porcherie *f*

pigtail ['pɪgˌteɪl] *n* : natte *f*

pile[1] ['paɪəl] *n* HEAP : pile *f,* tas *m*— ~ *v* **piled; piling** *vt* **1** STACK : empiler **2** LOAD : remplir — *vi* **1** *or* ~ **up** : s'accumuler **2** CROWD : s'empiler

pile[2] *n* NAP : poil *m* (d'un tapis, etc.)

pilfer ['pɪlfər] *vt* : chaparder *fam*

pilgrim ['pɪlgrəm] *n* : pèlerin *m,* -rine *f* — **pilgrimage** ['pɪlgrəmɪʤ] *n* : pèlerinage *m*

pill ['pɪl] *n* : pilule *f,* cachet *m*

pillage ['pɪlɪʤ] *n* : pillage *m* — ~ *vt* **-laged; -laging** : piller

pillar ['pɪlər] *n* : pilier *m*

pillow ['pɪˌlo:] *n* : oreiller *m* — **pillowcase** ['pɪloˌkeɪs] *n* : taie *f* d'oreiller

pilot ['paɪlət] *n* : pilote *m* — ~ *vt* : piloter — **pilot light** *n* : veilleuse *f*

pimple ['pɪmpəl] *n* : bouton *m*

pin ['pɪn] *n* **1** : épingle *f* **2** BROOCH : broche *f* **3** *or* **bowling** ~ : quille *f* — ~ *vt* **pinned; pinning 1** FASTEN : épingler **2** *or* ~ **down** : fixer

pincers ['pɪntsərz] *npl* : tenailles *fpl*

pinch ['pɪntʃ] *vt* **1** : pincer **2** STEAL : piquer — *vi* : serrer — ~ *n* **1** SQUEEZE : pincement *m* **2** LITTLE : pincée *f* **3 in a** ~ : à la rigueur

pine[1] ['paɪn] *n* : pin *m*

pine[2] *vi* **pined; pining 1** LANGUISH : languir **2** ~ **for** : désirer ardemment

pineapple ['paɪnˌæpəl] *n* : ananas *m*

pink ['pɪŋk] *adj* : rose — ~ *n* : rose *m*

pinnacle ['pɪnɪkəl] *n* : pinacle *m*

pinpoint ['pɪnˌpɔɪnt] *vt* : préciser

pint ['paɪnt] *n* : pinte *f*

pioneer [ˌpaɪə'nɪr] *n* : pionnier *m,* -nière *f*

pious ['paɪəs] *adj* : pieux

pipe ['paɪp] *n* **1** : tuyau *m* **2** : pipe *f* (pour fumer du tabac) — **pipeline** ['paɪpˌlaɪn] *n* : pipeline *m*

piquant ['pi:kənt, 'pɪkwənt] *adj* : piquant

pirate ['paɪrət] *n* : pirate *m*

pistachio [pə'stæʃiˌo:, -'stɑ-] *n, pl* **-chios** : pistache *f*

pistol ['pɪstəl] *n* : pistolet *m*

piston ['pɪstən] *n* : piston *m*

pit ['pɪt] *n* **1** HOLE : trou *m,* fosse *f* **2** MINE : mine *f* **3** : creux *m* (de l'estomac) **4** : noyau *m* (d'un fruit) — ~ *vt* **pitted; pitting 1** MARK : marquer **2** : dénoyauter (un fruit) **3** ~ **against** : opposer à

pitch ['pɪtʃ] *vt* **1** : dresser (une tente, etc.) **2** THROW : lancer — *vi* LURCH : tanguer (se dit d'un navire, etc.) — ~ *n* **1** DEGREE, LEVEL : degré *m,* niveau *m* **2** TONE : ton *m* **3** THROW : lancement *m* **4** *or* **sales** ~ : boniment *m* de vente — **pitcher** ['pɪtʃər] *n* **1** JUG : cruche *f* **2** : artilleur *m Can* (au baseball) — **pitchfork** ['pɪtʃˌfɔrk] *n* : fourche *f*

pitfall ['pɪtˌfɔl] *n* : piège *m*

pith ['pɪθ] *n* : moelle *f* — **pithy** ['pɪθi] *adj* **pithier; pithiest** : concis

pity ['pɪṭi] *n, pl* **pities 1** : pitié *f* **2 what a** ~**!** : quel dommage! — ~ *vt* **pitied; pitying** : avoir pitié de — **pitiful** ['pɪṭɪfəl] *adj* : pitoyable — **pitiless** ['pɪṭɪləs] *adj* : impitoyable

pivot ['pɪvət] *n* : pivot *m* — ~ *vi* : pivoter

pizza ['pi:tsə] *n* : pizza *f*

placard ['plækərd, -ˌkɑrd] *n* POSTER : affiche *f*

placate ['pleɪˌkeɪt, 'plæ-] *vt* **-cated; -cating** : calmer

place ['pleɪs] *n* **1** : place *f* **2** LOCATION : endroit *m,* lieu *m* **3 in the first** ~ : tout d'abord **4 take** ~ : avoir lieu — ~ *vt* **placed; placing 1** PUT, SET : placer, mettre **2** RECOGNIZE : remettre **3** ~ **an order** : passer une commande — **placement** ['pleɪsmənt] *n* : placement *m*

placid ['plæsəd] *adj* : placide

plagiarism ['pleɪʤəˌrɪzəm] *n* : plagiat *m* — **plagiarize** ['pleɪʤəˌraɪz] *vt* **-rized; -rizing** : plagier

plague ['pleɪg] *n* **1** : peste *f* **2** CALAMITY : fléau *m*

plaid ['plæd] *n* : tissu *m* écossais — ~ *adj* : écossais

plain ['pleɪn] *adj* **1** SIMPLE : simple **2** CLEAR : clair, évident **3** FRANK : franc

4 HOMELY : ordinaire — ~ *n* : plaine *f* — **plainly** [ˈpleɪnli] *adv* **1** SIMPLY : simplement **2** CLEARLY : clairement **3** FRANKLY : franchement

plaintiff [ˈpleɪntɪf] *n* : demandeur *m*, -deresse *f*; plaignant *m*, -gnante *f*

plan [ˈplæn] *n* **1** DIAGRAM : plan *m* **2** IDEA : projet *m* — ~ *v* **planned; planning** *vt* **1** INTEND : projeter **2** PREPARE : organiser — *vi* : faire des projets

plane[1] [ˈpleɪn] *n* **1** SURFACE : plan *m* **2** AIRPLANE : avion *m*

plane[2] *n or* **carpenter's ~** : rabot *m*

planet [ˈplænət] *n* : planète *f*

plank [ˈplæŋk] *n* : planche *f*

planning [ˈplænɪŋ] *n* : organisation *f*, planification *f*

plant [ˈplænt] *vt* : planter — ~ *n* **1** : plante *f* **2** FACTORY : usine *f*

plaque [ˈplæk] *n* : plaque *f*

plaster [ˈplæstər] *n* : plâtre *m* — ~ *vt* **1** : plâtrer **2** COVER : couvrir

plastic [ˈplæstɪk] *adj* **1** : de plastique, en plastique **2 ~ surgery** : chirurgie *f* esthétique — ~ *n* : plastique *m*

plate [ˈpleɪt] *n* **1** SHEET : plaque *f* **2** DISH : assiette *f* **3** ILLUSTRATION : planche *f* — ~ *vt* **plated; plating** : plaquer (avec un métal)

plateau [plæˈto:] *n, pl* **-teaus** *or* **-teaux** [-ˈto:z] : plateau *m*

platform [ˈplætˌfɔrm] *n* **1** STAGE : tribune *f*, estrade *f* **2** : quai *m* (d'une gare) **3** *or* **political ~** : plate-forme *f* (électorale)

platinum [ˈplætənəm] *n* : platine *m*

platoon [pləˈtu:n] *n* : section *f* (dans l'armée)

platter [ˈplæṭər] *n* : plat *m*

plausible [ˈplɔzəbəl] *adj* : plausible

play [ˈpleɪ] *n* **1** : jeu *m* **2** DRAMA : pièce *f* de théâtre — ~ *vi* : jouer — *vt* **1** : jouer à (un jeu, un sport) **2** : jouer de (un instrument de musique) **3** PERFORM : jouer **4 ~ down** : minimiser **5 ~ up** EMPHASIZE : souligner — **player** [ˈpleɪər] *n* : joueur *m*, joueuse *f* — **playful** [ˈpleɪfəl] *adj* : enjoué — **playground** [ˈpleɪˌgraʊnd] *n* : cour *f* de récréation — **playing card** *n* : carte *f* à jouer — **playmate** [ˈpleɪˌmeɪt] *n* : camarade *mf* de jeu — **play-off** [ˈpleɪˌɔf] *n* : match *m* crucial — **playpen** [ˈpleɪˌpɛn] *n* : parc *m* (pour bébés) — **plaything** [ˈpleɪˌθɪŋ] *n* : jouet *m* — **playwright** [ˈpleɪˌraɪt] *n* : dramaturge *mf*, auteur *m* dramatique

plea [ˈpli:] *n* **1** : défense *f* (en droit) **2** REQUEST : appel *m*, requête *f* — **plead** [ˈpli:d] *v* **pleaded** *or* **pled** [ˈplɛd]; **pleading** : plaider

pleasant [ˈplɛzənt] *adj* : agréable — **please** [ˈpli:z] *v* **pleased; pleasing** *vt* **1** GRATIFY : plaire à, faire plaisir à **2** SATISFY : contenter — *vi* : plaire, faire plaisir — ~ *adv* : s'il vous plaît — **pleasing** [ˈpli:zɪŋ] *adj* : agréable — **pleasure** [ˈplɛʒər] *n* : plaisir *m*

pleat [ˈpli:t] *n* : pli *m*

pledge [ˈplɛʤ] *n* **1** SECURITY : gage *m* **2** PROMISE : promesse *f* — ~ *vt* **pledged; pledging 1** PAWN : mettre en gage **2** PROMISE : promettre

plenty [ˈplɛnti] *n* **1** ABUNDANCE : abondance *f* **2 ~ of** : beaucoup de — **plentiful** [ˈplɛntɪfəl] *adj* : abondant

pliable [ˈplaɪəbəl] *adj* : flexible, malléable

pliers [ˈplaɪərz] *npl* : pinces *fpl*

plight [ˈplaɪt] *n* : situation *f* difficile

plod [ˈplɑd] *vi* **plodded; plodding 1** : marcher lourdement **2** LABOR : peiner

plot [ˈplɑt] *n* **1** LOT : lopin *m*, parcelle *f* (de terre) **2** STORY : intrigue *f* **3** CONSPIRACY : complot *m* — ~ *v* **plotted; plotting** *vt* : faire un plan de — *vi* CONSPIRE : comploter

plow *or* **plough** [ˈplaʊ] *n* **1** : charrue *f* **2** → **snowplow** — ~ *vt* **1** : labourer (la terre) **2** : déneiger

ploy [ˈplɔɪ] *n* : stratagème *m*

pluck [ˈplʌk] *vt* **1** : cueillir (une fleur) **2** : plumer (un oiseau) **3** : pincer (une corde) **4 ~ one's eyebrows** : s'épiler les sourcils

plug [ˈplʌg] *n* **1** STOPPER : bouchon *m*, tampon *m* **2** : prise *f* (électrique) — ~ *vt* **plugged; plugging 1** BLOCK : boucher **2** ADVERTISE : faire de la publicité pour **3 ~ in** : brancher

plum [ˈplʌm] *n* : prune *f*, pruneau *m Can*

plumb [ˈplʌm] *adj* : vertical, droit — **plumber** [ˈplʌmər] *n* : plombier *m* — **plumbing** [ˈplʌmɪŋ] *n* **1** : plomberie *f* **2** PIPES : tuyauterie *f*

plummet [ˈplʌmət] *vi* : tomber

plump [ˈplʌmp] *adj* : grassouillet, dodu

plunder [ˈplʌndər] *vt* : piller — ~ *n* : pillage *m*

plunge [ˈplʌnʤ] *v* **plunged; plunging** *vt* : plonger — *vi* **1** DIVE : plonger **2** DROP : chuter — ~ *n* **1** DIVE : plongeon *m* **2** DROP : chute *f* — **plunger** [ˈplʌnʤər] *n* : ventouse *f*

plural [ˈplʊrəl] *adj* : pluriel — ~ *n* : pluriel *m*

plus [ˈplʌs] *adj* : positif — ~ *n* **1** *or* ~

sign : plus *m* **2** ADVANTAGE : plus *m,* avantage *m* — ~ *prep* : plus — ~ *conj* AND : et

plush [ˈplʌʃ] *n* : peluche *f* — ~ *adj* : somptueux

Pluto [ˈplu:ţo:] *n* : Pluton *f*

plutonium [plu:ˈto:niəm] *n* : plutonium *m*

ply [ˈplaɪ] *vt* **plied; plying 1** USE : manier (un outil) **2** PRACTICE : exercer

plywood [ˈplaɪˌwʊd] *n* : contre-plaqué *m*

pneumatic [nʊˈmæţɪk, njʊ-] *adj* : pneumatique

pneumonia [nʊˈmo:njə, njʊ-] *n* : pneumonie *f*

poach[1] [ˈpo:ʧ] *vt* : pocher (des œufs)

poach[2] *vt or* ~ **game** : braconner le gibier — **poacher** [ˈpo:ʧər] *n* : braconnier *m,* -nière *f*

pocket [ˈpɑkət] *n* : poche *f* — ~ *vt* : empocher — **pocketbook** [ˈpɑkətˌbʊk] *n* PURSE : sac *m* à main, sacoche *f Can* — **pocketknife** [ˈpɑkətˌnaɪf] *n, pl* **-knives** : canif *m*

pod [ˈpɑd] *n* : cosse *f*

poem [ˈpo:əm] *n* : poème *m* — **poet** [ˈpo:ət] *n* : poète *mf* — **poetic** [poˈɛţɪk] *or* **poetical** [-ţɪkəl] *adj* : poétique — **poetry** [ˈpo:ətri] *n* : poésie *f*

poignant [ˈpɔɪnjənt] *adj* : poignant

point [ˈpɔɪnt] *n* **1** : point *m* **2** PURPOSE : utilité *f,* but *m* **3** TIP : pointe *f* **4** FEATURE : qualité *f* **5 at one** ~ : à un moment donné — ~ *vt* **1** AIM : braquer **2** *or* ~ **out** INDICATE : indiquer — **point–blank** [ˈpɔɪntˈblæŋk] *adv* : à bout portant — **pointer** [ˈpɔɪntər] *n* **1** ROD : baguette *f* **2** TIP : conseil *m* — **pointless** [ˈpɔɪntləs] *adj* : inutile — **point of view** *n* : point *m* de vue

poise [ˈpɔɪz] *n* **1** EQUILIBRIUM : équilibre *m* **2** COMPOSURE : assurance *f*

poison [ˈpɔɪzən] *n* : poison *m* — ~ *vt* : empoisonner — **poisonous** [ˈpɔɪzənəs] *adj* : vénéneux (se dit d'une plante), vénimeux (se dit d'un animal), toxique (se dit d'une substance)

poke [ˈpo:k] *v* **poked; poking** *vt* **1** JAB : pousser **2** THRUST : fourrer *fam* — ~ *n* JAB : coup *m*

poker[1] [ˈpo:kər] *n* : tisonnier *m* (pour le feu)

poker[2] *n* : poker *m* (jeu de cartes)

polar [ˈpo:lər] *adj* : polaire — **polar bear** *n* : ours *m* polaire, ours *m* blanc — **polarize** [ˈpo:ləˌraɪz] *vt* **-ized; -izing** : polariser

pole[1] [ˈpo:l] *n* ROD : perche *f*

pole[2] *n* : pôle *m* (en géographie)

police [pəˈli:s] *vt* **-liced; -licing** : surveiller — ~ *ns & pl* **the** ~ : la police — **policeman** [pəˈli:smən] *n, pl* **-men** [-mən, -ˌmɛn] : policier *m* — **police officer** *n* : agent *m* de police — **policewoman** [pəˈli:sˌwʊmən] *n, pl* **-women** [-ˌwɪmən] : femme *f* policier

policy [ˈpɑləsi] *n, pl* **-cies 1** : politique *f* **2** *or* **insurance** ~ : police *f* d'assurance

polio [ˈpo:liˌo:] *or* **poliomyelitis** [ˌpo:liˌo:ˌmaɪəˈlaɪţəs] *n* : polio *f,* poliomyélite *f*

polish [ˈpɑlɪʃ] *vt* **1** : polir **2** : cirer (se dit des chaussures, etc) — ~ *n* **1** LUSTER : poli *m,* éclat *m* **2** WAX : cire *f* (pour les meubles, etc.), cirage *m* (pour les chaussures) **3 nail** ~ : vernis *m* à ongles

polite [pəˈlaɪt] *adj* **-liter; -est** : poli — **politeness** [pəˈlaɪtnəs] *n* : politesse *f*

political [pəˈlɪţɪkəl] *adj* : politique — **politician** [ˌpɑləˈtɪʃən] *n* : politicien *m,* -cienne *f* — **politics** [ˈpɑləˌtɪks] *ns & pl* : politique *f*

polka [ˈpo:lkə, ˈpo:kə] *n* : polka *f* — **polka dot** *n* : pois *m,* picot *m Can*

poll [ˈpo:l] *n* **1** SURVEY : sondage *m* **2** ~**s** *npl* : urnes *fpl* — ~ *vt* **1** : obtenir (des voix) **2** CANVASS : sonder

pollen [ˈpɑlən] *n* : pollen *m*

pollute [pəˈlu:t] *vt* **-luted; -luting** : polluer — **pollution** [pəˈlu:ʃən] *n* : pollution *f*

polyester [ˈpɑliˌɛstər, ˌpɑliˈ-] *n* : polyester *m*

polymer [ˈpɑləmər] *n* : polymère *m*

pomegranate [ˈpɑməˌgrænət, ˈpɑmˌgræ-] *n* : grenade *f* (fruit)

pomp [ˈpɑmp] *n* : pompe *f* — **pompous** [ˈpɑmpəs] *adj* : pompeux

pond [ˈpɑnd] *n* : étang *m,* mare *f*

ponder [ˈpɑndər] *vt* : considérer — *vi* ~ **over** : réfléchir à, méditer sur

pontoon [pɑnˈtu:n] *n* : ponton *m*

pony [ˈpo:ni] *n, pl* **-nies** : poney *m* — **ponytail** [ˈpo:niˌteɪl] *n* : queue *f* de cheval

poodle [ˈpu:dəl] *n* : caniche *m*

pool [ˈpu:l] *n* **1** PUDDLE : flaque *f* (d'eau), mare *f* (de sang) **2** RESERVE : fonds *m* commun **3** BILLIARDS : billard *m* américain **4** *or* **swimming** ~ : piscine *f* — ~ *vt* : mettre en commun

poor [ˈpʊr, ˈpor] *adj* **1** : pauvre **2** INFERIOR : mauvais — **poorly** [ˈpʊrli, ˈpor-] *adv* BADLY : mal

pop[1] ['pap] *v* **popped; popping** *vt* **1** BURST : faire éclater **2** PUT : mettre — *vi* **1** BURST : éclater, exploser **2 ~ in** : faire une petite visite **3** *or* **~ out** : sortir **4 ~ up** APPEAR : surgir — **~** *n* **1** : bruit *m* sec **2** SODA : boisson *f* gazeuse — **~** *adj* : pop
pop[2] *n or* **~ music** : musique *f* pop
popcorn ['pap,kɔrn] *n* : pop-corn *m*
pope ['po:p] *n* : pape *m*
poplar ['paplər] *n* : peuplier *m*
poppy ['papi] *n, pl* **-pies** : coquelicot *m*
popular ['papjələr] *adj* : populaire — **popularity** [,papjə'lærəṭi] *n* : popularité *f* — **popularize** ['papjələ,raɪz] *vt* **-ized; -izing** : populariser
populate ['papjə,leɪt] *vt* **-lated; -lating** : peupler — **population** [,papjə'leɪʃən] *n* : population *f*
porcelain ['porsələn] *n* : porcelaine *f*
porch ['portʃ] *n* : porche *m*
porcupine ['pɔrkjə,paɪn] *n* : porc-épic *m*
pore[1] ['por] *vi* **pored; poring ~ over** : étudier de près
pore[2] *n* : pore *m*
pork ['pork] *n* : porc *m*
pornography [pɔr'nagrəfi] *n* : pornographie *f* — **pornographic** [,pɔrnə'græfɪk] *adj* : pornographique
porous ['porəs] *adj* : poreux
porpoise ['pɔrpəs] *n* : marsouin *m*
porridge ['pɔrɪdʒ] *n* : porridge *m France*, gruau *m Can*
port[1] ['port] *n* HARBOR : port *m*
port[2] *n or* **~ side** : bâbord *m*
port[3] *n or* **~ wine** : porto *m*
portable ['porṭəbəl] *adj* : portatif
porter ['porṭər] *n* : porteur *m*, -teuse *f*
portfolio [port'fo:li,o] *n, pl* **-lios** : portefeuille *m*
porthole ['port,ho:l] *n* : hublot *m*
portion ['porʃən] *n* : portion *f*
portrait ['portrət, -,treɪt] *n* : portrait *m*
portray [por'treɪ] *vt* DEPICT : représenter
Portuguese [,portʃə'gi:z, -'gi:s] *adj* : portugais — **~** *n* : portugais *m* (langue)
pose ['po:z] *v* **posed; posing** *vt* : poser — *vi* **1** : poser **2 ~ as** : se faire passer pour — **~** *n* : pose *f*
posh ['paʃ] *adj* : chic
position [pə'zɪʃən] *n* **1** : position *f* **2** JOB : poste *m* — **~** *vt* **1** PLACE : placer **2** ORIENT : positionner
positive ['pazəṭɪv] *adj* **1** : positif **2** SURE : sûr, certain
possess [pə'zɛs] *vt* : posséder — **possession** [pə'zɛʃən] *n* **1** : possession *f* **2 ~s** *npl* BELONGINGS : biens *mpl* — **possessive** [pə'zɛsɪv] *adj* : possessif
possible ['pasəbəl] *adj* : possible — **possibility** [,pasə'bɪləṭi] *n, pl* **-ties** : possibilité *f* — **possibly** ['pasəbli] *adv* : peut-être, possiblement *Can*
post[1] ['po:st] *n* POLE : poteau *m*
post[2] *n* POSITION : poste *m*
post[3] *n* MAIL : poste *f*, courrier *m* — **~** *vt* **1** MAIL : poster **2 keep ~ed** : tenir au courant — **postage** ['po:stɪdʒ] *n* : affranchissement *m* — **postal** ['po:stəl] *adj* : postal — **postcard** ['po:st,kard] *n* : carte *f* postale
poster ['po:stər] *n* : poster *m*, affiche *f*
posterity [pa'stɛrəṭi] *n* : postérité *f*
posthumous ['pastʃəməs] *adj* : posthume
postman ['po:stmən, -,mæn] *n, pl* **-men** [-mən, -,mɛn] → **mailman** — **post office** *n* : bureau *m* de poste
postpone [,po:st'po:n] *vt* **-poned; -poning** : remettre, reporter — **postponement** [,po:st'po:nmənt] *n* : renvoi *m*, remise *f*
postscript ['po:st,skrɪpt] *n* : post-scriptum *m*
posture ['pastʃər] *n* : posture *f*
postwar [,po:st'wɔr] *adj* : d'après-guerre
pot ['pat] *n* **1** SAUCEPAN : marmite *f*, casserole *f* **2** CONTAINER : pot *m*
potassium [pə'tæsiəm] *n* : potassium *m*
potato [pə'teɪṭo] *n, pl* **-toes** : pomme *f* de terre, patate *f fam*
potent ['po:tənt] *adj* **1** POWERFUL : puissant **2** EFFECTIVE : efficace
potential [pə'tɛntʃəl] *adj* : potentiel — **~** *n* : potentiel *m*
pothole ['pat,ho:l] *n* : nid-de-poule *m*
potion ['po:ʃən] *n* : potion *f*
pottery ['paṭəri] *n, pl* **-teries** : poterie *f*
pouch ['pautʃ] *n* **1** BAG : petit sac *m* **2** : poche *f* (des marsupiaux)
poultry ['po:ltri] *n* : volaille *f*
pounce ['paunts] *vi* **pounced; pouncing** : bondir
pound[1] ['paund] *n* **1** : livre *f* (unité de mesure) **2** : livre *f* sterling
pound[2] *n* SHELTER : fourrière *f*
pound[3] *vt* **1** CRUSH : piler **2** HAMMER : marteler **3** BEAT : battre — *vi* BEAT : battre
pour ['por] *vt* : verser — *vi* **1** FLOW : couler **2** RAIN : pleuvoir à verse
pout ['paut] *vi* : faire la moue — **~** *n* : moue *f*

poverty ['pɑvərṭi] *n* : pauvreté *f*
powder ['paʊdər] *vt* **1** : poudrer **2** CRUSH : pulvériser — ~ *n* : poudre *f* — **powdery** ['paʊdəri] *adj* : poudreux
power ['paʊər] *n* **1** AUTHORITY : pouvoir *m* **2** ABILITY : capacité *f* **3** STRENGTH : puissance *f* **4** CURRENT : courant *m* — ~ *vt* : faire fonctionner, faire marcher — **powerful** ['paʊərfəl] *adj* : puissant — **powerless** ['paʊərləs] *adj* : impuissant
practical ['præktɪkəl] *adj* : pratique — **practically** ['præktɪkli] *adv* : pratiquement
practice *or* **practise** ['præktəs] *v* **-ticed** *or* **-tised; -ticing** *or* **-tising** *vt* **1** : pratiquer **2** : exercer (une profession) — *vi* **1** : s'exercer **2** TRAIN : s'entraîner — ~ *n* **1** : pratique *f* **2** : exercice *m* (d'une profession) **3** TRAINING : entraînement *m* — **practitioner** [præk'tɪʃənər] *n* : praticien *m*, -cienne *f*
pragmatic [præg'mæṭɪk] *adj* : pragmatique
prairie ['prɛri] *n* : prairie *f*
praise ['preɪz] *vt* **praised; praising** : louer — ~ *n* : louange *f* — **praiseworthy** ['preɪz,wərði] *adj* : louable, digne d'éloges
prance ['prænts] *vt* **pranced; prancing** : caracoler (se dit d'un cheval), cabrioler (se dit d'une personne)
prank ['præŋk] *n* : farce *f*
prawn ['prɔn] *n* : crevette *f* (rose)
pray ['preɪ] *vi* : prier — **prayer** ['prɛr] *n* : prière *f*
preach ['pri:ʧ] *v* : prêcher — **preacher** ['pri:ʧər] *n* : pasteur *m*
precarious [prɪ'kæriəs] *adj* : précaire
precaution [prɪ'kɔʃən] *n* : précaution *f*
precede [prɪ'si:d] *vt* **-ceded; -ceding** : précéder — **precedence** ['prɛsədənts, prɪ'si:dənts] *n* **1** : préséance *f* **2** PRIORITY : priorité *f* — **precedent** ['prɛsədənt] *n* : précédent *m*
precinct ['pri:,sɪŋkt] *n* **1** DISTRICT : arrondissement *m* (en France), circonscription *f* (au Canada) **2** ~**s** *npl* : environs *mpl*
precious ['prɛʃəs] *adj* : précieux
precipice ['prɛsəpəs] *n* : précipice *m*
precipitate [pri'sɪpə,teɪt] *v* **-tated; -tating** : précipiter — **precipitation** [pri-,sɪpə'teɪʃən] *n* **1** HASTE : précipitation *f*, hâte *f* **2** : précipitations *fpl* (en météorologie)
precise [pri'saɪs] *adj* : précis — **precisely** [pri'saɪsli] *adv* : précisément — **precision** [pri'sɪʒən] *n* : précision *f*
preclude [pri'klu:d] *vt* **-cluded; -cluding** : empêcher
precocious [pri'ko:ʃəs] *adj* : précoce
preconceived [,pri:kən'si:vd] *adj* : préconçu
predator ['prɛdəṭər] *n* : prédateur *m*
predecessor ['prɛdə,sɛsər, 'pri:-] *n* : prédécesseur *m*
predicament [pri'dɪkəmənt] *n* : situation *f* difficile
predict [pri'dɪkt] *vt* : prédire — **predictable** [pri'dɪktəbəl] *adj* : prévisible — **prediction** [pri'dɪkʃən] *n* : prédiction *f*
predispose [,pri:dɪ'spo:z] *vt* : prédisposer
predominant [pri'dɑmənənt] *adj* : prédominant
preen ['pri:n] *vt* : lisser (ses plumes)
prefabricated [,pri:'fæbrə,keɪṭəd] *adj* : préfabriqué
preface ['prɛfəs] *n* : préface *f*
prefer [pri'fər] *vt* **-ferred; -ferring** : préférer — **preferable** ['prɛfərəbəl] *adj* : préférable — **preference** ['prɛfrənts, 'prɛfər-] *n* : préférence *f* — **preferential** [,prɛfə'rɛnʧəl] *adj* : préférentiel
prefix ['pri:,fɪks] *n* : préfixe *m*
pregnancy ['prɛgnəntsi] *n, pl* **-cies** : grossesse *f* — **pregnant** ['prɛgnənt] *adj* : enceinte
prehistoric [,pri:hɪs'tɔrɪk] *or* **prehistorical** [-ɪkəl] *adj* : préhistorique
prejudice ['prɛʤədəs] *n* **1** HARM : préjudice *m* **2** BIAS : préjugés *mpl* — ~ *vt* **-diced; -dicing 1** : porter préjudice à (en droit) **2 be** ~**d** : avoir des préjugés
preliminary [pri'lɪmə,nɛri] *adj* : préliminaire
prelude ['prɛ,lu:d, 'prel,ju:d; 'preɪ-,lu:d, 'pri:-] *n* : prélude *m*
premature [,pri:mə'tʊr, -'tjʊr, -'ʧʊr] *adj* : prématuré
premeditated [pri'mɛdə,teɪṭəd] *adj* : prémédité
premier [pri'mɪr, -'mjɪr; 'pri:miər] *adj* : premier — ~ *n* → **prime minister**
premiere [prɪ'mjɛr, -'mɪr] *n* : première *f* (d'un spectacle)
premise ['prɛmɪs] *n* **1** : prémisse *f* (d'un raisonnement) **2** ~**s** *npl* : lieux *mpl*
premium ['pri:miəm] *n* : prime *f*
preoccupied [pri'ɑkjə,paɪd] *adj* : préoccupé

prepare [prɪ'pær] *v* **-pared; -paring** *vt* : préparer — *vi* : se préparer — **preparation** [ˌprɛpə'reɪʃən] *n* **1** PREPARING : préparation *f* **2** **~s** *npl* ARRANGEMENTS : préparatifs *mpl* — **preparatory** [pri'pærəˌtori] *adj* : préparatoire

prepay [ˌpri:'peɪ] *vt* **-paid; -paying** : payer d'avance

preposition [ˌprɛpə'zɪʃən] *n* : préposition *f*

preposterous [pri'pɑstərəs] *adj* : absurde, insensé

prerequisite [pri'rɛkwəzət] *n* : préalable *m*

prerogative [prɪ'rɑgəṭɪv] *n* : prérogative *f*

prescribe [pri'skraɪb] *vt* **-scribed; -scribing** : prescrire — **prescription** [pri'skrɪpʃən] *n* : prescription *f*

presence ['prɛzənts] *n* : présence *f*

present[1] ['prɛzənt] *adj* **1** CURRENT : actuel **2** ATTENDING : présent — **~** *n* *or* **~ time** : présent *m*

present[2] ['prɛzənt] *n* GIFT : cadeau *m* — **~** [prɪ'zɛnt] *vt* : présenter — **presentation** [ˌpri:ˌzɛn'teɪʃən, ˌprɛzən-] *n* : présentation *f*

presently ['prɛzəntli] *adv* **1** SOON : bientôt **2** NOW : actuellement, en ce moment

preserve [pri'zərv] *vt* **-served; -serving** **1** PROTECT : préserver **2** MAINTAIN : conserver — **~** *n* **1** *or* **game ~** : réserve *f* **2** **~s** *npl* : confitures *fpl* — **preservation** [ˌprɛzər'veɪʃən] *n* : préservation *f*, maintien *m* — **preservative** [pri'zərvəṭɪv] *n* : agent *m* de conservation

president ['prɛzədənt] *n* : président *m* — **presidency** ['prɛzədəntsi] *n, pl* **-cies** : présidence *f* — **presidential** [ˌprɛzə'dɛntʃəl] *adj* : présidentiel

press ['prɛs] *n* : presse *f* — **~** *vt* **1** PUSH : presser, appuyer sur **2** IRON : repasser — *vi* **1** PUSH : appuyer **2** CROWD : se presser — **pressing** ['prɛsɪŋ] *adj* : urgent — **pressure** ['prɛʃər] *n* : pression *f* — **~** *vt* **-sured; -suring** : pousser, faire pression sur

prestige [prɛ'stiʒ, -'sti:ʤ] *n* : prestige *m* — **prestigious** [prɛ'stɪʤəs, -'sti-, prə-] *adj* : prestigieux

presume [pri'zu:m] *vt* **-sumed; -suming** : présumer — **presumably** [pri'zu:məbli] *adv* : vraisemblablement — **presumption** [prɪ'zʌmpʃən] *n* : présomption *f* — **presumptuous** [prɪ'zʌmptʃuəs] *adj* : présomptueux

pretend [pri'tɛnd] *vt* **1** PROFESS : prétendre **2** FEIGN : faire semblant de — *vi* : faire semblant — **pretense** *or* **pretence** ['pri:ˌtɛnts, pri'tɛnts] *n* **1** CLAIM : prétention *f* **2** PRETEXT : prétexte *m* — **pretentious** [pri'tɛntʃəs] *adj* : prétentieux

pretext ['pri:ˌtɛkst] *n* : prétexte *m*

pretty ['prɪṭi] *adj* **-tier; -est** : joli, beau — **~** *adv* FAIRLY : assez

pretzel ['prɛtsəl] *n* : bretzel *m*

prevail [pri'veɪl] *vi* : prévaloir — **prevalent** ['prɛvələnt] *adj* : répandu

prevent [pri'vɛnt] *vt* : empêcher — **prevention** [pri'vɛntʃən] *n* : prévention *f* — **preventive** [pri'vɛntɪv] *adj* : préventif

preview ['pri:ˌvju] *n* : avant-première *f*

previous ['pri:viəs] *adj* : antérieur, précédent — **previously** ['pri:viəsli] *adv* : antérieurement, auparavant

prey ['preɪ] *ns & pl* : proie *f* — **prey on** *vt* : faire sa proie de

price ['praɪs] *n* : prix *m* — **~** *vt* **priced; pricing** : fixer un prix sur — **priceless** ['praɪsləs] *adj* : inestimable

prick ['prɪk] *n* : piqûre *f* — **~** *vt* **1** : piquer **2** **~ up one's ears** : dresser l'oreille — **prickly** ['prɪkəli] *adj* **-lier; -est** : épineux

pride ['praɪd] *n* : fierté *f*, orgueil *m* — **~** *vt* **prided; priding ~ oneself on** : être fier de

priest ['pri:st] *n* : prêtre *m* — **priesthood** ['pri:stˌhʊd] *n* : prêtrise *f*

prim ['prɪm] *adj* **primmer; primmest** : guindé

primary ['praɪˌmɛri, 'praɪməri] *adj* **1** FIRST : primaire **2** PRINCIPAL : principal — **primarily** [praɪ'mɛrəli] *adv* : principalement

prime[1] ['praɪm] *vt* **primed; priming** **1** LOAD : charger **2** PREPARE : apprêter **3** COACH : préparer

prime[2] *n* **the ~ of life** : la force de l'âge — **~** *adj* **1** MAIN : principal **2** EXCELLENT : excellent — **prime minister** *n* : Premier ministre *m*

primer[1] ['praɪmər] *n* : apprêt *m*

primer[2] ['prɪmər] *n* : premier livre *m* de lecture

primitive ['prɪməṭɪv] *adj* : primitif

primrose ['prɪmˌro:z] *n* : primevère *f*

prince ['prɪnts] *n* : prince *m* — **princess** ['prɪntsəs, 'prɪnˌsɛs] *n* : princesse *f*

principal ['prɪntsəpəl] *adj* : principal — **~** *n* **1** DIRECTOR : directeur *m*, -trice *f* **2** : principal *m* (d'une dette), capital *m* (d'une somme)

principle ['prɪntsəpəl] *n* : principe *m*
print ['prɪnt] *n* **1** MARK : empreinte *f* **2** LETTER : caractère *m* **3** ENGRAVING : gravure *f* **4** : imprimé *m* (d'un tissu) **5** : épreuve *f* (en photographie) **6 in ~** : disponible — **~** *vt* : imprimer (un texte, etc.) — *vi* : écrire en lettres moulées — **printer** ['prɪntər] *n* **1** : imprimeur *m* (personne) **2** : imprimante *f* (machine) — **printing** ['prɪntɪŋ] *n* **1** : imprimerie *f* (technique) **2** IMPRESSION : impression *f* **3** LETTERING : écriture *f* en lettres moulées
prior ['praɪər] *adj* **1** : antérieur, précédent **2 ~ to** : avant — **priority** [praɪ'ɔrət̬i] *n, pl* **-ties** : priorité *f*
prison ['prɪzən] *n* : prison *f* — **prisoner** ['prɪzənər] *n* : prisonnier *m*, -nière *f*
privacy ['praɪvəsi] *n, pl* **-cies** : intimité *f* — **private** ['praɪvət] *adj* **1** : privé **2** PERSONAL : personnel — **~** *n* : (simple) soldat *m* — **privately** ['praɪvətli] *adv* : en privé
privilege ['prɪvlɪdʒ, 'prɪvə-] *n* : privilège *m* — **privileged** ['prɪvlɪdʒd, 'prɪvə-] *adj* : privilégié
prize ['praɪz] *n* : prix *m* — **~** *adj* : primé — **~** *vt* **prized; prizing** : priser — **prizewinning** ['praɪz,wɪnɪŋ] *adj* : primé, gagnant
pro ['pro:] *n* **1** → **professional 2 the ~s and cons** : le pour et le contre
probability [,prabə'bɪlət̬i] *n, pl* **-ties** : probabilité *f* — **probable** ['prabəbəl] *adj* : probable — **probably** [-bli] *adv* : probablement
probation [pro'beɪʃən] *n* : période *f* d'essai (d'un employé)
probe ['pro:b] *n* **1** : sonde *f* (en médecine) **2** INVESTIGATION : enquête *f* — **~** *vt* **probed; probing** : sonder
problem ['prabləm] *n* : problème *m*
procedure [prə'si:dʒər] *n* : procédure *f*
proceed [pro'si:d] *vi* **1** ACT : procéder **2** CONTINUE : continuer **3** ADVANCE : avancer, aller — **proceedings** [pro'si:dɪŋz] *npl* **1** EVENTS : événements *mpl* **2** *or* **legal ~** : poursuites *fpl* — **proceeds** ['pro:,si:dz] *npl* : recette *f*
process ['pra,sɛs, 'pro:-] *n, pl* **-cesses** ['pra,sɛsəz, 'pro:-, -səsəz, -sə,si:z] **1** : processus *m* **2** METHOD : procédé *m* **3 in the ~ of** : en train de — **~** *vt* : traiter — **procession** [prə'sɛʃən] *n* : procession *f*
proclaim [pro'kleɪm] *vt* : proclamer — **proclamation** [,praklə'meɪʃən] *n* : proclamation *f*
procrastinate [prə'kræstə,neɪt] *vi* **-nated; -nating** : remettre à plus tard
procure [prə'kjʊr] *vt* **-cured; -curing** : obtenir
prod ['prad] *vt* **prodded; prodding** : pousser
prodigal ['pradɪgəl] *adj* : prodigue
prodigious [prə'dɪdʒəs] *adj* : prodigieux
prodigy ['pradədʒi] *n, pl* **-gies** : prodige *m*
produce [prə'du:s, -'dju:s] *vt* **-duced; -ducing 1** : produire **2** SHOW : présenter **3** CAUSE : causer — **~** ['pra,du:s, 'pro:-, -,dju:s] *n* : produits *mpl* agricoles — **producer** [prə'du:sər, -'dju:-] *n* : producteur *m*, -trice *f* — **product** ['pra,dʌkt] *n* : produit *m* — **productive** [prə'dʌktɪv] *adj* : productif
profane [pro'feɪn] *adj* **1** SECULAR : profane **2** IRREVERENT : sacrilège — **profanity** [pro'fænət̬i] *n, pl* **-ties** : juron *m*
profess [prə'fɛs] *vt* : professer — **profession** [prə'fɛʃən] *n* : profession *f* — **professional** [prə'fɛʃənəl] *adj* : professionnel — **~** *n* : professionnel *m*, -nelle *f* — **professor** [prə'fɛsər] *n* : professeur *m*
proficiency [prə'fɪʃəntsi] *n, pl* **-cies** : compétence *f* — **proficient** [prə'fɪʃənt] *adj* : compétent
profile ['pro:,faɪl] *n* : profil *m*
profit ['prafət] *n* : profit *m*, bénéfice *m* — **~** *vi* **~ from** : tirer profit de — *vt* BENEFIT : profiter à — **profitable** ['prafət̬əbəl] *adj* : profitable
profound [prə'faʊnd] *adj* : profond
profuse [prə'fju:s] *adj* **1** ABUNDANT : abondant **2** LAVISH : prodigue — **profusion** [prə'fju:ʒən] *n* : profusion *f*
prognosis [prag'no:sɪs] *n, pl* **-ses** [-,si:z] : pronostic *m*
program *or Brit* **programme** ['pro:,græm, -grəm] *n* **1** : programme *m* **2 television ~** : émission *f* de télévision — **~** *vt* **-grammed** *or* **-gramed; -gramming** *or* **-graming** : programmer
progress ['pragrəs, -,grɛs] *n* **1** : progrès *m* **2 in ~** : en cours — **~** [prə'grɛs] *vi* : progresser — **progressive** [prə'grɛsɪv] *adj* **1** : progressiste (en politique, etc.) **2** : progressif
prohibit [pro'hɪbət] *vt* : interdire — **prohibition** [,pro:ə'bɪʃən, ,pro:hə-] *n* : prohibition *f*
project ['pra,dʒɛkt, -dʒɪkt] *n* : projet *m* — **~** [prə'dʒɛkt] *vt* : projeter — *vi*

PROTRUDE : faire saillie — **projectile** [prəˈdʒɛktəl, -ˌtaɪl] *n* : projectile *m* — **projection** [prəˈdʒɛkʃən] *n* **1** : projection *f* **2** BULGE : saillie *f* — **projector** [prəˈdʒɛktər] *n* : projecteur *m*

proliferate [prəˈlɪfəˌreɪt] *vi* **-ated; -ating** : proliférer — **proliferation** [prəˌlɪfəˈreɪʃən] *n* : prolifération *f* — **prolific** [prəˈlɪfɪk] *adj* : prolifique

prologue [ˈproːˌlɔg, -ˌlɑg] *n* : prologue *m*

prolong [prəˈlɔŋ] *vt* : prolonger

prom [ˈprɑm] *n* : bal *m* d'étudiants

prominent [ˈprɑmənənt] *adj* **1** : proéminent **2** IMPORTANT : important — **prominence** [ˈprɑmənənts] *n* **1** : proéminence *f* **2** IMPORTANCE : importance *f*

promiscuous [prəˈmɪskjuəs] *adj* : de mœurs légères

promise [ˈprɑməs] *n* : promesse *f* — **~** *v* **-mised; -mising** : promettre — **promising** [ˈprɑməsɪŋ] *adj* : prometteur

promote [prəˈmoːt] *vt* **-moted; -moting** : promouvoir — **promoter** [prəˈmoːt̬ər] *n* : promoteur *m*, -trice *f* — **promotion** [prəˈmoːʃən] *n* : promotion *f*

prompt [ˈprɑmpt] *vt* **1** INCITE : inciter **2** CAUSE : provoquer — **~** *adj* **1** QUICK : prompt **2** PUNCTUAL : ponctuel

prone [ˈproːn] *adj* **1** APT : sujet, enclin **2** FLAT : à plat ventre

prong [ˈprɔŋ] *n* : dent *f*

pronoun [ˈproːˌnaʊn] *n* : pronom *m*

pronounce [prəˈnaʊnts] *vt* **-nounced; -nouncing** : prononcer — **pronouncement** [prəˈnaʊntsmənt] *n* : déclaration *f* — **pronunciation** [prəˌnʌntsiˈeɪʃən] *n* : prononciation *f*

proof [ˈpruːf] *n* **1** EVIDENCE : preuve *f* **2** PRINT : épreuve *f* — **proofread** [ˈpruːfˌriːd] *vt* **-read** [-ˌrɛd]; **-reading** : corriger les épreuves de

prop [ˈprɑp] *n* **1** SUPPORT : étai *m* **2** **~s** *npl* : accessoires *mpl* — **~** *vt* **propped; propping 1** LEAN : appuyer **2 ~ up** SUPPORT : étayer

propaganda [ˌprɑpəˈgændə, ˌproː-] *n* : propagande *f*

propagate [ˈprɑpəˌgeɪt] *v* **-gated; -gating** *vt* : propager — *vi* : se propager

propel [prəˈpɛl] *vt* **-pelled; -pelling** : propulser — **propeller** [prəˈpɛlər] *n* : hélice *f*

propensity [prəˈpɛntsət̬i] *n, pl* **-ties** : propension *f*

proper [ˈprɑpər] *adj* **1** SUITABLE : convenable **2** REAL : vrai **3** CORRECT : correct **4 ~ name** : nom propre — **properly** [ˈprɑpərli] *adv* : correctement

property [ˈprɑpərt̬i] *n, pl* **-ties 1** POSSESSIONS : biens *mpl*, propriété *f* **2** REAL ESTATE : biens *mpl* immobiliers **3** QUALITY : propriété *f*

prophet [ˈprɑfət] *n* : prophète *m* — **prophecy** [ˈprɑfəsi] *n, pl* **-cies** : prophétie *f* — **prophesy** [ˈprɑfəˌsaɪ] *vt* **-sied; -sying** : prophétiser — **prophetic** [prəˈfɛt̬ɪk] *adj* : prophétique

proponent [prəˈpoːnənt] *n* : partisan *m*, -sane *f*

proportion [prəˈporʃən] *n* **1** : proportion *f* **2** SHARE : part *f* — **proportional** [prəˈporʃənəl] *adj* : proportionnel — **proportionate** [prəˈporʃənət] *adj* : proportionnel

proposal [prəˈpoːzəl] *n* : proposition *f*

propose [prəˈpoːz] *v* **-posed; -posing** *vt* : proposer — *vi* : faire une demande en mariage — **proposition** [ˌprɑpəˈzɪʃən] *n* : proposition *f*

proprietor [prəˈpraɪət̬ər] *n* : propriétaire *mf*

propriety [prəˈpraɪət̬i] *n, pl* **-ties** : convenance *f*

propulsion [prəˈpʌlʃən] *n* : propulsion *f*

prose [ˈproːz] *n* : prose *f*

prosecute [ˈprɑsɪˌkjuːt] *vt* **-cuted; -cuting** : poursuivre — **prosecution** [ˌprɑsɪˈkjuːʃən] *n* : poursuites *fpl* judiciaires — **prosecutor** [ˈprɑsɪˌkjuːt̬ər] *n* : procureur *m*

prospect [ˈprɑˌspɛkt] *n* **1** VIEW : vue *f* **2** POSSIBILITY : perspective *f* **3 ~s** : espérances *fpl* — **prospective** [prəˈspɛktɪv, ˈprɑˌspɛk-] *adj* : éventuel

prosper [ˈprɑspər] *vt* : prospérer — **prosperity** [prɑˈspɛrət̬i] *n* : prospérité *f* — **prosperous** [ˈprɑspərəs] *adj* : prospère

prostitute [ˈprɑstəˌtuːt, -ˌtjuːt] *n* : prostituée *f* — **prostitution** [ˌprɑstəˈtuːʃən, -ˈtjuː-] *n* : prostitution *f*

prostrate [ˈprɑˌstreɪt] *adj* **1** : allongé à plat ventre **2** STRICKEN : prostré

protagonist [proˈtægənɪst] *n* : protagoniste *mf*

protect [prəˈtɛkt] *vt* : protéger — **protection** [prəˈtɛkʃən] *n* : protection *f* — **protective** [prəˈtɛktɪv] *adj* : protecteur — **protector** [prəˈtɛktər] *n* : protecteur *m*, -trice *f*

protein [ˈproːˌtiːn] *n* : protéine *f*

protest [ˈproːˌtɛst] *n* **1** DEMONSTRATION

: manifestation *f* **2** OBJECTION : protestation *f* — ~ [pro'tɛst] *v* : protester — **Protestant** ['prɑtəstənt] *n* : protestant *m*, -tante *f* — **protester** *or* **protestor** ['pro:ˌtɛstər, prə'-] *n* : manifestant *m*, -tante *f*

protocol ['pro:təˌkɔl] *n* : protocole *m*

protrude [pro'tru:d] *vi* **-truded; -truding** : dépasser

proud ['praʊd] *adj* **1** : fier **2** ARROGANT : orgueilleux

prove ['pru:v] *v* **proved; proved** *or* **proven** ['pru:vən]; **proving** *vt* : prouver — *vi* : s'avérer, se montrer

proverb ['prɑˌvərb] *n* : proverbe *m*

provide [prə'vaɪd] *v* **-vided; -viding** *vt* : fournir — *vi* ~ **for** SUPPORT : subvenir aux besoins de — **provided** [prə'vaɪdəd] *or* ~ **that** *conj* : à condition que — **providence** ['prɑvədənts] *n* : providence *f*

province ['prɑvɪnts] *n* **1** : province *f* **2** SPHERE : domaine *m* — **provincial** [prə'vɪntʃəl] *adj* : provincial

provision [prə'vɪʒən] *n* **1** SUPPLYING : approvisionnement *m* **2** STIPULATION : stipulation *f* **3** ~**s** *npl* : provisions *fpl* — **provisional** [prə'vɪʒənəl] *adj* : provisoire

provoke [prə'vo:k] *vt* **-voked; -voking** : provoquer — **provocative** [prə'vɑkətɪv] *adj* : provocant, provocateur

prow ['praʊ] *n* : proue *f*

prowess ['praʊəs] *n* : prouesse *f*

prowl ['praʊl] *vi* : rôder — ~ *n* **be on the** ~ : rôder — **prowler** ['praʊlər] *n* : rôdeur *m*, -deuse *f*

proximity [prɑk'sɪməti] *n* : proximité *f* — **proxy** ['prɑksi] *n, pl* **proxies** : procuration *f*

prude ['pru:d] *n* : prude *f*

prudence ['pru:dənts] *n* : prudence *f* — **prudent** ['pru:dənt] *adj* : prudent

prune[1] ['pru:n] *n* : pruneau *m*

prune[2] *vt* **pruned; pruning** : élaguer, tailler

pry ['praɪ] *v* **pried; prying** *vi* ~ **into** : mettre son nez dans — *vt or* ~ **open** : forcer avec un levier

psalm ['sɑm, 'sɑlm] *n* : psaume *m*

pseudonym ['su:dəˌnɪm] *n* : pseudonyme *m*

psychiatry [sə'kaɪətri, saɪ-] *n* : psychiatrie *f* — **psychiatric** [ˌsaɪki'ætrɪk] *adj* : psychiatrique — **psychiatrist** [sə'kaɪətrɪst, saɪ-] *n* : psychiatre *mf*

psychic ['saɪkɪk] *adj* : psychique

psychoanalysis [ˌsaɪkoə'næləsɪs] *n* : psychanalyse *f* — **psychoanalyst** [ˌsaɪko'ænəlɪst] *n* : psychanalyste *mf* — **psychoanalyze** [ˌsaɪko'ænəlˌaɪz] *vt* **-lyzed; -lyzing** : psychanalyser

psychology [saɪ'kɑlədʒi] *n, pl* **-gies** : psychologie *f* — **psychological** [ˌsaɪkə'lɑdʒɪkəl] *adj* : psychologique — **psychologist** [saɪ'kɑlədʒɪst] *n* : psychologue *mf*

psychotherapy [ˌsaɪko'θɛrəpi] *n* : psychothérapie *f*

puberty ['pju:bərti] *n* : puberté *f*

public ['pʌblɪk] *adj* : public — ~ *n* : public *m* — **publication** [ˌpʌblə'keɪʃən] *n* : publication *f* — **publicity** [pə'blɪsəti] *n* : publicité *f* — **publicize** ['pʌbləˌsaɪz] *vt* **-cized; -cizing** : rendre public, faire connaître

publish ['pʌblɪʃ] *vt* : publier — **publisher** ['pʌblɪʃər] *n* **1** : éditeur *m*, -trice *f* **2** : maison *f* d'édition (entreprise)

puck ['pʌk] *n* : palet *m*, rondelle *f Can* (au hockey)

pucker ['pʌkər] *vt* : plisser — *vi* : se plisser

pudding ['pʊdɪŋ] *n* : pudding *m*, pouding *m*

puddle ['pʌdəl] *n* : flaque *f* (d'eau)

puff ['pʌf] *vi* **1** BLOW : souffler **2** PANT : haleter **3** ~ **up** SWELL : enfler — *vt or* ~ **out** : gonfler — ~ *n* **1** : bouffée *f* **2 cream** ~ : chou *m* à la crème **3** *or* **powder** ~ : houppette *f* — **puffy** ['pʌfi] *adj* **puffier; puffiest** : enflé, bouffi

pull ['pʊl, 'pʌl] *vt* **1** : tirer **2** STRAIN : se froisser **3** EXTRACT : arracher **4** DRAW : sortir **5** ~ **off** : enlever **6** ~ **oneself together** : se ressaisir **7** ~ **up** RAISE : remonter — *vi* **1** ~ **away** : se retirer **2** ~ **out of** : quitter **3** ~ **through** RECOVER : s'en tirer **4** ~ **together** COOPERATE : agir en concert **5** ~ **up** STOP : s'arrêter — ~ *n* **1** TUG : coup *m* **2** INFLUENCE : influence *f* — **pulley** ['pʊli] *n, pl* **-leys** : poulie *f* — **pullover** ['pʊlˌo:vər] *n* : chandail *m*, pull-over *m France*

pulmonary ['pʊlməˌnɛri, 'pʌl-] *adj* : pulmonaire

pulp ['pʌlp] *n* : pulpe *f*

pulpit ['pʊlˌpɪt] *n* : chaire *f*

pulsate ['pʌlˌseɪt] *vi* **-sated; -sating** **1** BEAT : palpiter **2** VIBRATE : vibrer — **pulse** ['pʌls] *n* : pouls *m*

pummel ['pʌməl] *vt* **-meled; -meling** : bourer de coups

pump[1] ['pʌmp] *n* : pompe *f* — ~ *vt* **1** : pomper (de l'eau) **2** ~ **up** : gonfler

pump[2] *n* SHOE : escarpin *m*
pumpernickel ['pʌmpər,nɪkəl] *n* : pain *m* noir
pumpkin ['pʌmpkɪn, 'pʌŋkən] *n* : citrouille *f*, potiron *m France*
pun ['pʌn] *n* : jeu *m* de mots
punch[1] ['pʌntʃ] *vt* **1** : donner un coup de poing à **2** PERFORATE : poinçonner — ~ *n* BLOW : coup *m* de poing
punch[2] *n* : punch *m* (boisson)
punctual ['pʌŋktʃʊəl] *adj* : ponctuel — **punctuality** [ˌpʌŋktʃʊ'æləṭi] *n* : ponctualité *f*
punctuate ['pʌŋktʃʊˌeɪt] *vt* **-ated; -ating** : ponctuer — **punctuation** [ˌpʌŋktʃʊ'eɪʃən] *n* : ponctuation *f*
puncture ['pʌŋktʃər] *n* **1** HOLE : perforation *f* **2** PRICK : piqûre *f* — ~ *vt* **-tured; -turing 1** PIERCE : perforer **2** : crever (un ballon, un pneu, etc.)
pungent ['pʌndʒənt] *adj* : âcre
punish ['pʌnɪʃ] *vt* : punir — **punishment** ['pʌnɪʃmənt] *n* : punition *f* — **punitive** ['pju:nəṭɪv] *adj* : punitif
puny ['pju:ni] *adj* **-nier; -est** : chétif
pup ['pʌp] *n* : chiot *m*, jeune animal *m*
pupil[1] ['pju:pəl] *n* STUDENT : élève *mf*
pupil[2] *n* : pupille *f* (de l'œil)
puppet ['pʌpət] *n* : marionnette *f*
puppy ['pʌpi] *n, pl* **-pies** : chiot *m*
purchase ['pərtʃəs] *vt* **-chased; -chasing** : acheter — ~ *n* : achat *m*
pure ['pjʊr] *adj* **purer; purest** : pur
puree [pjʊ'reɪ, -'ri:] *n* : purée *f*
purely ['pjʊrli] *adv* : purement
purgatory ['pərgəˌtori] *n, pl* **-ries** : purgatoire *m* — **purge** ['pərdʒ] *vt* **purged; purging** : purger — ~ *n* : purge *f*
purify ['pjʊrəˌfaɪ] *vt* **-fied; -fying** : purifier — **purifier** ['pjʊrəˌfaɪər] *n* : purificateur *m*
puritan ['pju:rətən] *n* : puritain *m*, -taine *f* — **puritanical** [ˌpju:rə'tænɪkəl] *adj* : puritain
purity ['pjʊrəṭi] *n* : pureté *f*
purple ['pərpəl] *adj* : violet, pourpre — ~ *n* : violet *m*, pourpre *m*
purpose ['pərpəs] *n* **1** AIM : intention *f*, but *m* **2** DETERMINATION : résolution *f* **3 on** ~ : exprès — **purposeful** ['pərpəsfəl] *adj* **1** MEANINGFUL : significatif **2** INTENTIONAL : réfléchi **3** DETERMINED : résolu — **purposely** ['pərpəsli] *adv* : exprès
purr ['pər] *n* : ronronnement *m* — ~ *vi* : ronronner
purse ['pərs] *n* **1** *or* **change** ~ : portemonnaie *m* **2** HANDBAG : sac *m* à main, sacoche *f Can*
pursue [pər'su:] *vt* **-sued; -suing** : poursuivre — **pursuer** [pər'su:ər] *n* : poursuivant *m*, -vante *f* — **pursuit** [pər'su:t] *n* **1** : poursuite *f* **2** OCCUPATION : activité *f*
pus ['pʌs] *n* : pus *m*
push ['pʊʃ] *vt* **1** : pousser **2** PRESS : appuyer sur **3** THRUST : enfoncer **4** ~ **away** : repousser — *vi* **1** : pousser **2** ~ **on** : continuer **3** ~ **(oneself)** : s'exercer — ~ *n* **1** SHOVE : poussée *f* **2** EFFORT : effort *m* — **pushy** ['pʊʃi] *adj* **pushier; pushiest** : arriviste
pussycat ['pʊsiˌkæt] *n* : minet *m*, minou *m fam*
put ['pʊt] *v* **put; putting** *vt* **1** : mettre **2** PLACE : placer, poser **3** EXPRESS : dire **4** ~ **forward** PROPOSE : avancer, proposer — *vi* ~ **up with** TOLERATE : supporter — **put away** *vt* **1** STORE : ranger **2** *or* ~ **aside** : mettre de côté — **put down** *vt* **1** : poser, déposer **2** WRITE : mettre (par écrit) — **put off** *vt* POSTPONE : remettre à plus tard, retarder — **put on** *vt* **1** ASSUME : prendre **2** PRESENT : monter (un spectacle, etc.) **3** WEAR : mettre — **put out** *vt* **1** EXTINGUISH, TURN OFF : éteindre **2** INCONVENIENCE : déranger — **put up** *vt* **1** BUILD : ériger **2** LODGE : loger **3** HANG : accrocher
putrefy ['pju:trəˌfaɪ] *v* **-fied; -fying** *vt* : putréfier — *vi* : se putréfier
putty ['pʌṭi] *n, pl* **-ties** : mastic *m*
puzzle ['pʌzəl] *vt* **-zled; -zling** CONFUSE : intriguer, laisser perplexe — ~ *n* **1** : casse-tête *m* **2** *or* **jigsaw** ~ : puzzle *m* **3** MYSTERY : énigme *f*, mystère *m*
pyjamas *Brit* → **pajamas**
pylon ['paɪˌlɑn, -lən] *n* : pylône *m*
pyramid ['pɪrəˌmɪd] *n* : pyramide *f*
python ['paɪˌθɑn, -θən] *n* : python *m*

Q

q [ˈkju:] *n, pl* **q's** *or* **qs** [ˈkju:z] : q *m,* dix-septième lettre de l'alphabet
quack[1] [ˈkwæk] *vi* : faire des coin-coin
quack[2] *n* CHARLATAN : charlatan *m*
quadruped [ˈkwɑdrəˌpɛd] *n* : quadrupède *m*
quadruple [kwɑˈdru:pəl, -ˈdrʌ-; ˈkwɑdrə-] *v* **-pled; -pling** : quadrupler — ~ *adj* : quadruple
quagmire [ˈkwægˌmaɪr, ˈkwɑg-] *n* : bourbier *m*
quail [ˈkweɪl] *n, pl* **quail** *or* **quails** : caille *f*
quaint [ˈkweɪnt] *adj* **1** ODD : bizarre **2** PICTURESQUE : pittoresque
quake [ˈkweɪk] *vi* **quaked; quaking** : trembler
qualify [ˈkwɑləˌfaɪ] *v* **-fied; -fying** *vt* **1** LIMIT : poser des conditions sur **2** AUTHORIZE : qualifier, autoriser **3** MODERATE : mitiger — *vi* : se qualifier — **qualification** [ˌkwɑləfəˈkeɪʃən] *n* **1** : qualification *f* **2** LIMITATION : réserve *f* **3** ABILITY : compétence *f* — **qualified** [ˈkwɑləˌfaɪd] *adj* : qualifié, compétent
quality [ˈkwɑləţi] *n, pl* **-ties** : qualité *f*
qualm [ˈkwɑm, ˈkwɑlm, ˈkwɔm] *n* : scrupule *m*
quandary [ˈkwɑndri] *n, pl* **-ries** : dilemme *m*
quantity [ˈkwɑntəţi] *n, pl* **-ties** : quantité *f*
quarantine [ˈkwɔrənˌti:n] *n* : quarantaine *f* — ~ *vt* **-tined; -tining** : mettre en quarantaine
quarrel [ˈkwɔrəl] *n* : dispute *f,* querelle *f* — ~ *vi* **-reled** *or* **-relled; -reling** *or* **-relling** : se quereller, se disputer — **quarrelsome** [ˈkwɔrəlsəm] *adj* : querelleur
quarry [ˈkwɔri] *n, pl* **-ries** EXCAVATION : carrière *f*
quart [ˈkwɔrt] *n* : quart *m* de gallon
quarter [ˈkwɔrţər] *n* **1** : quart *m* **2** : (pièce de) vingt-cinq cents *m* **3** DISTRICT : quartier *m* **4** : trimestre *m* (de l'année fiscale) **5** ~ **after three** : trois heures et quart **6** ~**s** *npl* LODGINGS : logement *m* — ~ *vt* : diviser en quatre — **quarterly** [ˈkwɔrţərli] *adv* : tous les trois mois, trimestriellement — ~ *adj* : trimestriel — ~ *n, pl* **-lies** : publication *f* trimestrielle
quartet [kwɔrˈtɛt] *n* : quatuor *m*
quartz [ˈkwɔrts] *n* : quartz *m*
quash [ˈkwɑʃ, ˈkwɔʃ] *vt* : étouffer, réprimer
quaver [ˈkweɪvər] *vi* : trembloter
quay [ˈki:, ˈkeɪ, ˈkweɪ] *n* WHARF : quai *m*
queasy [ˈkwi:zi] *adj* **-sier; -est** : nauséeux
Quebecer [kwɪˈbɛkər] *adj* : québécois
Quebecois *or* **Québécois** [kebeˈkwɑ:] *adj* : québécois
queen [ˈkwi:n] *n* : reine *f*
queer [ˈkwɪr] *adj* ODD : étrange, bizarre
quell [ˈkwɛl] *vt* SUPPRESS : réprimer
quench [ˈkwɛntʃ] *vt* **1** EXTINGUISH : éteindre **2** ~ **one's thirst** : étancher la soif
query [ˈkwɪri, ˈkwɛr-] *n, pl* **-ries** : question *f* — ~ *vt* **-ried; -rying** ASK : poser une question à
quest [ˈkwɛst] *n* : quête *f*
question [ˈkwɛstʃən] *n* : question *f* — ~ *vt* **1** ASK : poser une question à **2** INTERROGATE : questionner **3** DOUBT : mettre en doute — **questionable** [ˈkwɛstʃənəbəl] *adj* : discutable — **question mark** *n* : point *m* d'interrogation — **questionnaire** [ˌkwɛstʃəˈnær] *n* : questionnaire *m*
queue [ˈkju:] *n* LINE : queue *f,* file *f* — ~ *vi* **queued; queuing** *or* **queueing** : faire la queue
quibble [ˈkwɪbəl] *vi* **-bled; -bling** : chicaner — ~ *n* : chicane *f*
quick [ˈkwɪk] *adj* : rapide — ~ *adv* : rapidement, vite — **quicken** [ˈkwɪkən] *vt* : accélérer — ~ *vi* : s'accélérer — **quickly** [ˈkwɪkli] *adv* : rapidement, vite — **quickness** [ˈkwɪknəs] *n* : rapidité *f,* vitesse *f* — **quicksand** [ˈkwɪkˌsænd] *n* : sables *mpl* mouvants
quiet [ˈkwaɪət] *n* **1** : silence *m* **2** CALM : calme *m* — ~ *adj* **1** SILENT : silencieux **2** CALM : tranquille — ~ *vt* **1** SILENCE : faire taire **2** CALM : calmer — *vi or* ~ **down** : se calmer — **quietly** [ˈkwaɪətli] *adv* **1** SILENTLY : sans bruit, doucement **2** CALMLY : tranquillement
quilt [ˈkwɪlt] *n* : édredon *m*
quintet [kwɪnˈtɛt] *n* : quintette *m* — **quintuple** [kwɪnˈtu:pəl, -ˈtju:-, -ˈtʌ-; ˈkwɪntə-] *adj* : quintuple

quip [ˈkwɪp] *n* : raillerie *f*
quirk [ˈkwərk] *n* : bizarrerie *f* — **quirky** [ˈkwərki] *adj* **quirkier; quirkiest** : excentrique
quit [ˈkwɪt] *v* **quit; quitting** *vt* **1** LEAVE : quitter **2** STOP : arrêter — *vi* **1** GIVE UP : abandonner **2** RESIGN : démissionner
quite [ˈkwaɪt] *adv* **1** COMPLETELY : tout à fait **2** RATHER : assez **3** POSITIVELY : vraiment
quits [ˈkwɪts] *adj* **1** : quitte **2 we called it ~** : nous y avons renoncé
quiver [ˈkwɪvər] *vi* : trembler
quiz [ˈkwɪz] *n, pl* **quizzes** TEST : interrogation *f* — **~** *vt* **quizzed; quizzing** : questionner, interroger
quota [ˈkwoːt̬ə] *n* : quota *m*
quotation [kwoˈteɪʃən] *n* **1** CITATION : citation *f* **2** ESTIMATE : devis *m* — **quotation marks** *npl* : guillemets *mpl* — **quote** [ˈkwoːt] *vt* **quoted; quoting 1** CITE : citer **2** STATE : indiquer (un prix) **3** : coter (un prix à la Bourse) — **~** *n* **1** → **quotation 2 ~s** *npl* → **quotation marks**
quotient [ˈkwoːʃənt] *n* : quotient *m*

R

r [ˈɑr] *n, pl* **r's** *or* **rs** [ˈɑrz] : r *m*, dix-huitième lettre de l'alphabet
rabbi [ˈræˌbaɪ] *n* : rabbin *m*
rabbit [ˈræbət] *n, pl* **-bit** *or* **-bits** : lapin *m*, -pine *f*
rabies [ˈreɪbiːz] *ns & pl* : rage *f* — **rabid** [ˈræbɪd] *adj* **1** : enragé (se dit d'un chien) **2** FURIOUS : furieux
raccoon [ræˈkuːn] *n, pl* **-coon** *or* **-coons** : raton *m* laveur
race[1] [ˈreɪs] *n* **1** : race *f* **2 human ~** : genre *m* humain
race[2] *n* : course *f* (à pied, etc.) — **~** *vi* **raced; racing** : courir — **racehorse** [ˈreɪsˌhors] *n* : cheval *m* de course — **racetrack** [ˈreɪsˌtræk] *n* : hippodrome *m*
racial [ˈreɪʃəl] *adj* : racial — **racism** [ˈreɪˌsɪzəm] *n* : racisme *m* — **racist** [ˈreɪsɪst] *n* : raciste *mf*
rack [ˈræk] *n* **1** SHELF : étagère *f* **2 luggage ~** : porte-bagages *m* — **~** *vt* **1 ~ed with** : tourmenté par **2 ~ one's brains** : se creuser les méninges
racket[1] [ˈrækət] *n* : raquette *f* (de tennis, etc.)
racket[2] **1** DIN : vacarme *m* **2** SWINDLE : escroquerie *f*
racy [ˈreɪsi] *adj* **racier; -est** : osé, risqué
radar [ˈreɪˌdɑr] *n* : radar *m*
radiant [ˈreɪdiənt] *adj* : radieux — **radiance** [ˈreɪdiənts] *n* : éclat *m* — **radiate** [ˈreɪdiˌeɪt] *v* **-ated; -ating** *vt* : irradier — *vi* : rayonner — **radiation** [ˌreɪdiˈeɪʃən] *n* : rayonnement *m* — **radiator** [ˈreɪdiˌeɪt̬ər] *n* : radiateur *m*
radical [ˈrædɪkəl] *adj* : radical — **~** *n* : radical *m*, -cale *f*
radii → **radius**
radio [ˈreɪdiˌoː] *n, pl* **-dios** : radio *f* — **~** *vt* : transmettre par radio — **radioactive** [ˈreɪdioˈæktɪv] *adj* : radioactif
radish [ˈrædɪʃ] *n* : radis *m*
radius [ˈreɪdiəs] *n, pl* **radii** [-diˌaɪ] : rayon *m*
raffle [ˈræfəl] *vt* **-fled; -fling** : mettre en tombola — **~** *n* : tombola *f*
raft [ˈræft] *n* : radeau *m*
rafter [ˈræftər] *n* : chevron *m*
rag [ˈræg] *n* **1** : chiffon *m*, guenille *f Can* **2 in ~s** : en haillons
rage [ˈreɪʤ] *n* **1** : colère *f*, rage *f* **2 be all the ~** : faire fureur — **~** *vi* **raged; raging 1** : être furieux **2** : hurler (se dit du vent, etc.)
ragged [ˈrægəd] *adj* **1** UNEVEN : inégal **2** TATTERED : en loques
raid [ˈreɪd] *n* **1** : invasion *f*, raid *m* **2** *or* **police ~** : descente *f*, rafle *f* — **~** *vt* INVADE : envahir
rail[1] [ˈreɪl] *vi* **~ at** : invectiver contre
rail[2] *n* **1** BAR : barre *f* **2** HANDRAIL : balustrade *f* **3** TRACK : rail *m* **4 by ~** : par train — **railing** [ˈreɪlɪŋ] *n* **1** : rampe *f* (d'un escalier), balustrade *f* (d'un balcon) **2** RAILS : grille *f* — **railroad** [ˈreɪlˌroːd] *n* : chemin *m* de fer — **railway** [ˈreɪlˌweɪ] → **railroad**
rain [ˈreɪn] *n* : pluie *f* — **~** *vi* : pleuvoir — **rainbow** [ˈreɪnˌboː] *n* : arc-en-ciel *m* — **raincoat** [ˈreɪnˌkoːt] *n* : imperméable *m* — **rainfall** [ˈreɪnˌfɔl] *n* : précipitations *fpl* — **rainy** [ˈreɪni] *adj* **rainier; -est** : pluvieux
raise [ˈreɪz] *vt* **raised; raising 1** : lever **2** REAR : élever **3** GROW : cultiver **4** INCREASE : augmenter **5** : soulever (des objections) **6 ~ money** : collecter des fonds — **~** *n* : augmentation *f*
raisin [ˈreɪzən] *n* : raisin *m* sec

rake ['reɪk] *n* : râteau *m* — ∼ *vt* **raked; raking** : ratisser
rally ['ræli] *v* **-lied; -lying** *vi* : se rallier, se rassembler — *vt* : rallier, rassembler — ∼ *n, pl* **-lies** : ralliement *m*, rassemblement *m*
ram ['ræm] *n* : bélier *m* (mouton) — ∼ *vt* **rammed; ramming 1** CRAM : fourrer **2** *or* ∼ **into** : percuter
RAM ['ræm] *n* (*r*andom-*a*ccess *m*emory) : RAM *f*
ramble ['ræmbəl] *vi* **-bled; -ling 1** WANDER : se balader **2** *or* ∼ **on** : divaguer — ∼ *n* : randonnée *f*, excursion *f*
ramp ['ræmp] *n* **1** : rampe *f* **2** : passerelle *f* (pour accéder à un avion)
rampage ['ræm,peɪʤ] *vi* **-paged; -paging** : se déchaîner
rampant ['ræmpənt] *adj* : déchaîné
ramshackle ['ræm,ʃækəl] *adj* : délabré
ran → **run**
ranch ['ræntʃ] *n* : ranch *m*
rancid ['ræntsɪd] *adj* : rance
rancor *or Brit* **rancour** ['ræŋkər] *n* : rancœur *f*, rancune *f*
random ['rændəm] *adj* **1** : aléatoire **2 at** ∼ : au hasard
rang → **ring**
range ['reɪnʤ] *n* **1** : chaîne *f* (de montagnes) **2** STOVE : cuisinière *f* **3** VARIETY : gamme *f* **4** SCOPE : portée *f* — ∼ *vi* **ranged; ranging 1** EXTEND : s'étendre **2** ∼ **from ... to ...** : varier entre ... et ... — **ranger** ['reɪnʤər] *n or* **forest** ∼ : garde *m* forestier
rank[1] ['ræŋk] *adj* : fétide
rank[2] *n* **1** ROW : rang *m* **2** : grade *m* (militaire) **3** ∼**s** : simples soldats *mpl* **4 the** ∼ **and file** : la base — ∼ *vt* RATE : classer, ranger — *vi* : se classer, compter
rankle ['ræŋkəl] *vi* **-kled; -kling** : rester sur le cœur
ransack ['ræn,sæk] *vt* **1** SEARCH : fouiller **2** LOOT : saccager
ransom ['ræntsəm] *n* : rançon *f* — ∼ *vt* : payer une rançon pour
rant ['rænt] *vi or* ∼ **and rave** : fulminer
rap[1] ['ræp] *n* KNOCK : coup *m* sec — ∼ *v* **rapped; rapping** : cogner
rap[2] *n or* ∼ **music** : rap *m*
rapacious [rə'peɪʃəs] *adj* : rapace
rape ['reɪp] *vt* **raped; raping** : violer — ∼ *n* : viol *m*
rapid ['ræpɪd] *adj* : rapide — **rapids** ['ræpɪdz] *npl* : rapides *mpl*
rapture ['ræptʃər] *n* : extase *f*
rare ['rær] *adj* **rarer; rarest 1** FINE : exceptionnel **2** UNCOMMON : rare **3** : saignant (se dit de la viande) — **rarely** ['rærli] *adv* : rarement — **rarity** ['rærət̬i] *n, pl* **-ties** : rareté *f*
rascal ['ræskəl] *n* : polisson *m*, -sonne *f*
rash[1] ['ræʃ] *adj* : irréfléchi
rash[2] *n* : rougeurs *fpl*
raspberry ['ræz,bɛri] *n, pl* **-ries** : framboise *f*
rat ['ræt] *n* : rat *m*
rate ['reɪt] *n* **1** PACE : vitesse *f*, rythme *m* **2** : taux *m* (d'intérêt, etc.) **3** PRICE : tarif *m* **4 at any** ∼ : de toute manière — ∼ *vt* **rated; rating 1** REGARD : considérer **2** RANK : classer
rather ['ræðər, 'rʌ-, 'rɑ-] *adv* **1** FAIRLY : assez, plutôt **2 I'd** ∼ **decide** : je préférerais décider
ratify ['ræt̬ə,faɪ] *vt* **-fied; -fying** : ratifier — **ratification** [,ræt̬əfə'keɪʃən] *n* : ratification *f*
rating ['reɪtɪŋ] *n* **1** : classement *m*, cote *f* **2** ∼**s** *npl* : indice *m* d'écoute
ratio ['reɪʃio] *n, pl* **-tios** : rapport *m*, proportion *f*
ration ['ræʃən, 'reɪʃən] *n* **1** : ration *f* **2** ∼**s** *npl* : vivres *mpl* — ∼ *vt* **rationed; rationing** : rationner
rational ['ræʃənəl] *adj* : rationnel — **rationale** [,ræʃə'næl] *n* : logique *f*, raisons *fpl* — **rationalize** ['ræʃənə,laɪz] *vt* **-ized; -izing** : rationaliser
rattle ['ræt̬əl] *v* **-tled; -tling** *vi* : faire du bruit — *vt* **1** SHAKE : agiter **2** UPSET : déconcerter **3** ∼ **off** : débiter à toute vitesse — ∼ *n* **1** : succession *f* de bruits secs **2** *or* **baby's** ∼ : hochet *m* — **rattlesnake** ['ræt̬əl,sneɪk] *n* : serpent *m* à sonnettes
ravage ['rævɪʤ] *vt* **-aged; -aging** : ravager — **ravages** ['rævɪʤəz] *npl* : ravages *mpl*
rave ['reɪv] *vi* **raved; raving 1** : délirer **2** ∼ **about** : parler avec enthousiasme de
raven ['reɪvən] *n* : grand corbeau *m*
ravenous ['rævənəs] *adj* **1** HUNGRY : affamé **2** VORACIOUS : vorace
ravine [rə'vi:n] *n* : ravin *m*
ravishing ['rævɪʃɪŋ] *adj* : ravissant
raw ['rɔ] *adj* **rawer; rawest 1** UNCOOKED : cru **2** INEXPERIENCED : novice **3** CHAFED : à vif (se dit d'une plaie) **4** : cru et humide (se dit de la température) **5** ∼ **materials** : matières *fpl* premières
ray ['reɪ] *n* : rayon *m* (de lumière), lueur *f* (d'espoir, etc.)
rayon ['reɪ,ɑn] *n* : rayonne *f*

raze [ˈreɪz] *vt* **razed; razing** : raser, détruire

razor [ˈreɪzər] *n* : rasoir *m* — **razor blade** *n* : lame *f* de rasoir

reach [ˈri:ʧ] *vt* **1** : atteindre **2** *or* ~ **out** : tendre **3** : parvenir à (une entente, etc.) **4** CONTACT : rejoindre — *vi* EXTEND : s'étendre — ~ *n* **1** : portée *f*, proximité *f* **2 within** ~ : à portée de la main

react [riˈækt] *vi* : réagir — **reaction** [riˈækʃən] *n* : réaction *f* — **reactionary** [riˈækʃəˌnɛri] *adj* : réactionnaire — ~ *n, pl* **-ries** : réactionnaire *mf* — **reactor** [riˈæktər] *n* : réacteur *m*

read [ˈri:d] *v* **read** [ˈrɛd]; **reading** *vt* **1** : lire **2** INTERPRET : interpréter **3** SAY : dire **4** INDICATE : indiquer — *vi* : se lire — **readable** [ˈri:dəbəl] *adj* : lisible — **reader** [ˈri:dər] *n* : lecteur *m*, -trice *f*

readily [ˈrɛdəli] *adv* **1** WILLINGLY : volontiers **2** EASILY : facilement

reading [ˈri:dɪŋ] *n* : lecture *f*

readjust [ˌri:əˈʤʌst] *vt* : réajuster — *vi* : se réadapter

ready [ˈrɛdi] *adj* **readier; -est 1** : prêt, disposé **2** AVAILABLE : disponible **3 get** ~ : se préparer — ~ *vt* **readied; readying** : préparer

real [ˈri:l] *adj* **1** : véritable, réel **2** GENUINE : authentique — ~ *adv* VERY : très — **real estate** *n* : biens *mpl* immobiliers — **realistic** [ˌri:əˈlɪstɪk] *adj* : réaliste — **reality** [riˈæləṭi] *n, pl* **-ties** : réalité *f*

realize [ˈri:əˌlaɪz] *vt* **-ized; -izing 1** : se rendre compte de **2** ACHIEVE : réaliser

really [ˈrɪli, ˈrɪ:-] *adv* : vraiment

realm [ˈrɛlm] *n* **1** KINGDOM : royaume *m* **2** SPHERE : domaine *m*

reap [ˈri:p] *vt* : moissonner, récolter

reappear [ˌri:əˈpɪr] *vi* : réapparaître

rear[1] [ˈrɪr] *vt* : élever (des enfants, etc.)

rear[2] *n* : arrière *m*, derrière *m* — ~ *adj* : postérieur

rearrange [ˌri:əˈreɪnʤ] *vt* **-ranged; -ranging** : réarranger

reason [ˈri:zən] *n* : raison *f* — ~ *vi* : raisonner — **reasonable** [ˈri:zənəbəl] *adj* : raisonnable — **reasoning** [ˈri:zənɪŋ] *n* : raisonnement *m*

reassure [ˌri:əˈʃʊr] *vt* **-sured; -suring** : rassurer — **reassurance** [ˌri:əˈʃʊrənts] *n* : réconfort *m*

rebate [ˈri:ˌbeɪt] *n* : ristourne *f*

rebel [ˈrɛbəl] *n* : rebelle *mf* — ~ [rɪˈbɛl] *vi* **-belled; -belling** : se rebeller — **rebellion** [rɪˈbɛljən] *n* : rébellion *f* — **rebellious** [rɪˈbɛljəs] *adj* : rebelle

rebirth [ˌri:ˈbərθ] *n* : renaissance *f*

reboot [ˌri:ˈbu:t] *vt* : réamorcer, redémarrer (en informatique)

rebound [ˈri:ˌbaʊnd, rɪ:ˈbaʊnd] *vi* : rebondir — ~ [ˈri:ˌbaʊnd] *n* : rebond *m*

rebuff [rɪˈbʌf] *vt* : rabrouer — ~ *n* : rebuffade *f*

rebuild [ˌri:ˈbɪld] *vt* **-built** [-ˈbɪlt]; **-building** : reconstruire

rebuke [rɪˈbju:k] *vt* **-buked; -buking** : reprocher — ~ *n* : réprimande *f*

rebut [rɪˈbʌt] *vt* **-butted; -butting** : réfuter — **rebuttal** [rɪˈbʌṭəl] *n* : réfutation *f*

recall [rɪˈkɔl] *vt* **1** : rappeler (au devoir, etc.) **2** REMEMBER : se rappeler **3** REVOKE : annuler — ~ [rɪˈkɔl, ˈri:ˌkɔl] *n* : rappel *m*

recapitulate [ˌri:kəˈpɪʧəˌleɪt] *v* **-lated; -lating** : récapituler

recapture [ˌri:ˈkæpʧər] *vt* **-tured; -turing 1** : reprendre **2** RELIVE : revivre

recede [rɪˈsi:d] *vi* **-ceded; -ceding** : se retirer

receipt [rɪˈsi:t] *n* **1** : reçu *m* **2** ~**s** *npl* : recettes *fpl*

receive [rɪˈsi:v] *vt* **-ceived; -ceiving** : recevoir — **receiver** [rɪˈsi:vər] *n* : récepteur *m*, combiné *m*

recent [ˈri:sənt] *adj* : récent — **recently** [-li] *adv* : récemment

receptacle [rɪˈsɛptɪkəl] *n* : récipient *m*

reception [rɪˈsɛpʃən] *n* : réception *f* — **receptionist** [rɪˈsɛpʃənɪst] *n* : réceptionniste *mf* — **receptive** [rɪˈsɛptɪv] *adj* : réceptif

recess [ˈri:ˌsɛs, rɪˈsɛs] *n* **1** ALCOVE : recoin *m* **2** BREAK : récréation *f* (scolaire) — **recession** [rɪˈsɛʃən] *n* : récession *f*

recharge [ˌri:ˈʧɑrʤ] *vt* **-charged; -charging** : recharger — **rechargeable** [ˌri:ˈʧɑrʤəbəl] *adj* : rechargeable

recipe [ˈrɛsəˌpi:] *n* : recette *f*

recipient [riˈsɪpiənt] *n* : récipiendaire *mf*

reciprocal [rɪˈsɪprəkəl] *adj* : réciproque

recite [rɪˈsaɪt] *vt* **-cited; -citing 1** : réciter (un poème, etc.) **2** LIST : énumérer — **recital** [rɪˈsaɪṭəl] *n* : récital *m*

reckless [ˈrɛkləs] *adj* : imprudent — **recklessness** [ˈrɛkləsnəs] *n* : imprudence *f*

reckon [ˈrɛkən] *vt* : estimer, penser — **reckoning** [ˈrɛkənɪŋ] *n* : calculs *mpl*

reclaim [rɪˈkleɪm] *vt* : récupérer

recline [rɪˈklaɪn] *vi* **-clined; -clining** : s'allonger — **reclining** [rɪˈklaɪnɪŋ] *adj* : réglable (se dit d'un siège)
recluse [ˈrɛˌklu:s, rɪˈklu:s] *n* : reclus *m*, -cluse *f*
recognition [ˌrɛkɪgˈnɪʃən] *n* : reconnaissance *f* — **recognizable** [ˈrɛkəgˌnaɪzəbəl] *adj* : reconnaissable — **recognize** [ˈrɛkɪgˌnaɪz] *vt* **-nized; -nizing** : reconnaître
recoil [rɪˈkɔɪl] *vi* : reculer — **~** [ˈri:ˌkɔɪl, rɪˈ-] *n* : recul *m* (d'une arme à feu)
recollect [ˌrɛkəˈlɛkt] *v* : se souvenir — **recollection** [ˌrɛkəˈlɛkʃən] *n* : souvenir *m*
recommend [ˌrɛkəˈmɛnd] *vt* : recommander — **recommendation** [ˌrɛkəmənˈdeɪʃən] *n* : recommandation *f*
reconcile [ˈrɛkənˌsaɪl] *v* **-ciled; -ciling** *vt* **1** : réconcilier (des personnes), concilier (des dates, etc.) **2 ~ oneself to** : se résigner à — *vi* MAKE UP : se réconcilier — **reconciliation** [ˌrɛkənˌsɪliˈeɪʃən] *n* : réconciliation *f*
reconsider [ˌri:kənˈsɪdər] *vt* : reconsidérer
reconstruct [ˌri:kənˈstrʌkt] *vt* : reconstruire
record [rɪˈkɔrd] *vt* **1** : enregistrer **2** WRITE DOWN : noter — **~** [ˈrɛkərd] *n* **1** DOCUMENT : dossier *m* **2** REGISTER : registre *m* **3** HISTORY : passé *m* **4** : disque *m* (de musique) **5** *or* **police ~** : casier *m* judiciaire **6 world ~** : record *m* mondial — **recorder** [rɪˈkɔrdər] *n* **1** : flûte *f* à bec **2** *or* **tape ~** : magnétophone *m* — **recording** [rɪˈkɔrdɪŋ] *n* : enregistrement *m*
recount[1] [rɪˈkaʊnt] *vt* NARRATE : raconter
recount[2] [ˈri:ˌkaʊnt, ˌriˈ-] *vt* : recompter (des votes, etc.) — **~** *n* : décompte *m*
recourse [ˈri:ˌkɔrs, rɪˈ-] *n* **1** : recours *m* **2 have ~ to** : recourir à
recover [rɪˈkʌvər] *vt* : récupérer — *vi* RECUPERATE : se remettre, se rétablir — **recovery** [rɪˈkʌvəri] *n, pl* **-ries** : rétablissement *m*
recreation [ˌrɛkriˈeɪʃən] *n* : loisirs *mpl*, récréation *f* — **recreational** [ˌrɛkriˈeɪʃənəl] *adj* : récréatif
recruit [rɪˈkru:t] *vt* : recruter — **~** *n* : recrue *f* — **recruitment** [rɪˈkru:tmənt] *n* : recrutement *m*
rectangle [ˈrɛkˌtæŋgəl] *n* : rectangle *m* — **rectangular** [rɛkˈtæŋgjələr] *adj* : rectangulaire
rectify [ˈrɛktəˌfaɪ] *vt* **-fied; -fying** : rectifier
rector [ˈrɛktər] *n* : pasteur *m* — **rectory** [ˈrɛktəri] *n, pl* **-ries** : presbytère *m*
rectum [ˈrɛktəm] *n, pl* **-tums** *or* **-ta** [-tə] : rectum *m*
recuperate [rɪˈku:pəˌreɪt, -ˈkju:-] *v* **-ated; -ating** *vt* : récupérer — *vi* : se rétablir
recur [rɪˈkər] *vi* **-curred; -curring** : réapparaître — **recurrence** [rɪˈkərənts] *n* : répétition *f* — **recurrent** [rɪˈkərənt] *adj* : qui se répète
recycle [rɪˈsaɪkəl] *vt* **-cled; -cling** : recycler
red [ˈrɛd] *adj* : rouge — **~** *n* : rouge *m* — **redden** [ˈrɛdən] *v* : rougir — **reddish** [ˈrɛdɪʃ] *adj* : rougeâtre
redecorate [ˌri:ˈdɛkəˌreɪt] *vt* **-rated; -rating** : repeindre
redeem [riˈdi:m] *vt* : racheter, sauver — **redemption** [rɪˈdɛmpʃən] *n* : rédemption *f*
red–handed [ˈrɛdˈhændəd] *adv & adj* : la main dans le sac
redhead [ˈrɛdˌhɛd] *n* : roux *m*, rousse *f*
red–hot [ˈrɛdˈhɑt] *adj* : brûlant
redness [ˈrɛdnəs] *n* : rougeur *f*
redo [ˌri:ˈdu:] *vt* **-did** [-dɪd]; **-done** [-ˈdʌn]; **-doing** : refaire
red tape *n* : paperasserie *f*
reduce [rɪˈdu:s, -ˈdju:s] *vt* **-duced; -ducing** : réduire — **reduction** [rɪˈdʌkʃən] *n* : réduction *f*
redundant [rɪˈdʌndənt] *adj* : superflu
reed [ˈri:d] *n* : roseau *m*
reef [ˈri:f] *n* : récif *m*
reek [ˈri:k] *vi* : empester
reel [ˈri:l] *n* : bobine *f* (de fil, etc.) — **~** *vt* **~ in** : enrouler (une ligne de pêche), ramener (un poisson) — *vi* **1** STAGGER : tituber **2** SPIN : tournoyer
reestablish [ˌri:ɪˈstæblɪʃ] *vt* : rétablir
refer [riˈfər] *v* **-ferred; -ferring** *vt* DIRECT : renvoyer — *vi* **~ to 1** : faire allusion à **2** CONSULT : consulter
referee [ˌrɛfəˈri:] *n* : arbitre *m* — **~** *v* **-eed; -eeing** : arbitrer
reference [ˈrɛfrənts, ˈrɛfə-] *n* **1** : référence *f* **2 in ~ to** : en ce qui concerne
refill [ˌri:ˈfɪl] *vt* : remplir à nouveau — **~** [ˈri:ˌfɪl] *n* : recharge *f*, cartouche *f* (d'encre)
refine [rɪˈfaɪn] *vt* **-fined; -fining** : raffiner — **refined** [riˈfaɪnd] *adj* : raffiné — **refinement** [rɪˈfaɪnmənt] *n* : raffinement *m* — **refinery** [rɪˈfaɪnəri] *n, pl* **-eries** : raffinerie *f*

reflect [rɪˈflɛkt] *vt* : réfléchir (la lumière), refléter (une image, etc.) — *vi* **1** PONDER : réfléchir **2 ~ badly on** : faire du tort à — **reflection** [rɪˈflɛkʃən] *n* **1** : réflexion *f* **2** IMAGE : reflet *m*

reflex [ˈriːˌflɛks] *n* : réflexe *m*

reflexive [rɪˈflɛksɪv] *adj* : réfléchi

reform [rɪˈfɔrm] *vt* : réformer — **~** *n* : réforme *f* — **reformer** [rɪˈfɔrmər] *n* : réformateur *m*, -trice *f*

refrain[1] [rɪˈfreɪn] *vi* **~ from** : se retenir de

refrain[2] *n* : refrain *m* (en musique)

refresh [rɪˈfrɛʃ] *vt* : rafraîchir — **refreshments** [riˈfrɛʃmənts] *npl* : rafraîchissements *mpl*

refrigerate [rɪˈfrɪʤəˌreɪt] *vt* **-ated; -ating** : réfrigérer — **refrigeration** [rɪˌfrɪʤəˈreɪʃən] *n* : réfrigération *f* — **refrigerator** [rɪˈfrɪʤəˌreɪţər] *n* : réfrigérateur *m*

refuel [riːˈfjuːəl] *v* **-eled** *or* **-elled; -eling** *or* **-elling** *vt* : ravitailler en carburant — *vi* : se ravitailler

refuge [ˈrɛˌfjuːʤ] *n* : refuge *m*, abri *m* — **refugee** [ˌrɛfjʊˈʤiː] *n* : réfugié *m*, -giée *f*

refund [rɪˈfʌnd, ˈriːˌfʌnd] *vt* : rembourser — **~** [ˈriːˌfʌnd] *n* : remboursement *m*

refurbish [rɪˈfərbɪʃ] *vt* : remettre à neuf

refuse[1] [rɪˈfjuːz] *vt* **-fused; -fusing 1** : refuser **2 ~ to do sth** : se refuser à faire qqch — **refusal** [rɪˈfjuːzəl] *n* : refus *m*

refuse[2] [ˈrɛˌfjuːs, -ˌfjuːz] *n* : ordures *fpl*, déchets *mpl*

refute [rɪˈfjuːt] *vt* **-futed; -futing** : réfuter

regain [riːˈgeɪn] *vt* : retrouver

regal [ˈriːgəl] *adj* : royal, majestueux — **regalia** [rɪˈgeɪljə] *npl* : insignes *mpl*, vêtements *mpl* de cérémonie

regard [rɪˈgɑrd] *n* **1** : égard *m*, considération *f* **2** ESTEEM : estime *f* **3 ~s** *npl* : amitiés *fpl* **4 with ~ to** : en ce qui concerne — **~** *vt* **1** HEED : tenir compte de **2** ESTEEM : estimer **3 as ~s** : en ce qui concerne **4 ~ as** : considérer — **regarding** [rɪˈgɑrdɪŋ] *prep* : concernant — **regardless** [rɪˈgɑrdləs] *adv* : malgré tout — **regardless of** *prep* **1** : sans tenir compte de **2** IN SPITE OF : malgré

regime [reɪˈʒiːm, rɪ-] *n* : régime *m* — **regimen** [ˈrɛdʃəmən] *n* : régimen *m*

regiment [ˈrɛʤəmənt] *n* : régiment *m*

region [ˈriːʤən] *n* : région *f* — **regional** [ˈriːʤənəl] *adj* : régional

register [ˈrɛʤəstər] *n* : registre *m* — **~** *vt* **1** : inscrire, enregistrer **2** SHOW : exprimer **3** RECORD : indiquer (la température, etc.) **4** : immatriculer (un véhicule) — *vi* ENROLL : s'inscrire — **registration** [ˌrɛʤəˈstreɪʃən] *n* **1** : inscription *f*, enregistrement *m* **2 ~ number** : numéro *m* d'immatriculation — **registry** [ˈrɛʤəstri] *n, pl* **-tries** : registre *m*

regret [rɪˈgrɛt] *vt* **-gretted; -gretting** : regretter — **~** *n* **1** REMORSE : remords *m* **2** SORROW : regret *m* — **regrettable** [riˈgrɛţəbəl] *adj* : lamentable

regular [ˈrɛgjələr] *adj* **1** : régulier **2** CUSTOMARY : habituel — **~** *n* : habitué *m*, -tuée *f* — **regularity** [ˌrɛgjəˈlærəţi] *n, pl* **-ties** : régularité *f* — **regularly** [ˈrɛgjələrli] *adv* : régulièrement — **regulate** [ˈrɛgjəˌleɪt] *vt* **-lated; -lating** : régler — **regulation** [ˌrɛgjəˈleɪʃən] *n* **1** RULE : règlement *m*, règle *f* **2** CONTROL : réglementation *f*

rehabilitate [ˌriːhəˈbɪləˌteɪt, ˌriːə-] *vt* **-tated; -tating** : réhabiliter — **rehabilitation** [ˌriːhəˌbɪləˈteɪʃən, ˌriːə-] *n* : réhabilitation *f*

rehearse [rɪˈhərs] *vt* **-hearsed; -hearsing** : répéter — **rehearsal** [rɪˈhərsəl] *n* : répétition *f*

reign [ˈreɪn] *n* : règne *m* — **~** *vi* : régner

reimburse [ˌriːəmˈbərs] *vt* **-bursed; -bursing** : rembourser — **reimbursement** [ˌriːəmˈbərsmənt] *n* : remboursement *m*

rein [ˈreɪn] *n* : rêne *f*

reindeer [ˈreɪnˌdɪr] *n* : renne *m*

reinforce [ˌriːənˈfors] *vt* **-forced; -forcing** : renforcer — **reinforcement** [ˌriːənˈforsmənt] *n* : renfort *m*

reinstate [ˌriːənˈsteɪt] *vt* **-stated; -stating** : rétablir (dans ses fonctions)

reiterate [riˈɪţəˌreɪt] *vt* **-ated; -ating** : réitérer

reject [rɪˈʤɛkt] *vt* : rejeter — **rejection** [rɪˈʤɛkʃən] *n* : rejet *m*

rejoice [rɪˈʤɔɪs] *vi* **-joiced; -joicing** : se réjouir

rejuvenate [riˈʤuːvəˌneɪt] *vt* **-nated; -nating** : rajeunir

rekindle [ˌriːˈkɪndəl] *vt* **-dled; -dling** : raviver, ranimer

relapse [ˈriːˌlæps, riˈlæps] *n* : rechute *f* — **~** [riˈlæps] *vi* **-lapsed; -lapsing** : rechuter

relate [rɪˈleɪt] *v* **-lated; -lating** *vt* **1** TELL : raconter **2** ASSOCIATE : relier — *vi* **1 ~ to** : se rapporter à **2 ~ to** : s'entendre (avec) **3 ~ to** : apprécier, comprendre — **related** [rɪˈleɪt̬əd] *adj* **~ to** : apparenté à — **relation** [rɪˈleɪʃən] *n* **1** : rapport *m,* lien *m* **2** RELATIVE : parent *m,* -rente *f* **3 in ~ to** : par rapport à **4 ~s** *npl* : rapports *mpl,* relations *fpl* — **relationship** [rɪˈleɪʃənˌʃɪp] *n* **1** : rapport *m,* relations *fpl* **2** KINSHIP : liens *mpl* de parenté — **relative** [ˈrɛlət̬ɪv] *n* : parent *m,* -rente *f* — **~** *adj* : relatif — **relatively** [ˈrɛlət̬ɪvli] *adv* : relativement

relax [rɪˈlæks] *vt* : détendre — *vi* : se détendre — **relaxation** [ˌriːˌlækˈseɪʃən] *n* : détente *f,* relaxation *f*

relay [ˈriːˌleɪ] *n* **1** : relève *m* **2** *or* **~ race** : course *f* de relais — **~** [ˈriːˌleɪ, riˈleɪ] *vt* **-layed; -laying** : relayer, transmettre

release [riˈliːs] *vt* **-leased; -leasing 1** FREE : libérer, mettre en liberté **2** : relâcher (une bride, etc.) **3** EMIT : émettre **4** : publier (un livre), sortir (un nouveau film) — **~** *n* **1** : libération *f* **2** : sortie *f* (d'un film), parution *f* (d'un livre)

relegate [ˈrɛləˌgeɪt] *vt* **-gated; -gating** : reléguer

relent [rɪˈlɛnt] *vi* **1** GIVE IN : céder **2** ABATE : se calmer — **relentless** [rɪˈlɛntləs] *adj* : implacable

relevant [ˈrɛləvənt] *adj* : pertinent — **relevance** [ˈrɛləvənts] *n* : pertinence *f*

reliable [rɪˈlaɪəbəl] *adj* : fiable, sûr — **reliability** [rɪˌlaɪəˈbɪlət̬i] *n, pl* **-ties** : fiabilité *f* — **reliance** [rɪˈlaɪənts] *n* **1** : dépendance *f* **2** TRUST : confiance *f*

relic [ˈrɛlɪk] *n* : relique *f*

relief [rɪˈliːf] *n* **1** : soulagement *m* **2** AID : aide *f,* secours *m* **3** : relief *m* (d'une carte géographique) **4** REPLACEMENT : relève *f* — **relieve** [rɪˈliːv] *vt* **-lieved; -lieving 1** : soulager **2** REPLACE : relayer (qqn) **3 ~ s.o. of** : libérer qqn de

religion [rɪˈlɪʤən] *n* : religion *f* — **religious** [rɪˈlɪʤəs] *adj* : religieux

relinquish [rɪˈlɪŋkwɪʃ, -ˈlɪn-] *vt* : renoncer à

relish [ˈrɛlɪʃ] *n* **1** : condiment *m* à base de cornichons **2 with ~** : avec un plaisir évident — **~** *vt* : savourer

relocate [ˌriːˈloːˌkeɪt, ˌriːloˈkeɪt] *v* **-cated; -cating** *vt* : transférer — *vi* : déménager, s'établir ailleurs — **relocation** [ˌriːloˈkeɪʃən] *n* : déménagement *m*

reluctance [rɪˈlʌktənts] *n* : réticence *f* — **reluctant** [rɪˈlʌktənt] *adj* : réticent — **reluctantly** [rɪˈlʌktəntli] *adv* : à contrecœur

rely [rɪˈlaɪ] *vi* **-lied; -lying ~ on 1** : dépendre de **2** TRUST : se fier à

remain [rɪˈmeɪn] *vi* : rester — **remainder** [rɪˈmeɪndər] *n* : reste *m,* restant *m* — **remains** [rɪˈmeɪnz] *npl* : restes *mpl*

remark [rɪˈmɑrk] *n* : remarque *f,* observation *f* — **~** *vt* **1** : remarquer **2** SAY : mentionner — *vi* **~ on** : observer que — **remarkable** [rɪˈmɑrkəbəl] *adj* : remarquable

remedy [ˈrɛmədi] *n, pl* **-dies** : remède *m* — **~** *vt* **-died; -dying** : remédier à — **remedial** [rɪˈmiːdiəl] *adj* : de rattrapage

remember [rɪˈmɛmbər] *vt* **1** : se rappeler, se souvenir de **2 ~ to** : ne pas oublier de — *vi* : se rappeler, se souvenir — **remembrance** [rɪˈmɛmbrənts] *n* : souvenir *m*

remind [rɪˈmaɪnd] *vt* **~ s.o. of sth** : rappeler qqch à qqn — **reminder** [rɪˈmaɪndər] *n* : rappel *m*

reminisce [ˌrɛməˈnɪs] *vi* **-nisced; -niscing** : se rappeler le bon vieux temps — **reminiscent** [ˌrɛməˈnɪsənt] *adj* **~ of** : qui rappelle, qui fait penser à

remission [riˈmɪʃən] *n* : rémission *f*

remit [rɪˈmɪt] *vt* **-mitted; -mitting** : envoyer (de l'argent)

remnant [ˈrɛmnənt] *n* **1** : reste *m,* restant *m* **2** TRACE : vestige *m*

remorse [rɪˈmɔrs] *n* : remords *m* — **remorseful** [rɪˈmɔrsfəl] *adj* : plein de remords

remote [rɪˈmoːt] *adj* **-moter; -est 1** : lointain, éloigné **2** ALOOF : distant — **remote control** *n* : télécommande *f*

remove [rɪˈmuːv] *vt* **-moved; -moving 1** : enlever, ôter **2** DISMISS : renvoyer **3** ELIMINATE : supprimer, dissiper — **removable** [rɪˈmuːvəbəl] *adj* : amovible — **removal** [rɪˈmuːvəl] *n* : élimination *f*

remunerate [rɪˈmjuːnəˌreɪt] *vt* **-ated; -ating** : rémunérer

render [ˈrɛndər] *vt* : rendre

rendition [rɛnˈdɪʃən] *n* : interprétation *f*

renegade [ˈrɛnɪˌgeɪd] *n* : renégat *m,* -gate *f*

renew [rɪˈnuː, -ˈnjuː] *vt* **1** : renouveler **2** RESUME : reprendre — **renewal** [rɪˈnuːəl, -ˈnjuː-] *n* : renouvellement *m*

renounce [rɪˈnaʊnts] *vt* **-nounced; -nouncing** : renoncer à

renovate [ˈrɛnəˌveɪt] *vt* **-vated; -vating** : rénover — **renovation** [ˌrɛnəˈveɪʃən] *n* : rénovation *f*

renown [rɪˈnaʊn] *n* : renommée *f*, renom *m* — **renowned** [rɪˈnaʊnd] *adj* : renommé, célèbre

rent [ˈrɛnt] *n* **1** : loyer *m* (somme d'argent) **2 for ~** : à louer — **~** *vt* : louer — **rental** [ˈrɛntəl] *n* : location *f* — **~** *adj* : de location — **renter** [ˈrɛntər] *n* : locataire *mf*

renunciation [rɪˌnʌntsiˈeɪʃən] *n* : renonciation *f*

reorganize [ˌriːˈɔrgəˌnaɪz] *vt* **-nized; -nizing** : réorganiser — **reorganization** [ˌriːˌɔrgənəˈzeɪʃən] *n* : réorganisation *f*

repair [rɪˈpær] *vt* : réparer — **~** *n* **1** : réparation *f* **2 in bad ~** : en mauvais état

repay [rɪˈpeɪ] *vt* **-paid; -paying** : rembourser (un emprunt), rendre (une faveur, etc.)

repeal [rɪˈpiːl] *vt* : abroger, révoquer — **~** *n* : abrogation *f*, révocation *f*

repeat [rɪˈpiːt] *vt* : répéter — **~** *n* **1** : répétition *f* **2** : rediffusion *f* (se dit d'une émission) — **repeatedly** [rɪˈpiːţədli] *adv* : à plusieurs reprises

repel [rɪˈpɛl] *vt* **-pelled; -pelling** : repousser — **repellent** [rɪˈpɛlənt] *adj* : repoussant

repent [rɪˈpɛnt] *vi* : se repentir — **repentance** [rɪˈpɛntənts] *n* : repentir *m*

repercussion [ˌriːpərˈkʌʃən, ˌrɛpər-] *n* : répercussion *f*

repertoire [ˈrɛpərˌtwɑr] *n* : répertoire *m*

repetition [ˌrɛpəˈtɪʃən] *n* : répétition *f* — **repetitious** [ˌrɛpəˈtɪʃəs] *adj* : répétitif — **repetitive** [rɪˈpɛţəţɪv] *adj* : répétitif

replace [rɪˈpleɪs] *vt* **-placed; -placing 1** : remettre (à sa place) **2** SUBSTITUTE : remplacer **3** EXCHANGE : échanger — **replacement** [rɪˈpleɪsmənt] *n* **1** : remplacement *m* **2** SUBSTITUTE : remplaçant *m*, -çante *f* **3 ~ part** : pièce *f* de rechange

replenish [rɪˈplɛnɪʃ] *vt* **1** : réapprovisionner **2** : remplir (de nouveau)

replica [ˈrɛplɪkə] *n* : réplique *f*

reply [rɪˈplaɪ] *vi* **-plied; -plying** : répondre, répliquer — **~** *n, pl* **-plies** : réponse *f*, réplique *f*

report [rɪˈport] *n* **1** : rapport *m*, compte rendu *m* **2** *or* **news ~** : reportage *m* **3 weather ~** : bulletin *m* (météorologique) — **~** *vt* **1** RELATE : raconter **2 ~ an accident** : signaler un accident — *vi* **~ to s.o.** : se présenter à qqn — **report card** *n* : bulletin *m* scolaire — **reporter** [rɪˈporţər] *n* : journaliste *mf*, reporter *m*

reprehensible [ˌrɛpriˈhɛntsəbəl] *adj* : répréhensible

represent [ˌrɛprɪˈzɛnt] *vt* : représenter — **representation** [ˌrɛprɪˌzɛnˈteɪʃən, -zən-] *n* : représentation *f* — **representative** [ˌrɛprɪˈzɛntəţɪv] *adj* : représentatif — **~** *n* : représentant *m*, -tante *f*

repress [rɪˈprɛs] *vt* : réprimer — **repression** [riˈprɛʃən] *n* : répression *f*

reprieve [rɪˈpriːv] *n* : sursis *m*

reprimand [ˈrɛprəˌmænd] *n* : réprimande *f* — **~** *vt* : réprimander

reprint [riˈprɪnt] *vt* : réimprimer — **~** [ˈriːˌprɪnt, riˈprɪnt] *n* : réimpression *f*

reprisal [rɪˈpraɪzəl] *n* : représailles *fpl*

reproach [rɪˈproːʧ] *n* **1** : reproche *m* **2 beyond ~** : irréprochable — **~** *vt* : reprocher à — **reproachful** [rɪˈproːʧfəl] *adj* : de reproche

reproduce [ˌriːprəˈduːs, -ˈdjuːs] *v* **-duced; -ducing** *vt* : reproduire — *vi* : se reproduire — **reproduction** [ˌriːprəˈdʌkʃən] *n* : reproduction *f*

reptile [ˈrɛpˌtaɪl] *n* : reptile *m*

republic [rɪˈpʌblɪk] *n* : république *f* — **republican** [rɪˈpʌblɪkən] *n* : républicain *m*, -caine *f* — **~** *adj* : républicain

repudiate [rɪˈpjuːdiˌeɪt] *vt* **-ated; -ating** : répudier

repugnant [rɪˈpʌgnənt] *adj* : répugnant — **repugnance** [rɪˈpʌgnənts] *n* : répugnance *f*

repulse [rɪˈpʌls] *vt* **-pulsed; -pulsing** : repousser — **repulsive** [rɪˈpʌlsɪv] *adj* : repoussant

reputation [ˌrɛpjəˈteɪʃən] *n* : réputation *f* — **reputable** [ˈrɛpjəţəbəl] *adj* : de bonne réputation — **reputed** [rɪˈpjuːţəd] *adj* : réputé

request [rɪˈkwɛst] *n* : demande *f* — **~** *vt* : demander

require [rɪˈkwaɪr] *vt* **-quired; -quiring 1** CALL FOR : requérir **2** NEED : avoir besoin de — **requirement** [rɪˈkwaɪrmənt] *n* **1** NEED : besoin *m* **2** DEMAND : exigence *f* — **requisite** [ˈrɛkwəzɪt] *adj* : nécessaire

resale [ˈriːˌseɪl, ˌriːˈseɪl] *n* : revente *f*

rescind [rɪˈsɪnd] *vt* : annuler, abroger

rescue [ˈrɛsˌkjuː] *vt* **-cued; -cuing** : sauver, secourir — **~** *n* : sauvetage *m* — **rescuer** [ˈrɛsˌkjuːər] *n* : sauveteur *m*, secouriste *mf*

research [rɪˈsərʧ, ˈriːˌsərʧ] *n* : recherches *fpl* — ~ *vt* : faire des recherches sur — **researcher** [rɪ'sɑrʧər, 'ri:ˌ-] *n* : chercheur *m*, -cheuse *f*

resemble [rɪ'zɛmbəl] *vt* **-bled; -bling** : ressembler à — **resemblance** [rɪ'zɛmbləns] *n* : ressemblance *f*

resent [rɪ'zɛnt] *vt* : en vouloir à, s'offenser de — **resentful** [rɪ'zɛntfəl] *adj* : éprouver du ressentiment — **resentment** [rɪ'zɛntmənt] *n* : ressentiment *m*

reserve [rɪ'zərv] *vt* **-served; -serving** : réserver — ~ *n* : réserve *f* — **reservation** [ˌrɛzər'veɪʃən] *n* **1** : réserve *f* (indienne) **2** RESERVING : réservation *f* — **reserved** [rɪ'zərvd] *adj* : réservé, discret — **reservoir** ['rɛzərˌvwɑr, -ˌvwɔr, -ˌvɔr] *n* : réservoir *m*

reset [ˌri:'sɛt] *vt* **-set; -setting** : remettre à l'heure (une montre), remettre à zéro (un compteur)

residence ['rɛzədəns] *n* : résidence *f* — **reside** [rɪ'zaɪd] *vi* **-sided; -siding** : résider — **resident** ['rɛzədənt] *adj* : résidant — ~ *n* : résident *m*, -dente *f* — **residential** [ˌrɛzə'dɛnʧəl] *adj* : résidentiel

residue ['rɛzəˌdu:, -ˌdju:] *n* : résidu *m*

resign [ri'zaɪn] *vt* **1** QUIT : démissionner **2** ~ **oneself to** : se résigner à — **resignation** [ˌrɛzɪg'neɪʃən] *n* **1** : démission *f* **2** ACCEPTANCE : résignation *f*

resilient [rɪ'zɪljənt] *adj* **1** : résistant **2** ELASTIC : élastique — **resilience** [ri'zɪljəns] *n* **1** : résistance *f* **2** ELASTICITY : élasticité *f*

resin ['rɛzən] *n* : résine *f*

resist [rɪ'zɪst] *vt* : résister à — **resistance** [rɪ'zɪstənts] *n* : résistance *f* — **resistant** [ri'zɪstənt] *adj* : résistant

resolve [rɪ'zɑlv] *vt* **-solved; -solving 1** : résoudre **2** ~ **to do** : décider de faire — ~ *n* : résolution *f*, détermination *f* — **resolution** [ˌrɛzə'lu:ʃən] *n* : résolution *f* — **resolute** ['rɛzəˌlu:t] *adj* : résolu

resonance ['rɛzənənts] *n* : résonance *f* — **resonant** ['rɛzənənt] *adj* : résonant

resort [rɪ'zɔrt] *n* **1** : recours *m* **2** : centre *m* touristique, station *f* (de ski, etc.) — ~ *vi* ~ **to** : recourir à, avoir recours à

resound [rɪ'zaʊnd] *vi* : résonner, retentir — **resounding** [rɪ'zaʊndɪŋ] *adj* : retentissant

resource ['ri:ˌsors, ri'sors] *n* : ressource *f* — **resourceful** [rɪ'sorsfəl, -'zors-] *adj* : ingénieux, débrouillard

respect [rɪ'spɛkt] *n* **1** : respect *m* **2** ~**s** *npl* : respects *mpl*, hommages *mpl* **3 in** ~ **to** : en ce qui concerne **4 in some** ~**s** : à certains égards — ~ *vt* : respecter — **respectable** [ri'spɛktəbəl] *adj* : respectable — **respectful** [rɪ'spɛktfəl] *adj* : respectueux — **respective** [rɪ'spɛktɪv] *adj* : respectif — **respectively** [rɪ'spɛktɪvli] *adv* : respectivement

respiratory ['rɛspərəˌtori, rɪ'spaɪrə-] *adj* : respiratoire

respite ['rɛspɪt, rɪ'spaɪt] *n* : répit *m*, sursis *m*

response [rɪ'spɑnts] *n* : réponse *f* — **respond** [rɪ'spɑnd] *vi* : répondre — **responsibility** [rɪˌspɑntsə'bɪləti] *n, pl* **-ties** : responsabilité *f* — **responsible** [rɪ'spɑntsəbəl] *adj* : responsable — **responsive** [ri'spɑntsɪv] *adj* : réceptif

rest[1] ['rɛst] *n* **1** : repos *m* **2** SUPPORT : appui *m* **3** : silence *m* (en musique) **4** ~ **area** : aire *f* de repos, halte *f* routière *Can* — ~ *vi* **1** : se reposer **2** LEAN : s'appuyer **3** ~ **on** DEPEND : dépendre de — *vt* **1** : reposer **2** LEAN : appuyer

rest[2] *n* REMAINDER : reste *m*

restaurant ['rɛstəˌrɑnt, -rənt] *n* : restaurant *m*

restful ['rɛstfəl] *adj* : reposant, paisible

restless ['rɛstləs] *adj* : inquiet, agité

restore [rɪ'stor] *vt* **-stored; -storing 1** RETURN : retourner **2** REESTABLISH : rétablir **3** REPAIR : restaurer — **restoration** [ˌrɛstə'reɪʃən] *n* **1** : rétablissement *m* **2** REPAIR : restauration *f*

restrain [rɪ'streɪn] *vt* **1** : retenir **2** ~ **oneself** : se retenir — **restrained** [rɪ'streɪnd] *adj* : contenu, maîtrisé — **restraint** [rɪ'streɪnt] *n* **1** : restriction *f*, contrainte *f* **2** SELF-CONTROL : retenue *f*, maîtrise *f* de soi

restrict [rɪ'strɪkt] *vt* : restreindre — **restriction** [rɪ'strɪkʃən] *n* : restriction *f* — **restrictive** [rɪ'strɪktɪv] *adj* : restrictif

result [rɪ'zʌlt] *vi* **1** ~ **from** : résulter de **2** ~ **in** : avoir pour résultat — ~ *n* **1** : résultat *m* **2 as a** ~ **of** : à la suite de

resume [rɪ'zu:m] *v* **-sumed; -suming** : reprendre

résumé *or* **resume** *or* **resumé** ['rɛzəˌmeɪ, ˌrɛzə'-] *n* : curriculum *m* vitæ

resumption [rɪ'zʌmpʃən] *n* : reprise *f*

resurgence [rɪ'sərʤənts] *n* : réapparition *f*

resurrection [ˌrɛzə'rɛkʃən] *n* : résur-

rection *f* — **resurrect** [ˌrɛzə'rɛkt] *vt* : ressusciter
resuscitate [rɪ'sʌsəˌteɪt] *vt* **-tated; -tating** : réanimer
retail ['ri:ˌteɪl] *vt* : vendre au détail — ∼ *n* : vente *f* au détail — ∼ *adj* : de détail — ∼ *adv* : au détail — **retailer** ['ri:ˌteɪlər] *n* : détaillant *m*, -lante *f*
retain [rɪ'teɪn] *vt* : retenir
retaliate [rɪ'tæliˌeɪt] *vi* **-ated; -ating** : riposter — **retaliation** [rɪˌtæli'eɪʃən] *n* : riposte *f*, représailles *fpl*
retarded [ri'tɑrdəd] *adj* : arriéré
retention [rɪ'tɛntʃən] *n* : rétention
reticence ['rɛtəsənts] *n* : réticence *f* — **reticent** ['rɛtəsənt] *adj* : réticent, hésitant
retina ['rɛtənə] *n, pl* **-nas** *or* **-nae** [-ənˌi:, -ənˌaɪ] : rétine *f*
retire [rɪ'taɪr] *vi* **-tired; -tiring** **1** WITHDRAW : se retirer **2** : prendre sa retraite **3** : aller se coucher — **retirement** [rɪ'taɪrmənt] *n* : retraite *f*
retort [rɪ'tɔrt] *vt* : rétorquer, riposter — ∼ *n* : riposte *f*
retrace [ˌri:'treɪs] *vt* **-traced; -tracing** ∼ **one's steps** : revenir sur ses pas
retract [rɪ'trækt] *vt* **1** WITHDRAW : retirer **2** : rentrer (ses griffes, etc.) — **retractable** [rɪ'træktəbəl] *adj* : escamotable
retrain [ˌri:'treɪn] *vt* : recycler
retreat [rɪ'tri:t] *n* **1** : retraite *f* **2** REFUGE : refuge *m* — ∼ *vi* : se retirer, reculer
retribution [ˌrɛtrə'bju:ʃən] *n* : châtiment *m*
retrieve [rɪ'tri:v] *vt* **-trieved; -trieving** : retrouver, récupérer — **retrieval** [ri'tri:vəl] *n* : récupération *f*
retroactive [ˌrɛtro'æktɪv] *adj* : rétroactif
retrospect ['rɛtrəˌspɛkt] *n* **in** ∼ : avec le recul — **retrospective** [ˌrɛtrə'spɛktɪv] *adj* : rétrospectif
return [rɪ'tərn] *vi* **1** : retourner, revenir **2** REAPPEAR : réapparaître — *vt* **1** : rapporter, rendre **2** YIELD : produire — ∼ *n* **1** : retour *m* **2** YIELD : rapport *m*, rendement *m* **3 in** ∼ **for** : en échange de **4** *or* **tax** ∼ : déclaration *f* d'impôts — ∼ *adj* : de retour
reunite [ˌri:jʊ'naɪt] *vt* **-nited; -niting** : réunir — **reunion** [ri'ju:njən] *n* : réunion *f*
revamp [ˌri:'væmp] *vt* : retaper (une maison), réviser (un texte)
reveal [rɪ'vi:l] *vt* **1** : révéler **2** SHOW : laisser voir
revel ['rɛvəl] *vi* **-eled** *or* **-elled; -eling** *or* **-elling** ∼ **in** : se délecter de
revelation [ˌrɛvə'leɪʃən] *n* : révélation *f*
revelry ['rɛvəlri] *n, pl* **-ries** : festivités *fpl*, réjouissances *fpl*
revenge [rɪ'vɛndʒ] *vt* **-venged; -venging** : venger — ∼ *n* **1** : vengeance *f* **2 take** ∼ **on** : se venger sur
revenue ['rɛvəˌnu:, -ˌnju:] *n* : revenu *m*
reverberate [rɪ'vərbəˌreɪt] *vi* **-ated; -ating** : retentir, résonner
reverence ['rɛvərənts] *n* : révérence *f*, vénération *f* — **revere** [rɪ'vɪr] *vt* **-vered; -vering** : révérer, vénérer — **reverend** ['rɛvərənd] *adj* : révérend — **reverent** ['rɛvərənt] *adj* : respectueux
reverse [rɪ'vərs] *adj* : inverse, contraire — ∼ *v* **-versed; -versing** *vt* **1** : inverser **2** CHANGE : renverser, annuler — *vi* : faire marche arrière (se dit d'une voiture) — ∼ *n* **1** BACK : dos *m*, envers *m* **2** *or* ∼ **gear** : marche *f* arrière **3 the** ∼ : le contraire — **reversal** [rɪ'vərsəl] *n* **1** : renversement *m* **2** CHANGE : revirement *m* **3** SETBACK : revers *m* — **reversible** [rɪ'vərsəbəl] *adj* : réversible — **revert** [rɪ'vərt] *vi* ∼ **to** : revenir à
review [rɪ'vju:] *n* **1** : révision *f* **2** OVERVIEW : résumé *m* **3** : critique *f* **4** : revue *f* (militaire) — ∼ *vt* **1** EXAMINE : examiner **2** : repasser (une leçon) **3** : faire la critique de (un roman, etc.) — **reviewer** [rɪ'vju:ər] *n* : critique *mf*
revile [rɪ'vaɪl] *vt* **-viled; -viling** : injurier
revise [rɪ'vaɪz] *vt* **-vised; -vising** **1** : réviser, corriger **2** : modifier (une politique) — **revision** [rɪ'vɪʒən] *n* : révision *f*
revive [rɪ'vaɪv] *v* **-vived; -viving** *vt* **1** : ranimer, raviver **2** : réanimer (une personne) **3** RESTORE : rétablir — *vi* COME TO : reprendre connaissance — **revival** [rɪ'vaɪvəl] *n* : renouveau *m*, renaissance *f*
revoke [rɪ'vo:k] *vt* **-voked; -voking** : révoquer
revolt [ri'vo:lt] *vt* : révolter, dégoûter — *vi* ∼ **against** : se révolter contre — ∼ *n* : révolte *f*, insurrection *f* — **revolting** [rɪ'vo:ltɪŋ] *adj* : révoltant, dégoûtant
revolution [ˌrɛvə'lu:ʃən] *n* : révolution *f* — **revolutionary** [ˌrɛvə'lu:ʃənˌɛri] *adj* : révolutionnaire — ∼ *n, pl* **-aries** : révolutionnaire *mf* — **revolutionize**

[ˌrɛvəˈluːʃənˌaɪz] *vt* **-ized; -izing** : révolutionner
revolve [rɪˈvɑlv] *v* **-volved; -volving** *vt* : faire tourner — *vi* : tourner
revolver [rɪˈvɑlvər] *n* : revolver *m*
revulsion [rɪˈvʌlʃən] *n* : répugnance *f*
reward [rɪˈwɔrd] *vt* : récompenser — ~ *n* : récompense *f*
rewrite [ˌriːˈraɪt] *vt* **-wrote** [-ˈroːt]; **-written** [-ˈrɪtən]; **-writing** : récrire
rhetoric [ˈrɛt̬ərɪk] *n* : rhétorique *f* — **rhetorical** [rɪˈtɔrɪkəl] *adj* : rhétorique
rheumatism [ˈruːməˌtɪzəm, ˈrʊ-] *n* : rhumatisme *m*
rhino [ˈraɪˌnoː] *n, pl* **-no** *or* **-nos** → **rhinoceros** — **rhinoceros** [raɪˈnɑsərəs] *n, pl* **-noceroses** *or* **-noceros** *or* **-noceri** [-ˌraɪ] : rhinocéros *m*
rhubarb [ˈruːˌbɑrb] *n* : rhubarbe *f*
rhyme [ˈraɪm] *n* **1** : rime *f* **2** VERSE : vers *m* — ~ *vi* **rhymed; rhyming** : rimer
rhythm [ˈrɪðəm] *n* : rythme *m* — **rhythmic** [ˈrɪðmɪk] *or* **rhythmical** [-mɪkəl] *adj* : rythmique
rib [ˈrɪb] *n* : côte *f* (en anatomie) — ~ *vt* **ribbed; ribbing** : taquiner
ribbon [ˈrɪbən] *n* : ruban *m*
rice [ˈraɪs] *n* : riz *m*
rich [ˈrɪʧ] *adj* **1** : riche **2** ~ **meal** : repas *m* lourd — **riches** [ˈrɪʧəz] *npl* : richesses *fpl* — **richness** [ˈrɪʧnəs] *n* : richesse *f*
rickety [ˈrɪkət̬i] *adj* : branlant
ricochet [ˈrɪkəˌsheɪ] *n* : ricochet *m* — ~ *vi* **-cheted** [-ˌʃeɪd] *or* **-chetted** [-ˌʃɛt̬əd]; **-cheting** [-ˌʃeɪɪŋ] *or* **-chetting** [-ˌʃɛt̬ɪŋ] : ricocher
rid [ˈrɪd] *vt* **rid; ridding 1** : débarrasser **2** ~ **oneself of** : se débarrasser de — **riddance** [ˈrɪdənts] *n* **good** ~**!** : bon débarras!
riddle[1] [ˈrɪdəl] *n* : énigme *f*, devinette *f*
riddle[2] *vt* **-dled; -dling 1** : cribler **2** ~ **with** : plein de
ride [ˈraɪd] *v* **rode** [ˈroːd]; **ridden** [ˈrɪdən]; **riding** *vt* **1** : monter (à cheval, à bicyclette), prendre (le bus, etc.) **2** TRAVEL : parcourir — *vi* **1** *or* ~ **horseback** : monter à cheval **2** : aller (en auto, etc.) — ~ *n* **1** : tour *m*, promenade *f* **2** : manège *m* (à la foire) **3 give s.o. a** ~ : conduire qqn en voiture — **rider** [ˈraɪdər] *n* **1** : cavalier *m*, -lière *f* **2** CYCLIST : cycliste *mf*, motocycliste *mf*
ridge [ˈrɪʤ] *n* : chaîne *f* (de montagnes)
ridiculous [rəˈdɪkjələs] *adj* : ridicule — **ridicule** [ˈrɪdəˌkjuːl] *n* : ridicule *m*, dérision *f* — ~ *vt* **-culed; -culing** : ridiculiser
rife [ˈraɪf] *adj* **be** ~ **with** : être abondant en
rifle[1] [ˈraɪfəl] *vi* **-fled; -fling** ~ **through** : fouiller dans
rifle[2] *n* : carabine *f*, fusil *m*
rift [ˈrɪft] *n* **1** : fente *f*, fissure *f* **2** BREACH : désaccord *m*
rig[1] [ˈrɪg] *vt* : truquer (une élection)
rig[2] *vt* **rigged; rigging 1** : gréer (un navire) **2** EQUIP : équiper **3** *or* ~ **out** DRESS : habiller **4** *or* ~ **up** : bricoler — ~ *n* **1** : gréement *m* **2** *or* **oil** ~ : plateforme *f* pétrolière — **rigging** [ˈrɪgɪŋ, -gən] *n* : gréement *m*
right [ˈraɪt] *adj* **1** JUST : bien, juste **2** CORRECT : exact **3** APPROPRIATE : convenable **4** STRAIGHT : droit **5 be** ~ : avoir raison **6** → **right-hand** — ~ *n* **1** GOOD : bien *m* **2** ENTITLEMENT : droit *m* **3 on the** ~ : à droite **4** *or* ~ **side** : droite *f* — ~ *adv* **1** WELL : bien, comme il faut **2** EXACTLY : précisément **3** DIRECTLY : droit **4** IMMEDIATELY : tout de suite **5** COMPLETELY : tout à fait **6** *or* **to the** ~ : à la droite — ~ *vt* **1** RESTORE : redresser **2** ~ **a wrong** : réparer un tort — **right angle** *n* : angle *m* droit — **righteous** [ˈraɪʧəs] *adj* : juste, droit — **rightful** [ˈraɪt̬fəl] *adj* : légitime — **right-hand** [ˈraɪtˈhænd] *adj* **1** : du côté droit **2** ~ **man** : bras *m* droit — **right-handed** [ˈraɪtˈhændəd] *adj* : droitier — **rightly** [ˈraɪtli] **1** : à juste titre **2** CORRECTLY : correctement — **right-of-way** [ˌraɪt̬əˈweɪ, -əv-] *n, pl* **rights-of-way** : priorité *f* (sur la route) — **right-wing** [ˈraɪtˈwɪŋ] *adj* : de droite (en politique)
rigid [ˈrɪʤɪd] *adj* : rigide
rigor *or Brit* **rigour** [ˈrɪgər] *n* : rigueur *f* — **rigorous** [ˈrɪgərəs] *adj* : rigoureux
rim [ˈrɪm] *n* **1** EDGE : bord *m* **2** : jante *f* (d'une roue)
rind [ˈraɪnd] *n* : écorce *f* (de citron, etc.)
ring[1] [ˈrɪŋ] *v* **rang** [ˈræŋ]; **rung** [ˈrʌŋ]; **ringing** *vi* **1** : sonner **2** RESOUND : résonner — *vt* : sonner (une cloche, etc.) — ~ *n* **1** : son *m*, tintement *m* **2** CALL : coup *m* de téléphone
ring[2] *n* **1** : bague *f*, anneau *m* **2** CIRCLE : cercle *m* **3** *or* **boxing** ~ : ring *m* (de boxe) **4** NETWORK : réseau *m* (clandestin) — ~ *vt* **ringed; ringing** : encercler — **ringleader** [ˈrɪŋˌliːdər] *n* : meneur *m*, -neuse *f*
rink [ˈrɪŋk] *n* : piste *f*, patinoire *f*

rinse ['rɪnts] *vt* **rinsed; rinsing** : rincer — ~ *n* : rinçage *m*
riot ['raɪət] *n* : émeute *f* — ~ *vi* : faire une émeute — **rioter** ['raɪət̬ər] *n* : émeutier *m*, -tière *f*
rip ['rɪp] *v* **ripped; ripping** *vt* **1** : déchirer **2** ~ **off** : arracher — *vi* : se déchirer — ~ *n* : déchirure *f*
ripe ['raɪp] *adj* **riper; ripest** : mûr, prêt — **ripen** ['raɪpən] *v* : mûrir
ripple ['rɪpəl] *v* **-pled; -pling** *vi* : onduler (se dit de l'eau) — *vt* : rider — ~ *n* : ondulation *f*, ride *f*
rise ['raɪz] *vi* **rose** ['ro:z]; **risen** ['rɪzən]; **rising** **1** : se lever (se dit d'une personne, du soleil, etc.) **2** INCREASE : augmenter, monter **3** ~ **up** REBEL : se soulever (contre) — ~ *n* **1** ASCENT : montée *f* **2** INCREASE : augmentation *f* **3** INCLINE : pente *f* — **riser** ['raɪzər] *n* **1 early** ~ : lève-tôt *mf* **2 late** ~ : lève-tard *mf*
risk ['rɪsk] *n* : risque *m* — ~ *vt* : risquer — **risky** ['rɪski] *adj* **riskier; -est** : risqué, hasardeux
rite ['raɪt] *n* : rite *m* — **ritual** ['rɪtʃuəl] *adj* : rituel — ~ *n* : rituel *m*
rival ['raɪvəl] *n* : rival *m*, -vale *f* — ~ *adj* : rival — ~ *vt* **-valed** *or* **-valled; -valing** *or* **-valling** : rivaliser avec — **rivalry** ['raɪvəlri] *n, pl* **-ries** : rivalité *f*
river ['rɪvər] *n* : rivière *f*, fleuve *m* — ~ *adj* : fluvial
rivet ['rɪvət] *n* : rivet *m* — ~ *vt* **1** : river, fixer **2 be** ~**ed by** : être fasciné par
road ['ro:d] *n* **1** : route *f* **2** STREET : rue *f* **3** PATH : chemin *m* — **roadblock** ['ro:d,blɑk] *n* : barrage *m* routier — **roadside** ['ro:d,saɪd] *n* : bord *m* de la route — **roadway** ['ro:d,weɪ] *n* : chaussée *f*
roam ['ro:m] *vi* : errer
roar ['ror] *vi* **1** : rugir **2** ~ **with laughter** : éclater de rire — *vt* : hurler — ~ *n* **1** : rugissement *m* **2** : grondement *m* (d'un avion, etc.)
roast ['ro:st] *vt* : rôtir (de la viande, etc.), griller (des noix, etc.) — ~ *n* : rôti *m* — **roast beef** *n* : rosbif *m*
rob ['rɑb] *vt* **robbed; robbing** **1** : dévaliser (une banque), cambrioler (une maison) **2** STEAL : voler — **robber** ['rɑbər] *n* : voleur *m*, -leuse *f* — **robbery** ['rɑbəri] *n, pl* **-beries** : vol *m*
robe ['ro:b] *n* **1** : toge *f* (d'un juge) **2** → **bathrobe**
robin ['rɑbən] *n* : rouge-gorge *m*
robot ['ro:,bɑt, -bət] *n* : robot *m*
robust [ro'bʌst, 'ro:,bʌst] *adj* : robuste
rock[1] ['rɑk] *vt* **1** : bercer (un enfant), balancer (un berceau) **2** SHAKE : secouer — *vi* : se balancer — ~ *n or* ~ **music** : musique *f* rock
rock[2] *n* **1** : roche *f*, roc *m* **2** BOULDER : rocher *m* **3** STONE : pierre *f*
rocket ['rɑkət] *n* : fusée *f*
rocking chair *n* : fauteuil *m* à bascule
rocky ['rɑki] *adj* **rockier; -est** **1** : rocheux **2** SHAKY : précaire
rod ['rɑd] *n* **1** : baguette *f* (de bois), tige *f* (de métal) **2** *or* **fishing** ~ : canne *f* à pêche
rode → **ride**
rodent ['ro:dənt] *n* : rongeur *m*
rodeo ['ro:di,o:, ro'deɪ,o:] *n, pl* **-deos** : rodéo *m*
roe ['ro:] *n* : œufs *mpl* de poisson
roe deer *n* : chevreuil *m*
role ['ro:l] *n* : rôle *m*
roll ['ro:l] *n* **1** : rouleau *m* **2** LIST : liste *f* **3** BUN : petit pain *m* **4** : roulement *m* (de tambour) — ~ *vt* **1** : rouler **2** ~ **down** : baisser **3** ~ **out** : dérouler **4** ~ **up** : retrousser (ses manches) — *vi* **1** : (se) rouler **2** ~ **over** : se retourner — **roller** ['ro:lər] *n* : rouleau *m* — **roller coaster** ['ro:lər,ko:stər] *n* : montagnes *fpl* russes — **roller–skate** ['ro:lər,skeɪt] *vi* **-skated; -skating** : faire du patin à roulettes — **roller skates** *npl* : patins *mpl* à roulettes
Roman ['ro:mən] *adj* : romain — **Roman Catholic** *adj* : catholique
romance [ro'mænts, 'ro:,mænts] *n* **1** : roman *m* d'amour **2** AFFAIR : liaison *f* amoureuse
romantic [ro'mæntɪk] *adj* : romantique
roof ['ru:f, 'rʊf] *n, pl* **roofs** ['ru:fs, 'rʊfs; 'ru:vz, 'rʊvz] **1** : toit *m* **2** ~ **of the mouth** : palais *m* — **roofing** ['ru:fɪŋ, 'rʊfɪŋ] *n* : toiture *f* — **rooftop** ['ru:f,tɑp, 'rʊf-] *n* → **roof**
rook ['rʊk] *n* : tour *f* (aux échecs)
rookie ['rʊki] *n* : novice *mf*
room ['ru:m, 'rʊm] *n* **1** : chambre *f* (à coucher), salle *f* (de conférence) **2** SPACE : espace *m* **3** OPPORTUNITY : possibilité *f* — **roommate** ['ru:m,meɪt, 'rʊm-] *n* : camarade *mf* de chambre — **roomy** ['ru:mi, 'rʊmi] *adj* **roomier; -est** : spacieux
roost ['ru:st] *n* : perchoir *m* — ~ *vi* : se percher — **rooster** ['ru:stər, 'rʊs-] *n* : coq *m*
root[1] ['ru:t, 'rʊt] *n* **1** : racine *f* **2** SOURCE : origine *f* **3** CORE : fond *m*, cœur *m* — *vt* ~ **out** : extirper

root[2] *vi* ~ **for** SUPPORT : encourager
rope [ˈroːp] *n* : corde *f* — ~ *vt* **roped; roping 1** : attacher (avec une corde) **2** ~ **off** : interdire l'accès à
rosary [ˈroːzəri] *n, pl* **-ries** : chapelet *m*
rose[1] → **rise**
rose[2] [ˈroːz] *n* : rose *f* (fleur), rose *m* (couleur) — **rosebush** [ˈroːzˌbʊʃ] *n* : rosier *m*
rosemary [ˈroːzˌmɛri] *n, pl* **-maries** : romarin *m*
Rosh Hashanah [ˌrɑʃhɑˈʃɑnə, ˌroːʃ-] *n* : le Nouvel An juif
rostrum [ˈrɑstrəm] *n, pl* **-tra** [-trə] *or* **-trums** : tribune *f*
rosy [ˈroːzi] *adj* **rosier; -est 1** : rose, rosé **2** PROMISING : prometteur
rot [ˈrɑt] *v* **rotted; rotting** : pourrir — ~ *n* : pourriture *f*
rotary [ˈroːt̬əri] *adj* : rotatif — ~ *n* : rond-point *m*
rotate [ˈroːˌteɪt] *v* **-tated; -tating** *vi* : tourner — *vt* **1** : tourner **2** ALTERNATE : faire à tour de rôle — **rotation** [roˈteɪʃən] *n* : rotation *f*
rote [ˈroːt] *n* **by** ~ : par cœur
rotten [ˈrɑtən] *adj* **1** : pourri **2** BAD : mauvais
rouge [ˈruːʒ] *n* : rouge *m* à joues
rough [ˈrʌf] *adj* **1** COARSE : rugueux **2** RUGGED : accidenté **3** CHOPPY : agité **4** DIFFICULT : difficile **5** FORCEFUL : brusque **6** APPROXIMATE : approximatif **7** ~ **draft** : brouillon *m* — ~ *vt* **1** → **roughen 2** ~ **up** BEAT : tabasser *fam* — **roughage** [ˈrʌfɪʤ] *n* : fibres *mpl* alimentaires — **roughen** [ˈrʌfən] *vt* : rendre rugueux — **roughly** [ˈrʌfli] *adv* **1** : rudement **2** ABOUT : environ — **roughness** [ˈrʌfnəs] *n* : rugosité *f*
roulette [ˌruːˈlɛt] *n* : roulette *f*
round [ˈraʊnd] *adj* : rond — ~ *adv* → **around** — ~ *n* **1** : série *f* (de négociations, etc.) **2** : manche *f* (d'un match) **3** ~ **of applause** : salve *f* d'applaudissements **4** ~**s** *npl* : visites *fpl* (d'un médecin, etc.), rondes *fpl* (d'un policier, etc.) — ~ *vt* **1** TURN : tourner **2** ~ **off** : arrondir **3** ~ **off** *or* ~ **out** COMPLETE : compléter **4** ~ **up** GATHER : rassembler — ~ *prep* → **around** — **roundabout** [ˈraʊndəˌbaʊt] *adj* : indirect — **round–trip** [ˈraʊndˌtrɪp] *n* : voyage *m* aller et retour — **roundup** [ˈraʊndˌʌp] *n* : rassemblement *m*
rouse [ˈraʊz] *vt* **roused; rousing 1** AWAKEN : réveiller **2** EXCITE : susciter
rout [ˈraʊt] *n* : déroute *f* — ~ *vt* : mettre en déroute
route [ˈruːt, ˈraʊt] *n* **1** : route *f* **2** *or* **delivery** ~ : tournée *f* de livraison
routine [ruːˈtiːn] *n* : routine *f* — ~ *adj* : routinier
row[1] [ˈroː] *vi* : ramer
row[2] [ˈroː] *n* **1** : file *f* (de gens), rangée *f* (de maisons, etc.) **2 in a** ~ SUCCESSIVELY : de suite
row[3] [ˈraʊ] *n* **1** RACKET : vacarme *m* **2** QUARREL : dispute *f*
rowboat [ˈroːˌboːt] *n* : bateau *m* à rames
rowdy [ˈraʊdi] *adj* **-dier; -est** : tapageur
royal [ˈrɔɪəl] *adj* : royal — **royalty** [ˈrɔɪəlti] *n, pl* **-ties 1** : royauté *f* **2 royalties** *npl* : droits *mpl* d'auteur
rub [ˈrʌb] *v* **rubbed; rubbing** *vt* **1** : frotter **2** ~ **in** : faire pénétrer — *vi* **1** ~ **against** : frotter contre **2** ~ **off** : enlever (en frottant) — ~ *n* : friction *f*, massage *m*
rubber [ˈrʌbər] *n* : caoutchouc *m* — **rubber band** *n* : élastique *m* — **rubber stamp** *n* : tampon *m* (de caoutchouc) — **rubbery** [ˈrʌbəri] *adj* : caoutchouteux
rubbish [ˈrʌbɪʃ] *n* **1** : ordures *fpl*, déchets *mpl* **2** NONSENSE : bêtises *fpl*
rubble [ˈrʌbəl] *n* : décombres *mpl*
ruby [ˈruːbi] *n, pl* **-bies** : rubis *m*
rudder [ˈrʌdər] *n* : gouvernail *m*
ruddy [ˈrʌdi] *adj* **-dier; -est** : rougeaud
rude [ˈruːd] *adj* **ruder; rudest 1** IMPOLITE : grossier **2** ABRUPT : brusque — **rudely** [ˈruːdli] *adv* : grossièrement — **rudeness** [ˈruːdnəs] *n* : manque *m* d'éducation
rudiment [ˈruːdəmənt] *n* : rudiment *m* — **rudimentary** [ˌruːdəˈmɛntəri] *adj* : rudimentaire
ruffle [ˈrʌfəl] *vt* **-fled; -fling 1** : ébouriffer (ses cheveux), hérisser (ses plumes) **2** VEX : contrarier — ~ *n* : volant *m* (d'une jupe, etc.)
rug [ˈrʌg] *n* : tapis *m*, carpette *f*
rugged [ˈrʌgəd] *adj* **1** : accidenté (se dit d'un terrain), escarpé (se dit d'une montagne) **2** STURDY : robuste
ruin [ˈruːən] *n* : ruine *f* — ~ *vt* : ruiner
rule [ˈruːl] *n* **1** : règle *f*, règlement *m* **2** CONTROL : autorité *f* **3 as a** ~ : en général — ~ *v* **ruled; ruling** *vt* **1** GOVERN : gouverner **2** : juger, décider (d'un juge) **3** ~ **out** : écarter — *vi* : gouverner, régner — **ruler** [ˈruːlər] *n* **1** : dirigeant *m*, -geante *f*; souverain *m*, -raine *f* **2** : règle *f* (pour mesurer) — **ruling** [ˈruːlɪŋ] *n* VERDICT : décision *f*
rum [ˈrʌm] *n* : rhum *m*
rumble [ˈrʌmbəl] *vi* **-bled; -bling 1**

: gronder **2** : gargouiller (se dit de l'estomac) — **~** *n* : grondement *m*
rummage [ˈrʌmɪʤ] *vi* **-maged; -maging ~ in** : fouiller dans
rumor *or Brit* **rumour** [ˈru:mər] *n* : rumeur *f* — **~** *vt* **be ~ed that** : il paraît que
rump [ˈrʌmp] *n* **1** : croupe *f* (d'un animal) **2** *or* **~ steak** : romsteck *m*
run [ˈrʌn] *v* **ran** [ˈræn]; **run; running** *vi* **1** : courir **2** FUNCTION : marcher **3** LAST : durer **4** : déteindre (se dit des couleurs) **5** EXTEND : passer (se dit d'un câble) **6** : se présenter (comme candidat) **7 ~ away** : s'enfuir **8 ~ into** ENCOUNTER : rencontrer **9 ~ into** HIT : heurter **10 ~ late** : être en retard **11 ~ out of** : manquer de **12 ~ over** : écraser — *vt* **1** : courir **2** OPERATE : faire marcher **3** : faire couler (de l'eau) **4** MANAGE : diriger **5 ~ a fever** : faire de la température — **~** *n* **1** : course *f* **2** TRIP : tour *m*, excursion *f* **3** SERIES : série *f* **4 in the long ~** : à la longue — **runaway** [ˈrʌnəˌweɪ] *n* : fugitif *m*, -tive *f* — **~** *adj* : fugueur — **rundown** [ˈrʌnˌdaʊn] *n* : résumé *m* — **run–down** [ˈrʌnˈdaʊn] *adj* **1** : délabré **2** EXHAUSTED : fatigué
rung[1] → **ring**[1]
rung[2] [ˈrʌŋ] *n* : barreau *m* (d'une échelle, etc.)
runner [ˈrʌnər] *n* : coureur *m*, -reuse *f* — **runner–up** [ˌrʌnərˈʌp] *n*, *pl* **runners–up** : second *m*, -conde *f* — **running** [ˈrʌnɪŋ] *adj* **1** FLOWING : courant **2** CONTINUOUS : continuel **3** CONSECUTIVE : de suite
runway [ˈrʌnˌweɪ] *n* : piste *f* (d'envol ou d'atterrissage)
rupture [ˈrʌpʧər] *n* : rupture *f* — **~** *v* **-tured; -turing** *vt* : rompre — *vi* : se rompre
rural [ˈrʊrəl] *adj* : rural
ruse [ˈru:s, ˈru:z] *n* : ruse *f*, stratagème *m*
rush[1] [rʌʃ] *n* **1** : jonc *m* (plante) **2 in a ~** : pressé
rush[2] *vi* : se précipiter — *vt* **1** : presser, bousculer **2** ATTACK : prendre d'assaut **3** : transporter d'urgence (à l'hôpital, etc.) — **~** *n* **1** : hâte *f*, empressement *m* **2** : bouffée *f* (d'air), torrent *m* (d'eau) — **rush hour** *n* : heure *f* de pointe
russet [ˈrʌsət] *adj* : roux
Russian [ˈrʌʃən] *adj* : russe — **~** *n* : russe (langue)
rust [ˈrʌst] *n* : rouille *f* — **~** *vi* : se rouiller — *vt* : rouiller
rustic [ˈrʌstɪk] *adj* : rustique, champêtre
rustle [ˈrʌsəl] *vi* **-tled; -tling** bruire — **~** *n* : bruissement *m*
rusty [ˈrʌsti] *adj* **rustier; -est** : rouillé
rut [ˈrʌt] *n* **1** : ornière *f* **2 be in a ~** : s'enliser dans une routine
ruthless [ˈru:θləs] *adj* : impitoyable, cruel
rye [ˈraɪ] *n* : seigle *m*

S

s [ˈɛs] *n*, *pl* **s's** *or* **ss** [ˈɛsəz] : s *m*, dix-neuvième lettre de l'alphabet
Sabbath [ˈsæbəθ] *n* **1** : sabbat *m* (judaïsme) **2** : dimanche *m* (christianisme)
sabotage [ˈsæbəˌtɑʒ] *n* : sabotage *m* — **~** *vt* **-taged; -taging** : saboter
sack [ˈsæk] *n* : sac *m* — **~** *vt* **1** FIRE : virer *fam* **2** PLUNDER : saccager
sacred [ˈseɪkrəd] *adj* : sacré
sacrifice [ˈsækrəˌfaɪs] *n* : sacrifice *m* — **~** *vt* **-ficed; -ficing** : sacrifier
sad [ˈsæd] *adj* **sadder; saddest** : triste — **sadden** [ˈsædən] *vt* : attrister
saddle [ˈsædəl] *n* : selle *f* — **~** *vt* **-dled; -dling** : seller
sadistic [səˈdɪstɪk] *adj* : sadique
sadness [ˈsædnəs] *n* : tristesse *f*
safari [səˈfɑri, -ˈfær-] *n* : safari *m*
safe [ˈseɪf] *adj* **safer; safest 1** : sûr **2** UNHARMED : en sécurité **3** CAREFUL : prudent **4 ~ and sound** : sain et sauf — **~** *n* : coffre-fort *m* — **safeguard** [ˈseɪfˌgɑrd] *n* : sauvegarde *f* — **~** *vt* : sauvegarder — **safely** [ˈseɪfli] *adv* **1** : sûrement **2 arrive ~** : bien arriver — **safety** [ˈseɪfti] *n*, *pl* **-ties** : sécurité *f* — **safety belt** *n* : ceinture *f* de sécurité — **safety pin** *n* : épingle *f* de sûreté
sag [ˈsæg] *vi* **sagged; sagging** : s'affaisser
sage[1] [ˈseɪʤ] *n* : sauge *f* (plante)
sage[2] *n* : sage *m*
said → **say**
sail [ˈseɪl] *n* **1** : voile *f* (d'un bateau) **2 go for a ~** : faire un tour en bateau **3 set ~** : prendre la mer — **~** *vi* : nav-

iguer — *vt* **1** : manœuvrer (un bateau) **2 ~ the seas** : parcourir les mers — **sailboat** ['seɪl,bo:t] *n* : voilier *m* — **sailor** ['seɪlər] *n* : marin *m*, matelot *m*
saint ['seɪnt, *before a name* ,seɪnt *or* sənt] *n* : saint *m*, sainte *f*
sake ['seɪk] *n* **1 for goodness' ~!** : pour l'amour de Dieu! **2 for the ~ of** : pour le bien de
salad ['sæləd] *n* : salade *f*
salary ['sæləri] *n, pl* **-ries** : salaire *m*
sale ['seɪl] *n* **1** : vente *f* **2 for ~** : à vendre **3 on ~** : en solde — **salesman** ['seɪlzmən] *n, pl* **-men** [-mən, -,mɛn] : vendeur *m*, représentant *m* — **saleswoman** ['seɪlz,wʊmən] *n, pl* **-women** [-,wɪmən] : vendeuse *f*, représentante *f*
salient ['seɪljənt] *adj* : saillant
saliva [sə'laɪvə] *n* : salive *f*
salmon ['sæmən] *ns & pl* : saumon *m*
salon [sə'lɑn, 'sæ,lɑn] *n* : salon *m*
saloon [sə'lu:n] *n* : bar *m*
salt ['sɔlt] *n* : sel *m* — **~** *vt* : saler — **saltwater** ['sɔlt,wɔt̬ər, -,wɑ-] *adj* : de mer — **salty** ['sɔlti] *adj* **saltier; -est** : salé
salute [sə'lu:t] *vt* **-luted; -luting** : saluer — **~** *n* : salut *m*
salvage ['sælvɪʤ] *vt* **-vaged; -vaging** : sauver, récupérer
salvation [sæl'veɪʃən] *n* : salut *m*
salve ['sæv, 'sɑv] *n* : onguent *m*, pommade *f*
same ['seɪm] *adj* **1** : même **2 be the ~ (as)** : être comme **3 the ~ thing (as)** : la même chose (que) — **~** *pron* **1 all the ~** : pareil **2 the ~** : le même — **~** *adv* **the ~** : pareil
sample ['sæmpəl] *n* : échantillon *m* — **~** *vt* **-pled; -pling** : essayer
sanctify ['sæŋktə,faɪ] *vt* **-fied; -fying** : sanctifier
sanction ['sæŋkʃən] *n* : sanction *f* — **~** *vt* : sanctionner
sanctuary ['sæŋktʃʊ,ɛri] *n, pl* **-aries** : sanctuaire *m*
sand ['sænd] *n* : sable *m* — **~** *vt* **1** : sabler (une route) **2** : poncer (du bois)
sandal ['sændəl] *n* : sandale *f*
sandpaper ['sænd,peɪpər] *n* : papier *m* de verre — **~** *vt* : poncer
sandwich ['sænd,wɪtʃ] *n* : sandwich *m* — **~** *vt* **~ between** : mettre entre
sandy ['sændi] *adj* **sandier; -est** : sablonneux
sane ['seɪn] *adj* **saner; -est 1** : sain d'esprit **2** SENSIBLE : raisonnable
sang → **sing**
sanitary ['sænətɛri] *adj* **1** : sanitaire **2** HYGIENIC : hygiénique — **sanitary napkin** *n* : serviette *f* hygiénique — **sanitation** [,sænə'teɪʃən] *n* : système *m* sanitaire
sanity ['sænət̬i] *n* : équilibre *m* mental
sank → **sink**
Santa Claus ['sæntə,klɔz] *n* : père *m* Noël
sap[1] ['sæp] *n* : sève *f* (d'un arbre)
sap[2] *vt* **sapped; sapping** : saper, miner
sapphire ['sæ,faɪr] *n* : saphir *m*
sarcasm ['sɑr,kæzəm] *n* : sarcasme *m* — **sarcastic** [sɑr'kæstɪk] *adj* : sarcastique
sardine [sɑr'di:n] *n* : sardine *f*
sash ['sæʃ] *n* : large ceinture *f* (d'une robe), écharpe *f* (d'un uniforme)
sat → **sit**
satellite ['sæt̬ə,laɪt] *n* : satellite *m*
satin ['sætən] *n* : satin *m*
satire ['sæ,taɪr] *n* : satire *f* — **satiric** [sə'tɪrɪk] *or* **satirical** [-ɪkəl] *adj* : satirique
satisfaction [,sæt̬əs'fækʃən] *n* : satisfaction *f* — **satisfactory** [,sæt̬əs'fæktəri] *adj* : satisfaisant — **satisfy** ['sæt̬əs,faɪ] *vt* **-fied; -fying** : satisfaire — **satisfying** ['sæt̬əs,faɪɪŋ] *adj* : satisfaisant
saturate ['sætʃə,reɪt] *vt* **-rated; -rating 1** : saturer **2** DRENCH : tremper
Saturday ['sæt̬ər,deɪ, -di] *n* : samedi *m*
Saturn ['sæt̬ərn] *n* : Saturne *f*
sauce ['sɔs] *n* : sauce *f* — **saucepan** ['sɔs,pæn] *n* : casserole *f* — **saucer** ['sɔsər] *n* : soucoupe *f*
Saudi ['saʊdɪ] *or* **Saudi Arabian** ['saʊdɪə'reɪbɪən] *adj* : saoudien
sauna ['sɔnə, 'saʊnə] *n* : sauna *m*
saunter ['sɔntər, 'sɑn-] *vi* : se promener
sausage ['sɔsɪʤ] *n* : saucisse *f* (crue), saucisson *m* (cuit)
sauté [sɔ'teɪ, so:-] *vt* **-téed** *or* **-téd; -téing** : faire revenir
savage ['sævɪʤ] *adj* : sauvage, féroce — **~** *n* : sauvage *mf* — **savagery** ['sævɪʤri, -ʤəri] *n, pl* **-ries** : férocité *f*
save ['seɪv] *vt* **saved; saving 1** RESCUE : sauver **2** RESERVE : garder **3** : gagner (du temps), économiser (de l'argent) **4** : sauvegarder (en informatique) — **~** *prep* EXCEPT : sauf
savior ['seɪvjər] *n* : sauveur *m*
savor ['seɪvər] *vt* : savourer — **savory** ['seɪvəri] *adj* : savoureux

saw[1] → **see**
saw[2] ['sɔ] *n* : scie *f* — ~ *vt* **sawed; sawed** *or* **sawn** ['sɔn]; **sawing** : scier — **sawdust** ['sɔˌdʌst] *n* : sciure *f* — **sawmill** ['sɔˌmɪl] *n* : scierie *f*
saxophone ['sæksəˌfo:n] *n* : saxophone *m*
say ['seɪ] *v* **said** ['sɛd]; **saying; says** ['sɛz] *vt* **1** : dire **2** INDICATE : indiquer (se dit d'une montre, etc.) — *vi* **1** : dire **2 that is to ~** : c'est-à-dire — ~ *n, pl* **says** ['seɪz] **1 have no ~** : ne pas avoir son mot à dire **2 have one's ~** : dire son mot — **saying** ['seɪɪŋ] *n* : dicton *m*
scab ['skæb] *n* **1** : croûte *f*, gale *f* *Can* **2** STRIKEBREAKER : jaune *mf*
scaffold ['skæfəld, -ˌfo:ld] *n* : échafaudage *m* (en construction)
scald ['skɔld] *vt* : ébouillanter
scale[1] ['skeɪl] *n* : pèse-personne *m*, balance *f*
scale[2] *n* : écaille *f* (d'un poisson, etc.) — ~ *vt* **scaled; scaling** : écailler
scale[3] *n* : gamme *f* (en musique), échelle *f* (salariale)
scallion ['skæljən] *n* : ciboule *f*, échalote *f*
scallop ['skɑləp, 'skæ-] *n* : coquille *f* Saint-Jacques
scalp ['skælp] *n* : cuir *m* chevelu
scam ['skæm] *n* : escroquerie *f*
scan ['skæn] *vt* **scanned; scanning 1** EXAMINE : scruter **2** SKIM : lire attentivement **3** : balayer (en informatique)
scandal ['skændəl] *n* : scandale *m* — **scandalous** ['skændələs] *adj* : scandaleux
Scandinavian [ˌskændə'neɪviən] *adj* : scandinave
scant ['skænt] *adj* : insuffisant
scapegoat ['skeɪpˌgo:t] *n* : bouc *m* émissaire
scar ['skɑr] *n* : cicatrice *f* — ~ *v* **scarred; scarring** *vt* : laisser une cicatrice sur — *vi* : se cicatriser
scarce ['skɛrs] *adj* **scarcer; scarcest** : rare — **scarcely** ['skɛrsli] *adv* : à peine — **scarcity** ['skɛrsəṭi] *n, pl* **-ties** : pénurie *f*
scare ['skɛr] *vt* **scared; scaring 1** : faire peur à **2 be ~d of** : avoir peur de — ~ *n* **1** FRIGHT : peur *f* **2** PANIC : panique *f* — **scarecrow** ['skɛrˌkro:] *n* : épouvantail *m*
scarf ['skɑrf] *n, pl* **scarves** ['skɑrvz] *or* **scarfs** : écharpe *f*, foulard *m*
scarlet ['skɑrlət] *adj* : écarlate — **scarlet fever** *n* : scarlatine *f*
scary ['skɛri] *adj* **scarier, -est** : qui fait peur
scathing ['skeɪðɪŋ] *adj* : cinglant
scatter ['skæṭər] *vt* **1** STREW : éparpiller **2** DISPERSE : disperser — *vi* : se disperser
scavenger ['skævənʤər] *n* : charognard *m*, -gnarde *f*
scenario [sə'næriˌo:, -'nɑr-] *n, pl* **-ios** : scénario *m*
scene ['si:n] *n* **1** : scène *f* **2 behind the ~s** : dans les coulisses — **scenery** ['si:nəri] *n, pl* **-eries 1** : décor *m* **2** LANDSCAPE : paysages *mpl* — **scenic** ['si:nɪk] *adj* : pittoresque
scent ['sɛnt] *n* **1** : arôme *m* **2** PERFUME : parfum *m* **3** TRAIL : piste *f* — **scented** ['sɛntəd] *adj* : parfumé
sceptic ['skɛptɪk] → **skeptic**
schedule ['skɛˌʤu:l, -ʤəl, *esp Brit* 'ʃɛdˌju:l] *n* **1** : programme *m* **2** TIMETABLE : horaire *m* **3 behind ~** : en retard **4 on ~** : à l'heure — ~ *vt* **-uled; -uling** : prévoir
scheme ['ski:m] *n* **1** PLAN : plan *m* **2** PLOT : intrigue *f* — ~ *vi* **schemed; scheming** : conspirer
schizophrenia [ˌskɪtsə'fri:niə, ˌskɪzə-, -'frɛ-] *n* : schizophrénie *f*
scholar ['skɑlər] *n* : savant *m*, -vante *f*; érudit *m*, -dite *f* — **scholarship** ['skɑlərˌʃɪp] *n* : bourse *f*
school[1] ['sku:l] *n* : banc *m* (de poissons)
school[2] *n* **1** : école *f*, lycée *m* **2** COLLEGE : université *f* **3** DEPARTMENT : faculté *f* — ~ *vt* : instruire — **schoolboy** ['sku:lˌbɔɪ] *n* : écolier *m* — **schoolgirl** ['sku:lˌgərl] *n* : écolière *f*
science ['saɪənts] *n* : science *f* — **scientific** [ˌsaɪən'tɪfɪk] *adj* : scientifique — **scientist** ['saɪəntɪst] *n* : scientifique *mf*
scissors ['sɪzərz] *npl* : ciseaux *mpl*
scoff ['skɑf] *vi* ~ **at** : se moquer de
scold ['sko:ld] *vt* : gronder, réprimander
scoop ['sku:p] *n* **1** : pelle *f* **2** : exclusivité *f* (en journalisme) — ~ *vt* **1** : enlever (avec une pelle) **2 ~ out** : évider **3 ~ up** : ramasser
scooter ['sku:ṭər] *n* **1** : trottinette *f* **2** *or* **motor ~** : scooter *m*
scope ['sko:p] *n* **1** RANGE : étendue *f*, portée *f* **2** OPPORTUNITY : possibilités *fpl*
scorch ['skɔrʧ] *vt* : roussir
score ['skor] *n, pl* **scores 1** : score *m*, pointage *m* *Can* (aux sports) **2** RATING : note *f*, résultat *m* **3** : partition *f* (en

musique) **4 keep ~** : marquer les points — **~** *vt* **scored; scoring 1** : marquer (un point) **2** : obtenir (une note)
scorn ['skɔrn] *n* : mépris *m,* dédain *m* — **~** *vt* : mépriser, dédaigner — **scornful** ['skɔrnfəl] *adj* : méprisant
scorpion ['skɔrpiən] *n* : scorpion *m*
scotch ['skɑtʃ] *n or* **~ whiskey** : scotch *m* — **Scottish** ['skɑṭɪʃ] *adj* : écossais
scoundrel ['skaundrəl] *n* : chenapan *m*
scour ['skauər] *vt* **1** SCRUB : récurer **2** SEARCH : parcourir
scourge ['skərdʒ] *n* : fléau *m*
scout ['skaut] *n* : éclaireur *m,* -reuse *f;* scout *m,* scoute *f*
scowl ['skaul] *vi* : faire la grimace — **~** *n* : air *m* renfrogné
scram ['skræm] *vi* **scrammed; scramming** : filer *fam*
scramble ['skræmbəl] *vt* **-bled; -bling** : brouiller, mêler — **~** *n* : bousculade *f,* ruée *f* — **scrambled eggs** *npl* : œufs *mpl* brouillés
scrap ['skræp] *n* **1** PIECE : bout *m* **2** *or* **~ metal** : ferraille *f* **3 ~s** *npl* LEFTOVERS : restes *mpl* — **~** *vt* **scrapped; scrapping** : mettre au rebut
scrapbook ['skræp,buk] *n* : album *m* de coupures de journaux
scrape ['skreɪp] *v* **scraped; scraping** *vt* **1** : racler **2** : s'écorcher (le genou, etc.) **3** *or* **~ off** : enlever en grattant — *vi* **1 ~ against** : érafler **2 ~ by** : se débrouiller — **~** *n* **1** : éraflure *f* **2** PREDICAMENT : pétrin *m fam* — **scraper** ['skreɪpər] *n* : grattoir *m*
scratch ['skrætʃ] *vt* **1** : égratigner **2** MARK : rayer **3** : se gratter (la tête, etc.) **4 ~ out** : biffer — **~** *n* **1** : éraflure *f,* égratignure *f* **2 from ~** : à partir de zéro
scrawny ['skrɔni] *adj* **-nier; -niest** : maigre
scream ['skri:m] *vi* : hurler, crier — **~** *n* : hurlement *m,* cri *m*
screech ['skri:tʃ] *n* **1** : cri *m* perçant **2** : crissement *m* (de pneus, etc.) — **~** *vi* **1** : pousser un cri **2** : crisser (se dit des pneus, etc.)
screen ['skri:n] *n* **1** : écran *m* (de télévision, etc.) **2** PARTITION : paravent *m* **3** *or* **window ~** : moustiquaire *f* — **~** *vt* **1** SHIELD : protéger **2** HIDE : cacher **3** EXAMINE : passer au crible
screw ['skru:] *n* : vis *f* — **~** *vt* **1** : visser **2 ~ up** RUIN : bousiller — **screwdriver** ['skru:,draɪvər] *n* : tournevis *m*
scribble ['skrɪbəl] *v* **-bled; -bling** : gribouiller, griffonner — **~** *n* : gribouillage *m*
script ['skrɪpt] *n* : scénario *m* (d'un film, etc.)
scroll ['skro:l] *n* : rouleau *m* (de parchemin) — **~** *vi* : défiler (en informatique)
scrub ['skrʌb] *vt* **scrubbed; scrubbing** SCOUR : récurer — **~** *n* : nettoyage *m*
scruple ['skru:pəl] *n* : scrupule *m* — **scrupulous** ['skru:pjələs] *adj* : scrupuleux
scrutiny ['skru:təni] *n, pl* **-nies** : analyse *f* attentive
scuffle ['skʌfəl] *n* : bagarre *f*
sculpture ['skʌlptʃər] *n* : sculpture *f* — **sculptor** ['skʌlptər] *n* : sculpteur *m*
scum ['skʌm] *n* : écume *f*
scurry ['skəri] *vi* **-ried; -rying** : se précipiter
scuttle ['skʌṭəl] *vt* **-tled; -tling** : saborder (un navire)
scythe ['saɪð] *n* : faux *f*
sea ['si:] *n* **1** : mer *f* **2 at ~** : en mer — **~** *adj* : de mer — **seafood** ['si:,fu:d] *n* : fruits *mpl* de mer — **seagull** ['si:,gʌl] *n* : mouette *f*
seal[1] ['si:l] *n* : phoque *m*
seal[2] *n* **1** STAMP : sceau *m* **2** CLOSURE : fermeture *f* (hermétique) — **~** *vt* : sceller, cacheter
seam ['si:m] *n* : couture *f*
search ['sərtʃ] *vt* : fouiller — *vi* **~ for** : chercher — **~** *n* **1** : recherche *f* **2** EXAMINATION : fouille *f*
seashell ['si:,ʃɛl] *n* : coquillage *m* — **seashore** ['si:,ʃor] *n* : bord *m* de la mer — **seasick** ['si:,sɪk] *adj* **be ~** : avoir le mal de mer — **seasickness** ['si:,sɪknəs] *n* : mal *m* de mer
season ['si:zən] *n* : saison *f* — **~** *vt* : assaisonner, épicer — **seasonal** ['si:zənəl] *adj* : saisonnier — **seasoned** ['si:zənd] *adj* : expérimenté — **seasoning** ['si:zənɪŋ] *n* : assaisonnement *m*
seat ['si:t] *n* **1** : siège *m* **2** : fond *m* (de pantalon) **3 take a ~** : asseyez-vous — **~** *vt* **1 be ~ed** : s'asseoir **2 the bus ~s 30** : l'autobus peut accueillir 30 personnes — **seat belt** *n* : ceinture *f* de sécurité
seaweed ['si:,wi:d] *n* : algue *f* marine
secede [sɪ'si:d] *vi* **-ceded; -ceding** : faire sécession
secluded [sɪ'klu:dəd] *adj* : isolé — **seclusion** [sɪ'klu:ʒən] *n* : isolement *m*
second ['sɛkənd] *adj* : second, deu-

xième — ~ *or* **secondly** ['sɛkəndli] *adv* : deuxièmement — ~ *n* **1** : deuxième *mf;* second *m,* -conde *f* **2** MOMENT : seconde *f* **3 have ~s** : prendre une deuxième portion (de nourriture) — ~ *vt* : affirmer, appuyer — **secondary** ['sɛkən,dɛri] *adj* : secondaire — **secondhand** ['sɛkənd'hænd] *adj* : d'occasion — **second–rate** ['sɛkənd'reɪt] *adj* : médiocre

secret ['si:krət] *adj* : secret — ~ *n* : secret *m* — **secrecy** ['si:krəsi] *n, pl* **-cies** : secret *m*

secretary ['sɛkrə,tɛri] *n, pl* **-taries 1** : secrétaire *mf* **2** : ministre *m* (du gouvernement)

secrete [sɪ'kri:t] *vt* **-creted; -creting** : sécréter

secretive ['si:krəʈɪv, sɪ'kri:ʈɪv] *adj* : cachottier — **secretly** ['siɪkrətli] *adv* : en secret

sect ['sɛkt] *n* : secte *f*

section ['sɛkʃən] *n* : section *f,* partie *f*

sector ['sɛktər] *n* : secteur *m*

secular ['sɛkjələr] *adj* : séculier, laïque

secure [sɪ'kjʊr] *adj* **-curer; -est** : sûr, en sécurité — ~ *vt* **-cured; -curing 1** FASTEN : attacher **2** GET : obtenir — **security** [sɪ'kjʊrəʈi] *n, pl* **-ties 1** : sécurité *f* **2** GUARANTEE : garantie *f* **3 securities** *npl* : valeurs *fpl*

sedan [sɪ'dæn] *n* : berline *f*

sedative ['sɛdəʈɪv] *n* : calmant *m,* sédatif *m*

sedentary ['sɛdən,tɛri] *adj* : sédentaire

seduce [sɪ'du:s, -'dju:s] *vt* **-duced; -ducing** : séduire — **seduction** [sɪ'dʌkʃən] *n* : séduction *f* — **seductive** [sɪ'dʌktɪv] *adj* : séduisant

see ['si:] *v* **saw** ['sɔ]; **seen** ['si:n]; **seeing** *vt* **1** : voir **2** UNDERSTAND : comprendre **3** ESCORT : accompagner **4 ~ through** : mener à terme **5 ~ you later** : au revoir — *vi* **1** : voir **2** UNDERSTAND : comprendre **3 let's ~** : voyons **4 ~ to** : s'occuper de

seed ['si:d] *n, pl* **seed** *or* **seeds 1** : graine *f* **2** SOURCE : germe *m* — **seedling** ['si:dlɪŋ] *n* : semis *m,* jeune plant *m* — **seedy** ['si:di] *adj* **seedier; seediest** SQUALID : miteux

seek ['si:k] *v* **sought** ['sɔt]; **seeking** *vt* **1** *or* **~ out** : chercher **2** REQUEST : demander — *vi* : rechercher

seem ['si:m] *vi* : paraître, sembler, avoir l'air

seep ['si:p] *vi* : suinter

seesaw ['si:,sɔ] *n* : balançoire *f,* bascule *f*

seethe ['si:ð] *vi* **seethed; seething** : bouillonner (de rage)

segment ['sɛgmənt] *n* : segment *m*

segregate ['sɛgrɪ,geɪt] *vt* **-gated; -gating** : séparer — **segregation** [,sɛgrɪ'geɪʃən] *n* : ségrégation *f*

seize ['si:z] *vt* **seized; seizing 1** GRASP : saisir **2** CAPTURE : prendre — **seizure** ['si:ʒər] *n* : attaque *f,* crise *f* (en médecine)

seldom ['sɛldəm] *adv* : rarement

select [sə'lɛkt] *adj* : privilégié — ~ *vt* : choisir, sélectionner — **selection** [sə'lɛkʃən] *n* : sélection *f*

self ['sɛlf] *n, pl* **selves** ['sɛlvz] **1** : moi *m* **2 her better ~** : son meilleur côté — **self–addressed** [,sɛlfə'drɛst] *adj* **~ envelope** : enveloppe *f* affranchie — **self–assured** [,sɛlfə'ʃʊrd] *adj* : sûr de soi — **self–centered** [,sɛlf'sɛntərd] *adj* : égocentrique — **self–confidence** [,sɛlf'kɑnfədents] *n* : confiance *f* en soi — **self–confident** [,sɛlf'kɑnfədənt] *adj* : sûr de soi — **self–conscious** [,sɛlf'kɑntʃəs] *adj* : gêné, timide — **self–control** [,sɛlfkən'tro:l] *n* : maîtrise *f* de soi — **self–defense** [,sɛlfdɪ'fɛnts] *n* : autodéfense *f* — **self–employed** [,sɛlfɪm'plɔɪd] *adj* : qui travaille à son compte — **self–esteem** [,sɛlfɪ'sti:m] *n* : amour-propre *m* — **self–evident** [,sɛlf'ɛvədənt] *adj* : qui va de soi — **self–explanatory** [,sɛlfɪk'splænə,tori] *adj* : explicite — **self–help** [,sɛlf'hɛlp] *n* : initiative *f* personnelle — **self–important** [,sɛlfɪm'pɔrtənt] *adj* : vaniteux — **self–interest** [,sɛlf'ɪntrəst, -tə,rɛst] *n* : intérêt *m* personnel — **selfish** ['sɛlfɪʃ] *adj* : égoïste — **selfishness** ['sɛlfɪʃnəs] *n* : égoïsme *m* — **self–pity** [,sɛlf'pɪʈi] *n, pl* **-ties** : apitoiement *m* sur soi-même — **self–portrait** [,sɛlf'pɔrtrət] *n* : autoportrait *m* — **self–respect** [,sɛlfrɪ'spɛkt] *n* : amour *m* propre — **self–righteous** [,sɛlf'raɪtʃəs] *adj* : suffisant — **self–service** [,sɛlf'sərvɪs] *n* : libre-service *m* — **self–sufficient** [,sɛlfsə'fɪʃənt] *adj* : autosuffisant — **self–taught** [,sɛlf'tɔt] *adj* : autodidacte

sell ['sɛl] *v* **sold** ['so:ld]; **selling** *vt* : vendre — *vi* : se vendre — **seller** ['sɛlər] *n* : vendeur *m,* -deuse *f*

selves → **self**

semantics [sɪ'mæntɪks] *ns & pl* : sémantique *f*

semblance ['sɛmbləntś] *n* : semblant *m,* apparence *f*

semester [sə'mɛstər] *n* : semestre *m*

semicolon ['sɛmi,ko:lən, 'sɛ,maɪ-] *n* : point-virgule *m*
semifinal ['sɛmi,faɪnəl, 'sɛ,maɪ-] *n* : demi-finale *f*
seminary ['sɛmə,nɛri] *n, pl* **-naries** : séminaire *m* — **seminar** ['sɛmə,nɑr] *n* : séminaire *m*
senate ['sɛnət] *n* : sénat *m* — **senator** ['sɛnəṭər] *n* : sénateur *m*
send ['sɛnd] *vt* **sent** ['sɛnt]; **sending 1** : envoyer, expédier **2 ~ away for** : commander **3 ~ back** : renvoyer (de la marchandise, etc.) **4 ~ for** : appeler, faire venir — **sender** ['sɛndər] *n* : expéditeur *m*, -trice *f*
Senegalese [,sɛnəgə'li:z, -'li:s] *adj* : sénégalais
senile ['si:,naɪl] *adj* : sénile — **senility** [sɪ'nɪləṭi] *n* : sénilité *f*
senior ['si:njər] *n* **1** SUPERIOR : supérieur *m* **2** : étudiant *m*, -diante *f* de dernière année (en éducation) **3** *or* **~ citizen** : personne *f* du troisième âge **4 be s.o.'s ~** : être plus âgé que qqn — **~** *adj* **1** : haut placé **2** ELDER : aîné, plus âgé — **seniority** [,si:'njɔrəṭi] *n* : ancienneté *f*
sensation [sɛn'seɪʃən] *n* : sensation *f* — **sensational** [sɛn'seɪʃənəl] *adj* : sensationnel
sense ['sɛnts] *n* **1** : sens *m* **2** FEELING : sensation *f* **3** COMMON SENSE : bon sens *m* **4 make ~** : être logique — **~** *vt* **sensed; sensing** : sentir — **senseless** ['sɛntsləs] *adj* : insensé — **sensible** ['sɛntsəbəl] *adj* : raisonnable, pratique — **sensibility** [,sɛntsə'bɪləṭi] *n, pl* **-ties** : sensibilité *f* — **sensitive** ['sɛntsəṭɪv] *adj* **1** : sensible **2** TOUCHY : susceptible — **sensitivity** [,sɛntsə'tɪvəṭi] *n, pl* **-ties** : sensibilité *f* — **sensor** ['sɛn,sɔr, 'sɛntsər] *n* : détecteur *m* — **sensual** ['sɛntʃuəl] *adj* : sensuel — **sensuous** ['sɛnʃuəs] *adj* : sensuel
sent → **send**
sentence ['sɛntənts, -ənz] *n* **1** : phrase *f* **2** JUDGMENT : sentence *f*, condamnation *f* — **~** *vt* **-tenced; -tencing** : condamner
sentiment ['sɛntəmənt] *n* **1** : sentiment *m* **2** BELIEF : opinion *f*, avis *m* — **sentimental** [,sɛntə'mɛntəl] *adj* : sentimental — **sentimentality** [,sɛntə,mɛn'tæləṭi] *n, pl* **-ties** : sentimentalité *f*
sentry ['sɛntri] *n, pl* **-tries** : sentinelle *f*
separation [,sɛpə'reɪʃən] *n* : séparation *f* — **separate** ['sɛpə,reɪt] *v* **-rated; -rating** *vt* **1** : séparer **2** DISTINGUISH : distinguer — *vi* : se séparer — **~** ['sɛprət, 'sɛpə-] *adj* **1** : séparé **2** DETACHED : à part **3** DISTINCT : distinct — **separately** ['sɛprətli, 'sɛpə-] *adv* : séparément
September [sɛp'tɛmbər] *n* : septembre *m*
sequel ['si:kwəl] *n* : continuation *f*, suite *f*
sequence ['si:kwənts] *n* **1** ORDER : ordre *m*, suite *f* **2** : série *f*, succession *f* (de nombres)
serene [sə'ri:n] *adj* : serein, calme — **serenity** [sə'rɛnəṭi] *n* : sérénité *f*
sergeant ['sɑrdʒənt] *n* : sergent *m*
serial ['sɪriəl] *adj* : en série — **~** *n* : feuilleton *m* — **series** ['sɪr,i:z] *n, pl* : série *f*
serious ['sɪriəs] *adj* : sérieux — **seriously** ['sɪriəsli] *adv* **1** : sérieusement **2** GRAVELY : gravement **3 take ~** : prendre au sérieux
sermon ['sərmən] *n* : sermon *m*
serpent ['sərpənt] *n* : serpent *m*
servant ['sərvənt] *n* : domestique *mf*
serve ['sərv] *v* **served; serving** *vi* **1** : servir **2 ~ as** : servir de — *vt* **1** : servir (une personne, etc.), desservir (une région, etc.) **2 ~ time** : purger une peine — **server** ['sərvər] *n* **1** WAITER : serveur *m*, -veuse *f* **2** : serveur *m* (en informatique)
service ['sərvəs] *n* **1** : service *m* **2** CEREMONY : office *m* (en religion) **3** MAINTENANCE : entretien *m* **4 armed ~s** : forces *fpl* armées — **~** *vt* **-viced; -vicing** : réviser (un véhicule, etc.) — **serviceman** ['sərvəs,mæn, -mən] *n, pl* **-men** [-mən, -,mɛn] : militaire *m* — **service station** *n* : station-service *f*, poste *m* d'essence — **serving** ['sərvɪŋ] *n* : portion *f*, ration *f*
session ['sɛʃən] *n* : séance *f*, session *f*
set ['sɛt] *n* **1** : ensemble *m*, série *f*, jeu *m* **2** : set *m* (au tennis) **3** *or* **stage ~** : scène *f*, plateau *m* **4** *or* **television ~** : poste *m* de télévision — **~** *v* **set; setting** *vt* **1** *or* **~ down** : mettre, placer **2** : régler (une montre) **3** FIX : fixer (un rendez-vous, etc.) **4 ~ fire to** : mettre le feu à **5 ~ free** : mettre en liberté **6 ~ off** : déclencher (une alarme), faire détoner (une bombe) **7 ~ out to do sth** : se proposer de faire qqch **8 ~ up** ASSEMBLE : installer **9 ~ up** ESTABLISH : établir — *vi* **1** : prendre (se dit de la gélatine, etc.) **2** : se coucher (se dit du soleil) **3 ~ in** BEGIN : commencer **4 ~ off** *or* **~ out** : partir (en voyage) — **~** *adj* **1** FIXED

: fixe **2** READY : prêt — **setback** ['sɛt-ˌbæk] *n* : revers *m* — **setting** ['sɛtɪŋ] *n* **1** : réglage *m* (d'une machine) **2** MOUNTING : monture *f* (d'un bijou) **3** SCENE : décor *m*

settle ['sɛtəl] *v* **settled; settling** *vi* **1** : se poser (se dit d'un oiseau), se déposer (se dit de la poussière) **2 ~ down** RELAX : se calmer **3 ~ for** : se contenter de **4 ~ in** : s'installer — *vt* **1** DECIDE : fixer, décider **2** RESOLVE : résoudre **3** PAY : régler (un compte) **4** CALM : calmer **5** COLONIZE : coloniser — **settlement** ['sɛtəlmənt] *n* **1** PAYMENT : règlement *m* **2** COLONY : colonie *f,* village *m* **3** AGREEMENT : accord *m* — **settler** ['sɛtələr] *n* : colonisateur *m,* -trice *f;* colon *m*

seven ['sɛvən] *n* : sept *m* — **~** *adj* : sept — **seven hundred** *adj* : sept cents — **seventeen** [ˌsɛvən'ti:n] *n* : dix-sept *m* — **~** *adj* : dix-sept — **seventeenth** [ˌsɛvən'ti:nθ] *n* **1** : dix-septième *mf* **2 April ~** : le dix-sept avril — **~** *adj* : dix-septième — **seventh** [ˌsɛvənθ] *n* **1** : septième *mf* **2 July ~** : le sept juillet — **~** *adj* : septième — **seventieth** ['sɛvəntiəθ] *n* : soixante-dixième *mf* — **~** *adj* : soixante-dixième — **seventy** ['sɛvənti] *n, pl* **-ties** : soixante-dix *m* — **~** *adj* : soixante-dix

sever ['sɛvər] *vt* **-ered; -ering 1** : couper **2** BREAK : rompre

several ['sɛvrəl, 'sɛvə-] *adj & pron* : plusieurs

severance ['sɛvrənts, 'sɛvə-] *n* **1** : rupture *f* **2 ~ pay** : indemnité *f* de départ

severe [sə'vɪr] *adj* **-verer; -verest 1** : sévère **2** SERIOUS : grave — **severely** [sə'vɪrli] *adv* **1** : sévèrement **2** SERIOUSLY : gravement

sew ['so:] *v* **sewed; sewn** ['so:n] *or* **sewed; sewing** : coudre

sewer ['su:ər] *n* : égout *m* — **sewage** ['su:ɪʤ] *n* : eaux *fpl* d'égout

sewing ['so:ɪŋ] *n* : couture *f*

sex ['sɛks] *n* **1** : sexe *m* **2** INTERCOURSE : relations *fpl* sexuelles — **sexism** ['sɛkˌsɪzəm] *n* : sexisme *m* — **sexist** ['sɛksɪst] *adj* : sexiste — **sexual** ['sɛkʃuəl] *adj* : sexuel — **sexuality** [ˌsɛkʃu'æləṭi] *n* : sexualité *f* — **sexy** ['sɛksi] *adj* **sexier; sexiest** : sexy

shabby ['ʃæbi] *adj* **-bier; -biest 1** WORN : miteux **2** UNFAIR : mal, injuste

shack ['ʃæk] *n* : cabane *f*

shackles ['ʃækəlz] *npl* : fers *mpl,* chaînes *fpl*

shade ['ʃeɪd] *n* **1** : ombre *f* **2** : ton *m* (d'une couleur) **3** NUANCE : nuance *f* **4** *or* **lampshade** : abat-jour *m* **5 window ~** : store *m* — **~** *vt* **shaded; shading** : protéger de la lumière — **shadow** ['ʃædo:] *n* : ombre *f* — **shadowy** ['ʃædowi] *adj* INDISTINCT : vague — **shady** ['ʃeɪdi] *adj* **shadier; shadiest 1** : ombragé **2** DISREPUTABLE : suspect

shaft ['ʃæft] *n* **1** : tige *f* (d'une flèche, etc.) **2** HANDLE : manche *m* **3** AXLE : arbre *m* **4** *or* **mine ~** : puits *m*

shaggy ['ʃægi] *adj* **-gier; -est** : poilu

shake ['ʃeɪk] *v* **shook** ['ʃuk]; **shaken** ['ʃeɪkən]; **shaking** *vt* **1** : secouer **2** MIX : agiter **3 ~ hands with s.o.** : serrer la main à qqn **4 ~ one's head** : secouer la tête **5 ~ up** UPSET : ébranler — *vi* : trembler — **~** *n* **1** : secousse *f* **2** → **handshake** — **shaker** ['ʃeɪkər] *n* **1 salt ~** : salière *f* **2 pepper ~** : poivrière *f* — **shaky** ['ʃeɪki] *adj* **shakier; shakiest 1** : tremblant **2** UNSTABLE : peu ferme

shall ['ʃæl] *v aux, past* **should** ['ʃud]; *pres sing & pl* **shall 1** (*expressing volition or futurity*) → **will 2** (*expressing possibility or obligation*) → **should 3 ~ we go?** : nous y allons?

shallow ['ʃælo:] *adj* **1** : peu profond **2** SUPERFICIAL : superficiel

sham ['ʃæm] *n* : faux-semblant *m*

shambles ['ʃæmbəlz] *ns & pl* : désordre *m*

shame ['ʃeɪm] *n* **1** : honte *f* **2 what a ~!** : quel dommage! — **~** *vt* **shamed; shaming** : faire honte à — **shameful** ['ʃeɪmfəl] *adj* : honteux

shampoo [ʃæm'pu:] *vt* : se laver (les cheveux) — **~** *n, pl* **-poos** : shampooing *m*

shan't ['ʃænt] (*contraction of* **shall not**) → **shall**

shape ['ʃeɪp] *v* **shaped; shaping** *vt* **1** : façonner **2** DETERMINE : déterminer **3 be ~d like** : avoir la forme de — *vi or* **~ up** : prendre forme — **~** *n* **1** : forme *f* **2 get in ~** : se mettre en forme — **shapeless** ['ʃeɪpləs] *adj* : informe

share ['ʃɛr] *n* **1** : portion *f,* part *f* **2** : action *f* (d'une compagnie) — **~** *v* **shared; sharing** *vt* **1** : partager **2** DIVIDE : diviser — *vi* : partager — **shareholder** ['ʃɛrˌho:ldər] *n* : actionnaire *mf*

shark ['ʃɑrk] *n* : requin *m*

sharp ['ʃɑrp] *adj* **1** : affilé **2** POINTY

: pointu 3 ACUTE : aigu 4 HARSH : dur, sévère 5 CLEAR : net 6 : dièse (en musique) — ~ *adv* **at two o'clock ~** : à deux heures pile — ~ *n* : dièse *m* (en musique) — **sharpen** ['ʃɑrpən] *vt* : aiguiser (un couteau, etc.), tailler (un crayon) — **sharpener** ['ʃɑrpənər] *n* **1** *or* **knife ~** : aiguisoir *m* **2** *or* **pencil ~** : taille-crayon *m* — **sharply** ['ʃɑrpli] *adv* : brusquement

shatter ['ʃæṭər] *vt* **1** : briser, fracasser **2** DEVASTATE : détruire — *vi* : se briser, se fracasser

shave ['ʃeɪv] *v* **shaved; shaved** *or* **shaven** ['ʃeɪvən]; **shaving** *vt* **1** : raser **2** SLICE : couper — *vi* : se raser — ~ *n* : rasage — **shaver** ['ʃeɪvər] *n* : rasoir *m*

shawl ['ʃɔl] *n* : châle *m*

she ['ʃi:] *pron* : elle

sheaf ['ʃi:f] *n, pl* **sheaves** ['ʃi:vz] : gerbe *f* (de céréales), liasse *f* (de papiers)

shear ['ʃɪr] *vt* **sheared; sheared** *or* **shorn** ['ʃorn]; **shearing** : tondre — **shears** ['ʃɪrz] *npl* : cisailles *fpl*

sheath ['ʃi:θ] *n, pl* **sheaths** ['ʃi:ðz, 'ʃi:θs] : fourreau *m* (d'épée), gaine *f* (de poignard)

shed[1] ['ʃɛd] *v* **shed; shedding** *vt* **1** : verser (des larmes) **2** : perdre (ses poils, etc.) **3 ~ light on** : éclairer — *vi* : perdre ses poils, muer

shed[2] *n* : abri *m*, remise *f*

she'd ['ʃi:d] (*contraction of* **she had** *or* **she would**) → **have, would**

sheen ['ʃi:n] *n* : lustre *m*, éclat *m*

sheep ['ʃi:p] *n, pl* **sheep** : mouton *m* — **sheepish** ['ʃi:pɪʃ] *adj* : penaud

sheer ['ʃɪr] *adj* **1** PURE : pur **2** STEEP : escarpé

sheet ['ʃi:t] *n* **1** : drap *m* (de lit) **2** : feuille *f* (de papier) **3** : plaque *f* (de glace, etc.)

shelf ['ʃɛlf] *n, pl* **shelves** ['ʃɛlvz] : étagère *f*, rayon *m*

shell ['ʃɛl] *n* **1** : coquillage *m* **2** : carapace *f* (d'un crustacé, etc.) **3** : coquille *f* (d'œuf, etc.) **4** POD : cosse *f* **5** MISSILE : obus *m* — ~ *vt* **1** : décortiquer (des noix), écosser (des pois) **2** BOMBARD : bombarder

she'll ['ʃi:l, 'ʃɪl] (*contraction of* **she shall** *or* **she will**) → **shall, will**

shellfish ['ʃɛl,fɪʃ] *n* : crustacé *m*

shelter ['ʃɛltər] *n* **1** : abri *m*, refuge *m* **2 take ~** : se réfugier — ~ *vt* **1** PROTECT : protéger **2** HARBOR : abriter

shepherd ['ʃɛpərd] *n* : berger *m*

sherbet ['ʃərbət] *n* : sorbet *m*

sheriff ['ʃɛrɪf] *n* : shérif *m*

sherry ['ʃɛri] *n, pl* **-ries** : xérès *m*

she's ['ʃi:z] (*contraction of* **she is** *or* **she has**) → **be, have**

shield ['ʃi:ld] *n* : bouclier *m* — ~ *vt* : protéger

shier, shiest → **shy**

shift ['ʃɪft] *vt* : bouger, changer — *vi* **1** : se déplacer, bouger **2** CHANGE : changer **3** *or* **~ gears** : changer de vitesse — ~ *n* **1** : changement *m* **2** : équipe *f* (au travail)

shimmer ['ʃɪmər] *vi* : briller, reluire

shin ['ʃɪn] *n* : tibia *m*

shine ['ʃaɪn] *v* **shone** ['ʃo:n, *esp Brit and Can* 'ʃɒn] *or* **shined; shining** *vi* : briller — *vt* POLISH : cirer (des chaussures) — ~ *n* : éclat *m*

shingle ['ʃɪŋgəl] *n* : bardeau *m* — **shingles** ['ʃɪŋgəlz] *npl* : zona *m*

shiny ['ʃaɪni] *adj* **shinier; shiniest** : brillant

ship ['ʃɪp] *n* : bateau *m*, navire *m* — ~ *vt* **shipped; shipping** : expédier (par bateau), transporter (par avion) — **shipbuilding** ['ʃɪp,bɪldɪŋ] *n* : construction *f* navale — **shipment** ['ʃɪpmənt] *n* : cargaison *f*, chargement *m* — **shipping** ['ʃɪpɪŋ] *n* : transport *m* (maritime) — **shipwreck** ['ʃɪp,rɛk] *n* : naufrage *m* — ~ *vt* **be ~ed** : faire naufrage — **shipyard** ['ʃɪp,jɑrd] *n* : chantier *m* naval

shirt ['ʃərt] *n* : chemise *f*

shiver ['ʃɪvər] *vi* : frissonner — ~ *n* : frisson *m*

shoal ['ʃo:l] *n* : banc *m* (de poissons, etc.)

shock ['ʃɑk] *n* **1** : choc *m* **2** *or* **electric ~** : décharge *f* (électrique) — ~ *vt* : choquer, scandaliser — **shock absorber** *n* : amortisseur *m* — **shocking** ['ʃɑkɪŋ] *adj* : choquant

shoddy ['ʃɑdi] *adj* **-dier; -est** : de mauvaise qualité

shoe ['ʃu:] *n* : chaussure *f*, soulier *m* — **shoelace** ['ʃu:,leɪs] *n* : lacet *m* — **shoemaker** ['ʃu:,meɪkər] *n* : cordonnier *m*, -nière *f*

shone → **shine**

shook → **shake**

shoot ['ʃu:t] *v* **shot** ['ʃɑt]; **shooting** *vt* **1** : tirer (une balle, etc.) **2** : lancer (un regard) **3** PHOTOGRAPH : photographier **4** FILM : tourner — *vi* **1** : tirer **2 ~ by** : passer en trombe — ~ *n* : rejeton *m*, pousse *f* (d'une plante) — **shooting star** *n* : étoile *f* filante

shop ['ʃɑp] *n* **1** : magasin *m,* boutique *f* **2** WORKSHOP : atelier *m* — **~** *vi* **shopped; shopping 1** : faire des courses **2 go shopping** : faire les magasins — **shopkeeper** ['ʃɑp,ki:pər] *n* : commerçant *m,* -çante *f;* marchand *m,* -chande *f* — **shoplift** ['ʃɑp,lɪft] *vt* : voler à l'étalage — **shoplifter** ['ʃɑp,lɪftər] *n* : voleur *m,* -leuse *f* à l'étalage — **shopper** ['ʃɑpər] *n* : personne *f* qui fait ses courses

shore ['ʃor] *n* : rivage *m,* bord *m*

shorn → **shear**

short ['ʃort] *adj* **1** : court **2** : petit, de petite taille **3** CURT : brusque **4 a ~ time ago** : il y a peu de temps **5 be ~ of** : être à court de — **~** *adv* **1 fall ~** : ne pas atteindre **2 stop ~** : s'arrêter net — **shortage** ['ʃɔrtɪʤ] *n* : manque *m,* carence *f* — **shortcake** ['ʃɔrt,keɪk] *n* : tarte *f* sablée — **shortcoming** ['ʃɔrt,kʌmɪŋ] *n* : défaut *m* — **shortcut** ['ʃɔrt,kʌt] *n* : raccourci *m* — **shorten** ['ʃɔrtən] *vt* : raccourcir — **shorthand** ['ʃɔrt,hænd] *n* : sténographie *f* — **short–lived** ['ʃɔrt'lɪvd, -'laɪvd] *adj* : éphémère — **shortly** ['ʃɔrtli] *adv* : bientôt — **shortness** ['ʃɔrtnəs] *n* **1** : petite taille *f* **2 ~ of breath** : manque *m* de souffle — **shorts** *npl* : short *m,* pantalons *mpl* courts — **shortsighted** ['ʃɔrt,saɪṭəd] → **nearsighted**

shot ['ʃɑt] *n* **1** : coup *m* (de feu) **2** : coup *m,* tir *m* (aux sports) **3** ATTEMPT : essai *m,* tentative *f* **4** PHOTOGRAPH : photo *f* **5** INJECTION : piqûre *f* **6** : verre *m* (de liqueur) —**shotgun** ['ʃɑt,gʌn] *n* : fusil *m*

should ['ʃʊd] *past of* **shall 1 if she ~ call** : si elle appelle **2 I ~ have gone** : j'aurais dû y aller **3 they ~ arrive soon** : ils devraient arriver bientôt **4 what ~ we do?** : qu'allons nous faire?

shoulder ['ʃo:ldər] *n* **1** : épaule *f* **2** : accotement *m* (d'une chaussée) — **shoulder blade** *n* : omoplate *f*

shouldn't ['ʃʊdənt] (*contraction of* **should not**) → **should**

shout ['ʃaʊt] *v* : crier — **~** *n* : cri *m*

shove ['ʃʌv] *vt* **shoved; shoving** : pousser, bousculer — **~** *n* **give s.o. a ~** : pousser qqn

shovel ['ʃʌvəl] *n* : pelle *f* — **~** *vt* **-veled** *or* **-velled; -veling** *or* **-velling** : pelleter

show ['ʃo:] *v* **showed; shown** ['ʃo:n] *or* **showed; showing** *vt* **1** : montrer **2** TEACH : enseigner **3** PROVE : démontrer **4** ESCORT : accompagner **5** : passer (une émission, un film, etc.) **6 ~ off** : faire étalage de — *vi* **1** : se voir **2 ~ off** : faire le fier **3 ~ up** ARRIVE : arriver — **~** *n* **1** : démonstration *f* **2** EXHIBITION : exposition *f* **3** : spectacle *m* (de théâtre), émission *f* (de télévision, etc.) — **showdown** ['ʃo:,daʊn] *n* : confrontation *f*

shower ['ʃaʊər] *n* **1** : douche *f* **2** : averse *f* (de pluie, etc.) **3** PARTY : fête *f* — **~** *vt* **1** SPRAY : arroser **2 ~ s.o. with** : couvrir qqn de — *vi* : prendre une douche

showy ['ʃo:i] *adj* **showier; showiest** : tape-à-l'œil

shrank → **shrink**

shrapnel ['ʃræpnəl] *ns & pl* : éclats *mpl* d'obus

shred ['ʃrɛd] *n* **1** : brin *m,* parcelle *f* **2 in ~s** : en lambeaux — **~** *vt* **shredded; shredding 1** : déchirer **2** GRATE : râper

shrewd ['ʃru:d] *adj* : astucieux

shriek ['ʃri:k] *vi* : pousser un cri perçant — **~** *n* : cri *m* perçant

shrill ['ʃrɪl] *adj* : perçant, strident

shrimp ['ʃrɪmp] *n* : crevette *f*

shrine ['ʃraɪn] *n* : lieu *m* saint

shrink ['ʃrɪŋk] *v* **shrank** ['ʃræŋk]; **shrunk** ['ʃrʌŋk] *or* **shrunken** ['ʃrʌŋkən]; **shrinking** : rétrécir

shrivel ['ʃrɪvəl] *vi* **-eled** *or* **-elled; -eling** *or* **-elling** *or* **~ up** : se dessécher, se rider

shroud ['ʃraʊd] *n* **1** : linceul *m* **2** VEIL : voile *m* — **~** *vt* : envelopper

shrub ['ʃrʌb] *n* : arbuste *m,* arbrisseau *m*

shrug ['ʃrʌg] *vi* **shrugged; shrugging** : hausser les épaules

shrunk → **shrink**

shudder ['ʃʌdər] *vi* : frissonner, frémir — **~** *n* : frisson *m*

shuffle ['ʃʌfəl] *v* **-fled; -fling** *vt* : mélanger (des papiers), battre (des cartes) — *vi* : marcher en traînant les pieds

shun ['ʃʌn] *vt* **shunned; shunning** : éviter, esquiver

shut ['ʃʌt] *v* **shut; shutting** *vt* **1** CLOSE : fermer **2** → **turn off 3 ~ up** CONFINE : enfermer — *vi* **1** *or* **~ down** : fermer **2 ~ up** : se taire — **shutter** ['ʃʌṭər] *n or* **window ~** : volet *m* (d'une fenêtre)

shuttle ['ʃʌṭəl] *n* **1** : navette *f* (à l'aéroport, etc.) **2** → **space shuttle** — **~** *vt*

-tled; -tling : transporter — **shuttlecock** [ˈʃʌt̬əlˌkɑk] *n* : volant *m*

shy [ˈʃaɪ] *adj* **shier** *or* **shyer** [ˈʃaɪər]; **shiest** *or* **shyest** [ˈʃaɪəst] : timide, gêné — ~ *vi* **shied; shying** *or* ~ **away** : éviter — **shyness** [ˈʃaɪnəs] *n* : timidité *f*

sibling [ˈsɪblɪŋ] *n* : frère *m*, sœur *f*

sick [ˈsɪk] *adj* **1** : malade **2 be** ~ VOMIT : vomir **3 be** ~ **of** : en avoir assez de **4 feel** ~ : avoir des nausées — **sicken** [ˈsɪkən] *vt* DISGUST : écœurer — **sickening** [ˈsɪkənɪŋ] *adj* : écœurant — **sick leave** *n* : congé *m* de maladie

sickle [ˈsɪkəl] *n* : faucille *f*

sickly [ˈsɪkli] *adj* **-lier; -est** : maladif — **sickness** [ˈsɪknəs] *n* : maladie *f*

side [ˈsaɪd] *n* **1** : bord *m* **2** : côté *m* (d'une personne), flanc *m* (d'un animal) **3** : côté *m*, camp *m* (de l'opposition, etc.) **4** ~ **by** ~ : côte à côte **5 take** ~**s** : prendre parti — ~ *adj* : latéral — *vi* ~ **with** : prendre le parti de — **sideboard** [ˈsaɪdˌbord] *n* : buffet *m* — **sideburns** [ˈsaɪdˌbərnz] *npl* : favoris *mpl* — **side effect** *n* : effet *m* secondaire — **sideline** [ˈsaɪdˌlaɪn] *n* : travail *m* d'appoint — **sidewalk** [ˈsaɪdˌwɔk] *n* : trottoir *m* — **sideways** [ˈsaɪdˌweɪz] *adv & adj* : de côté — **siding** [ˈsaɪdɪŋ] *n* : revêtement *m* extérieur

siege [ˈsiːʤ, ˈsiːʒ] *n* : siège *m*

sieve [ˈsɪv] *n* : tamis *m*, crible *m*

sift [ˈsɪft] *vt* **1** : tamiser **2** *or* ~ **through** : examiner

sigh [ˈsaɪ] *vi* : soupirer — ~ *n* : soupir *m*

sight [ˈsaɪt] *n* **1** : vue *f* **2** SPECTACLE : spectacle *m* **3** : centre *m* d'intérêt (touristique) **4 catch** ~ **of** : apercevoir — **sightseer** [ˈsaɪtˌsiːər] *n* : touriste *mf*

sign [ˈsaɪn] *n* **1** : signe *m* **2** NOTICE : panneau *m*, enseigne *f* — ~ *vt* : signer (un chèque, etc.) — *vi* **1** : signer **2** ~ **up** ENROLL : s'inscrire

signal [ˈsɪgnəl] *n* : signal *m* — ~ *v* **-naled** *or* **-nalled; -naling** *or* **-nalling** *vt* **1** : faire signe à **2** INDICATE : signaler — *vi* **1** : faire des signes **2** : mettre son clignotant (dans un véhicule)

signature [ˈsɪgnəˌʧʊr] *n* : signature *f*

significance [sɪgˈnɪfɪkənts] *n* **1** : signification *f*, sens *m* **2** IMPORTANCE : importance *f* — **significant** [sɪgˈnɪfɪkənt] *adj* **1** : significatif **2** IMPORTANT : considérable — **significantly** [sɪgˈnɪfɪkəntli] *adv* : sensiblement — **signify** [ˈsɪgnəˌfaɪ] *vt* **-fied; -fying** : signifier — **sign language** *n* : langage *m* des signes — **signpost** [ˈsaɪnˌpoːst] *n* : poteau *m* indicateur

silence [ˈsaɪlənts] *n* : silence *m* — ~ *vt* **-lenced; -lencing** : faire taire — **silent** [ˈsaɪlənt] *adj* **1** : silencieux **2** : muet (se dit d'un film, etc.)

silhouette [ˌsɪləˈwɛt] *n* : silhouette *f*

silicon [ˈsɪlɪkən, -ˌkɑn] *n* : silicium *m*

silk [ˈsɪlk] *n* : soie *f* — **silky** [ˈsɪlki] *adj* **silkier; -est** : soyeux

sill [ˈsɪl] *n* : rebord *m* (d'une fenêtre), seuil *m* (d'une porte)

silly [ˈsɪli] *adj* **-lier; -est** : stupide, bête

silt [ˈsɪlt] *n* : limon *m*

silver [ˈsɪlvər] *n* **1** : argent *m* **2** → **silverware** — ~ *adj* : d'argent, en argent — **silverware** [ˈsɪlvərˌwær] *n* : argenterie *f*, coutellerie *f Can* — **silvery** [ˈsɪlvəri] *adj* : argenté

similar [ˈsɪmələr] *adj* : semblable, pareil — **similarity** [ˌsɪməˈlærət̬i] *n, pl* **-ties** : ressemblance *f*, similarité *f*

simmer [ˈsɪmər] *vi* : mijoter

simple [ˈsɪmpəl] *adj* **-pler; -plest 1** : simple **2** EASY : facile — **simplicity** [sɪmˈplɪsət̬i] *n* : simplicité *f* — **simplify** [ˈsɪmpləˌfaɪ] *vt* **-fied; -fying** : simplifier — **simply** [ˈsɪmpli] *adv* **1** : simplement **2** ABSOLUTELY : absolument

simulate [ˈsɪmjəˌleɪt] *vt* **-lated; -lating** : simuler

simultaneous [ˌsaɪməlˈteɪniəs] *adj* : simultané

sin [ˈsɪn] *n* : péché *m* — ~ *vi* **sinned; sinning** : pécher

since [ˈsɪnts] *adv* **1** *or* ~ **then** : depuis **2 long** ~ : il y a longtemps — ~ *conj* **1** : depuis que **2** BECAUSE : puisque, comme **3 it's been years** ~ ... : il y a des années que ... — ~ *prep* : depuis

sincere [sɪnˈsɪr] *adj* **-cerer; -cerest** : sincère — **sincerely** [sɪnˈsɪrli] *adv* : sincèrement — **sincerity** [sɪnˈsɛrət̬i] *n* : sincérité *f*

sinful [ˈsɪnfəl] *adj* : immoral

sing [ˈsɪŋ] *v* **sang** [ˈsæŋ] *or* **sung** [ˈsʌŋ]; **sung; singing** : chanter

singer [ˈsɪŋər] *n* : chanteur *m*, -teuse *f*

single [ˈsɪŋgəl] *adj* **1** : seul, unique **2** UNMARRIED : célibataire **3 every** ~ **day** : tous les jours **4 every** ~ **time** : chaque fois — ~ *vt* **-gled; -gling** ~ **out 1** SELECT : choisir **2** DISTINGUISH : distinguer

singular [ˈsɪŋgjələr] *adj* : singulier — ~ *n* : singulier *m*

sinister ['sɪnəstər] *adj* : sinistre
sink ['sɪŋk] *v* **sank** ['sæŋk] *or* **sunk** ['sʌŋk]; **sunk; sinking** *vi* **1** : couler **2** DROP : baisser, tomber — *vt* **1** : couler **2 ~ sth into** : enfoncer qqch dans — **~** *n* **1** *or* **bathroom ~** : lavabo *m* **2** *or* **kitchen ~** : évier *m*
sinner ['sɪnər] *n* : pécheur *m*, -cheresse *f*
sip ['sɪp] *vt* **sipped; sipping** : boire à petites gorgées, siroter *fam* — **~** *n* : petite gorgée *f*
siphon ['saɪfən] *n* : siphon *m* — **~** *vt* : siphonner
sir ['sər] *n* **1** (*as a form of address*) : monsieur *m* **2** (*in titles*) : sir *m*
siren ['saɪrən] *n* : sirène *f*
sirloin ['sər,lɔɪn] *n* : aloyau *m*
sissy ['sɪsi] *n, pl* **-sies** : poule *f* mouillée *fam*
sister ['sɪstər] *n* : sœur *f* — **sister–in–law** ['sɪstərɪn,lɔ] *n, pl* **sisters–in–law** : belle-sœur *f*
sit ['sɪt] *v* **sat** ['sæt]; **sitting** *vi* **1** *or* **~ down** : s'asseoir **2** LIE : être, se trouver **3** MEET : siéger **4** *or* **~ up** : se redresser — *vt* : asseoir
site ['saɪt] *n* **1** : site *m*, emplacement *m* **2** LOT : terrain *m*
sitting room → **living room**
situated ['sɪtʃʊ,eɪṭəd] *adj* : situé — **situation** [,sɪtʃʊ'eɪʃən] *n* : situation *f*
six ['sɪks] *n* : six *m* — **~** *adj* : six — **six hundred** *adj* : six cents — **sixteen** [sɪks'ti:n] *n* : seize *m* — **~** *adj* : seize — **sixteenth** [sɪks'ti:nθ] *n* **1** : seizième *mf* **2 October ~** : le seize octobre — **~** *adj* : seizième — **sixth** ['sɪksθ, 'sɪkst] *n* **1** : sixième *mf* **2 March ~** : le six mars — **~** *adj* : sixième — **sixtieth** ['sɪksṭiəθ] *n* : soixantième *mf* — **~** *adj* : soixantième — **sixty** ['sɪksṭi] *n, pl* **-ties** : soixante *m* — **~** *adj* : soixante
size ['saɪz] *n* **1** : taille *f* (d'un vêtement), pointure *f* (de chaussures, etc.) **2** EXTENT : ampleur *f* — **~** *vt* **sized, sizing** *or* **~ up** : jauger, évaluer
sizzle ['sɪzəl] *vi* **-zled; -zling** : grésiller
skate ['skeɪt] *n* : patin *m* — **~** *vi* **skated; skating** : patiner, faire du patin — **skateboard** ['skeɪt,bord] *n* : planche *f* à roulettes — **skater** ['skeɪṭər] *n* : patineur *m*, -neuse *f*
skeleton ['skɛlətən] *n* : squelette *m*
skeptical ['skɛptɪkəl] *adj* : sceptique
sketch ['skɛtʃ] *n* : esquisse *f*, croquis *m* — **~** *vt* : esquisser
skewer ['skju:ər] *n* : brochette *f*, broche *f*
ski ['ski:] *n, pl* **skis** : ski *m* — **~** *vi* **skied; skiing** : faire du ski
skid ['skɪd] *n* : dérapage *m* — **~** *vi* **skidded; skidding** : déraper, patiner
skier ['ski:ər] *n* : skieur *m*, skieuse *f*
skill ['skɪl] *n* **1** : habileté *f*, dextérité *f* **2** TECHNIQUE : technique *f* **3 ~s** *npl* : compétences *fpl* — **skilled** ['skɪld] *adj* : habile
skillet ['skɪlət] *n* : poêle *f* (à frire)
skillful *or Brit* **skilful** ['skɪlfəl] *adj* : habile, adroit
skim ['skɪm] *vt* **skimmed; skimming 1** : écumer (de la soupe), écrémer (du lait) **2** : effleurer (une surface) **3** *or* **~ through** : parcourir (un livre, etc.) — **~** *adj* : écrémé
skimpy ['skɪmpi] *adj* **skimpier; skimpiest 1** : maigre (se dit d'une portion) **2** : étriqué (se dit d'un vêtement)
skin ['skɪn] *n* **1** : peau *f* **2** : pelure *f* (de pomme, etc.) — **~** *vt* **skinned; skinning 1** : dépouiller (un animal) **2** : s'écorcher (le genou, etc.) — **skin diving** *n* : plongée *f* sous-marine — **skinny** ['skɪni] *adj* **-nier; -est** : maigre
skip ['skɪp] *v* **skipped; skipping** *vi* : sautiller — *vt* OMIT : sauter — **~** *n* : petit saut *m*, petit bond *m*
skirmish ['skərmɪʃ] *n* : escarmouche *f*
skirt ['skərt] *n* : jupe *f*
skull ['skʌl] *n* : crâne *m*
skunk ['skʌŋk] *n* : mouffette *f*
sky ['skaɪ] *n, pl* **skies** : ciel *m* — **skylight** ['skaɪ,laɪt] *n* : lucarne *f* — **skyline** ['skaɪ,laɪn] *n* : horizon *m* — **skyscraper** ['skaɪ,skreɪpər] *n* : gratte-ciel *m*
slab ['slæb] *n* : dalle *f*, bloc *m*
slack ['slæk] *adj* **1** LOOSE : mou, lâche **2** CARELESS : négligent — **slacks** ['slæks] *npl* : pantalon *m* — **slacken** ['slækən] *vt* : relâcher
slain → **slay**
slam ['slæm] *n* : claquement *m* (de porte) — **~** *v* **slammed; slamming** *vt* **1** : claquer (une porte, etc.) **2** *or* **~ down** : flanquer **3** *or* **~ shut** : fermer brusquement — *vi* **~ into** : heurter
slander ['slændər] *vt* : calomnier, diffamer — **~** *n* : calomnie *f*, diffamation *f*
slang ['slæŋ] *n* : argot *m*
slant ['slænt] *n* : pente *f*, inclinaison *f* — **~** *vi* : pencher, s'incliner
slap ['slæp] *vt* **slapped; slapping** : gi-

fler, donner une claque à — ~ *n* : gifle *f*, claque *f*
slash [ˈslæʃ] *vt* : entailler
slat [ˈslæt] *n* : lame *f*, lamelle *f*
slate [ˈsleɪt] *n* : ardoise *f*
slaughter [ˈslɔt̬ər] *n* : massacre *m* — ~ *vt* **1** : abattre (des animaux) **2** MASSACRE : massacrer — **slaughterhouse** [ˈslɔt̬ərˌhaʊs] *n* : abattoir *m*
slave [ˈsleɪv] *n* : esclave *mf* — **slavery** [ˈsleɪvəri] *n* : esclavage *m*
sled [ˈslɛd] *n* : traîneau *m*, luge *f*
sledgehammer [ˈslɛʤˌhæmər] *n* : masse *f*
sleek [ˈsli:k] *adj* : lisse, luisant
sleep [ˈsli:p] *n* **1** : sommeil *m* **2 go to ~** : s'endormir — ~ *vi* **slept** [ˈslɛpt]; **sleeping** : dormir — **sleeper** [ˈsli:pər] *n* **be a light ~** : avoir le sommeil léger — **sleepless** [ˈsli:pləs] *adj* **have a ~ night** : passer une nuit blanche — **sleepwalker** [ˈsli:pˌwɔkər] *n* : somnambule *mf* — **sleepy** [ˈsli:pi] *adj* **sleepier; -est 1** : somnolent **2 be ~** : avoir sommeil
sleet [ˈsli:t] *n* : grésil *m* — ~ *vi* : grésiller
sleeve [ˈsli:v] *n* : manche *f* — **sleeveless** [ˈsli:vləs] *adj* : sans manches
sleigh [ˈsleɪ] *n* : traîneau *m*, carriole *f Can*
slender [ˈslɛndər] *adj* : svelte, mince
slept → **sleep**
slice [ˈslaɪs] *vt* **sliced; slicing** : trancher — ~ *n* : tranche *f*, rondelle *f*
slick [ˈslɪk] *adj* SLIPPERY : glissant
slide [ˈslaɪd] *v* **slid** [ˈslɪd]; **sliding** [ˈslaɪdɪŋ] *vi* : glisser — *vt* : faire glisser — ~ *n* **1** : glissoire *f* **2** : toboggan *m* (dans un terrain de jeu) **3** : diapositive *f* (en photographie) **4** DECLINE : baisse *f*
slier, sliest → **sly**
slight [ˈslaɪt] *adj* **1** SLENDER : mince **2** MINOR : léger — ~ *vt* : offenser — **slightly** [ˈslaɪtli] *adv* : légèrement, un peu
slim [ˈslɪm] *adj* **slimmer; slimmest 1** : svelte **2 a ~ chance** : une faible chance — ~ *v* **slimmed; slimming** : maigrir
slime [ˈslaɪm] *n* MUD : vase *f*, boue *f*
sling [ˈslɪŋ] *vt* **slung** [ˈslʌŋ]; **slinging** THROW : lancer — ~ *n* **1** : fronde *f* **2** : écharpe *f* (en médecine) — **slingshot** [ˈslɪŋˌʃɑt] *n* : lance-pierres *m*
slip[1] [ˈslɪp] *v* **slipped; slipping** *vi* **1** SLIDE : glisser **2 ~ away** : partir furtivement **3 ~ up** : faire une gaffe — *vt* **1** : glisser **2 ~ into** : enfiler (un vêtement, etc.) — ~ *n* **1** MISTAKE : erreur *f* **2** : jupon *m* **3 a ~ of the tongue** : un lapsus
slip[2] *n* **~ of paper** : bout *m* (de papier)
slipper [ˈslɪpər] *n* : pantoufle *f*
slippery [ˈslɪpəri] *adj* **-perier; -est** : glissant
slit [ˈslɪt] *n* **1** OPENING : fente *f* **2** CUT : incision *f* — ~ *vt* **slit; slitting** : couper
slither [ˈslɪðər] *vi* : ramper
sliver [ˈslɪvər] *n* : éclat *m* (de bois)
slogan [ˈslo:gən] *n* : slogan *m*
slope [ˈslo:p] *vi* **sloped; sloping** : pencher — ~ *n* : pente *f*
sloppy [ˈslɑpi] *adj* **-pier; -piest 1** CARELESS : peu soigné **2** UNKEMPT : débraillé
slot [ˈslɑt] *n* **1** : fente *f* **2** GROOVE : rainure *f*
sloth [ˈslɔθ, ˈslo:θ] *n* : paresse *f*
slouch [ˈslaʊʧ] *vi* : marcher avec les épaules rentrées
slow [ˈslo:] *adj* **1** : lent **2 be ~** : retarder (se dit d'une horloge) — ~ *adv* → **slowly** — ~ *vt* : retarder — *vi or* **~ down** : ralentir — **slowly** [ˈslo:li] *adv* : lentement — **slowness** [ˈslo:nəs] *n* : lenteur *f*
slug [ˈslʌg] *n* : limace *f* (mollusque)
sluggish [ˈslʌgɪʃ] *adj* : lent
slum [ˈslʌm] *n* : taudis *m*
slumber [ˈslʌmbər] *vi* : sommeiller — ~ *n* : sommeil *m*
slump [ˈslʌmp] *vi* **1** DROP : baisser, chuter **2** COLLAPSE : s'effondrer — ~ *n* : crise *f* (économique)
slung → **sling**
slur[1] [ˈslər] *n* : calomnie *f*, diffamation *f*
slur[2] *vt* **slurred; slurring** : mal articuler (ses mots)
slurp [ˈslərp] *v* : boire bruyamment
slush [ˈslʌʃ] *n* : neige *f* fondue, gadoue *f Can*
sly [ˈslaɪ] *adj* **slier** [ˈslaɪər]; **sliest** [ˈslaɪəst] **1** : rusé, sournois **2 on the ~** : en cachette
smack[1] [ˈsmæk] *vi* **~ of** : sentir
smack[2] *vt* **1** : donner une claque à **2** KISS : donner un baiser à — ~ *n* **1** SLAP : claque *f*, gifle *f* **2** KISS : gros baiser *m* — ~ *adv* : juste, exactement
small [ˈsmɔl] *adj* : petit — **smallpox** [ˈsmɔlˌpɑks] *n* : variole *f*
smart [ˈsmɑrt] *adj* **1** : intelligent **2** STYLISH : élégant
smash [ˈsmæʃ] *n* **1** COLLISION : choc *m* **2** BANG, CRASH : fracas *m* — ~ *vt*

BREAK : fracasser — *vi* **1** SHATTER : se briser **2 ~ into** : s'écraser contre
smattering ['smæţərɪŋ] *n* : notions *fpl* vagues
smear ['smɪr] *n* : tache *f* — **~** *vt* **1** : barbouiller, faire des taches sur **2 ~ sth on** : enduire qqch de
smell ['smɛl] *v* **smelled** ['smɛld] *or* **smelt** ['smɛlt]; **smelling** : sentir — **~** *n* **1** : odorat *m* **2** ODOR : odeur *f* — **smelly** ['smɛli] *adj* **smellier; -est** : qui sent mauvais
smile ['smaɪl] *vi* **smiled; smiling** : sourire — **~** *n* : sourire *m*
smirk ['smərk] *n* : petit sourire *m* satisfait
smitten ['smɪtən] *adj* **be ~ with** : être épris de
smock ['smɑk] *n* : blouse *f*, sarrau *m*
smog ['smɑg, 'smɔg] *n* : smog *m*
smoke ['smo:k] *n* : fumée *f* — **~** *v* **smoked; smoking** : fumer — **smoke detector** *n* : détecteur *m* de fumée — **smoker** ['smo:kər] *n* : fumeur *m*, -meuse *f* — **smokestack** ['smo:k-ˌstæk] *n* : cheminée *f* — **smoky** ['smo:ki] *adj* **smokier; -est** : enfumé
smolder ['smo:ldər] *vi* : couver
smooth ['smu:ð] *adj* : lisse (se dit d'une surface, etc.), calme (se dit de la mer), doux (se dit de la peau, etc.) — **~** *or* **~ out** *vt* : défroisser — **smoothly** ['smu:ðli] *adv* : sans heurts
smother ['smʌðər] *vt* **1** : recouvrir (un feu) **2** : étouffer (qqn)
smudge ['smʌʤ] *vt* **smudged; smudging** : salir, faire des taches sur — **~** *n* : tache *f*, bavure *f*
smug ['smʌg] *adj* **smugger; smuggest** : suffisant
smuggle ['smʌgəl] *vt* **-gled; -gling** : faire passer en contrebande — **smuggler** ['smʌgələr] *n* : contrebandier *m*, -dière *f*
snack ['snæk] *n* : casse-croûte *m*, collation *f*
snag ['snæg] *n* : accroc *m* — **~** *vt* **snagged; snagging** : faire un accroc à (un bas)
snail ['sneɪl] *n* : escargot *m*
snake ['sneɪk] *n* : serpent *m*
snap ['snæp] *v* **snapped; snapping** *vi* **1** BREAK : se casser, se briser **2 ~ at** : répondre brusquement à — *vt* **1** BREAK : casser, briser **2 ~ one's fingers** : claquer des doigts **3 ~ open/shut** : s'ouvrir, se fermer d'un coup sec — **~** *n* **1** : claquement *m* **2** FASTENER : bouton-pression *m* **3 be a ~** : être facile — **snappy** ['snæpi] *adj* **-pier; -piest 1** FAST : vite **2** STYLISH : élégant — **snapshot** ['snæpˌʃɑt] *n* : instantané *m*
snare ['snær] *n* : piège *m*
snarl[1] ['snɑrl] *vi* TANGLE : enchevêtrer
snarl[2] *vi* GROWL : grogner — **~** *n* : grognement *m*
snatch ['snæʧ] *vt* : saisir
sneak ['sni:k] *vi* : se glisser, se faufiler — *vt* : faire furtivement — **sneakers** ['sni:kərz] *npl* : tennis *mpl France*, espadrilles *fpl Can* — **sneaky** ['sni:ki] *adj* **sneakier; -est** : sournois
sneer ['snɪr] *vi* : ricaner — **~** *n* : ricanement *m*
sneeze ['sni:z] *vi* **sneezed; sneezing** : éternuer — **~** *n* : éternuement *m*
snide ['snaɪd] *adj* : sarcastique
sniff ['snɪf] *vi* : renifler — **~** *n* : inhalation *f* — **sniffle** ['snɪfəl] *vi* **-fled; -fling** : renifler — **sniffles** ['snɪfəlz] *npl* **have the ~** : être enrhumé
snip ['snɪp] *n* : coup *m* de ciseaux — **~** *vt* **snipped; snipping** : couper
snivel ['snɪvəl] *vi* **-eled** *or* **-elled; -eling** *or* **-elling** : pleurnicher *fam*
snob ['snɑb] *n* : snob *mf* — **snobbish** ['snɑbɪʃ] *adj* : snob
snoop ['snu:p] *vi or* **~ around** : fouiner
snooze ['snu:z] *vi* **snoozed; snoozing** : sommeiller — **~** *n* : petit somme *m*, sieste *f*
snore ['snor] *vi* **snored; snoring** : ronfler — **~** *n* : ronflement *m*
snort ['snɔrt] *vi* : grogner (se dit d'un cochon, d'une personne) — **~** *n* : grognement *m*
snout ['snaʊt] *n* : museau *m*, groin *m*
snow ['sno:] *n* : neige *f* — **~** *vi* : neiger — **snowbank** ['sno:ˌbæŋk] *n* : banc *m* de neige *Can* — **snowfall** ['sno:ˌfɔl] *n* : chute *f* de neige — **snowflake** ['sno:-ˌfleɪk] *n* : flocon *m* de neige — **snowman** ['sno:ˌmæn] *n* : bonhomme *m* de neige — **snowplow** ['sno:ˌplaʊ] *n* : chasse-neige *m* — **snowshoe** ['sno:-ˌʧu:] *n* : raquette *f* — **snowstorm** ['sno:ˌstɔrm] *n* : tempête *f* de neige — **snowy** ['sno:i] *adj* **snowier; -est 1** : neigeux **2** : enneigé (se dit d'une montagne, etc.)
snub ['snʌb] *vt* **snubbed; snubbing** : rabrouer — **~** *n* : rebuffade *f*
snuff ['snʌf] *vt or* **~ out** : moucher (une chandelle)
snug ['snʌg] *adj* **snugger; snuggest 1** : confortable, douillet **2** TIGHT

: ajusté — **snuggle** ['snʌgəl] *vi* **-gled; -gling** : se blottir

so ['so:] *adv* **1** LIKEWISE : aussi **2** THUS : ainsi **3** THEREFORE : alors **4** *or* **~ much** : tant **5** *or* **~ very** : si **6 and ~ on** : et cetera **7 I think ~** : je pense que oui **8 I told you ~** : je te l'avais bien dit — **~** *conj* **1** THEREFORE : donc **2** *or* **~ that** : pour que **3 ~ what?** : et alors? — **~** *adj* TRUE : vrai — **~** *pron* **or ~** : plus ou moins

soak ['so:k] *vt* **1** : tremper **2 ~ up** : absorber — **~** *n* : trempage *m*

soap ['so:p] *n* : savon *m* — **~** *vt* **~ up** : savonner — **soapy** ['so:pi] *adj* **soapier; -est** : savonneux

soar ['sor] *vi* **1** : planer **2** INCREASE : monter (en flèche)

sob ['sab] *vi* **sobbed; sobbing** : sangloter — **~** *n* : sanglot *m*

sober ['so:bər] *adj* **1** : sobre **2** SERIOUS : sérieux — **sobriety** [sə'braɪəṭi, so-] *n* **1** : sobriété *f* **2** SERIOUSNESS : sérieux *m*

so-called ['so:'kɔld] *adj* : présumé

soccer ['sakər] *n* : football *m France,* soccer *m Can*

social ['so:ʃəl] *adj* : social — **~** *n* : réunion *f* — **sociable** ['so:ʃəbəl] *adj* : sociable — **socialism** ['so:ʃəˌlɪzəm] *n* : socialisme *m* — **socialist** ['so:ʃəlɪst] *n* : socialiste *mf* — **~** *adj* : socialiste — **socialize** ['so:ʃəˌlaɪz] *v* **-ized; -izing** *vt* : socialiser — *vi* **~ with** : fréquenter des gens — **society** [sə'saɪəṭi] *n, pl* **-eties** : société *f* — **sociology** [ˌso:si'alədʒi] *n* : sociologie *f*

sock[1] ['sak] *n, pl* **socks** *or* **sox** : chaussette *f*

sock[2] *vt* : donner un coup de poing à

socket ['sakət] *n* **1** *or* **electric ~** : prise *f* de courant **2** *or* **eye ~** : orbite *f*

soda ['so:də] *n* **1** *or* **~ pop** : boisson *f* gazeuse, soda *m France,* liqueur *f Can* **2** *or* **~ water** : soda *m*

sodium ['so:diəm] *n* : sodium *m*

sofa ['so:fə] *n* : canapé *m*

soft ['sɔft] *adj* **1** : mou **2** SMOOTH : doux — **softball** ['sɔftˌbɔl] *n* : balle-molle *f Can* — **soft drink** *n* : boisson *f* non alcoolisée, boisson *f* gazeuse — **soften** ['sɔfən] *vt* **1** : amollir, ramollir **2** EASE : adoucir, atténuer — *vi* **1** : se ramollir **2** EASE : s'adoucir — **softly** ['sɔftli] *adv* : doucement — **softness** ['sɔftnəs] *n* : douceur *f* — **software** ['sɔftˌwær] *n* : logiciel *m*

soggy ['sagi] *adj* **-gier; -est** : détrempé

soil ['sɔɪl] *vt* : salir, souiller — **~** *n* DIRT : terre *f*

solace ['saləs] *n* : consolation *f*

solar ['so:lər] *adj* : solaire

sold → **sell**

solder ['sadər, 'sɔ-] *n* : soudure *f* — **~** *vt* : souder

soldier ['so:ldʒər] *n* : soldat *m*

sole[1] ['so:l] *n* : sole *f* (poisson)

sole[2] *n* : plante *f* (du pied), semelle *f* (d'un soulier)

sole[3] *adj* : seul — **solely** ['so:li] *adv* : uniquement

solemn ['saləm] *adj* : solennel — **solemnity** [sə'lɛmnəṭi] *n, pl* **-ties** : solennité *f*

solicit [sə'lɪsət] *vt* : solliciter

solid ['saləd] *adj* **1** : solide **2** UNBROKEN : continu **3 ~ gold** : or massif **4 two ~ hours** : deux heures de suite — **~** *n* : solide *m* — **solidarity** [ˌsalə'dærəṭi] *n* : solidarité *f* — **solidify** [sə'lɪdəˌfaɪ] *v* **-fied; -fying** *vt* : solidifier — *vi* : se solidifier — **solidity** [sə'lɪdəṭi] *n, pl* **-ties** : solidité *f*

solitary ['saləˌtɛri] *adj* : solitaire — **solitude** ['saləˌtu:d, -ˌtju:d] *n* : solitude *f*

solo ['so:ˌlo:] *n, pl* **-los** : solo *m* — **soloist** ['so:loɪst] *n* : soliste *mf*

solution [sə'lu:ʃən] *n* : solution *f* — **soluble** ['saljəbəl] *adj* : soluble — **solve** ['salv] *vt* **solved; solving** : résoudre — **solvent** ['salvənt] *n* : solvent *m*

somber ['sambər] *adj* : sombre

some ['sʌm] *adj* **1** (*of unspecified identity*) : un **2** (*of an unspecified amount*) : de, un peu de **3** (*of an unspecified number*) : certains **4** SEVERAL : quelques **5 that was ~ game!** : ça c'était un match! — **~** *pron* **1** SEVERAL : certains, quelques-uns **2 do you want ~?** : en voulez vous? — **~** *adv* **~ twenty people** : une vingtaine de personnes — **somebody** ['sʌmbədi, -ˌbadi] *pron* : quelqu'un — **someday** ['sʌmˌdeɪ] *adv* : un jour — **somehow** ['sʌmˌhaʊ] *adv* **1** : pour quelque raison **2 ~ or other** : d'une manière ou d'une autre — **someone** ['sʌmˌwʌn] *pron* : quelqu'un

somersault ['sʌmərˌsɔlt] *n* : culbute *f*

something ['sʌmθɪŋ] *pron* **1** : quelque chose **2 ~ else** : autre chose — **sometime** ['sʌmˌtaɪm] *adv* **1** : un jour, un de ces jours **2 ~ next month** : dans le courant du mois à venir — **sometimes** ['sʌmˌtaɪmz] *adv*

: quelquefois, parfois — **somewhat** [ˈsʌmˌhwʌt, -ˌhwɑt] *adv* : un peu — **somewhere** [ˈsʌmˌhwɛr] *adv* **1** : quelque part **2 ~ around** : autour de **3 ~ else** → **elsewhere**

son [ˈsʌn] *n* : fils *m*

song [ˈsɔŋ] *n* : chanson *f*

son-in-law [ˈsʌnɪnˌlɔ] *n, pl* **sons-in-law** : gendre *m*, beau-fils *m*

soon [ˈsu:n] *adv* **1** : bientôt **2** SHORTLY : sous peu **3 as ~ as** : aussitôt que **4 ~ after** : peu après **5 ~er or later** : tôt ou tard **6 the ~er the better** : le plus tôt sera le mieux

soot [ˈsʊt, ˈsu:t, ˈsʌt] *n* : suie *f*

soothe [ˈsu:ð] *vt* **soothed; soothing 1** : calmer, apaiser **2** RELIEVE : soulager

sophisticated [səˈfɪstəˌkeɪţəd] *adj* **1** : perfectionné **2** WORLDLY : sophistiqué

sophomore [ˈsɑfˌmor, ˈsɑfəˌmor] *n* : étudiant *m*, -diante *f* de deuxième année

soprano [səˈpræˌno:] *n, pl* **-nos** : soprano *mf*

sorcerer [ˈsɔrsərər] *n* : sorcier *m* — **sorcery** [ˈsɔrsəri] *n* : sorcellerie *f*

sordid [ˈsɔrdɪd] *adj* : sordide

sore [ˈsor] *adj* **sorer; sorest 1** : douloureux **2 ~ loser** : mauvais perdant **3 ~ throat** : mal *m* de gorge — **~** *n* : plaie *f* — **sorely** [ˈsorli] *adv* : grandement — **soreness** [ˈsornəs] *n* : douleur *f*

sorrow [ˈsɑrˌo:] *n* : chagrin *m*, peine *f*

sorry [ˈsɑri] *adj* **-rier; -est 1** PITIFUL : lamentable **2 feel ~ for** : plaindre **3 I'm ~** : je suis désolé, je regrette

sort [ˈsɔrt] *n* **1** : genre *m*, sorte *f* **2 a ~ of** : une espèce de — **~** *vt* : trier, classer — **sort of** *adv* **1** SOMEWHAT : plutôt **2** MORE OR LESS : plus ou moins

SOS [ˌɛsˌo:ˈɛs] *n* : S.O.S. *m*

so-so [ˈso:ˈso:] *adv* : comme ci comme ça — **~** *adj* : moyen

soufflé [su:ˈfleɪ] *n* : soufflé *m*

sought → **seek**

soul [ˈso:l] *n* **1** : âme *f* **2 not a ~** : pas un chat

sound[1] [ˈsaʊnd] *adj* **1** HEALTHY : sain **2** FIRM : solide **3** SENSIBLE : logique **4 a ~ sleep** : un sommeil profond **5 safe and ~** : sain et sauf

sound[2] *n* **1** : son *m* **2** NOISE : bruit *m* — **~** *vt* : sonner, retentir — *vi* **1** : sonner **2** SEEM : sembler, paraître

sound[3] *n* CHANNEL : détroit *m* — **~** *vt* : sonder

soundproof [ˈsaʊndˌpru:f] *adj* : insonorisé

soup [ˈsu:p] *n* : soupe *f*

sour [ˈsaʊər] *adj* : aigre — **~** *vt* : aigrir

source [ˈsors] *n* : source *f*, origine *f*

south [ˈsaʊθ] *adv* : au sud, vers le sud — **~** *adj* : (du) sud — **~** *n* : sud *m* — **southeast** [saʊˈθi:st] *adv* : au sud-est, vers le sud-est — **~** *adj* : (du) sud-est — **~** *n* : sud-est *m* — **southeastern** [saʊˈθi:stərn] *adj* → **southeast** — **southerly** [ˈsʌðərli] *adv & adj* : (du) sud — **southern** [ˈsʌðərn] *adj* : du sud, méridional — **southwest** [saʊθˈwest] *adv* : au sud-ouest, vers le sud-ouest — **~** *adj* : (du) sud-ouest — **~** *n* : sud-ouest *m* — **southwestern** [saʊθˈwestərn] *adj* → **southwest**

souvenir [ˌsu:vəˈnɪr, ˈsu:vəˌ-] *n* : souvenir *m*

sovereign [ˈsɑvərən] *n* : souverain *m*, -raine *f* — **~** *adj* : souverain — **sovereignty** [ˈsɑvərənti] *n, pl* **-ties** : souveraineté *f*

sow[1] [ˈsaʊ] *n* : truie *f*

sow[2] [ˈso:] *vt* **sowed; sown** [ˈso:n] *or* **sowed; sowing** : semer

sox → **sock**

soybean [ˈsɔɪˌbi:n] *n* : graine *f* de soja

spa [ˈspɑ] *n* : station *f* thermale

space [ˈspeɪs] *n* **1** : espace *m* **2** ROOM, SPOT : place *f* — **~** *vt* **spaced; spacing** *or* **~ out** : espacer — **spaceship** [ˈspeɪsˌʃɪp] *n* : vaisseau *m* spatial — **space shuttle** *n* : navette *f* spatiale — **spacious** [ˈspeɪʃəs] *adj* : spacieux, ample

spade[1] [ˈspeɪd] *n* SHOVEL : bêche *f*, pelle *f*

spade[2] *n* : pique *f* (aux cartes)

spaghetti [spəˈgɛţi] *n* : spaghetti *mpl*

span [ˈspæn] *n* **1** PERIOD : espace *m* **2** : travée *f* (d'un pont) — **~** *vt* **spanned; spanning 1** : couvrir (une période) **2** CROSS : s'étendre sur

spaniel [ˈspænjəl] *n* : épagneul *m*

Spanish [ˈspænɪʃ] *adj* : espagnol — **~** *n* : espagnol *m* (langue)

spank [ˈspæŋk] *vt* : donner une fessée à

spare [ˈspær] *vt* **spared; sparing 1** PARDON : pardonner **2** SAVE : épargner **3 can you ~ a dollar?** : avez-vous un dollar à me prêter? **4 I can't ~ the time** : je n'ai pas le temps **5 ~ no expense** : ne pas ménager ses efforts — **~** *adj* **1** : de rechange **2** EXCESS : de trop — **~** *n or* **~ part** : pièce *f* de rechange — **spare time** *n* : temps *m*

libre — **sparing** [ˈspærɪŋ] *adj* : économe
spark [ˈspɑrk] *n* : étincelle *f* — ~ *vt* : éveiller, susciter — **sparkle** [ˈspɑrkəl] *vi* **-kled; -kling** : étinceler, scintiller — ~ *n* : scintillement *m* — **spark plug** *n* : bougie *f*
sparrow [ˈspæro:] *n* : moineau *m*
sparse [ˈspɑrs] *adj* **sparser; sparsest** : clairsemé, épars — **sparsely** [ˈspɑrsli] *adv* : peu
spasm [ˈspæzəm] *n* : spasme *m*
spat[1] [ˈspæt] → **spit**
spat[2] *n* QUARREL : prise *f* de bec
spatter [ˈspæt̬ər] *vt* : éclabousser
spawn [ˈspɔn] *vi* : frayer — *vt* : engendrer, produire — ~ *n* : frai *m*
speak [ˈspi:k] *v* **spoke** [ˈspo:k]; **spoken** [ˈspo:kən]; **speaking** *vi* **1** : parler **2** ~ **out against** : dénoncer **3** ~ **up** : parler plus fort **4** ~ **up for** : défendre — *vt* **1** : dire **2** : parler (une langue) — **speaker** [ˈspi:kər] *n* **1** : personne *f* qui parle (une langue) **2** ORATOR : orateur *m*, -trice *f* **3** LOUDSPEAKER : haut-parleur *m*
spear [ˈspɪr] *n* : lance *f* — **spearhead** [ˈspɪrˌhɛd] *n* : fer *m* de lance — ~ *vt* : mener, être à la tête de — **spearmint** [ˈspɪrˌmɪnt] *n* : menthe *f* verte
special [ˈspɛʃəl] *adj* : spécial, particulier — **specialist** [ˈspɛʃəlɪst] *n* : spécialiste *mf* — **specialize** [ˈspɛʃəˌlaɪz] *vi* **-ized; -izing** : se spécialiser — **specially** [ˈspɛʃəli] *adv* : spécialement — **specialty** [ˈspɛʃəlt̬i] *n, pl* **-ties** : spécialité *f*
species [ˈspi:ˌʃi:z, -ˌsi:z] *ns & pl* : espèce *f*
specify [ˈspɛsəˌfaɪ] *vt* **-fied; -fying** : spécifier — **specific** [spɪˈsɪfɪk] *adj* : précis, explicite — **specifically** [spɪˈsɪfɪkli] *adv* **1** : spécialement **2** EXPLICITLY : expressément
specimen [ˈspɛsəmən] *n* : spécimen *m*, échantillon *m*
speck [ˈspɛk] *n* **1** SPOT : tache *f* **2** BIT : brin *m* — **speckled** [ˈspɛkəld] *adj* : tacheté, moucheté
spectacle [ˈspɛktɪkəl] *n* **1** : spectacle *m* **2** ~**s** *npl* GLASSES : lunettes *fpl* — **spectacular** [spɛkˈtækjələr] *adj* : spectaculaire — **spectator** [ˈspɛkˌteɪt̬ər] *n* : spectateur *m*, -trice *f*
specter *or* **spectre** [ˈspɛktər] *n* : spectre *m*
spectrum [ˈspɛktrəm] *n, pl* **-tra** [-trə] *or* **-trums** **1** : spectre *m* **2** RANGE : gamme *f*
speculation [ˌspɛkjəˈleɪʃən] *n* : conjectures *fpl*, spéculations *fpl*
speech [ˈspi:ʧ] *n* **1** : parole *f* **2** ADDRESS : discours *m* — **speechless** [ˈspi:ʧləs] *adj* : muet
speed [ˈspi:d] *n* **1** : vitesse *f* **2** VELOCITY : rapidité *f* — ~ *v* **sped** [ˈspɛd] *or* **speeded; speeding** *vi* **1** : faire un excès de vitesse **2** ~ **off** : aller à toute vitesse — *vt or* ~ **up** : accélérer — **speed limit** *n* : limitation *f* de vitesse — **speedometer** [spɪˈdɑmət̬ər] *n* : compteur *m* (de vitesse) — **speedy** [ˈspi:di] *adj* **speedier; -est** : rapide
spell[1] [ˈspɛl] *vt* **1** : écrire, orthographier **2** *or* ~ **out** : épeler **3** MEAN : signifier
spell[2] *n* ENCHANTMENT : sortilège *m*
spell[3] *n* : période *f* (de temps)
spellbound [ˈspɛlˌbaʊnd] *adj* : captivé
spelling [ˈspɛlɪŋ] *n* : orthographe *f*
spend [ˈspɛnd] *vt* **spent** [ˈspɛnt]; **spending** **1** : dépenser (de l'argent) **2** : passer (ses vacances, etc.)
sperm [ˈspərm] *n, pl* **sperm** *or* **sperms** : sperme *m*
sphere [ˈsfɪr] *n* : sphère *f* — **spherical** [ˈsfɪrɪkəl, ˈsfɛr-] *adj* : sphérique
spice [ˈspaɪs] *n* : épice *f* — ~ *vt* **spiced; spicing** : assaisonner — **spicy** [ˈspaɪsi] *adj* **spicier; -est** : épicé, piquant
spider [ˈspaɪdər] *n* : araignée *f*
spigot [ˈspɪgət, -kət] *n* : robinet *m*
spike [ˈspaɪk] *n* **1** : gros clou *m* **2** POINT : pointe *f* — **spiky** [ˈspaɪki] *adj* **-kier; -est** : pointu
spill [ˈspɪl] *vt* : renverser, répandre — *vi* : se répandre
spin [ˈspɪn] *v* **spun** [ˈspʌn]; **spinning** *vi* : tourner, tournoyer — *vt* **1** : faire tourner **2** : filer (de la laine) — ~ *n* **1** : tour *m* **2** **go for a** ~ : faire une balade (en auto)
spinach [ˈspɪnɪʧ] *n* : épinards *mpl*
spinal cord [ˈspaɪnəl] *n* : moelle *f* épinière
spindle [ˈspɪndᵊl] *n* : fuseau *m* (en textile)
spine [ˈspaɪn] *n* **1** : colonne *f* vertébrale **2** : piquant *m* (d'un animal) **3** : dos *m* (d'un livre)
spinster [ˈspɪntstər] *n* : vieille fille *f*
spiral [ˈspaɪrəl] *adj* : en spirale — ~ *n* : spirale *f* — ~ *vi* **-raled** *or* **-ralled; -raling** *or* **-ralling** : aller en spirale
spire [ˈspaɪr] *n* : flèche *f*
spirit [ˈspɪrət] *n* **1** : esprit *m* **2** **in good** ~**s** : de bonne humeur **3** ~**s** *npl*

: spiritueux *mpl* — **spirited** ['spɪrət̬əd] *adj* : animé — **spiritual** ['spɪrɪʧʊəl, -ʧəl] *adj* : spirituel — **spirituality** [ˌspɪrɪʧʊ'æləṭi] *n* : spiritualité *f*

spit¹ ['spɪt] *n* : broche *f*

spit² *v* **spit** *or* **spat** ['spæt]; **spitting** : cracher — ~ *n* SALIVA : salive *f*

spite ['spaɪt] *n* **1** : rancune *f* **2 in ~ of** : malgré — ~ *vt* **spited; spiting** : contrarier — **spiteful** ['spaɪtfəl] *adj* : rancunier

splash ['splæʃ] *vt* : éclabousser — *vi or* **~ about** : patauger — ~ *n* **1** : éclaboussement *m* **2** : plouf *m* (bruit)

splatter ['splæṭər] → **spatter**

spleen ['spli:n] *n* : rate *f* (organe)

splendid ['splɛndəd] *adj* : splendide — ~ **splendor** *or Brit* **splendour** ['splɛndər] *n* : splendeur *f*

splint ['splɪnt] *n* : attelle *f*

splinter ['splɪntər] *n* : éclat *m* — ~ *vi* : se briser en éclats

split ['splɪt] *v* **split; splitting** *vt* **1** : fendre (du bois), déchirer (un pantalon) **2** *or* **~ up** : diviser — *vi* **~ up** : se séparer — ~ *n* **1** CRACK : fente *f* **2** *or* **~ seam** : déchirure *f*

splurge ['splərʤ] *vi* **splurged; splurging** : faire des folles dépenses

spoil ['spɔɪl] *vt* **spoiled** *or* **spoilt** ['spɔɪlt]; **spoiling** **1** RUIN : gâcher **2** PAMPER : gâter — **spoils** ['spɔɪlz] *npl* : butin *m*

spoke¹ ['spo:k] → **speak**

spoke² *n* : rayon *m* (d'une roue)

spoken → **speak**

spokesman ['spo:ksmən] *n, pl* **-men** [-mən, -ˌmɛn] : porte-parole *m* — **spokeswoman** ['spo:ksˌwʊmən] *n, pl* **-women** [-ˌwɪmən] : porte-parole *f*

sponge ['spʌnʤ] *n* : éponge *f* — ~ *vt* **sponged; sponging** : éponger — **spongy** ['spʌnʤi] *adj* **spongier; -est** : spongieux

sponsor ['spɑntsər] *n* : parrain *m* (d'une cause, etc.) — ~ *vt* : patronner — **sponsorship** ['spɑntsərˌʃɪp] *n* : parrainage *m*, patronage *m*

spontaneity ['spɑntə'ni:əṭi, -'neɪ-] *n* : spontanéité *f* — **spontaneous** [spɑn'teɪniəs] *adj* : spontané

spooky ['spu:ki] *adj* **spookier; -est** : qui donne la chair de poule

spool ['spu:l] *n* : bobine *f*

spoon ['spu:n] *n* : cuillère *f* — **spoonful** ['spu:nˌfʊl] *n* : cuillerée *f*

sporadic [spə'rædɪk] *adj* : sporadique

sport ['sport] *n* **1** : sport *m* **2 be a good ~** : avoir l'esprit d'équipe — **sportsman** ['sportsmən] *n, pl* **-men** [-mən, -ˌmɛn] : sportif *m* — **sportswoman** ['sportsˌwʊmən] *n, pl* **-women** [-ˌwɪmən] : sportive *f* — **sporty** ['sporṭi] *adj* **sportier; -est** : sportif

spot ['spɑt] *n* **1** : tache *f* **2** DOT : pois *m* **3** PLACE : endroit *m*, lieu *m* **4 in a tight ~** : dans l'embarras **5 on the ~** INSTANTLY : immédiatement — ~ *vt* **spotted; spotting** **1** STAIN : tacher **2** DETECT, NOTICE : apercevoir, repérer — **spotless** ['spɑtləs] *adj* : impeccable — **spotlight** ['spɑtˌlaɪt] *n* **1** : projecteur *m*, spot *m* **2 be in the ~** : être le centre de l'attention — **spotty** ['spɑ'ṭi] *adj* **-tier; -est** : irrégulier

spouse ['spaʊs] *n* : époux *m*, épouse *f*

spout ['spaʊt] *vi* : jaillir — ~ *n* : bec *m* (d'une cruche)

sprain ['spreɪn] *n* : entorse *f*, foulure *f* — ~ *vt* : se faire une entorse à, se fouler (la cheville, etc.)

sprawl ['sprɔl] *vi* **1** : être affalé (dans un fauteuil, etc.) **2** EXTEND : s'étendre — ~ *n* : étendue *f*

spray¹ ['spreɪ] *n* BOUQUET : gerbe *f*, bouquet *m*

spray² *n* **1** MIST : gouttelettes *fpl* fines **2** *or* **aerosol ~** : vaporisateur *m*, bombe *f* **3** *or* **~ bottle** : atomiseur *m* — ~ *vt* : vaporiser, pulvériser

spread ['sprɛd] *v* **spread; spreading** *vt* **1** : propager (une nouvelle), répandre (de l'information) **2** *or* **~ out** : écarter **3** : étaler, tartiner (avec de la confiture, etc.) — *vi* **1** : se propager (se dit d'une maladie) **2** *or* **~ out** : s'étendre (se dit d'un feu) — ~ *n* **1** : propagation *f*, diffusion *f* **2** PASTE : pâte *f* à tartiner — **spreadsheet** ['sprɛdˌʃi:t] *n* : tableur *m*

spree ['spri] *n* **go on a spending ~** : faire de folles dépenses

sprightly ['spraɪtli] *adj* **-lier; -est** : vif, alerte

spring ['sprɪŋ] *v* **sprang** ['spræŋ] *or* **sprung** ['sprʌŋ]; **sprung; springing** *vi* **1** : sauter, bondir **2 ~ from** : surgir de — *vt* **1** ACTIVATE : actionner **2 ~ sth on s.o.** : surprendre qqn avec qqch — ~ *n* **1** : puits *m* **2** : printemps *m* (saison) **3** LEAP : bond *m*, saut *m* **4** RESILIENCE : élasticité *f* **5** : ressort *m* (mécanisme) **6** *or* **bedspring** : sommier *m* — **springboard** ['sprɪŋˌbord] *n* : tremplin *m* — **springtime** ['sprɪŋˌtaɪm] *n* : printemps *m* — **springy** ['sprɪŋi] *adj* **springier; -est** : élastique

sprinkle ['sprɪŋkəl] *v* **-kled; -kling** *vt* **1** : arroser **2** DUST : saupoudrer — ~ *n* : petite averse *f* — **sprinkler** ['sprɪŋk'lər] *n* : arroseur *m*
sprint ['sprɪnt] *vi* : courir — ~ *n* : sprint *m* (aux sports)
sprout ['spraʊt] *vi* : germer, pousser — ~ *n* : pousse *f*
spruce[1] ['spru:s] *vt* **spruced; sprucing ~ up** : embellir
spruce[2] *n* : épicéa *m*
spun → **spin**
spur ['spər] *n* **1** : éperon *m* **2** STIMULUS : incitation *f* **3 on the ~ of the moment** : sur le coup — ~ *vt* **spurred; spurring 1** *or* **~ on** : éperonner (un cheval) **2 ~ on** MOTIVATE : motiver
spurn ['spərn] *vt* : repousser, rejeter
spurt[1] ['spərt] *vi* : jaillir — ~ *n* : jaillissement *m*, jet *m*
spurt[2] *n* **1** : sursaut *m* (d'énergie, etc.) **2 work in ~s** : travailler par à-coups
spy ['spaɪ] *vi* **spied; spying ~ on** : espionner — ~ *n* : espion *m*
squabble ['skwabəl] *n* : dispute *f*, querelle *f* — ~ *vi* **-bled; -bling** : se disputer, se chamailler
squad ['skwad] *n* : peloton *m* (militaire), brigade *f* (de police)
squadron ['skwadrən] *n* : escadron *m* (de soldats), escadre *f* (de navires ou d'avions)
squalid ['skwalɪd] *adj* : sordide
squalor ['skwalər] *n* : conditions *fpl* sordides
squander ['skwandər] *vt* : gaspiller
square ['skwær] *n* **1** : carré *m* **2** : place *f* (d'une ville) — ~ *adj* **squarer; squarest 1** : carré **2** EVEN : quitte — ~ *vt* **squared; squaring** : carrer (un nombre) — **square root** *n* : racine *f* carrée
squash[1] ['skwaʃ, 'skwɔʃ] *vt* : écraser, aplatir
squash[2] *n, pl* **squashes** *or* **squash** : courge *f*
squat ['skwat] *vi* **squatted; squatting** : s'accroupir — ~ *adj* **squatter; squattest** : trapu
squawk ['skwɔk] *n* : cri *m* rauque — ~ *vi* : pousser des cris rauques
squeak ['skwi:k] *vi* : grincer — ~ *n* : grincement *m*
squeal ['skwi:l] *vi* **1** : pousser des cris aigus **2** : crisser (se dit des pneus), grincer (se dit des freins) **3 ~ on** : dénoncer — ~ *n* : petit cri *m* aigu
squeamish ['skwi:mɪʃ] *adj* : impressionnable, délicat
squeeze ['skwi:z] *vt* **squeezed; squeezing 1** : presser, serrer **2** : extraire (du jus) — ~ *n* : pression *f*, resserrement *m*
squid ['skwɪd] *n, pl* **squid** *or* **squids** : calmar *m*
squint ['skwɪnt] *vi* : loucher
squirm ['skwərm] *vi* : se tortiller
squirrel ['skwərəl] *n* : écureuil *m*
squirt ['skwərt] *vt* : lancer un jet de — *vi* : jaillir — ~ *n* : jet *m*
stab ['stæb] *n* **1** : coup *m* de couteau **2 ~ of pain** : élancement *m* **3 take a ~ at sth** : tenter de faire qqch — ~ *vt* **stabbed; stabbing 1** KNIFE : poignarder **2** THRUST : planter
stable ['steɪbəl] *n* **1** : étable *f* (pour le bétail) **2** *or* **horse ~** : écurie *f* — ~ *adj* **-bler; -est** : stable — **stability** [stə'bɪləţi] *n, pl* **-ties** : stabilité *f* — **stabilize** ['steɪbəˌlaɪz] *vt* **-lized; -lizing** : stabiliser
stack ['stæk] *n* : tas *m*, pile *f* — ~ *vt* : entasser, empiler
stadium ['steɪdiəm] *n, pl* **-dia** [-diə] *or* **-diums** : stade *m*
staff ['stæf] *n, pl* **staffs** ['stæfs, 'stævz] *or* **staves** ['stævz, 'steɪvz] **1** : bâton *m* **2** *pl* **staffs** PERSONNEL : personnel *m*
stag ['stæg] *n, pl* **stags** *or* **stag** : cerf *m*
stage ['steɪʤ] *n* **1** : scène *f* (au théâtre) **2** PHASE : étape *f* **3 the ~** : le théâtre — ~ *vt* **staged; staging 1** : mettre en scène **2** ORGANIZE : organiser
stagger ['stægər] *vi* : tituber, chanceler — *vt* **1** : échelonner **2 be ~ed by** : être stupéfié par — **staggering** ['stægərɪŋ] *adj* : stupéfiant
stagnant ['stægnənt] *adj* : stagnant — **stagnate** ['stægˌneɪt] *vi* **-nated; -nating** : stagner
stain ['steɪn] *vt* **1** : tacher **2** : teindre (du bois) — ~ *n* **1** : tache *f* **2** DYE : teinture *f* — **stainless steel** ['steɪnləs] *n* : acier *m* inoxydable
stair ['stær] *n* **1** STEP : marche *f* **2 ~s** *npl* : escalier *m* — **staircase** ['stærˌkeɪs] *n* : escalier *m* — **stairway** ['stærˌweɪ] *n* : escalier *m*
stake ['steɪk] *n* **1** POST : poteau *m*, pieu *m*, piquet *m* **2** INTEREST : intérêts *mpl* **3 be at ~** : être en jeu — ~ *vt* **staked; staking 1** BET : miser, parier **2 ~ a claim to** : revendiquer
stale ['steɪl] *adj* **staler; stalest 1** : rassis **2** OLD : vieux **3** STUFFY : vicié
stalk[1] ['stɔk] *n* : tige *f* (d'une plante)
stalk[2] *vt* : traquer, suivre
stall[1] ['stɔl] *n* **1** : stalle *f* (d'un cheval,

etc.) 2 STAND : stand *m*, kiosque *m* — ~ *vi* : caler (se dit d'un moteur)
stall[2] *vt* : retarder
stallion ['stæljən] *n* : étalon *m*
stalwart ['stɔlwərt] *adj* 1 STRONG : robuste 2 ~ **supporter** : partisan *m* inconditionnel
stamina ['stæmənə] *n* : résistance *f*
stammer ['stæmər] *vi* : bégayer — ~ *n* : bégaiement *m*
stamp ['stæmp] *n* 1 SEAL : cachet *m* 2 MARK : tampon *m* 3 *or* **postage** ~ : timbre *m* — ~ *vt* 1 : affranchir (une lettre, etc.) 2 IMPRINT : estamper 3 MINT : frapper (la monnaie) 4 ~ **one's feet** : taper des pieds
stampede [stæm'pi:d] *n* : débandade *f*, ruée *f*
stance ['stænts] *n* : position *f*
stand ['stænd] *v* **stood** ['stʊd]; **standing** *vi* 1 : être debout 2 BE : être, se trouver 3 CONTINUE : rester valable 4 LIE, REST : reposer 5 ~ **back** : reculer 6 ~ **out** : ressortir 7 *or* ~ **up** : se mettre debout — *vt* 1 PLACE : mettre 2 ENDURE : supporter 3 ~ **a chance** : avoir de bonnes chances — **stand by** *vt* 1 : s'en tenir à (une promesse, etc.) 2 SUPPORT : appuyer — **stand for** *vt* 1 MEAN : signifier 2 PERMIT : tolérer — **stand up** *vi* 1 ~ **for** : défendre 2 ~ **up to** : tenir tête à — **stand** *n* 1 RESISTANCE : résistance *f* 2 STALL : stand *m* 3 BASE : pied *m* 4 POSITION : position *f* 5 ~**s** *npl* : tribune *f*
standard ['stændərd] *n* 1 : norme *f* 2 BANNER : étendard *m* 3 CRITERION : critère *m* 4 ~ **of living** : niveau *m* de vie — ~ *adj* : standard
standing ['stændɪŋ] *n* 1 RANK : position *f*, standing *m* 2 DURATION : durée *f*
standpoint ['stænd,pɔɪnt] *n* : point *m* de vue
standstill ['stænd,stɪl] *n* 1 **be at a** ~ : être paralysé 2 **come to a** ~ : s'arrêter
stank → **stink**
stanza ['stænzə] *n* : strophe *f*
staple[1] ['steɪpəl] *n* : produit *m* de base — ~ *adj* : principal, de base
staple[2] *n* : agrafe *f* — ~ *vt* **-pled; -pling** : agrafer — **stapler** ['steɪplər] *n* : agrafeuse *f*
star ['stɑr] *n* : étoile *f* — ~ *v* **starred; starring** *vt* FEATURE : avoir pour vedette — *vi* ~ **in** : être la vedette de
starboard ['stɑrbərd] *n* : tribord *m*
starch ['stɑrtʃ] *vt* : amidonner — ~ *n* 1 : amidon *m* 2 : fécule *f* (aliment)
stardom ['stɑrdəm] *n* : célébrité *f*
stare ['stær] *vi* **stared; staring** : regarder fixement — ~ *n* : regard *m* fixe
starfish ['stɑr,fɪʃ] *n* : étoile *f* de mer
stark ['stɑrk] *adj* 1 PLAIN : austère 2 HARSH : sévère, dur
starling ['stɑrlɪŋ] *n* : étourneau *m*
starry ['stɑri] *adj* **-rier; -est** : étoilé
start ['stɑrt] *vi* 1 : débuter, commencer 2 SET OUT : partir 3 JUMP : sursauter 4 *or* ~ **up** : démarrer — *vt* 1 : commencer 2 CAUSE : provoquer 3 *or* ~ **up** ESTABLISH : établir 4 *or* ~ **up** : mettre en marche (un moteur, etc.) — ~ *n* 1 : commencement *m*, début *m* 2 **get an early** ~ : commencer tôt 3 **give s.o. a** ~ : faire sursauter qqn — **starter** ['stɑrt̬ər] *n* : démarreur *m* (d'un véhicule)
startle ['stɑrt̬əl] *vt* **-tled; -tling** : surprendre
starve ['stɑrv] *v* **starved; starving** *vi* : mourir de faim — *vt* : affamer — **starvation** [stɑr'veɪʃən] *n* : faim *f*
state ['steɪt] *n* 1 : état *m* 2 **the States** : les États-Unis — ~ *vt* **stated; stating** 1 SAY : déclarer 2 REPORT : exposer — **statement** ['steɪtmənt] *n* 1 : déclaration *f* 2 *or* **bank** ~ : relevé *m* de compte — **statesman** ['steɪtsmən] *n, pl* **-men** [-mən, -,mɛn] : homme *m* d'État
static ['stæt̬ɪk] *adj* : statique — ~ *n* : parasites *mpl* (en radio, etc.)
station ['steɪʃən] *n* 1 : gare *f* (de train) 2 : chaîne *f* (de télévision), poste *m* (de radio) 3 → **fire station, police station** — ~ *vt* : poster, placer — **stationary** ['steɪʃə,nɛri] *adj* : stationnaire
stationery ['steɪʃə,nɛri] *n* : papeterie *f*, papier *m* à lettres
station wagon *n* : familiale *f*
statistic [stə'tɪstɪk] *n* : statistique *f*
statue ['stæ,tʃu:] *n* : statue *f*
stature ['stætʃər] *n* : stature *f*, taille *f*
status ['steɪt̬əs, 'stæ-] *n* 1 : statut *m* 2 *or* **marital** ~ : situation *f* (de famille) 3 *or* **social** ~ : rang *m* (social)
statute ['stæ,tʃu:t] *n* : loi *f*, règle *f*
staunch ['stɔntʃ] *adj* : dévoué
stay[1] ['steɪ] *vi* 1 REMAIN : rester, demeurer 2 LODGE : séjourner 3 ~ **awake** : rester éveillé 4 ~ **in** : rester à la maison — ~ *n* : séjour *m*
stay[2] *n* SUPPORT : soutien *m*
stead ['stɛd] *n* **in s.o.'s** ~ : à la place de qqn — **steadfast** ['stɛd,fæst] *adj* 1 FIRM : ferme 2 LOYAL : fidèle — **steady** ['stɛdi] *adj* **steadier; -est** 1

FIRM, SURE : ferme, stable **2** FIXED : fixe **3** CONSTANT : constant — ~ *vt* **steadied; steadying** : stabiliser
steak ['steɪk] *n* : bifteck *m*, steak *m*
steal ['sti:l] *v* **stole** ['sto:l]; **stolen** ['sto:lən]; **stealing** : voler
stealthy ['stɛlθi] *adj* **stealthier; -est** : furtif
steam ['sti:m] *n* **1** : vapeur *f* **2 let off** ~ : se défouler — *vt* **1** : cuire à la vapeur **2** *or* ~ **up** : s'embuer
steel ['sti:l] *n* **1** : acier *m* **2** ~ **industry** : sidérurgie — ~ *adj* : en acier, d'acier
steep[1] ['sti:p] *adj* : raide, à pic
steep[2] *vt* : infuser (du thé, etc.)
steeple ['sti:pəl] *n* : clocher *m*, flèche *f*
steer[1] ['stɪr] *n* : bœuf *m*
steer[2] *vt* **1** : conduire (une voiture, etc.), gouverner (un navire) **2** GUIDE : diriger — **steering wheel** *n* : volant *m*
stem ['stɛm] *n* : tige *f* (d'une plante), pied *m* (d'un verre) — ~ *vi* ~ **from** : provenir de
stench ['stɛntʃ] *n* : puanteur *f*
step ['stɛp] *n* **1** : pas *m* **2** RUNG, STAIR : marche *f* **3** ~ **by** ~ : petit à petit **4 take** ~**s** : prendre des mesures **5 watch your** ~ : faites attention (à la marche) — ~ *vi* **stepped; stepping 1** : faire un pas **2** ~ **back** : reculer **3** ~ **down** RESIGN : se retirer **4** ~ **in** : intervenir **5** ~ **out** : sortir (pour un moment) **6** ~ **this way** : par ici — **step up** *vt* INCREASE : augmenter
stepbrother ['stɛp,brʌðər] *n* : beau-frère *m* — **stepdaughter** ['stɛp,dɔṭər] *n* : belle-fille *f* — **stepfather** ['stɛp,fɑðər, -,fa-] *n* : beau-père *m*
stepladder ['stɛp,lædər] *n* : escabeau *m*
stepmother ['stɛp,mʌðər] *n* : belle-mère *f* — **stepsister** ['stɛp,sɪstər] *n* : belle-sœur *f* —**stepson** ['stɛp,sʌn] *n* : beau-fils *m*
stereo ['stɛri,o:, 'stɪr-] *n, pl* **stereos** : stéréo *f* — ~ *adj* : stéréo
stereotype ['stɛrio,taɪp, 'stɪr-] *vt* **-typed; -typing** : stéréotyper — ~ *n* : stéréotype *m*
sterile ['stɛrəl] *adj* : stérile — **sterility** [stə'rɪləṭi] *n* : stérilité *f*— **sterilization** [,stɛrələ'zeɪʃən] *n* : stérilisation *f* — **sterilize** ['stɛrə,laɪz] *vt* **-ized; -izing** : stériliser
sterling silver ['stərlɪŋ] *n* : argent *m* fin
stern[1] ['stərn] *adj* : sévère
stern[2] *n* : poupe *f*
stethoscope ['stɛθə,sko:p] *n* : stéthoscope *m*
stew ['stu:, 'stju:] *n* : ragoût *m* — ~ *vi* **1** : cuire **2** FRET : être préoccupé
steward ['stu:ərd, 'stju:-] *n* **1** : administrateur *m*, -trice *f* **2** : steward *m* (d'un avion, etc.) — **stewardess** ['stu:ərdəs, 'stju:-] *n* : hôtesse *f*
stick[1] ['stɪk] *n* **1** : bâton *m* **2** WALKING STICK : canne *f*
stick[2] *v* **stuck** ['stʌk]; **sticking** *vt* **1** : coller **2** STAB : enfoncer **3** PUT : mettre **4** ~ **out** : sortir, tirer (la langue) — *vi* **1** : se coller **2** JAM : se bloquer **3** ~ **around** : rester **4** ~ **out** PROTRUDE : dépasser **5** ~ **up for** : défendre — **sticker** ['stɪkər] *n* : autocollant *m* — **sticky** ['stɪki] *adj* **stickier; -est** : collant
stiff ['stɪf] *adj* **1** RIGID : rigide, raide **2** STILTED : guindé **3** : courbaturé (se dit des muscles) — **stiffen** ['stɪfən] *vt* : renforcer, raidir — *vi* : se durcir, se raidir — **stiffness** ['stɪfnəs] *n* : raideur *f*, rigidité *f*
stifle ['staɪfəl] *vt* **-fled; -fling** : étouffer
stigmatize ['stɪgmə,taɪz] *vt* **-tized; -tizing** : stigmatiser
still ['stɪl] *adj* **1** : immobile **2** SILENT : tranquille — ~ *adv* **1** : encore, toujours **2** NEVERTHELESS : quand même, tout de même **3 sit** ~**!** : reste tranquille! — ~ *n* : quiétude *f*, calme *m* — **stillness** ['stɪlnəs] *n* : calme *m*, silence *m*
stilt ['stɪlt] *n* : échasse *f* — **stilted** ['stɪltəd] *adj* : forcé
stimulate ['stɪmjə,leɪt] *vt* **-lated; -lating** : stimuler — **stimulant** ['stɪmjələnt] *n* : stimulant *m* — **stimulation** [,stɪmjə'leɪʃən] *n* : stimulation *f* — **stimulus** ['stɪmjələs] *n, pl* **-li** [-,laɪ] : stimulant *m*
sting ['stɪŋ] *v* **stung** ['stʌŋ]; **stinging** : piquer — ~ *n* : piqûre *f* — **stinger** ['stɪŋər] *n* : dard *m*, aiguillon *m*
stingy ['stɪnʤi] *adj* **stingier; -est** : avare, pingre — **stinginess** ['stɪnʤinəs] *n* : avarice *f*
stink ['stɪŋk] *vi* **stank** ['stæŋk] *or* **stunk** ['stʌŋk]; **stunk; stinking** : puer — ~ *n* : puanteur *f*
stint ['stɪnt] *vi* ~ **on** : lésiner sur — ~ *n* : période *f* (de travail)
stipulate ['stɪpjə,leɪt] *vt* **-lated; -lating** : stipuler — **stipulation** [,stɪpjə'leɪʃən] *n* : stipulation *f*
stir ['stər] *v* **stirred; stirring** *vt* **1** : agiter, remuer **2** MOVE : émouvoir **3**

INCITE : inciter **4** *or* **~ up** PROVOKE : susciter — *vi* : remuer, bouger — **~** *n* COMMOTION : émoi *m*
stirrup ['stərəp, 'stɪr-] *n* : étrier *m*
stitch ['stɪʧ] *n* : point *m* (en couture, en médecine) — **~** *v* : coudre
stock ['stɑk] *n* **1** INVENTORY : réserve *f*, stock *m* **2** SECURITIES : actions *fpl*, valeurs *fpl* **3** ANCESTRY : lignée *f*, souche *f* **4** BROTH : bouillon *m* **5 out of ~** : épuisé **6 take ~ of** : évaluer — **~** *vt* : approvisionner — *vi* **~ up on** : s'approvisionner en — **stockbroker** ['stɑk,bro:kər] *n* : agent *m* de change
stocking ['stɑkɪŋ] *n* : bas *m*
stock market *n* : Bourse *f*
stocky ['stɑki] *adj* **stockier; -est** : trapu
stodgy ['stɑʤi] *adj* **stodgier; -est 1** DULL : lourd **2** OLD-FASHIONED : vieux-jeu
stoic ['sto:ɪk] *n* : stoïque *mf* — **~** *or* **stoical** [-ɪkəl] *adj* : stoïque
stoke ['sto:k] *vt* **stoked; stoking** : alimenter (un feu, etc.)
stole[1] ['sto:l] → **steal**
stole[2] *n* : étole *f*
stolen → **steal**
stomach ['stʌmɪk] *n* : estomac *m* — **~** *vt* : supporter, tolérer — **stomachache** ['stʌmɪk,eɪk] *n* : mal *m* de ventre
stone ['sto:n] *n* **1** : pierre *f* **2** : noyau *m* (d'un fruit) — **~** *vt* **stoned; stoning** : lapider — **stony** ['sto:ni] *adj* **stonier; -est** : pierreux
stood → **stand**
stool ['stu:l] *n* : tabouret *m*
stoop ['stu:p] *vi* **1** : se baisser, se pencher **2 ~ to** : s'abaisser à
stop ['stɑp] *v* **stopped; stopping** *vt* **1** PLUG : boucher **2** PREVENT : empêcher **3** HALT : arrêter, mettre fin à **4** CEASE : cesser de — *vi* **1** : s'arrêter, stopper **2** CEASE : cesser **3 ~ by** : passer — **~** *n* **1** : arrêt *m*, halte *f* **2 come to a ~** : s'arrêter **3 put a ~ to** : mettre fin à — **stoplight** ['stɑp,laɪt] *n* : feu *m* rouge — **stopper** ['stɑpər] *n* : bouchon *m*
store ['stor] *vt* **stored; storing** : emmagasiner, entreposer — **~** *n* **1** SUPPLY : réserve *f*, provision *f* **2** SHOP : magasin *m* — **storage** ['storɪʤ] *n* : entreposage *m* — **storehouse** ['stor,haus] *n* : entrepôt *m* — **storekeeper** ['stor,ki:pər] *n* : commerçant *m*, -çante *f* — **storeroom** ['stor,ru:m, -,rum] *n* : magasin *m*, réserve *f*
stork ['stɔrk] *n* : cigogne *f*
storm ['stɔrm] *n* : orage *m*, tempête *f* — **~** *vi* **1** RAGE : tempêter **2 ~ out** : partir furieux — *vt* ATTACK : prendre d'assaut — **stormy** ['stɔrmi] *adj* **stormier; -est** : orageux
story[1] ['stori] *n, pl* **stories 1** TALE : conte *m* **2** ACCOUNT : histoire *f*, récit *m* **3** RUMOR : rumeur *f*
story[2] *n* FLOOR : étage *m*
stout ['staut] *adj* **1** RESOLUTE : tenace **2** STURDY : fort **3** FAT : corpulent
stove ['sto:v] *n* **1** : poêle *m* (pour chauffer) **2** RANGE : cuisinière *f*
stow ['sto:] *vt* **1** : ranger **2** LOAD : charger — *vi* **~ away** : voyager clandestinement
straddle ['strædəl] *vt* **-dled; -dling** : s'asseoir à califourchon sur
straggle ['strægəl] *vi* **-gled; -gling** : traîner — **straggler** ['strægələr] *n* : traînard *m*, -narde *f*
straight ['streɪt] *adj* **1** : droit **2** : raide (se dit des cheveux) **3** HONEST : franc — **~** *adv* **1** DIRECTLY : (tout) droit, directement **2** FRANKLY : carrément — **straightaway** [,streɪtə'weɪ] *adv* : immédiatement — **straighten** ['streɪtən] *vt* **1** : redresser, rendre droit **2** *or* **~ up** : ranger — **straightforward** [streɪt-'fɔrwərd] *adj* **1** FRANK : franc, honnête **2** CLEAR : clair, simple
strain ['streɪn] *vt* **1** : se forcer (la voix), se fatiguer (les yeux), se froisser (un muscle) **2** FILTER : égoutter **3 ~ oneself** : faire un grand effort — *vi* : s'efforcer — **~** *n* **1** STRESS : stress *m*, tension *f* **2** SPRAIN : foulure *f* — **strainer** ['streɪnər] *n* : passoire *f*
strait ['streɪt] *n* **1** : détroit *m* **2 in dire ~s** : aux abois
strand[1] ['strænd] *vt* **be left ~ed** : être abandonné
strand[2] *n* : fil *m*, brin *m*
strange ['streɪnʤ] *adj* **stranger; strangest 1** : étrange, bizarre **2** UNFAMILIAR : inconnu — **strangely** ['streɪnʤli] *adv* : étrangement — **strangeness** ['streɪnʤnəs] *n* : étrangeté *f* — **stranger** ['streɪnʤər] *n* : étranger *m*, -gère *f*
strangle ['stræŋgəl] *vt* **-gled; -gling** : étrangler
strap ['stræp] *n* **1** : courroie *f*, sangle *f* **2** *or* **shoulder ~** : bretelle *f* — **~** *vt* **strapped; strapping** : attacher — **strapless** ['stræpləs] *n* : sans bretelles — **strapping** ['stræpɪŋ] *adj* : robuste, costaud *fam*

strategy [ˈstræṭədʒi] *n, pl* **-gies** : stratégie *f* — **strategic** [strəˈtiːdʒɪk] *adj* : stratégique

straw [ˈstrɔ] *n* **1** : paille *f* **2 the last ~** : le comble

strawberry [ˈstrɔˌbɛri] *n, pl* **-ries** : fraise *f*

stray [ˈstreɪ] *n* : animal *m* errant — **~** *vi* **1** : errer, vagabonder **2** DEVIATE : s'écarter — **~** *adj* : errant, perdu

streak [ˈstriːk] *n* **1** : raie *f,* bande *f* **2** VEIN : veine *f*

stream [ˈstriːm] *n* **1** : ruisseau *m* **2** FLOW : flot *m,* courant *m* — **~** *vi* : couler — **streamer** [ˈstriːmər] *n* **1** : banderole *f* **2** : serpentin *m* (de papier) — **streamlined** [ˈstriːmˌlaɪnd] *adj* **1** : aérodynamique **2** EFFICIENT : efficace

street [ˈstriːt] *n* : rue *f* — **streetcar** [ˈstriːtˌkɑr] *n* : tramway *m* — **streetlight** [ˈstriːtˌlaɪt] *n* : réverbère *m*

strength [ˈstrɛŋkθ] *n* **1** : force *f* **2** TOUGHNESS : résistance *f* **3** INTENSITY : intensité *f* **4 ~s and weaknesses** : qualités et faiblesses — **strengthen** [ˈstrɛŋkθən] *vt* **1** : fortifier **2** REINFORCE : renforcer **3** INTENSIFY : intensifier

strenuous [ˈstrɛnjʊəs] *adj* **1** : énergique **2** ARDUOUS : ardu — **strenuously** [ˈstrɛnjʊəsli] *adv* : vigoureusement

stress [ˈstrɛs] *n* **1** : stress *m,* tension *f* **2** EMPHASIS : accent *m* — **~** *vt* **1** EMPHASIZE : mettre l'accent sur **2** *or* **~ out** : stresser — **stressful** [ˈstrɛsfəl] *adj* : stressant

stretch [ˈstrɛtʃ] *vt* **1** : étirer (des muscles, un élastique, etc.) **2** EXTEND : tendre **3 ~ the truth** : exagérer — *vi* **1** : s'étirer **2 ~ out** EXTEND : s'étendre — **~** *n* **1** : étirement *m* **2** EXPANSE : étendue *f* **3** : période *f* (de temps) — **stretcher** [ˈstrɛtʃər] *n* : civière *f,* brancard *m*

strew [ˈstruː] *vt* **strewed; strewed** *or* **strewn** [ˈstrun]; **strewing** : éparpiller

stricken [ˈstrɪkən] *adj* **~ with** : affligé de (une émotion), atteint de (une maladie)

strict [ˈstrɪkt] *adj* : strict — **strictly** *adv* **~ speaking** : à proprement parler

stride [ˈstraɪd] *vi* **strode** [ˈstroːd]; **stridden** [ˈstrɪdən]; **striding** : marcher à grandes enjambées — **~** *n* **1** : grand pas *m,* enjambée *f* **2 make great ~s** : faire de grands progrès

strident [ˈstraɪdənt] *adj* : strident

strife [ˈstraɪf] *n* : conflit *m*

strike [ˈstraɪk] *v* **struck** [ˈstrʌk]; **struck; striking** *vt* **1** HIT : frapper **2** *or* **~ against** : heurter **3** *or* **~ out** DELETE : rayer **4** : sonner (l'heure) **5** IMPRESS : impressionner **6** : découvrir (de l'or, du pétrole) **7 it ~s me that ...** : il m'apparaît que ... **8 ~ up** START : commencer — *vi* **1** : frapper **2** ATTACK : attaquer **3** : faire grève — **~** *n* **1** BLOW : coup *m* **2** : grève *f* (des transports, etc.) **3** ATTACK : attaque *f* **4** : prise *f Can* (au baseball) — **striker** [ˈstraɪkər] *n* : gréviste *mf* — **striking** [ˈstraɪkɪŋ] *adj* : frappant, saisissant

string [ˈstrɪŋ] *n* **1** : ficelle *f* **2** SERIES : suite *f* **3 ~s** *npl* : cordes *fpl* (d'un orchestre) — **~** *vt* **strung** [ˈstrʌŋ]; **stringing** : enfiler — **string bean** *n* : haricot *m* vert

stringent [ˈstrɪndʒənt] *adj* : rigoureux, strict

strip[1] [ˈstrɪp] *v* **stripped; stripping** *vt* REMOVE : enlever — *vi* UNDRESS : se déshabiller

strip[2] *n* : bande *f*

stripe [ˈstraɪp] *n* : rayure *f,* bande *f* — **striped** [ˈstraɪpt, ˈstraɪpəd] *adj* : rayé, à rayures

strive [ˈstraɪv] *vi* **strove** [ˈstroːv]; **striven** [ˈstrɪvən] *or* **strived; striving 1 ~ for** : lutter pour **2 ~ to** : s'efforcer de

strode → **stride**

stroke [ˈstroːk] *vt* **stroked; stroking** : caresser — **~** *n* : attaque *f* (cérébrale)

stroll [ˈstroːl] *vi* : se promener — **~** *n* : promenade *f* — **stroller** [ˈstroːlər] *n* : poussette *f* (pour enfants)

strong [ˈstrɔŋ] *adj* : fort, robuste — **stronghold** [ˈstrɔŋˌhoːld] *n* : bastion *m* — **strongly** [ˈstrɔŋli] *adv* **1** DEEPLY : profondément **2** TOTALLY : totalement **3** VIGOROUSLY : énergiquement

strove → **strive**

struck → **strike**

structure [ˈstrʌktʃər] *n* : structure *f* — **structural** [ˈstrʌktʃərəl] *adj* : structural

struggle [ˈstrʌgəl] *vi* **-gled; -gling 1** : lutter, se débattre **2** STRIVE : s'efforcer — **~** *n* : lutte *f*

strung → **string**

strut [ˈstrʌt] *vi* **strutted; strutting** : se pavaner

stub [ˈstʌb] *n* : mégot *m* (de cigarette), bout *m* (de crayon, etc.), talon *m* (de chèque) — **~** *vt* **stubbed; stubbing ~ one's toe** : se cogner le doigt de pied

stubble ['stʌbəl] *n* : barbe *f* de plusieurs jours
stubborn ['stʌbərn] *adj* **1** : têtu, obstiné **2** PERSISTENT : tenace
stuck → **stick** — **stuck–up** ['stʌk'ʌp] *adj* : prétentieux
stud[1] ['stʌd] *n* : étalon *m*
stud[2] *n* **1** NAIL : clou *m* **2** : montant *m* (en construction)
student ['stu:dənt, 'stju:-] *n* : élève *m*, élève *f* (au primaire); étudiant *m*, -diante *f* (universitaire) — **studio** ['stu:di,o:, 'stju:-] *n, pl* **-dios** : studio *m*, atelier *m* — **study** ['stʌdi] *n, pl* **studies** **1** : étude *f* **2** OFFICE : bureau *m* — ~ *v* **studied; studying** : étudier — **studious** ['stu:diəs, 'stju:-] *adj* : studieux
stuff ['stʌf] *n* **1** : affaires *fpl*, choses *fpl* **2** MATTER, SUBSTANCE : chose *f* — ~ *vt* **1** FILL : rembourrer **2** CRAM : fourrer — **stuffing** ['stʌfɪŋ] *n* : rembourrage *m* — **stuffy** ['stʌfi] *adj* **stuffier; -est** **1** STODGY : ennuyeux **2** : bouché (se dit du nez) **3** ~ **rooms** : pièces *fpl* mal aérées
stumble ['stʌmbəl] *vi* **-bled; -bling** **1** : trébucher **2** ~ **across** *or* ~ **upon** : tomber sur
stump ['stʌmp] *n* **1** : moignon *m* (d'un membre) **2** *or* **tree** ~ : souche *f* — ~ *vt* : laisser perplexe
stun ['stʌn] *vt* **stunned; stunning** **1** : assommer (avec un coup) **2** ASTONISH : étonner
stung → **sting**
stunk → **stink**
stunning ['stʌnɪŋ] *adj* **1** : incroyable, sensationnel **2** STRIKING : frappant
stunt[1] ['stʌnt] *vt* : rabougrir
stunt[2] *n* : prouesse *f* (acrobatique)
stupid ['stu:pəd, 'stju:-] *adj* **1** : stupide **2** SILLY : bête — **stupidity** [stʊ'pɪdəṭi, stjʊ-] *n, pl* **-ties** : stupidité *f*
sturdy ['stərdi] *adj* **-dier; -est** **1** : fort, résistant **2** ROBUST : robuste — **sturdiness** ['stərdinəs] *n* : solidité *f*
stutter ['stʌṭər] *vi* : bégayer — ~ *n* : bégaiement *m*
sty ['staɪ] *n* **1** *pl* **sties** PIGPEN : porcherie *f* **2** *pl* **sties** *or* **styes** : orgelet *m*
style ['staɪl] *n* **1** : style *m* **2** FASHION : mode *f* — ~ *vt* **styled; styling** : coiffer (les cheveux) — **stylish** ['staɪlɪʃ] *adj* : chic, élégant
suave ['swɑv] *adj* : raffiné et affable
subconscious [,sʌb'kɑntʃəs] *adj* : subconscient — ~ *n* : subconscient *m*
subdivision ['sʌbdə,vɪʒən] *n* : subdivision *f*
subdue [səb'du:, -'dju:] *vt* **-dued; -duing** **1** CONQUER : subjuguer **2** CONTROL : dominer **3** SOFTEN : atténuer — **subdued** [səb'du:,d, -'dju:d] *adj* : atténué
subject ['sʌbʤɪkt] *n* **1** : sujet *m* **2** TOPIC : matière *f* — ~ *adj* **1** : asservi **2** ~ **to** : sujet à — ~ [səb'ʤɛkt] *vt* ~ **to** : soumettre à — **subjective** [səb'ʤɛktɪv] *adj* : subjectif
subjunctive [səb'ʤʌnktɪv] *n* : subjonctif *m*
sublet ['sʌb,lɛt] *vt* **-let; -letting** : souslouer
sublime [sə'blaɪm] *adj* : sublime
submarine ['sʌbmə,ri:n, ,sʌbmə'-] *n* : sous-marin *m*
submerge [səb'mərʤ] *vt* **-merged; -merging** : submerger
submit [səb'mɪt] *v* **-mitted; -mitting** *vi* **1** YIELD : se rendre **2** ~ **to** : se soumettre à — *vt* : soumettre — **submission** [səb'mɪʃən] *n* : soumission *f* — **submissive** [səb'mɪsɪv] *adj* : soumis
subordinate [sə'bɔrdənət] *adj* : subordonné — ~ *n* : subordonné *m*, -née *f* — ~ [sə'bɔrdən,eɪt] *vt* **-nated; -nating** : subordonner
subpoena [sə'pi:nə] *n* : assignation *f*
subscribe [səb'skraɪb] *vi* **-scribed; -scribing** ~ **to** : s'abonner à (un magazine, etc.) — **subscriber** [səb'skraɪbər] *n* : abonné *m*, -née *f* — **subscription** [səb'skrɪpʃən] *n* : abonnement *m*
subsequent ['sʌbsɪkwənt, -sə,kwɛnt] *adj* **1** : subséquent, suivant **2** ~ **to** : postérieur à — **subsequently** ['sʌbsɪ,kwɛntli, -,kwənt-] *adv* : par la suite
subservient [səb'sərvIənt] *adj* : servile
subside [səb'saɪd] *vi* **-sided; -siding** : s'atténuer
subsidiary [səb'sɪdi,ɛri] *adj* : secondaire — ~ *n, pl* **-aries** : filiale *f*
subsidy ['sʌbsədi] *n, pl* **-dies** : subvention *f* — **subsidize** ['sʌbsə,daɪz] *vt* **-dized; -dizing** : subventionner
subsistence [səb'sɪstənts] *n* : subsistance *f* — **subsist** [səb'sɪst] *vi* : subsister
substance ['sʌbstənts] *n* : substance *f*
substandard [,sʌb'stændərd] *adj* : inférieur
substantial [səb'stæntʃəl] *adj* : substantiel — **substantially** [səb'stæntʃəli] *adv* : considérablement
substitute ['sʌbstə,tu:t, -,tju:t] *n* **1** : remplaçant *m*, -çante *f*; suppléant *m*,

-pléante *f* **2 :** succédané *m* (d'une chose) — ∼ *vt* **-tuted; -tuting** : substituer, remplacer
subtitle ['sʌbˌtaɪtəl] *n* : sous-titre *m*
subtle ['sʌtəl] *adj* **-tler; -tlest** : subtil — **subtlety** ['sʌtəlti] *n, pl* **-ties** : subtilité *f*
subtraction [səb'trækʃən] *n* : soustraction *f* — **subtract** [səb'trækt] *vt* : soustraire
suburb ['sʌˌbərb] *n* **1 :** quartier *m* résidentiel **2 the** ∼**s** : la banlieue — **suburban** [sə'bərbən] *adj* : de banlieue
subversive [səb'vərsɪv] *adj* : subversif
subway ['səbˌweɪ] *n* : métro *m*
succeed [sək'si:d] *vt* : succéder à — *vi* : réussir — **success** [sək'sɛs] *n* : réussite *f,* succès *m* — **successful** [sək'sɛsfəl] *adj* : réussi — **successfully** [sək'sɛsfəli] *adv* : avec succès
succession [sək'sɛʃən] *n* **1 :** succession *f* **2 in** ∼ : successivement, de suite — **successive** [sək'sɛsɪv] *adj* : successif — **successor** [sək'sɛsər] *n* : successeur *m*
succinct [sək'sɪŋkt, sə'sɪŋkt] *adj* : succinct
succumb [sə'kʌm] *vi* : succomber
such ['sʌtʃ] *adj* **1 :** tel, pareil **2** ∼ **as** : comme **3** ∼ **a pity! :** quel dommage! — ∼ *pron* **1 :** tel **2 as** ∼ : comme tel — ∼ *adv* **1** VERY : très **2** ∼ **a nice man! :** un homme si gentil! **3** ∼ **that :** de façon à ce que
suck ['sʌk] *vt* **1** *or* ∼ **on** : sucer **2** *or* ∼ **up :** absorber (un liquide), aspirer (avec une machine) — **suckle** ['sʌkəl] *v* **-led; -ling** *vt* : allaiter — *vi* : téter — **suction** ['sʌkʃən] *n* : succion *f*
sudden ['sʌdən] *adj* **1 :** soudain, subit **2 all of a** ∼ : tout à coup — **suddenly** ['sʌdənli] *adv* : soudainement, subitement
suds ['sʌdz] *npl* : mousse *f* (de savon)
sue ['su:] *vt* **sued; suing** : poursuivre en justice
suede ['sweɪd] *n* : daim *m,* suède *m*
suet ['su:ət] *n* : graisse *f* de rognon
suffer ['sʌfər] *vi* : souffrir — **suffering** ['sʌfərɪŋ] *n* : souffrance *f*
suffice [sə'faɪs] *vi* **-ficed; -ficing** : être suffisant, suffir — **sufficient** [sə'fɪʃənt] *adj* : suffisant — **sufficiently** [sə'fɪʃəntli] *adv* : suffisamment
suffix ['sʌˌfɪks] *n* : suffixe *m*
suffocate ['sʌfəˌkeɪt] *v* **-cated; -cating** *vt* : asphyxier, suffoquer — *vi* : s'asphyxier, suffoquer
suffrage ['sʌfrɪʤ] *n* : suffrage *m*
sugar ['ʃʊgər] *n* : sucre *m* — **sugarcane** ['ʃʊgərˌkeɪn] *n* : canne *f* à sucre — **sugarhouse** ['ʃʊgərˌhaʊs] *n* : cabane *f* (à sucre) *Can*
suggestion [səg'ʤɛstʃən, sə-] *n* : suggestion *f,* proposition *f* — **suggest** [səg'ʤɛst, sə-] *vt* **1 :** proposer, suggérer **2** INDICATE : laisser supposer
suicide ['su:əˌsaɪd] *n* **1 :** suicide *m* **2 commit** ∼ : se suicider — **suicidal** [ˌsu:ə'saɪdəl] *adj* : suicidaire
suit ['su:t] *n* **1 :** complet *m* (d'homme), tailleur *m* (de femme) **2 :** couleur *f* (aux cartes) — ∼ *vt* : convenir à, aller à — **suitable** ['su:təbəl] *adj* : convenable, approprié — **suitcase** ['su:tˌkeɪs] *n* : valise *f*
suite ['swi:t] *n* : suite *f*
suitor ['su:tər] *n* : prétendant *m*
sulfur *or Brit* **sulphur** ['sʌlfər] *n* : soufre *m*
sulk ['sʌlk] *vi* : bouder — **sulky** ['sʌlki] *adj* **sulkier; -est** : boudeur
sullen ['sʌlən] *adj* : maussade, morose
sulphur *Brit* → **sulfur**
sultry ['sʌltri] *adj* **-trier; -est 1 :** étouffant, lourd **2** SENSUAL : sensuel
sum ['sʌm] *n* : somme *f* — ∼ *vt* **summed; summing** ∼ **up** : résumer — **summarize** ['sʌməˌraɪz] *v* **-rized; -rizing** *vt* : résumer — *vi* : se résumer — **summary** ['sʌməri] *n, pl* **-ries** : sommaire *m,* résumé *m*
summer ['sʌmər] *n* : été *m*
summit ['sʌmət] *n* : sommet *m,* cime *f*
summon ['sʌmən] *vt* **1 :** appeler (qqn), convoquer (une réunion) **2 :** citer (en droit) — **summons** ['sʌmənz] *n, pl* **summonses** SUBPOENA : assignation *f*
sumptuous ['sʌmptʃʊəs] *adj* : somptueux
sun ['sʌn] *n* : soleil *m* — **sunbathe** ['sʌnˌbeɪ] *vi* **-bathed; -bathing** : prendre un bain de soleil — **sunburn** ['sʌnˌbərn] *n* : coup *m* de soleil
Sunday ['sʌnˌdeɪ, -di] *n* : dimanche *m*
sunflower ['sʌnˌflaʊər] *n* : tournesol *m*
sung → **sing**
sunglasses ['sʌnˌglæsəz] *npl* : lunettes *fpl* de soleil
sunk → **sink**
sunlight ['sʌnˌlaɪt] *n* : (lumière *f* du) soleil *m* — **sunny** ['sʌni] *adj* **-nier; -est** : ensoleillé — **sunrise** ['sʌnˌraɪz] *n* : lever *m* du soleil — **sunset** ['sʌnˌsɛt] *n* : coucher *m* du soleil — **sunshine** ['sʌnˌʃaɪn] *n* : (lumière *f* du) soleil *m* — **suntan** ['sʌnˌtæn] *n* : hâle *m,* bronzage *m*

super ['su:pər] *adj* : super *fam,* génial
superb [sʊ'pərb] *adj* : superbe
superficial [ˌsu:pər'fɪʃəl] *adj* : superficiel
superfluous [sʊ'pərfluəs] *adj* : superflu
superintendent [ˌsu:pərɪn'tɛndənt] *n* **1** : commissaire *m* (de police) **2** *or* **building ~** : concierge *mf* **3** *or* **school ~** : inspecteur *m,* -trice *f*
superior [sʊ'pɪriər] *adj* : supérieur — **~** *n* : supérieur *m,* -rieure *f* — **superiority** [sʊˌpɪri'ɔrət̬i] *n, pl* **-ties** : supériorité *f*
superlative [sʊ'pərlət̬ɪv] *n* : superlatif *m*
supermarket ['su:pərˌmɑrkət] *n* : supermarché *m*
supernatural [ˌsu:pər'nætʃərəl] *adj* : surnaturel
superpower ['su:pərˌpaʊər] *n* : superpuissance *f*
supersede [ˌsu:pər'si:d] *vt* **-seded; -seding** : remplacer, supplanter
superstition [ˌsu:pər'stɪʃən] *n* : superstition *f* — **superstitious** [ˌsu:pər'stɪʃəs] *adj* : superstitieux
supervise ['su:pərˌvaɪz] *vt* **-vised; -vising** : surveiller, superviser — **supervision** [ˌsu:pər'vɪʒən] *n* : surveillance *f,* supervision *f* — **supervisor** ['su:pərˌvaɪzər] *n* : surveillant *m,* -lante *f*
supper ['sʌpər] *n* : dîner *m,* souper *m Can*
supplant [sə'plænt] *vt* : supplanter
supple ['sʌpəl] *adj* **-pler; -plest** : souple
supplement ['sʌpləmənt] *n* : supplément *m* — **~** ['sʌpləˌmɛnt] *vt* : compléter, augmenter
supply [sə'plaɪ] *vt* **-plied; -plying** **1** : fournir **2 ~ with** : approvisionner en — **~** *n, pl* **-plies** **1** : provision *f,* réserve *f* **2 ~ and demand** : l'offre et la demande **3 supplies** *npl* : provisions *fpl,* vivres *mpl* **4 supplies** *npl* : fournitures *fpl* (de bureau, etc.) — **supplier** [sə'plaɪər] *n* : fournisseur *m,* -seuse *f*
support [sə'port] *vt* **1** BACK : soutenir, appuyer **2** : subvenir aux besoins de (une famille, etc.) **3** PROP UP : supporter — **~** *n* **1** : appui *m,* soutien *m* **2** PROP : support *m* — **supporter** [sə'port̬ər] *n* **1** : partisan *m,* -sane *f* **2** FAN : supporter *m*
suppose [sə'po:z] *vt* **-posed; -posing** **1** : supposer **2 be ~d to do sth** : être censé faire qqch — **supposedly** [sə'po:zədli] *adv* : soi-disant
suppress [sə'prɛs] *vt* **1** : réprimer **2** WITHHOLD : supprimer
supreme [sʊ'pri:m] *adj* : suprême — **supremacy** [sʊ'prɛməsi] *n, pl* **-cies** : suprématie *f*
sure ['ʃʊr] *adj* **surer; surest** **1** : sûr **2 make ~ that** : s'assurer que — **~** *adv* **1** OF COURSE : bien sûr **2 it ~ is hot!** : quelle chaleur! — **surely** ['ʃʊrli] *adv* : sûrement
surfing ['sərfɪŋ] *n* : surf *m*
surface ['sərfəs] *n* **1** : surface *f* **2** AREA : superficie *f* — **~** *vi* **-faced; -facing** : faire surface, remonter à la surface — *vt* : revêtir (une chaussée)
surfboard ['sərfˌbord] *n* : planche *f* de surf
surfeit ['sərfət] *n* : excès *m*
surfing ['sərfɪŋ] *n* : surf *m*
surge ['sərʤ] *vi* **surged; surging** : déferler — **~** *n* **1** : déferlement *m* (de la mer), ruée *f* (de personnes, etc.) **2** INCREASE : augmentation *f* (subite)
surgeon ['sərʤən] *n* : chirurgien *m,* -gienne *f* — **surgery** ['sərʤəri] *n, pl* **-geries** : chirurgie *f* — **surgical** ['sərʤɪkəl] *adj* : chirurgical
surly ['sərli] *adj* **-lier; -est** : revêche, bourru
surname ['sərˌneɪm] *n* : nom *m* de famille
surpass [sər'pæs] *vt* : surpasser
surplus ['sərˌplʌs] *n* : excédent *m,* surplus *m*
surprise [sə'praɪz, sər-] *n* **1** : surprise *f* **2 take by ~** : prendre au dépourvu — **~** *vt* **-prised; -prising** : surprendre — **surprising** [sə'praɪzɪŋ, sər-] *adj* : surprenant
surrender [sə'rɛndər] *vt* : rendre, céder — *vi* : se rendre — **~** *n* : capitulation *f,* reddition *f*
surround [sə'raʊnd] *vt* : entourer — **surroundings** [sə'raʊndɪŋz] *npl* : environs *mpl,* alentours *mpl*
surveillance [sər'veɪlənts, -'veɪljənts, -'veɪənts] *n* : surveillance *f*
survey [sər'veɪ] *vt* **-veyed; -veying** **1** : arpenter (un terrain) **2** INSPECT : inspecter **3** POLL : sonder — **~** ['sərˌveɪ] *n, pl* **-veys** **1** INSPECTION : inspection *f* **2** POLL : sondage *m* — **surveyor** [sər'veɪər] *n* : arpenteur *m,* -teuse *f*
survive [sər'vaɪv] *v* **-vived; -viving** *vi* : survivre — *vt* : survivre à — **survival** [sər'vaɪvəl] *n* : survie *f* — **survivor** [sər'vaɪvər] *n* : survivant *m,* -vante *f*
susceptible [sə'sɛptəbəl] *adj* **~ to** : prédisposé à

suspect [ˈsʌsˌpɛkt, səˈspɛkt] *adj* : suspect — ∼ [ˈsʌsˌpɛkt] *n* : suspect *m*, -pecte *f* — ∼ [səˈspɛkt] *vt* **1** : douter de, se méfier de **2** ∼ **s.o. of** : soupçonner qqn de

suspend [səˈspɛnd] *vt* : suspendre — **suspenders** [səˈspɛndərz] *npl* : bretelles *fpl* — **suspense** [səˈspɛnts] *n* **1** : incertitude *f* **2** : suspense *m* (au cinéma, etc.)

suspicion [səˈspɪʃən] *n* : soupçon *m* — **suspicious** [səˈspɪʃəs] *adj* **1** QUESTIONABLE : suspect **2** DISTRUSTFUL : soupçonneux

sustain [səˈsteɪn] *vt* **1** SUPPORT : soutenir **2** NOURISH : nourrir **3** SUFFER : subir

swagger [ˈswægər] *vi* : se pavaner

swallow[1] [ˈswɑlo:] *vt* **1** : avaler **2** *or* ∼ **up** : engloutir — ∼ *n* : gorgée *f*

swallow[2] *n* : hirondelle *f*

swam → **swim**

swamp [ˈswɑmp] *n* : marais *m*, marécage *m* — ∼ *vt* : inonder — **swampy** [ˈswɑmpi] *adj* **swampier; -est** : marécageux

swan [ˈswɑn] *n* : cygne *m*

swap [ˈswɑp] *vt* **swapped; swapping** : échanger — ∼ *n* : échange *m*

swarm [ˈswɔrm] *n* : essaim *m* (d'abeilles, etc.) — ∼ *vi* ∼ **with** : grouiller de

swat [ˈswɑt] *vt* **swatted; swatting** : écraser (un insecte)

sway [ˈsweɪ] *n* **1** : balancement *m* **2** INFLUENCE : influence *f* — ∼ *vi* : se balancer — *vt* : influencer

swear [ˈswær] *v* **swore** [ˈswor]; **sworn** [ˈsworn]; **swearing** *vi* CURSE : jurer — *vt* VOW : jurer — **swearword** [ˈswærˌwərd] *n* : juron *m*

sweat [ˈswɛt] *vi* **sweat** *or* **sweated; sweating** : transpirer — ∼ *n* : sueur *f*, transpiration *f*

sweater [ˈswɛt̬ər] *n* : pull-over *m France*, chandail *m*

sweaty [ˈswɛt̬i] *adj* **sweatier; -est** : en sueur

sweep [ˈswi:p] *v* **swept** [ˈswɛpt] **sweeping** *vt* **1** : balayer **2** *or* ∼ **aside** : écarter — *vi* : balayer — ∼ *n* **1** : coup *m* de balai **2** SCOPE : étendue *f* — **sweeping** [ˈswi:pɪŋ] *adj* **1** WIDE : large **2** EXTENSIVE : de grande portée

sweet [ˈswi:t] *adj* **1** : doux, sucré **2** PLEASANT : agréable, gentil — ∼ *n* : bonbon *m*, dessert *m* — **sweeten** [ˈswi:tən] *vt* : sucrer — **sweetener** [ˈswi:tənər] *n* : édulcorant *m* — **sweetheart** [ˈswi:tˌhɑrt] *n* **1** : petit ami *m*, petite amie *f* **2** (*used as a term of address*) : chéri *m*, -rie *f* — **sweetness** [ˈswi:tnəs] *n* : douceur *f* — **sweet potato** *n* : patate *f* douce

swell [ˈswɛl] *vi* **swelled; swelled** *or* **swollen** [ˈswo:lən, ˈswʌl-]; **swelling 1** *or* ∼ **up** : enfler, gonfler **2** INCREASE : augmenter — ∼ *n* : houle *f* (de la mer) — **swelling** [ˈswɛlɪŋ] *n* : enflure *f*, gonflement *m*

sweltering [ˈswɛltərɪŋ] *adj* : étouffant

swept → **sweep**

swerve [ˈswərv] *vi* **swerved; swerving** : faire une embardée — ∼ *n* : embardée *f*

swift [ˈswɪft] *adj* : rapide — **swiftly** [ˈswɪftli] *adv* : rapidement

swim [ˈswɪm] *vi* **swam** [ˈswæm]; **swum** [ˈswʌm]; **swimming 1** : nager **2** REEL : tourner — ∼ *n* **1** : baignade *f* **2 go for a** ∼ : aller se baigner — **swimmer** [ˈswɪmər] *n* : nageur *m*, -geuse *f*

swindle [ˈswɪndəl] *vt* **-dled; -dling** : escroquer — ∼ *n* : escroquerie *f* — **swindler** [ˈswɪndələr] *n* : escroc *m*

swine [ˈswaɪn] *ns & pl* : porc *m*

swing [ˈswɪŋ] *v* **swung** [ˈswʌŋ]; **swinging** *vt* : balancer, faire osciller — *vi* **1** : se balancer, osciller **2** SWIVEL : tourner — ∼ *n* **1** : va-et-vient *m*, balancement *m* **2** : balançoire *f* (dans un terrain de jeu) **3 be in full** ∼ : battre son plein

swipe [ˈswaɪp] *vt* **swiped; swiping 1** : passer dans un lecteur de cartes **2** STEAL : piquer *fam*

swirl [ˈswərl] *vi* : tourbillonner — ∼ *n* : tourbillon *m*

swish [ˈswɪʃ] *vi* RUSTLE : faire un bruit léger

Swiss [ˈswɪs] *adj* : suisse

switch [ˈswɪʧ] *n* **1** CHANGE : changement *m* **2** : interrupteur *m* (d'électricité), bouton *m* (d'une radio ou d'une télévision) — ∼ *vt* **1** CHANGE : changer de **2** ∼ **on** : ouvrir, allumer **3** ∼ **off** : couper, fermer, éteindre — *vi* SWAP : échanger — **switchboard** [ˈswɪʧˌbord] *n or* **telephone** ∼ : standard *m*

swivel [ˈswɪvəl] *vi* **-eled** *or* **-elled; -eling** *or* **-elling** : pivoter

swollen → **swell**

swoop [ˈswu:p] *vi* ∼ **down on** : s'abattre sur — ∼ *n* : descente *f* en piqué

sword [ˈsɔrd] *n* : épée *f*

swordfish [ˈsɔrdˌfɪʃ] *n* : espadon *m*

swore, sworn → **swear**

swum → **swim**
swung → **swing**
syllable [ˈsɪləbəl] *n* : syllabe *f*
syllabus [ˈsɪləbəs] *n, pl* **-bi** [-ˌbaɪ] *or* **-buses** : programme *m* (d'études)
symbol [ˈsɪmbəl] *n* : symbole *m* — **symbolic** [sɪmˈbɑlɪk] *adj* : symbolique — **symbolism** [ˈsɪmbəˌlɪzəm] *n* : symbolisme *m* — **symbolize** [ˈsɪmbəˌlaɪz] *vt* **-ized; -izing** : symboliser
symmetry [ˈsɪmətri] *n, pl* **-tries** : symétrie *f* — **symmetrical** [səˈmɛtrɪkəl] *adj* : symétrique
sympathy [ˈsɪmpəθi] *n, pl* **-thies 1** COMPASSION : sympathie *f* **2** UNDERSTANDING : compréhension *f* **3** CONDOLENCES : condoléances *fpl* — **sympathetic** [ˌsɪmpəˈθɛṭɪk] *adj* **1** COMPASSIONATE : compatissant **2** UNDERSTANDING : compréhensif — **sympathize** [ˈsɪmpəˌθaɪz] *vi* **-thized; -thizing ~ with 1** PITY : plaindre **2** UNDERSTAND : comprendre
symphony [ˈsɪmpfəni] *n, pl* **-nies** : symphonie *f*
symposium [sɪmˈpoːziəm] *n, pl* **-sia** [-ziə] *or* **-siums** : symposium *m*
symptom [ˈsɪmptəm] *n* : symptôme *m*
synagogue [ˈsɪnəˌɡɑɡ, -ˌɡɔɡ] *n* : synagogue *f*
synchronize [ˈsɪŋkrəˌnaɪz, ˈsɪn-] *vt* **-nized; -nizing** : synchroniser
syndrome [ˈsɪnˌdroːm] *n* : syndrome *m*
synonym [ˈsɪnəˌnɪm] *n* : synonyme *m* — **synonymous** [səˈnɑnəməs] *adj* : synonyme
syntax [ˈsɪnˌtæks] *n* : syntaxe *f*
synthesis [ˈsɪnθəsɪs] *n, pl* **-ses** [-ˌsiːz] : synthèse *f* — **synthetic** [sɪnˈθɛṭɪk] *adj* : synthétique
syringe [səˈrɪndʒ, ˈsɪrɪndʒ] *n* : seringue *f*
syrup [ˈsərəp, ˈsɪrəp] *n* : sirop *m*
system [ˈsɪstəm] *n* **1** : système *m* **2** BODY : organisme *m* **3 digestive ~** : appareil *m* digestif — **systematic** [ˌsɪstəˈmæṭɪk] *adj* : systématique

T

t [ˈtiː] *n, pl* **t's** *or* **ts** [ˈtiːz] : t *m*, vingtième lettre de l'alphabet
tab [ˈtæb] *n* **1** FLAP : languette *f* **2 keep ~s on** : surveiller
table [ˈteɪbəl] *n* : table *f* — **tablecloth** [ˈteɪbəlˌklɔθ] *n* : nappe *f* — **tablespoon** [ˈteɪbəlˌspuːn] *n* : cuillère *f* à soupe
tablet [ˈtæblət] *n* **1** : bloc-notes *m* **2** PILL : comprimé *m*
tabloid [ˈtæˌblɔɪd] *n* : quotidien *m* populaire, tabloïde *m*
taboo [təˈbuː, tæ-] *adj* : tabou — **~** *n, pl* **-boos** : tabou *m*
tacit [ˈtæsɪt] *adj* : tacite
taciturn [ˈtæsɪˌtərn] *adj* : taciturne
tack [ˈtæk] *vt* **1** ATTACH : clouer **2 ~ on** ADD : ajouter
tackle [ˈtakəl] *n* **1** GEAR : équipement *m*, matériel *m* **2** : plaquage *m* (au football) — **~** *vt* **-led; -ling 1** : plaquer (au football) **2** CONFRONT : s'attaquer à
tacky [ˈtæki] *adj* **tackier; tackiest 1** STICKY : collant **2** GAUDY : de mauvais goût
tact [ˈtækt] *n* : tact *m* — **tactful** [ˈtæktfəl] *adj* : plein de tact
tactical [ˈtæktɪkəl] *adj* : tactique — **tactic** [ˈtæktɪk] *n* : tactique *f* — **tactics** [ˈtæktɪks] *ns & pl* : tactique *f*
tactless [ˈtæktləs] *adj* : qui manque de tact
tadpole [ˈtædˌpoːl] *n* : têtard *m*
tag[1] [ˈtæɡ] *n* LABEL : étiquette *f* — **~** *v* **tagged; tagging** *vt* LABEL : étiqueter — *vi* **~ along** : suivre
tag[2] *vt* : toucher (au jeu de chat)
tail [ˈteɪl] *n* **1** : queue *f* **2 ~s** *npl* : pile *f* (d'une pièce de monnaie) — **~** *vt* FOLLOW : suivre
tailor [ˈteɪlər] *n* : tailleur *m* — **~** *vt* **1** : faire sur mesure (un vêtement) **2** ADAPT : adapter
taint [ˈteɪnt] *vt* : entacher, souiller
Taiwanese [ˌtaɪwəˈniːz, -ˈniːs] *adj* : taiwanais
take [ˈteɪk] *v* **took** [ˈtʊk]; **taken** [ˈteɪkən]; **taking** *vt* **1** : prendre **2** BRING : emmener **3** CARRY : porter **4** REQUIRE : demander **5** ACCEPT : accepter **6** BEAR : supporter **7** : passer (un examen) **8 I ~ it that** : je suppose que **9 ~ a walk** : se promener **10 ~ apart** DISMANTLE : démonter **11 ~ back** : retirer **12 ~ in** ALTER : reprendre **13 ~ in** UNDERSTAND : saisir **14 ~ in** DECEIVE : tromper **15 ~ off** REMOVE : enlever **16 ~ on** : assumer (une responsabilité) **17 ~ over** : prendre le pouvoir **18 ~ place** : avoir lieu **19**

~ **up** SHORTEN : raccourcir **20** ~ **up** OCCUPY : prendre — *vi* **1** WORK : faire effet **2** ~ **off** DEPART : s'en aller **3** ~ **off** : décoller (se dit d'un avion) — ~ *n* **1** PROCEEDS : recette *f* **2** : prise *f* (au cinéma) — **takeoff** ['teɪk,ɔf] *n* : décollage *m* (d'un avion) — **takeover** ['teɪk,o:vər] *n* : prise *f* de contrôle (d'une compagnie)

talcum powder ['tælkəm] *n* : talc *m*

tale ['teɪl] *n* : conte *m*, histoire *f*

talent ['tælənt] *n* : talent *m* — **talented** ['tæləntəd] *adj* : talentueux, doué

talk ['tɔk] *vt* **1** : parler **2** ~ **about** : parler de **3** ~ **to/with** : parler avec — *vi* **1** SPEAK : parler **2** ~ **over** : parler de, discuter — ~ *n* **1** CONVERSATION : entretien *m*, conversation *f* **2** SPEECH : discours *m*, exposé *m* — **talkative** ['tɔkət̬ɪv] *adj* : bavard

tall ['tɔl] *adj* **1** : grand **2 how** ~ **are you?** : combien mesures-tu?

tally ['tæli] *n, pl* **-lies** : compte *m* — ~ *v* **-lied; -lying** *vt* RECKON : calculer — *vi* MATCH : correspondre

tambourine [,tæmbə'ri:n] *n* : tambourin *m*

tame ['teɪm] *adj* **tamer; tamest 1** : apprivoisé **2** : docile — ~ *vt* **tamed; taming** : apprivoiser, dompter

tamper ['tæmpər] *vi* ~ **with** : forcer (une serrure), falsifier (un document)

tampon ['tæm,pɑn] *n* : tampon *m* (hygiénique)

tan ['tæn] *v* **tanned; tanning** *vt* : tanner (du cuir) — *vi* : bronzer — ~ *n* **1** SUNTAN : bronzage *m* **2** : brun *m* clair (couleur)

tang ['tæŋ] *n* : goût *m* piquant

tangent ['tændʒənt] *n* : tangente *f*

tangerine ['tændʒə,ri:n, ,tændʒə'-] *n* : mandarine *f*

tangible ['tændʒəbəl] *adj* : tangible

tangle ['tæŋgəl] *v* **-gled; -gling** *vt* : enchevêtrer — *vi* : s'emmêler — ~ *n* : enchevêtrement *m*

tango ['tæŋ,go:] *n, pl* **-gos** : tango *m*

tank ['tæŋk] *n* **1** : réservoir *m*, cuve *f* **2** : char *m* (militaire) — **tanker** ['tæŋkər] *n* **1** *or* **oil** ~ : pétrolier *m* **2** *or* ~ **truck** : camion-citern *m*

tantalizing ['tæntə,laɪzɪŋ] *adj* : alléchant

tantrum ['tæntrəm] *n* **throw a** ~ : piquer une crise

tap[1] ['tæp] *n* FAUCET : robinet *m* — ~ *vt* **tapped; tapping** : mettre sur écoute

tap[2] *v* **tapped; tapping** *vt* TOUCH : tapoter, taper — *vi* : taper légèrement — ~ *n* : petit coup *m*

tape ['teɪp] *n or* **adhesive** ~ : ruban *m* adhésif — ~ *vt* **taped; taping 1** : coller avec un ruban adhésif **2** RECORD : enregistrer — **tape measure** *n* : mètre *m* ruban

taper ['teɪpər] *vi* **1** : s'effiler **2** *or* ~ **off** : diminuer

tapestry ['tæpəstri] *n, pl* **-tries** : tapisserie *f*

tar ['tɑr] *n* : goudron *m* — ~ *vt* **tarred; tarring** : goudronner

tarantula [tə'ræntʃələ, -'ræntələ] *n* : tarentule *f*

target ['tɑrgət] *n* **1** : cible *f* **2** GOAL : objectif *m*, but *m*

tariff ['tærɪf] *n* : tarif *m* douanier

tarnish ['tɑrnɪʃ] *vt* : ternir — *vi* : se ternir

tarpaulin [tɑr'pɔlən, 'tɑrpə-] *n* : bâche *f*

tart[1] ['tɑrt] *adj* SOUR : aigre

tart[2] *n* : tartelette *f*

tartan ['tɑrtən] *n* : tartan *m*, tissu *m* écossais

task ['tæsk] *n* : tâche *f*

tassel ['tæsəl] *n* : gland *m*

taste ['teɪst] *v* **tasted; tasting** *vt* : goûter (à) — *vi* ~ **like** : avoir le goût de — ~ *n* : goût *m* — **tasteful** ['teɪstfəl] *adj* : de bon goût — **tasteless** ['teɪstləs] *adj* **1** FLAVORLESS : sans goût **2** COARSE : de mauvais goût — **tasty** ['teɪsti] *adj* **tastier; tastiest** : savoureux

tattered ['tæt̬ərd] *adj* : en lambeaux

tattle ['tæt̬əl] *vi* **-tled; -tling** ~ **on s.o.** : dénoncer qqn

tattoo [tæ'tu:] *vt* : tatouer — ~ *n* : tatouage *m*

taught → **teach**

taunt ['tɔnt] *n* : raillerie *f* — ~ *vt* : railler

taut ['tɔt] *adj* : tendu

tavern ['tævərn] *n* : taverne *f*

tax ['tæks] *vt* **1** : imposer (une personne), taxer (de l'argent, des marchandises) **2** STRAIN : mettre à l'épreuve — ~ *n* : taxe *f*, impôt *m* — **taxable** ['tæksəbəl] *adj* : imposable — **taxation** [tæk'seɪʃən] *n* : taxation *f*, imposition *f* — **tax–exempt** ['tæksɪg'zɛmpt, -ɛg-] *adj* : exempt d'impôts

taxi ['tæksi] *n, pl* **taxis** : taxi *m*

taxpayer ['tæks,peɪər] *n* : contribuable *mf*

tea ['ti:] *n* : thé *m*

teach ['ti:tʃ] *v* **taught** ['tɔt]; **teaching** *vt* **1** : enseigner (un sujet) **2** ~ **s.o. to**

: apprendre qqn à — *vi* : enseigner — **teacher** ['ti:ʧər] *n* : instituteur *m*, -trice *f* (à l'école primaire); professeur *m* — **teaching** ['ti:ʧɪŋ] *n* : enseignement *m*

teacup ['ti:ˌkʌp] *n* : tasse *f* à thé

team ['ti:m] *n* : équipe *f* — ~ *vi* ~ **up with** : faire équipe avec — ~ *adj* : d'équipe — **teammate** ['ti:mˌmeɪt] *n* : coéquipier *m*, -pière *f* — **teamwork** ['ti:mˌwərk] *n* : travail *m* d'équipe

teapot ['ti:ˌpɑt] *n* : théière *f*

tear[1] ['tær] *v* **tore** ['tor]; **torn** ['torn]; **tearing** *vt* **1** RIP : déchirer **2** ~ **down** : démolir **3** ~ **off** *or* ~ **out** : arracher **4** ~ **up** : déchirer — *vi* **1** : se déchirer **2** RUSH : se précipiter — ~ *n* : déchirure *f*

tear[2] ['tɪr] *n* : larme *f* — **tearful** ['tɪrfəl] *adj* : larmoyant

tease ['ti:z] *vt* **teased; teasing** : taquiner — ~ *n* : taquin *m*, -quine *f*

teaspoon ['ti:ˌspu:n] *n* : petite cuillère *f*, cuillère *f* à café

technical ['tɛknɪkəl] *adj* : technique — **technicality** [ˌtɛknəˈkæləṭi] *n*, *pl* **-ties** : détail *m* technique — **technician** [tɛkˈnɪʃən] *n* : technicien *m*, -cienne *f*

technique [tɛkˈni:k] *n* : technique *f*

technological [ˌtɛknəˈlɑʤɪkəl] *adj* : technologique — **technology** [tɛkˈnɑləʤi] *n*, *pl* **-gies** : technologie *f*

tedious ['ti:diəs] *adj* : fastidieux — **tedium** ['ti:diəm] : ennui *m*

teem ['ti:m] *vi* ~ **with** : foisonner de, abonder en

teenage ['ti:nˌeɪʤ] *or* **teenaged** [-ˌeɪʤd] *adj* : adolescent, d'adolescence — **teenager** ['ti:nˌeɪʤər] *n* : adolescent *m*, -cente *f* — **teens** ['ti:nz] *npl* : adolescence *f*

teepee → **tepee**

teeter ['ti:ṭər] *vi* : chanceler

teeth → **tooth** — **teethe** ['ti:ð] *vi* **teethed; teething** : faire ses dents

telecommunication [ˌtɛləkəˌmju:nəˈkeɪʃən] *n* : télécommunication *f*

telegram ['tɛləˌgræm] *n* : télégramme *m*

telegraph ['tɛləˌgræf] *n* : télégraphe *m*

telephone ['tɛləˌfo:n] *n* : téléphone *m* — ~ *v* **-phoned; -phoning** *vt* : téléphoner à — *vi* : appeler, téléphoner

telescope ['tɛləˌsko:p] *n* : télescope *m*

televise ['tɛləˌvaɪz] *vt* **-vised; -vising** : téléviser — **television** ['tɛləˌvɪʒən] *n* **1** : télévision *f* **2** *or* ~ **set** : téléviseur *m*

tell ['tɛl] *v* **told** ['to:ld]; **telling** *vt* **1** : dire **2** RELATE : raconter **3** DISTINGUISH : distinguer **4** ~ **s.o. off** : réprimander qqn — *vi* **1** : dire **2** KNOW : savoir **3** SHOW : se faire sentir **4** ~ **on s.o.** : dénoncer qqn — **teller** ['tɛlər] *n or* **bank** ~ : caissier *m*, -sière *f*

temp ['tɛmp] *n* : intérimaire *mf; occasionnel m*, -nelle *f Can*

temper ['tɛmpər] *vt* MODERATE : tempérer — ~ *n* **1** MOOD : humeur *f* **2 lose one's** ~ : se mettre en colère — **temperament** ['tɛmpərmənt, -prə-, -pərə-] *n* : tempérament *m* — **temperamental** [ˌtɛmpərˈmɛntəl, -prə-, -pərə-] *adj* : capricieux — **temperate** ['tɛmpərət] *adj* **1** MILD : tempéré **2** MODERATE : modéré

temperature ['tɛmpərˌʧur, -prə-, -ʧər] *n* **1** : température *f* **2 have a** ~ : avoir de la température

temple ['tɛmpəl] *n* **1** : temple *m* **2** : tempe *f* (en anatomie)

tempo ['tɛmˌpo:] *n*, *pl* **-pi** [-ˌpi:] *or* **-pos** **1** : tempo *m* **2** PACE : rythme *m*

temporarily [ˌtɛmpəˈrɛrəli] *adv* : temporairement — **temporary** ['tɛmpəˌrɛri] *adj* : temporaire

tempt ['tɛmpt] *vt* : tenter — **temptation** [tɛmpˈteɪʃən] *n* : tentation *f*

ten ['tɛn] *n* : dix *m* — ~ *adj* : dix

tenacious [təˈneɪʃəs] *adj* : tenace — **tenacity** [təˈnæsəṭi] *n* : ténacité *f*

tenant ['tɛnənt] *n* : locataire *mf*

tend[1] ['tɛnd] *vt* : s'occuper de

tend[2] *vi* ~ **to** : avoir tendance à — **tendency** ['tɛndəntsi] *n*, *pl* **-cies** : tendance *f*

tender[1] ['tɛndər] *adj* **1** : tendre **2** PAINFUL : douloureux

tender[2] *vt* : présenter — ~ *n* **1** : soumission *f* **2 legal** ~ : cours *m* légal

tenderloin ['tɛndərˌlɔɪn] *n* : filet *m* (de porc, etc.)

tenderness ['tɛndərnəs] *n* : tendresse *f*

tendon ['tɛndən] *n* : tendon *m*

tenet ['tɛnət] *n* : principe *m*

tennis ['tɛnəs] *n* : tennis *m*

tenor ['tɛnər] *n* : ténor *m*

tense[1] ['tɛnts] *n* : temps *m* (en grammaire)

tense[2] *v* **tensed; tensing** *vt* : tendre — *vi or* ~ **up** : se raidir — ~ *adj* **tenser; tensest** : tendu — **tension** ['tɛnʧən] *n* : tension *f*

tent ['tɛnt] *n* : tente *f*

tentacle ['tɛntɪkəl] *n* : tentacule *m*

tentative ['tɛntəṭɪv] *adj* **1** HESITANT : hésitant **2** PROVISIONAL : provisoire

tenth [ˈtɛnθ] *n* **1** : dixième *mf* **2 September ~** : le dix septembre — **~** *adj* : dixième
tenuous [ˈtɛnjʊəs] *adj* : ténu
tepee [ˈti:ˌpi:] *n* : tipi *m*
tepid [ˈtɛpɪd] *adj* : tiède
term [ˈtərm] *n* **1** WORD : terme *m* **2** : trimestre *m* (scolaire) **3 be on good ~s** : être en bons termes — **~** *vt* : appeler, nommer
terminal [ˈtərmənəl] *adj* : terminal — **~** *n* **1** : borne *f* (en électricité) **2** *or* **computer ~** : terminal *m* **3** : terminus *m* (de train, de bus)
terminate [ˈtərməˌneɪt] *v* **-nated; -nating** *vi* : se terminer — *vt* : terminer — **termination** [ˌtərməˈneɪʃən] *n* : fin *f*
terminology [ˌtərməˈnɑləʤi] *n, pl* **-gies** : terminologie *f*
termite [ˈtərˌmaɪt] *n* : termite *m*
terrace [ˈtɛrəs] *n* : terrasse *f*
terrain [təˈreɪn] *n* : terrain *m*
terrestrial [təˈrɛstriəl] *adj* : terrestre
terrible [ˈtɛrəbəl] *adj* : terrible, épouvantable — **terribly** [ˈtɛrəbli] *adv* : terriblement
terrier [ˈtɛriər] *n* : terrier *m*
terrific [təˈrɪfɪk] *adj* **1** FRIGHTFUL : terrible **2** EXCELLENT : formidable
terrify [ˈtɛrəˌfaɪ] *vt* **-fied; -fying** : terrifier — **terrifying** [ˈtɛrəˌfaɪɪŋ] *adj* : terrifiant
territory [ˈtɛrəˌtori] *n, pl* **-ries** : territoire *m* — **territorial** [ˌtɛrəˈtoriəl] *adj* : territorial
terror [ˈtɛrər] *n* : terreur *f* — **terrorism** [ˈtɛrərˌɪzəm] *n* : terrorisme *m* — **terrorist** [ˈtɛrərɪst] *n* : terroriste *mf* — **terrorize** [ˈtɛrərˌaɪz] *vt* **-ized; -izing** : terroriser
terse [ˈtərs] *adj* **terser; tersest** : concis, succinct
test [ˈtɛst] *n* **1** TRIAL : épreuve *f* **2** EXAM : examen *m*, test *m* **3 blood ~** : analyse *f* de sang — **~** *vt* **1** TRY : essayer **2** QUIZ : examiner, tester **3** : analyser (le sang, etc.), examiner (les yeux, etc.)
testament [ˈtɛstəmənt] *n* **1** WILL : testament *m* **2 the Old/New Testament** : l'Ancien, le Nouveau Testament
testicle [ˈtɛstɪkəl] *n* : testicule *m*
testify [ˈtɛstəˌfaɪ] *v* **-fied; -fying** : témoigner
testimony [ˈtɛstəˌmo:ni] *n, pl* **-nies** : témoignage *m*
test tube *n* : éprouvette *f*
tetanus [ˈtɛtənəs] *n* : tétanos *m*
tether [ˈtɛðər] *vt* : attacher
text [ˈtɛkst] *n* : texte *m* — **textbook** [ˈtɛkstˌbʊk] *n* : manuel *m* scolaire
textile [ˈtɛkˌstaɪl, ˈtɛkstəl] *n* : textile *m*
texture [ˈtɛksʧər] *n* : texture *f*
than [ˈðæn] *conj* : que — **~** *prep* : que, de
thank [ˈθæŋk] *vt* **1** : remercier **2 ~ you** : merci — **thankful** [ˈθæŋkfəl] *adj* : reconnaissant — **thankfully** [ˈθæŋkfəli] *adv* **1** : avec reconnaissance **2** FORTUNATELY : heureusement — **thankless** [ˈθæŋkləs] *adj* : ingrat — **thanks** [ˈθæŋks] *npl* **1** : remerciements *mpl* **2 ~ to** : grâce à
Thanksgiving [θæŋksˈgɪvɪŋ, ˈθæŋksˌ-] *n* : jour *m* d'Action de Grâces
that [ˈðæt] *pron, pl* **those** [ˈðo:z] **1** : cela, ce, ça **2** (*more distant*) : celui-là, celle-là, ceux-là, celles-là **3** WHO : qui **4** (*used to introduce relative clauses*) : que **5 is ~ you?** : c'est toi? **6 ~ is** : c'est-à-dire — **~** *conj* **1** : que **2 in order ~** : afin que — **~** *adj, pl* **those** **1** : ce, cet, cette, ces **2 ~ one** : celui-là, celle-là — **~** *adv* VERY : tellement, très
thaw [ˈθɔ] *vt* : dégeler (des aliments) — *vi* **1** : se dégeler **2** MELT : fondre — **~** *n* : dégel *m*
the [ðə, *before vowel sounds usu* ði:] *art* **1** : le, la, l', les **2** PER : le, la **3 ~ English** : les Anglais — **~** *adv* **1** : le **2 ~ sooner ~ better** : le plus tôt sera le mieux
theater *or* **theatre** [ˈθi:əʈər] *n* : théâtre *m* — **theatrical** [θiˈætrɪkəl] *adj* : théâtral
theft [ˈθɛft] *n* : vol *m*
their [ˈðɛr] *adj* : leur — **theirs** [ˈðɛrz] *pron* **1** : le leur, la leur, les leurs **2 some friends of ~** : des amis à eux
them [ˈðɛm] *pron* **1** (*used as direct object*) : les **2** (*used as indirect object*) : leur **3** (*used as object of a preposition*) : eux, elles
theme [ˈθi:m] *n* : thème *m*
themselves [ðəmˈsɛlvz, ðɛm-] *pron* **1** (*used reflexively*) : se **2** (*used emphatically*) : eux-mêmes, elles-mêmes **3** (*used after a preposition*) : eux, elles, eux-mêmes, elles-mêmes **4 by ~** : tous seuls, toutes seules
then [ˈðɛn] *adv* **1** : alors **2** NEXT : ensuite, puis **3** BESIDES : et puis — **~** *adj* : d'alors, de l'époque
theology [θiˈɑləʤi] *n, pl* **-gies** : théologie *f*
theorem [ˈθi:ərəm, ˈθɪrəm] *n* : théorème *m* — **theoretical** [ˌθi:əˈrɛtɪkəl]

adj : théorique — **theory** [ˈθi:əri, ˈθɪri] *n, pl* **-ries** : théorie *f*

therapeutic [ˌθɛrəˈpju:t̬ɪk] *adj* : thérapeutique — **therapist** [ˈθɛrəpɪst] *n* : thérapeute *mf* — **therapy** [ˈθɛrəpi] *n, pl* **-pies** : thérapie *f*

there [ˈðær] *adv* **1** *or* **over ~** : là-bas **2 down/up ~** : là-dessous, là-haut **3 in ~** : là-dedans **4 ~, it's done!** : voilà, c'est fini! **5 who's ~?** : qui est là? — **~** *pron* **1 ~ is/are** : il y a **2 ~ are three of us** : nous sommes trois — **thereabouts** *or* **thereabout** [ðærəˈbauts, -ˈbaut, ˈðærəˌ-] *adv* : dans les environs, par là — **thereafter** [ðærˈæftər] *adv* : par la suite — **thereby** [ðærˈbaɪ, ˈðærˌbaɪ] *adv* : ainsi — **therefore** [ˈðærˌfor] *adv* : donc, par conséquent

thermal [ˈθərməl] *adj* : thermal, thermique

thermometer [θərˈmɑmət̬ər] *n* : thermomètre *m*

thermos [ˈθərməs] *n* : thermos *mf*

thermostat [ˈθərməˌstæt] *n* : thermostat *m*

thesaurus [θɪˈsɔrəs] *n, pl* **-sauri** [-ˈsɔrˌaɪ] *or* **-sauruses** [-ˈsɔrəsəz] : dictionnaire *m* analogique, dictionnaire *m* des synonymes

these → **this**

thesis [ˈθi:sɪs] *n, pl* **theses** [ˈθiˌsi:z] : thèse *f*

they [ˈðeɪ] *pron* **1** : ils, elles **2 as ~ say** : comme on dit **3 there ~ are** : les voici — **they'd** [ˈðeɪd] (*contraction of* **they had** *or* **they would**) → **have, would** — **they'll** [ˈðeɪl, ˈðel] (*contraction of* **they shall** *or* **they will**) → **shall, will** — **they're** [ˈðɛr] (*contraction of* **they are**) → **be** — **they've** [ˈðeɪv] (*contraction of* **they have**) → **have**

thick [ˈθɪk] *adj* **1** : épais **2** DENSE : bête **3 a ~ accent** : un accent prononcé **4 two inches ~** : deux pouces d'épaisseur — **~** *n* **in the ~ of** : au plus fort de — **thicken** [ˈθɪkən] *vt* : épaissir (une sauce, etc.) — **~** *vi* : s'épaissir — **thicket** [ˈθɪkət] *n* : fourré *m* — **thickness** [ˈθɪknəs] *n* : épaisseur *f*, grosseur *f*

thief [ˈθi:f] *n, pl* **thieves** [ˈθi:vz] : voleur *m*, -leuse *f*

thigh [ˈθaɪ] *n* : cuisse *f*

thimble [ˈθɪmbəl] *n* : dé *m* à coudre

thin [ˈθɪn] *adj* **thinner; thinnest 1** : mince **2** SPARSE : clairsemé **3** WATERY : clair (se dit d'une soupe, etc.) — **~** *v* **thinned; thinning** *vt* DILUTE : diluer — *vi* : s'éclaircir

thing [ˈθɪŋ] *n* **1** : chose *f* **2 ~s** *npl* BELONGINGS : affaires *fpl* **3 for one ~** : en premier lieu **4 how are ~s?** : comment ça va? **5 the important ~ is...** : l'important c'est...

think [ˈθɪŋk] *v* **thought** [ˈθɔt]; **thinking** *vt* **1** : penser **2** BELIEVE : croire **3 ~ up** : inventer — *vi* **1** : penser **2 ~ about** *or* **~ of** CONSIDER : penser à **3 ~ of** REMEMBER : se rappeler

thinness [ˈθɪnnəs] *n* : minceur *f*

third [ˈθərd] *adj* : troisième — **~** *or* **thirdly** [-li] *adv* : troisième, troisièmement — **~** *n* **1** : troisième *mf* (dans une série) **2** : tiers *m* (en mathématiques) **3 December ~** : le trois décembre — **Third World** *n* : le tiers-monde

thirst [ˈθərst] *n* : soif *f* — **thirsty** [ˈθərsti] *adj* **thirstier; thirstiest 1** : assoiffé **2 be ~** : avoir soif

thirteen [ˌθərˈti:n] *n* : treize *m* — **~** *adj* : treize — **thirteenth** [ˌθərˈti:nθ] *n* **1** : treizième *mf* **2 January ~** : le treize janvier — **~** *adj* : treizième

thirty [ˈθərt̬i] *n, pl* **-ties** : trente *m* — **~** *adj* : trente — **thirtieth** [ˈθərt̬iəθ] *n* **1** : trentième *mf* **2 May ~** : le trente mai — **~** *adj* : trentième

this [ˈðɪs] *pron, pl* **these 1** : ce, ceci **2** (*in comparisons*) : celui-ci, celle-ci, ceux-ci, celles-ci **3 ~ is your room** : voici ta chambre — **~** *adj, pl* **these** [ˈði:z] **1** : ce, cet, cette, ces **2 ~ one** : celui-ci, celle-ci **3 ~ way** : par ici — **~** *adv* : si, aussi

thistle [ˈθɪsəl] *n* : chardon *m*

thorn [ˈθɔrn] *n* : épine *f* — **thorny** [ˈθɔrni] *adj* **thornier; thorniest** : épineux

thorough [ˈθəˌro:] *adj* **1** : consciencieux **2** COMPLETE : complet — **thoroughly** [ˈθəroli] *adv* **1** : à fond **2** COMPLETELY : absolument — **Thoroughbred** [ˈθəroˌbrɛd] *n* : pur-sang *m* — **thoroughfare** [ˈθəroˌfær] *n* : voie *f* publique

those → **that**

though [ˈðo:] *conj* : bien que, quoique — **~** *adv* **1** : cependant, pourtant **2 as ~** : comme si

thought [ˈθɔt] → **think** — **~** *n* **1** : pensée *f* **2** IDEA : idée *f* — **thoughtful** [ˈθɔtfəl] *adj* **1** : pensif **2** KIND : aimable — **thoughtless** [ˈθɔtləs] *adj* **1** : irréfléchi **2** RUDE : manquer d'égard (envers qqn)

thousand ['θaʊzənd] *n, pl* **-sands** *or* **-sand** : mille *m* — **~** *adj* : mille — **thousandth** ['θaʊzəntθ] *n* : millième *mf* — **~** *adj* : millième
thrash ['θræʃ] *vi or* **~ about** : se débattre
thread ['θrɛd] *n* : fil *m* — **~** *vt* : enfiler (une aiguille, des perles, etc.) — **threadbare** ['θrɛd'bær] *adj* : usé
threat ['θrɛt] *n* : menace *f* — **threaten** ['θrɛtən] *v* : menacer — **threatening** ['θrɛtənɪŋ] *adj* : menaçant
three ['θri:] *n* : trois *m* — **~** *adj* : trois — **three hundred** *adj* : trois cent
threshold ['θrɛʃˌho:ld, -ˌo:ld] *n* : seuil *m*
threw → **throw**
thrift ['θrɪft] *n* : économie *f* — **thrifty** ['θrɪfti] *adj* **thriftier; thriftiest** : économe
thrill ['θrɪl] *vt* : transporter (de joie) — **~** *n* : frisson *m* — **thriller** ['θrɪlər] *n* : thriller *m* — **thrilling** ['θrɪlɪŋ] *adj* : excitant
thrive ['θraɪv] *vi* **throve** ['θro:v] *or* **thrived; thriven** ['θrɪvən] **1** FLOURISH : réussir **2** PROSPER : prospérer
throat ['θro:t] *n* : gorge *f*
throb ['θrɑb] *vi* **throbbed; throbbing 1** : battre, palpiter **2** VIBRATE : vibrer **3** **~ with pain** : lanciner
throes ['θro:z] *npl* **1** : agonie *f* **2 in the ~ of** : en proie à
throne ['θro:n] *n* : trône *m*
throng ['θrɔŋ] *n* : foule *f*
through ['θru:] *prep* **1** : à travers **2** BECAUSE OF : à cause de **3** BY : par **4** DURING : pendant **5 Monday ~ Friday** : du lundi au vendredi **6** → **throughout** — **~** *adv* **1** : à travers **2** COMPLETELY : complètement **3 let ~** : laisser passer — **~** *adj* **1 be ~** : avoir terminé **2 ~ traffic** : trafic en transit — **throughout** [θru:'aʊt] *prep* **1** : partout dans **2** DURING : pendant
throw ['θro:] *vt* **threw** ['θru:]; **thrown** ['θro:n]; **throwing 1** : lancer (une balle, etc.) **2** CONFUSE : déconcerter **3** **~ a party** : organiser une fête **4 ~ away** *or* **~ out** : jeter — **~** *n* TOSS : lancer *m*, jet *m* — **throw up** *vt* : vomir, renvoyer *Can fam*, restituer *Can fam*
thrush ['θrʌʃ] *n* : grive *f* (oiseau)
thrust ['θrʌst] *vt* **thrust; thrusting 1** : enfoncer, planter **2 ~ upon** : imposer à — **~** *n* : poussée *f*
thud ['θʌd] *n* : bruit *m* sourd
thug ['θʌg] *n* : voyou *m*
thumb ['θʌm] *n* : pouce *m* — **~** *vt or* **~ through** : feuilleter — **thumbnail** ['θʌmˌneɪl] *n* : ongle *m* du pouce — **thumbtack** ['θʌmˌtæk] *n* : punaise *f*
thump ['θʌmp] *vt* : cogner — *vi* : battre fort (se dit du cœur) — **~** *n* : bruit *m* sourd
thunder ['θʌndər] *n* : tonnerre *m* — **~** *vi* : tonner — **~** *vt* SHOUT : vociférer — **thunderbolt** ['θʌndərˌbo:lt] *n* : foudre *f* — **thunderous** ['θʌndərəs] *adj* : étourdissant — **thunderstorm** ['θʌndərˌstorm] *n* : orage *m*
Thursday ['θərzˌdeɪ, -di] *n* : jeudi *m*
thus ['ðʌs] *adv* **1** : ainsi, donc **2 ~ far** : jusqu'à présent
thwart ['θwɔrt] *vt* : contrecarrer
thyme ['taɪm, 'θaɪm] *n* : thym *m*
thyroid ['θaɪˌrɔɪd] *n* : thyroïde *f*
tic ['tɪk] *n* : tic *m* (nerveux)
tick[1] ['tɪk] *n* : tique *f* (insecte)
tick[2] *n* **1** : tic-tac *m* (bruit) **2** CHECK : coche *f* — **~** *vi* : faire tic-tac — *vt* **1** *or* **~ off** CHECK : cocher **2 ~ off** ANNOY : agacer
ticket ['tɪkət] *n* **1** : billet *m* (d'avion, de train, etc.), ticket *m* (d'autobus, de métro) **2** *or* **parking ~** : contravention *f*
tickle ['tɪkəl] *v* **-led; -ling** *vt* **1** : chatouiller **2** AMUSE : amuser — *vi* : chatouiller — **~** *n* : chatouillement *m* — **ticklish** ['tɪkəlɪʃ] *adj* : chatouilleux
tidal wave ['taɪdəl] *n* : raz-de-marée *m*
tidbit ['tɪdˌbɪt] *n* : détail *m* intéressant
tide ['taɪd] *n* : marée *f* — **~** *vt* **tided; tiding ~ over** : dépanner
tidy ['taɪdi] *adj* **-dier; -est** NEAT : propre — **~** *vt* **-died; -dying** *or* **~ up** : ranger
tie ['taɪ] *n* **1** : attache *f*, cordon *m* **2** BOND : lien *m* **3** : match *m* nul (aux sports) **4** NECKTIE : cravate *f* — **~** *v* **tied; tying** *or* **tieing** *vt* **1** : attacher **2** **~ a knot** : faire un nœud — *vi* : faire match nul, être ex æquo
tier ['tɪr] *n* : étage *m*, gradin *m* (d'un stade)
tiger ['taɪgər] *n* : tigre *m*
tight ['taɪt] *adj* **1** : serré, étroit **2** TAUT : tendu **3** STINGY : avare **4 a ~ seal** : une fermeture étanche — **~** *adv* **closed ~** : bien fermé — **tighten** ['taɪtən] *vt* : serrer, resserrer — **tightly** ['taɪtli] *adv* : fermement, bien — **tightrope** ['taɪtˌro:p] *n* : corde *f* raide — **tights** ['taɪts] *npl* : collants *mpl*
tile ['taɪl] *n* : carreau *m*, tuile *f* — **~** *vt*

tiled; tiling : carreler, poser des tuiles sur

till[1] ['tɪl] *prep & conj* → **until**

till[2] *vt* : labourer

till[3] *n* : tiroir-caisse *m*

tilt ['tɪlt] *n* **1** : inclinaison *f* **2 at full ~** : à toute vitesse — **~** *vt* : pencher, incliner — *vi* : se pencher, s'incliner

timber ['tɪmbər] *n* **1** : bois *m* de construction **2** BEAM : poutre *f*

time ['taɪm] *n* **1** : temps *m* **2** AGE : époque *f* **3** : rythme *m* (en musique) **4 at ~s** : parfois **5 at this ~** : en ce moment **6 for the ~ being** : pour le moment **7 from ~ to ~** : de temps à autre **8 have a good ~** : amusez-vous bien **9 on ~** : à l'heure **10 several ~s** : plusieurs fois **11 ~ after ~** : à maintes reprises **12 what ~ is it?** : quelle heure est-il? — **~** *vt* **timed; timing 1** SCHEDULE : prévoir, fixer **2** : chronométrer (une course, etc.) — **timeless** ['taɪmləs] *adj* : éternel — **timely** ['taɪmli] *adj* **-lier; -est** : opportun — **timer** ['taɪmər] *n* : minuteur *m* (en cuisine) — **times** ['taɪmz] *prep* **3 ~ 4 is 12** : 3 fois 4 égale 12 — **timetable** ['taɪm,teɪbəl] *n* : horaire *m*

timid ['tɪmɪd] *adj* : timide

tin ['tɪn] *n* **1** : étain *m* (métal) **2** *or* **~ can** : boîte *f* — **tinfoil** ['tɪn,fɔɪl] *n* : papier *m* d'aluminium

tinge ['tɪndʒ] *vt* **tinged; tingeing** *or* **tinging** ['tɪndʒɪŋ] : teinter — **~** *n* : teinte *f*

tingle ['tɪŋgəl] *vi* **-gled; -gling** : picoter — **~** *n* : picotement *m*

tinker ['tɪŋkər] *vi* **~ with** : bricoler

tinkle ['tɪŋkəl] *vi* **-kled; -kling** : tinter — **~** *n* : tintement *m*

tint ['tɪnt] *n* : teinte *f* — **~** *vt* : teinter

tiny ['taɪni] *adj* **-nier; -niest** : minuscule

tip[1] ['tɪp] *v* **tipped; tipping** *vt* **1** TILT : incliner **2** *or* **~ over** : renverser — *vi* : pencher

tip[2] *n* END : pointe *f,* bout *m* (d'un crayon)

tip[3] *n* ADVICE : conseil *m,* tuyau *m fam* — **~** *vt* **~ off** : prévenir

tip[4] *vt* : donner un pourboire à — **~** *n* GRATUITY : pourboire *m*

tipsy ['tɪpsi] *adj* **-sier; -est** : gris *fam,* éméché *fam*

tiptoe ['tɪp,to:] *n* **on ~** : sur la pointe des pieds — **~** *vi* **-toed; -toeing** : marcher sur la pointe des pieds

tire[1] ['taɪr] *n* : pneu *m*

tire[2] *v* **tired; tiring** *vt* : fatiguer — *vi* : se fatiguer — **tired** ['taɪrd] *adj* **1** : fatigué **2 be ~ of** : en avoir assez de — **tiresome** ['taɪrsəm] *adj* : ennuyeux

tissue ['tɪ,ʃu:] *n* **1** : tissu *m* (en biologie) **2** : mouchoir *m* en papier, papier *m* mouchoir *Can*

title ['taɪṭəl] *n* : titre *m* — **~** *vt* **-tled; -tling** : intituler

to ['tu:] *prep* **1** : à **2** TOWARD : vers **3** IN ORDER TO : afin de, pour **4** UP TO : jusqu'à **5 a quarter ~ three** : trois heures moins le quart **6 be nice ~ him** : sois gentil envers lui **7 ten ~ the box** : dix par boîte **8 two ~ four years old** : entre deux et quatre ans **9 want ~ do** : vouloir faire — **~** *adv* **1 come ~** : reprendre connaissance **2 go ~ and fro** : aller et venir

toad ['to:d] *n* : crapaud *m*

toast ['to:st] *vt* **1** : griller (du pain), toaster *Can* **2** : boire à la santé de (une personne) — **~** *n* **1** : toast *m,* pain *m* grillé, rôtie *f* **2 drink a ~ to** : porter un toast à — **toaster** ['to:stər] *n* : grille-pain *m*

tobacco [tə'bæko:] *n, pl* **-cos** : tabac *m*

toboggan [tə'bɑgən] *n* : toboggan *m,* traîne *f Can*

today [tə'deɪ] *adv* : aujourd'hui — **~** *n* : aujourd'hui *m*

toddler ['tɑdələr] *n* : bambin *m,* -bine *f*

toe ['to:] *n* : orteil *m,* doigt *m* de pied — **toenail** ['to:,neɪl] *n* : ongle *m* d'orteil

together [tə'gɛðər] *adv* **1** : ensemble **2 ~ with** : ainsi que

toil ['tɔɪl] *n* : labeur *m* — **~** *vi* : peiner

toilet ['tɔɪlət] *n* BATHROOM : toilettes *fpl,* toilette *f Can* — **toilet paper** *n* : papier *m* hygiénique — **toiletries** ['tɔɪlətriz] *npl* : articles *mpl* de toilette

token ['to:kən] *n* **1** SIGN : signe *m,* marque *f* **2** : jeton *m* (pour le métro, etc.)

told → **tell**

tolerable ['tɑlərəbəl] *adj* : tolérable — **tolerance** ['tɑlərənts] *n* : tolérance *f* — **tolerant** ['tɑlərənt] *adj* : tolérant — **tolerate** ['tɑlə,reɪt] *vt* **-ated; -ating** : tolérer

toll[1] ['to:l] *n* **1** : péage *m* **2 death ~** : nombre *m* de morts **3 take a ~ on** : affecter

toll[2] *v* RING : sonner

tomato [tə'meɪṭo, -'mɑ-] *n, pl* **-toes** : tomate *f*

tomb ['tu:m] *n* : tombeau *m* — **tombstone** ['tu:m,sto:n] *n* : pierre *f* tombale

tomorrow [tə'mɑro] *adv* : demain — **~** *n* : demain *m*

ton ['tən] *n* : tonne *f*
tone ['to:n] *n* **1** : ton *m* **2** BEEP : tonalité *f* — ~ *vt* **toned; toning** *or* ~ **down** : atténuer
tongs ['taŋz, 'tɔŋz] *npl* : pinces *fpl*
tongue ['tʌŋ] *n* : langue *f*
tonic ['tanɪk] *n* : tonique *m*
tonight [tə'naɪt] *adv* : ce soir — ~ *n* : ce soir, cette nuit
tonsil ['tantsəl] *n* : amygdale *f*
too ['tu:] *adv* **1** ALSO : aussi **2** VERY : très
took → **take**
tool ['tu:l] *n* : outil *m* — **toolbox** ['tu:l-ˌbaks] *n* : boîte *f* à outils
toot ['tu:t] *vi* : klaxonner — ~ *n* : coup *m* de klaxon
tooth ['tu:θ] *n, pl* **teeth** ['ti:θ] : dent *f* — **toothache** ['tu:θˌeɪk] *n* : mal *m* de dents — **toothbrush** ['tu:θˌbrʌʃ] *n* : brosse *f* à dents — **toothpaste** ['tu:θˌpeɪst] *n* : dentifrice *m*
top[1] ['tap] *n* **1** : haut *m* **2** SUMMIT : cime *f* **3** COVER : couvercle *m* **4 on** ~ **of** : sur — ~ *vt* **topped; topping 1** COVER : couvrir **2** SURPASS : dépasser — ~ *adj* **1** : de haut, du haut **2** LEADING : premier, principal **3 the** ~ **floor** : le dernier étage
top[2] *n* : toupie *f* (jouet)
topic ['tapɪk] *n* : sujet *m* — **topical** ['tapɪkəl] *adj* : d'actualité
topple ['tapəl] *v* **-pled; -pling** *vi* : basculer — *vt* : renverser
torch ['tɔrtʃ] *n* : torche *f*
tore → **tear**[1]
torment ['tɔrˌmɛnt] *n* : tourment *m* — ~ ['tɔrˌmɛnt, tɔr'-] *vt* : tourmenter
torn → **tear**[1]
tornado [tɔr'neɪdo] *n, pl* **-does** *or* **-dos** : tornade *f*
torpedo [tɔr'pi:do] *n, pl* **-does** : torpille *f* — ~ *vt* : torpiller
torrent ['tɔrənt] *n* : torrent *m*
torrid ['tɔrɪd] *adj* : torride
torso ['tɔrˌso:] *n, pl* **-sos** *or* **-si** [-ˌsi:] : torse *m*
tortoise ['tɔrtəs] *n* : tortue *f* — **tortoiseshell** ['tɔrtəsˌʃɛl] *n* : écaille *f*
tortuous ['tɔrtʃuəs] *adj* : tortueux
torture ['tɔrtʃər] *n* : torture *f* — ~ *vt* **-tured; -turing** : torturer
toss ['tɔs, 'tas] *vt* : tirer, lancer — *vi* ~ **and turn** : se tourner et se retourner — ~ *n* : lancer *m*
tot ['tat] *n* : petit enfant *m*
total ['to:təl] *adj* : total — ~ *n* : total *m* — ~ *vt* **-taled** *or* **-talled; -taling** *or* **-talling** : totaliser, additionner
totalitarian [ˌto:ˌtælə'tɛriən] *adj* : totalitaire
touch ['tʌtʃ] *vt* **1** : toucher **2** AFFECT : émouvoir **3** ~ **up** : retoucher — *vi* : se toucher — ~ *n* **1** : toucher *m* (sens) **2** HINT : touche *f* **3 a** ~ **of** : un peu de **4 keep in** ~ : demeurer en contact — **touchdown** ['tʌtʃˌdaʊn] *n* **1** : atterrissage *m* (d'un avion) **2** : but *m* (au football américain) — **touchy** ['tʌtʃi] *adj* **touchier; touchiest 1** : susceptible **2 a** ~ **subject** : un sujet épineux
tough ['tʌf] *adj* **1** : dur **2** STRONG : solide **3** STRICT : sévère **4** DIFFICULT : difficile — **toughen** ['tʌfən] *vt or* ~ **up** : endurcir — *vi* : s'endurcir — **toughness** ['tʌfnəs] *n* : dureté *f*
tour ['tʊr] *n* **1** : tour *m* (d'une ville, etc.), visite *f* (d'un musée, etc.) **2 go on** ~ : faire une tournée — ~ *vi* **1** TRAVEL : voyager **2** : être en tournée (se dit d'une équipe, etc.) — *vt* : visiter — **tourist** ['tʊrɪst, 'tər-] *n* : touriste *mf*
tournament ['tərnəmənt, 'tʊr-] *n* : tournoi *m*
tousle ['taʊzəl] *vt* **-sled; -sling** : ébouriffer (les cheveux)
tout ['taʊt] *vt* : vanter les mérites de
tow ['to:] *vt* : remorquer — ~ *n* : remorquage *m*
toward ['tord, tə'wɔrd] *or* **towards** ['tordz, tə'wɔrdz] *prep* : vers
towel ['taʊəl] *n* : serviette *f*
tower ['taʊər] *n* : tour *f* — ~ *vi* ~ **over** : dominer — **towering** ['taʊərɪŋ] *adj* : imposant
town ['taʊn] *n* **1** VILLAGE : village *m* **2** CITY : ville *f* — **township** ['taʊnˌʃɪp] *n* **1** : municipalité *f* **2** : canton *m Can* (division territoriale)
tow truck ['to:ˌtrʌk] *n* : dépanneuse *f*, remorqueuse *f Can*
toxic ['taksɪk] *adj* : toxique
toy ['tɔɪ] *n* : jouet *m* — ~ *vi* ~ **with** : jouer avec
trace ['treɪs] *n* : trace *f* — ~ *vt* **traced; tracing 1** : tracer, calquer (un dessin) **2** FOLLOW : suivre **3** LOCATE : retrouver
track ['træk] *n* **1** : piste *f* **2** FOOTPRINT : trace *f* **3** *or* **railroad** ~ : voie *f* ferrée **4 keep** ~ **of** : suivre — ~ *vt* : suivre la trace de, suivre la piste de
tract[1] ['trækt] *n* **1** EXPANSE : étendue *f* **2** : appareil *m* (en physiologie)
tract[2] *n* LEAFLET : brochure *f*
traction ['trækʃən] *n* : traction *f*
tractor ['træktər] *n* **1** : tracteur *m* **2** *or* **tractor–trailer** : semi-remorque *m*

trade [ˈtreɪd] *n* **1** PROFESSION : métier *m* **2** COMMERCE : commerce *m* **3** INDUSTRY : industrie *f* **4** EXCHANGE : échange *m* — ~ *v* **traded; trading** *vi* : faire du commerce — *vt* ~ **sth for** : échanger qqch pour — **trademark** [ˈtreɪdˌmɑrk] *n* : marque *f* de fabrique

tradition [trəˈdɪʃən] *n* : tradition *f* — **traditional** [trəˈdɪʃənəl] *adj* : traditionnel

traffic [ˈtræfɪk] *n* **1** : circulation *f* (routière) **2 drug** ~ : trafic *m* de drogue — ~ *vi* **-ficked; -ficking** : trafiquer — **traffic light** *n* : feu *m* (de signalisation)

tragedy [ˈtræʤədi] *n, pl* **-dies** : tragédie *f* — **tragic** [ˈtræʤɪk] *adj* : tragique

trail [ˈtreɪl] *vi* **1** DRAG : traîner **2** LAG : être à la traîne **3** ~ **off** : s'estomper — *vt* **1** : traîner **2** PURSUE : suivre la piste de — ~ *n* **1** : trace *f*, piste *f* **2** PATH : sentier *m*, chemin *m* — **trailer** [ˈtreɪlər] *n* **1** : remorque *f* **2** CAMPER : caravane *f*, roulotte *f Can*

train [ˈtreɪn] *n* **1** : train *m* **2** : traîne *f* (d'une robe) **3** SERIES : suite *f*, série *f* **4** ~ **of thought** : fil *m* des pensées — ~ *vt* **1** : former, entraîner (un athlète, etc.) **2** AIM : braquer — *vi* : s'entraîner (aux sports) — **trainer** [ˈtreɪnər] *n* **1** : entraîneur *m*, -neuse *f* (aux sports) **2** : dresseur *m*, -seuse *f* (d'animaux)

trait [ˈtreɪt] *n* : trait *m*

traitor [ˈtreɪt̬ər] *n* : traître *m*, -tresse *f*

tramp [ˈtræmp] *vi* : marcher (d'un pas lourd) — ~ *n* VAGRANT : clochard *m*, -charde *f*

trample [ˈtræmpəl] *vt* **-pled; -pling** : piétiner

trampoline [ˌtræmpəˈliːn, ˈtræmpəˌ-] *n* : trampoline *m*

trance [ˈtrænts] *n* : transe *f*

tranquillity *or* **tranquility** [trænˈkwɪlət̬i] *n* : tranquillité *f* — **tranquilizer** [ˈtræŋkwəˌlaɪzər] *n* : tranquillisant *m*

transaction [trænˈzækʃən] *n* : transaction *f*

transcribe [trænˈskraɪb] *vt* **-scribed; -scribing** : transcrire — **transcript** [ˈtrænˌskrɪpt] *n* : transcription *f*

transfer [træntsˈfər, ˈtræntsˌfər] *v* **-ferred; -ferring** *vt* **1** : transférer **2** : muter (un employé) — *vi* **1** : être transféré **2** : changer (d'université) — ~ [ˈtræntsˌfər] *n* **1** : transfert *m*, mutation *f* **2** : virement *m* (de fonds)

transform [træntsˈfɔrm] *vt* : transformer — **transformation** [ˌtræntsfərˈmeɪʃən] *n* : transformation *f*

transfusion [træntsˈfjuːʒən] *n* : transfusion *f*

transgression [træntsˈgrɛʃən, trænz-] *n* : transgression *f* — **transgress** [træntsˈgrɛs, trænz-] *vt* : transgresser

transient [ˈtræntʃənt, ˈtrænsiənt] *adj* : transitoire, passager

transit [ˈtræntsɪt, ˈtrænzɪt] *n* **1** : transit *m* **2** TRANSPORTATION : transport *m* — **transition** [trænˈsɪʃən, -ˈzɪʃ-] *n* : transition *f* — **transitive** [ˈtræntsət̬ɪv, ˈtrænzə-] *adj* : transitif — **transitory** [ˈtræntsəˌtori, ˈtrænzə-] *adj* : transitoire, passager

translate [træntsˈleɪt, trænz-; ˈtræntsˌ-, ˈtrænzˌ-] *vt* **-lated; -lating** : traduire — **translation** [træntsˈleɪʃən, trænz-] *n* : traduction *f* — **translator** [træntsˈleɪt̬ər, trænz-; ˈtræntsˌ-, ˈtrænzˌ-] *n* : traducteur *m*, -trice *f*

translucent [træntsˈluːsənt, trænz-] *adj* : translucide

transmit [træntsˈmɪt, trænz-] *vt* **-mitted; -mitting** : transmettre — **transmission** [træntsˈmɪʃən, trænz-] *n* : transmission *f* — **transmitter** [træntsˈmɪt̬ər, trænz-; ˈtræntsˌ-, ˈtrænsˌ-] *n* : émetteur *m*

transparent [træntsˈpærənt] *adj* : transparent — **transparency** [træntsˈpærəntsi] *n, pl* **-cies** : transparence *f*

transplant [træntsˈplænt] *vt* : transplanter — ~ [ˈtræntsˌplænt] *n* : transplantation *f*

transport [træntsˈport, ˈtræntsˌ-] *vt* : transporter — ~ [ˈtræntsˌport] *n* : transport *m* — **transportation** [ˌtræntspərˈteɪʃən] *n* : transport *m*

transpose [træntsˈpoːz] *vt* **-posed; -posing** : transposer

trap [ˈtræp] *n* : piège *m* — ~ *vt* **trapped; trapping** : prendre au piège, attraper — **trapdoor** [ˈtræpˈdor] *n* : trappe *f*

trapeze [træˈpiːz] *n* : trapèze *m*

trappings [ˈtræpɪŋz] *npl* SIGNS : attributs *mpl*

trash [ˈtræʃ] *n* : déchets *mpl*, ordures *fpl*

trauma [ˈtrɔmə, ˈtraʊ-] *n* : traumatisme *m* — **traumatic** [trəˈmæt̬ɪk, trɔ-, traʊ-] *adj* : traumatisant

travel [ˈtrævəl] *vi* **-eled** *or* **-elled; -eling** *or* **-elling 1** : voyager **2** SPREAD : circuler, se répandre **3** MOVE : aller, rouler — ~ *n* : voyages *mpl* — **travel-**

er *or* **traveller** ['trævələr] *n* : voyageur *m*, -geuse *f*

trawl ['trɔl] *vi* : pêcher au chalut — **trawler** ['trɔlər] *n* : chalutier *m*

tray ['treɪ] *n* : plateau *m*

treachery ['trɛtʃəri] *n, pl* **-eries** : traîtrise *f* — **treacherous** ['trɛtʃərəs] *adj* **1** : traître **2** DANGEROUS : dangereux

tread ['trɛd] *v* **trod** ['trɑd]; **trodden** ['trɑdən] *or* **trod; treading** *vt* **~ water** : nager sur place — *vi or* **~ on** : marcher sur — **~** *n* **1** STEP : pas *m* **2** : bande *f* de roulement (d'un pneu) — **treadmill** ['trɛd,mɪl] *n* : exerciseur *m*

treason ['tri:zən] *n* : trahison *f*

treasure ['trɛʒər, 'treɪ-] *n* : trésor *m* — **~** *vt* **-sured; -suring** : tenir beaucoup à — **treasurer** ['trɛʒərər, 'treɪ-] *n* : trésorier *m*, -rière *f* — **treasury** ['trɛʒəri, 'treɪ-] *n, pl* **-suries 1** : trésorerie *f* **2 Treasury** : ministère *m* des Finances

treat ['tri:t] *vt* **1** : traiter **2 ~ s.o. to sth** : offrir qqch à qqn — **~** *n* : régal *m*, plaisir *m*

treatise ['tri:təs] *n* : traité *m*

treatment ['tri:tmənt] *n* : traitement *m*

treaty ['tri:ti] *n, pl* **-ties** : traité *m*

treble ['trɛbəl] *adj* **1** TRIPLE : triple **2** : de soprano (en musique) — **treble clef** *n* : clé *f* de sol

tree ['tri:] *n* : arbre *m*

trek ['trɛk] *n* : randonnée *f*

trellis ['trɛlɪs] *n* : treillis *m*, treillage *m*

tremble ['trɛmbəl] *vi* **-bled; -bling** : trembler

tremendous [trɪ'mɛndəs] *adj* **1** HUGE : énorme **2** EXCELLENT : formidable

tremor ['trɛmər] *n* : tremblement *m*

trench ['trɛntʃ] *n* : tranchée *f*

trend ['trɛnd] *n* **1** : tendance *f* **2** FASHION : mode *f* — **trendy** ['trɛndi] *adj* **trendier; trendiest** : à la mode

trepidation [,trɛpə'deɪʃən] *n* : inquiétude *f*

trespass ['trɛspəs, -,pæs] *vi* : s'introduire illégalement

trial ['traɪəl] *n* **1** HEARING : procès *m* **2** TEST : essai *m* **3** ORDEAL : épreuve *f* — **~** *adj* : d'essai

triangle ['traɪ,æŋgəl] *n* : triangle *m* — **triangular** [traɪ'æŋgjələr] *adj* : triangulaire

tribe ['traɪb] *n* : tribu *f* — **tribal** ['traɪbəl] *adj* : tribal

tribulation [,trɪbjə'leɪʃən] *n* : tourment *m*

tribunal [traɪ'bju:nəl, trɪ-] *n* : tribunal *m*

tribute ['trɪb,ju:t] *n* : hommage *m* — **tributary** ['trɪbjə,tɛri] *n, pl* **-taries** : affluent *m*

trick ['trɪk] *n* **1** PRANK : farce *f*, tour *m* **2** KNACK : truc *m*, astuce *f* — **~** *vt* : duper — **trickery** ['trɪkəri] *n* : tromperie *f*

trickle ['trɪkəl] *vi* **-led; -ling** DRIP : dégouliner — **~** *n* : filet *m* (d'eau)

tricky ['trɪki] *adj* **trickier; trickiest 1** SLY : rusé **2** DIFFICULT : difficile

tricycle ['traɪsəkəl, -,sɪkəl] *n* : tricycle *m*

trifle ['traɪfəl] *n* : bagatelle *f*, rien *m* — **trifling** ['traɪflɪŋ] *adj* : insignifiant

trigger ['trɪgər] *n* : détente *f*, gâchette *f* — **~** *vt* : déclencher

trillion ['trɪljən] *n* : billion *m*

trilogy ['trɪlədʒi] *n, pl* **-gies** : trilogie *f*

trim ['trɪm] *vt* **trimmed; trimming 1** CUT : tailler **2** ADORN : décorer — **~** *adj* **trimmer; trimmest 1** SLIM : mince **2** NEAT : soigné — **~** *n* **1** HAIRCUT : coupe *f* **2** DECORATION : garniture *f* — **trimmings** ['trɪmɪŋs] *npl* : garniture *f*

Trinity ['trɪnəti] *n* : Trinité *f*

trinket ['trɪŋkət] *n* : babiole *f*

trio ['tri:,o:] *n, pl* **trios** : trio *m*

trip ['trɪp] *v* **tripped; tripping** *vi* : trébucher, s'enfarger *Can* — *vt* **1** : faire trébucher (une personne) **2** ACTIVATE : déclencher — **~** *n* **1** : voyage *m* **2** STUMBLE : trébuchement *m*

tripe ['traɪp] *n* : tripes *fpl* (d'un animal)

triple ['trɪpəl] *v* **-pled; -pling** : tripler — **~** *n* : triple *m* — **~** *adj* : triple — **triplets** ['trɪpləts] *npl* : triplés *mpl* — **triplicate** ['trɪplɪkət] *n* **in ~** : en trois exemplaires

tripod ['traɪ,pɑd] *n* : trépied *m*

trite ['traɪt] *adj* **triter; tritest** : banal

triumph ['traɪəmpf] *n* : triomphe *m* — **~** *vi* : triompher — **triumphal** [traɪ'ʌmpfəl] *adj* : triomphal — **triumphant** [traɪ'ʌmpfənt] *adj* : triomphant

trivial ['trɪviəl] *adj* : insignifiant — **trivia** ['trɪviə] *ns & pl* : futilités *fpl* — **triviality** [,trɪvi'æləti] *n, pl* **-ties** : insignifiance *f*

trod, trodden → **tread**

trolley ['trɑli] *n, pl* **-leys** : tramway *m*

trombone [trɑm'bo:n] *n* : trombone *m*

troop ['tru:p] *n* **1** GROUP : bande *f*, groupe *m* **2 ~s** *npl* : troupes *fpl* — **trooper** ['tru:pər] *n* **1** : soldat *m* **2** *or* **state ~** : gendarme *m France*, policier *m*

trophy ['tro:fi] *n, pl* **-phies** : trophée *m*

tropic ['trɑpɪk] *n* **1** : tropique *m* **2 the ~s** : les tropiques *mpl* — **~** *or* **tropical** ['trɑpɪkəl] *adj* : tropical
trot ['trɑt] *n* : trot *m* — **~** *vi* **trotted; trotting** : trotter
trouble ['trʌbəl] *vt* **-bled; -bling 1** WORRY : inquiéter **2** BOTHER : déranger — **~** *n* **1** PROBLEMS : ennuis *mpl* **2** EFFORT : mal *m,* peine *f* **3 be in ~** : avoir des ennuis **4 I had ~ doing it** : j'ai eu du mal à le faire — **troublemaker** ['trʌbəl,meɪkər] *n* : fauteur *m,* -trice *f* de troubles — **troublesome** ['trʌbəlsəm] *adj* : gênant, pénible
trough ['trɔf] *n, pl* **troughs** ['trɔfs, 'trɔvz] **1** : abreuvoir *m* (pour les animaux) **2** *or* **feeding ~** : auge *f*
trousers ['traʊzərz] *npl* : pantalon *m*
trout ['traʊt] *ns & pl* : truite *f*
trowel ['traʊəl] *n* : truelle *f* (pour le mortier), déplantoir *m* (pour le jardinage)
truant ['tru:ənt] *n* : élève *mf* absentéiste
truce ['tru:s] *n* : trêve *f*
truck ['trʌk] *n* : camion *m* — **trucker** ['trʌkər] *n* : camionneur *m,* -neuse *f;* routier *m*
trudge ['trʌʤ] *vi* **trudged; trudging** : marcher péniblement
true ['tru:] *adj* **truer; truest 1** FACTUAL : vrai **2** LOYAL : fidèle **3** GENUINE : authentique
truffle ['trʌfəl] *n* : truffe *f*
truly ['tru:li] *adv* : vraiment
trump ['trʌmp] *n* : atout *m*
trumpet ['trʌmpət] *n* : trompette *f*
trunk ['trʌŋk] *n* **1** STEM, TORSO : tronc *m* **2** : trompe *f* (d'un éléphant) **3** : coffre *m* (d'une voiture) **4** SUITCASE : malle *f* **5 ~s** *npl* : maillot *m* de bain
trust ['trʌst] *n* **1** CONFIDENCE : confiance *f* **2** HOPE : espoir *m* **3** : trust *m* (en finances) **4 in ~** : par fidéicommis — **~** *vi* **1** HOPE : espérer **2 ~ in** : faire confiance à — *vt* **1** ENTRUST : confier **2 I ~ him** : j'ai confiance en lui — **trustee** [,trʌs'ti:] *n* : fidéicommissaire *mf* — **trustworthy** ['trʌst,wərði] *adj* : digne de confiance
truth ['tru:θ] *n, pl* **truths** ['tru:ðz, 'tru:θs] : vérité *f* — **truthful** ['tru:θfəl] *adj* : sincère, vrai
try ['traɪ] *v* **tried; trying** *vt* **1** ATTEMPT : essayer **2** : juger (un accusé) **3** TEST : éprouver, mettre à l'épreuve **4** TASTE : goûter — *vi* : essayer — **~** *n, pl* **tries** : essai *m* — **trying** ['traɪɪŋ] *adj* : pénible — **tryout** ['traɪ,aʊt] *n* : essai *m*
tsar ['zɑr, 'tsɑr, 'sɑr] → **czar**
T-shirt ['ti:,ʃərt] *n* : tee-shirt *m,* t-shirt *m*
tub ['tʌb] *n* **1** VAT : cuve *f* **2** CONTAINER : pot *m* **3** BATHTUB : baignoire *f*
tuba ['tu:bə, 'tju:-] *n* : tuba *m*
tube ['tu:b, 'tju:b] *n* **1** : tube *m* **2** *or* **inner ~** : chambre *f* à air **3 the ~** : la télé
tuberculosis [tʊ,bərkjə'lo:səs, tjʊ-] *n, pl* **-loses** [-,si:z] : tuberculose *f*
tubing ['tu:bɪŋ, 'tju:-] *n* : tubes *mpl* — **tubular** ['tubjələr, 'tju:-] *adj* : tubulaire
tuck ['tʌk] *vt* **1** *or* **~ away** : ranger **2 ~ in** : rentrer (une chemise, etc.) — **~** *n* : pli *m*
Tuesday ['tu:z,deɪ, 'tju:z-, -di] *n* : mardi *m*
tuft ['tʌft] *n* : touffe *f* (de cheveux, d'herbe, etc.)
tug ['tʌg] *vt* **tugged; tugging** *or* **~ at** : tirer sur — **~** *n* : petit coup *m* — **tugboat** ['tʌg,bo:t] *n* : remorqueur *m* — **tug-of-war** [,tʌgə'wɔr] *n, pl* **tugs-of-war** : lutte *f* à la corde
tuition [tʊ'ɪʃən, 'tju:-] *n* : frais *mpl* de scolarité
tulip ['tu:lɪp, 'tju:-] *n* : tulipe *f*
tumble ['təmbəl] *vi* **-bled; -bling** : tomber — **~** *n* : chute *f* — **tumbler** ['tʌmblər] *n* : verre *m* droit
tummy ['tʌmi] *n, pl* **-mies** : ventre *m*
tumor *or Brit* **tumour** ['tu:mər, 'tju:-] *n* : tumeur *f*
tumult ['tu:,mʌlt 'tju:-] *n* : tumulte *m* — **tumultuous** [tʊ'mʌlʧʊəs, tjʊ:-] *adj* : tumultueux
tuna ['tu:nə 'tju:-] *n, pl* **-na** *or* **-nas** : thon *m*
tune ['tu:n, 'tju:n] *n* **1** MELODY : air *m* **2 in ~** : accordé, juste **3 out of ~** : désaccordé, faux — **~** *v* **tuned; tuning** *vt* **1** : accorder (un piano, etc.) **2** *or* **~ up** : régler (un moteur) — *vi* **~ in** : se mettre à l'écoute — **tuner** ['tu:nər, 'tju:-] *n* : accordeur *m* (de pianos, etc.)
tunic ['tu:nɪk, 'tju:-] *n* : tunique *f*
Tunisian [tu:'ni:ʒən, tju:'nɪziən] *adj* : tunisien
tunnel ['tʌnəl] *n* : tunnel *m* — **~** *vi* **-neled** *or* **-nelled; -neling** *or* **-nelling** : creuser un tunnel
turban ['tərbən] *n* : turban *m*
turbine ['tərbən, -,baɪn] *n* : turbine *f*
turbulent ['tərbjələnt] *adj* : turbulent — **turbulence** ['tərbjələnts] *n* : turbulence *f*

turf ['tərf] *n* : gazon *m*
turkey ['tərki] *n, pl* **-keys** : dinde *f*
Turkish ['tərkɪʃ] *adj* : turc — ~ *n* : turc *m* (langue)
turmoil ['tər,mɔɪl] *n* : désarroi *m*, confusion *f*
turn ['tərn] *vt* **1** : tourner **2** SPRAIN : tordre **3** ~ **down** REFUSE : refuser **4** ~ **down** LOWER : baisser **5** ~ **in** : rendre **6** ~ **into** : convertir en **7** ~ **off** : éteindre (la lumière, etc.), couper (le contact, etc.) **8** ~ **out** EXPEL : expulser **9** ~ **out** PRODUCE : produire **10** ~ **out** → **turn off 11** *or* ~ **over** FLIP : retourner **12** ~ **over** TRANSFER : remettre **13** ~ **s.o.'s stomach** : soulever le cœur à qqn **14** ~ **up** RAISE : augmenter — *vi* **1** ROTATE : tourner **2** BECOME : devenir **3** SOUR : tourner **4** CHANGE : se transformer **5** HEAD : se diriger **6** *or* ~ **around** : se retourner **7** ~ **in** RETIRE : se coucher **8** ~ **in** DELIVER : livrer **9** ~ **into** : se changer en **10** ~ **out** COME : venir **11** ~ **out** RESULT : se terminer **12** ~ **out to be** : s'avérer, se révéler **13** ~ **up** APPEAR : se présenter — ~ *n* **1** ROTATION : tour *m* **2** CHANGE : changement *m* **3** CURVE : virage *m* **4** DEED : service *m* **5 wait your** ~ : attendez votre tour
turnip ['tərnəp] *n* : navet *m*
turnout ['tərn,aʊt] *n* : participation *f* — **turnover** ['tərn,o:vər] *n* **1** REVERSAL : renversement *m* **2** : roulement *m* (du personnel) **3 apple** ~ : chausson *m* aux pommes — **turnpike** ['tərn,paɪk] *n* : autoroute *f* à péage — **turntable** ['tərn,teɪbəl] *n* : platine *f*
turpentine ['tərpən,taɪn] *n* : térébenthine *f*
turret ['tərət] *n* : tourelle *f*
turtle ['tərtəl] *n* : tortue *f* — **turtleneck** ['tərtəl,nɛk] *n* : col *m* roulé, col *m* montant
tusk ['tʌsk] *n* : défense *f* (d'un animal)
tutor ['tu:ṭər, 'tju:-] *n* : précepteur *m*, -trice *f;* professeur *m* particulier — ~ *vt* : donner des cours particuliers à
tuxedo [,tək'si:,do:] *n, pl* **-dos** *or* **-does** : smoking *m*
TV [,ti:'vi:, 'ti:,vi:] → **television**
twang ['twæŋ] *n* : ton *m* nasillard (de la voix)
tweed ['twi:d] *n* : tweed *m*
tweet ['twi:t] *n* : pépiement *m* — ~ *vi* : pépier
tweezers ['twi:zərz] *ns & pl* : pince *f* à épiler
twelve ['twɛlv] *n* : douze *m* — ~ *adj* : douze — **twelfth** ['twɛlfθ] *n* **1** : douzième *mf* **2 February** ~ : le douze février — ~ *adj* : douzième
twenty ['twʌnti, 'twɛn-] *n, pl* **-ties** : vingt *m* — ~ *adj* : vingt — **twentieth** ['twʌntiəθ, 'twɛn-] *n* **1** : vingtième *mf* **2 March** ~ : le vingt mars — ~ *adj* : vingtième
twice ['twaɪs] *adv* **1** : deux fois **2** ~ **as much** : deux fois plus
twig ['twɪg] *n* : brindille *f*
twilight ['twaɪ,laɪt] *n* : crépuscule *m*
twin ['twɪn] *n* : jumeau *m*, -melle *f* — ~ *adj* : jumeau
twine ['twaɪn] *n* : ficelle *f*
twinge ['twɪndʒ] *n* : élancement *m* (de douleur)
twinkle ['twɪŋkəl] *vi* **-kled; -kling 1** : scintiller (se dit des étoiles, etc.) **2** : pétiller (se dit des yeux) — ~ *n* : scintillement *m* (des étoiles), pétillement *m* (des yeux)
twirl ['twərl] *vt* : faire tournoyer — *vi* : tournoyer — ~ *n* : tournoiement *m*
twist ['twɪst] *vt* **1** TURN : tourner **2** SPRAIN : tordre **3** DISTORT : déformer — *vi* **1** : serpenter (se dit d'une route) **2** COIL : s'enrouler **3** ~ **and turn** : se tortiller **4** ~ **off** : dévisser — ~ *n* **1** TURN : tour *m* **2** BEND : tournant *m* **3 a** ~ **of fate** : un coup du sort — **twister** ['twɪstər] → **tornado**
twitch ['twɪtʃ] *vi* : se contracter — ~ *n* *or* **nervous** ~ : tic *m* (nerveux)
two ['tu:] *n, pl* **twos** : deux *m* — ~ *adj* : deux — **twofold** ['tu:'fo:ld] *adj* : double — ~ *adv* : doublement — **two hundred** *adj* : deux cents
tycoon [taɪ'ku:n] *n* : magnat *m*
tying → **tie**
type ['taɪp] *n* **1** KIND : type *m* **2** : caractère *m* (d'imprimerie) — ~ *v* **typed; typing** : taper (à la machine) — **typewriter** ['taɪp,raɪṭər] *n* : machine *f* à écrire, dactylo *f Can*
typhoon [taɪ'fu:n] *n* : typhon *m*
typical ['tɪpɪkəl] *adj* : typique — **typify** ['tɪpə,faɪ] *vt* **-fied; -fying** : être typique de
typist ['taɪpɪst] *n* : dactylo *mf*
typography [taɪ'pɑgrəfi] *n* : typographie *f*
tyranny ['tɪrəni] *n, pl* **-nies** : tyrannie *f* — **tyrant** ['taɪrənt] *n* : tyran *m*
tzar ['zɑr, 'tsɑr, 'sɑr] → **czar**

U

u [ˈju:] *n, pl* **u's** *or* **us** [ˈju:z] : u *m,* vingt et unième lettre de l'alphabet
udder [ˈʌdər] *n* : pis *m*
UFO [ˌjuːˌɛfˈoɪ, ˈjuːˌfoɪ] *n* (*unidentified flying object*), *pl* **UFO's** *or* **UFOs** : ovni *m*
ugly [ˈʌgli] *adj* **-lier; -est** : laid — **ugliness** [ˈʌglinəs] *n* : laideur *f*
ulcer [ˈʌlsər] *n* : ulcère *f*
ulterior [ˌʌlˈtɪriər] *adj* **~ motive** : arrière-pensée *f*
ultimate [ˈʌltəmət] *adj* **1** : ultime, final **2** SUPREME : suprême — **ultimately** [ˈʌltəmətli] *adv* **1** : finalement, en fin de compte **2** EVENTUALLY : par la suite
ultimatum [ˌʌltəˈmeɪṭəm, -ˈmɑ-] *n, pl* **-tums** *or* **-ta** [-ṭə] : ultimatum *m*
ultraviolet [ˌʌltrəˈvaɪələt] *adj* : ultraviolet
umbilical cord [ˌʌmˈbɪlɪkəl] *n* : cordon *m* ombilical
umbrella [ˌʌmˈbrɛlə] *n* : parapluie *m*
umpire [ˈʌmˌpaɪr] *n* : arbitre *m* — **~** *vt* **-pired; -piring** : arbitrer
umpteenth [ˈʌmpˌtinθ, ˌʌmpˈ-] *adj* : énième
unable [ˌʌnˈeɪbəl] *adj* **1** : incapable **2** **be ~ to** : ne pas pouvoir
unabridged [ˌʌnəˈbrɪʤd] *adj* : intégral
unacceptable [ˌʌnɪkˈsɛptəbəl] *adj* : inacceptable
unaccountable [ˌʌnəˈkaʊntəbəl] *adj* : inexplicable
unaccustomed [ˌʌnəˈkʌstəmd] *adj* **be ~ to** : ne pas avoir l'habitude de
unadulterated [ˌʌnəˈdʌltəˌreɪṭəd] *adj* : pur, naturel
unaffected [ˌʌnəˈfɛktəd] *adj* **1** : indifférent **2** NATURAL : sans affectation
unafraid [ˌʌnəˈfreɪd] *adj* : sans peur
unaided [ˌʌnˈeɪdəd] *adj* : sans aide
unanimous [jʊˈnænəməs] *adj* : unanime
unannounced [ˌʌnəˈnaʊnst] *adj* : inattendu, sans se faire annoncer
unarmed [ˌʌnˈɑrmd] *adj* : non armé, sans armes
unassuming [ˌʌnəˈsu:mɪŋ] *adj* : modeste
unattached [ˌʌnəˈtæʧt] *adj* **1** : détaché **2** UNMARRIED : libre
unattractive [ˌʌnəˈtræktɪv] *adj* : peu attrayant
unauthorized [ˌʌnˈɔθəˌraɪzd] *adj* : non autorisé
unavailable [ˌʌnəˈveɪləbəl] *adj* : indisponible
unavoidable [ˌʌnəˈvɔɪdəbəl] *adj* : inévitable
unaware [ˌʌnəˈwær] *adj* **1** : ignorant **2** **be ~ of** : ignorer, ne pas être conscient de
unbalanced [ˌʌnˈbælən*t*st] *adj* : déséquilibré
unbearable [ˌʌnˈbærəbəl] *adj* : insupportable
unbelievable [ˌʌnbəˈli:vəbəl] *adj* : incroyable
unbending [ˌʌnˈbɛndɪŋ] *adj* : inflexible
unbiased [ˌʌnˈbaɪəst] *adj* : impartial
unborn [ˌʌnˈbɔrn] *adj* : qui n'est pas encore né
unbreakable [ˌʌnˈbreɪkəbəl] *adj* : incassable
unbroken [ˌʌnˈbro:kən] *adj* **1** INTACT : intact **2** CONTINUOUS : continu
unbutton [ˌʌnˈbʌtən] *vt* : déboutonner
uncalled–for [ˌʌnˈkɔldˌfɔr] *adj* : déplacé, injustifié
uncanny [ənˈkæni] *adj* **1** STRANGE : mystérieux, troublant **2** REMARKABLE : remarquable
unceasing [ˌʌnˈsi:sɪŋ] *adj* : incessant
uncertain [ˌʌnˈsərtən] *adj* : incertain — **uncertainty** [ˌʌnˈsərtənti] *n, pl* **-ties** : incertitude *f*
unchanged [ˌʌnˈʧeɪnʤd] *adj* : inchangé — **unchanging** [ˌʌnˈʧeɪnʤɪŋ] *adj* : immuable
uncivilized [ˌʌnˈsɪvəˌlaɪzd] *adj* : barbare
uncle [ˈʌŋkəl] *n* : oncle *m*
unclear [ˌʌnˈklɪr] *adj* : peu clair
uncomfortable [ˌʌnˈkʌm*p*fərṭəbəl] *adj* **1** : inconfortable **2** AWKWARD : mal à l'aise
uncommon [ˌʌnˈkɑmən] *adj* : rare, peu commun
uncompromising [ˌʌnˈkɑmprəˈmaɪzɪŋ] *adj* : intransigeant
unconcerned [ˌʌnkənˈsərnd] *adj* : indifférent
unconditional [ˌʌnkənˈdɪʃənəl] *adj* : inconditionnel
unconscious [ˌʌnˈkɑnʃəs] *adj* : inconscient

uncontrollable [ˌʌnkənˈtro:ləbəl] *adj* : incontrôlable
unconventional [ˌʌnkənˈvɛntʃənəl] *adj* : peu conventionnel
uncouth [ˌʌnˈku:θ] *adj* : grossier
uncover [ˌʌnˈkʌvər] *vt* : découvrir
undecided [ˌʌndɪˈsaɪdəd] *adj* : indécis
undeniable [ˌʌndɪˈnaɪəbəl] *adj* : indéniable
under [ˈʌndər] *adv* **1** : en dessous **2** LESS : moins **3** *or* **~ anesthetic** : sous anesthésie — **~** *prep* **1** BELOW, BENEATH : sous, en dessous de **2** ACCORDING TO : d'après, selon
underage [ˌʌndərˈeɪdʒ] *adj* : mineur
underclothes [ˈʌndərˌklo:z, -ˌklo:ðz] *npl* → **underwear**
undercover [ˌʌndərˈkʌvər] *adj* : secret
underdeveloped [ˌʌndərdɪˈvɛləpt] *adj* : sous-développé
underestimate [ˌʌndərˈɛstəˌmeɪt] *vt* **-mated; -mating** : sous-estimer
undergo [ˌʌndərˈgo:] *vt* **-went** [-ˈwɛnt]; **-gone** [-ˈgɔn]; **-going** : subir, éprouver
undergraduate [ˌʌndərˈgrædʒuət] *n* : étudiant *m*, -diante *f* de premier cycle; étudiant *m*, -diante *f* qui prépare une licence *France*
underground [ˌʌndərˈgraʊnd] *adv* : sous terre — **~** [ˈʌndərˌgraʊnd] *adj* **1** : souterrain **2** SECRET : clandestin — **~** [ˈʌndərˌgraʊnd] *n* SUBWAY : métro *m*
undergrowth [ˈʌndərˈgro:θ] *n* : sous-bois *m*, broussailles *fpl*
underhanded [ˌʌndərˈhændəd] *adj* SLY : sournois
underline [ˈʌndərˌlaɪn] *vt* **-lined; -lining** : souligner
underlying [ˌʌndərˈlaɪɪŋ] *adj* : sous-jacent
undermine [ˌʌndərˈmaɪn] *vt* **-mined; -mining** : saper, miner
underneath [ˌʌndərˈni:θ] *prep* : sous, au-dessous de — **~** *adv* : en dessous, dessous
underpants [ˈʌndərˌpænts] *npl* : caleçon *m*, slip *m France*
underpass [ˈʌndərˌpæs] *n* : voie *f* inférieure (de l'autoroute), passage *m* souterrain (pour piétons)
underprivileged [ˌʌndərˈprɪvlɪdʒd] *adj* : défavorisé
undershirt [ˈʌndərˌʃərt] *n* : maillot *m* de corps
understand [ˌʌndərˈstænd] *vt* **-stood** [-ˈstʊd]; **-standing** **1** : comprendre **2** BELIEVE : croire — **understandable** [ˌʌndərˈstændəbəl] *adj* : compréhensible — **understanding** [ˌʌndərˈstændɪŋ] *n* **1** : compréhension *f* **2** AGREEMENT : entente *f*, accord *m* — **~** *adj* : compréhensif
understudy [ˈʌndərˌstʌdi] *n, pl* **-dies** : doublure *f* (au théâtre)
undertake [ˌʌndərˈteɪk] *vt* **-took** [-ˈtʊk]; **-taken** [-ˈteɪkən]; **-taking** : entreprendre (une tâche), assumer (une responsabilité) — **undertaker** [ˈʌndərˌteɪkər] *n* : entrepreneur *m* de pompes funèbres — **undertaking** [ˈʌndərˌteɪkɪŋ, ˌʌndərˈ-] *n* : entreprise *f*
undertone [ˈʌndərˌto:n] *n* : voix *f* basse
undertow [ˈʌndərˌto:] *n* : courant *m* sous-marin
underwater [ˌʌndərˈwɔt̬ər, -ˈwɑ-] *adj* : sous-marin — **~** *adv* : sous l'eau
under way [ˌʌndərˈweɪ] *adv* : en cours, en route
underwear [ˈʌndərˌwær] *n* : sous-vêtements *mpl*
underwent → **undergo**
underworld [ˈʌndərˌwərld] *n or* **criminal ~** : milieu *m*, pègre *f*
undesirable [ˌʌndɪˈzaɪrəbəl] *adj* : indésirable
undisputed [ˌʌndɪˈspju:t̬əd] *adj* : incontesté
undo [ˌʌnˈdu:] *vt* **-did; -done; -doing** **1** UNFASTEN : défaire, détacher **2** **~ a wrong** : réparer un tort
undoubtedly [ˌʌnˈdaʊt̬ədli] *adv* : sans aucun doute
undress [ˌʌnˈdrɛs] *vt* : déshabiller — *vi* : se déshabiller
undue [ˌʌnˈdu:, -ˈdju:] *adj* : excessif, démesuré
undulate [ˈʌndʒəˌleɪt] *vi* **-lated; -lating** : onduler
unduly [ˌʌnˈdu:li] *adv* : excessivement
unearth [ˌʌnˈɛrθ] *vt* : déterrer
uneasy [ˌʌnˈi:zi] *adj* **1** : mal à l'aise, gêné **2** WORRIED : inquiet **3** UNSTABLE : précaire — **uneasily** [ˌʌnˈi:zəli] *adv* : avec inquiétude — **uneasiness** [ˌʌnˈi:zinəs] *n* : inquiétude *f*
uneducated [ˌʌnˈɛdʒəˌkeɪt̬əd] *adj* : sans éducation
unemployed [ˌʌnɪmˈplɔɪd] *adj* : en chômage, sans travail — **unemployment** [ˌʌnɪmˈplɔɪmənt] *n* : chômage *m*
unequal [ˌʌnˈi:kwəl] *adj* : inégal
uneven [ˌʌnˈi:vən] *adj* **1** : inégal **2** ODD : impair
unexpected [ˌʌnɪkˈspɛktəd] *adj* : inattendu, imprévu
unfailing [ˌʌnˈfeɪlɪŋ] *adj* **1** CONSTANT

: infaillible **2** INEXHAUSTIBLE : inépuisable
unfair [ˌʌnˈfær] *adj* : injuste — **unfairly** [ˌʌnˈfærli] *adj* : injustement — **unfairness** [ˌʌnˈfærnəs] *n* : injustice *f*
unfaithful [ˌʌnˈfeɪθfəl] *adj* : infidèle — **unfaithfulness** [ˌʌnˈfeɪθfəlnəs] *n* : infidélité *f*
unfamiliar [ˌʌnfəˈmɪljər] *adj* **1** : inconnu, peu familier **2 be ∼ with** : mal connaître
unfasten [ˌʌnˈfæsən] *vt* : déboucler (une ceinture)
unfavorable [ˌʌnˈfeɪvərəbəl] *adj* : défavorable
unfeeling [ˌʌnˈfi:lɪŋ] *adj* : insensible
unfinished [ˌʌnˈfɪnɪʃd] *adj* : inachevé
unfit [ˌʌnˈfɪt] *adj* : inapte, impropre
unfold [ˌʌnˈfo:ld] *vt* **1** : déplier **2** REVEAL : dévoiler — *vi* : se dérouler
unforeseen [ˌʌnforˈsi:n] *adj* : imprévu
unforgettable [ˌʌnfərˈgɛt̬əbəl] *adj* : inoubliable
unforgivable [ˌʌnfərˈgɪvəbəl] *adj* : impardonnable
unfortunate [ˌʌnˈfɔrʧənət] *adj* **1** UNLUCKY : malheureux **2** REGRETTABLE : regrettable, fâcheux — **unfortunately** [ˌʌnˈfɔrʧənətli] *adv* : malheureusement
unfounded [ˌʌnˈfaʊndəd] *adj* : sans fondement
unfurl [ˌʌnˈfərl] *vt* : déployer
unfurnished [ˌʌnˈfərnɪʃt] *adj* : non meublé
ungainly [ˌʌnˈgeɪnli] *adj* : gauche
ungodly [ˌʌnˈgɑdli, -ˈgɑd-] *adj* UNSEEMLY : indu, impossible
ungrateful [ˌʌnˈgreɪtfəl] *adj* : ingrat
unhappy [ˌʌnˈhæpi] *adj* **-pier; -est 1** SAD : malheureux, triste **2** DISSATISFIED : mécontent — **unhappiness** [ˌʌnˈhæpinəs] *n* : tristesse *f*
unharmed [ˌʌnˈhɑrmd] *adj* : indemne
unhealthy [ˌʌnˈhɛlθi] *adj* **-healthier; -healthiest 1** : insalubre, malsain **2** SICKLY : malade, maladif
unheard-of [ˌʌnˈhərdəv] *adj* : sans précédent, inconnu
unhook [ˌʌnˈhʊk] *vt* **1** REMOVE : décrocher **2** UNFASTEN : dégrafer
unhurt [ˌʌnˈhərt] *adj* : indemne
unicorn [ˈju:nəˌkɔrn] *n* : licorne *f*
unification [ˌju:nəfəˈkeɪʃən] *n* : unification *f*
uniform [ˈju:nəˌfɔrm] *adj* : uniforme — **∼** *n* : uniforme *m* — **uniformity** [ˌju:nəˈfɔrmət̬i] *n, pl* **-ties** : uniformité *f*
unify [ˈju:nəˌfaɪ] *vt* **-fied; -fying** : unifier
unilateral [ˌju:nəˈlæt̬ərəl] *adj* : unilatéral
uninhabited [ˌʌnɪnˈhæbət̬əd] *adj* : inhabité
union [ˈju:njən] *n* **1** : union *f* **2** *or* **labor ∼** : syndicat *m*
unique [jʊˈni:k] *adj* : unique — **uniquely** [jʊˈni:kli] *adv* : exceptionnellement
unison [ˈju:nəsən, -zən] *n* **in ∼** : à l'unisson
unit [ˈju:nɪt] *n* **1** : unité *f* **2** GROUP : groupe *m*
unite [jʊˈnaɪt] *v* **united; uniting** *vt* : unir — *vi* : s'unir — **unity** [ˈju:nət̬i] *n, pl* **-ties** : unité *f*
universe [ˈju:nəˌvərs] *n* : univers *m* — **universal** [ˌju:nəˈvərsəl] *adj* : universel
university [ˌju:nəˈvərsət̬i] *n, pl* **-ties** : université *f*
unjust [ˌʌnˈʤʌst] *adj* : injuste — **unjustified** [ˌʌnˈʤʌstəˌfaɪd] *adj* : injustifié
unkempt [ˌʌnˈkɛmpt] *adj* : en désordre, négligé
unkind [ˌʌnˈkaɪnd] *adj* : peu aimable, pas gentil — **unkindness** [ˌʌnˈkaɪndnəs] *n* : méchanceté *f*
unknown [ˌʌnˈno:n] *adj* : inconnu
unlawful [ˌʌnˈlɔfəl] *adj* : illégal
unless [ənˈlɛs] *conj* : à moins que, à moins de
unlike [ˌʌnˈlaɪk] *adj* : différent — **∼** *prep* **1** : différent de **2** : contrairement à — **unlikelihood** [ˌʌnˈlaɪkliˌhʊd] *n* : improbabilité *f* — **unlikely** [ˌʌnˈlaɪkli] *adj* **-lier; -liest** : improbable
unlimited [ˌʌnˈlɪmət̬əd] *adj* : illimité
unload [ˌʌnˈlo:d] *vt* : décharger
unlock [ˌʌnˈlɑk] *vt* : ouvrir, débarrer *Can* (une porte, etc.)
unlucky [ˌʌnˈlʌki] *adj* **-luckier; -luckiest 1** : malchanceux **2** : qui porte malheur (se dit d'un numéro)
unmarried [ˌʌnˈmærid] *adj* : célibataire
unnecessary [ˌʌnˈnɛsəˌsɛri] *adj* : inutile
unnerving [ˌʌnˈnərvɪŋ] *adj* : déconcertant
unnoticed [ˌʌnˈno:t̬əst] *adj* : inaperçu
unoccupied [ˌʌnˈɑkjəˌpaɪd] *adj* **1** IDLE : inoccupé **2** EMPTY : libre
unofficial [ˌʌnəˈfɪʃəl] *adj* : officieux, non officiel
unpack [ˌʌnˈpæk] *vi* : défaire ses bagages

unparalleled [ˌʌnˈpærəˌlɛld] *adj* : sans égal, sans pareil
unpleasant [ˌʌnˈplɛzənt] *adj* : désagréable
unplug [ˌʌnˈplʌg] *vt* **-plugged; -plugging 1** UNCLOG : déboucher **2** DISCONNECT : débrancher
unpopular [ˌʌnˈpɑpjələr] *adj* : impopulaire
unprecedented [ˌʌnˈprɛsəˌdɛntəd] *adj* : sans précédent
unpredictable [ˌʌnprɪˈdɪktəbəl] *adj* : imprévisible
unprepared [ˌʌnpriˈpærd] *adj* : mal préparé
unqualified [ˌʌnˈkwɑləˌfaɪd] *adj* : non qualifié
unquestionable [ˌʌnˈkwɛsʧənəbəl] *adj* : incontestable
unravel [ˌʌnˈrævəl] *vt* **-eled** *or* **-elled; -eling** *or* **elling** : démêler, dénouer
unreal [ˌʌnˈri:l] *adj* : irréel — **unrealistic** [ˌʌnˌri:əˈlɪstɪk] *adj* : irréaliste
unreasonable [ˌʌnˈri:zənəbel] *adj* : déraisonnable
unrecognizable [ˌʌnˈrɛkəgˌnaɪzəb'l] *adj* : méconnaissable
unrelated [ˌʌnrɪˈleɪţəd] *adj* : sans rapport
unrelenting [ˌʌnrɪˈlɛntɪŋ] *adj* : implacable
unreliable [ˌʌnrɪˈlaɪəbəl] *adj* : peu fiable, peu sûr
unrepentant [ˌʌnrɪˈpɛntənt] *adj* : impénitent
unrest [ˌʌnˈrɛst] *n* : agitation *f,* troubles *mpl*
unripe [ˌʌnˈraɪp] *adj* : pas mûr, vert
unrivaled *or* **unrivalled** [ˌʌnˈraɪvəld] *adj* : sans égal, incomparable
unroll [ˌʌnˈro:l] *vt* : dérouler
unruly [ˌʌnˈru:li] *adj* : indiscipliné
unsafe [ˌʌnˈseɪf] *adj* : dangereux
unsatisfactory [ˌʌnˌsætəsˈfæktəri] *adj* : peu satisfaisant
unscrew [ˌʌnˈskru:] *vt* : dévisser
unseemly [ˌʌnˈsi:mli] *adj* **-lier; -est** : inconvenant
unseen [ˌʌnˈsi:n] *adj* : invisible
unsettle [ˌʌnˈsɛţəl] *vt* **-tled; -tling** DISTURB : perturber — **unsettled** [ˌʌnˈsɛţəld] *adj* **1** UNSTABLE : instable **2** DISTURBED : troublé
unsightly [ˌʌnˈsaɪtli] *adj* : laid
unskilled [ˌʌnˈskɪld] *adj* : non spécialisé — **unskillful** [ˌʌnˈskɪlfəl] *adj* : malhabile
unsound [ˌʌnˈsaʊnd] *adj* : peu judicieux
unspeakable [ˌʌnˈspi:kəbəl] *adj* **1** : indicible **2** TERRIBLE : atroce
unstable [ˌʌnˈsteɪbəl] *adj* : instable
unsteady [ˌʌnˈstɛdi] *adj* **1** : instable **2** SHAKY : tremblant
unsuccessful [ˌʌnsəkˈsɛsfəl] *adj* **1** : infructueux **2 be ~** : échouer
unsuitable [ˌʌnˈsu:ţəbəl] *adj* : qui ne convient pas, inapproprié — **unsuited** [ˌʌnˈsu:ţəd] *adj* : inapte
unsure [ˌʌnˈʃʊr] *adj* **1** : incertain **2 be ~ of oneself** : manquer de confiance en soi
unsuspecting [ˌʌnsəˈspɛktɪŋ] *adj* : qui ne se doute de rien
unthinkable [ˌʌnˈθɪŋkəbəl] *adj* : impensable, inconcevable
untidy [ˌʌnˈtaɪdi] *adj* **-dier; -est** : en désordre
untie [ˌʌnˈtaɪ] *vt* **-tied; -tying** *or* **-tieing** : dénouer, défaire
until [ˌʌnˈtɪl] *prep* **1** UP TO : jusqu'à **2** BEFORE : avant — **~** *conj* : jusqu'à ce que, avant que, avant de
untimely [ˌʌnˈtaɪmli] *adj* **1** : prématuré **2** INOPPORTUNE : déplacé
untoward [ˌʌnˈtɔrd, -ˈto:ərd, -təˈwɔrd] *adj* : fâcheux
untroubled [ˌʌnˈtrʌbəld] *adj* **1** : tranquille **2 be ~ by** : ne pas être affecté par
untrue [ˌʌnˈtru:] *adj* : faux
unused *adj* [ˌʌnˈju:zd, *in sense 1 usually* -ˈju:st] **1** UNACCUSTOMED : pas habitué **2** NEW : neuf, nouveau
unusual [ˌʌnˈju:ʒuəl] *adj* : peu commun, rare — **unusually** [ˌʌnˈju:ʒuəli] *adv* : exceptionnellement
unveil [ˌʌnˈveɪl] *vt* : dévoiler
unwanted [ˌʌnˈwɑntəd] *adj* : non désiré
unwarranted [ˌʌnˈwɔrəntəd] *adj* : injustifié
unwelcome [ˌʌnˈwɛlkəm] *adj* : inopportun
unwell [ˌʌnˈwɛl] *adj* : indisposé
unwieldy [ˌʌnˈwi:ldi] *adj* : encombrant
unwilling [ˌʌnˈwɪlɪŋ] *adj* : peu disposé — **unwillingly** [ˌʌnˈwɪlɪŋli] *adv* : à contrecœur
unwind [ˌʌnˈwaɪnd] *v* **-wound; -winding** *vt* : dérouler — *vi* **1** : se dérouler **2** RELAX : se détendre
unwise [ˌʌnˈwaɪz] *adj* : imprudent
unworthy [ˌʌnˈwərði] *adj* **~ of** : indigne de
unwrap [ˌʌnˈræp] *vt* **-wrapped; -wrapped** : déballer
up [ˈʌp] *adv* **1** ABOVE : en haut **2** UP-

WARDS : vers le haut **3 farther ~** : plus loin **4 go ~** : augmenter, monter **5 speak ~** : parler plus fort **6 stand ~** : se lever **7 ~ until** : jusqu'à — **~** *adj* **1** AWAKE : levé **2** INCREASING : qui augmente **3** UP-TO-DATE : au courant, à jour **4** FINISHED : fini **5 be ~ for** : être pret pour **6 what's ~?** : qu'est-ce qui se passe? — **~** *prep* **1** : en haut de **2 go ~** : monter **3 sail ~ the river** : remonter la rivière en bateau **4 ~ to** : jusqu'à — **~** *v* **upped; upping** *vt* : augmenter — *vi* **~ and leave** : partir sans mot dire

upbringing ['ʌpˌbrɪŋɪŋ] *n* : éducation *f*

upcoming [ˌʌp'kʌmɪŋ] *adj* : prochain, à venir

update [ˌʌp'deɪt] *vt* **-dated; -dating** : mettre à jour — **~** ['ʌpˌdeɪt] *n* : mise *f* à jour

upgrade ['ʌpˌgreɪd, ˌʌp'-] *vt* **-graded; -grading 1** IMPROVE : améliorer **2** PROMOTE : promouvoir

upheaval [ˌʌp'hi:vəl] *n* : bouleversement *m*

uphill [ˌʌp'hɪl] *adv* **go ~** : monter — **~** ['ʌpˌhɪl] *adj* **1** ASCENDING : qui monte **2** DIFFICULT : pénible

uphold [ˌʌp'ho:ld] *vt* **-held; -holding** : soutenir, maintenir

upholstery [ˌʌp'ho:lstəri] *n, pl* **-steries** : rembourrage *m*

upkeep ['ʌpˌki:p] *n* : entretien *m*

upon [ə'pɔn, ə'pɑn] *prep* **1** : sur **2 ~ leaving** : en partant

upper ['ʌpər] *adj* : supérieur

upper class *n* : aristocratie *f*

upper hand *n* **have the ~** : avoir le dessus

uppermost ['ʌpərˌmo:st] *adj* : le plus haut, le plus élevé

upright ['ʌpˌraɪt] *adj* : droit — **~** *n* : montant *m* (en construction)

uprising ['ʌpˌraɪzɪŋ] *n* : soulèvement *m*

uproar ['ʌpˌro:r] *n* : tumulte *m*

uproot [ˌʌp'ru:t, -'rʊt] *vt* : déraciner

upset [ˌʌp'sɛt] *vt* **-set; -setting 1** OVERTURN : renverser **2** DISRUPT : déranger **3** ANNOY : ennuyer — **~** *adj* **1** DISTRESSED : bouleversé **2** ANNOYED : ennuyé, vexé **3 have an ~ stomach** : avoir l'estomac dérangé — **~** ['ʌpˌsɛt] *n* : bouleversement *m*

upshot ['ʌpˌʃɑt] *n* : résultat *m*

upside down *adv* **1** : à l'envers **2 turn ~** : mettre sens dessus dessous — **upside-down** [ˌʌpˌsaɪd'daʊn] *adj* : à l'envers

upstairs [ˌʌp'stærz] *adv* : en haut — **~** ['ʌpˌstærz, ˌʌp'-] *adj* : d'en haut, à l'étage — **~** ['ʌpˌstærz, ˌʌp'-] *ns & pl* : étage *m*

upstart ['ʌpˌstɑrt] *n* : arriviste *mf*

upstream ['ʌp'stri:m] *adv* : en amont

up-to-date [ˌʌptə'deɪt] *adj* **1** : à jour **2** MODERN : moderne

uptown ['ʌp'taʊn] *adv* : dans les quartiers résidentiels

upturn ['ʌpˌtərn] *n* : amélioration *f*, reprise *f* (économique)

upward ['ʌpwərd] *or* **upwards** [-wərdz] *adv* **1** : vers le haut **2 ~ of** : plus de — **upward** *adj* : ascendant

uranium [jʊ'reɪniəm] *n* : uranium *m*

Uranus [jʊ'reɪnəs, 'jʊrənəs] *n* : Uranus *f*

urban ['ərbən] *adj* : urbain

urbane [ˌər'beɪn] *adj* : raffiné, courtois

urge ['ərʤ] *vt* **urged; urging** : pousser, inciter — **~** *n* **1** DESIRE : envie *f* **2** IMPULSE : pulsion *f* — **urgency** ['ərʤəntsi] *n, pl* **-cies** : urgence *f* — **urgent** ['ərʤənt] *adj* **1** : urgent **2 be ~** : presser

urinal ['jʊrənəl, *esp Brit* jʊr'aɪnəl] *n* : urinoir *m*

urine ['jʊrən] *n* : urine *f* — **urinate** ['jʊrəˌneɪt] *vi* **-nated; -nating** : uriner

urn ['ərn] *n* : urne *f*

us ['ʌs] *pron* : nous

usable ['ju:zəbəl] *adj* : utilisable

usage ['ju:sɪʤ, -zɪʤ] *n* : usage *m*

use ['ju:z] *v* **used** ['ju:zd; *in phrase "used to" usually* 'ju:stu:]; **using** *vt* **1** : employer, utiliser, se servir de **2** CONSUME : consommer **3 ~ up** : épuiser — *vi* **she ~d to dance** : elle dansait avant — **~** ['ju:s] *n* **1** : emploi *m*, usage *m* **2** USEFULNESS : utilité *f* **3 in ~** : occupé **4 what's the ~?** : à quoi bon? — **used** ['ju:zd] *adj* **1** SECONDHAND : d'occasion **2 be ~ to** : avoir l'habitude de, être habitué à — **useful** ['ju:sfəl] *adj* : utile, pratique — **usefulness** ['ju:sfəlnəs] *n* : utilité *f* — **useless** ['ju:sləs] *adj* : inutile — **user** ['ju:zər] *n* : usager *m;* utilisateur *m*, -trice *f*

usher ['ʌʃər] *vt* **1** : conduire, accompagner **2 ~ in** : inaugurer — **~** *n* : huissier *m* (à un tribunal); placeur *m*, -ceuse *f* (au théâtre)

usual ['ju:ʒʊəl] *adj* **1** : habituel **2 as ~** : comme d'habitude — **usually** ['ju:ʒʊəli] *adv* : habituellement, d'habitude

usurp [jʊ'sərp, -'zərp] *vt* : usurper

utensil [jʊˈtɛntsəl] *n* : ustensile *m*
uterus [ˈjuːt̬ərəs] *n, pl* **uteri** [-ˌraɪ] : utérus *m*
utility [juːˈtɪlət̬i] *n, pl* **-ties 1** : utilité *f* **2** *or* **public ~** : service *m* public
utilize [ˈjuːt̬əlˌaɪz] *vt* **-lized; -lizing** : utiliser
utmost [ˈʌtˌmoːst] *adj* **1** FARTHEST : extrême **2 of ~ importance :** de la plus haute importance — **~** *n* **do one's ~** : faire tout son possible
utopia [jʊˈtoːpiə] *n* : utopie *f* — **utopian** [jʊˈtoːpiən] *adj* : utopique
utter[1] [ˈʌtər] *adj* : absolu, total
utter[2] *vt* : émettre (un son), pousser (un cri) — **utterance** [ˈʌt̬ərənts] *n* : déclaration *f*, paroles *fpl*
utterly [ˈʌtərli] *adv* : complètement

V

v [ˈviː] *n, pl* **v's** *or* **vs** [ˈviːz] : v *m*, vingt-deuxième lettre de l'alphabet
vacant [ˈveɪkənt] *adj* **1** AVAILABLE : libre **2** UNOCCUPIED : vacant — **vacancy** [ˈveɪkəntsi] *n, pl* **-cies 1** : chambre *f* disponible **2** : poste *m* vacant **3 no ~** : complet
vacate [ˈveɪˌkeɪt] *vt* **-cated; -cating** : quitter
vacation [veɪˈkeɪʃən, və-] *n* : vacances *fpl*
vaccination [ˌvæksəˈneɪʃən] *n* : vaccination *f* — **vaccinate** [ˈvæksəˌneɪt] *vt* **-nated; -nating** : vacciner — **vaccine** [vækˈsiːn, ˈvækˌ-] *n* : vaccin *m*
vacuum [ˈvæˌkjuːm, -kjəm] *n, pl* **vacuums** *or* **vacua** [ˈvækjʊə] : vide *m* — **~** *vt* : passer l'aspirateur sur — **vacuum cleaner** *n* : aspirateur *m*, balayeuse *f Can*
vagina [vəˈʤaɪnə] *n, pl* **-nae** [-ˌniː, -ˌnaɪ] *or* **-nas** : vagin *m*
vagrant [ˈveɪgrənt] *n* : vagabond *m*, -bonde *f*
vague [ˈveɪg] *adj* **vaguer; vaguest** : vague
vain [ˈveɪn] *adj* **1** FUTILE : vain **2** CONCEITED : vaniteux
valentine [ˈvælənˌtaɪn] *n* : carte *f* de Saint-Valentin
valiant [ˈvæljənt] *adj* : vaillant
valid [ˈvæləd] *adj* : valable, valide — **validate** [ˈvæləˌdeɪt] *vt* **-dated; -dating** : valider
valley [ˈvæli] *n, pl* **-leys** : vallée *f*
valor *or Brit* **valour** [ˈvælər] *n* : bravoure *f*
value [ˈvælˌjuː] *n* : valeur *f* — **~** *vt* **valued; valuing 1** : estimer, évaluer **2** APPRECIATE : apprécier — **valuable** [ˈvæljʊəbəl, -jəbəl] *adj* **1** : de valeur **2** WORTHWHILE : précieux — **valuables** [ˈvæljʊəbəlz, -jəbəlz] *npl* : objets *mpl* de valeur
valve [ˈvælv] *n* : valve *f* (d'un pneu), soupape *f*
vampire [ˈvæmˌpaɪr] *n* : vampire *m*
van [ˈvæn] *n* : camionnette *f*, fourgonnette *f*
vandal [ˈvændəl] *n* : vandale *mf* — **vandalism** [ˈvændəlˌɪzəm] *n* : vandalisme *m* — **vandalize** [ˈvændəlˌaɪz] *vt* **-ized; -izing** : saccager
vane [ˈveɪn] *n or* **weather ~** : girouette *f*
vanguard [ˈvænˌgɑrd] *n* : avant-garde *f*
vanilla [vəˈnɪlə, -ˈnɛ-] *n* : vanille *f*
vanish [ˈvænɪʃ] *vi* : disparaître
vanity [ˈvænət̬i] *n, pl* **-ties** : vanité *f*
vantage point [ˈvæntɪʤ] *n* : point *m* de vue
vapor [ˈveɪpər] *n* : vapeur *f*
variable [ˈvɛriəbəl] *adj* : variable — **~** *n* : variable *f* — **variant** [ˈvɛriənt] *n* : variante *f* — **variation** [ˌvɛriˈeɪʃən] *n* : variation *f* — **varied** [ˈvɛrid] *adj* : varié, divers — **variety** [vəˈraɪət̬i] *n, pl* **-eties 1** DIVERSITY : variété *f* **2** SORT : espèce *f*, sorte *f* — **various** [ˈvɛriəs] *adj* : divers, varié
varnish [ˈvɑrnɪʃ] *n* : vernis *m* — **~** *vt* : vernir
vary [ˈvɛri] *v* **varied; varying** : varier
vase [ˈveɪs, ˈveɪz, ˈvɑz] *n* : vase *m*
vast [ˈvæst] *adj* : vaste — **vastness** [ˈvæstnəs] *n* : immensité *f*
vat [ˈvæt] *n* : cuve *f*, bac *m*
vault [ˈvɔlt] *n* **1** ARCH : voûte *f* **2** *or* **bank ~** : chambre *f* forte
VCR [ˌviːˌsiːˈɑr] *n* (videocassette recorder) : magnétoscope *m*
veal [ˈviːl] *n* : veau *m*
veer [ˈvɪr] *vi* : virer
vegetable [ˈvɛʤtəbəl, ˈvɛʤət̬ə-] *adj* **1** : végétal **2 ~ soup** : soupe *f* aux légumes — **~** *n* : légume *m* — **vegetarian** [ˌvɛʤəˈtɛriən] *n* : végétarien *m*, -rienne *f* — **vegetation** [ˌvɛʤəˈteɪʃən] *n* : végétation *f*

vehement [ˈviːəmənt] *adj* : véhément
vehicle [ˈviəkəl, ˈviːˌhɪkəl] *n* : véhicule *m*
veil [ˈveɪl] *n* : voile *m* — ~ *vt* : voiler
vein [ˈveɪn] *n* **1** : veine *f* **2** : filon *m* (d'un minéral, etc.) **3** : nervure *f* (d'une feuille)
velocity [vəˈlɑsət̬i] *n, pl* **-ties** : vélocité *f*
velvet [ˈvɛlvət] *n* : velours *m* — **velvety** [ˈvɛlvət̬i] *adj* : velouté
vending machine [ˈvɛndɪŋ-] *n* : distributeur *m* automatique
vendor [ˈvɛndər] *n* : vendeur *m*, -deuse *f*
veneer [vəˈnɪr] *n* **1** : placage *m* (de bois) **2** FACADE : vernis *m*
venerable [ˈvɛnərəbəl] *adj* : vénérable — **venerate** [ˈvɛnəˌreɪt] *vt* **-ated; -ating** : vénérer
venereal [vəˈnɪriəl] *adj* : vénérien
venetian blind [vəˈniːʃən] *n* : store *m* vénitien
vengeance [ˈvɛnʤənts] *n* **1** : vengeance *f* **2 take ~ on** : se venger sur — **vengeful** [ˈvɛnʤfəl] *adj* : vengeur, vindicatif
venison [ˈvɛnəsən, -zən] *n* : venaison *f*
venom [ˈvɛnəm] *n* : venin *m* — **venomous** [ˈvɛnəməs] *adj* : venimeux
vent [ˈvɛnt] *vt* : décharger — ~ *n* **1** : orifice *m*, conduit *m* **2** *or* **air ~** : bouche *f* d'aération — **ventilate** [ˈvɛntəlˌeɪt] *vt* **-lated; -lating** : ventiler — **ventilation** [ˌvɛntəlˈeɪʃən] *n* : ventilation *f*
venture [ˈvɛnʧər] *v* **-tured; -turing** *vt* RISK : risquer — *vi or* **~ out** : s'aventurer — ~ *n* : entreprise *f*
Venus [ˈviːnəs] *n* : Vénus *f*
veranda *or* **verandah** [vəˈrændə] *n* : véranda *f*
verb [ˈvərb] *n* : verbe *m* — **verbal** [ˈvərbəl] *adj* : verbal — **verbatim** [vərˈbeɪt̬əm] *adv & adj* : mot pour mot
verdict [ˈvərdɪkt] *n* : verdict *m*
verge [ˈvərʤ] *n* **1** EDGE : bordure *f* **2 on the ~ of** : sur le point de
verify [ˈvɛrəˌfaɪ] *vt* **-fied; -fying** : vérifier
vermin [ˈvərmən] *ns & pl* : vermine *f*
versatile [ˈvərsət̬əl] *adj* : polyvalent
verse [ˈvərs] *n* **1** STANZA : strophe *f* **2** POETRY : vers *mpl* **3** : verset *m* (de la Bible) — **versed** [ˈvərst] *adj* **be well ~ in** : être versé dans
version [ˈvərʒən] *n* : version *f*
versus [ˈvərsəs] *prep* : contre
vertebra [ˈvərtəbrə] *n, pl* **-brae** [-ˌbreɪ, -ˌbriː] *or* **-bras** : vertèbre *f*
vertical [ˈvərtɪkəl] *adj* : vertical — ~ *n* : verticale *f*
vertigo [ˈvərtɪˌgoː] *n, pl* **-goes** *or* **-gos** : vertige *m*
very [ˈvɛri] *adv* **1** : très **2 ~ much** : beaucoup — ~ *adj* **1** EXACT : même **2 at the ~ least** : tout au moins **3 the ~ thought!** : quelle idée!
vessel [ˈvɛsəl] *n* **1** : vaisseau *m* **2** CONTAINER : récipient *m*
vest [ˈvɛst] *n* : gilet *m*
vestige [ˈvɛstɪʤ] *n* : vestige *m*
veteran [ˈvɛt̬ərən, ˈvɛtrən] *n* : vétéran *m*, ancien combattant *m*
veterinarian [ˌvɛt̬ərəˈnɛriən, ˌvɛt̬rə-] *n* : vétérinaire *mf*
veto [ˈviːt̬o] *n, pl* **-toes** : veto *m* — ~ *vt* : mettre son veto à
vex [ˈvɛks] *vt* **vexed; vexing** : vexer, contrarier
via [ˈvaɪə, ˈviːə] *prep* : via, par
viable [ˈvaɪəbəl] *adj* : viable
vial [ˈvaɪəl] *n* : ampoule *f*
vibrant [ˈvaɪbrənt] *adj* : vibrant — **vibrate** [ˈvaɪˌbreɪt] *vi* **-brated; -brating** : vibrer — **vibration** [vaɪˈbreɪʃən] *n* : vibration *f*
vicar [ˈvɪkər] *n* : vicaire *m*
vice [ˈvaɪs] *n* : vice *m*
vice president *n* : vice-président *m*, -dente *f*
vice versa [ˌvaɪsɪˈvərsə, ˌvaɪsˈvər-] *adv* : vice versa
vicinity [vəˈsɪnət̬i] *n, pl* **-ties** : environs *mpl*
vicious [ˈvɪʃəs] *adj* **1** SAVAGE : brutal **2** MALICIOUS : méchant
victim [ˈvɪktəm] *n* : victime *f*
victor [ˈvɪktər] *n* : vainqueur *m* — **victorious** [vɪkˈtoːriəs] *adj* : victorieux — **victory** [ˈvɪktəri] *n, pl* **-ries** : victoire *f*
video [ˈvɪdiˌoː] *n* : vidéo *f* — ~ *adj* : vidéo — **videocassette** [ˌvɪdiokəˈsɛt] *n* : vidéocassette *f* — **videotape** [ˈvɪdioˌteɪp] *n* : bande *f* vidéo — ~ *vt* **-taped; -taping** : enregistrer (sur magnétoscope)
vie [ˈvaɪ] *vi* **vied; vying** [ˈvaɪɪŋ] **~ for** : lutter pour
Vietnamese [viˌɛtnəˈmiːz, -ˈmiːs] *adj* : vietnamien
view [ˈvjuː] *n* **1** : vue *f* **2** OPINION : opinion *f*, avis *m* **3 come into ~** : apparaître **4 in ~ of** : vu, étant donné — ~ *vt* **1** : voir **2** CONSIDER : considérer — **viewer** [ˈvjuːər] *n or* **television ~** : téléspectateur *m*, -trice

f — **viewpoint** [ˈvju:ˌpɔɪnt] *n* : point *m* de vue
vigil [ˈvɪʤəl] *n* : veille *f* — **vigilance** [ˈvɪʤələnts] *n* : vigilance *f* — **vigilant** [ˈvɪʤələnt] *adj* : vigilant, attentif
vigor *or Brit* **vigour** [ˈvɪgər] *n* : vigueur *f* — **vigorous** [ˈvɪgərəs] *adj* : vigoureux
vile [ˈvaɪl] *adj* **viler; vilest** **1** BASE : vil **2** AWFUL : abominable, exécrable
villa [ˈvɪlə] *n* : villa *f*
village [ˈvɪlɪʤ] *n* : village *m* — **villager** [ˈvɪlɪʤər] *n* : villageois *m*, -geoise *f*
villain [ˈvɪlən] *n* : scélérat *m*, -rate *f*; méchant *m*, -chante *f*
vindicate [ˈvɪndəˌkeɪt] *vt* **-cated; -cating** : justifier
vindictive [vɪnˈdɪktɪv] *adj* : vindicatif
vine [ˈvaɪn] *n* : vigne *f*
vinegar [ˈvɪnɪgər] *n* : vinaigre *m*
vineyard [ˈvɪnjərd] *n* : vignoble *m*
vintage [ˈvɪntɪʤ] *n* **1** *or* **~ wine** : vin *m* de grand cru **2** *or* **~ year** : millésime *m*
vinyl [ˈvaɪnəl] *n* : vinyle *m*
violate [ˈvaɪəˌleɪt] *vt* **-lated; -lating** : violer — **violation** [ˌvaɪəˈleɪʃən] *n* : violation *f*
violence [ˈvaɪələnts] *n* : violence *f* — **violent** [ˈvaɪələnt] *adj* : violent
violet [ˈvaɪələt] *adj* : violet — **~** *n* **1** : violette *f* (plante) **2** : violet *m* (couleur)
violin [ˌvaɪəˈlɪn] *n* : violon *m* — **violinist** [ˌvaɪəˈlɪnɪst] *n* : violoniste *mf*
VIP [ˌvi:ˌaɪ:ˈpi:] *n, pl* **VIPs** [-ˈpi:z] (*v*ery *i*mportant *p*erson) : personnage *m* de marque
viper [ˈvaɪpər] *n* : vipère *f*
virgin [ˈvərʤən] *adj* : vierge — **~** *n* : vierge *f* — **virginity** [vərˈʤɪnəṭi] *n, pl* **-ties** : virginité *f*
virile [ˈvɪrəl, -ˌaɪl] *adj* : viril
virtual [ˈvərʧʊəl] *adj* : virtuel (en informatique) — **virtually** [ˈvərʧʊəli] *adv* : pratiquement
virtue [ˈvərˌʧu:] *n* **1** : vertu *f* **2 by ~ of** : en raison de
virtuoso [ˌvərʧʊˈo:ˌso:, -ˌzo:] *n, pl* **-sos** *or* **-si** [-ˌsi:, -ˌzi:] : virtuose *mf*
virtuous [ˈvərʧʊəs] *adj* : vertueux
virulent [ˈvɪrələnt, -jələnt] *adj* : virulent
virus [ˈvaɪrəs] *n* : virus *m*
visa [ˈvi:zə, -sə] *n* : visa *m*
viscous [ˈvɪskəs] *adj* : visqueux
vise *or Brit* **vice** [ˈvaɪs] *n* : étau *m*
visible [ˈvɪzəbəl] *adj* : visible — **visibility** [ˌvɪzəˈbɪləṭi] *n, pl* **-ties** : visibilité *f*
vision [ˈvɪʒən] *n* : vision *f* — **visionary** [ˈvɪʒəˌnɛri] *adj* : visionnaire
visit [ˈvɪzət] *vt* : rendre visite à (qqn), visiter (un lieu) — **~** *n* : visite *f* — **visitor** [ˈvɪzəṭər] *n* : visiteur *m*, -teuse *f*
visor [ˈvaɪzər] *n* : visière *f*
vista [ˈvɪstə] *n* : vue *f*
visual [ˈvɪʒʊəl] *adj* : visuel — **visualize** [ˈvɪʒʊəˌlaɪz] *vt* **-ized; -izing** : visualiser
vital [ˈvaɪṭəl] *adj* **1** : vital **2** ESSENTIAL : essentiel — **vitality** [vaɪˈtæləṭi] *n, pl* **-ties** : vitalité *f*
vitamin [ˈvaɪṭəmən] *n* : vitamine *f*
vivacious [vəˈveɪʃəs, vaɪ-] *adj* : vif, animé
vivid [ˈvɪvəd] *adj* : vivant, vif
vocabulary [vo:ˈkæbjəˌlɛri] *n, pl* **-laries** : vocabulaire *m*
vocal [ˈvo:kəl] *adj* **1** : vocal **2** OUTSPOKEN : franc — **vocal cords** *npl* : cordes *fpl* vocales — **vocalist** [ˈvo:kəlɪst] *n* : chanteur *m*, -teuse *f*
vocation [voˈkeɪʃən] *n* **1** : vocation *f* (religieuse) **2** OCCUPATION : profession *f*, métier *m* — **vocational** [voˈkeɪʃənəl] *adj* : professionnel
vodka [ˈvɑdkə] *n* : vodka *m*
vogue [ˈvo:g] *n* **1** : vogue *f*, mode *f* **2 be in ~** : être à la mode
voice [ˈvɔɪs] *n* : voix *f* — **~** [ˈvɔɪs] *vt* **voiced; voicing** : exprimer, formuler
void [ˈvɔɪd] *adj* **1** NULL : nul **2 ~ of** : dépourvu de — **~** *n* : vide *m* — **~** *vt* ANNUL : annuler
volatile [ˈvɑləṭəl] *adj* : volatil, instable
volcano [vɑlˈkeɪˌno:, vɔl-] *n, pl* **-noes** *or* **-nos** : volcan *m* — **volcanic** [vɑlˈkænɪk, vɔl-] *adj* : volcanique
volley [ˈvɑli] *n, pl* **-leys** : volée *f* — **volleyball** [ˈvɑliˌbɔl] *n* : volley-ball *m*
volt [ˈvo:lt] *n* : volt *m* — **voltage** [ˈvo:ltɪʤ] *n* **1** : voltage *m* **2 high ~** : de haute tension
volume [ˈvɑljəm, -ju:m] *n* : volume *m*
voluntary [ˈvɑlənˌtɛri] *adj* **1** : volontaire **2** UNPAID : bénévole — **volunteer** [ˌvɑlənˈtɪr] *n* : volontaire *mf* — **~** *vt* : offrir — *vi* : se porter volontaire
voluptuous [vəˈlʌpʧʊəs] *adj* : voluptueux
vomit [ˈvɑmət] *n* : vomi *m* — **~** *v* : vomir
voracious [vɔˈreɪʃəs, və-] *adj* : vorace
vote [ˈvo:t] *n* **1** : vote *m* **2** SUFFRAGE : droit *m* de vote — **~** *v* **voted; voting** : voter — **voter** [ˈvo:ṭər] *n* : électeur *m*, -trice *f* — **voting** [ˈvo:ṭɪŋ] *n* : scrutin *m*, vote *m*

vouch [ˈvaʊʧ] *vi* **~ for** : répondre de — **voucher** [ˈvaʊʧər] *n* : bon *m*
vow [vaʊ] *n* : vœu *m,* serment *m* — **~** *vt* : jurer
vowel [ˈvaʊəl] *n* : voyelle *f*
voyage [ˈvɔɪɪʤ] *n* : voyage *m*
vulgar [ˈvʌlgər] *adj* **1** COMMON : vulgaire **2** CRUDE : grossier — **vulgarity** [ˌvʌlˈgærət̬i] *n, pl* **-ties** : vulgarité *f*
vulnerable [ˈvʌlnərəbəl] *adj* : vulnérable — **vulnerability** [ˌvʌlnərəˈbɪlət̬i] *n* : vulnérabilité *f*
vulture [ˈvʌlʧər] *n* : vautour *m*
vying → **vie**

W

w [ˈdʌbəlˌju:] *n, pl* **w's** *or* **ws** [-ˌju:z] : w *m,* vingt-troisième lettre de l'alphabet
wad [ˈwɑd] *n* : tampon *m* (d'ouate, etc.), liasse *f* (de billets)
waddle [ˈwɑdəl] *vi* **-dled; -dling** : se dandiner
wade [ˈweɪd] *v* **waded; wading** *vi* : patauger — *vt or* **~ across** : traverser
wafer [ˈweɪfər] *n* : gaufrette *f*
waffle [ˈwɑfəl] *n* : gaufre *f*
waft [ˈwɑft, ˈwæft] *vi* : flotter
wag [ˈwæg] *vt* **wagged; wagging** : agiter, remuer
wage [ˈweɪʤ] *n or* **wages** *npl* : salaire *m,* paie *f* — **~** *vt* **waged; waging ~ war** : faire la guerre
wager [ˈweɪʤər] *n* : pari *m* — **~** *v* : parier
wagon [ˈwægən] *n* : chariot *m*
wail [ˈweɪl] *vi* : se lamenter — **~** *n* : lamentation *f*
waist [ˈweɪst] *n* : taille *f* — **waistline** [ˈweɪstˌlaɪn] *n* : taille *f*
wait [ˈweɪt] *vi* : attendre — *vt* **1** AWAIT : attendre **2 ~ tables** : servir à table — **~** *n* **1** : attente *f* **2 lie in ~ for** : guetter — **waiter** [ˈweɪt̬ər] *n* : serveur *m,* garçon *m* — **waiting room** *n* : salle *f* d'attente — **waitress** [ˈweɪtrəs] *n* : serveuse *f*
waive [ˈweɪv] *vt* **waived; waiving** : renoncer à
wake[1] [ˈweɪk] *v* **woke** [ˈwo:k]; **woken** [ˈwo:kən] *or* **waked; waking** *vi or* **~ up** : se réveiller — *vt* : réveiller — **~** *n* : veillée *f* funèbre
wake[2] *n* **1** : sillage *m* (laissé par un bateau) **2 in the ~ of** : à la suite de
waken [ˈweɪkən] *vt* : réveiller — *vi* : se réveiller
walk [ˈwɔk] *vi* **1** : marcher, aller à pied **2** STROLL : se promener — *vt* **1** : faire à pied **2** : raccompagner (qqn), promener (un chien) — **~** *n* **1** : marche *f,* promenade *f* **2** PATH : chemin *m* **3** GAIT : démarche *f* (d'une personne) — **walker** [ˈwɔkər] *n* : marcheur *m,* -cheuse *f;* promeneur *m,* -neuse *f* — **walking stick** *n* : canne *f* — **walkout** [ˈwɔkˌaʊt] *n* STRIKE : grève *f* — **walk out** *vi* **1** STRIKE : faire la grève **2** LEAVE : partir, sortir **3 ~ on** : quitter, abandonner
wall [ˈwɔl] *n* **1** : mur *m* (extérieur), paroi *f* (intérieure) **2** : remparts *mpl* (d'une ville)
wallet [ˈwɑlət] *n* : portefeuille *m*
Walloon [wɑˈlu:n] *adj* : wallon
wallop [ˈwɑləp] *vt* : donner une raclée à — **~** *n* : raclée *f*
wallow [ˈwɑˌlo:] *vi* **1** : se vautrer **2 ~ in** : s'apitoyer sur
wallpaper [ˈwɔlˌpeɪpər] *n* : tapisserie *f* — **~** *vt* : tapisser
walnut [ˈwɔlˌnʌt] *n* **1** : noyer *m* (arbre) **2** : noix *f* (fruit)
walrus [ˈwɔlrəs, ˈwɑl-] *n, pl* **-rus** *or* **-ruses** : morse *m*
waltz [ˈwɔlts] *n* : valse *f* — **~** *vi* : valser
wan [ˈwɑn] *adj* **wanner; wannest** : blême, pâle
wand [ˈwɑnd] *n* : baguette *f* (magique)
wander [ˈwɑndər] *vi* **1** : se promener, se balader **2** STRAY : errer — *vt* : parcourir — **wanderer** [ˈwɑndərər] *n* : vagabond *m,* -bonde *f*
wane [ˈweɪn] *vi* **waned; waning** : diminuer — **~** *n* **be on the ~** : être sur le déclin
want [ˈwɑnt, ˈwɔnt] *vt* **1** DESIRE : vouloir **2** NEED : avoir besoin de **3** LACK : manquer de **4 ~ed** : recherché par la police — **~** *n* **1** NEED : besoin *m* **2** LACK : manque *m* **3** DESIRE : désir *m* **4 for ~ of** : faute de — **wanting** [ˈwɑntɪŋ, ˈwɔn-] *adj* **be ~** : manquer
wanton [ˈwɑntən, ˈwɔn-] *adj* **1** LEWD : lascif **2 ~ cruelty** : cruauté *f* gratuite
war [ˈwɔr] *n* : guerre *f*
ward [ˈwɔrd] *n* **1** : salle *f* (d'un hôpital, etc.) **2** : circonscription *f* électorale **3 ~ of the court** : pupille *f* — **~** *vt or*

~ off : parer, éviter — **warden** [ˈwɔrdən] *n* **1** : gardien *m*, -dienne *f* **2** *or* **prison ~** : directeur *m*, -trice *f* de prison

wardrobe [ˈwɔrd,ro:b] *n* **1** CLOSET : armoire *f*, penderie *f* **2** CLOTHES : garde-robe *f*

warehouse [ˈwær,haʊs] *n* : entrepôt *m*, magasin *m* — **wares** [ˈwærz] *npl* : marchandises *fpl*

warfare [ˈwɔr,fær] *n* : guerre *f*

warhead [ˈwɔr,hɛd] *n* : ogive *f*

warily [ˈwærəli] *adv* : avec précaution

warlike [ˈwɔr,laɪk] *adj* : guerrier, belliqueux

warm [ˈwɔrm] *adj* **1** : chaud **2** LUKEWARM : tiède **3** CARING : chaleureux **4 I feel ~** : j'ai chaud — **~** *vt or* **~ up** : chauffer, réchauffer — *vi* **1** *or* **~ up** : se réchauffer **2 ~ to** : se prendre de sympathie pour (qqn), s'enthousiasmer pour (qqch) — **warm–blooded** [ˈwɔrmˈblʌdəd] *adj* : à sang chaud — **warmhearted** [ˈwɔrmˈhɑrţəd] *adj* : chaleureux — **warmly** [ˈwɔrmli] *adv* **1** : chaleureusement **2 dress ~** : s'habiller chaudement — **warmth** [ˈwɔrmpθ] *n* **1** : chaleur *f* **2** AFFECTION : affection *f*

warn [ˈwɔrn] *vt* **1** : avertir **2** INFORM : aviser — **warning** [ˈwɔrnɪŋ] *n* **1** : avertissement *m* **2** NOTICE : avis *m*

warp [ˈwɔrp] *vt* **1** : voiler (bois, etc.) **2** DISTORT : déformer

warrant [ˈwɔrənt] *n* **1** : autorisation *f* **2 arrest ~** : mandat *m* d'arrêt — **~** *vt* : justifier — **warranty** [ˈwɔrənti, ,wɔrənˈti:] *n, pl* **-ties** : garantie *f*

warrior [ˈwɔriər] *n* : guerrier *m*, -rière *f*

warship [ˈwɔr,ʃɪp] *n* : navire *m* de guerre

wart [ˈwɔrt] *n* : verrue *f*

wartime [ˈwɔr,taɪm] *n* : temps *m* de guerre

wary [ˈwæri] *adj* **warier; -est 1** : prudent, circonspect **2 be ~ of** : se méfier de

was → **be**

wash [ˈwɔʃ, ˈwɑʃ] *vt* **1** : laver, se laver **2 ~ away** : emporter — *vi* : se laver — **~** *n* **1** : lavage *m* **2** LAUNDRY : linge *m* sale — **washable** [ˈwɔʃəbəl, ˈwɑ-] *adj* : lavable — **washcloth** [ˈwɔʃ,klɔθ, ˈwɑʃ-] *n* : gant *m* de toilette, débarbouillette *f Can* — **washed–out** [ˈwɔʃtˈaʊt, ˈwɑʃt-] *adj* **1** : décoloré **2** EXHAUSTED : épuisé — **washer** [ˈwɔʃər, ˈwɑ-] *n* **1** → **washing machine 2** : rondelle *f*, joint *m* — **washing machine** *n* : machine *f* à laver — **washroom** [ˈwɔʃ,ru:m, ˈwɑʃ-, -,rʊm] *n* : toilettes *fpl*

wasn't [ˈwʌzənt] (*contraction of* **was not**) → **be**

wasp [ˈwɑsp] *n* : guêpe *f*

waste [ˈweɪst] *v* **wasted; wasting** *vt* : gaspiller, perdre — *vi or* **~ away** : dépérir — **~** *adj* : de rebut — **~** *n* **1** : gaspillage *m* (d'argent), perte *f* (de temps) **2** RUBBISH : déchets *mpl*, ordures *fpl* — **wastebasket** [ˈweɪst,bæskət] *n* : corbeille *f* à papier — **wasteful** [ˈweɪstfəl] *adj* : gaspilleur — **wasteland** [ˈweɪst,lænd, -lənd] *n* : terre *f* inculte

watch [ˈwɑtʃ] *vi* **1** : regarder **2** *or* **keep ~** : faire le guet **3 ~ out** : faire attention — *vt* **1** : regarder **2** *or* **~ over** : veiller — **~** *n* **1** : montre *f* **2** SURVEILLANCE : surveillance *f* — **watchdog** [ˈwɑtʃ,dɔg] *n* : chien *m* de garde, chienne *f* de garde — **watchful** [ˈwɑtʃfəl] *adj* : vigilant — **watchman** [ˈwɑtʃmən] *n, pl* **-men** [-mən, -,mɛn] : gardien *m*

water [ˈwɔţər, ˈwɑ-] *n* : eau *f* — **~** *vt* **1** : arroser (un jardin, etc.) **2** *or* **~ down** DILUTE : diluer, couper (du vin, etc.) — *vi* **1** : larmoyer (se dit des yeux) **2 my mouth is ~ing** : j'ai l'eau à la bouche — **watercolor** [ˈwɔţər,kʌlər, ˈwɑ-] *n* : aquarelle *f* — **watercress** [ˈwɔţər,krɛs, ˈwɑ-] *n* : cresson *m* — **waterfall** [ˈwɔţər,fɔl, ˈwɑ-] *n* : chute *f* (d'eau), cascade *f* — **water lily** *n* : nénuphar *m* — **watermark** [ˈwɔţər,mɑrk, ˈwɑ-] *n* : filigrane *m* — **watermelon** [ˈwɔţər,mɛlən, ˈwɑ-] *n* : pastèque *f*, melon *m* d'eau — **waterproof** [ˈwɔţər,pru:f, ˈwɑ-] *adj* : imperméable — **watershed** [ˈwɔţər,ʃɛd, ˈwɑ-] *n* **1** : ligne *m* de partage des eaux **2** : moment *m* critique — **water-skiing** [ˈwɔţər,ski:ɪŋ, ˈwɑ-] *n* : ski *m* nautique — **watertight** [ˈwɔţər,taɪt, wɑ-] *adj* : étanche — **waterway** [ˈwɔţər,weɪ, ˈwɑ-] *n* : cours *m* d'eau navigable — **waterworks** [ˈwɔţərˈwərks, wɑ-] *npl* : système *m* hydraulique — **watery** [ˈwɔţəri, ˈwɑ-] *adj* **1** : larmoyant (se dit des yeux) **2** DILUTED : trop liquide, dilué

watt [ˈwɑt] *n* : watt *m* — **wattage** [ˈwɑţɪdʒ] *n* : puissance *f* en watts

wave [ˈweɪv] *v* **waved; waving** *vi* **1** : faire un signe de la main **2** : flotter au vent (se dit d'un drapeau) — *vt* **1** SHAKE : agiter, brandir **2** CURL : onduler 3 SIGNAL : faire signe à — ~ *n* 1 : vague *f* (d'eau) 2 CURL : ondulation *f* 3 : onde *f* (en physique) 4 : geste *m* de la main 4 SURGE : vague *f* — **wavelength** [ˈweɪvˌlɛŋkθ] *n* : longueur *f* d'onde

waver [ˈweɪvər] *vi* : vaciller, chanceler

wavy [ˈweɪvi] *adj* **wavier; -est** : ondulé

wax[1] [ˈwæks] *vi* : croître (se dit de la lune)

wax[2] *n* : cire *f* — ~ *vt* : cirer (le plancher, etc.), farter (des skis) — **waxy** [ˈwæksi] *adj* **waxier; -est** : cireux

way [ˈweɪ] *n* 1 : chemin *m* 2 MEANS : façon *f*, manière *f* 3 **by the ~** : à propos 4 **by ~ of** : par, via 5 **come a long ~** : faire de grands progrès 6 **get in the ~** : gêner le passage 7 **get one's own ~** : arriver à ses fins 8 **out of the ~** REMOTE : éloigné, isolé 9 **which ~ did he go?** : où est-il passé?

we [ˈwi:] *pron* : nous

weak [ˈwi:k] *adj* : faible — **weaken** [ˈwi:kən] *vt* : affaiblir — *vi* : s'affaiblir, faiblir — **weakling** [ˈwi:klɪŋ] *n* : mauviette *f* — **weakly** [ˈwi:kli] *adv* : faiblement — **weakness** [ˈwi:knəs] *n* 1 : faiblesse *f* 2 FLAW : défaut *m*

wealth [ˈwɛlθ] *n* 1 : richesse *f* 2 **a ~ of** : une profusion de — **wealthy** [ˈwɛlθi] *adj* **wealthier; -est** : riche

wean [ˈwi:n] *vt* : sevrer (un bébé)

weapon [ˈwɛpən] *n* : arme *f*

wear [ˈwær] *v* **wore** [ˈwor]; **worn** [ˈworn]; **wearing** *vt* 1 : mettre, porter 2 **~ oneself out** : s'épuiser 3 *or* **~ out** : user — *vi* 1 LAST : durer 2 **~ off** : diminuer 3 **~ out** : s'user, se détériorer — ~ *n* 1 USE : usage *m* 2 CLOTHES : vêtements *mpl* — **wear and tear** : usure *f*

weary [ˈwɪri] *adj* **-rier; -est** : fatigué, las — ~ *vt* **-ried; -rying** : lasser, fatiguer — **weariness** [ˈwɪrinəs] *n* : lassitude *f* — **wearisome** [ˈwɪrisəm] *adj* : fastidieux

weasel [ˈwi:zəl] *n* : belette *f*

weather [ˈwɛðər] *n* 1 : temps *m* 2 **be under the ~** : ne pas être dans son assiette — ~ *vt* OVERCOME : surmonter — **weather–beaten** [ˈwɛðərˌbi:tən] *adj* 1 : battu, usé (par les intempéries) 2 : hâlé (se dit d'un visage) — **weatherman** [ˈwɛðərˌmæn] *n, pl* **-men** [-mən, -ˌmɛn] : météorologiste *mf* — **weather vane** *n* : girouette *f*

weave [ˈwi:v] *v* **wove** [ˈwo:v] *or* **weaved; woven** [ˈwo:vən] *or* **weaved; weaving** *vt* 1 : tisser 2 **~ one's way through** : se faufiler à travers — *vi* : tisser — ~ *n* : tissage *m*

web [ˈwɛb] *n* 1 : toile *f* (d'araignée) 2 : palmure *f* (d'un oiseau) 3 NETWORK : réseau *m* 4 **Web** → **World Wide Web**

webbed [ˈwɛbd] *adj* : palmé

webmaster [ˈwɛbˌmæstər] *n* : webmestre *m*

wed [ˈwɛd] *v* **wedded; wedding** *vt* : se marier à, épouser — *vi* : marier

we'd [ˈwi:d] (*contraction of* **we had, we should,** *or* **we would**) → **have, should, would**

wedding [ˈwɛdɪŋ] *n* : mariage *m*, noces *fpl*

wedge [ˈwɛʤ] *n* 1 : cale *f* 2 PIECE : morceau *m* (de fromage), part *m* (de gâteau, etc.) — ~ *vt* **wedged; wedging** 1 : caler, fixer 2 CRAM : enfoncer

Wednesday [ˈwɛnzˌdeɪ, -di] *n* : mercredi *m*

wee [ˈwi:] *adj* 1 : très petit 2 **in the ~ hours** : aux petites heures (du matin)

weed [ˈwi:d] *n* : mauvaise herbe *f* — ~ *vt* 1 : désherber 2 **~ out** : se débarrasser de

week [ˈwi:k] *n* : semaine *f* — **weekday** [ˈwi:kˌdeɪ] *n* : jour *m* de semaine — **weekend** [ˈwi:kˌɛnd] *n* : fin *f* de semaine, week-end *m* — **weekly** [ˈwi:kli] *adv* : à la semaine, chaque semaine — ~ *adj* : hebdomadaire — ~ *n, pl* **-lies** : hebdomadaire *m*

weep [ˈwi:p] *vi* **wept** [ˈwɛpt]; **weeping** : pleurer — **weeping willow** *n* : saule *m* pleureur — **weepy** [ˈwi:pi] *adj* **weepier; -est** : au bord des larmes

weigh [ˈweɪ] *vt* 1 : peser 2 CONSIDER : considérer 3 **~ down** : accabler — *vi* 1 : peser 2 **~ on s.o.'s mind** : préoccuper qqn

weight [ˈweɪt] *n* 1 : poids *m* 2 IMPORTANCE : influence *f* 3 **gain ~** : engraisser 4 **lose ~** : maigrir — **weighty** [ˈweɪṭi] *adj* **weightier; -est** 1 HEAVY : pesant, lourd 2 IMPORTANT : de poids

weird [ˈwɪrd] *adj* 1 : mystérieux 2 STRANGE : étrange, bizarre

welcome [ˈwɛlkəm] *vt* **-comed; -coming** : accueillir, souhaiter la bienvenue à — ~ *adj* 1 : bienvenu 2 **you're ~** : de rien, je vous en prie — ~ *n* : accueil *m*

weld [ˈwɛld] *vt* : souder — ~ *n* : soudure *f*

welfare [ˈwɛlˌfær] *n* 1 WELL-BEING

: bien-être *m* **2** AID : aide *f* sociale, assistance *f* publique
well[1] ['wɛl] *n* : puits *m* (d'eau, de pétrole, etc.) — **~** *vi or* **~ up** : monter, jaillir
well[2] *adv* **better** ['bɛţər]; **best** ['bɛst] **1** : bien **2 as ~** : aussi — **~** *adj* : bien — **~** *interj* **1** (*used to introduce a remark*) : bon, bien, enfin **2** (*used to express surprise*) : ça alors!, eh bien!
we'll ['wi:l, wɪl] (*contraction of* **we shall** *or* **we will**) → **shall, will**
well–being ['wɛl'bi:ɪŋ] *n* : bien-être *m* — **well–bred** ['wɛl'brɛd] *adj* : bien élevé, poli — **well–done** ['wɛl'dʌn] *adj* **1** : bien fait **2** : bien cuit (se dit de la viande, etc.) — **well–known** ['wɛl'no:n] *adj* : bien connu — **well–meaning** ['wɛl'mi:nɪŋ] *adj* : bien intentionné — **well–off** ['wɛl'ɔf] *adj* : prospère — **well–rounded** [cwelcraundəd] *adj* : complet — **well–to–do** [ˌwɛltə'du:] *adj* : riche, aisé
Welsh ['wɛlʃ] *adj* : gallois — **~** *n* : gallois *m* (langue)
welt ['wɛlt] *n* : zébrure *f*, marque *f* (sur la peau)
went → **go**
wept → **weep**
were → **be**
we're ['wɪr, 'wər, 'wi:ər] (*contraction of* **we are**) → **be**
weren't ['wərənt, 'wərnt] (*contraction of* **were not**) → **be**
west ['wɛst] *adv* : à l'ouest, vers l'ouest — **~** *adj* : ouest, d'ouest — **~** *n* **1** : ouest *m* **2 the West** : l'Ouest *m*, l'Occident *m* — **westerly** ['wɛstərli] *adv* : vers l'ouest — **~** *adj* : à l'ouest, d'ouest — **western** ['wɛstərn] *adj* **1** : ouest, de l'ouest, occidental **2 Western** : de l'Ouest, occidental — **Westerner** ['wɛstərnər] *n* : habitant *m*, -tante *f* de l'Ouest — **westward** ['wɛstwərd] *adv & adj* : vers l'ouest
wet ['wɛt] *adj* **wetter; wettest 1** : mouillé **2** RAINY : pluvieux **3 ~ paint** : peinture *f* fraîche — **~** *vt* **wet** *or* **wetted; wetting** : mouiller, humecter
we've ['wi:v] (*contraction of* **we have**) → **have**
whack ['*h*wæk] *vt* : donner une claque à — **~** *n* : coup *m*, claque *f*
whale ['*h*weɪl] *n, pl* **whales** *or* **whale** : baleine *f*
wharf ['*h*wɔrf] *n, pl* **wharves** ['*h*wɔrvz] : quai *m*
what ['*h*wɑt, '*h*wʌt] *adj* **1** (*used in questions and exclamations*) : quel **2** WHATEVER : tout — **~** *pron* **1** (*used in questions*) : qu'est-ce que, qu'est-ce qui **2** (*used in indirect statements*) : ce que, ce qui **3 ~ does it cost?** : combien est-ce que ça coûte? **4 ~ for?** : pourquoi? **5 ~ if** : et si — **whatever** [*h*wɑţ'ɛvər, ˌ*h*wʌţ-] *adj* **1** : n'importe quel **2 there's no chance ~** : il n'y a pas la moindre possibilité **3 nothing ~** : rien du tout — **~** *pron* **1** ANYTHING : (tout) ce que **2** (*used in questions*) : qu'est-ce que, qu'est-ce qui **3 ~ it may be** : quoi que ce soit — **whatsoever** [ˌ*h*wɑtso'ɛvər, ˌ*h*wʌt-] *adj & pron* → **whatever**
wheat ['*h*wi:t] *n* : blé *m*
wheedle ['*h*wi:dəl] *vt* **-dled; -dling** : enjôler
wheel ['*h*wi:l] *n* **1** : roue *f* **2** *or* **steering ~** : volant *m* — **~** *vt* : pousser (quelque chose sur des roulettes) — **wheelbarrow** ['*h*wi:lˌbærˌo:] *n* : brouette *f* — **wheelchair** ['*h*wi:lˌʧær] *n* : fauteuil *m* roulant
wheeze ['*h*wi:z] *vi* **wheezed; wheezing** : respirer bruyamment
when ['*h*wɛn] *adv* : quand — **~** *conj* **1** : quand, lorsque **2 the days ~ I go to the bank** : les jours où je vais à la banque — **~** *pron* : quand — **whenever** [*h*wɛn'ɛvər] *adv* : quand (donc) — **~** *conj* **1** : chaque fois que **2 ~ you like** : quand vous voulez
where ['*h*wɛr] *adv* **1** : où **2 ~ are you going?** : où vas-tu? — **~** *conj & pron* : où — **whereabouts** ['*h*wɛrəˌbaʊts] *adv* : où (donc) — **~** *ns & pl* **know s.o.'s ~** : savoir où se trouve qqn
whereas [*h*wɛr'æz] *conj* : alors que, tandis que
wherever [*h*wɛr'ɛvər] *conj* **1** : n'importe où **2** WHERE : où, où donc
whet ['*h*wɛt] *vt* **whetted; whetting 1** : affûter, aiguiser (un couteau) **2 ~ one's appetite** : ouvrir l'appétit
whether ['*h*wɛðər] *conj* **1** : si **2 we doubt ~ he'll show up** : nous doutons qu'il vienne **3 ~ you like it or not** : que cela te plaise ou non
which ['*h*wɪʧ] *adj* **1** : quel **2 in ~ case** : auquel cas — **~** *pron* **1** (*used in questions*) : lequel, quel **2** (*used in relative clauses*) : qui, que — **whichever** [*h*wɪʧ'ɛvər] *adj* : peu importe quel — **~** *pron* : quel que
whiff ['*h*wɪf] *n* **1** PUFF : bouffée *f* **2** SMELL : odeur *f*
while ['*h*waɪl] *n* **1** : temps *m*, moment

m **2 be worth one's ~** : valoir la peine **3 in a ~** : sous peu — **~** *conj* **1** : pendant que **2** WHEREAS : tandis que, alors que **3** ALTHOUGH : bien que — **~** *vt* **whiled; whiling ~ away** : (faire) passer

whim ['*h*wɪm] *n* : caprice *m,* lubie *f*

whimper ['*h*wɪmpər] *vi* : gémir, pleurnicher *fam* — **~** *n* : gémissement *m*

whimsical ['*h*wɪmzɪkəl] *adj* : capricieux, fantasque

whine ['*h*waɪn] *vi* **whined; whining 1** WHIMPER : gémir **2** COMPLAIN : se plaindre — **~** *n* : gémissement *m*

whip ['*h*wɪp] *v* **whipped; whipping** *vt* **1** : fouetter **2** BEAT : battre (des œufs, etc.) — *vi* FLAP : battre, claquer — **~** *n* : fouet *m*

whir ['*h*wər] *vi* **whirred; whirring** : ronronner, vrombir

whirl ['*h*wərl] *vi* : tourner, tourbillonner — **~** *n* : tourbillon *m* — **whirlpool** ['*h*wərl,pu:l] *n* : tourbillon *m* (d'eau) — **whirlwind** ['*h*wərl,wɪnd] *n* : tourbillon *m* (de vent)

whisk ['*h*wɪsk] *vt* **1** : fouetter (des œufs) **2** *or* **~ away** : enlever — **~** *n* : fouet *m* (en cuisine)

whisker ['*h*wɪskər] *n* **1** : poil *m* de barbe **2 ~s** *npl* : barbe *f* (d'un homme), moustaches *fpl* (d'un chat, etc.)

whiskey *or* **whisky** ['*h*wɪski] *n, pl* **-keys** *or* **-kies** : whisky *m*

whisper ['*h*wɪspər] *v* : chuchoter — **~** *n* : chuchotement *m*

whistle ['*h*wɪsəl] *v* **-tled; -tling** : siffler — **~** *n* **1** : sifflement *m* (son) **2** : sifflet *m* (objet)

white ['*h*waɪt] *adj* **whiter; -est** : blanc — **~** *n* **1** : blanc *m* (couleur) **2** *or* **~ person** : Blanc *m,* Blanche *f* — **white–collar** ['*h*waɪt'kɑlər] *adj* : de bureau — **whiten** ['*h*waɪtən] *v* : blanchir — **whiteness** ['*h*waɪtnəs] *n* : blancheur *f* — **whitewash** ['*h*waɪt-,wɔʃ] *n* : lait *m* de chaux

whittle ['*h*wɪtəl] *vt* **-tled; -tling ~ down** : réduire

whiz *or* **whizz** ['*h*wɪz] *vi* **whizzed; whizzing 1** BUZZ : bourdonner **2 ~ by** : passer à toute vitesse — **~** *or* **whizz** *n, pl* **whizzes** : expert *m,* as *m* — **whiz kid** *n* : jeune prodige *m*

who ['hu:] *pron* **1** (*used in direct and indirect questions*) : qui, qui est-ce qui **2** (*used in relative clauses*) : qui — **whoever** [hu:'ɛvər] *pron* **1** : qui que ce soit, quiconque **2** (*used in questions*) : qui

whole ['ho:l] *adj* **1** : entier **2** INTACT : intact **3 a ~ lot** : beaucoup — **~** *n* **1** : tout *m,* ensemble *m* **2 as a ~** : dans son ensemble **3 on the ~** : en général — **wholehearted** ['ho:l-'hɑrṭəd] *adj* : sincère — **wholesale** ['ho:l,seɪl] *n* : vente *f* en gros — **~** *adj* : de gros — **~** *adv* : en gros — **wholesaler** ['ho:l,seɪlər] *n* : grossiste *mf* — **wholesome** ['ho:lsəm] *adj* : sain — **whole wheat** *adj* : de blé entier — **wholly** ['ho:li] *adv* : entièrement

whom ['hu:m] *pron* **1** (*used in direct and indirect questions*) : qui, à qui **2** (*used in relative clauses*) : que

whooping cough ['hu:pɪŋ] *n* : coqueluche *f*

whore ['hor] *n* : prostituée *f*

whose ['hu:z] *adj* **1** (*used in questions*) : de qui, à qui **2** (*used in relative clauses*) : dont — **~** *pron* : à qui

why ['*h*waɪ] *adv* : pourquoi — **~** *n, pl* **whys** : pourquoi *m* — **~** *conj* : pourquoi — **~** *interj* (*used to express surprise*) : mais!, tiens!

wick ['wɪk] *n* : mèche *f*

wicked ['wɪkəd] *adj* **1** : méchant **2** MISCHIEVOUS : espiègle **3** TERRIBLE : terrible — **wickedness** ['wɪkədnəs] *n* : méchanceté *f*

wicker ['wɪkər] *n* : osier *m*

wide ['waɪd] *adj* **wider; widest 1** : de large, de largeur **2** VAST : étendu, vaste — **~** *adv* **1 ~ apart** : très écarté **2 far and ~** : partout **3 open ~** : ouvrir grand (la bouche) — **wide–awake** ['waɪdə'weɪk] *adj* : éveillé, alerte — **widely** ['waɪdli] *adv* : largement — **widen** ['waɪdən] *vt* : élargir — **widespread** ['waɪd'sprɛd] *adj* : généralisé

widow ['wɪ,do:] *n* : veuve *f* — **~** *vt* : devenir veuf — **widower** ['wɪdowər] *n* : veuf *m*

width ['wɪdθ] *n* : largeur *f*

wield ['wi:ld] *vt* **1** : manier **2** EXERT : exercer

wife ['waɪf] *n, pl* **wives** ['waɪvz] : femme *f,* épouse *f*

wig ['wɪg] *n* : perruque *f*

wiggle ['wɪgəl] *v* **-gled; -gling** *vi* : remuer — *vt* : faire bouger (ses orteils, etc.)

wigwam ['wɪg,wɑm] *n* : wigwam *m*

wild ['waɪld] *adj* **1** : sauvage **2** UNRULY : indiscipliné **3** RANDOM : au hasard **4** FRANTIC : frénétique **5** OUTRAGEOUS : extravagant — **~** *adv* **1** → **wildly 2**

run ∼ : se déchaîner — **wild boar** *n* : sanglier *m* — **wilderness** [ˈwɪldərnəs] *n* : région *f* sauvage — **wildfire** [ˈwaɪld,faɪr] *n* **1** : feu *m* de forêt **2 spread like ∼** : se répandre comme une traînée de poudre — **wildflower** [ˈwaɪld,flaʊər] *n* : fleur *f* des champs — **wildlife** [ˈwaɪld,laɪf] *n* : faune *f* — **wildly** [ˈwaɪldli] *adv* **1** FRANTICALLY : frénétiquement **2** EXTREMELY : extrêmement

will[1] [ˈwɪl] *v, past* **would** [ˈwʊd]; *pres sing & pl* **will** *vt* WISH : vouloir — *v aux* **1 tomorrow we ∼ go shopping** : demain nous irons faire les magasins **2 he ∼ get angry over nothing** : il se fâche pour des riens **3 I ∼ go despite them** : j'irai malgré eux **4 I won't do it** : je ne le ferai pas **5 that ∼ be the mailman** : ça doit être le facteur **6 the back seat ∼ hold three people** : le siège arrière peut accommoder trois personnes **7 accidents ∼ happen** : les accidents arrivent **8 you ∼ do as I say** : je t'ordonne de faire ce que je te dis

will[2] *n* **1** : volonté *f* **2** TESTAMENT : testament *m* **3 free ∼** : de son propre gré — **willful** *or* **wilful** [ˈwɪlfəl] *adj* **1** OBSTINATE : volontaire **2** INTENTIONAL : délibéré — **willing** [ˈwɪlɪŋ] *adj* **1** : complaisant **2 be ∼ to** : être prêt à, être disposé à — **willingly** [ˈwɪlɪŋli] *adv* : volontiers, de bon cœur — **willingness** [ˈwɪlɪŋnəs] *n* : bonne volonté *f*

willow [ˈwɪ,lo:] *n* : saule *m*

willpower [ˈwɪl,paʊər] *n* : volonté *f*

wilt [ˈwɪlt] *vi* : se faner

wily [ˈwaɪli] *adj* **wilier; -est** : rusé, malin

win [ˈwɪn] *v* **won** [ˈwʌn]; **winning** *vi* : gagner — *vt* **1** : gagner, remporter **2 ∼ over** : convaincre — **∼** *n* : victoire *f*

wince [ˈwɪnts] *vi* **winced; wincing** : tressaillir — **∼** *n* : tressaillement *m*

winch [ˈwɪntʃ] *n* : treuil *m*

wind[1] [ˈwɪnd] *n* **1** : vent *m* **2** BREATH : souffle *m* **3** : gaz *mpl* intestinaux **4 get ∼ of** : apprendre

wind[2] [ˈwaɪnd] *v* **wound** [ˈwaʊnd]; **winding** *vi* : serpenter — *vt* **1** COIL : enrouler **2 ∼ a clock** : remonter une horloge

wind down *vi* RELAX : se détendre

windfall [ˈwɪnd,fɔl] *n* : bénéfice *m* inattendu

winding [ˈwaɪndɪŋ] *adj* : sinueux

wind instrument *n* : instrument *m* à vent

windmill [ˈwɪnd,mɪl] *n* : moulin *m* à vent

window [ˈwɪn,do:] *n* : fenêtre *f* (d'une maison), vitre *f* (d'une voiture), guichet *m* (dans une banque, etc.), vitrine *f* (d'un magasin) — **windowpane** [ˈwɪn,do:,peɪn] *n* : vitre *f*, carreau *m* — **windowsill** [ˈwɪndo,sɪl] *n* : rebord *m* de fenêtre

windpipe [ˈwɪnd,paɪp] *n* : trachée *f*

windshield [ˈwɪnd,ʃi:ld] *n* **1** : pare-brise *m* **2 ∼ wiper** : essuie-glace *m*

wind up [ˈwaɪnd,ʌp] *vt* : terminer, conclure — *vi* : finir

windy [ˈwɪndi] *adj* **windier; -est 1** : venteux **2 it's ∼** : il vente

wine [ˈwaɪn] *n* : vin *m* — **wine cellar** *n* : cave *f* à vin

wing [ˈwɪŋ] *n* : aile *f*

wink [ˈwɪŋk] *vi* : faire un clin d'œil — **∼** *n* **1** : clin *m* d'œil **2 not sleep a ∼** : ne pas fermer l'œil

winner [ˈwɪnər] *n* : gagnant *m*, -gnante *f* — **winning** [ˈwɪnɪŋ] *adj* : gagnant — **winnings** [ˈwɪnɪŋz] *npl* : gains *mpl*

winter [ˈwɪntər] *n* : hiver *m* — **∼** *adj* : d'hiver — **wintergreen** [ˈwɪntər,gri:n] *n* : gaulthérie *f* — **wintertime** [ˈwɪntər,taɪm] *n* : hiver *m* — **wintry** [ˈwɪntri] *adj* **-trier; -est** : hivernal

wipe [ˈwaɪp] *vt* **wiped; wiping 1** : essuyer **2 ∼ away** : effacer (un souvenir) **3 ∼ out** : détruire — **∼** *n* : coup *m* d'éponge

wire [ˈwaɪr] *n* **1** : fil *m* métallique **2** : câble *m* (électrique ou téléphonique) — **∼** *vt* **wired; wiring 1** : faire l'installation électrique de **2** BIND : relier, attacher — **wireless** [ˈwaɪrləs] *adj* : sans fil — **wiring** [ˈwaɪrɪŋ] *n* : installation *f* électrique — **wiry** [ˈwaɪri] *adj* **wirier** [ˈwaɪriər]; **-est** : mince et musclé

wisdom [ˈwɪzdəm] *n* : sagesse *f* — **wisdom tooth** *n* : dent *f* de sagesse

wise [ˈwaɪz] *adj* **wiser; wisest 1** : sage **2** SENSIBLE : prudent — **wisecrack** [ˈwaɪz,kræk] *n* : vanne *f* — **wisely** [ˈwaɪzli] *adv* : sagement

wish [ˈwɪʃ] *vt* **1** : souhaiter, désirer **2 ∼ s.o. well** : souhaiter le meilleur à qqn — *vi* **1** : souhaiter, vouloir **2 as you ∼** : comme vous voulez — **∼** *n* **1** : souhait *m*, désir *m*, vœu *m* **2 best ∼es** *npl* : meilleurs vœux *mpl* — **wishful** [ˈwɪʃfəl] *adj* **1** : désireux **2 ∼ thinking** : illusions *fpl*

wishy-washy ['wɪʃi,wɔʃi, -,wɑʃi] *adj* : faible, insipide
wisp ['wɪsp] *n* **1** : mèche *f* (de cheveux) **2** HINT : trace *f*, soupçon *m*
wistful ['wɪstfəl] *adj* : mélancolique
wit ['wɪt] *n* **1** CLEVERNESS : ingénuosité *f* **2** HUMOR : esprit *m* **3 at one's ~'s end** : désespéré **4 scared out of one's ~s** : mort de peur
witch ['wɪtʃ] *n* : sorcière *f* — **witchcraft** ['wɪtʃ,kræft] *n* : sorcellerie *f*
with ['wɪð, 'wɪθ] *prep* **1** : avec **2 I'm going ~ you** : je vais avec toi **3 it varies ~ the season** : ça varie selon la saison **4 the girl ~ red hair** : la fille aux cheveux roux **5 ~ all his faults, he's still my friend** : malgré tous ses défauts, il est quand même mon ami
withdraw [wɪð'drɔ, wɪθ-] *v* **-drew** [-'dru:]; **-drawn** [-'drɔn]; **-drawing** *vt* : retirer, rétracter (une parole, etc.) — *vi* LEAVE : se retirer — **withdrawal** [wɪð'drɔəl, wɪθ-] *n* : retrait *m* — **withdrawn** [wɪð'drɔn, wɪθ-] *adj* : renfermé, replié sur soi-même
wither ['wɪðər] *vi* : se faner, se flétrir
withhold [wɪθ'ho:ld, wɪð-] *vt* **-held** [-'hɛld]; **-holding** : retenir (des fonds), refuser (la permission, etc.)
within [wɪð'ɪn, wɪθ-] *adv* : à l'intérieur — **~** *prep* **1** : dans, à l'intérieur de **2** (*in expressions of distance*) : à moins de **3** (*in expressions of time*) : en moins de **4 ~ reach** : à (la) portée de la main
without [wɪð'aut, wɪθ-] *adv* **do ~** : se passer de — **~** *prep* : sans
withstand [wɪθ'stænd, wɪð-] *vt* **-stood** [-'stud]; **-standing 1** BEAR : supporter **2** RESIST : résister à
witness ['wɪtnəs] *n* **1** : témoin *m* **2** EVIDENCE : témoignage *m* **3 bear ~** : témoigner — **~** *vt* **1** SEE : être témoin de **2** : servir de témoin lors de (une signature)
witty ['wɪṭi] *adj* **-tier; -est** : ingénieux
wives → **wife**
wizard ['wɪzərd] *n* **1** : magicien *m*, sorcier *m* **2 a math ~** : un génie en mathématiques
wobble ['wɑbəl] *vi* **-bled; -bling 1** : branler, osciller **2** : trembler (se dit de la voix, etc.) — **wobbly** ['wɑbəli] *adj* : bancal
woe ['wo:] *n* **1** : affliction *f* **2 ~s** *npl* TROUBLES : peines *fpl* — **woeful** ['wo:fəl] *adj* : triste
woke, woken → **wake**
wolf ['wulf] *n, pl* **wolves** ['wulvz] : loup *m*, louve *f* — **~** *vt or* **~ down** : engloutir, engouffrer
woman ['wumən] *n, pl* **women** ['wɪmən] : femme *f* — **womanly** ['wumənli] *adj* : féminin
womb ['wu:m] *n* : utérus *m*
won → **win**
wonder ['wʌndər] *n* **1** MARVEL : merveille *f* **2** AMAZEMENT : émerveillement *m* — **~** *vi* : penser, songer — *vt* : se demander — **wonderful** ['wʌndərfəl] *adj* : merveilleux, formidable
won't ['wo:nt] (*contraction of* **will not**) → **will**
woo ['wu:] *vt* **1** COURT : courtiser, faire la cour à **2** : rechercher les faveurs de (un client, etc.)
wood ['wud] *n* **1** : bois *m* (matière) **2** *or* **~s** *npl* FOREST : bois *m* — **~** *adj* : de bois, en bois — **woodchuck** ['wud,tʃʌk] *n* : marmotte *f* d'Amérique — **wooded** ['wudəd] *adj* : boisé — **wooden** ['wudən] *adj* : en bois, de bois — **woodpecker** ['wud,pɛkər] *n* : pic *m* — **woodwind** ['wud,wɪnd] *n* : bois *m* (en musique) — **woodwork** ['wud,wərk] *n* : boiseries *fpl* (en menuiserie)
wool ['wul] *n* : laine *f* — **woolen** *or* **woollen** ['wulən] *adj* **1** : de laine, en laine **2 ~s** *npl* : lainages *mpl* — **woolly** ['wuli] *adj* **-lier; -est** : laineux
woozy ['wu:zi] *adj* **-zier; -est** : qui a la tête qui tourne
word ['wərd] *n* **1** : mot *m* **2** NEWS : nouvelles *fpl* **3 ~s** *npl* : texte *m*, paroles *fpl* (d'une chanson, etc.) **4 have a ~ with s.o.** : parler avec qqn **5 keep one's ~** : tenir sa parole — **~** *vt* : formuler, rédiger — **wording** ['wərdɪŋ] *n* : termes *mpl* (d'un document) — **word processing** *n* : traitement *m* de texte — **word processor** *n* : machine *f* à traitement de textes — **wordy** ['wərdi] *adj* **wordier; -est** : prolixe
wore → **wear**
work ['wərk] *n* **1** LABOR : travail *m* **2** EMPLOYMENT : travail *m*, emploi *m* **3** : œuvre *f* (d'art, etc.) **4 ~s** *npl* FACTORY : usine *f* **5 ~s** *npl* MECHANISM : rouages *mpl* (d'une horloge, etc.) — **~** *v* **worked** ['wərkt] *or* **wrought** ['rɔt]; **working** *vt* **1** : faire travailler (qqn) **2** OPERATE : faire marcher — *vi* **1** : travailler **2** FUNCTION : fonctionner **3** SUCCEED : réussir — **workbench** ['wərk,bɛntʃ] *n* : établi *m* — **worked**

up *adj* : nerveux — **worker** ['wərkər] *n* : travailleur *m*, -leuse *f*; employé *m*, -ployée *f* — **working** ['wərkɪŋ] *adj* **1** : qui travaille (se dit d'une personne), de travail (de sit d'un vêtement, etc.) **2 be in ~ order** : en état de marche — **working class** *n* : classe *f* ouvrière — **workman** ['wərkmən] *n, pl* **-men** [-mən, -ˌmɛn] : ouvrier *m* — **workmanship** ['wərkmənˌʃɪp] *n* : habileté *f*, dextérité *f* — **workout** ['wərkˌaʊt] *n* : exercices *mpl* physiques — **work out** *vt* **1** DEVELOP : élaborer **2** SOLVE : résoudre — *vi* **1** TURN OUT : marcher **2** SUCCEED : fonctionner, bien tourner **3** EXERCISE : s'entraîner, faire de l'exercice — **workshop** ['wərkˌʃɑp] *n* : atelier *m* — **work up** *vt* **1** EXCITE : stimuler **2** GENERATE : produire

world ['wərld] *n* **1** : monde *m* **2 think the ~ of s.o.** : tenir qqn en haute estime — **~** *adj* : du monde, mondial — **worldly** ['wərldli] *adj* : matériel, de ce monde — **worldwide**['wərld'waɪd] *adv* : partout dans le monde — **~** *adj* : mondial, universel

World Wide Web *n* : Web *m*

worm ['wərm] *n* **1** : ver *m* **2 ~s** *npl* : vers *mpl* (intestinaux)

worn → **wear** — **worn–out** ['worn'aʊt] *adj* **1** USED : usé, fini **2** EXHAUSTED : épuisé, éreinté

worry ['wəri] *v* **-ried; -rying** *vt* : inquiéter, préoccuper — *vi* : s'inquiéter — **~** *n, pl* **-ries** : inquiétude *f*, souci *m* — **worried** ['wəri:d] *adj* : inquiet — **worrisome** ['wərisəm] *adj* : inquiétant

worse ['wərs] *adv* (*comparative of* **bad** *or of* **ill**) : moins bien, plus mal — **~** *adj* (*comparative of* **bad** *or of* **ill**) **1** : pire, plus mauvais **2 get ~** : s'empirer — **~** *n* **1 the ~** : le pire **2 take a turn for the ~** : s'aggraver, empirer — **worsen** ['wərsən] *vi* : empirer, rempirer *Can fam* — *vt* : aggraver

worship ['wərʃəp] *v* **-shiped** *or* **-shipped; -shiping** *or* **-shipping** *vt* : adorer, vénérer — *vi* : pratiquer une religion — **~** *n* : adoration *f*, culte *m* — **worshiper** *or* **worshipper** ['wərləpər] *n* : fidèle *mf* (en religion)

worst ['wərst] *adv* (*superlative of* **ill** *or of* **bad** *or* **badly**) : plus mal — **~** *adj* (*superlative of* **bad** *or of* **ill**) : pire, plus mauvais — **~** *n* **the ~** : le pire

worth ['wərθ] *n* **1** : valeur *f* (monétaire) **2** MERIT : mérite *m* **3 ten dollars' ~ of gas** : dix dollars d'essence — **~** *prep* **1 be ~ doing** : valoir l'effort **2 it's ~ $ 10** : cela vaut 10 $ — **worthless** ['wərθləs] *adj* **1** : sans valeur **2** USELESS : inutile — **worthwhile** [wərθ'hwaɪl] *adj* : qui en vaut la peine — **worthy** ['wərði] *adj* **-thier; -est** : digne

would ['wʊd] *past of* **will 1 he ~ often take his children to the park** : il amenait souvent ses enfants au parc **2 I ~ go if I had the money** : j'irais si j'avais les moyens **3 I ~ rather go alone** : je préférerais y aller seul **4 she ~ have won if she hadn't tripped** : elle aurait gagné si elle n'avait pas trébuché **5 ~ you kindly help them?** : auriez-vous la gentillesse de les aider? — **wouldn't** ['wʊd-'nt] (*contraction of* **would not**) → **would**

wound[1] ['wu:nd] *n* : blessure *f* — **~** *vt* : blesser

wound[2] ['waʊnd] → **wind**

wove, woven → **weave**

wrangle ['ræŋgəl] *vi* **-gled; -gling** : se disputer

wrap ['ræp] *vt* **wrapped; wrapping 1** : envelopper, emballer **2** *or* **~ up** FINISH : conclure — **~** *n* → **wrapper** — **wrapper** ['ræpər] *n* : papier *m*, emballage *m* — **wrapping** ['ræpɪŋ] *n* : emballage *m*

wrath ['ræθ] *n* : furie *f*, colère *f*

wreath ['ri:θ] *n, pl* **wreaths** ['ri:ðz, 'ri:θs] : couronne *f* (de fleurs, etc.)

wreck ['rɛk] *n* **1** WRECKAGE : épave *f* (d'un navire) **2** ACCIDENT : accident *m* (de voiture), écrasement *m* (d'avion) **3 be a nervous ~** : être à bout — **~** *vt* : détruire (une automobile), faire échouer (un navire) — **wreckage** ['rɛkɪʤ] *n* **1** : épave *f* (d'un navire) **2** : décombres *mpl* (d'un édifice)

wren ['rɛn] *n* : roitelet *m*

wrench ['rɛntʃ] *vt* PULL : tirer brusquement — **~** *n* **1** TUG : secousse *f* **2** *or* **monkey ~** : clef *f*

wrestle ['rɛsəl] *vi* **-tled; -tling** : lutter, pratiquer la lutte (aux sports) — **wrestler** ['rɛsələr] *n* : lutteur *m*, -teuse *f* — **wrestling** ['rɛsəlɪŋ] *n* : lutte *f* (sport)

wretch ['rɛtʃ] *n* : pauvre diable *m* — **wretched** ['rɛtʃəd] *adj* **1** : misérable **2 ~ weather** : temps *m* affreux

wriggle ['rɪgəl] *vi* **-gled; -gling** : gigoter

wring ['rɪŋ] *vt* **wrung** ['rʌŋ]; **wringing 1** *or* **~ out** : essorer (du linge) **2** TWIST : tordre

wrinkle ['rɪŋkəl] *n* : ride *f* — ~ *v* **-kled; -kling** *vt* : rider — *vi* : se rider
wrist ['rɪst] *n* : poignet *m* — **wristwatch** ['rɪst,wɑʧ] *n* : montre-bracelet *f*
writ ['rɪt] *n* : ordonnance *f* (en droit)
write ['raɪt] *v* **wrote** ['ro:t]; **written** ['rɪtən]; **writing** : écrire — **write down** *vt* : mettre par écrit, noter — **write off** *vt* CANCEL : annuler — **writer** ['raɪţər] *n* : écrivain *m*, écrivaine *f Can*
writhe ['raɪð] *vi* **writhed; writhing** : se tordre, se tortiller
writing ['raɪţɪŋ] *n* : écriture *f*
wrong ['rɔŋ] *n* **1** : mal *m* **2** INJUSTICE : tort *m* — ~ *adj* **wronger; wrongest 1** : mal **2** UNSUITABLE : inapproprié **3** INCORRECT : mauvais, faux **4 be ~** : se tromper, avoir tort **5 what's ~?** : qu'est-ce qui ne va pas? — ~ *adv* **1** : à tort **2** INCORRECTLY : mal — ~ *vt* **wronged; wronging** : faire du tort à — **wrongful** ['rɔŋfəl] *adj* **1** UNJUST : injustifié **2** UNLAWFUL : illégal — **wrongly** ['rɔŋli] *adv* : à tort
wrote → **write**
wrought iron ['rɔt] *n* : fer *m* forgé
wrung → **wring**
wry ['raɪ] *adj* **wrier** ['raɪər]; **wriest** ['raɪəst] : narquois

XYZ

x ['ɛks] *n, pl* **x's** *or* **xs** ['ɛksəz] : x *m*, vingt-quatrième lettre de l'alphabet
xenophobia [,zɛnə'fo:biə, ,zi:-] *n* : xénophobie *f*
Xmas ['krɪsməs] → **Christmas**
X ray ['ɛks,reɪ] *n* **1** : rayon *m* X **2** *or* **~ photograph** : radiographie *f* — **x-ray** *vt* : radiographier
xylophone ['zaɪlə,fo:n] *n* : xylophone *m*
y ['waɪ] *n, pl* **y's** *or* **ys** ['waɪz] : y *m*, vingt-cinquième lettre de l'alphabet
yacht ['jɑt] *n* : yacht *m*
yam ['jæm] *n* SWEET POTATO : patate *f* douce
yank ['jæŋk] *vt* : tirer d'un coup sec — ~ *n* : coup *m* sec
yap ['jæp] *vi* **yapped; yapping 1** : japper **2** CHATTER : jacasser — ~ *n* : jappement *m*
yard ['jɑrd] *n* **1** : yard *m*, verge *f Can* (unité de mesure) **2** COURTYARD : cour *f* **3** : jardin *m* (d'une maison) — **yardstick** ['jɑrd,stɪk] *n* **1** : mètre *m* **2** CRITERION : critère *m*
yarn ['jɑrn] *n* **1** : fil *m* (à tisser) **2** TALE : histoire *f*
yawn ['jɔn] *vi* : bâiller — ~ *n* : bâillement *m*
year ['jɪr] *n* **1** : an *m*, année *f* **2 he's ten ~s old** : il a dix ans **3 I haven't seen them in ~s** : je ne les ai pas vus depuis des années — **yearbook** ['jɪr,bʊk] *n* : recueil *m* annuel, annuaire *m* — **yearly** ['jɪrli] *adv* **1** : annuellement **2 three times ~** : trois fois par an — ~ *adj* : annuel
yearn ['jərn] *vi* **~ for** : désirer ardemment — **yearning** ['jərnɪŋ] *n* : désir *m* ardent
yeast ['ji:st] *n* : levure *f*
yell ['jɛl] *vi* : crier — *vt* : crier, hurler — ~ *n* : cri *m*, hurlement *m*
yellow ['jɛlo] *adj* : jaune — ~ *n* : jaune *m* — ~ *v* : jaunir — **yellowish** ['jɛloɪʃ] *adj* : jaunâtre
yelp ['jɛlp] *n* : glapissement *m* — ~ *vi* : glapir
yes ['jɛs] *adv* **1** : oui **2 you're not ready, are you? ~, I am** : vous n'êtes pas prêt? mais si, je le suis — ~ *n* : oui *m*
yesterday ['jɛstər,deɪ, -di] *adv* : hier — ~ *n* **1** : hier *m* **2 the day before ~** : avant-hier *m*
yet ['jɛt] *adv* **1** : encore **2 has he come ~?** : est-il déjà arrivé? **3 not ~** : pas encore **4 ~ more problems** : encore des problèmes **5** NEVERTHELESS : néanmoins — ~ *conj* : mais
yield ['ji:ld] *vt* **1** PRODUCE : produire, rapporter **2 ~ the right of way** : céder le passage — *vi* **1** GIVE : céder **2** SURRENDER : se rendre — ~ *n* : rendement *m*, rapport *m*
yoga ['jo:gə] *n* : yoga *m*
yogurt ['jo:gərt] *n* : yaourt *m*, yogourt *m*
yoke ['jo:k] *n* : joug *m*
yolk ['jo:k] *n* : jaune *m* (d'œuf)
you ['ju:] *pron* **1** (*used as subject — singular*) : tu (familier), vous (forme polie) **2** (*used as subject — plural*) : vous **3** (*used as the direct or indirect object of a verb*) : te (familier), vous (forme polie), vous (pluriel) **4** (*used as the object of a preposition*) : toi (familier), vous (forme polie), vous (pluriel) **5 ~ never know** : on ne sait

jamais — **you'd** ['juɪd, 'jʊd] (*contraction of* **you had** *or* **you would**) → **have, would** — **you'll** ['ju:l, 'jʊl] (*contraction of* **you shall** *or* **you will**) → **shall, will**

young ['jʌŋ] *adj* **younger** ['jʌŋgər]; **youngest** [-gəst] **1** : jeune **2 my ~er brother** : mon frère cadet **3 she is the ~est** : elle est la plus jeune — **~** *npl* : jeunes *mfpl* (personnes), petits *mpl* (animaux) — **youngster** ['jʌŋkstər] *n* **1** : jeune *mf* **2** CHILD : enfant *mf*

your ['jʊr, 'jo:r, jər] *adj* **1** (*familiar singular*) : ta, ton **2** (*formal singular*) : votre **3** (*familiar plural*) : tes **4** (*formal plural*) : vos **5 on ~ left** : à votre gauche

you're ['jʊr, 'joɪr, 'jər, 'juɪər] (*contraction of* **you are**) → **be**

yours ['jʊrz, 'jo:rz] *pron* **1** (*familiar singular*) : le tien, la tienne **2** (*formal singular*) : le vôtre, la vôtre **3** (*familiar plural*) : les tiens, les tiennes **4** (*formal plural*) : les vôtres

yourself [jər'sɛlf] *pron, pl* **yourselves** [jər'sɛlvz] **1** (*used reflexively*) : tu (familier), vous (forme polie), vous (pluriel) **2** (*used for emphasis*) : toi-même (familier), vous-même (forme polie), vous-mêmes (pluriel)

youth ['ju:θ] *n, pl* **youths** ['ju:ðz, 'ju:θs] **1** : jeunesse *f* **2** BOY : jeune *m* **3 today's ~** : les jeunes d'aujourd'hui — **youthful** ['ju:θfəl] *adj* **1** : juvénile, de jeunesse **2** YOUNG : jeune

you've ['ju:v] (*contraction of* **you have**) → **have**

yowl ['jæʊl] *vi* : hurler (se dit d'un chien ou d'une personne) — **~** *n* : hurlement *m*

yule ['ju:l] *n* : Noël *m* — **yuletide** ['juɪl-ˌtaɪd] *n* : temps *m* de Noël

z ['zi:] *n, pl* **z's** *or* **zs** : z *m*, vingt-sixième lettre de l'alphabet

zany ['zeɪni] *adj* **-nier; -est** : farfelu *fam*

zeal ['zi:l] *n* : zèle *m*, ferveur *f* — **zealous** ['zɛləs] *adj* : zélé

zebra ['zi:brə] *n* : zèbre *m*

zed ['zɛd] *Brit* → **z**

zenith ['zi:nəθ] *n* : zénith *m*

zero ['zi:ro, 'zɪro] *n, pl* **-ros** : zéro *m* — **~** *adj* : zéro, nul

zest ['zɛst] *n* **1** : enthousiasme *m*, entrain *m* **2** FLAVOR : piquant *m*

zigzag ['zɪgˌzæg] *n* : zigzag *m* — **~** *vi* **-zagged; -zagging** : zigzaguer

zinc ['zɪŋk] *n* : zinc *m*

zip ['zɪp] *v* **zipped; zipping** *vt or* **~ up** : fermer avec une fermeture à glissière — *vi* SPEED : filer à toute allure — **zip code** *n* : code *m* postal — **zipper** ['zɪpər] *n* : fermeture *f* à glissière

zodiac ['zo:diˌæk] *n* : zodiaque *m*

zone ['zo:n] *n* : zone *f*

zoo ['zu:] *n, pl* **zoos** : zoo *m* — **zoology** [zo'ɑlədʒi, zu:-] *n* : zoologie *f*

zoom ['zu:m] *vi* : passer comme une trombe — **~** *n or* **~ lens** : zoom *m*

zucchini [zʊ'ki:ni] *n, pl* **-ni** *or* **-nis** : courgette *f*

Common French Abbreviations

FRENCH ABBREVIATION AND EXPANSION		ENGLISH EQUIVALENT	
AB, Alb.	Alberta	**AB, Alta.**	Alberta
ALÉNA	Accord de libre-échange nord-américain	**NAFTA**	North American Free Trade Agreement
AP	assistance publique (France)	—	welfare services
ap. J.-C.	après Jésus-Christ	**AD**	anno Domini
a/s	aux soins de	**c/o**	care of
av.	avenue	**ave.**	avenue
av. J.-C.	avant Jésus-Christ	**BC**	before Christ
avr.	avril	**Apr.**	April
BC	Colombie-Britannique	**BC, B.C.**	British Columbia
bd	boulevard	**blvd.**	boulevard
BD	bande dessinée	—	comic strip
BN	Bibliothèque nationale	—	national library
BP	boîte postale	**P.O.B.**	post office box
B.S.	bien-être social (Canada)	—	welfare services
c	centime	**c, ct.**	cent
C	centigrade, Celsius	**C**	centigrade, Celsius
CA	comptable agréé (Canada)	**CPA**	certified public accountant
CA	courant alternatif	**AC**	alternating current
c.-à-d.	c'est-à-dire	**i.e.**	that is
C.-B.	Colombie-Britannique	**BC, B.C.**	British Columbia
CC	courant continu	**DC**	direct current
CE	Communauté européenne	**EC**	European Community
CEE	Communauté européenne économique	**EEC**	European Economic Community
cg	centigramme	**cg**	centigram
Cie	compagnie	**Co.**	company
cm	centimètre	**cm**	centimeter
C.P.	case postale (Canada)	**P.O.B**	post office box
CV	curriculum vitae	**CV**	curriculum vitae
déc.	décembre	**Dec.**	December
dép., dépt.	département	**dept.**	department
DG	directeur général	**CEO**	chief executive officer
dim.	dimanche	**Sun.**	Sunday
dir.	directeur	**dir.**	director
DOM	Département(s) d'outre-mer	—	French overseas department
dr.	droite	**rt.**	right

FRENCH ABBREVIATION AND EXPANSION		ENGLISH EQUIVALENT	
Dr	docteur	**Dr.**	doctor
E	Est, est	**E**	East, east
ECG	électrocardiogramme	**EKG**	electrocardiogram
éd.	édition	**ed.**	edition
EPS	éducation physique et sportive	**PE**	physical education
etc.	et caetera, et cetera	**etc.**	et cetera
É.-U.	États-Unis	**US**	United States
F	Fahrenheit	**F**	Fahrenheit
F	franc	**fr.**	franc
FAB	franco à bord	**FOB**	free on board
févr.	février	**Feb.**	February
FMI	Fonds monétaire international	**IMF**	International Monetary Fund
g	gauche	**l., L**	left
g	gramme	**g**	gram
h	heure(s)	**hr.**	hour
HS	hors service	**—**	out of order
i.e.	c'est-à-dire	**i.e.**	that is
IPC	indice des prix à la consommation	**CPI**	consumer price index
Î.P.-É	île-du-Prince-Édouard	**PE, P.E.I.**	Prince Edward Island
janv.	janvier	**Jan.**	January
jeu.	jeudi	**Thurs.**	Thursday
juill.	juillet	**Jul.**	July
kg	kilogramme	**kg**	kilogram
km	kilomètre	**km**	kilometer
l	litre	**l**	liter
lun.	lundi	**Mon.**	Monday
m	mètre	**m.**	meter
M.	monsieur	**Mr.**	mister
mar.	mardi	**Tues.**	Tuesday
MB, Man.	Manitoba	**MB, Man.**	Manitoba
mer.	mercredi	**Wed.**	Wednesday
MLF	mouvement de libération des femmes	**—**	—
Mlle	Mademoiselle	**Ms., Miss**	—
Mme	Madame	**Ms., Mrs.**	—
MST	maladie sexuellement transmissible	**STD**	sexually transmitted disease
N	Nord, nord	**N**	North, north
N°, n°	numéro	**no.**	number
NB, N.-B.	Nouveau-Brunswick	**NB, N.B.**	New Brunswick
n.d.	non disponible	**NA**	not available

FRENCH ABBREVIATION AND EXPANSION		ENGLISH EQUIVALENT	
NL, T.-N.-L.	Terre-Neuve et Labrador	**NL**	Newfoundland and Labrador
nov.	novembre	**Nov.**	November
NS, N.-É.	Nouvelle-Écosse	**NS, N.S.**	Nova Scotia
NT	Territoires du Nord-Ouest	**NT, N.T.**	Northwest Territories
NU	Nunavut	**Nu**	Nunavut
O	Ouest, ouest	**W**	West, west
oc	ondes courtes	**s-w**	short wave
oct.	octobre	**Oct.**	October
OIT	Organisation internationale du travail	**ILO**	International Labor Organization
OMS	Organisation mondiale de la santé	**WHO**	World Health Organization
ON, Ont.	Ontario	**ON, Ont.**	Ontario
ONG	organisation non gouvernementale	**NGO**	nongovernmental organization
ONU	Organisation des Nations Unies	**UN**	United Nations
OTAN	Organisation du traité de l'Atlantique Nord	**NATO**	North Atlantic Treaty Organization
OVNI, ovni	objet volant non identifié	**UFO**	unidentified flying object
p.	page	**p.**	page
PCV	paiement contre vérification	—	collect call
PDG	président-directeur général	**CEO**	chief executive officer
PE	Île-du-Prince-Édouard	**PE, P.E.I.**	Prince Edward Island
p. ex.	par exemple	**e.g.**	for example
PIB	produit intérieur brut	**GDP**	gross domestic product
PNB	produit national brut	**GNP**	gross national product
P.-S.	post-scriptum	**P.S.**	postscript
QC	Québec	**QC, Que.**	Quebec
QG	quartier général	**HQ**	headquarters
QI	quotient intellectuel	**IQ**	intelligence quotient
R-D	recherche-développement	**R and D**	research and development
réf.	référence	**ref.**	reference
RF	République Française	—	France
RN	route nationale	—	interstate highway
RV	rendez-vous	**rdv., R.V.**	rendezvous
s.	siècle	**c., cent.**	century
S	Sud, sud	**S, so.**	South, south
SA	société anonyme	**Inc.**	incorporated (company)

FRENCH ABBREVIATION AND EXPANSION		ENGLISH EQUIVALENT	
sam.	samedi	**Sat.**	Saturday
SARL	société à responsabilité limitée	**Ltd.**	limited (corporation)
Sask.	Saskatchewan	**SK, Sask.**	Saskatchewan
SDF	sans domicile fixe	**—**	homeless (person)
sept.	septembre	**Sept.**	September
SK	Saskatchewan	**SK, Sask.**	Saskatchewan
SM	Sa Majesté	**HM**	His Majesty, Her Majesty
SME	Système monétaire européen	**—**	European Monetary System
St	saint	**St.**	Saint
Ste	sainte	**St.**	Saint
SVP	s'il vous plaît	**pls.**	please
t	tonne	**t., tn.**	ton
tél.	téléphone	**tel.**	telephone
T.-N.	Terre-Neuve	**NF, Nfld.**	Newfoundland
T.N.-O.	Territoires du Nord-Ouest	**NT, N.T.**	Northwest Territories
TVA	taxe à valeur ajoutée	**VAT**	value-added tax
UE	Union européenne	**EU**	European Union
univ.	université	**U., univ.**	university
V., v.	voir	**vid.**	see
ven.	vendredi	**Fri.**	Friday
vol.	volume	**vol.**	volume
VPC	vente par correspondance	**—**	mail-order selling
W-C	water closet	**w.c.**	water closet
YT, Yuk.	Yukon	**YT, Y.T.**	Yukon Territory